From the Office of
FRANK GALBAVI

Diesel Engine and Fuel System Repair

Diesel Engine and Fuel System Repair

Fourth Edition

John F. Dagel

Co-owner, DK Diesel Injection, Inc.
Watertown, South Dakota

Robert N. Brady

Vancouver Community College and
HiTech Consulting Limited

Prentice Hall
Upper Saddle River, New Jersey
Columbus, Ohio

Library of Congress Cataloging-in-Publication Data

Dagel, John F.
  Diesel engine and fuel system repair / John F. Dagel. — 4th ed /
written by R.N. Brady.
      p.   cm.
  ISBN 0-13-399692-1
    1. Diesel motor—Maintenance and repair.   2. Diesel motor—Fuel
systems—Maintenance and repair.   I. Brady, Robert N.   II. Title.
TJ799.D33   1998
621.43'68—dc21   97-8259
                                                             CIP

Cover art: Detroit Diesel, series 149
Editor: Ed Francis
Production Editor: Sheryl Glicker Langner
Production Coordination: Tally Morgan, WordCrafters Editorial Services, Inc.
Design Coordinator: Karrie M. Converse
Cover Designer: Raymond Hummons
Production Manager: Laura Messerly
Electronic Text Management: Karen L. Bretz
Marketing Manager: Danny Hoyt

This book was set in Palatino and Eras by TCSystems and was printed and bound by Courier/Kendallville, Inc.
The cover was printed by Phoenix Color Corp.

© 1998, 1994, 1988, 1982 by Prentice-Hall, Inc.
Simon & Schuster/A Viacom Company
Upper Saddle River, New Jersey 07458

Printed in the United States of America

10 9 8 7 6 5 4

ISBN: 0-13-399692-1

Prentice-Hall International (UK) Limited, *London*
Prentice-Hall of Australia Pty. Limited, *Sydney*
Prentice-Hall of Canada, Inc., *Toronto*
Prentice-Hall Hispanoamericana, S. A., *Mexico*
Prentice-Hall of India Private Limited, *New Delhi*
Prentice-Hall of Japan, Inc., *Tokyo*
Simon & Schuster Asia Pte. Ltd., *Singapore*
Editora Prentice-Hall do Brasil, Ltda., *Rio de Janeiro*

Especially for Linda, Alanna, Alicia, Scott, Tracy and Adele!

To all of the creative individuals who have allowed me to gain knowledge and skills from their benchmark experiences and to the many motivated students, friends and SAE colleagues within the diesel and automotive industry who have shared their standards of excellence. This book is a reflection of a diversity of backgrounds of truly remarkable people who provided me with their time and support. I trust that the finished product meets your high standards and expectations.

Preface

As a published author of 11 textbooks for Prentice-Hall since 1981 in the automotive and diesel field, I was very pleased to be asked to undertake preparing and writing the fourth edition of John Dagel's text, *Diesel Engine and Fuel System Repair.*

John is now in semiretirement, and enjoying his leisure time immensely. His efforts in the first three editions of this text are recognized and appreciated.

Some of the material contained within this fourth edition encapsulates some of John's earlier material which is still relevant to some aspects of diesel engine repair, specifically those engines still in use equipped with mechanical fuel systems and governors. New material has been added to highlight the latest technology currently in use by all of the major diesel engine OEM's worldwide, particularly the new designs of engine component parts, electronic fuel injection systems and electronic governor controls.

Each chapter was reviewed, updated and added to where appropriate to reflect the latest technology. A wide range of new illustrations and photographs has been incorporated to help the reader understand the intent of the accompanying text. My thanks to reviewers Richard Lazorchick, Steel Center A.V.T.S.; Kemp Pheley, Montana State University/Billings; and Dr. Michael Henich, Linn Benton Community College.

The beginning diesel technician, student and apprentice today faces the challenge of ever-changing technology, with an emphasis on a solid foundation in electronics. Individuals who choose to enter the diesel engineering field must dedicate their efforts to lifelong learning if they are to acquire a standard of excellence in their chosen profession, and to be capable of passing on their many skills to future generations. Major OEM dealers now demand that personnel have the minimum prerequisite of a grade 12 education, and prefer-ably some time at a community college associated with university entrance in physics, math, science, and English. They must also be conversant with the operation of various desktop, laptop and notebook computers, as well as knowing how to use software programs such as Windows.

Future field service technicians, service managers, fleet service management and sales application engineering personnel also need to be skilled in human resource and conflict management if they hope to become managers.

In the United States, the General Accounting Office (GAO) recently conducted a detailed study of over one hundred highly skilled professions. They determined that the needed skill levels of both automotive and diesel technicians were on a par with X-ray technicians and computer programmers.

No textbook of this type can truly reflect the wishes and needs of everyone within the diesel industry without the support, encouragement and assistance which I received from many of my colleagues. I trust that the finished product is reflective of their commitment to excellence, and that John Dagel is pleased with my efforts to bring this fourth edition up to date.

I wish you well in your pursuit of new knowledge, since your study of this book, coupled with hands-on tasks, will enhance your ability to understand, service and diagnose the latest electronically controlled diesel engines and fuel systems. These skills will make you a very valuable employee, and will provide you with a rewarding, challenging and fulfilling career for many years to come.

Robert N. Brady

About the Author

Robert N. Brady has been involved in the automotive, heavy-duty truck and equipment field since 1959, having served a recognized five-year apprenticeship as both an automotive and heavy-duty truck and equipment technician. He is a graduate of Stow College of Engineering in Glasgow, Scotland, with a degree in Mechanical Engineering Technology. He holds degrees both from the University of British Columbia and the University of Alberta in Adult Education. He is a certified automotive, commercial transport and heavy-duty equipment technician.

His experience includes positions as a shop foreman and service manager with Kenworth; fleet maintenance superintendent with North American Van Lines; factory service trainer for Canada; service representative and sales application engineer with Detroit Diesel; Diesel Engineering and Diesel Mechanic/Technician college instructor; and college department head at Vancouver Community College. He is a director and Past President of the VCC Faculty Association. In 1987, he formed his own company, HiTech Consulting Ltd., specializing in technical training program design/implementation aimed specifically at heavy-duty, on- and off-highway equipment. He has designed and implemented training programs for a number of large truck fleets as well as for mining companies. He has set up fleet maintenance programs and been a speaker at a number of adult education seminars.

He is author of ten automotive, diesel, and heavy-duty truck books for Simon & Schuster's Prentice Hall college division, where he has also been a book series editor. He has also written numerous technical articles for publication in local and national technical magazines. He is a member of SAE (Society of Automotive Engineers) International, in which he has held positions as the past chair of the local British Columbia Section. In 1989–1990, under his leadership, the section was presented an SAE Award of Merit for outstanding technical meetings. At the International level of SAE, he served three years on the Sections Board, and was both Vice-Chair and Chair. He co-chaired the 1992 Section Officers Leadership Seminar held in Warrendale, PA., for worldwide section officers, and returned in 1993 as Chair. Other activities within SAE at the Sections Board level include: Chair of the Executive Committee; Past Chair of the Administrative Committee; member of the Section Evaluation and Awards Committee and the Section Activities; Chair of the Brazil Ad Hoc Committee and subsequently Chair of the International Sections and Affiliates Committee; member of the Regional Coordinators Committee where he was responsible for the provinces of British Columbia, Alberta and Manitoba, as well as an acting RC for the NW/Spokane-Intermountain and Oregon sections; and member of the Total Quality Management Committee. He was appointed to the Board of Directors for SAE International for a three-year term covering 1994 to 1997, where he has been involved as a member of the DPCC (Development Project Coordinating Committee), the Appeals Board, and member of the Total Life Cycle Committee.

He was one of two SAE Board of Director members appointed to the Ad Hoc Committee which developed the STS (Service Technician Society), March 1996, under the auspices of SAE. STS is now a rapidly developing society catering to the many diversified needs of service technicians in all areas of Land, Sea, Air and Space.

He is the technical editor for Canada's National Trucking Newspaper and Equipment Buyer's Guide, where he writes a monthly technical column dealing with new technology and maintenance items.

His military background includes service with the Army Emergency Reserve of the British Army in both the Paratroop Regiment and the R.E.M.E. (Royal Electrical Mechanical Engineers). He is a former Scottish amateur boxing champion, semi-professional soccer player, a very active long-distance cyclist and skier, and enjoys restoring older cars. He is currently coaching a select soccer team of teenagers in his local area.

Contents

Diesel Engine and Fuel System Repair

1

Development of the Diesel Engine

OVERVIEW

With this chapter we begin our study of the diesel engine from a short historical perspective, review general characteristics and main component function and requirements, look at main design features, and briefly review the latest concepts now in use.

HISTORICAL BACKGROUND

A diesel engine is an internal combustion engine. This means that combustion (burning) of fuel occurs within the engine cylinder. Diesel engines are available in many cylinder arrangements and sizes. Since 1895, when the first practical diesel engine was developed by Rudolf Diesel, diesel engines have been a source of reliable, efficient, long-lasting power.

The modern-day diesel engine is a direct result of developmental work that started in 1794 when an inventor named Street developed the internal combustion engine. His basic ideas were further developed in 1824 by a young French engineer named Sadi Carnot. Although Carnot did not actually build an engine, he presented ideas that were utilized in building the diesel engine. He stated that highly compressed air created by a compression ratio of 15 : 1 would generate enough heat to ignite dry wood. He also suggested that the air used for combustion be highly compressed before ignition. Engines had previously used air for combustion at atmospheric pressure. He also suggested that the cylinder walls should be cooled, since the heat from combustion would make them very hot, affecting the operation of the engine.

In 1876, Nicholaus Otto constructed the first four-stroke cycle internal combustion engine, which ran on gasoline using flame ignition. This engine used ideas suggested, but not tried, by other engineers. It was successful and became the model for all succeeding four-stroke cycle engines, gas as well as diesel.

In 1892, Rudolph Diesel, a young German engineer, patented a compression ignition engine. Called the rational heat motor, this engine was to use a compression ratio higher than any other engine had utilized. Based on his early calculations, Diesel estimated that this engine would have a thermal efficiency of 73%. Most engineers of the day declared that it was impossible to build such an engine. Diesel, certain that his engine would work, convinced the Maschinenfabrik Augsburg Company to build an engine for test purposes.

It was decided early on that his original projections of compression pressures of 200 atm (atmospheres) or 2900 psi (pounds per square inch) were too high, and much testing and redesigning were done, resulting in an engine with a compression ratio of 18.4 : 1. Next began the search for a suitable fuel. The original patent called for coal dust, but early tests were performed with lamp petroleum (kerosene). Injecting the fuel into the cylinder at the correct time in the correct amounts with a sufficient degree of atomization proved to be a huge and almost insurmountable task. Many tests, many heartbreaking and discouraging results were endured before a workable system resulted. The first running engine utilized compressed air to blow the fuel charge into the cylinder under high pressure. This design was not what Diesel originally had in mind, because it required an engine-driven air compressor, which subtracted from the engine horsepower. Further testing eliminated some of the complicated and bulky air-injection system, but the engine continued to use compressed air as the primary means of injecting fuel.

1

In 1897 the engine was ready for production, and the right to build under license was sold to many firms, many of which still build diesel engines today. The development and utilization of the diesel engine as we presently know it was under way.

The catalyst that provided the initiative for continued research and development of the diesel engine was the same in the early 1900s as it is today; that is, the search for a more fuel-efficient engine because of the high cost of fuel. In the early 1900s the gas engine, or "petrol engine" as it was known, had been king. With the successful operation of Diesel's compression ignition fuel burning engine, a new era dawned. Application of this new engine as the prime mover in applications where the petrol engine had been used was not an easy task. The huge size and tremendous weight of the diesel made it impossible to use in any but stationary situations.

The development of a small compact fuel injection system by the German inventor Robert Bosch in 1927 helped to free the diesel engine from one of its major limitations, the fuel system's size. It was compact (barely larger than a carburetor), lightweight, and contained a built-in governor. Now all the bulky compressors, reservoirs, lines, and control valves used by the previous air-injection systems could be eliminated. Engine control under varying loads and speed conditions was equal to or better than the carburetor used on petrol engines.

With this major limitation removed, engine manufacturers began seriously considering the diesel engine as a power source. Work began in earnest to further simplify and refine the diesel engine.

As the diesel came to the United States, engines manufactured by Cummins, Caterpillar, General Motors, and others started to impress vehicle owners by their ruggedness and fuel economy. For many years the engine stayed in the heavy equipment and large-truck market, gaining popularity and proving in the face of skepticism that it was a dependable engine.

In the 1950s the development of a smaller rotary lightweight pump by Vernon Roosa paved the way for the diesel's entry into another major field of application, farm tractors. Almost overnight farm tractors around the world became diesel powered. The diesel engine has continued to be developed, entering new markets and experiencing greater usage.

Another example of diesel engine development is the addition of a small lightweight turbocharger (an exhaust-driven air pump that pumps air into the intake manifold). This allowed further reduction of engine weight and a decrease in exhaust smoke, making the engine what it is today, a highly efficient, lightweight, pollution-free engine.

Modern diesels are found in every application and play an important part in our daily lives. Diesel engines resemble gas engines in many ways. The diesel engine's external appearance is nearly the same as a gas engine, and at first glance the engine's internal parts resemble those of a gas engine; however, closer inspection reveals that most internal parts are made stronger and heavier to withstand the greater pressures within the diesel engine. The major difference between the two engines is the ignition and fuel systems. Earlier-model gas engines employ a carburetor, distributor, and spark plugs. Later gasoline engines employ fuel-injection, distributorless ignition systems and electronic controls. A diesel engine is a compression ignition engine using a fuel injection pump, injection nozzles or injectors, and electronic controls.

DIESEL ENGINE CHARACTERISTICS

Diesel engines run by using air, fuel, and ignition just like gasoline engines. Differences between gas and diesel engines are:

1. *Type of fuel.* Diesel fuel is a less volatile fuel than gasoline but possesses a greater number of Btu (British thermal units) per gallon. As a result, more total horsepower is obtained from a gallon of diesel fuel than from a gallon of gasoline.

2. *Type of ignition.* The fuel and air mixture in a gas engine cylinder is ignited by a spark plug. In a diesel engine the mixture is ignited by the heat from compression.

3. *Fuel and air mixing.* In gasoline engines the fuel and air are mixed in the carburetor and intake manifold or injected through either a throttle body or injectors located in the intake manifold close to the intake valve(s). In a diesel engine the diesel fuel is mixed with the air when the fuel is injected into the cylinder compressed air charge.

NOTE   Diesel engines have combustion chambers that are specially designed to aid in the mixing of fuel and air. Since mixing must be done immediately following injection of the fuel, combustion chamber design and manufacture are very important factors in the effective operation of a diesel engine.

DIESEL ENGINE COMPONENTS

To understand the diesel engine and how it works, the nomenclature of all engine parts must be known and understood. Figure 1–1 shows an exploded view of a diesel engine and its working parts. A part-by-part description follows:

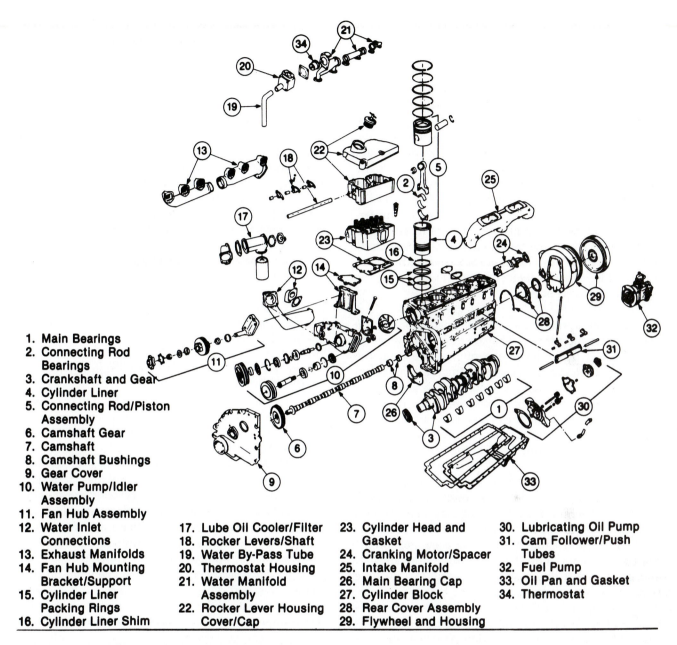

1. Main Bearings
2. Connecting Rod Bearings
3. Crankshaft and Gear
4. Cylinder Liner
5. Connecting Rod/Piston Assembly
6. Camshaft Gear
7. Camshaft
8. Camshaft Bushings
9. Gear Cover
10. Water Pump/Idler Assembly
11. Fan Hub Assembly
12. Water Inlet Connections
13. Exhaust Manifolds
14. Fan Hub Mounting Bracket/Support
15. Cylinder Liner Packing Rings
16. Cylinder Liner Shim

17. Lube Oil Cooler/Filter
18. Rocker Levers/Shaft
19. Water By-Pass Tube
20. Thermostat Housing
21. Water Manifold Assembly
22. Rocker Lever Housing Cover/Cap

23. Cylinder Head and Gasket
24. Cranking Motor/Spacer
25. Intake Manifold
26. Main Bearing Cap
27. Cylinder Block
28. Rear Cover Assembly
29. Flywheel and Housing

30. Lubricating Oil Pump
31. Cam Follower/Push Tubes
32. Fuel Pump
33. Oil Pan and Gasket
34. Thermostat

FIGURE 1–1 Components of a diesel engine. (Courtesy of Cummins Engine Company, Inc.)

1. *Cylinder block.* This is considered the "backbone" of an internal combustion engine, to which all other engine parts are bolted or connected. The block has many drilled and tapped holes for capscrews, which allow other parts to be connected. Also contained in the block are:

   a. Bores or saddles for supporting the crankshaft

   b. Drilled bores for supporting the camshaft

   c. Cylinder holes for the cylinder sleeves

2. *Crankshaft and main bearings.* A crankshaft is a long shaft inserted in the bottom of the block with offset crankpin journals or throws formed onto it. It is used to change up-and-down motion of the pistons and rods to rotary motion. Contained within the crankshaft are drilled passageways that supply oil to the main and rod bearings. The main bearings are friction bearings that support the crankshaft in the block.

3. *Cylinder sleeves or liners.* Most diesel engines use a replaceable cylinder sleeve so that if the sleeve becomes worn it can be replaced easily without rebor-

ing the cylinder or replacing the block. Cylinder sleeves will be one of two types:

    a.   *Dry type.* A sleeve fitted into a bored hole in the block with no O-rings or other sealing devices on it. It is sometimes called a *replacement cylinder*.

    b.   *Wet type.* A cylinder sleeve that fits into the block and comes in contact with the coolant water. Since water is allowed to circulate around it, the sleeve must be sealed at the top and bottom. Sealing is accomplished on the top end by fitting the sleeve into a counterbore cut into the block. O-rings made of oil- and water-resistant neoprene (a synthetic) are fitted to the bottom of the sleeve and prevent the coolant water from leaking into the crankcase or oil pan.

4.   *Piston, rings, and connecting rod.* The function of the piston and the rings that are fitted in grooves on the piston is the transmission of pressure from the burning fuel and air to the connecting rod that is connected to the crankshaft. The connecting rod's function is as the name implies: connecting the piston to the crankshaft. Holding the piston and connecting rod together is the piston pin, usually a full floating type (this means that the pin floats in both the piston and the rod).

5.   *Camshaft and timing gears.* The camshaft in a diesel engine operates the intake and exhaust valves, the injectors in some engines and may drive the oil pump and injection pump. The camshaft drive gear is meshed with and is timed to the crankshaft gear on the front or rear of the crankshaft. This drives the camshaft and ensures that the engine valves will stay in time with the crankshaft and pistons.

6.   *Cam followers.* The cam followers (sometimes called lifters) mounted in drilled holes in the block ride on the cam lobes. Inserted into the cam followers are rods or hollow tubes (pushrods) which operate the valves and injectors (no pushrods are used on overhead camshaft engines).

7.   *Cylinder head and valves.* The cylinder head's main function is to provide a cap for the cylinder. In addition, it provides passageways that allows air into the cylinder and exhaust gases to pass out. The ports are opened and closed by poppet valves that fit into guides in the cylinder head.

8.   *Rocker arms and pushrods.* The rocker arms are mounted on a shaft with one end on the valves and the other end on a pushrod. Movement of the pushrod causes the arm to rock on its pivot shaft, hence the name *rocker arm*. Pushrods transmit the rotary camshaft motion into reciprocating (up and down) motion, to activate the rocker arms.

9.   *Oil pan.* A pan-shaped cover that bolts onto the bottom of the block and acts as a reservoir for the engine oil.

10.   *Lubricating oil pump.* Generally a positive-displacement gear pump that delivers a given quantity of oil every revolution. Resistance to flow supplies oil under pressure to the engine.

11.   *Water pump.* A nonpositive-displacement centrifugal pump (a pump that does not deliver a given amount of water every revolution). It aids the flow of coolant water through the engine block and radiator. The pump is generally mounted on the front of the engine block, and is either gear or belt driven from the crankshaft, and connected to the cooling system with rubber hoses.

12.   *Radiator.* A device designed to allow water to flow through it, thereby cooling the water by radiation.

13.   *Oil cooler.* A device used to cool the engine oil during engine operation. The construction of the cooler allows coolant water and engine oil to circulate through the cooler simultaneously without being mixed. Heat is removed by convection between the hotter oil and the engine coolant.

14.   *Flywheel housing.* A round circular housing bolted to the back of the engine that serves as an engine and transmission mount. Enclosed in the flywheel housing is the flywheel.

15.   *Flywheel.* A heavy metal wheel bolted onto the rear of the crankshaft that provides a place to mount the starter ring gear and the transmission clutch. Engine power impulses are absorbed and stored in the heavy metal wheel that is mounted on the rear end of the crankshaft. This flywheel provides inertia or constant rotary motion.

16.   *Torsional vibration damper.* The main function of the vibration damper is to dampen out torsional twisting vibration that occurs when the engine runs. The damper is mounted on the front of the crankshaft.

17.   *Intake manifold.* Bolted to the cylinder head or intake port, the intake manifold provides passageways for the passage of clean air from the air cleaner to the engine.

18.   *Exhaust manifold.* Connected to the engine exhaust outlets, the exhaust manifold provides a means for collecting the exhaust gases and routing them to turbocharger and then the muffler.

19.   *Fuel system.* The fuel system delivers the correct amount of fuel to the engine cylinders at the correct time, depending on the engine load and speed.

20.   *Starter.* An auxiliary motor used to rotate the flywheel and crankshaft for starting the engine. It may be electric, air, or hydraulically powered.

21.   *Alternator.* Used to charge the storage batteries and supply current for vehicle lights and other accessories.

22. *Turbocharger.* An exhaust-driven air pump that supplies air to the engine under pressure. This pressure boost, called *supercharging*, increases the engine's efficiency.

DIESEL ENGINE DESIGNS AND CLASSIFICATIONS

The majority of diesel engine manufacturers lean toward a four-stroke-cycle operating concept, while Detroit Diesel Corporation offers both four- and two-stroke-cycle diesel engines. Detroit Diesel is the largest manufacturer of two-stroke-cycle diesel engines in the world. In the United States, truck and bus diesel engine design since the late 1970s has concentrated on increased power output and reliability; however, the major consideration in the 1990s is for control of engine exhaust emissions to comply with the stringent U.S. EPA (Environmental Protection Agency) exhaust smoke emissions standards while providing lower specific fuel economy. This has resulted in all heavy-duty high-speed diesel truck engines being equipped with turbochargers as a means of achieving desired power outputs, engine responsiveness under load, and acceptable fuel economy. To control exhaust emissions, fuel consumption goals and improved engine life between overhauls, the adoption of electronic fuel injection systems is now well under way on such major North American engines as Caterpillar, Cummins, and Detroit Diesel Corporation products.

All midheavy and heavy-duty high-speed engines employ the DI (direct-injection) open-combustion-chamber design, where the injector sprays fuel directly into the cylinder, with the combustion chamber being formed basically by the shape of the piston crown. The injectors used with all of these engines are of the multihole variety.

For many years the inline six-cylinder configuration diesel engine has been a standard design. Nevertheless, V-type engine configurations have also been solid performers in many well-known engines. V-engine designs reduce both the length and the overall dimensions of a comparable six-cylinder inline engine that would produce the same horsepower characteristics. V-engines are commonly available in all types of applications from V6 through V20. Some manufacturers of V-engines have adopted a range of engines with a standardized bore and stroke range to allow many common parts to be used in both their V- and inline engine configurations. Several examples are Detroit Diesel with its line of 71, 92, and 149 series two-stroke-cycle engines; Caterpillar's 3400, 3500, and 3600 series; Cummins' K series; and Mercedes-Benz with its 400 engine series.

Some of the major features of a typical six-cylinder inline engine for a heavy-duty high-speed electronically controlled unit injector Detroit Diesel series 60 truck engine are illustrated in Figure 1–2. This engine, along with its four-cylinder series 50 model, has an overhead camshaft design, two-piece crosshead pistons, a pulse recovery exhaust manifold, and high-efficiency turbocharger with a ceramic turbine wheel, injector rocker arms with ceramic rollers, and a silicon nitride rocker arm that produces fuel injector spray-in pressures of 28,000 psi or 193,060 kilopascal (kPa). Air-to-air-charge cooling is a standard feature on these engines in on-highway truck applications. Figure 1–3 is a line drawing of a cross-sectional view of the 3406E Caterpillar engine, which also employs an overhead camshaft and electronic unit injectors. These engines, along with the Volvo VE D12, the Isuzu 12-L 6WA1TC, the Deere 10.5 and 12.5L units, and Cummins Apex are inline six-cylinder engines with overhead camshaft design and electronic injector controls, features that make them leaders in their field.

The following list summarizes the general advantages and design features of an inline engine in comparison to a V-engine.

- Many years of successful design experience and manufacture.
- Ease of servicing and repair as well as usually being less expensive to overhaul than a V of the same horsepower.
- Generally ease of accessibility to auxiliary drive items, which can be mounted on the side of the engine block easier than on a V.
- Ease of installation due to a narrower width than a V.
- Engine that can be mounted horizontally or vertically in a bus application, for example.
- Fewer moving parts in a six-cylinder than in a comparable V8 engine of the same power output.
- Manufacturing costs that may be lower than those of a V.
- Ease of crankshaft balancing due to the firing order of the engine.
- Easy to turbocharge, due to the cylinder arrangement and large crankshaft bearing area.
- Good main and camshaft bearing life because of the accessible bearing surface area and space availability.
- Fuel and oil consumption as well as exhaust emissions that are normally lower than those of a comparable V8 engine, due to fewer cylinders in the inline engine.
- A noise level that although not necessarily lower does tend to be so compared with a V8 engine configuration.

Viewed from Any Angle... the Series 60 is a World Class Engine

High Efficiency Turbocharger—*uses a pulse-recovery exhaust manifold that provides increased heat flow energy to the state-of-the-art turbocharger.*

Short Ports—*This unique configuration allows for very short intake and exhaust ports for efficient air flow, low pumping losses and reduced heat transfer.*

Iron Crosshead Pistons—*They allow the top ring to be placed much closer to the top of the piston. This reduces the dead volume above the top ring and improves fuel economy.*

Gasket Eliminator—*reduces engine service time since it is not necessary to get a separate gasket to complete a repair.*

Cylinder Liner, Flanges and Bores—*Plateau honing minimizes piston ring break-in and allows quicker ring seal. Flanges at the liner upper end seat in counterbores in the block deck and project slightly above it to compress the head gasket for a good seal. Cylinder bores feature replaceable, wet-type cylinder liners.*

Isolators—*reduce engine noise.*

Crankshaft, Main and Rod Bearings—*Crankshaft is forged, induction hardened steel for high strength, and features computer positioned oil passages to promote a thick oil film in the highest loaded sections. Large main and rod bearings increase bearing life and tolerance to wear.*

FIGURE 1–2 Major design features of a DDEC II (Detroit Diesel Electronic Controls, second generation) series 60 four-stroke-cycle heavy-duty truck engine employing electronic fuel injection and governing, an overhead camshaft, and AAAC (air-to-air aftercooling). (Courtesy of Detroit Diesel Corporation.)

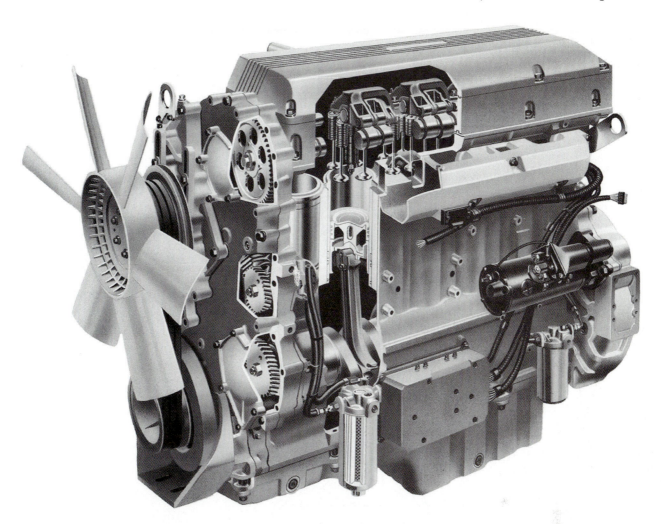

Fluid Weep Hole—*is provided in the unlikely occurrence of an upper seal water leak. It will leak externally instead of internally to the crankcase. This also allows easy identification of a problem before damage can occur.*

Overhead Camshaft—*design eliminates parts, is easy to inspect and service and optimizes intake and exhaust air passages in the cylinder head for easier engine breathing, and minimizes valve train losses.*

Eight Head Bolts per Cylinder—*provide a uniform load on the gasket and liner to reduce stress on the liner flange and block counterbore.*

Strong Cylinder Block—*block is extensively ribbed and contoured for maximum rigidity and sound reduction, without excessive weight.*

Redundant Internal Seals—*provide an extra seal in the event of primary seal malfunction.*

Grade Eight Metric Fasteners—*are stronger than are commonly used on heavy-duty engines, thus improving gasket loads and decreasing likelihood of breaking. Flanged fasteners eliminate washers.*

Generally speaking, the inline engine configuration is cheaper to produce for a given horsepower output. In no way can the inline six-cylinder engine be categorically characterized as better than a V configuration, or vice versa. In North America, however, the trend seems to be away from V8 engines in heavy-duty trucks to the long-used inline six-cylinder four-stroke-cycle direct-injection engine design. Mack Trucks with its E7 series; Caterpillar with its 3406 and 3176, C10, and C12 models; Cummins with its L10, M11, and 14-L series; Detroit Diesel with its series 60; and Volvo with its VE D12 have all chosen to use the inline six-cylinder engine configuration.

All midheavy and heavy-duty high-speed engines employ the direct-injection open-combustion-chamber design, where the injector sprays fuel directly into the cylinder and the combustion chamber is formed basically by the shape of the piston crown. The injectors used with all these engines are of the multi-hole variety.

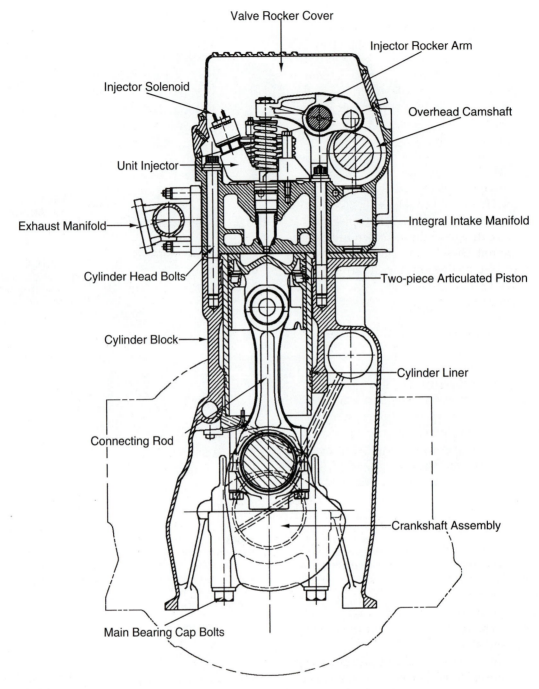

FIGURE 1–3 *Design features of a 3406E Caterpillar heavy-duty truck engine that employs an overhead camshaft, electronically controlled unit injectors and governing, and AACC (air-to-air charge cooling). (Courtesy of Capterpillar, Inc.)*

PISTON DESIGNS

One of the most important components in the engine that has a direct bearing on the combustion process is the actual design of the piston crown and the number and types of piston rings used. With the strict U.S. EPA

exhaust smoke emissions, let's look at some of the more prominent piston and ring shapes now in use in heavy-duty high-speed truck engines.

Many pistons used with four-stroke-cycle diesel engines are manufactured from an aluminum alloy. The exception to this would be those used in DDC's series 60 engine, which uses a pearlitic malleable iron piston material similar to that found in DDC's two-stroke-cycle engines. A one-piece trunk-type piston is used in such well-known engines as Volvo, Mercedes-Benz, Ford, Detroit Diesel's 8.2-L, and some Cummins engines, while in others, such as Detroit Diesel's 71 and 92 two-stroke models and their more recent series 60 four-stroke-cycle model, two-piece crosshead pistons are used. Caterpillar also uses a two-piece articulated piston in their 3176, C10, C12, and 3406E engines, as does Mack in their inline six-cylinder E7 engines. Cummins employs two-piece articulated pistons in its L10, M11, and N 14-L model truck engines. Celect engine models employ articulated pistons that are similar in basic design to those shown in this section for both Detroit Diesel and Caterpillar engines. The heavy-duty 14-L engine employs a ferrous metal piston crown with an aluminum alloy skirt. Smaller model Cummins engines employ an aluminum one-piece trunk piston.

Although the one-piece trunk piston is still used by many major manufacturers of high-speed heavy-duty truck diesel engines, the move not only to higher brake mean effective pressures (BMEPs) on the piston crown to increase horsepower and reduce exhaust emissions, but the need to control lube oil consumption into the combustion chamber more closely, as well as to minimize the escape of pressurized combustion gases into the engine crankcase, has resulted in a number of engine manufacturers choosing to employ a two-piece crosshead or articulated piston design. This piston meets all the design considerations discussed above, but it also minimizes side thrust on the piston as it changes direction at the top of its stroke, particularly during the power stroke, when the force of the expanding gases are greatest. The use of a two-piece piston where the dome or crown of the piston is separate from the skirt allows each piece to act independent of the other. The result is less side thrust to both the piston rings and skirt.

Figure 1–4 illustrates a crosshead piston concept that is used by Detroit Diesel Corporation in its lineup of two- and four-stroke heavy-duty diesel engines. These two-piece pistons are made from pearlitic malleable iron for increased strength. Detroit Diesel was the first manufacturer of high-speed diesel engines to use the crosshead piston concept, which was introduced in the 1970s. Figure 1–5 illustrates the two-piece articulated piston used by Caterpillar in its 10L, 12L, 3176B, and 3406E series inline six-cylinder electronically controlled unit injector engine model. The two-piece articulated piston features a forged steel crown and a forged aluminum skirt. The piston has a three-

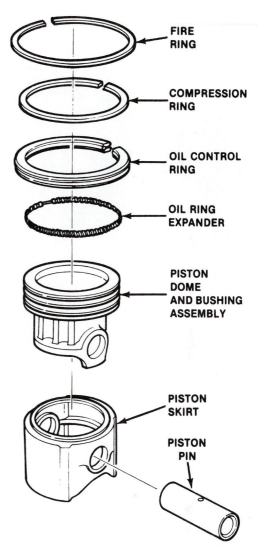

FIGURE 1–4 *Two-piece crosshead piston design used on the DDC series 60 four-stroke cycle engine with a three-ring piston stackup arrangement. Note that the top fire ring is only 3.8 mm (0.150 in.) from the top of the piston crown. (Courtesy of Detroit Diesel Corporation.)*

ring pack with the top ring only 0.200 in. (5 mm) from the top of the crown. Mack employs a two-piece piston similar to that shown for the Caterpillar 3176 engine. Mack has employed this concept since the 1970s. Major advantages of using a two-piece piston are as follows:

1. Engine life and reliability are increased.
2. Running clearances are better controlled, due to less distortion of the skirt.
3. The piston skirt therefore maintains its designed shape, due to less thermal (heat) distortion.
4. Piston ring and piston ring groove wear is re-

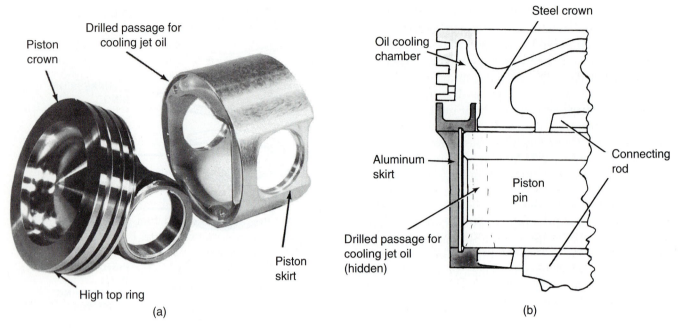

FIGURE 1–5 *(a) Caterpillar 3176, C10, and C12 engine two-piece articulated piston that features a forged steel crown and forged aluminum skirt. A three-ring stackup is used with the top (fire) ring being only 5 mm (0.200 in.) from the top of the piston crown. (b) Cross section of 3176 piston assembly showing the drilled passage for pressurized lube oil flow to the underside of the piston crown. (Courtesy of Caterpillar, Inc.)*

duced as a result of less piston crown motion. Tighter control of piston ring to liner clearances can therefore be maintained, which results in less engine oil seeping into the combustion chamber area. This results in tighter control of exhaust emissions.

5. Since the top compression (fire) ring can be placed much closer to the top of the piston crown with this design, there is less dead airspace between the fire ring and the side of the piston crown. This results in an increase in the effective volume of the combustion chamber, thereby improving combustion efficiency and fuel economy as well as lowering overall exhaust emissions.

6. Increased lubrication and cooling of the piston crown is achieved. For example, on DDC's piston, pressurized engine lube oil is directed up through the rifle-drilled connecting rod and into casting struts within the underside of the piston crown. This results in a "cocktail shaker" action of the lube oil for lower piston crown operating temperatures.

7. Improved piston pin and bearing life, due to the increased piston pin bearing area through the design of the one-piece slipper bearing over a conventional piston pin bore bushing concept.

8. Less bending stress on the piston pin, due to increased bearing area.

One-piece trunk-type aluminum alloy pistons are

used in many midrange and heavy-duty high-speed diesel engines. The cast aluminum alloy piston is used in the 3406B Caterpillar engine, Cummins Band C models, and some models of the 855-in.[3] (14-L) Cummins Big Cam series engines. It is also important to note that aluminum alloy pistons require the use of a cast-in Ni-resist (nickel) insert in the area that supports the top compression ring. Some engines employ integrally cast and bonded iron bands for both compression rings, such as Caterpillar's 3406B engines, resulting in longer wear life and increased piston reuse potential at major overhaul.

Recent advances in aluminum alloy piston technology allow top ring groove reinforcement by applying a high-strength aluminum alloy using either the TIG or MIG welding process, which reduces the overall weight of the piston since a separate cast-in and bond Ni-resist insert is not required. Without this stronger material, the aluminum alloy piston would be unable to stand up to the pressures and temperatures developed during the combustion phase of operation.

Other major features of heavy-duty engines such as those used in class 8 trucks is that they employ under-piston oil cooling. Oil under pressure from the engine lubricating system is directed through piston cooling oil nozzles located in the block, such as those used by Caterpillar, Cummins, and Mack, or by rifle-drilled connecting rods such as those found in DDC's two-stroke-cycle series engines and four-stroke-cycle series 50 and 60 engines. The use of cooling oil is necessary due to the high BMEP values created throughout the engine's power stroke; otherwise, piston overheating and subsequent failure would result.

PISTON RINGS

Prior to 1988, many heavy-duty high-speed diesel truck engines employed a top compression ring on the piston that was positioned between 1/2 and 3/4 in. (12.7 to 19 mm) below the crown. These engines were designed to develop maximum firing pressures of approximately 1800 psi (12,411 kPa). However, post-1988 heavy-duty truck engines are now developing firing pressures as high as 2300 psi (15,858 kPa). These higher firing pressures are a result of engine design changes to meet the stringent U.S. EPA exhaust smoke emissions standards. Consequently, the top compression, or fire ring as it is more commonly referred to, on post-1988 engines is located much closer to the top of the piston crown, to minimize the dead airspace that previously existed above the top ring. For example, Caterpillar's 3176 engine has its top piston ring only 0.200 in. (5 mm) from the top of the piston crown and DDC's series 60 top ring is only 0.150 in. (3.8 mm) from the top of the piston. This dimension is typical of what is found on most heavy-duty high-speed direct-injected diesel engines today.

The number of piston rings contained on the piston will vary between three and four in most high-speed heavy-duty diesel engines. When the top compression ring is placed very close to the top of the piston crown, it is commonly referred to as a *fire ring* since, in effect, it is subjected to the flames generated during the combustion cycle. Improvements in piston ring materials and design have allowed many engines to reduce their ring pack from four rings to three, resulting in less friction (Figure 1–6). Most fire rings use a *keystone* design, which is a ring with its sides tapered approximately 15°. In addition, the face of the ring is usually barrel shaped against the liner surface to provide a uniform coating of oil on the cylinder liner wall to improve ring life. The material used on the fire ring face can include conventional electroplated or inlaid chrome with no groove being used, such as you might find on some earlier design rings. Other ring facings can include plasma-sprayed complex chromium irons and molybdenum for severe-duty applications. Another advantage of the barrel-shaped ring is that it reduces overall friction, due to there being less overall surface contact with the liner, and results in greater resistance to liner scuffing even under severe operating conditions. Less friction also results in improved engine fuel economy. The second and third compression rings may be either keystone shaped or rectangular and are also chrome plated in many instances. Improvements in piston ring manufacturing processes have resulted in a new method of prestressing the rings to provide a more uniform and complete stress-relief feature. Piston rings have a free diameter greater than that of the cylinder bore; therefore, when they are compressed in the cylinder, they are placed under stress. With manufacturing improvements that allow a much closer fit to the cylinder liner shape, lower-tension oil ring expanders can be used not only to reduce friction but also to provide a more uniform oil film, resulting in improved fuel economy as well as longer cylinder component life. Figure 1–6 illustrates the three-ring piston arrangement used by DDC on their two-piece piston used in the four-stroke-cycle series 60 heavy-duty engine.

Piston rings play a major part in sealing the combustion gases within the cylinder as well as limiting

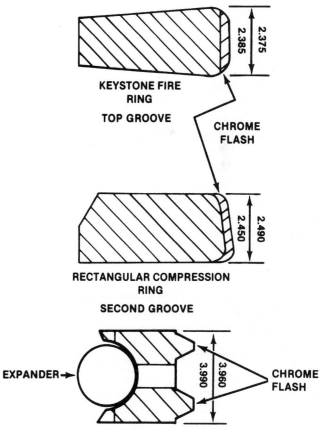

FIGURE 1–6 *Typical arrangement of a three-ring piston stackup for a heavy-duty series 60 truck direct injection diesel engine that uses prestressed rings in both the top fire ring and the compression ring (second groove). (Courtesy of Detroit Diesel Corporation.)*

the amount of engine lube oil that will seep past the rings and be burned within the combustion chamber. Much research and development continues in an effort to produce a piston ring pack that will meet all the conditions desired in heavy-duty high-speed engines. Although major improvements have been made to engine components to meet the ever-more-stringent EPA exhaust emissions levels, the piston rings' ability to seal against lube oil does much to improve the overall exhaust emissions emanating from the combustion process. One way in which engine and lube oil manufacturers have coordinated their efforts is in the recommendation that high-speed heavy-duty truck engines use 15W-40 engine oils rather than the long used SAE 30 oils. Tests have shown conclusively that the use of a 15W-40 engine oil can provide up to a 30% lower engine oil consumption rate. In addition, the use of 1% ash oils can further reduce oil consumption by as much as 35% over 1.5% ash-type oils.

VALVES

Four-valve cylinder heads are commonly found in all class 8 engines, with two intake and two exhaust valves being used on four-stroke-cycle models, while DDC's two-stroke-cycle engines employ four exhaust valves per cylinder on their 71 and 92 series models. The use of four valve heads improves the engine's volumetric efficiency or ability to breathe more easily. This results in a better charge of air to the cylinder as well as allowing smoother flow out of the exhaust system. Many current heavy-duty high-speed truck engines employ cross-flow cylinder heads, where the inlet and exhaust manifolds are located on opposite sides of the engine. This feature improves the flow of air and exhaust gases into and out of the cylinder. One unique configuration now in use is that employed by DDC in their series 60 four-stroke engine, known as *parallel port configuration*. Figure 1–7 illustrates this design concept. Using four valves per cylinder (two intake and two exhaust), the four valves per cylinder are located 90° from the setup used on traditional engines. The parallel port configuration allows for very short, unobstructed intake and exhaust ports for more efficient airflow, lower pumping losses, and reduced heat transfer, thereby allowing the engine to breathe more freely and to run cooler under load.

Another popular valve design concept, used by Caterpillar on their 3176 model engine, is shown in Figure 1–8. In this design the intake and exhaust ports are located on one side of the cylinder head to form what is commonly referred to as a *uniflow design*. The quiescent intake ports of adjacent cylinders are siamesed to one of three large plenums and there are

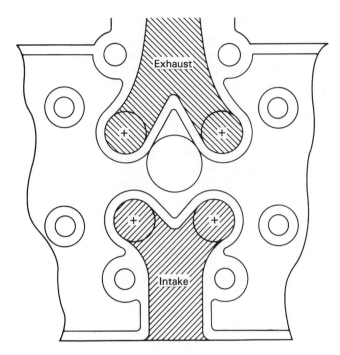

FIGURE 1–7 Unique design of the crossflow intake and exhaust valve arrangement used on DDC's series 60 engine. (Courtesy of Detroit Diesel Corporation.)

individual exhaust ports for each cylinder. The four-valve-per-cylinder arrangement is skewed to shorten the exhaust port length, which reduces heat rejection and minimizes the flow interference between the exhaust valves in each port.

AFTERCOOLING

Most heavy-duty high-speed diesel truck engines today are designed from their inception to accept not only turbocharging, but also to offer some form of aftercooling. Initially, turbocharging was used to increase the power output of a given-displacement engine design; however, in these days of stringent exhaust emission legislation, turbocharging is used to improve combustion efficiency and lower the fuel consumption and engine noise level; in addition, the excess air supply from turbocharging can be used to clean or water down the exhaust gases, enabling easier control of exhaust smoke emission levels. Consequently, both tuned intake and exhaust system manifolds are now being used to improve the overall performance of heavy-duty high-speed diesel truck and bus engines. Air-to-air aftercooling provides a 3 to 5% improvement in fuel economy and reduced exhaust emissions.

Aftercooling, or *charge air cooling* as it is commonly called, is the process of lowering the pressur-

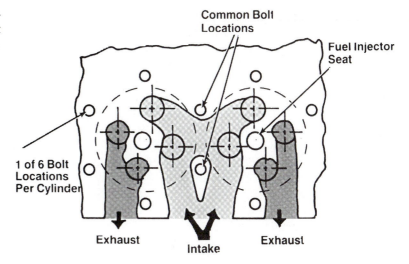

FIGURE 1–8 *Intake and exhaust valve airflow arrangement used on the 3176 Cat engine. (Courtesy of Caterpillar, Inc.)*

Common Bolt Locations

Fuel Injector Seat

1 of 6 Bolt Locations Per Cylinder

Exhaust   Intake   Exhaust

ized air charge, leaving the outlet side of the turbocharger to provide a more dense air charge. Cooler pressurized air supplied to the engine results not only in greater volumetric efficiency (ability to inhale and retain the oxygen charge) in the cylinder, but in a more thermally efficient engine (better fuel economy), or the ability of the engine to increase its power output.

In the most prominently used system, shown in Figure 1–9, which is the AAAC (air-to-air aftercooling) design, turbocharger air pressure is routed through a cooler core mounted in front of the radiator where the ram-air effect of the wind as the vehicle moves along the highway is capable of lowering the turbo air from 300°F (149°C) to approximately 110°F (43°C), resulting

in the greatest reduction in turbocharger air temperature prior to it entering the intake manifold on a four-stroke-cycle engine, or the blower on a Detroit Diesel two-stroke-cycle engine.

The term *aftercooling* is also referred to as *intercooling,* and since the combustion process starts at a lower temperature, both peak temperatures and peak pressures are reduced. This results in an increase in engine power output without increasing the thermal and mechanical loads on the engine as well as lowering the emitted smoke levels from the engine, specifically the reduction of nitrogen oxides, which is the element that causes smog to form in the atmosphere as a yellowish-brown haze.

FIGURE 1–9 *Basic design concept of an AAAC (air-to-air aftercooled) engine. (Courtesy of Detroit Diesel Corporation.)*

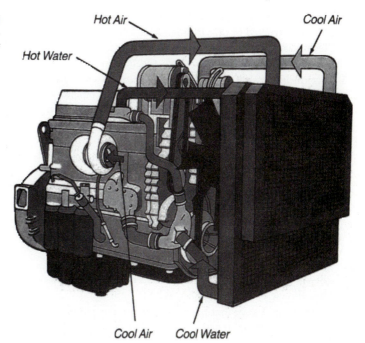

Hot Air

Cool Air

Hot Water

Cool Air   Cool Water

As we head into the late 1990s, all major truck diesel engine manufacturers are switching over to an electronically controlled unit injector or unit pump system. The major reason for this is that inline pump injection systems are incapable of producing high-enough injection pressures to allow the combustion phase to emit a minimum amount of exhaust pollutants. Detroit Diesel Corporation was the first major engine manufacturer to release electronically controlled fuel injection in 1985; Caterpillar followed suit in 1987 and Cummins in 1989. Robert Bosch Corporation now uses electronically controlled injection so that engine users will be able to meet the strict exhaust emissions regulations.

SUMMARY

Within this chapter we have provided general information for you to use to begin your study of the diesel engine: basic facts, a background history of the compression ignition engine, a concept of the major parts required and their function, and the purpose of an aftercooling system. Other chapters will supply you with more details and give you specific knowledge of the various engine systems.

SELF-TEST QUESTIONS

1. Technician A says that the concept of the internal combustion engine was developed in 1794 by a person named Street. Technician B says that Rudolf Diesel, in concert with Sadi Carnot, developed this engine in 1824. Who is right?

2. The four-stroke-cycle internal combustion engine was first constructed in 1876 by Nicholaus Otto according to technician A. Technician B says that it was developed by Rudolf Diesel in 1895. Who is right?

3. Technician A says that the first practical diesel engine was developed in 1927 by Robert Bosch. Technician B says that a patent was issued in 1892 for a compression ignition engine to Rudolf Diesel, who later developed a running engine in 1895. Who is right?

4. Technician A says that diesel engines did not actually compete successfully with gasoline engines until Robert Bosch invented and produced the compact fuel injection system in 1927. Technician B says that it was the early 1950s before Bosch developed the compact fuel system. Who is correct?

5. Technician A says that the first rotary/distributor diesel fuel injection pump was developed by Robert Bosch in the early 1950s. Technician B says that it was developed by Vernon Roosa. Who is right?

6. Technician A says that the term *compression ignition engine* is used in reference to the gasoline engine. Technician B says that it is related solely to the diesel combustion system. Who understands this term best?

7. Technician A says that diesel fuel contains a higher heat value in Btu per gallon or liter than that of gasoline. Technician B says that gasoline contains much more heat. Which technician knows his theory best?

8. Technician A says that in a diesel engine, only air is inhaled during the intake stroke. Technician B says that both air and diesel fuel must be taken into the cylinder on the intake stroke. Which technician best understands the basic theory of operation?

9. Technician A says that to initiate combustion in a diesel engine, a hot glow plug must be used. Technician B says that the fuel is ignited by the heat of the compressed air. Which technician is correct?

10. Technician A says that the majority of diesel engines now in use employ a direct-injection principle. Technician B says that a precombustion chamber with a glow plug is more common. Who is right?

11. Technician A says that current heavy-duty high-speed diesel engines used in trucks employ turbochargers, air-to-air-charge-cooling, and electronically controlled injection systems. Technician B says that only high-performance gasoline engines use these features. Which technician is correct?

12. Technician A says that current heavy-duty high-speed diesel engines now employ two-piece piston assemblies, often referred to as either crosshead or articulated in design. Technician B says that only large-bore slow-speed diesel engines use this design concept. Which technician is correct?

13. Technician A says that Detroit Diesel Corporation was the first major engine OEM to offer crosshead pistons in their line of diesel engines. Technician B says that Caterpillar was the first major OEM to offer two-piece pistons. Who is correct?

14. Technician A says that *fire ring* is a term used to indicate the bottom compression ring on a piston. Technician B says that the fire ring is the top compression ring on the piston assembly. Who is right?

15. Technician A says that a one-piece piston assembly is commonly referred to as an articulated design. Technician B says that it is known as a trunk-type piston. Who is right?

16. Technician A says that all diesel pistons are manufactured from an aluminum alloy. Technician B says that some pistons are aluminum, while others employ steel crowns and alloy skirts. Which technician knows the theory best?

17. Technician A says that typical firing pressures in current heavy-duty high-speed diesel engines range between 1800 and 2300 psi (12,411 and 15,858 kPa). This figure is far too high according to technician B, who believes that this would destroy the engine. Is technician A or B correct?

18. Technician A says that in a crossflow cylinder head valve arrangement the intake and exhaust valves are on opposite sides of the head. Technician B says that both the intake and exhaust manifolds are on the same side of the head. Which technician is correct?

19. Technician A says that the term *aftercooling* refers to a system used to reduce the temperature of the air on a naturally aspirated engine. Technician B says that an aftercooler is used only on turbocharged engines to reduce the temperature of the air entering the cylinder. Which technician knows the theory best?

20. Technician A says that typical engine full-load compressed air temperatures leaving the outlet side of the turbocharger are close to 300°F (149°C). Technician B says that they would be closer to 900°F (482°C) and that is why an aftercooler is required. Which technician is correct?

21. Technician A says that NO_x (nitrogen oxides) emitted from internal combustion engines cause smog to form in the atmosphere. Technician B disagrees, saying that it is carbon monoxide that causes smog. Which technician is correct?

Diesel Engine Operating Fundamentals

OVERVIEW

In this chapter we discuss the operating fundamentals of two- and four-stroke-cycle diesel engines. This discussion will provide you with a solid foundation on which to pursue the other engineering characteristics relative to the diesel engine. Direct- and indirect-injection designs are described along with the characteristics and formulas for such concepts as horsepower, torque, piston speed, brake mean effective pressure, thermal efficiency, volumetric efficiency, mechanical efficiency, work, power, and energy.

DIESEL ENGINE CLASSIFICATIONS

Diesel engines can be classified by two major characteristics: their operating cycle design and the type of combustion chamber they employ. By this we simply mean that the engine can operate on either the two- or four-stroke-cycle design. In addition, either one of these types of engine can be designed to operate on what is commonly referred to as the DI (direct-injection) open-combustion-chamber concept, or alternatively, on the IDI (indirect-injection) closed-combustion-chamber design. All heavy-duty high-speed diesel engines now in use operate on the direct injection principle. Figure 2–1 briefly illustrates the difference between DI and IDI combustion chamber design; combustion chambers are discussed in more detail in Chapter 4.

An understanding of the operation of two- and four-stroke-cycle diesel engines will facilitate your efforts when troubleshooting engines and fuel systems. The operating characteristics of each type of design

will exhibit problems common only to that style of engine. The majority of high-speed diesel engines manufactured today are of the four-stroke-cycle design, so we begin with a study of its basic operating cycle. The fundamental operation of both four-stroke-cycle gasoline and diesel engines is the same: they require two complete revolutions of the engine crankshaft, or 720°, to complete the four piston strokes involved in one complete cycle of events.

FOUR-STROKE-CYCLE OPERATION

There are two major differences between a gasoline and a diesel engine:

1. A diesel engine requires a much higher compression ratio, because with no spark plug to initiate combustion, the heat generated by compressing the air in the cylinder is what causes the high-pressure injected diesel fuel to ignite.

2. On the intake stroke of a diesel engine, only air is supplied to the cylinder, whether the engine is naturally aspirated or turbocharged. In a gasoline engine a mixture of air and gasoline is taken into the cylinder on the intake stroke and then compressed. A spark plug then initiates combustion of this premixed fuel charge.

The four piston strokes in a four-stroke-cycle diesel engine are commonly known as (1) the intake stroke, (2) the compression stroke, (3) the power or expansion stroke, and (4) the exhaust stroke. Figure 2–2 illustrates the four piston strokes in schematic form in a direct-injection engine. Next, we consider the sequence of events involved in one complete cycle of operation of the four-stroke-cycle engine.

Intake Stroke
During the intake stroke, the exhaust valves are closed but the inlet valves are open; therefore, the down-

Direct injection (a) defines the category where the fuel is injected directly into the combustion chamber volume formed between the cylinder head and the top of the piston. Mixing is achieved by using a multi-hole fuel injection nozzle and/or causing the intake air to swirl. High injection pressures are required (18,000–30,000 psi) (124110–206850 kPa) for fine atomization which promotes good contact between air and fuel.

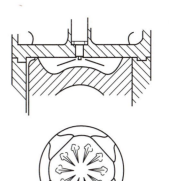

(a)

Indirect Injection (b) occurs where fuel is injected into a pre-chamber which communicates with the cylinder through a narrow passage. During the compression stroke, air enters the pre-chamber, which is usually about one half of the total compression volume. Mixing is achieved by spraying fuel into the turbulent air in the pre-chamber (generally with a single-hole pintle nozzle) where ignition occurs. The burning air-fuel mixture then enters the cylinder where it mixes with the remaining air to complete the combustion. This chamber has a small throat area so that inflow and exit velocities are high. Low injection pressures (5000–14,000 psi) (34475–96530 kPa) are used and the chamber is not as sensitive to the degree of fuel atomization.

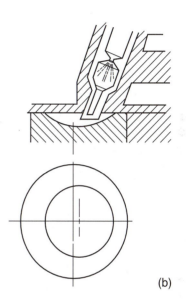

(b)

FIGURE 2–1   *Principles of DI (direct-injection) and IDI (indirect-injection) combustion chamber designs. [Reprinted with permission from Chevron Research and Technology Company, a division of Chevron U.S.A. Inc.; copyright Chevron Research Company, 1995.]*

ward-moving piston induces a flow of air into the cylinder. This air pressure will be less than atmospheric on a naturally aspirated engine, whereas on a turbocharged or blower-equipped engine, this air pressure will be higher than atmospheric. Basically, the intake stroke accounts for 180° of piston movement, which is one-half of a crankshaft revolution. During this time the piston has completed one complete stroke down the length of the cylinder. The weight or percentage of air that is retained in the cylinder during this time is known as volumetric efficiency (VE). In most naturally aspirated engines that rely only on piston movement to inhale air, VE is between 85 and 90% of atmospheric pressure. In turbocharged or gear-driven blower engines, the VE is always greater than atmospheric or 100%; therefore, VE val-

ues between 120 and 200% are common on these engines. The power output of any engine depends on the cylinder air charge at the end of the intake stroke. The engine crankshaft and flywheel have rotated through approximately 180°.

Compression Stroke
During the compression stroke, both the intake and exhaust valves are closed as the piston moves up the cylinder. The upward-moving piston causes the trapped air to be placed under compression to approximately 450 to 550 psi (3103 to 3792 kPa) and 1000 to 1200°F (538 to 649°C) as a mean average. Both pressures and temperatures vary based on the actual engine design and compression ratio. Cylinder compression pressures and temperatures are affected by the

4 CYCLE

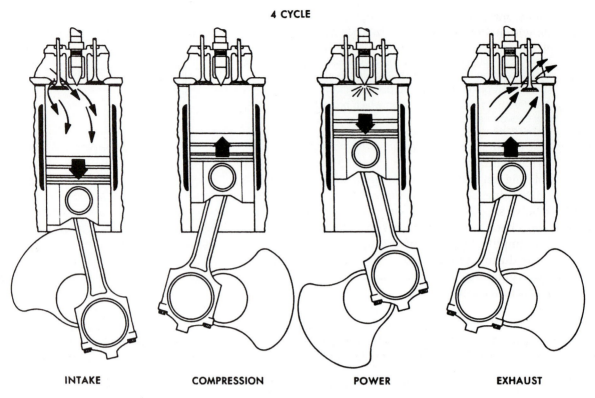

| INTAKE | COMPRESSION | POWER | EXHAUST |

FIGURE 2–2 Sequence of individual piston and valve events for a four-stroke-cycle diesel engine. (Courtesy of Detroit Diesel Corporation.)

ambient air temperature, turbocharger boost pressure, engine compression ratio, valve timing, and engine speed and load. Consequently, some engines may exhibit compression pressures into the 600s, with their air temperature being at the high end of the figures quoted above. Just before the piston reaches the top of the cylinder, high-pressure diesel fuel is injected into this hot air mass and fuel is ignited, causing a substantial pressure and temperature rise within the combustion chamber. Fuel is injected continually to maintain this high pressure, with the number of degrees of injection being related to engine load and speed as well as to the specific model and type of engine being used. Once again the piston has completed approximately 180° of crankshaft rotation. Added to the crankshaft rotation from the intake stroke, the engine crankshaft and the flywheel have now rotated through approximately 360° or one full turn of rotation within the cycle of events.

Power or Expansion Stroke
The combustion chamber of the cylinder is formed between the space that exists between the top of the piston (crown) and the cylinder head. The pressure released by the burning fuel in the combustion chamber forces the piston down the cylinder. The peak cylinder

firing pressures on today's high-speed heavy-duty truck engines can range between 1800 and 2300 psi (12,411 to 15,856 kPa), with temperatures between 3000 and 4000°F (1649 to 2204°C) for very short time periods. This motion is transferred through the piston, the piston pin, and the connecting rod to the engine crankshaft and flywheel. Therefore, the straight-line motion of the piston is converted to rotary motion at the crankshaft and flywheel from the connecting rod. The length of the power stroke is controlled by how long the exhaust valves remain closed. Basically, the piston has moved down the cylinder from the top to the bottom and in so doing traveled through approximately 180°. Therefore, added to the already completed intake and the compression strokes, the crankshaft and flywheel have rotated through approximately 540° of the cycle of events.

Exhaust Stroke
The engine camshaft has now opened the cylinder exhaust valves; therefore, the exhaust gases, which are at a higher pressure than atmospheric, will start to flow out of the open exhaust valves. The upward-moving piston will positively displace these burned gases out of the cylinder as it moves from the bottom of its stroke to the top. This involves another 180° of crank-

shaft and flywheel rotation, which will complete the cycle of events within 720°, or two complete revolutions. Four piston strokes were involved to achieve one power stroke from this individual cylinder. The sequence of events will be repeated once again.

Valve Timing

During the four-stroke cycle of events just described, the opening and closing of the intake and exhaust valves are accomplished by the action of the gear-driven and rotating engine camshaft. Each engine manufacturer determines during the design phase just how long each valve should remain open to obtain the desired operating characteristics from that specific engine model. One simplified example of the sequence of events that occurs during a four-stroke-cycle engine's operation for one cylinder of a turbocharged engine is shown in a basic schematic in Figure 2–3.

NOTE The valve timing diagram shown in Figure 2–3 represents 720° of crankshaft rotation. For simplicity, two complete circles have been superimposed on one another.

To ensure complete scavenging of all the exhaust gases from the cylinder at the end of the exhaust stroke and prior to the start of the intake stroke, the engine manufacturer actually has the camshaft open the intake valve before the upward-moving piston has completed its exhaust movement. The action of the burned gases flowing out of the exhaust valve ports allows a ram-air effect to occur once the intake valve is opened. This ensures complete removal of the exhaust gases. When the piston has reached TDC (top dead center) on its exhaust stroke and the piston starts to move down on its intake stroke, the exhaust valves remain open to ensure complete scavenging of any remaining exhaust gases caused by the inrushing air through the intake valve ports. The exhaust valves are closed a number of degrees ATDC (after top dead center) by the camshaft lobe action. The fact that the intake valves are opened before the piston reaches TDC on its exhaust stroke and the exhaust valves do not close until the piston is moving down on its intake stroke creates a condition known as *positive valve overlap*, which simply means that both the intake and exhaust valves are open at the same time for a specified number of crankshaft rotation degrees. For example, if the intake valves open 16° BTDC (before top dead center) and the exhaust valves

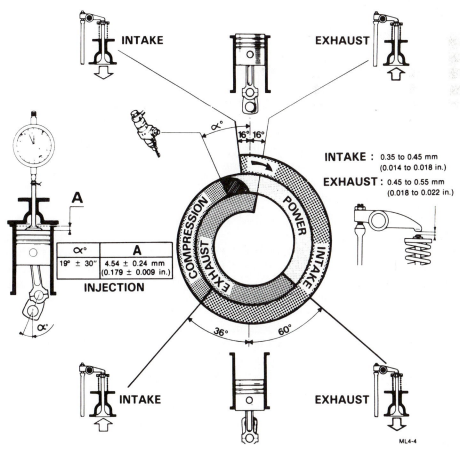

FIGURE 2–3 *Typical four-stroke-cycle diesel engine polar valve timing diagram showing the relative piston strokes, intake, compression, power, and exhaust. Specific degrees are also shown for the duration of each stroke as well as the actual start of fuel injection BTDC (before top dead center). (Courtesy of Mack Trucks, Inc.)*

INTAKE   EXHAUST

INTAKE : 0.35 to 0.45 mm
(0.014 to 0.018 in.)

EXHAUST : 0.45 to 0.55 mm
(0.018 to 0.022 in.)

16° 16°

α°	A
19° ± 30"	4.54 ± 0.24 mm (0.179 ± 0.009 in.)

INJECTION

36°   60°

INTAKE   EXHAUST

ML4-4

do not close until 16° ATDC, the valve overlap condition is said to be 32°.

The downward-moving piston would reach BDC and start its upward stroke for the compression cycle. However, note in Figure 2–3 that the intake valves do not close until a number of degrees ABDC (after bottom dead center). This ensures that a full charge of air will be retained in the cylinder. Remember that the greater the air retained at the start of the compression stroke, the greater the engine's volumetric efficiency and power output capability. Simply put, VE is the difference in the weight of air contained in the cylinder with the piston at BDC with the engine stopped versus what it would be with the piston at BDC with the engine running.

The compression stroke begins only when the intake valves close (exhaust valves are already closed). Fuel is injected BTDC by the fuel injector or nozzle, depending on the type of fuel injection system used. Again, the start of fuel injection is determined by the engine manufacturer, based on the load and speed requirements of the engine. Fuel injection will begin earlier (farther away from TDC) with an increase in speed and load, whereas it will begin later (closer to TDC) under low speed and load conditions.

When the piston is forced down the cylinder by the pressure of the expanding and burning gases (air and fuel), the power stroke will continue until such times as the engine camshaft opens the exhaust valves. In the simplified diagrams shown in Figures 2–2 and 2–3, the exhaust valves open BBDC (before bottom dead center) to allow the burned gases to start moving out and through the exhaust ports, exhaust manifold, exhaust piping, and muffler. When the piston turns at BDC and starts to come back up the cylinder, it will positively expel all of the burned exhaust gases from the cylinder. As the piston approaches TDC, the camshaft once again opens the intake valves for the cylinder, and the sequence of events is repeated over again.

Figure 2–3 illustrates one example of the duration of degrees involved in each piston stroke of a typical four-stroke-cycle Mack MIDS06.20.30 Midliner truck diesel engine. Such a diagram is commonly referred to as a *polar valve timing diagram,* since both TDC and BDC are always shown. The positions of both TDC and BDC are similar to that of the north and south poles on a globe of the earth, hence the technical term *polar valve timing.* Keep in mind that the actual number of degrees varies between engine makes and models. Typical stroke degrees for a high-speed diesel engine may include the following four conditions:

1. *Intake stroke.* Valves open at 16° BTDC and close at 36° ABDC; total duration is 232° of crankshaft rotation.
2. *Power stroke.* Starts at TDC and continues until the exhaust valves open at 60° BBDC; total duration is 120°.
3. *Compression stroke.* Occurs when the intake valves close at 36° ABDC until TDC; total duration is 144°.
4. *Exhaust stroke.* Values open at 60° BBDC and close at 16° ATDC; total duration is 256° of crankshaft rotation.

Piston Positions

The sequence of events just described represented the cycle of events in one cylinder of a multicylinder engine. In a six-cylinder four-stroke-cycle engine application, for example, six cylinders are in various stages of events while the engine is running. The technician must understand what one cylinder is doing in relation to another at any given position of the crankshaft, because often when timing an injection pump to the engine or when adjusting exhaust valves or timing unit injectors, a specific sequence of adjustment must be followed. Knowing the firing order of the engine and what piston/cylinder is on what stroke can save you a lot of time when performing timing and valve adjustments. We mentioned earlier that the sequence of one cycle occurs within two complete revolutions of the crankshaft, or 720° of rotation of the engine. Therefore, in a six-cylinder four-stroke-cycle engine each piston would be 120° apart in the firing stroke. Simply put, we would have six power strokes occurring within two crankshaft revolutions on a six-cylinder engine.

To demonstrate such an example, refer to Figure 2-4, which simplifies the complete cycle of events and where each piston would be and on what stroke when piston 1 is at TDC starting its power stroke. For simplicity we have shown the 720° of crankshaft rotation in two individual circles as well as in one sketch that shows both circles superimposed on top of one another, which is the commonly accepted method in the industry. The example shows a firing order of 1–5–3–6–2–4 for an engine that rotates CW (clockwise) when viewed from the front.

TWO-STROKE-CYCLE OPERATION

The largest manufacturer of two-stroke-cycle high-speed heavy-duty diesel engines in the world is Detroit Diesel, owned by Roger Penske. Although there are two-stroke-cycle engines that do not employ

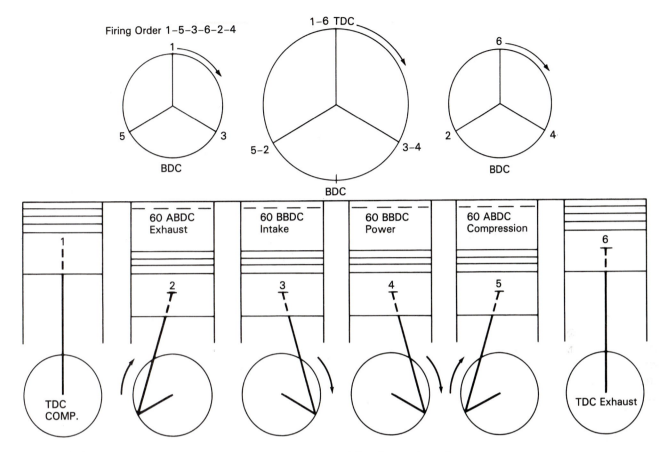

FIGURE 2–4 *Relative piston firing positions for a six-cylinder inline four-stroke-cycle engine throughout 720° of crankshaft rotation; firing order is 1–5–3–6–2–4.*

valves but operate on ports only, Detroit Diesel two-stroke-cycle engines employ a set of intake ports located around the center of the cylinder liner, with conventionally operated pushrod-type exhaust valves at the top of each cylinder. The operation of the two-stroke-cycle engine is illustrated in Figure 2-5, which depicts the layout of a V-configuration engine. The only difference between the V and inline two-stroke Detroit Diesel engines is in the basic cylinder arrangement.

In a four-stroke-cycle engine, 720 crankshaft degrees or two complete revolutions, plus four piston movements, are required to complete the intake, compression, power, and exhaust strokes. On a two-stroke-cycle engine, this sequence of events is completed in only one complete turn of the crankshaft, or 360° of rotation involving only two piston movements. This is accomplished basically by eliminating the separate intake and exhaust strokes, which are a necessary part of four-stroke-cycle operation. During the intake and exhaust piston movements of the four-stroke cycle, the engine basically acts as an air pump by drawing air in and pumping burned exhaust gases out.

To achieve the elimination of these two specific strokes in the two-cycle engine requires the use of a gear-driven, positive-displacement blower assembly, commonly known as a Roots-type blower. This blower supplies the airflow necessary for several actions:

- Scavenging of exhaust gases from the cylinder.
- Cooling of internal engine components, such as the cylinder liner, the piston, and exhaust valves. Approximately 30% of the engine cooling is achieved by airflow from the blower and turbocharger.
- Combustion purposes.
- Crankcase ventilation by controlled leakage of air past the oil control rings when the piston is at TDC.

Most models of Detroit Diesel two-stroke-cycle engines are equipped with both a gear-driven blower and an exhaust-gas-driven turbocharger. The blower supplies a positive displacement of air, which is required at idle and light-load operation since the turbocharger does not receive a high enough exhaust gas

FIGURE 2–5 Two-stroke-cycle diesel engine principle of operation. (Courtesy of Detroit Diesel Corporation.)

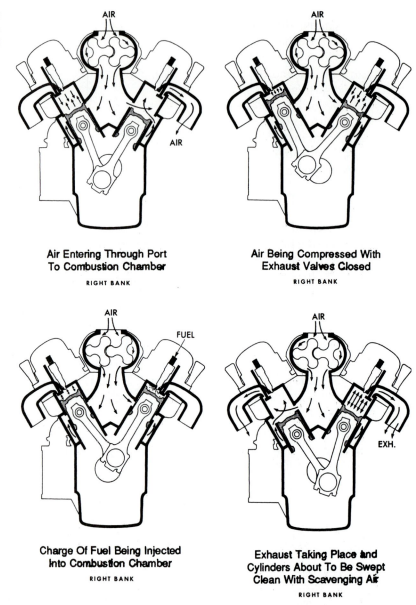

Air Entering Through Port To Combustion Chamber

RIGHT BANK

Air Being Compressed With Exhaust Valves Closed

RIGHT BANK

Charge Of Fuel Being Injected Into Combustion Chamber

RIGHT BANK

Exhaust Taking Place and Cylinders About To Be Swept Clean With Scavenging Air

RIGHT BANK

pressure/flow to cause it to supply sufficient air to the engine. The blower is capable of producing approximately 4 to 7 psi (27 to 48 kPa) throughout the engine speed range. Under heavy loads the turbocharger boost will increase and supply between approximately 40 and 50 in. of mercury (in. Hg) or between 20 and 25 psi (140 to 172 kPa) to the intake ports in the cylinder liners. When the engine is operating under load, a bypass valve built into the gear-driven blower end plate opens and allows the air pressure on both sides of the blower (inlet and outlet) to equalize. In this way the horsepower required to drive the blower is reduced, and basically the airflow is being supplied by the exhaust-gas-driven turbocharger.

Two-stroke-cycle Detroit Diesel engines are equipped with exhaust valves only, with four per cylinder being used for better scavenging purposes. The cylinder liner is arranged so that it has a series of ports cast and machined around the liner circumference approximately halfway down its length. These ports act basically as intake valves.

The engine block is designed so that all liners are surrounded by an *air box* that runs the length of the block. The air box is somewhat like a plenum chamber, where the blower air is pumped into to ensure that there will always be an adequate volume for the four functions listed. Any time that a piston in a cylinder has uncovered the liner ports, the air box pressure is free to flow into and through a cylinder. The operational events are described next.

Scavenging

During scavenging the liner ports are uncovered by the piston and the exhaust valves are open. The angled ports in the liner provides a unidirectional flow of pressurized air into and through the cylinder to scavenge the exhaust gases through the open exhaust valves. This action also cools the internal components, such as the piston, liner, and valves, with approximately 30% of engine cooling provided by this airflow. This leaves the cylinder full of clean, cool fresh air for combustion purposes when the piston covers the liner ports.

Compression

Compression begins when the piston moves up from BDC and covers the previously open liner intake ports. The exhaust valves are timed to close a few degrees after this occurs, to ensure positive scavenging along with a positive charge of fresh air for combustion purposes.

Power

The initial start of fuel injection varies between series of engines and the year of manufacture; however, generally speaking, this is between 12 and 15° BTDC, with the engine running at an idle speed between 500 and 600 rpm. Advancement of injection occurs automatically through throttle movement via a helical cut plunger in non-DDEC-equipped engines, or electronically in DDEC (Detroit Diesel Electronic Control) systems as the engine speed is increased.

When the unit injector sprays fuel into the combustion chamber, there is a small delay before ignition occurs; then the intense heat generated by combustion of the fuel increases both the temperature and pressure of the air/fuel charge. Injection continues for a number of degrees and the resultant force of the high-pressure gases drives the piston down the cylinder on its power stroke. The length of the power stroke in Detroit Diesel two-stroke-cycle engines will vary slightly, but at 90 to 95° ATDC, the exhaust valves will start to open. Compare this to a power stroke of between 120 and 140° on a four-stroke-cycle engine. But although the power stroke is shorter on the two-cycle engine, there are twice as many of them. When the piston is at TDC, a regulated amount of air box pressure is designed to leak past the oil control ring drain holes of the piston to ensure positive crankcase ventilation.

Exhaust

Exhaust occurs when the exhaust valves start to open by camshaft and rocker arm action. The power stroke, therefore, effectively ends at this point, as the burned gases escape into the exhaust manifold either to drive a turbocharger or to flow freely to a muffler. The exhaust valves have to open before the piston uncovers the liner ports; otherwise, the higher pressure of the exhaust gases would blow back into the air box against the much lower blower pressure.

Once the piston crown uncovers the liner ports, usually about 60° BBDC, the air box pressure is higher than the exhaust pressure and scavenging begins again. This continues until the piston has reached BDC and starts back up in the cylinder and ends when the piston has again recovered the liner ports to start the compression stroke once more.

Therefore, every upstroke of the piston in a two-stroke-cycle engine is basically a compression stroke, and every downstroke is a power stroke. The intake and exhaust events occur only during the time that the exhaust valves and liner ports are open. Scavenge blowthrough (liner ports open) takes place through approximately 120° of crankshaft rotation, although keep in mind that the exhaust valves open at about 90 to 95° ATDC and close several degrees after the piston has recovered the liner ports as it moves upward. The exhaust valves are therefore open for approximately 155 to 160° of crankshaft rotation.

Valve Timing

The polar valve timing diagram shown in Figure 2–6 illustrates one example of the various degrees of port opening, valves opening, and closure for a two-stroke-cycle non-DDEC-equipped Detroit Diesel V92 engine. The specific year of manufacture of the engine, the particular engine series, specific model, and application as well as the fuel delivery rate can result in different degrees of valve timing as well as injection duration.

If you compare this valve timing diagram with that shown in Figure 2-3 for the four-stroke-cycle engine, you will see that there are substantial differences in the duration of the various strokes and the number of crankshaft degrees involved. A thorough understanding of the differences between the two- and four-stroke operating cycles will serve you well when considering their operation and when attempting to troubleshoot the engine in some cases.

Piston Positions

In Figure 2-4 we considered an example of the relative piston positions for a six-cylinder four-stroke-cycle engine. This diagram allowed us to visually interpret where each piston is in relation to the others as well as what stroke each piston is on. Now assume that in the two-stroke-cycle Detroit Diesel engines we are to consider where each piston is at a given time and what stroke it is on. Most of us would simply assume that since the sequence of events occurs in 360 crankshaft

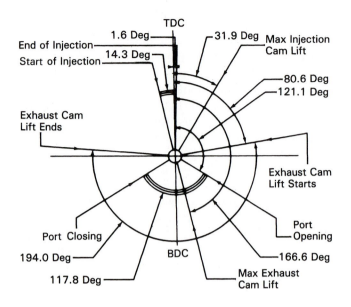

8V–92TA With Standard Cam
9A90 Injector with 1.480 Timing

TDC
1.6 Deg
End of Injection
14.3 Deg
Start of Injection
31.9 Deg   Max Injection
Cam Lift
80.6 Deg
121.1 Deg

Exhaust Cam
Lift Ends

Exhaust Cam
Lift Starts

Port
Opening

Port Closing
194.0 Deg
117.8 Deg
BDC
166.6 Deg
Max Exhaust
Cam Lift

.014 Hot Lash   .016 Cold Lash

Exhaust Valve Lift Starts–   98.2 Deg ATDC   98.9 Deg ATDC
Exhaust Valve Lift Ends–   246.0 Deg ATDC   243.0 Deg ATDC

Max. Injection Cam Lift– .2755
Max. Exhaust Cam Lift – .3270

FIGURE 2–6 *Example of a typical two-stroke-cycle diesel engine polar valve timing diagram. (Courtesy of Detroit Diesel Corporation.)*

degrees, we can divide the degrees by the number of cylinders and we would know where each piston was. If we were to consider an 8V-71 or 92 series model, logic would tell us to divide 360° by 8 = 45°. This conclusion would be reasonable if the engine were a 90° V configuration; in fact, however, these engines have a 63.5° angle between the banks. Therefore, the firing impulses between two cylinders has to add up to 90°. Figure 2–7 illustrates how Detroit Diesel does this on these series of engines for a right-hand rotation model with a firing order of 1L–3R–3L–4R–4L–2R–2L–1R. Keep in mind that the manufacturer determines the engine rotation from the front and identifies the left and right cylinder banks from the flywheel end, although it numbers the cylinders on each bank from the front of the engine. If we assume that cylinder 1 on the left bank is at TDC compression, the other cylinders would be spaced 26.5°, 63.5°, 26.5°, and so on, throughout the firing order. By referring to Figure 2-6, which illustrates a typical example of a two-stroke 8V-92TA (turbocharged and aftercooled) engine polar valve timing diagram, you can determine exactly what stroke each piston is on in Figure 2-7.

COMPARISON OF TWO- AND FOUR-STROKE-CYCLE DESIGNS

Although the two-stroke-cycle engine has twice as many power strokes as that of its four-cycle counterpart, it does not produce twice the power output at the engine crankshaft or flywheel. This is due, in part, to the fact that the length of the power stroke is much shorter in the two-stroke than in the four-stroke engine. Average power stroke length in the two-cycle engine can be between 90 and 95 crankshaft degrees, while the four-cycle engine tends to have a power stroke of between 120 and 140°.

The two-stroke-cycle engine, however, generally delivers more power for the same weight and cylinder displacement, or the same basic horsepower, from a smaller-displacement engine size. We can compare the power differences as follows:

1. In a four-stroke-cycle engine, there is a longer period available for the scavenging of exhaust gases and the separation of the exhaust and inlet strokes. In addition, with a shorter valve overlap period versus the port/valve concept in the two-stroke engine, there tends to be a purer air charge at the start of the compression stroke in a four-cycle engine than in a conventional blower-air-supplied two-stroke engine. However, once a turbocharger is added to the two-stroke engine, the airflow delivery rate is increased substantially; therefore, two-stroke-cycle engines such as Detroit Diesel's 71 and 92 series highway truck engines equipped with both a blower and a turbocharger match the characteristics of the four-stroke engine.

2. Both four- and two-stroke-cycle engines have pumping losses. The four-stroke-cycle losses occur during the intake and the exhaust strokes, whereas in the two-stroke-cycle engine the power losses required to drive the gear-driven blower reduce the net engine power output. In addition, two-stroke engines require a much larger airflow capacity to operate since the purpose of the airflow is to (a) scavenge the burned exhaust gases from the cylinder in a short interval (usually between 100 and 150°); (b) cool the internal engine components, such as the cylinder liner, the piston crown, and the exhaust valves (approximately 30% of the cooling of a two-stroke-cycle engine is done by airflow); (c) supply fresh air for combustion purposes; and (d) provide air leakage for positive crankcase ventilation.

3. Pumping losses occur in a four-stroke-cycle engine during the intake and exhaust strokes. Equivalent losses to drive the gear-driven blower exist in the two-stroke engine, plus as much as 40% of the engine

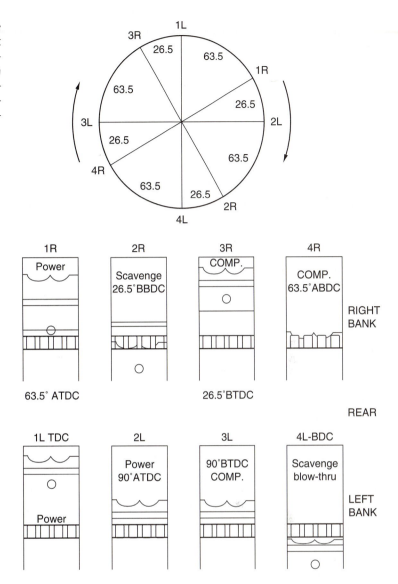

FIGURE 2–7 Example of the firing order and piston placement in degrees for a DDC two-stroke-cycle 63. 5° V8 diesel engine with a right-hand firing order of 1L–3R–3L–4R–4L–2R–2L–1R, determined from the front of the engine.

friction. However, this has been reduced substantially in current Detroit Diesel two-cycle engines by the use of a bypass blower to reduce pumping losses once the turbocharger boost increases to a predetermined level. Generally, on a nonturbocharged two-cycle engine the blower power loss is less than the four-cycle pumping losses when the engines are operating at less than 50% of their rated speed. From 50% up to rated speed, however, the four-cycle engines' pumping losses tend to be about two-thirds that for the two-cycle engine. Two-cycle engines that employ both a turbocharger and a bypass blower, such as Detroit Diesel 71, 92, and 149 series engines, have changed this ratio substantially.

4. The thermal (heat) loading on the piston, valves, cylinder head, and cylinder liner tend to be lower on a four-stroke-cycle engine because the power stroke occurs only once every two crankshaft revolutions versus once per revolution on a two-stroke engine.

5. It is easier to lubricate the pistons, rings, and liners in a four-cycle engine, due to the absence of ports that are required in the two-cycle liner.

6. The two-cycle engine tends to have a slightly higher fuel consumption curve due to its double-power-stroke principle throughout the same 720° for a four-cycle engine.

7. Generally, the two-stroke-cycle engine can produce more power per cubic inch (cubic centimeter) of displacement than that for a four-cycle engine when high-power applications are required, such as in high-output marine and off-highway mining trucks. In heavy-duty on-highway truck applications, one example is the Detroit Diesel 8V-92TA-DDEC model rated at 500 bhp (373 kW) at 2100 rpm from 736 in³ (12.1 L). This same engine can pump out up to 765 bhp (571 kW) in high-output marine applications, which is more than 1 hp/in³ of displacement. The Cat 3406E at

500 bhp has a displacement of 893 in^3 or 14.6 L, while the Cummins N14 at 500 bhp has a displacement of 855 in^3 (14 L). Mack's six-cylinder E7 model at 454 bhp (339 kW) from 728 in^3 (12 L), however, is a good example of high power from small displacement in a four-stroke-cycle engine.

8. The CR (compression ratio) on four-stroke engines tends to be lower than that on an equivalent-rated two-cycle engine. Consider that the Caterpillar 3406E engine has a CR of 16.25:1; the Cummins N14 has a CR of 16.2:1, Detroit Diesel's series 60 12.7-L and series 50 each have a CR of 15:1 while its two-cycle 92 has a CR of 17:1. However, Volvo's VE D12 electronically controlled six-cylinder four-stroke model has a CR of 17.5:1.

9. The BMEP (brake mean effective pressure), which is the average pressure exerted on the piston crown during the power stroke, is generally lower on a two-cycle engine. Consider that a Detroit Diesel 92 series engine rated at 450 bhp (336 kW) at 2100 would have a BMEP of 115 psi (793 kPa); the same engine at 500 bhp (373 kW) would have a BMEP of 128 psi (883 kPa). Compare this to the four-stroke-cycle engine models in the same general power rating category. The Caterpillar 3406E rated at 475 bhp (354 kW) at 1800 rpm would have a BMEP of 234 psi (1613 kPa), and at the peak torque point of 1200 rpm, its BMEP climbs to 295 psi (2037 kPa). A Cummins N14 at 500 bhp at 2100 rpm would develop a BMEP of 221 psi (1524 kPa). A Detroit Diesel series 60 12.7L rated at 370 bhp (276 kPa) at 1800 rpm would develop a BMEP of 210 psi (1460 kPa); the same engine at 470 bhp (351 kW) would have a BMEP of 229 psi (1579 kPa). Mack's E7-454 bhp (339 kW) model has a BMEP of 274 psi (1890 kPa), while its E9 V8 rated at 500 bhp (373 kW) develops a BMEP of 209 psi (1440 kPa). Volvo's latest six-cylinder electronically controlled VE D12 rated at 415 bhp (310 kW) at 1900 rpm develops a BMEP of 234 psi (1612 kPa). As you can see, four-cycle engines tend to have BMEPs almost twice that for the two-cycle engines rated at the same horsepower. You may have noticed that the smaller the four-cycle engine displacement, the higher the BMEP value will be. In Chapter 3 we discuss in more detail and describe how to determine the BMEP of any engine.

10. The BSFC (brake specific fuel consumption) of a two-stroke-cycle engine tends to be higher than that for a comparably rated four-cycle engine. BSFC is simply the ratio of fuel burned to the actual horsepower produced. Engine manufacturers always show their projected BSFC for an engine at different loads and speeds in their sales literature. Later in this chapter we discuss BSFC in more detail; examples of BSFC for several well-known engine makes and models are illustrated and discussed. Electronically controlled heavy-duty diesel engines are capable of returning fuel economy superior to mechanical models, which confirms that these engines have a higher *thermal efficiency* (heat efficiency) as well as the ability to meet the stringent exhaust emissions regulations of the U.S. EPA.

We can summarize the two cycles by considering that the piston operation is divided into closed and open periods. The *closed period* occurs during the power stroke and the *open period* during the time the inlet and exhaust strokes are occurring. Consider the following sequence:

Two-Stroke Cycle

- Closed period
  a–b: compression of trapped air
  b–c: heat created by the combustion process
  c–d: expansion or power stroke
- Open period
  d–e: blowdown or escape of pressurized exhaust gases
  e–f: scavenging of exhaust gases by the blower and/or blower–turbocharger combination
  f–g: air supply for the next compression stroke

All of the events above occur within 360°, one complete turn of the engine crankshaft/flywheel.

Four-Stroke Cycle

- Closed period
  a–b: compression of trapped air
  b–c: heat created by the combustion process
  c–d: expansion or power stroke
- Open period
  d–e: blowdown or escape of pressurized exhaust gases
  e–f: exhaust stroke
  f–g: inlet and exhaust valve overlap
  g–h: induction stroke
  h–i: compression

All of these events require 720° of crankshaft/flywheel rotation, in contrast to the 360° in the two-cycle engine.

ENGINE FIRING ORDERS

The number of cylinders and the engine configuration (inline versus V) and the directional rotation of the engine determine the actual firing order. In Chapter 8 we discuss in detail the purpose and function of crankshaft counterweights, engine balance shafts, and vibration dampers in the overall balance of a running engine. Every cylinder in an engine produces what are commonly referred to as *disturbing forces* that act along the axis of each cylinder as a result of the acceleration and deceleration of the rotating connecting rod and piston assembly as the individual cranks rotate through 360°.

The actual firing order of an engine, and therefore the position of the individual cranks on the shaft, can be established today by computerized analysis. The following parameters must be considered:

- Main bearing loads when adjacent cylinders fire in sequence
- Engine balance

- Torsional vibrations of the crankshaft
- In some special cases, the airflow interference in the intake manifold

Figure 2–8 illustrates typical firing orders used for various engines with differing numbers of cylinders for both two- and four-stroke-cycle engines. Two-stroke crankshaft arrangements tend to be more complicated than those in a four-cycle engine, because the two-stroke engine must fire all cylinders in one crankshaft rotation (360° versus 720°). It is common in four-cycle engines to repeat, or "mirror," the two halves of

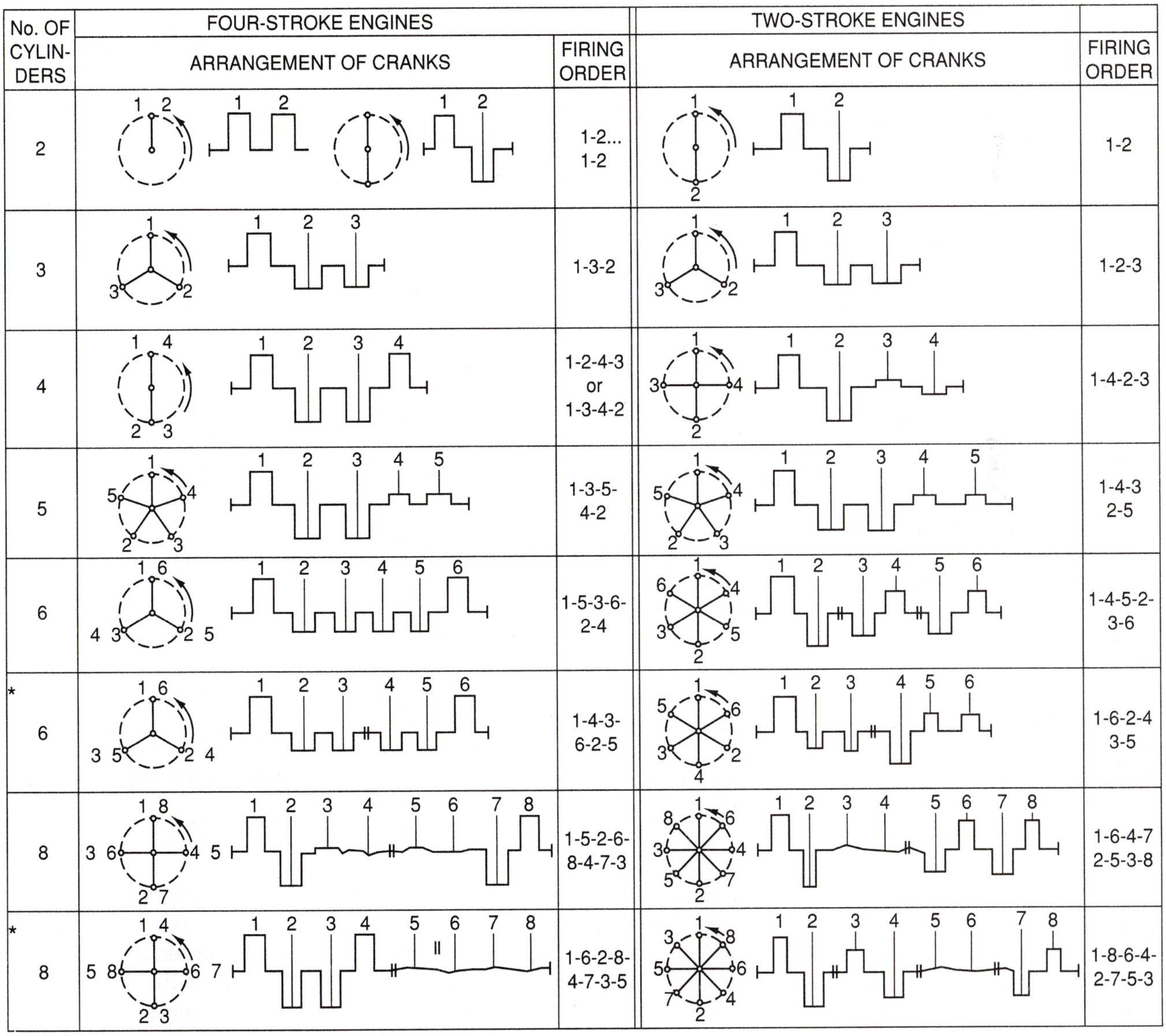

No. OF CYLINDERS	FOUR-STROKE ENGINES		TWO-STROKE ENGINES	
	ARRANGEMENT OF CRANKS	FIRING ORDER	ARRANGEMENT OF CRANKS	FIRING ORDER
2		1-2... 1-2		1-2
3		1-3-2		1-2-3
4		1-2-4-3 or 1-3-4-2		1-4-2-3
5		1-3-5-4-2		1-4-3-2-5
6		1-5-3-6-2-4		1-4-5-2-3-6
* 6		1-4-3-6-2-5		1-6-2-4-3-5
8		1-5-2-6-8-4-7-3		1-6-4-7-2-5-3-8
* 8		1-6-2-8-4-7-3-5		1-8-6-4-2-7-5-3

FIGURE 2–8 *Typical crankshaft throw arrangements for both four- and two-cycle models for engines with between two- and eight-cylinder designs.*

the crankshaft to eliminate coupling forces (equal masses positioned opposite one another). This also often allows a number of firing orders to be obtained from a single crankshaft arrangement. The discussion of crankshaft balance and the forces involved is a specialized area in its own right, so we will not delve into details here. In many current high-speed V-configuration engines the desired firing order is often achieved by employing offset con-rod (connecting rod) journals on the same throw of the crankshaft.

The most widely used six-cylinder firing order for a CW-rotation (from the front) two- or four-stroke-cycle engine is 1–5–3–6–2–4. If the engine rotation is reversed, such as for some twin-engine marine applications, a typical firing order might be 1–4–2–6–3–5. When V-engine configurations are employed, the firing order is determined based on the engine rotation and whether it is a two- or four-stroke-cycle type. Most engine OEMs identify cylinder numbering from the front of the engine; however, in some cases the cylinder number is determined from the rear. In addition, on V-engines most manufacturers identify the left and right cylinder banks from the flywheel end.

Standard rotation on many engines is based on the SAE (Society of Automotive Engineers) technical standard in which rotation is determined from the flywheel end. Normally, this is CCW (counterclockwise), which results in a CW rotation when viewing the engine from the front. Opposite rotation according to the SAE is still viewed from the flywheel end; however, the engine crankshaft would rotate CCW when viewed from the front. Note that Caterpillar numbers its engine cylinders from the front to the rear, with cylinder 1 being on the right side and cylinder 2 on the left side when viewed from the rear. This means that the left and right engine banks on a V model are determined from the flywheel end. For example, a four-cycle V12 Caterpillar 3512 engine model with a standard SAE rotation would have a firing order of 1–12–9–4–5–8–11–2–3–10–7–6; the cylinder numbering system would appear as illustrated in Figure 2–9. This same engine running in SAE opposite rotation would have a firing order of 1–4–9–8–5–2–11–10–3–6–7–12.

A two-stroke-cycle V configuration, such as those manufactured by Detroit Diesel in V6, V8, V12, V16, and V20 models, determines left and right cylinder banks from the flywheel end, with the cylinders being numbered from the front to rear on each bank, as illustrated in Figure 2–10 for a series of V models. In addition, Detroit Diesel engines determine the crankshaft rotation from the front of the engine, *not* from the flywheel end. Anytime the engine rotation is changed from CW (right hand) to CCW (left hand), the engine firing order is always different, as indicated in Figure 2-10.

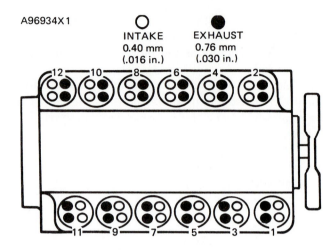

CYLINDER AND VALVE LOCATION

FIGURE 2–9 *Cylinder and valve location for a model 3512 (V12) four-stroke-cycle engine. (Courtesy of Caterpillar, Inc.)*

SUMMARY

This chapter has provided you with a solid understanding of the concept of operation for both two- and four-stroke cycle engines. You have also been provided with the concept of operation for both IDI and DI engine designs. Engine firing orders, relative piston positions and valve timing information will all contribute to your ability to set and adjust both the intake and exhaust valve clearances, and to be able to discuss and compare the advantages and disadvantages of different types of internal combustion engines.

SELF-TEST QUESTIONS

1. Technician A says that the piston strokes in a four-stroke-cycle diesel or gasoline engine involve intake, compression, power, and exhaust. Technician B says that the order is compression, intake, power, and exhaust. Who is correct?

2. Technician A says that a four-stroke-cycle diesel engine requires 720° (two full turns) of crankshaft rotation to produce one power stroke. Technician B says that two power strokes are produced within 720°. Which technician is correct?

3. Technician A says that during the intake stroke on a gasoline engine, both air and fuel are mixed. Technician B says that only air is inhaled into the cylinder. Who is correct?

4. Technician A says that on a diesel engine, only air is inhaled on the intake stroke. Technician B says that both air and fuel are taken into the cylinder on the intake stroke. Who is right?

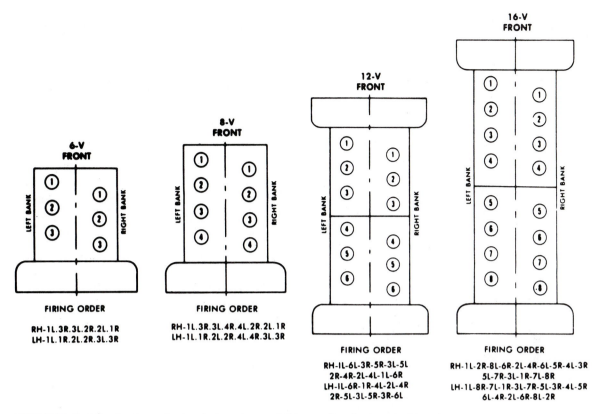

FIGURE 2-10 *Engine cylinder designation and firing orders for two-stroke-cycle 6V, 8V, 12V, and 16V models. (Courtesy of Detroit Diesel Corporation.)*

5. Technician A says that the term *volumetric efficiency* (VE) refers to the weight of air retained in the cylinder at the end of the intake stroke. Technician B says that it is the pressure of the air at the end of the compression stroke. Which technician is correct?

6. Technician A says that in naturally aspirated engines, the VE will always be less than 100%. Technician B says that the engine would starve for air if this were the case, and therefore it must have at least a VE of 100% (atmospheric pressure).

7. Technician A says that atmospheric pressure at sea level is approximately 14.7 psi (101.3 kPa). Technician B says that it is closer to 16 psi (110.3 kPa). Who is correct?

8. Technician A says that the VE in turbocharged engines is always greater than atmospheric pressure, or higher than 100%. Technician B says that no engine can run at VEs in excess of 100%, due to frictional losses. Which technician is correct?

9. Technician A says that typical cylinder pressures at the end of the compression stroke (prior to injection of fuel) range between 1000 and 1200 psi (6895 to 8274 kPa). Technician B says that they would be closer to the range 450 to 600 psi (2758 to 4137 kPa). Which technician is right?

10. Technician A says that typical compression temperatures range between 1000 and 1200°F (538 to 649°C). Technician B says that they would be closer to 2000°F (1093°C). Who is correct?

11. Technician A says that peak cylinder firing pressures in electronically controlled high-speed heavy-duty diesel engines range between 1200 and 1400 psi (8274 to 9653 kPa). Technician B believes that they are closer to 1800 and 2300 psi (12,411 and 15,856 kPa). Who is correct?

12. Technician A says that the intake valves open at BTDC and close at ABDC. Technician B says that they open at TDC and close at BDC. Who is right?

13. Technician A says that the term *positive valve overlap* indicates that both the intake and exhaust valves are open for a given number of degrees before and after TDC. Technician B says that both the intake and exhaust valves are open before and after BDC. Which technician is correct?

14. Technician A says that a polar valve timing diagram indicates the duration of all strokes. Technician B says that it only indicates the duration of the power stroke. Who is right?

15. Technician A says that two-stroke-cycle DDC engine models employ both intake and exhaust valves. Technician B says that only exhaust valves are used in these engines since the cylinder liners are designed with a row of intake ports. Which technician is correct?

16. Which of the following two strokes are eliminated from a two-stroke-cycle engine?
    a. intake and exhaust
    b. compression and exhaust

c. intake and compression
d. compression and power

17. Technician A says that in a two-stroke-cycle DDC engine, every upstroke of the piston produces compression, and every downstroke produces power. Technician B says that this is impossible since the engine would not run without both an intake and an exhaust stroke. Which technician is correct?

18. Technician A says that a two-stroke engine has a longer power stroke in crankshaft degrees than that of a four-cycle engine model. Technician B says that the four-stroke-cycle engine has a longer power stroke. Which technician is correct?

19. A typical firing order for a six-cylinder four-stroke-cycle engine would be
    a. 1–5–2–4–6–3
    b. 1–5–3–6–2–4
    c. 1–4–2–6–3–5

20. Technician A says that in a two-stroke-cycle DDC engine, the gear-driven blower is used to supply the air required for both the scavenging and intake strokes. Technician B says that the blower is used to supercharge the engine. Which technician is correct?

21. Technician A says that a supercharged engine is any engine that has pressurized air added to it or any engine that uses a turbocharger or blower. Technician B disagrees and says that to supercharge an engine, you must close the valves early enough to trap the high-pressure turbo or blower air in the cylinder; therefore, a supercharged engine is any engine that takes air into the cylinder at higher than atmospheric pressure and then compresses it. Which technician is correct?

22. Technician A says that all DDC two-cycle engines must be supercharged since they employ a gear-driven blower. Technician B disagrees and says that the blower air is simply used to scavenge exhaust gases and supply fresh air for combustion purposes. Which technician is correct?

23. Technician A says that approximately 30% of the engine cooling in a two-stroke-cycle DDC engine is achieved by blower airflow. Technician B believes that possibly 10% cooling might be achieved by blower airflow. Which technician is correct?

24. Technician A says that on two-cycle DDC engines, the blower supply air pressure is between 20 and 25 psi (138 to 172 kPa). Technician B says that it ranges between 4 and 7 psi (28 to 48 kPa). Who is right?

25. Technician A says that average turbocharger boost pressures on both two- and four-cycle heavy-duty high-speed diesel engines range between 40 and 50 in. (102 to 127 cm) of mercury, or approximately 20 to 25 psi (138 to 172 kPa). Technician B says that it is closer to 8 to 10 psi (55 to 69 kPa). Who is right?

26. Technician A says that scavenge blowthrough of the cylinder liners in two-stroke-cycle DDC engines occurs when the piston is approximately 40° ABDC. Technician B says that it occurs approximately 60° BBDC until about 60° ABDC, for a duration of 120°. Which technician is correct?

27. Technician A says that two-cycle DDC 71 and 92 series V-configuration engines are designed with a 63.5° angle between the banks. Technician B says that they are 90° Vs. Who is correct?

28. Technician A says that the average duration of a two-stroke-cycle engine power stroke is about 90 to 95°. Technician B says that they are closer to between 120 and 140°. Who is right?

29. Technician A says that pumping losses occur in all two-stroke-cycle engines during the intake and exhaust strokes. These losses occur in a four-stroke-cycle engine according to technician B. Who is correct?

30. Technician A says that the compression ratio tends to be higher on four-cycle engines than it does on two-cycle models. Not so, says technician B, it is the other way around. Who is right?

31. Technician A says that the BMEP is lower on two-cycle engines than on four-cycle models. Technician B says that it is the exact opposite to technician A's statement. Who is right?

32. Technician A says that the BSFC tends to be higher for a two-cycle engine. Not so, says technician B; the four-cycle engine uses more fuel than the two-stroke engine. Who is correct?

33. True or False: Standard engine rotation according to SAE (Society of Automotive Engineers) standards is clockwise from the flywheel end.

34. Technician A says that the cylinder number for most engines is determined from the front end of the engine. Technician B says that cylinder numbers are always determined from the flywheel end. Which technician is correct?

35. Technician A says that most OEMs determine the left and right banks on a V-configuration engine from the flywheel end. Technician B says that they are determined from the front. Who is right?

Understanding Horsepower and Related Terms

OVERVIEW

Within this chapter we discuss the technical concepts and basic engineering knowledge needed by a diesel technician in day-to-day service operations, and how a thorough understanding of these engine working concepts will assist you to read and interpret OEM engine performance brochures. You will be able to compare gasoline to diesel engine performance, and understand why different makes of engines perform at different levels.

DIESEL ENGINEERING FUNDAMENTALS

This section deals with many of the more commonly used terms and operating conditions related to engine performance. No attempt is made to discuss the more advanced formulas that are required when designing an internal combustion engine, since these are not normally needed in a diesel technician's day-to-day duties.

Energy, force, work, power, horsepower, torque; if these terms are confusing to you as a beginning technician, you are *not* alone, because many technicians and people who work with diesel-powered vehicles every day have the same problems.

As either a diesel technician or engineering student studying heat engines or thermodynamics, your knowledge of these widely used terms will help you to understand and appreciate the operating philosophies of how a diesel engine operates. A thorough understanding of these terms, along with a solid knowledge

of the various operating principles discussed herein, will facilitate discussion of these concepts with your colleagues. When analyzing and troubleshooting current mechanical or electronic engines, a mental picture of what actually occurs within the engine cylinders will allow you to recognize and trace possible problem areas.

In this section, English and metric equivalents have been used as much as possible. Use the English/metric conversion chart (Table 3–1) to review or convert from either system. After using the chart for a short period of time, you will find that you will remember many of the more common conversion factors.

UNDERSTANDING POWER TERMS

Energy
The *first law of thermodynamics* states that energy can be neither created nor destroyed. Only the form in which energy exists can be changed; for example, heat can be transformed into mechanical energy. All internal combustion engines apply the same principle by burning a fuel within the cylinder to produce heat. The high-pressure gases created due to combustion force the piston down the cylinder on its expansion or power stroke. The heat energy is converted into mechanical energy through the piston and connecting rod, which in turn rotates the engine crankshaft and flywheel to supply the power needed.

The *second law of thermodynamics* states that heat cannot be completely converted to another form of energy. For example, in an engine mechanical energy can be produced from a fuel, because heat passes only from a warmer to a colder body. The reverse of this process is possible only if energy is supplied.

TABLE 3–1   Metric conversion chart

Common metric prefixes

kilo (k) = 1000	milli (m) = 0.001
centi (c) = 0.01	micro (μ) = 0.000001

Multiply	By	To get	Multiply	By	To get
Length					
inches (in.)	25.4	millimeters (mm)		0.03937	inches (in.)
inches (in.)	2.54	centimeters (cm)		0.3937	inches (in.)
feet (ft)	0.3048	meters (m)		3.281	feet (ft)
yards (yd)	0.9144	meters (m)		1.094	yard (yd)
mile (mi)	1.609	kilometers (km)		0.6214	mile (mi)
microinch (μin.)	0.0254	micron (μm)		39.37	microinch (μin.)
micron (μm)	0.000001	meters (m)		1,000,000	micron (μm)
microinch (μin.)	0.000001	inches (in.)		1,000,000	microinch (μin.)
Area					
square inches (in^2)	645.16	square millimeters (mm^2)		0.00155	square inches (in^2)
square inches (in^2)	6.452	square centimeters (cm^2)		0.155	square inches (in^2)
square feet (ft^2)	0.0929	square meters (m^2)		10.764	square feet (ft^2)
Volume					
cubic inches (in^3)	16,387.0	cubic millimeters (mm^3)		0.000061	cubic inches (in^3)
cubic inches (in^3)	16.387	cubic centimeters (cm^3)		0.06102	cubic inches (in^3)
cubic inches (in^3)	0.01639	liters (L)		61.024	cubic inches (in^3)
quarts (qt)	0.94635	liters (L)		1.0567	quarts (qt)
gallons (gal)	3.7851	liters (L)		0.2642	gallons (gal)
cubic feet (ft^3)	28.317	liters (L)		0.03531	cubic feet (ft^3)
cubic feet (ft^3)	0.02832	cubic meters (m^3)		35.315	cubic feet (ft^3)
Weight/force					
ounces (av) (oz)	28.35	grams (g)		0.03527	ounces (av) (oz)
pounds (av) (lb)	0.454	kilograms (kg)		2.205	pounds (av) (lb)
U.S. tons (t)	907.18	kilograms (kg)		0.001102	U.S. tons (t)
U.S. tons (t)	0.90718	metric tons (t)		1.1023	U.S. tons (t)
Power					
horsepower (hp)	0.7457	kilowatts (kW)		1.341	horsepower (hp)
Torque/Work Force					
inch-pounds (lb-in.)	0.11298	newton-meters (N · m)		8.851	inch-pound (lb-in.)
foot-pounds (lb-ft)	1.3558	newton-meters (N · m)		0.7376	foot-pound (lb-ft)
Speed					
miles/hour (mph)	1.609	kilometers/hour (km/h)		0.6214	miles/hour (mph)
kilometers/hour (km/h)	0.27778	meters/sec (m/s)		3.600	kilometers/hr (km/h)
miles/hour (mph)	0.4470	meters/sec (m/s)		2.237	miles/hour (mph)
Pressure					
pounds per square inch (psi)	0.069	bar		14.50	pounds per square inch (psi)
pounds per square inch (psi)	6.895	kilopascal (kPa)		0.14503	pounds per square inch (psi)

Subtract	From	To get	Multiply	By	To get
Temperature					
32	Fahrenheit (°F) and divide by 1.8	Celsius (°C)		1.8 and add 32	Fahrenheit (°F)

Fuel consumption

$$\frac{235}{\text{miles per gallon (mpg) U.S.}} = \text{liters/100 kilometers (L/100 km)}$$

$$\frac{235}{\text{liters/100 kilometers (L/100 km)}} = \text{miles per gallon (mpg) U.S.}$$

$$\frac{282}{\text{miles per gallon (mpg) Imp.}} = \text{liters/100 kilometers (L/100 km)}$$

$$\frac{235}{\text{liters/100 kilometers (L/100 km)}} = \text{miles per gallon (mpg) Imp.}$$

Force

Force can be defined as push or pull on an object (Figure 3–1). As the diesel fuel within the engine cylinder is burned, it expands and exerts force on the piston head. This force causes the piston to move downward and exerts force onto the engine crankshaft connecting rod throw, causing the crankshaft to turn. The amount of force is controlled by the amount of fuel burned. It can be seen then that the chemical burning of fuel provides the mechanical energy that creates force so that the engine can do work.

Work

Work is done when a force travels through a distance (Figure 3–2). If force is exerted and no movement occurs, no work is being done. Work is also done in "braking" or slowing down a vehicle such as a tractor or truck.

Force and *distance* can easily be measured in most cases, so the amount of work can be calculated by using the following formulas:

- English measurement

$$\text{Work} = \text{force (pounds)} \times \text{distance (feet)}$$
$$= 330 \text{ pounds} \times 100 \text{ feet}$$
$$= 33{,}000 \text{ foot-pounds}$$

- Metric measurement

$$\text{Work (joules)} = \text{force (newtons)} \times \text{distance (meters)}$$
$$(1 \text{ N} = 4448 \text{ pounds-force})$$
$$330 \text{ lb-ft} \times 4.448 = 1468 \text{ N}$$
$$\text{work} = 1468 \text{ newtons} \times 30.5 \text{ meters}$$
$$= 44{,}774 \text{ joules (J) or newton-meters}$$
$$(\text{N} \cdot \text{m})$$

Work, along with energy and force, is the beginning of determining power. Since the only kind of work we have discussed so far has been accomplished by pulling or pushing, we need to look at another kind of work, that which is developed by rotating motion such as an engine crankshaft. The amount of work done is still determined by multiplying the force in pounds times the distance the weight is moved in feet.

Power

The term *power* is used to describe how much work has been done in a given period of time. The rate at which work can be done is measured in terms of power, or how many units of work (ft-lb) have been done in a unit of time. We can show this simply as

$$\text{power} = \frac{\text{work}}{\text{time}}$$

Normally, power is expressed as how many foot-pounds of work is done per minute. If enough work is performed in a given period of time, we can start to compare it to the word *horsepower*, which is used to describe the power output of all internal combustion engines (see Figure 3-1). A detailed description of horsepower follows.

Horsepower

What is horsepower? The term *horsepower* is peculiar to the U.S. customary system. In the SI system, *watt* is the term used for power.

$$1 \text{ horsepower} = 746 \text{ watts}$$

The term *horsepower* was introduced by James Watt when he observed how much power one horse could develop. He found that a medium-sized draft horse could pull 330 pounds a distance of 100 feet in 1 minute. This became a standard *unit of measure*, one that he used to rate his steam engine. By multiplying 330 lb times 100 ft, he set 33,000 ft-lb/min as defining 1 horsepower. The formula for horsepower thus is

$$\text{horsepower} = \frac{\text{force (pounds)} \times \text{distance (feet)}}{\text{time (minutes)} \times 33{,}000}$$

Thus, 1 horsepower is the ability to do 33,000 ft-lb of work in 1 minute, or 550 ft-lb of work in 1 second (33,000 divided by 60 seconds equals 550).

Note that in Figure 3–2 the horse is lifting a 330-lb weight to a height of 100 ft in 1 minute. Using the formula the number of horsepower represented is determined as follows:

$$\text{horsepower} = \frac{330 \text{ lb} \times 100 \text{ ft}}{1 \text{ min} \times 33{,}000}$$
$$= 33{,}000$$
$$= 1$$

FIGURE 3–1 *The horse is applying force against the rock, but the rock is not moving. Therefore, no work is being done. (Courtesy of the American Association for Vocational Instructional Materials.)*

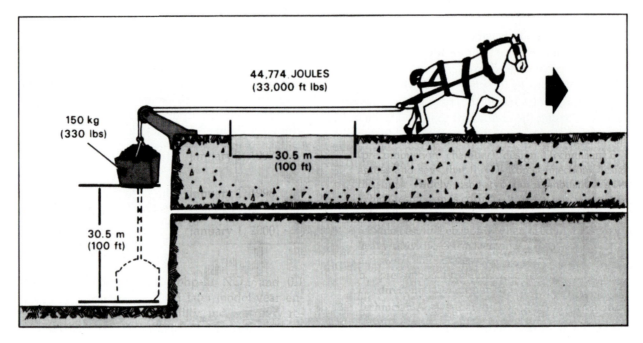

FIGURE 3–2 If a force moves an object from a state of rest, work is done. (Courtesy of the American Association for Vocational Instructional Materials.)

In Figure 3–3a the horse is dragging at the rate 100 ft/min a weight that requires 330 lb of pull to move it. In this example it is not necessary to know the value of the weight. The pulling force is determined by how difficult the weight is to pull. You apply the horsepower formula as follows:

$$\text{horsepower} = \frac{330 \text{ lb} \times 100 \text{ ft}}{1 \text{ min} \times 33,000}$$
$$= \frac{33,000}{33,000}$$
$$= 1$$

This is typical of how you determine the *drawbar horsepower* of a tractor.

In Figure 3–3b, force by pulling is replaced by force by turning a shaft (rotating force). This is the way power is measured at the engine flywheel and at the PTO (power takeoff) shaft of tractors. If we assume that it takes 1 minute to lift the 330-lb weight to a height of 100 ft, you can determine horsepower as follows:

$$\text{horsepower} = \frac{330 \text{ lb} \times 100 \text{ ft}}{1 \text{ min} \times 33,000}$$
$$= \frac{33,000}{33,000}$$
$$= 1$$

Let us consider the work that is produced by mov-

ing a weight of 100 lb (45.36 kg) through a distance of 10 ft (3 m) in a time of 4 seconds (sec or s). The power expended would be

$$\text{power} = \frac{\text{work}}{\text{time}} = \frac{1000 \text{ ft-lb}}{4 \text{ sec}} = 250 \text{ ft-lb/sec}$$

How much horsepower have we expended in doing this work? One horsepower is considered as being 550 ft-lb/sec, 33,000 ft-lb/min, or 1,980,000 ft-lb/hr. Therefore, we can compute horsepower as follows:

$$\text{horsepower} = \frac{250 \text{ ft-lb/sec}}{550 \text{ ft-lb/sec}} = 0.45 \text{ hp} \ (0.33 \text{ kW})$$

If this work were expended continually for a period of 1 min, the energy produced would be

$$\text{power} = \frac{\text{work}}{\text{time}} = \frac{1000 \text{ ft-lb}}{1 \text{ min}} = 1000 \text{ ft-lb/min}$$

and the horsepower produced would be

$$\text{horsepower} = \frac{1000 \text{ ft-lb/min}}{33,000 \text{ ft-lb/min}} = 0.030 \text{ hp}$$

You can see that if work is performed at a slower rate, less horsepower is produced; therefore, we can safely say that the word *horsepower* is an expression of how fast work can be done. In an internal combustion engine this work is produced within the cylinder due to the expanding gases. The faster the engine speed, the quicker the work is produced.

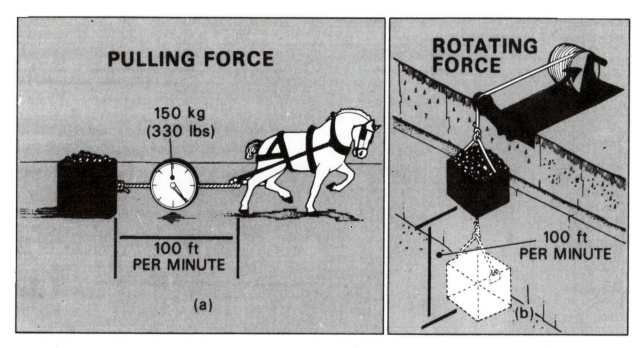

FIGURE 3–3 *Horsepower is measured by the amount of work accomplished. Whether you are lifting, (a) pulling, or (b) using rotating force, it takes 1 minute at 1 horsepower to lift or move the 330-pound weight a distance of 100 feet. (Courtesy of the American Association for Vocational Instructional Materials.)*

Metric Horsepower

In the metric system, power is expressed by the word *kilowatt* (kW), used initially to express the power of electrical machinery, where 1 hp is considered equal to 746 watts (W) in the English equivalent. (A watt is an ampere $\times$ a volt; an ampere is a measure of volume/quantity and a volt is a measure of electrical pressure.) Since 1 kW equals 1000 W, we can show 1 electrical hp as being equivalent to 0.746 kW. Conversely, 1 kW equals 1.341 hp. This 746 W of measurement is an American equivalent; in the metric system 1 hp is considered as being 735.5 W, or 75 kg · m/s. The German abbreviation for this unit of measurement is PS (*Pferdestärke*), where 1 PS (European horsepower) = 0.986 hp. The French equivalent is CV (*cheval vapeur*), where 1 ch = 1 PS = 0.07355 kW. This means that metric horsepower is approximately 1.5% less than the American unit of measurement! Other measures that you will encounter have been established by the ISO (International Standardization Organization), DIN (Deutsches Institut für Normung—German Institute for Standardization), and SAE (Society of Automotive Engineers), headquartered in Warrendale (Pittsburgh), Pennsylvania.

Horsepower Formulas

Work is done when a force is exerted over a distance. This can be defined mathematically as work equals distance (*D*) multiplied by a force (*F*). As horsepower is a measure of the rate (speed) at which the work is done, we can show this mathematically as

$$\text{horsepower} = \frac{D \times F}{33,000}$$

where the 33,000 is a constant figure determined by analysis and observation by James Watt when he studied the average rate of work for a horse with respect to the work his steam engine could do. He determined that the average horse could produce a work rate equal to 33,000 ft-lb/min (0.7457 kW/min), which he equated to 1 hp/min, or 550 ft-lb/sec (0.0124 kW/s).

Horsepower is generally considered as being one of two types:

1. *Brake horsepower* (bhp). This is the actual useful horsepower developed at the crankshaft/flywheel. It can be determined by a known formula, but certain data must be readily available, such as the dynamometer information (weight on a brake arm $\times$ distance). Without the dynamometer information, this type of horsepower cannot be readily determined unless the engine is run on a dynamometer with suitable horsepower, torque, and speed gauges. Many dynamometers also have a formula and data included on a

riveted plate to allow you to compute the engine power being produced.

2. *Indicated horsepower* (ihp). This is the power developed within a cylinder based on the amount of heat released but does not take into account any frictional losses. The cylinder's mean indicated pressure can be monitored by installing a special test gauge to record the maximum firing pressure. If a maximum pressure indicator gauge is available and the cylinder pressure is known, you can factor out indicated horsepower using a formula.

Horsepower Performance Curves

One easy way to show engine performance curves is to view an OEM (Original Equipment Manufacturers) sales specification sheet. These sheets include graphs indicating the horsepower, torque and fuel performance curves for various engine models. Figure 3–4 shows a number of engine ratings for Detroit Diesel's four-stroke cycle, 12.7L Series 60, electronically controlled heavy duty truck engine. By picking an engine rpm along the horizontal line of each graph, we can draw a vertical line upwards until it bisects the fuel

Performance Curves

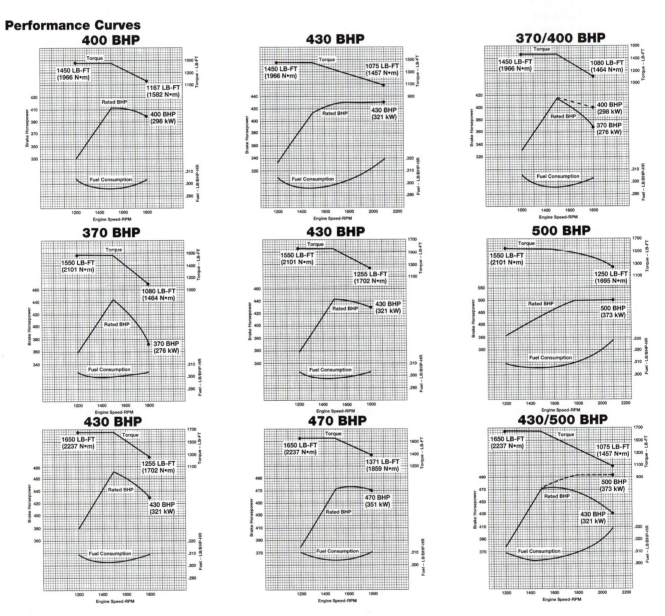

FIGURE 3–4   (Courtesy of Detroit Diesel Corporation.)

consumption curve, the horsepower curve, and the torque curve, where we can read the respective values desired. Note that there are three 430 hp (321 kW) ratings shown. One of these develops this horsepower at 2100 rpm, while the other two develop this same power, but at 1800 rpm. One of the 430 hp, 1800 rpm engines has a higher torque rating than the other at 1200 rpm. This is achieved through electronic programming of the engine ECM (electronic control module). Note also that the fuel performance curve is higher on the 1650 lb ft (2237 N · m) rated 430 hp model than it is on the other two. On the 370/400 bhp (276/298 kW) model, the engine can be programmed to provide 370 hp at rated speed, climbing to 400 hp at 1500 rpm. This feature allows the operator to run the vehicle in a cruise mode at a lower engine speed, which also provides a lower brake specific fuel consumption, but with a higher horsepower at this lower speed. The 430/500 hp (321/373 kW) model also offers a higher horsepower setting down to 1800 rpm, while the vehicle operates in the cruise control mode. Programming electronic engines to produce their best power at a lower speed results in a gear-fast-run-slow concept (lower numerical axle ratio). This, coupled with higher power and torque curves, provides better vehicle performance overall. Some of the performance graphs in Figure 3-4 illustrate a fairly flat power line, commonly known as a constant horsepower curve, since there is no loss of power with a reduction in engine speed for several hundred rpm.

NOTE   Horsepower is related to BMEP but is also influenced by both the speed of the engine and the cylinder/engine displacement.

Figure 3–5 illustrates the performance curve and relative information for the Caterpillar 3406E electronically controlled unit injector truck engine. Figure 3–6 illustrates an engine performance curve for a Cummins N14-460E electronically controlled heavy-duty truck engine. Note in this example and others that the engine brake horsepower performance curve is tailored so that the maximum power and best fuel economy are achieved at a speed within the operating range where most driving is done on a heavy-duty truck application. Cummins refers to the point on the engine performance curve where this occurs as the *command point*. In Figure 3–7 note how the engine horsepower begins to drop as the operator revs the engine beyond 1700 rpm. Also note in Figure 3–6 that the engine torque starts to decrease fairly quickly beyond 1500 rpm and the fuel consumption starts to increase.

This design feature "forces" the truck driver to use what is known as a *progressive shift pattern*. This means that the engine is accelerated only high enough to get the vehicle rolling; then a shift is made to the next higher gear. By using this shifting technique, not only does the higher engine *torque* move the vehicle gradually up to road speed, but it also keeps the engine within the most fuel efficient curve, as you can see from the BSFC line in Figures 3–4, 3–5, and 3–6. Most heavy-duty electronically controlled diesel engine-mounted ECMs (electronic control modules) are programmed to provide this type of operational response. The fuel consumption and torque curves are discussed in detail later in the chapter.

The performance curves of brake horsepower we have been discussing are typical of most of the newer electronically controlled unit injector heavy-duty truck engines manufactured by Caterpillar, Cummins, Detroit Diesel, Mack, Isuzu, and Volvo. On mechanically governed and injected engines, however, the horsepower generally tends to decrease with a reduction in engine speed (rpm) from the full-load-rated setting as the engine rpm is reduced due to an increasing load, since the rate/speed of doing the work is slower. Electronic controls provide tremendous flexibility for tailoring engine performance that is not possible with mechanical controls. Proper selection of turbocharging and air-to-air-charge cooling, high top piston rings, piston bowl geometry, and the use of low-sulfur diesel fuel all help to provide this improvement in engine performance and reduce the exhaust emissions so that they can comply with the EPA-mandated limits.

Regardless of the type of horsepower calculated, most diesel technicians in the field choose to use the following simplified formula to determine horsepower, particularly when the engine torque and speed are known:

$$hp = \frac{torque \times rpm}{5252}$$

Brake Horsepower
The formula for brake horsepower can be stated as

$$bhp = \frac{2 \times \pi \times r \times rpm \times w}{33,000}$$

where π (*pi*) = 3.1416

r = distance between the centerline of the engine crankshaft and the application of a weight on a brake arm, in feet or meters

rpm = speed of the engine, in revolutions per minute

w = effective weight on a brake arm, in pounds or kilograms

3406E

Truck Engine Performance

475 (354) @ 1800 rpm

DM0479-00

1750 Peak Torque
50 State

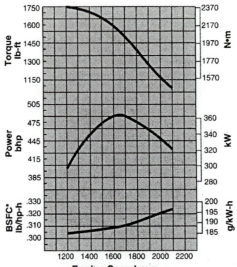

	Rated	English			Maximum		Rated	Metric			Maximum	
	475 hp				**485 hp**		**354 kW**				**362 kW**	
Engine Speed rpm	Engine Power w/o fan hp	Engine Torque lb ft	Engine BMEP psi	S Fuel Consum lb/hp-h	Fuel Rate gph		Engine Speed rpm	Engine Power w/o fan kW	Engine Torque N•m	Engine BMEP kPa	S Fuel Consum g/kW-h	Fuel Rate l/hr
2100	431	1078	182	.324	20.0		2100	322	1462	1254	197	75.6
2000	447	1173	198	.322	20.5		2000	333	1590	1364	196	77.7
1900	461	1275	215	.319	21.0		1900	344	1729	1483	194	79.5
1800	475	1387	234	.316	21.3		1800	354	1880	1613	192	80.8
1700	485	1499	253	.311	21.5		1700	362	2033	1745	189	81.3
1600	485	1593	269	.309	21.3		1600	362	2160	1854	188	80.8
1500	472	1653	279	.309	20.8		1500	352	2241	1923	188	78.9
1400	455	1705	288	.307	20.0		1400	339	2312	1984	187	75.7
1300	430	1738	293	.306	18.7		1300	321	2356	2022	186	70.9
1200	400	1751	295	.304	16.9		1200	298	2374	2037	185	64.0

Engine Speed rpm	Intake Manif Temp °F	Intake Manif Pres in-Hg	Intake Air Flow cfm	Exh Manif Temp °F	Exh Stk Temp °F	Exh Gas Flow cfm	Engine Speed rpm	Intake Manif Temp °C	Intake Manif Pres kPa	Intake Air Flow m³/min	Exh Manif Temp °C	Exh Stk Temp °C	Exh Gas Flow m³/min
2100	110	45.4	1164	911	671	2441	2100	43	153	33.0	488	355	69.2
2000	114	47.2	1168	938	695	2498	2000	45	159	33.1	503	368	70.8
1900	114	49.2	1161	965	717	2537	1900	45	166	32.9	518	381	71.9
1800	113	51.3	1143	993	741	2547	1800	45	173	32.4	533	393	72.2
1700	113	53.1	1108	1018	765	2519	1700	45	179	31.4	548	407	71.4
1600	112	54.1	1055	1041	790	2452	1600	44	182	29.9	561	421	69.5
1500	110	53.6	988	1061	815	2343	1500	43	181	28.0	571	435	66.4
1400	107	51.7	906	1080	840	2198	1400	41	174	25.7	582	449	62.3
1300	103	48.1	811	1099	871	2011	1300	39	162	23.0	593	466	57.0
1200	98	41.7	688	1121	914	1767	1200	36	140	19.5	605	490	50.1

Conditions

This engine performance data is typical of the engines approved by the Environmental Protection Agency (EPA) and the California Air Resources Board (CARB) for the calendar year 1994. This engine is approved for use in Canada. This data may change, subject to EPA and CARB approved engineering changes

* Brake Specific Fuel Consumption

Tolerance

Curves represent typical values obtained under lug conditions. Ambient air conditions and fuel used will affect these values. Each of the values may vary in accordance with the following tolerances.

Exhaust Stack Temperature	± 75°F ± 42°C	Power	±3%
Intake Manifold Pressure-Gage	± 3 in. Hg ± 10 kPa	BSFC*	± 010 lb/hp-h ± 6 g/kW-h
Torque	± 3%	Fuel Rate	± 5%

FIGURE 3–5 *Model performance operating conditions for electronically controlled 3406E truck engine rated 475 hp (345 kW). (Courtesy of Caterpillar, Inc.)*

Indicated Horsepower

The commonly accepted formula to determine indicated horsepower is

$$ihp = \frac{P \times L \times A \times N}{33,000}$$

where P = indicated brake mean effective pressure
L = length of the piston stroke, in feet
A = area of the piston crown, in square inches
N = number of power strokes per cylinder per minute

In two-stroke-cycle engines, N is the number of cylinders × rpm, while for four-stroke-cycle engines, N is the number of cylinders × rpm/2, since there are only half as many power strokes in the four-cycle engine. Using the formula, let's determine the ihp developed from a four-cycle six-cylinder engine with a bore of 5.4 in. (137 mm) and a stroke of 6.5 in. (165 mm) that develops an IMEP (indicated mean effective pressure) of 234 psi (1613 kPa) when operating at 1800 rpm.

$$ihp = \frac{PLAN}{33,000} = \frac{234 \times 6.5 \times 22.9 \times 1800 \times 6}{12 \times 33,000 \times 2}$$
$$= 474.96 \text{ ihp (354 kW)}$$

The number 12 in the formula is needed to convert the piston stroke into feet; however, if the stroke were 6 in. (152.4 mm) we could simply enter it on the upper line as 0.5 and remove the number 12 from the lower line. The answer, 474.96 ihp, is actually the horsepower listed for the Cat 3406E electronically controlled unit injector engine shown in Figure 3-5.

If we were to use the same formula but apply it to a two-stroke-cycle engine such as a Detroit Diesel 6V-92 series engine with a bore of 4.84 in. (123 mm), a stroke of 5 in. (127 mm), and a BMEP of 137 psi (944.6 kPa) running at 2100 rpm, what would be the ihp?

$$ihp = \frac{PLAN}{33,000} = \frac{137 \times 5 \times 18.39 \times 2100 \times 6}{12 \times 33,000}$$
$$= 400.81 \text{ ihp (299 kW)}$$

Some people prefer to use these optional formulas for determining indicated horsepower:

- Two-stroke cycle

$$ihp = \frac{PLANK}{23,000 \times 12} \text{ or } \frac{PLANK}{396,000}$$

- Four-stroke cycle

$$ihp = \frac{PLANK}{33,000 \times 12 \times 2} \text{ or } \frac{PLANK}{792,000}$$

where n is the rpm and k is the number of cylinders.

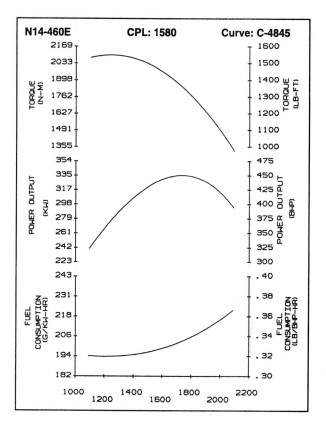

FIGURE 3–6   *Performance curves for N14-460E (855 in³ displacement) electronically controlled Celect engine. (Courtesy of Cummins Engine Company, Inc.)*

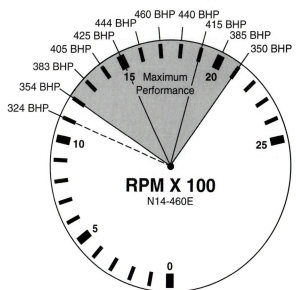

FIGURE 3–7   *Performance graph of typical horsepower output versus engine speed for an electronically controlled heavy-duty N14 engine. (Courtesy of Cummins Engine Company, Inc.)*

Horsepower Ratings

Now that we are familiar with how to determine horsepower, let's discuss horsepower ratings applied to engines when installed in various applications. If you consider the same model engine in different applications the horsepower ratings may not be the same because of the loads and speed variation that an engine is subjected to during a typical working day. An engine in a heavy-duty on-highway truck tends to be exposed to what is known as an *intermittent–continuous duty cycle* as the operator revs the engine up and down during upshifting and downshifting of the transmission as a result of the geography and terrain in which the vehicle is operating. On the other hand, a diesel generator set is designed to start and run at a fixed speed, possibly with a fixed load or an alternating load based on the demands for electrical power. Consequently, the horsepower (kW) rating for the genset (generator set) would be lower than that for the truck, because it is possible that the gen-set engine might run 24 hours a day, 7 days a week for a month or longer. To ensure optimum engine life and fuel economy, as well as factoring in some possible temporary overload capability into the gen-set application, most OEMs will derate this engine to 70% of maximum rated horsepower.

NOTE All current heavy-duty diesel engines are equipped with either an engine identification plate or a series of stick-on decals attached to the rocker cover(s) that list the horsepower output at rated speed. In addition, an EPA compliance sticker confirms that the engine meets the mandated exhaust emissions limits for the year in which the engine was manufactured. Other information on these decals indicates the engine model, family and displacement, fuel injector delivery rate, initial injection timing, and intake and exhaust valve clearances. All specifications—even on U.S.-built engines—are now adopting the metric standard of measurement!

Basically, there are seven general classifications of horsepower ratings with which you should be familiar:

1. *Rated horsepower* is the net horsepower available from the engine with a specified injector fuel rate and engine speed, which is guaranteed within (±5% of that shown in OEM sales literature according to the SAE standard ambient conditions, elevation, and air density. This is usually stated in the literature, such as 77°F (25°C) and 29.31 in. Hg (99 kPa) barometer (dry).

2. *Intermittent rated horsepower* is used for variable speed and load applications where full output is required for short intervals. To obtain optimum life expectancy, the average load should not exceed 60% (turbo) and 70% (nonturbo) of full load at the average operating speed. Typical examples for this rating are a crew boat, crane, shovel, railcar, railyard switcher, front-end loader, earthmoving scraper, and off-highway rear-dump truck.

3. *Intermittent maximum horsepower* is a rating used for applications in which maximum output is desirable and long engine life between overhauls is of secondary importance, or in which the average load does not exceed 35% of the full load at the average operating speed. Typical examples include a bow thruster used for docking purposes on marine vessels, standby gen-set, and standby fire pump.

4. *Continuous horsepower* is a rating given to an engine running under a constant load for long periods without a reduction in speed or load. This rating gives the range of optimum fuel economy and longest engine life. The maximum speed for this rating is generally shown on a performance curve chart. The pump or injectors may or may not have reserve capacity for momentary overload demands. The average load should not exceed the continuous rating of the engine. Typical examples include a stationary air compressor, quarry-rock crusher, marine dredge, gen-set, and mud pump in oil-well drilling applications.

5. *Intermittent continuous horsepower* is a rating used for applications that are primarily continuous but have some variations in load and/or speed. Average fuel consumption at this rating should not exceed that of the continuous rating. The injectors or pump may or may not have reserve capacity for momentary overload demands. Typical applications include a steering bow thruster on marine vessels, workboat, portable air compressor, dredge, gen-set, railroad locomotive, and bottom-dump earthmoving truck.

6. *Shaft horsepower* is the net horsepower available at the output shaft of an application, for example, the horsepower measured at the output flange of a marine gearbox.

7. *Road horsepower* is a rating of the power available at the drive wheels, for example, on a truck after losses due to the transmission, driveline, and so on.

Engine Torque

Torque can be defined as an effort that produces or tends to produce rotation. Generally, this effort is produced by force acting on a lever. Torque, a twisting and turning force that is developed at the engine crankshaft, is a measure of the engine's capacity to do work. Torque is expressed in pound-feet (lb-ft), or newton-meters (N · m) in the metric system. Smaller quantities of torque can be expressed in pound-inches (lb-in.) or N · m.

When measuring torque, the length of the lever arm and force applied are important. To obtain torque, multiply pounds of force times the length of the lever arm.

To further develop your understanding of torque, note the differences in torque shown in Figure 3–8. To determine the torque in Figure 3–8a, use the following formula:

torque = force × length of lever arm

- US: Torque = 330 lb × 1 ft
      = 330 foot-pounds
- SI: Torque = 1468 N × 0.305 m
      = 447.7 newton-meters

If the length of the lever arm is doubled as in Figure 3-8b, the result is

- US: Torque = 330 × 2
      = 660 foot-pounds
- SI: Torque = 1468 N × 0.61 m
      = 895.5 newton-meters

If 330 foot-pounds of torque is all that is needed, you can reduce the amount of force because the length of the lever arm has been increased (Figure 3-8c).

- US: Torque = 165 × 2
      = 330 foot-pounds

- SI: Torque = 734 N × 0.61 m
      = 447.7 newton-meters

Torque produced at the engine flywheel is developed by energy from the burning fuel, which has expanded and produced force. This force causes the engine piston to move downward and transmit force through the connecting rod to the crankshaft connecting rod journal on the crankshaft throw. The throw then becomes the lever that transmits the force to the engine crankshaft, causing it to turn and develop torque.

As you accelerate the engine in a truck or tractor under load, notice that the engine block has a tendency to turn in the direction opposite to the flywheel.

Figure 3–9 illustrates how this happens. In Figure 3-9a the engine is not running and remains level on its mounts. With the engine running and a light load applied to the engine flywheel, the engine tips slightly to the left in the direction opposite to the flywheel rotation. As the load on the engine is increased, the engine leans farther to the left as a result of the increased torque.

Figure 3–10 illustrates the conditions related to the development of torque, which is produced by a force (expanding high-pressure gases) pushing down on top of the piston crown. This force is measured in pounds per square inch (or in the metric system of measurement, kilopascal). The force on the piston is transferred through a lever (length and throw of the connecting rod), which in turn is connected to the crankshaft journal. The force exerted on the top

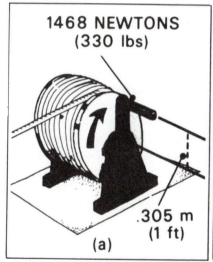
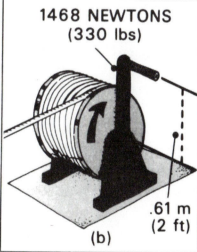
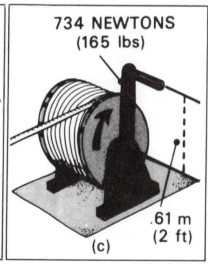

FIGURE 3–8 *Torque is determined by multiplying the force in pounds times the length of the lever arm in feet. (Courtesy of the American Association for Vocational Instructional Materials.)*

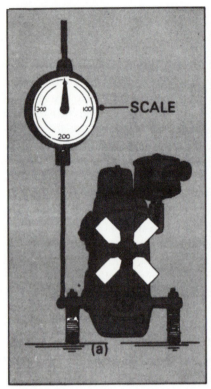

FIGURE 3–9 *How torque develops. (a) There is no torque applied when the engine is not running. (b) At a light load the engine begins to develop torque, as shown on the scale. (c) As the load is increased, torque increases, thus causing the engine to lean farther to the left. (Courtesy of the American Association for Vocational Instructional Materials.)*

(crown) of the piston decreases as the piston moves down the cylinder; this energy is used up in rotating the crankshaft. Torque depends on BMEP as well as engine cylinder displacement; therefore, BMEP is the average pressure exerted on each square inch (square millimeter) of the piston crown throughout the actual power stroke within the cylinder multiplied by the area of the piston crown. This force (F) = area $\times$ BMEP.

The length of the connecting rod (lever) is shown in Figure 3-10. Torque can therefore be described as the force (F) multiplied by the length of the lever (L) and is best defined as

$$\text{torque } (T) = \frac{\text{hp} \times 5252}{\text{rpm}}$$

The number 5252 is a mathematical constant derived from the basic horsepower (kilowatt) formula:

$$\text{hp} = \frac{DF}{33,000T}$$

An easy way to understand torque is to consider that as a heavy-duty truck is forced to move up a hill and the road speed and engine speed are decreased by

the grade, the horsepower (rate of doing work) is slower but the engine torque increases with a reduction in speed. Therefore, it is the torque that keeps the crankshaft turning and actually pulls the truck up the hill. Similarly, when a tandem-axle dump truck is up to its axles in mud, it isn't horsepower that pulls it out (high hp occurs at elevated speed, so revving the engine simply results in wheel slippage with no appreciable movement); once again it is the torque.

An attempt to move a heavily loaded truck from a parked position on a hill involves *gradeability* (percentage of hill steepness). What the vehicle needs is the ability to produce enough torque or *work power* to get moving and stay moving at a slow vehicle speed. Therefore, the engine torque multiplied through the transmission and rear-axle ratios determines the truck's ability to overcome resistance to soft terrain or an uphill working position.

We can determine the torque produced in a given engine if we know some of the other specifications of the engine. The formula for torque,

$$T = \frac{5252 \times \text{hp}}{\text{rpm}}$$

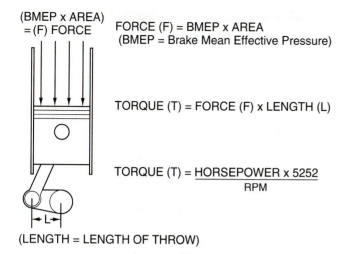

FIGURE 3–10 *Characteristics involved in determining engine torque.*

is the simplest method to use when you want to determine the torque from an engine at a certain operational speed. From our earlier discussion of horsepower, we know that heavy-duty electronically controlled engines are designed to produce their best power and fuel consumption at a midrange rpm value. Figure 3–6 is one example, a Cummins N14 Celect engine rated at 460 hp at 1700 rpm. What is important here is that the torque drops off fairly quickly as the engine speed is increased beyond this range. On the other hand, as the rpm is reduced, the torque increases until at 1200 rpm it reaches its *peak torque point,* which in this example is 1550 lb-ft (2101 N · m). The 1995-N14-460E+ was recalibrated to produce 1650 lb-ft (2237 N · m) at 1200 rpm.

Refer now to Figure 3–5 which lists all the operational data for the 3406E Caterpillar engine rated at 475 bhp at 1800 rpm. Using our torque formula we can confirm if the horsepower and torque are as stated in the figure. Let's see if the torque at full-load rated speed and the peak torque point checkout by using the formula

$$T = \frac{5252 \times hp}{rpm} = \frac{5252 \times 475}{1800}$$
$$= 1386\ lb{-}ft\ (1879\ N \cdot m)$$

Another method is commonly used and can be applied to determine the torque from two- and four-stroke-cycle engines if the engine displacement and BMEP are known.

- Two-stroke cycle

$$\text{Torque} = \frac{\text{BMEP} \times \text{displacement}}{75.4}$$

- Four-stroke cycle

$$\text{Torque} = \frac{\text{BMEP} \times \text{displacement}}{150.8}$$

In both of these formulas the numbers 75.4 and 150.8 are constants derived from a mathematical procedure.

Once again refer to Figure 3–5 and determine the torque at rated and peak torque speeds using the four-stroke-cycle engine formula.

$$\text{Torque at rated speed } (T) = \frac{\text{BMEP} \times \text{displacement}}{150.8}$$
$$= \frac{234 \times 893}{150.8} = 1385.68\ \text{lb-ft}\ (1879\ \text{N} \cdot \text{m})$$

$$\text{Peak torque at 1200 rpm } (T) = \frac{\text{BMEP} \times \text{displacement}}{150.8}$$
$$= \frac{295 \times 893}{150.8} = 1747\ \text{lb-ft}\ (2369\ \text{N} \cdot \text{m})$$

As you can see from these calculations, there are minor variations in the final answer, but we have determined that these formulas do work!

Torque Rise

You will encounter the term *torque rise* often in reference to most of today's electronically controlled diesel engines, particularly with respect to heavy-duty on-highway truck applications. This term simply expresses as a percentage the increase in engine torque as the engine speed is reduced from its maximum full load rpm or rated speed. For example, an engine develops 1000 lb-ft (1356 N · m) of torque at its rated speed of 2100 rpm, and this torque increases to 1500 lb-ft (2034 N · m) when the rpm is reduced to 1200 rpm (known as the peak torque point); the rate of torque rise is equal to 50%. If this 50% torque increase is divided by the 900-rpm drop from rated to peak torque rpm, this engine develops 5.55% torque rise for every 100-rpm decrease. Such a situation might occur when a heavy-duty truck is forced to climb a hill without the operator downshifting the transmission or changing the throttle position. Before the introduction of electronically controlled unit injector and pump–line–nozzle systems, OEMs employed various mechanical devices, such as *torque springs* or two belleville washers within the governor, which could be adjusted to tailor the actual rate of torque rise of the engine. This function can now be programmed into the ECM on the engine to allow fine control of both the horsepower and torque curves. If the engine has been tailored for a high rate of torque rise with a decrease in engine speed, the operator downshifts the transmission less often. The engine, in truck driver jargon, "is able to hang onto the load a lot longer," such as when moving up a hill.

We can use the following formula to determine torque rise:

$$\text{torque rise} = \frac{\text{peak torque} - \text{torque at rated speed}}{\text{torque at rated speed}}$$

In Figure 3–5 note that the 3406E Caterpillar electronically controlled engine rated at 475 hp (354 kW) at 1800 rpm produces a torque of 1387 lb-ft (1880 N · m). The torque increases to 1751 lb-ft (2374 N · m) at 1200 rpm. Therefore, we can determine the torque rise of this engine:

$$\text{torque rise} = \frac{1751 - 1387}{1387} = \frac{364}{1387} = 26.24\%$$

BMEP Formula

BMEP, the brake mean effective pressure, is the average pressure exerted on the piston crown during the working or power stroke. This factor is often described in terms of the performance capability of an engine model, because the BMEP is a measurement of how efficiently an engine is using its piston displacement to do work. Torque depends on BMEP as well as engine cylinder displacement. Horsepower is a value related to BMEP but it is also influenced by engine speed as well as displacement. Therefore, for a constant BMEP condition, torque increases in direct relation to the piston displacement of the engine. BMEP is actually difficult to define accurately since it is a parameter that doesn't specifically exist. It is the *theoretical* mean effective pressure developed during each power stroke, which would in turn develop a power equal to a given horsepower or kilowatt figure.

BMEP is also equal to the IMEP (indicated mean effective pressure) times the mechanical efficiency of the engine. The BMEP must be calculated after the bhp or torque of the engine is known, and it can be determined using the conventional ihp formula stated earlier in this chapter. In the following formula, the BMEP (P_b) and bhp are used in place of IMEP (P_i) and ihp.

$$\text{bhp} = \frac{P_b L A n}{33,000} \quad \text{or} \quad P_b = \frac{33,000 \text{ bhp}}{L A n}$$

where P_b = BMEP = brake mean effective pressure in psi or kPa
L = piston stroke, in feet or meters
A = piston crown area, in square inches or square millimeters
n = number of power strokes per minute

The total piston displacement (D) in cubic inches (or cubic centimeters or liters) of an engine is equal to the area of one piston times the stroke times the number of cylinders. So the formula can be simplified somewhat for both two- and four-stroke-cycle engines as follows:

- Four-stroke cycle

$$P_b = \frac{792,000 \text{ bhp}}{DN}$$

- Two-stroke cycle

$$P_b = \frac{396,000 \text{ bhp}}{DN}$$

where D is the total piston displacement of the engine, in either in^3 or cm^3, N is the engine speed, in rpm.

For example, using the formula above for a four-stroke-cycle Cummins engine with a displacement of 855 in^3 (14,011 cm^3, 14.011 L) developing 460 bhp at 1800 rpm, the BMEP would be

$$P_b = \frac{792,000 \text{ bhp}}{DN} = \frac{792,000 \times 460}{855 \times 1800}$$

$$= 236.72 \text{ psi, (1632 kPa)}$$

Using the same dimensions for a two-stroke-cycle engine, the BMEP would be

$$P_b = \frac{396,000 \text{ bhp}}{DN} = \frac{396,000 \times 460}{855 \times 1800}$$

$$= 118.36 \text{ psi (816.1 kPa)}$$

Note that the two-stroke-cycle engine has a BMEP close to half that of a four-cycle model, even when running at the same horsepower setting. This is due to the fact that approximately only half as much fuel is injected for each power stroke in the two-stroke model as in the four-stroke model. Keep in mind, however, that the two-cycle model has about twice as many power strokes as the four-cycle engine. For example, a 400 hp Detroit Diesel 92 series engine running at full load would have approximately 90 mm^3 of fuel injected for each stroke of the injector plunger. The four-cycle engine set at the same horsepower rating would have approximately 180 mm^3 of fuel injected on every stroke of the injector plunger. This does not mean that the two-cycle model is more fuel efficient than the four-cycle model. Generally, the two-cycle engine tends to be a little more thirsty than its four-stroke counterpart.

More simplified formulas can be used to determine BMEP if the engine torque and the engine displacement are known, for example:

- Two-stroke cycle

$$\text{BMEP} = \frac{75.4 \times \text{torque}}{\text{displacement}}$$

- Four-stroke cycle

$$\text{BMEP} = \frac{150.8 \times \text{torque}}{\text{displacement}}$$

Refer again to Figure 3–5. You will see that the BMEP at the rating and speed of 475 hp (354 kW) at 1800 rpm is 234 psi (1613 kPa). Take careful note that in any engine as the engine rpm is reduced under full-load operation toward the peak torque point, the BMEP increases accordingly. In the 475-hp (354-kW) 3406E engine, notice that the BMEP climbs to 295 psi (2037 kPa) at 1200 rpm. Using our formulas, let's determine if the BMEP is as listed for both the rated and 1200-rpm peak torque speeds.

- Rated speed (1800 rpm)

$$\text{BMEP} = \frac{150.8 \times \text{torque}}{\text{displacement}}$$
$$= \frac{150.8 \times 1387}{893}$$
$$= 234.22 \text{ psi } (1614.96 \text{ kPa})$$

- Peak torque speed (1200 rpm)

$$\text{BMEP} = \frac{150.8 \times 1751}{893} = 295.6 \text{ psi } (2039 \text{ kPa})$$

Compare these answers to the values listed in Figure 3–5—they agree.

Piston Speed Formula

The speed of the piston within the cylinder is to some degree a measure of the wear rate within the cylinder and the wear rate of the piston ring. Piston speed can be determined by the following formula:

$$\text{piston speed} = \frac{L \times \text{rpm} \times 2}{12} \text{ or } \frac{\text{stroke (in.)} \times \text{rpm}}{6}$$

The number 2 appears in the first formula because the piston moves up and down for each crankshaft revolution. The number 12 is to convert the speed to feet per minute. In the second formula we have simply substituted the number 6 and removed the 2. In either case the formula produces the same result. If an engine had a stroke of 6.5 in. (165 mm), what would its piston speed be in feet per minute (meters per minute) with the engine running at 1800 rpm?

$$\frac{L \times \text{rpm} \times 2}{12} = \frac{6.5 \text{ in. (165 mm)} \times 1800 \times 2}{12}$$
$$= 1950 \text{ ft/min } (594 \text{ m/min})$$

BSFC Formula

BSFC, brake specific fuel consumption, is always listed on engine manufacturers' sales data literature and is usually shown in either lb/bhp-hr or g/kWh (grams/kilowatthour). One lb/hp-hr is equal to 608.277 g/kWh. Figure 3-5 illustrates an example of the BSFC for a Caterpillar 3406E model heavy-duty truck engine rated at 475 hp (354 kW) at 1800 rpm and a peak torque at 1200 rpm of 1750 lb-ft (2373 N · m). As you can readily see on the graph for BSFC, fuel consumption is approximately 0.316 lb/hp-hr (192 g/kWh) for a fuel rate of 21.3 U.S. gallons (80.8 L/h) when running at 1800 rpm. At the peak torque rating of 1200 rpm, the fuel rate is 0.304 lb/hp-hr (185 g/kWh) for a fuel consumption rate of 16.9 U.S. gallons (64 L/h). This same chart lists the various other important specifications and operating conditions for this engine rating, which can actually produce a maximum horsepower rating of 485 bhp (362 kW) at approximately 1650 rpm, for example, during a cruise control mode.

In the OEM's sales data for BSFC in Figure 3–5, the U.S. gallons per hour, or fuel rate in liters per hour, is determined as follows. Let's consider the example listed with an engine speed of 1800 rpm and 475 hp (354 kW), where the BSFC is shown as 0.316 lb/hp-hr (192 g/kWh). If we multiply 475 × 0.316, we get 150.1 lb/hr of fuel consumed, which is listed in the chart as being equivalent to 21.3 U.S. gallons/hr (80.8 L/h). If we divide 150.1 lb by 21.3, the weight of the fuel per U.S. gallon is 7.046 lb (3.196 kg). Table 16-1 indicates that this fuel has an API (American Petroleum Institute) gravity rating of approximately 36. The API rating of the fuel determines its heat value and therefore the Btu (British thermal unit) of heat content available from a pound or a gallon.

Based on the foregoing information, we can use the following formula to determine BSFC:

$$\text{BSFC} = \frac{\text{pounds of fuel per hour}}{\text{bhp}}$$
$$= \frac{150.1}{475} = 0.316 \text{ lb/hp-hr } (192 \text{ g/kWh})$$

SPECIAL NOTE All on-highway diesel engines sold in the United States must comply with the EPA exhaust emissions standards for the year in which they were manufactured. Information relative to the EPA standards for engine power output, fuel delivery rate, rpm, valve lash, and so on, can be found on a stick-on decal attached to the engine or its rocker cover area.

If manufacturers' information is not readily available, the BSFC could be determined by noting the fuel injection rate listed on the engine decal. If we were to assume that this was 249.36 mm^3 per stroke of the injector, we could multiply this times the number of engine power strokes over a 1-hour period. In the 3406E Cat engine described in Figure 3–5, we can calculate the total power strokes as follows:

$$\frac{1800 \times 6 \times 60}{2} = 324{,}000 \text{ power strokes per hour}$$

A cubic millimeter is 1/1000 of a cubic centimeter; therefore, each injector will deliver 0.24936 cm^3 per stroke (249.36 mm^3). To determine the fuel used, multiply 324,000 × 0.24936 cm^3, which equals 80,792 cm^3 or 80.792 L/h, or 21.34 U.S. gallons/hr. The data listed in Figure 3–5 have been rounded off to show 80.8 L/h (21.3 U.S. gallons/hr).

Refer again to the information for the 3406E engine in Figure 3–5. Notice that the BSFC actually decreases, or improves, as the engine speed is reduced by load down to its peak torque of 1200 rpm (fewer injection cycles) where it is shown to be 0.304 lb/hp-hr (185 g/kWh). Usually, this occurs because the volumetric efficiency of the engine tends to increase with a reduction in engine speed due to the fact that the intake valves are open for a longer time at this lower speed and the intake manifold temperature is also usually lower.

Two-stroke-cycle engines tend to be a little more thirsty than their four-stroke-cycle counterparts. The two-stroke engine, however, is generally a faster accelerating and decelerating engine because of its power stroke every 360° (versus 720° in the four-stroke cycle). In addition, most two-stroke engines produce equal or greater horsepower from a smaller-displacement engine. Often, they tend to be more compact and lighter, but there are exceptions when we factor in the latest design of four-cycle models that use new lightweight materials and electronic controls. We already know what a typical electronic four-cycle engine (Caterpillar 3406E) will consume in fuel through reference to Figure 3–5. Similarly, Figure 3–4 indicates that the Detroit Diesel series 60 engine has outstanding BSFC. Now let us consider the BSFC for an equivalent two-stroke engine such as the DDC 92 series with electronic controls and in the same basic horsepower rating category as the four-stroke series 60 and the 3406E from the BSFC charts in Figures 3–4 and 3–5. We can see that the series 60, 370/400 bhp, 400 and 430 hp model has a BSFC of 0.297 lb/hp-hr (181 g/kWh) at a 1400 to 1450 rpm rate, which is better than that listed for the 3406E at the same speed and 475 bhp (354 kW), where the BSFC is 0.307 lb/hp-hr (187 g/kWh). We must be careful, though, when reading such BSFC ratings, because they cannot be considered as completely accurate during normal day-to-day operation due to the many variables encountered. The 1994 series 60 Detroit Diesel with a BSFC of 0.297 lb/hp-hr (181 g/kWh) was the world's first high-speed heavy-duty engine to break the 0.300 lb/hp-hr (182.9 g/kWh) BSFC barrier, followed closely by the Volvo VE D12 model with a BSFC of 0.300 lb/hp-hr at the 370 bhp (276 kW) variable torque rating.

Information for the two-stroke 8V-92TA DDEC engine rated at 500 bhp at 2100 rpm illustrated in Figure 3–11 indicates a BSFC of approximately 0.378 lb/hp-hr (0.230 g/kWh). To be fair, this engine produces 475 bhp at a speed of approximately 1740 rpm, with a BSFC of approximately 0.344 lb/hp-hr (209 g/kWh). At the peak torque speed of 1200 rpm, the 92 engine has a BSFC of 0.348 lb/hp-hr (212 g/kWh) versus 0.304 (185) for the 3406E and 0.303 (184) for the series 60. What this means is that if all engines were run at the speeds that produced this 470 to 475 bhp (351 to 354 kW) for 1 hour on a dynamometer under carefully controlled and equal conditions, we might expect each engine to consume the following amounts of fuel:

- Detroit Diesel 475-bhp 8V-92TA-DDEC at 1740 rpm = 475 × 0.344 = 163.4 lb/hr (74.11 kg) divided by its API 36 gravity rating of approximately 7.046 lb/U.S. gallon; this engine will burn 23.19 U.S. gallons/hr (87.78 L).
- DDC series 60 at 470 bhp at 1800 rpm = 470 × 0.304 = 142.88 lb/hr (64.81 kg) divided by an API rating of 36 at 7.046 lb/U.S. gallon; this engine will burn 20.27 U.S. gallons/hr (76.76 L).
- Caterpillar 3406E at 475 bhp at 1800 rpm = 475 × 0.316 = 150.1 lb/hr (68.08 kg) divided by an API 36 fuel rating of 7.046 lb/U.S. gallon; the fuel consumption rate is 21.3 U.S. gallons/hr (80.63 L).

As you can see, the two-stroke-cycle engine would burn 2.92 U.S. gallons/hr (11.05 L) more than its Detroit Diesel series 60 counterpart, and 1.89 U.S. gallons/hr (7.15 L) more than the 3406E Caterpillar engine.

SPECIAL NOTE   The BSFC curves shown at full-load conditions in OEM sales literature are *not* true indicators of fuel-tank mileage or fuel con-

Performance Curves

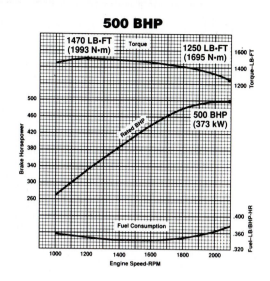

Rating Explanation

RATED BHP is the power rating for variable speed and load applications where full power is required intermittently.
FUEL CONSUMPTION CURVE shows fuel used in pounds per brake horsepower hour.

· POWER OUTPUT guaranteed within 5% at rated ambient conditions.
THIS RATING does not include power requirements for accessory and standard equipment.

FIGURE 3–11 *Sample horsepower (kW), torque, and BSFC (brake specific fuel comsumption) performance curves for a two-stroke-cycle model 8V-92TA DDEC-equipped diesel engine rated at 450 hp (336 kW) and 500 hp (373 kW) at 2100 rpm. (Courtesy of Detroit Diesel Corporation.)*

sumption over a 1-hour period, because the engine spends only a portion of time operating on the full-load curve. A significant amount of time is spent at various part-load conditions; therefore, full-load BSFC curves cannot be used to accurately reflect fuel-tank mileage or economy. Nevertheless, published figures can be used to approximate what the fuel economy might be under varying operating conditions—if the operator has a record of a typical daily operating cycle!

If an engine is being operated on a gaseous fuel such as LNG (liquid natural gas) or CNG (compressed natural gas), the BSFC is determined by the following formula:

$$BSFC = \frac{ft^3 \text{ of gas burned} \times \text{heating value} \times 60}{\text{length of test (min)} \times bhp}$$

For example, if an engine rated at 300 bhp (224 kW) used a gaseous fuel with a heating value of 1100 Btu/cu ft (31 m³), and consumed 400 ft³ (11.3 m³) of gas in 15 min, what would its BSFC be?

$$BSFC = \frac{400 \times 1100 \times 60}{15 \times 300} = \frac{26,400,000}{4500}$$
$$= 5867 \text{ Btu/bhp-hr}$$

Thermal Efficiency

TE (thermal efficiency) represents the *heat efficiency* of an internal combustion engine. Diesel and gasoline engines can consume either a liquid or a gaseous fuel that is normally injected into the combustion chamber. The heat that is released as the fuel burns creates the high-pressure gases required to force the piston down the cylinder and rotate the engine crankshaft. The API fuel rating determines the Btu heat content contained within a given volume of fuel (see Table 16-1).

Let's determine the TE of the 3406E Caterpillar engine rated at 475 hp (354 kW) listed in Figure 3–5. We know from the information in the chart that at 1800 rpm this engine consumes 0.316 lb/hp-hr (192 g/kWh); therefore, if we multiply the horsepower by the fuel, we have 475 × 0.316 = 150.1 lb/hr (68 kg/h) of fuel consumed. We need to know the heat value of the fuel used, and we can determine this from Table 16-1; earlier we determined under the BSFC for this engine that it was in fact using an API fuel rated at 36. Each pound of this fuel contains a LHV (low heat value—see Chapter 16 for a description) of approximately 18,410 Btu; therefore, if we multiply the Btu value by the total fuel consumed in 1 hour, which was 150.1 lb, the total heat released into the engine combustion chambers was 150.1 × 18,410 = 2,763,341 Btu/hr. Divide this total heat released by the available horsepower of 475 and we can determine that to produce each horsepower in this engine required 5817.56 Btu (2,763,341 ÷ 475 hp). Mathematical information indicates that a perfect engine requires 2545 Btu/hp-hr, so if we divide 2545 by 5817.56, which is what our engine used, we find that we have a thermal efficiency of 43.74%. If we were to use the HHV (high heat value) figure for this fuel, we would have a TE of 40.99%. In other words, for every dollar of fuel that we poured through this engine, we received approximately a LHV TE of 43.74 cents of a return at the flywheel.

All of the step-by-step procedures just described can be pulled into a simplified BTE (brake thermal efficiency) formula:

$$BTE = \frac{2545}{BSFC \times Btu/lb}$$

Using this formula, we can calculate the 3406E engine TE as follows using the LHV for this 36 API fuel of 18,414 Btu/lb:

$$BTE = \frac{2545}{0.316 \times 18,414} = \frac{2545}{5817.56} = 43.74\%$$

Keep in mind that these TE percentages have been determined under controlled test lab conditions as shown in Figure 3–5. In actual field operating conditions where changing speeds and loads are experienced along with ambient air temperatures and other factors, the TE may be lower. Notice in Figure 3–5 that for the 3406E engine the BSFC is quoted as being accurate within ±010 lb/hp-hr (±6 g/kWh), and the fuel rate is listed as being acceptable within ±5% of that shown. This means that the TE for the LHV could be as low as 40.99% less 5% (2.04%) = 38.95%, or for the HHV rating, 43.74% less 5% (2.187%) = 41.55%. These are impressive figures for TE. All of the latest electronically controlled DI (direct-injection) unit injector diesel engines from Caterpillar, Cummins, Detroit Diesel, Mack, and Volvo have thermal efficiencies in the same basic range. See the next section for more information on thermal efficiency.

Heat Losses

Let us continue to use the TE example for the 3406E Caterpillar engine rated at 475 hp (354 kW). If we assume that our TE was in fact 43.74%, it means that we lost 100 − 43.74 = 56.26% of the heat that was released into the cylinders. Where did this heat loss go? This heat loss can be related to four factors:

1. Cooling system (approximately 23 to 27%)
2. Exhaust system (approximately 23 to 27%)
3. Friction losses (approximately 7 to 9%)
4. Heat radiation (approximately 3%)

If we assume that we lost 23% to the cooling system, 23% to the exhaust (turbocharger driven), 7.26% to friction, and 3% to radiation, the total accounts for our heat losses of 56.26%. We calculated that this engine needed 5817.56 Btu to produce 1 hp-hr and that 2545 Btu of this was needed to produce that 1 hp-hr. Therefore, by multiplying each of the system's heat loss percentages by 5817.56, we expended the heat injected into the engine as follows:

Cooling	= 5817.56 × 0.23	= 1338 Btu
Exhaust	= 5817.56 × 0.23	= 1338 Btu
Friction	= 5817.56 × 0.0726	= 422.35 Btu
Radiation	= 5817.56 × 0.03	= 174.52 Btu
	1 horsepower/hr	= 2545 Btu
	Total Btu of heat	= 5817.87 Btu

The heat losses chosen for the 3406E Cat engine are examples only and are not specific to this engine. Nevertheless, they can be considered as fairly typical for high-speed heavy-duty electronically controlled unit injector diesel engines in use today.

Engine Speed Droop

All diesel engines use mechanical (weights versus a spring) or electronic (magnetic pickup) governors to control the idle and maximum speeds, or all speed ranges when desired. Unless the engine is equipped with an *isochronous* or *zero-droop* governor, the engine speed is always lower when operating under load than when it is running with no load. This speed difference is described in Chapter 17. The difference between these two operating speed conditions commonly referred to as *governor droop*, can be determined as follows:

$$\frac{speed}{droop} = \frac{rpm\ at\ MNL\ speed - rpm\ at\ MFL\ speed}{rpm\ at\ MFL\ speed}$$

NOTE   MNL = maximum no-load speed, often referred to as *high idle;* MFL = maximum full-load speed, often referred to as *rated.*

Joule's Equivalent

A common measure for determining the amount of work available from an engine based on its fuel heat value in Btu is Joule's equivalent, which states that 1 Btu is capable of releasing the equivalent of 778 ft-lb of work, or 1 ft-lb = 0.001285 Btu. Therefore, the horsepower-hour (kWh) is the measure of 1 hp for a 1-hr period. Since we know that the amount of work required to produce a horsepower is equal to 550 lb-ft/sec, 33,000 ft-lb/min, or 1,980,000 ft-lb/hr, we can determine that a perfect engine with no heat losses would require 2545 Btu/hr to produce 1 hp by using the following formula:

$$1 \text{ hp/hr} = \frac{1,980,000}{778} = 2545 \text{ Btu}$$

Gasoline versus Diesel Engines

The thermal efficiency, or heat efficiency, of a diesel engine is superior to that of the spark-ignited gasoline (Otto cycle) engine. As we know from information discussed earlier in this chapter, the diesel engine employs compression ratios much higher than those of a gasoline engine. This is necessary to create a high-enough cylinder air temperature for the injected diesel fuel to vaporize and start to burn. The much higher combustion pressures and temperatures allow a greater expansion rate and more energy to be extracted from the fuel. Tremendous improvements have occurred in gasoline spark-ignited engines, particularly in the 1990s when fuel consumption improvements due to changes in engine component design, combustion improvements, and electronic control of distributor-less ignition and fuel injection systems have resulted in thermal efficiencies in the area of 35 to 39%. Gasoline engines tend to return better fuel economy when held at a steady speed, such as during highway driving, but they suffer in city-driving cycles because of the intake manifold air-throttling effect and pumping losses that occur at lower speeds.

Diesel engines, on the other hand, do not suffer from a throttled air supply and operate with a stratified air charge in the cylinder under all operating conditions. The net result of the unthrottled air in the diesel engine is that at idle rpm and light loads, the air/fuel ratio in the cylinder is very lean (90 : 1 to 120 : 1). This excess air supply lowers the average specific heat of the cylinder gases, which in turn increases the indicated work obtained from a given amount of fuel.

To comply with EPA exhaust emissions standards, automotive gasoline engines have to operate close to a *stoichiometric* air/fuel ratio, which is approximately 14 : 1. In other words, about 14 kg of air is required to completely combust 1 kg of fuel. Another way to look at this is that approximately 10,000 L of air is required to burn 1 L of gasoline. Even under full-load operating conditions the diesel engine operates with an excess air factor of at least 10 to 20%, which usually results in air/fuel ratios in the region 20 : 1 to 25 : 1. To meet exhaust emissions standards the gasoline engine relies on an exhaust-gas oxygen sensor to constantly monitor the "richness" or "leanness" of the exhaust gases after combustion. This oxygen sensor signal sends update information continuously to the on-board ECM (electronic control module) to allow operation in what is commonly known as a *closed-loop* operating mode. Failure of the oxygen sensor results in the engine falling back into an *open-loop* mode (no signal to the ECM), and the ECM automatically resorts to a "limp-home" condition that allows the engine to run but at a reduced performance. Because of their excess air factor of operation, most diesel engines at this time do not need an exhaust-gas oxygen sensor, or a catalytic converter, although some light- and midrange mechanically controlled truck engines are equipped with converters (see the section "Exhaust Emissions Limits" in Chapter 4).

Another advantage that the diesel engine enjoys over its gasoline counterpart is that the diesel fuel contains about 11% more Btu per unit volume than that in gasoline. Therefore, the diesel engine would have a better return per dollar spent on fuel.

Mechanical Efficiency

The ME (mechanical efficiency) of an internal combustion engine is determined by comparing the actual usable hp (bhp) to the cylinder hp (ihp). The higher the mechanical efficiency of the engine, the lower the fuel consumption. The ME of an engine can be determined from the following formula:

$$\text{ME} = \frac{\text{bhp}}{\text{ihp}}$$

If an engine produced 280 bhp with an ihp of 350, its ME would be

$$\frac{\text{bhp}}{\text{ihp}} = \frac{280}{350} = 80\%$$

Volumetric Efficiency

The power that can be extracted from an internal combustion piston engine is related to the amount of air that can be consumed or fed into the engine cylinders and retained. The higher the percentage of air retained, the larger the quantity of fuel that can be injected and burned to completion.

VE (volumetric efficiency) is the weight of air retained in the engine cylinder at the start of the compression stroke. In NA (naturally aspirated) nonturbocharged or blower-equipped engines that rely on atmospheric air pressure to force its way into the cylinder, the resistance to airflow caused by the intake ducting (such as the diameter, number of bends, length, and air-cleaner restriction) and intake manifold design lower the VE. The VE of an NA engine is therefore always less than atmospheric pressure (14.7 psi or 101.35 kPa) at sea level. Most NA engines have a VE in the region of 85 to 90% of atmospheric pressure, or between 12.49 and 13.23 psi (86.1 to 91.2 kPa).

When a turbocharger or gear-driven blower is added to a two- or four-stroke cycle engine, the VE can be greater than atmospheric pressure (that is, 100%). The critical factor in determining the cylinder air pressure before the start of the compression stroke is the timing of the intake valve closing on a four-stroke-cycle engine or the liner port and exhaust valve closing on a two-stroke-cycle Detroit Diesel engine. As an example refer to Figure 3–5, which lists operating conditions for Caterpillar's 3406E engine. Note that at 1800 rpm under full load this engine has an intake manifold pressure of 51.3 in. Hg. This is equivalent to 25.2 psi (173.7 kPa) and is supplied by the exhaust gas-driven turbocharger on this four-cycle engine. As the engine speed is reduced under load, note that the turbocharger boost pressure at the peak torque point of 1200 rpm reduces to 41.7 in. Hg (20.5 psi or 141.2 kPa). The reason behind this is that with a slower-running engine, the exhaust gas flow rate has decreased to 1767 cubic feet per minute (cfm), or 50 cubic meter per minute (cm³/min), from 2547 cfm (or 72 cm³/min) at 1800 rpm. Therefore, although the engine cylinder receives air at a pressure well above atmospheric, the valve timing is the final determining factor of what the trapped cylinder air pressure will be. On turbocharged engines, this can range anywhere between 130 and 200% higher than atmospheric.

People often talk about an engine as being "supercharged" and believe that as soon as an engine is fitted with a turbocharger or gear-driven blower that it automatically becomes so. Keep in mind that in technical classifications the intake valve timing on a four-cycle engine and the port and exhaust valve timing on a two-cycle model determine if the engine is actually supercharged. If the cylinder air pressure at the start of the compression stroke is higher than atmospheric, the engine is basically supercharged. The degree of supercharging, however, is directly related to the actual cylinder air pressure charge!

Engine Displacement and Compression Ratio

Although there are many electronically controlled unit injector diesel engines on the market today with similar horsepower (kW) ratings, the torque developed by some of these engines is higher or lower than that of others in some instances. The displacement of the engine cylinders and the compression ratio are factors that can affect the developed torque at a given engine speed.

Displacement

The displacement of an engine can be determined from OEM sales or service literature. In the absence of this information, a cylinder's displacement can be determined by the following formulas. To determine the cubic inch or cubic centimeter displacement of a cylinder, we need to know the bore and stroke dimensions. For example, let's assume that an engine has a bore and stroke of 5.12 × 6.30 in. (130 × 160 mm). The first thing we need to do is compute the area of the piston crown from the known bore size of 5.12 in. (130 mm). Use this formula: area = πR^2, where π = 3.1416 and R is the radius of the bore squared. In our example, area = 3.1416 × 2.56 × 2.56 = 20.58 in^2 (132.83 cm^2). Now if we multiply the area of the piston by the stroke, we can determine the cylinder volume or displacement: 20.58 × 6.30 in. = 129.7 in^3 (2125.39 cm^3, or 2.125 L).

If the engine were a six-cylinder model, we would have an engine displacement of 6 × 129.7 = 778 in^3 (12,752 cm^3, or 12.7 L). Using the same formula for the 3406E engine in Figure 3–5, we would find a piston crown area of 22.9 in^2 (148 cm^2) multiplied by a stroke of 6.5 in. (165 mm) for a cylinder displacement of 148.85 in^3 (2349.2 cm^3). Since it is a six-cylinder engine, the total engine displacement is 893.1 in^3 (14.6 L).

To determine the *airflow requirements* of an engine, we need to be able to calculate the approximate volume of air required per minute in either cubic feet per minute (cfm), or cubic meters per minute (m³/min) in the metric system of measurement. This can be determined by knowing the volume swept by all the pistons during one stroke for each cycle, which can be determined simply by knowing the number of cylinders times the area of the piston crown in square feet (square meters) times the stroke in feet (meters) times the number of cycles per cylinder per minute:

$$\text{engine displacement per minute} = N \times A \times S \times n \text{ (cfm)}$$

where N = number of cylinders
A = piston area, in ft^2 (m^2)
S = stroke, in ft (m)
n = cycles per min for one cylinder
= rpm for two-cycle engines
= rpm/2 for four-cycle engines

Let's assume that we want to calculate the airflow requirements for the 3406E engine discussed in Figure 3–5—a six-cylinder four-stroke-cycle engine with a bore of 5.4 in. (137 mm), a stroke of 6.5 in. (165 mm), and horsepower (kW) rated at 1800 rpm:

engine displacement per minute

$$= \frac{6 \times \pi}{4 \times 0.45^2 \times 0.541} \times \frac{1800}{2}$$

$$= 6 \times 0.7854 \times 0.202 \times 0.541 \times 900 = 464 \text{ cfm}$$

This airflow requirement is for a nonturbocharged engine model. Once we turbocharge the engine and add an air-to-air aftercooler system and electronic fuel injection controls to meet the mandated limits for exhaust emissions, the engine airflow requirement demands generally increase by turbocharger boost pressure ratios on the order of 2 : 1 and 3 : 1 in high-speed high-output models. In the case of the 3406E engine, note in Figure 3–5 that the specification for intake airflow calls for 1143 cfm (32.4 m³/min) at 1800 rpm. Note also that the exhaust gas flow rate at 1800 rpm with the engine producing 475 bhp (354 kW) is quoted as 2547 cfm (72 m³/min). Therefore, the 3406E engine actually requires an airflow rate that is 1143 cfm divided by 464 cfm (from the simplified formula calculation), which yields a ratio difference for this turbocharged and aftercooled engine that is 2.463 times greater than that for a naturally aspirated engine of the same displacement.

An alternative method to determine the airflow requirements is to use this formula:

$$\frac{\text{cubic inch displacement} \times \text{rpm}}{3456}$$

$$\times \text{volmetric efficiency} = \text{cfm}$$

Inserting the same data for the 3406E engine results in the following:

$$\frac{893 \times 1800}{3456} = 465 \text{ cfm} \times \text{VE} = \text{demand flow air}$$

We know from the specification sheet that this engine requires 2.46 times the air that a naturally aspirated model would require. In Chapter 13 we discuss the airflow requirements for two- and four-stroke-cycle engines in more detail.

Compression Ratio

CR (compression ratio) is used to compare the difference in cylinder volume when the piston is at BDC (bottom dead center) and when the piston is at TDC. Figure 3–12 is a CR comparison of a low-compression gas engine and a diesel engine. Most gasoline engines operate with CR values between 8 : 1 and 10.5 : 1, whereas diesel engines operate with much higher CR values, averaging between 14 : 1 and 17.5 : 1 on most current high-speed heavy-duty electronically controlled models of the DI (direct-injection) design. However, a number of IDI (indirect-injection) models run CRs as high as 23 : 1. Figure 3–12 indicates that the volume of air in the cylinder for the gasoline engine has been compressed to one-sixth its volume with the piston at TDC; in the diesel example, the volume has been reduced to one-sixteenth its volume with the piston at TDC.

The higher CR in diesel engines is one of the reasons that diesel engines are more thermally efficient than their gasoline counterparts. Higher CR results in greater expansion of the gases in the cylinder after combustion; therefore, a higher percentage of fuel energy is converted into useful work. Since a diesel engine does not use a spark plug for ignition of the fuel charge, the high CR raises the trapped cylinder air to a temperature that is above the self-ignition point of the

FIGURE 3–12 This example of how the compression ratio is estimated shows that a gasoline engine operates with a much lower CR than does a diesel engine.

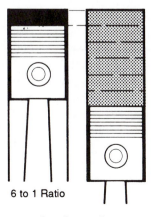

6 to 1 Ratio

Gasoline engine

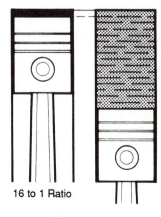

16 to 1 Ratio

Diesel engine

injected diesel fuel. Typical CRs are 15.0 : 1 for the Detroit Diesel series 50 8.5L and series 60 12.7L (16 : 1 for the series 60 11.1L model); 16.2 : 1 for the Cummins N14, and 16.25 : 1 for the 3406E Caterpillar model. Since we know that the engine displacement for the 12.7-L series 60 is 774 in^3/6 = 129 in^3 (2114 cm^3) divided by the CR of 15.0 : 1, the clearance volume (CV) between the piston crown and the underside of the cylinder head at TDC would be 129 divided by 15 = 8.6 in^3 (141 cm^3). The series 60 11.1-L model CV is 7 in^3 (115.5 cm^3). For the N14, with a displacement of 855 in^3 (14 L), the CV is 8.79 in^3 (144 cm^3). The 3406E, with a displacement of 893 in^3 (14.6 L) would have a CV of 9.16 in^3 (150.2 cm^3).

Keep in mind that both the engine torque and the horsepower of an engine are related to engine displacement, BMEP, and speed. Thus the different torque figures that are listed on OEM sales sheets for engines of the same speed and horsepower settings are controlled by the variables of engine displacement, BMEP, valve timing, injector timing, turbocharger boost, air inlet temperature, air swirl, fuel injection spray-in pressure, distribution, and so on.

Compression Temperature
Engine compression ratio has a bearing on the final temperature of the cylinder air charge before injection of fuel. The temperature of the compressed air (boost) flowing from the turbocharger on high-speed heavy-duty engines at full-load operating conditions is usually in the region of 300°F (149°C). This air temperature drastically lowers the denseness of the air charge and affects the power output of the engine as well as its ability to meet mandated exhaust emissions standards. Therefore, an ATAAC (air-to-air aftercooler) is widely used on heavy-duty highway trucks, and industrial, off-highway, and marine engines employ JWAC (jacket water aftercooling) systems. These systems are described in Chapters 12 and 13. The ATAAC system lowers the turbo boost air to between 100 and 110°F (38 and 43°C). Typical high-speed heavy-duty diesel engines generate compression pressures in the range 450 to 500 psi (3103 to 3792 kPa), which create cylinder air temperatures in the region of 900 to 1000°F (482 to 538°C). The relationship of temperature and pressure during the compression cycle can be considered to be in the region of about 2 : 1 and 3 : 1; the figure can be higher or lower depending on the engine compression ratio, air turbulence created during the upward movement of the piston, and of course the turbocharger boost ratio and the temperature of the air entering and being trapped within the cylinder. Final pressures and temperatures created during the power stroke are relative to the compression pressures and the quantity of fuel injected based on the load/speed of the engine.

Engines operating with boost pressure ratios in the region of 3 : 1 and ATAAC experience BMEPs between 180 and 295 psi (1241 to 2034 kPa) on most four-stroke-cycle engines for rated speed and peak torque rpm outputs, respectively. Because of their double power stroke, two-cycle engines have BMEP that are normally about 100 psi (690 kPa) lower than that of an equivalent four-stroke model. Keep in mind, however, from the information shown in Figure 3–5, that peak cylinder pressures experienced in current high-speed heavy-duty engines can be between 1800 and 2300 psi (12,411 to 15,856 kPa).

HEATING VALUE EQUIVALENTS

Typical heat value equivalents and their metric units for some of the more commonly used fuels are listed next.

Fuel	Imperial units	Metric units
Diesel	162,000 Btu/gallon	0.0377 GJ/L
Gasoline	146,000 Btu/gallon	0.0340 GJ/L
Propane	110,000 Btu/gallon	0.0255 GJ/L
	21,570 Btu/lb	0.0515 GJ/kg
Natural gas	1000 Btu/ft^3	0.0372 GJ/m^3
Coal	8500 to 15,000 Btu/lb	20 to 35 GJ/tonne
Electricity	3412 Btu/kWh	0.0036 GJ/kWh

GJ represents gigajoules, used to describe the metric quantity in billions (giga).

These heat values in Btu are average readings only and will vary in actual heat content of the gas or crude oil used. In the case of diesel fuel, refer to Chapter 16, which has a chart dealing with API (American Petroleum Institute) Btu heat values based on the fuels' API rating.

ISO STANDARDS

Not long ago the North American automotive, truck, and manufacturing industry regarded the European quality standards ISO 9000 with disdain; now it has embraced the standards as the core of a new global scheme to measure the performance of suppliers. Many manufactured products now contain a decal indicating that the component or item has been manufactured to ISO 9000 standards. This rating system is the core quality gauge for frontline parts makers to meet a set of industry-specific sets of standards.

ISO 9000 means global quality standards. Although *ISO* stands for International Standardization

Organization, the term is used as a variant of the Greek word *isos,* meaning equal, and is pronounced *ice-oh.* The choice of the number 9000 was arbitrary. The North American manufacturing industry does not want variations in supplier standards within a country or between countries; rather, the industry demands consistency of an agreed-on standard at all levels. Since most ISO standards will be common, suppliers and OEMs will save time and money.

We have discussed the ISO 9000 standards, but there are others. The ISO standards can be grouped into the following categories:

- ISO 9000: an overview and introduction to the other standards, including definitions of terms and concepts related to quality that are used in the other standards
- ISO 9001: comprehensive general standard for quality assurance in product design, development, manufacturing, installation, and servicing
- ISO 9002: standards that focus on manufacturing and installation of products
- ISO 9003: standards that cover final inspection and testing
- ISO 9004: guidelines for managing a quality control system; more details on managing the quality systems that are called for in the other standards; intended for use in auditing quality systems

SUMMARY

The information provided within this chapter gives you a solid foundation from which to discuss the detailed engineering operating concepts of a diesel engine. These concepts will help you to compare various types and models of engines, and to see how the design features of a specific engine can be altered to improve its overall performance in a given application.

SELF-TEST QUESTIONS

1. List the strokes involved in one complete cycle of operation for a four-stroke diesel engine.
2. The four strokes in Question 1 involve
   a. 270° of crankshaft rotation
   b. 360° of crankshaft rotation
   c. 600° of crankshaft rotation
   d. 720° of crankshaft rotation
3. What are the two strokes that are effectively eliminated from a two-stroke-cycle diesel engine?
4. The working strokes of a two-stroke-cycle diesel engine are completed in the following number of crankshaft degrees:
   a. 180
   b. 360
   c. 540
   d. 720
5. Typical compression ratios used in heavy-duty high-speed diesel engines range between
   a. 8 and 10 : 1
   b. 10 and 13 : 1
   c. 14 and 17 : 1
   d. 19 and 22 : 1
6. Typical compression pressures produced in heavy-duty high-speed diesel truck engines run between
   a. 250 and 300 psi (1724 to 2068 kPa)
   b. 350 and 425 psi (2413 to 2930 kPa)
   c. 450 and 550 psi (3103 to 3792 kPa)
   d. 600 and 800 psi (4137 to 5516 kPa)
7. Technician A says that the term *thermal efficiency* is an expression of the mechanical efficiency of the engine, whereas technician B says that it is an indicator of the heat efficiency of the engine. Who is correct?
8. Thermal efficiency of a diesel truck engine generally runs between
   a. 24 and 28%
   b. 30 and 34%
   c. 34 and 38%
   d. 38 and 42%
9. Typical fuel performance figures for current high-speed heavy-duty diesel engines average between
   a. 0.380 and 0.395 lb/bhp-hr (231 to 240 g/kWh)
   b. 0.350 and 0.370 lb/bhp-hr (213 to 225 g/kWh)
   c. 0.315 and 0.340 lb/bhp-hr (192 to 207 g/kWh)
   d. 0.300 and 0.315 lb/bhp-hr (183 to 192 g/kWh)
10. One gallon of U.S. fuel is equal to
    a. 4.256 L
    b. 3.900 L
    c. 3.785 L
    d. 3.600 L
11. True or False: *Btu* means *British thermal unit.*
12. How many Btu are required to produce 1 hp in a perfect engine over a 1-hr period?
    a. 2040
    b. 2250
    c. 2415
    d. 2545
13. Technician A says that the term *work* is computed by multiplying the force times the distance. Technician B disagrees. Who is correct?
14. Technician A says that horsepower keeps the piston moving and is a measure of how fast work can be done by the engine. Technician B says that torque is the ability to move a load or do work. Who is correct?
15. Horsepower is accepted as being a given amount of work developed in a given period. In English-speaking countries this is generally accepted as being equal to
    a. 28,000 ft-lb/min
    b. 33,000 ft-lb/min
    c. 35,550 ft-lb/min
    d. 37,300 ft-lb/min

16. Torque is a twisting and turning force that is developed at the
    a. piston
    b. connecting rod
    c. crankshaft
    d. flywheel

17. True or False: A constant-horsepower engine maintains a steady horsepower over a wider speed band than does a conventional diesel engine.

18. Technician A says that all diesel truck engines develop their greatest torque value at about 65% of their rated speed under full loads, for example, 1200 rpm versus 1950 rpm. Technician B says that the greatest torque is developed at the rated speed and horsepower setting, for example, 1950 rpm and 400 hp. Which technician knows what he or she is talking about here?

19. Technician A says that torque is what pulls a truck up a hill with a decrease in speed. Technician B says that horsepower is what pulls the truck up the hill as the engine and road speed drop off. Who is right here?

20. Technician A says that a high-torque-rise diesel engine will allow fewer transmission shifts to have to be made over a conventional diesel engine–equipped truck. Technician B says that there is no difference as long as the engine speed is kept at the rated value. Who is correct?

21. Technician A says that torque in the metric system is expressed in newton-meters (N · m), whereas technician B says that it is expressed in kilopascal (kPa). Who is correct?

22. Horsepower is expressed in kilowatts in the metric system of measurement, with 1 kilowatt equal to 1000 watts. Technician A says that 1 hp is higher in value than 1 kW. Technician B says that 1 hp is less than 1 kW. Is technician A or technician B correct?

23. A horsepower is equivalent to
    a. 0.674 kW
    b. 0.746 kW
    c. 0.940 kW
    d. 1.341 kW

24. Technician A says that brake mean effective pressure (BMEP) is the average pressure developed on the piston crown during the power stroke, whereas technician B says that it is the maximum pressure developed when the injected diesel fuel ignites. Who is correct?

25. Many heavy-duty highway-truck diesel engines use aftercooling to increase the horsepower of the engine. Technician A says that aftercooling reduces the exhaust heat loss of the engine and allows more heat for power. Technician B says that aftercooling lowers the temperature of the pressurized air from the turbocharger so that a denser charge is supplied to the engine cylinders, thereby producing more power. Is technician A or technician B correct?

26. Technician A says that the exhaust temperatures developed at the full-load-rated rpm speed of an engine will be lower than that produced at the peak torque engine speed. Technician B disagrees. Who is correct?

27. Technician A says that the exhaust temperatures on a two-stroke-cycle engine tend to be slightly higher than those produced on an equivalent-horsepower four-stroke-cycle engine at rated rpm. Technician B says that he has this reversed; exhaust temperatures are cooler on the two-stroke-cycle engine. Who is correct?

28. True or False: The duration of the power stroke in crankshaft degrees is longer on a two-cycle diesel engine than it is on a four-cycle engine.

29. What is the principle on which the gasoline or Otto cycle engine is said to operate?

30. On what principle does the compression ignition or diesel engine operate?

31. True or False: Caterpillar manufactures both two- and four-stroke cycle engines.

32. To convert cubic inches to cubic centimeters, multiply by
    a. 6.895
    b. 12.7
    c. 16.387
    d. 22.32

33. A Caterpillar 3176 model engine has a displacement per cylinder of 1.7 L. How many in^3 is this? Give the engine's total displacement in in^3 and L.

34. How many cubic centimeters make 1 L?

35. How many millimeters make 1 in.?

36. How many cubic inches make 1 L?

37. Determine the total in^3 displacement of a six-cylinder engine with a bore of 5.5 in. (139.7 mm) and a stroke of 6 in. (152 mm); then convert this answer to cm^3 and L.

38. One micron is equal to one millionth of a meter. This can be expressed in decimal form as
    a. 0.03937 in.
    b. 0.003937 in.
    c. 0.0003937 in.
    d. 0.00003937 in.

39. To convert engine torque from lb-ft to its metric equivalent, by what should you multiply?

40. Describe briefly the definition of a supercharged engine.

41. Draw a circle and sketch in the duration of each individual stroke for a four-stroke-cycle diesel engine. Show the start and end of injection at an idle speed as well as the positive valve overlap condition that exists.

42. Repeat the process described in Question 41 for a two-stroke-cycle diesel engine.

43. Sketch and show the relative piston firing positions for a six-cylinder CW-rotation four-stroke-cycle engine with a firing order of 1–5–3–6–2–4 using the degrees created in Question 41, and describe where each piston is and what stroke it is on.

44. Repeat the process that was described in Question 43 for a two-stroke-cycle engine.

45. Typical full-load-rated horsepower air temperature leaving the outlet side of the turbocharger on high-speed diesel engines is approximately
    a. 65.5°C (150°F)
    b. 93°C (200°F)
    c. 149°C (300°F)
    d. 204°C (400°F)

46. True or False: VE (volumetric efficiency) refers to the weight of air contained in the cylinder with the piston at BDC stopped versus what it would be at BDC running.

47. True or False: Ihp (indicated horsepower) refers to usable power at either the engine crankshaft or flywheel.

48. Technician A states that 1 hp is considered equal to 33,000 lb-ft (44,741 N · m) of work per minute. Technician B states that it is equivalent to 550 lb-ft (746 N · m) of work per second. Is only one technician correct or are both correct?

49. One Btu (kJ/kg) of released heat within a combustion chamber is capable of producing the following amount of mechanical work:
    a. 710 ft-lb (963 N · m)
    b. 758 ft-lb (1028 N · m)
    c. 778 ft-lb (1055 N · m)
    d. 876 ft-lb (1188 N · m)

50. Technician A states that current high-speed DI diesel engines develop peak firing pressures between 1200 and 1400 psi (6895 to 8274 kPa). Technician B says that this is too low and that peak pressures run between 1800 and 2300 psi (12,411 to 15,858 kPa). Who is correct?

51. List the advantages and disadvantages of a two-stroke-cycle engine in comparison to an equivalent four-cycle model.

52. Determine the following information for a six-cylinder four-stroke-cycle engine running at 1800 rpm:

    a. ihp; then convert it into kW; bore of 5.5 in. (140 mm) and a stroke of 6 in. (152 mm); a BMEP of 237 psi (1634 kPa)
    b. piston speed in feet/minute (m/min); then convert it to mph and km/h
    c. torque in lb-ft; then into N · m
    d. convert BMEP to its metric equivalent of kPa
    e. thermal efficiency using a fuel consumption rate of 0.316 lb/bhp-hr (g/kWh) with a calorific value of 19,100 Btu/lb (kJ/kW)

53. Determine the BMEP of a 365-bhp (272-kW) four-stroke-cycle engine using the formula

    $$BMEP = \frac{792{,}000 \times bhp}{D \times N}$$

    where D is the total piston displacement of the engine in in^3 and/or cm^3. Employ the displacement from your answer in Question 52; $N = 2100$ rpm.

54. If an engine develops a torque of 1650 lb-ft (2237 N · m) at 1200 rpm, what horsepower (kW) would it produce?

55. If an engine develops 470 bhp (351 kW) at 1800 rpm, what torque would it produce in lb-ft and N · m?

56. Fuel injector spray-in pressures on several current high-speed electronically controlled diesel engines can range as high as
    a. 15,000 psi (103,425 kPa)
    b. 20,000 psi (137,900 kPa)
    c. 24,000 psi (165,480 kPa)
    d. 28,000 psi (193,060 kPa)

57. Technician A says that current heavy-duty high-speed DI diesel engines employ single-hole pintle-type injection nozzles. Technician B says that they employ multi-hole nozzles/injectors for better fuel distribution and penetration. Who is correct?

4 Combustion Systems

OVERVIEW

In this chapter we introduce and describe the fundamentals of internal combustion. As a result of contemporary environmental concerns, combustion has undergone major changes to ensure that diesel engines can comply with the stringent exhaust emissions regulations in the United States. We discuss the characteristics of air and fuel and the engine combustion chamber and piston designs that have been introduced to improve the exhaust emissions and fuel economy of the engine.

THE COMBUSTION PROCESS

The combustion phase of engine operation is the period during which the high-pressure diesel fuel is injected into the compressed airmass in the cylinder, then ignited to produce a high-temperature, and high-pressure rise in the combustion chamber. The pressure created by the expanding gases forces the piston down the cylinder. The chemical energy released from the burning diesel fuel and air mixture is then converted to mechanical energy through the piston, connecting rod, and crankshaft to power the flywheel.

TYPES OF COMBUSTION CHAMBERS

The vintage of a diesel engine and its original equipment manufacturer (OEM) determine the type of combustion chamber used. The three main types of combustion chambers that have been employed fit into three main designs:

1. PC (precombustion chamber)
2. Turbulence or energy cell
3. DI (direct injection)

For many years mechanical fuel-injected and governed engines employed either the precombustion or turbulence chamber design. Both of these systems allowed use of an electrically heated glow plug to facilitate ease of starting, particularly in cold-weather operation. Heavy-duty diesel engines with both types of systems employed pistons that had a lower compression ratio than that used in direct-injection models. They also employed lower injection pressures than did the DI models. Both the PC and turbulence chamber models due to their design features were less reliant on higher-grade fuels and would emit lower exhaust emissions when using these lower-grade fuels than would a DI engine model. However, they were harder to start than a higher-compression-ratio DI engine, and if one or more glow plugs were faulty, both hard starting and rough combustion would be evident until the engine reached normal operating temperature. In addition, the PC and turbulence chamber engines tended to consume between 10 and 15% more fuel than did the DI model engine. In automotive diesel engines, due to the need for power output and performance somewhat similar to a gasoline engine, high compression ratios of between 21 and 23 : 1 were required; therefore, the PC chamber model was chosen initially due to its quieter operation. However, many modern automotive diesel engines now employ the DI design concept, with some models also employing a glow plug simply to facilitate quick and rapid starts in cold weather along with smoother operation. One example using this DI and glow plug design concept is the Navistar International 7.3 L/444 in^3 HEUI (hydraulically actuated electronic unit injector) engine model used in both Ford and Navistar truck products.

Precombustion Chambers

The precombustion chamber (Figure 4–1) differs from the energy cell in that fuel is injected into the prechamber rather than the main chamber as in the case of the energy cell. The precombustion chamber will contain approximately 20 to 35% of the combustion chamber's total top dead center (TDC) volume. Prechambers are connected to the main chamber by a direct passageway.

Precombustion chambers are used on many modern diesel engines and have many advantages, such as less exhaust emission and adaptability to various grades of fuel; they also require less atomization of injected fuel. Disadvantages include hard starting and less efficiency. Most prechamber engines are equipped with a cylinder-type glow plug for easier starting.

Components

1. A single- or two-piece chamber either screwed into the cylinder head or held in place by the injection nozzle
2. A piston head designed with a concave section
3. In many cases a glow plug that is threaded into the nozzle body or holder and protrudes into the prechamber

Precombustion Chamber Operation

As the piston reaches the top of its compression stroke, heated air is trapped in the main chamber and in the prechamber. At this point fuel is injected into the pre-combustion chamber. Although the mixture (fuel and air) in the prechamber is excessively rich at the point of injection, burning begins and the rapidly expanding fuel and air rush through the connecting passageway into the main chamber, where burning is completed. As can be seen, the fuel and air mixture rushing from the prechamber into the main chamber causes a high degree of turbulence and creates a mixture of air and fuel that will burn evenly and cleanly.

Type of Injection Nozzle or Injector Used

Precombustion chamber engines use a single- or double-hole nozzle, since atomization requirements are not great. Nozzle opening pressure can be greatly reduced also. Common opening pressures are 1800 to 2000 psi (127 to 141 kg/cm^2) as opposed to 2500 to 3000 psi (176 to 211 kg/cm^2) in direct-injection mechanically governed engines.

Turbulence Chambers

A turbulence chamber (Figure 4–2) is very similar to a precombustion chamber in that it is a separate, smaller chamber connected to the main chamber. It differs in that it usually contains approximately 50 to 75% of the TDC cylinder volume and is connected to the main chamber with a passageway that may run at right angles to the main chamber.

Components

1. Turbulence chambers may be an integral part of the cylinder head or, like the precombustion chamber, may be a separate part that is installed into the cylinder head.
2. They usually have flat-top pistons, since the fuel and air mixture does not strike the piston at a

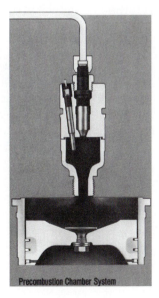

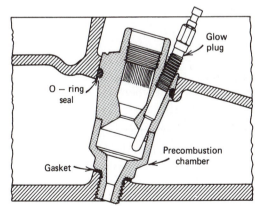

FIGURE 4–1 (A) Precombustion chamber and its connection to the main cylinder; (B) Details of a typical PC chamber located in the cylinder head.

Precombustion Chamber System

Glow plug

O — ring seal

Gasket

Precombustion chamber

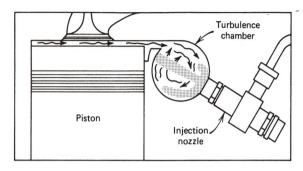

FIGURE 4–2 Turbulence chamber. (Courtesy of Deere & Co.)

right angle when it leaves the chamber. In most cases the passageway is designed so that the fuel and air mixture will enter the chamber parallel to the top of the piston or at a 15 to 20° angle.

3.   Engines with this type of turbulence chamber may use a cylinder glow plug for ease in starting.

Turbulence Chamber Operation
As the piston reaches the top of its compression stroke, air is trapped in the turbulence chamber and the main combustion chamber. Fuel is injected into the turbulence chamber, where burning occurs immediately, and the resulting expansion forces the air and fuel mixture into the main chamber with considerable force and speed. Because of the design of the passageway connecting the chamber with the main combustion chamber, the fuel and air mixture enters the main chamber at an angle and creates a high degree of turbulence in the main chamber. This turbulence aids in mixing the fuel with the air, enabling complete combustion.

Type of Injection Nozzle or Injector Used
A single- or double-hole nozzle is used in most turbulence chamber engines. This chamber is somewhat similar in operation to the precombustion chamber. A high degree of atomization is not required. Nozzle opening pressure is usually in the range 1800 to 2000 psi (127 to 141 kg/cm^2).

Direct Injection
Although the IDI design was used for many years in some diesel engines, the DI system is dominant in today's heavy-duty high-speed diesel engines. In the DI system the fuel is injected directly into an open combustion chamber formed by the shape of the piston crown or bowl and the underside of the cylinder head fire deck. In the typical DI system shown in Figure 4–3, the injection nozzle is located in the cylinder head and extends directly into the engine cylinder. Note that the piston crown is shaped in such a manner that, in effect,

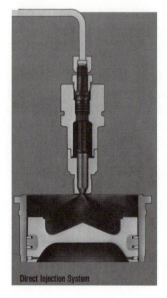

FIGURE 4–3 Direct-injection system.

it will form the combustion chamber when the piston approaches top dead center and fuel is injected.

Two main piston crown designs are used today in DI diesel engines:

1.   The Mexican hat–shaped piston shown in Figure 4-3 is the basic shape used by Detroit Diesel, Caterpillar, Cummins, and Mack, with minor variations among them.

2.   The in-bowl piston shape (illustrated in Figure 4–4) is often referred to as the MAN system, since much research was undertaken by this German engine company in perfecting this shape. Others who use this type of piston crown shape include Perkins, Caterpillar, Cummins, and Detroit Diesel in their 8.2-L four-stroke-cycle engines.

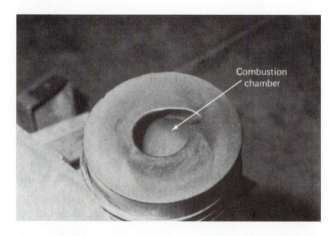

FIGURE 4–4 MAN-type combustion chamber.

Piston-Induced Swirl or Squish

As the intake valve closes and the piston starts upward on its compression stroke, the design on the piston, the Mexican hat, forces the trapped air to rotate or swirl very rapidly by the time the piston reaches the end of its compression stroke. Highly atomized fuel is then injected into the combustion chamber containing the rapidly swirling heated air, and combustion occurs immediately.

Type of Injection Nozzle or Injection Used

A multi-hole injection combustion chamber design is needed to distribute the fuel throughout the cylinder and to atomize it. Nozzle opening pressures are usually in the average range 2500 to 4000 psi (176 to 281 kg/cm^2).

COMBUSTION DYNAMICS

Pressure–Volume Curve

Figure 4–5 will help you understand the processes that occur within the engine cylinder and combustion chamber. The figure illustrates what actually transpires during the two most important strokes in a four-stroke-cycle diesel engine. The PV (pressure–volume) diagram represents the piston from a position corresponding to 90° BTDC (before top dead center) as it moves up the cylinder on its compression stroke to 90° ATDC (after TDC) on its power stroke. The vertical lines in the diagram represent cylinder pressure, which can vary substantially between makes and models of engines.

Typical cylinder pressures within the cylinder and combustion chamber at the start of injection would be approximately 550 to 600 psi (3793 to 4137 kPa) and the compressed air would be anywhere between 900 and 1100°F (482 to 593°C). Both the pressures and temperatures can, of course, vary with different compression ratios and engine design characteristics. Once the diesel fuel has been injected and starts to burn, peak cylinder pressures can run between 1800 and 2300 psi (12,411 to 15,859 kPa), with temperatures peaking to between 3500 and 4000°F (1927 to 2204°C) on high-speed heavy-duty truck direct-injected diesel engines.

In Figure 4-5 the dashed line represents the increase in cylinder pressure BTDC and prior to fuel being injected when the engine is cranked over on the starter motor. For our close study of the actual four phases of combustion, we are concerned with the solid black line shown on the PV diagram. When the fuel is injected at point A, the liquid-atomized fuel leaving the injector spray tip must vaporize and mix first to initiate combustion, due to the heat contained within the compressed air charge. The higher the cylinder pressure and temperature, the faster the fuel will vaporize and the quicker ignition will begin.

The ignition delay period extends from point A to point B; normal ignition delay periods range from 0.001 to 0.003 second. When the injected fuel ignites at point B, a rapid rise in both pressure and temperature occurs within the cylinder. This phase is known as the *uncontrolled burning* or *flame propagation* period. The uncontrolled burning period ends at point C, which is followed by a controlled combustion period from

FIGURE 4–5 *Pressure–volume curve diesel engine combustion operating principle. (Courtesy of Zexel USA. Technology and Information Division.)*

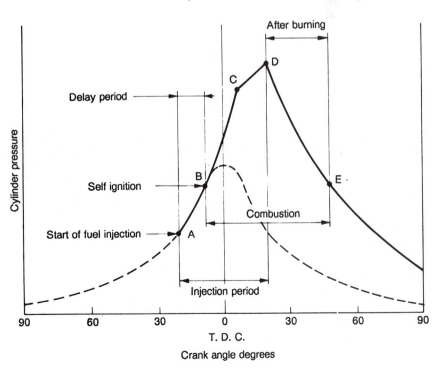

point C to point D as the remaining fuel is injected. This action creates a gradual increase in cylinder pressure. The engine manufacturer determines through engineering analysis the actual rate of injection for this period. The actual rate of injection is simply the quantity or volume of diesel fuel injected in terms of either the injection pump camshaft angle degrees (multiple-plunger inline pump), or the engine camshaft angle degrees in a unit injector fuel system.

Note that between points B and C the piston has actually attained its TDC position and is being pushed down the cylinder by the pressure of the expanding gases. In this example the fuel injection duration ends at point D, with the piston being approximately 18 to 20° ATDC. The last droplets of fuel that were cut off at point D and any remaining unburned fuel particles will continue to burn between points D and E, thereby creating an afterburning period that produces the pressures to keep the piston moving on its power stroke. Note, however, that if the afterburning period takes too long due to poor mixing of the fuel and air, combustion temperatures will increase, with a subsequent decrease in the engine's thermal efficiency (heat efficiency). Thermal efficiency is discussed in more detail later in the chapter. One other problem of a long afterburn period is the generation of soot in the exhaust, as a result of incomplete combustion.

In the diesel engine, air only is drawn into the cylinder and subsequently compressed during the upward-moving piston compression stroke. Table 4–1 lists the properties of air. The diesel engine always operates with an excess air/fuel ratio due to the unthrottled entry of air. A diesel engine mechanically or electronically regulates the fuel flow and is therefore a leaner-burning engine than its gasoline counterpart. At an idle rpm, the diesel engine tends to operate at an extremely lean air/fuel ratio with the excess air running between 600 and 1000%; at the high-speed end of the operating range, the diesel still has an excess air/fuel ratio of about 10 to 15% over its gasoline counterpart when producing its maximum horsepower. This excess air percentage can be shown as: excess air = lambda (λ) + 1.1–1.15, for the combustion to remain within acceptable exhaust smoke limits. The point at

which fuel is injected directly into the compressed air varies between engines and with the load and speed on the engine, similar to the way the spark plug firing point varies in a gasoline engine through the advance mechanism.

Compression ratios in the automotive precombustion chamber diesel engine average between 20 and 23 : 1, with resultant compression pressures from as low as 275 to 490 psi (1896 to 3378 kPa). Heavy duty high-speed DI diesel engines used in highway trucks with compression ratios between 14 and 17 : 1, which are turbocharged and air-to-air aftercooled, obtain average compression pressures between 435 and 600 psi (30 to 41 bar) and compression temperatures before fuel is injected of between 700 and 900°C (1292 to 1652°F). Peak cylinder pressures and temperatures after the fuel is injected range anywhere between 1200 psi (8274 kPa) to as high as 2300 psi (15,858 kPa) on direct-injected high-speed heavy-duty diesel engines. Temperatures can peak as high as 2204°C (4000°F). The fuel injection pressures will depend on the type of system used, with pump–line–nozzle systems being incapable of delivering as high an injection pressure as the compact unit injector system. The fuel pressure required to open the nozzle needle valve in a pump line system generally ranges between 1800 and 3950 psi (12,411 to 27,235 kPa), although there are some that are capable of slightly higher pressure peaks. When this high-pressure fuel, or what is known as *nozzle lift* or *release pressure*, is forced through the very small holes in the tip, there is a fuel pressure increase similar to placing your thumb over a garden hose without a nozzle. The result is an increase in spray pressure and a reduction in volume so that spray-in pressure ranges between 18,000 and 19,600 psi (124,110 to 135,142 kPa). The number of holes in the spray tip and their diameter determine the fuel droplet size. Both have an impact on fuel vaporization times, combustion rate, and exhaust emissions levels. Generally, the fuel droplets range in size from 10 to 100 microns (μm) for a typical light distillate diesel fuel. Recall that 1 micron is 1 millionth of a meter; it can be written as a decimal: 0.00003937 in. Consequently, the fuel droplet size in inches would be 0.0003937 in. for a 10-μm droplet and 0.003937 in. for a 100-μm fuel droplet size. The final pressure at which the nozzle or unit injector needle valve opens depends on the compressive force of the needle valve spring and the area on which the increasing fuel pressure operates. However, many holes or orifices in the tip are usually between 0.005 and 0.010 in. (0.127 to 0.254 mm) in diameter on multiple-hole nozzles used in high-speed heavy-duty diesel engines.

The unit injector system is capable of producing spray-in pressures between 26,000 and 28,000 psi

TABLE 4–1   *Nitrogen and oxygen content of air.*

	By volume		By weight	
	Percent	Ratio	Percent	Ratio
Nitrogen	79	3.76	76.8	3.32
Oxygen	21	1.00	23.2	1.00
Total	100		100	

(179,270 to 193,060 kPa). The speed of penetration of the fuel leaving the injector tip can approach velocities as high as 780 mph (1255 km/h), which is faster than the speed of sound. The fact that the pump–line–nozzle systems cannot obtain as high a pressure for injection and control of exhaust emissions has forced fuel injection manufacturers to move toward adoption of the superior unit injector system. Detroit Diesel Corporation, which has always used unit injectors, has now been joined by Caterpillar, Cummins, Volvo, and Robert Bosch in using this type of injection system.

The injected fuel (atomized) is basically in a liquid state; therefore, for ignition to take place, the fuel must vaporize (known as distillation temperature). This means that the fuel must penetrate the airmass (high-pressure air/high temperature) to allow the fuel molecules to mix with the oxygen molecules within the combustion chamber. Unlike a gasoline engine, where the air/fuel mix has already taken place during the intake and compression strokes, the diesel fuel must achieve this after injection. For the fuel actually to reach a state of ignition, there is a time delay from the point of injection to the point of ignition. This time delay is approximately 0.001 second and results in a slower-igniting fuel. The longer this time delay before the initial fuel that was injected takes to ignite, the greater the volume of injected fuel that will be collected within the combustion chamber. When this volume of fuel does ignite, there is a pressure increase within the combustion chamber. A time delay of longer than approximately 0.003 second would be an excessively long ignition delay period and would therefore result in a rough-running engine (knocking). This knocking occurs at the start of combustion in a diesel engine instead of at the end of combustion in a gasoline engine.

In a DI diesel engine, fuel that is injected and mixed during the ignition delay period will have a direct effect on the shape of the cylinder/combustion chamber pressure rise pulse. Fuel that is burned before the cylinder pressure reaches its peak value controls the peak height value developed within the cylinder. In other words, the peak rate of heat release determines the rapid rise in cylinder pressure that occurs immediately after ignition of the fuel. The peak in the heat release results from the rapid combustion of the diesel fuel, which was injected and premixed with the high-temperature cylinder air during the delay period. This rapid pressure rise after ignition contributes to the noise from the diesel combustion process that is characteristic of all diesel engines. A reduction in the cetane number of the diesel fuel being used increases the ignition delay period and contributes to a noisier combustion sound.

Fuel that is premixed during the ignition delay period, and therefore the peak rate of heat release and the peak rate of cylinder pressure increase in the combustion chamber, depends on the ignition delay and the quantity of fuel injected and mixed with the air. Ignition delay is affected by five factors:

1. The duration in crankshaft degrees of the actual delay period from the start of fuel injection until the fuel vaporizes and ignites, more commonly known as *ignition delay*
2. The temperature and pressure of the intake air
3. Engine compression ratio
4. The heat absorbed by the open-cylinder air charge during the intake stroke and during the closed compression stroke from various surrounding engine surfaces
5. The cetane number of the fuel; the higher the rating, the shorter the ignition delay period

Ignition lag will increase if the injection timing is either very late or very early, because the fuel will be injected into an airmass that has lost a lot of its compression heat (late timing) or not yet attained it through early injection timing. Since the injector will continue to inject fuel into this already burning mass, the pressure will rise to a peak pressure as the piston attains the TDC position. As the piston starts down into its power stroke, this additional injected fuel maintains a steady pressure as it starts to burn, thereby providing the diesel engine with the term *constant-pressure cycle*. In some engines, the fuel is cut off just BTDC, others may cut off fuel at TDC, while still, others may not cut fuel off until after TDC. Because of the fact that diesel fuel continues to be injected into the already burning fuel of the combustion chamber as the piston moves down the cylinder on its power stroke, the cylinder pressure is said to remain constant during the combustion process.

With the gasoline engine, the instantaneous ignition concept produces a very rapid rise in cylinder pressure with a very fast burn rate, resulting in a hammerlike blow on the piston crown. In the diesel cycle, the pressure rise is sustained for a longer period, resulting in a more gradual and longer push on the piston crown than that in the gasoline engine. Rudolf Diesel's original concept more than 100 years ago was that his engine would continue to have fuel injected during the power stroke and that no heat losses would occur in his uncooled engine. This concept was known as an *adiabatic diesel engine*, which in the true sense of the term meant that there would be no loss of heat to the cylinder walls while the piston moved up on its compression stroke. In addition, no cooling system would be used, resulting in the transfer of waste heat to the exhaust for a gain in thermal efficiency. Since no cooling system would be required, no frictional losses would occur through having to use a gear-driven water pump, and so on. We know this was impossible to achieve; however, Diesel's original idea of producing a true constant-pressure cycle, although never achieved, did attain some measure of success in the engines that now bear his name.

There is no internal combustion engine today that operates on either a true constant-pressure or constant-volume cycle under varying operating conditions, because they all require a few degrees of crankshaft rotation to complete combustion with a subsequent rise in cylinder pressure.

FUEL INJECTION TIMING

Engine manufacturers determine the best fuel injection timing point by experimentation in a test cell with the engine on a dynamometer. Actual fuel injection timing is then determined after consideration of the following factors:

- Horsepower output
- Fuel consumption
- Engine noise
- Exhaust gas denseness due to incomplete combustion (black soot)
- Exhaust gas temperatures
- Exhaust gas emissions with respect to NO_x (nitric oxides), HC (hydrocarbons), CO (carbon monoxide), CO_2 (carbon dioxide), and PM (particulate matter)

The actual start of fuel injection varies among makes and models of engines due to design differences; at an idle speed the variance can be anywhere between 5 and 15° BTDC. As the engine speed is increased and a greater volume of fuel is injected, timing must be advanced to allow the fuel to burn to completion because of the now-faster-moving piston, since there will be less time available. Consider that in an engine having a piston stroke of 6 in. (152.4 mm), at an idle speed of 600 rpm the speed of the piston will be 2 × 6 in., since the piston will move up the cylinder once and down the cylinder once for every 360° or each complete turn of the crankshaft. Therefore, piston speed can be determined by the following formula:

$$\text{piston speed} = \frac{2 \times \text{stroke length} \times \text{rpm}}{12}$$

So at a 600-rpm idle speed, the piston will travel 600 ft/min, or 60 × 600 in 1 hr. In 1 hr the piston travels 36,000 ft; if we divide by 5280 ft we can determine its

speed in miles per hour, which in this case is 6.81 mph (11 km/h). At a maximum engine speed of 2100 rpm, the piston will travel at 2100 ft/min or 23.86 mph (38.39 km/h). If the start of fuel pressurization within the fuel injection pump barrel was to occur at the same number of degrees BTDC at the high-speed as at the low-speed setting, then, as you can see in Figure 4–6, the piston would be closer to the top of its stroke before fuel injection actually began, while running at the higher speed. The start of fuel injection has therefore been retarded (begins later in the compression stroke of the upward-moving piston) at the higher speed. It becomes necessary to advance the start of fuel injection (inject fuel earlier) in the cylinder with an increase in engine speed. Figure 4-6 shows the actual beginning of fuel pressurization (beginning of compression) within the pumping plunger and barrel bore. In an inline multiple-plunger injection pump that uses long fuel lines to transfer the fuel from the pump to the injector and nozzle, there is also a time delay required to create a high-enough pressure in this long column of fuel before the nozzle will open and allow fuel injection to begin. This is important to understand since the speed of the engine/pump affects the actual start of injection.

Figure 4–7 illustrates a typical inline injection pump plunger and barrel assembly with the spring-loaded delivery valve assembled above the barrel. The connecting high-pressure fuel line and fuel nozzle are shown on the right-hand side. Once the upward-moving plunger has closed the fuel supply and discharge ports in the barrel, trapped fuel is placed under pressure or compression. The fuel must be at a high enough pressure to overcome the fuel line residual pressure and the spring-loaded delivery valve above the barrel. T_1 is the time from the start of fuel pressurization/compression until the delivery valve actually opens. T_2 in the diagram is the time required for transmission of the high-pressure fuel inside the fuel pipe to the nozzle. T_2 is determined by the speed of the pressure wave transmission and the pipe length. In most high-speed diesel engines using inline pumps, this pressure wave transmission speed is approximately 1350 to 1400 m/s (4429 to 4593 ft/sec), which is a fuel speed of between 3020 and 3132 mph (4860 to 5040 km/h). Note that T_2 remains constant regardless of injection pump speed. The time required for the residual pressure in the injection pipe to reach a high enough level that it can open the nozzle delivery valve is pressure T_3. Keep in mind that nozzle release pressures are adjustable by either an internal screw adjustment or by the use of shims. In both cases you effectively change the compressive force of the nozzle valve spring. This allows the same nozzle to be used in more

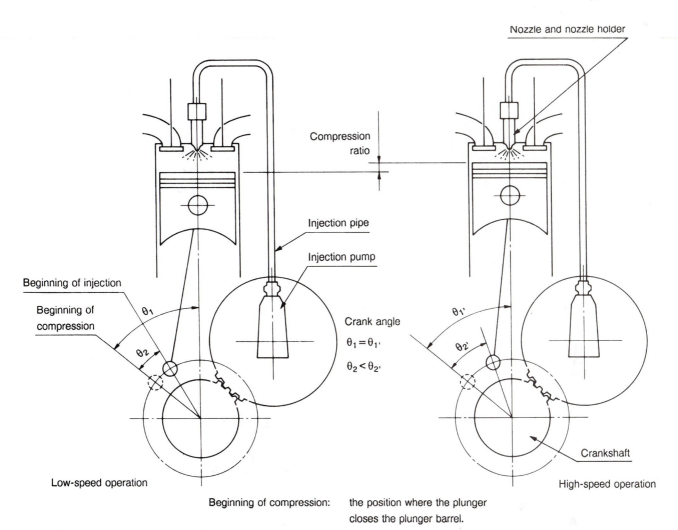

Beginning of compression: the position where the plunger closes the plunger barrel.

Beginning of injection: the position where the fuel oil is injected from the nozzle into the cylinder.

FIGURE 4–6 How the start of fuel injection into the combustion chamber must be advanced as the engine speed is increased. (Courtesy of Zexel USA, Technology and Information Division.)

than one particular model of engine. Pressure T_3 decreases as the injection pump speed increases, and increases (longer lag time) when the residual pressure in the fuel line decreases.

The injection lag time in a unit injector fuel system is shorter than that in an inline pump system because there is no long fuel line as a result of the fuel pressure being developed within the body of the unit injector. To give you an appreciation of just how short a time is involved in the fuel injection period, refer to Figure 4–8 which illustrates the time in milliseconds (thousandths of a second) required to complete the injection period in a typical high-speed diesel engine running at different rpm levels.

If an engine idling at 500 rpm requires 15° of engine crankshaft rotation to inject its desired quantity of fuel, the actual time to complete this process will be 5 milliseconds. If injection started at 15° BTDC at 2000 rpm, the time available for injection drops to approximately 1.75 milliseconds. The same engine running at a speed of 2000 rpm starting injection at 30° BTDC will have only 3 milliseconds for the completion of the injected fuel to burn, which includes the actual injection time and the mixing of the atomized fuel with the compressed air charge, plus the vaporization of the fuel followed by burning. Advancement of the start of fuel injection can be obtained through either mechanical or electronic means.

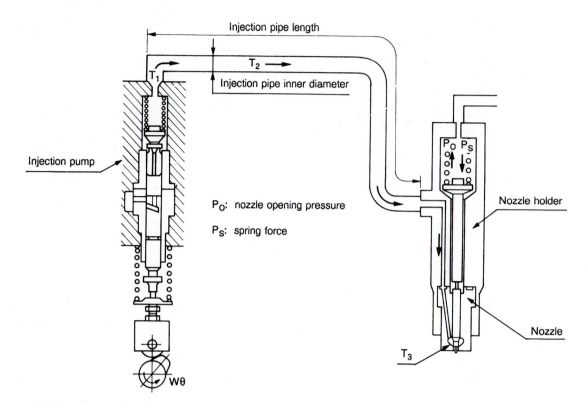

FIGURE 4-7 *Three major areas that create injection lag in a multiple-plunger inline injection pump. (Courtesy of Zexel USA,, Technology and Information Division.)*

RETARDED VERSUS ADVANCED TIMING

The reason that a variable injection/engine timing system is required on today's heavy-duty diesel engines, particularly in on-highway vehicles, is that the strin-

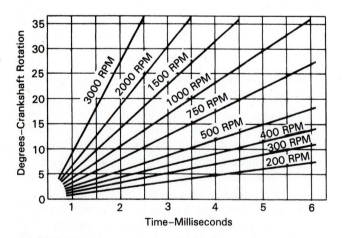

FIGURE 4-8 *Graph illustrating the very short time period, in milliseconds (thousandths of a second), available for fuel injection purposes related to engine speed and the point at which injection begins BTDC (before top dead center).*

gent exhaust emissions legislation mandated through the EPA in the United States was designed to reduce pollutants in the air that we breathe. In addition to limiting the exhaust emissions from the engine exhaust stack, however, the engine manufacturers want to improve the fuel economy and performance of their products. The two main culprits that EPA wants controlled are hydrocarbons and nitrogen oxides.

Just what are hydrocarbons? Unburned or partially burned fuel in the combustion chamber results in hydrocarbons—basically soot produced from the carbon in the diesel fuel. Nitrogen oxides, on the other hand, are what create the yellowish-brown smog that is so noticeable in cities such as Los Angeles. Nitrogen oxides are created when combustion chamber temperatures exceed 3000°F (1649°C), due to oxygen and nitrogen combining during this high-temperature phase. Since both oxygen and nitrogen are constituent parts of the air that we breathe, it is pretty hard to avoid these conditions completely.

EXHAUST EMISSIONS LIMITS

Both gasoline and diesel engines in North America are manufactured so that they *must* comply with the U.S. EPA exhaust emissions standards for the year in which they are produced. For heavy-duty on-highway diesel engines, these exhaust emissions fall into various categories that deal with hydrocarbons, carbon monoxide, nitrogen oxides, and particulate matter.

Exhaust gases have several major constituents.

- Carbon dioxide (CO_2), although nonpoisonous, does contribute to *global warming*. Complete combustion produces CO_2 and water.

- Carbon monoxide (CO) is a colorless, odorless, and tasteless gas. Inhalation of as little as 0.3% by volume can cause death within 30 minutes. The exhaust gas from spark ignition engines at an idle speed has a high CO content. For this reason, *never* allow the engine to run in enclosed spaces such as a closed garage.

- Oxides of nitrogen (NO_x) have two classes. Nitrogen monoxide (NO) is a colorless, odorless, and tasteless gas that is rapidly converted into nitrogen dioxide (NO_2) in the presence of oxygen. NO_2 is a yellowish- to reddish-brown poisonous gas with a penetrating odor that can destroy lung tissue. NO and NO_2 are customarily treated together and referred to as oxides of nitrogen (NO_x).

- Hydrocarbons (HC) of many different types are present in exhaust gas. In the presence of nitrogen oxide and sunlight, they form oxidants that irritate the mucous membranes. Some hydrocarbons are considered to be carcinogenic. Incomplete combustion produces unburned hydrocarbons.

- Particulate matter (PM), in accordance with U.S. legislation, includes all substances (with the exception of unbound water) that under normal conditions are present as solids (ash, carbon) or liquids in exhaust gases.

Federal emissions standards for diesel truck and bus exhaust in g/bhp-hr are shown here for 1994 and 1998:

Year	HC	CO	NO_x	PM	Fuel sulfur weight (%)
1994	1.3	15.5	5.0	0.1	0.05
1998	1.3	15.5	4.0	0.1	0.05

The only difference for urban buses is that the PM is 0.05 g/bhp-hr (for 1994 and 1998).

Future EPA regulations also extend into off-highway diesel equipment as well as marine applications (see tables 4–2 and 4–3). California, which has the strictest internal combustion engine exhaust emissions in the world, usually sets standards that are then followed by the EPA. California has enacted emission levels that extend to utility engines such as lawn mowers and garden equipment (gas or diesel). Separate standards are in place for hand-held engines. Non-hand-held engines have to meet two standards (three for diesels): total hydrocarbon plus nitrogen oxide level, carbon monoxide level, and for diesels, a particulate matter limit.

The CARB (California Air Resources Board) now has laws in place covering all types of internal combustion engines in almost all types of applications; these laws cover retrofitted engines as well. The CARB requires certification test procedures and emission standards for heavy-duty (40 hp, 30 kW, and over) construction and farm equipment for the 1995 model year and beyond. Also beginning in 1995, all new and heavy-duty off-highway engines must certify to emission standards of 1.3 g/bhp-hr for HC; 5.0 g/bhp-hr for NO_x, and 0.25 g/bhp-hr for PM. For the year 1999, all new heavy-duty off-highway engines must certify

TABLE 4–2   Projected EPA off-highway exhaust emissions standards. (Courtesy of Diesel & Gas Turbine Publications.)

Net power kW (Hp)	HC g/kW-hr (g/bHp-hr)	CO g/kW-hr (g/bHp-hr)	NO_x g/kW-hr (g/bHp-hr)	PM g/kW-hr (g/bHp-hr)	Smoke A/L/P* (%)
130 (175)	1.3 (1.0)	11.4 (8.5)	9.2 (6.9)	0.54 (0.4)	20/15/50
≥75 to <130 (100 to <175)	—	—	9.2 (6.9)	—	20/15/50
≥37 to <75 (50 to <100)	—	—	9.2 (6.9)	—	20/15/50

* Smoke opacity standards are reported in terms of percent opacity during an acceleration mode, a lug mode, and the peak opacity on either the acceleration or lug modes.

TABLE 4–3   EPA's implementation timetable for off-highway engine exhaust emissions. (Courtesy of Diesel & Gas Turbine Publications.)

Engine size kW (Hp)	Implementation date
≥130 to <560 (≥175 to <750)	January 1, 1996
≥75 to <130 (≥100 to <175)	January 1, 1997
≥37 to <75 (≥50 to <100)	January 1, 1998
>560 (>750)	January 1, 2000

to 0.60 g/bhp-hr HC, 2.0 g/bhp-hr NO_x, and 0.1 g/bhp-hr for PM. All 1995 and later-model-year engines must comply with durability and warranty requirements similar to those imposed for on-highway engines in the state. All 1991 heavy-duty diesel engines rebuilt after 1995 must comply with a capping standard of 10 g/bhp-hr for HC and NO_x.

To reduce exhaust emissions from diesel engines, particularly heavy-duty on-highway models, engine advancements and after-treatment technologies have been adopted to ensure that all engines are in compliance with EPA standards. Exhaust emissions standards have become more stringent over the years; the latest major limits came into affect in 1994. By 1998 NO_x must drop by 20% from the 1994 limits to 4.0 g/bhp-hr. Most of the 1994 heavy-duty on-highway engines were able to meet the regulations through higher injection pressures, high top ring pistons, tailored intake and exhaust systems, and closely designed turbochargers using air-to-air-charge cooling systems. In addition, in October 1993 in the United States, legislation reduced the allowable sulfur content in diesel fuel to 0.05%, which has also helped in reducing emissions because 98% of the sulfur is combusted to sulfur dioxide and the rest is combusted to sulfates. This low-sulfur fuel still leaves about 0.01 g/bhp-hr sulfate in the raw exhaust. Diesel fuel contains molecules with between 8 and 15 carbon atoms, and engine lube oils tend to have molecules with more than 15 carbon atoms; diesel fuel and engine lube oil differ in molecular size.

SUMMARY

Your knowledge acquired through details given in this chapter will provide you with a thorough understanding of the phases of combustion within the diesel engine. This knowledge will help you when trouble-shooting an engine with unusual exhaust smoke color, poor fuel economy, hard starting and rough running.

SELF-TEST QUESTIONS

1. Technician A says that the most popular type of combustion chamber design for heavy-duty high-speed diesel truck engines is the IDI (indirect-injection) or PC (precombustion chamber) design. Technician B disagrees and says that the DI (direct-injection) design is the most widely used type of combustion system. Which technician is correct?

2. Which of the following combustion chamber designs offers the best fuel economy when used in midheavy and heavy-duty diesel truck engines?
   a. swirl chamber design
   b. precombustion chamber design
   c. direct-injection design

3. Technician A says that a glow plug is not required for startup of a precombustion chamber design engine. Technician B disagrees, stating that it is the direct-injection engine type that does not require the use of a glow plug system for startup. Who is right?

4. The MAN M-type combustion chamber design is one whereby
   a. the combustion chamber bowl is contained within the crown of the piston
   b. the combustion chamber is in fact a small antechamber contained within the cylinder head
   c. the combustion chamber is located to the side of the main chamber

5. Technician A says that current cylinder firing pressures in high-speed heavy-duty engines average 1000 to 1200 psi (6895 to 8274 kPa). Technician B says this is too low and that pressures between 1800 and 2300 psi (12,411 to 15,858 kPa) are more common. Who is correct?

6. Technician A says that fuel injection pressures now in use in heavy-duty highway truck engines range between 19,000 and 28,000 psi (131,005 to 193,060 kPa). Technician B says this is impossible because such pressures would blow the engine apart. Is technician A or technician B correct?

7. Technician A says that the diesel engine operates on the constant-volume principle. Technician B disagrees, saying that the diesel engine operates on the constant-pressure cycle. Who is correct?

8. When the diesel fuel is injected into the combustion chamber, it is broken down into very fine particles. The term to describe this process is
   a. vaporization
   b. injection
   c. cetane explosion
   d. atomization

9. Ignition delay in a diesel engine is
   a. the time lag from initial injection to actual ignition
   b. the time required to raise the fuel pressure high

enough to overcome the compression pressure in the cylinder

c. the time delay required for the glow plug to reach its red-hot state

d. the time lag for the injected vaporized fuel actually to atomize

10. Technician A says that a long ignition delay period would result in a rough-running engine. Technician B says that a long ignition delay period would result in an engine knocking sound, due to the high pressures created within the combustion chamber. Who is correct?

11. Technician A says that combustion in a diesel engine can take place only when the carbon and hydrogen molecules are atomized, whereas technician B says that the carbon and hydrogen must mix with the oxygen in the combustion chamber in a vaporized state to initiate successful combustion. Who is correct?

12. Air used in a diesel engine for combustion is made up of oxygen and nitrogen. Technician A says that by volume, there is more nitrogen than oxygen in a given amount of air. Technician B says that there has to be more oxygen to sustain combustion. Which technician knows his or her basic chemistry?

13. Technician A says that a by-product of combustion is carbon dioxide, whereas technician B says that carbon monoxide is formed as a by-product of combustion. Who is right?

14. Technician A says that a diesel engine operates with an air/fuel ratio of approximately 25 : 1 under full load, whereas technician B states that it is closer to 100 : 1 under all conditions of operation. Who is correct?

15. List and describe briefly the four stages of combustion that occur in a diesel engine to achieve complete burning of the injected fuel.

16. List the main factors that affect the ignition delay period in the combustion chamber.

17. Technician A says that the letters EPA mean "European Protection Association," whereas technician B says that they mean "Environmental Protection Agency." Who is correct?

18. List the four main culprits that EPA wants controlled as a by-product of the combustion process in the exhaust of heavy-duty diesel engines.

19. Technician A says that when an engine is running at normal injection timing (nonadvanced), the injection of fuel will be later than it would be when running in an advanced timing mode. Technician B says that under normal timing, the fuel is injected earlier in the injection cycle. Who is correct?

20. True or False: During advanced injection timing, the fuel is injected earlier (piston is farther away from TDC). This means that the air pressure and temperature in the cylinder are lower, resulting in an increased ignition delay period.

21. Technician A says that during normal injection timing a lower nitrogen oxide content is produced at the exhaust but a higher percentage of hydrocarbons is produced. Technician B says that this is incorrect; instead, at normal injection timing there is a higher nitrogen oxide content but a lower hydrocarbon content. Who is correct?

22. True or False: Sulfur dioxide, which is a by-product of combustion, is caused by the sulfur content of the diesel fuel.

5 Engine Disassembly

OVERVIEW

In this chapter we discuss general engine overhaul procedures that can be applied to the many diesel engines used in thousands of applications worldwide. The purpose of the chapter is not to describe details relative to specific engine makes or models, but rather to consider the most appropriate and safest method to employ for any engine overhaul process. In this process it is extremely important to avoid removing any damaging marks that may indicate one or more reasons for failure. Also, care must be exercised so that no additional damage to the components is introduced.

OVERHAUL PROCEDURES

The physical size and application/installation of a diesel engine will determine the best process to employ during repair. Often it is not possible to completely remove the engine from its application/installation because of its size, for example, the very large slow-speed engines used in large marine or industrial applications. These engines are overhauled in place by removal of component parts as necessary. In addition, in some pleasure craft, workboat marine applications, or mobile equipment such as heavy duty trucks, maintenance management personnel may choose to complete an in-frame overhaul rather than a major overhaul that requires complete removal of the engine from its application. If the engine assembly can be removed from its application, a more thorough cleaning, inspection, and repair can be performed.

In many large fleets, it is customary to stock one or more overhauled engines, so that when required, an engine can be removed from a piece of equipment and quickly replaced with a like model. In this way, equipment downtime is kept to a minimum, and the efficiency of the equipment is maintained. This practice is common in long-distance on-highway trucks and in mobile mining equipment applications. In these cases the engine is usually mounted on a subframe assembly that facilitates quick and easy removal. The removed engine can then be systematically disassembled and overhauled to an as-new condition.

Engine disassembly is a very important part of being a proficient diesel technician; teardown should be accomplished rapidly but not haphazardly. Much can and should be learned about the engine during teardown, such as: Did it fail prematurely? Was failure operator or maintenance oriented? Also, by the time the technician has completed teardown, he or she should have a good idea of what parts will be needed for repair or rebuilding the engine. It can be seen, therefore, that engine teardown or disassembly is one of the most important parts of engine overhaul. The decision to disassemble an engine for overhaul should be based on fact, not assumptions, and must be made by the technician before any disassembly takes place. To assist in making this decision the engine should be run or operated in some manner, preferably with a dynamometer.

NOTE   In the case of a truck or agricultural tractor, most shops will have a dynamometer with which the engine can be tested. If no dynamometer is available, make an effort to run the engine under load by operating it.

Engine Diagnosis and Inspection before Disassembly

Discuss the engine operation with the operator. Is the engine being overhauled as a matter of routine because of mileage or hours, or is it being overhauled because of a particular problem such as oil consumption or engine noise? In discussing the engine operation with the operator you may discover that the engine does not need an overhaul; it is possible that an incorrect assumption has been made by the owner or operator. An example of this is excessive engine oil consumption, which may be caused by many things besides worn piston rings.

A thorough check of the following items should be made before the engine is overhauled:

1. *Engine valve seals* (if used). Seals may be broken, worn out, or improperly installed.
2. *Engine front and rear main seals.* Check for leakage during operation.
3. *Air systems and air compressor* (if used). Check air tank for oil accumulation.
4. *Engine turbocharger*
   a. Remove the pipe or hose that connects the turbocharger to the intake manifold. Oil accumulation in this pipe indicates a turbo seal leak.
   b. Oil dripping out the exhaust side of the turbocharger indicates a turbo seal leak.
5. *Engine blower*
   a. Remove air inlet pipe to blower (Detroit Diesel two-cycle engines).
   b. Blower rotors should not be wet with oil; if they are, oil seal leak is indicated.

NOTE The examples above should point out the possibility of a mistake in assuming an engine needs an overhaul just because it may be using an excessive amount of oil. Many times engines are overhauled needlessly because someone did not first check the engine closely or diagnose the problem thoroughly.

After discussing the engine to be overhauled with the owner/operator, the technician should make a test run to determine if there are any unusual engine conditions that will require special attention during overhaul. The engine should be checked for:

1. *Engine Noises.* Noises such as rod bearing noise or piston slap are generally removed during a complete overhaul. Other noises that come from timing gears and piston pin bushings should be noted so that they are completely checked during engine overhaul.

2. *Engine oil pressure.* Engine oil pressure must be considered one of the vital signs of engine condition. For example, if engine oil pressure is low, particular attention must be given to the following items during engine rebuild:

   a. Oil level
   b. Oil filters
   c. Oil pump pickup
   d. Oil pump
   e. Crankshaft journal size and condition
   f. Pressure relief valves
   g. Oil filter bypass valves
   h. Oil cooler bypass valves
   i. Camshaft journals and camshaft bearings

NOTE Although normal rebuild procedures should return all of these engine parts to like-new condition, in some cases, if a part such as a relief valve spring looks acceptable, it might be put back into the engine as long as no low-oil-pressure problems had been encountered. If it had been known in advance that a low-oil-pressure problem existed, the technician would have replaced the spring to ensure correct operation.

---

3. Engine temperature. If the engine temperature is abnormal (higher or lower) during operation, the following items should be given a close check during engine overhaul:

   a. Coolant level
   b. Gauge condition
   c. Radiator flow and condition
   d. Water pump condition
   e. Thermostats and shutters (if used)
   f. Thermostat seals

4. *Engine operation.* Check engine operation for:

a. Excessive smoke
   ▪ Air cleaner may be restricted.
   ▪ Injectors or injection nozzles are clogged or incorrectly adjusted.
   ▪ Fuel system may be improperly calibrated.

b. Low power, no smoke
   ▪ Fuel starvation is indicated.
   ▪ Pump may be improperly calibrated.
   ▪ Fuel filter may be dirty or clogged.

Types of Engine Overhaul

Engine overhaul usually falls into one of two categories: overhaul with the engine in the vehicle or overhaul with the engine removed from the vehicle.

Overhaul with the Engine in the Vehicle

Very often engines are overhauled (in the frame major) with the engine left in the vehicle.

Advantages

1. Time is saved by not having to remove engine.
2. The vehicle serves as a place to mount the engine so that it can be worked on without additional stands or brackets.
3. Cost to the customer is reduced. As much as 16 hours (two days' working time) may be saved by not removing and reinstalling the engine.

Disadvantages

1. All engine seals and gaskets are harder to replace, such as front and rear main seals.
2. It is harder to inspect some engine components such as the camshaft.

3. The block is not thoroughly cleaned as it would be if it were removed from the vehicle and cleaned in a chemical tank. In particular, the water jacket would be cleaned much better if it were cleaned in a chemical tank.
4. The technician may have to climb up on a crawler tractor (for instance), causing considerable inconvenience and awkward work access.

Overhaul with the Engine Removed from the Vehicle

Most complete overhauls are done with the engine removed from the vehicle.

Advantages

1. The engine can be completely disassembled and all gaskets and seals replaced.
2. The engine can be mounted on an engine stand, which provides easy access (Figure 5-1).

Disadvantages

1. It takes more time than in-the-vehicle overhaul.
2. Heavy lifting stands and brackets are required to remove engine from the vehicle.

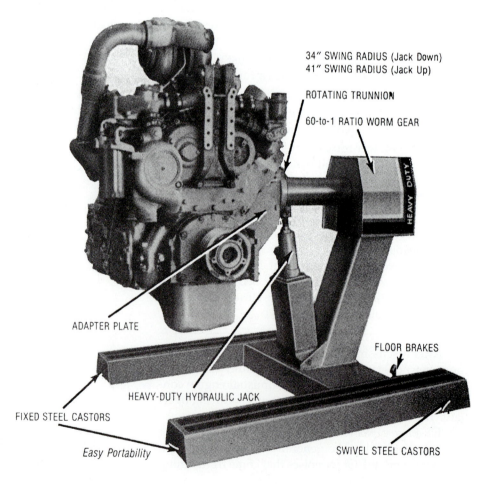

FIGURE 5–1 *Commonly used mounting stand for overhaul or repair of heavy-duty diesel engines. (Courtesy of Kent-Moore Division, SPX Corporation.)*

34" SWING RADIUS (Jack Down)
41" SWING RADIUS (Jack Up)

ROTATING TRUNNION

60-to-1 RATIO WORM GEAR

ADAPTER PLATE

HEAVY-DUTY HYDRAULIC JACK

FIXED STEEL CASTORS

Easy Portability

FLOOR BRAKES

SWIVEL STEEL CASTORS

NOTE   The decision to remove the engine from the vehicle is often based on the condition of the crankshaft and the customer's decision. A worn crankshaft must be removed from the engine to be reconditioned. This cannot be done with the engine in the vehicle. Common practice in this case is to drop the engine pan and inspect the shaft before making a decision.

Engine Removal

These procedures are intended to supplement the service manual.

1. Remove hood, side panels, or tilt the cab if engine is in a cab-over truck.

CAUTION   Before tilting the cab of a truck, check the inside of the cab for any loose articles that may fall through the windshield as the cab tilts. Many cabs have hydraulic lifts, so that one person can easily lift the cab; others have no lifts and require two people to tilt them. Before tilting or raising a cab, read the instructions on the cab near the lift or ask the owner/operator.

NOTE   After the cab has been raised, make sure the safety catch is in place and the transmission is in neutral before you start to work on the engine.

2. Visually inspect the engine for oil and water leaks. This may help you in making a repair decision later.

3. Steam clean or pressure wash the engine and vehicle in the engine area.

4. Drain the coolant from the radiator and engine block. Dispose of used antifreeze according to safety regulations!

5. Remove the radiator and all connecting hoses if required.

6. Disconnect any oil lines that lead to oil filters or gauges. Drain and dispose of used engine oil.

NOTE   If the engine to be removed is in a farm tractor, splitting stands of some type are required. Check with your instructor or service manual for the proper stand to use.

7. Disconnect all air lines that lead to the engine.

8. Disconnect the transmission or remove as required. Refer to your instructor.

9. Remove the intake and exhaust pipes.

10. Disconnect all electrical connections from the vehicle to the engine. Most technicians identify the electrical connections in some manner so that after the engine is reinstalled there is no question about where to hook them up. This can be done with various colors of spray paint, masking tape, or tags. Any method that you have available will save considerable time later.

11. Remove any other items that in your opinion may get in the way of engine removal, including linkages and any engine accessories.

12. Attach a lifting chain or bracket to the engine.

13. Move the hoist over the engine and connect the chain to the hoist.

NOTE   Make sure that the hoist and chain have sufficient capacity to lift the engine being removed. Diesel engines are *Heavy!* A common diesel engine may weigh 2500 lb (1100 kg). BE CAREFUL. Refer to Figure 5-2.

14. Lift the engine from the vehicle.

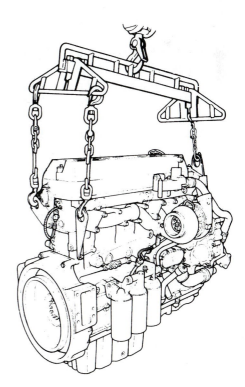

FIGURE 5–2   *Recommended sling arrangement for lifting a heavy-duty engine using chain falls and a spreader bar.* (Courtesy of Detroit Diesel Corporation.)

CAUTION   Lift the engine high enough to clear the frame only and make sure that no one is standing under it.

15.   Place the engine on the floor with blocks to level it or on an engine stand in preparation for disassembly (Figure 5-1).

Engine Disassembly

Since engine disassembly with the engine removed from the vehicle is the most complete disassembly procedure, it will be discussed in detail in this section. If the engine is to be disassembled in the vehicle, the procedures need only be altered to omit the engine components that are not going to be removed, such as the crankshaft. If the engine has not been cleaned by steaming or high-pressure washer previous to removal, it should be cleaned at this time. Place the engine on a suitable stand or cart for disassembly.

NOTE   The following disassembly procedure is general in nature and should be used with the engine service manual. Keep in mind that much of the engine disassembly procedure is determined by the technician doing the job. In most cases no set procedure must be followed. As you gain experience you will acquire or develop your own procedure for disassembly. You will soon see that in diagnosing engine problems, engine disassembly is the one area that requires the most knowledge. Remember, the faster you tear down the engine, the more time you gain on the flat rate, enabling you to meet or exceed the recommended time.

CAUTION   Do not disassemble the engine in a manner that damages component parts.

To aid you in becoming a professional technician, many visual checks that you should make as a matter of practice have been included in the following disassembly procedures. Refer to Figure 1-1.

Rocker Covers

Remove the bolts from the cover and remove the cover; place the bolts back into the cover. Note the condition of the oil clinging to the underside of the rocker cover. A white-colored scum or film of oil clinging to the cover may indicate water leakage into the engine by any of the following:

1. Cracked block
2. Cracked head (other than combustion chamber area)
3. Leaking sleeve seal rings (if wet-type sleeve engine)
4. Leaking oil cooler.

Intake Manifold

NOTE   On some engines the fuel injection lines may have to be removed before the intake manifold can be removed.

1.   Remove the capscrews or bolts that hold the intake manifold on, and remove the intake manifold.

NOTE   At this time decide what is to be done with the capscrews and bolts as they are removed. Experienced technicians usually place them in a basket for cleaning or storage; however, beginners often have trouble finding the correct bolts when reassembling the engine. A time-saving suggestion for the beginner would be to place the bolts with the part or parts taken off.

2.   Inspect the manifold for accumulation of dust or oil.

a. Dust or dirt in the manifold would indicate a faulty air cleaner or inlet pipe. (Check it closely before engine reassembly!)

b. A wet, oily film in the intake manifold would indicate leaking turbocharger or blower seals. If the engine is not equipped with a turbo or blower, the air cleaner could be overfull (oil bath type of air cleaner).

3.   Check the manifold for cracks (visual).

Rocker Arms or Rocker Box Assemblies and Pushrods (Figure 5-3)

NOTE   Before removing rocker arm assemblies or rocker boxes, the injector (if used) and valve adjusting screws and locknuts should be loosened and backed out. This is done to prevent damage to valves or pushrods when the rocker arm assemblies are replaced during reassembly.

(A)

(B)

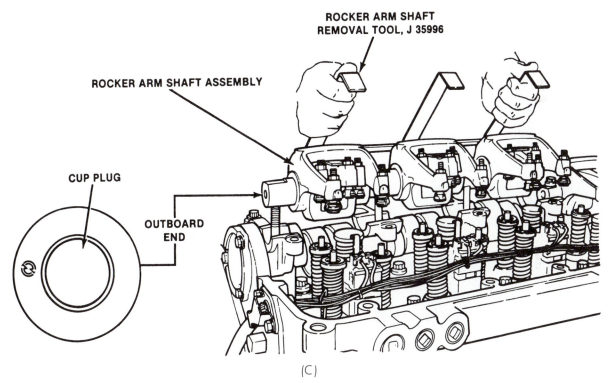

(C)

FIGURE 5–3 *Removal of rocker arm assemblies and pushrods from (a) and (b) 3406 CAT and (c) series 60 Detroit engines. (Courtesy of Detroit Diesel Corporation.)*

1. Inspect the rocker arm assemblies for worn bushings.

   a. This can be done by grasping the rocker arm with a Vise Grip or pliers and attempting to tip it sideways. Excessive rocking indicates a worn bushing.

   b. Another check on rocker arm conditions can be performed by disassembling the rocker arm assembly and visually inspecting the bushing and shaft.

2. Inspect pushrods for straightness.

Water Manifold and Thermostat Housing (if Used)

1. Remove the bolts that attach it to the engine head or block.

2. Inspect the water manifold for cracks or rusted spots that may cause water leakage.

Turbocharger (if Used)

1. Remove the turbocharger hold-down bolts and any other support brackets.

2. Remove oil inlet and return lines.

3. Inspect turbo outlet for traces of oil film. (This may indicate that the turbo needs an overhaul.)

Exhaust Manifold

1.   On some engines, lock plates (plates that hold the bolts in place) will have to be straightened before the manifold-retaining bolts can be removed.

2.   Check the manifold for cracks.

Injection Nozzles or Injectors and Fuel Lines (Figures 5-4 and 5-5)

1.   On engines using injection nozzles, remove the fuel lines from the nozzles and pump. Place plastic caps or plugs on all openings to prevent the entry of dirt.

2.   Inspect the fuel lines for worn spots that may cause leakage.

3.   Loosen and remove hold-down capscrew or screws.

FIGURE 5–5   Fuel line removal, 3406 CAT.

(a)

(b)

FIGURE 5–4   Removing (a) 3176 CAT electronic UI (unit injector); and (b) Mack diesel engine nozzle.

4.   Grasp the nozzle and attempt to turn it back and forth, pulling up at the same time. This will remove many nozzles.

5.   If stud bolts are used to hold the nozzle in, it cannot be turned; in this case, use a pry bar or similar tool. Wedge it under the nozzle to move it upward out of the cylinder head. Visually inspect nozzle for damage to the tip.

CAUTION   Care must be used in prying the nozzle upward, as damage to the nozzle could result. (Pencil nozzles manufactured by Stanadyne Diesel Systems are easily bent and extreme care must be taken.)

---

a.   Since nozzles are often stuck in the cylinder head, a puller or slide hammer must be used to pull them.

b.   Some nozzles require special pullers. Consult the manufacturer's service manual for more information.

6.   Remove the injectors (Cummins—Detroit).

a.   Loosen and remove hold-down capscrew or nut.

b.   Using a rolling head pry bar or special removal tool. Remove injector by pulling or prying it upward.

c.   Visually inspect injector tip for damage. Make sure that injector openings are all capped or plugged, and store injectors in a place where they will not be damaged.

Water Pump

1. Remove drive belts if used.
2. Check the drive belts for cracks.
3. Remove capscrews that hold the water pump to block or cylinder head and remove the water pump.
4. Visually check the water pump impeller for erosion.
5. If the fan was bolted to the water pump drive pulley, check it closely for cracks and bent blades.

All Accessories

Remove fuel filter housings, hoses, oil and water filters attached to the engine.

Injection Pump (Figure 5-6)

1. Prior to removal, center the rack on CAT PLN systems. On Bosch PLN systems, rotate the crankshaft to place No. 1 piston at TDC—compression.
2. Remove all bolts that hold the injection pump to the engine and remove pump.
3. Visually inspect the pump for broken mounting flange and stripped or cross-threaded fittings.

Cylinder Head or Heads

1. Before you remove the cylinder head, open and/or remove drain plugs to make sure that all coolant has been drained from the block. Although the cooling system radiator may have been drained before the engine was removed from the vehicle, some coolant may have remained in the block.
2. Loosen all cylinder head hold-down bolts. (See Figure 5-7 for a typical sequence.)

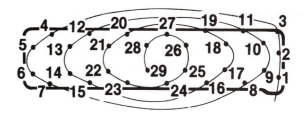

FIGURE 5–7 *Recommended cylinder head loosening sequence for studs, bolts, or nuts. (Courtesy of GMC Trucks.)*

3. Lift out the cylinder head bolts, checking each one for erosion and rust. Eroded or rusted bolts should not be reused.
4. Lift the cylinder head from the block:

a. Using a lifting bracket and hoist (Figure 5-8).

(A)

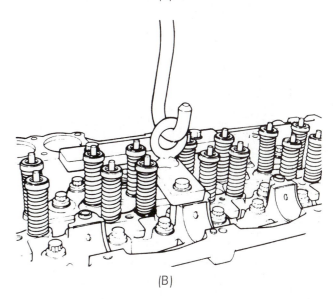

(B)

FIGURE 5–8 (A) Chain sling cylinder head removal; (B) one example of a special lifting bracket used to safely remove a cylinder head assembly from the engine block. [(B) Courtesy of Detroit Diesel Corporation.]

FIGURE 5–6 *3406 CAT injection pump removal.*

b.   Manually. Single or two-cylinder heads, DDC 149 and Series 55, Cummins and Mack, etc., can be lifted off by hand or by a sling.

5.   Inspect the cylinder head combustion chamber surface closely for:

a.   Cracks
b.   Pitting
c.   Signs of gasket leakage

NOTE   If the head is badly cracked or pitted, now is the time to make a decision about replacement or repair. Items such as cylinder heads may not be stocked on a routine basis and may have to be ordered.

---

6.   Inspect the cylinder gasket closely, especially around water holes. Areas that are blackened or burned out may indicate a warped head or block.

7.   Inspect the top of piston for injection nozzle tracks or pitting.

NOTE   Fuel injected into the cylinder generally leaves light carbon or soot tracks on the pistons. This "track" or pattern indicates how well the injection nozzle or injector tip is aligned and if any plugged holes exist. See (Figure 2-1a).

---

8.   Place the cylinder head on blocks or cardboard to protect it from damage.

9.   If you wish to disassemble the cylinder head at this time, (refer to Chapter 7) before further engine disassembly.

Clutch and Flywheel

1.   Before removing the clutch pressure plate and clutch disc, mark the pressure plate by placing "match marks" on the pressure plate and flywheel. Match marking is usually done with a center punch and a hammer or a metal marker pen.

2.   Remove the bolts that secure the pressure plate to the flywheel.

CAUTION   Some flywheels are recessed and the clutch pressure plate will stay on the flywheel after the bolts are removed. Others are not recessed, and as the last bolt is removed, the pres-

---

sure plate will have to be held by hand to prevent it from dropping to the floor.

---

3.   Lift the pressure plate and clutch disc from the flywheel using proper lifting equipment.

4.   Inspect the pressure plate for:

a.   Cracks, distortion, or warpage with a straightedge
b.   Wear on release fingertips and loose release finger pivot pins

5.   Inspect the clutch disc (follow OSHA asbestos dust regulations). Lining is worn excessively if the rivets that hold it on the disc are flush with the lining surface. On new clutch plates the rivets will be recessed about 1/16 in. (1.6 mm).

6.   Match-mark the flywheel (if not marked by manufacturer). Match marking of the flywheel is done by marking the flywheel and crankshaft if accessible. If the crankshaft cannot be reached with the flywheel installed, sometimes a punch mark can be put on the flywheel and flywheel dowel pin. Many flywheels are marked or so designed at the factory for correct assembly in one of the following ways:

a.   Offset bolt holes
b.   Offset dowel pin holes
c.   Match marks or timing marks. In any event, match marking the flywheel ensures that you will reinstall it the same way it was installed previously. If there is any doubt about flywheel timing when reinstalling the flywheel, double check the engine service manual!

7.   Loosen the flywheel attaching bolts and remove the flywheel (Figure 5-9).

CAUTION   If the flywheel does not have dowel pins, use caution when removing the last bolt, since the flywheel may fall on the floor and injure you or a fellow worker.

---

8.   Check the flywheel for the following:

a.   Cracks
b.   Warpage or distortion (use a straight edge)
c.   Pilot bearing fit (pilot bearing should be a hammer tap fit into the flywheel)

FLYWHEEL
LIFT TOOL

(A)

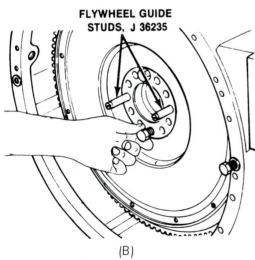

FLYWHEEL GUIDE
STUDS, J 36235

(B)

FIGURE 5–9 (A) Using a special lifting tool to either remove or install the flywheel safely; (B) using two guide studs
threaded into the rear mounting flange of the crankshaft to
facilitate removal or installation of the flywheel assembly.
(Courtesy of Detroit Diesel Corporation.)

d. Bolt holes for oblong-shaped and missing or
stripped threads (pressure plate bolt holes)

e. Starter ring gear for damaged or missing teeth

Oil Pan (Figure 1-1)

1. Remove the bolts that secure the engine oil
pan to block.

2. Remove the oil pan.

NOTE   The oil pan gasket may cause the oil pan
to stick to the engine block, requiring you to
wedge a small screwdriver or putty knife between the block and the oil pan to break it loose.
Use caution when prying on the pan to prevent
damage to block or oil pan. Striking the pan with
a rubber mallet can help dislodge the pan without damage.

Oil Pump and Pickup Screen (Figure 5-10)

1. Unlock the oil pump bolts that hold the oil
pump to the engine block.

2. Remove the oil pump hold-down bolts and
remove the pump.

3. Inspect the screen for blockage.

4. Inspect the pickup tube for cracks or bends.

NOTE   Some engines, such as Cummins, have
an externally mounted oil pump. This type of oil
pump can be removed without removing the
pan. See Item 30 in Figure 1-1.

At this time turn the engine over to allow further disassembly to take place (Figure 5-1). If the engine is mounted on an engine stand, this is no problem; simply rotate the engine by turning the crank on
the engine stand. If the engine is situated on the
floor, lift the engine with a hoist to tip it over or lay
it down.

CAUTION   When lifting or moving the engine
with a hoist, get someone to help you. Make it
safe. Use correctly rated slings.

Vibration Damper (Figure 5-11)

The vibration dampers on most engines require a special puller for removal.

1. Remove the bolt or bolts that secure the crankshaft damper to the crankshaft.

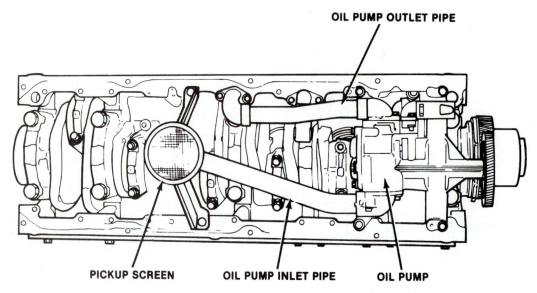

OIL PUMP OUTLET PIPE

PICKUP SCREEN   **OIL PUMP INLET PIPE**   **OIL PUMP**

FIGURE 5–10 View of the underside of a series 60 four-stroke-cycle engine with the oil pan removed. Note the inlet and outlet pipes to and from the oil pump. (Courtesy of Detroit Diesel Corporation.)

2.   Select the correct puller for removal or as indicated by your instructor.

CAUTION   Most dampers have puller holes to allow them to be removed. Connect the puller only at this point, or serious damage to the damper may result. Do not remove it by striking with a hammer!

---

3.   After removal of the damper, check it visually for:

FIGURE 5–11 Vibration damper removal with special puller.

a.   Worn areas where engine front seal rides

b.   Nicks or marks on the flywheel part of damper

4.   For further information and checks to be made on the damper, refer to Chapter 8.

Timing Gear Cover (Figure 5-12)

1.   Remove the bolts that hold the timing gear cover to the engine block.

2.   Remove the timing cover by tapping it with a plastic hammer.

3.   If the cover cannot be removed by tapping with a plastic hammer, a screwdriver may be wedged between the cover and block to "break" it loose.

CAUTION   Care must be exercised when wedging or driving a screwdriver between the cover and the block, as damage to the cover may result.

Flywheel Housing (Bell Housing) (Figure 5-13)

1.   Remove the bolts from the flywheel housing.

2.   Remove the housing and inspect it for cracks.

NOTE   Most flywheel housings are aligned to the block with dowel pins and may require the

FIGURE 5–12 Timing gear cover removal.

use of a plastic hammer to jar them loose. If the hammer does not loosen the housing, you may have to use a bar or a screwdriver to pry it off.

CAUTION Care must be used when prying the housing off, or damage to the housing may result.

Pistons and Connecting Rods

NOTE If the engine block is not on an engine stand, enabling you to rotate the engine, have someone help you tip it over or use a hoist. The engine block can be in the horizontal or vertical position when removing the pistons. If the engine block is mounted on an engine stand, it can be rotated easily so that pistons can be removed (Figure 5-1).

1. Before attempting to remove the pistons, the carbon and/or ridge should be removed from the top of the cylinder bore. If only carbon is at the top of the bore, it can be removed easily with emery paper or a carbon scraper. If a ridge is worn at the top of the cylinder, a ridge reamer must be used to remove it (Figure 6-23).

FIGURE 5–13 Flywheel housing removal. (Courtesy of Detroit Diesel Corporation.)

NOTE Most diesel engines using sleeves have very little or no ridge, regardless of the time on the engines. This is a result of the lubricating quality of diesel fuel, and since sleeves are generally replaced during a major overhaul, ridge removal is necessary only on engines that do not have sleeves.

2. Check the rod bearing caps and rods for match marks. If the rods have not been factory marked, mark them with a punch or number marking set to ensure that the rod cap and rod are placed together during inspection and reassembly.

3. Remove the rod cap bolts and remove the rod caps (Figure 5-14).

FIGURE 5–14 Removing rod caps.

4.   Push the piston and rod assembly out with a wooden driver or plastic hammer handle (Figure 5-15).

CAUTION   Do not attempt to drive connecting rod and piston assemblies out with a metal driver. Serious damage to the connecting rod may occur.

5.   Keep bearings with rods for inspection.

Main Bearing Caps and Crankshaft
1.   Remove the main bearing bolts.
2.   Check the main bearing caps for match marks or numbers. If the caps are not marked, use a punch or number marking set and mark the caps in relationship to the block to ensure that the caps are reinstalled in the same manner.

3.   After match marking or checking the factory marks, remove the main bearing caps (Figure 5-16).

NOTE   In many cases the main bearing caps have an interference fit with the block and will require a slight tap with a plastic hammer to remove. If this does not remove the cap, insert a main bearing bolt into the cap partway and tip sideways on the bolt. This will cause the cap to tip. Continue working the cap from side to side in this manner to allow you to remove it easily. Use slide hammers on caps equipped with tapped holes.

4.   After the main bearing caps have been removed, inspect the main bearings in an effort to detect any unusual wear patterns that may indicate problems with the block or crankshaft. For a detailed explanation of bearing failures, see Chapter 8.
5.   Remove the crankshaft using a lifting hook and hoist (Figure 5-17) or web slings.

NOTE   In cases where a small inline or V8 engine is being worked on, the crankshaft can be removed easily by hand. Have someone help you lift the shaft straight up and out.

6.   Lay the crankshaft on the floor to support it or stand it on end and secure it to a workbench or other solid structure.

NOTE   If the crankshaft is to be laid on the floor, it should be placed on a clean piece of plywood and in an area where no damage can occur.

FIGURE 5–15 Removing piston and connecting rod from engine.

FIGURE 5–16 Removing main bearing caps.

FIGURE 5–17 *Removing crankshaft.*

7. Visually inspect the crankshaft for ridging and roughness.

An evaluation should be made at this time regarding the condition of the crankshaft, since it may have to be sent out for inspection and grinding, which takes a considerable amount of time. This decision should be made now to prevent holding up reassembly of the engine at a later date. See Chapter 8 for more detailed information on how to check and evaluate the condition of the crankshaft.

Camshaft and Timing Gears

1. Remove the bolts that secure the camshaft retainer to the block and remove the camshaft (Figure 5-18).

FIGURE 5–18 *Camshaft removal.*

2. Visually inspect the camshaft for worn lobes or bearing journals.

3. Inspect the timing gear or gears for wear.

Cam Followers or Cam Follower Boxes

1. Remove cam followers by lifting them from the bores in the block (Figure 5-19, 3406 CAT engine).

NOTE   Most engines (except Cummins and Detroit Diesel) have cam followers that ride in holes bored in the block and can be removed simply by lifting them out of the bore. Cummins engines have the cam followers anchored to a plate called a box, which is bolted to the side of the engine. To remove this box requires the removal of the six bolts that hold it in place. See item 31 in Figure 1-1.

---

2. Visually inspect the cam followers for wear, pitting, and flaking. For more detailed information on checking cam followers, see Chapter 10.

Other Brackets, Pulley, and Miscellaneous Items
To prepare the block for cleaning and inspection, all other brackets and soft plugs and cylinder liner sleeves (for cylinder sleeve removal instructions, see Chapter 6) should be removed before placing the block in the chemical tank.

ENGINE CLEANING PROCEDURES

All U.S. states and Canadian provinces currently have in place regulations about the disposal of hazardous chemicals. The concerned diesel technician today should be familiar with the local laws concerning the use and disposal of any cleaning agent that is com-

FIGURE 5–19 *Cam follower removal.*

monly used in maintaining diesel-powered equipment, regardless of the application. Failure to follow the regulations can result in serious environmental damage as well as danger to the user. Substantial monetary fines are levied against companies and individuals who fail to follow responsible disposal practices.

Proper cleaning of assemblies and individual parts is essential when servicing and rebuilding engine and accessory drive components such as manual gearshift, automatic and powershift transmissions, marine gears, power pumps, generator sets, and so forth. Proper cleaning is especially critical for parts with operating components that cannot be completely disassembled. Also, partly disassembled components, such as tapered roller bearing cones and cups and planetary gear pinions that are often left mounted in a housing or on a shaft, require special procedures for thorough cleaning.

When it becomes necessary to perform an overhaul or repair of an engine or major drive component, the main objective in removing and disassembling any component is to replace or repair damaged and worn parts. Therefore, all parts must be cleaned thoroughly before they are inspected to determine their suitability for reuse. Any varnish, sludge, dirt, and other foreign material must be removed from usable parts before a component is reassembled.

The skilled diesel technician must be aware that to prevent damage to certain components, the correct cleaning method and chemicals must be used. Adopting the wrong cleaning method or agent can be as harmful as no cleaning at all. Bearing races and rollers, polished shafts, or gear teeth exposed to moisture, acids, or caustic solutions during the cleaning process can quickly water spot, stain, rust, or corrode. Returning such parts to the engine can cause rapid wear and premature failure. The methods discussed herein are general in nature and should not be considered an all encompassing guide for cleaning and degreasing components. Specific cleaning methods and cleaning agents required for a particular component or assembly are usually available from commercial chemical cleaning companies; information is also available in the service literature of engine manufacturers.

SAFE WORK HABITS WHEN CLEANING

Some alkalis, detergents, and solvents can irritate the skin or be harmful to the eyes. Adequate ventilation is a must when working around and with cleaning chemicals. When working with potentially harmful substances, carefully read and heed the cautions and warnings on the product labels. *Always* wear safety

equipment such as safety glasses, a face shield, gloves, and apron. Exercise extreme care when spraying to prevent injury to other personnel and to avoid an accident! Components such as cylinder liners, oil cooler cores, and radiators usually require special treatment when cleaned.

Steam Cleaning

Steam cleaning should be done only to remove heavy deposits of dirt and grease from exterior surfaces of the engine block and major drive components. Heavy grease deposits should first be scraped and brushed away. Internal engine components should not be steam cleaned, because the process may remove the protective oil film and cause the parts to water spot and rust. During an in-frame overhaul, if no other cleaning agent is readily available, steam cleaning may be done but cautiously, and all parts should be thoroughly flushed, blown-dry with compressed air, and quickly relubricated to prevent rusting.

Pressurized Oil Sprays

Oil-based mineral solvents and fuel oils under pressure can be used to flush varnish, sludge, and dirt from cylinder block internal passages and surfaces of component part housings. Drain holes or other openings through which these solvents can be flushed must be adequate to carry away dirt and flushing oils. All flushing oils must be drained completely from the components to prevent contamination from lubricants added to the reassembled components.

Heated Solvents

Many smaller engine and drive assembly components can be thoroughly and safely cleaned by flushing, soaking, or mechanically agitating them in heated petroleum solvents. Oils and solvents used for this purpose, however, must be capable of being heated to the required temperature without producing safety or health hazards from volatile or harmful vapors. Naphtha, white gas, varnish remover, and similar solvents obviously should not be heated under any circumstances.

Small parts such as bearings and gears can be suspended on metal wires, or placed in wire baskets, and submerged in the heated solvent tank to soak off grease, varnish, and sludge. Mechanical agitation of the solvent or parts will increase the effectiveness of the cleaning solvents. Extremely tough scale and varnish can be brushed loose. Exercise care to keep loose brush bristles out of assembled parts.

After cleaning all parts, machined and polished surfaces of components, bores, housings, and their internal parts should be protected from rust and corrosion with a coating of oil or light grease. Small parts can be kept in shallow pans and covered with oil until needed. Larger parts should be coated with grease or oil and wrapped in polyethelene film or oil-proof paper.

Hot Tank Cleaning

Hot tank cleaning is a method commonly used for all ordinary cast iron or steel engine parts, and it is usually required when heavy scale buildup is evident within the engine block coolant passages. However, many companies that rebuild engines now employ glass or walnut beads to clean off engine blocks. The engine block is placed in an enclosure with a rotating table. The doors of the enclosure are then securely closed and the table is rotated with the engine bolted securely in place. The engine block or parts are bombarded by the beading agent to clean the part effectively without having to use chemicals.

Generally, a hot tank can be filled with a variety of commercially available cleaning chemicals; selection and strength are determined by the type of metal to be cleaned. One of the most commonly used cleaning agents for both cast iron and steel parts consists of a commercial heavy-duty alkaline solvent with a tank big enough to accept the largest engine block or component part to be cleaned. To increase the effectiveness of the cleaning process, the engine block can be lowered onto a steel grade below the level of the alkaline; then the solvent is heated to approximately 160°F (71°C) and a mechanically driven device moves the grate backward and forward to create an agitating action. In some cases, air can also be injected into the solution.

The time required to clean a component part in the alkaline solvent hot tank is determined by the degree of scale and so forth that has to be removed and the type of chemical being used. It can be as short as 20 minutes or as long as an overnight soak. For example, cylinder blocks and cylinder heads that are heavily scaled may require extra cleaning by agitating the parts in a bath of inhibited commercial pickling acid and leaving them in the acid until the bubbling action stops, which is usually between 20 and 30 minutes.

CAUTION When using commercial pickling acid, take care to prevent electrolysis between dissimilar metals such as aluminum, copper, and other nonferrous metals with the cast iron or steel engine block or head(s). These metals should be removed from the parts before they are treated with acid. Two examples are alu-

minum square head plugs and the injector copper tubes that are used within the cylinder head area.

After the bubbling action stops, lift the parts, allow them to drain, then reimmerse them for another 10 minutes. Repeat as necessary to completely remove all scale from the block or head coolant passages. Rinse all parts thoroughly in clean, hot water or with steam. Neutralize any remaining acid by immersing the parts in an alkali bath. Finally, rinse the parts in clean, hot water or with steam; dry the parts with compressed air; and oil all machined surfaces to prevent rusting.

Cold Tank Solvent Cleaning

Cold tank solvent cleaning can be used for most of the steel and aluminum parts of the engine. Make sure that the strength of the chemical solvent will not attack tin-coated parts such as those found on some pistons and/or liners. Cold tank cleaning is also good for removing the rustproofing compound from service replacement parts. In addition to solvents, diesel fuel oil can also be used for cleaning purposes, particularly when working with injector components. To clean a part using the cold tank method, follow these three steps:

1. Immerse and agitate the part in a suitable tank.
2. Use a soft-bristle brush to go over and through oil and water passages so that all deposits are removed.
3. When parts are thoroughly clean, rinse them in clean fuel oil and allow them to air dry, or carefully use compressed air for this purpose.

Cleaning Aluminum Parts

Aluminum parts can be cleaned safely in diesel fuel or in a detergent solution, but *never* one containing an *alkali!* Detergents can be used at room temperature, in a heated tank with mechanical agitation, or in a steam cleaner. To detergent-clean aluminum parts follow these five steps:

1. Prepare a solution of heavy-duty detergent in a hot tank, cold tank, or a steam cleaner.
2. Agitate the parts in the detergent or steam clean with the detergent–water solution until all grease and dirt are removed.
3. Rinse the parts thoroughly in a tank of hot water, with a high-pressure hot water rinse, or with steam.

4. Dry all parts with compressed air.
5. If further cleaning is required, perform each of the following steps:
   a. Brush on a commercial, chlorinated solvent suitable for aluminum and leave it on the part for several hours.
   b. Steam clean the part with a solution of detergent and water.
   c. Rinse the part in clean water and dry with compressed air.

SUMMARY

This completes the general disassembly of the engine. If the recommended visual inspections were made as the engine was disassembled, you should know the general condition of the engine and you have some idea of what parts will be needed to repair it. At this time further component inspection and repair check should take place so that a complete parts listing can be compiled. Components such as cylinder head, oil pump, and fuel injection pumps are covered separately in other chapters of this book.

SELF-TEST QUESTIONS

1. True or False: When degreasing or cleaning dirty engines and equipment, you can dump or drain oil and filters into a city drain.
2. Technician A says that heavy-duty ball or roller bearing assemblies can be cleaned safely by submerging them into a hot tank of caustic solution. Technician B disagrees strongly, saying that this can cause water spotting and acid etching of the components and should not be attempted; it is better to wash the components carefully in a clean solvent. Who is correct?
3. After a ball or roller bearing has been cleaned, technician A says that it is acceptable to spin the bearing with compressed air to ensure that all dirt particles have been removed. Technician B says that this action can severely damage the bearing and in some cases cause the bearing to disintegrate. Which technician knows safe work habits?
4. Technician A says that regardless of what type of cleaning agent is being used, you should always work in a well-ventilated area and wear safety glasses, an eye shield, gloves, and an apron. Technician B says that this is necessary only when using a caustic solution in a hot tank. Who is correct?
5. Technician A says that you should never heat naphtha, white gas, varnish remover, and similar solvents under any cleaning condition. Technician B says that as long as you do not exceed 93°C (200°F) there is no danger. Who is correct?
6. Technician A says that after any cleaning procedure, all machined surfaces should be oiled lightly to prevent rust and corrosion from forming. Technician B says that this is a bad idea because the oil tends to attract dust. Who is correct?
7. True or False: A common hot tank cleaning solution for use with both cast iron and steel parts consists of a commercial heavy-duty alkaline solvent solution.
8. Technician A says that when using a commercial pickling acid in a hot tank it is not necessary to remove nonferrous metals such as copper and aluminum engine parts. Technician B says that if you do not remove these parts, an electrolytic action between dissimilar metals will cause them to be eaten away. Who is right?
9. True or False: The time required to clean a component part of scale accumulation depends on the strength of the cleaning solution.
10. True or False: After hot tank cleaning all parts should be thoroughly rinsed with clean hot water or steam and dried with compressed air, and machined surfaces should be lightly oiled.
11. True or False: Aluminum parts should never be cleaned in a solution containing alkali.
12. Technician A says that an in-frame engine overhaul is just as effective as a complete rebuild that involves removing the engine from its application. Technician B says that you cannot achieve as successful a job of internal cleaning of the engine block with an in-frame repair. Who is correct?
13. Technician A says that during an in-frame overhaul the crankshaft main bearings can be changed by rolling them in and out by use of a special pin inserted into the crankshaft journal oil hole. Technician B says that this is impossible and that the crankshaft *must* be removed to do this. Who is right?
14. If an engine block is to be steam cleaned externally for any reason, Technician A says that the engine should always be running to allow equal distribution of the heat from the engine block. Technician B says that this is unsafe: Steam heat applied to an aluminum injection pump housing can result in severe distortion of the housing; internal plunger-to-barrel clearances can be affected, thereby causing scuffing or scoring. Which technician knows safe working procedures best?
15. Technician A says that when disassembling an engine, you should follow a systematic procedure that allows you to minimize damage to components and to get to other components as required. Technician B says that it doesn't matter how you pull the engine apart, because most components will be replaced anyway. Who is correct?
16. To facilitate and assist the technician in determining the possible cause for an engine failure, technician A says that all mating parts should be carefully labeled and identified. In addition, care should be taken not to scratch, score, or damage the parts during disassembly. Technician B says that this is not necessary—why waste

time since new parts will be installed. Which technician has better standards of excellence?

17. After reassembly of an engine and prior to initial startup, technician A says that you should place the throttle at full fuel to facilitate start-up and to allow a higher oil pump flow to quickly lubricate the internal parts. Technician B says that you should always prelube the main oil gallery and oil filter to ensure a minimum time delay for the oil to start flowing through the engine. Who is a better technician?

18. True or False: Once the engine has started after being rebuilt, you should leave the turbocharger oil supply line loose to ensure that it is receiving an adequate flow of oil. If no oil flow is visible after 20 to 30 sec, you should shut down the engine.

19. True or False: After initial engine start-up, the engine should be run at fast idle rather than wide open throttle.

20. During initial engine running after a rebuild, what signs should the technician be checking for? On a separate sheet of paper, list major checks that you would perform.

21. Technician A says that all engine parts that are not already marked by the manufacturer should be match-marked to allow reinstallation in the same position. Technician B says that this doesn't matter since all parts will be cleaned anyway and position does not make any difference. Which technician is correct?

22. Technician A says that intake and exhaust valves can be match-marked to their respective valve guide by using a sharp center punch to dot the head of the valve with its number. Technician B says that it is better to use a metal marker to do this and/or place the respective valves in a numbered wooden or cardboard valve holder. Which technician is correct?

23. On a separate sheet of paper, list the four major procedural steps required in a failure analysis.

24. Technician A says that it is extremely important that all nuts and bolts be correctly torqued and that the same-size diameter bolt have the same torque value as a taperlock stud. Technician B disagrees, saying that taperlock studs do not have as high a torque rating as a nut or bolt. Which technician is correct?

6

The Cylinder Block

OVERVIEW

This chapter describes the main function and features of the major structural part of the diesel engine: the engine block. Both dry and wet-type cylinder liners, the necessary disassembly, inspection and cleaning of the block, and the service repair tasks required at major overhaul are discussed.

CYLINDER BLOCK STRUCTURE

Most modern diesel engines use a cylinder block similar in construction to the one pictured in Figure 6-1. The cylinder block may be described as the largest single part and the main structure, or "backbone," of the diesel engine. All other engine parts are bolted or connected to the cylinder block in some way.

Contained within the cylinder block are the following:

1. Coolant passages and water jacket
2. Holes or bores for the piston and sleeve assembly
3. Bores or supports for the cam bushings and camshaft
4. Main bearing bores that hold the main bearings and support the crankshaft
5. Drilled or cored passageways for the engine lubrication system
6. Holes or bores in the water jacket that allow insertion of the freeze or expansion plugs
7. Many drilled and tapped holes utilizing vari-

ous types of threads that allow the cylinder head or heads and other engine parts to be bolted or connected to it with some type of fastener or bolt

DIESEL ENGINE CYLINDER BLOCKS

Diesel engine cylinder blocks may be one of four types: wet sleeve, dry sleeve, bored without a sleeve (parent bore), or air cooled.

Wet Sleeve Block
A wet sleeve or liner block is designed with a number of large holes in which the cylinder sleeves are inserted (Figure 6-1). These holes are designed so that the coolant will be circulated around the cylinder sleeve or liner. The coolant is prevented from leaking into the crankcase of the engine by O-ring seals at the bottom of the liner. At the top of the block a counterbore is cut into the block for the lip or flange of the sleeve to fit onto and prevent coolant leakage. The uppermost part of this lip may be slightly larger than the lower part. This larger diameter provides an interference fit with the block when the sleeve is installed.

Advantages

1. The major advantage is the contact of coolant directly with the sleeve, enabling rapid and positive heat transfer from the combustion chamber to the coolant.
2. Sleeves are easily removed and installed during engine rebuild to bring the cylinder block back to like-new condition.
3. Cylinder sleeves may be replaced individually if they become worn or damaged prematurely.

FIGURE 6-1 Diesel engine cylinder block and related parts. (Courtesy of Cummins Engine Company, Inc.)

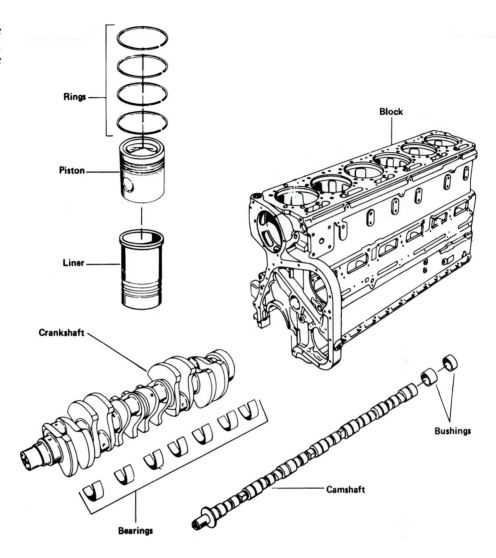

Disadvantages

1. The major disadvantages are the problems encountered in maintaining a coolant seal between the bottom of the sleeve and the block. The seals used (O-ring and crevice seals) sometimes do not have the same longevity as might be expected from the engine.

2. This seal leakage generally occurs at the bottom of the sleeve and contaminates the lube oil.

Dry Sleeve Block

A *dry sleeve* block (Figure 6-2) is designed with a bored or honed hole in the block that allows no coolant contact with the cylinder sleeve. The sleeve is inserted into the bored hole or it can be either a "slip or press-fit." A counter-bore is bored into the block to accommodate the sleeve lip and to help position the sleeve as in the wet sleeve type. The sleeve is held in place by the cylinder head gasket and cylinder head bolted onto the block.

Advantages

1. The dry sleeve type does not have coolant in contact with the cylinder sleeve, since the sleeve is fitted into a bored hole in the block. This is a major advantage in that sealing the sleeve at the bottom is not required.

2. There is no lube oil contamination as a result of the leaking of coolant by the sleeve seals.

3. The block can be brought back to like-new condition easily by the installation of new sleeves.

4. Cylinder sleeves may be replaced individually if they become worn prematurely or damaged.

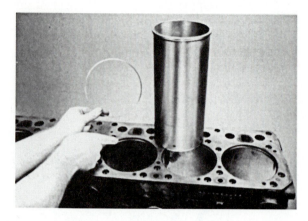

FIGURE 6–2 Dry press-fit cylinder liner showing the liner flange shim used to obtain the correct flange protrusion. (Courtesy of Mack Trucks, Inc.)

Disadvantages

1. Since the coolant is not in direct contact with the sleeve, heat transfer from the combustion chamber to the coolant water is not as rapid as it would be with a wet-type sleeve.
2. This slow heat transfer may result in short engine life and cylinder damage.

No-Sleeve Block

A *parent-bore* or *no-sleeve* block has holes bored for the cylinder with the pistons and piston rings inserted directly into this hole. No provision in the block for wet- or dry-type sleeves is made.

Advantages

1. The major advantage is the initial cost of construction in that the machining and fitting of sleeves is not required.
2. No provision has to be made for O-ring grooves and no contact area is needed.
3. The block can be made lighter because of thin cylinder wall construction.

Disadvantages

1. A major disadvantage of this type of block is that during rebuild or repair of the engine a worn cylinder must be rebored or honed.
2. Reboring requires special equipment and the engine must be disassembled completely.
3. Reduced engine block life.

Air-Cooled Block

A *air-cooled* block is similar to a parent-bore block in that it does not have cylinder sleeves but bored holes

for the piston. It has no coolant passageways or water jackets; fins have been added to the cylinder block to dissipate heat. Cooling then is accomplished by the passage of air around the fins.

Advantages

1. It is much lighter in weight because the water jackets have been eliminated.
2. No coolant is required, which in itself eliminates problems that go with liquid-cooled engines, such as leakage, freezing, rust formation, and inadequate cooling.
3. This eliminates the need for a radiator, water pump, and thermostat.

Disadvantages

1. It generally does not have sleeves, making replacement or reboring necessary if one cylinder becomes worn or damaged.
2. It has no coolant with which to operate hot water heaters used in trucks, and in tractors with cabs.
3. It needs some type of cooling fan, usually belt driven.
4. Cooling fans around cylinders can become clogged by dirt and engine oil, creating an overheated cylinder.

DISASSEMBLY, INSPECTION, AND CLEANING OF THE CYLINDER BLOCK

At this point all major components and accessories should have been removed from the block. If not, refer to Chapter 5. Further disassembly should include removal of the following:

1. *Oil galley or passageway plugs*
2. *All cover plates (oil and water)*
3. *Expansion plugs (soft plugs).* Removal of expansion plugs can be accomplished quickly and easily by:
    a. Driving a sharp punch or chisel through them
    b. Twisting or turning them sideways
    c. Prying them from block with a bar, using caution not to damage the block, which will prevent a new plug from sealing
    d. Inspecting the expansion plugs after removal in an attempt to determine if the engine coolant was being properly maintained

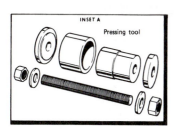
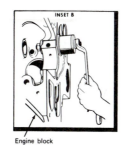

(A)

(B)

FIGURE 6–3 *(A) Nonadjustable cam bushing installation tool; (B) adjustable cam bushing installation tool. [(A) Courtesy of J.I. Case Co.]*

NOTE   If expansion plugs show signs of high corrosive action within the cooling system, a check should be made of the water filter or conditioner.

---

4. *Oil pressure relief valves*
    a. Remove the valve and spring.
    b. Make sure that the valve moves freely in its bore and that the spring is not broken.

Removing the Cam Bushing

Removal of cam bushings or bearings should not be attempted without special bushing drivers, or damage to the cam bearing bore in the block may result. Two types of bushing installation and removal tools are common in most shops: the solid nonadjustable type (Figure 6-3) made to fit one size bushing or the adjustable type (Figure 6-3) which can be adjusted to fit any size bushing within a given range.

Before removal of the cam bushings, inspect them to determine if normal wear has occurred or if some malfunction or lubrication problem exists. Also check all oil supply holes before removal of the bushings so that no question exists about the proper alignment when installing the bushing. The cam bushings should be removed as follows:

1. Select the correct-size bushing driver.
2. Place the bushing driver into the bushing to be removed.
3. Place the driver guide cone on the driving bar and insert the assembly into the block and bushing driver.
4. Make sure that the guide cone is held securely into another bushing or bushing bore so that no misalignment of driving bar can occur.
5. Hold the bar with one hand and strike it on the driving end with solid, firm hits with a large hammer.
6. Drive the bushing until it clears the block bore.
7. Follow the procedure above and remove all the cam bushings.

Removing the Cylinder Sleeves

Cylinder sleeves must be pulled or pushed out of the block with a sleeve puller. The most common type of sleeve puller in use is similar to the one shown in Figure 6-4.

Pulling Wet Sleeves from the Block

1. Select the adapter plate that will fit the sleeve.
2. Make sure that the plate fits snugly in the sleeve (to prevent cocking) and that the outside diam-

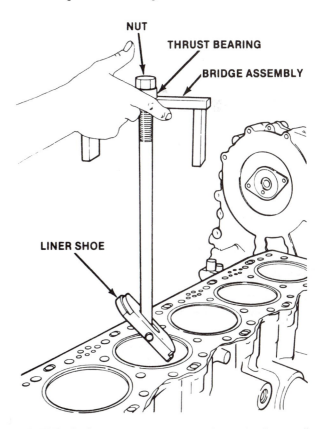

FIGURE 6–4 *Pivoting shoe type of cylinder liner puller with its bridge assembly and puller screw, Kent-Moore part J35791. (Courtesy of Detroit Diesel Corporation.)*

eter of the puller plate is not larger than the sleeve out-side diameter. (An adapter plate larger than the sleeve may damage the block.)

3.   Attach the adapter plate to the through bolt.

NOTE   If the adapter plate is the type that can be installed from the top of the sleeve, it will have a cutaway or milled area on each side (Figure 6-4). This, along with the swivel on the bottom of the through bolt, allows the plate to be tipped slightly and inserted from the top, eliminating the need to install the adapter plate in the bottom of the sleeve and then insert the through bolt and attach the nut.

---

4.   After the adapter plate and through bolt have been installed in the sleeve, hold the through bolt and adapter plate firmly in the sleeve with one hand and install the support bracket with the other hand.

5.   Screw the through-bolt nut down on the through bolt until it contacts the support bracket. This will hold the adapter plate and through bolt snugly in place.

CAUTION   Before tightening the sleeve puller nut, make sure the sleeve puller supports or legs are positioned on a solid part of the block. Tighten the nut with the ratchet; the sleeve should start to move upward. If it does not and the puller nut becomes hard to turn, stop and recheck your puller installation before proceeding.

By using an air-impact wrench to rotate the hex nut on top of the tool, quick liner removal is assured. A tool such as this allows the technician to pull six stubborn wet liners in less than 4 minutes. By means of adapters, this tool can be made to fit a wide variety of diesel engine cylinder liners.

6.   On wet sleeves, after the sleeve has been pulled from the block far enough to clear the O-rings, tip or swivel the sleeve puller adapter plate and remove the sleeve puller assembly.

7.   The sleeve can now be lifted out by hand.

NOTE   Engines with tight-fitting dry sleeves may require a special hydraulic puller.

Pulling Dry Sleeves with a Hydraulic Puller

1.   Select an adapter plate to fit the sleeve. (See note in "Pulling Wet Sleeve from the Block.")

2.   Assemble the through-bolt plate and hydraulic ram.

3.   Adjust the through-bolt nut so that the adapter plate fits snugly in the sleeve and the hydraulic ram sits firmly on the supports or legs.

CAUTION   Make sure that the legs or supports are positioned on a solid part of the block to prevent cracking the block.

---

4.   Pump the hydraulic hand pump connected to the hydraulic ram.

5.   Make sure that the puller plate is seated correctly in the sleeve.

6.   Operate the hand pump until the sleeve is removed.

NOTE   If the sleeve does not move upward after considerable hydraulic pressure has been applied, it may be necessary to tap the sleeve adapter plate from the bottom, using a bar and hammer to break it loose.

CAUTION   Under no circumstances should a hydraulic ram or hand pump be overloaded by using an extension handle on the hand pump. This may cause a hydraulic hose to burst, resulting in serious injury to the operator from high-pressure hydraulic fluid escaping.

---

7.   Pump the hydraulic hand pump until the puller cylinder has moved its full length.

8.   If the sleeve cannot be moved using this procedure, another procedure used by some technicians is to use an electric welder and weld several beads vertically inside the full length of the sleeve from top to bottom. This heating and cooling of the sleeve may shrink it enough to allow removal.

9.   In some cases, press-fit dry sleeves cannot be removed successfully using any one or all of the procedures outlined above. If this is the case, the cylinder block must be taken to an automotive machine shop and the sleeve bored out.

Once the liner has been removed, write the cylinder number on its outer surface with a liquid metal marker or Dykem, and tag any shims from below the liner flange to ensure that they will be used with the same liner. This will allow you to retain the same cylinder liner protrusion or intrusion, depending on the type of liner used. Should the liner be removed due to failure, use match marks and numbers so that upon closer inspection, the technician or factory service representative can determine the cause of failure.

Inspecting The Cylinder Liner

When a wet cylinder liner has been removed at major overhaul or because of leaking liner seal rings, consider whether the liner might be used again. If so, it must be thoroughly cleaned and then inspected. After removing the liner seal rings, wash the liner in detergent soap and warm water and clean the inside diameter with a stiff nonmetallic brush to remove dirt and impurities. Use a high-quality steel wire brush to clean the liner flange seating area. If the outside diameter of the liner is scaled from coolant, check to see how thick the scale buildup is. Use a wire brush on the liner to remove the scale, since using a strong caustic solution could leave stains on the machined inside diameter of the liner. Then use a steam cleaner or solvent in a tank to clean the liner. Dry the liner with compressed air and lightly lubricate the machined surfaces to prevent any possibility of rusting. This also allows the oil to work its way into the surface finish.

SERVICE TIP If the liners are not going to be inspected or used right away, always store them in an upright position until ready for use. Experience has shown that liners left on their sides for any length of time can become egg shaped and distorted, thereby making reinstallation in the block bores very difficult—sometimes even impossible.

Once a liner has been cleaned thoroughly, closely inspect it to determine if it has the following characteristics:

1. *Surface finish and/or crosshatch irregularities.* Refer to Figure 6-5 (left-hand side) and check for a moderate polish. A moderate polish means a bright mirror finish exists only in areas that are worn and some traces of the original hone marks, or an indication of an etch pattern, are still visible. The right-hand side of the diagram illustrates a near-mirrorlike finish in the worn area with no traces of the original hone marks or an etch pattern. Replace the liner if a heavy polish is visible over 20% of the piston ring travel area or if 30% of the ring travel area has both a moderate and a heavy polish while the other half shows a heavy polish.

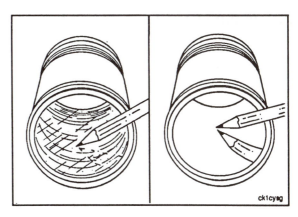

FIGURE 6–5 *Used cylinder liner. Left-hand side shows signs of a moderate polish yet still exhibits some traces of the original hone marks and an indication of the etch pattern. Right-hand side exhibits a near mirror-like finish on the surface of the liner with no traces of the original hone or etch marks. (Courtesy of Cummins Engine Company, Inc.)*

2. *Scuffing, scoring, gouging, or low spots on the inside diameter.* If your fingernail catches in a scratch, the liner should be replaced.

3. *Taper, wear, and ovality on the inside diameter.* This is determined by using a dial bore gauge.

4. *Signs of cracking, particularly at the flange, and around the port belt area of two-stroke-cycle engines.* (It may be necessary to employ a nondestructive magnetic particle, fluorescent magnetic particle, and a black light, or a fluorescent penetrant method similar to that described for checking an engine block or crankshaft, if cracks cannot be seen clearly with the naked eye.)

5. *Additional flange irregularities.* Check for smoothness and flatness on the top and bottom surfaces.

6. *A smooth and flat hardened liner insert, if used below the flange.* Replace the insert if it shows signs of indentations.

7. *Cavitation erosion, severe corrosion, or pitting on the outside surface of wet liners.* Reject the liner if deep pits are visible or if the corrosion cannot be removed with a fine emery cloth.

8. *Dark spots, stains, or low-pressure areas on the outside diameter of dry liners.* This indicates poor liner-to-block contact.

9. *Shiny areas on the outside diameter or flange area.* These usually indicate liner movement (wet or dry type).

10. *Fretting on the outside diameter of the liner, particularly below the ports on two-cycle engines.* This is the result of slight movement of the liner during engine operation, causing block metal to adhere to the liner. These metal particles can be removed from the surface of the liner with a coarse, flat stone.

Inspecting the Cylinder Block

After all sleeves have been removed, a preliminary visual inspection should be made to determine if the block can be repaired and reused or if it requires replacement. Items to check at this point are:

1. Visual cracks in water jacket internally and externally
2. Cored or drilled passageways for cracks
3. Main bearing and cylinder head bolt holes for cracked or broken threads
4. Block top surface for excessive erosion around water holes, head gasket wear, or cracks
5. Main bearing caps and saddles for cracks

After determining that the block will be reusable, all gasket material and heavy accumulation of grease or oil should be scraped or wiped off. It is common practice at this time to soak the block in a hot or cold tank of cleaning solution, which should remove all carbon, grease, scale, and lime deposits. After the block is removed from the tank, it can be cleaned with a steam cleaner, high-pressure washer, or water hose. During steaming of all passageways, oil galleys, and water jackets, use a stiff bristle brush or other suitable device to dislodge all foreign material that may be lodged or caked in the block. Also at this time the block should be visually checked again for cracks that may have opened up in the hot tank.

NOTE   Special attention should be given to the removal of scale or sludge accumulations within the water jackets because they will act like insulation and prevent heat from traveling into the coolant water. Poor heat transfer may cause scuffing or scoring of the cylinder and rings and excessive oil consumption. Consideration of what caused the sludge formation should be given at this point. Is it a normal accumulation, or has the cooling system maintenance been neglected?

It is recommended that after the block has been steamed it be sprayed with a light coat of preservative or rust preventive oil or solution.

FINAL INSPECTION, TESTING, RECONDITIONING, AND ASSEMBLY

At this time it is suggested that the block be placed on a suitable engine stand so that it can be rotated and tilted to allow access to all areas. If an engine stand is not available, a clean workbench will be sufficient.

NOTE   It is also suggested that the block be checked with an electric crack detector if it is available. Every attempt should be made at this point to ensure that the block is not cracked, since in the following steps the block is being readied for reassembly.

Checking and/or Resurfacing the Block-Top Surface

The cylinder block top must be checked for straightness throughout its length and for erosion around water outlets, using the following procedures.

NOTE   Erosion can be checked only after the block has been thoroughly cleaned.

---

1. Clean the top machined surface of the block by hand with sandpaper or with an electric or air-driven sander.
2. To determine the extent of erosion damage, use a new head gasket. Lay the gasket on the block. Visually check to see whether erosion will interfere with the gasket sealing.
3. If the erosion around water holes is excessive, the block top surface must be resurfaced or the water holes sleeved. No further checks can or should be made until the top surface has been resurfaced. (Resurfacing or machining the block top surface requires special equipment and should not be attempted in a general repair shop.) Most automotive machine shops have equipment to perform the resurfacing operation. If the water holes are to be sleeved, refer to the engine service manual for the correct procedure.
4. If the top surface has not been resurfaced and is considered usable because of lack of erosion, it should be checked for straightness both lengthwise and crosswise as well as diagonally.
5. Using an accurate straightedge, check the block by setting the straightedge on the top of the block (Figure 6-6).
6. Hold the straightedge with one hand. Using a 0.0015- to 0.002-in. (0.04- to 0.05-mm) feeler gauge, try to insert the feeler gauge between the block and straightedge. Most engine manufacturers recommend that if the block is warped 0.004 in. (.10 mm) or more, it should be remachined.
7. Inspect and tap all bolt holes to ensure that the threads are clean and usable.

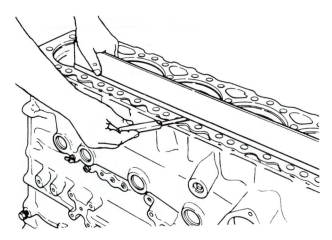

FIGURE 6–6 *Checking cylinder block with straight edge. (Courtesy of Detroit Diesel Corporation.)*

Checking the Main Bearing Bore Size and Alignment

Checking the main bearing bore is a very important step in engine or block rebuild. The main bearing bore should be checked for correct diameter and out-of-roundness using either a dial bore gauge or telescoping holegauge, as shown in Figure 6-7. In addition to this check, many manufacturers recommend the use of a master bar (Figure 6-8) to check the main bearing bore alignment.

NOTE Some technicians do not make main bearing bore alignment checks on engines that have a tendency to have a problem with bore alignment. The main bearing bore is simply redone whenever the engine is rebuilt, as a matter of routine. With

this in mind, check with your instructor or someone who has had experience with engine rebuilding. If in doubt about main bearing bore alignment, send the block to a shop that has the capability to check and/or bore the main bearing bores.

Checking and/or Reconditioning the Cylinder Sleeve Counterbore

1. The block counterbore and packing ring area must be cleaned of all rust, scale, and grease and should not have any rough, eroded areas that might cut or ruin a sleeve, O-ring, or crevice seal.

   a. Check the sleeve counterbore closely for cracks; if cracks are found, the block can be salvaged by resleeving the counterbore. Resleeving the counterbore should be attempted only by experienced technicians using the correct equipment.

2. Cleaning the block packing ring area and liner flange counterbore lip can be done by hand with a small piece of crocus cloth, wet–dry sandpaper, or emery paper of 100 to 120 grit (Figure 6-9).

3. The block counterbore top depth must be measured to ensure that sleeve protrusion will be correct after the sleeve is installed. The counterbore should also be uniform in depth around the circumference of the bore.

4. Measurement of the block counterbore should be done with a depth micrometer or dial indicator mounted on a machined sled fixture (Figure 6-10). If a depth micrometer is used, make sure that the micrometer is held firmly on the block surface when making measurements.

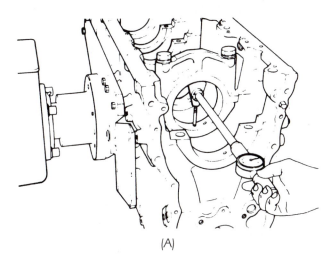

(A)

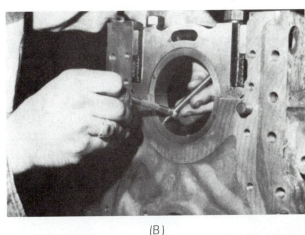

(B)

FIGURE 6–7 *(A) Gauging the engine block crankshaft main bearing bores with a precision dial bore gauge; (B) checking main bearing bore for out-of-roundness. [(A) Courtesy of Detroit Diesel Corporation.]*

FIGURE 6–8 *Using master bar to check main bearing bore alignment. (Courtesy of Cummins Engine Company, Inc.)*

5. The counterbore depth should be checked in at least four positions around the circumference of the counterbore to determine if the depth is within specifications. The counterbore depth should not vary more than 0.001 in. (0.025 mm) at all four positions.

6. After measuring the counterbore depth, the sleeve lip or flange should be measured with an outside micrometer.

NOTE   Use a new sleeve for this measurement or check the service manual.

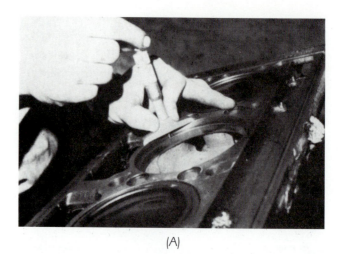

(A)

(B)

FIGURE 6–10 *(A) Measuring block sleeve counterbore with depth micrometer; (B) checking the depth of the cylinder block liner flange counterbore with a dial indicator mounted on a sled gauge. [(B) Courtesy of Detroit Diesel Corporation.]*

FIGURE 6–9 *Cleaning block counterbore before sleeve installation.*

The block counterbore depth can then be subtracted from this figure to obtain an estimated sleeve protrusion of 0.001 to 0.005 in. (0.025 to 0.127 mm).

7. If the counterbore does not meet the manufacturer's specifications, it should be reworked. On many engines, reworking the counterbore is a simple operation that can be accomplished easily if the correct tools are available. The counterbore tool is designed to fit into the block and recut the counterbore to a uniform depth (Figure 6-11). If the block counterbore cannot be

FIGURE 6–11 Using a power-driven Porta-Matic tool for an in-frame repair of a cracked or damaged counterbore area of the cylinder block liner. (Courtesy of Kent-Moore Division, SPX Corporation.)

reworked within your shop, many automotive machine shops can perform this type of work. Since correct sleeve protrusion determined by block counterbore depth and condition is vitally important to correct head gasket sealing, the block counterbore must be correct before engine reassembly can continue.

NOTE After recutting, the counterbore depth has been increased in depth. As a result, the sleeve protrusion will not be correct. This can be remedied by placing shims of the proper thickness on the sleeve to make up for the metal that has been removed from the block. Not all sleeves fit in the block with protrusion. Some engine sleeves when installed are below the top surface of the block. Check the sleeve position according to the manufacturer's specifications.

After you have completed the checks outlined above, the block is ready for reassembly.

Block Machining
Cylinder block checks, inspection, and measurements may indicate the following problems:

1. Warpage of the top deck.
2. Cylinder bores distorted (taper, ovality, wear). Parent bore engines do not employ a cylinder liner; the piston rides directly in the cylinder block bore.
3. Cylinder liner block counterbore slope or damage.
4. Lower block bore damage at the base of the liner seal ring area on wet liners.
5. Camshaft bore damage.
6. Crankshaft bore misalignment.
7. Erosion around water passage holes.
8. Blower mounting pad distortion (two-cycle engine models).

Any of these conditions would necessitate the need for machining of the top deck, power honing or boring of the cylinder liner parent bores, machining and sleeving of the liner counterbore or lower bore area, or camshaft or crankshaft line boring/honing of the crankshaft main bearing caps. This requires special equipment such as that shown in Figure 6-12 to remachine the top of the block. Figure 6-13 shows the equipment needed either to power-hone the block liner bores, or to rebore the cylinder bore to accept an oversized-outside-diameter cylinder liner. In dry liners, a damaged block bore larger than the biggest available outside-diameter liner can be resalvaged by machining the bore oversize, fitting a press-fit sleeve into the block, then power honing or boring the sleeve back to the standard outside diameter of the new liner (Figure 6-14). In addition, if the cylinder liner counter-

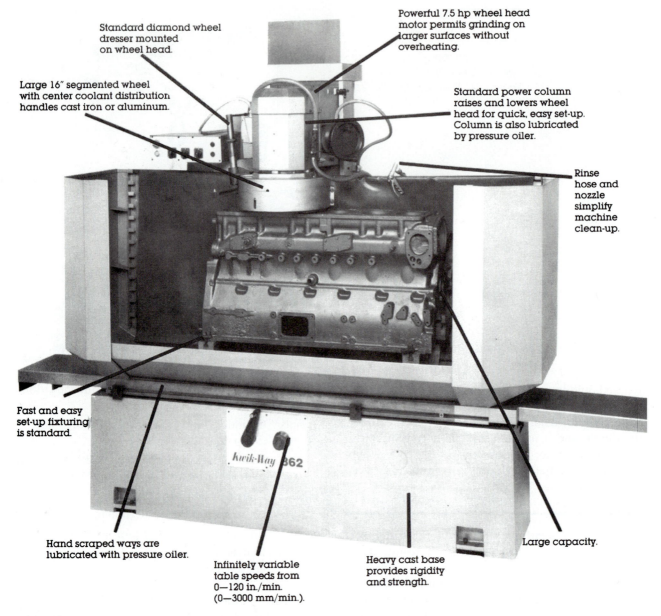

Standard diamond wheel dresser mounted on wheel head.

Powerful 7.5 hp wheel head motor permits grinding on larger surfaces without overheating.

Large 16" segmented wheel with center coolant distribution handles cast iron or aluminum.

Standard power column raises and lowers wheel head for quick, easy set-up. Column is also lubricated by pressure oiler.

Rinse hose and nozzle simplify machine clean-up.

Fast and easy set-up fixturing is standard.

Hand scraped ways are lubricated with pressure oiler.

Infinitely variable table speeds from 0–120 in./min. (0–3000 mm/min.).

Heavy cast base provides rigidity and strength.

Large capacity.

FIGURE 6–12 *Diesel engine securely mounted and precision leveled to allow a grinding and milling machine to resurface the top deck of the engine block. This same type of a machine can be used to resurface the cylinder head. (Courtesy of Kwik-Way Manufacturing Co.)*

bores (top of block) are damaged, they can also be remachined using the cutter tool shown in Figure 6-11, and if necessary, a press-fit sleeve can be installed. If the crankshaft bores are out of alignment, either machining or power honing with the tooling shown in Figure 6-15 can be employed. Normally, the main bearing caps must be machined flat at the parting line first, then the power hone run through the bores after torquing the retaining bolts to specifications.

Installing the Cam Bushing

Installation of cam bushings requires a special bushing driver or drivers, as described in the removal section (see Figure 6-3).

CAUTION Particular attention must be given to bushing alignment during installation to ensure lubrication to various parts of the engine.

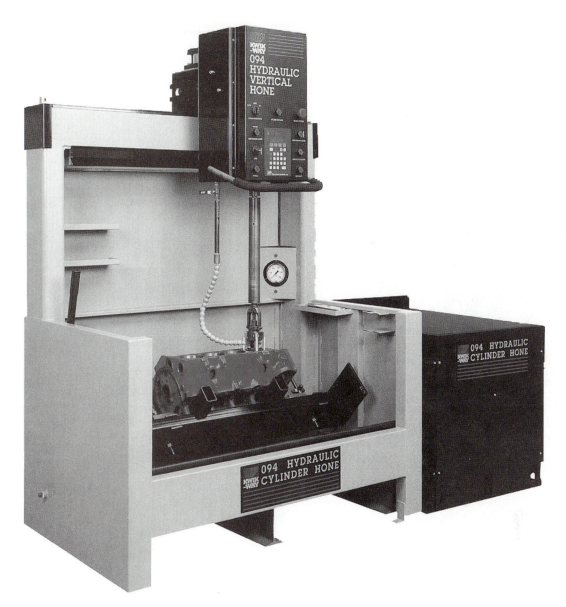

FIGURE 6-13 *Power honing machine used to hone a cylinder block bore to accept either an oversized liner or piston assembly. (Courtesy of Kwik-Way Manufacturing Co.)*

Many engines pump oil to the cam bushings and then to the rocker arms via a drilled passageway. Alignment of the bushing oil feed hole with the passageway is critical.

Before bushing installation, check all cam bushing bores in the block for nicks, scratches, and rust. Most bushing bores are tapered or chamfered slightly on one or both sides to make bushing installation easier. Make sure that the taper has no nicks or burrs that may damage the new bushing. Select bushings and de-termine their proper location in the block. Cam bushings may be of different widths and of different internal and external diameters in any one given engine.

1. Place the bushing on the driver without the driver bar.

2. Place the bushing and driver in front of the hole or bore that the bushing is supposed to be driven into.

3. Make sure that the bushing is aligned with the block oil holes.

4. Mark the bushing driver in line with the lube hole in the bushing.

5. Mark the block in line with the lube hole in the bushing bore, using a Magic Marker or similar device.

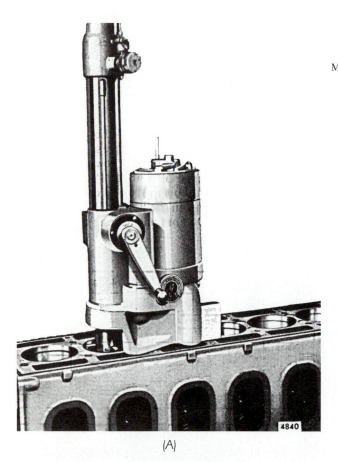

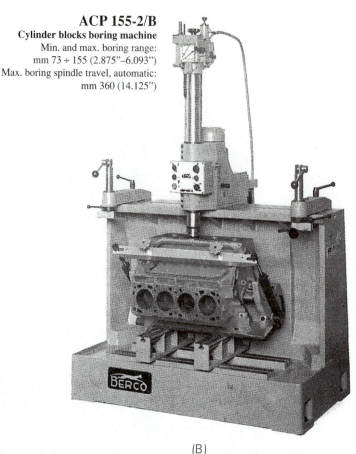

ACP 155-2/B
Cylinder blocks boring machine
Min. and max. boring range:
mm 73 ÷ 155 (2.875"–6.093")
Max. boring spindle travel, automatic:
mm 360 (14.125")

(A)

(B)

FIGURE 6–14 (A) Cylinder block portable boring bar mounted on the top surface of the engine block in preparation for boring the cylinder bores to accept oversize outside diameter dry-type slip-fit liners; (B) example of an engine block bolted securely into a precision floor-mounted boring machine. [(A) Courtesy of Detroit Diesel Corporation.]

6.   Insert a driving bar with a driving cone into bushing and driver.

7.   Tap the driving bar lightly to start the bushing into the bore, recheck alignment, and then drive the bushing into place with firm, solid hits with the hammer.

CAUTION   When driving cam bushings into a block, use care to prevent the bushing from tipping sideways; this could ruin the bushing.

Cam bushings can also be installed using a puller tool (Figure 6-3). This tool is very similar to the one mentioned previously; the main difference is that the bushings are not driven in with a hammer but pulled in. The driving rod or through bolt has been threaded and the bushings can be pulled or pushed in place by tightening a nut screw onto the threaded through bolt. This particular type of puller has an advantage because very little or no damage is done to the cam bush-

ing, which sometimes happens when a driving-type installer is used.

Installing the Galley Plugs, Expansion Plugs, Cover Plates, and Oil Pressure Relief Valves

---

NOTE   Select a suitable sealer such as Permatex, pipe joint sealer, or 3-M compound.

---

1.   Apply sealer to the galley plugs in small amounts and tighten the plugs securely.

2.   Apply sealer to the expansion plugs and, using a driver, drive into the block with a hammer.

a.   Cup plugs can be driven in with a bushing or seal driver that just fits into the plug (Figure 6-16).

b.   A convex plug can be expanded when in place by striking with a ball peen hammer and driver to deflect it into position.

FIGURE 6–15 *Cylinder block crankshaft line honing repair tools and equipment installed into the engine to correct for misalignment. (Courtesy of Sunnen Products Company.)*

Block Bore Diameter

The cylinder block must be checked with a dial bore gauge to determine if taper and out-of-round (ovality) readings are within worn limit specifications. The number of readings taken and their spacing throughout the block bore length depend on whether the block has been designed as a *parent bore* (no liner), a dry liner, or a wet liner. In dry liner engines,

FIGURE 6–16 *Cup expansion plug driver.*

or engines with a parent bore, measure the bore diameter throughout its length at five or six places and at 90° to each other for taper and ovality dimensions and compare to service manual specs. On a four-stroke-cycle wet liner engine, dial reading checks are taken at three positions, A, B, and C, as illustrated in Figure 6-17 for a series 50 or 60 DDC model. On two-stroke-cycle DDC engines, only the upper half of the liner is directly in contact with the engine coolant (above the cylinder liner ports–port belt area); therefore, dial bore checks would be taken as shown in Figure 6-18.

In blocks using either dry or wet liners, any physical damage to the liner surface usually requires installation of a new cylinder liner. In DDC two-stroke-cycle series 71 engines, a dry slip-fit liner is used; so if the liner inside diameter is lightly scuffed or scored, or the liner outside diameter exhibits some discoloration (dark spots), contact is not occurring. The cylinder block can be lightly cleaned with a fixed hone to accept a 0.001-in. (0.0254-mm) oversize-outside-diameter liner. If boring is required, oversize-outside-diameter liners are readily available from DDC in 0.005, 0.010, 0.020, or 0.030 in. (0.125, 0.254, 0.508, or 0.762 mm) outside diameter *only*. No liners with larger inside diame-

MAXIMUM ALLOWABLE CYLINDER BLOCK BORE DIAMETER

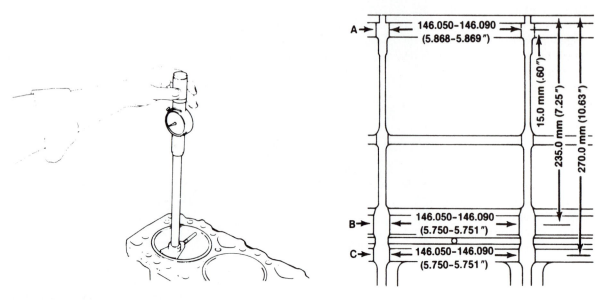

FIGURE 6–17 *Using a precision dial bore gauge to determine wear, ovality, and taper within a cylinder block bore. (Courtesy of Detroit Diesel Corporation.)*

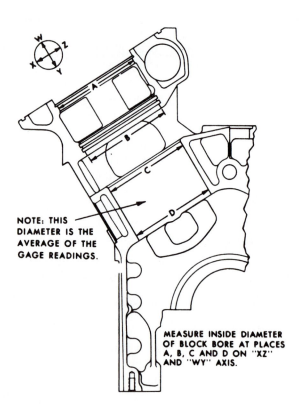

FIGURE 6–18 *Recommended positions used to check a cylinder block bore in a two-stroke-cycle DDC 92 series engine with a precision dial bore gauge or inside micrometer. (Courtesy of Detroit Diesel Corporation.)*

ter are available; therefore, a standard-diameter piston is always used.

In some light- and medium-duty diesel engines, no cylinder liners are used, and the piston operates directly within the engine block (parent bore). Visually inspect the block bore for any signs of scuffing or scoring; if there are signs, the block bore may have to be power honed or bored to take an oversize piston. If the block bore requires boring beyond the largest size of oversize piston available, a replacement press-fit sleeve could be obtained to salvage the block. The block must be bored to accept the outside diameter of the sleeve (allow a press fit of 0.002 to 0.003 in or 0.0508 to 0.0762 mm). Then rebore the inside diameter of the sleeve after pressing it into the block to bring it back to the replacement piston size.

Honing versus Reboring

Any service technician involved in major engine repairs must be well versed in the various techniques of honing the cylinder block bore and liner, including knowing when to hone and when to correct the block bore by remachining with a boring tool. In all cases, the initial use of a cylinder hone is simply to remove minor imperfections from the block or liner inside diameter before employing a dial gauge to determine bore or liner condition for reuse with respect to diameter, out-of-round condition, and taper. Cylinder liners that fall outside specifications should be replaced automatically with new liners. Honing can also be done to break any cylinder wall glaze, so that new piston rings can be seated on a nonpolished surface.

A hone or ridge reamer is also required to remove any minor ridge (Figure 6-19) at the top of the block bore or cylinder liner formed by the old piston ring travel. Attempting to hand-hone a cylinder block to accept oversize liners in excess of 0.001 in. (0.0254 mm) or oversize pistons, which generally are available in 0.010, 0.020, and 0.030 in. (0.254, 0.508, and 0.762 mm) sizes, can be done correctly only by using a boring bar. A portable boring bar such as the one illustrated in Figure 6-14A can be used to perform an in-frame repair; or at major engine overhaul, the block assembly can be mounted and clamped into a floor-mounted model such as the one illustrated in Figure 6-14B. An optional method that is widely used to prepare a cylinder block to accept oversize-outsize-diameter liners, or oversize pistons in a parent bore block, is to use a *power hone* similar to the one illustrated in Figure 6-13.

Attempting to enlarge a cylinder bore with a hand hone powered by an air or electric drill motor would require considerable time; in addition, the hone would tend to follow the existing imperfections in the block bore. If reboring is necessary in any parent block bore, or to accept an oversize-outside-diameter liner, only remove enough material to clean up the bore and to accept the first oversize piston or liner available; in this way, future reboring at major overhaul is possible. If you are boring to accept an oversize piston, determine from service information just what piston-to-block clearance is specified. For example, if the piston-to-liner clearance for an aluminum piston is specified as being between 0.006 and 0.007 in. (0.152 to 0.177 mm), bore to within 0.002 to 0.003 in. (0.050 to 0.076 mm) or slightly less to allow finishing by honing the block bore. This would allow you to obtain the proper crosshatch pattern and surface finish on the cylinder wall.

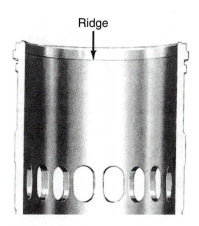

Ridge

FIGURE 6–19 *Wear ridge on a used cylinder liner or block bore. (Courtesy of Detroit Diesel Corporation.)*

Some engine manufacturers do *not* offer oversize-diameter pistons for some of their engines. One example is the Caterpillar 3116 truck engine. Caterpillar determined that it was not practical to rebore the blocks for oversize pistons. In this case the procedure to salvage a cylinder block with major cylinder bore damage is to bore the cylinder oversize and employ a press-in sleeve, which can then be rebored to produce the correct-size bore while leaving enough material to allow for a properly honed crosshatch pattern.

CYLINDER HONES

A power honing machine can be used for cylinder block reconditioning. Major tool and equipment suppliers offer hones in a variety of styles. Basically, however, there are three main types of hand-operated hones used to recondition cylinder block bores or liners:

1. A spring-loaded hone (Figure 6-20) can be adjusted to suit different bore sizes. This type of hone tends to follow the contours of a worn bore due to the spring pressure exerted on the stones; therefore, it is used to quickly deglaze a bore or a liner. Do not use this type of equipment when attempting to hone a just completed cylinder block bore to achieve the correct piston-to-liner clearance as well as the correct surface finish crosshatch pattern.

2. A ball-type hone or flexi-hone (Figure 6-21) is also used mainly to create effective cylinder wall deglazing or to clean a used liner by lightly roughening up the surface to facilitate new piston ring seating.

3. A fixed-type hone (Figure 6-22) can be set to a specific diameter by rotating a knurled knob above the stones until the expanding mechanism (stones) make firm but light contact with the cylinder wall. This type is used to hone a cylinder or block bore after reboring to achieve the correct crosshatch pattern and desired piston-to-liner clearance.

Reasons for Honing

It is *not* necessary to hone a new cylinder liner to modify its inside-diameter surface finish. The liner has already undergone a machine-honing process at the factory, and any change to the crosshatch pattern will adversely affect the seating of the piston rings. When reusing liners, some engine manufacturers support honing and others are opposed to it. By way of background information, Detroit Diesel, Mack, and a number of major European and Japanese diesel engine manufacturers are in favor of honing used liners if they are to be reused. There are several reasons why many engine manufacturers recommend honing a liner prior to reuse:

Range 2" to 7"

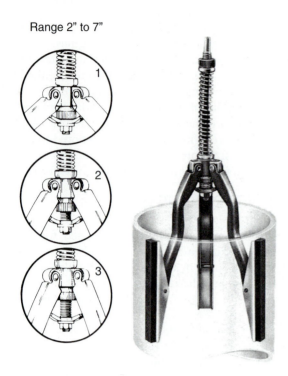

3-Stone Glaze Breaker Hone
ADJUSTABLE TENSION

Full range 2" to 7" diameter. Fully adjustable for both diameter and tension. Rugged construction. Flexible drive shaft. Equipped with three 220 grit stones recommended for ring seating.

Spreader Limiter permits easy insertion in the cylinder bore or when changing from cylinder to cylinder.
1. Spread Limiter adjustment nut shown in position to allow hone to open to full capacity.
2. Spread Limiter adjustment shown turned up on shaft to limit arm diameter to open to about half capacity of the hone.
3. Spread Limiter adjustment nut turned up on shaft to limit the arm's diameter to open for a smaller diameter job.

FIGURE 6–20   Spring-loaded adjustable cylinder liner hone that can be employed to lightly clean or to deglaze a liner. (Courtesy of Hastings Manufacturing Co.).

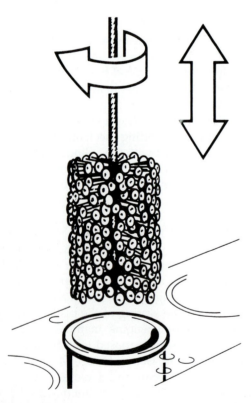

FIGURE 6–21   Ball-type hone, or flexi-hone, used mainly to deglaze cylinder liners or to clean up a used liner to provide a seat for new piston rings.

- To break any glaze and to obtain the correct surface roughness so that the piston rings can seat against the cylinder wall as quickly as possible with minimum wear; otherwise, the piston ring seating time will be lengthened or piston rings may fail to seat correctly.
- To obtain a surface structure that allows optimum adhesion of the lube oil, so that a film of oil is maintained between the piston rings and the liner.
- To create a crosshatch pattern on the inside diameter of the liner. This will optimize the distribution and removal of oil from the cylinder wall when the piston moves down. Too steep a crosshatch pattern can lead to excessive oil consumption, whereas too narrow a pattern can lead to scuffing of the rings, inadequate lubrication, and damage to the cylinder kit.
- Any deep ridge at the top of the liner similar to that illustrated in Figure 6-19 would invariably render the liner unfit for further use. You may need to use a ridge reamer (Figure 6-23) to remove this ridge before attempting to pull the piston and rings from the liner or block bore in a press-fit liner. A small ridge formed at the top of the liner by the piston rings can be removed with a hone; if it is not removed, interference with the travel of the new rings may result in actual compression ring breakage.

(A)

(B)

FIGURE 6–22 *(A) Installing an adjustable hone set into the cylinder liner or block bore; (B) adjusting the hone to a fixed position within the cylinder liner to obtain a specific cross-hatch finish on either the cylinder liner or block bore after machining. [(A) Courtesy of Sunnen Products Company; (B) courtesy of Cummins Engine Company, Inc.]*

FIGURE 6–23 *Clamshell-design ridge reamer tool that can be adjusted to cut the worn ridge within a cylinder liner or cylinder block bore. (Courtesy of Hastings Manufacturing Co.)*

Holding Fixture

You cannot effectively hone a liner when it is outside the engine block without using a suitable holding fixture. Ideally, a scrap cylinder block makes the best fixture! If you choose to install the liner in a cylinder block that is to be reused, the block should be dismantled and then cleaned thoroughly after the liner honing process. The type of hone recommended and the stone grit required to successfully hone a liner depend on the liner material used. Cast iron liners, hardened cast iron, steel, and even aluminum cylinders dictate the honing stones and materials that should be used. Major manufacturers of hones and stones for all facets of the automotive and diesel industry, such as Sunnen Products Company, include with their products honing instructions for reconditioning cylinders and liners. Refer to these directions along with the engine manufacturer's service manual procedure prior to honing. For best results, thoroughly wash out all cylinders before honing.

Liner Surface Finish

Correct honing procedures produce a cylinder liner surface finish that exhibits a crosshatch pattern similar to that illustrated in Figure 6-24 which shows a 20 to 25° and a 40 to 50° example. This illustration is magnified many times for instructional purposes. Each engine manufacturer specifies in its service manual what angle of crosshatch pattern and what surface finish are desired. Surface finish is usually stated as being in the region of 20 to 35 RMS (root mean square), which is

Ridge Reamers

QUICK-CUT–FEED UP

This extra-sturdy, extra-durable ridge reamer will handle all modern engines with bores including canted and most short stroke types. Tool sits solidly in the cylinder, with holding blades maintaining hook wall contact for smooth cut. Cutter head guide plate locks on both sides. Tungsten carbide Saf-T-Blade will not overcut, chatter or dig in. Smooth cutting action of this ridge reamer is attained by fine-thread feed-up. Accuracy maintained by heavy, heat-treated center bolt. Steel collar on center bolt protects threads from wrench damage. Three position setting of spring-loaded cutter head permits change from one cylinder to another without adjusting cutter head assembly.

Clamshell package

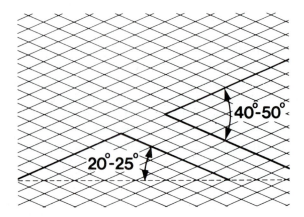

FIGURE 6–24 *Example of how to identify a cylinder liner or block bore surface finish crosshatch pattern in degrees. (Courtesy of Cummins Engine Company, Inc.)*

| Liner material | Stone type used | | | | | |
| | 70 grit | 150 grit | 220 grit | 280 grit | 400 grit | 600 grit |
	Liner microinch surface finish					
Cast iron	100	32	20	12	6	3
Hardened sleeve	25	20	—	12	5	1
Steel sleeve	—	35	—	20	7	2

simply a mathematical term indicating the average irregularity in millionths of an inch (0.000001 in.). This angle of surface finish is usually referred to as a *microinch finish* because the actual surface finish on the liner inside diameter would appear to the naked eye similar to that shown in Figure 6-25.

The actual microinch surface finish is controlled by the proper selection of honing stone used—the grit. For example, both roughing and finishing stones are available with grits ranging from 70 to 600: the 70 grit stones are regarded as roughing types, 150 grit as finishing, 220 grit as a medium finishing set, 280 grit as a polishing set, 400 grit as a fine set, and 600 grit as an extrafine finishing set. Keep in mind that the rougher the stone grit used, the larger will be the microinch surface finish. Consider the finish on a liner or sleeve surface from the following information:

FIGURE 6–25 *Example of a properly finished crosshatch liner surface pattern. (Courtesy of Cummins Engine Company, Inc.)*

Hone Driving Power and Adjustment

When using a hone, the drive motor (air or electric) must be set to rotate the assembly in a clockwise direction at speeds between 250 and 450 rpm. The size of drive motor required depends on the diameter of stones being used. It is advisable to use a 1/2-in. (12.7-mm)-capacity drill motor for bore sizes up to 3 in. (76.2 mm), a 5/8-in. (16-mm) motor for up to 4.75 in. (121 mm), and a 3/4-in. (19-mm) motor for bore sizes larger than 4.75 in. (121 mm).

A ball-type hone offers no adjustment, but it does come in a range of sizes to suit different-diameter bores and liners. Some spring-loaded hones can be adjusted, and all fixed hones are equipped with an adjustment knob to allow expansion of the stones until they have a firm but light drag on the cylinder wall. Figure 6-22 illustrates placement of a fixed, adjustable Sunnen hone into the cylinder or liner. The pinion is raised about 1/4 in. (6 mm), then turned counterclockwise to set the stones to the approximate diameter of the cylinder and liner. Push the pinion down until it engages with the outside gear on the hone body. Expand the combination of two stones and two guides firmly against the cylinder-liner wall by turning the hone ring wrench clockwise (Figure 6-22). While making this adjustment, the tops of the stones and guides should not extend more than 1/2 in. (12.7 mm) out of the top of the liner.

Honing Process

Honing stones can be used either dry or wet. When used dry, stones cut faster; when used wet, a honing oil must be employed. Metal removal can be achieved faster in a cast iron liner when dry honing is done; honing oil is recommended when a 280-, 400-, or 600-grit stone is used. Honing oil should always be used when honing steel or aluminium. Use a squirt can or brush to apply a continuous flow to the stones and cylinder. If a recommended honing oil is not readily available, smear vegetable shortening liberally on the cylinder and the stones.

It is important to inspect liners thoroughly before honing to avoid wasting time on those that are damaged severely or are worn and in an out-of-round condition beyond acceptable service manual specifications. The smaller the amount of material that can be removed from the used liner to clean it up lightly, the better. However, avoid casual roughing up of the cylinders, since too coarse a crosshatch pattern will show deep scratches that will permit leakage between the rings and cylinder wall as well as wearing the new rings excessively. If wear limits published in the engine service manual are exceeded after honing, new rings will not have sufficient wall tension due to the size increase, and new liners will be required.

The purpose of honing a used cylinder liner is simply to deglaze the surface with minimal removal of metal. The intent is not to enlarge the bore size. Consequently, it takes very little effort and time to accomplish this procedure. Always exercise care when honing to avoid removing excess material from the cylinder or liner.

With the honing tool fixture (with the correct stone grit) inserted into and adjusted to the cylinder or liner bore size, connect the top of the hone drive shaft to a drive motor. Using the chuck key, tighten the chuck securely.

SERVICE TIP Support the drive motor on an overhead support bracket similar to the one illustrated in Figure 6-26. This tool allows you to adjust a stroking rod to prevent the hone from moving too far through the cylinder at the bottom; otherwise, the stones can strike the lower end of the block strengthening struts, resulting in breakage of the stones and damage to the hone.

The speed at which you manually push/pull (stroke) the drive motor and hone the cylinder up and down will determine the finished crosshatch angle. The stone grit determines the RMS surface finish. You need to use short up-and-down overlapping strokes equal to about one stroke per second. Detroit Diesel recommends a 120-grit stone set when honing its four-stroke-cycle series 50 and 60 engine cylinder liners, while Mack recommends a stone set between 150 and 250 grit to "glaze bust" its dry liners. Cummins recommends a 280-grit stone set to deglaze and clean the cylinder bores of its B series engines that do not use a liner. Cummins further recommends that a fine-grit ball hone and a mixture of equal parts of mineral spirits and SAE 30W engine oil be used.

Remember these two steps when honing. First, on used liners or bores, always start stroking at the bottom or least worn section of the liner or bore using short strokes to concentrate honing in the smallest di-

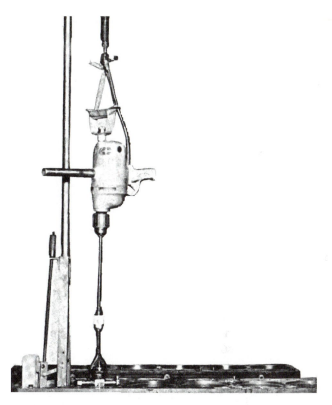

FIGURE 6–26 Special honing fixture to support a heavy-duty variable-speed drill motor used to drive the honing stones when cleaning up a liner or block bore. (Courtesy of Cummins Engine Company, Inc.)

ameter of the cylinder. Gradually lengthen the stroke as metal is removed and the stones make contact higher up the cylinder. Allow the stones to extend about 1/2 in. (13 mm) from the cylinder at the top of its stroke.

Second, work the hone up and down the full length of the liner with the drive motor running at between 300 and 400 rpm. Do this a few times (about 15 seconds maximum) or after about 10 full strokes of the hone. The result should be a crisscross pattern that produces hone marks on an axis stated by the engine manufacturer in the respective engine service manual. For example, DDC states that the liner should be honed to produce between a 22 and 32° crisscross (crosshatch) pattern in its series 50 and 60 cylinder liners, while Mack recommends that a diamond crisscross pattern of 20- to 35-μin. RMS finish be achieved. On Cummins B series engines that use no liner, the block bore finish should be honed to produce a correctly deglazed surface and crosshatched appearance with the lines at a 15 to 25° angle with the top of the cylinder block (or a 30 to 50° included angle). When bringing the drive motor to a stop *do not* allow the hone to come to a stop in the same position.

Keep it moving so that no one area of the bore ends up with too narrow a crosshatch pattern. In addition, to avoid vertical scratches up and down the length of the cylinder, relieve the tension on the hone before removing it from the cylinder. Otherwise, these vertical scratches can form a path for combustion gases to blow by.

Cleaning the Liner or Block after Honing

The ideal liquid for washing or cleaning a liner or cylinder block may seem to be gasoline, diesel fuel, or solvent. Tests have shown, however, that on liner surfaces cleaned in this manner, too much grinding and honing dust is left in the crosshatch surface grooves. Subsequently, this will cause damage to the liner and the piston rings. After honing, wash the inside surface of the liner with a solution of household laundry detergent and scrub with a stiff nonmetallic bristle brush to remove as much of the honing debris as possible. Rinse with hot water and blow dry. After the bore is dry, coat it with clean engine oil and allow it to soak in for 10 minutes. Wipe the lube oil from the bore with a clean white cloth or white paper towel. If the cloth or towel shows evidence of gray or darker stains, honing debris is still present on the cylinder liner surface. Repeat the oil application and wiping procedure until no evidence of stain appears on the cloth or towel. Use a brass or steel wire brush to clean the top of the liner flange.

NOTE   If you are honing an engine block with no liner (that is, where the piston runs directly in the block bore), after the honing procedure is complete and before engine reassembly, thoroughly clean the cylinder block, oil galleries, and cylinder bores using a solution of strong detergent and water. Incomplete cleaning will lead to piston seizure or rapid wear of the cylinder bores or sleeves, pistons, and rings!

Installing a Wet Liner

A wet liner can be installed on its own or as part of a cylinder pack that includes the assembled piston, piston rings, and connecting rod. (The cylinder pack is described in detail in Chapter 9).

If the measurements of the outside diameter and thickness of the liner flange area are outside specifications, the liner will have to be replaced. If the cylinder block counterbore is damaged, remachine it and/or install a sleeve. Many engine manufacturers supply liners of oversized flange diameter and thickness to allow reuse of an engine block. For example, in the Cummins

NT-855 (14-L) engine series, you can obtain liners with a 0.020-in. (0.51-mm) larger outside-diameter flange and liners with a 0.010-in. (0.25-mm) thicker flange. You can install a wet liner into the cleaned block bore minus any of the seal rings, pull the liner into position and secure it in place with liner hold-down clamps, and check the flange protrusion. Then you can add or delete liner flange shims to obtain the correct specifications.

Follow this procedure to install a wet liner:

1.   Engine manufacturers suggest that you lubricate the liner crevice and seal rings shown in Figures 6-27 to 6-29. These seals are installed into respective machined grooves on the liner; however, on Detroit Diesel's two-stroke wet-liner models, the liner seal rings are installed into the cylinder block bore machined grooves located above the liner port area. Refer to Figure 6-18. Check the service manual for your engine since the liner seal material will usually dictate the type of lubricant to use. Consider the following suggested lubricants:

- *Cummins NT-855 (14-L) engine liner:* vegetable oil
- *Cummins L10 engine liner:* 15W-40 engine oil
- *Detroit Diesel two-stroke 92 series:* clean engine oil
- *Detroit Diesel four-stroke-cycle series 50 and 60 engine liners:* clean petroleum jelly
- *Caterpillar 3176 engine:* clean engine oil
- *Caterpillar 3406 engine liner:* liquid soap on early O-ring seals, engine oil on the crevice seal and later O-rings

---

CAUTION   Many engine manufacturers oppose the use of hydrogenated vegetable shortening as a seal lubricant because of the adverse effects that it has on the seal ring material.

---

2.   Some engine manufacturers suggest that you apply a bead of RTV (room-temperature vulcanizing) sealant on either the cylinder block counterbore or on the underside of the liner flange. The diameter of the bead should be between 3/64 in. (0.047 in., or 1.19 mm) and 1/16 in. (0.0625 in., or 1.58 mm). Figure 6-30 illustrates where to apply this sealer bead. Note that the liner *must* be installed within 5 minutes, maximum, after bead installation; otherwise, the RTV sealer will have dried out and may not seal effectively.

3.   Manually insert the liner carefully into the block bore (align the previous match marks to the block) and push it down squarely as far as you can.

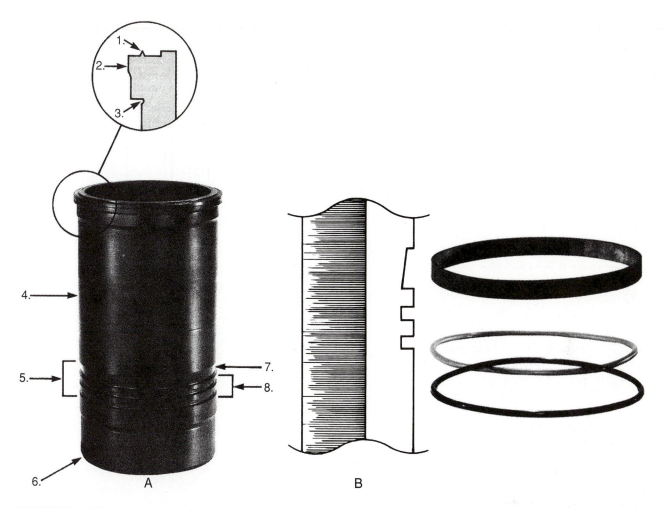

FIGURE 6–27 *Features of a typical wet cylinder liner assembly and the seal rings required to retain the engine coolant within the engine block passages and around the outside diameter of the liner. 1, Bead; 2, press fit; 3, relief; 4, wall; 5, sealing area; 6, chamfer; 7, crevice seal groove; 8, packing ring grooves. (Courtesy of Cummins Engine Company, Inc.)*

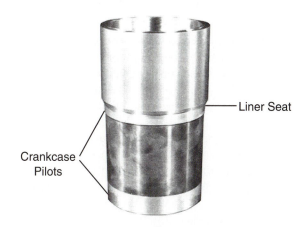

FIGURE 6–28 *Midstop design cylinder liner employed by Cat in its 3176 engine model. (Courtesy of Caterpillar, Inc.)*

4. Using a properly sized cylinder liner diameter driver and handle, gently tap the liner all the way into the block counterbore. When the liner reaches bottom you will hear a dull thud. If you have a suitable liner installer similar to that illustrated in Figure 6-31, you can pull the liner squarely into position, or use a liner driver tool, shown in Figure 6-32. This allows you to recheck the liner protrusion with a dial gauge (Figure 6-33), which clearly shows where cylinder liner protrusion is measured in relation to the top machined surface of the engine block. If a liner press is not available, once the liner has been driven home, you may have to install a cylindrical liner clamping plate bolted to the cylinder block upper deck to ensure that the liner is completely bottomed in the block counterbore.

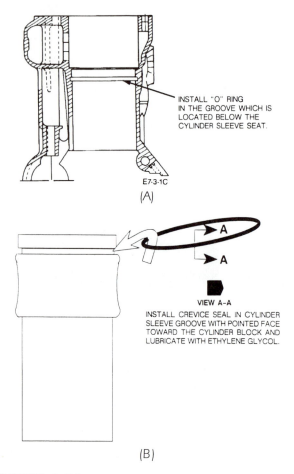

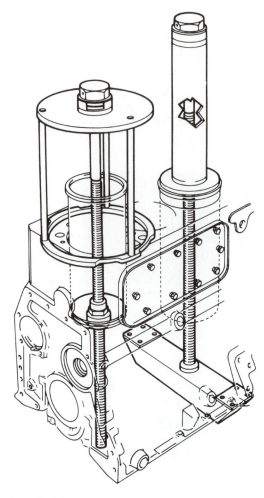

FIGURE 6–29 (A) Mack E-7 engine wet/dry liner O-ring groove; (B) Mack E-7 liner crevice seal groove. (Courtesy of Mack Trucks, Inc.)

FIGURE 6–31 Installation tooling used to install a cylinder liner assembly into the block bore when it is a press fit or interference fit. (Courtesy of DAF Trucks, Eindhoven, The Netherlands.)

Recheck the liner protrusion with either a dial sled gauge, or a straightedge and feeler gauges, at four points 90° apart. If the protrusion is not within the service manual specifications, try reshimming; or, the liner may have to be repulled and both the liner flange and block counterbore rechecked for possible problems.

5. Some engine manufacturers recommend that once protrusion has been checked, you should use a feeler gauge to measure the clearance between the liner and its lower bore to ensure that no distortion has occurred during installation. Figure 6-34 illustrates this particular check where one manufacturer's spec calls for a clearance of 0.002 to 0.006 in. (0.05 to 0.15 mm).

6. Take a dial bore gauge and recheck the liner inside diameter for out-of-roundness at five points throughout the liner length. Then take another set of readings at a 90° axis to the first.

7. If the liner protrusion, lower liner block check with the feeler gauge, or the liner bore out-of-round

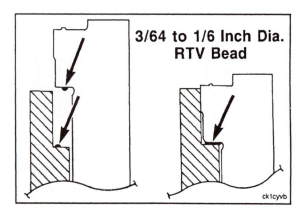

FIGURE 6–30 Where to apply a bead of RTV (room-temperature vulcanizing) sealant between the cylinder liner flange and engine block counterbore. (Courtesy of Cummins Engine Company, Inc.)

FIGURE 6–32 *Driving sleeve in place with driver. (Courtesy Cummins Engine Company, Inc.)*

condition are not within specs, repull the liner and check for possible rolled or twisted seal rings, or clean the liner flange or cylinder block counterbore.

8. On Detroit Diesel two-stroke-cycle engines, once the liner has been installed, use a liner hold-down clamp and check the distance (intrusion) of the liner below the cylinder block machined surface. Figure 6-35 illustrates that these engines employ a hardened steel insert in the block counterbore on which the liner flange sits and an individual cylindrical sealing gasket that sits on the liner flange. When the cylinder head is torqued down, this gasket is compressed and acts as a seal between the combustion chamber, liner, head, and block.

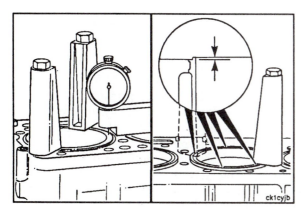

FIGURE 6–33 *Employing two cylinder liner hold-down clamps while using a sled-mounted dial gauge to check liner protrusion. (Courtesy of Cummins Engine Company, Inc.)*

FIGURE 6–34 *Using a feeler gauge around the bottom circumference of a wet cylinder liner after installation to check for any signs of liner distortion due to rolled or twisted seal rings. (Courtesy of Cummins Engine Company, Inc.)*

Installing a Dry Slip-Fit Liner

Detroit Diesel's two-stroke 71 series engine model has a dry cylinder liner that is a slip-fit design in the engine block bore. The service manual specification calls for a liner-to-block bore clearance of between 0.0005 and 0.0025 in. (0.0127 to 0.0635 mm) on used parts. Before removing a liner from the block, matchmark it with a metal marker to ensure that when it is reinstalled it will be inserted into the same position. If the

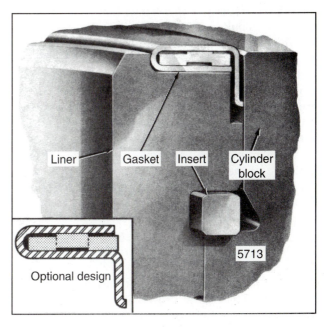

FIGURE 6–35 *Example of a hardened steel insert in the cylinder liner block counterbore and the placement of the individual sealing gasket employed by Detroit Diesel on its 71 series engine models that use a dry slip-fit liner. (Courtesy of Detroit Diesel Corporation.)*

cylinder block has to be lightly honed at overhaul, Detroit Diesel supplies 0.001-in. (0.0254-mm) oversize-outside-diameter liners to allow a closer fit to the block bore. If, however, the cylinder block has to be rebored oversize, oversize-*outside-diameter-only* liners will be required. These liners are available in 0.001, 0.005, 0.010, 0.020, and 0.030 in. oversize (0.0254, 0.127, 0.254, 0.508, and 0.762 mm). Take careful note that the liners are *only* available in oversized outside diameter, and *no* oversized pistons are available! If a liner is replaced, it can be reused with a used or a new standard-diameter piston assembly. Liner-to-block clearances after-reboring should fall within 0.0005 to 0.0015 in. (0.013 to 0.038 mm). The oversize dimension of the liner is etched on its outside diameter.

Installing a Dry Press-Fit Liner

Dry liners that are press fit or interference fit into the cylinder block are between 0.0004 and 0.0008 in. (0.010 to 0.020 mm) larger on their outside diameter than the block bore. Follow these steps to achieve proper installation of the liner:

1. Select a hydraulic or mechanical press and suitable guide adapters that can be inserted across the liner at the top. Figure 6-31 is a mechanical puller arrangement. The left side of the figure shows removal of the liner; the right side shows the tooling required to press the liner back into place.

2. Refer to Figure 6-2 and make sure that any shims from under the liner flange that were removed when it was pulled from the block bore are reinstalled into the block counterbore prior to installation.

3. Position the liner squarely with the machined surface of the top of the engine block. Although this can be determined visually, if you use a small try square placed at 90° intervals around the liner outside diameter prior to installation, you can lightly hand bump the liner to square it up.

4. Apply a small amount of light lube oil to the top edge of the block bore if necessary. Be careful—excessive amounts can create heat transfer problems between the outside diameter of the block bore and the liner during normal operation.

5. Carefully press the liner into the block bore. Then check the liner flange protrusion height above the machined surface of the block as illustrated in Figure 6-33. Obtain this specification from the engine service manual. Then you can lay a small straightedge across the top of the liner and gauge the protrusion with a feeler gauge, although the use of a dial indicator mounted on a sled gauge as illustrated is preferable. Securely hold the liner in position during the protrusion check with two cylinder liner hold-down clamps, which are shown in Figure 6-33. Liner protru-

sion is needed to allow the cylinder head gasket to seal correctly. If the liner protrusion is not within published specs, you will have to pull it back out. By using different liner-to-block counterbore shims, proper protrusion can be achieved. However, you may have to clean or remachine the counterbore to square it up again.

NOTE Press-fit dry-liner installation can be made easier by chilling the liner. Pack in dry ice for 35 to 45 minutes to allow it to cool before installation. If you choose this method, *be very careful* to avoid serious injury when handling dry ice or parts that have been chilled. Dry ice can cause skin burns and eye injury if not handled properly. Always wear safety gloves and goggles. Never seal dry ice in an airtight container because it may cause the container to explode or burst. Follow these two steps:

1. When removing the liner from the dry ice, *do not* wrap a shop cloth or towel around it, because it may stick to the liner surface.

2. Using safety gloves, quickly insert the liner into the block bore; make sure that it is square to the top of the block. Then pull the liner into position as shown in Figure 6-31 (right-hand side) or by using a hydraulic press.

Final Testing of the Block for Water Leaks after Sleeves (Wet Type) Have Been Installed

Testing the cylinder block for water leaks before final assembly is recommended by some manufacturers.

NOTE This procedure is rarely used in the field, since if the block is in good condition and the sleeves are installed correctly, water leaks rarely occur.

Many methods of checking blocks for water leaks are used in the field, dictated primarily by the equipment available. Two methods are listed here. Select the method that is recommended by the engine manufacturer or that the equipment is available for.

1. Fill the block with antifreeze after sleeves and expansion plugs have been installed. If equipment is available, pressurize with compressed air and check for leaks. (Figure 6-36).

2. Pressurize the block water jacket with air and immerse the block in a tank of hot water. Check for bubbles. Any area leaking air should be checked. The

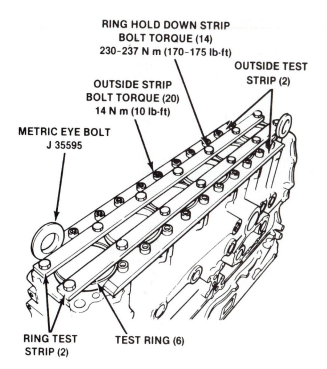

FIGURE 6–36 *Preparing a cylinder block for a pressure test to determine if any cracks are evident. Test strips are bolted as shown to seal off the coolant passages. (Courtesy of Detroit Diesel Corporation.)*

block should now be ready for further assembly of engine parts and complete engine assembly.

Dry-liner engines should have a maximum air pressure applied to them of 40 psi (276 kPa), whereas wet-liner engines should never have air pressure in excess of 20 psi (138 kPa) applied to them. Allow the air pressure to be maintained for at least 2 hours. At the end of the test period, carefully inspect the outside diameter of wet-liner flanges and the underside of the block on Cummins or Caterpillar engines for any signs of liner O-seal ring leakage. Note, however, that on Detroit Diesel series 50 and 60 engines (see Figure 6-37) coolant weep holes located alongside the engine block allow any coolant that leaks past the top liner seal ring to exit at the holes. Check the various oil passages, crankcase, and exterior of the block for any signs of water and antifreeze leakage, which would confirm that either the block is cracked or a liner seal ring is leaking. Most manufacturers recommend that a cracked block be replaced with a new one. There are, however, methods that are sometimes used to repair a small crack that is not located in an area close to either the cylinder liner or cylinder head sealing surfaces.

NOTE   If a block is to be stored for a time before further engine assembly, it should be protected from rusting by first covering any openings and then painting the block. A heavy coat of oil or grease should be applied to the inside of cylinder liners as a rust preventive and preservative measure.

SUMMARY

The information gleaned from the detailed service descriptions described in this chapter will permit you to systematically perform an inspection, analysis, and repair of the engine cylinder block and liners at major overhaul. This skill will broaden your understanding of the importance of the block and its components, and assist you in both the service/repair and effective troubleshooting of the engine.

SELF-TEST QUESTIONS

1. Technician A says that most high-speed diesel engine cylinder blocks are made from aluminum alloy. Technician B disagrees, stating that gray cast iron alloys with a fairly high silicon content ensure superior durability. Who is correct?

2. Technician A states that all high-speed diesel engines employ one-piece cylinder blocks. Technician B says

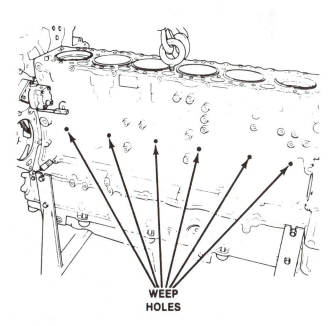

FIGURE 6–37 *Example of cylinder-block-located weep holes which indicate when engine coolant leaks past the upper liner seal ring of a series 60 four-stroke-cycle electronically controlled engine. (Courtesy of Detroit Diesel Corporation.)*

that a number of larger high-speed engines employ two- and even three-piece bolted blocks. Who knows the product information best?

3. True or False: The most widely used high-speed engine cylinder block is a six-cylinder inline configuration.

4. Technician A says that when cylinder block bores become worn, the block should be replaced. Technician B says that the block can be rebored or a new cylinder sleeve (liner) can be used. Who is correct?

5. True or False: A square engine block design means that the bore and stroke are the same dimension.

6. Technician A says that when overhauling an engine, it is very important to remove any scale buildup from the internal coolant passages to prevent overheating during operation. Technician B says that as long as you steam clean these passages thoroughly, there should be no problem. Which technician has higher standards of excellence?

7. Technician A says that it is not necessary to pressure test a cylinder block at major overhaul if no visible cracks are apparent during inspection when you are using nondestructive testing methods. Technician B says that you should always perform a pressure check to confirm that no cracks exist, since you cannot always detect hairline cracks using the nondestructive method. Which technician is correct?

8. True or False: All machined surfaces of an engine block should always be checked with a straightedge and a feeler gauge for any signs of distortion.

9. True or False: Cylinder block crankshaft bore alignment should be checked at major overhaul even if no bearing damage is evident.

10. True or False: If a cylinder block crankshaft bore is misaligned, the block should be replaced.

11. True or False: Signs of fretting at the main bearing cap parting line are indicative of movement of the main bearing cap.

12. True or False: A dry cylinder liner is always press fit in the block bore.

13. Technician A says that a dry press-fit cylinder liner can normally be pressed in the block bore by hand. Not so says technician B; a hydraulic press is necessary to install it. Which technician is correct?

14. Technician A says that to recondition a cylinder block bore, either an adjustable/fixed power hone (see Figure 6-13) can be used, or a boring bar can be used. Technician B says that a boring bar should be used to enlarge the block bore and that a hone should be used only to finish the bore crosshatch. Which technician is correct?

15. List the conditions for which cylinder block counterbores should always be checked.

16. Damaged cylinder liner block counterbores can be remachined to repair them, according to technician A. Technician B says that the block would have to be replaced. Who is correct?

17. Technician A says that when remachining of the top deck of the cylinder block is necessary, you are limited to how much metal can be removed and should be guided by the dimension from the centerline of the

crankshaft to the top of the deck. Technician B says that you can remove as much metal as necessary from the top deck surface; simply employ a thicker cylinder head gasket to offset the removed deck metal. Which one of these technicians would you follow?

18. Cylinder block camshaft bores can also be remachined at engine overhaul if necessary, according to technician A. Technician B says that the block would require replacement. Who is right?

19. To determine if the cylinder block bore is within the allowable limits regarding wear, ovality, and taper, use
   a. a precision dial indicator
   b. inside calipers
   c. an inside micrometer
   d. a tape measure

20. List the three most commonly used types of cylinder liners.

21. True or False: All cylinder liners are press fit in the cylinder block bore.

22. A common material used to cast cylinder liners is
   a. chrome
   b. cast gray iron
   c. molybdenum
   d. aluminum alloy

23. Which current high-speed heavy-duty diesel engine manufacturer employs telltale weep holes along the side of its engine block to indicate that coolant is leaking past the first liner seal O-ring?

24. True or False: A number of cylinder liners are chrome plated on their inside diameter.

25. Technician A says that cylinder liners should not only be numbered but should be match-marked before removal to ensure that they are reinstalled in the same cylinder bore. Technician B says that numbering is required, but it doesn't matter where you reinsert the liner. Which technician is correct, and why?

26. Technician A says that liners should be stored horizontally before and after inspection. Technician B says that they should be stored vertically (standing up); otherwise, they can become egg shaped or distorted after a period of time. Which technician is correct?

27. What condition is indicated by a very high glasslike polish on the inside surface of a liner?

28. The condition existing in Question 27 is usually caused by what operating parameters?

29. Technician A says that to repair the condition in Question 27 successfully, you need to rebore the block or liner. Technician B says that by using a fine-grit ball hone and a mixture of equal parts of mineral spirits and 30 weight engine oil you can correct this condition. Which technician is correct?

30. When inspecting a used cylinder liner bore, a bright mirror finish in certain areas is indicative of
   a. wear
   b. glazing
   c. scuffing
   d. scoring

31. Liners should always be checked with a dial bore gauge to determine what three conditions?

32. Cavitation corrosion on the outside surface of a wet-type liner is usually caused by what operating condition(s)?

33. Dark spots, stains, or low-pressure areas on the outside diameter of dry liners generally indicate what type of a condition?

34. Shiny spots or areas on the outside diameter or flange area of a cylinder liner are usually indicative of
    a. movement during engine operation
    b. overheating
    c. coolant leakage
    d. distortion

35. Cracking of a cylinder liner flange can usually be attributed to
    a. sloping counterbores in the block
    b. liner movement
    c. overheating
    d. light-load operation

36. True or False: A liner crosshatch pattern can be established to produce any surface angle finish.

37. Cylinder liner glaze must be broken using
    a. emery cloth
    b. glass beading
    c. reboring
    d. cylinder hone

38. List the three basic types of cylinder hones that are widely used.

39. Technician A says that a honing stone of any grade grit can be used to finish the desired crosshatch pattern on the inside diameter of a block bore or liner assembly. Not so, says technician B; the type of block or liner material determines the grit of stone that would be used. Who is correct?

40. True or False: Honing stones should always be used dry.

41. If a cylinder block bore requires that an oversized liner be used, technician A says that a boring machine must be employed. Technician B says that a power hone could also be used. Are both technicians correct in their statements?

42. True or False: In Question 41, if a boring machine is used, you still need to employ a fixed hone to produce the correct liner surface crosshatch pattern.

43. Technician A says that too steep a crosshatch pattern on a block bore or liner surface would result in scuffing and tearing of the new piston rings. Technician B believes that it would result in pumping oil. Which technician is correct?

44. Technician A says that too shallow a crosshatch pattern in a block bore or liner would result in pumping oil, while technician B says that too shallow a crosshatch angle in a block bore or liner surface would result in tearing and scuffing of the rings. Which technician is correct?

45. True or False: To achieve the desired crosshatch pattern in the block bore or liner, the speed at which you stroke the honing stones up and down is the key factor.

46. True or False: If a plateau finish is required on the block bore or cylinder liner surface, you should use a 200-grit honing stone and hone for about 20 seconds per cylinder.

47. True or False: Honing debris is best removed by submerging the liners in a tank with hot caustic solution.

48. Describe how you would best remove all traces of honing dust from a liner or block bore.

49. Technician A says that liners should always be clamped down prior to checking the liner flange protrusion limit. Technician B says that this isn't necessary since most liners are press fit at the flange area anyway. Which technician is correct?

50. Too much cylinder liner protrusion would result in (possibly more than one correct answer)
    a. liner movement
    b. cracking of the liner flange
    c. cracking of the cylinder head
    d. head gasket leakage

51. Insufficient cylinder liner protrustion would result in (possibly more than one correct answer)
    a. liner movement
    b. head gasket leakage
    c. liner distortion
    d. liner flange cracking

52. To correct for insufficient liner protrusion, what remedy would you use?

53. If too much liner protrusion existed, what remedy would you use?

54. True or False: Wet cylinder liner seals should usually be lubricated prior to liner installation in the block. If your answer is *true*, what lubricant would you use? If your answer is *false*, why so?

55. Some engine manufacturers suggest that you apply a thin bead of RTV sealant to what two areas of the cylinder liner during installation?

56. After you install a wet-type cylinder liner, the lower inside bore of the liner indicates some distortion. What condition do you think might cause this problem?

57. Technician A says that cylinder liners are available in both oversized inside and outside diameter. Technician B disagrees, stating that all cylinder liners retain a standard inside bore diameter and are oversized only on their outside diameter. Which technician is correct?

58. True or False: Most cylinder liners require removal and installation by use of a special liner puller.

7

The Cylinder Head and Components

OVERVIEW

This chapter will provide you with details of the purpose and function of the cylinder head assembly. Various designs are discussed, and the service repair tasks required to ensure successful performance of the engine intake and exhaust system, as well as an analysis of specialized equipment needed to perform these various service/repair functions, are discussed. The individual components within the cylinder head are featured and discussed along with the service/repair tasks necessary.

CYLINDER HEAD STRUCTURE AND FUNCTION

Diesel engine cylinder heads are similar in structure to the one shown in Figure 7-1. The cylinder head's main function is to provide a head or cap to the engine cylinder. Cylinder heads may be found in different configurations depending on the number of cylinders they cover. Different configurations are designed to deal with such factors as weight, warpage, and ease of handling. It is common to find cylinder heads that are designed for one, two, three, four, and six cylinders.

The diesel engine cylinder head (see Figure 7-1) consists of:

1. A single-piece casting (1) that may cover one or more cylinders
2. Valve guides (3) that guide the valves as they are opened and closed
3. Passageways or ports (11) that are opened and closed by the valves
4. Drilled bores or seats for the injectors or injection nozzles, water passageways, ports for intake air, and exhaust gases

5. Special steel alloy inserts or seats (4) for the valves
6. Precombustion chambers (some heads)

In modern diesel engines, cylinder head service must be an important part of major engine overhaul. Cylinder head service is sometimes performed hastily and with little consideration of the important functions the cylinder head must perform. Along with the cylinder and rings, the cylinder head aids in the development of compression and oil control. It is recommended then that the cylinder head service be performed with care and accuracy to provide long hours of trouble-free engine operation. If the cylinder head is being repaired, if a routine major overhaul is being done, or if the head has experienced a premature valve failure, all the following service recommendations should be performed.

SERVICE RECOMMENDATIONS

Disassembling the Cylinder Head

Assume that the cylinder head or heads have been removed from the engine and are ready to be disassembled and reconditioned. If not, refer to Chapter 5 on engine disassembly. Before disassembly of cylinder head, all loose grease and dirt should be removed by using either a steam cleaner or high-pressure washer.

CAUTION All injectors or injection nozzles should be removed before the head is steamed or washed.

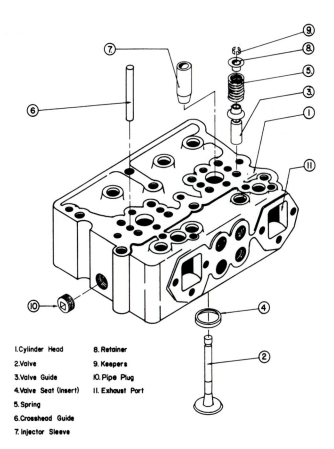

1. Cylinder Head
2. Valve
3. Valve Guide
4. Valve Seat (Insert)
5. Spring
6. Crosshead Guide
7. Injector Sleeve
8. Retainer
9. Keepers
10. Pipe Plug
11. Exhaust Port

FIGURE 7-1 Typical diesel engine cylinder head.

A visual inspection should be made to determine if the head is usable. Any visible cracks in the cylinder head will make the head unfit for further use.

NOTE There are some situations where small cracks in the cylinder head are not damaging or detrimental to the operation of the engine. Each engine design may have some peculiarity in this regard. If the technician does not have experience with a particular model of cylinder head, it must be taken to a shop or repair station that has been rebuilding or servicing cylinder heads of that type. Figure 7-2 shows a cracked cylinder head that is no longer usable.

Cracked cylinder heads are often repaired by welding or pinning, and in many cases they have proven to be dependable. A firm that has considerable experience should be selected if the cylinder head is to be repaired, since a rebuilt head that does not stand up in service may ruin the rest of the engine by allowing coolant to leak into the engine lube oil. If a cracked head is discovered during a major rebuild, the head

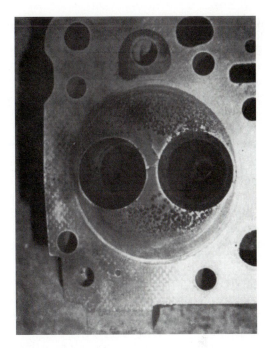

FIGURE 7-2 Cracked diesel engine cylinder head showing the effects of water in the combustion chamber.

should be replaced with a new one. The increased cost will be offset in the long run by increased engine life and dependability. If there is some question about rebuilding or replacing a cylinder head, check with your instructor.

The valve springs, keepers, and retainer should be removed with a valve spring compressor. Many types of compressors can be used, but the most common one in the field is the C-clamp type (Figure 7-3).

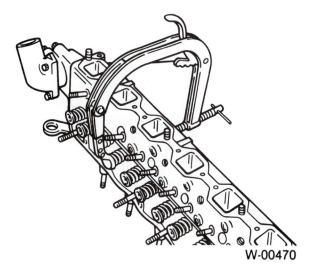

W-00470

FIGURE 7-3 Using an adjustable C-clamp tool to compress the valve spring during either removal or installation. (Courtesy of GMC Trucks.)

1. With the valve spring compressor in the open position, place it on the valve and valve spring.

2. Adjust the spring end jaws with the adjusting screw so that the jaws clamp snugly on the valve spring retainer.

3. Compress the spring by closing the valve spring compressor.

NOTE   It may be impossible to break the retainer loose from the retaining clips and compress the spring with the force exerted by the valve spring compressor. A slight tap with a hammer on the retainer while attempting to compress the spring will aid in loosening the retainer.

---

4. When the valve spring retainer is loosened, compress the spring far enough to remove keepers and retainer.

5. Loosen the compressor and remove the spring and valve from the cylinder head.

6. Visually inspect the valves and valve seats for signs of damage and wear.

7. Remove any other part or parts from the cylinder head, such as water plates, thermostat housings, and brackets.

Precombustion Chamber Inspection

Prechambers require some special attention when the engine is being serviced, since they are a part of the cylinder head. Many of them are fitted into the water jacket and have O rings and copper gaskets that must be replaced whenever the chamber is removed. Special tools are required to remove and/or replace most prechambers. Check your service manual or ask your instructor for the proper procedures.

Cleaning the Cylinder Head

1. Immerse the cylinder head into a dip or soak type of cleaning tank and allow it to soak until all baked-on grease, oil, and paint have been removed. In most cases 2 hours will be sufficient.

2. Remove the cylinder head from the cleaning tank and steam clean or rinse with hot water.

3. Blow out all passageways with compressed air.

4. Place the head on some type of suitable stand or bench and sand the cylinder head gasket surface with a sander.

Testing and Checking the Cylinder Head for Cracks

At this time the cylinder head must be checked for cracks that may not have been detected during visual inspection. Cylinder head cracks can be caused by sev-

eral factors: improper torque sequence used in securing head to block during assembly, difference in cylinder sleeve height or protrusion, or overheating.

Overheating is a primary cause of cylinder head cracks that are usually found in the combustion chamber between the valves or between a valve and an injector or nozzle. A buildup of scale from the cooling system of 1/16 in. has the insulating effect equal to 4 in. of cast iron. Therefore, if a cylinder head shows signs of cracking, it will be necessary to inspect and service the cooling system to prevent a recurrence. The three most common methods available to perform this check are described below.

Electromagnetic Crack Detector

An electromagnetic crack detector is a U-shaped device that is set on the surface of the cylinder head and energized with an electrical power source (Figure 7-4). Metal filings are sprinkled around the detector and, if the head has a crack, the crack will attract the metal filings, making the crack visible.

Pressure Testing

Plates or plugs to cover all water inlets and outlets must be available to pressure test a cylinder head. After plates have been bolted on, connect air pressure to the head with appropriate fittings and immerse in a tank of water. Any cracks will be pinpointed by the air bubbles escaping from them. Identify the source of the bubbles to make sure they are not coming from the plates or the plugs being used to seal the head. Partic-

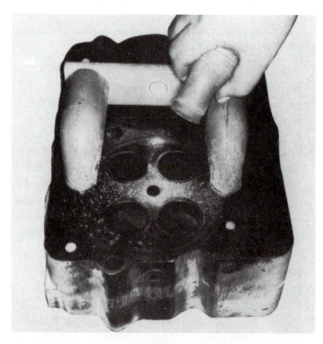

FIGURE 7–4   Checking a cylinder head for cracks using electromagnetic tester. (Courtesy of Cummins Engine Company, Inc.)

ular attention must be given to the area around the valve seats and injector sleeves. Mark the leaking sleeves for replacement.

The pressure checking method is widely used since it is fairly easy to perform and is very effective not only in determining if a crack(s) exists but also if there are coolant leaks at the injector sleeves. Different heads require special blank-off plates and gaskets, although many service technicians employ sheet rubber or neoprene gaskets and steel plates to seal off the various coolant passages (Figure 7-5A). One of the blank-off plates must be drilled and tapped to accept a compressed air fitting such as at the sealing plate bolted in place over the thermostat housing cover opening with a quick-couple connector for an air hose attachment.

Figure 7-5B illustrates another pressure test example where two metal test strips and gaskets are assembled to the cylinder head. The test strips are bolted to the head using the cylinder head bolts and nuts. If the cylinder head has been descaled, install all of the removed plugs. If new plugs are used, they are usually precoated with a sealer. If the old plugs are being reused, coat the plugs with Loctite, pipe sealant, or Teflon tape and torque them to the spec listed in the service manual. If new cup plugs or frost plugs are used, coat them with a good grade of non-hardening sealant such as Loctite 620 or equivalent. Similarly, if injector sleeves (tubes) have been removed, new ones have to be installed prior to the pressure check.

Minor variations will exist between engines and models, follow these basic steps in the pressure check method:

1. Install the coolant passage blank-off plates along with a compressed air fitting into a coolant passage.

2. Install dummy injectors into position in each injector bore sleeve (tube). If dummy injectors are not

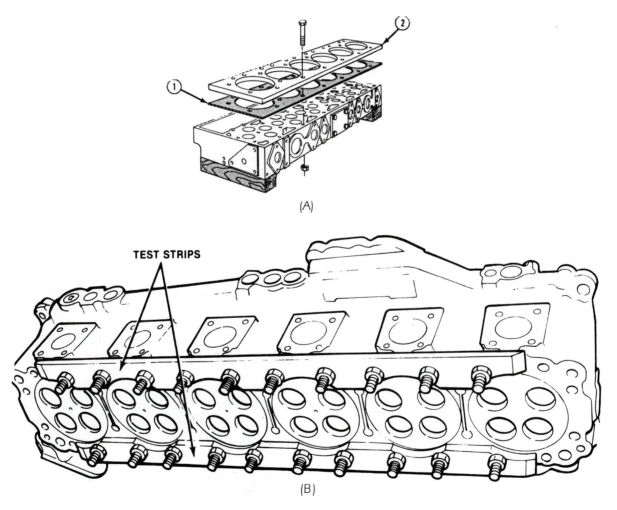

(A)

TEST STRIPS

(B)

FIGURE 7–5 (A) Using a sealing gasket (1) and thick steel plate (2) bolted to the underside of an L10 cylinder head in preparation for a pressure test; (B) test strips and suitable gaskets bolted to the underside of a series 60 cylinder head in preparation for a pressure test. [(A) Courtesy of Cummins Engine Company Inc.; (B) courtesy of Detroit Diesel Corporation.]

readily available, use old scrap ones torqued into place. If an injector sleeve holding tool kit similar to the one illustrated in Figure 7-6A for a Cummins L10 engine model is available, install and tighten these components in place for each cylinder as shown.

3. Use one of these two methods to check the cylinder head.

a. Submerge the head in a tank of preheated water usually at a temperature between 82 and 93°C (180 to 190°F). Apply the recommended air pressure to the coolant water jacket for at least a 20-minute period (Figure 7-6B).

b. If a tank is not available, fill the coolant jackets with a mixture of antifreeze and water; bolt the blank-off plates into position; apply the recommended regulated air pressure to the air fitting and leave it under pressure for 1

to 2 hours to allow the antifreeze mixture to penetrate any cracks.

NOTE The air pressure applied to the cylinder head will vary depending on the type of injector and sleeve used. On replaceable sleeves (tubes) that are surrounded by coolant, the recommended air pressure is between 30 and 40 psi (207 to 276 kPa). However, some designs of cylinder heads suggest air test pressure of between 80 and 100 psi (552 to 690 kPa). *Always* closely check the engine manufacturer's service literature to ensure that you do not exceed the recommended pressure!

---

4. Air bubbles appearing when the head is submerged in a tank of heated water are indicative of cracks (Figure 7-6B). Closely inspect the area to ensure that any leak is not from one of the gaskets and blank-off plates. If so, the head may be distorted and require remachining.

5. Note any signs of leakage of antifreeze mixture which would indicate a crack in the cylinder head.

Dye Penetrant

Dye penetrant is a crack-detecting method that requires no special equipment with the exception of a can of spray-type penetrant and a can of spray developer. When using the dye penetrant, spray the area to be checked and wipe off or remove all excess dye. Spray on the developer. It will draw the dye penetrant from the crack, making it visible.

Of the three types of crack detection discussed here, the electromagnetic and dye penetrant would be used in areas where they can be seen. The pressure testing method should be used where there is a possibility of a crack in an area that cannot be seen, such as valve ports, combustion chambers, and all other areas not visible.

Although cylinder heads can be repaired by welding, and a number of specialty shops offer this service, most engine manufacturers suggest that all cracked heads be replaced.

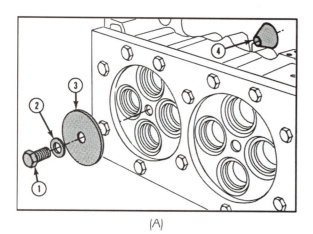

(A)

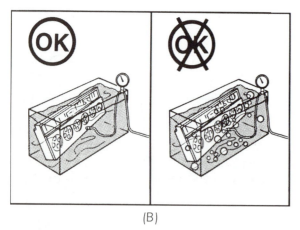

(B)

FIGURE 7–6 (A) Installing special injector retaining sleeve tooling to an L10 cylinder head prior to pressure checking. 1, Capscrew; 2, flat washer; 3, ST-1179-4 anvil; 4, ST-1179-2 mandrel. (B) L10 cylinder head submerged in a tank of hot water with a fitting attached to a compressed air line supply; signs of air bubbles indicate a cracked head, assuming that no leaks are evident at the sealing plates and gaskets. (Courtesy of Cummins Engine Company, Inc.)

Testing the Cylinder Head for Warpage

Check the cylinder head for warpage using a straightedge and a 0.004-in. (0.10-mm) feeler gauge (Figure 7-7). The feeler gauge must not pass between the straightedge and cylinder head at any point. If it does, the cylinder head must be resurfaced.

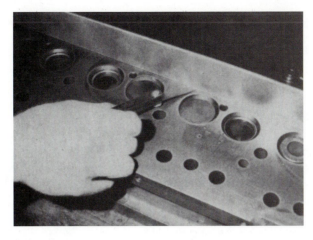

(a)

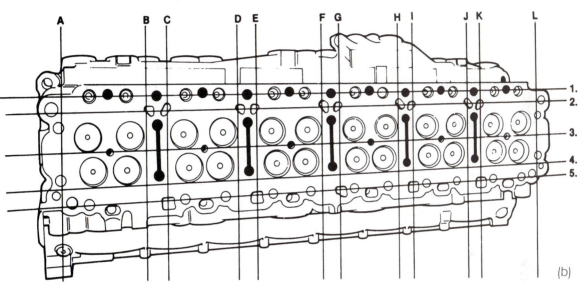

(b)

FIGURE 7-7 *Checking a cylinder head for warpage by using a feeler gauge and a straightedge. Checks should be made at points indicated in illustration (b). [(b) Courtesy of Detroit Diesel Corporation.)*

NOTE   Engine manufacturers may vary in their recommendations as to what point during the cylinder head rebuild the head should be resurfaced. Check the engine service manual for instructions at this point. Most automotive machine shops have the necessary equipment to resurface the cylinder head.

Checking and/or Replacing the Valve Guide

After the cylinder head has been checked or resurfaced and is considered usable, the valve guides should be checked for wear as follows: Check the guide inside diameter with a snap, ball, or dial gauge in three different locations throughout the length of the guide (Figure 7-8).

NOTE   Experienced technicians can usually determine if the valve guide is worn excessively by inserting a new or unworn valve into the guide within approximately 1/4 in. (7 mm) of the cylinder head or valve seat and moving it from side to side. The method of measurement used will be determined by the technician's experience and the degree of accuracy desired.

SPECIAL NOTE   If you suspect excessive valve guide wear, but want to confirm this before removing the cylinder head, follow these steps: Remove the rocker cover(s), rotate the engine to TDC on one cylinder at a time, depress the valve

Small Hole Gages

Extra long for gaging deep and shallow holes, slots and similar work.

J 26900-14
Set of 4 Small Hole Gages

- Gaging surface is a full-round with a flat bottom; permits use in smallest of shallow holes, slots and grooves, etc.
- Knurled knob at end of handle is used for size adjustment. Hole size is obtained by measuring over the contact points with a micrometer.
- Gauging surface is fully hardened to insure long tool life.
- Supplied 4 gages in a fitted case.

Range		Overall	Probe
English	Metric	Length	Depth (L)
.125" - .200"	(3-5MM)	3 5/8"	.880:
.200" - .300"	(5-7.5MM)	3 7/8"	1.200"
.300" - .400"	(7.5-10MM)	4"	1.600"
.400" - .500"	(10-13MM)	4 1/4"	1.600

FIGURE 7–8 *Small-hole gauges have a split ball at one end that can be expanded by turning the upper knurled knob. Typically used to measure intake and exhaust valve guides for wear, the ball dimension is checked by means of an outside micrometer. (Courtesy of Kent-Moore Division, SPX Corporation.)*

spring, and remove the valve locks (keepers) and spring. Refer to Figure 7-9 and place a dial indicator tip against the valve stem. Rotate and rock the valve to determine the stem-to-guide wear and compare it to the service manual specifications.

With the cylinder head removed and disassembled, use a small valve guide bore cleaning brush of nylon or wire construction attached to a drill motor to remove all gum, varnish, or carbon deposits. Then carefully inspect the guide for signs of cracks, chipping, scoring, or excessive wear. Use a small hole (ball) adjustable gauge (see Figure 7-10) within the guide bore and adjust the gauge to produce a slight drag; then remove the gauge, check it with an outside micrometer, and compare the dimension to the service manual specs. Check the guide diameter in three places (top, middle, and bottom) and the measurements at 90° to one another. Check the diameter of the valve stem with an outside micrometer to the published specs, and compare the valve stem diameter with that of its mating guide to determine the actual valve stem-to-guide wear. Clearances beyond worn limits require that the valve guide be replaced on most diesel engines. How-

ever, some engine manufacturers (mainly light-duty automotive) offer oversized-outside-diameter valve stems to bring the clearance within specs.

One method that can be used with integral guides

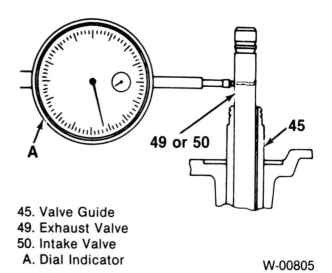

45. Valve Guide
49. Exhaust Valve
50. Intake Valve
A. Dial Indicator

W-00805

FIGURE 7–9 *One method of checking valve stem-to-guide clearance with the cylinder head still in position on the engine. Place a dial indicator as illustrated against the valve stem while rocking the valve back and forth. (Courtesy of GMC Trucks.)*

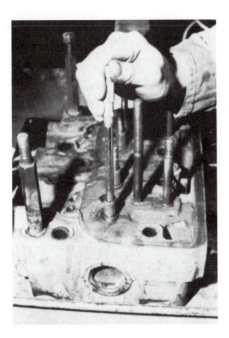

FIGURE 7-10 *Measuring a valve guide with a ball gauge.*

is to *knurl* the inside diameter of the guide with special equipment, or to bore the worn guide and install a bronze valve guide liner. In both cases, a reamer is used to resize the guide after this procedure. Knurling is a process that basically cuts a spiral screw thread within the bore of the guide. Figure 7-11 illustrates the procedure that can be used to bore and install a bronze

guide liner as well as how to use the optional guide spiral (knurling) and finish ream the guide insert.

Replacement valve guides are press fit within their mating bore in the cylinder head. To remove the valve guides, you can use one of several methods: a hammer and properly sized shouldered punch, a mechanical threaded guide puller, a hydraulic press, or an air impact hammer and chisel arrangement similar to that illustrated in Figure 7-12. Removal or installation of the guide with the air chisel hammer requires that you employ special tools that must be held vertical to the cylinder head and forced tight against the guide to prevent pounding of the end of the guide.

Drive or press the guide out of the cylinder head, making sure that the driver is driven or pressed straight (Figure 7-13). If it is not pressed straight, damage to the valve guide or cylinder head may result. After the guide has been removed, check the guide bore for scoring. Use a stiff-wire brush similar to that used to clean the inside of the guide; run the brush through the bore in the cylinder head to remove any minor imperfections. A badly scored guide bore may have to be reamed out to accommodate the next-larger-size guide. After guide bore is checked, select the correct guide (intake or exhaust) and insert it in guide bore.

NOTE   Guide insertion can be made easier by the use of a press-fit lubricant such as that supplied by Sunnen Manufacturing Company.

Installation Procedure

BORING GUIDE OVERSIZE

Select proper tooling and bore out old guide. Both H.S. and Carbide Boring Tools are available

INSTALLING "BRONZE LINER' IN GUIDE

Lube guide, push guide-liner into holder, select guide driver and hammer into place.

TRIMMING BRONZE LINER

Insert tool point into the seam, push down to guide top and turn once to remove excess material.

I.D. FINISHING METHODS

BALL BROACH   **SPIRAL & FINISH REAM**

FINISH SIZE OPERATION

To finish I.D., select appropriate Ball Broach and drive through guide. Flex-hone with high RPM drill.

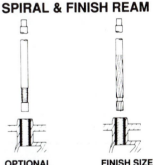

OPTIONAL GUIDE SPIRAL

For closer than normal stem to guide clearance, spiraling is suggested for added lubrication.

FINISH SIZE OPERATION

To finish ream, lubricate reamer with bronze-lube and run through guide. Both H.S. and Carbide Reamers are available.

FIGURE 7-11   *Installation and finishing procedures required for successful and accurate reconditioning of a worn valve guide by the insertion of a precision wear sleeve. (Courtesy of Hastings Manufacturing Co.)*

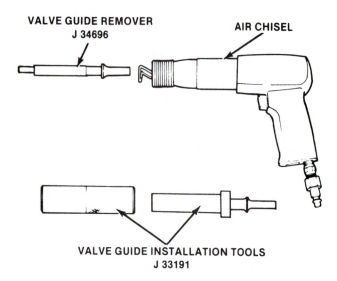

VALVE GUIDE REMOVER
J 34696

AIR CHISEL

VALVE GUIDE INSTALLATION TOOLS
J 33191

FIGURE 7-12 *Special air chisel and adapter tools required to remove or install a valve guide. (Courtesy of Detroit Diesel Corporation.)*

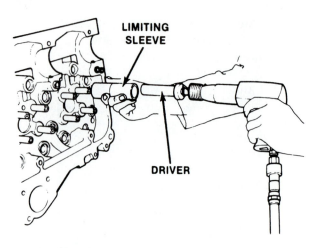

LIMITING
SLEEVE

DRIVER

FIGURE 7-14 *Using a special air chisel and tooling to install a new valve guide into the cylinder head. (Courtesy of Detroit Diesel Corporation.)*

Insert the chamfered end of the new valve guide into its bore from the top side of the cylinder head. Then make sure that you have the correct guide installer, as shown in the example in Figure 7-14, and use the air impact chisel to drive the guide into place in the cylinder head from the top side.

NOTE   If you do not have the correct guide installation tools, take extreme care when installing a new guide. Do not drive the guide too far into the head bore. Either measure the height of a guide that is still in place or refer to the service manual to ensure that you install the new guide to its specified height above the cylinder head using a vernier caliper as shown in Figure 7-15.

FIGURE 7-13 *Removing a valve guide from cylinder head with a press.*

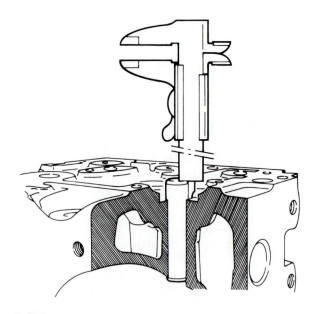

3-2-4

FIGURE 7-15 *Using a vernier caliper to measure the installation height of a valve guide. (Courtesy of DAF Trucks, Eindhoven, The Netherlands.)*

In some engines employing aluminum alloy cylinder heads, a nonferrous valve guide is used. Often, this means that you must heat the head in boiling water or a temperature-controlled oven to safely remove the guide. To install the new guide safely, the head can be preheated and the guide chilled before installation.

Many manufacturers recommend that a new guide be hand reamed after installation to ensure that the guide inside diameter did not change during the installation process.

NOTE   Some engine manufacturers have guides that are manufactured by a special process to make them wear longer; these guides should not be reamed. Check engine manufacturer's recommendation closely in this area.

Checking and Reconditioning the Valve Seat

After guides have been replaced or reconditioned, valve seat checking and reconditioning should be done. Valve seats must be checked for looseness by tapping the seat lightly with the peen end of a ball peen hammer. A loose seat will produce a sound different from the sound produced while tapping on the cylinder head. In some cases a loose seat can be seen to move while tapping on it. If the seat is solid, check it for cracks and excessive width. If the seat passes all checks, it should be reconditioned as outlined, using a specially designed valve seat grinder.

Reconditioning or Grinding the Valve Seat
First select the proper mandrel pilot.

NOTE   The mandrel pilot is selected by measuring the valve stem with a micrometer or caliper or by referring to the manufacturer's specifications. After experience has been gained in this area, selection of the pilot is easily done by a visual check.

Pilots are usually one of two types full-measure, expandable or tapered. An expandable pilot (Figure 7-16A) is inserted into the guide and then expanded by tightening the expanding screw on the pilot until it is tight in the guide. Expandable pilots are not considered as accurate as tapered pilots and should be used only when a tapered pilot is not available. Some technicians prefer expandable pilots because they compensate for guide wear better than does a tapered pilot; by

FIGURE 7-16   (A) Expandable pilot; (B) tapered pilot.

expanding into the guide, the pilot tightens and adjusts to the guide size or wear. A tapered pilot (Figure 7-16B) does not have an expanding screw and relies on the taper of the pilot to tighten it into the guide.

After the pilot has been selected and inserted into the guide (Figure 7-17), the grinding wheel or stone must be selected. Selection of the grinding wheel is made by determining the valve seat angle, diameter, and the seat material.

1.   Use a *concentric grinder*, one in which the grinding stone contacts the full-seat face width.

2.   Use an *eccentric grinder* and stone, similar to Figure 7-18, which is designed so that the rotating

FIGURE 7-17   Tapered pilot inserted into the valve guide.

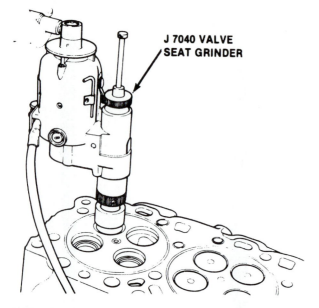

FIGURE 7–18 *Grinding a valve seat insert within the cylinder head using an eccentric valve seat grinder and stone. (Courtesy of Detroit Diesel Corporation.)*

grinding wheel contacts the seat at only one point at any time as it rotates around the seat. A micrometer feed on the handle of the drive motor permits very fine adjustment of the amount of material to be removed.

3. Use an adjustable seat cutter employing tungsten carbide blades that can cut thousands of seats before showing wear and can produce a very fine surface finish. This system is superior to a grinding stone, which requires refacing and or replacing much more frequently.

Although the concentric and eccentric valve seat grinders have been used for many years, they do have some drawbacks. The concentric valve seat stone grinder that contacts the full-seat circumference at one time tends to retain the fine grinding dust during the grinding process and can actually pound these filings back into the seat. Consequently, it does not produce as fine a seat surface finish as the eccentric grinder shown in Figure 7-18, which contacts only one part of the seat at any given time as it rotates off-center around the valve seat. The eccentric grinder does, however, take longer to grind the seat than does a concentric grinder. Both concentric and eccentric valve seat grinders employ grinding stones and holders that are threaded onto the end of the drive motor chuck. Stones are readily available in a wide variety of diameters and seat angles. Stones can be reground using a diamond point tool attachment when worn. Stones are available in different grits and colors; their makeup is relative to the type of material to be ground. Cast iron heads and regular steel inserts usually employ a gray-

colored stone, whereas hardened Stellite inserts require a white stone.

The main advantage of a seat cutter with a tungsten carbide blade shown in Figure 7-19 is that it does not require regular resharpening as a grinding stone does. It retains seat-to-guide concentricity much better, and it can grind thousands of seats with one set of blades, which are replaceable when required. This type of seat cutter can cut a seat in the same time that it takes to dress a stone, plus it cuts in far fewer revolutions and produces a true flat seat at an exact angle with a superior finish.

NOTE   To establish an interference angle between valve and valve seat, one must be ground at a different angle to provide a sharp or narrow seat to valve contact. For example, seat ground at 45° with valve ground at 44° (Figure 7-20).

This interference angle with its narrow contact area aids in seating the valve during starting by helping to cut through the carbon particles that may accumulate on the valve seat. Interference angles are not recommended for valves that have rotators, as the rotating valve will remove any carbon that may accumulate on the seat or valve face.

The important part of the valve seat grinding process is to ensure that the insert, when finish ground, will produce the desired valve seat contact width along with the proper location on the valve face. The width required on the valve face-to-seat contact area is determined by the overall valve head diameter and is specified by the engine manufacturer in the service literature. For example a 2-in. (50.8-mm)-diameter valve might call for a face width of 0.060 to 0.090 in.

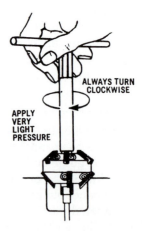

FIGURE 7–19 *Using a valve seat insert cutter tool to restore a worn seat. (Courtesy of Neway Manufacturing, Inc.)*

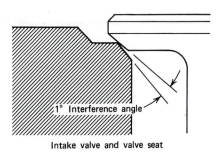

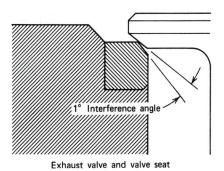

Intake valve and valve seat

Exhaust valve and valve seat

FIGURE 7–20 Interference angle between valve and valve seat. (Courtesy of J.I. Case Co.)

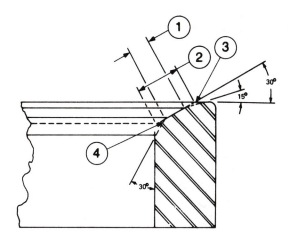

FIGURE 7–21 Illustration of a 30° valve seat insert. The minimum seat width is shown as item 1; item 2 shows the maximum recommended seat width. The seat width and its location to the valve face can be achieved by using a 15° stone to remove metal from the top side at position 3, a method known as undercutting. Position 4 at the throat area can be overcut by using a 60° stone. (Courtesy of Cummins Engine Company, Inc.)

(1.5 to 2.25 mm). The seat face contact should start at about the midpoint of the valve face and move toward the head of the valve but stop short of the rim (margin). To achieve this accurately, often you must use a *three-angle cutting sequence* on the valve seat insert in the cylinder head by employing three stones (cutters) ground or adjusted to these three separate angles. This allows you to perform what is commonly referred to as *overcutting or undercutting* to position the seat on the desired location of the valve face. In addition, the cutting sequence allows you to obtain the recommended face seat width accurately.

To effectively produce a three-angle valve seat, the technician can employ a 15°, 30°, and 60° cutter set. This tooling is designed to produce a three-angle cut using a carbide tip tool that cuts all three valve seat angles at once. The tooling allows manual operation by hand or an electric cutting motor drive assembly. It features a carbide pilot and articulated spindle holder with a ball-mounted spindle for self-aligning tooling.

When cutting a three-angle valve seat as shown in Figure 7-21, note that area 4 has been cut with a 60° cutter or stone, while area 3 has been cut with a 15° stone. Item 1 in the diagram is the *minimum* valve seat width, which in this example is 0.060 in (1.5 mm); item 2 is the *maximum* seat width of 0.090 in. (2.25 mm). Both items 1 and 2 have a 30° angle. Once the seat has been initially cut or ground to 30°, it should not require recutting if the service technician applied the 15°

and 60° cutters or stones very gently to obtain the desired seat width and location on the valve face when checked with Prussian Blue paste.

If you are using a grinding stone, refer to Figure 7-18, which illustrates an eccentric seat grinder supported on a valve guide pilot. By adjusting the drive motor micrometer handle, the stone will automatically be lowered onto the seat, and the internal drive mechanism will allow the stone to slowly rotate around the seat until it has finished the rotation. If you are using a concentric grinding stone, you control how hard the stone contacts the seat (downward pressure) and for how long. Therefore, be very careful that you do not remove too much stock from the seat. Start the drive motor and lightly and quickly allow the stone to contact the seat; then inspect it to see how much material has been removed. Carefully continue to grind the seat until it is cleaned up completely.

If you are using a valve seat cutter with tungsten carbide blades, you can select a cutter of the same basic diameter as the valve head that has been set to the correct angle. Refer to Figure 7-19 and place the cutter over the valve guide pilot. Slowly lower the cutter to the valve seat face, since dropping it can damage the cutter blade and seat. Place a T-handle or motor-driven power unit over the hex drive of the cutter, and while maintaining a centered light downward pressure, rotate the cutter clockwise through several complete revolutions. Carefully remove the cutter and inspect the seat surface as shown in Figure 7-22 to

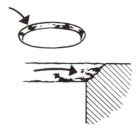

FIGURE 7-22 *Close inspection of the valve seat insert to determine how much material needs to be removed to square up the seat. (Courtesy of Neway Manufacturing, Inc.)*

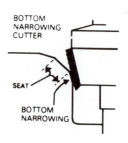

FIGURE 7-24 *Overcutting a seat insert by using a 60° cutter to raise the bottom edge of the valve face seat contact surface. (Courtesy of Neway Manufacturing, Inc.)*

determine the condition of the surface finish. This procedure will allow you to gauge just how much material needs to be removed to square up the seat.

Whether you are using a grinding stone or a cutter arrangement, once the seat has been cleaned to satisfaction, remove the tooling, apply Prussian Blue paste to the valve as shown in Figure 7-23, and inspect the valve face for the seat width and location. Normally, if you have used only one stone (cutter) set to the recommended angle (30°, for example), the seat width will normally be too wide. You will have to *overcut* or *undercut* to raise or lower the seat location and to achieve the desired seat width.

Figure 7-24 illustrates that by using a stone (cutter) with a steeper angle (overcutting 60°, for example), you can successfully raise the bottom edge of the seat contact surface, since the removed material no longer contacts the valve face. This is known as a *bottom narrowing cut*.

Figure 7-25 illustrates that by using a narrower stone (cutter)—undercutting 15°, for example—you can remove valve seat insert material from the top edge of the seat contact surface area, thereby lowering the top edge of the valve face seat. This is known as a *top narrowing cut*.

If the top and bottom narrowing cuts have been performed very lightly and with adequate care, the seat will be centered between both cuts as illustrated in Figure 7-26. If the seat width is too narrow, you will have to use the 30° stone (cutter) again. If the seat is too wide, or the seat location is too high or too low, you may have to overcut or undercut to achieve the correct seat location and width.

Always confirm the seat width and location by use of Prussian Blue paste on the valve face as described earlier. Refer to Figure 7-27 and gently tap the valve up and down slightly. Apply finger pressure to the top of the valve head and to the stem tip until you have achieved a clean valve face seat contact area. If an *intereference angle* is being used, the valve face seat contact area will appear as a *ring mark* or narrow line, rather than the wider seat that occurs when no interference angle is used. The ring mark should appear about one-third of the way down the valve face from the rim (margin). If the mark is too high, cut the top narrowing angle slightly to lower the mark. If the mark is too low, cut the seat angle at the bottom to raise the mark. If an open spot appears on the valve face seat contact area and it is greater than 12.7 mm (1/2 in.), reuse the seat stone (cutter) over the pilot and gently attempt to blend it in by turning the stone (cutter) by hand only. Small noncontact spots on the valve seat face tend to peen themselves into a full-face con-

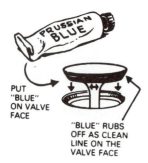

FIGURE 7-23 *Use of Prussian Blue paste spread lightly across the valve face. Bounce the valve once on its seat, then carefully remove it and check the seat contact area and width. (Courtesy of Neway Manufacturing, Inc.)*

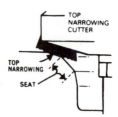

FIGURE 7-25 *Undercutting a seat insert by using a 15° cutter to lower the valve face seat contact surface. (Courtesy of Neway Manufacturing, Inc.)*

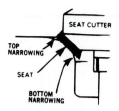

FIGURE 7–26 Centering of the valve seat insert to the valve face contact surface by narrowing both the top and bottom seat areas. (Courtesy of Neway Manufacturing, Inc.)

tact pattern within a very short time after initial engine startup.

After any valve seat cutting (grinding) procedure, install a small dial gauge on a pilot (as illustrated in Figure 7-28) with its extension point resting against the valve seat. Set the gauge to zero and gently rotate it at least one complete turn to determine the runout that exists between the valve guide and seat insert. This will indicate if the valve seat is concentric to the guide; although stated in the engine-service manual specs, the maximum reading is usually 0.05 mm (0.002 in.), but check the engine service manual specs. Excessive runout readings can be traced to a worn valve guide or grinding equipment that has not been set up or used properly.

SPECIAL NOTE   Any time that the valve seats or the valves have been reground, it is very important that you check the *valve head recess* which can be done by using a dial indicator mounted onto a sled gauge as illustrated in Figure 7-29. Always check the engine service manual to determine the allowable dimension! If the valve head is too low in its seat, *valve guttering* will occur. In other words, the valve will fail to open wide enough and may result in a restriction to both the air inlet and exhaust gas flow to and from the com-

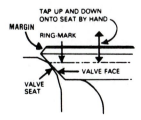

FIGURE 7–27 Determining the contact location of the valve face to valve seat insert by tapping the valve onto the seat by hand. After removal, check the Prussian Blue paste as described in Figure 7-23 to determine seat width and actual location. (Courtesy of Neway Manufacturing, Inc.)

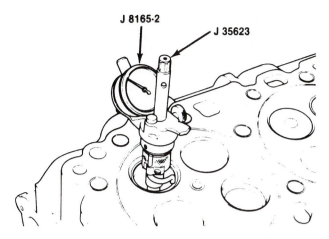

FIGURE 7–28 Using a special dial gauge and adapter to check the concentricity (runout) of the valve guide to the valve seat insert. (Courtesy of Detroit Diesel Corporation.)

bustion chamber and cylinder. Rough engine operation will result along with low power, poor fuel economy, smoke at the exhaust stack, incomplete combustion, and carbon buildup around the neck of the valves. In some cases where both a new valve and seat insert are being used, the seat insert *may* require grinding to lower the valve head sufficiently to avoid contact with the piston crown. This situation can occur when a cylinder head fire deck has been resurfaced and new standard thickness inserts have been installed. Reduced thickness inserts of 0.010, 0.020, and 0.030 in. (0.254, 0.5, and 0.75 mm) should be installed to handle the same amount of material ground from the fire deck. Note that maxi-

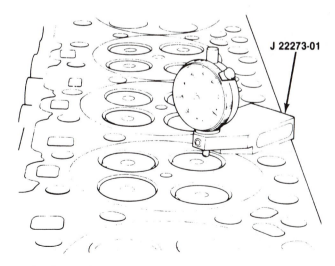

FIGURE 7–29 Using a dial indicator mounted on a sled to determine the valve head protrusion or intrusion. (Courtesy of Detroit Diesel Corporation.)

mum values for valve *protrusion* and *intrusion* are specified. If the valve sits too high above the fire deck, regrind the seat insert. If it sits too far below the fire deck, replace the insert. If the valve head rim (margin) is too thin, replace the valve.

Replacing the Valve Seat

If it is determined that the valve seat must be replaced because of cracks or excessive width, the following procedure should be used:

　1.　Using a removing tool (Figure 7-30), remove the seat carefully to prevent damage to the cylinder head.

NOTE　Use extreme caution when removing the valve seat. Damage to the cylinder head in the valve seat area may render the head unfit for further use.

　2.　Clean the valve port and seat area with a carbon brush and compressed air.

NOTE　It is recommended that after removal of a valve seat, the seat counterbore be enlarged to allow installation of an oversized seat. Although this practice is used most often, with additional experience the technician will be able to determine the type of cylinder heads that will allow the successful replacement of valve seats without enlargement of the counterbore. A slightly oversized valve seat (0.005 to 0.010 in., 0.013 to 0.25 mm) is generally available and may be used to ensure a good seat fit in the counterbore if the counterbore is not recut.

CAUTION　Valve guides must be in good condition or replaced before any attempt to cut valve seat counterbore or replace valve seats.

　3.　If it is decided to enlarge the valve seat counterbore or to cut a counterbore in a head not originally equipped with valve seats, a cutting tool or reseater similar to the one shown should be used (Figure 7-31). Many types of counterbore cutting tools are available. Follow operating instructions of cutter being used to eliminate damage to the cylinder head.

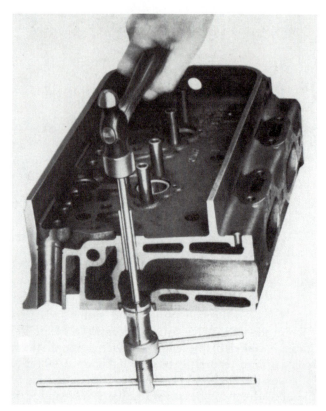

A

B

FIGURE 7–30　*Valve seat removing tool. (Courtesy of Detroit Diesel Corporation.)*

FIGURE 7–31 *Valve seat counterbore cutter.*

Installing the Valve Seats

1. After the valve seat counterbore has been enlarged or considered usable, select a mandrel pilot for the insert that will fit snugly in the valve guide.

2. Obtain a new valve seat insert that will fit the counterbore using the engine parts manual as reference or using the chart supplied with the valve seat insert cutting tool set.

3. Visually inspect the counterbore, making sure that it is free from metal particles and rough edges. Select a driver that has an outside diameter slightly smaller than the seat.

4. Place a ring insert over the driver pilot onto the cylinder head counterbore.

5. Place the driver onto the pilot, and with a hammer drive the valve seat into the counterbore using sharp, hard blows.

NOTE   Alternative methods of valve seat installations are (1) shrinking valve seats by cooling and then driving them in, or (2) warming the cylinder head in hot water and then installing the seat.

CAUTION   Safety glasses should be worn during this operation, as valve seat inserts are very brittle and may shatter, causing eye damage.

---

6. After driving the seat in place, it is recommended that the seat be staked or knurled in place (Figure 7-32). If a knurling or staking tool is not available, a 1/4-in. (7-mm) round-end punch may be used to stake insert around its outer circumference.

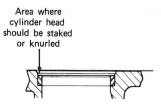

FIGURE 7–32 *Area of cylinder head that should be staked or knurled to hold valve seat insert.*

NOTE   If the seat is cast iron, no knurling or staking is necessary, as the seat has the same coefficient of expansion as the cylinder head. Seats that are made of steel alloy require staking, since their expansion rate does not match that of cast iron. As a result, they may fall out during engine warm-up.

Valve Inspection, Cleaning, and Refacing
Valve Inspection
A decision must be made at this time to replace or reface the valves (Figure 7-33). To determine if the valves are reusable, they should be inspected for:

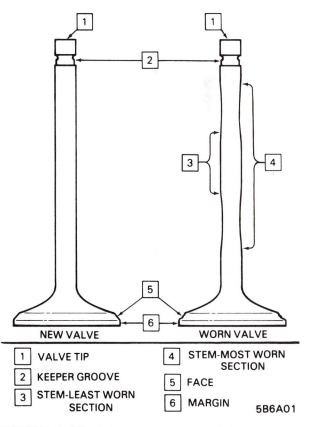

1	VALVE TIP	4	STEM-MOST WORN SECTION
2	KEEPER GROOVE	5	FACE
3	STEM-LEAST WORN SECTION	6	MARGIN

5B6A01

FIGURE 7–33 *Typical areas to inspect for valve wear at major overhaul. (Courtesy of GMC Trucks.)*

1.   Carbon buildup on the underside of the head. A buildup of carbon indicates that oil has been leaking into the combustion chamber between the valve stem and the valve guide.

2.   Stretched stem or cupped head. Valves that are badly cupped or stretched should not be reused, as they could break and ruin the engine. Cupped or stretched valves are usually caused by excessive heat, excessive tappet clearance, engine overspeeding, or weak valve springs.

3.   Nicks or marks in the head. Valves with nicks or marks in the head indicate the valve was in a cylinder that had metal particles in it. Metal particles in a cylinder usually come from broken piston rings, broken pistons, or broken valves. Replace all valves that show any sign of damage.

4.   Burned or pitted area in face. Burning or pitting is caused by tight tappet adjustment, dirty inlet air, or engine over-fueling.

5.   Worn keeper (collet) grooves (recesses).

6.   Scored or worn stem (Figure 7-33). Stem diameter should be checked with micrometer.

7.   Margin width.

8.   Worn stem end.

Valve Cleaning

1.   If the valve passes all the checks listed above, it must be cleaned thoroughly using a wire buffing wheel.

CAUTION   Do not press the valve against the wire wheel too hard, as damage to the valve may result. Safety glasses must be worn during valve buffing.

A much preferred method of valve cleaning is the glass bead blaster, if it is available.

2.   After cleaning, the valve must be checked for warpage. Experienced technicians usually check valves for warpage by inserting them into the valve-refacing machine. If the valve is warped, it can easily be seen when the valve is moved up to the grinding wheel.

Valve Refacing

Valve refacing is done on a valve-refacing machine similar to the one shown in Figure 7-34.

1.   Determine at what angle the valve face is ground by visual inspection or by checking the manufacturer's specifications.

2.   Adjust valve chuck head to correspond with the valve face angle (Figure 7-34). If an interference angle is recommended by the engine manufacturer, set

the valve chuck head at that angle at this time. Although the valve is generally ground with an interference angle, some manufacturers recommend grinding the valve seat to establish the interference angle.

3.   With valve-grinding machine stopped, install and adjust the grinding wheel dresser so that it will just touch the grinding wheel (Figure 7-34). Start the machine and move the diamond dresser back and forth across the face of the grinding wheel until the wheel surface is smooth and flat all the way across. Remove the dressing attachment.

CAUTION   Safety glasses must be worn during valve refacing.

---

4.   Place the valve in the machine chuck (Figure 7-35) and adjust the valve stop so that the valve will be positioned in the chuck on the uppermost portion of the machined area on the stem.

5.   Tighten the chuck on the valve stem.

6.   With the machine stopped and grinding stone backed slightly away from valve face, adjust the valve table stop nut (Figure 7-34) so that the stone does not touch the valve stem.

7.   Start the machine; adjust cooling oil flow with adjusting valve on coolant hose or pump so that an adequate flow of oil is established. Move the grinding wheel toward the valve until it just touches. Move the valve back and forth across the face of the stone with table control lever, moving the stone closer to the valve with the stone feed control as the valve is ground (Figure 7-36).

8.   When the valve appears to be ground or refaced so that it is smooth and free from pits and/or burned spots, back the stone away from the valve and move the valve table and valve clear of grinding stone, using controls mentioned previously.

CAUTION   Do not move the valve table away from the grinding stone until the stone has been backed away from the valve, as damage to the valve face may result.

---

9.   Visually check the valve carefully for pits and face condition. If the valve face still has pits and wear marks, continue grinding until the valve face is completely smooth and free of burned spots and pits.

CAUTION   Do not remove the valve from the chuck until the grinding or refacing is completed.

Wheel head
Sealed, lubricated ball bearings, pre-loaded to eliminate end play. Features two wheels mounted back to back. One for grinding valve faces. One for valve butts and rocker arm pads. Special wheel for stellite valve faces is supplied standard. (Optional fixtures required for butt grinding and rocker arm pads.)

Wheel Drive
Two speeds for maximum versatility.

Diamond wheel dresser
Mounted on machine...in position for use without removing valve from chuck. Pops up and down for fast wheel dressing.

Self-contained circulating oil system
Features a long-life impeller pump in easy to clean drawer type reservoir. Capacity: 3 gallons (11.3 liters). Water-soluble grinding fluid assures stress-free cutting action. Captures grit and chips.

Workhead
"Ground in assembly" workhead with sealed, pre-lubricated ball bearings pre-loaded to eliminate end play. Air actuated, hardened and ground collets, with adjustable end stop, handle any stem diameter from .175" to .800" (4.5 mm to 20.3 mm). **Two-speed drive** provides correct rotation speeds for head diameters up to 4" (102 mm).

Valve face angle adjustment
Can be set and locked at any angle from 0 to 75

Feed screw
Turns in ball bearing and oilite bushing. Feed nut and screw bearing are end loaded to eliminate back-lash. Feed screw and nut are sealed off from dirt and chips. In-feed graduated in .001" increments.

FIGURE 7–34 Model VR-6500 precision valve refacer is used to grind metal from the valve face with a rotating grinding wheel (stone). (Courtesy of Sunnen Products Company.)

Once the valve is removed from the chuck, it is impossible to install it in the same position in the chuck. As a result, the valve will require additional grinding, which would have been unnecessary if it had remained in the chuck. Following removal of the valve from the machine chuck, check the valve margin (Figure 7-33).

NOTE   The valve margin is the distance from the valve head or top to the valve face. This margin must be held within the manufacturer's specifications to prevent premature burning and subsequent failure. If it is not within the manufacturer's specifications, the valve should be replaced.

Refacing the Valve Stem End
After the valve has been refaced, the stem end of the valve should be ground to ensure that it is flat. Use the following procedure:

1. Start the machine; using the dressing diamond, dress the stone (Figure 7-34).
2. Clamp the valve in the holding bracket.
3. With the valve-grinding machine operating, move the valve across the stone, removing only enough metal to "true" up or flatten the end of the valve (Figure 7-35, bottom left).
4. Remove the valve from the holder and install a taper or chamfer tool in holder. Start the machine and grind the taper (Figure 7-35, top right).

NOTE   The taper does not have to be very large; 1/32 to 1/16 in. (0.79 to 1.59 mm) is considered sufficient.

Checking the Valve Springs
Valve springs are very important to the life of the valve as well as to efficient engine operation. They must be checked before reassembling the cylinder head. The valve spring should be checked for straightness, ten-

Air-actuated hardened and ground collets speed production, assure pinpoint chucking of valves.

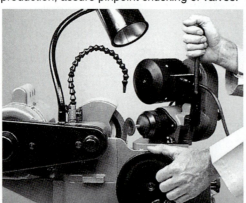

Valve butt chamfering attachment (standard) removes sharp edges after grinding process.

Valve butt grinding attachment (optional) has quick action cam lock and micrometer feed.

Rocker arm grinding attachment (optional) grinds pad parallel to the bore of shaft type rocker arms.

FIGURE 7–35 *Four of the common grinding jobs that can be performed to a valve and rocker arm using the model VR-6500 valve refacer machine. (Courtesy of Sunnen Products Company.)*

sion, and breaks by using the following tools and methods:

1. *Straightness.* Use a T-square or similar device (Figure 7-37).

2. *Tension and free length.* Insert the valve spring in a spring tension gauge to test unloaded or free length and tension at loaded length (Figure 7-38).

3. *Breaks.* By visual inspection check the valve spring carefully after it is cleaned for cracked or broken coils. If any evidence of breaks or cracks is indicated, the valve spring must be replaced.

Valve Rotators and Keepers

Valve rotators can be one of two types, either the free release or mechanical, positive type. Valve rotators are attached to the valves to make them rotate during engine operation. This rotation ensures that no carbon

will collect on the valve face or seat and cause valve burning.

The free valve or release type of rotator is designed so that every time the valve is opened and closed, the valve has no spring tension on it (Figure 7-39). This release of spring tension allows the valve to be rotated by the outgoing exhaust gases or engine vibration. The free valve rotator must be visually checked closely for wear during reassembly and all worn parts replaced.

The positive rotator is a mechanical device that mechanically rotates the valve every time it is opened and closed by the rocker arm. The positive-type rotator can be checked by tapping with a plastic hammer after the valve spring rotator and keepers have been installed. (Tapping with a hammer simulates engine operation.)

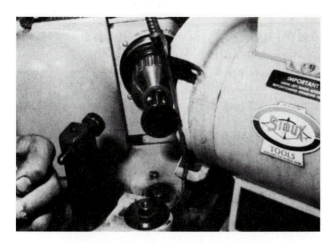

FIGURE 7–36 Grinding valve face.

NOTE   Although all valve rotators may pass the tests or checks and be considered usable, it is good practice during a major engine overhaul to replace all valve rotators to ensure a long period of trouble-free operation.

The valve keepers must be checked closely for wear and replaced if any wear is evident.

Preparing for Cylinder Head Assembly

After the cylinder head has been given a final cleaning (rinsed with cleaning fluid and blown off with compressed air), it should be placed in or on a suitable stand for final assembly.

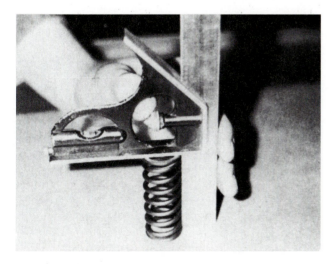

FIGURE 7–37 Checking a valve spring with a T-square.

FIGURE 7–38 Checking valve springs with a spring tester.

Checking the Valve Seat-to-Valve Contact

Install the valves in the head one at a time and check seat-to-valve contact with one of the following methods:

1. *Prussian Blue.* When Prussian Blue is being used to check valve seating, apply the bluing to the valve face (Figure 7-23). Insert the valve into the valve guide and snap it lightly against the seat. Remove the valve and inspect the face. The bluing should have an even seating mark all the way around the valve face. If not, the valve seat is not concentric and must be reground.

2. *A lead pencil or felt-tip marking pen.* When a lead pencil or felt-tip marker is being used to check the valve-to-seat contact, place pencil marks about 1/8 in. (3 mm) apart all the way around valve face (Figure

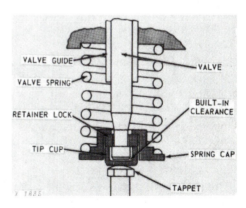

FIGURE 7–39 Free valve rotator.

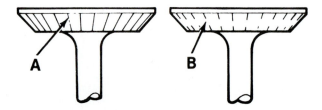

FIGURE 7–40 (A) Placing lead pencil marks across the valve face prior to face-to-seat checking; (B) inspection of the valve face-to-seat contact area after proper contact. (Courtesy of GMC Trucks.)

7-40). After the valve face is marked, place the valve in the guide and snap it against the valve seat. Remove the valve and inspect the marks made on the face. If the valve-to-seat contact is good, all marks will be broken. If all marks are not broken, the valve seat is not concentric and it must be reground. After checking the valve-to-seat contact, make sure that the lead is wiped from the valve.

NOTE   Lapping or seating of the valve with a lapping compound is not required if the valve and seat have been ground properly. Lapping is not recommended by most engine manufacturers.

Checking the Valve Head Height
If the valve head height (distance the valve protrudes above or below the machined surface of the cylinder head) has not been checked previously, it should be checked at this time. It should be checked as follows:

1. Place a straightedge across the cylinder head and use a feeler gauge to measure the distance between the valve head and the straightedge. Compare this reading to the manufacturer's specifications.

2. As indicated, some valves may protrude above the surface of the cylinder head; if this is the case, place the straightedge across the valve and use a feeler gauge to measure the distance from the valve head to the cylinder head machined surface.

Selecting the Valve Seals
After all valves and seals have been checked, the next step in the head assembly is to determine what type of valve seals (if any) are to be used.

NOTE   Some engines do not use valve seals because the valve guides have been tapered to prevent oil loss at this point.

Valve seals fit around the valve and prevent oil from running down the valve stem into the combustion chamber, causing oil consumption. Valve seals come in many types and configurations (Figure 7-41). If the cylinder head was originally equipped with valve seals, the engine overhaul gasket set will generally contain the valve seals. If the cylinder head was not originally equipped with valve seals, select either the positive or umbrella type of valve seal for intake and exhaust valves.

NOTE   Although some cylinder heads may have been equipped with valve seals, it may be desirable to select a more modern or positive type of seal for installation on the cylinder head.

The most common types of seals are the rubber umbrella or Teflon insert type that clamps onto the valve stem (Figure 7-42). Umbrella oil deflectors will generally not require guide top machining. Positive seals will require machining if the cylinder head was not originally equipped with them. A valve guide machining tool must be used to machine the guide.

Valve Guide Machining and Seal Installation
1. Select the correct cutting tool by referring to the seal manufacturer's application data.
2. Install the cutting tool in a 1/2-in. electric drill and machine the top of the guide, using a firm pressure on the drill to prevent cutting a wavy or uneven top on the guide (Figure 7-43).

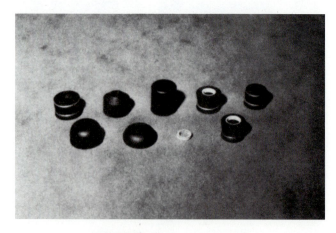

FIGURE 7–41 Valve seals.

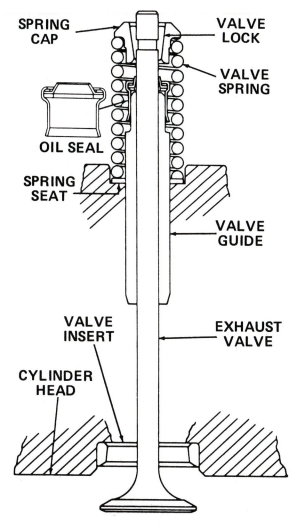

FIGURE 7–42 *Details of a typical valve, spring, and seat configuration. (Courtesy of Detroit Diesel Corporation.)*

SPRING CAP

VALVE LOCK

VALVE SPRING

OIL SEAL

SPRING SEAT

VALVE GUIDE

VALVE INSERT

EXHAUST VALVE

CYLINDER HEAD

NOTE The guide should be machined to the height specified in the instruction sheet provided by the seal manufacturer.

After all guides are machined, all metal chips must be thoroughly cleaned from the cylinder head.

3. Blow out all intake and exhaust ports with compressed air to ensure that no chips or particles remain.

4. Install valves and valve seals.

Testing and Replacing the Injector Sleeves

Many diesel engine cylinder heads have a copper sleeve into which the injector is installed. This copper sleeve is installed directly into the water jacket and must be sealed at the top and bottom. If leakage occurs at the copper sleeve, water may leak into the combustion chamber. As a result, the sleeve seal must be checked carefully during cylinder head repair for water leakage. Leakage testing of the injector sleeves will involve pressurizing the coolant passageways as outlined under pressure testing of the cylinder head.

If it is found that the injector sleeves leak and they are to be replaced, the following procedure should be followed:

1. Remove the injector sleeve following the manufacturer's instructions. Most engine manufacturers provide specially designed tools to install and remove the injector sleeves (Figure 7-44).

2. Before sleeve installation is attempted, the bore in the cylinder head that the sleeve fits into must be thoroughly cleaned, using compressed air or by sanding with emery paper.

FIGURE 7–43 *Machining valve guide.*

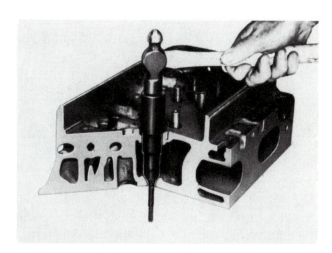

FIGURE 7–44 *Installing an injector copper sleeve. (Courtesy of Detroit Diesel Corporation.)*

NOTE   Many cylinder heads use O-rings in the sleeve bore to help seal the sleeve to the cylinder head. During cleaning of the sleeve bore, make sure that the O-ring grooves are cleaned.

3.   Install the new sleeve on the installation tool and insert a sleeve and installation tool in the cylinder head. Some sleeves are simply driven in place (Figure 7-44), while others must be rolled over on the combustion chamber end and reamed (Figure 7-45) after installation. Refer to the OEM service manual.

4.   After injector sleeves have been installed, it is recommended that the cylinder head be pressure checked to ensure that a leaktight seal has been established to prevent water leakage around the sleeves.

5.   After a new injector sleeve has been installed, injector tip protrusion should be checked and compared to the manufacturer's specifications. Injector tip protrusion is the distance the injector tip protrudes below the surface of the cylinder head gasket surface. Too much or too little protrusion may cause the injector spray to strike the piston in the wrong place or strike the cylinder wall. This incorrect positioning of the injector spray can cause incorrect cylinder operation (combustion).

Final Cylinder Head Assembly
Complete the head assembly using the following procedures:

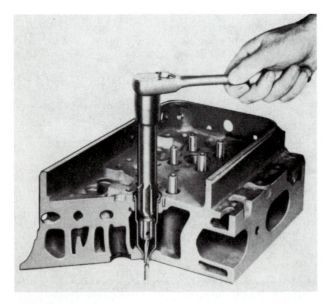

FIGURE 7–45 *Reaming a copper sleeve after installation. (Courtesy of Detroit Diesel Corporation.)*

1.   Install a spring over the valve and valve seal.
2.   Install a spring retainer on the valve spring.
3.   Using the valve spring compressor, compress the spring just far enough to install keepers (Figure 7-3).
4.   If the cylinder head is to be stored for some time before it is installed, the intake and exhaust ports must be plugged or covered with tape to prevent anything from getting into them until final engine assembly.

Assembling the Cylinder Head onto the Engine
The assembly of the cylinder head or heads onto the engine block will involve many different procedures that are peculiar to a given engine. The following procedures are general in nature and are offered to supplement the manufacturer's service manual.

1.   Before attempting to install the cylinder head, make sure that the cylinder head and block surface are free from all rust, dirt, old gasket materials, and grease or oil.

NOTE   Before placing the head gasket on the block, make sure that all bolt holes in the block are free of oil and dirt by blowing them out with compressed air.

2.   Select the correct head gasket and place it on the cylinder block (Figure 7-46), checking it closely for an "up" or "top" mark that some head gaskets may have on them.

NOTE   In most cases head gaskets will be installed dry with no sealer, although in some situations an engine manufacturer may recommend applying sealer to the gasket before cylinder head installation. Take particular note of the recommendations in the service manual or ask your instructor.

3.   After placing the head gasket on the block, place water and oil O-rings (if used) in the correct positions.

Some head gaskets will be a one-piece solid composition type, while others will be made of steel and composed of several sections or pieces. Detroit Diesel two-cycle engines, for example, use a circular tin ring that fits on top of the cylinder sleeve to seal the compression (See Figure 6-35). In addition to this sleeve

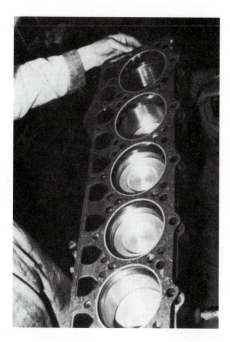

FIGURE 7–46 *Installing a head gasket on a block.*

seal are numerous O-rings that seal the coolant and lubricating oil, making up the head gasket.

NOTE The installation of some head gaskets requires the use of threaded guide studs that are screwed in the head bolt holes to hold the head gasket in place during head installation. Guide studs can be made from bolts by sawing off the heads and grinding a taper on the end. Most modern engines will have dowels or locating pins in the block to aid in holding the cylinder head gasket in place during cylinder head assembly.

---

4. After gasket and all O-rings are in place, check the cylinders to make sure that no foreign objects have been left in them, such as O-rings and bolts.

5. Place head or heads on the cylinder block carefully to avoid damage to the head gasket.

6. On in-line engines with three separate heads that do not use dowel pins, it may be necessary to line up heads by placing a straightedge across the intake or exhaust manifold surfaces.

7. Clean and inspect all head bolts or capscrews for erosion or pitting. Clean bolts that are very rusty and dirty with a wire wheel.

CAUTION Do not force or push the threaded part of the bolt into the wire wheel, as damage to the threads may result.

NOTE Any bolt that shows any signs of stretching or pitting should be replaced. A broken head bolt can ruin a good overhaul job.

---

8. Coat bolt threads and heads with light oil or International Compound no. 2 and place the bolts or capscrews into the bolt holes in the head and block.

CAUTION Before placing bolts into the engine, be sure that each bolt has a washer (if used). Some engines do not use washers under the head bolts. CHECK! Be sure that you have the correct bolt and/or washer combination.

---

9. Using a speed handle wrench and the appropriate-sized socket, start at the center of the cylinder head and turn the bolts down snug, which is until the bolt touches the head and increased torque is required to turn it.

10. When all bolts have been tightened this far, continue to tighten each bolt one-fourth to one-half turn at a time with a torque wrench until the recommended torque is reached.

NOTE Bolt tightening must be done according to the sequence supplied by the engine manufacturer when available (Figure 7-47). If sequence is not available, tighten the head starting with the center bolts, working outward toward the ends in a circular sequence.

Checking and Installing the Pushrod (Tube)

After the cylinder heads have been torqued to the correct amount, the pushrods or tubes and rocker arm assemblies may be installed.

1. Check all pushrods and tubes for straightness by rolling them on a flat surface.

NOTE Straightening of push tubes is discouraged. Bent ones should be replaced with new.

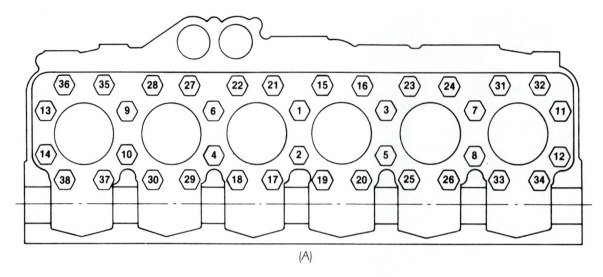

(A)

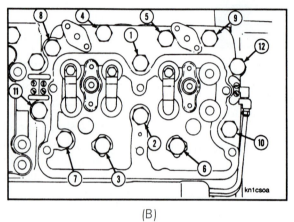

(B)

FIGURE 7–47 (A) Example of a cylinder head bolt tightening sequence for a series 60 engine model; (B) cylinder head bolt tightening sequence for a model N14 (855 in³) engine. [(A) Courtesy of Detroit Diesel Corporation; (B) courtesy of Cummins Engine Company, Inc.]

Push tubes must be checked for wear, breaks or cracks where the ball socket on either end has been fitted into the tube.

---

2. Place rods or tubes in the engine, making sure that they fit into the cam followers or tappets.

Checking and Installing the Rocker Arm

The rocker arm assembly or rocker arm is one component part of the engine that is occasionally overlooked during a diesel engine overhaul. Some technicians have the mistaken assumption that rocker arms wear very little or not at all. This is not true. Rocker arm wear may account for increased engine oil consumption. Oil consumption occurs because the increased clearance allows an excessive amount of oil to splash or leak on the valve stem. This oil will run down the valve and end up in the combustion chamber.

Rocker Arm Checks

The rocker arms and rocker arm assembly should be visually checked for the following:

1. Rocker arm bushing wear
2. Rocker arm shaft wear

Although some manufacturers may give a dimension for the shaft and bushing, the decision to replace should not rest entirely on dimension. The appearance of the shaft and bushing is a factor in determining if a replacement should take place. Look for:

1. Scoring.
2. Pitting. It must also be kept in mind that a bushing may be acceptable now but not after an additional 2000 hours of operation.
3. Magnetic inspection. Some manufacturers recommend that the rocker arms be checked

for cracks using a magnetic-type tester. If equipment is available, it is recommended that this check be made.

Installing and Adjusting the Rocker Arm
Place rocker arm assembly or housing on engine, making sure that rocker arm sockets engage the push rods. See Chapter 10 for more details.

NOTE   Rocker arm assemblies on some engines may be built into a separate housing called a rocker box. These box assemblies will require the installation of gaskets between them and the cylinder head.

CAUTION   If rocker arm or tappet adjusting screws were not loosened during engine disassembly, they should be loosened at this time. This ensures that no damage will result to the valves or valve train when the rocker arm assembly is pulled in place with the hold-down bolts.

Install rocker arm hold-down bolts and torque them to specifications.

NOTE   Some rocker arms may be held in place with bolts that serve as head bolts in addition to holding the rocker arms. These bolts will be tightened to the same torque as the head bolts.

Checking the Valve Crossheads (Bridges) and Guides

Valve crossheads are used on some types of diesel engines that use *four-valve heads*. Four-valve heads used on four-stroke cycle engines have two intake and two exhaust valves per cylinder. Two-stroke cycle engines such as Detroit Diesel use four exhaust valves in each cylinder. The crosshead is a bracket or bridgelike device that allows a single rocker arm to open two valves at the same time (Figure 7-48).

The crossheads (bridge) must be checked for wear as follows:

1. Check the crosshead for cracks visually and with magnetic crack detector if available.
2. Check the crosshead inside diameter for out-of-roundness and excessive diameter.

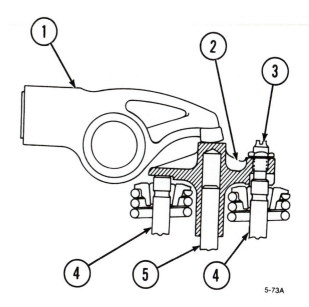

FIGURE 7–48 *Close-up view of a four-valve-head rocker arm (1), yoke/bridge/crosshead (2), yoke adjusting screw (3), valve stem (4), and yoke guide pin (5). (Courtesy of Mack Trucks, Inc.)*

3. Visually check for wear at the point of contact between rocker lever and crosshead.
4. Check the adjusting screw threads for broken or worn threads.
5. Check the crosshead guide pin for diameter with micrometer.
6. Check the crosshead guide pin to ensure that it is at right angles to head-milled surface.
7. If the guide pin requires replacement, check the engine service manual for the correct procedure.

Valve and Injector Adjustment

All of the intake and exhaust valves should now be adjusted along with the mechanical or electronic unit injector assembly timing height. The correct sequence to use will depend on the engine firing order. Refer to the information contained in Chapters 21, 22, and 23, which describe in detail how best to adjust valve clearances and injector timing heights.

After valve and injector adjustment, install the rocker arm covers. New gaskets should be used on the cover or covers and glued to the cover with a gasket adhesive. Install the intake manifold, exhaust manifold, generator or alternator, thermostat housing, and any other accessory that could not be installed before the heads were installed. After this final assembly, recheck all hose connections and electrical connections to ensure that all connections are completed and tight.

SUMMARY

Details within this chapter have provided you with information and knowledge necessary to successfully service/repair the cylinder head assembly. This will increase your level of expertise in successfully diagnosing, analyzing and effectively troubleshooting performance complaints of this major engine component.

SELF-TEST QUESTIONS

1. List the five major functions of the cylinder head.
2. Cylinder heads are generally cast from what type of materials?
3. Material strengths for cylinder heads are generally about
   a. 100 MPa
   b. 175 MPa
   c. 250 MPa
   d. 300 MPa
4. Technician A says that the term *four-valve head* refers to an engine with a total of four valves within the cylinder head. Technician B says the term means that each cylinder covered by the head contains four valves. Who is correct?
5. Technician A says that the term *crossflow cylinder head* means that the intake manifold is on one side while the exhaust manifold is on the opposite side. Technician B says that the term means that the inlet air enters one side of the head, flows across the piston crown, and flows back out of the same side to induce swirl to the exhaust gases during the valve overlap cycle. Which technician is correct?
6. Technician A says that all DDC two-stroke-cycle engines only use exhaust valves. Technician B says that all engines need both intake and exhaust valves to operate. Which technician knows engine operating theory best?
7. Technician A says that Detroit Diesel, Caterpillar, and Cummins employ individual cylinder heads on their larger-displacement engines. Technician B says that the only engine manufacturers that employ these feature are those that build very-large-displacement slow-speed engines such as those for marine applications. Which technician is correct?
8. List the advantages of using four valves per cylinder over two valves.
9. True or False: A parallel port valve configuration in a cylinder head means that the valves are located 90° from the position used on traditional engines.
10. The Caterpillar 3406E engine has a stainless steel sleeve at the exhaust port within the cylinder head. What is the purpose of this feature?
11. True or False: Water or coolant directional nozzles within the cylinder head are designed to increase the velocity (speed and direction) of the block coolant entering the head to improve the coolant flow around the valve and injector areas.
12. Technician A says that most high-speed heavy-duty diesel engine injectors are screwed into the cylinder head. Not so, says technician B; they are held in place by a hold-down clamp arrangement. Which technician is correct?
13. True or False: Most unit injectors are inserted into a copper or stainless steel injector tube within the cylinder head to allow for adequate cooling of the injector assembly.
14. The shape of the intake and exhaust valves in diesel engines is commonly referred to as a
    a. reed valve
    b. poppet valve
    c. gate valve
    d. rotating valve
15. Exhaust valves in diesel engines are exposed to average operating temperatures as hot as
    a. 600°C (1112°F)
    b. 700°C (1292°F)
    c. 800°C (1472°F)
    d. 900°C (1652°F)
16. List some of the common metal alloys from which exhaust valves are manufactured.
17. List some of the more common materials from which intake valves are made.
18. How do intake and exhaust valves manage to dissipate their absorbed heat?
19. What does a Stellite valve seat insert material consist of, and why would it be used?
20. Technician A says that both the intake and exhaust valves are retained in place in the cylinder head by the use of split locks (keepers). Technician B says that the spring retainer performs this function. Who is correct?
21. What is the purpose of a positive valve rotator assembly?
22. Describe the method you would use to determine if a positive valve rotator assembly was operating correctly in an engine.
23. Technician A says that faulty valve stem seals will result in combustion blowby, low compression, and hard starting. Technician B says that oil will be pulled down the valve guide, resulting in burning of oil and blue smoke in the exhaust gas. Which technician is correct?
24. Technician A says that worn valve guides can cause a rocking action as the valve opens and closes, resulting in poor valve face-to-seat contact and early valve failure from burning. Technician B says that oil pulled down the guides will cause blue smoke in the exhaust gas. Are both statements correct?
25. Technician A says that worn valve guides can sometimes be repaired by a knurling procedure. Technician B says that when worn, all valve guides must be replaced. Who is correct?
26. Technician A says that if a cylinder head does not con-

tain replaceable valve guides, when the head is worn it must be replaced. Technician B says that the head can be machined to accept press-fit valve guide assemblies. Which technician is correct?

27. True or False: Valve seat inserts are shrink fit in the cylinder head.

28. Technician A says that all valves should be marked at removal to ensure that they will be replaced into the same guide position upon reassembly. Technician B says that it doesn't matter where they are placed after repair. Which technician is correct?

29. Technician A says that if injectors are being reused at an engine rebuild, they can be serviced and then replaced into any cylinder. Technician B believes that it is good policy to always reinstall an injector into the same cylinder. Does it matter? If no, why not? If yes, give your reasons.

30. Technician A says that most intake and exhaust valves are machined with a 30° angle on their faces. Not so, says technician B; a 45° angle is much more common. Who is correct?

31. True or False: If a cylinder head is being removed with the injectors in place, the head should not be placed on a bench; it should be supported on wooden blocks or a head support bracket.

32. Technician A says that cylinder head bolts should be loosened off in the reverse order that they were torqued in, which is from the outside of the head toward the center. Technician B disagrees, saying that you should always start by loosening the head bolts from the center and working outward. Which technician is correct?

33. Technician A says that when remachining the fire deck of the cylinder head, you are limited to how much metal can be taken off. Therefore, refer to the engine manufacturer's specs for the minimum head thickness. Technician B says that it doesn't matter how much metal you remove; you can always use a thicker cylinder head gasket. Which technician knows the overhaul procedure best?

34. True or False: Heavy coolant scale buildup can result in cylinder head cracking due to overheating.

35. List the four methods that can be used to check a cylinder head for signs of cracks at engine overhaul.

36. Cleaning and polishing of the cylinder head fire deck can be performed using emery cloth with a grit rating of between
    a. 120 and 180
    b. 240 and 400
    c. 400 and 600
    d. 600 and 800

37. True or False: Cylinder head flatness can be checked by visually looking at the surface condition.

38. Technician A says that valve guide wear can be determined without removing the cylinder head by following a set procedure, which includes using a dial indica-

tor. Technician B says that the only way to determine valve guide wear is to remove and disassemble the cylinder head assembly. Which technician is correct?

39. True or False: Some engine manufacturers supply valves with oversized valve stems to avoid having to replace the valve guides.

40. To check valve face-to-seat contact, the best method to use is to lightly coat the face with
    a. blue layout ink
    b. Prussian Blue paste
    c. Never-seize
    d. line pencil marks

41. Technician A says that the best way to remove valve seat inserts is to use a small, sharp chisel and a hammer to split them. Technician B says that you should employ a special puller assembly. Which technician is correct?

42. Technician A says that when installing new valve seat inserts, you can heat the head in a temperature-controlled oven and chill the insert for best results, or use a guided installer and press or tap (hammer) the insert into place. Technician B says that you can simply drive the insert into the head with a hammer by working around the outer circumference of the insert. Who is correct?

43. If the cylinder head fire deck has to be remachined, technician A says that you should consider using thinner valve seat inserts. Technician B says that you can simply machine the hardened inserts during the head resurfacing procedure. Which technician is correct?

44. Technician A says that valve face seat contact width and placement are very important when regrinding valves and seats. Technician B says that it doesn't matter where the seat contact is as long as a good, wide seat exists to help to dissipate valve head heat. Which technician has a better understanding of the valve and seat grinding procedure?

45. True or False: The terms *overcutting* and *undercutting* refer to the procedure used when it is necessary to use a grinding stone or cutter with a larger or smaller angle.

46. The term *three-angle grinding* is often used by high-performance cylinder head rebuild shops. Describe what this term means.

47. What kinds of problems would exist if a valve had too much head protrusion?

48. What kinds of problems would exist if a valve had too much intrusion?

49. Too wide a valve seat face contact surface usually results in what types of problems?

50. Too narrow a valve seat face contact area usually results in what kinds of problems?

51. Technician A says that if a cylinder head has worn valve guides, these should be replaced before attempting to regrind the valve seat inserts. Technician B says that replacement will have no bearing on the finished valve seat grind quality, because either a grinding stone or cutter will be used. Which technician understands the

factors behind a good valve seat reconditioning procedure?

52. Technician A believes that using a grinding stone produces a better valve seat insert finish than using a valve seat cutter with blades. What do you think? Give your reasons.

53. How would you check a valve to determine if it is bent when you cannot see that it is bent?

54. After regrinding a valve face, you discover that the head margin is too thin. What types of problems would occur if you reused the valve?

55. What is an interference angle between a valve and its seat insert? Does this feature provide any advantages?

56. Technician A says that when employing an interference angle the valve face is always ground at a smaller angle than the seat. Technician B says that it is the seat insert that has the smaller angle. Which technician knows theory of operation best?

57. Technician A says that an interference angle of the valve face to seat cannot be used when employing positive valve rotators. Technician B says it can be used. Which technician is correct and why?

58. Technician A says that all valves should be lapped into their seats after grinding to produce a smooth finish. Technician B says that lapping should only be used, and very lightly, if a sealing test indicates poor seat-to-face contact. Which technician is correct?

59. Technician A says that to check for tight valve face-to-seat sealing, you can employ a vacuum pump and suction cup over the valve head, or you can turn the cylinder head on its side and fill the intake and exhaust ports with diesel fuel and check for signs of fluid leakage. Technician B says that you should seal off both the intake and exhaust ports on the cylinder head with bolted plates drilled to take a compressed air fitting to check for effective valve seat sealing. Which technician knows the correct procedure?

60. List the checks required on all valve springs when performing a cylinder head rebuild.

61. Technician A says that all new cylinder head gaskets have to be coated with a suitable sealer prior to installation. Technician B says that most new gaskets are already coated and do not require additional sealant. Who is correct?

62. Technician A says that cylinder head gaskets are designed to be installed one way only. Technician B says that they can be installed in any direction since there is no top or bottom. Which technician is correct?

63. Technician A says that cylinder heads should be retorqued from the ends of the heads working toward the center. Technician B says that you should start the torquing sequence from the center of the head and work outward in a CW direction. Which technician knows the procedure best?

64. Technician A says that all cylinder heads should be retorqued after a rebuilt engine has been run on a dy-

namometer or has accumulated a given number of hours or miles (kilometers). Technician B says that this is not necessary, unless specified by the engine manufacturer. Which technician is correct?

65. Technician A says that if you are installing a cylinder head and locating dowels are used on the cylinder block fire deck, it isn't necessary to use guide studs. Technician B says that you should always employ two guide studs to facilitate installation. Which technician knows good work practices?

66. Technician A says that cylinder head retaining bolts should be lightly coated with clean engine oil or International Compound No. 2 or equivalent on the threads, as well as underneath the hex head to provide for a more uniform torque loading of the bolt. Technician B says that you should flood the cylinder block oil hole with clean engine oil to ensure that proper torque is achieved. Which technician is correct, and why?

67. Overtorquing of a cylinder head can result in
   a. bolt breakage
   b. head distortion
   c. head cracking
   d. coolant leakage into the cylinder
   e. all of the above

68. Undertorquing of a cylinder head can result in
   a. head gasket leakage
   b. head cracking
   c. valve breakage
   d. injector siezure

69. Torquing of very large engine cylinder head nuts is usually achieved by using a
   a. socket and long bar extension on the torque wrench
   b. gear-driven torque multiplier
   c. hydraulic tensioner
   d. portable hydraulic jack on the end of the torque wrench

70. Technician A says that cylinder head nuts and bolts should be taken to their final value in one step after snugging up. Technician B says that you should torque these up in incremental values using two to three steps because this procedure will provide a more even torque. Which technician is correct?

71. Technician A says that overtightening a unit injector type hold-down clamp bolt on a mechanical rack model can result in a sticking or binding rack condition. Technician B says that it will result in coolant leakage from the injector tube into the cylinder. Who is correct?

72. True or False: The valve bridge (crosshead, yoke) is designed to allow two valves to be opened at the same time.

73. Technician A says that valve bridges require occasional adjustment. Technician B disagrees, stating that no adjustment is provided or required. Which technician is correct?

74. Technician A says that if the rocker arm pallet (comes in

contact with the valve stem or bridge) is worn, you can regrind the surface on a valve grinding machine. Technician B says that this would weaken the rocker arm and should not be attempted. Which technician is correct?

75. True or False: Cracks in rocker arms require replacement of the assembly.

76. Technician A says that many rocker arm pedestal hold-down bolts are T-drilled to carry pressurized lube oil to the rocker arm shaft. Technician B says that this would weaken the bolt and that splash lubrication is more common. Which technician is correct?

8

Crankshaft, Main Bearings, Vibration Damper, and Flywheel

OVERVIEW

This chapter deals with the largest rotating component and one of the most expensive within the engine: the crankshaft. Its function and operation are interlinked with the connecting rods, pistons, vibration damper and flywheel to effectively transfer the chemical energy released within the combustion chamber, and convert this energy into useful work at the flywheel. Service and repair details will provide the skills and knowledge to maintain heavy duty diesel engines in active service.

CRANKSHAFT STRUCTURE AND FUNCTION

The crankshaft in a diesel engine is used to change the up-and-down motion of the pistons and connecting rods to usable rotary motion at the flywheel. It is called a crankshaft because it is made with cranks or throws (an offset portion of the shaft), with a rod journal (that connects rod-bearing surfaces) machined or manufactured on the end. Different designs and different throw arrangements are used, determined by the number of engine cylinders and engine configurations, such as inline or V design. On one end, generally the rear of the shaft, a flywheel (a heavy metal wheel) will be attached. Attached to the opposite end will be the vibration damper. This assembly (Figure 8-1) is mounted on the bottom of the engine block by the main bearings and caps.

Within the diesel engine the pressure developed during operation by the burning fuel and air is trapped in the cylinder by the pistons and rings that are connected to the crankshaft by the connecting rods. The crankshaft then transmits this pressure or power to the flywheel for use outside the engine. To increase this power and produce torque, the crankshaft has been designed with the addition of cranks or throws. These throws extend from the center line of the shaft outward. The distance that they extend outward is determined by the engine manufacturer and is called the stroke of the crankshaft. The crankshaft will have one throw for every cylinder in an inline engine and one throw for every two cylinders in a V-design engine. Throw arrangement or spacing plays a very important part in helping to balance the engine. Figure 8-2 shows typical throw arrangements found in engines used today.

Since the crankshaft must rotate at different speeds over a wide speed range, it must be balanced precisely to avoid vibration. In addition, counterweights must be added to offset the inertia forces generated by the up-and-down movement of the piston-and-rod assembly. Most crankshafts will be constructed with counterweights on them, while others may be bolted on.

The crankshaft must be solidly supported in the block to absorb the power from the engine cylinders. This is done by the main bearings, friction-type bearings (made from steel, copper, and lead) that fit into machined bores or saddles in the block. Main bearings are constructed in a way similar to connecting rod bearings and are of the same material. For a more detailed description of bearing material construction, see Chapter 9. Since the main and rod bearings are friction-type bearings, adequate lubrication must be maintained at all times.

Lubrication for the crankshaft and main bearings is provided by engine oil supplied by the oil pump to

144

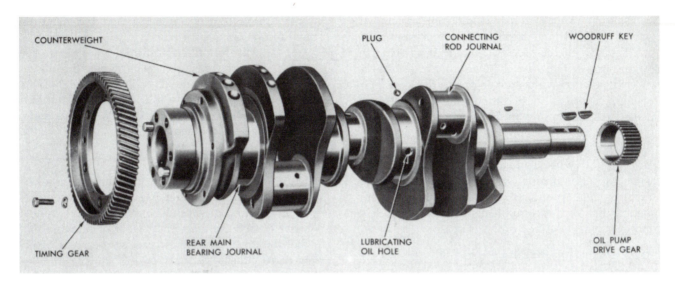

FIGURE 8-1   Typical diesel engine crankshaft. (Courtesy of Detroit Diesel Corporation.)

the oil galleries that are connected to the main bearings. After reaching the bearings, it flows through drillings in the crankshaft to the rod bearing journals. It then provides lubrication for the rod bearings and is allowed to drip off into the oil pan.

Mounted on the rear of the crankshaft is the flywheel. This flywheel helps to smooth out the power impulses developed within the engine and provides a place for the attached transmission clutch (a transmission connecting and disconnecting device).

Since the crankshaft now has a heavy flywheel mounted on the back, the free or front end must have a torsional (twisting) vibration damper to prevent twisting of the crankshaft by power impulses as they occur in the engine. This damper is smaller in size than the flywheel and is especially designed to prevent

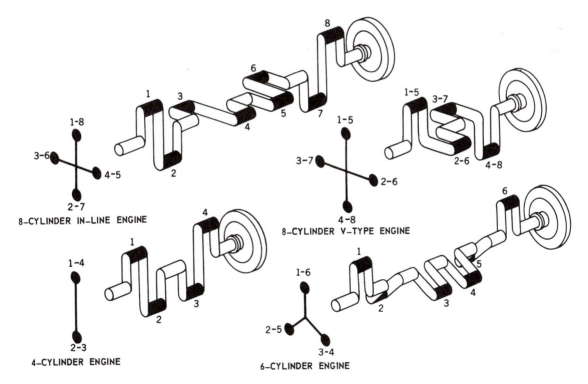

FIGURE 8-2   Typical crankshaft throw arrangement in a diesel engine. (Courtesy of Deere & Co.)

crankshaft breakage that may result from torsional vibrations created in the engine during operation.

The flywheel, crankshaft, main bearings, and vibration damper make up the team that transmits the power developed within the engine to the load. During engine overhaul these components require careful, detailed inspection and reconditioning if they are to give many hours of trouble-free service.

Unfortunately, components such as the vibration damper and flywheel sometimes receive at best only a casual inspection during a major rebuild and, as a result, bring about premature engine failure. It is recommended that all the components be checked and reconditioned as described in this chapter.

CRANKSHAFT CLEANING AND INSPECTION

Before any measurements are made on the crankshaft, it should be thoroughly cleaned.

Cleaning Procedure

The best cleaning method is the hot chemical cleaning tank. Before placing the crankshaft in the hot tank you should:

1. Remove all oil passageway plugs.
2. Remove all seal wear sleeves if present.
3. Remove transmission pilot bearing or bushing (if mounted in crankshaft).

After removal from hot tank, the crankshaft should be cleaned further by:

1. Using a stiff bristle brush to clean oil passageways and drillings
2. Using a steam cleaner or high-pressure washer to clean the entire shaft
3. Using compressed air to blow out all oil passageways and blow dry entire crankshaft

Visual Inspection

Crankshaft should be visually inspected at this time for the following:

1. Check for cracked or worn front hub woodruff key slots.
2. Check the rod and main bearing journals visually for excessive scoring and bluing.
3. Check the crankshaft dowel pin holes for:

   a. Cracks
   b. Size (oversize or oblong)

4. Check the dowel pins for wear or damage and snug fit into crankshaft.
5. Check around all oil supply holes for cracks.
6. Check the area on the shaft where the oil seals ride (front and rear). If the wear sleeve is not used and the shaft has a deep groove in it, the groove should be smoothed out with emery paper, and a wear sleeve and oversize seal installed.

NOTE If at this point you find that the crankshaft is unfit for further use or needs reconditioning, an effort should be made to determine what caused the crankshaft wear or damage so that the problem can be remedied before a new or reground shaft is installed.

The following steps should be used to determine what may have caused the damage to the crankshaft and main bearings:

7. Inspect both the main and connecting rod bearings, using the illustrations later in this chapter as a guide.
8. Check the bearings and shaft for evidence of insufficient lubrication.
9. Check the bearings and shaft for evidence of improper assembly.
10. Check the block line bore as outlined in the block section (see Figure 6-3).
11. If the crankshaft was broken, carefully check the vibration damper.

NOTE If the crankshaft does not appear to be worn or damaged beyond repair, the following checks should be made to accurately determine if the shaft needs to be reconditioned.

Inspection by Measurement

Accurate measurement of crankshaft rod and main bearing journals must be made with a micrometer in the following manner:

1. *Out-of-roundness.* Check by measuring in at least two different places around the journal diameter with a micrometer as shown in Figure 8-3. Usually if the journal diameter is 0.001 to 0.002 in. (0.025 to 0.050 mm) smaller (less) than manufacturer's specifications, the crankshaft should be reground.

NOTE The manufacturer's specifications should be checked for allowable crankshaft wear.

FIGURE 8–3 *Measuring connecting-rod journal.*

2. *Journal taper.* Check by measuring the connecting rod and main bearing journal diameter with a micrometer. Measure near one edge of the journal next to the crank cheek and then move across the journal, checking the diameter in the middle and opposite edge. If the diameters are different and in excess of OEM specs, the crankshaft must be reground.

3. *Crankshaft thrust surfaces.* The crankshaft thrust surfaces should be checked for:

a. Scoring (visually)
b. Measurement with an inside micrometer (Figure 8-4)

FIGURE 8–4 *Checking crankshaft thrust width with an inside micrometer. (Courtesy of Cummins Engine Company, Inc.)*

NOTE   Thrust surfaces may be reconditioned or reground if they are scored or rough. Most shops that are equipped to regrind crankshafts can perform this repair. It must be remembered that after the thrust surface has been reground, an oversize thrust bearing will be required.

If the crankshaft is to be reconditioned, it should be taken to an automotive machine shop specializing in this type of work. It is recommended that a shop be selected that can grind the fillets (area between the crank cheek and journal) in addition to the crankshaft journals and that can make some type of magnetic or electrical check for cracks.

CAUTION   All diesel engine crankshafts must be fillet ground to prevent breakage of the crankshaft (Figure 8-5). See OEM specifications!

Crack Detection

One of several methods may be employed by repair shops to check for cracks in a crankshaft. In most cases, crack detecting will be done by the shop doing the grinding. Explanation of two popular methods used is given at this point in case a repair shop does not have the equipment and capability to perform the checks.

Magnetic Particle Method

This method uses some type of electrical magnet to magnetize either a small section or the whole crankshaft at a time. A fine metallic powder is then sprayed on the crankshaft. If the crankshaft is cracked, a small magnetic field forms at the crack and the metal particles are concentrated or gathered at this point.

Spray Penetrant Method

This method uses a spray penetrant dye, which is sprayed on the crankshaft and the excess wiped off. The shaft is then sprayed with a developer that draws the penetrant out of the cracks, making them visible.

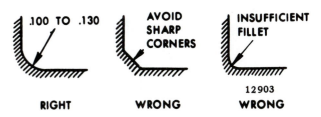

FIGURE 8–5 *Fillet area of a diesel engine crankshaft (Courtesy of Detroit Diesel Corporation.)*

MAIN BEARING DEFECTS AND REMEDIES

Main bearings are generally replaced with new ones during a major engine overhaul or rebuild. As indicated earlier in this chapter, the bearings should be inspected closely for wear and damage to determine if some abnormal condition such as low oil pressure or main bore misalignment exists within the engine that must be corrected before the engine is reassembled.

The following information and illustrations should be used when inspecting main bearings to determine if the bearing wear is normal or if conditions exist within the engine that may cause premature bearing failure. Premature bearing failures are caused by:

- Dirt: 44.9%
- Misassembly: 13.4%
- Misalignment: 12%
- Insufficient lubrication: 10.8%
- Overloading: 9.5%
- Corrosion: 4.2%
- Other: 4.5%

Surface Fatigue (Figure 8-6)

Appearance.   Small irregular areas of surface material are missing from the bearing lining.

Damaging Action.   Heavy pulsating loads imposed on the bearing by a reciprocating engine cause the bearing surface to crack due to metal fatigue, as illustrated in Figure 8-7. Fatigue cracks widen and deepen perpendicular to the bond line. Close to the bond line, fatigue cracks turn and run parallel to the bond line, eventually joining and causing pieces of the surface to flake out.

Possible Causes.   Bearing failure due to surface fatigue is usually the result of the normal life span of the bearing being exceeded.

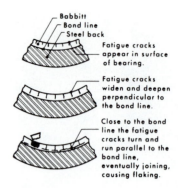

FIGURE 8–7   *Bearing cross section showing internal damage caused by fatigue. (Courtesy of Clevite Industries, Inc.)*

Corrective Action

1. If the service life for the old bearing was adequate, replace with the same type of bearing to obtain a similar service life.
2. If the service life of the old bearing was too short, replace with a heavier-duty bearing to obtain a longer life.
3. Replace all other bearings (main, connecting rod and camshaft), as their remaining service life may be short.
4. Recommend that the operator avoid "hot rodding" and lugging, as these tend to shorten bearing life.

Foreign Particles in the Lining (Figure 8-8)

Appearance.   Foreign particles are embedded in the bearing. Scrape marks may also be visible on the bearing surface.

Damaging Action. Dust, dirt, abrasives, and/or metallic particles present in the oil supply embed in

FIGURE 8–6   *Bearing surface showing effects of surface fatigue. (Courtesy of Clevite Industries Inc.)*

FIGURE 8–8   *Foreign particles embedded in bearing lining. (Courtesy of Clevite Industries, Inc.)*

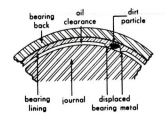

FIGURE 8–9 *Bearing cross section showing how dirt particles are embedded in bearing material. (Courtesy of Clevite Industries, Inc.)*

the soft babbitt-bearing lining, displacing metal and creating a high spot (Figure 8-9).

A high spot may be large enough to make contact with the journal, causing a rubbing action that can lead to the eventual breakdown and rupture of the bearing lining. Foreign particles may embed only partially and the protruding portion may come in contact with the journal and cause a grinding wheel action.

Possible Causes. Three factors can lead to bearing failure due to foreign particles.

1. Improper cleaning of the engine and parts prior to assembly.
2. Road dirt and sand entering the engine through the air-intake manifold.
3. Wear of other engine parts, resulting in small fragments of these parts entering the engine's oil supply.

Corrective Action

1. Install new bearings, being careful to follow proper cleaning procedures.
2. Grind journal surfaces if necessary.

3. Recommend that the operator have the oil changed at proper intervals and have air filter, oil filter, and crankcase breather-filter cleaned as recommended by the manufacturer.

Foreign Particles on the Bearing Back (Figure 8-10)

Appearance. A localized area of wear can be seen on the bearing surface. Also, evidence of foreign particle(s) may be visible on the bearing back or bearing seat directly behind the area of surface wear.

Damaging Action. Foreign particles between the bearing and its housing prevent the entire area of the bearing back from being in contact with the housing base (Figure 8-11). As a result, the transfer of heat away from the bearing surface is not uniform and causes localized heating of the bearing surface, which reduces the life of the bearing.

Also, an uneven distribution of the load causes an abnormally high pressure area on the bearing surface, increasing localized wear on this material.

Possible Causes. Dirt, dust, abrasives, and/or metallic particles either present in the engine at the time of assembly or created by a burr-removal operation can become lodged between the bearing back and bearing seat during engine operation.

Corrective Action

1. Install new bearings following proper cleaning and burr-removal procedures for all surfaces.
2. Check the journal surfaces and regrind if excessive wear is discovered.

FIGURE 8–10 *Results of bearing being installed with dirt on back side. (Courtesy of Clevite Industries, Inc.)*

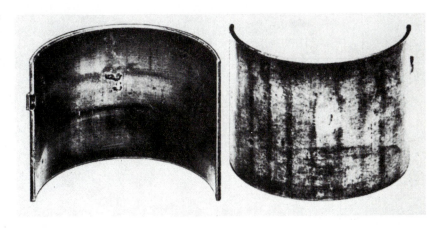

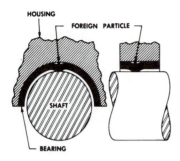

FIGURE 8-11 *Cross section showing dirt under bearing. (Courtesy of Clevite Industries, Inc.)*

Insufficient Crush (Figure 8-12)

Appearance. Highly polished areas are visible on the bearing back and/or on the edge of the parting line.

Damaging Action. When a bearing with insufficient crush is assembled in an engine, it is loose and therefore free to work back and forth within its housing. Because of the loss of radial pressure, there is inadequate contact with the bearing seat, thus impeding heat transfer away from the bearing. As a result, the bearing overheats, causing deterioration of the bearing surface.

Possible Causes. There are four possible causes of insufficient crush:

1. Bearing parting faces were filed down in a mistaken attempt to achieve a better fit, thus removing the crush.
2. Bearing caps were held open by dirt or burrs on the contact surface.
3. Insufficient torquing during installation (be certain bolt does not bottom in a blind hole).

FIGURE 8-12 *Bearing showing effects of insufficient crush. (Courtesy of Clevite Industries, Inc.)*

4. The housing bore was oversize or the bearing cap was stretched, thus minimizing the crush.

Corrective Action

1. Install new bearings using correct installation procedures (never file parting faces).
2. Clean the mating surfaces of bearing caps prior to assembly.
3. Check the journal surfaces for excessive wear and regrind if necessary.
4. Check the size and condition of the housing bore and recondition if necessary.
5. Correct the shim thickness (if applicable).

Shifted Bearing Cap (Figure 8-13)

Appearance. Excessive wear areas can be seen near the parting lines on opposite sides of the upper and lower bearing shells.

Damaging Action. The bearing cap has been shifted, causing one side of each bearing-half to be pushed against the journal at the parting line. The resulting metal-to-metal contact and excessive pressure cause deterioration of the bearing surface and above-normal wear areas.

Possible Causes. These are five factors that can cause a shifted bearing cap:

1. Using too large a socket to tighten the bearing cap. In this case, the socket crowds against the cap, causing it to shift.
2. Reversing the position of the bearing cap.

FIGURE 9.13 *Damage caused to bearing by a shifted or misaligned bearing cap. (Courtesy of Clevite Industries, Inc.)*

3. Inadequate dowel pins between bearing shell and housing (if used), allowing the shell to break away and shift.
4. Improper torquing of cap bolts, resulting in a "loose" cap that can shift positions during engine operation.
5. Enlarged cap bolt holes or stretched cap bolts, permitting greater-than-normal play in the bolt holes.

Corrective Action

1. Check journal surfaces for excessive wear and regrind if necessary.
2. Install the new bearing, being careful to use the correct size socket to tighten the cap and the correct-size dowel pins (if required).
3. Alternate torquing from side to side to assure proper seating of the cap.
4. Check the bearing cap and make sure that it is in its proper position.
5. Use new bolts to assure against overplay within the bolt holes.

Distorted Crankcase (Figure 8-14)

Appearance.   A wear pattern is visible on the upper or lower halves of the complete set of main bearings. The degree of wear varies from bearing to bearing depending on the nature of the distortion. The center bearing usually shows the greatest wear.

Damaging Action.   A distorted crankcase imposes excessive loads on the bearing with the point of greatest load being at the point of greatest distortion. These excessive bearing loads cause excessive bearing wear. Also, oil clearance is reduced and metal-to-metal contact is possible at the point of greatest distortion.

Possible Causes.   Alternating periods of engine heating and cooling during operation are a prime cause of crankcase distortion. As the engine heats the crankcase expands, and as it cools the crankcase contracts. This repetitive expanding and contracting cause the crankcase to distort in time.

Distortion may also be caused by extreme operating conditions (for example, hot-rodding and lugging) or improper torquing procedure for cylinder head bolts.

Corrective Action

1. Determine if distortion exists by use of Prussian Blue or visual methods.
2. Align bore the housing (if applicable).
3. Install new bearings.

Bent Crankshaft (Figure 8-15)

Appearance.   A wear pattern is visible on the upper and lower halves of the complete set of main bearings. The degree of wear varies from bearing to bearing de-

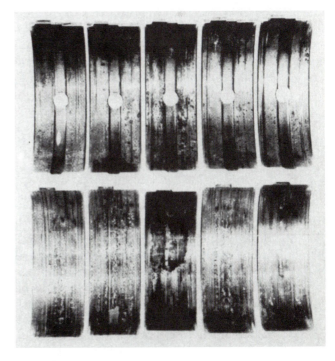

FIGURE 8-14 *Bearings damaged by a distorted crankcase. (Courtesy of Clevite Industries, Inc.)*

FIGURE 8–15 *Bearings damaged by a bent crankshaft. (Courtesy of Clevite Industries, Inc.)*

pending upon the nature of the distortion. The center bearing usually shows the greatest wear.

Damaging Action.   A distorted crankshaft subjects the main bearings to excessive loads, with the greatest load being at the point of greatest distortion (Figure 8-16). The result is excessive bearing wear. Also, the oil clearance spaces between journals and bearings are reduced, making it possible for metal-to-metal contact to occur at the point of greatest distortion.

Possible Causes.   A crankshaft is usually distorted due to extreme operating conditions, such as hot-rodding and lugging.

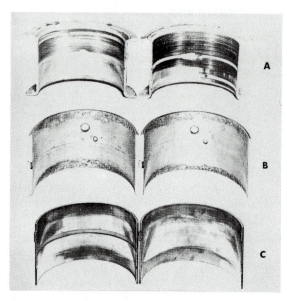

FIGURE 8–17 *Damage to bearings caused by out-of-shape journal. (Courtesy of Clevite Industries, Inc.)*

Corrective Action

1. Determine if distortion exists by means of Prussian Blue or visual methods.
2. Install a new or reconditioned crankshaft.
3. Install new bearings.

Out-of-Shape Journal (Figure 8-17)

Appearance.   In general, if a bearing has failed because of an out-of-shape journal, an uneven wear pattern is visible on the bearing surface. Specifically, however, these wear areas can be in any one of three patterns: in Figure 8-17 photo A shows the wear pattern caused by a tapered journal. Photo B shows the wear pattern caused by an hourglass-shaped journal. Photo C shows the pattern of a barrel-shaped journal. See also Figure 8-18.

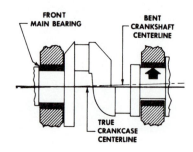

FIGURE 8–16 *Cross section showing how bent crankshaft fits into block. (Courtesy of Clevite Industries, Inc.)*

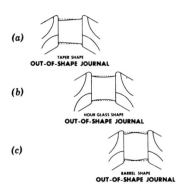

FIGURE 8–18 *Various journal shapes caused by wear. (Courtesy of Clevite Industries, Inc.)*

FIGURE 8-19 *Bearing damaged caused by fillet wear. (Courtesy of Clevite Industries, Inc.)*

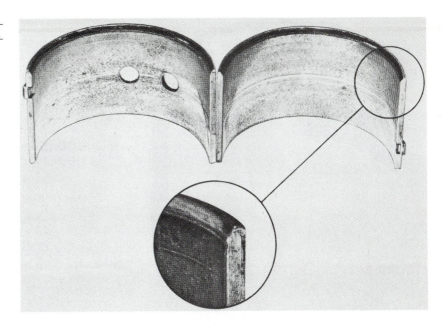

Damaging Action.   An out-of-shape journal imposes an uneven distribution of the load on the bearing surface, increasing heat generated and thus accelerating bearing wear. An out-of-shape journal also affects the bearing's oil clearance, making it insufficient in some areas and excessive in others, thereby upsetting the proper functioning of the lubrication system.

Possible Causes.   If the journal is tapered, there are two possible causes.

1.   Uneven wear at the journal during operation (misaligned rod)
2.   Improper machining of the journal at some previous time

If the journal is hourglass or barrel shaped, this is always the result of improper machining.

Corrective Action.   Regrinding the crankshaft can best remedy out-of-shape-journal problems. Then install new bearings in accordance with proper installation procedures.

Fillet Ride (Figure 8-19)
Appearance.   When fillet ride has caused a bearing to fail, areas of excessive wear are visible on the extreme edges of the bearing surface (Figure 8-20).

Damaging Action.   If the radius of the fillet at the corner where the journal blends into the crank is larger than required, it is possible for the edge of the engine bearing to make metal-to-metal contact and ride on this oversize fillet.

This metal-to-metal contact between the bearing and fillet causes excessive wear, leading to premature bearing fatigue.

Possible Causes.   Fillet ride results if excessive fillets are left at the edges of the journal at the time of crankshaft machining.

Corrective Action

1.   Regrind the crankshaft, paying particular attention to allowable fillet radii (Figure 8-5).

NOTE   Be careful not to reduce fillet radius too much, since this can weaken the crankshaft at its most critical point.

---

2.   Install new bearings.

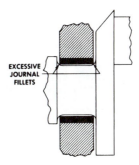

EXCESSIVE JOURNAL FILLETS

FIGURE 8-20 *Cross section of crankshaft and bearing showing fillet ride. (Courtesy of Clevite Industries, Inc.)*

FIGURE 8–21 *Bearing damage caused by oil starvation. (Courtesy of Clevite Industries, Inc.)*

Oil Starvation

Appearance. When a bearing has failed due to oil starvation, its surface is usually very shiny. In addition, there may be excessive wear of the bearing surface due to the wiping action of the journal (Figure 8-21).

Damaging Action. The absence of a sufficient oil film between the bearing and the journal permits metal-to-metal contact. The resulting wiping action causes premature bearing fatigue (Figure 8-22).

Possible Causes. Any one of the following conditions could cause oil starvation:

1. Insufficient oil clearance—usually the result of utilizing a replacement bearing that has too great a wall thickness. In some cases the journal may be oversize.
2. Broken or plugged oil passages, prohibiting proper oil flow.
3. A blocked oil suction screen or oil filter.
4. A malfunctioning oil pump or pressure relief valve.

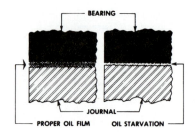

FIGURE 8–22 *How oil starvation would damage engine during operation. (Courtesy of Clevite Industries, Inc.)*

FIGURE 8–23 *Locating lugs not nested. (Courtesy of Clevite Industries, Inc.)*

5. Misassembling main bearings blocking off an oil supply hole.

Corrective Action

1. Double-check all measurements taken during the bearing selection procedure to catch any errors in calculation.
2. Check to be sure that the replacement bearing you are about to install is the correct one for the application (that it has the correct part number).
3. Check the journals for damage and regrind if necessary.
4. Check the engine for possible blockage of oil passages, oil suction screen, and oil filter.
5. Check the operation of the oil pump and pressure relief valve.
6. Be sure that the oil holes are properly indexed when installing the replacement bearings.
7. Advise the operator about the results of engine lugging.

Misassembly

Engine bearings will not function properly if they are installed wrong. In many cases misassembly will result in premature failure of the bearing.

Figures 8-23 to 8-25 show typical assembly errors most often made in the installation of engine bearings.

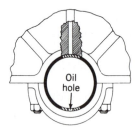

FIGURE 8–24 *Bearing halves reversed, oil hole in wrong place. (Courtesy of Clevite Industries, Inc.)*

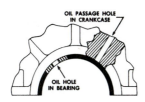

FIGURE 8-25 *Bearing oil hole not aligned with oil passage hole. (Courtesy of Clevite Industries, Inc.)*

MAIN BEARING SPECIFICATIONS AND CRANKSHAFT TOLERANCES

Main bearings for many engines are supplied in standard, 0.001-, 0.010-, 0.020-, 0.030-, and 0.040-in. sizes. Other engine manufacturers do not recommend that the crankshaft be ground; as a result, no undersize bearings are supplied. After the crankshaft has been reconditioned, the correct-size main bearings must be selected to give the recommended running or oil clearance. For example, a crankshaft may be ground to a 0.020 undersize (the correct main bearing then is a 0.020 undersize).

If specifications are not available for the crankshaft on which you are working, the following general specifications may be referred to when you are measuring the crankshaft.

General specifications for main bearings and crankshaft tolerances are as follows:

1. Crankshaft finish: 20 μin or more.
2. Diameter tolerance:
   a. 0.0005 in. for journals up to 1 1/2 in. in diameter
   b. 0.001 in. for journals 1 1/2 to 10 in. in diameter
3. Out of round: 0.002 in. maximum. (Never use a medium out-of-round journal with a maximum out-of-round bore.)
4. Taper should not exceed:
   a. 0.0002 in. for journals up to 1 in. wide
   b. 0.0004 in. for journals from 1 to 2 in. wide
   c. 0.0005 in. for journals 2 in. and wider
5. Hourglass or barrel-shaped condition: use same specifications.
6. Oil holes must be well blended into journal surface and have no sharp edges.

MAIN BEARING AND CRANKSHAFT INSTALLATION

It is assumed that the cylinder block has been checked, cleaned, and reconditioned. If not, refer to block re-conditioning in Chapter 6 before attempting to install main bearings or crankshaft.

1. Put the cylinder block on a clean workbench or engine stand in the inverted position.
2. Install the main bearing top half (shells) of proper size carefully in cylinder block, making sure that the bearing locating lug is aligned correctly with the matching slot in the block or cap (Figure 8-26).

CAUTION Make sure that all main bearing feed holes are lined up with holes in the main bearings. Also make sure that the block and bearings are clean.

---

3. Install the rear main bearing seal into the block if a split seal is used. Most one-piece rear main seals in engines are made of neoprene and may be coated with grease before the crankshaft is installed to prevent damage to the seal on initial engine startup (check OEM specs).
4. Blow out all oil passageways and remove any protective grease or preservative from crankshaft.
5. Install crankshaft using a lifting sling or bracket as in Figure 8-27.
6. If the timing gears and camshaft are installed in the block, index the timing mark on the crankshaft gear with the appropriate mark.
7. Main bearing clearance should be checked at this time using Plastigage.

NOTE Plastigage is a plastic thread that is broken into the correct length and placed on the main or rod journal or in the rod cap on the bearing. When the bearing cap is installed and torqued, the plastic thread is flattened out between the journal

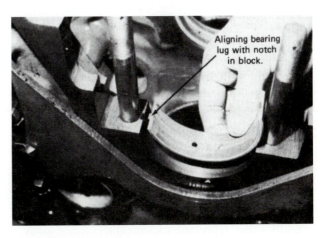

FIGURE 8-26 *Aligning bearing lug with slot in engine block or connecting rod.*

FIGURE 8–27 *Lifting crankshaft with a sling.*

and bearing. The cap is then removed and the width of the Plastigage compared to various widths pictured on the package that contained the Plastigage. By this comparison the rod bearing clearance can be determined. Carefully clean the Plastigage from the rod journal and bearing.

8. Break off a piece of Plastigage the same width as the crankshaft journal and place it on the crankshaft journal of one main bearing.

9. Carefully place the appropriate main bearing and cap on the journal (check number) and tighten down evenly with a torque wrench to specs.

CAUTION Do not drive main bearing caps in place with a hammer, since this may dislodge the bearing shell and distort the bearing when the cap is drawn into place.

NOTE Do not turn the crankshaft after the main bearing cap is torqued with Plastigage in place, because damage to Plastigage will result.

10. Loosen the main bearing cap bolts completely and remove caps.

11. Measure the Plastigage by comparing it to the pictures on the envelope that it came in (Figure 8-28).

NOTE The envelope is marked off in various widths that represent various thicknesses, such as 0.001, 0.002, 0.003 in. (and also 0.025 mm, 0.050 mm, 0.075 mm, etc.).

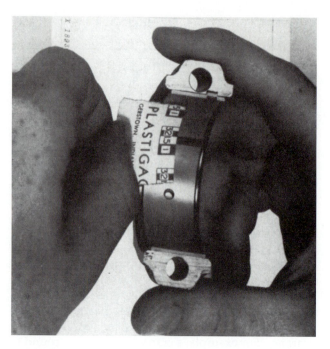

FIGURE 8–28 *Comparing Plastigage against envelope. (Courtesy of Deere & Co.)*

12. If the clearance is as recommended by the manufacturer, clean the Plastigage from the bearing and journal. If the clearance is not as recommended, check the bearing for correct size with respect to the crankshaft. If the bearing clearance is incorrect, remove the bearing and check for dirt or metal particles that may have been lodged under it.

13. All main bearings should be checked as outlined, then lubricated with engine oil or acceptable lubricant and the caps installed and torqued to specs.

NOTE In most cases the main bearing cap bolts are torqued using a torque wrench to a specified torque value. Some engine OEMs now recomment using the template or torque turn method to tighten main bolts. (Consult your engine service manual for details.)

14. As each main bearing cap is tightened, turn the crankshaft and check for binding. If the shaft does not turn freely, loosen the cap to determine what is causing the binding.

REAR MAIN SEAL INSTALLATION

If the rear main seal is not of the split, two-piece type and has not been installed in the block as outlined in step 3, it should be installed at this time. Most modern engines use a single-piece, lip-type, rear main seal (Figure 8-29).

1. A main bearing seal like the one shown in Figure 8-30 will be mounted into a seal housing that is bolted to the block and holds the seal in place.

NOTE   The rear main seal housing that is bolted to the engine block must be centered (sometimes called run out) carefully on the crankshaft seal flange or wear sleeve. Many engine manufacturers use dowel pins to center the housing; others have no dowel pins and the housing must be centered using a dial indicator or other centering device.

---

2. If the wear sleeve has not been replaced, replace it at this time using the following procedure.

   a. Remove the old wear sleeve by cutting it with a sharp chisel or center punch.

FIGURE 8–30 *Seal and seal housing in place on cylinder block, Cummins N14 engine.*

CAUTION   Use extreme caution when cutting old sleeve to prevent damage to the crankshaft.

---

   b. Clean the crankshaft flange.

   c. Install a wear sleeve using a special driver or installer.

3. If the rear seal housing uses dowel pins for centering, the seal can be installed into the seal housing before the housing is installed onto the engine block. Install the seal using a driver to prevent damage to the seal.

4. Install the housing onto the block, tapping it on the dowel pins with a plastic hammer.

NOTE   Special attention should be paid to the seal if it is installed in the housing to ensure that the seal lip is installed on the crankshaft flange without damage and is pointing toward the crankshaft, not the flywheel.

FIGURE 8–29 *Typical rear main seal. (Courtesy of Detroit Diesel Corporation.)*

5. If the rear seal housing does not have dowel pins for centering:

   a. Install the housing with a new gasket onto the block and install all bolts finger tight.

   b. Mount a dial indicator on the crankshaft flywheel flange with the plunger end of the indicator riding on the inside of the seal housing (Figure 8-31).

FIGURE 8–31 *Centering main bearing seal housing with a dial indicator. (Courtesy of Cummins Engine Company, Inc.)*

c. If no dial indicator is available or another method is desired, a piece of round stock (a round piece of metal similar to a bolt) may be used to center the housing.

NOTE   To determine what size round stock should be used, measure the crankshaft seal flange to obtain the diameter. Next measure the inside diameter of the seal housing and subtract the flange diameter from it. Divide the answer by 2 to determine the stock size.

d. With the seal housing bolted to the block finger tight, insert stock between crankshaft seal flange and seal housing. Roll the stock around the entire circumference of the crankshaft. This will center the seal housing.

e. Carefully tighten the seal housing bolts to the recommended torque.

f. Using a seal driver or installer, install the seal into the housing.

CAUTION   Oversize seals and sleeves should be installed as an assembled unit using special tooling; otherwise seal lip leakage will result.

VIBRATION DAMPERS

Vibration dampers used on diesel engines are designed to help dampen the torsional vibrations created within the crankshaft when the engine is running. The vibration damper is usually connected or mounted onto the free end of the crankshaft opposite the flywheel. It may be made up of two round steel cast rings bonded together by a rubber element or employ a flywheel encased within a viscous silicone fluid (Figure 8-32).

Bonded Rubber Dampers

The inner hub unit of the damper construction is hublike to fit the crankshaft, while the outer unit or ring is designed to fit over the hub with the rubber element in between. The entire assembly is held together by the molded rubber.

Inspecting a Bonded Rubber Damper

Although vibration dampers appear to be a solid unit that requires little if any inspection, they must be checked before use on a rebuilt engine.

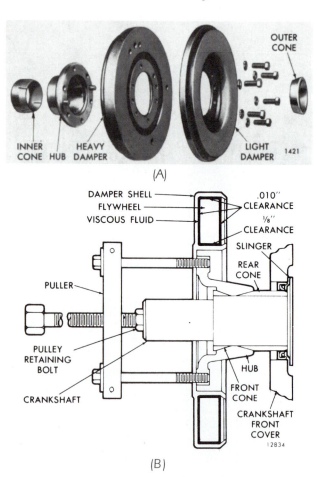

FIGURE 8–32 *(A) Typical rubber vibration damper; (B) special puller assembly to remove a viscous crankshaft vibration damper. (Courtesy of Detroit Diesel Corporation.)*

Some rubber element dampers have index marks that should be checked for mark alignment. If the marks do not line up, the damper should be replaced.

It should also be checked for wobble (lateral run out) after it has been mounted on the crankshaft. (A dial indicator is used on the inner surface.) If wobble exceeds the manufacturer's specifications, a new damper should be installed.

Viscous Dampers

The viscous damper, Figure 8-32B, is of a two-piece design. The fluid in the housing provides the resistance so that the flywheel unit absorbs the twisting motion of the crankshaft.

Inspecting a Viscous Damper

Viscous dampers should be checked for nicks, cracks, or bulges. Bulges or cracks may indicate that the fluid has ignited and expanded the damper case.

NOTE Many engine manufacturers recommend that the viscous dampers be replaced during a major engine overhaul or rebuild. The manufacturer's suggestions and recommendations concerning replacement should be followed closely in this area to prevent crankshaft breakage.

FLYWHEELS

The engine flywheel is a component that, like the vibration damper, sometimes does not get a close inspection during an engine rebuild. The flywheel has several important functions to perform. Some of these are to:

- Provide a true machined surface on which to mount the clutch or power takeoff
- Provide a place to mount the clutch pilot bearing
- Provide a place to mount the starter ring gear (a steel ring gear into which the starter motor pinion gear meshes)
- Help balance the engine
- Provide momentum to keep the engine running under heavy load between firing impulses.

Inspecting the Flywheel and Starter Ring Gear

The flywheel should be closely inspected during an engine rebuild for the following:
1. Check the contact surface (face) for:

a. Straightness (using a straightedge)

NOTE If the flywheel contact surface is not straight or true, it can be machined and reused.

---

b. Heat cracks or checks

NOTE Small heat cracks in the face of a flywheel are common and are not a reason for discarding the flywheel.

---

2. Check the flywheel and ring gear.

a. Dowel pin holes in the flywheel and bolt holes.
b. Condition of the flywheel ring gear. Ring gear teeth should not be worn or chipped. If they are, replace.

NOTE The flywheel ring gear is a replaceable gear that fits onto the outside of the flywheel and can be replaced by supporting the flywheel on a wood block with the face or clutch side up. The blocks used to support the flywheel must be smaller than the inside diameter of the ring gear to allow the ring gear to pass over them.

Removing and Replacing the Ring Gear
1. Heat the ring gear to approximately 300°F (150°C) evenly around the entire circumference with an acetylene torch (Figure 8-33).

FIGURE 8-33 Heat flywheel ring gear with torch.

NOTE   Some manufacturers do not recommend heating the ring for removal, but slight heating of the flywheel ring gear before removal will make the gear come off much more easily. Use Tempilstik chalked on the ring gear to avoid overheating!

2.   Using a drift and a hammer, drive the ring gear from the flywheel.

NOTE   The position or direction of the flywheel gear chamfer should be noted during removal for reference when reinstalling the new gear.

3.   Turn the flywheel over (ring gear side up) and support it on a flat surface.
4.   Heat the new ring gear evenly around its entire circumference.

CAUTION   Ring gear should not be heated in excess of 300 to 400°F (149 to 204°C). The temperature can be checked with Tempilstick or soft solder. Simply touch the Tempilstick or solder to the heated gear; if it melts the gear is at about 300 to 400°F or (149 to 204°C) (Figure 8-34).

5.   Grasp the ring gear with pliers and place on the flywheel recess with the chamfered side of the teeth facing the same way that the old ring gear faced.
6.   Tap the ring gear into place with a drift or large punch and hammer.

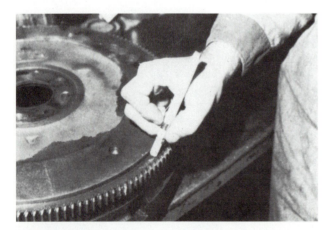

FIGURE 8–34 Checking temperature of flywheel ring gear with Tempilstick.

Flywheel Installation

Before attempting to install the flywheel, a method of lifting it into place should be selected. In many cases the flywheel is lifted by hand; in other cases the mechanic may select a hoist of some type to lift it into place (see Figure 5-9). Before attempting to install the flywheel, you should:

1.   Place guide studs or dowels in the crankshaft flange. (Guide studs can easily be made from bolts by sawing off the heads and slotting the end.)
2.   Determine if the flywheel can be installed in more than one position relative to the crankshaft. This is called flywheel timing.

NOTE   Flywheel timing is very important because the flywheel may have marks on it that will be used later on to set valves, injectors, and/or time injection pump.

3.   Install the flywheel and crankshaft capscrews, then torque the capscrews to the recommended torque.

NOTE   If guide studs were used to guide the flywheel in place, they should be removed and replaced with bolts at this time.

4.   If a bolt lockplate is utilized, it should be locked or bent now.
Installation of the crankshaft, main bearings, vibration damper, and flywheel should be complete at this time.

SUMMARY

As noted throughout this chapter, the components mentioned, such as the crankshaft, vibration damper, and flywheel, are given a very quick and casual inspection by some technicians. It cannot be emphasized enough that a complete, extensive check should be made on these components, because it will prevent costly and embarrassing premature engine failure. We cannot always anticipate engine parts failing because the normal life span has been exceeded. Thus a technician must not simply be a "replacer of parts" but, like a doctor, must be capable of diagnosing the engine to determine why the part failed. Study the failure analysis section of this chapter so that you become proficient in recognizing the telltale signs of engine bearing problems; this will enable you to correct them before they can cause engine damage or failure.

SELF-TEST QUESTIONS

1. Technician A says that there is generally one more main bearing journal than there are cylinder numbers. Technician B says that the crankshaft must have the same number of main bearing journals and cylinders. Who is correct?

2. True or False: Crankshaft counterweights are employed to produce greater torque when the engine is running.

3. True or False: Most high-speed engine crankshafts are manufactured from a one-piece forged alloy steel billet.

4. True or False: Built or semibuilt crankshafts are sectional crankshafts that are used on larger slow-speed engines.

5. True or False: The crankshaft fillet radius is used to relieve the stresses at each journal by spreading the load across a greater cross-sectional area.

6. Technician A says that crankshaft main and con-rod journals are always induction hardened to fairly shallow depths. Technician B says that all journals are hardened all the way through. Which technician is correct?

7. True or False: Offset crankshaft journal oil holes are designed to provide a 50% thicker oil film during engine operation.

8. What washers maintain crankshaft end float or end play?

9. Give three ways to minimize flexing of main bearing caps during engine operation.

10. Technician A says that crankshaft oil passages can be cleaned effectively by removing the Allen-head screws and using a stiff-bristle brush pushed and pulled through the oil hole drillings. Technician B says that it is better to submerge the crankshaft in a tank of hot caustic solution. Who is correct?

11. On a separate sheet of paper, list the various checks and tests that you would perform on a crankshaft at overhaul.

12. Technician A says that minor imperfections on crankshaft journals can be removed only by regrinding. Technician B says that this can be done by polishing the crankshaft in a metal lathe using fine emery cloth and diesel fuel as a lubricant. Which technician is correct?

13. When a crankshaft is reground, technician A says that you would want to use *oversized* bearings to account for the metal that has been removed. Technician B says that you would want to use *undersized* bearings in this case. Which technician understands the philosophy behind this procedure?

14. True or False: If the crankshaft thrust surfaces have been reground, you usually have to employ thicker thrust washers to maintain the correct end float.

15. Technician A says that to maintain crankshaft end float within specs, it is acceptable to use either thicker or thinner thrust washers on either side of the crankshaft. Technician B says that this cannot be done; instead, the same thickness thrust washers are required on both sides of the thrust surfaces. Which technician is correct?

16. True or False: If a crankshaft requires regrinding, both the main and connecting-rod journals must have the same amount of material removed from their surfaces.

17. Generally, a high-speed crankshaft is reground to a diameter that is smaller by one of three sizes. List the three sizes.

18. Most high-speed engine manufacturers specify that the maximum amount of metal that can be removed from a crankshaft journal be limited to
   a. 0.762 mm (0.030 in.)
   b. 1.000 mm (0.03937 in.)
   c. 1.500 mm (0.060 in.)

19. When measuring a crankshaft journal with a micrometer, it should be checked at how many different positions and how many axes?

20. True or False: To determine taper on a crankshaft journal, you should compare the readings from one axis with those of another.

21. True or False: To determine ovality on a crankshaft journal, you should compare readings along one axis.

22. True or False: If either a front or rear crankshaft oil seal surface is badly worn, the crankshaft can be repaired using a Speedi-Sleeve and an oversized oil seal assembly.

23. True or False: To determine if the crankshaft webs are misaligned or overflexed, a dial indicator inserted between the webs can be used.

24. Crankshafts can be checked for signs of cracks using what three nondestructive methods?

25. If a crankshaft suffers a break, list the two types of breaks that can occur and the angle at which they usually occur.

26. Crankshaft failures can generally be categorized into four main areas. What are these?

27. When installing a crankshaft with new bearings that are properly lubricated and main bearing caps torqued to spec, technician A says that if the crankshaft rotates freely, you do not need to check each individual bearing for the proper clearance. Is this an acceptable service procedure? Explain why or why not.

28. Crankshaft bearing clearance can be accurately checked by using
   a. wire solder
   b. Plastigage
   c. layout ink
   d. Prussian Blue

29. The majority of high-speed diesel engines employ main and con-rod bearings that are generally referred to as
   a. ball bearings
   b. roller bearings
   c. shell bearings
   d. needle bearings

30. True or False: Some high-speed diesel engines employ ball bearings to support the engine crankshaft.

31. Most shell bearings consist of five layers of material. List the layers and their materials.

32. True or False: Normally, the size of a shell bearing is stamped on the back face of the bearing assembly.

33. Shell bearings are prevented from spinning during engine rotation by the use of a
    a. locating tang
    b. dowel pin
    c. retaining bolt

34. Shell bearings dissipate their heat by being compressed into the cap or saddle; this is known as
    a. free diameter
    b. bearing crush
    c. press fit
    d. slip fit

35. True or False: All shell bearings can be installed in either the upper or lower position without any problems occurring.

36. True or False: Upper main shell bearings can be removed and replaced during an in-frame overhaul by the use of a roll pin.

37. When inspecting shell bearings at overhaul, bright or shiny spots appearing on the back side of the bearing are usually indicative of
    a. overheating
    b. bearing shell movement
    c. insufficient bearing clearance
    d. too much bearing clearance

38. Excessive main bearing clearance will result in
    a. low oil pressure
    b. high oil pressure
    c. aeration of the oil
    d. engine vibration

39. Bearing shells can be checked for thickness using a
    a. dial indicator
    b. depth micrometer
    c. vernier caliper
    d. ball micrometer

40. True or False: A properly fitted and operating shell bearing usually appears dull gray in color after a reasonable period of service.

41. Technician A says that a main bearing noise is usually more evident when the engine is loaded. Technician B says that a connecting-rod bearing noise is generally more noticeable when the engine is unloaded. Do you agree with both of these statements? Explain why or why not.

42. True or False: Worn main and connecting-rod bearings are usually accompanied by lower than normal oil pressure, excessive oil consumption, and blue smoke in the exhaust.

43. Severe scratches or scoring on the surface of a shell bearing is usually indicative of
    a. lack of oil
    b. overheating

c. metal-to-metal contact between the bearing and journal
d. dirt or foreign particles in the oil

44. The most common cause of shell bearing damage can usually be attributed to
    a. overloading
    b. dirt and foreign particles
    c. corrosion
    d. lack of lubrication

45. True or False: Technician A says that a typical cause of main bearing failure can be traced to fast/dry starts after an engine oil filter change.

46. Technician A says that many new crankshaft oil seals are precoated with a special lubricant and should not, therefore, have the lip prelubricated with oil. Technician B says that you should always coat the oil seal lip with clean engine lube oil. Who is correct?

47. The most effective type of engine crankshaft vibration damper on high-speed diesel engines is the
    a. single-rubber type
    b. double-rubber type
    c. viscous type

48. Flywheels and housings are available in different diameters that are manufactured to meet standards set by which one of the following associations?
    a. ASTM
    b. API
    c. SAE
    d. ISO

49. True or False: No. 1 size flywheel is smaller than a No. 4.

50. Technician A says that the starter ring gear is usually pinned or bolted to the flywheel assembly. Technician B says that the ring gear is a shrink fit to the flywheel. Who is correct?

51. Technician A says that to replace the flywheel ring gear you have to remove the flywheel from the crankshaft. Technician B says that you simply have to unbolt it and replace it with a new ring gear. Who is correct?

52. Technician A says that a scuff plate used on a flywheel is designed to prevent scuffing of the machined surface by a clutch assembly. Technician B says that the scuff plate is used as a self-locking plate for the retaining bolts. Who is correct?

53. True or False: One of the functions of the mass contained in the flywheel is to store energy and return it to the crankshaft during engine operation. This maintains a steady engine speed between the firing impulses of the cylinders.

54. Technician A says that all engine flywheels contain engine timing marks to facilitate in-service checks. Technician B disagrees, saying that two-cycle Detroit Diesel engines do not use any flywheel timing marks, since they are not necessary when a unit injector fuel system is used. Who is correct?

55. True or False: All flywheels are mounted on the rear of the engine and supported on dowel pins as well as being bolted onto the rear of the engine crankshaft.

56. Technician A says that many engine flywheels can be installed in only one position to align the retaining bolt holes. Technician B says that flywheels can be installed in any position, because the bolt holes are always drilled the same center-to-center distance apart. Who is correct?

57. True or False: If a flywheel is capable of being installed in any of several positions, you should manually rotate the crankshaft over to place the No. 1 piston at TDC; then install the flywheel so that the No. 1 TDC mark is aligned with the stationary pointer.

58. True or False: Slight discoloration and a series of small cracks on the machined surface of a flywheel that employs a heavy-duty clutch or PTO requires that the flywheel be replaced.

59. Technician A says that a worn flywheel pilot bearing can be replaced without having to remove the flywheel from the engine crankshaft. Technician B says that this is not possible; you must remove the flywheel assembly. Who is correct?

60. True or False: Using excessive heat on a flywheel ring gear can destroy the surface hardness of the teeth.

61. Technician A says that to prevent overheating a flywheel ring gear, you can use a heat-indicating crayon or install the ring gear into a temperature-controlled oven. Technician B says that heat should never be applied to a flywheel ring gear. Who is correct?

62. Technician A says that it is advisable to thread two guide studs into the rear of the crankshaft mounting flange when installing the flywheel and to use a suitable lifting bracket and sling to facilitate installation. Technician A says that it is easier to manually lift the flywheel into position and rotate it to line up the bolt holes. Which technician knows safer work habits?

63. True or False: Many engine manufacturers recommend that flywheel bolts be changed at major overhaul regardless of the visible condition of the bolts.

64. Technician A says that flywheel retaining bolts that thread into "blind" holes should be heavily lubricated prior to installation. Technician B says that this can cause a hydrostatic lock in the hole; therefore, only a light coating of oil should be used on the threads, plus a small amount of oil under the bolt head. Who is correct?

65. Technician A says that when flywheel retaining bolts are to be tightened, they should be pulled up in increments using a diagonal tightening sequence until the correct torque is obtained. Technician B says that most high-speed engine manufacturers specify that the flywheel bolts be tightened using the torque-turn method, which is more accurate. Which technician is correct?

66. True or False: Flywheel housing concentricity or runout should always be checked with a dial indicator gauge after tightening the retaining bolts.

67. Technician A says that a flywheel housing bore that is not concentric after installation can cause oil leakage from the rear oil seal. Technician B disagrees, saying that this could not happen since the oil seal is press fit in the bore. Which technician is correct?

68. After flywheel installation, what runout checks would you perform using a dial indicator?

69. Technician A says that excessive flywheel runout can lead to complaints of engine vibration and heavy-duty clutch problems. Technician B says that this is not possible if the flywheel is torqued to the right spec. Who is correct?

70. True or False: Distortion of the machined flywheel face surface could cause clutch slippage.

71. Technician A says that if the rear crankshaft oil seal which is press fit in the flywheel housing bore leaks, the flywheel must be removed to replace the seal. Technician B says that the problem can be solved in place by drilling two small holes in the seal housing, inserting two self-tapping screws, and using a slide hammer to remove the seal. Which technician is correct?

9

Pistons, Piston Rings, and Connecting-Rod Assembly

■ ■ ■

OVERVIEW

Pistons and connecting rods link the chemical energy released within the combustion chamber and the conversion of this energy into mechanical work at the engine crankshaft and flywheel. This chapter describes the structure and function of these important components. Details are also provided on the inspection, cleaning, and service repair tasks necessary to ensure a smooth running engine and effective sealing of combustion gases within the cylinder.

SYSTEM STRUCTURE AND FUNCTION

The piston rings, piston pin, and connecting rod assembly make up what are considered the major parts in a reciprocating diesel engine (Figure 9-1). The piston and ring assembly provide the plug or seal for the pressure developed by the burning fuel and air within the cylinder. The piston pin attaches the piston and ring assembly to the connecting rod, which in turn is connected to the crankshaft. Power developed within the cylinder is transferred to the crankshaft by this assembly.

The piston, piston rings, and connecting-rod assembly is one of the most unique and important assemblies within the diesel engine. Probably no other part of the diesel engine is subjected to the extreme heat, pressure, and force that are encountered by the piston, which is the central or main part of this assembly. During normal engine operation the piston is subjected to temperatures of 1200 to 1300°F (650 to 700°C), while during shutdown it may be at ambient tempera-

ture (temperature surrounding engine, or atmospheric temperature).

To accept this extreme temperature change many times through its normal lifetime without failing, the piston must be made from a very durable material. Most diesel engine pistons are made from aluminum alloy, a mixture of copper, silicon, magnesium, manganese, iron, and lead. An exception to this would be Detroit Diesel two-stroke-cycle pistons, which are constructed from pearlitic malleable iron and plated with tin.

NOTE Aluminum is most commonly used in four-stroke-cycle diesel engines because of its ability to transfer heat quickly, thereby allowing the piston to run cooler than one made from cast iron. In addition, aluminum is much lighter, making the total reciprocating weight within the engine less; this decreases the inertia (the tendency of a body in motion to stay in motion). Inertia is generated at the top and bottom of the piston stroke by rapid start and stop. Less inertia helps to create a better-balanced and smoother-running engine.

Some diesel engine pistons are one-piece of the trunk type (Figure 9-2), although many diesel engines now use the crosshead type of piston. The design of the crosshead piston (Figure 9-3) is such that it almost eliminates any side or thrust load on the piston, thereby decreasing wear and increasing ring life.

The trunk type of piston is made up of piston head, piston pin boss (bearing area), ring grooves, groove lands, and piston skirt. Because trunk-type aluminum pistons are constructed with more metal in the

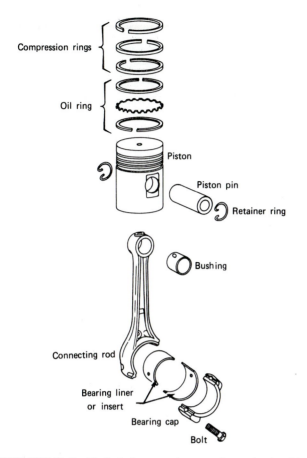

FIGURE 9–1 *Typical piston and connecting-rod assembly.*

piston pin boss area to support the piston pin, provision must be made for the uneven expansion that results from this design. To ensure that the piston will be round after expansion from the heat of combustion, aluminum pistons are cam ground or egg shaped (elliptical) (Figure 9-4).

Careful consideration must be given to the clearance of the piston within the cylinder. Excessive clearance will allow the piston to pound or knock against the cylinder wall after engine startup until the piston becomes hot. Too little clearance can cause scoring of the piston when it is hot because no clearance remains for lubricating oil between the piston and cylinder wall. It can be seen then that a clearance that gives little or no piston noise during cold operation and provides lubrication clearance during hot operation is the clearance desired. This clearance is generally built into the piston by the manufacturer. For example, a 4-in. (101.60-mm)-diameter cylinder might be fitted with an aluminum piston 0.001 to 0.002 in. (0.025 to 0.05 mm) smaller in diameter than the cylinder. Clearance between the piston and cylinder depends a great deal on the diameter of the piston and the type of material, as a large piston must have more room for expansion when it becomes hot during engine operation.

The head of the piston may contain (depending on engine design) the cylinder combustion chamber (Figure 9-5). The combustion chamber is designed to

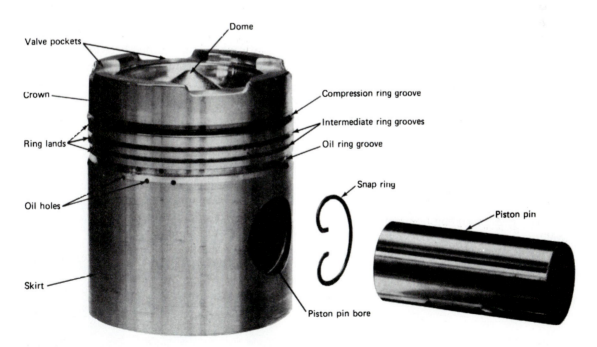

FIGURE 9–2 *Typical trunk piston (identified). (Courtesy of Cummins Engine Company, Inc.)*

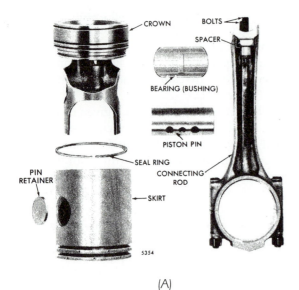

(A)

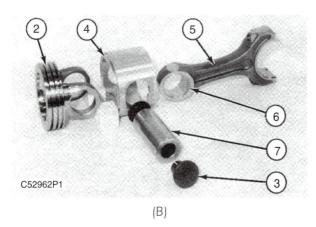

(B)

FIGURE 9–3 *(A) Crosshead diesel engine piston; (B) components of a 3176B Cat articulated piston: 2, piston crown; 3, piston retaining plug; 4, articulated piston skirt; 5, connecting rod; 6, bearing; 7, piston pin. [(A) Courtesy of Detroit Diesel Corporation; (B) courtesy of Caterpillar, Inc.)]*

aid in mixing the fuel and air together so that complete combustion (burning of the fuel) can occur.

NOTE   Complete combustion in a diesel engine is the ultimate goal of all engine manufacturers. How well it is achieved depends on factors such as the design of the combustion chamber, injection nozzle opening pressure, injection nozzle hole size, and compression ratio. This subject is discussed in detail in Chapter 4.

The piston pin boss (bearing area) is the part of the piston that provides the support for the piston pin that connects the piston to the connecting rod. The pis-

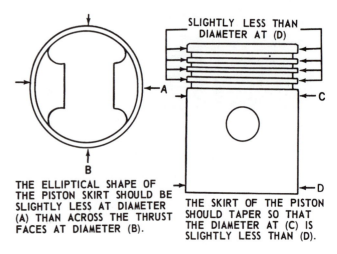

FIGURE 9–4 *Cam ground piston. (Courtesy of Deere & Co.)*

ton boss is made as part of the piston and supported also by ribs or bars on the inside of the piston.

Guiding and supporting the piston within the cylinder are the piston skirts (side walls of the piston below the ring area). When combustion occurs and force is exerted on the piston, it is held straight in the cylinder by the piston skirts in contact with the cylinder wall.

NOTE   In reality, piston skirts do not make contact with the cylinder wall, since a film of lubricating oil is maintained between wall and piston at all times during engine operation.

FIGURE 9–5 *Diesel engine piston head design.*

Cut in the piston immediately below the head are the ring grooves. These ring grooves are designed or shaped the same as the rings that are fitted into them. Many aluminum pistons have an iron or Ni-resist insert in the top ring groove. The Ni-resist area of the piston, in which the ring groove is cut, will be made from a harder metal such as nickel-chrome-iron to increase the wear qualities of the ring groove.

Installed into the ring grooves to aid the piston in reducing power loss due to blowby are the piston rings (circular, springlike steel devices) (Figure 9-1). Between each ring, supporting them, are the ring lands.

Piston rings are designed with an uninstalled or free diameter larger than the cylinder bore, so that when the ring is installed, radial pressure is applied to the cylinder wall.

The piston will normally have several different types of rings on it (Figure 9-6). Here are three examples:

1. Compression ring (top position). The top or compression ring seals the compression and pressure from combustion in the combustion chamber.

2. Combination compression and oil scraper ring (second groove). This second ring is generally a combination compression and oil scraper ring, aiding in controlling combustion loss and oil control.

3. Oil control ring (third or fourth groove depending on how many rings are on the piston). The oil control ring is designed to control the flow of oil onto the cylinder wall on the upstroke of the piston for lubrication and scrape the oil back off on the downstroke.

Not all pistons will have three rings. The number of rings is determined by the engine manufacturer, taking into consideration factors such as bore size, engine speed, and engine configuration (inline or V).

Shown are several different pistons with their respective ring combinations (Figure 9-7).

One of the most critical wear areas in the engine is the piston rings and pistons because they are subjected to the tremendous heat of combustion and possible dirt-laden air supplied to the cylinder. To ensure a long, trouble-free period of operation, particular attention must be given to regular oil, oil filter, and air filter changes. In addition, it is very important during engine overhaul or rebuild that strict attention be paid to detail and manufacturer's recommendations to ensure that a quality job can be done.

As stated earlier in this chapter, the pistons and ring combination are connected to the connecting rod by the piston pin, which is held in place by the retainer rings. The piston pin bushing is supported in the end of the connecting rod by a bushing made from brass, bronze, steel, or aluminum. The connecting rod is composed of very strong steel alloy shaped like an I-beam with a hole in one end for the piston pin (Figure 9-8). The other end of the rod has a larger hole or bore with a removable cap so that the rod may be connected to the rod journal. Installed in this hole will be a sleeve-type friction bearing (Figure 9-9) comprised of two halves, one half in the connecting rod and the other half in the rod cap. Connecting rod bearings are specially designed to meet the following requirements imposed on them during engine operation:

1. *Fatigue resistance.* The bearing must be able to withstand intermittent loading to which it may be subjected.

2. *Conformability.* The bearing material must be able to creep or flow slightly to compensate for any unavoidable misalignment between the shaft and bearing.

FIGURE 9–6 *Several types of piston rings. (Courtesy of Deere & Co.)*

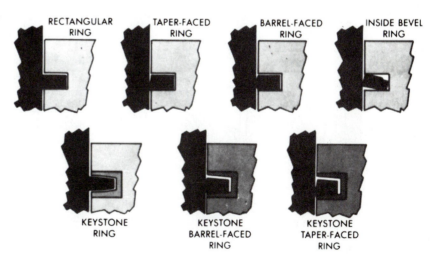

RECTANGULAR RING   TAPER-FACED RING   BARREL-FACED RING   INSIDE BEVEL RING

KEYSTONE RING   KEYSTONE BARREL-FACED RING   KEYSTONE TAPER-FACED RING

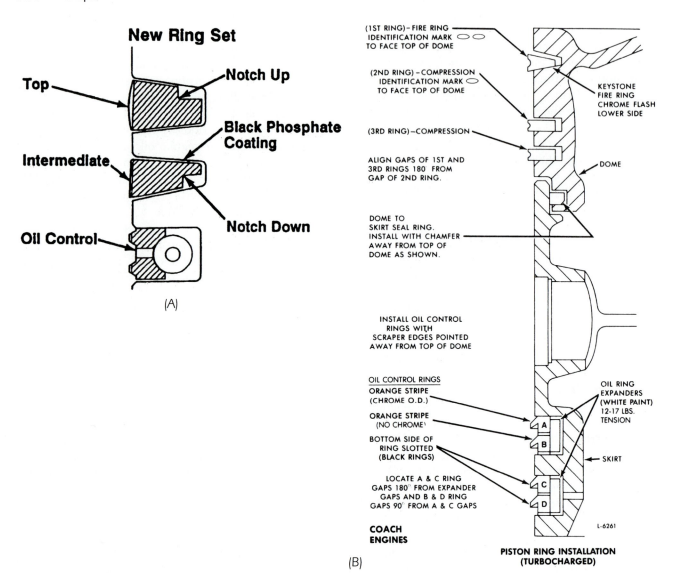

FIGURE 9–7 (A) Example of the three-ring arrangement used on Cummins L10, M11, and N14 engine models; (B) example of piston ring stackup used by DDC on its V92 series of two-stroke-cycle transit bus engines. [(A) Courtesy of Cummins Engine Company, Inc.; (B) Courtesy of Detroit Diesel Corporation.]

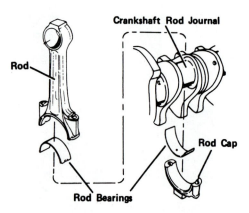

FIGURE 9–8 Diesel engine connecting rod. (Courtesy of Cummins Engine Company, Inc.)

3. *Embeddability.* The ability of the bearing material to absorb foreign abrasive particles that might otherwise scratch the shaft that the bearing is supporting.

4. *Surface action.* The ability of a bearing to resist seizure if the bearing and shaft make contact during engine operation. This situation may occur when an extreme load squeezes the oil film out of the clearance space between the shaft and bearing.

5. *Corrosive resistance.* A bearing characteristic that resists chemical corrosion caused by acids that are the by-product of combustion.

6. *Temperature strength.* How well the bearing will carry its load at engine-operating temperature without flowing out of shape or breaking up.

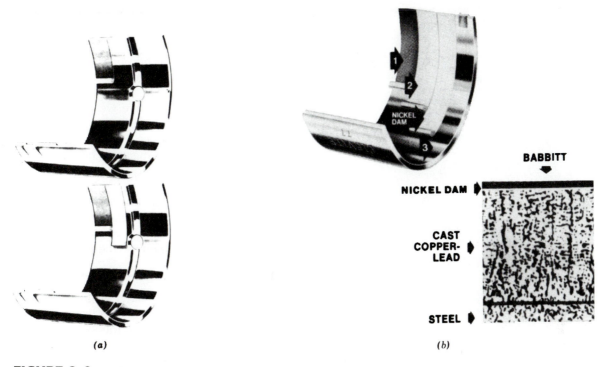

FIGURE 9–9   (a) Sleeve type friction bearing; (b) trimetal cast copper–lead bearing. (Courtesy of Clevite Industries Inc.)

7. Thermal conductivity. The ability of a bearing material to absorb heat and transfer it from the bearing surface to the housing. An important factor in bearing longevity.

To meet all the requirements, engine bearings are designed with a steel backing (Figure 9-9) and a liner of bearing material. The bearing surface is the part of a journal bearing that performs the basic antifriction function and thus is considered to be of primary importance. The most common metals used are copper and lead with a thin overlay (0.001 in. thick) of babbitt on some bearings.

Babbitt is added to the surface of some bearings because it provides a low co-efficient of friction, the softness required to permit a reasonable amount of foreign particles to embed themselves, and the conformability characteristics necessary so that shaft and bearing will conform to each other.

There are four common materials used in modern engine bearings. *Babbitt* is divided into two categories, conventional and micro or thin babbitt. It may be a tin- or lead-base material. Conventional babbitt bearings differ from micro bearings by the amount of babbitt laminated on the steel back. *Sintered copper lead* is made by sintering metal powders on a steel strip. *Cast copper lead,* a copper–lead alloy cast on a steel strip, is available with or without an overlay. Aluminum is a widely available and corrosion-resistant material obtainable in solid, bimetal, and trimetal construction.

The rod bearing is lubricated by engine oil supplied under pressure through a drilling in the crank-shaft journal (Chapter 11). Since there is clearance between the connecting rod bearing and the crankshaft journal, the oil used for lubrication is allowed to leak off into the oil pan or crankcase area of the engine.

INSPECTION, CLEANING, AND REMOVAL OF THE PISTONS

Visual Inspection of the Piston

Place the piston and rod assembly in a vise as shown in Figure 9-10 and clamp it securely.

NOTE   It is recommended that a vise with brass jaw protectors or a rag be used to protect the rod when it is clamped into the vise.

Make a visual inspection of the piston rings, land, and skirt area to determine if the piston is reusable. The piston should be checked for:

1. Scored skirt area
2. Cracked skirt
3. Uneven wear (skirt area)
4. Broken ring lands
5. Stuck or broken rings

FIGURE 9–10 *Correct procedure for clamping rod and piston in a vise.*

6. Worn piston pin bores
7. Burned or eroded areas in head

After inspecting the piston as mentioned above, it must be determined what caused the piston damage (if any). The condition that caused the piston damage must be corrected before the engine is reassembled.

Piston skirt scoring (Figure 9-11) can be caused by any of the following: engine overheating, excessive fuel settings, improper piston clearance, insufficient lubrication, or improper injection nozzle or injector.

Piston cracking or ring land breakage can be caused by excessive use of starting fluid, excessive piston clearance, or foreign objects in the cylinder.

Piston skirt wear can be caused by normal engine

operation, dirty lubricating oil, too little piston clearance, or dirty intake air.

Piston burning or erosion can be caused by plugged nozzle or injection orifices, excessive engine load during cold operation, and water leakage into the cylinder.

Piston pin bearing bore wear can be caused by normal engine operation, dirty engine oil, or insufficient lubrication.

Pistons with stuck rings may be the result of overheating, insufficient lubrication, or excessive fuel settings.

If the piston fails this inspection, it should be removed from the rod and discarded (see section on rod removal). If the decision is made to use the piston again, it should be left on the rod for now.

NOTE Leaving the piston on the rod will provide a means for holding the piston during the cleanup and inspection to follow.

Rings can be easily removed by using a ring installation removal tool (Figure 9-12).

Normally, pistons and rings are discarded and replaced with new ones during a major overhaul, but there are exceptions. For example, a new engine with very few hours on it may be disassembled because of excessive oil consumption. Normally, engine manufacturers recommend replacing the rings only, not the pistons. Pistons may also be used again in an older engine that, after overhaul, is to be only used occasionally or for a short number of hours. Given these circumstances, rings must be replaced and the piston or pistons may be used over again if they pass inspection.

Cleaning the Ring Grooves

1. A ring groove cleaner (Figure 9-13) should be used to clean all the carbon from the ring grooves so they may be checked for wear.

FIGURE 9–11 *Scored piston. (Courtesy of Detroit Diesel Corporation.)*

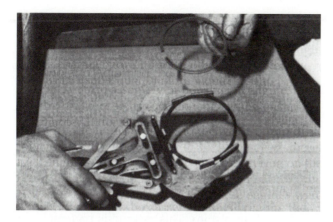

FIGURE 9–12 *Ring installation and removal tool.*

2. Select the tool bit that fits the ring groove and install the cleaner on the piston in the ring groove.

3. Operate the groove cleaner by twisting or turning it around the piston.

4. Clean the grooves until all carbon has been removed.

CAUTION Care must be exercised when using the groove cleaner to prevent any metal from being removed from the bottom of the ring grooves or piston surface by continuing to turn the cleaner after all the carbon has been cleaned away.

NOTE   If a ring groove cleaner is not available, a top compression ring may be broken in half, the end filed square and used as a ring groove cleaner.

FIGURE 9–13 *Piston ring groove cleaner.*

Measuring the Ring Groove

The ring grooves can now be checked for wear to determine if the pistons will be reusable. Use the following procedure:

1. Check the top and second ring grooves with a ring groove gauge if available (Figure 9-14).

2. If a ring groove gauge is not available, a new ring and a feeler gauge may be used. If the ring and groove are straight, the ring need not be installed on the piston. If the ring and groove are of the keystone type, the ring must be installed on the piston and the ring pushed flush with the piston ring land. Using a 0.006-in. (0.015-mm) feeler gauge, try to insert the gauge between the ring and piston ring land (Figure 9-15). If the feeler gauge can be inserted and removed easily, the ring groove is worn excessively and the piston must be replaced.

Removing the Piston

Once it has been determined that the piston ring grooves are in usable condition, the piston can now be removed from the connecting rod for further checking. The piston may be removed as follows:

1. Remove the piston pin retaining rings using a pair of circlip pliers (Figure 9-16).

NOTE   When removing Detroit Diesel (two-stroke) piston pin retainers (a thin spring steel-like cap holds the pin in); see Figure 9-3A. A hole

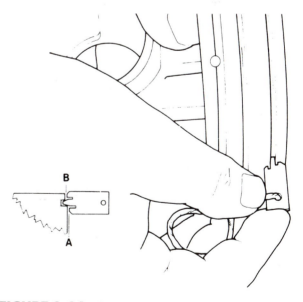

FIGURE 9–14 *Checking a piston fire (top) ring groove for wear with the aid of special keystone gauges. If gauge shoulder contacts piston at position A or B, replace piston. (Courtesy of Detroit Diesel Corporation.)*

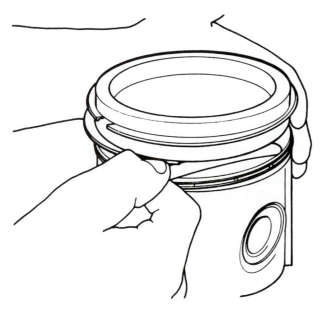

FIGURE 9-15 *Using a feeler gauge to measure and check piston ring side clearance. (Courtesy of Detroit Diesel Corporation.)*

should be made in the retainer with a chisel or punch; then insert a bar and pry the pin retainer from the piston. The pin can now easily be pushed from the piston and rod by hand. See also the retainer in Figure 9-3B for a 3176 Cat.

CAUTION Piston pins must never be driven from an aluminum piston without first heating the piston to approximately 200°F (93°C) in hot water. If this procedure is not followed, serious

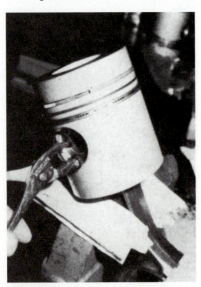

FIGURE 9-16 Removing piston pin retaining rings

damage to the piston may result. After the piston is heated, the piston pin can be tapped out using a driver and a hammer. Detroit Diesel iron pistons will not require heating and the piston pin can easily be pushed from the piston after removal of the piston pin retainers.

2.   After the piston has been removed from the connecting rod and if the piston is to be used again, it should be given a final cleaning in a commercial parts cleaner or a strong detergent and water. Many automotive machine shops use glass bead cleaning machines to clean pistons. This method is preferable if it is available.

3.   After final cleaning, the piston should be given a critical final inspection for cracks.

4.   Store pistons in a clean, dry area where they will be protected from dirt and possible damage until reassembly.

INSPECTING THE CONNECTING RODS

The connecting-rod bearings should be removed from the rod and rod cap in preparation for inspection. After removal of bearings the rod cap should be installed on the rod and cap bolts torqued to specifications. After torquing the cap, the rod should be checked as follows:

Measuring the Rod Small End Bore for Out-of-Roundness with a Snap Gauge and Outside Micrometer

1.   Place a snap or telescoping gauge into the rod bore and determine the bushing diameter (Figure 9-17).

2.   Remove the snap gauge and use the outside micrometer to measure the snap gauge size.

3.   This measurement is the bushing size expressed in thousandths of an inch.

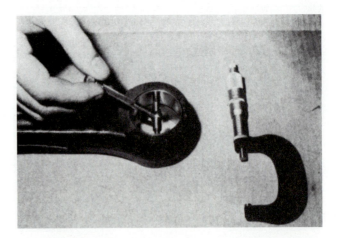

FIGURE 9-17 Measuring piston pin bushing in rod.

NOTE   Although measurement of the piston pin bushing is recommended by most manufacturers to determine if it is worn beyond reusable replacement limits, experience has proven that piston pin bushings should be replaced as a matter of practice during a major overhaul on a high-mileage or high-time engine. If piston bushings are not replaced during a major overhaul when a new piston, sleeve, and rings are installed, the load on the piston pin bushing will be increased and this may cause an old pin bushing to break up or wear excessively during engine break-in. In addition, if the pin bushing is not replaced, it may fail before the engine is due for another major overhaul.

Completing the Rod Inspection

The rod big end bore should be measured with a snap gauge and inside micrometer in the same manner that the small end bore was measured. If the rod big end bore does not meet specifications, it should be reconditioned or replaced.

NOTE   Major rod reconditioning, such as honing the big end bore or straightening, is generally not attempted in a general repair shop because this procedure requires special equipment.

If the rod big end bore passes the checks outlined above, the rod can then be checked for straightness using a rod alignment device (Figures 9-18 and 9-19). If the rod is not straight, it should be replaced or reconditioned.

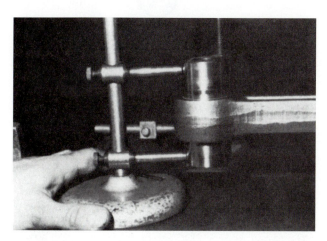

FIGURE 9–18 Checking connecting rod for straightness on a surface table with an adjustable pin and sled gauge using a piston pin or mandrel.

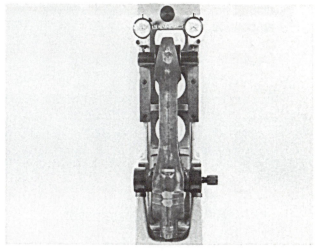

(A)

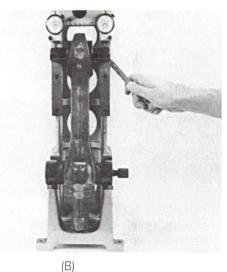

(B)

FIGURE 9–19 Using a special connecting-rod checker with two dial gauges to check for (A) bends and (B) twists in a connecting rod. (Courtesy of Cummins Engine Company, Inc.)

NOTE   Again, if the correct equipment is not available to straighten and check the rod for cracks using a magna-flux machine, the rod should be taken to a shop that specializes in this type of repair.

PISTON PIN INSPECTION

The piston pin should be measured with an outside micrometer at both ends and in the middle (Figure 9-20). The measurement should agree with the manufacturer's specifications. If not, the pin should be replaced.

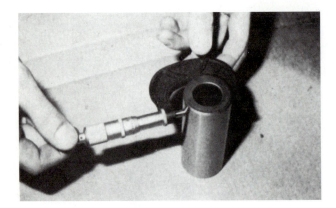

FIGURE 9–20 Piston pin measurement.

NOTE This check may be omitted if new sleeves and pistons are being installed, since most sleeve and piston kits contain a new piston pin.

FINAL ASSEMBLY OF PISTONS, PISTON RINGS, AND CONNECTING RODS

1. Install the piston on the rod by inserting the piston pin through the rod and piston. Then install the piston pin retainer rings.

NOTE The piston pin can be inserted through an aluminum piston very easily by hand if the piston has been preheated to 200°F (93°C) using hot water.

2. Install the piston pin retainers.

NOTE After driving piston pin retainers into Detroit Diesel trunk- or crosslead-type pistons, it is critical that an inspection be made to ensure that it will seal oil out of the combustion chamber. A special vacuum pump and adapter can be used for this purpose. Do not make only a visual inspection (Figure 9-21).

3. Using a rag or some other suitable protector for the rod, clamp the piston and connecting-rod assembly into a vise.

4. Allow the piston to rest on the vise jaws, in preparation for piston ring installation onto the piston.

5. Before installing the piston rings on the piston, it is good practice to check the rings in the cylinder for correct end gap.

(A)

(B)

FIGURE 9–21 (A) Installing a solid piston pin retainer into a two-stroke-cycle DDC engine piston; (B) using a hand-operated vacuum pump and gauge to check that the solid piston pin retainer is seated properly and will not leak. (Courtesy of Detroit Diesel Corporation.)

NOTE   Insufficient ring end gap will not allow the ring to expand when heated and may cause ring scuffing and scoring, resulting in compression loss, excessive blowby, and oil consumption.

6.   Insert rings vertically one at a time into the cylinder with the end gap up. Tip the ring into the horizontal position and place a piston without rings head first into cylinder bore, pushing it down onto the ring, leveling it.

7.   With a feeler gauge, measure the gap between the ends of the ring (Figure 9-22). The ring gap should be within specifications provided by the manufacturer. A general specification for the ring end gap is 0.004 in. (0.1 mm) for every 1 in. (25 mm) of cylinder diameter. If the ring gap does not meet specifications, check the ring set to ensure that the correct set is being used. All rings in the set should be checked as indicated above.

8.   Carefully read the instructions included with the piston rings before attempting to install them.

NOTE   Installation of piston rings on the piston is a very important step and allows no room for error. Follow instructions to the letter in this critical area.

9.   The following instructions are general but are very similar to the instructions included with most ring sets.

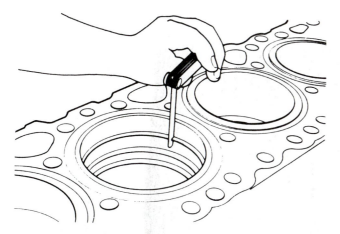

FIGURE 9–22 *Measuring piston ring gap with a feeler gauge after installing the rings into the cylinder and squaring them up with a piston inserted upside down. (Courtesy of Detroit Diesel Corporation.)*

a.   With the piston and rod assembly clamped in a vise, place the oil ring expander (if used) (Figure 9-23) in the piston groove where the oil ring will be installed.

CAUTION   On two-piece oil rings, do not allow the expander (a spring device that fits under the ring, holding it out against the cylinder wall) ends to overlap. This could cause broken rings or excessive oil consumption.

NOTE   Since the oil control ring, or rings, is the ring nearest the bottom of the piston, it should be installed first. If the top rings were installed first, it would be impossible to install the lower rings unless they were installed from the bottom up. Although this can be done, most technicians prefer to install the rings on the piston starting with the lowest ring and working upward, installing the top ring last.

b.   Select the oil ring that fits into the lowest groove on the piston and carefully inspect it to determine which side goes up. This can be easily determined if the ring is marked with a dot or "top" (Figure 9-24). If the ring is not marked, refer to the installation instructions. Some oil rings may be tapered, with the taper installed to the top. Others may not have any taper or mark and can be installed either way.

c.   Place the ring in a ring installation tool. Expand the ring so that it will slide down over the piston easily and install it over the ring

FIGURE 9–23 *Installing ring expander.*

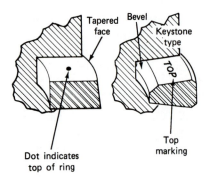

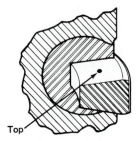

FIGURE 9-24 Typical ring markings.

expander. Place the ring end gap at a 90° angle from the expander butt joint.

CAUTION Do not expand the ring any more than is absolutely needed to slide it over the piston, as this may permanently warp, damage, or break the ring.

---

d. After installation of the oil ring, select and install the ring immediately above it, paying close attention to the top mark.

e. Continue installing the remaining rings, using the installation instructions as a reference, until all rings are installed.

This completes assembly of the piston, rings, and rod assembly. The assembly is now ready to be in-

FIGURE 9-26 Heavy-duty clamp piston ring compressor (Courtesy of Kent-Moore Division, SPX Corporation.)

FIGURE 9-25 Adjustable steel band clamp piston ring compressor for bore sizes in the range 2.125 to 5 in. (54 to 127 mm). (Courtesy of Kent-Moore Division, SPX Corporation.)

stalled in the engine. (See "Installing the Piston and Connecting-Rod Assembly.") If assembly is not to be installed in the engine immediately, it should be placed in a rack or in some suitable place so that no damage to rings or piston will result.

Installing the Piston and Connecting-Rod Assembly

Installation of the piston and rod assembly into the sleeve or cylinder bore requires a special tool called a ring compressor. The ring compressor is a device that fits around the piston and compresses the rings so that they may be inserted into the cylinder or sleeve without breakage or damage. Ring compressors are usually of the compression (Figure 9-25), clamp type (Figure 9-26), or tapered sleeve type (Figure 9-27).

A sleeve-type ring compressor resembles an engine sleeve but has a taper cut into one end. When the piston and rod assembly is inserted into the sleeve, the rings contact the taper and are compressed into position as the piston is pushed into the compressor. This type of ring compressor can be made for any engine by obtaining and machining a taper on one end of an old sleeve. This type of ring compressor is preferred

FIGURE 9–27 *Tapered-sleeve ring compressor. (Courtesy of Kent-Moore Division, SPX Corporation.)*

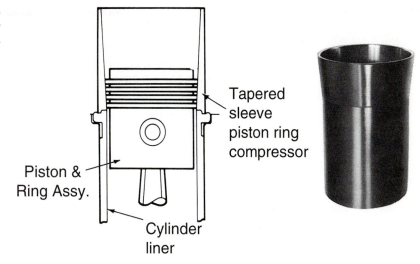

Tapered sleeve piston ring compressor

Piston & Ring Assy.

Cylinder liner

by many technicians, since it is easier to install on the piston and eliminates the possibility of ring breakage during piston installation into the cylinder. The primary disadvantage is that it will work for only one engine or cylinder size, requiring the technician who works on many engines to have a ring compressor for each one.

After selection of a ring compressor, the piston and rod assembly may be installed in the following steps:

1. With the piston and rod assembly clamped in the vise, remove the rod bolts and rod cap from the connecting rod.

2. Determine what size rod bearing must be used from earlier measurement of the crankshaft rod journal with a micrometer. Select and insert the bearing top half into the connecting rod, paying particular attention to the bearing locating lug and the slot in the connecting rod (Figure 9-28).

CAUTION   Make sure that a final check is made of the rod bearing insert to ensure that it is the correct size. Size markings are found on the back on the rod bearing insert. Standard-sized bearings may or may not be marked indicating their size: 0.010 in., 0.020 in. (0.25 mm, 0.50 mm).

3. Lubricate the rod bearing with engine oil or light grease.

4. Lubricate rings and pistons liberally with engine oil.

5. Position rings around piston so that the gaps do not line up. A common recommendation is to stagger ring gaps 90 to 180° apart around the piston (Figure 9-29).

NOTE   Positioning the rings in this manner will prevent excessive blowby during the initial startup that would result if all the ring gaps were in line.

6. If a clamp or band ring compressor is to be used, expand it and place on the piston (Figure 9-30).

7. If a tapered sleeve ring compressor is being used, the piston and rod assembly must be removed from the vise and inserted into the sleeve compressor (Figure 9-31).

8. After installation of the ring compressor on the piston and rod assembly, it can now be inserted into the cylinder sleeve or cylinder bore; the rod number should face the camshaft on six-cylinder engines and the outside of blocks on V8 engines. The rods are numbered to indicate which cylinder they fit into.

FIGURE 9–28 *Aligning bearing lug with slot in engine block or connecting rod. (Courtesy of Clevite Industries, Inc.)*

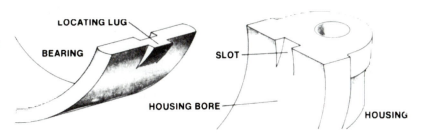

LOCATING LUG
BEARING
HOUSING BORE
SLOT
HOUSING

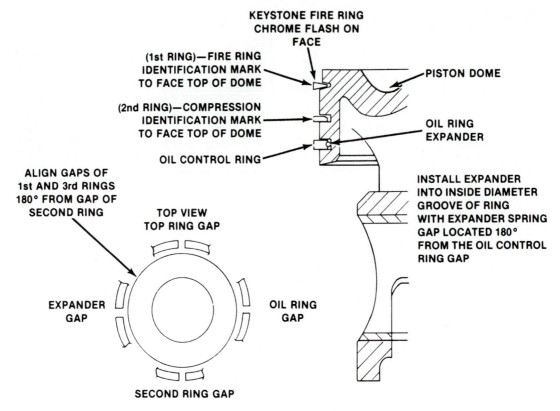

FIGURE 9–29 *Piston ring identification markings and individual location of the piston ring gaps during installation for a series 50 or 60 engine. (Courtesy of Detroit Diesel Corporation.)*

CAUTION   Before inserting the piston and rod assembly in the cylinder bore, the crankshaft should be positioned so that the rod journal of the pistons being installed is in the bottom deadcenter position.

NOTE   Some engine manufacturers (Detroit Diesel and Cat-3176) recommend installing the piston and rod assembly into the sleeve before the sleeve is installed into the block (Figure 9-32).

9.   Using a hammer handle, tap or push down on the piston, inserting it into the cylinder (Figure 9-30).

CAUTION   When pushing the piston into the cylinder, make sure that the rod is lined up with the rod journal. Failure to do this may result in damage to the rod journal by the rod. If the rod

bolts are in the rod, it is a good practice to put a plastic cap or piece of rubber hose on each bolt to protect the rod journal.

10.   After the piston and rod assembly is in place with the rod and bearing firmly seated on the rod journal, the rod bearing clearance should be checked using Plastigage (Figure 8-28).

NOTE   Plastigage is thin plastic thread that can be broken into the correct length and placed on the rod journal or in the rod cap on the bearing. When the rod cap is installed and torqued, the plastic thread is flattened out to the clearance between the rod journal and rod bearing. The cap is then removed, and the width of the Plastigage compared to various widths pictured on the package that contained the Plastigage. By this comparison the rod bearing clearance can be determined. Carefully clean the Plastigage from the rod journal and bearing.

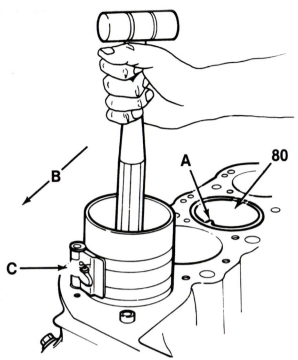

80. Piston
A. "Front" Mark
B. Front of Engine
C. Piston Ring Compressor Tool   W-00508

FIGURE 9–30 *Using a hammer handle to push the piston assembly down into the cylinder bore and free of the piston ring compressor band. (Courtesy of GMC Trucks.)*

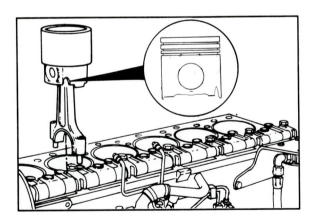

FIGURE 9–31 *Preparing to install the piston and installed ring compressor into the engine cylinder liner bore. Make sure that the numbered side of the connecting rod is facing the correct side of the engine block. (Courtesy of Cummins Engine Company, Inc.)*

FIGURE 9–32 *Piston and sleeve assembly ready for installation. (Courtesy of Detroit Diesel Corporation.)*

11. Lubricate the rod bearing with the lubricant recommended by the manufacturer and install the rod cap, making sure that the number on the rod and cap match and are on the same side (Figure 9-33).

12. Torque the rod cap bolts to specifications and, if used, lock the lock plates. Then with a feeler gauge, check for the correct rod side clearance between the connecting rod and the crank journal flange. *Turn the crankshaft after each rod and piston assembly has been installed to make sure that it moves freely.* If the crankshaft does not turn after torquing the rod cap, recheck the rod for alignment-bearing clearance and rod side clearance to determine the problem. Install all rods and rod caps in the same manner, as described above. Install liner retainer clamps on top of the block to prevent possible liner movement when turning the crankshaft!

Recheck all rod torques and numbers, making sure that rods and pistons are in the correct cylinders

FIGURE 9–33 *Rod markings (match marks).*

and rod caps are matched to the correct rod. After this final check the engine is ready for further assembly.

SUMMARY

This chapter has covered the correct procedures for removing, checking, cleaning, and reassembling pistons, connecting rods, and piston rings. If you have any further questions concerning the piston and connecting-rod assembly, consult the engine service manual or your instructor.

SELF-TEST QUESTIONS

1. Describe the major purpose of a piston.
2. A trunk-type piston is a
   a. one-piece assembly
   b. two-piece assembly
3. Many heavy-duty high-speed engines in use today employ two-piece pistons. What are they called?
4. Technician A says that a trunk-type piston exerts less side thrust on the piston rings and cylinder wall than does a two-piece piston design. Technician B says that the two-piece piston design accomplishes this much better. Which technician understands piston design better?
5. List the advantages of a two-piece piston design over a single-piece design.
6. Technician A says that some aluminum alloy pistons are ground in an elliptical or barrel shape to provide a better piston-to-liner fit. Technician B says that this would lead to excessive ring blowby and piston slap when the engine was at normal operating temperature. Which technician understands the concept better?
7. The top of the piston is usually referred to as the
   a. crown
   b. skirt
   c. slipper bearing
   d. boss area
8. Aluminum alloy pistons normally employ a Ni-resist insert at the top and sometimes the second ring belt area. Describe this material and state the reason for its use.
9. Technician A states that when two-piece piston assemblies are used the crown is manufactured from a forged aluminum alloy to allow for greater expansion and better sealing, while the skirt is made from forged steel. Technician B says the reverse: the crown is steel and the skirt is aluminum alloy. Which technician is correct?
10. True or False: Since aluminum weighs approximately one-third that of cast iron and steel, an aluminum piston would be one-third of the weight of an equivalent steel model.
11. High-speed heavy-duty direct injection diesel engines normally employ pressurized under-piston lube oil cooling, according to technician A. Technician B says that this would result in unacceptable lube oil temperatures; therefore, an air intake system aftercooler is used instead. Which technician knows basic engine design theory better?
12. The letters SCFR mean that a piston, in addition to being manufactured from aluminum alloy, is
    a. special chrome ferrous-reinforced
    b. squeeze-cast fiber-reinforced
13. The advantage of using SCFR in the manufacture of a piston is to
    a. improve fatigue strength
    b. provide better piston-to-liner clearance
    c. provide longer piston ring life
    d. improve piston scuffing characteristics
14. One of the coatings that is sometimes used on pearlitic malleable iron piston skirts to improve scuff resistance is
    a. tin
    b. solder
    c. chrome
    d. copper
15. One of the coatings sometimes used on aluminum alloy piston skirts to improve scuff resistance is
    a. graphite
    b. tin
    c. solder
    d. powdered cast iron
16. True or False: Two-piece pistons generally have a piston pin bearing that is referred to as a slipper bearing.
17. Current high-speed heavy-duty diesel engines tend to employ a piston crown that is shaped similar to a
    a. saucer
    b. Mexican hat (concave)
    c. bowl-in-crown
18. List the advantages of using the piston design selected in your answer for Question 17.
19. Some heavy-duty high-speed diesel engines use a piston crown shape that is known as a *reentrant chamber*. What are the advantages of this design?
20. Technician A says that a piston crown with a quiescent combustion chamber shape does not impart a suitable swirling action to the air for use in high-speed engines. Technician B says that the quiescent design is most often used in slower running engines which operate with a large quantity of excess air. Are both technicians correct in their statements?
21. Technician A says that the average operating temperature in the center of the piston crown of a heavy-duty high-speed diesel engine is in the range of 475 to 600°F (246 to 315°C). Technician B says that the temperature has to be higher than this and suggests that it is closer to 1000 to 1200°F (538 to 649°C). Which technician is closer to reality?
22. True or False: The thermal (heat) conductivity of steel is slower than that of aluminum; consequently, a higher cooling oil flow is required to prevent oil aging when a steel crown is used.

23. True or False: Some very-high-output-horsepower high-speed diesel engines employ ceramic-coated piston crown assemblies.

24. The most widely used design of piston pin in high-speed heavy-duty diesel engines is
    a. semifloating
    b. fixed
    c. fully floating

25. True or False: A hollow piston pin is more widely used than a solid pin.

26. Piston pin retainers are generally of what type?

27. Technician A says that two-stroke-cycle DDC engines employ solid piston pin retainers because the oil control rings are located toward the base of the piston skirt. Technician B says the solid retainers are strictly to prevent the fully floating piston pin from striking the ports in the cylinder liner. Which technician knows theory better?

28. Technician A says that piston crowns tend to be manufactured with a taper that increases toward the top of the piston. Technician B disagrees, saying that only the piston skirt is tapered to allow for expansion. Which technician is correct?

29. True or False: Prior to removing a piston from the cylinder, you may have to use a ridge reamer.

30. Failure to perform the task in Question 29 can lead to damage of the piston, particularly in what area?

31. True or False: Pistons should always be identified as to cylinder number to ensure they will be replaced in the same position.

32. Technician A says that the best way to clean a piston of carbon at overhaul is to glass bead the complete assembly. Technician B disagrees, saying that this procedure would remove any protective coating from the piston skirt and should be avoided. Technician B says crushed walnut shells in a glass-bead-type machine are better for cleaning carbon from the piston ring belt area. Which technician is correct?

33. Technician A says that careful inspection of the injector spray pattern on the crown of the piston can indicate plugged nozzle orifices or injector overspray. Technician B says that you have to remove and test the injector to confirm any nozzle wear. Which technician is correct?

34. Aluminum alloy pistons employing fully floating piston pins should be preheated to facilitate piston pin hand insertion or removal, according to technician A. Technician B disagrees, saying that the pin should be pressed or hammered in or out. Which technician is correct?

35. True or False: The term *fire ring* in relation to a piston ring means that it is the top ring on the piston.

36. True or False: The purpose of placing the top ring very close to the piston crown on high-speed heavy-duty engines is to reduce the dead air space that exists with lower-positioned rings. This results in more effective combustion.

37. True or False: Piston rings should always be removed using a special piston ring expander.

38. Most high-speed heavy-duty diesel engines now employ rings shaped in a
    a. keystone design
    b. rectangular design
    c. square design
    d. bevel-faced design

39. The advantage of using the ring in your answer to Question 38 is that it tends to minimize
    a. combustion gas blowby
    b. ring sticking
    c. pumping oil
    d. ring scuffing

40. The ring in your answer to Question 38 generally has sides that are
    a. flat
    b. oval
    c. tapered
    d. convex

41. True or False: Aluminum alloy pistons can be checked for cracks by using a magnetic particle detection procedure.

42. True or False: Forged steel piston crowns can be checked for cracks only by using a dye penetrant method.

43. Technician A says that all piston rings have a free diameter that is greater than the cylinder bore. Technician B says that this is not true; the rings would not fit into the cylinder when assembled onto the piston. Which technician is correct?

44. Name the two main piston ring clearances.

45. Piston ring wear groove gauges are generally used to check the following design of piston ring:
    a. Square
    b. Rectangular
    c. Bevel faced
    d. Keystone

46. An insufficient piston ring gap can result in
    a. ring breakage
    b. combustion blowby
    c. piston land damage
    d. scoring of the liner
    e. all of the above

47. True or False: Insufficient piston ring side clearance can result in ring sticking.

48. True or False: A prestressed piston ring results in lower overall ring stress and a more rugged piston ring.

49. To offer scuff and corrosion resistance, top piston rings are generally coated with
    a. molybdenum
    b. chrome
    c. graphite
    d. nickel

50. Technician A says that during piston ring installation, you must look for a dot, part number, the word *top*, or

a black phosphate coating to determine how to install the ring. Technician B says that the ring can be installed in any direction without any problems. Which technician is correct?

51. Technician A says that to inspect for piston ring damage on a two-cycle engine, you can remove the block air box inspection covers. Technician B says that you need to pull out the piston assembly to determine this. Who is correct?

52. True or False: Cylinder combustion gas pressures are the same on all piston rings during engine operation.

53. A *high modulus of elasticity* is a desired feature on a piston ring. What does this term mean?

54. Technician A says that the purpose of an oil control ring is to prevent oil from being burned in the combustion chamber. Technician B says that it is designed to distribute oil across the face of the cylinder wall on the upstroke and to scrape it off on the downstroke. Which technician is correct?

55. Name two commonly used types of oil ring expanders.

56. What condition is most likely to cause very early ring failure after a rebuild resulting in low compression, hard starting, and burning of oil?
    a. Dust-out through unfiltered air
    b. Use of the wrong grade of oil
    c. Insufficient ring gap
    d. Too much ring gap

57. Using the wrong grade of oil and light-load operation after new piston rings have been installed will usually result in
    a. cylinder liner glazing
    b. stuck rings
    c. broken rings
    d. siezed pistons and liners

58. List the causes that might lead to surface scuffing of the piston ring and cylinder liner.

59. When checking piston rings to determine the difference between a cold- and a hot-stuck condition, what features should you look for?

60. Technician A says that piston rings must be staggered around the piston so that their gaps are not aligned. Technician B says that since the rings rotate during engine operation, it doesn't matter where you place the individual ring gaps. Which technician is better trained?

61. Technician A says that on some pistons the design of the crown makes it necessary that the piston be installed facing in only one direction. Technician B says that pistons can be installed in any position. Which technician is correct?

62. Technician A says that the cylinder liner must be installed into the block bore before the piston and rings can be installed. Technician B says that on many engines the piston and liner can be installed as a complete assembly. Which technician is correct?

63. True or False: All connecting rods are designed to trans-

mit the reciprocating or straight-line motion at the piston to rotary motion at the crankshaft.

64. True or False: On four-stroke-cycle engines during the compression and power strokes, the rod is placed under tension, while during the last part of the exhaust stroke and the beginning of the intake stroke, the rod is placed under the forces of compression.

65. True or False: On two-stroke-cycle engines, the con-rod is less highly stressed than in a four-cycle engine.

66. List the two types of con-rods that are widely used in high-speed diesel engines.

67. What is the purpose of rifle-drilling some connecting rods?

68. True or False: Technician A says that all con-rods are balanced, so you should never mix the caps and rods on an engine. Technician B says that since all rods are balanced, it wouldn't make any difference. Who is correct?

69. Con-rods are generally manufactured from a single forging. What metals are used in their construction?

70. What alphabetical letter would best describe the cross-sectional shape of a typical con-rod?
    a. I-beam
    b. H-beam
    c. O-section
    d. A-beam

71. Steel used in bridge construction usually has a built-in safety factor of 5. What is the safety factor in a con-rod?

72. Technician A says that bolts used with con-rods are normally grade 5 or 6. Technician B says that grade 8 or higher should always be used. Which technician is correct?

73. True or False: Rod bolts or nuts should be replaced automatically at each major overhaul.

74. Dark spots in the bearing cap or saddle area of a con-rod are usually indications of
    a. bearing movement
    b. poor bearing contact
    c. insufficient bearing-to-journal clearance
    d. too much bearing-to-journal clearance

75. Shiny areas at the parting line of the con-rod cap to rod are indicative of
    a. cap movement
    b. bearing movement
    c. insufficient bearing clearance
    d. too much bearing clearance

76. True or False: All con-rods are subjected to stretch during engine operation; therefore, if the rod cap bore end is tapered or oval, the rod should be replaced.

77. Rehoning of a con-rod on a power honing machine at overhaul involves what specific steps to recondition it, particularly at the crankshaft journal end?

78. If a con-rod is honed at its crank journal end, does this have any effect on the compression ratio in that cylinder?

79. If con-rods are honed at overhaul, does this action have any effect on the weight of the finished product and therefore the balance of the other con-rods?

80. List the procedure(s) that can be used at the time of overhaul to determine if a con-rod is twisted or bent.

81. One of the more common conditions that leads to bending of a con-rod is
    a. a hydrostatic lock (water in the cylinder)
    b. overspeeding of the engine
    c. uneven cylinder balance
    d. trapped fuel or oil in the cylinder

82. What might cause the condition to the answer you chose in Question 81?

83. Con-rods can be checked for cracks at inspection or rebuilt by using what type of nondestructive testing procedure?

84. Technician A says that minor nicks or burns on the con-rod can be relieved by grinding to produce proper blending of the ground area to form a smooth surface. Technician B says that the con-rod should be discarded if any such irregularities are discovered. Which technician is correct?

85. Most diesel engines use bushings in the piston pin bore area of the con-rod that are replaceable. If no bushing is used, are oversized pins available?

86. Technician A says that the top and bottom bearing of the con-rod are identical. Not so, says technician B, and if the wrong bearing is used, the oil hole through the rifle-drilled con-rod can be blocked. Is there any validity in technician B's statement of concern?

87. True or False: Con-rod bearings can be identified in regard to size and position by etched or stamped numbers on the backside.

88. What gauge should you use to check con-rod bearing clearances?

89. True or False: When installing con-rods and pistons into an engine cylinder, the numbered sides of the rod and cap should always face one another.

90. Technician A says that once a con-rod has been installed over the crankshaft journal and its bolts have been torqued to spec, you should always check the rod side clearance with a feeler gauge. Technician B says that as long as the engine crankshaft can be rotated manually, this check is not necessary. Which technician is correct?

91. In V-type engines where two con-rods are located on one journal, a lack of side clearance between the rods could be caused by
    a. bent rods
    b. twisted rods
    c. one rod installed backward on the journal

92. Technician A says that the numbers on the con-rod of an inline engine are usually designed to face a specific side of the engine block, such as the camshaft or oil cooler side. Technician B says the way the numbers face makes no difference. Which technician is correct, and why?

93. In engines using two-piece crosshead or articulated pistons, the con-rod has an open saddle at the piston pin end. How are the piston and pin attached to the rod?

94. True or False: Main bearing wear results in oil starvation of the con-rod bearings.

95. Technician A says that if the crankshaft con-rod journals are in need of regrinding to a smaller diameter, the main bearing journals also have to be reground to the same size. Not so says technician B; only the rod journals need to be reground. Which technician is correct?

96. True or False: A properly fitted and operating con-rod shell bearing usually appears dull gray in color after a reasonable period of service.

97. Technician A says that a con-rod bearing noise is generally more noticeable when the engine is unloaded; technician B says the noise is more noticeable when the engine is loaded. Who is correct?

10 Camshaft, Cam Followers, Pushrods, Rocker Arms, and Timing Gear Train

OVERVIEW

This chapter describes the components required to activate the intake and exhaust valves, as well as the fuel injector assembly. Service and repair tasks are described and highlighted. This knowledge provides a detailed understanding of valve timing, and how incorrect valve timing can affect engine performance.

SYSTEM STRUCTURE AND FUNCTION

During engine operation the camshaft (a long shaft with cams on it), cam followers, pushrods, and timing gears (Figure 10-1) work together to open and close the intake and exhaust valves. As the valves open and close, intake air is admitted into the cylinder on the intake stroke and exhaust gases are allowed to move out of the cylinder on the exhaust stroke, allowing the engine to breathe. In addition to providing the mechanism to operate the valves, the camshaft and timing gear train may also be utilized to operate the fuel transfer pump (sometimes called a lift pump), injection pump, and the engine oil pump. The enblock camshaft shown in Figure 10-1 fits into the engine block in bores (drilled holes) fitted with sleeve-type bearings or is mounted in bearing supports on top of the cylinder head (overhead camshaft engines; Figure 10-2). Lubrication is provided by splash in some engines, while in others it is provided to the cam bushings or bearings under pressure from the oil pump.

The camshaft in a diesel engine is used to operate the intake and exhaust valves. In most diesel engines this camshaft will have two lobes per cylinder to operate the intake and exhaust valves.

NOTE On unit injector engines such as Detroit Diesel, Cat, Volvo, and Cummins, an additional lobe or cam on the camshaft is used to operate the injector. In these engines the camshaft will have three lobes per cylinder, as in Figure 10-3, which illustrates an overhead camshaft design.

Working with the camshaft to operate the valves are:

1. Cam followers. Sleevelike plungers that fit into bored holes in the block and ride on the camshaft. They are also called lifters (Figure 10-4).

2. Pushrods. Long, hollow, or solid rods that fit into the cam followers on one end with the other end fitting into a ball socket arrangement on the rocker arm (Figure 10-4).

3. Rocker arms and rocker arm shaft (Figure 10-5). The rocker arms provide the pivot point between the pushrod and valve or injector. Generally mounted on a shaft that is supported by brackets bolted to the cylinder head, the rocker arms are pushed up on one end by the pushrod and rock on the shaft much like a lever. The opposite end pushes the valve down against the spring pressure, allowing air into the cylinder or exhaust gases out. Most rocker arms have an adjusting screw and locknut that are used to adjust the clearance from rocker arm to valve (tappet).

The power required to turn the camshaft and operate the valves is supplied by the crankshaft through the timing gear train. The time when the valves open and close is called valve timing and is controlled by

FIGURE 10–1 (A) Typical location of an in-block camshaft design for an L10 model engine showing its drive gear in relation to the engine gear train; (B) flat follower, pushrod, and rocker arm assembly used with an in-block camshaft design. (Courtesy of Cummins Engine Company, Inc.)

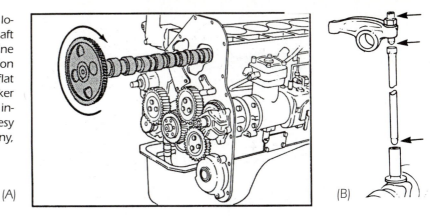

(A)

(B)

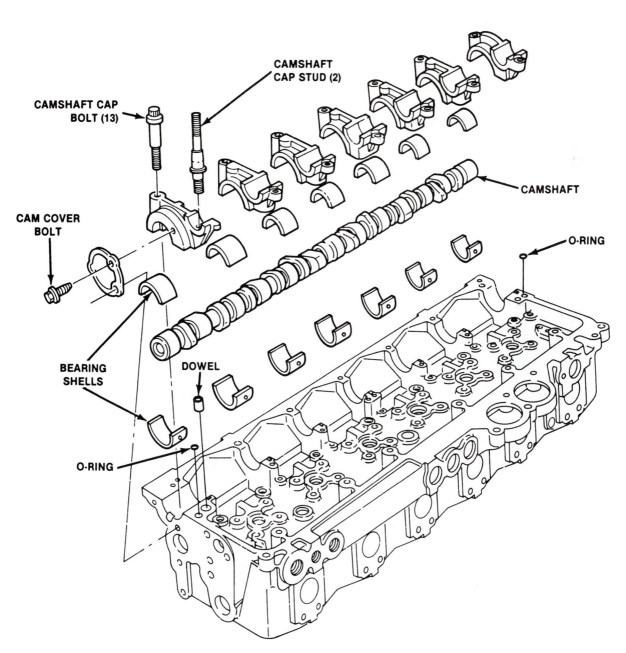

FIGURE 10–2 Series 60 Detroit Diesel overhead camshaft bearing arrangement. (Courtesy of Detroit Diesel Corporation.)

185

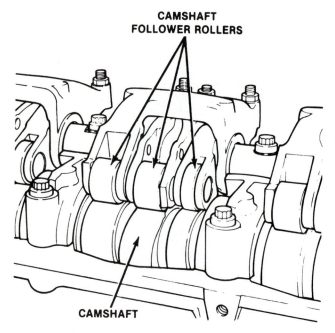

CAMSHAFT FOLLOWER ROLLERS

CAMSHAFT

FIGURE 10–3 Close-up showing the series 50 and 60 overhead camshaft design and the roller followers. The two outer ones operate the intake and exhaust valves, while the center roller follower operates the unit injector. (Courtesy of Detroit Diesel Corporation.)

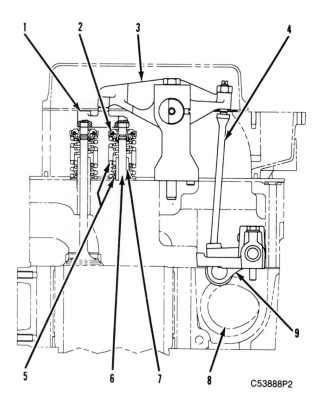

FIGURE 10–4 Cat model 3176 engine valve operating mechanism. 1, Intake bridge; 2, rotocoil; 3, intake rocker arm; 4, pushrod; 5, valve springs (inner and outer); 6, intake valves; 7, valve guide; 8, camshaft; 9, lifter. (Courtesy of Caterpillar, Inc.)

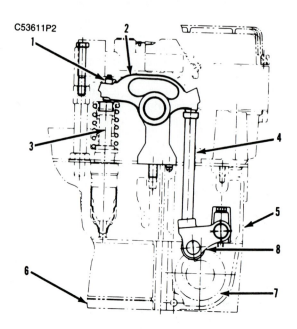

C53611P2

FIGURE 10–5 Cat model 3176 engine electronically controlled, but mechanically actuated, unit injector operating mechanism. 1, Adjusting nut; 2, rocker arm assembly; 3, electronically controlled unit injector; 4, pushrod; 5, cylinder head; 6, spacer block; 7, camshaft; 8, lifter. (Courtesy of Caterpillar, Inc.)

the timing gears (the cam lobes and their placement on the camshaft). This valve timing becomes a very critical part of the engine design, since engine fuel efficiency, power, and smooth operation are dependent upon it. Since valve timing does play a very important part in the operation of the engine, all component parts related to it must be checked as follows during an engine overhaul.

CAMSHAFT CLEANING AND INSPECTION

It is assumed at this time that the camshaft has been removed. If not, refer to Chapter 6. Since the camshaft is an internal engine part that constantly runs in lubricating oil within the engine, it does not require much cleanup. Generally, it can be cleaned by rinsing it in a cleaning solvent of the type used in a shop cleaning tank or by steaming with a steam cleaner.

NOTE If the camshaft has oil galleries or oil passageways, clean them with a wire brush and compressed air.

After cleaning, blow dry with compressed air. Then visually inspect the shaft, cam lobes, and bearing surfaces. This visual inspection must include the following:

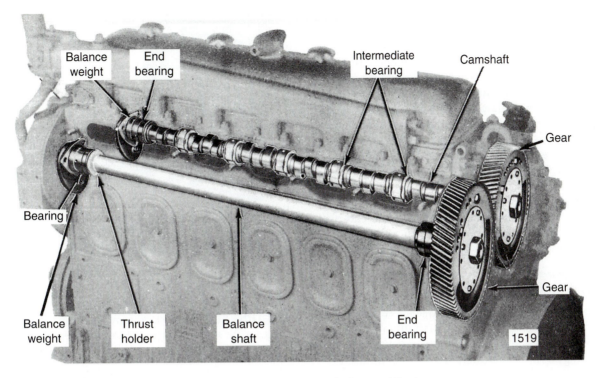

FIGURE 10–6 *Location of the camshaft and the balance shaft assemblies in a series 6-71 model two-stroke-cycle engine. (Courtesy of Detroit Diesel Corporation.)*

1. Inspection of the cam lobes for pitting, scoring, or wear
2. Inspection of cam bearing journals for scoring, bluing, or wear
3. Inspection of cam drive gear keyway for cracks or distortion

---

NOTE Detroit Diesel two-cycle engines use a unique camshaft-bearing (bushing) arrangement (Figure 10-6) made up of two bearing halves that when fitted together around the camshaft journal make up the camshaft bearing. Holding the bearing together until it and the camshaft are installed into the block is a spring ring. After installation in the block, the bearing is secured with a setscrew. See the engine repair manual or consult your instructor for correct removal procedures.

If the camshaft does not pass this visual inspection, it must be discarded and replaced with a new one. If the camshaft does pass visual inspection, it must be inspected further, using a micrometer to measure the cam lobes and bearing journals. Measure the cambearing journals as shown in Figure 10-7 using a micrometer and comparing the measurement to specifications supplied by the engine manufacturer. Since engine manufacturers recommend many different ways to check camshaft lobes, the service manual must be consulted

before making the cam lobe measurement. In addition, to perform an accurate check, you must have a thorough understanding of cam lobe design. Study the cam lobe shown in Figure 10-8 before making any checks.

Listed below are several procedures that can be used to check a cam lobe:

1. Measure with a micrometer from heel to toe

FIGURE 10–7 *Measuring cam bearing journals using an outside micrometer.*

with the outside micrometer to determine if the cam is worn sufficiently to affect lift. (Refer to specifications.)

2.   Measure with a micrometer at the base circle, then heel to toe, and subtract the base circle from the heel-toe measurement. This answer is called the cam lift.

3.   Measure the cam lobe for wear using a feeler gauge and piece of hard square stock slightly longer than the lobe width. Lay the stock across the cam lobe and attempt to insert the feeler gauge as shown (Figure 10-9). The cam lobe should not be worn in excess of 0.003 in. (0.076 mm).

4.   Measure the cam lobe from heel to toe and compare with specifications.

5.   Some engine manufacturers recommend placing the camshaft in V-blocks and using a dial indicator to check runout.

NOTE   If the equipment is not available to do step 5, a close check on the camshaft runout can be made by inserting the camshaft into its bore in the block. If the camshaft turns freely without binding, it can be assumed that it is straight.

When the foregoing checks have been completed and the camshaft is considered usable, closely check each lobe for roughness or burrs on the cam lobe surface. These small surface imperfections can be removed by sanding with a fine crocus cloth.

Inspecting With the Camshaft in the Engine

In some situations it may become necessary to check the cam lobe lift with the camshaft installed in the engine. This can be done by using a dial indicator in the following manner:

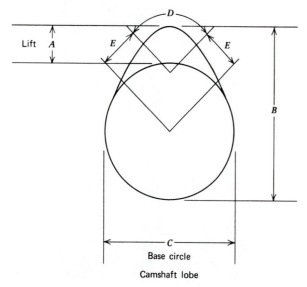

FIGURE 10–8   Camshaft lobe design. A = lift, B = lift + base circle dimension, C = base circle, D = nose, E = flank.

FIGURE 10-9   Checking cam lobes using a feeler gauge and square stock. (Courtesy of Detroit Diesel Corporation.)

1.   Remove the rocker arm assembly and place the dial indicator on the engine as shown in Figure 10-10, with the plunger of indicator on the pushrod.

2.   Turn the engine until the pushrod has bottomed (dial indicator will stop moving). This indicates that the cam follower is on the base circle or heel of the cam lobe. Zero the indicator at this point.

3.   Turn the engine until the dial indicator needle stops moving in one direction (clockwise, for example) and begins to move in the opposite direction. This indicates that the cam follower has moved up on the cam to the point of highest travel and is starting to drop off (or recede).

NOTE   It may be necessary to back the engine up for a quarter-turn and then turn it back in the direction of rotation to reestablish the point of maximum rise.

---

4.   Record the dial indicator travel from zero to maximum rise. This represents the cam lobe lift and should be compared to the manufacturer's specifications.

5.   If the cam lobe lift is less then the manufacturer's specifications, the camshaft must be replaced.

CAM FOLLOWER INSPECTION

As explained previously, the cam followers are round, sleeve-shaped devices that ride on the camshaft lobes in a bored guide hole in the block. The followers guide and support the pushrods.

FIGURE 10–10 *Measuring cam lobe lift with dial indicator. (Courtesy of Navistar International Transportation Corp.)*

NOTE Some cam followers have a roller attached to the end of the sleeve. This roller rolls on the camshaft lobes and aids in the reduction of friction (Figure 10-11).

Sleeve-type cam followers must be checked on the thrust face for pitting and scoring. Roller-type cam followers must be disassembled so that a check of the roller, roller bushing, and roller pin can be performed. Consult the engine repair manual before attempting to disassemble roller and pin from a cam follower. Most manufacturers recommend special procedures and fixtures for removal of the pin and roller. If this procedure is not followed, damage to the cam follower may result.

If roller bushing and pin are worn excessively or beyond the manufacturer's specifications, they should be replaced with new ones.

NOTE The foregoing procedures apply in general to overhead valve engines (those with pushrods and cam followers). Some diesel engines may have overhead camshaft arrangements. Engines with this type of arrangement will have different cam followers that require different checking procedures. The service manual must be consulted when working on these engines.

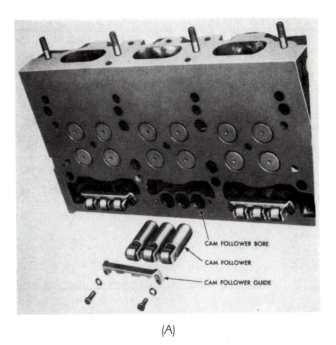

(A)

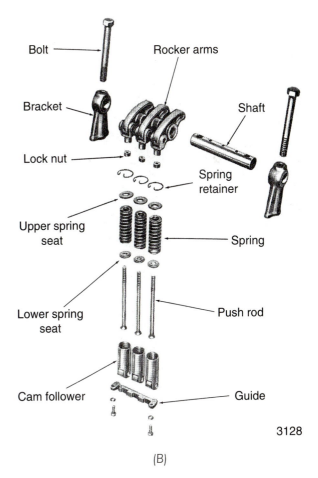

(B)

3128

FIGURE 10–11 *(A) Cam followers equipped with rollers; (B) valve and mechanical unit injector operating mechanism used on 53, 71, and 92 series DDC two-stroke-cycle engines. (Courtesy of Detroit Diesel Corporation.)*

PUSHROD INSPECTION

The long metal rod or tube that rides in the cam fol-lower and extends upward to the rocker arm is a very important part of the valve operating mechanism. In normal service very few problems are associated with the pushrod. Pushrod damage generally occurs when the rocker arms are incorrectly adjusted or the engine is overspeeded.

When the pushrods are removed as a result of en-gine service, they should be checked for the following:

- Straightness by rolling on a flat surface or with a straightedge
- Ball and socket wear, usually with a magnifying glass or as recommended by the manufacturer

NOTE   Hollow push tubes such as used by Cummins should be checked to determine if they are full of oil by tapping them lightly on a hard surface. A hollow sound should result. If not, the tube is full of oil and indicates that the ball pressed into the tube is loose. Replace the push tube if this condition is found.

ROCKER ARM INSPECTION

Rocker arms should be inspected and checked as out-lined in Chapter 7.

INSPECTION, REPLACEMENT, AND ASSEMBLY OF THE TIMING GEAR TRAIN

The timing gear train will include all gears that drive the camshaft and will generally be the crankshaft gear, idler gear, and camshaft gear (Figure 10-12). All the

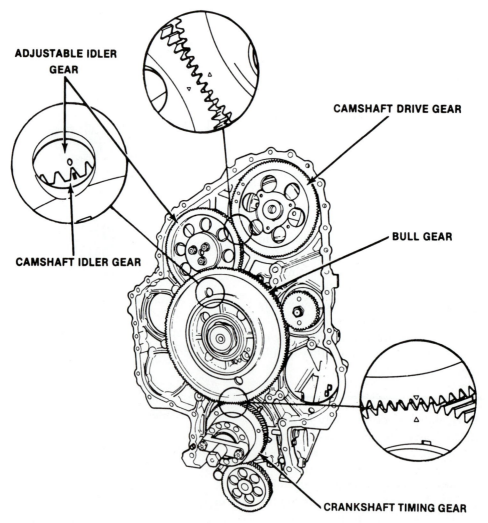

FIGURE 10–12   Timing gear train series 60 Detroit. (Courtesy of Detroit Diesel Corporation.)

gears in the timing gear train should be checked when the camshaft or cam gear is serviced, since any wear on an associated gear in the train may have an adverse effect on the camshaft gear and/or engine timing. In addition, worn gears may cause a knocking noise in the engine or fail after a few hours of operation.

Inspecting the Timing Gears
The timing gears should be visually inspected for the following:

- Chipped teeth
- Pitted teeth
- Burred teeth

NOTE   Often a close visual inspection of the timing gears will reveal a slight roll or lip on each gear tooth caused by wear. A gear worn with this type of wear should be replaced.

Removing the Camshaft Gear
If the camshaft gear is to be replaced, it must be removed from the camshaft using either a press or a puller. If a press is to be used, follow these general rules:

1. Make sure that the gear is supported on the center hub next to the shaft to prevent cracking or breaking.
2. Place a shaft protector on the end of the camshaft to protect the shaft.
3. Press shaft from gear (Figure 10-13).

FIGURE 10–13 *Pressing camshaft gear from camshaft.* (Courtesy of Detroit Diesel Corporation.)

CAUTION   Safety glasses should be worn when the press is being used, and the engine service manual should be checked to determine if any special pullers, supports, or procedures are to be used.

NOTE   If failure of the timing gear train has occurred, it is very important at this point to determine what may have caused it; for example, lack of lubrication, gear misalignment or overloading, wrong gear for the application, or normal wear. Make sure that you know what caused the failure before you reassemble the gear train.

Replacing the Camshaft Gear
Replacement of the camshaft gear on the camshaft requires strict attention to detail, because damage to the gear and camshaft may result if proper procedures are not followed. After consulting the engine service manual, the following general procedures must be followed when assembling the camshaft gear to the camshaft:

1. Install a new key in the camshaft keyway.

NOTE   Some engines may require offset keys to advance the camshaft timing. (Check your service manual carefully.)

2. Check and install the thrust plate or wear washer, if used. Some engines will not require a wear washer, since the back of the camshaft gear rides directly against the block.

NOTE   If not done previously, the thrust plate or wear washer should be checked for wear visually and with a micrometer.

3. If the gear is to be pressed on the shaft, apply grease to the end of the shaft.
4. Support the camshaft in an arbor press to prevent damage to the camshaft. This can be done by using two flat pieces of metal on the press table. Insert the camshaft between them until the shoulder of the camshaft rests firmly on them.
5. Set the gear on the shaft, paying close attention to alignment with a woodruff key.
6. Select a sleeve or piece of pipe that will fit over the shaft and place it on the gear.

NOTE   This sleeve or pipe must have an inside diameter at least 1/16 in. (1.58 mm) larger than the camshaft diameter.

7.   Press the gear onto the camshaft until the gear contacts the shoulder of the camshaft.

8.   If the gear is to be heated and then installed on the camshaft, the following procedure is to be followed:

NOTE   Heating of the gear is recommended by some engine manufacturers. Consult your service manual.

a.   Heat the camshaft gear to 300 to 400°F (150 to 200°C), using an oven or a heating torch.

NOTE   A 400°F Tempilstick may be used to check the gear temperature. If a Tempilstick is not available, a piece of soft solder of 50% lead and 50% tin melts at approximately 350 to 400°F (175 to 200°C) and can be used to check gear temperature. Touch the gear with the Tempilstick or solder to check the temperature.

b.   With a plier or tongs, place the gear on the camshaft. Tap slightly with a hammer to ensure that it is installed all the way onto the camshaft.

c.   Install the retaining nut, if used.

CAUTION   Gear should not be overheated and should be allowed to cool normally. *Do not* use cold water to cool the gear, as it may shrink the gear and cause it to break.

9.   When camshaft and gear are assembled, the camshaft can be inserted into the block and timing marks indexed or lined up (Figure 10-12).

NOTE   If camshaft bushings have not been replaced and are worn, refer to "Installing the Cam Bushing" in Chapter 6.

10.   Check timing gear backlash to ensure that the gears have the correct clearance between the gear teeth. Too little clearance will cause a whining noise, while too much clearance may cause a knocking noise.

NOTE   Two methods of checking gear backlash are acceptable: the dial indicator method and the feeler gauge method.

11.   If the dial indicator method is to be used, attach the dial indicator to the engine block by clamping or with magnetic base.

12.   Position the indicator plunger on a gear tooth and zero indicator.

13.   Rock the gear forward and back by hand, observing the dial indicator movement (Figure 10-14).

NOTE   Gear backlash is measured between mating gears only, so that one gear must remain stationary during checking.

14.   If the feeler gauge method is to be used in checking, select feeler ribbons of the correct thickness as indicated in the engine repair manual. If, after insertion of a correct-thickness feeler gauge, there is still gear backlash, the gears are worn excessively and must be replaced.

15.   After the camshaft and timing gears have been installed and all timing marks checked, recheck all retaining bolts for proper torque; lock all lock plates if used.

16.   If an oil slinger is used, install it on the crankshaft.

NOTE   It is a good practice at this point to review and check the oil supply system for the tim-

FIGURE 10-14   Gear backlash.

ing gears. Most engines lubricate the timing gear train with splash oil; others may employ pressure lubrication through a nozzle or oil passage. If a complete engine overhaul is being performed, all passageways should have been checked during block cleaning and inspection. *Double-check it now*, before the front cover is installed.

Installing the Front Timing Cover

When a final check has been made of the timing mark alignment, lock plates, bolt torques, and oil slinger installation, the engine is ready for installation of the front cover.

1. If not done previously, clean the cover thoroughly and remove the old crankshaft oil seal and cover gasket.

2. Install a new seal into the front cover using a seal driver (Figure 10-15).

3. Glue a new cover gasket onto the cover with a good gasket sealer.

NOTE On some engines the camshaft will have a retaining device of some type other than a plate that is bolted to the block to hold the camshaft in place. It may be a thrust plate in the cover or a spring-loaded plunger in the end of the camshaft. This (hold-in device) must be checked carefully before installation of the front cover for the proper adjustment or installation procedures.

---

4. Install the front cover, starting it onto the dowel pins (if used) and tapping in place. Install and tighten the bolts.

5. Install the vibration damper or front pulley in this manner:

FIGURE 10–15 *Installing front seal in front cover.*

a. Install the woodruff key in the crankshaft slot if used.

b. Start the damper or pulley on the shaft, making sure that the slot in the pulley lines up with the woodruff key in the crankshaft.

c. Install the retaining bolt with a washer into the end of the crankshaft and tighten, pulling the damper in place.

NOTE Some dampers may not slide onto the shaft far enough so that the retaining bolt can be started into the crankshaft. If this condition exists, a long bolt may be used to pull the damper in place.

CAUTION Do not drive on the damper with a hammer, as damage may result that would cause it to have excess runout or be out of balance.

---

6. Install all other components, such as water pump, alternator, and fan brackets.

SUMMARY

This chapter has presented a detailed explanation of cam lobe nomenclature and valve timing to assist you in understanding the function of the camshaft and timing gear train. In addition, information concerning camshaft, cam followers, pushrods, rocker arms, and timing gear train inspection and assembly has been provided to assist you in repair or replacement of the timing gears and camshaft components. If questions still exist concerning the procedures and recommendations, consult your instructor.

SELF-TEST QUESTIONS

1. Technician A says that camshafts on high-speed heavy-duty diesel engines are generally belt or chain driven. Technician B says that camshafts are gear driven on high-speed heavy-duty diesel engines. Who is correct?

2. Technician A says that the camshaft on electronically controlled unit injector diesel engines is only required to operate the intake and exhaust valves, since the injector is controlled from the ECM. Technician B disagrees, stating that the camshaft is needed to operate the injector plunger to create the high pressures required for injection. Which technician is correct?

3. Technician A says that the highest point on the camshaft is generally referred to as the *nose*; technician B says that it is called the *base circle*. Who is right?

4. True or False: A camshaft that is located within the engine block rather than in the cylinder head is known as an *overhead camshaft.*

5. List four high-speed heavy-duty diesel engines that employ an overhead camshaft design.

6. Which one of the four engines listed in question 5 employs a silicon nitride cam follower roller in its injector rocker arm assembly?

7. On a separate sheet of paper, list six advantages of using an overhead camshaft versus an in-block type.

8. Technician A says that the camshaft on a four-stroke-cycle engine is driven at half the speed of the crankshaft, while on a two-cycle engine it is driven at the same speed. Technician B disagrees, stating that the camshaft on the two-cycle must turn twice crankshaft speed since there is a power stroke every crankshaft revolution. Who is correct?

9. True or False: Many larger diesel engines employ segmented, or bolted together, camshaft sections.

10. Technician A says that on two-stroke-cycle DDC 71 and 92 engine models, only one camshaft is used to operate the valves and injectors, similar to that commonly found on V8 gasoline engines. Technician B disagrees, saying that each cylinder bank has its own camshaft assembly. Who is right here?

11. Technician A says that in addition to aligning the timing marks between the camshaft and idler or crankshaft gear, several major engine manufacturers use offset camshaft gear keys to allow specific camshaft timing arrangements. Technician B says that all camshaft gear keys are straight and that any camshaft timing advancement must be made by the engagement of the cam and crank gear timing marks. Who is correct?

12. What make and model of high-speed heavy-duty diesel engine can have its camshaft timing altered by adding or removing cam follower box gaskets?

13. In Question 12, technician A says that adding gaskets retards the camshaft timing, whereas removing gaskets advances the timing. Technician B says that A has this backwards; instead, adding gaskets advances timing, and removing gaskets retards the timing. Which technician is correct?

14. True or False: To alter the camshaft timing on a Cummins L10 or M11, you can add or remove cam follower box gaskets.

15. Technician A states that to check the camshaft timing on a Cummins N14, L10, M11, or K series engine you need to remove an injector and set up two dial indicator gauges so that both the piston travel and the injector pushrod travel can be monitored. Not so, says technician B; you only have to use one dial gauge to check the piston travel and compare its position with the marks on the accessory drive pulley at the front of the engine. Which technician knows the material best?

16. Technician A says there are no flywheel timing marks on two-cycle DDC engine models for timing reference purposes. Technician B says all engines need flywheel and/or pulley marks to allow for engine timing checks. Which technician knows the products better?

17. True or False: Most Caterpillar engines are equipped with a flywheel timing bolt that can be inserted to lock the engine at TDC for the No. 1 cylinder.

18. Technician A says that when an in-block camshaft lobe is suspected of being worn, you can check it by placing a dial indicator gauge on top of the valve spring retainer and setting the rocker arm for zero lash (or on the injector follower), rotating the engine over, and comparing the cam lift to specs. Technician B says that you need to remove the camshaft from the block to check its worn lobe condition. Who is correct?

19. Technician A says that to effectively clean a camshaft after removal, you should soak it in a hot tank of caustic solution. Technician B says that you should clean it with either diesel fuel or solvent and dry it with compressed air and lint-free rags. Who is correct?

20. Technician A says to quickly check a removed camshaft for individual lobe lift, place it between two vee blocks and employ a dial indicator. Technician B says place it into a metal lathe self-centering chuck and use a dial gauge. Are both technicians correct in their statements?

21. Technician A says that to replace the camshaft bushings on an in-block design, the engine needs to be completely disassembled. Technician B says that once the engine gear train or front cover has been removed, you can pull the camshaft and employ an expandable bearing (bushing) puller to replace them. Which technician is correct?

22. True or False: When replacing camshaft bushings, you can install them in any position without aligning locating notches.

23. Technician A says that camshaft end float must be checked in a manner similar to that used for a crankshaft. Technician B says that this isn't necessary, since the camshaft end play is controlled by the gear lash that exists between the various gears in mesh. Which technician is correct?

24. Technician A says that inline model two-stroke DDC engine models have a balance shaft driven from the oil pump drive gear. Technician B disagrees, saying that the balance shaft is located on the side of the block opposite the camshaft. Who is correct?

25. True or False: DDC two-cycle engines employ balance weights within the cam and balance shaft gears to produce a force that is equal and opposite to that developed by the uneven firing impulses of the pistons.

26. Which make of engine uses VS (valve set) timing marks located on the accessory drive pulley at the front of the engine and the letters A, B, and C?

27. Make a list of the items you would check on a flat or mushroom-type lifter (follower) at overhaul.

28. Make a list of the items you would inspect and check on a roller-type cam follower at overhaul.

29. List two methods for determining if a pushrod is bent.

Lubrication Systems and Lube Oil

OVERVIEW

It is important for the service technician to understand the types of lube oils that should be used in different engine makes and applications, recommended service requirements, and problems that can occur through neglect and poor maintenance practices. This chapter provides you with details of lube oils and systems, and the service/repair tasks needed to keep this important engine system trouble free.

LUBRICATION SYSTEM FUNCTION

Most diesel engine lubrication systems are similar to the one shown in Figure 11-1. The system is composed of oil galleries, oil cooler, oil filter, oil pump, and oil pan or oil sump.

The oil pan or sump will be filled with engine oil. This oil is supplied by the lubrication system throughout the engine to all points of lubrication during engine operation. Without this supply of oil the engine would quickly be destroyed.

The diesel engine lubrication system provides pressurized lubrication throughout the engine during operation to reduce friction. Other functions of the lube system are:

1. *Dissipate (get rid of) engine heat.* The heat generated by friction within the engine must be controlled to avoid engine damage.

2. *Clean; prevent rust and corrosion.* By-products of combustion (water, acids) must be removed from the engine by the lube system and lube oil so that parts such as pistons, rings, and bearings remain clean

throughout the engine life. In addition, the lube oil must prevent rust and corrosion from occurring, especially during long periods of engine shutdown.

3. *Provide a seal between the piston rings and cylinder wall or cylinder sleeve.* The piston and ring assembly would not be capable of providing a gas-tight seal without the aid of the lube oil provided by the lube system. Excessive blowby would result if this seal did not exist, resulting in the loss of compression and a poor-running engine.

4. *Absorb thrust or shock loads.* As the engine operates, many parts throughout the engine are subjected to shock- or thrust-type loads that must be absorbed or reduced to prevent engine noise and damage. An example of this would be the force exerted on the connecting rod journal by the connecting rod and piston assembly during the engine power stroke. At full load this force may be as much as 5000 psi (350 kg/cm^2). Without the cushioning effect of lube oil, the rod bearings would be destroyed quickly.

5. *Reduce friction.* The lube system reduces friction by providing and maintaining an oil film between all moving parts. The oil film between two sliding surfaces (such as the rod bearing and the crankshaft journal) has two characteristics that make us realize how very important the lubrication of engine parts is.

a. Oil molecules shaped like very small ball bearings slide over one another freely.

b. The oil molecules adhere to the bearing and crankshaft surfaces more readily than to each other.

Figure 11-2 shows the resulting effect. The top layer of oil molecules clings to the surface of the moving metal and moves with it. In so doing, it slides over

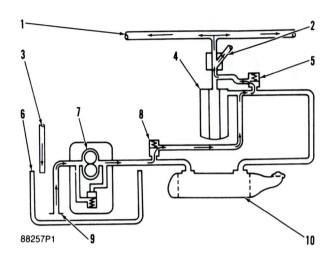

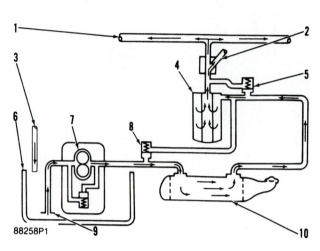

(A)

(B)

Flow Of Oil (Engine Cold)
(1) Oil manifold in cylinder block. (2) Oil supply line to turbocharger. (3) Oil return line from turbocharger. (4) Oil filter. (5) Bypass valve for the oil filter. (6) Oil pan. (7) Oil pump. (8) Bypass valve for the oil cooler. (9) Suction bell. (10) Oil cooler.

Flow Of Oil (Engine Warm)
(1) Oil manifold in cylinder block. (2) Oil supply line to turbocharger. (3) Oil return line from turbocharger. (4) Oil filter. (5) Bypass valve for the oil filter. (6) Oil pan. (7) Oil pump. (8) Bypass valve for the oil cooler. (9) Suction bell. (10) Oil cooler.

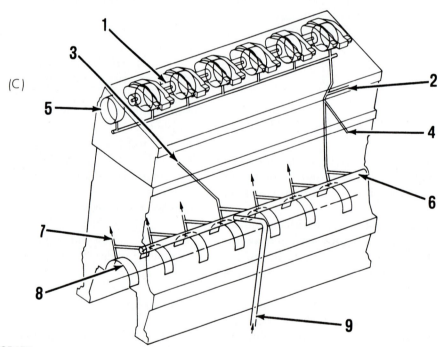

(C)

C57654P1

(c) Engine Oil Flow Schematic (1) Rocker arm shaft. (2) Oil passage to adjustable idler gear. (3) Oil passage to air compressor. (4) Oil passage to cluster idler gear. (5) Camshaft bearing journals. (6) Oil manifold. (7) Piston cooling passage. (8) Main bearings. (9) Oil passage from the oil filter.

FIGURE 11–1 Oil flow in a Cat 3406E engine model. (Courtesy of Caterpillar, Inc.)

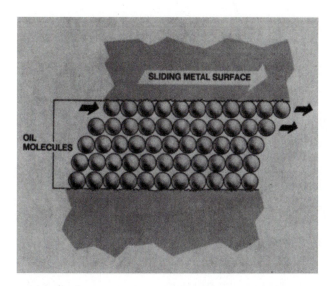

FIGURE 11–2 *Layers of oil molecules between two metal surfaces. (Courtesy of Clevite Industries, Inc.)*

the second layer of oil molecules to some degree, but does exert some drag that causes the second layer to move, but at a much slower rate. In like manner, the second layer slides over and drags the third layer at a slower speed. This continues through all the layers of oil molecules until the bottom layer is reached. The bottom layer clings to the stationary piece of metal and remains stationary. This action by the lubricant greatly reduces friction and increases bearing life.

SYSTEM DESIGN

The system must be designed to fulfill all the engine requirements for many hours of operation without failure. Three basic systems have been used in internal combustion engines over the years.

1. *Splash lubrication system.* This system utilizes the movement of engine parts to supply splash oil to all moving parts during engine operation. This type of system has many drawbacks, since lubrication is provided to those engine parts within the engine crankcase only. No pressure or flow is developed by which oil could be supplied to areas of the engine such as rocker arms or external engine accessories.

2. *Forced-feed lubrication system.* This system supplies oil to most of the engine rotating or rocking parts under pressure supplied by an oil pump. This oil pump is located within the engine crank-case on some engines, while on others it may be located externally. All pumps are driven by the engine timing gear train or camshaft. This type of system is used on many diesel engines.

3. *Full-force-feed lubrication system.* This system is very similar in design to the force-feed system, with the exception that it supplies oil through a rifle drilling

in the connecting rod to the piston pin and underside of the piston. This oil, sprayed on the underside of the piston head, aids in cooling, especially if the engine is turbocharged.

SYSTEM COMPONENTS

Lubrication system components vary greatly in design, but little difference exists between component function from engine to engine. A typical full-force-feed system will have the following components:

1. *Reservoir* (oil pan), generally located at the bottom of the engine to hold and collect engine oil. Oil is distributed to the various lubrication points from this pan by the oil pump.

2. *The pickup screen or suction strainer* (Figure 11-3), is located on the inlet side of the pump to prevent large dirt particles or other foreign material from entering the pump. This strainer in many engines is nothing more than fine metal screen; in others it may be a cloth or fabric strainer.

3. *Oil pump*, considered the heart of the lubrication system. A sufficient flow of oil to maintain oil pressure to all lubrication points must be supplied by this positive-displacement pump. Engine lube oil pumps for high-speed diesel engines are generally of two types:

    a. *External gear pumps* (Figure 11-4) are most commonly used. This pump consists of two meshed gears, one driving the other, a body or housing in which they are enclosed, and an inlet and outlet. As the gears are turned, oil is drawn in the inlet side and is carried in the space between the teeth and the pump housing. As the gears continue to turn, the oil is carried around to the outlet port of the pump and forced out by the meshing of the gear teeth.

    b. *Internal gear or crescent pumps* (Figure 11-5) are designed with one gear rotating inside another gear. The smaller gear drives the larger-diameter gear and is offset from the center of the large gear so that the gear teeth are in mesh. As the gears turn, oil is picked up and carried by the space between the large gear teeth. When the gears come into mesh, the oil is forced out the pump outlet by the intermeshing of gears.

NOTE   As the impeller turns, oil is trapped in the space between the vane and pump body. Continued turning forces the oil into a progressively

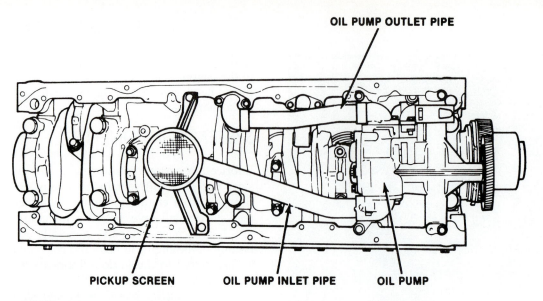

FIGURE 11–3 View of the underside of a series 60 four-stroke-cycle engine with the oil pan removed. Note the inlet and outlet pipes to and from the oil pump. (Courtesy of Detroit Diesel Corporation.)

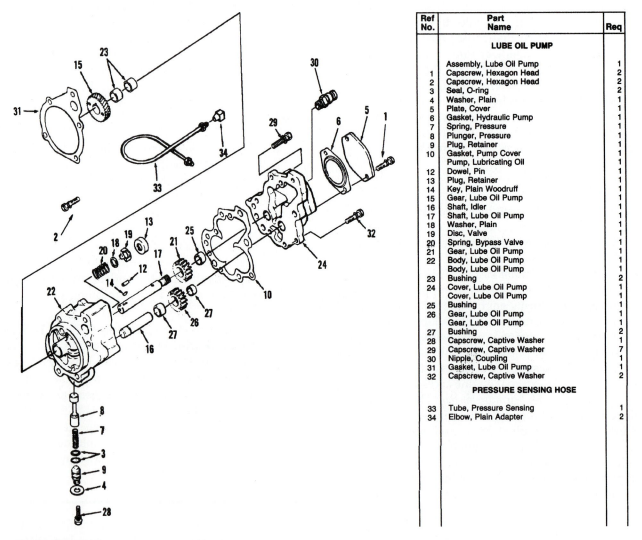

Ref No.	Part Name	Req
	LUBE OIL PUMP	
	Assembly, Lube Oil Pump	1
1	Capscrew, Hexagon Head	2
2	Capscrew, Hexagon Head	2
3	Seal, O-ring	2
4	Washer, Plain	1
5	Plate, Cover	1
6	Gasket, Hydraulic Pump	1
7	Spring, Pressure	1
8	Plunger, Pressure	1
9	Plug, Retainer	1
10	Gasket, Pump Cover	1
	Pump, Lubricating Oil	1
12	Dowel, Pin	1
13	Plug, Retainer	1
14	Key, Plain Woodruff	1
15	Gear, Lube Oil Pump	1
16	Shaft, Idler	1
17	Shaft, Lube Oil Pump	1
18	Washer, Plain	1
19	Disc, Valve	1
20	Spring, Bypass Valve	1
21	Gear, Lube Oil Pump	1
22	Body, Lube Oil Pump	1
	Body, Lube Oil Pump	1
23	Bushing	2
24	Cover, Lube Oil Pump	1
	Cover, Lube Oil Pump	1
25	Bushing	1
26	Gear, Lube Oil Pump	1
	Gear, Lube Oil Pump	1
27	Bushing	2
28	Capscrew, Captive Washer	1
29	Capscrew, Captive Washer	7
30	Nipple, Coupling	1
31	Gasket, Lube Oil Pump	1
32	Capscrew, Captive Washer	2
	PRESSURE SENSING HOSE	
33	Tube, Pressure Sensing	1
34	Elbow, Plain Adapter	2

FIGURE 11–4 Oil pump details for a Cummins N14 engine model. (Courtesy of Cummins Engine Company, Inc.)

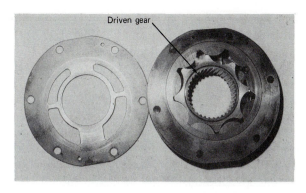

FIGURE 11–5 *Internal gear pump.*

smaller area and finally discharges it out of the pump outlet.

4. *Filters.* Oil filters generally are one of two common types: partial or full flow (Figure 11-6).

a. *Partial or bypass.* The partial flow filter, as the name implies, filters only a certain percentage of the oil (approximately 30 to 40%). It is connected to the engine oil gallery in such a manner that oil does not have to pass through the filter before entering the engine. In fact, oil flows through the filter and then back to the oil pump or oil pan. Most engine manufacturers no longer use this type of filter because of its low cleaning efficiency.

b. *Full flow.* Most modern diesel engines use the full-flow filter. In this filter all oil pumped by the oil pump must pass through the oil filter before it enters the engine oil gallery. Since 100% of the oil is filtered before it is used for lubrication, this filter's efficiency in dirt removal is much greater, resulting in its widespread use.

Either type of filter, partial or full flow, may be a shell and element type (Figure 11-6) with a replaceable element or a replaceable type of metal can (Figure 11-7) that has the element sealed into it, commonly referred to as a *spin-on* model. The replaceable cartridge for the element type may be constructed in one of two different ways:

a. Cotton waste (an absorbent or depth type of filter), which absorbs impurities in the oil.

b. Treated pleated paper (more common). The treated paper filter element is considered an adsorbent (or surface) type. It filters from the oil passing through it all dirt particles larger than the porous holes in the paper.

NOTE As the filter continues to catch dirt, it becomes more efficient, since the collection of dirt particles on its surface allows smaller and smaller particles to pass through it. Eventually, however, the filter becomes completely plugged and must be replaced with a new cartridge.

5. *Pressure regulator and bypass valves.* Pressure within the lubrication system must be regulated as the viscosity of the oil changes. Also, because of temperature changes, filters such as the full flow filter must have an automatic bypass system to prevent engine damage in the event that the filter becomes clogged.

Both of these requirements are fulfilled by both a pressure regulator valve and a bypass valve. Design of these valves may be one of two common types:

a. Ball (spring loaded)

b. Plunger (spring loaded) (Figure 11-6)

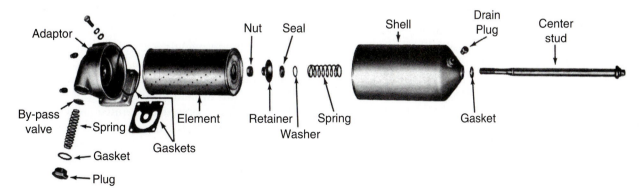

FIGURE 11–6 *Details of a full-flow oil filter of the shell and element type with a replaceable filter. Shell must be cleaned in solvent and dried at filter replacement. (Courtesy of Detroit Diesel Corporation.)*

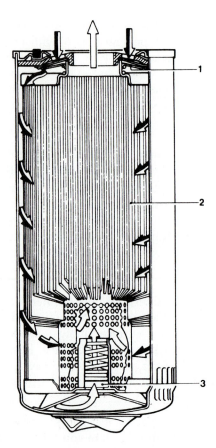

FIGURE 11-7 *Typical oil flow through a spin-on type of full-flow lube oil filter assembly. 1, Nonreturn valve; 2, treated and pleated paper element filter; 3, pressure relief valve which opens when the filter is plugged allowing oil to bypass the filter and enter the lube system unfiltered. (Courtesy of DAF Trucks, Eindhoven, The Netherlands.)*

The main job of the pressure-regulating valve is to prevent excessive oil pressure within the system; in a sense, it becomes a safety valve or limiting valve. Oil pumps are designed to maintain sufficient flow at normal engine temperature and speed. As a result, when oil temperature is low and viscosity is high, excess pressure will be developed. A regulating valve is then used to dump off the excess flow to maintain correct pressure.

Since most modern diesel engines have a full flow filter, a bypass valve is designed into the filter or filter base so that the engine receives a sufficient oil supply at all times in the event that a filter cartridge or element becomes plugged. This "safety device" is in the normally closed position during engine operation unless the filter becomes clogged.

6. *Oil coolers* (warmers). Oil coolers in many diesel engines are of the oil-to-water type. Coolers of this type resemble a small radiator enclosed in a hous-ing. Water is pumped around the copper core or element and oil is circulated through it (Figure 11-8).

In most situations during engine operation, the oil is hotter than the coolant water, resulting in heat transfer from oil to water, keeping the oil at a safe operating temperature. Normal oil temperature in most engines will be about 220 to 230°F (104 to 110°C).

Cooling is not the main job of the oil cooler at all times. During operation following a cold start, engine water will reach operating temperature much sooner than engine lube oil. In this situation the oil cooler warms the oil rather than cools it.

Supplementary Components

1. *Pressure gauge or indicator light.* The oil pressure gauge is calibrated in pounds per square inch (psi) or in kPa (kilopascal). It is used by the operator to determine if the engine oil pressure is correct. Pressure gauges can be one of two types:

a. *Mechanical.* The mechanical type (sometimes called the Bourdon type) (Figure 11-9) is connected to an oil pressure gallery by a tube that transmits the pressure to the gauge mounted on the operator's instrument panel.

b. *Electrical.* The electrical type (Figure 11-10) is made up of an indicating gauge (similar to the one used on the Bourdon tube), which is a wire and pressure-sending unit that is screwed into the engine oil gallery at a convenient takeoff port. Engine oil pressure pushing against the diaphragm in the sending unit moves a sliding wiper arm across a resistor (Figure 11-11), changing the resistance value of the sending unit, since the sending unit provides the ground for the gauge circuit. The amount of current passing through the gauge, which causes needle movement, will be determined by the amount of ground that the sending unit is providing.

Many modern engines employ an indicating light system in place of a pressure gauge. Making up the system are an indicator light, electrical wire, and sending unit. In this system, the sending unit inserted into the oil gallery is a pressure-operated switch that operates the lamp circuit. During engine shutdown with no oil pressure, the sending unit is closed, providing a ground for the lamp circuit. With the ignition switch in the ON position, power is supplied to the lamp to illuminate it. After the engine is started and oil pressure opens the sending unit by pushing against the diaphragm, the lamp circuit ground is lost and the light goes out, indicating to the operator that the engine has

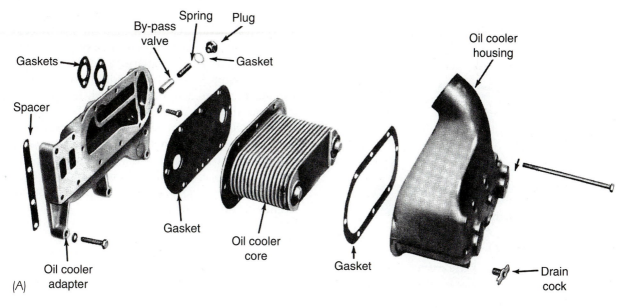

(A)

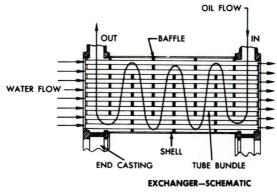

(B)

FIGURE 11–8 (A) Details of a plate oil cooler assembly; (B) typical lube oil flow through a tube oil cooler. (Courtesy of Detroit Diesel Corporation.)

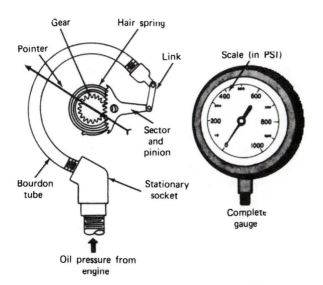

FIGURE 11–9 Bourdon oil pressure gauge. (Courtesy of Deere & Co.)

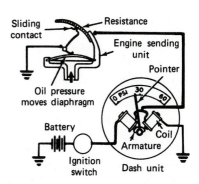

FIGURE 11–10 Electric oil pressure gauge. (Courtesy of Deere & Co.)

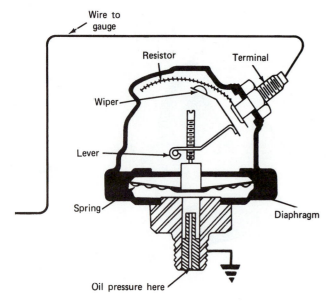

FIGURE 11-11 *Electrical sending unit.* (Courtesy of Deere & Co.)

oil pressure. This system has a built-in disadvantage in that it gives the operator no indication of the amount of oil pressure being developed.

2. *Dipstick.* The most simple and most widely used method of checking the oil in the crankcase is the dipstick. The dipstick is constructed of a long piece of flat steel that fits into a tube inserted into the engine oil pan from the top, allowing easy operator access.

ENGINE LUBE OIL

The lubrication system is not complete without lube oil. Lube oil is a petroleum product made up of carbon and hydrogen along with other additives to make a lubricant that can meet the specifications supplied by engine manufacturers. In general, diesel engine lube oil should meet the following requirements. It must:

1. Be viscous enough at all engine temperatures to keep two highly loaded surfaces apart
2. Remain relatively stable at all engine temperatures
3. Act as a coolant and cleaner
4. Prevent rust and corrosion

Hundreds of commercially available engine oils are produced worldwide, and labeling terminology and grading differ among suppliers. Some marketers of engine lube oils may claim that their lubricant is suitable for all makes of diesel engines. Such claims should be checked with the recommendations of a specific engine's manufacturer. Engines manufactured

in North America require a lube oil that is selected based on SAE (Society of Automotive Engineers) viscosity grade and API (American Petroleum Institute) service designations, although OEM and U.S. military specifications are also often quoted. In Europe, military specifications and the CCMC (The Comité des Constructeurs du Marché Commun) represent the requirements of European lube oil manufacturers for engine oil quality. In North America both the SAE and API standards are displayed, and only oils meeting these recommended properties should be considered as suitable for a given engine. Figure 11-12 illustrates a typical oil can symbol that indicates the lube oil meets an enhanced level of lubricant performance of the API CF-4 category.

NOTE In January 1995, the API began voluntarily licensing of API CG-4 lubricating oils for use in on-highway truck engines. To conform with this change, it is now recommended that heavy-duty electronically controlled diesel engines operating on low-sulfur fuel (0.05%) use API CG-4-designated lube oils. The phase-in of API CG-4 oils was not immediate; therefore, API CF-4 oils may continue to be used until CG-4 products become available.

The use of CG-4 lube oils is recommended by Detroit Diesel in both its series 50 and 60 four-cycle engine models; other engine OEMs are scheduled to follow this same recommendation. The recommended lube oil viscosity grade continues to be 15W-40 for heavy-duty high-speed on-highway truck engines manufactured by all of the major OEMs. The use of a CG-4 lubricant does not permit extension of normal oil drain intervals. CG-4 lube oil does have several advantages:

- Better control of engine deposits and prevention of corrosive wear
- Reduced oil consumption and improved oil viscosity control
- Control of combustion soot dispersancy, oxidation, and lube oil shear

Viscosity of Oils

Oils are classified by a numbering system to indicate basic viscosity grading. For example, in Figure 11-12 note that the oil is a 15W-40 grade, which is a multiviscosity lubricant. The 15W indicates that the oil has a viscosity of 15 when cold (W = winter). The 40 indicates that when the oil is hot, its additives allow it to

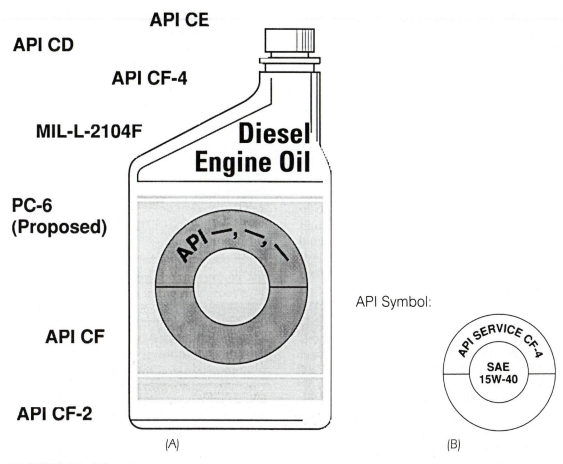

FIGURE 11–12 *API and SAE symbols on a typical lube oil container. (Reprinted with permission from Chevron Research and Technology Company, a division of Chevron U.S.A. Inc.; copyright Chevron Research Company, 1995.)*

thicken to an equivalent viscosity of 40 weight oil. Some oils may be labeled as a single-weight lubricant such as 30, 40, or 50. Various alphabetical letters have appeared on oil containers for years; these letters have changed as lubricating oils have improved. Letters on an oil can such as, SA, SB, SC, SD, SE, SF, or SG signify that the oil has been designed for S (spark ignition) internal combustion engines. Diesel engine lubricant containers have the letters CA, CB, CC, CD, CD-11, CE, CF, or CG to signify that the oil is intended for a C (compression ignition)-type diesel engine.

Engine oil viscosity was first defined by Isaac Newton as a measure of the resistance offered when one layer of the fluid moves relative to an adjacent layer. The higher the viscosity or thickness of the fluid film, the greater is the internal resistance to motion. Newton discovered that the viscosity of a fluid or lube oil will remain constant if both the temperature and pressure are held constant. Within an engine subjected to changing operating conditions, however, these two "constants" are regularly subjected to change. Most single-grade lube oils such as a 30, 40, or 50 are some-

times referred to as being Newtonian, whereas multi-grade oils are non-Newtonian because they don't obey the basic law, as we shall see. Several factors affect lube oil viscosity:

- Composition of the refined oil with its additives
- Operating temperature of the oil
- Pressure (loads) between two lubricated parts

The ASTM (American Society for Testing and Materials) created a method to provide a number called the VI (viscosity index). The VI is related to the amount of change for a given oil compared to two reference oils over a range of 40 to 100°C (104 to 212°F). On the ASTM scale, most engine oils have a VI of 90 or more, although it is not uncommon for light, multigrade oils to have a VI approaching 200 due to the additive packages used with them. Single-weight oils are more successful in some engine designs than others, but they have the disadvantage of having a much higher drag when cranking the engine over in cold-weather operation. Non-W-grades of lube oil are based only on their viscosities at 100°C (212°F). Multiviscosity oils are formulated to meet the W-grade criterion of a relatively thin oil at a particular low temperature, yet meet the standards for a thicker, non-W-grade oil at a higher temperature [usually 100°C (212°F)].

1. *Viscosity:* resistance to flow of a liquid. The molecules of a more viscous oil have greater cohesion (stick together more firmly) than a less viscous oil. The higher the number given to the oil, the greater its viscosity (resistance to flow) will be. Temperatures also greatly affect the viscosity of an oil. Hotter oil will flow more rapidly than colder oil.

2. *Pour point:* lowest temperature at which an oil will still be thin enough to pour.

3. *Flash point:* temperature at which the oil will be sufficiently vaporized to ignite.

Oil Recommendations

Engine manufacturers recommend engine oils based on their experience with oil viscosities. Manufacturers do not always specifically state that a certain *brand name* lube oil be used. Rather, the key is that the oil brand selected meet the minimum specs stated in the engine manufacturer's technical data.

Although some OEMs offer engine oils under their own name, any brand name engine oil can be used as long as it meets the standards and specifications specified by the engine manufacturer regarding sulfated ash and so on. Always refer to the engine service manual, operator manual, or lube oil spec sheets to ensure that the oil you choose for a certain engine make and model does in fact comply with the specs of the OEM. Failure to do so could have a detrimental effect on engine oil consumption and engine life and MAY void the existing warranty for the engine.

Some typical lube oil recommendations as specified by engine manufacturers follow:

- *Caterpillar:* Cat diesel engine oil CF-4, CE/SG (15W-40, 10W-30), CD11 (15W-40), CD/SD (10W, 30, 40). For Cat natural gas engine operation use NGEO (natural gas engine oil) SAE 30 or 40.
- *Cummins:* Cummins Premium Blue SAE 15W-40, CE, CF-4, SF, Cummins NTC-400, and Cummins NTC-444. Cummins Premium Blue 2000 SAE 15W-40 meeting Cummins Engineering Standard 20066 may be used where CF-4 oils are required.
- *Mack:* Bulldog Premium EO-L (engine oil lube) meeting the T-8 engine test.
- *Detroit Diesel:* DDC manufactures two- and four-stroke-cycle engines; therefore, its recommended lube oil viscosities are that a single-weight lube oil be used in its two-cycle models. SAE 40 is typically used in series 71 and 92 engines; for 149 se-

ries and high-output 71 and 92 engines, SAE 50 is recommended. For series 50, 55, and 60 engines, 15W-40 oil is the base oil, and current engines have a decal on the rocker cover recommending the use of a 15W-40 Mobil Delvac 1300 Super product. In all DDC engines, any engine oil that meets the company's specifications for CG-4 lubricants can be used.

To avoid possible engine damage, do not use single-grade (monograde) lubricants in Detroit Diesel four-cycle series 50, 55, and 60 engines, regardless of API classification.

Synthetic Lube Oils

The history of synthetic oils dates back to World War II when they were developed to meet the critically high standards of the aviation industry. Synthetic oils have been used in various forms for diesel truck applications since the early to mid-1960s, particularly for differentials and transmissions. Because of their superior cooling quality and service life much longer than that of mineral oils, they have found favor in severe-duty service off-road operations for diesel engines. Although more expensive than mineral oils, synthetic lubricants can be the ideal choice under heavy loads and steep operating grades. Synthetic oil is a far more refined, purer product than mineral oil, which is one reason it costs more. In addition, synthetic oil tends to be stickier than mineral oil and provides a better oil wedge between gear teeth on differentials and transmissions. As stricter emissions standards become a fact of life, synthetic engine oils are on the horizon for heavy-duty diesel engines as well as for gasoline-powered passenger cars.

Exhaust Emissions and Lube Oil

Electronically controlled diesel engines now operate in an era dominated by low-emissions fuels. Engine lube oil plays an important role in meeting stringent exhaust limits. Engine oils are being formulated to handle the side effects of EPA mandates.

Low-sulfur fuel (0.05%), which was introduced in October 1993, does allow the engine to burn cleaner, but it also affects key engine parts. To meet the strict standards for diesel particulate emissions, engine manufacturers have changed their piston designs by moving the rings closer to the top of the piston crown; thus the crevice volume (area above the top ring and piston crown) is reduced, but the rings are subjected to hotter temperatures. To protect the engines, lubricants have to control deposits at elevated temperatures. Since the top piston rings now operate in a much hotter environment, top ring groove deposits may increase, as well as oil viscosity. Improved additive packages help to minimize these new deposit configurations, thereby reducing wear and oil consumption. Improved oxidation inhibitors keep the oil viscosity within its designed grade level for longer periods.

To reduce nitrogen oxide emissions, many new engines use retarded injection timing, a feature that can substantially increase soot loading in the oil film on the cylinder walls. Advanced dispersancy additives help to keep this extra load of soot suspended instead of attaching internally to key engine parts. When the oil is drained, the soot is removed with the used oil. Dispersed soot is what makes the engine oil "black," and it can also cause the oil to thicken in time. Dispersancy-type oil additives provide reduced abrasive wear, fewer plugged filters, cleaner engines, and excellent pumpability during cold-weather startup. Much of the particulate exhaust emissions in the newer diesel engines consist of unburned oil escaping through the exhaust gases.

The new characteristics of the widely used 15W-40 oils in high-speed heavy-duty engines also offer fleets the possibility of extending oil drain intervals without suffering any loss of performance. An oil drain interval of 30,000 miles (48,279 km) is not uncommon in many of today's newer engines. Accumulated mileages of between 800,000 and 1 million miles (1,287,440 to 1,609,300 km) are becoming standard practice between overhauls. The 15W-40 multiviscosity oil is also designed to be compatible with oil oxidation catalysts that will be required on many smaller, high-speed diesel engines throughout the 1990s.

The main elements of these new engine oils is that there is only 1% ash content, which is held in check by ashless dispersants, and that the TBN (total base number) is 9. TBN is an indication of the depletion rate of the oil's additive package. Low ash in lube oils is key to reducing deposits in the piston top ring groove area; any such deposits can cause ring sticking, blowby, and high oil consumption.

Oil Change Intervals

During use, engine lubricating oil undergoes deterioration from combustion by-products and contamination by the engine. Certain components in a lubricant additive package are designed to deplete with use. For this reason, regardless of the oil formulation, regular oil drain intervals are necessary. These intervals may vary in length, depending on engine operation, fuel quality, and lubricant quality. Generally, shorter oil drain intervals extend engine life through prompt replenishment of the protection qualities in the lubricant.

Should it be determined that the oil drain interval is unacceptably short, then the selection of a lubricant with a Total Base Number (TBN per ASTM D 2896) above 10 may be appropriate. Experience has shown, however, that a higher TBN oil with a longer oil change interval is not as effective in protecting the engine from wear. Use the intervals listed until the best practical oil drain interval can be established by oil analysis.

Proper drain intervals for engine oil require that the oil be drained before the contaminant load becomes so great that the oil's lubricating function is impaired or heavy deposits of suspended contaminants occur. Oil and filter change intervals are usually recommended by each engine manufacturer for various operating conditions. This information is usually contained in service manual literature as well as operator manuals (engine, vehicle, equipment) and is provided simply as a general guide. Engine operating environments, speeds, loads, idling time, ambient air temperature, grades encountered with mobile equipment, and airborne dust all affect the lube oil life cycle.

Regardless of the type of oil used, it is always wise to have a schedule for oil sampling in a fleet operation to determine the best mileage (hours, time) at which to change the engine lube oil and filter(s). Another method for determining the oil and filter change interval if no service literature is available is to use kilometers (miles), hours, or months—whichever comes first. On industrial and marine engine applications, oil change intervals are normally based on accumulated engine hours; the type of application, loads, and speeds play a large part in determining the recommended oil drain period. The type of diesel fuel used and the sulfur content also are relevant. Because of the many factors involved, the change interval can range from as low as 50 hours to 500 hours or 6 months maximum.

As can be seen from the preceding information, the lube system and the lube oil in it deserve more than a casual consideration, especially in oil selection. Engine oil must be changed at regular intervals to keep the internal engine parts clean, since in most cases dirt is the engine's primary enemy. Keep the engine clean and it will not wear out.

In addition, the lube system must be closely inspected during an engine overhaul if it is to function correctly for many hours of operation. All too often the components of the system are taken for granted and overlooked during engine overhaul. The result in many cases is a newly overhauled engine with less oil pressure than it should have. It is recommended that all lubrication system components be checked thoroughly during engine overhaul.

INSPECTION AND OVERHAUL OF COMPONENTS

It is assumed that the oil pump has been removed from the engine at this time. If not, refer to Chapter 6 on engine disassembly.

Oil Pump Disassembly

1. Remove the pump cover from the pump body (external gear-type pump).
2. Inspect the cover for wear.

NOTE   If the cover is worn, it should be machined or replaced with a new cover.

---

3. Remove the idler gear and driven gear from the pump housing.

NOTE   In most cases the idler gear can be lifted from its supporting shaft (idler shaft) and removed. The drive gear will be keyed to the drive shaft with a woodruff key (half moon) or roll pin (spring steel pin) and may have to be pressed from the shaft. If the drive gear must be pressed from the drive shaft, the drive shaft should be removed from the pump body before attempting to remove the gear. In many cases the pump drive shaft will have the oil pump drive gear pressed onto it. This must be removed before the drive shaft and drive gear can be removed from the pump housing. (Check your engine service manual or with your instructor.)

---

4. Check the idler and drive gear closely for pitted and worn teeth. Teeth should be checked closely at the points shown in Figure 11-13.
5. Check the gear width (parallel with the center hole) with a micrometer.
6. Check the drive shaft diameter at the bushing contact with a micrometer. This diameter should meet the manufacturer's specifications.
7. Check the pump housing internally for wear as shown in Figure 11-14.
8. Check the drive shaft bushing (if used) with a snap gauge. Compare with specifications.

NOTE   Some pumps have replaceable bushings that can be renewed. Others require replacement of the pump body. If bushings are to be replaced

FIGURE 11–13 Areas where oil pump gears should be checked for wear.

in the pump body, check the service manual closely for installation and boring instructions.

9. Check all mating surfaces (such as where the cover fits onto the pump body). Surfaces should not be nicked or burred. If there are nicks or burrs, remove them with a small, flat file.

CAUTION   Care must be exercised when filing on a pump body, as it can easily be ruined. If the body is warped excessively, replace it with a new one.

Oil Pump Reassembly (General)

After all parts have been inspected, repaired, or replaced, the pump can be reassembled.

FIGURE 11–14 Areas to check when checking oil pump housing for wear.

1. Insert the oil pump drive shaft with the driven gear installed on it into the pump body.

NOTE   To install the pump drive gear, the pump drive shaft must be supported on the opposite end while the pump drive gear is installed. You must do this before the pump cover is installed.

---

2. Support the drive shaft on the drive gear end and press the pump drive gear in place (Figure 11-15).

CAUTION   Make sure that the woodruff key or roll pin is installed, securing the gear to the shaft, to prevent gear from turning on the shaft during operation.

---

3. Install the idler gear on the idler shaft.
4. Turn the drive shaft, checking for binding or interference as the shaft is turned.

NOTE   Any binding is usually caused by nicks on gears. Remove the gears and file or stone off nicks.

---

5. When the pump drive shaft and gears have been rotated without binding, pump cover-to-gear clearance should be checked with Plastigage as follows:

a.   Place Plastigage across the face of the gears.

NOTE   Plastigage is a thin plastic thread that can be broken into the correct length and used to check the clearance between two closely fitted parts.

---

b.   Install the cover and tighten to specifications.

CAUTION   Do not turn the pump drive gear with Plastigage on it.

---

c.   Remove the cover and check the width of the Plastigage against the Plastigage envelope (Figure 8-28) to determine the clearance between the cover and gears.
d.   If the clearance is excessive or does not meet specifications, it must be corrected by replacing the gears or pump as needed. [General specifications for oil pump gear-to-cover clearance are 0.003 to 0.005 in. (0.076 to 0.127 mm).]

NOTE   Many oil pumps will contain a bypass or regulating valve that should be checked during pump overhaul as outlined in the following section.

Inspection and Repair of Oil Pressure Regulation and Bypass Valves

Because of different systems' designs and requirements, the regulator or bypass valves may be located anywhere in the engine or oil pump. Regardless of where they are located or what their function is, all valves must be disassembled and inspected as follows:

1. Remove the valve spring cap retainer.
2. Remove the spring, inspect for worn or twisted coils, and check the free length and spring pressure with a spring tester.
3. If the valve is the plunger type, check the plunger and plunger seat for scoring and wear. Replace all valves that show excessive wear.
4. Ball valves should be checked for pitting and wear and replaced if found defective.
5. Check the valve seat visually for pitting and uneven wear.

NOTE   Some valve seats are replaceable and can be replaced without replacing the valve assembly. Other types of valves will require replacement of the entire valve body or pump assembly, which includes the valve seat.

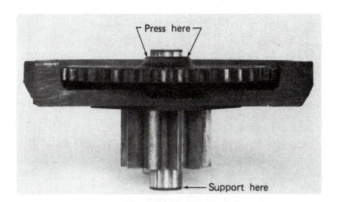

FIGURE 11–15 *Pressing drive shaft and drive gear together. (Courtesy of Cummins Engine Company, Inc.)*

Checking the Oil Filter Housing or Mounting

Regardless of the type of filter used, element or cartridge type, the base or filter mount must be checked carefully during engine overhaul as follows:

1. If a bypass valve is incorporated into the housing, it should be removed and checked as outlined in the regulator valve section.
2. Check the housing for cracks.
3. Check all gasket surfaces for straightness and nicks.
4. If using an element filter, which uses a can or shell with a center bolt, make sure that the center bolt threads are usable.
5. Make sure that springs, gaskets, and spacers (as outlined in the service manual or parts book) are in place in element-type filters.
6. Check the can for signs of collapse on the closed end.
7. Check for cracks around the bolt hole and elsewhere.
8. Check housing passageways, making sure that all are open and free of obstructions.

Oil Cooler Testing and Repair

Since oil and water both flow through the oil cooler simultaneously, it becomes very important that mixing of oil and water at this point does not occur due to a leak or crack in the cooler. Two types of coolers are found on modern diesel engines, plate type and tube type. Many variations of these basic types will be found.

> NOTE   Complete servicing of the oil cooler should be done on a routine basis during a major engine overhaul. In addition, the cooler may occasionally fail between engine overhaul periods. Indications of cooler failure are oil in the water or water in the oil pan. In either case the following service instructions will apply.

Servicing of the oil cooler assembly should include complete disassembly and cleaning of the core section with a solution recommended by the engine manufacturer. In most cases the cooler core can be cleaned using an oakite-type solution or muriatic acid.

> CAUTION   Some cores contain aluminum, a nonferrous metal that cannot be cleaned as outlined above. In this type of situation, use a normal parts cleaning solution. After cleaning, inspect all parts as follows.

1. Check the core visually for

a. Cracks or breaks in welded joints
b. Bulges or bent tubes

2. If the core does not pass visual inspection, replace it with a new one.
3. If the core passes visual checks, it should be checked by pressurizing with air in the following manner:

a. If a test fixture is available, mount the core in the fixture in preparation for testing.

> NOTE   If a test fixture is not available, a plate or plates can be made to test the cooler core. In general, the plate should be designed so that air pressure can be supplied to one side (oil or water) of the cooler only (Figure 11-16).

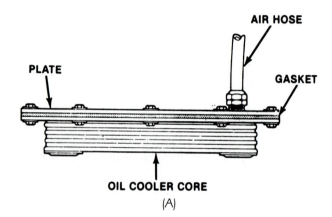

(A)

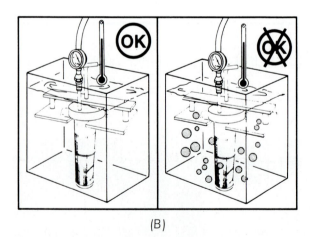

(B)

FIGURE 11-16   (A) Preparing a plate oil cooler for pressure checking; (B) submerging a tubular oil cooler core into a container of heated water to check for signs of air bubbles from the compressed air supply. [(A) Courtesy of Detroit Diesel Corporation; (B) courtesy of Cummins Engine Company, Inc.]

b. After the plates have been attached to the core, pressurize it with 35 to 40 psi (2.5 to 2.8 kg/cm²) and immerse it in water.

c. Inspect carefully for air leaks.

4. If core passes all the checks outlined above, clean the housing and install new O-rings or gaskets and reassemble the core to the cooler.

NOTE   Generally, cooler assembly will be a simple matter of installing the core in the cooler housing, using new gaskets or O-rings. An exception to this is the Cummins tube-type cooler, which requires indexing (timing) in the housing during assembly. Figure 11-17 is an example of index marking.

---

5. Before the cooler assembly is installed onto the engine, the bypass valve should be checked as outlined under the regulator valve section.

6. Using new gaskets, mount the cooler on the engine and tighten all bolts.

SYSTEM TESTING

Testing the lube oil system involves testing the pressure at various engine speeds and temperatures. In general, testing is done at the following times:

1. *After an engine overhaul.* The lube system must be thoroughly checked and monitored during engine start-up and rebuild. Proper oil pressure is vital to long engine life.

2. *Lube system problems between engine overhauls.* Many times low lube oil pressure will occur long before the engine is due for a major rebuild. The cause of the problem can be found only by testing and checking the lube system.

3. *Before an overhaul.* Many technicians like to check lube oil pressure before the engine is disassembled for rebuild as an indication of what to be especially alert for during rebuild. (For example, if lube pressure is low, the clearances throughout the engine should be carefully checked and held within recommendations.)

TESTING AND TROUBLESHOOTING THE LUBE SYSTEM

To accurately test and determine the condition of a lubrication system, the following procedure should be followed:

1. Test the oil level and check the oil for correct weight, viscosity, and possible dilution. If any doubt exists about the condition of the lube oil, it should be replaced before proceeding with further tests.

2. Change the lube oil filter and inspect the old filter for metal particles.

NOTE   If a can type of spin-on filter is used, it may be necessary to cut it apart to check for metal particles. If the filter is filled with many particles of bearing material, it is a good possibility that a worn or damaged bearing is causing the low oil pressure. In most cases the engine bearings should be checked before proceeding with further testing of the lube system.

---

3. Warm the engine thoroughly by driving the vehicle or by loading the engine on a dynamometer.

4. Install a master pressure gauge somewhere in the system where it will indicate system pressure.

CAUTION   Make sure that the gauge is calibrated-scaled to handle the highest expected oil pressure or damage to the gauge may result.

---

5. Discuss the complaint with the customer if the condition is customer oriented. Make a mental note of causes that may be creating problems.

6. Determine from the engine service manual what correct oil pressure should be and at what speed

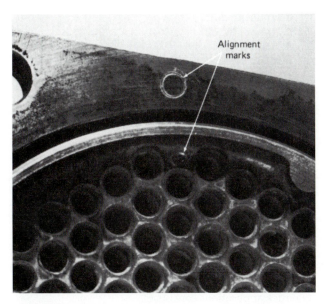

FIGURE 11–17   *Oil cooler index markings. (Courtesy of Cummins Engine Company, Inc.)*

testing should be done. [Many engines require a minimum of 40 psi (2.8 kg/cm^2) at either rated load or high idle, for example], refer to OEM specs.

7.   Run the engine and check the oil pressure.

8.   If the engine oil pressure meets specifications, no further checks need be made. If not, proceed with step 9.

9.   If the oil pressure was too low or too high, an attempt should be made to determine what the cause might be.

NOTE   Some engines will have a pressure regulator adjustment for oil pressure. If your engine is so equipped, make the adjustment to bring the oil pressure into the specified range.

10.   If the oil pressure cannot be adjusted and does not meet specifications, the system pressure regulating valve should be checked.

NOTE   The order and the type of checks that will be made are largely dependent on the technician and the condition of the engine. For example, a newly rebuilt engine would be tested knowing that all clearances and regulator valves were checked during assembly. A key item to look for in rebuilt engines is improperly installed or incorrect gaskets at such places as the oil filter base, oil pump mounting, blower mounting, and other places where pressure oil could be routed incorrectly. In contrast to this would be an engine that had been performing correctly with good oil pressure for many hours and then developed low oil pressure. Troubleshooting of this engine must be approached with the idea that it was correct at one time, but wear or malfunction of some part has created a low-pressure situation.

11.   If the pressure regulator valve and spring are in good condition, check all the bypass valves used on oil filters and oil coolers.

12.   Check the oil pump. In most cases the engine oil pan will have to be removed to gain access to the oil pump.

13.   If no problem exists with the oil pump, the main and rod bearings should be checked by removing the caps and checking the bearings for wear, scoring, and clearance with Plastigage.

14.   If the main and rod bearing clearances are all right, check the camshaft bushings.

NOTE   Since checking the camshaft bushings requires an extensive amount of engine teardown, a decision should be made at this time about the engine condition. Perhaps a complete engine overhaul should be done at this time. This decision would be dependent on the overall general condition of the engine, number of hours in use, and the owner's wishes.

15.   At this time most of the points within the engine that contribute to low oil pressure have been indicated. If the problem has not been remedied, a thorough study of the engine lubrication system should be undertaken, considering any peculiarity the engine being worked on may have.

SUMMARY

This chapter has covered the lube oil and system requirements in a diesel engine. The function, operation, testing, and overhaul or replacement of each component are covered in sufficient detail to allow you to understand, test, and repair the system. When troubleshooting, it is very important to view the lube oil, lube system, and its components as a complete unit, using common sense and a systematic simple-to-complex method of checking to isolate and repair problems.

SELF-TEST QUESTIONS

1.   Refined crude oil is commonly referred to as a
    a.   base stock
    b.   mineral oil
    c.   vegetable oil
    d.   additive package

2.   List some of the more commonly used oil additives and the reasons for their use.

3.   Technician A says that oxidation of engine lube oil can lead to viscosity increases, engine deposits, and corrosion. Technician B says that the oxidation would decrease the oil viscosity, reduce engine oil pressure, and increase the oil temperature. Which technician is correct?

4.   Technician A says that viscosity improvers and wear inhibitors prevent thinning of the oil and therefore wear of bearings. Technician B says that they prevent foaming of the oil as well as act as friction modifiers. Which technician knows the purpose of these two additives?

5.   A typical dosage of an additive package in a typical heavy-duty diesel engine lube oil used in automotive or truck applications consists of
    a.   0.5% to 2% by weight
    b.   3% to 5% by weight

c. 3% to 16% by weight

d. 10% to 30% by weight

6. What percentage of the following items constitutes a typical lube oil package?
   a. base stock crude
   b. additive package
   c. viscosity index improver
   d. various inhibitors

7. Lube oils in North America are manufactured to various standards set down by these organizations. What do the letters represent?
   a. SAE
   b. API
   c. ASTM

8. Technician A says that letters appearing on any oil container that begin with S indicate a diesel engine lubricant. Technician B says that the letter C indicates a diesel engine lubricant, since the letter S is used for gasoline spark-ignited engines. Which technician is correct?

9. True or False: Oil viscosity rating is a measure of the oil's resistance when one layer of the fluid moves relative to an adjacent layer.

10. True or False: An oil referred to as Newtonian (Isaac Newton) is a multiviscosity weight (grade) lube oil.

11. True or False: An oil referred to as non-Newtonian is a straight-weight (grade) lube oil.

12. True or False: An oil with a higher viscosity number means that the thickness of the fluid film is greater.

13. Multiviscosity oils are identified by an alphabetical letter following the first number. This letter is
    a. C
    b. F
    c. S
    d. W

14. True or False: The viscosity of multigrade oils is based on their ability to meet an ASTM W-grade standard of a relatively thin oil at a particular low temperature, while also meeting the standards for a thicker, non-W-grade oil at a higher temperature [usually 100°C (212°F)].

15. True or False: Base stocks used to formulate multigrade oils are of low viscosity and are thickened with additive packages called VI (viscosity index) improvers.

16. True or False: The term *polymerization* refers to the chemical linking together of giant molecules to a large number of smaller ones.

17. The most frequently recommended oil grade for use in heavy-duty high-speed four-stroke-cycle engines such as those of Caterpillar, Cummins, Detroit Diesel, Volvo, Mack, and Navistar is
    a. 5W-20
    b. 10W-30
    c. 10W-40
    d. 15W-40

18. Why does the two-cycle DDC engine require a different oil grade than that for the DDC four-cycle models?

19. The engine oil recommended for two-stroke-cycle Detroit Diesel engines is

    a. 10W-30
    b. 15W-40
    c. 30
    d. 40 or 50

20. List the problems that will occur if a lube oil with too thick a viscosity grade is used.

21. List the problems that will occur if a lube oil with too thin a viscosity grade is used.

22. Technician A says that synthetic lube oils are far more refined and therefore a purer product than mineral oils. Technician B says that synthetic oil tends to be stickier than mineral oil and that is why synthetic oils are more expensive. Is one of the technicians correct, or are both statements valid?

23. Technician A says that the reason that diesel engine oil tends to appear much blacker than the oil used in gasoline engines over the same hours (miles, kilometers) is that they are subjected to much greater pressures and stresses. Technician B disagrees, saying that the dispersed soot from the combustion phase is the cause. Which technician is correct?

24. Technician A says that the newer electronic engines use retarded injection timing to meet the more stringent EPA exhaust emissions regulations and to reduce NO_x emissions. Technician B says that injection timing has been advanced to reduce NO_x. Who is right?

25. Based on your answer to Question 24, does this feature increase or decrease soot loading on the cylinder walls?

26. True or False: The letters TBN stand for total base number.

27. Technician A says that TBN means the oil has started to thicken and should be changed more frequently. Technician B says that TBN is an indication of the depletion rate of the oil's additive package. Which technician is correct?

28. True or False: An oil with a high ash content helps to reduce deposits in the piston top ring groove area, which can cause ring sticking, blowby, and high oil consumption.

29. List three methods that could be used to determine the best point at which to change the engine lube oil and filter.

30. Describe how a lube oil analysis program can help determine when internal engine components are wearing prematurely or are close to a failure level.

31. Why has the use of electronic fuel injection been able to reduce metallic iron wear in engines compared to that normally found in mechanically governed and controlled engines?

32. Technician A says that the typical oil temperature in a high-speed heavy-duty diesel engine is normally 230°F (110°C). Technician B says that oil temperature should be closer to 195°F (91°C). Who is correct?

33. Maximum engine lube oil temperatures should not exceed
    a. 200°F (93°C)
    b. 215°F (102°C)

c. 235°F (113°C)

d. 250°F (121°C)

34. Name the two spring-loaded valves within the lube oil system that control normal and maximum operating pressures.

35. What prevents starvation of lube oil to the engine if and when the full-flow oil filter(s) becomes plugged?

36. If the engine oil cooler becomes plugged, what device would still allow oil to flow to the engine components?

37. True or False: Most oil pumps are gear driven from the crankshaft.

38. The word *gerotor* describes an oil pump that is a combination of

a. gear and rotor

b. piston and gear

c. piston and rotor

d. dual gears

39. Technician A says that a scavenge pump is used to supply lube oil to the opposite end of the oil pan in engine applications that operate at steep angles. Technician B says that this pump is used on large engines to supply half of the oil flow throughout the engine. Which technician is correct?

40. High-speed diesel engine full-flow oil filters are generally rated for a micron filtration size of approximately

a. 30

b. 25

c. 20

d. 10

41. Bypass oil filters that filter approximately 10% of the total oil flow are rated in the range

a. 20 to 30 μm

b. 20 to 25 μm

c. 15 to 20 μm

d. 10 to 15 μm

42. Technician A says that when a duplex filtration system is used one or more filters can be changed while the engine is running. Technician B says that the engine must be stopped to change an oil filter. Who is correct?

43. True or False: The appearance of sludge is an indication that the oil and filter should be changed more frequently.

44. True or False: Thin black oil is an indication of fuel in the oil.

45. True or False: Milky discoloration of the oil is an indication of coolant in the oil.

46. Overtightening of a spin-on lube oil filter can result in what type of a problem?

47. Shell and element lube oil filters should be drained and washed in clean solvent and dried with compressed air. What other service items need to be replaced with this type of a filter assembly?

48. Describe the basic theory of operation of a Tattle Tale filter used on heavy-duty engines.

49. True or False: The difference in temperature between the engine cooling system and the oil is generally within the range of 30 to 40°F (17 to 23°C).

50. Name the two types of engine oil coolers that are used on heavy-duty diesel engines.

51. Technician A says that a leaking oil cooler core during engine operation will result in water in the oil. Not so, says Technician B, who believes that lube oil would enter the cooling system instead. Who is correct and state your reasons why.

52. Describe what method you would use to clean an oil cooler core.

53. Describe how you would perform a pressure check on an oil cooler core.

54. The crankcase ventilation system ensures that harmful crankcase vapors can be recirculated through the engine. How would you determine if high crankcase pressure existed, and how would you check it?

55. Describe what conditions can lead to a crankcase explosion on a large-displacement diesel engine. What component is employed to prevent this condition from happening?

56. Describe how you would prelubricate an engine.

12 Cooling Systems

OVERVIEW

This chapter covers cooling system functions and heat loads, coolant treatment, the relationship of coolant to cylinder liner pitting, the effects of antifreeze, coolant testing, and scale buildup. Specific features of the coolant system are highlighted: for example, filters, radiators, and thermostats.

COOLING SYSTEM FUNCTION

All internal combustion engines require treated water within a radiator system, heat exchanger, keel cooler, or cooling tower to prevent the engine from overheating and boiling over. Documented studies have shown that more than 40% of all engine problems are directly or indirectly related to improper maintenance of the cooling system.

The basic function of a cooling system is to dissipate a portion of the heat created within the engine combustion chamber. Heat absorbed by the pistons, rings, liners, cylinder heads, and cylinder block during engine operation that is not directly converted into useful power at the flywheel must be handled by the cooling system. A properly designed cooling system must maintain the coolant operating temperature within a fairly narrow band to ensure proper combustion, minimize blowby, and allow the engine lube oil to function correctly. Tests have proven that wear on cylinder walls can be up to eight times greater with a coolant temperature of 100°F (38°C) compared to one of 180°F (82°C). Normal engine operating temperatures are generally controlled by one or more temperature regulators or thermostats. Typical coolant temperatures under loaded engine conditions fall within 180 to 200°F (82 to 93°C).

Component Description, Operation, and Function

All liquid-type cooling systems have basically the same components except for the temperature controls, such as fan clutches, shutters, and thermostats. A typical liquid cooling system will have the following components:

1. *Radiator.* A device that performs two important functions:

    a. Provides a storage tank for the engine coolant.

    b. Provides a surface where engine heat can be dissipated to the surrounding air.

        (1) Radiator cores (the radiator surface that dissipates the heat) are generally tube and fin type (Figure 12-1).

2. *Water jackets.* Water jackets surround the engine block and provide a storage area for the coolant. They also provide a place for the coolant to circulate through the block and pick up the excess engine heat.

3. *Water pump.* A centrifugal nonpositive-displacement pump used to pump the water through the block (water jacket) and radiator. It may be driven by a gear or pulley and belt arrangement.

4. *Thermostat.* A temperature-controlled valve that regulates the flow of coolant through the engine and radiator. This flow regulation maintains engine temperature.

5. *Fan and fan drives.* The fan is mounted on the water pump drive pulley hub or on a separate fan hub driven by a V- or serpentine belt. It provides air movement across the radiator so that heat can be dissipated. On some diesel engines (especially trucks), the fan can be driven by a fluid clutch, which is controlled by the

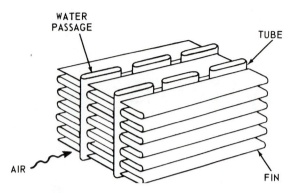

FIGURE 12–1 Tube-and-fin radiator.

temperature of the air passing over it. Depending on the temperature, the fan will run fast or slow.

NOTE Viscous fan drives reduce fan speed when the engine and coolant water are cold, while electric clutch fan drives disconnect the fan from the drive hub entirely and the fan is not driven at all when the engine is cold.

Clutch fan drives save fuel and horsepower, since the fan does not run at all, or its speed is substantially reduced when the engine is cold.

6. *Temperature gauge.* A gauge that tells the operator what the engine coolant temperature is. It can be one of two types:

a. *Electric* (Figure 12-2). An electric temperature gauge has a sending unit threaded into the water jacket or manifold to sense engine temperature. This sending unit provides the

ground for the gauge circuit that includes the indicator gauge. Current is supplied to the circuit from the battery via the ignition switch. When the coolant is cold, the sensing unit provides no ground for the circuit; when it heats up, a ground is provided, causing current to flow in the gauge circuit and to indicate a reading on the gauge.

b. *Expansion* (Figure 12-3). The Bourdon expansion gauge unit is made up of a gauge, a long copper or steel tube with a protective cover, and a sensing unit or bulb that fits in the block or water manifold. The tube and gauge expansion unit are filled with a liquid that expands rapidly when heated. When the coolant warms up, the sensing unit and the liquid in it warm up and the gauge mechanism is operated, showing coolant temperature.

7. *Shutters.* Shutters are louverlike panels that are mounted in front of the radiator and, when closed, prevent airflow across the radiator. This restricted airflow decreases warm-up time after a cold engine start and provides a means for regulating water temperature during engine operation. Most shutters are air closed and spring opened, while some may be operated by a thermostat through direct linkage.

8. *Radiator cap.* A cap that maintains a given pressure within the cooling system. This pressure allows coolant temperatures to run hotter without boiling. (Every pound of pressure exerted on the coolant

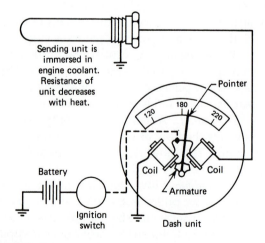

FIGURE 12–2 Electric temperature gauge. (Courtesy of Deere & Co.)

FIGURE 12–3 Expansion temperature gauge.

increases the boiling point by $3\frac{1}{2}°F$.) Included in the cap is a vacuum valve that allows air to enter the system when the coolant cools and contracts. If the cap did not have a vacuum valve, pressure inside the radiator might fall so low that outside air pressure might cause the radiator and hoses to collapse.

9. *Water conditioner and filter.* A filter containing an element that conditions the coolant and prevents it from becoming too acidic. An over-acid coolant can cause cavitation that can erode the sleeves and cylinder block.

10. *Coolant.* The coolant is generally a water and antifreeze mixture. Even in climates where freezing is not a problem, antifreeze and water are the most popular coolant because of the antifreeze's rust-inhibitor capabilities. Antifreeze and water are generally installed in the cooling system in a 50:50 ratio.

11. *Shutterstat.* The shutterstat is an air control valve that is operated by coolant temperature and controls the air supply to the shutter operating cylinder.

12. *Hoses.* The hoses that direct the flow of water from the block to the radiator are made from neoprene, a rubberlike material, and may be of the molded type, straight type, or flexible type. The straight-type hose can be used where a straight line exists between the two hose connections. If the hose has to make a bend, a molded or flexible hose must be utilized. Lower radiator hoses, the ones that connect the lower water pump elbow with the lower radiator connections, usually have a coiled wire in them so that they do not collapse or suck shut during operation.

13. *Clamps.* Many different types of clamps are used when attaching the hoses to the radiator and block inlet and outlets.

ENGINE HEAT LOADS

Heat dissipated to the coolant at rated power and peak torque engine speeds is used to define the heat load that must be dissipated by the cooling system, either to a radiator or heat exchanger system such as that found in industrial and marine applications. The energy distribution from combustion of the injected fuel can be split into four categories:

1. Useful work or power available after frictional losses
2. Exhaust gases (which recapture some heat energy to drive a turbocharger)
3. Cooling system (which recaptures some energy, for example, as an in-cab heater and defroster)
4. Heat radiation from the engine

Exact heat loads vary in specific makes of engines. In modern electronically controlled engines, TE (thermal efficiency), or the heat efficiency and useful work from the engine, approaches 40 to 42%. Typical heat rejection values for today's engines can range from as high as 14,000 Btu (10,440 kW) per minute in high-output electronically controlled engines to as little as 4000 Btu (2,983 kW) per minute in low-horsepower engines. Average heat rejection to the cooling system is usually in the range of 30 to 35 Btu/hp-min for a basic engine. The addition of accessories to the coolant system, such as transmission and marine gear oil coolers, can increase the cooling system heat load to between 40 and 50 Btu/min.

Assume that an engine is rated at 450 bhp (335.6 kW) with a heat load of 14,000 Btu (10,440 kW) per minute. If we divide the heat load by 450 bhp (335.6 kW), the cooling system would have to absorb 31 Btu/hp-min. In a smaller engine rated at only 150 bhp (112 kW) with a heat load of 4000 Btu/min, the cooling system has to absorb 27 Btu/hp (0.471 kW) per minute. As you can see, there isn't too much of a difference between the cooling system heat absorption requirements of the smaller and larger rated engines. For example, the 3176B Caterpillar inline six-cylinder four-stroke-cycle engine which has electronically controlled unit injectors is a 10.3-L (629-in^3) displacement engine. Although initially designed for heavy-duty truck applications, it is now used in a variety of applications. Total heat rejection on this engine is 27 Btu/hp-min, with 17 Btu from the engine cooling jacket and 10 Btu from the ATAAC (air-to-air aftercooler) charge air system.

Thermal efficiency (or heat efficiency) simply means that if the engine has a 42% TE, for every $1 of fuel injected into the combustion chamber, there is a 42-cent return at the flywheel as usable power. This means that approximately 58% of the heat developed from combustion is wasted and dissipated to the cooling, exhaust, friction, and radiation areas. If we assume that our example engine is rated at 450 bhp (335.6 kW) and the cooling system handles 14,000 Btu (10,440 kW) per minute, in 1 hour the cooling system has to handle $60 \times 14,000 = 840,000$ Btu. If we divide this figure by 450 bhp (335.6 kW), the cooling system load is 1866.66 Btu/hp-hr.

From the discussion in Chapter 3 we know that a perfect engine incurring no heat losses would require enough injected fuel to release 2545 Btu of heat within the cylinder to produce 1 hp (0.746 kW) over a 1-hour period. If this 2545 Btu/hp-hr represents usable power with a 42% TE value, we can factor out the remaining Btu heat losses. If the engine has a fuel consumption of 0.310 lb/bhp-hr (188.5 g/kWh), at a rating of

450 bhp (335.6 kW) in 1 hour the engine consumes 450 × 0.310 = 139.5 lb (63.27 kg) of fuel. If the fuel has an API rating of 38, it weighs 6.95 lb/U.S. gallon (3.15 kg/3.78 L). The engine consumes, therefore, 20.07 U.S. gallons/hr (75.97 L/h). A 38 API fuel contains 137,000 Btu HHV (high heat value) per U.S. gallon, so in 1 hour the total heat released into the engine cylinders is 137,000 × 20.07 = 2,749,590 Btu. If we divide this total heat released by the power rating of 450 bhp (335.6 kW), the engine requires 6110.2 Btu to produce 1 hp over a 1-hour period. We know that only 2545 Btu of this heat was actually useful power; therefore, 6110.2 − 2545 = 3565.2 Btu was lost to the cooling system, exhaust, friction, and radiation. The 1866.66 Btu/hp-hr is equal to 30.54% of the total heat used (6110.2 Btu). Added to the 42% TE, we have now accounted for 42 + 30.54 = 72.54% of the fuel heat released into the combustion chamber. This means that the remaining 27.46% of dissipated heat losses was accounted for by the exhaust and friction and radiation area, which represents 1698.54 Btu.

RADIATORS

A radiator is a form of heat exchanger that is designed to allow hot coolant from the engine to flow through a series of tubes or cores to dissipate its heat. The heat is dissipated by air being drawn through the radiator fins when the vehicle is stationary by an engine-driven suction fan; when the vehicle is moving, ambient ram (forced or pushed) air passes through the radiator. When a radiator is used on a stationary piece of equipment such as a portable air compressor, a *blower fan* pulls ambient air from below the unit and forces it through the radiator core in the opposite direction to what occurs on a car, truck, or piece of mobile equipment capable of being driven at a reasonable speed. There are three main types of radiators in use:

1. In a *downflow* design, the coolant flows from the top to the bottom of the radiator core. The effect of gravity in this type of system generally minimizes the restriction to the suction side of the water pump. Figure 12-4 illustrates a downflow system. Typical heavy-duty class 8 diesel trucks employ radiators with a frontal area ranging from 1000 to 1700 in^2 (6451 to 10,967 cm^2) depending on the engine power rating and the required heat loads.

2. In another design the hot coolant from the thermostat housing enters either the top or bottom of the radiator first and circulates through a series of tubes and liquid-tight baffles in a crossflow, downward, or upward loop. The number of passes of the coolant through these types of radiators depends on the heat transfer level required. Figure 12-5 illustrates a two-pass crossflow radiator, and Figure 12-6 illustrates a two-pass counterflow design. A greater number of coolant passes increases the velocity of the coolant. In recent years, a two-pass design commonly referred to as LFC (low-flow-cooling) has been used

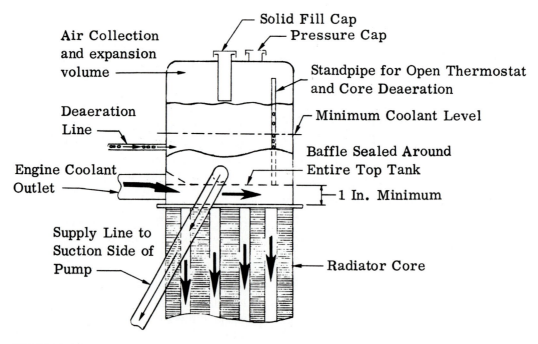

FIGURE 12–4 Typical design of a heavy-duty downflow tube and fin radiator highlighting the baffled top tank. (Courtesy of Detroit Diesel Corporation.)

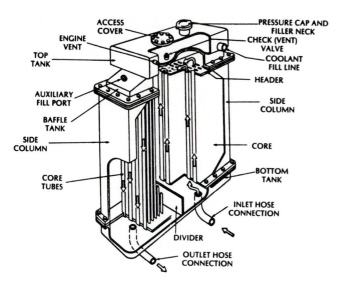

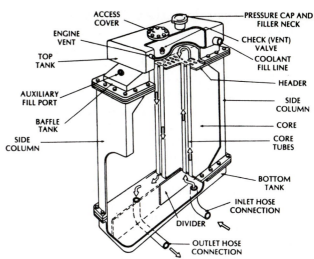

FIGURE 12-5 Coolant flow through a two-pass cross-flow heavy-duty truck radiator. (Courtesy of Cummins Engine Company, Inc.)

FIGURE 12-6 Coolant flow through a heavy-duty truck two-pass counterflow radiator. (Courtesy of Cummins Engine Company, Inc.)

by Cummins on a number of its truck engines. Figure 12-7 illustrates the basic flow from the engine to and through this system for a 14-L engine. The main difference between an LFC system and a traditional system is that the LFC design has a reduced coolant flow rate through the radiator and usually operates with a higher-pressure cap, since system pressures can exceed 40 psi (276 kPa). The two-pass LFC radiator di-

rects the engine coolant down one side of the core and up the other to increase tube velocity and keep the coolant in the radiator as long as possible. This results in a lower-temperature coolant to the water-cooled engine aftercooler, which lowers the charge temperature of the pressurized air flowing from the turbocharger to the engine. This in turn provides a denser air charge to the cylinders, resulting in improved fuel economy and

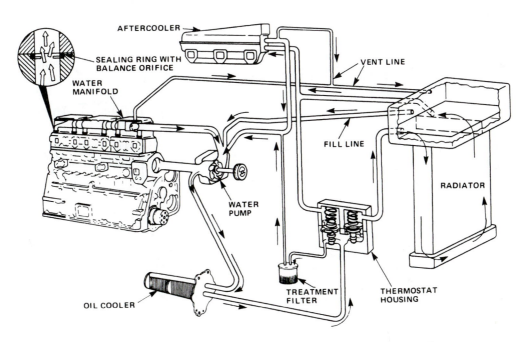

FIGURE 12-7 Coolant flow paths through a Cummins NTC (14-L) engine low-flow cooling system. (Courtesy of Cummins Engine Company, Inc.)

lower exhaust emissions. The LFC system is generally not required on engines employing AAACs (air-to-air aftercoolers).

3. In a *crossflow* design the coolant enters the radiator along one of the side headers and flows horizontally through the core to the opposite side. Figure 12-8 illustrates a typical crossflow radiator design for an inline engine. In Vee-type engines two thermostat housings would be connected together, or alternatively, have two outlets to the radiator. The crossflow design allows a lower overall hood height, which is often necessary with aerodynamic truck styling.

RADIATOR SHUTTERS

Some heavy-duty trucks and tractors have a venetian-blind type of mechanism mounted directly in front of the radiator core. This device is known as a *shutter assembly*, and it is designed to control cooling airflow across the radiator. Certain truck models may install the radiator shutters behind the radiator core. Figure 12-9 illustrates both types of systems. Both shutter assemblies have horizontal vanes, but some crossflow radiator designs employ vertical vanes. The shutter assembly is designed to maintain and control the operating temperature of the engine coolant within a given range. It is commonly used on trucks operating in cold ambient conditions.

CAUTION Shutters are commonly used on trucks that employ JWAC systems. Shutters should not be used on engines equipped with AAAC systems unless the installation provides for mounting the shutter between the AAAC core and the radiator core. Mounting a shutter assembly in front of the AAAC core will result in hot air from the turbocharger compressor entering the engine. This can cause short valve and piston life as well as poor fuel economy and a reduction in engine power.

Shutters are only used in conjunction with a clutch fan. With the shutters in the closed position, a fan would be highly stressed in attempting to pull air through a closed radiator core. To prevent this condition from occurring, a thermally operated fan clutch is used, which can be disengaged until the radiator shutters are opened. The actual engine coolant temperature at which the shutters and thermatic fan engage depends on the opening temperature of the engine coolant thermostat. The basic sequence of events for a heavy-duty class 8 truck equipped with 82°C (180°F) coolant thermostats, shutters, and a thermatic clutch fan is presented in Figure 12-10. The vanes, or individual blinds, of the shutter assembly are connected by

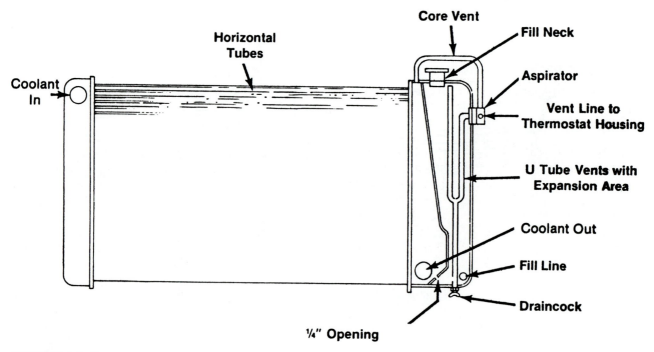

FIGURE 12–8 Identification of components of a crossflow radiator system. (Courtesy of Cummins Engine Company, Inc.)

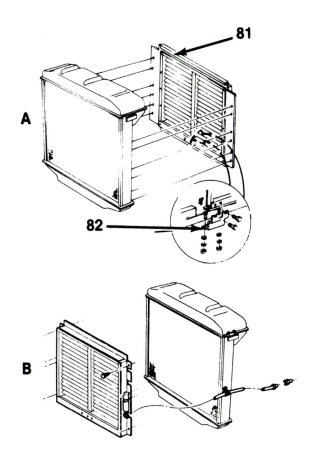

81. Shutter Assembly
82. Bracket
A. Rear Installation
B. Front Installation

F-03883

FIGURE 12–9 *Heavy-duty radiator shutter arrangement showing (A) the shutter assembly located behind the radiator core and (B) the shutter located in front of the radiator core. (Courtesy of GMC Trucks.)*

mechanical rod linkage so that they can be opened or closed to suit engine operating temperature conditions.

The power unit that rotates the vanes is an air cylinder which operates on compressed air from the vehicle air brake reservoir. The shutters are either fully open or fully closed. To prevent overheating of the engine in the event of a system malfunction, the shutters are normally held open by spring pressure and closed by air pressure.

THERMOSTATS

Purpose and Function
Although the radiator or heat exchanger system absorbs and dissipates the rejected heat to the cooling system, to maintain a steady coolant temperature under all operating conditions, all internal combustion engines employ temperature-controlled thermostats (stats) or regulators. The thermostat(s) is normally located within a bolted housing at the top front of the engine block as illustrated in Figure 12-11. To perform effectively, a stat must operate as follows:

- Start to open at a specified temperature
- Be fully open at a specified number of degrees above the *start-to-open* temperature
- Allow a specified amount of coolant under pressure to flow when the stat is fully open
- Block all coolant flow to the radiator when in the closed position

As you can see in Figure 12-11B, all engine coolant flows through a bypass pipe (hose) back to the suction side of the water pump at temperatures below the opening point of the stat. Additional coolant requirements of the pump during this period are supplied through a makeup or fill line. When the engine coolant reaches the stat opening temperature, engine coolant flows through the open stat to the top radiator hose as shown in Figure 12-12 to the baffle area of the radiator top tank. This hot coolant then passes through the radiator tubes where it gives up its heat to the airflow moving through the radiator fins.

Types
Depending on the cooling system design three basic types of thermostats can be used in diesel engines: full blocking, nonblocking, and partial blocking. Let's look more closely at each one of these types.

Figure 12-13 illustrates the full-blocking type of stat. Figure 12-12 depicts the actual flow of coolant through the stat to the radiator HE (heat exchanger) as well as the bypass circuit. During engine warm-up, all engine coolant flows through the bypass circuit, thereby preventing any coolant from being exposed to heat loss by flowing through the radiator or HE. This provides for a faster warm-up period. As the thermostat begins to open, increasing amounts of engine coolant flow to the radiator or HE, and bypass flow is correspondingly reduced. At approximately 15 to 20°F (8 to 11°C) above the opening temperature of the stat, the bypass opening is fully blocked and the total flow of coolant is directed into the radiator or HE.

The partial blocking type of stat shown in Figure 12-14 directs coolant to a bypass passage connected to the water pump when cold (closed), but directs all coolant flow to the radiator or HE when hot (open). Figure 12-15 illustrates a partial blocking, or shielded stat assembly as it would actually appear.

Figure 12-16 illustrates a nonblocking (choke or

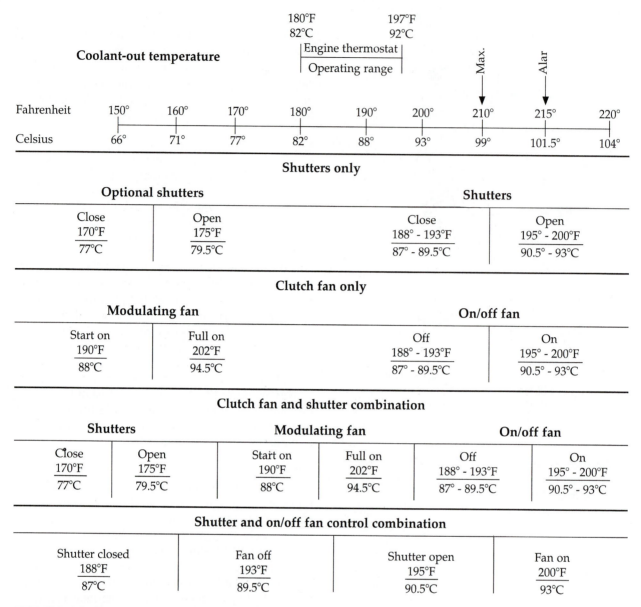

FIGURE 12–10 Heavy-duty truck cooling system operating temperatures for various components when using a 180°F opening thermostat(s).

poppet-type) thermostat which will always bypass some coolant down the bypass line to the water pump while the stat is open or closed.

Construction and Operation

Engine coolant is corrosive even when properly maintained and treated with antifreeze and SCAs. Stats, therefore, are normally made from brass or brass-coated materials. The stat consists of a brass cup filled with a heat-expansive, waxlike material (sometimes referred to as beeswax) retained within the cup by an elastomeric seal. The stat valve is connected to a piston that is held on the elastomer by a spring. Figure 12-17 illustrates the basic construction and operation of a thermostat.

A stat can be vented or nonvented. The *vent* refers to the deaeration capability of the cooling system. The design of the cooling system determines whether the stat is vented. In a vented system, venting is accomplished by drilling a small hole in the stat valve or notching the valve at its seat (see the design shown in Figure 12-13). Nonvented stats should only be installed in cooling systems of the positive deaeration type. This is usually the case if one or more deaeration lines (hoses) extend from the stat housing area to the radiator or HE top tank.

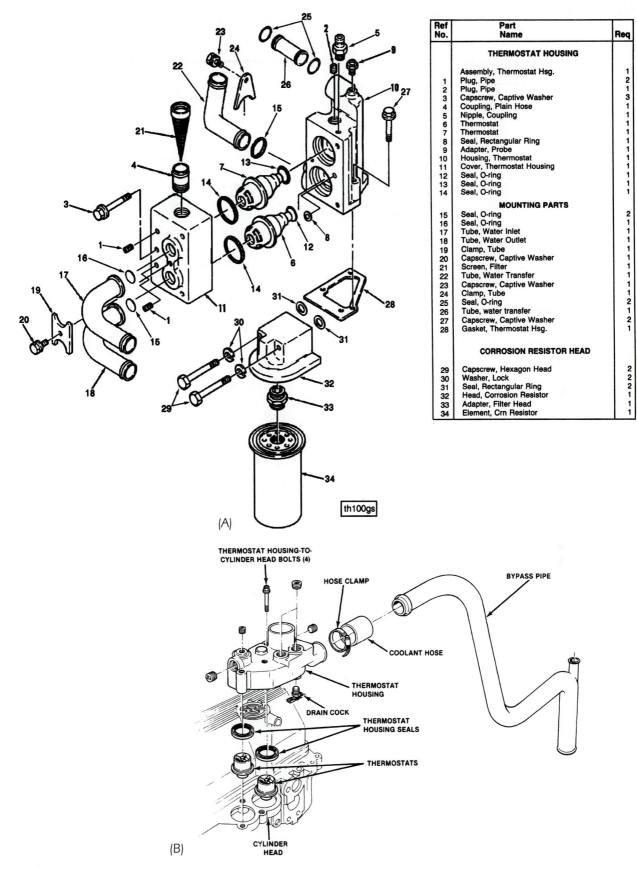

Ref No.	Part Name	Req
	THERMOSTAT HOUSING	
	Assembly, Thermostat Hsg.	1
1	Plug, Pipe	2
2	Plug, Pipe	1
3	Capscrew, Captive Washer	3
4	Coupling, Plain Hose	1
5	Nipple, Coupling	1
6	Thermostat	1
7	Thermostat	1
8	Seal, Rectangular Ring	1
9	Adapter, Probe	1
10	Housing, Thermostat	1
11	Cover, Thermostat Housing	1
12	Seal, O-ring	1
13	Seal, O-ring	1
14	Seal, O-ring	1
	MOUNTING PARTS	
15	Seal, O-ring	2
16	Seal, O-ring	1
17	Tube, Water Inlet	1
18	Tube, Water Outlet	1
19	Clamp, Tube	1
20	Capscrew, Captive Washer	1
21	Screen, Filter	1
22	Tube, Water Transfer	1
23	Capscrew, Captive Washer	1
24	Clamp, Tube	1
25	Seal, O-ring	2
26	Tube, water transfer	1
27	Capscrew, Captive Washer	2
28	Gasket, Thermostat Hsg.	1
	CORROSION RESISTOR HEAD	
29	Capscrew, Hexagon Head	2
30	Washer, Lock	2
31	Seal, Rectangular Ring	2
32	Head, Corrosion Resistor	1
33	Adapter, Filter Head	1
34	Element, Crn Resistor	1

FIGURE 12–11 (A) Exploded view of the component parts of the thermostat housing used on N14 model engines; (B) thermostats and related parts for a series 60 DDC engine model. [(A) Courtesy of Cummins Engine Company, Inc.; (B) Courtesy of Detroit Diesel Corporation.]

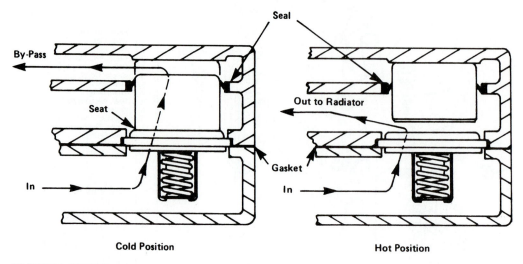

FIGURE 12-12 Coolant flow to the bypass pipe and to the radiator in the cold and hot positions when using a fully blocking type of thermostat. (Courtesy of Cummins Engine Company, Inc.)

Designs

Engine manufacturers employ various types of stats and locate one or more within a housing similar to that shown in Figure 12-11. For example, in the Cummins optimized JWAC and LFC radiator cooling system, two stats are used within a common housing; one stat is a bypass type while the other is a radiator type. At engine startup, the bypass stat is wide open and the radiator stat is closed. Coolant flows through the stat housing to the JWAC aftercooler inlet to allow the gradually warming coolant to heat the intake air for more efficient combustion. When the coolant temperature reaches 160°F (71°C), flow to the aftercooler decreases as the bypass stat begins to close. At coolant temperatures below 175°F (79°C), there is no coolant flow through the radiator core; all of the coolant flows through the bypass stat to the aftercooler. Take careful note that at 175°F (79°C) the radiator stat begins to open and some coolant begins to flow to the radiator; therefore, between 175 and 185°F (79 to 85°C), the two stats operate together to control the flow and temperature of coolant flow to the aftercooler and the radiator.

At engine coolant temperatures above 185°F (85°C), the bypass stat to the JWAC is fully closed. The radiator stat continues to open until it is fully open at 195°F (91°C) or higher and all engine coolant flows to and through the radiator as illustrated in Figure 12-7.

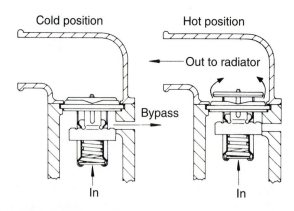

FIGURE 12-13 Weir fully blocking thermostat design. (Courtesy of Detroit Diesel Corporation.)

FIGURE 12-14 Coolant flow through a partial blocking thermostat. (Courtesy of Detroit Diesel Corporation.)

FIGURE 12-15 *Partial or semiblocking (shielded) thermostat. (Courtesy of Detroit Diesel Corporation.)*

The maximum allowable coolant temperature in these engines is 212°F (100°C). Depending on the Cummins engine model in use, 10 to 20 U.S. gpm (38 to 76 L) of coolant flows through the radiator stat to the low-flow radiator.

Removal and Inspection

In cases of engine or coolant overheating, many service personnel remove the thermostats. This should only be done, however, as a temporary measure to allow possible relocating of the vehicle or equipment when all else fails. Stat removal normally should *not* be done. Operating an engine without a stat is not recommended because the engine will run too cool,

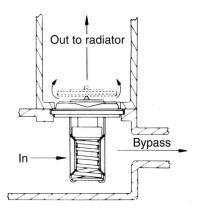

FIGURE 12-16 *Coolant flow through a nonblocking (choke or poppet) thermostat. (Courtesy of Detroit Diesel Corporation.)*

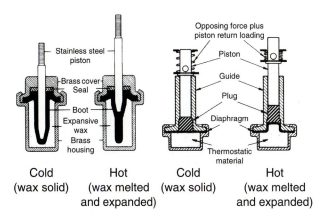

FIGURE 12-17 *Construction and operation of a typical thermostat assembly. (Courtesy of Detroit Diesel Corporation.)*

thereby causing condensation of water and incomplete combustion, which results in corrosive acids and sludge forming in the lube oil. This can restrict lube oil flow and accelerate engine wear. In addition, poor combustion causes rough idling and increased amounts of exhaust pollutants and white smoke (water vapor). When using full- or partial-blocking stats that fail to open fully (or stick closed), the bypass system will remain open and prevent a sufficient flow of coolant to the radiator or HE. As a result, the engine coolant temperature may rise even higher.

Opening Temperature and Distance

Each stat is designed and constructed to start to open at a specific temperature, which is stamped on the stem or housing area. The stat control section moves through a set distance to its fully open position. For example, Figure 12-15 shows that this stat should move through a distance of 23.36 ± 0.76 mm (0.920 ± 0.030 in.). Failure of the stat to open fully will restrict the engine coolant from reaching the rad or HE. For example, a 180°F (82°C) stat would have a start-to-open temperature in the range of 177 to 183°F (81 to 83°C) and should be fully open at approximately 197°F (92°C).

Operational Check

Never apply direct flame heat to a stat to cause it to open. Do not allow the stat to sit directly against the bottom of a metal container filled with water during the test. Ideally, the stat should be suspended in a container of clean water as shown in Figure 12-18 along with a suspended thermometer. Some stat test kits include a small drive motor that spins a propeller to agitate the water constantly. If this is not available, stir the water during the heating process.

Follow these steps as part of your operational check of a thermostat:

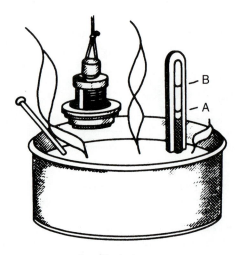

A – Starts to open
B – Fully open

FIGURE 12–18 *Test equipment needed to perform a thermostat operational check. (Courtesy of Detroit Diesel Corporation.)*

1. Note the temperature stamped on the stat.
2. Carefully record the temperature at which the stat starts to open. It may take 10 minutes for some stats to reach their full open condition.
3. Carefully watch the thermometer; the stat should be *fully open* at approximately 15 to 20°F (8 to 11°C) above the stamped value on the stat.
4. Using vernier calipers, carefully measure the distance that the stat has moved from closed to open. Figure 12-15 shows one example of a stat opening distance. Refer to the engine service literature for the spec relative to your engine make and model.
5. Replace a stat that fails to open at the correct temperature or fails to open fully.

Stats can become damaged from an overheated engine condition, which may be due to restriction to coolant flow through the radiator or HE (scale, hardened gel), collapsed or weak hoses, slipping fan belts, coolant leaks, or aerated coolant. Stats that are stuck open prevent the engine from reaching its normal operating temperature. A stat that does not open, or only opens partially, can cause engine overheating. Prior to replacing stats, make sure that the stat housing seating/seal and gasket areas are cleaned of rust and scale buildup. When installing a new seal (Figure 12-11), make certain that the seal is installed in the proper direction and use a seal driver so that the seal is not kinked or installed off square when driven into the housing(s). Apply a small amount of clean engine oil to lubricate the seal lips before pushing the stats into position. Some engines employ horizontally installed stats and seals, whereas others have vertically in-stalled stats and seals. When installing the stat housing gasket, be careful not to apply excessive amounts of gasket cement. Cement can damage the seal lip or accumulate on the stat. If a stat housing drain cock or vent cock is used, apply a coating of Loctite Pipe Sealer with Teflon or equivalent to the threads.

ANTIFREEZE

The AF (antifreeze) used in diesel engines can be of the EG (ethylene glycol) type or the aqueous PG (propylene glycol) type. PG is essentially EG with a methyl group attached to one end, and its chemistry is similar to that of EG. PG is propylene oxide combined with water to form the glycol.

One of the major advantages of PG is that the U.S. Food and Drug Administration has classified it as GRAS (generally regarded as safe). EG, however, is frequently responsible for poisoning cats and dogs who are drawn to its sweet taste. Consider also that 32 fluid ounces (950 milliliters) of ingested PG can be fatal to a 150-lb (68-kg) person, while less than 4 fluid ounces (100 mL) of EG is fatal. In the United States, the Clean Air Act considers EG a hazardous air pollutant. In addition, the U.S. Occupational Safety and Health Administration (OSHA), which regulates workplace safety, has placed an 8-hour average exposure standard for EG at 50 ppm. On the other hand, PG has not been considered dangerous enough to require safety legislation standards. In the face of increasing environmental concerns regarding EG, the adoption of PG-based antifreezes can be expected in heavy-duty diesel trucks and equipment.

All AFs must be disposed of in a safe manner. Most local regulations consider used AF a hazardous waste due to the heavy metals that accumulate. Because of their high biochemical oxygen demands, neither EG or PG can be disposed of in sewer systems. Check with local, state, provincial, or federal agencies for the proper disposal guidelines. Take careful note that both EG and PG antifreeze can now be cleaned and recycled, and both are biodegradable. A variety of portable AF recycling machines are available from most major equipment and tool suppliers.

Tests have shown that PG used with the same SCA package that is used with EG provides extra cavitation corrosion protection equivalent to at least 20 to 40%. Thus it offers significant advantages to users of heavy-duty diesel engines.

Antifreeze is used for boil-over protection, freeze protection, and some corrosion protection. AF solutions should be used year-round to provide a stable environment for seals and hoses. The freeze protection value depends on the concentration of AF used. A 40%

AF-to-water mix offers freeze protection to about −10°F (−23°C), while a 60% AF-to-water mix offers protection to about −65°F (−55°C). Never use more than a 67% maximum AF–water solution; more than that can adversely affect coolant freezing and boiling temperatures, increase silicate levels, and reduce heat transfer. A 50% glycol mix is considered optimal. Table 12-1 illustrates various cooling system capacities in U.S. gallons and the freeze protection offered when using EG-type AF based on the volume of AF that is added to the system. The cooling system capacity is generally listed in the engine or vehicle service literature. When adding or topping off coolant, never use a 100% AF solution as makeup coolant or straight water; always mix AF with water to provide the same concentration as the initial fill. Otherwise, dilution or possible overconcentration of the system coolant can occur.

Heavy-duty diesel engine antifreeze consists of a number of chemicals and is formulated with a balance of nitrite, nitrate, borate, small amounts of sodium silicate, and azoles to protect soft metals. These additives provide a very effective corrosion inhibitor, particularly for aluminum components. As sodium silicate depletes over time, it can "drop out" of the coolant solution through a process called catalytic polymerization. In this process, individual silicate molecules unite in the presence of engine heat and form larger particles that precipitate in the form of gel, which can plug coolant passages.

TESTING THE COOLANT

Fleet service technicians are charged with the responsibility of maintaining the cooling system. Typical coolant should be maintained with a 50 to 67% antifreeze precharged with 3% Nalcool; then a Need Release filter should be installed to safeguard the system. This coolant mix will establish a recommended inhibitor level for cost-effective protection. Two technologies are dominant in heavy-duty diesel engine cooling systems today:

1. Nalcool 3000, distributed through the Power Fleet Division, Penray Companies, Inc., is the primary SCA (supplemental coolant additive) used by Caterpillar and Detroit Diesel.
2. DCA-4 (diesel coolant additive, fourth generation) is the primary SCA used by Cummins, which owns Fleetguard.

SPECIAL NOTE Since most heavy-duty diesel engines employ either the Penray Nalcool or Fleetguard SCA products, a conversion factor of recommended SCA levels from Nalcool to Fleetguard DCA units, and vice versa, is required. One DCA unit is equivalent to 2.0 volume percent Nalcool measured as 800 ppm (parts per million) nitrite.

The SCAs must be checked closely and analyzed to ensure that the coolant mix is within levels recommended by engine manufacturers. Control of the SCAs is one of the major reasons for field and lab analysis of heavy-duty diesel engine coolants; therefore, it is very important that the diesel technician understand this test procedure.

Most SCAs are formulated for use with both EG and PG antifreeze. Nevertheless, if you are using PG check with the SCA supplier to make sure that its package will work with PG. Remember, using an SCA package that is not suitable for PG will result in coolant dropout.

Overconcentration of SCAs causes a high level of solids to gather in the cooling system. Chemical deposits at the water pump seal weep hole are usually an indication of overconcentration. Underconcentration of SCAs can result in pitting of liner surfaces. Checking for overconcentration of SCAs can be done by testing reserve alkalinity and conductivity, but checking usually requires special kits or a coolant sample taken to a lab for analysis. Overconcentration of SCAs can lead to these conditions:

- Deposits on heat transfer surfaces and fouling of the cooling system with precipitated additives
- Water pump seal leaks
- Plugging of coolant passages from solder bloom/corrosion or silicate gelation

To effectively test the condition of the coolant for glycol and nitrite as well as TDS (total dissolved solids), a number of coolant test kits are available commercially. These kits allow the technician to test the coolant for proper SCA concentration as well as TDS and pH level, which is a measure of the degree of alkalinity or acidity of the coolant. The optimum pH is generally within the range 7.5 to 11.0. A reading below 7.5 pH indicates acidity, while one above 11.0 pH indicates an alkaline concentration. Consider the following cooling pH scale:

0	7.5	11	14
Acidic corrosion of iron, steel, copper, brass	Optimum coolant pH range	Alkaline corrosion of aluminum and solder	

TABLE 12–1   Selection guide for cooling system freeze protection[a]

[c]	2[b]	3	4	5	6	7	8	9	10	11	12	13	14	15	16	17	18
7	6°[d]	−17°	−54°														
8	10°	−7°	−34°	−62°													
9	14°	0°	−21°	−50°													
10	16°	4°	−12°	−34°	−62°												
11	18°	8°	−6°	−23°	−47°	−62°											
12	19°	10°	0°	−15°	−34°	−57°											
13	21°	13°	3°	−9°	−25°	−45°	−62°										
14		15°	6°	−5°	−18°	−34°	−54°										
15		16°	8°	0°	−12°	−26°	−43°	−62°									
16		17°	10°	2°	−8°	−19°	−34°	−52°	−62°								
17		18°	12°	5°	−4°	−14°	−27°	−42°	−58°								
18		19°	14°	7°	0°	−10°	−21°	−34°	−50°	−62°							
19		20°	15°	9°	2°	−7°	−16°	−28°	−42°	−56°							
20			16°	10°	4°	−3°	−12°	−22°	−34°	−48°	−62°						
21			17°	12°	6°	0°	−9°	−17°	−28°	−41°	−54°	−62°					
22			18°	13°	8°	2°	−6°	−14°	−23°	−34°	−47°	−59°					
23			19°	14°	9°	4°	−3°	−10°	−19°	−29°	−40°	−52°	−62°				
24			19°	15°	10°	5°	0°	−8°	−15°	−24°	−34°	−46°	−58°				
25			20°	16°	12°	7°	1°	−5°	−12°	−20°	−29°	−40°	−52°	−62°			
26			21°	17°	13°	8°	3°	−3°	−9°	−16°	−25°	−34°	−45°	−57°			
27				17°	14°	9°	4°	0°	−6°	−13°	−22°	−30°	−38°	−50°	−62°		
28				18°	15°	10°	6°	1°	−5°	−11°	−18°	−27°	−34°	−44°	−55°	−62°	
29				18°	15°	11°	7°	3°	−2°	−8°	−15°	−23°	−30°	−38°	−48°	−58°	
30				19	16°	12°	8°	4°	0°	−6°	−12°	−19°	−26°	−34°	−43°	−53°	−62°

Source: Peterbilt Motors Company, Division of PACCAR.

[a] Ethylene glycol-base antifreeze

Ethylene glycol-base antifreeze	25%	33%	40%	50%	60%
Protects to:	10°	0°	−12°	−34°	−62°

[b] Gallons of ethylene glycol–base antifreeze required.
[c] Cooling system capacity in gallons.
[d] Degrees of temperature in Fahrenheit.

Note: 60% ethylene glycol–base antifreeze and 40% water by volume gives maximum protection. *Never* use concentrated ethylene glycol–base antifreeze, as it will freeze at approximately 0°F.

Acids can form when glycol degrades or gases bleed past gaskets into the coolant. The Nalcool/Penray two-way test strip kit includes directions on the strip container to guide the technician on how to interpret and compare the nitrite and glycol content, as well as the acidity or alkaline level of the coolant. After dipping a test strip into the coolant and removing it, the color change on the test strip is compared with the colored blocks on the container to determine coolant SCA condition. Another test kit is used to check for MBT (mercaptobenzothiazole) and nitrite in a coolant sample. Directions in this container describe how to draw a small sample of coolant and how to mix the solutions in the various plastic bottles until a specific color change to the coolant is noted. Record the number of drops of solution required to cause a coolant color change; then refer to the directions to determine if additional SCAs need to be added. If you are using a Cummins Fleetguard test kit, note that this same procedure will indicate how many DCA-4s are required. Too much SCA can lead to silicate dropout, while too little SCA can create corrosion and cavitation. A TDS (total dissolved solids) tester can quickly indicate the solid particle percentage in the coolant when dipped into the radiator top tank by measuring the conductivity between two probes of the tester. The level of dissolved solids in the coolant water should generally not exceed 340 ppm (20 grams per gallon). The higher a coolant's TDS, the greater the amount of corrosion and scale buildup that will occur.

SCALE BUILDUP

All engines radiate a great deal of heat, which is normally removed by the coolant as it flows through the engine. Scale or rust developed in the coolant passages acts as an insulator and blocks heat transfer. Scale occurs when magnesium and calcium (always present in tap water) are deposited on the heated metal surfaces inside the cooling system. Normally, scale occurs where temperatures are highest, such as at the cylinder head and the outside of wet liners, as well as in heat exchanger or radiator cores. Depending on the water used (hardness, alkalinity, acidity, and so on), scale tends to form a hard white crust. Scale deposits on the outside of a wet liner can cause it to expand unevenly, and the liner metal can actually bulge inward in the areas of hot spots. As the pistons and rings move up and down within the liners, irregular ring and liner wear occur. This causes metal scuffing to take place between the rings, pistons, and the liner surface. Eventually, metal scoring occurs, which is an advanced stage of scuffing. The tearing metal creates stuck or broken rings, piston damage, and possible piston-to-liner seizure. Cylinder head cracking is another inevitable result.

COOLANT FILTERS

Many heavy-duty engines employ coolant filter conditioners that have two basic functions: to provide the most effective way of controlling the addition of SCAs and to provide the benefits of mechanical filtration. These filters, which are the bypass type, are plumbed into the system so that coolant under pressure from the engine block enters the inlet side of the filter assembly and returns to a low-pressure side of the coolant system (back toward the suction side of the water pump). Two shutoff valves allow the technician to prevent any coolant loss from the block when changing the coolant filter.

Figure 12-19 illustrates a typical coolant filter for a heavy-duty high-speed engine. This particular Need Release filter assembly, which is manufactured by Penray/Nalcool, is designed to release the correct amount of SCAs into the coolant during engine operation to provide complete cooling system protection for up to 1 year or 120,000 miles (193,116 km). As the chemically balanced SCAs (inhibitors) within the coolant deplete, the metal alloy membranes within the filter cartridge detect the need for additional corrosion protection. Before the system reaches a corrosive condition, the *Need Release membranes* release the exact amount of treatment necessary to adjust the system to the proper level of corrosion protection.

FLUSHING THE SYSTEM

The cooling system should be flushed at a recommended time interval as stated by the engine manufacturer in the service literature. Suggested mileage or time was discussed in the "Antifreeze" section of this chapter. After draining and flushing the system, follow the manufacturer's recommendation for precharging the cooling system.

CAUTION   Service personnel often back, or reverse, flush the cooling system. In this procedure a pressurized water hose is connected to the bottom radiator hose or heat exchanger to force liquid out of the top hose outlet. This reverse flushing procedure should only be considered a salvage operation. Back flushing can loosen scale formations that cause the cooling system to clog at a later date during the operation.

Each time that the antifreeze is changed, the coolant system should be cleaned (flushed) with Nalprep 2001, Fleetguard Restore, or an equivalent to

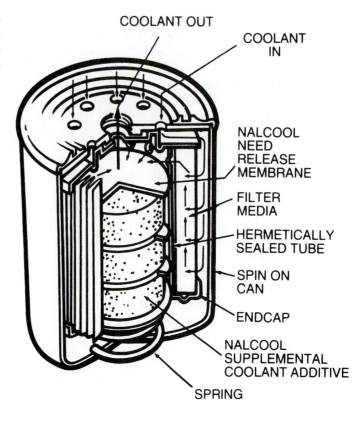

FIGURE 12-19 Cutaway view of a typical coolant system filter assembly. (Courtesy of Power Fleet Division, The Penray Companies, Inc.)

COOLANT OUT

COOLANT IN

NALCOOL NEED RELEASE MEMBRANE

FILTER MEDIA

HERMETICALLY SEALED TUBE

SPIN ON CAN

ENDCAP

NALCOOL SUPPLEMENTAL COOLANT ADDITIVE

SPRING

ensure that the system is thoroughly clean before adding Nalcool 3000 or equivalent, followed by a water antifreeze mix. Follow these steps when flushing the system:

1. Thoroughly power flush the complete cooling system using a flushing kit. Limit the air pressure to 138 kPa (20 psi) because excess pressure applied to the water can damage the radiator, thermostat, and water pump seals. Back, or reverse, flushing the cooling system can be considered a salvage operation if after using a commercially available chemical cleaner the radiator core is still partially dirty. Figure 12-20 illustrates how to reverse flush the radiator core using hot water forced through the system in the opposite direction to normal coolant flow.

CAUTION Reverse flushing can cause small loosened scale particles to damage internal seals within the water pump and thermostat areas. It is better to remove the radiator and have it repaired at a radiator shop.

---

2. Add 2 L of Nalprep 2001 or equivalent for every 30 L of water. If using Fleetguard Restore, add 1 U.S. gallon (3.8 L) for each 10 to 15 U.S. gallons (38 to 57 L) of water.

3. Start and run the engine for 1.5 to 2 hours.

This can be done in the shop or yard area, or the vehicle can be road tested to ensure circulation of the cleaner from all cooling system surfaces and passages.

4. Allow the engine to cool, then drain the cooling system and flush it with fresh water, or fill the system with clean fresh water and run the engine for 5 minutes at high idle with the coolant temperature above 185°F (85°C).

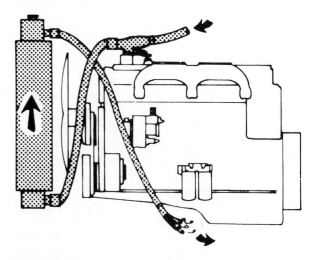

FIGURE 12-20 Hookup procedure used to reverse, or back flush, a radiator. (Courtesy of Cummins Engine Company, Inc.)

NOTE If the cooling system has already started to overheat due to severe gelling problems, a longer cleaning period may be required. Proceed to step 5 if this is the case.

5. Perform steps 1 and 2. Then leave the cleaner, such as Nalprep 2001 or equivalent, in the cooling system for 250 hours, 30 days, or 16 to 20,000 km (9942 to 12,428 miles), whichever comes first. Nalprep 2001 will not harm cooling system metals, seals, or hoses. It will not cause deterioration of cooling system sealants as some high PH cleaners will.

6. Completely drain the coolant from the engine and flush with fresh water as in step 4. Add Nalcool 3000 (with Stabil-Aid) or equivalent; then add a mixture of antifreeze and water to the cooling system. On a Cummins engine, install a new *initial charge* coolant filter and a 50-50 mix of antifreeze to ensure the correct DCA-4 concentration.

PRESSURE CAPS

There are two descriptive terms that you may come across when dealing with cooling systems regardless of whether a radiator or heat exchanger system is being used. The first term is *A/W* (air-to-water differential) and is the difference between engine *coolant out*, or the top tank temperature, and the ambient air temperature. For example, with a stabilized top tank temperature of 185°F (85°C), and with air entering the radiator at 100°F (38°C), the differential is 85°F (29°C). The second term is *ATB* (air-to-boil) and represents the ambient air temperature at which top tank boiling occurs. The boiling point should always be considered as 212°F (100°C). For example, consider the same engine operating at 185°F (85°C) with air at 100°F (38°C): 212°F (100°C) − 185°F (85°C) = 27°F (15°C) + 100°F (38°C) ambient = 127°F (53°C) air-to-boil.

All cooling systems are able to handle a specific heat load from a given engine and are designed to prevent engine overheating at sea level without the use of a pressure cap. A pressure cap, illustrated in Figure 12-21 is used to protect against boiling at above baseline elevations. System pressure is required to maintain water pump performance at elevated coolant temperature, to prevent loss of coolant at low-boiling-point altitudes, and to reduce coolant loss due to after boil at engine shutdown. Each pound of pressure applied to the cooling system raises the boiling point of the coolant by approximately 3°F (1.7°C); therefore, a 7-lb (48-kPa) pressure cap on a cooling system will raise the boiling point of the coolant from 212°F (100°C) at sea level to 232.5°F (111°C). For each 1000 ft (305 m) in altitude, the boiling point decreases by approximately 1.25°F (0.5°C). The opening pressure for all pressure caps is stamped or inscribed on the top of the cap in psi (kPa). For example, a number 12 indicates a 12-psi (83-kPa) cap.

Figure 12-21 illustrates a typical pressure cap for a cooling system. When the coolant pressure acting on

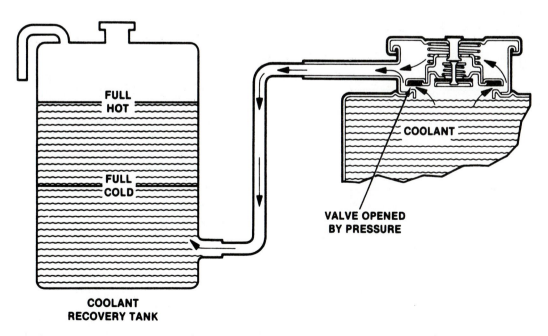

FULL HOT

FULL COLD

COOLANT

VALVE OPENED BY PRESSURE

COOLANT RECOVERY TANK

FIGURE 12–21 *Process of radiator pressure cap opening and directing expanded coolant to a recovery tank. (Courtesy of Detroit Diesel Corporation.)*

the underside of the pressure cap seal against the spring becomes high enough, the valve unseats and hot coolant is normally routed to a surge tank to prevent any loss of coolant. When the spring pressure is greater than that developed in the cooling system, the valve closes. When an engine is shut down and the coolant starts to lose its temperature, it contracts, thereby reducing the pressure within the radiator, surge tank, or bottle and cooling system. To prevent collapse of hoses and other nonsupported components, a second and smaller valve within the pressure cap assembly opens as this vacuum is created. Figure 12-22 illustrates the action of this small valve, which usually opens at approximately 5/8 lb (4.3 kPa). The vacuum created as the fluid cools, sucks fluid from the radiator overflow line, which is normally connected to a separate surge tank or plastic bottle, and replenishes the radiator coolant volume.

To check the operating condition of the pressure cap, refer to Figure 12-23 which shows a hand tester installed on the cap. Pump up the pressure to the value stamped on the cap and note the rate of decrease on the gauge. If the pressure doesn't hold for approximately 10 seconds, replace the cap.

PRESSURE CHECKING THE COOLING SYSTEM

When coolant loss or overheating is a problem, the cooling system can be pressurized to help determine the location of the leak and to determine the causes of overheating under various operating conditions. Check the following areas:

Components that leak	Reasons for overheating
Hoses and clamps	Thermostat problem
Radiator cap	Aeration
Head and gasket	Shutter control thermostat
Water pump	Thermatic (thermally activated) fan thermostat
Cylinder liner O-rings or counterbore	
Radiator, oil cooler, aftercooler and heater cores	Clogged radiator fins
	Plugged radiator tubes
	Faulty water pump (slipping belt, broken impeller, or spinning of the impeller on its shaft)

A pressure check of the system can be performed in the following situations:

- During an engine rebuild when wet liners are replaced and before the oil pan is installed to check that the liner O-rings are not leaking
- During engine service when coolant is found in the engine oil and the liner O-rings may be the cause

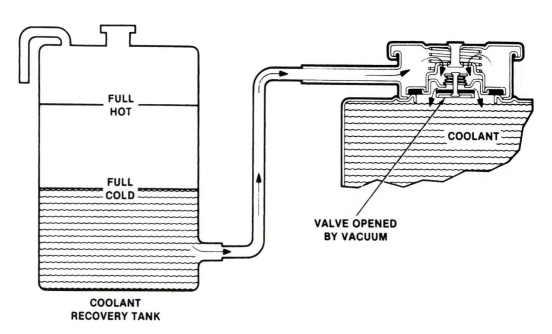

FULL HOT

FULL COLD

COOLANT

VALVE OPENED BY VACUUM

COOLANT RECOVERY TANK

FIGURE 12–22 Opening of radiator cap vacuum valve as the engine cools to allow coolant to be recovered from the expansion tank, thereby preventing collapse of radiator hoses. (Courtesy of Detroit Diesel Corporation.)

- Suspected leak of a cylinder head water seal ring or gasket
- Suspected leak of an injector sleeve
- Suspected leak of fluid by the external engine cooling system components
- Checking the radiator or heat exchanger pressure cap for its opening pressure as well as the vacuum portion of the cap when the engine is shut down

Figure 12-23 illustrates a standard cooling system pressure tester kit, which consists of a special graduated pressure gauge mounted to a hand-operated pump, a radiator filler neck adapter, a pressure cap adapter, a rubber filler neck plug, and a hose assembly. Some models of cooling system analyzer kits come with a temperature probe to allow the technician to check the exact temperature of the cooling system while under pressure. The kit also allows troubleshooting of thermostat openings, thermatic fan operating range, and electronic temperature sensors, and it monitors new and rebuilt engines through warm-up cycles. The cooling system is easily checked for pressure by hooking up the shop-regulated air supply to a pressure probe and dialing in the desired test pressure. Unlike a hand-operated pump test system, by using shop air the cooling system can be left pressurized for an extended period of time to find difficult and intermittent leaks. In addition, with the kit pressure probe, the cylinder head can be diagnosed for cracks, blown head gaskets, and leaking piston sleeves.

Attach the hand pump shown in Figure 12-23 to the radiator expansion/surge tank cap neck to check the cooling system for suspected leaks. Build up the system pressure by viewing the gauge until it registers the release pressure stamped on the radiator cap. The

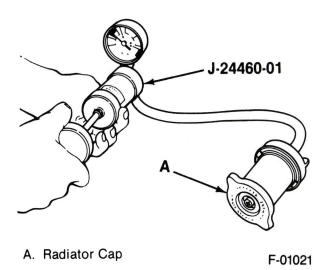

A. Radiator Cap   F-01021

FIGURE 12–23 *Using a pressure pump to establish the opening pressure of the radiator cap. (Courtesy of GMC Trucks.)*

system should hold pressure for about 2 minutes; if it doesn't, check for signs of external or internal leaks.

EXPANSION TANKS AND HEAT EXCHANGERS

In stationary gen-set or marine engine applications, the radiator and fan cooling system is replaced by an ET (expansion tank) and HE (heat exchanger) core. The ET is a large cast iron receptacle that acts as a header tank; it is similar to the top tank and/or ET used in a radiator and fan system (Figure 12-24). Note that the expansion tank on high-performance marine engines illustrated in Figure 12-24 is used in conjunction with deaerators on 3408/3412 Caterpillar engines. The deaerators shown in Figure 12-25 are designed to remove tiny air bubbles from the coolant. Excessive air bubbles can lead to water pump cavitation and reduced coolant flow; therefore, proper deaeration is mandatory. This is achieved by means of two swirl chamber air separator housings on V-model engines from each cylinder bank. These deaerators allow a much smaller expansion tank to be used, and they are designed to operate on the principle of a centrifuge. As the hot coolant enters the chamber, it begins to swirl and forces the coolant to the outside and onto the heat exchanger. The air bubbles move to the center of the deaerator and exit through a short hose to the expansion tank as can be seen in Figure 12-25.

Directly below the ET is a tubular-type heat exchanger assembly with an engine-driven raw water pump connection (Figure 12-24). The coolant pump flow through the 3606 engine is quoted as being 228 U.S. gallons per minute (880 L) at 1000-rpm engine speed; for the 3616 model, it is 546 U.S. gallons per minute (2100 L) at 1000-rpm engine speed. The ET has a filler cap that may or may not contain a spring-loaded pressure cap. An overflow tube is generally plumbed into the ET; the tube can be routed to a receptacle, or it may vent directly into the bilge on a marine installation. The ET provides a means of filling the engine cooling system as well as providing space for fluid expansion of the coolant as its temperature rises.

In the HE system, the engine is filled with a fresh water coolant mixture similar to that used in a radiator system. To cool the hot, fresh engine coolant, raw seawater, city water, or lake water can be pumped through the HE core in a direction opposite to the flow of the fresh water. The raw water is circulated by the action of a gear- or belt-driven raw water pump (described later in this chapter). The sealed HE ensures that both the engine coolant and raw water flows never mix, since they are plumbed through separate tubing or cores. This can be seen in Figure 12-26 where the hot engine coolant flows from the cylinder head

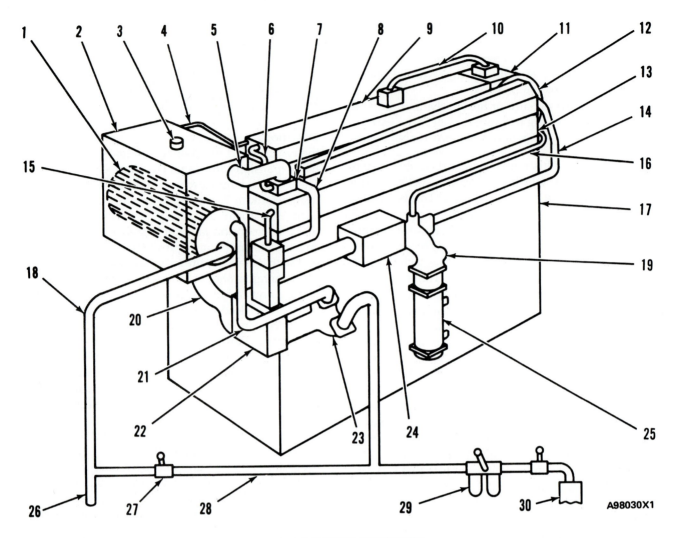

COOLING SYSTEM SCHEMATIC

1. Heat exchanger. 2. Expansion tank. 3. Pressure cap. 4. Vent line. 5. Outlet line. 6. Outlet line. 7. Regulator housing. 8. Aftercooler inlet line. 9. Water cooled manifold. 10. Outlet line. 11. Water cooled turbocharger. 12. Aftercooler housing. 13. Cylinder head. 14. Aftercooler outlet line. 15. Internal bypass (shunt) line. 16. Turbocharger inlet line. 17. Cylinder block. 18. Outlet line. 19. Bonnet. 20. Inlet line. 21. Inlet line. 22. Water pump. 23. Sea water pump. 24. Engine oil cooler. 25. Auxiliary oil cooler. 26. Outlet for sea water circuit. 27. Bypass valve. 28. Bypass line. 29. Duplex strainer. 30. Inlet for sea water circuit.

FIGURE 12–24 Flow path through a marine engine heat exchanger cooling system with a JWAC feature to reduce the temperature of the turbocharger boost air. (Courtesy of Caterpillar, Inc.)

water manifold through the thermostat(s) to the ET. The coolant then flows vertically through the cells of the HE core. The raw water flowing horizontally between the cells of the HE core lowers the temperature of the engine coolant as it passes through the cells. This engine coolant can then flow over a marine gear oil cooler and the engine oil cooler to lower the operating temperature of these two lubricants. The coolant is then directed into the suction side of the engine fresh water pump and is circulated through the engine block and cylinder head.

Smaller-horsepower (kW) high-speed marine in-

stallations have a cellular-type HE assembly that is usually contained within the expansion tank. Some larger applications may employ a tubular type of HE that is bracket mounted alongside the engine. To ensure proper filling of the HE cooling system, an air-bleed hose must be installed between the top of each thermostat housing and the top of the expansion tank.

Two raw water pumps on large V-model engines supply the raw water flow to and through the HEs. The warm raw water is then plumbed overboard on a marine application. In some industrial HE applications, a raw water cooling tank is used to recirculate

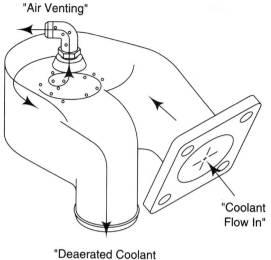

FIGURE 12-25 *Swirl chamber design of coolant deaerator housing used with a heat exchanger cooling system. (Courtesy of Caterpillar, Inc.)*

the raw city water to and through the HE system to minimize water usage.

Zinc Electrodes

To counteract electrolysis or galvanic action within the cooling system, zinc electrodes are normally screwed into and located in the HE inlet cover and the raw

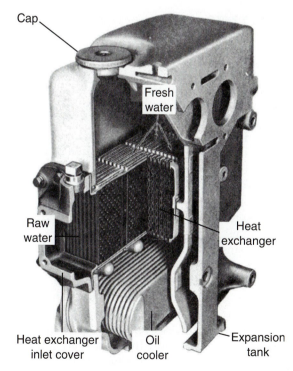

FIGURE 12-26 *Combination heat exchanger and expansion tank arrangement also showing the engine oil cooler. (Courtesy of Detroit Diesel Corporation.)*

water pump(s) inlet elbow. Most electrodes can be identified by their square brass head, which allows removal with a wrench. These electrodes act as sacrificial elements within the cooling system; that is, the electrolysis tends to corrode them rather than the other metal components within the cooling system.

Electrodes should be removed at given service intervals and inspected after cleaning with a wire brush. If an electrode is worn excessively, it should be replaced. To determine the condition of a used electrode, strike it sharply against a hard metal surface; a weakened electrode will break.

Cleaning the Heat Exchanger Core

As with a radiator cooling system, after many hours of operation, scale deposits can accumulate within the core of the heat exchanger, thereby reducing its efficiency. Soft water plus a good grade of antifreeze should be used as an engine coolant. At major engine overhaul, or if the heat exchanger fails to maintain the fresh engine coolant within its designed range, the HE may require cleaning. Follow these steps:

1. Drain the cooling system.
2. Remove the heat exchanger housing and/or core.

NOTE   To prevent drying and hardening of accumulated foreign substances, the HE core must be cleaned as soon as possible after removing it from service. The core can be cleaned at a commercial facility that has an ultrasound cleaning system, or use step 3 as follows.

---

3. Immerse the HE core in a scale solvent consisting of one-third muriatic acid and two-thirds water to which $1/2$ lb (0.226 kg) of oxalic acid has been added to each $2\frac{1}{2}$ U.S. gallons (9.5 L) of solution.
4. Remove the core when foaming and bubbling stops, which normally is about 30 to 60 seconds.
5. Flush the core thoroughly with clean hot water under pressure.

RAW WATER PUMPS

When a heat exchanger cooling system is used on an industrial or marine installation, a water pump(s) is required to circulate cooling raw water through the HE core. Most RWP (raw water pumps) are gear driven on diesel engines, but it is possible for these units to be belt driven. The RWP drive location varies in different makes and models of engines. Figure 12-27, a view across the center of the RWP, shows the normal flow of raw water. Note that both the inlet and outlet passages are located on the top of the pump housing. Because

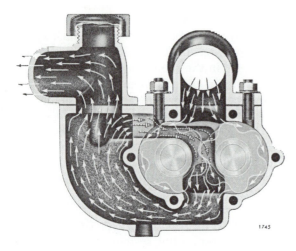

FIGURE 12–27 *View across the center of a Jabsco raw water pump illustrating the normal flow of water and recirculation of priming water through the channel at the rear of the pump housing. (Courtesy of Detroit Diesel Corporation.)*

these pumps are widely used in marine applications with salt water, the pump housing is usually manufactured from a bronze or brass material, and the impeller is manufactured from a rubber or neoprene material. In applications where the vessel may be running in frigid waters, a special impeller material must be used to avoid cracking of the impeller blades.

Figure 12-28 is a cutaway view of a typical RWP manufactured by Jabsco. The pump drive shaft (213) is supported by a prelubricated, shielded, double-row ball bearing (222). An oil seal (247 and 249) prevents oil leakage from the bearing compartment and a rotary seal (256) prevents water leakage along the shaft. A rubber/neoprene impeller (220) is splined to the end of the drive shaft (213) and is self-lubricated by the pumped water. Never run the pump any longer than required for the pump to prime itself; otherwise, impeller damage can occur. A wear plate (255) in the impeller compartment prevents wear of the pump housing and can be reversed if wear on the plate becomes excessive. A slot machined in the outer periphery of the wear plate registers with a dowel in the pump housing, thereby preventing the plate from rotating with the shaft assembly.

The flexible impeller allows these pumps to be operated in either a clockwise or counterclockwise direction. The pump end cover is marked with an arrow and the letters RH or LH to show the outlet port for either of these rotations. Once the pump has been operated in one direction, attempting to reverse its rotation will result in the impeller cracking at the base of the individual blades (vanes). Within the pump housing is an offset cam (250) designed to direct the flow within the housing. This cam causes the impeller to take up a set

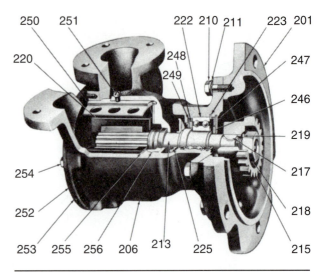

201. Adaptor – pump	225. Oil slinger – shaft
206. Housing – pump	246. Washer – felt
210. Bolt – housing to adaptor	247. Seal – bearing
	248. Washer – felt
211. Lock washer	249. Seal – bearing
213. Shaft – drive	250. Cam – offset
215. Gear – drive	251. Bolt – cam
217. Key – woodruff	252. Cover
218. Nut – gear retaining	253. Gasket – cover
219. Lock washer	254. Bolt – cover
220. Impeller	255. Wear plate
222. Ball bearing	256. Seal assy.
223. Retainer – bearing	

FIGURE 12–28 *Identification of components of a Jabsco raw water pump. (Courtesy of Detroit Diesel Corporation.)*

curvature during pump operation. Any time you attempt to manually rotate the engine over, keep this caution in mind: Turning the engine opposite its normal rotation more than about one-eighth of a turn can result in impeller damage. If you have to rotate the engine in a direction opposite to its normal rotation beyond this limit, disconnect the RWP from the engine.

The seal parts of a RWP may be replaced without removing the pump from the engine as follows:

1. Remove the pump cover screws and take off the cover and gasket.

2. Using two pliers, grasp an impeller blade at each side and pull the impeller from the shaft. The spline plug will come out with the impeller.

3. Insert two wires with a hook fashioned into each end and insert between the pump housing and the seal with the hooks over the edge of the carbon seal. Pull the seal assembly from the shaft.

4. Remove the seal and gasket in the same manner if they require replacement.

5. Assemble the carbon seal, seal ring, and

washer in the correct relative positions and slide them over the shaft and against the seal seat. Make sure the seal ring is contained snugly within the ferrule.

6. Install the Marcel washer (deformed one) next to the flat washer.

7. Compress the impeller blades to clear the off-set cam and press the impeller onto the splined shaft; then install the spline plug.

8. Manually rotate the impeller several turns in the direction that it will normally run to position the blades correctly.

9. Install a new gasket between the pump housing and cover.

KEEL COOLING SYSTEMS

In many marine applications where dirty raw water makes the use of a heat exchanger system impractical, a keel cooling system such as that illustrated in Figure 12-29 can be used. This cooling system is similar to the HE system just described: however, the heat transfer of the engine fresh water coolant occurs in a nest of tubes that are mounted to the hull of the ship below the waterline rather than in the HE core mounted in the engine ET. The ET used can be the same as that for an HE system.

In this example, when the thermostat(s) is open,

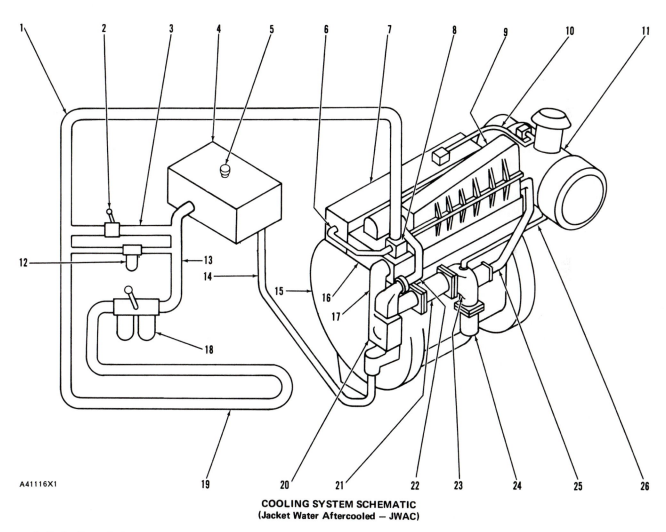

COOLING SYSTEM SCHEMATIC
(Jacket Water Aftercooled — JWAC)

1. Outlet line. 2. Bypass valve. 3. Bypass line. 4. Expansion tank. 5. Pressure cap. 6. Outlet line. 7. Water cooled manifold. 8. Regulator housing. 9. Aftercooler housing. 10. Outlet line. 11. Water cooled turbocharger. 12. Bypass filter. 13. Inlet line. 14. Inlet line. 15. Cylinder block. 16. Cylinder head. 17. Internal bypass (shunt) line. 18. Duplex strainer. 19. Keel cooler tubes. 20. Water pump. 21. Engine oil cooler. 22. Aftercooler inlet line. 23. Bonnet. 24. Auxiliary oil cooler. 25. Aftercooler outlet line. 26. Turbocharger inlet line.

FIGURE 12-29 *Schematic of a marine keel cooling system featuring JWAC to reduce the temperature of the turbocharger boost air supply. (Courtesy of Caterpillar, Inc.)*

the engine coolant flows to the keel cooling tubes or coils where it transfers its heat to the surrounding seawater. The return coolant is drawn through the vertical pipes and the ET by the engine water pump. When the thermostat(s) is closed, coolant entering the stat housing is bypassed directly to the engine water pump inlet where it remixes with the coolant from the water-cooled exhaust manifold jacket. The coolant is then circulated through the engine cylinder block and head. A percentage of the coolant leaving the head is routed through pipes or hoses to the hollow core exhaust manifold to minimize heat radiation into the engine room. This hot coolant leaving the exhaust manifold is then routed to the expansion tank. Since no engine coolant passes to the keel cooler with closed thermostats, a fairly rapid warm-up of the engine is assured.

SUMMARY

This chapter has highlighted the function and operation of the cooling system and its associated components. The cooling system is one of the most important and expensive engine and equipment downtime areas due to improper and regular maintenance. In this chapter, the reader is given the knowledge and skills to effectively maintain, service, and troubleshoot various types of engine cooling systems.

SELF-TEST QUESTIONS

1. Technician A says that typical coolant system temperatures should be between 140 and 165°F (60 to 74°C). Technician B disagrees, stating that normal coolant temperature should be between 185 and 200°F (85 to 93°C). Which technician do you believe?

2. True or False: Wear on cylinder walls can be up to eight times greater with a coolant temperature of 100°F (38°C) than one of 180°F (82°C).

3. Describe by approximate percentage the heat losses from an engine from the injected fuel used to produce power.

4. Technician A says that in a perfect engine with no heat losses 3300 Btu (966 W) is needed to produce 1 hp (0.746 kW) per hour. Technician B states that a perfect engine requires 2545 Btu/hp (746 W) per hour. Which technician knows heat engine theory better?

5. The average heat rejection to the cooling system in current high-speed high-output engines is approximately
   a. 30 to 35 Btu/hp (9 to 10 W/kW per minute)
   b. 40 to 50 Btu/hp (12 to 15 W/kW per minute)
   c. 50 to 60 Btu/hp (15 to 18 W/kW per minute)
   d. 60 to 70 Btu/hp (18 to 20 W/kW per minute)

6. True or False: Electronically controlled diesel engines are more thermally efficient than mechanically controlled models.

7. Calculate the heat load in Btu (W) that a Caterpillar 3176B EUI engine cooling system would have to absorb and dissipate from the following information: Engine is rated at 350 bhp (261 kW); fuel used has a LHV of 18,390 Btu/lb (42,780 kJ/kg) and weighs 7.001 lb/U.S. gal (839 g/L). Fuel consumption is 0.319 lb/hp-hr (194 g/kW-h). The engine has a TE of 43.38%; the cooling system absorbs 27.61% of the total heat load. Determine the total heat that this engine would produce in 1 hour; then calculate how many Btu/hp (W/kW) per minute the cooling system would handle.

8. From your answer to Question 7, and using information in Chapter 12, determine the coolant flow rate that would be required through this Cat engine with a water inlet temperature to the engine of 170°F (77°C) and a thermostat outlet temperature of 195°F (90.5°C).

9. From the information in Chapter 12, how many ppm (parts per million) hardness content, or corrosive chemicals of chloride or sulfate, would make water unfit for cooling system usage?

10. What does the chemical symbol pH represent in relation to coolant? Allowable pH is generally within the range
    a. 3.5 to 5
    b. 5 to 7
    c. 7.5 to 11
    d. 12 to 16.5

11. What is the purpose of using SCAs in a cooling system?

12. Describe what actually causes wet-type cylinder liner pitting. What can be done to minimize this condition?

13. Name the two common types of permanent antifreeze used in modern engines.

14. Which one of the two antifreezes listed in your answer for Question 13 is considered by the U.S. EPA to be a hazardous air pollutant?

15. True or False: Antifreeze is considered to be a nonhazardous waste.

16. Technician A says that used antifreeze must be disposed of once it is drained from an engine. Technician B says that all types of antifreeze can be cleaned and recycled. Which technician is aware of current technology?

17. Which one of the two types of antifreeze listed in your answer to Question 13 offers improved protection against cavitation corrosion, particularly in wet-liner engines?

18. Technician A says that too great a concentration of antifreeze can result in gelling of the coolant. Technician B believes that in very low ambient operating conditions, the greater the percentage of antifreeze used the better. Which technician is correct?

19. The maximum recommended concentration of antifreeze should never exceed
    a. 50%
    b. 57%

c.   63%

d.   67%

20. What additive in antifreeze acts as a corrosion inhibitor?

21. When maintenance personnel talk about silicate *dropout* in a coolant, what actually transpires and what problems occur from this action?

22. A widely used antifreeze spec is the General Motors standard GM-6038-M, which is listed on the antifreeze container. What does this standard limit, and to what percentage?

23. What antifreeze additive actually causes plugging of internal cooling passages and when allowed to dry appears as a white powdery substance?

24. Technician A says that if an engine overheating problem and coolant passage plugging can be traced to a silicate dropout condition, you would have to disassemble the radiator and engine to effectively clean the system. Technician B believes that you can use a commercially available nonacidic cleaner to remove the silica gel from the system without disassembling the engine. Which technician knows cooling system maintenance better?

25. If the procedure used in Question 24 doesn't work successfully, what would you do next? Describe the method(s) that would have to be employed.

26. True or False: Antifreeze protection level can be checked quickly by using a hydrometer or a refractometer similar to that for a battery.

27. List the problems that would occur to engine components if an antifreeze concentration was below 30%.

28. List the problems associated with using an antifreeze concentration above the maximum recommended level.

29. True or False: Chemical deposits at the water pump seal weep hole are usually an indication of possible overconcentration of SCAs.

30. True or False: SCA concentration must be checked regularly with a kit to determine the condition of the coolant.

31. When checking SCA concentration, what two additives relate directly to cylinder liner pitting concentration?

32. Scale buildup within a cooling system insulates and blocks heat transfer. What chemicals in tap water promote scale buildup?

33. Technician A says that 0.0625 in. (1.58 mm) of mineral scale deposit on a cylinder liner is equivalent to 1 in. of additional cast iron in insulating quantity. Technician B suggests that this amount of scale on the liner walls would be equivalent to approximately 4.25 in. (108 mm) of additional cast iron in insulating quality. Which technician is correct?

34. Name one cooling system corrosion inhibitor and stabilizer product that contains a patented scale suppressant to help prevent scale deposits.

35. One of the most effective ways to control coolant system SCAs is
   a.   using a coolant filter
   b.   flushing the system regularly
   c.   changing the antifreeze mixture twice a year
   d.   using a thermostat with a high opening temperature

36. List the various functions of a coolant filter assembly.

37. When radiators become plugged and have to be cleaned, the most popular method in use today is
   a.   boiling the radiator in a caustic solution
   b.   cleaning by ultrasonic methods
   c.   using solvent and rod cleaning brushes
   d.   pressure steam cleaning or using high-pressure hot water

38. Describe what the term *reverse flushing* means.

39. What is the main reason for using a radiator pressure cap (other than to prevent a loss of coolant)?

40. Technician A says that the term *ATB* represents the difference between engine coolant out, or the top tank temperature, and the ambient air temperature. Technician B says that it is the ambient temperature at which radiator top tank boiling occurs. Who is correct?

41. True or False: Each radiator or cooling system pressure cap has the opening pressure stamped on the cap.

42. What prevents the radiator or cooling system hoses from collapsing when the engine is stopped and the coolant begins to cool, thereby creating a partial vacuum?

43. How can a radiator pressure cap be checked to determine if it is operating correctly?

44. True or False: All radiators in use today are of the downflow type.

45. What major engine manufacturer employs LFC (low-flow cooling) systems on some of its engines?

46. True or False: All radiators employ one-pass coolant flow.

47. What feature of radiator design determines its rated cooling capacity?

48. What two materials are most widely used in the construction of heavy-duty truck radiators?

49. When radiator fins become soft or rotted, what is the usual cause?

50. True or False: The top tank of heavy-duty truck radiators contains two tanks within one, separated by a baffle arrangement.

51. Technician A says that cleaning radiator fins should never be done by employing high-pressure washers because this will damage the fins. Technician B says that high-pressure washer cleaning is required to dislodge bugs and other debris from the fins and is a recommended practice. Which technician is correct?

52. What types of problems does aerated coolant cause?

53. Describe how you would check a cooling system to determine if coolant is being aerated.

54. Technician A says that in cold-weather operation, all heavy-duty trucks should employ winterfronts that can be completely closed to keep the engine coolant operating temperature within specs. Technician B says that closing the winterfront completely could cause serious problems with the air-to-air aftercooler system. Which technician understands the theory of operation better?

55. AJWAC usually lowers the turbocharger boost air temperature under full-load conditions from approximately 300°F (149°C) to about
    a. 250°F (121°C)
    b. 200°F (93°C)
    c. 160°F (71°C)
    d. 110°F (43°C)

56. ALCC (advanced liquid charge cooling) is capable of lowering turbocharger boost temperatures down to which one of the answers in Question 55?

57. What is the difference between JWAC and ALCC?

58. Describe how you would clean or service either a JWAC or an ALCC system.

59. What are the three common types of thermostats used in diesel engines?

60. Describe how a thermostat actually opens and closes.

61. Operating an engine without a thermostat is not recommended. Give the reasons why.

62. What is the purpose of using thermostat seals, and what problems exist if they leak?

63. Describe how you would check a thermostat for effective operation. List the specific checks to confirm whether a thermostat is good or bad.

64. Why would a truck or stationary engine application use shutterstats?

65. Describe briefly how a shutterstat system operates.

66. List the operational checks that you would follow to check a shutterstat for correct operation on an engine.

67. Provide an example of the opening temperatures for a heavy-duty truck engine that employs a thermostat, a shutterstat, and a thermatic fan.

68. What would be the approximate fan airflow requirements for an engine rated at 470 hp (351 kW) with a 35 Btu/hp (10.25 W) per minute heat rejection to the cooling system?

69. Technician A says that radiator fans on highway trucks are normally required for only between 5 and 10% of engine operating time. Technician B says that the fan must operate most of the time to keep the engine coolant within the designed operating temperature. Which technician knows cooling theory best?

70. The horsepower required to drive a truck fan should not exceed which of the following percentages of the engine's developed horsepower?
    a. 2%
    b. 4%
    c. 6%
    d. 9%

71. True or False: A suction fan is designed to blow air through the radiator core.

72. True or False: A blower fan is designed to pull air through the radiator core.

73. For the amount of power expended to drive a fan, technician A says that the suction fan is more effective. Technician B believes that the blower fan is more effective. Give the reasons why you believe that technician A or B is correct.

74. On a portable application such as a trailer or skid-mounted unit with a large diesel-driven air compressor, would the engine-driven fan be of the suction or blower type? Why?

75. Describe the three commonly used designs of fan shrouds.

76. Why is a fan shroud a widely used item? Describe the main reason for employing one.

77. Technician A says that a fan should always be mounted as close as possible to the radiator core. Do you agree or disagree with this statement? Give reasons for your answer.

78. True or False: All thermatically operated fans use air pressure to function.

79. Technician A says that thermatic fans must have their hub belt driven from the engine crankshaft. Technician B says that no belt drive is necessary. Which technician is correct?

80. Technician A says that a Bendix and Kysor/Cadillac thermatic fan hub assembly is applied by spring pressure; technician B says the assembly is applied by air pressure. Who is correct?

81. True or False: A thermomodulated fan hub assembly relies on coolant temperature within the engine block to activate it.

82. True or False: Fan belts should always be adjusted using a fan belt tensioner gauge.

83. Technician A says that when multiple belts are used to drive a fan hub assembly, if one belt requires replacing, all of the belts should be changed since they are a matched set. Not so, says technician B; you only need to change the damaged, worn, or broken belt. Who is correct?

84. True or False: Marine engine applications use raw seawater routed through the engine cooling system and plumb fresh water through the heat exchanger to cool the hot, raw seawater.

85. True or False: Raw water pumps usually employ a special rubber or neoprene type of impeller.

86. The purpose of zinc electrodes in marine engine cooling systems is to
    a. counteract electrolysis
    b. prevent scale buildup
    c. maintain the correct pH control level
    d. prevent silica dropout in the antifreeze

87. How would you clean a marine engine heat exchanger core?

88. Describe briefly how a marine engine keel cooling system operates.

13

Air Inlet and Exhaust Systems

OVERVIEW

In this chapter the air inlet and exhaust system is explained in terms of its importance to the combustion system. In addition to operational aspects of the system, we discuss the major components that contribute to air and exhaust flow into and from the engine cylinders.

THE AIR SUPPLY

All internal combustion engines need an adequate supply of air that is clean, dry, filtered, fresh, and cool. Damp air contains less oxygen than dry air, thus it reduces engine power. The power loss is usually neg-ligible unless conditions of very high humidity are encountered in warm countries. On naturally aspirated (non-turbocharged) and particularly on turbocharged engines, air is as necessary to successful operation as is the quality of the fuel used. Lack of sufficient airflow to an engine can result in these conditions:

- High air inlet restriction
- Low turbocharger or blower boost pressure
- Higher exhaust temperatures
- Incomplete combustion
- Lower fuel economy
- Lack of power
- Smoke at the exhaust stack
- Increased exhaust emissions
- Shorter valve and piston life
- Noisier operation
- Increased lube oil use

Heavy-duty diesel engines with electronically controlled unit injectors are designed to provide minimum exhaust emissions, superior fuel economy, and high power outputs. Most of these engines are equipped with a variety of engine sensors. The air inlet system is equipped with one or more of the following sensors: ambient air pressure sensor for altitude compensation, intake manifold temperature sensor, and turbocharger boost pressure sensor. These three sensors can quickly determine a problem and cause the engine ECM to reduce speed and power. The sensors are normally mounted on the intake manifold. See chapters 21, 22 and 23 for specific OEM examples and sensor locations.

Black exhaust smoke pouring from any engine, particularly from a mechanically governed one, is a direct indication of either air starvation or engine overfueling. Unburned fuel doesn't all flow from the exhaust stack! Some of it actually washes down the cylinder wall and causes lube oil dilution. Some unburned fuel changes to carbon, which can stick to pistons, rings, and valves as well as plug the orifice holes in the injector tip.

Unfiltered air can rapidly wear out an engine—a condition often referred to as *dusting out* an engine. This condition is particularly noticeable when an engine has been overhauled but after a short period of time loses compression and power and emits heavy smoke at the exhaust stack. Tests by major diesel engine manufacturers have shown that as little as two tablespoons of dirt can dust out an engine within a very short time. All air contains small particles of dirt and abrasive material that are not always visible to the naked eye. Dirty intake air is the main cause today for wear on pistons, rings, liners, valves, and other internal engine components.

INTAKE AND EXHAUST SYSTEM FLOW

Four-Cycle Engines

Figure 13-1 illustrates the flow of the air in a turbocharged engine. The pressurized air flows into the cylinders through the open intake valve. The exhaust gases flow from the cylinder through the open exhaust valve(s) through the manifold and piping to the muffler assembly. This same airflow pattern is typical of turbocharged *intercooled* high-output heavy-duty engine models.

The intake charge is routed through a cast intake manifold bolted to the cylinder head. The manifold is designed and contoured to provide a minimum restriction to the airflow. In addition, most high-performance diesel engines employ four valve heads (two intake and two exhaust) in what is known as a cross-flow head design. See Figure 1-7 which shows that the air enters one side of the cylinder head and exits on the opposite side. This configuration provides for very short, unobstructed intake and exhaust ports for efficient airflow, low pumping losses, and reduced heat transfer, so the engine breathes more freely and runs cooler.

Two-Cycle Engines

The largest engine manufacturer of two-cycle heavy-duty engines is Detroit Diesel. The two-stroke-cycle engine differs from the four-cycle model in that it does not use intake valves. All poppet-type valves contained in the cylinder head are *exhaust only;* usually, there are four valves per cylinder on high-speed heavy-duty models.

Basic airflow through a V-design DDC engine is illustrated in Figure 2-5. Note that a gear-driven blower is used to force the pressurized air into an *airbox* which completely surrounds each cylinder. The cylinder liner contains a row of helically shaped ports to create high air turbulence as air flows into the cylinder. These ports serve as the intake system. The conventional intake and exhaust strokes of four-stroke-cycle engines are eliminated in the two-stroke engine. Every piston upstroke is compression, and every downstroke is power.

AIR CLEANERS

A large number of different air cleaner (filter) models are in use. We can categorize them into three general types: oil bath (seldom used), single-stage dry element, and two-stage dry element.

The oil bath air cleaner is seldom used now because it is less efficient at lower engine speeds when the airflow entering the engine is lower. This lower airflow reduces the agitation of the oil within the air cleaner sump and, therefore, does not trap airborne dust or dirt as well. In addition, overfilling an oil bath air cleaner can result in engine oil pullover, which causes engine overspeed. In cold weather, the oil can freeze; the result is high air inlet restriction and/or

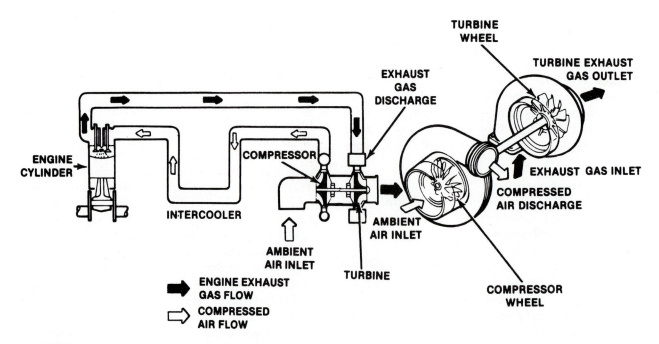

FIGURE 13–1   Schematic of the air and exhaust flow for a heavy-duty high-speed turbocharged and intercooled diesel engine. (Courtesy of Detroit Diesel Corporation.)

poor dust/dirt trapping ability. Operating a piece of equipment at steep angles can result in air restriction problems and possible oil pullover. An oil bath air cleaner must be serviced more frequently than a dry type, and the process is more time consuming. In addition, the oil bath air cleaner offers a higher initial restriction to airflow.

Dry Air Cleaners

The major advantage of a dry air filter is that it allows much longer periods between service intervals. Up to 160,930 km (100,000 miles) is not uncommon on heavy-duty on-highway trucks. The dry filter is capable of trapping dust or dirt with equal efficiency throughout the speed range. The filter element is made from treated paper that has been pleated and assembled into a continuous V-form throughout its circumference. In some filter models, this pleated paper element can be opened to a full length of 12 to 18 m (40 to 60 ft). The dry filter element increases in efficiency as the dirt load builds up a cake or bed in the valley of the V pleats—upward from a minimum efficiency of

99.5% to as high as 99.99%—and remains constant throughout the engine speed range.

The paper element is surrounded and protected by a perforated steel mesh screen (shell). Dry filters are available in either a cylindrical or square/rectangular panel shape. Figure 13-2 illustrates a Donaldson dual-filter element—composite, dry and horizontally mounted—which has primary and secondary units. In composite filters, dirty air enters through the inlet opening, where it travels through a plastic ring of vanes (called a precleaner) around the outside of the element. These vanes are designed to create a *cyclonic twist* to the air to throw the heavier dust and dirt particles outward by centrifugal force and downward into the dust cup area. The dust cup is held in place by a large heavy-duty clamp. On the composite heavy-duty, vertical-tube type shown in Figure 13-3, dirty air passes through the inlet and flows onto a series of tubes that are vertically mounted inside the air cleaner. The hard-plastic tubes contain vanes, which create a cyclonic twist similar to that described for the single and dual elements. Centrifugal action throws the

FIGURE 13–2 (A) Dual-filter air cleaner, which is a composite, dry, and horizontally mounted unit featuring a vacuator valve to expel 90%+ of the inlet laden dust or dirt by a centrifuge design; (B) same air filter assembly but in exploded view. (Courtesy of Donaldson Co., Inc.)

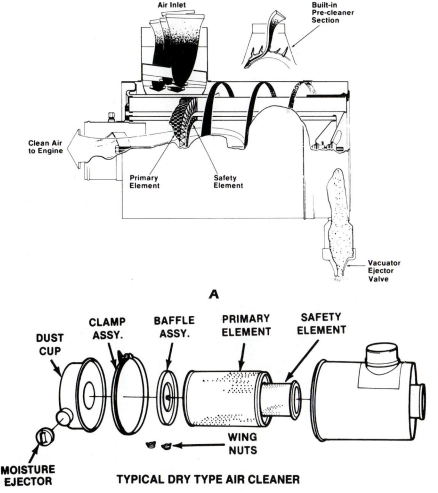

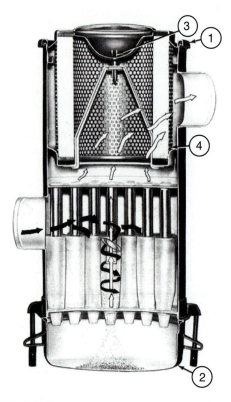

FIGURE 13–3 *Vertically mounted, composite, cyclonic type of heavy-duty air cleaner. 1, Top cover; 2, dust cup; 3, wing bolt; 4, filter element. (Courtesy of Donaldson Co., Inc.)*

heavier dust or dirt particles to the outside of the tube, where they drop downward to the removable dust cup. The clean air then passes upward through the center of the tubes and into the air filter, where minute dust and dirt particles can be removed.

An optional dust removal design is shown in Figure 13-2. In addition to the cyclonic action described, the dust that has been spun outward along the wall of the cleaner is directed toward a *Vacuator* dust ejector. This filter design can be mounted horizontally, as shown, or vertically with the Vacuator located at the base of the dust cup.

Precleaners and Screens

In heavy dust conditions, for example in situations involving off-highway trucks and equipment, precleaners such as those shown in Figure 13-4 are often used. These precleaners reduce the frequency of service by spinning the dust-laden air outward as shown in Figure 13-4. This dust is trapped and stored in a heavy-duty, hard, clear plastic bowl and cover assembly. When the dirt reaches the level indicated by a painted arrow on the bowl, remove the cover by loosening the wing nut, lift off the plastic body, and empty the dust.

Many engines and equipment operate in areas where coarse or fuzzy material such as chaff, lint, or leaves is continually airborne. To prevent any of this

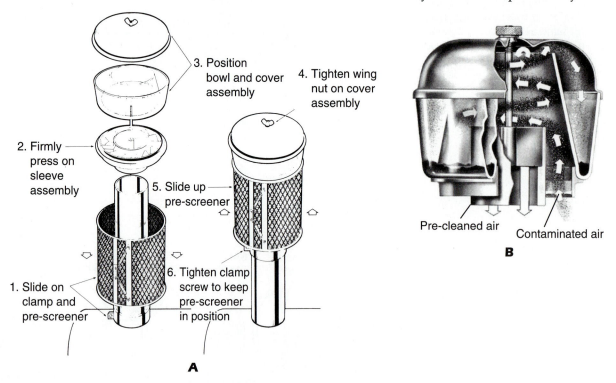

FIGURE 13–4 *(A) Features of a snap-on prescreener for a heavy-duty air cleaner assembly; (B) airflow diagram highlighting the spinning action imparted to the incoming air in the precleaner assembly to centrifuge and trap dust or dirt in the clear plastic bowl and cover assembly. (Courtesy of Donaldson Co., Inc.)*

FIGURE 13–5 Features of a heavy-duty on-highway truck DynaCell air cleaner assembly. (Courtesy of Farr Company.)

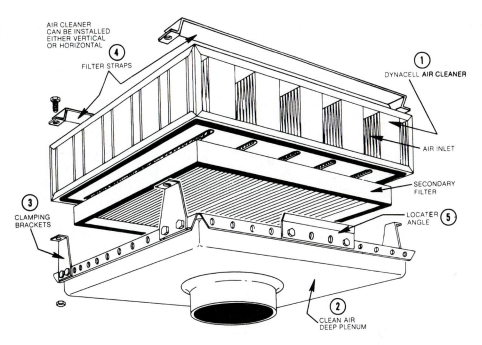

material from entering the engine, a snap-on pre-screener can be used (Figure 13-4). Equipment applications using dry filters that fight forest fires or operate in municipal garbage dumps where sparks from burning debris are often airborne, a fine prefilter screen is necessary. This screen prevents sparks from being pulled into the air cleaner and damaging the plastic cyclonic tubes.

Many heavy-duty Class 8 on-highway trucks have air cleaner assemblies mounted on the engine intake manifold (Figure 13-5). Another very popular air cleaner for on-highway as well as stationary industrial engine applications is the ECO series manufactured by the Farr Company. Figure 13-6 illustrates this model, which is a spin-on disposable unit. The air filter has a tapered offset cone design and can be mounted either horizontally or vertically. This design feature ensures that airflow distribution and dirt loading are uniform throughout the core, resulting in lower overall restriction, between three to five times longer filter life, and better fuel economy. The air inlet shown at the top can also be at the side if desired.

Cartridge Panel Air Cleaners

In the cartridge panel air cleaner shown in Figure 13-7 the filter element is square or rectangular in shape rather than round. These types of filters are more commonly used on larger equipment such as mining trucks, graders, and bottom-dump scrapers, where extremely heavy dust and dirt conditions are regularly encountered. Most of these designs employ an exhaust gas aspirator assembly, which is also illustrated in Figure 13-7. This system directs exhaust gas flow through

the piping to the aspirator funnel which creates a constant suction to the base of the dustbin located at the bottom of the centrifugal air cleaner panel. Heavily laden dusty air is spun outward as shown in Figure 13-8A by the shape of the deflector vanes at the inlet tubes, and 90% of the dirt is drawn off through the dustbin which is constantly subjected to the exhaust aspirator suction. Protecting the exhaust system from rain, fog, and other moisture is important to prevent corrosion of the exhaust piping. Either a balanced rain cap or smooth elbow-design raincap should be used on the end of the aspirator as illustrated in Figure

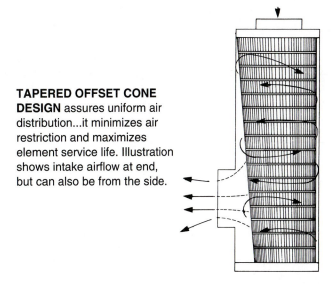

TAPERED OFFSET CONE DESIGN assures uniform air distribution...it minimizes air restriction and maximizes element service life. Illustration shows intake airflow at end, but can also be from the side.

FIGURE 13–6 Design of an Ecolite air cleaner with a tapered offset cone filter assembly. (Courtesy of Farr Company.)

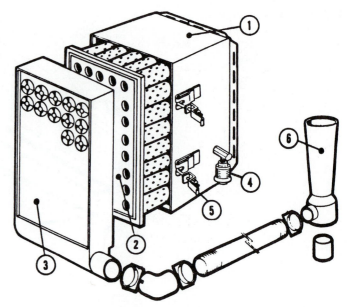

FIGURE 13-7 *Component parts of a two-stage dry air cleaner featuring an exhaust gas aspirator to withdraw and expel 90%+ of the dust-laden intake air. (Courtesy of Farr Company.)*

Mounting flanges are an integral part of all Series-D housings.

BASIC TWO-STAGE KIT INCLUDES

1. Air Cleaner Housing
2. Pamic Filter
3. Pre-Cleaner
4. Service Indicator
5. Fasteners
6. Aspirator Kit

13-8B. An optional dust ejector system shown in Figure 13-9 uses a supply of vehicle compressed air to bleed airflow through a nozzle in the Rotopamic or ultraheavy-duty model precleaner panel.

In applications where moisture is a continuing problem (for example, on marine applications or in coastal logging equipment), a moisture eliminator prescreen can be used. The moisture eliminator is fitted in front of the filter cartridge to attract moisture and dust. The coils of the eliminator cause the moisture-laden air to be trapped and drain by gravity to the base of the precleaner eliminator, which has a series of horizontal slots to allow the accumulated water to drain.

In heavy-duty off-highway equipment applications such as 170- and 200-ton mining vehicles, multiple air cleaners are required to handle the large airflow requirements of engines rated at 1600 to 2300 hp (1194 to 1716 kW). Figure 13-10 illustrates four UHD (ultraheavy-duty) Farr air cleaners mounted on the forward bulkhead of a typical mining truck. These particular air cleaner models offer three stages of filtration for large trucks, drill rigs, shovels, and so on. The first stage of UHD filtration occurs through the *superclone* precleaner. This precleaner operates similarly to the one shown in Figure 13-8 where up to 93% of the dirt and 90% of any water entering the system are removed. The UHD air cleaner uses a small amount of vehicle compressed air to provide bleed airflow for self-cleaning action in the precleaner section, which is located in the swing-away heavy-gauge forward metal grid that protects the precleaner section (see Figure 13-9). The compressed air source can be supplied from the air compressor, the pressure side of the turbocharger, or the air box of naturally aspirated two-cycle engines. The second stage employs a primary filter to remove 99.9% of the dirt that gets through the precleaner (see Figure 13-8A). The third-stage safety filter is designed to trap the small amount of dirt or dust that may get past the primary filter, so that the total system efficiency of 99.99% will be maintained.

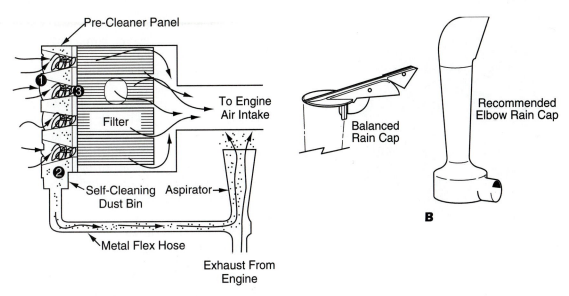

Pre-Cleaner Panel

❶

❸

Filter

To Engine
Air Intake

❷

Self-Cleaning
Dust Bin

Aspirator

Metal Flex Hose

Exhaust From
Engine

Balanced
Rain Cap

Recommended
Elbow Rain Cap

B

❶ Air enters pre-cleaner panel and is spun
to remove 90% of dust particles.

❷ The separated dust falls into dust bin
and is drawn out through aspirator.

❸ Pre-cleaned air now enters Pamic
after-cleaner for second-stage cleaning.

A

FIGURE 13–8 (A) Operational schematic of the two-stage Rotopamic heavy-duty
air cleaner equipped with an exhaust gas aspirator; (B) outlet options for the Rotopamic
heavy-duty air cleaner exhaust aspirator.

FIGURE 13–9 Features of a
compressed air aspirator bleed-
tube option used with a heavy-
duty Rotopamic air cleaner. (Courtesy of Farr Company.)

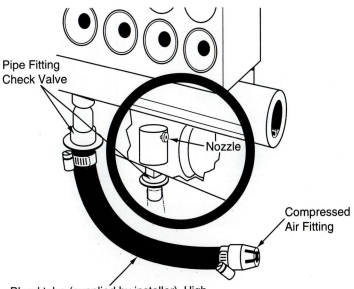

Pipe Fitting
Check Valve

Nozzle

Compressed
Air Fitting

Bleed tube (supplied by installer). High
temperature silicone hose capable of
handling positive pressure is
recommended.

FIGURE 13–10 *Location of four ultraheavy-duty dry air cleaner assemblies on the front of a large mining truck. (Courtesy of Farr Company.)*

Servicing the UHD air cleaner simply involves loosening the three latches on the side of the air cleaners to open the swing-away protective grate door. The primary element is held in place by two vertical straps. After loosening off the bolt at the top and bottom of each strap, swing the strap away. Insert the fingers of both hands into the access holes of the air cleaner element and pull it straight out. Thoroughly wipe out the housing with a clean cloth. If the safety element requires changing (normally only at engine overhaul), note that it is held in place by a bolt and tab at each

corner. Each bolt has a safety wire through its head to discourage unnecessary tampering. Cut the safety wires and remove the bolts. Grasp the element and pull it straight out of the housing.

In applications that operate in conditions of severe dust, it is extremely important to ensure that all ducting and piping to the air cleaner and engine are dust tight. Leaky connections, holes in piping, or other system faults must be avoided. Since only a couple of tablespoons of dust wear an engine out, several air cleaner manufacturers offer *dust detector kits* that are installed to engine duct work in the actual air cleaner.

Restriction Indicators

The most effective methods of determining when to service a dry filter element are by measuring the AIR (air inlet restriction) with a water manometer or by employing an air cleaner service indicator. Both gauges operate when there is a vacuum condition, that is, when the pressure within the air cleaner and ducting on the suction side of the turbocharger is less than atmospheric pressure. Consequently, a vacuum gauge can also be used to monitor AIR.

The restriction indicator gauge can be attached to the air cleaner housing or remotely mounted on the dash area of a heavy-duty truck or piece of equipment. A small-bore plastic tube connects the indicator with a fitting on the ducting at the engine. Figure 13-11 illustrates a common type of restriction indicator (Filter

5" to 10"
Normal clean filter. (Initial restriction varies with each system design.)

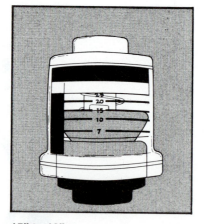

15" to 18"
The filter element is loading up with contaminants, but still has much useful life left. Fuel consumption is probably increasing.

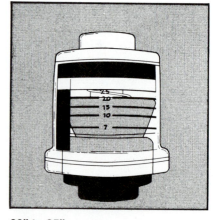

20" to 25"
The filter element should be replaced. The engine is probably using more fuel with slight loss of power. This upper limit will vary depending on whether equipment is diesel or gasoline fueled, and your fuel consumption experience.

FIGURE 13–11 *Graduated Filter Minder air restriction indicator which reads in inches of water to indicate to the operator or service technician the degree of air filter plugging. (Courtesy of Farr Company.)*

Minder). This model contains a clear plastic window so that when the air filter becomes plugged, the restriction (vacuum) pulls a small float gauge into view within the small inspection window. Once the system has been serviced, the gauge can be reset by pushing a small release button on the bottom of the gauge. The restriction gauge shown actually allows the operator or technician to visually determine the degree of AIR based on the graduated scale on the Filter Minder gauge. Restriction gauges are calibrated in inches of water and are available for different maximum settings.

Servicing Air Cleaners

Nothing will wear out an engine faster than unfiltered air entering the system. The finest lapping compound in the world is a combination of fine dust mixed with oil on the cylinder walls. Think also of the continuous rubbing action of the piston rings against the liner surface and you can readily appreciate the rapid wear condition that is present.

Although oil bath air cleaners are *seldom* found on modern diesel engines, you may be faced with servicing one of these older assemblies. The oil sump must be removed and the dirty oil disposed of safely. The oil sump can be washed in solvent, and the internal wire-mesh filter assembly can be washed in solvent and blown dry with an air hose. Using a steam cleaner tends to pack dirt tighter into the wire-mesh screen. Check all gaskets and seals for an air- and oil-tight fit. Refill the oil reservoir with the same grade of oil that is used in the engine. *Do not* overfill the air cleaner sump; check the sump for the oil level *full* mark. Overfilling an oil bath air cleaner can cause oil pullover and engine overspeed.

On dry-type filters, check the manufacturer's specifications and service recommendations closely prior to service, since *not all* dry filter elements can be washed. A filter restriction indicator lets you know when the filter and system require servicing. When restriction readings indicate that the filter element is plugged, perform the following procedure:

1. Clean off the access cover before removing any clamps or bolts.

2. Remove the necessary clamps, bolts, or wing nuts to gain access to the air cleaner filter. Dust cups should be dumped when they are two-thirds full by removing the large clamp at the base of the filter housing. Precleaners can be dumped when the dust reaches the level indicated on the clear heavy-duty plastic bowl (Figure 13-4). On cleaners equipped with the Donaldson Vacuator valve (Figure 13-2), make sure the valve is not damaged or plugged. Is the cup joint sealing?

3. On heavy-duty air cleaners that have cyclonic tubes, light dust plugging can be removed as illustrated in Figure 13-12 by using a stiff-fiber brush. If heavy plugging with fibrous material is evident, re-

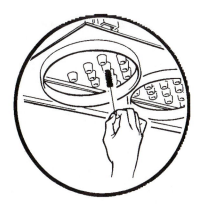

FIGURE 13–12 *Using a stiff-bristle brush to clean out the cyclonic tubes of a heavy-duty air cleaner assembly. (Courtesy of Donaldson Co., Inc.)*

move the lower body section for cleaning with compressed air and warm water at a temperature not exceeding 71°C (160°F). Avoid steam cleaning cyclonic tubes because the heat can melt the plastic.

4. Remove the filter by loosening off the large wing nut that retains it. On square and rectangular models, there are usually four or more large external wing nuts. On cartridge-type filters, carefully insert several fingers into the tube holes and work the element free from the housing as shown in Figure 13-13.

5. On reusable dry filter elements, take care not to pound, tap, or rap the dust out of them as severe damage can result. Dust and loose dirt can be removed by directing compressed air through the element in the opposite direction to normal airflow.

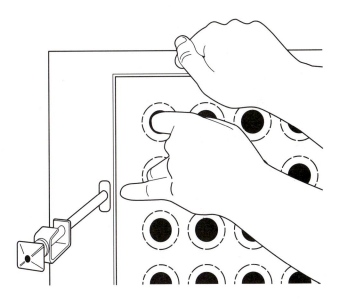

FIGURE 13–13 *Removal of the molded air filter element from a heavy-duty cartridge air cleaner assembly. (Courtesy of Farr Company.)*

FIGURE 13–14 Using a pressurized air nozzle to remove excess warm fresh water that was used to rinse the dry air filter element after cleaning in a sudsy solution. Never use more than 276 kPa (40 psi) of air pressure, and never place the air nozzle directly against the filter to avoid tearing (rupturing) the element. (Courtesy of Donaldson Co., Inc.)

CAUTION Do not allow the air nozzle to touch the element paper directly since this can rupture it. Keep the nozzle at least 51 mm (2 in.) away from the filter element. Reduced air pressure should be used, in the range of 345 to 414 kPa (50 to 60 psi), although some manufacturers allow up to 690 kPa (100 psi).

6. Thoroughly clean the filter with warm water. Many filter manufacturers offer a sudsy cleaning solution that can be mixed with warm water for cleaning purposes. The filter element should be soaked for at least 15 minutes in a large receptacle of the cleaning solution. Rinse it in clean warm water; then use a pressure air hose with a maximum of 276 kPa (40 psi) to remove excess water. Refer to Figure 13-14.

7. Once a filter element has been cleaned, dry it using warm flowing air at a maximum temperature of 71°C (160°F). This can be accomplished by setting the filter on a drying rack or placing it in a temperature-controlled oven.

8. Once the filter has been dried, inspect it for rips or tears. This is a *very important* step. The best method to use is to place the filter over a vertically mounted light bulb and rotate it slowly. You can also use a Trouble-light, as illustrated in Figure 13-15, to look for signs of damage.

9. Check all air cleaner system seals and gaskets and replace if damaged. Look for dust trails, which in-

FIGURE 13–15 Using a Trouble-light inserted inside the air filter element to check for signs of paper damage, tears, or ruptures. (Courtesy of Donaldson Co., Inc.)

dicate leaky gaskets. Many heavy-duty round air filters have a soft rubber compressible seal glued to one or both ends. This seal can permanently compress (set) so that it flattens out; the result is that when the air cleaner cover is installed, it does not produce a dust-tight seal. Compare the height of this seal with that of a new filter element. If the seal is badly set, replace the filter element. If starting aid fittings are used, inspect them to make sure they are tight and free of leaks.

10.   On square or rectangular cartridge-type air filters, the filter elements are encased in a heavy molded rubber or neoprene casing. When the filter is changed, therefore, a new seal is assured automatically. Prior to installing the new filter, always clean out the air cleaner housing using a damp cloth to pick up any dirt or dust. Do not blow pressurized air into the housing unless a safety element is in position; otherwise, dirt may enter the turbocharger and/or engine intake manifold. Figure 13-13 illustrates the replacement of a rectangular cartridge-type filter element.

11.   On air cleaner systems employing exhaust gas aspirators, ensure that the aspirator tube (piping) is not plugged. Plugging of these tubes can cause exhaust gas recirculation to melt the cyclonic tubes in the filter assembly. If components are melted, it is also possible that the assembly is located too close to an exhaust pipe. In addition, engine exhaust can rapidly plug dry filter elements, so make sure that exhaust gases are directed above and away from the air inlet system.

Remember that using a badly restricted (plugged) filter element results in excessive fuel consumption, loss of power, increased engine operating temperature, and shortened cylinder kit life. Using a damaged filter element results in rapid piston, ring, and cylinder wear and severe damage to the engine.

AIR DUCTING INSPECTION

The air induction piping functions with the air cleaner to carry clean air into the turbocharger and engine. In addition to servicing the air cleaner filter assembly, it is extremely important to check the piping hoses, elbows, and clamps for looseness, tears, or ruptures. Ignoring these components can lead to unfiltered air entering the system and destroying the engine in a very short time. Every time you service the air filter, inspect the intake ducting (piping) and elbows. Typical piping and connecting hose are illustrated in Figure 13-16A. Molded heavy-duty rubber elbows, which are approximately 6.25 mm (¼ in.) thick with ribbed reinforcement, are widely used and secured by T-bolt hose clamps. Metal tubing should be spaced at least 19 mm (¾ in.) apart from the hose clamps.

To check heavy-duty elbows and hoses, depress

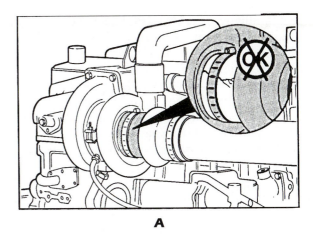

A

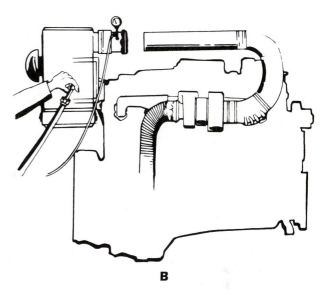

B

FIGURE 13–16 (A) Inspection of air inlet ducting heavy-duty elbows for signs of cracking, looseness, or damage; (B) sealed air inlet ducting being pressurized to check for signs of air leaks. (Courtesy of Cummins Engine Company, Inc.)

the hose where it is secured by the clamp and visually inspect it for signs of cutting or cracking as shown in Figure 13-16A. If you suspect that the tubing is not airtight, disconnect it at both the air cleaner outlet and the turbocharger inlet. Install heavy plastic shipping caps or light metal blanking plugs at each end and clamp them into position. Drill and tap one sealing plate, or use the air inlet restriction pipe plug, to adapt an air pressure fitting. Connect a hand pump or use a low-pressure regulator at a wall valve to limit the pressure to 14 kPa (2 psi). Apply liquid spray soap or use a brush and apply sudsy soap solution to each joint. Air bubbles indicate a leak.

If you suspect that the air cleaner assembly is pulling in unfiltered air, remove the dry filter element and install a dummy one, or install a prewrapped one for the test. Refer to Figure 13-16B. Clamp a rubber sheet tightly over the air cleaner inlet and outlet connections. Prepare an air fitting connection on the air cleaner, or clamp a used tire tube with its Schraeder valve over the inlet or outlet connection. Use liquid spray soap on the inlet and outlet connections as well as at the dust cup of the cleaner. Apply 14 kPa (2 psi) maximum and look for signs of air bubbles, which would indicate a leak. Clean the inside of piping and flexible connectors before replacing them on the engine.

AFTERCOOLERS

As the U.S. EPA exhaust emissions standards have become stringent, an area of engine design that has received more attention involves the temperature of the air that leaves the turbocharger and enters the engine intake manifold. One of the most important components in use today on electronically controlled high-speed heavy-duty diesel engines is the turbocharger-pressurized-air *aftercooler*.

Ideal air temperature for operating engines is usually in the region of 35 to 38°C (95 to 100°F). An engine rated at 187 kW (250 hp) would lose approximately 7.5 kW (10 hp) if the intake air temperature were allowed to rise to 54°C (130°F). The higher the ambient air temperature, the greater the expansion of the air; therefore, a loss of engine power always results. Depending on the rise in ambient air temperature and the engine design features, an engine can lose between 0.15 and 0.7% horsepower per cylinder for every 6°C (10°F) rise beyond 32°C (90°F), or approximately 1% power loss for each 6°C (10°F) of intake temperature rise above 32°C (90°F).

There are four basic types of aftercoolers:

1. Intercooler–aftercooler combination often used on high-output marine engines. This system uses raw sea or lake water to cool the intercooler, while the aftercooler is cooled by fresh engine coolant.
2. JWAC (jacket water aftercooler).
3. ALCC (advanced liquid charge cooling).
4. AAAC (air-to-air aftercooler).

The terms *intercooler* and *aftercooler* are interchangeable descriptions used by engine manufacturers. The word *inter* means in between the turbocharger and engine intake manifold; the word *after* means that a cooler is located after the pressurized air leaves the cold end of the turbocharger. Both words indicate that the pressurized turbocharger air is cooled by directing it through a cooler system, which can be either air or water cooled. Figure 13-1 shows the general location of an intercooler, while Figure 13-17 shows a charge air cooler system mounted in front of the radiator. Pressurized turbocharger air that is directed through the charge air cooler core is cooled by forced air as a vehicle moves along the highway. Most heavy-duty highway trucks powered by Caterpillar, Cummins, Detroit Diesel, Mack, and Volvo engines now use a system similar to that shown in Figure 13-17, where the charge air cooler is mounted in front of the radiator assembly. Some very-high-output marine engine applications employ both an intercooler and an aftercooler. The pressurized turbocharger air is intercooled before it enters the gear-driven blower. Once it passes through the blower, it is directed through an aftercooler and into the air box of two-stroke-cycle engines.

Water Aftercooling
Water-type inlet air aftercoolers employ fresh engine coolant routed through its water jacket to reduce the temperature of the pressurized air flowing through it from the turbocharger. A JWAC is capable of lowering the full-load engine turbocharger boost air from a temperature of about 149°C (300°F) down to approximately 93°C (200°F). The ALCC system is capable of lowering the turbo boost air temperature down to approximately 74°C (165°F).

Air-to-Air Aftercooling
The most efficient and widely used turbocharger boost air aftercooler on heavy-duty trucks and buses is the AAAC, or ATAAC as some engine manufacturers refer to it. The engine turbocharger is driven by hot pressurized exhaust gases flowing from the exhaust manifold into the turbine side. These gases drive the turbine wheel at speeds in excess of 100,000 rpm, where they then leave the system at the exhaust piping and flow through the muffler system. Inlet air is pulled through the air cleaner, compressed, and heated by the compressor wheel (cold side); then it is pushed through the AAAC core and it then moves to the engine intake manifold.

Cooling of the pressurized intake air increases combustion efficiency, which in turn lowers fuel consumption, increases horsepower, and helps to minimize exhaust emissions. The AAAC system increases the engine fuel economy by approximately 4% over a JWAC engine. Today, high BMEPs, high torque rise, and maximum engine power are being developed at midrange engine speeds, particularly on heavy-duty truck engines. Without the AAAC, the pressurized air leaving the turbocharger under full-load operation, at temperatures as high as 149°C (300°F), and entering the cylinder would result in short valve and piston

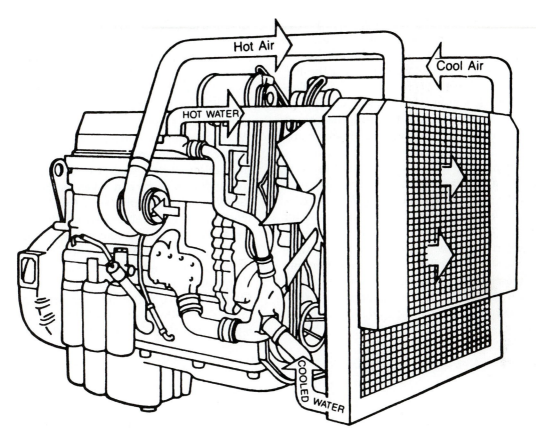

FIGURE 13–17 Design of a heavy-duty highway truck engine ATAAC (air-to-air after-cooler) which is mounted in front of the radiator. (Courtesy of Detroit Diesel Corporation.)

crown life, since there would be insufficient cooling airflow. In addition, the reduction in air density would lower the mass air charge for the combustion process resulting in a loss of power. This problem would be more severe on a two-stroke-cycle engine model where approximately 30% of the engine cooling is performed by the mass airflow rate.

Figure 13-17 illustrates a typical AAAC located in front of the radiator. Ambient air is moved across the aftercooler core and then the radiator core by means of the engine fan and also by the ram-air effect created when a truck is moving along the highway at vehicle speed. Consequently, the use of radiator shutters and/or snap-on winterfronts should be avoided. Any airflow restriction to the aftercooler core can cause higher exhaust temperatures, power loss, excessive fan usage, and a reduction in fuel economy. In cases where heavy-duty trucks operate in extremely cold weather conditions and a winterfront must be used, it should *never* be closed completely. Generally, a minimum of 20% airflow to the AAAC core must remain. When used with a viscous fan assembly, there should be at least a 203-mm (8-in.) diamond permanently open in the winterfront. This opening should be cen-

tered on the radiator, not at the top, bottom, or other off-center position. If more than one opening is used in the winterfront, these should be the same size at the top and bottom, or on the left and right sides, to produce a balanced airflow across the AAAC core as well as the fan blades. Winterfronts should always be completely removed when operating in ambient air temperatures above 4.5°C (40°F). Also, never install a winterfront directly against the AAAC core or radiator core or shutter. Install it in front of the truck grill with at least 51 mm (2 in.) of air space between the winterfront and the AAAC or radiator core to ensure sufficient bypass cooling in the event that the winterfront is not fully opened in warming temperatures. When winterfronts are fully open, the airflow passage should be equal to or greater than 40% of the radiator core area.

Pressurized turbocharger air flowing through the AAAC core assembly dissipates its heat to the cooler ram air entering the grill at the front of the vehicle. This design of aftercooler reduces the turbocharger air temperature from 149°C (300°F) to between 38 and 43°C (100 to 110°F) before it flows into the intake manifold. Note that the AAAC has no water or coolant running through it. The aftercooler core consists of a series of tubes surrounded by metal fins somewhat similar to a radiator. The fins disperse the cooling air much more effectively around the tubes through which the turbocharger boost air flows. On a heavy-duty truck, flexible rubber elbows, couplings, and hose clamps are used to secure the duct work to the turbocharger, aftercooler inlet and outlet, and also at the intake manifold.

Heavy-duty electronically controlled diesel engines employ a number of sensors to accurately control the exhaust emissions levels, fuel consumption, and engine power. A number of sensors are used for the air system. An ambient air pressure (barometric pressure) sensor, an intake manifold air temperature sensor, and a turbocharger boost sensor are commonly used to monitor the airflow system. These three sensors are usually mounted directly on the intake manifold or mounted on brackets close to the intake manifold.

Checking AAAC Types

The AAAC does not have coolant flowing through it, so it can be checked using the test equipment illustrated in Figure 13-18. The core of the aftercooler should be kept free of bugs, dust, dirt, and antifreeze spilled from the radiator cooling system. Antifreeze forms a sticky substance that can attract dust and dirt. When cleaning the aftercooler core, always blow air through the core from the back side, since blowing it from the front will push it farther into the aftercooler core and the radiator core when mounted on the vehicle. Regulate the air supply to 172 to 207 kPa (25 to 30 psi) when cleaning the core. Examine the core fins for external damage, debris, and corrosion from road salt.

To check the AAAC core for leaks, refer to Figure 13-18. Fabricate air inlet adaptor plugs to fit into the charge air cooler inlet and outlet connections. Fit a 0 to 414 kPa (0 to 60 psi) gauge and open/close air valve, preferably with an adjustable air-inlet control knob to regulate the air pressure to 172 kPa (25 psi). With the

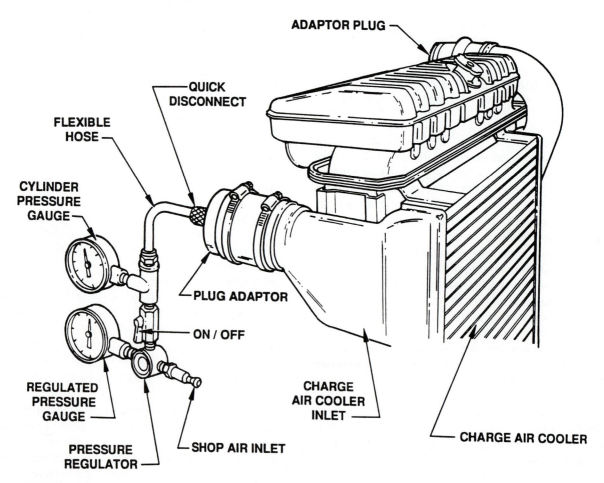

FIGURE 13–18 Charge air cooler pressure, test hookup. (Courtesy of Detroit Diesel Corporation.)

test equipment in position, apply 172 kPa (25 psi) to the cooler core. Apply a water–soap spray solution to each hose connection across the face of the charge air cooler and also at the intake manifold-head mating area. Closely check all welds on the charge air cooler and the tube header areas for stress cracks and signs of air bubbles, which would indicate a leak in the system. If the cooler core can hold 172 kPa (25 psi) with less than a 35-kPa (5-psi) loss in 15 seconds after the air supply hand valve is turned off, the core should be considered acceptable for use.

On heavy-duty trucks that employ air brakes, the engine-driven air compressor often draws its air supply from the engine intake manifold. The system *air dryer* can also be checked for correct operation while pressure checking the aftercooler core as just described. Use shop air to recharge the truck air brake reservoirs to 827 kPa (120 psi) so that you can force the air compressor governor to the unloaded position. This will allow charge air pressure to be directed to the air dryer through the air compressor. If the air dryer is leaking, it should be repaired as soon as possible.

TURBOCHARGERS

The key factor to increasing the power output of a given displacement engine model is to trap a greater airmass and density of charge air in the cylinders. The main advantage of using a TC (turbocharger) assembly is that it allows more air to be packed into the engine cylinders, thereby increasing the VE (volumetric efficiency). The higher the VE, the greater is the quantity of fuel that can be injected and burned to completion. This results in a more thermally efficient engine, and one that can produce substantial increases in both engine power and torque characteristics over its naturally aspirated or nonturbocharged sibling.

There are several methods by which the mass of trapped air within the engine cylinders can be increased. One method is to use an engine gear-driven assembly similar to the *Roots blower*, which is widely used by Detroit Diesel and the General Motors Electro-Motive Division on their two-stroke-cycle engine models. The power requirements needed to drive the blower are not required, however, when an exhaust-gas-driven turbocharger is used. Virtually all of the exhaust energy leaving the cylinders is available to drive the TC turbine wheel shown in Figure 13-1. Only about 5% is lost to heat transfer of the surrounding components, and even less is lost when water-cooled exhaust manifolds are employed as in marine engine applications. The blower does have the advantage of producing a positive airflow at lower speeds and light loads, when the pressure and flow rate of the engine

exhaust gases are lower than at rated full-load speed. The response time of the TC is generally slower than a gear-driven blower due to the small time lag involved when additional fuel must be injected until the higher pressure and flow of exhaust gases are available to drive the turbine.

Either one of these systems delivers boost air to the engine cylinders that is in excess of atmospheric pressure. The greater the air charge that can be retained within the engine cylinders at the start of the compression stroke, then the larger is the fuel volume that can be injected to produce a higher horsepower (kW). The pressure of the trapped air within the cylinders is controlled by the TC airflow capacity and, most important, by the intake and exhaust valve timing. The basic term for an engine that uses any device to increase the cylinder air charge is *supercharged*. A supercharged engine is an engine that takes air under pressure into the cylinders during the intake stroke and then compresses it. The degree of supercharging depends on the valve timing, since this controls when the intake valves close as the piston moves up the cylinder from BDC. Generally, gear-driven blowers are referred to as superchargers, while the exhaust-driven TC is simply called by the descriptive term *turbocharger*. Keep in mind, however, that both devices are capable of supplying air pressure to the engine cylinders that is higher than atmospheric pressure.

Each TC model is designed for a given displacement engine. The performance of a TC is defined by the pressure ratio, mass airflow rate, and the efficiency characteristics of both the compressor and turbine, as well as the mechanical efficiency of the bearing support assembly of the rotating components. The TC identification tag riveted on the center housing usually indicates the name of the manufacturer, the model and part number, and an A/R ratio—the area over the radius of the turbine housing. The letter A is the area of the exhaust gas inlet to the turbine wheel, and the letter R is the radius of the spiral of the turbine housing. This A/R number is very important because each number indicates that a slightly different housing is determined by turbocharger efficiency, airflow through the engine, engine application and speed range, and engine load (the unit injector size, or on inline injection pumps, the rack setting dimension).

Typical TC pressure ratios for high-speed diesel engines usually fall within the range of 2 to 2.5:1. The engine TC maximum boost pressures are determined by using a mercury (Hg) manometer connected to the inlet manifold (described later in this chapter). This is usually stated in inches of Hg at full-load rated speed in the engine service manual.

Turbocharger Types

The two main types of turbocharging are the CPTC (*constant-pressure turbocharging*) model and the PTC (*pulse turbocharging*) model. In the CPTC system, the exhaust ports from all cylinders are connected to a single exhaust manifold whose volume is large enough to provide a near constant pressure feed to the TC turbine housing inlet. This system has the advantage of providing a near constant gas flow rate; therefore, the TC can be matched to operate at optimum efficiency at specified engine operating conditions, particularly on applications that run at fairly constant loads and speeds. The disadvantage is that the energy entering the turbine is low because the pulsing energy of the gases leaving each cylinder in firing order sequence is damped out through the single exhaust manifold assembly. This represents a loss of potential energy to the turbine.

The majority of high-speed heavy-duty diesel engines in use today, particularly the electronically controlled unit injector models of Caterpillar, Cummins, and Detroit Diesel, favor the pulse turbocharging design. In addition, they employ specially designed exhaust manifolds to increase the efficiency of the exhaust gases flowing into the TC turbine housing. Figure 13-19 illustrates the DDC series 50 and 60 pulse recovery exhaust manifold, which improves TC efficiency at low engine speeds.

Pressure waves are generated in the manifold by the exhaust gases rushing past the valves as they begin to open. The length of these passages is tuned to create a response within the manifold that directs the pressure waves to the hot turbine wheel where some of the kinetic energy is recovered. Tuned TCs also improve white smoke cleanup by producing higher engine intake air boost pressure at lower engine speeds, as well as improved TC bearing temperature control. In addition, turbocharger designs are usually of the type described as a single-stage radial flow compressor, and a radial flow turbine with both components mounted to the same shaft.

Figure 13-1 illustrates a typical TC system and the air and exhaust flow passages to and from the engine cylinders. Basically, the TC consists of a housing, illustrated in Figure 13-20, that is a bolted unit with both a turbine and a compressor housing. The turbine end of the TC is often referred to as the *hot* side since the exhaust gases enter here. The compressor end is often referred to as the *cold* end, because this is where the intake air from the air cleaner system enters the housing.

In the center housing of the TC is a one-piece support shaft that has a vaned turbine and compressor wheel pressed onto each end. The compressor wheel is usually retained by a self-locking nut, while the turbine wheel is often part of the support shaft assembly. The rotating components are supported within the TC housing by bearings (bushings) that are pressure lubricated by engine oil directed to the center housing by a hydraulic or steel-braided hose. This allows a constant reservoir of oil to be maintained in the center housing. The pressurized oil supply actually results in the rotating shaft and components being supported on

FIGURE 13–19 *Turbocharger with a ceramic turbine wheel and pulse recovery exhaust manifold used with the series 50 8 5-L four-cylinder electronically controlled engine model. (Courtesy of Detroit Diesel Corporation.)*

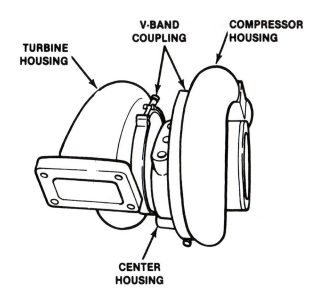

FIGURE 13–20 Major components of a typical turbocharger assembly. (Courtesy of Detroit Diesel Corporation.)

an oil film during high-speed engine operation. Therefore, the term *floating bearings* is often used to describe this type of system. Figure 13-21 illustrates these floating bearings on the support shaft. The bearings also act as thrust surfaces to absorb the thrust loads as the rotating assembly changes position during engine operation. Figure 13-22 illustrates the TC lubrication sup-

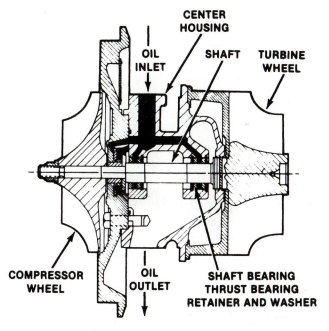

FIGURE 13–21 Sectional view of a turbocharger identifying the major components and showing the pressurized inlet oil flow and the low-pressure drain line. (Courtesy of Detroit Diesel Corporation.)

ply and drain lines, while Figure 13-21 shows the actual pressurized oil flow within the TC center housing. The large drain line allows hot oil to return to the engine crankcase. On some TC models, oil drains directly through a passageway in the engine block or through the blower end plate on some DDC two-stroke-cycle engines where the TC is mounted directly to the gear-driven blower.

The easiest way to understand TC operation is to view it as a large air pump. The hot pressurized exhaust gases leaving the exhaust manifold are directed into the turbine area. As these gases expand through the housing to the atmosphere, they cause rotation of the turbine wheel and shaft. The compressor wheel mounted on the opposite end of the support shaft is driven at the same speed. This speed of rotation averages about 100,000 rpm; speeds may be higher or lower depending on the design characteristics of the TC assembly. The compressor wheel draws air in through the air cleaner system, compresses it, and delivers it to the engine intake manifold on four-stroke-cycle models. On two-stroke-cycle DDC engines, the TC delivers its airflow to the gear-driven engine Roots blower. The TC responds to engine airflow demands by reacting to the flow of exhaust gases. As the power demands of the engine increase and the operator depresses the throttle, the exhaust gas flow increases, causing an increase in the speed of the rotating components. Since the TC relies on exhaust gas flow, there is always a small time lag between the additional injected fuel and the actual TC response. This time has been reduced to almost an unnoticeable point on new TCs by use of smaller and lighter rotating components that are often made of ceramics rather than aluminum alloy metals. Many diesel TCs employ engine coolant passages cast within the center housing to assist in maintaining the lube oil below the *coking* temperature. Otherwise, hot oil (particularly after engine shutdown) can actually boil and create carbon buildup within the lube oil passages and eventual plugging of the lube oil supply to the TC support bearings.

When air is pressurized, its temperature increases and its mass (density) decreases accordingly. Either JWAC or AAAC systems are widely employed on modern engines to reduce the temperature of the pressurized air entering the engine intake manifold or the two-stroke-cycle air box.

Wastegate Turbochargers

Many current high-speed on-highway truck diesel engines have wastegate turbochargers. Examples are the 5.9-L Cummins engine used in the Dodge Ram pickup truck, the 7.3-L Navistar engine used in Ford and Navistar trucks, and the 6.5-L GMC V8 diesel. Heavier-

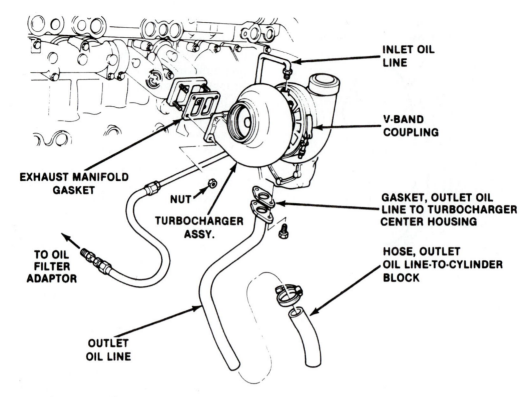

FIGURE 13–22 *Location of the turbocharger oil supply and drain lines for a heavy-duty high-speed engine. (Courtesy of Detroit Diesel Corporation.)*

duty engines using this TC include the Cat 3116 and the Cat 3406E—ratings of 435 bhp (325 kW) and higher. Engines rated below 435 bhp use a fixed, non-ceramic wheel that spins 6% faster than the 3406C engine model TC. A wastegate TC is designed to improve engine low-end performance and transient response, limit peak cylinder pressures, lower heat rejection and turbo speed, and reduce exhaust emissions. In addition, use of a wastegate allows very close matching to either an overdrive or manual transmission used in vehicles. The wastegate system can be adjusted to limit the maximum amount of boost depending on specific application needs, and the system provides improved throttle response at both the low-end and midrange loads.

An example of the location of a turbocharger wastegate can be seen in Figure 13-23 on a Cat 3406E series engine. A hose is connected to the body of the wastegate from the cold end of the outlet of the turbo assembly. Pressurized air (turbo boost) is routed into the wastegate control housing where it works against a spring-loaded diaphragm and linkage connected to the housing at the hot side (exhaust gas outlet) of the turbocharger. When the air pressure exceeds the spring setting in the control housing, the wastegate linkage shifts a small butterfly-type valve within the exhaust manifold porting area. This routes the exhaust

gas flow around the turbine wheel, thereby bypassing, or *wasting*, the heat energy around the turbine housing and back into the upstream side of the exhaust manifold piping. When the boost pressure within the intake manifold of the engine is reduced, the spring within the turbo wastegate control housing automatically reopens the wastegate valve to redirect the hot exhaust gases back into the turbine wheel area of the turbo, allowing boost to once again be delivered to the engine. There is usually an adjustable pushrod, as shown in Figure 13-23, that must be set to ensure that the butterfly valve within the wastegate remains in either the fully open or fully closed position.

Turbocharger Back Pressure Device

Another unique design feature in use on some turbochargers in high-speed diesel engines is the exhaust gas back pressure device. It is being used on the Navistar 7.3-L T 444E V8 engine that employs hydraulically actuated electronic unit injectors. Since this is a direct-injection design engine, less heat is rejected to the coolant than in an indirect-injection engine. To provide rapid warm-up in cold ambient conditions, an exhaust gas back pressure device is employed within the turbocharger (Figure 13-24). This device consists of a butterfly valve controlled and actuated by a solenoid and actuator piston. The butterfly valve is powered bocharger to restrict the exhaust flow. This action increases the exhaust back pressure and consequently the pumping effort required by the engine. This back pressure is monitored by a pressure sensor in the exhaust manifold. Thus, an electronic closed-loop strategy ensures that the exhaust back pressure is held at levels that will not affect drivability under varying speed, load, and acceleration conditions over a limited range of engine temperatures.

Turbocharger Maintenance

Properly maintained TCs should provide trouble-free service between engine overhauls. The three key maintenance items that affect the life of a turbocharger are excessive AIR (air inlet restriction), high EBP (exhaust back pressure), and lubrication of bearings. Unfiltered air entering the TC can cause fine lapping of the rotating components, and high AIR can cause lube oil to be drawn past the seals. On mechanically governed engines, high AIR and high EBP can create incomplete combustion which leads to carbon buildup on the rotating turbine wheel. This, in turn, can create an imbalance condition of the rotating components and the turbine blading may actually come into contact with the housing. On electronically controlled diesel engines, the various intake system sensors prevent the engines from being overfueled as a result of a high AIR condition.

A

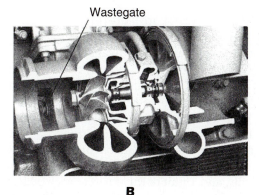

Wastegate

B

FIGURE 13–23 (A) Design features of the high-tech turbocharger used by Caterpillar on its 3406E engine models. Note linkage connection to the wastegate to bypass exhaust gases around the turbine in order to limit the turboboost pressure supply. (B) Cutaway view of wastegate turbocharger which improves transient response, limits peak cylinder pressure, and lowers heat rejection and turbo speed. (Courtesy of Caterpillar, Inc.)

hydraulically with engine oil supplied to the turbocharger bearings. The valve is only operational at idle and light load, when engine temperature and ambient temperature are low; therefore, once the engine is warmed up, the device is turned off. At temperatures below approximately 3°C, the device is activated by the electronic control unit on the vehicle, which is a variant of Ford Motor Company's EEC-IV control module. A signal from the control module opens an oil passage to charge the actuator cylinder, which in turn moves the actuator piston and closes the butterfly valve located in the exhaust outlet area of the tur-

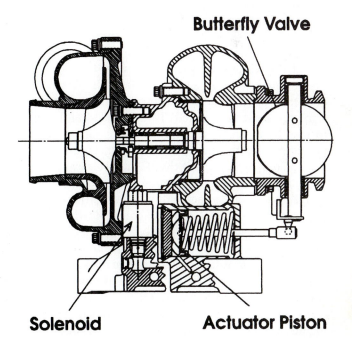

Butterfly Valve

Solenoid   **Actuator Piston**

FIGURE 13–24 Concept of an exhaust gas back pressure device used on the Navistar 7.3-L T444E V8 hydraulically actuated electronic unit injector engine model. (Reprinted with permission from SAE publication SP-930629, copyright 1994, Society of Automotive Engineers, Inc., Warrendale, PA.)

Leaks at the TC exhaust gaskets can prevent the rotating components from reaching the proper speed under load. This, in turn, reduces the boost pressure to the engine cylinders. Leaking gaskets or intake manifold seal rings on the outlet side of the TC compressor wheel can create a high-pitched whistle, particularly under load as the boost pressure forces its way past these areas.

TC inspection is best performed with the engine stopped and the intake ducting removed. Check for dirt and dust buildup on the compressor wheel impeller and in the housing. Excessive signs of dirt suggest that the air inlet ducting is not airtight, so perform the checks discussed earlier in this chapter and shown in Figure 13-16. You can also disconnect the exhaust piping to inspect the hot end of the turbo. Pay particular attention to the condition of the carbon buildup on the turbine vanes. Light carbon usually is indicative of light-load operation and/or excessive periods of idling. Do not attempt to remove carbon buildup from the vanes without removing the TC from the engine and disassembling it. Any signs of physical damage to either the compressor or turbine wheels are sufficient reason for immediate removal and replacement of these rotating assemblies. If damaged TC blading disintegrated during engine operation and the parts were inhaled into the engine cylinders, complete engine failure might be the result.

With the engine stopped, rotate the turbine wheel by hand to check for smooth and free operation. Any tight spots or signs of turbine or compressor wheel contact with their respective housings require TC removal and disassembly. Also examine the TC compressor intake area for signs of oil leaks. If oil is found, both the *axial* and *radial* clearances of the rotating assembly should be checked. These checks can be performed by means of a dial indicator gauge assembly mounted over the TC as illustrated in Figures 13-25 and 13-26. When checking the TC radial clearance with a dial gauge, use an offset gauge plunger as shown so that it comes into contact with the shaft through the oil inlet hole. Grasp the TC main shaft and slowly move it up and down while reading the dial gauge. To check the axial clearance (end to end), install and preload the dial gauge so that its pointer rests against the end of the shaft as shown in Figure 13-26. Push and pull the shaft backward and forward to record the end play.

Compare the radial and axial readings obtained to the specifications listed in the TC or engine service manual literature. Both of these clearances are fairly small on high-speed engine TCs. Radial clearances are usually in the range 0.15 to 0.53 mm (0.006 to 0.021 in.); axial clearances usually run between 0.025

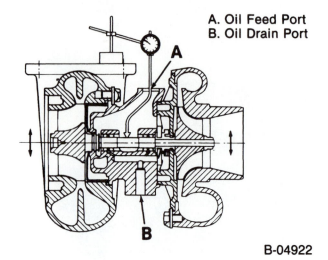

A. Oil Feed Port
B. Oil Drain Port

B-04922

FIGURE 13–25 *Using a dial indicator gauge to check the turbocharger bearing radial clearance. (Courtesy of GMC Trucks.)*

and 0.35 mm (0.001 to 0.014 in.), although specific models may allow greater clearances than these. If a dial indicator is not readily available, radial clearance can be checked by using a wire-type feeler gauge between the vanes and housing. Hold the TC shaft toward the feeler gauge to check this dimension.

When a suspected oil leak at the TC seal from the hot end (turbine) cannot be confirmed on a stopped engine, a commercially available fluorescent tracer liquid additive can be mixed with the engine lube oil. Normally, add 1 unit of the tracer to each 38 L (10 U.S. gallons) of engine lube oil. Refer to the packaging for specific directions.

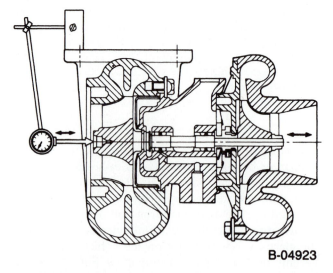

B-04923

FIGURE 13–26 *Dial indicator mounting required to check the turbocharger rotating assembly axial (end) play. (Courtesy of GMC Trucks.)*

CAUTION Under certain engine and turbocharger running test conditions, it may be necessary to remove the inlet ducting. If this is the case, refer to Figure 13-27 and *always* install a TC inlet shield to prevent the possibility of foreign objects or loose clothing being pulled into the rotating components. *Never* run a TC engine with this shield removed since serious personal injury can result.

To test a TC seal for leakage, follow these steps:

1. Start and run the engine until normal operating temperature is reached.

2. Stop the engine and add the recommended amount of fluorescent tracer to the engine oil.

3. Start and operate the engine at low idle for 10 minutes.

4. Stop the engine.

5. Allow the turbocharger to cool and remove the exhaust pipe from the hot end (turbine) of the housing.

6. Use a high-intensity *black light* to inspect the turbine outlet for oil.

7. A dark-blue glow usually indicates a raw fuel leak, while a yellow glow is indicative of a lube oil leak.

8. Remove the TC oil drain line and check it carefully. Lube oil leaks may be traced back to restrictions within this drain line. Clean any restrictions and/or replace a damaged or collapsed drain line or hose.

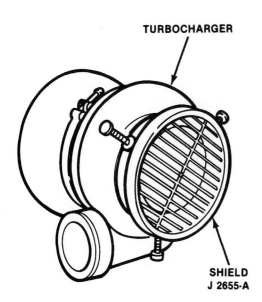

TURBOCHARGER

SHIELD
J 2655-A

FIGURE 13–27 *Installation of a turbocharger safety shield when running the engine with the air inlet piping disconnected. (Courtesy of Detroit Diesel Corporation.)*

64. Compressor Housing
65. Clamp
66. Lock Plate
67. Bolt
68. Center Assembly
69. Turbine Housing

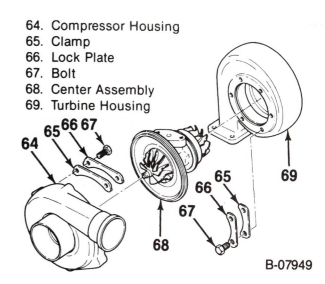

B-07949

FIGURE 13–28 *Three main components of a typical turbocharger assembly. (Courtesy of GMC Trucks.)*

9. Check for restrictions in the engine breather or tube, because high crankcase pressure can also cause the TC seals to leak.

Turbocharger Removal and Disassembly

Removal of the TC from the engine is a fairly straightforward process. Refer to Figure 13-22 and note that the TC hot-end housing flange is bolted to a mating flange on the engine exhaust manifold. A gasket is located between the mating surfaces. The cold end of the TC is usually connected to the air inlet piping or ducting by use of a heavy-duty thick-walled rubber hose and clamp arrangement. In addition, the various lube oil supply and drain lines must be disconnected. Carefully sling the TC with a suitable lifting tackle prior to removing the retaining bolts that hold it to the exhaust manifold.

If it is necessary to disassemble the TC assembly, always match-mark the hot and cold ends of the housing to the center housing assembly to allow reinstallation of the components in the same position. Figure 13-28 illustrates the three main TC components split apart after either loosening off the special band clamps or removing the bolts on some models. Most service facilities simply replace a damaged TC with a new or rebuilt one, since special equipment is required to overhaul and rebalance the rotating components. If, however, the TC is to be disassembled, the self-locking retaining nut on the compressor wheel end of the assembly must be removed and the back side of the compressor wheel must be supported on a hydraulic press: Use an old nut over the threads while applying pressure to it so that the shaft and turbine wheel assembly pop from the compressor wheel. Special pliers are usually required to remove the snap rings to reach the seals and bearings (bushings). In some cases a series of small bolts at the center housing must also be removed to access these components.

Carefully inspect all disassembled components. Compare all dimensions of the parts with those in the service manual. Replace all worn or damaged components. When reassembling the TC, make sure to align the match marks that were applied during the disassembly procedure.

Reinstall the TC assembly onto the engine using the reverse procedure of removal. Always use new self-locking nuts to retain the TC to the exhaust manifold. Remember that a new or rebuilt TC must be prelubricated before engine startup. Refer to Figure 13-29 and pour clean engine oil into the bearing housing cavity while turning the rotating assembly by hand to lubricate all of the internal components. With the turbo guard shown in Figure 13-27 in position, start the engine and run at an idle speed; do not use a WOT (wide-open throttle) condition. It is also usually good practice to leave the oil supply line slightly loose on engine startup, until you can confirm that a steady flow of lube oil is reaching the TC center housing. If no lube oil is evident within 30 seconds maximum, shut the engine down and determine the cause.

Once the engine has warmed up, carefully listen for any unusual metallic rattles or scraping sounds. After the engine has been stopped, the TC should coast freely and smoothly to a stop. Any signs of a jerky or sudden stop should be investigated and corrected.

Troubleshooting Turbochargers

Generally, when a turbocharged engine lacks power, emits black smoke, or shows signs of oil (blue smoke) at the exhaust stack, the turbocharger may not be at fault. Often the cause is TC related, but other factors can cause or contribute to these symptoms. Spend a few minutes first in checking possible causes before you start to remove the TC from the engine.

One of the easiest and most useful methods is to *listen, look, and feel* as described next.

Listen

Since the turbocharger is a standard item on most heavy-duty diesel engines manufactured today, most of us know what a normal-running turbocharger sounds like. Unusual TC operating sounds that you should be aware of include these:

1. A high-pitched whine, particularly under load, can be created by an exhaust gas leak or by a leak in the air induction piping between the TC and the engine intake manifold.

2. A sharp high-pitched scream is generally indicative of worn bearings or possibly that the turbine or compressor wheel is rubbing on its housing.

3. A cycling up and down in sound pitch can indicate air starvation or blockage in the air inlet duct system, a restricted air cleaner, or a buildup in dirt on the compressor wheel or diffuser vanes within the TC housing.

Look

One of the most important tools for troubleshooting is sight. Disconnect the exhaust and inlet piping from the TC housing assembly. Then make the following visual determinations:

1. Use either a flashlight or Trouble-light and carefully look into the turbine and compressor end of the TC. Are there any signs of rubbing marks (polishing) on either the wheels or the housing?

2. Are any of the blades (vanes) on the turbine or compressor wheels bent or damaged?

3. Is there heavy dirt buildup on the compressor wheel? This would indicate unfiltered air, possibly coming from a leak in the air ducting, or poor filter maintenance intervals.

4. Check for signs of heavy carbon or soot buildup on the vanes of the turbine wheel. This is indicative of incomplete combustion or burning oil (possibly from TC seals).

5. If heavy oil accumulations are noticeable, check for the possible source. Oil may be from TC seals, although oil in the compressor inlet may not necessarily be coming from the TC seals. Also check that the engine air compressor is not pumping oil.

6. Oil at the turbine end usually indicates an engine fault rather than a TC problem. Check the exhaust manifold for signs of engine oil accumulations, which may be from worn or broken rings on the pistons or worn valve guides. On two-stroke-cycle DDC models,

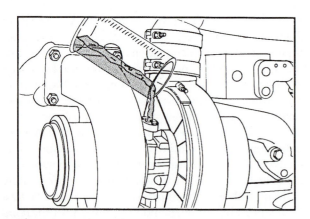

FIGURE 13–29 *Priming the turbocharger oil reservoir with clean engine oil prior to engine startup after installation of a new or rebuilt unit. (Courtesy of Cummins Engine Company, Inc.)*

leaking blower seals could contribute to the oil accumulations as well as leaking solid piston pin retainers or operation of the engine for long idle periods or under light-load conditions.

7. Turbochargers generally use metal piston seal rings rather than lip seals that are used on crankshafts. Therefore, the oil sealing on the TC is known as *dynamic sealing*. Oil slingers keep the oil away from the seal ring areas. Check these common causes of leaking TC seals: excessive engine idling, plugged crankcase breather system (high crankcase pressure), sludge buildup or accumulations within the center housing of the TC, high air inlet restriction conditions, plugged or kinked TC oil drain line, damage to the TC bearings or wheels, and worn piston rings in the engine (blowby).

Heavy carbon buildup on the turbine wheel can be cleaned once the end housing has been removed to allow access. Use a noncorrosive cleaning solvent and a soft-bristle brush. Avoid the use of a wire brush, screwdriver, or gasket scraper which could scratch, damage, or nick the blades. It is important that carbon be thoroughly removed; if not, an imbalance condition could lead to the wheel striking the housing once the engine is started. If the TC has to be completely disassembled to clean the carbon, a glass-beading machine can be used. Make sure that you use only the recommended material for cleaning, for example, walnut shells.

Feel

To avoid personal injury, make sure that the engine is stopped and the TC has been allowed to cool off. Then perform the following checks:

1. Slowly rotate the turbo wheels by hand. They should turn easily and smoothly.

2. Push inward against each wheel one at a time as you rotate it by hand. Once again, it should rotate smoothly and freely.

3. Determine if there are any signs of rubbing or scraping; these indicate a major problem.

4. Determine if the TC rotates smoothly and freely; if it does not, a major problem is indicated.

5. After replacing a new or rebuilt TC, always prelube the turbo as shown in Figure 13-29. Check the intake and exhaust system ducting (piping) for any signs of foreign objects. Check the TC oil supply and return line and the air filter ducting to ensure that all connections are airtight. Do the same on the exhaust system.

Figure 13-30 lists typical operational conditions that you may experience when dealing with turbochargers along with possible causes and suggested corrections.

EXHAUST MUFFLERS AND PARTICULATE TRAPS

Mufflers used on diesel engines can vary tremendously in physical size and design. Their purpose, however, is the same: to allow the escaping exhaust gases, which are under pressure, to expand within the muffler, thereby reducing the noise emitted as they exit into the atmosphere. Exhaust noise is caused by sound pressure waves that cause small changes in atmospheric pressure. The frequency, or pitch, of sound pressure waves is measured in cycles per second. Typical noise levels from a heavy-duty highway truck or trailer are usually within the 80 to 86 decibels (dB range).

Two typical muffler designs are illustrated in Figure 13-31. In the straight-through design, baffles located between the inlet and outlet cause the pressurized exhaust gases to follow a given path through connecting tubes. In the reverse-flow muffler design, the gases flow through connecting tubes. The muffler can be mounted either horizontally or vertically, as is the case on many heavy-duty on- and off-highway trucks and equipment.

Sometimes a small, round *spark arrestor* is added to the pipe exiting from the muffler assembly. This spark arrestor traps most incendiary sparks, thereby reducing any fire hazard, which is important in logging equipment, for example. The venting of glowing carbon particles blown out with the exhaust gases can retain sufficient heat to ignite surrounding materials. Stainless steel vanes inside the inlet tube spin exhaust gases and solid particles. Centrifugal force throws particles to the periphery of the tube where they move in an ascending spiral. When the particles pass the end of the inlet tube, they are thrown out of the gas stream into the outer chamber of the spark arrestor where they fall through a baffle and are collected in the carbon trap where they remain until the unit is serviced. The trap can be serviced by removing a clean-out plug located on the underside of the body. Any crust that has been formed over the hole can be broken with a screwdriver. Start the engine and run it at high idle to blow collected particles out of the clean-out hole. Replace the plug when finished.

A fairly widely used exhaust silencer is the *COWL* spiral silencer manufactured by Phillips & Temro (Figure 13-32). The exhaust gases are routed through an aluminum-coated 14- or 16-gauge cold-rolled steel housing. This type of a silencer is much more compact than the conventional exhaust muffler system and offers superior noise reduction. The COWL silencer consists of a spiral passage of constant cross-sectional area. The spiral is partially lined with noise absorbing stainless steel wool. The exhaust gases can pass from

(OPERATIONAL)

Engine lacks power	Black exhaust smoke	Excessive engine oil consumption	Blue exhaust smoke	Turbocharger noisy	Cyclic sound from turbocharger	Oil leak from compressor seal	Oil leak from turbine seal	CAUSE	CORRECTION
•	•		•	•		•		Clogged air filter element	Replace element according to engine service manual recommendations
	•	•	•	•	•	•		Obstructed air intake duct to turbo compressor	Remove obstruction or replace damaged parts as required
•	•		•					Obstructed air outlet duct from compressor to intake/manifold	Remove obstruction or replace damaged parts as required
•	•		•					Obstructed intake/manifold	Refer to engine service manual & remove obstruction
			•					Air leak in duct from air cleaner to compressor	Correct leak by replacing seals or tightening fasteners as required
•	•	•	•	•				Air leak in duct from compressor to intake/manifold	Correct leak by replacing seals or tightening fasteners as required
•	•	•	•	•				Air leak at intake/manifold engine inlet	Refer to engine service manual & replace gaskets or tighten fasteners as required
•	•	•	•	•		•		Obstruction in exhaust manifold	Refer to engine service manual & remove obstruction
•	•			•				Obstruction in muffler or exhaust stack	Remove obstruction or replace faulty components as required
•	•		•					Gas leak in exhaust manifold to engine connection	Refer to engine service manual & replace gaskets or tighten fasteners as required
•	•		•	•				Gas leak in turbine inlet to exhaust manifold connection	Replace gasket or tighten fasteners as required
			•					Gas leak in ducting after the turbine outlet	Refer to engine service manual & repair leak
	•	•				•	•	Obstructed turbocharger oil drain line	Remove obstruction or replace line as required
	•	•				•	•	Obstructed engine crankcase vent	Refer to engine service manual, clean obstruction
	•	•				•	•	Turbocharger center housing sludged or coked	Change engine oil & filter, overhaul or replace turbo as required
•	•							Fuel injectors incorrect output	Refer to engine service manual — replace or adjust faulty component(s) as required
•	•							Engine camshaft timing incorrect	Refer to engine service manual & replace worn parts
•	•	•	•			•	•	Worn engine piston rings or liners (blowby)	Refer to engine service manual & repair engine as required
•	•	•	•			•	•	Internal engine problem (valves, pistons)	Refer to engine service manual & repair engine as required
•	•	•	•	•	•	•	•	Dirt caked on compressor wheel and/or diffuser vanes	Clean using a *Non-Caustic* cleaner & *Soft Brush*. Find & correct source of unfiltered air & change engine oil & oil filter
•	•	•	•	•		•	•	Damaged turbocharger	Analyze failed turbocharger, find & correct cause of failure, overhaul or replace turbocharger as required

FIGURE 13–30 Turbocharger troubleshooting chart. (Courtesy of Detroit Diesel Corporation.)

(BEARINGS)

Slight wear or scratches	Moderate to heavy grooving on O.D. only	Moderate to heavy grooving on O.D. & I.D.	Extruded, or pounded. (May be stuck in ctr. hsg.)	Smooth undersized O.D.	Cracked or broken	Deep groove around center of O.D.	Oil holes fully or partially closed	Oil holes plugged with carbon	Polished looking O.D.	I.D. Polished & worn oversize	Melted (aluminum bearing)	CONDITION	PROBABLE CAUSE
•												Normal Use	Acceptable operating & maintenance procedures
	•											Contaminated oil (dirt in oil)	Engine oil & oil filter(s) not changed frequently enough, unfiltered air entering engine intake, malfunction of oil filter bypass valve
		•		•								Severely contaminated (dirty oil)	
			•		•	•						Pounded by eccentric shaft motion	Foreign object damage, coked or loose housing, excessive bearing clearance due to lube problem
				•			•					Center housing bearing bores, rough finish	Incorrect cleaning of center housing during overhaul of turbo. (Wrong chemicals, bores sand or bead blasted)
					•							Metal or large particle oil contamination	Severe engine wear. i.e., Bearing damage, camshaft or lifter wear, broken piston
						•			•			Lack of lube, oil lag, insufficient lube	Low oil level, high speed shutdowns, lube system failure, turbo plugged with hose fitting sealants
								•				Coking	Hot shutdowns, engine overfueled, restricted or leaking air intake/inlet
					•				•	•		Fine particles in oil (contaminated oil)	See contaminated oil
										•		Rough bearing journals on shaft	Bearing journals not protected from sand or bead blast cleaning during overhaul

GLOSSARY OF TERMS

ALIGNMENT — Proper position of parts.

BURR — Sharp metal.

COLD END — Compressor end of turbocharger.

CONTAINER — A box used to hold material.

DISCOLORATION — Change in color.

DISSIPATED — Dispersing or dispelling of heat.

DO NOT REUSE — Excessive damage - part requires replacement or possible remanufacturing.

EROSION — Gradual wear of material.

EXCESSIVE — Too much.

GLASS BEADING — Procedure used to clean parts where air under pressure is used to force small glass particles at a high rate of speed against the surface of the part.

HOT SHUTDOWN — Shutdown at high rpm will cause the turbocharger to continue spinning after the lubricant supply from the oil pump has stopped. Bearings will not be adequately lubricated or cooled.

HOT SIDE — Turbine side of turbocharger.

NICK — Small notch.

PITTING — Wear that causes holes in the material.

POLISH — To clean and smooth the surface.

REUSE — Parts that require inspection and reconditioning according to published specifications.

ROTATING UNIT — Compressor wheel-shaft-turbine assembly.

RUBBING — Contact between two parts.

SEVERELY — To a large degree.

SLIGHTLY — To a small degree.

STRAIGHTEN — Make straight.

WARP — To twist or bend out of shape.

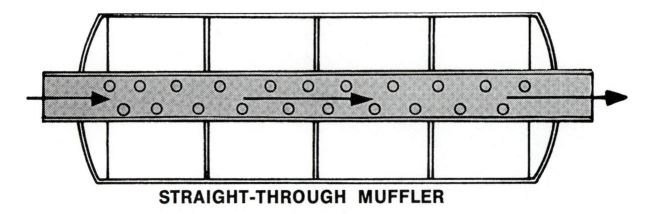

STRAIGHT-THROUGH MUFFLER

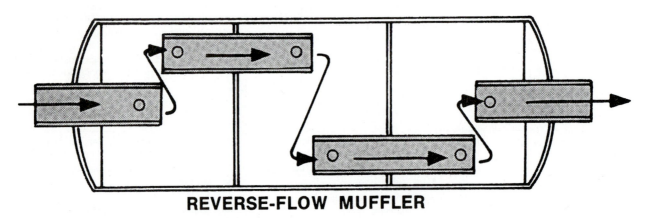

REVERSE-FLOW MUFFLER

FIGURE 13–31 Exhaust gas flow through two typical muffler assemblies.

FIGURE 13–32 Features of a COWL spiral exhaust silencer. (Courtesy of Temro Division, Budd Canada Inc.)

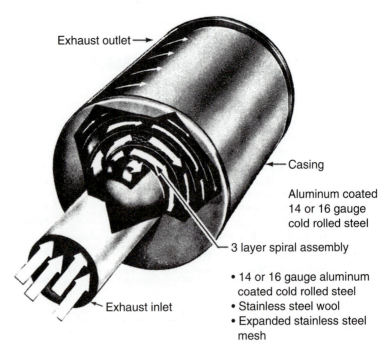

Exhaust outlet →

Casing

Aluminum coated 14 or 16 gauge cold rolled steel

3 layer spiral assembly

• 14 or 16 gauge aluminum coated cold rolled steel
• Stainless steel wool
• Expanded stainless steel mesh

Exhaust inlet

one spiral passage to another through bleed holes within the spiral body. Since sound waves travel in straight lines at a speed much higher than the speed of the exhaust gases passing through the silencer, they are continually bounced off the smooth wall of the spiral. Some of these sound waves are reflected into the wool-covered wall, where they are diffused. Other sound waves pass through the bleed holes, progressively attenuating the sound by wave cancellation as the gases pass through the multiple turns of the spiral. Any contaminants flowing into the silencer are centrifugally forced to the smooth outer surface and pass through the silencer, thus ensuring that no buildup of deposits occurs.

GEAR-DRIVEN BLOWERS

Figure 2-5 illustrates airflow through the engine of a V-model DDC engine. On larger models, two blowers are used, and on the DDC 20V-149 engine model three blower assemblies are needed since this engine consists of a V6–V8–V6 arrangement bolted together. The major function of the blower in two-stroke engines is to supply air at pressures between 4 and 7 psi (27 to 48 kPa) to the engine *air box* area, which acts as a reservoir for a header of charged air. Remember, in a two-cycle engine the intake and exhaust strokes are physically eliminated, so pressurized air is needed and is used for several purposes:

- Supply fresh air for combustion
- Cool the cylinder liner, piston crown, and exhaust valves
- Scavenge waste exhaust gases from the cylinder
- Allow a controlled amount of air leakage past the piston oil control rings when at TDC to provide for positive crankcase ventilation

Blower Construction

The basic construction of the blower illustrated in Figure 13-33 consists of an aluminum housing, two end plates, and two aluminum three-lobe rotors supported on ball and roller bearings within the end plates. As the blower rotates, air is trapped between the lobes and the housing to produce a positive air displacement into the engine air box. Figure 13-33 illustrates the major parts of a typical blower assembly used on a DDC V92 series engine. The blower is mounted on a machined pad on top of the engine block between both cylinder heads and is bolted in position. A splined shaft driven from the rear of the engine (gear train end) is also splined into a blower drive gear at the rear end of the right-hand rotor. On mechanically governed engines, the front end plate of the blower supports and drives the fuel transfer pump as well as the governor assembly.

On DDEC two-cycle engine models, the blower front end plate simply supports the fuel pump, since all engine governing is controlled from the engine ECM.

Blower Operation

The airflow rates of blowers depend on their physical size and speed of rotation. Typical engine airflow rates depend on displacement and speed. The power required to rotate a gear- or belt-driven blower can be substantial; for example, average power is between 25 and 30 hp on many high-speed automotive truck engines when running at maximum rated speed. To reduce this parasitic power loss, Detroit Diesel uses a bypass blower arrangement on its two-stroke-cycle engine models, which are also equipped with a turbocharger assembly. Recall that a turbocharger only provides pressurized airflow once the engine is running and under load. It is necessary, therefore, on two-cycle engines to employ a gear-driven blower so that a positive air displacement can be supplied to the engine for starting purposes and light-load operation. Once the engine is placed under load, the hot pressurized exhaust gases allow the turbocharger to supply all the necessary air requirements for the engine, and the gear-driven blower becomes unnecessary.

The principle employed by DDC to disengage the blower is a *bypass valve*. This bypass valve and its location are shown in Figure 13-34 and the concept of operation is illustrated in Figure 13-35. The spring-loaded bypass relief valve contained within the rear end plate of the blower is held closed during engine startup and also during low-rpm and light-load conditions. When the engine speed is increased and load is applied, the turbocharger boost air pressure increases to raise the air pressure within the engine air box area. On 6V and 8V-92 model DDC engines, when this air box pressure reaches approximately 6 psi (12 in. Hg/305 mm manometer fluid displacement) or 41 kPa, the spring-loaded bypass valve opens. Under this valve-open condition, turbocharger boost air is free to bypass the blower rotors and enter the engine air box. The blower is gear driven, so it will continue to rotate, but since the bypass valve is wide open, all the required air pressure is being supplied from the turbocharger assembly and the pressure rise across the blower (inlet to outlet) is greatly reduced. During this bypass mode of operation (reduced pumping losses) the blower requires very little power to drive it; therefore, a substantial improvement occurs in brake specific fuel consumption.

Blower Removal

The blower must be removed if a major overhaul of the engine is to be performed or if the blower assembly requires major servicing. The blower assembly has either

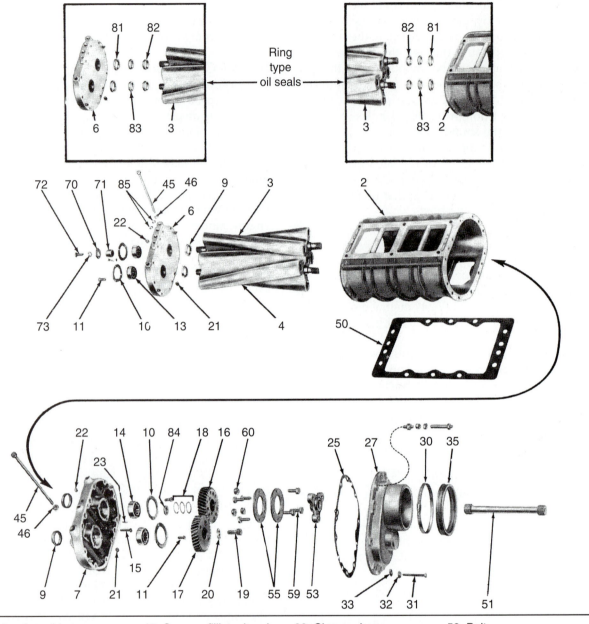

FIGURE 13–33 Exploded view illustrating the component parts of a gear-driven blower assembly for a DDC two-stroke-cycle engine. (Courtesy of Detroit Diesel Corporation.)

2. Housing – blower
3. Rotor Assy. – R.H. helix
4. Rotor Assy. – L.H. helix
6. Plate – blower front end
7. Plate – blower rear end
9. Seal – oil
10. Retainer – blower bearing
11. Retainer – lock screw
13. Bearing – blower rotor front (roller)
14. Bearing – blower rotor rear (ball)
15. Screw – fillister head
16. Gear – R.H. helix rotor
17. Gear – L.H. helix rotor
18. Shim – blower gear
19. Bolt – blower gear
20. Washer
21. Strainer – end plate oil passage
22. Plug – oil passage
23. Orifice – oil passage
25. Gasket – cover
27. Cover – rear end plate
30. Clamp – hose
31. Bolt – cover
32. Lock washer
33. Washer – special flat
35. Hose – blower drive cover
45. Bolt – blower mounting
46. Lock washer
50. Gasket
51. Shaft – blower drive
53. Hub – drive
55. Plate – flexible
59. Bolt
60. Spacer
70. Disc – fuel pump drive
71. Spacer – fuel pump drive disc
72. Bolt – drive disc
73. Lock washer
81. Collar – blower end plate
82. Carrier – seal ring
83. Ring – seal (piston type)
84. Spacer
85. Seal ring

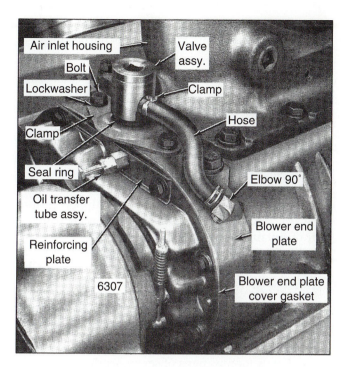

FIGURE 13–34 *Location of the gear-driven blower by-pass valve assembly used on DDC two-stroke-cycle engine models. (Courtesy of Detroit Diesel Corporation.)*

lip-type oil seals (item 9) or hook-type piston seal rings (item 83, Figure 13-33) in both the front and rear end plates. These seals are required to prevent pressurized lube oil on V engines, or drain oil on inline models, which lubricate the rotor support bearings from entering the blower rotor housing. In addition, they prevent blower air pressure from entering the engine

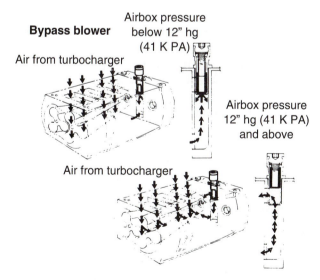

FIGURE 13–35 *Schematic illustrating the airflow through a mini-bypass gear-driven blower assembly. (Courtesy of Detroit Diesel Corporation.)*

crankcase and creating high crankcase pressure. If the seals are suspected of leaking, check them as follows:

1. Make sure that the engine is stopped.
2. Remove the air inlet housing from the blower.
3. Remove the blower safety screen if used.
4. Start and run the engine at idle. Exercise extreme care to prevent any loose clothing or foreign objects from entering the blower.
5. If the seals are leaking, use a Trouble-light or flashlight and look into the housing; you will see oil spiral along the length of the rotors.

In addition to the seal check, note if there are signs of rotor-to-rotor contact throughout their length. Contact is an indication that the bearings (items 13 and 14 in Figure 13-33) are worn and/or that excessive gear backlash might exist in the drive and driven gears. Perform one more check before removing the blower. With the engine stopped, grasp one blower rotor and push the other one downward, then let it go; it should spring back slightly. This indicates that the blower drive hub and flex coupling are operating correctly. Any looseness detected in the rotors during this check indicates damage to the blower drive hub assembly.

When removing a DDC blower assembly, remember that minor variations will exist between a mechanically governed engine and an electronically controlled one, since there are no injector control tubes or fuel rods in the DDEC system. Nevertheless, the basic removal procedure can be considered common for most engines.

Blower Overhaul

The blower must be disassembled in a systematic way using some special tools. Figure 13-33 is an exploded view of all of the component parts of a typical DDC V92 engine blower. Always match-mark each end plate to the blower housing to ensure that they are replaced in the same position.

NOTE   Refer to the exploded view in Figure 13-33 for the individual items listed in the following dissassembly procedure.

---

1. Once the blower accessories and front and rear cover plates (item 27) have been removed, refer to Figure 13-36 and jam a soft folded rag between the rotors (items 3 and 4). This will allow you to loosen and remove the gear retaining bolts that are threaded into each rotor. The blower drive and driven gears shown in Figure 13-36 *must* be removed using the two special

J 6270-1

FIGURE 13–36 *Using two Kent-Moore gear pullers to remove the drive and driven gears from the rear of a two-stroke-cycle engine blower assembly. (Courtesy of Detroit Diesel Corporation.)*

Kent-Moore pullers which have been bolted to the rear of each gear.

2. Leave the folded rag between the rotors as you tighten the puller center bolts; otherwise, the rotors would continue to spin during this tightening process. Alternately tighten each puller bolt so that the helical cut gears do not bind into one another.

3. Once the gears have been removed, take careful note of the hardened spacers and shims (item 18) behind each gear. Tie or wire these together so that they can be reinstalled in the same position upon reassembly.

4. Remove the three bearing retainer screws from each retainer at the front and rear of the blower. Remove the retainers (item 10).

5. Using the same pullers that were employed in Figure 13-36, attach the pullers to the blower end plate with bolts threaded into the bearing retainer holes.

6. Remove the two fillister heads (large slotted screws, item 15) that are located diagonally opposite one another in the end plate.

7. Jam the rotors with a soft folded rag and tighten the puller center bolts alternately to remove the end plate with its bearings from the blower housing.

8. At the front end plate on mechanically governed engines, remove the fuel pump drive bolt (item 72), washer, and spacer, as well as the two fillister head end plate retaining screws.

9. Using the same pullers that were employed in Figure 13-36, repeat the same procedure to remove the front end plate (item 6) and bearings (item 13) from the housing.

NOTE   The rotors can be pulled with the end plate and then pressed from the bearings, or they

can be separated by leaving the fillister head screws in position and pushed out of the bearings.

---

10. Remove the end plate bearings and seals from the front and rear plates by supporting the plate on wooden blocks or an arbor press and using suitable pressing stub shafts. Take note that the front end plate bearings (item 13) are of a roller design, while the rear end plate (gear end) has double-row radial and thrust ball bearings (item 14).

11. On turbocharged engines, the blower rotors employ seal ring carriers (item 82) that support piston type seal rings (item 83). Remove these seals using a pair of suitable snap-ring pliers.

12. If the seal ring carrier is damaged, remove it using a Kent-Moore puller similar to those shown in Figure 13-36.

Blower Inspection

After washing all parts in clean fuel oil, dry them with compressed air and lint-free rags. Carefully inspect the blower parts for any signs of severe scoring on the rotors, the end plates, the blower end plate mounting surface, and inside the blower housing. Minor imperfections can be removed using fine emery cloth in all areas. Note, however, that each blower end plate is bolted directly to the blower housing without a gasket, although a nonhardening sealer can be used. Any scoring, nicks, or burrs at either the end plate or housing can lead to leakage of air from the end plate to housing. Severely scored or damaged end plates should be replaced.

If the rotor support shaft serrations are worn or damaged, they can be replaced. The shafts are short-stub shafts that are pressed into and pinned to the hollow rotor lobes. Carefully inspect the end plate bearings for signs of pitting, flaking, or corrosion. *Never spin a ball or roller bearing using air pressure because bearing damage can occur.* Lubricate each bearing lightly with clean engine oil, and while holding the inner race from rotation, manually rotate the outer race slowly by hand to determine if any rough spots exist. The gear end plate double-row ball bearings are preloaded and so have no end play. A new bearing thus will have a certain amount of resistance to motion when rotated by hand. Check the oil seal rings, carriers, and collars for wear or scoring and replace them if worn excessively. When liptype oil seals are used, oversized oil seals and spacers can be employed on worn or grooved rotor shafts. Carefully examine the inside serrations on each blower gear for signs of wear or damage. If the gears are worn so that gear backlash is in excess of 0.004 in. (0.1 mm), both gears must be replaced as a set.

Blower Assembly

Each hollow aluminum alloy rotor is supported by bearings in each end plate. The rotors are designed to turn freely on these bearings so that at no time do the rotors actually come into contact with one another, the end plates, or the blower housing. When the blower is being reassembled, use the reverse procedure that was used for disassembly. Important points to remember during reassembly are listed next.

    1. Note that the rotors are machined so that one is a right-hand helix, and the other is a left-hand helix.

    2. The right-hand helix rotor is marked *gear end;* the left-hand rotor is the end with the serrated shaft. When viewing the blower from the drive end, the right-hand helix rotor is on the right and the left-hand helix rotor is on your left.

    3. The rotors must be timed to one another. This is achieved by placing the rotors in mesh with the omitted serrations (Figure 13-37) on the rotor stub shaft in a horizontal position and facing to the left as viewed from the gear end. Failure to time the rotors correctly will result in binding of the assembly when you attempt to turn it.

    4. Support the front end plate on two wooden blocks, similar to Figure 13-38 that are high enough to prevent the rotor shafts from contacting the benchtop. Always install the rotors into the front end plate first. Use seal protectors (lip-type seals), or take care when compressing the piston-type seal rings (lightly lubricated with oil) on the rotors as you push them into the end plate.

    5. Apply a light coating of permatex Form-A-Gasket No. 2 or an equivalent sealant to the mating

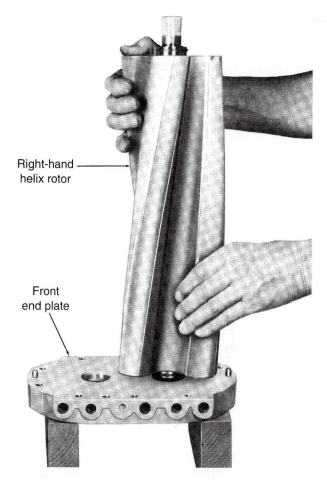

FIGURE 13-38 *Installing the blower rotor in the front end plate. (Courtesy of Detroit Diesel Corporation.)*

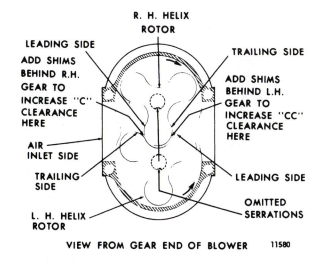

FIGURE 13-37 *Diagram showing the areas of the blower that must be checked for correct clearances and the location of selective thickness shims required to correct rotor lobe clearances. (Courtesy of Detroit Diesel Corporation.)*

surfaces of the end plate and the blower housing (no gasket is used here).

    6. Lower the blower housing over the top of the two rotors which are supported in the front end plate horizontally.

    7. Install the rear end plate, and insert and tighten the fillister head screws to retain each end plate to the blower housing.

    8. Install the front and rear end plate bearings (roller type in the front plate; double row in the rear). Lubricate the bearings with engine oil, and with the numbered side facing up toward you, use a suitable bearing driver and hammer to tap them into the housing bore over the rotor shafts.

    9. Install the bearing retainers and tighten their screws.

    10. Take the previously tied (wired) together shims that were removed earlier and install them behind the correct gear along with the hardened spacer.

    11. Place both of the rotor-omitted spline serrations in a horizontal position to the left. Align the omit-

ted serrated spline on each gear hub with the one on each rotor shaft. A center punch mark in the end of each rotor shaft at the omitted serration will assist you in aligning the gears on the shafts. Gently push and tap each gear onto the shaft. Use a rubber mallet to drive each gear on by alternating between them.

12.   Jam a soft folded rag between the rotors and tighten the gear retaining bolts to the recommended torque for your blower model. Torque on these bolts for DDC V 92 engines is between 100 and 110 lb-ft (136 to 150 N.m).

13.   Refer to Figure 13-39, which illustrates the location of the various minimum clearances for the blower rotor to housing. These are identified as A, B, C, CC, D, and E, and they are checked by inserting a long feeler gauge into the various positions illustrated in the clearance diagram. These dimensions are not the same for every model of engine blower. For example, they might be as follows:

A   0.007 in. (0.177 mm)
B   0.012 in. (0.304 mm)
C   0.010 in. (0.254 mm)
CC   0.006 in. (0.152 mm)
D   0.015 in. (0.381 mm)
E   0.005 in. (0.127 mm)

It is usually easier to use several feeler gauges stacked together when checking clearances in excess of 0.005 in. (0.127 mm). However, major tool suppliers can supply you with a specially designed feeler gauge set for this purpose.

14.   If the various clearances are outside of the stated limits, refer to Figure 13-37. The figure indicates the proper location of shims to alter a given dimension.

15.   When more or fewer shims are required be-

hind a gear to alter the rotor clearances, both gears must be removed using the special pullers shown earlier in Figure 13-36. In addition, both gears must be installed together to prevent binding between the helical gear teeth.

16.   To alter the rotor clearance, place a 0.003-in. (0.076-mm) shim behind a rotor gear to revolve the rotor approximately 0.001 in. (0.025 mm). This is achieved because of the helical design of the rotor. Shims force one rotor ahead of and rotate it away from the opposite rotor to effect a change in the clearance.

17.   Reinstall any accessory items, such as the fuel pump drive. Install new gaskets between the end plates and the end covers.

18.   Install a new blower-to-block gasket.

19.   Use guide studs to align the blower to the block and to keep the gasket in position. Lower the blower into position. Install all the items removed during blower removal, and tighten (torque) all bolts into position.

MARINE ENGINE APPLICATIONS

Air Silencers

Many marine applications, such as workboats, tugs, and logging boom boats, are equipped with conventional types of air cleaners. In certain applications they may even employ a *moisture eliminator*, described earlier in this chapter. Some pleasure craft may also employ some form of air filter/cleaner system; however, many such marine applications often use what is commonly called an *air silencer*. These may take the form of a rectangular device or be similar to the system illustrated in Figure 13-40. Although servicing is not required on the air silencers shown, the air cleaner has to be removed to perform other service operations. Some

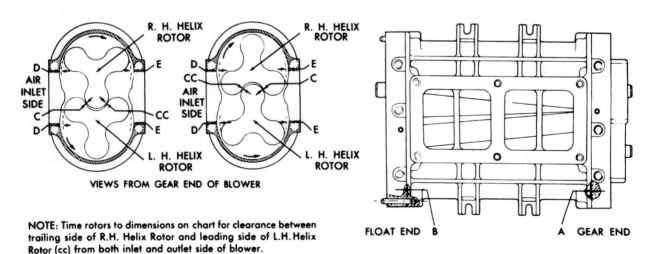

VIEWS FROM GEAR END OF BLOWER

NOTE: Time rotors to dimensions on chart for clearance between trailing side of R.H. Helix Rotor and leading side of L.H. Helix Rotor (cc) from both inlet and outlet side of blower.

FIGURE 13-39 Diagram illustrating where all the blower clearances must be checked. (Courtesy of Detroit Diesel Corporation.)

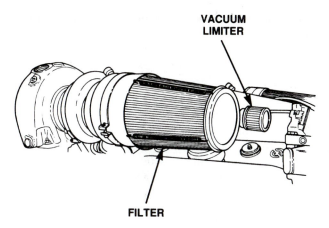

FIGURE 13–40 *Air silencer showing location of air separator and vacuum limiter. (Courtesy of Detroit Diesel Corporation.)*

silencers contain a perforated steel partition welded into place parallel with the outside faces, thereby dividing the silencer into two sections. Between the outer wall and the perforated partition (internal), sound-absorbent flameproof felted cotton waste is used.

The air separator filter element (or closed crankcase vapor collector) illustrated in Figure 13-40 is now common in pleasure craft marine applications. To operate efficiently, air separator filters and vacuum limiters must be maintained properly. Generally, there are three service intervals recommended for these systems:

1. Every 250 hours of engine service, clean and reoil the air separator filter elements and vacuum limiters.

2. Every 500 hours of engine operation, or once a year, replace the filter elements. The vacuum limiter can be replaced every two years or every 1000 hours of engine operation.

3. Clean and reoil filter elements and vacuum limiters any time that the restriction gauge shows red, or if so equipped, anytime that the restriction indicator gauge reaches its designed limit.

Servicing of these elements is similar to that for dry-type heavy-duty air filters. Once the precleaner element has been removed from the air separator, tap it gently to dislodge any large embedded dirt particles. Then gently clean the outside of the element with a soft-bristle brush. To clean the element, obtain and spray a commercially available liquid such as Walker solution onto the element and allow it to soak in for at least 20 minutes. *Never* use gasoline, steam, high-pressure water, compressed air cleaners, caustic solutions, strong detergents, or cleaning solvents. If you

do, filter damage is more than likely to occur! Rinse the element with clean, fresh water from the inside toward the outside. Shake off excess water after rinsing and allow the element to dry in ambient air. *Do not* use compressed shop air to dry the element since this may rupture it. Also, avoid using temperature-controlled ovens or heat dryers to dry the element because heat will shrink the cotton filter. Finally, reoil the element by squeezing Walker air filter oil out of the application bottle and into the valley of each filter pleat; make only one pass per pleat. Do not use a fluid such as engine oil, diesel fuel, WD-40, transmission fluid, or other lightweight oil because they can damage the filter element. Allow the oil to soak into the element for approximately 15 to 20 minutes; then reoil any dry (white) spots on the element. Reinstall it.

Clean the vacuum limiter after removing the complete assembly (do not detach the filter element). Use the same service procedure as that for the air filter element.

Water-Cooled Exhaust Manifolds

A water-cooled exhaust manifold is necessary because of the high heat radiation from the engine of marine applications into the engine room. Basically, the manifold consists of an integral casting that contains a hollow jacket surrounding the regular exhaust manifold. This type of a manifold is, therefore, substantially larger in diameter than a conventional air-cooled design. Figure 13-41 illustrates one example of a water-cooled exhaust manifold for either an industrial or marine application. Note that both an inlet line and outlet line are connected at opposite ends of the manifold to allow constant coolant circulation through the integral water jacket that surrounds the manifold. The coolant

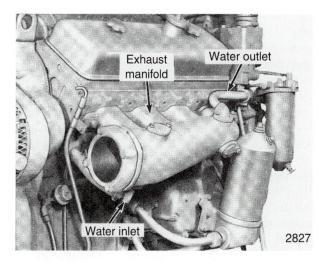

FIGURE 13–41 *Example of a water-cooled exhaust manifold. (Courtesy of Detroit Diesel Corporation.)*

flow is directed from the engine water jacket system under pressure, with a constant bypass into the exhaust manifold(s). The coolant leaves the forward end of the exhaust manifold and is discharged toward the thermostat housing area where the hot coolant can circulate through an expansion tank and heat exchanger or keel-cooled system. A drain plug is normally located below the exhaust manifold to allow water drainage when required; another drain plug allows moisture condensed from exhaust gases to be drained.

TROUBLESHOOTING USING MANOMETERS

All internal combustion engines require an adequate supply of clean filtered air to operate. Once combustion takes place, the exhaust gases exit the cylinders and normally expend their stored energy in driving a turbocharger. So both the *inlet* and the *exhaust* systems must be fairly free-flowing to avoid possible restrictions to either the air supply or the exhaust gases. Engine models operate at a given rpm where they are designed to produce a specific rated horsepower. If the airflow into the engine is affected in any way, not only will poor combustion result, but a number of other problem areas can surface: visible exhaust smoke, carbon deposits within the cylinders, high exhaust temperatures, a lack of power, and poor fuel economy.

The engine manufacturer usually places a limit on the amount of AIR (air inlet restriction) that the engine can handle without a loss in performance. This restriction within the air system occurs at maximum airflow requirement operating conditions of rated full load. On a naturally aspirated engine, the maximum airflow occurs at the maximum no-load or high-idle speed without regard to engine power. On turbocharged engines, the maximum airflow only occurs at the full-load (rated) engine speed, since the rotative speed of the turbocharger only produces maximum boost under this operating condition. Most engine manufacturers suggest a maximum restriction of between 510 and 635 mm (20 to 25 in.) of water for diesel engines; the allowable level is printed in the service manual or literature.

Generally, the maximum allowable AIR for naturally aspirated engines is 510 mm (20.0 in.) of water; for turbocharged engines, 635 mm (25 in.) is fairly standard. Excessive restriction affects the flow of air to the cylinders. On mechanically governed engine models, this will result in poor combustion and lack of power; the engine will tend to overheat; the exhaust, coolant, and oil temperatures will climb; and fuel economy will increase. On electronically controlled engines, the turbo boost sensor will limit the unit injector PWM (pulse-width modulated) signal, thereby limiting the amount of fuel delivered. This will result in a controlled loss of engine power and speed. If the engine oil temperature drifts outside of the preset parameters, a further reduction in engine power will occur. Excessively high oil temperatures will result in an automatic engine shutdown.

Manometer Use

When dealing with air inlet and exhaust systems, a number of air restriction (vacuum) and air pressure values can be determined by using both a water (H_2O) and mercury (Hg) *manometer* assembly. A manometer allows the service technician to determine the following engine operating conditions quickly and accurately:

- AIR (air inlet restriction): H_2O manometer
- Turbocharger boost pressure (two- or four-cycle): Hg manometer
- ABP (air box pressure on a two-cycle only): Hg manometer
- EBP (exhaust back pressure): Hg manometer
- Crankcase pressure: H_2O manometer

These manometers consist of a slack or solid tube formed into a U-shape as illustrated in Figure 13-42. A sliding scale allows the technician to calibrate the gauge to *zero* before use. At the top of each tube is a screw valve that allows the water or mercury within the tube to be retained when not in use and when transporting the manometers in service trucks or toolboxes. Before using a manometer, both valves at the top of the U-shaped tubes must be screwed open (one-half to one turn) to allow atmospheric air pressure to balance the fluid within each side of the tube.

Note in Figure 13-42 that the liquid within the two manometer tubes takes opposite shapes. Mercury, which is heavier than water, will not wet the inside of the tube and it forms what is commonly called a *convex miniscus*. Water, on the other hand, does wet the inside of the tube and forms a *concave miniscus*. Therefore, when zeroing-in the manometer prior to use, open both valves at the top of each tube and carefully move the sliding scale until the zero (0) on the ruler is opposite the fluid. During a manometer test, read the water type by sighting horizontally between the bottom of the concave water surface and the scale. Read a mercury manometer by sighting horizontally between the top of the convex mercury surface and the scale. Both sides of the displaced fluid are added together when using a *full-scale* model where the distance on the scale is equal to that found on a ruler or tape measure. On half-scale manometer models, read only one side of the displaced fluid scale.

If one column of fluid travels farther than the other disregard. Minor variations within the inside diameter of the tube (particularly when heavy duty clear plastic models are used) are the cause. The accu-

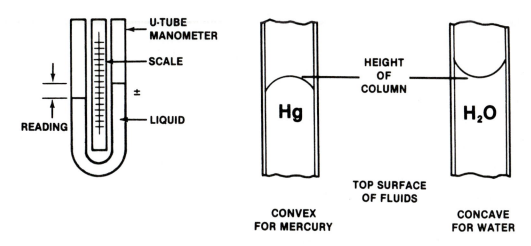

FIGURE 13–42 *Comparison of column height for both a mercury and a water manometer. (Courtesy of Detroit Diesel Corporation.)*

racy of the reading will not be impaired. Depending on the particular make and model of engine, the connection tap point for the manometer fitting will vary, but it is common for most engines. Check the AIR, EBP, ABP, and turbo boost at the following recommended positions:

1. Figure 13-43 illustrates where the AIR can be checked. AIR is checked using a water manometer at a point between 101 and 203 mm (4 to 8 in.) away from the turbocharger air inlet by removing a small pipe plug screwed into the inlet piping. Install a suitable brass fitting to which you can connect a small flexible rubber hose; the opposite end should fit over one of the open manometer valves. Note that the manometer has been *zeroed* by opening both valves and moving the sliding scale. If possible, operate the engine on a chassis or engine dyno at WOT and full-rated horsepower. Refer to Figure 13-44, which illustrates the water displacement on both sides of the manometer. On full-scale manometers, add both sides together; on a half-scale manometer, read only one side. A loss of 6.895 kPa (1 psi) of suction air pressure due to restriction in a system would be equivalent to a displacement of 27.7 in. (704 mm) on the H_2O manometer. Therefore, when the engine manufacturer's limit of say, 25 in. (635 mm) H_2O of restriction is reached, this means that the air pressure within the air inlet ducting to the suction side of the turbocharger is 0.9 psi (6.2 kPa) lower than atmospheric pressure. Compare your reading with that listed in the service manual.

2. Check turbocharger boost pressure using a Hg manometer. Remove a small plug located in the intake manifold or at the outlet side of the turbocharger assembly. Install a suitable brass fitting with a small-bore rubber hose connected between the fitting and the manometer. Repeat the same procedure as de-

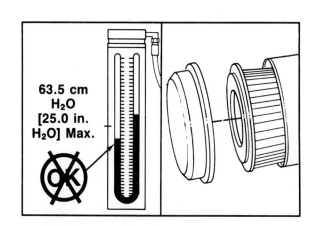

FIGURE 13–44 *Fluid displacement in a water manometer during a running engine test to check the air inlet restriction. In this example the maximum allowable restriction is quoted as being 25 in. (63.5 cm) H_2O. Add both sides of the manometer together when using a full-scale model; read only one side when using a one-half-scale model. (Courtesy of Cummins Engine Company, Inc.)*

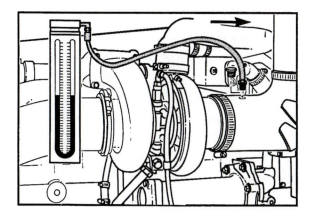

FIGURE 13–43 *Water manometer hookup to the air inlet ducting on the suction side of the turbocharger to check the air inlet restriction. (Courtesy of Cummins Engine Company, Inc.)*

scribed for the AIR check and compare your results to the service manual specs. Failure to fully load the engine during this test will result in a low turbocharger boost reading. On two-stroke-cycle DDC engine models, ABP can be checked using an Hg manometer by connecting a tight-fitting rubber hose over one end of the engine block air box drain tube and the opposite end to the manometer valve. EBP is checked using an Hg manometer connected into a brass fitting installed in the exhaust piping approximately 152 mm (6 in.) from the exhaust outlet from the turbocharger. Always use a brass fitting and make sure that the pipe plug that is installed into the hot exhaust at the completion of the test is *brass* not steel, since a steel plug will tend to freeze in position. Figure 13-45 illustrates an Hg manometer connected to the exhaust system to measure the EBP. Repeat the same procedure described for the AIR check and compare your results to specs.

3. Engine crankcase pressure can be checked using an H_2O manometer connected to one of several sources. You can place a small-bore tight-fitting hose over the oil level dipstick shroud; if the shroud extends below the oil level in the pan, however, you will not be able to record a reading. You can usually gain access to and remove a small pipe plug located in the side of the engine block above the pan rail. On some engine makes and models, the oil filler cap can be removed from a rocker cover, and an expandable rubber plug can be installed and tightened into position. A small connection on the adaptor plug can be used to connect a small-bore rubber hose to the H_2O manometer. Once again, a more accurate reading can be obtained by running the engine or vehicle on a dynamometer.

Manometer Specifications

Each engine manufacturer lists the allowable specifications for its engine manometers in the service manuals. These values are normally listed for a given engine rpm and also in inches of water or mercury. For example, you might find the following engine operating conditions listed for a given turbocharged engine:

	1800 rpm	2100 rpm
Air inlet restriction [kPa (in. water)]		
Full-load maximum, dirty air cleaner	5 (20)	Same
Full-load maximum, clean air cleaner	3 (12)	Same
Air inlet manifold pressure [kPa (in. Hg)]		
Minimum at full load	159 (47)	152 (45)
Crankcase pressure [kPa (in Hg)]	0.5 (2)	Same
Exhaust back pressure [kPa (in. Hg)]		
Maximum value, full load	10.1	(3)

Often it is necessary to convert the manometer reading into other units of measurement. Use the following pressure conversion values:

1 in. (25.4 mm) water	= 0.0735 in. Hg/1.86 mm Hg
1 in. (25.4 mm) water	= 0.0361 psi/0.248 kPa
1 in. (25.4 mm) mercury	= 13.60 in. H_2O/345.44 mm H_2O
1 in. (25.4 mm) mercury	= 0.491 psi/3.385 kPa
1 psi (6.895 kPa)	= 27.70 in. H_2O/703.6 mm H_2O
1 psi (6.895 kPa)	= 2.036 in. Hg/52 mm Hg
Note: 1 psi	= 6.895 kPa; 1 kPa
	= 0.145 psi

Causes for High or Low Manometer Readings

After you perform an AIR check, a turbocharger boost check, an EBP check, or a crankcase pressure check, you may find that the manometer values you obtained are higher or lower than those listed in the engine service manual. The only value that could be both high or low is the turbocharger boost value. The typical causes for high manometer readings in the AIR, EBP, and crankcase pressure operating conditions are described next.

High Air Inlet Restriction

High AIR results in poor combustion, lack of power, poor fuel economy, and higher than normal exhaust temperatures, particularly on two-stroke-cycle DDC

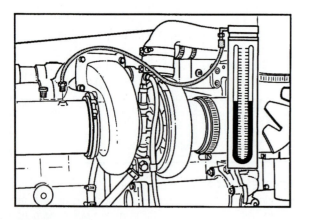

FIGURE 13–45 *Connection between the exhaust manifold and an Hg (mercury) manometer required to measure the exhaust back pressure. (Courtesy of Cummins Engine Company, Inc.)*

engine models where approximately 30% of the engine cooling is achieved by airflow through the ported cylinders. The following conditions are typical of those that might cause high AIR:

- Plugged or dirty air cleaner (precleaner or main element)
- Too small an air filter assembly (improperly sized to pass the required ft^3/min of air)
- Intake piping diameter too small
- Intake piping too long
- Intake piping containing too many elbows or bends
- Crushed intake piping (hole free)
- Damaged air cleaner assembly
- Collapsed rubber hoses in intake piping
- Water-soaked paper filter element (employ a moisture eliminator assembly when operating in heavy rainfall and high humidity areas)
- Coal dust plugging in mine sites (short filter life; use two-stage filters and exhaust gas aspirators)

Low Turbocharger Boost Pressure

Many of the causes of low turbocharger boost pressure are similar for two- and four-stroke-cycle engines. Some causes, however, are unique to the two-stroke cycle models because they employ a gear-driven blower assembly in addition to the exhaust-gas-driven turbocharger. Strategically placed small pipe plugs on the engine can be accessed to isolate the TC boost pressure from the air box pressure on two-cycle engines such as the DDC models. Reasons for low boost pressure can usually be traced to the following conditions:

- Anything that creates a high AIR condition
- High EBP condition
- Exhaust gas leaks feeding to turbo from engine
- Leaking fittings, connections, or intake manifold gasket from outlet side of turbo (usually accompanied by a high-pitched whistle under load due to pressurized air leaks)
- Plugged turbocharger safety screen if used on the inlet or outlet side
- Plugged or damaged air system aftercooler
- Possible turbocharger internal damage (visually check the condition of the turbine and compressor blading vanes for damage with the engine stopped)
- Leaking gasket between direct-mounted TC and the blower housing on a DDC two-cycle engine
- Low air box pressure on a two-cycle DDC engine caused by any of the foregoing conditions plus leaking hand-hole inspection covers on the block, leaking cylinder block-to-end-plate gaskets, a clogged blower inlet screen, or a partially stuck closed emergency air system shutdown valve
- Defective or damaged blower on a two-cycle DDC engine

- High air box pressure on a DDC two-cycle engine usually traced to high exhaust back pressure or partially plugged cylinder liner ports (normally related to carbon buildup)

High Exhaust Back Pressure

A slight pressure in the exhaust system is normal, but excessive EBP will seriously affect operation of the engine. Some of the causes of high EBP are these:

- Stuck rain cap at the end of a vertical exhaust stack
- Crushed exhaust piping
- Crushed or damaged muffler
- Too small a muffler
- Exhaust piping diameter too small
- Exhaust piping too long
- Exhaust piping with too many elbows or bends
- Excessive carbon buildup in exhaust system
- Obstruction in exhaust system or piping

High Crankcase Pressure

Crankcase pressure indicates the amount of compression leakage and/or air box pressure leakage between the piston rings. All engines operate with a slight crankcase pressure, which is highly desirable since low pressure prevents the entrance of dust as well as keeps any dust or dirt within suspension so that it can flow through the crankcase and be trapped in the engine breather system. Any signs of engine lube oil escaping from the engine breather tube, crankcase ventilator, dipstick tube hole, crankshaft oil seals, or air box drain tubes on two-cycle DDC engines may be a positive indicator of high crankcase pressure. Causes of high crankcase pressure can usually be traced to the following conditions:

- Too much oil in crankcase (check level after adequate drain-back time after engine shutdown)
- Plugged crankcase breather or tube system
- High EBP
- Excessive cylinder blowby (worn rings, scored liner, cracked piston, or a hole)
- On two-stroke DDC engine models, loose piston pin retainers, worn or damaged blower oil seals, leaking cylinder block-to-end-plate gaskets, or a defective blower

EXHAUST BRAKE DEVICES

An exhaust gas pressure engine retarding device is a widely used option found on many light- and medium-duty truck applications, both gasoline and diesel powered. The two common types currently in use are illustrated in Figure 13-46. The device shown in Figure 13-46A uses a sliding-gate type of valve, while the model in part B employs a butterfly valve assembly.

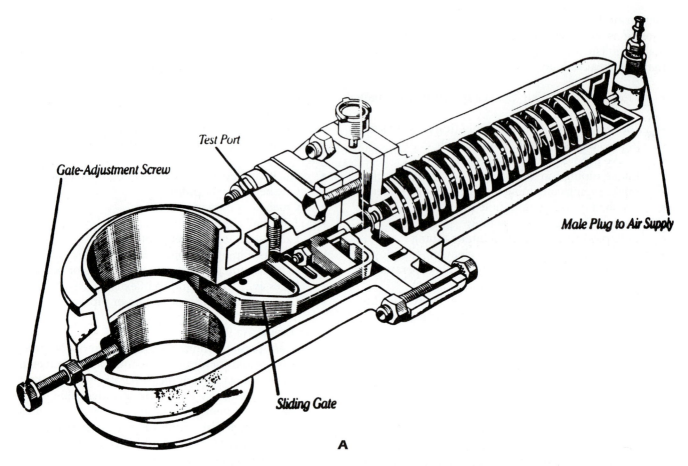

Gate-Adjustment Screw

Test Port

Male Plug to Air Supply

Sliding Gate

A

FIGURE 13–46 (A) Sliding-gate exhaust valve brake; B) Butterfly exhaust valve brake. [(A) Courtesy of Williams Controls, Dana Corporation; (B) courtesy of Cummins Engine Company, Inc.]

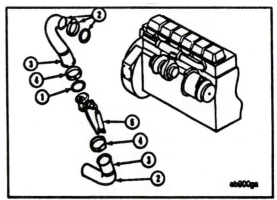

1. Gasket 2. Original Equipment 3. Exhaust Sleeve 4. V Clamp 5. EXTARDER Assembly

B

The exhaust brake, which is installed as shown in Figure 13-46, restricts engine exhaust flow when it is activated, thereby slowing the vehicle by increasing the pressure acting on the upward-moving pistons during the regular exhaust stroke. This action tends to transform the engine into a low-pressure air compressor.

The brake is installed in the exhaust pipe downstream from the turbocharger and before the catalytic converter and muffler. The exhaust brake valve can be actuated by either a pneumatic cylinder with air from the onboard air system of the vehicle for trucks equipped with air brakes or by an auxiliary 12-V electric air system supply. Typical exhaust brake actuation and release time is approximately two-tenths of a second. ON/OFF controls are normally mounted on the dashboard and activated through a rocker switch. When the rocker switch is placed in the ON position, the accelerator pedal is in the idle position, the clutch pedal is up (clutch engaged), the exhaust brake circuit is activated, and compressed air flows to the actuating cylinder to move either the sliding-gate or butterfly valve to the closed position. If the accelerator pedal is depressed past the normal idle position, the brake will be released automatically by breaking the electrical circuit to the brake actuating controls. Some exhaust brake manufacturers offer either hand or foot controls where the normal service brake is synchronized with the use of the exhaust brake. In addition, exhaust brake actuation can be wired to illuminate the stoplights of the vehicle during operation.

Minimum supply pressure of the exhaust brake compressed air is generally 85 psi (586 kPa) to overcome the force of the valve return spring. Maximum supply pressure is usually set at the same value as that for the air compressor governor, thereby limiting excessive supply pressure. Material used in the construction of the exhaust brake is usually ductile iron; in the operating cylinder the common material is anodized aluminum.

The exhaust brake restriction created affects the degree of braking that occurs. On butterfly-type valves, a factory drilled orifice (size depends on engine make and model) is used to maintain exhaust back pressure within limits set by the OEM. For example, this is limited to below 60 psi (414 kPa) on Cummins six-cylinder B5.9 engines and to below 65 psi (448 kPa) on Cummins six-cylinder C8.3 engine models. The Caterpillar 3116 engine is limited to 55 psi (379 kPa), the Detroit Diesel series 60 is limited to 45 psi (310 kPa), and the Navistar DTA-466 is limited to 28 psi (193 kPa). The braking horsepower generated depends on several factors:

- Engine design and the allowable back pressure it can withstand
- Engine displacement
- Speed of the engine during exhaust brake activation
- Transmission and axle gear ratios
- Placement and model of exhaust brake in use

To obtain maximum performance from the exhaust brake, the truck operator should select a gear that will cause the engine to operate at its normal governed rpm, consistent with the road conditions and engine rpm limits.

CAUTION   When driving on wet, slick, or icy roads, keep the exhaust brake control switch in the OFF position.

When an exhaust brake with an automatic transmission (such as an Allison model) is used, maximum braking will occur only if the transmission is equipped with a torque converter lockup clutch. The brake can still be used in an automatic transmission without a lockup clutch; however only 70 to 75% efficiency will be obtained due to the normal hydraulic slippage that occurs within the torque converter.

SUMMARY

The air inlet and exhaust systems are two of the most important systems in the engine, since they control the induction and supply of air to the engine cylinders, and permit hot exhaust gases to flow freely to the turbocharger assembly in order to provide the needed boost of pressurized air to the cylinders to produce combustion power. This chapter has highlighted the function and operation of both systems, and has provided details on the service, maintenance, repair and effective troubleshooting diagnosis needed to ensure consistent engine performance.

SELF-TEST QUESTIONS

1. List the problems associated with lack of sufficient airflow to an engine.

2. On electronically controlled high-speed heavy-duty diesel engines, list the various sensors used to monitor air system operating conditions.

3. True or False: An equivalent reduction of airflow on a two-cycle Detroit Diesel engine will affect the engine operating temperature more adversely than will a similar reduction in coolant flow.

4. List the four functions of the airflow on a two-stroke-cycle DDC engine.

5. What does the term *dusting-out* of an engine mean?

6. Technician A says that as little as 2 tablespoons of unfiltered air can severely damage an engine. Technician B says that it would take several pounds. Which technician is correct?

7. Diesel engines perform best at air inlet temperatures between
   a. 40 and 60°F (4.5 to 15.5°C)
   b. 60 and 90°F (15.5 to 32°C)
   c. 90 and 115°F (32 to 46°C)
   d. 120 and 150°F (49 to 65°C)

8. Technician A says that an air inlet temperature that is too cold allows the engine to produce more power due to a more dense air charge. Technician B says that this would result in a longer ignition delay once the fuel is injected. Which technician knows thermodynamics theory best?

9. A reduction in ambient air inlet temperature from 80°F (27°C) in summer operation to −20°F (−29°C) in the winter will severely affect the air temperature at the end of the compression stroke. The amount of variation depends on the piston crown shape and the turbulence that is created. Usually, the heat loss is approximately
   a. 100 to 130°F (38 to 54°C)
   b. 150 to 180°F (65 to 82°C)

c.   190 to 220°F (88 to 104°C)

d.   230 to 300°F (110 to 149°C)

10. Because of the problems associated with the answer to Question 9, diesel fuel characteristics must be altered when operating in winter conditions. Refer to Chapter 16 for information on how fuels vary between summer and winter. What characteristics would be altered?

11. Make a list of the visible and audible changes that result when the air inlet charge is too cold, such as during winter operation.

12. Technician A says that in cold-weather operation, engine air can be drawn from underhood or from within the engine compartment. Technician B says that this would result in air starvation. Which technician is correct?

13. True or False: Air inlet temperature that is too hot results in an engine power loss.

14. Technician A says that on nonturbocharged engines, there will be a power loss of approximately 1% for every 100 m (328 ft) in operating altitude. Technician B believes that the power loss will be greater—closer to 5%. Which technician is correct?

15. Describe the meaning of the term *volumetric efficiency*.

16. Determine the airflow requirements for a two-stroke-cycle blower and turbocharged engine with a displacement of 736 in^3 (12.06 L) at 2100 rpm.

17. Determine the airflow requirements for a four-stroke-cycle turbocharged and aftercooled engine with a displacement of 855 in^3 (14 L) at 2100 rpm.

18. Technician A says that oil bath air cleaners have been almost totally replaced by dry designs. Technician B says that there are more oil bath air cleaners in use than there are dry types. Which technician is up to date?

19. List and compare the advantages and disadvantages of using an oil bath versus a dry air cleaner assembly.

20. True or False: Dry air filters cannot be cleaned when service is required.

21. Technician A says that ultra-heavy-duty air cleaner systems used in mining and off-highway equipment employ a three-stage cleaning process. Technician B believes that it is only a two-stage cleaning process. Which technician is correct?

22. True or False: Some heavy-duty off-highway air cleaner systems offer a dust sight glass to determine if unfiltered air is entering the system.

23. The purpose of an air system restriction indicator is to warn the operator or service technician of

a.   high exhaust back pressure

b.   high turbo boost pressure

c.   high crankcase pressure

d.   high air inlet restriction

24. The maximum allowable air system flow restriction on high-speed heavy-duty diesel engines is normally within the range of

a.   10 to 15 in. water

b.   10 to 15 in. mercury

c.   20 to 25 in. water

d.   20 to 25 in. mercury

25. Technician A says that when servicing dry-type air filters or when drying a cleaned filter, it is acceptable to use up to 120 psi (827 kPa) of air pressure. Technician B says that this much air pressure would rupture the paper element; instead, air pressures should normally be reduced to a level between 50 and 60 psi (345 to 414 kPa). Which technician is correct?

26. Describe the best method to inspect a dry air filter element for signs of holes or tears.

27. List the sequential steps that you would employ to fully service a heavy-duty dry-type filter assembly.

28. Technician A says that some models of two- and three-stage air filter assemblies employ either an exhaust gas aspirator or a pressurized air supply to help to remove up to 90% of the initial stage of air filtration. Technician B says that exhaust gases would burn the filter and that air pressure would rupture the element. Which technician is correct?

29. List the engine problems that would be associated by continuing to operate with a high air inlet restriction condition.

30. Describe how you would inspect and check the air inlet ducting for signs of unfiltered air.

31. List the problems that can occur to the engine through excessive use of starting fluid, particularly in cold-weather operation.

32. Technician A says that an intercooler and aftercooler are basically designed to cool the turbocharger boost air before it enters the intake manifold. Technician B says that an intercooler is designed to cool the air charge, while an aftercooler is used to cool the exhaust gases. Which technician understands the purpose and function of the coolers?

33. Describe the three basic types of aftercoolers/intercoolers and the features of each.

34. Name the most common type of aftercooler used on heavy-duty high-speed engines in on-highway vehicles.

35. Describe a situation where both an intercooler and aftercooler might be employed on the same engine and discuss the function and purpose of each.

36. True or False: In an AAAC system the use of fully closed winterfronts should be avoided in cold-weather operation. Describe the reasons for your answer.

37. Technician A says that approximately 10% of the cooling on a DDC two-stroke-cycle engine is achieved by turbo blower airflow. Technician B says that it is closer to 30%. Which technician knows the product best?

38. True or False: If an AAAC system is employed, radiator shutterstats cannot be used.

39. Describe the method that you would use to check an AAAC core for possible leakage on a truck application.

40. List the three ways to perform an engine cylinder compression check on different types of diesel engines.

41. What conditions might cause low cylinder compression?

42. How does a cylinder leak-down check differ from an engine compression check?

43. Technician A says that most heavy-duty high-speed engine turbochargers are designed to rotate at speeds close to, and in some cases in excess of, 100,000 rpm. Impossible, says technician B; at this elevated speed the turbocharger would disintegrate. Which technician is correct?

44. The turbocharger is
    a. exhaust gas driven
    b. gear driven
    c. belt driven
    d. chain driven

45. What does the term *supercharged* engine mean?

46. True or False: All DDC two-stroke-cycle engines that employ a Roots blower are supercharged.

47. DDC engines that use Roots blowers are normally
    a. belt driven
    b. chain driven
    c. exhaust gas driven
    d. gear driven

48. True or False: Roots blowers can produce a more positive airflow at a lower speed than can a turbocharger.

49. Describe what the term *A/R ratio* means in relation to a turbocharger.

50. Describe what problems would exist on an engine fitted with the wrong model of *A/R* turbocharger.

51. What is the basic conceptual difference between a constant-pressure TC and a pulse turbocharger?

52. Typical engine full-load turbocharger boost pressures on heavy-duty high-speed engines usually ranges between
    a. 10 and 12 psi (69 to 83 kPa)
    b. 17 and 22 psi (117 to 152 kPa)
    c. 28 and 30 psi (193 to 207 kPa)
    d. 36 and 42 psi (248 to 289 kPa)

53. True or False: Some newer heavy-duty high-speed diesel engines employ ceramic turbine wheels in the turbocharger.

54. Technician A says that tuned intake manifolds and TCs are designed to improve white smoke cleanup by producing higher intake manifold air boost pressures at lower engine speeds. Technician B says that this design feature is used primarily to reduce intake air restriction. Which technician is correct?

55. Technician A says that the turbocharger rotating components are supported on pressure-lubricated ball bearings. Not so, says technician B; they use pressure-lubricated bushings. Which technician is correct?

56. True or False: Exhaust gas temperatures on a four-cycle engine are generally higher than those for a two-cycle engine.

57. Technician A says that a TC wastegate is employed to bypass exhaust gas flow around the turbine wheel to limit the maximum amount of boost pressure. Technician B believes that the wastegate is used to recirculate exhaust gases to lower combustion chamber temperatures and therefore improve exhaust gas emissions. Which technician is correct?

58. Can a TC wastegate be adjusted to control its opening pressure?

59. Describe how a TC wastegate differs from a TC back pressure device that is used on the Navistar 7.3-L 444E V8 engine model.

60. List the three key maintenance items that affect the life of a turbocharger.

61. A TC with no physical signs of damage has a high-pitched whine noise while the engine is under load. This is probably due to
    a. lack of oil to the TC bearings
    b. leaking intake or exhaust piping (hoses) on the outlet side of the TC
    c. high exhaust gas back pressure
    d. high air inlet restriction

62. A sharp high-pitched scream from a TC is usually indicative of one or more of the following problems:
    a. exhaust gas leakage
    b. turbo boost air leakage
    c. worn TC bearings
    d. turbine or compressor wheel rubbing on the housing

63. A speed cycling sound from a TC could indicate which one or more of the following problems:
    a. high air inlet restriction
    b. high exhaust back pressure
    c. dirt buildup on the compressor wheel

64. With the engine stopped and the intake and exhaust piping removed from the TC, how would you check to see if the TC bearings were worn?

65. You are using a fluorescent tracer liquid engine oil additive to inspect a TC at the hot exhaust outlet side along with a black light. A yellow glow would indicate a(n)
    a. raw fuel leak
    b. engine oil leak
    c. coolant leak from a cracked cylinder head
    d. high-pressure air leak

66. Following the same procedure as in Question 65, a dark-blue glow usually indicates a(n)
    a. raw fuel leak
    b. engine oil leak
    c. coolant leak
    d. high-pressure air leak

67. Describe in list form how you would disassemble a turbocharger assembly and the necessary precautions required.

68. When a new or rebuilt turbocharger is installed back onto the engine, what should be done before cranking and immediately after engine startup?

69. Signs of oil at the TC inlet side could be caused by leaking oil seals according to technician A. Technician B

says that they may be caused by an air compressor pumping oil. Is only one of the technicians correct, or are both correct?

70. True or False: Signs of engine oil at the turbine (hot end) of the TC usually indicate an engine fault rather than a TC seal problem.

71. List the most common causes of leaking TC seals.

72. Typical noise levels from a heavy-duty tractor or trailer moving along the highway at regulated speed levels are usually within the range
    a. 54 to 64 dB
    b. 65 to 70 dB
    c. 74 to 79 dB
    d. 80 to 86 dB

73. List some diesel engines that use exhaust gas after-treatment devices to comply with the 1994 EPA exhaust emissions limits.

74. The type of blower assembly used by DDC in its two-stroke-cycle engines is known as a
    a. Roots type
    b. pulse type
    c. constant-pressure type
    d. supercharger

75. True or False: Rotors used in DDC blowers never touch each other or the housing since they are supported on fully floating bearings.

76. True or False: Signs of oil flowing along the blower rotors when the engine is running are indicative of leaking blower oil seals.

77. The DDC blower assembly on current model engines employs a bypass blower design. Describe what this actually means and how it operates.

78. Average air delivery pressure available from the gear-driven blower on DDC two-cycle engines is in the range
    a. 4 to 7 psi (27 to 48 kPa)
    b. 8 to 12 psi (55 to 83 kPa)
    c. 15 to 19 psi (103 to 131 kPa)
    d. 21 to 24 psi (145 to 165 kPa)

79. True or False: Signs of rotor-to-rotor lobe contact on a DDC blower usually indicate that the blower bearings are worn.

80. Technician A says that the DDC two-cycle engine blower is usually gear driven at the same speed as the engine crankshaft. Technician B believes that the blower is driven at approximately twice engine speed. Which technician is right?

81. True or False: The blower rotors on DDC engines must be timed to one another during reassembly.

82. True or False: DDC blower rotor clearances are obtained by using selective shims behind the drive or driven gear of the assembly.

83. Describe the service required on a marine engine air separator and vacuum limiter filter assemblies.

84. True or False: Most marine engines employ dry-type exhaust manifolds.

85. What two types of manometers are widely used to troubleshoot diesel engines?

86. List what engine system checks you could perform with manometers and indicate the type of manometer you would use for each check.

87. True or False: Fluid displacement in an H_2O manometer is equal to 2.036 in. (52 mm) for every 1 psi (6.895 kPa) of air pressure applied to it.

88. True or False: Fluid displacement in an Hg manometer is equal to 27.7 in. (704 mm) for every 1 psi (6.895 kPa) of pressure applied to it.

89. List the causes of a high AIR condition.

90. List the causes of low TC boost pressure.

91. List the causes of low ABP on a DDC two-stroke-cycle engine.

92. List the causes of high EBP.

93. List the causes of high crankcase pressure.

14

Types of Fuel Systems

■ ■ ■

OVERVIEW

The diesel fuel injection system is the heart of the diesel engine. To ensure that high speed heavy duty diesel engines can comply with the stringent EPA exhaust emissions limits, technological advancements in engine design and controls now rely heavily on electronic fuel injection and governing systems. There are still many diesel engines in operation equipped with mechanical fuel systems. This chapter highlights the main types of fuel systems, both mechanically and electronically controlled. Basic fuel injection concepts, discussed here, can be studied in greater detail in respective OEM chapters throughout this book.

SYSTEM TYPES

This chapter provides an overview of the various types of fuel injection systems currently in use on various models and sizes of diesel engines. Details on different model fuel systems are provided in the appropriate chapters.

A number of different types of diesel fuel injection systems are in use today. Because of the move to strict control of engine exhaust emissions, most OEMs now produce electronically controlled fuel injection systems. Although these new fuel systems will dominate the rest of the 1990s and beyond, there are still millions of diesel engines in use with mechanically operated and controlled fuel injection systems that will continue to operate for years. In this chapter we discuss these mechanical systems briefly. This knowledge will prepare us to understand and appreciate the differences between mechanical and electronically controlled systems.

Basic fuel system types can be categorized as follows:

- Individual unit jerk pumps
- PLN (pump–line–nozzle) systems
- Distributor pump systems
- Unit injector fuel systems
- Cummins PT (pressure–time) fuel systems
- Electronically controlled fuel systems, which can be applied to all of the mechanical systems described above

A more detailed description of each one of the foregoing fuel systems follows; however, for complete details on each system, refer to specific chapters throughout this book.

Individual Unit Jerk Pumps

This concept is shown in simplified form in Figure 14-1, where fuel at low pressure from a transfer pump is delivered to the individual cylinder pumping units. Where a supply pump is unnecessary, a gravity-feed system can be used. Within the individual pump housings, a pumping plunger is forced upward by a camshaft as shown in Figure 14-2, to raise the trapped fuel to a high-enough pressure to be suitable for injection purposes. Figure 14-3 shows a single-cylinder Bosch jerk pump. The letter P in PF stands for "pump" and the F for "foreign camshaft drive" (no camshaft within the pump). The pump is engine mounted and a flat adjustable tappet is lifted by the pump camshaft lobe within the engine block. PFR indicates that a roller rather than a flat tappet is used. See Figure 14-4 for a cross section of a PFR pump. The engine-driven

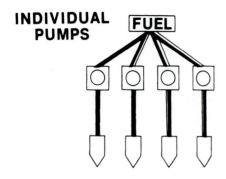

FIGURE 14–1   *Typical slow-speed engine fuel system.*

camshaft forces the roller (8) upward to allow the pumping plunger (4) to raise the fuel to a high-enough pressure to open the spring-loaded delivery valve (2). Fuel under pressure is then sent through a steel line to the injection nozzle located in the cylinder head. Within the nozzle is a valve held closed by spring pressure. When the fuel pressure is high enough, it opens the needle valve against spring pressure to allow fuel to be sprayed from a series of small holes (orifices) drilled in the nozzle spray tip into the combustion chamber. This provides higher injection pressures and good atomization of the fuel. See Chapter 18 for more specific details on injection nozzles.

PLN (Pump–Line–Nozzle) Systems

The PLN fuel injection pump employs a design where all of the individual pumping plungers are located within a common housing. This concept is shown in

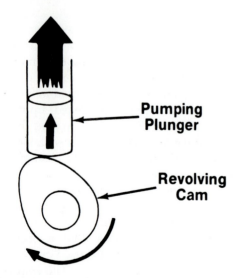

FIGURE 14–2   *Basic operation of a jerk pump system.*

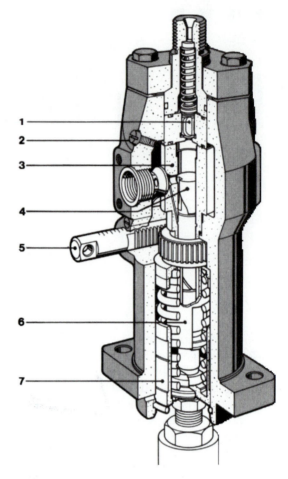

FIGURE 14–3   *Component I.D. for a Bosch model PF-1D jerk pump. (Courtesy of Robert Bosch Corporation).*

simplified form in Figure 14-5 and is one of the most widely used types of fuel systems for high-speed diesel engines.

Figure 14-6 shows the basic layout of the fuel system for a high-speed heavy-duty diesel engine. A small transfer or supply pump delivers low-pressure fuel to the injection pump housing for operation. The injection pump is timed to the engine gear train. In addition, the injection pump functions to pressurize, meter, and atomize the fuel for combustion purposes. See Chapter 19 for more details on these types of injection systems, which are also available with electronic controls on current engines. Robert Bosch Corp., Lucas Industries, Zexel (Diesel Kiki), and Nippondenso are just four major injection pump OEMs who now offer electronic controls on their products.

Distributor Pump Systems

The distributor pump system basic concept is shown in Figure 14-7. The pump is so named because it functions similar to an ignition distributor in a gasoline engine, in that a spinning internal rotor distributes

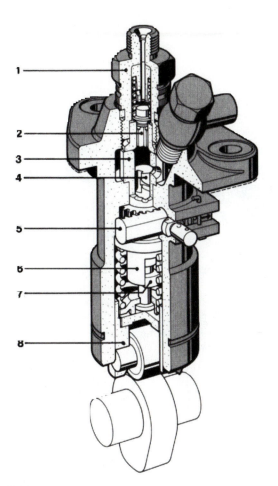

FIGURE 14-4 Section through type PFR 1 K. 1, Delivery-valve holder; 2, Delivery valve; 3, pump barrel; 4, pump plunger; 5, control rod; 6, control sleeve; 7, plunger control arm; 8, roller tappet.

high-pressure diesel fuel to the individual combustion chambers in engine firing-order sequence. Distributor pumps contain approximately only 35 to 40% of the parts of a PLN system; therefore, they are smaller and lighter. Consequently, they are limited in the quantity

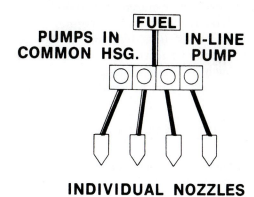

FIGURE 14-5 Medium- and high-speed diesel injection pump layout.

of fuel that they can deliver, as well as producing lower injection pressures than in a PLN system. However, distributor pumps are used extensively on smaller-displacement high-speed automotive and lighter commercial diesel engines.

Figure 14-8 illustrates a typical distributor pump fuel injection system for a V8 diesel engine for a pickup truck application. In this system a fuel lift pump delivers fuel at low pressures between 3 and 5 psi (21 to 34 kPa) to a vane pump housed within the end of the injection pump housing. The vane pump typically produces fuel supply pressures to the pumping chamber between 90 and 130 psi (621 to 896 kPa). Distributor pumps are also available with electronic controls from such well-known OEMs as Robert Bosch Corp., Zexel (Diesel Kiki), Nippondenso, and Lucas Industries.

Unit Injector Systems

The unit injector system has been widely used by Detroit Diesel Corporation (DDC) since 1937 when they first released their two-stroke cycle engine models and is used on both two- and four-stroke cycle DDC engines. Basically, a unit injector fuel system (shown in simplified form in Figure 14-9) combines the pump and nozzle in a single body. The fuel is supplied to each DDC injector at between 50 and 70 psi (345 to 483 kPa) from a gear fuel pump, shown in Figure 14-10. A common inlet manifold feeds all injectors simultaneously. The unit injector functions to time, atomize, meter, and pressurize the fuel for combustion purposes. Fuel used for cooling and lubrication purposes is directed through a common return manifold and restricted fitting back to the fuel tank. A similar system has also been in use for many years by the Electro Motive Division of General Motors Corporation in their large-displacement two-cycle engines used in railroad locomotives, marine, and industrial engine applications. The unit injector system is available in both MUI (mechanical unit injector) and EUI (electronic unit injector) design, with the MUI being used on nonelectronic fuel systems. Since the late 1980s and early 1990s, Caterpillar, Cummins, and Volvo have also adopted forms of both MUI and EUI systems in their product lines. See Chapter 21 for more details on both the MUI and EUI systems.

Cummins PT Fuel Pumps

The PT (pressure–time) fuel system which is unique to Cummins engines, employs a gear-type fuel supply pump along with a governor plunged and operator-controlled throttle to distribute fuel to the individual

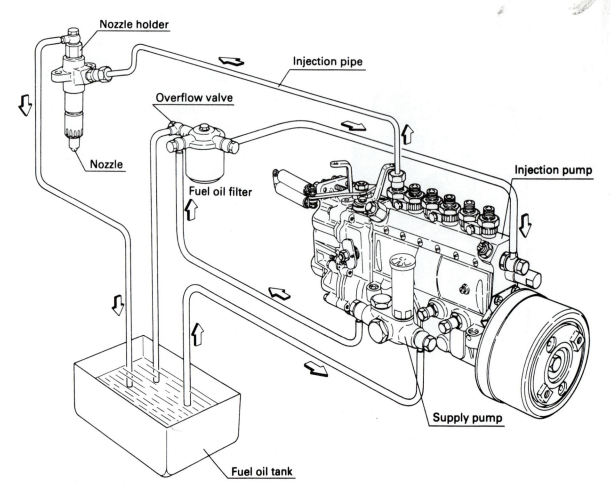

FIGURE 14–6 *Typical fuel system schematic for a six-cylinder inline multiple-plunger injection pump system. (Courtesy of Zexel Corporation, USA.)*

injectors. The speed of the engine determines the gear pump pressure curve and the available time during which the injector can meter the fuel required for injection purposes. For more details on the PT system, see Chapter 22.

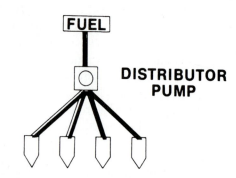

FIGURE 14–7 *Distributor injection pump.*

EUI Systems

Electronically controlled unit injector fuel systems are now widely used by many major engine OEMs, with Detroit Diesel, Caterpillar, Cummins, and Volvo offering these advanced control systems. At this time, the injector pumping plunger is activated mechanically by a rocker arm; however, in the HEUI (hydraulically actuated electronic unit injection) system (pronounced "Hughie") no rocker arm is necessary, since high-pressure oil is used to activate the injector pumping plunger. Refer to Chapter 23 for details on the HEUI system, which is currently being used by both Caterpillar and Navistar International in a number of their engines.

BASIC FUEL SYSTEM LAYOUT

The basic fuel system consists of the fuel tank(s) and a fuel transfer pump, which can be a separate engine-driven pump or can be mounted onto or inside the injection pump assembly, depending on the type of fuel

FIGURE 14-8 Distributor fuel injection pump system schematic flow.

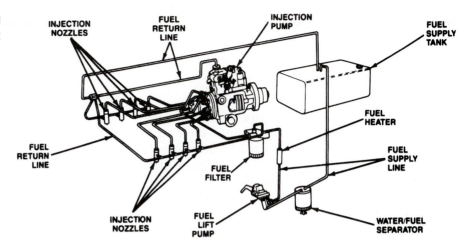

system in use (Figures 14-6, 14-8, and 14-10). In addition, the system uses two fuel filters: a primary filter located between the tank and the transfer pump, plus a secondary fuel filter located after the transfer pump to remove all impurities from the diesel fuel before it enters the injection pump, or flows onto the unit injectors in a low-pressure fuel system or to the nozzles on a high-pressure system. An optional item that is widely used today is a fuel filter/water separator located between the fuel tank and the transfer pump assembly. Generally, this unit contains an internal filter as well as a water trap. See Chapter 16 for more information on filters.

When two tanks are used, they are connected by a balance line between them, which may or may not contain a shut-off valve to allow isolation of one fuel tank. In many cases the fuel supply is pulled from one tank, while the return fuel is directed to the opposite tank.

A well-designed fuel tank will contain a drain plug in its base to allow fuel tank drainage. This allows the fuel to be drained from the tank prior to removal for any service reason. In addition, the tank should be drained periodically (once per year) to remove any traces of water.

The fuel tank filler cap is constructed with both a pressure relief valve and a vent valve. The filler cap

should be lubricated every couple of months with a few drops of light engine oil. The vent valve is designed to seal when fuel enters it due to causes such as overfilling, vehicle operating angle, or sudden shock that would cause fuel slosh within the tank. Although some fuel will tend to seep from the vent cap under certain operating conditions, this leakage rate should not exceed 1 ounce per minute in any vehicle operating position. To inspect the vent valve to determine that it is in fact operating correctly, clean around the valve before removal. Once removed, clean the valve of all dirt and fuel; hold the valve upright and locate the notches on the wrench flats. Cover one notch tightly with your finger while applying suction to the other. If the vent cap is operating correctly, it should allow flow and the ball inside should spin freely. If this

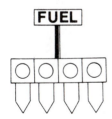

COMBINED
PUMP-NOZZLES

FIGURE 14-9 Unit fuel injector concept.

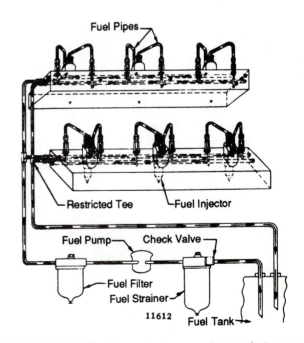

FIGURE 14-10 Schematic diagram of typical fuel system.

does not happen, shake the vent and repeat the process. Replace the valve if defective.

FUNCTIONS OF A FUEL INJECTION SYSTEM

You have probably heard the statement that "the fuel injection system is the actual heart of the diesel engine." When you consider that indeed a high-speed diesel could not be developed until an adequate fuel injection system was designed and produced, and that even Rudolf Diesel ran into problems basically associated with lack of a good injection system, this statement takes on a much broader and stronger meaning. Prior to delving into the specifics of individual injection pumps, let us consider what the actual demands and functions of a good injection system are.

HIGH- VERSUS LOW-PRESSURE FUEL SYSTEMS

The term *high pressure* versus *low pressure* in relation to a fuel injection system refers to the type of injection pump used on the system. If an engine employs an inline multiple-plunger injection pump such as that found on many six-cylinder four-stroke-cycle diesel engines, or uses a distributor-type pump, the metering and timing of the fuel is all done within the injection pump. Fuel is then delivered to each cylinder nozzle in engine firing-order sequence through a steel fuel line since the delivery pressure will normally range between 1800 and 4000 psi (12,411 to 27,580 kPa). This is where the term *high-pressure fuel system* originates.

High-pressure fuel injection pumps of the inline variety are capable of delivering higher fuel pressures than those available from a smaller distributor-type pump assembly. The fuel pressure delivered to the cylinder nozzle at 3000 psi (20,685 kPa), for example, is then forced through a series of very small orifices (holes) in the nozzle tip, which causes an increase in the injected fuel pressure. This action can be compared to a garden hose that is turned on with no spray nozzle on its end. The result will be substantial volume flow but little pressure other than that supplied by the city water mains. However, if you now place your finger, thumb, or a nozzle connection over the end of the hose, there is an immediate increase in velocity (speed and direction of the water) but a subsequent decrease in volume flow. At the nozzle, the same situation occurs, resulting in fuel spray-in pressures on the latest models of Robert Bosch and Caterpillar inline pump systems approaching 19,000 psi (1292 atm). Distributor pumps have spray-in pressures that are usually limited to between 11,000 and 14,000 psi (748 to 952 atm).

A low-pressure fuel system is one that delivers fuel to the injectors at pressures between 50 and 200 psi (345 to 1379 kPa). Typical fuel systems that use this type of system are Detroit Diesel Corporation and Cummins. Although the fuel delivery pressure is moderately low in comparison to the inline or distributor-type injection pump systems, a rocker-arm-activated injector plunger raises this supply pressure of 50 to 70 psi (345 to 483 kPa) in DDC's unit injector to between 2200 and 3300 psi (15,169 to 22,754 kPa) average. The fuel pressure then lifts the injector's needle valve from its seat against the spring pressure and allows fuel to be injected into the combustion chamber. In a unit injector, or in Cummins' PT system, there is no need to create a long column of pressurized fuel oil between the pump and the nozzle as you must do on a high-pressure fuel system; therefore, the resultant injection pressures on a unit injector system are higher than those for an inline high-pressure pump system. The spray-in pressures can run between 26,000 and 28,000 psi (1769 to 1905 atm) on the unit injector system. This produces a finer fuel spray (atomization), greater penetration into the compressed cylinder airmass, and usually shortens the ignition delay period. Consequently, mechanical or electronic unit injector systems are now also being used on diesel engines by Caterpillar, Cummins, Volvo, Deere, and Robert Bosch.

The requirements of a fuel injection system can be summarized as follows:

1. To receive equal power from all cylinders, the amount of fuel injected must remain constant from cycle to cycle, and obviously from cylinder to cylinder. A smooth-running engine is dependent on even fuel distribution to each cylinder throughout the speed range; otherwise, cylinder balance will be upset and some cylinders will be working harder than others. Overloading and overheating would result. This function is commonly referred to as *metering*.

   a. *Meter (measure).* The fuel injection system must measure the fuel supplied to the engine very accurately, since fuel requirements vary greatly with engine speed. Fuel is measured within the injection pump or injector by measuring it as it fills the pumping chamber (inlet metering) or as it leaves the pumping element (outlet metering). Although many variations of these two concepts exist, the basic principles have changed very little.

   b. *Time.* The timing of fuel injected into the cylinder is very important during engine starting, full load, and high-speed operation.

2. As engine load and speed vary owing to application and operating conditions, the point of actual

injection for a given load and speed will vary with this condition. Therefore, the injection system has to adjust the timing or point of injection to the fluctuating demands of engine operation. In summary, the injection system must *inject fuel* at the correct point in the cycle regardless of the engine *speed* and *load*. Many modern injection pumps have an automatic timing device built into them that changes the timing automatically as the engine speed changes.

Since fuel is compressible, there is a time lag between the actual beginning of delivery by the pump and the actual beginning of discharge from the nozzle; also, the rate of delivery from the pump is not identical with the rate of discharge from the nozzle. Therefore, by controlling the rate at which fuel is injected, the performance of many engines can be improved. One of the most important characteristics is the spray duration, particularly at full load, since it directly affects engine power, fuel consumption, and exhaust smoke. The type of nozzle used can to some extent control the actual rate of injection. In summation, the injection system must inject fuel at a rate necessary to control combustion and the rate of pressure rise *during combustion*. See Chapter 18 for more details on nozzles.

3. *Pressurize*. The fuel system must pressurize the fuel to open the injection nozzle (a spring-loaded valve) or the injector. In addition to the pressure required to open the nozzle, some pressure is required to inject fuel into the combustion chamber to offset the pressure of compression, which can range between 450 and 625 psi (32 to 45 kg/cm^2). The pressure setting of the injection nozzle or injector is directly related to the degree of atomization required. As the fuel is pumped through the holes in the tip (multihole nozzle) or around the pintle nozzle at high pressure of 1500 to 4000 psi (105 to 280 kg/cm^2), atomization occurs.

4. *Atomize* (the breaking up of fuel into small particles). The fuel must be atomized when it is injected into the combustion chamber, since unatomized fuel will not burn easily. This atomization can be compared to the atomization that occurs when you attach a spray nozzle to the end of a garden hose. The degree of atomization required will vary from engine to engine depending on the combustion chamber design. Good combustion is related to the degree of fuel atomization; therefore, the type of combustion chamber and engine speed affect these requirements. The type and size of nozzle plus the injection pressure will control the degree of atomization.

5. *Distribute*. Closely related to timing, the distribution of fuel must be accurate and according to the engine's firing order. Distributor pumps deliver fuel to each pump outlet in succession, and the lines are hooked to the cylinders in the correct firing order,

much like a distributor used on a gas engine. Inline pumps have the camshaft designed to permit the pump outlets to fire in the required engine cylinder firing order. Along with distributing the fuel to the various cylinders, the fuel system must distribute the fuel within the combustion chamber during initial injection. The fuel must be injected throughout the chamber so that all the air within the chamber is utilized. This requirement is fulfilled by the injection nozzle or injector, its hole size, and angle.

6. *Control start-and-stop injection*. Injection of fuel must start quickly and end quickly. Any delay in injection beginning will alter the pump-to-engine timing, causing hard-starting and poor-running engines. Any delay in injection ending can cause a smoky exhaust and irregular exhaust sound. The end of injection should be instantaneous, with no dribbling or secondary injections. In many systems this is accomplished by a valve called a delivery valve or retraction valve. Other pumps have a camshaft designed with a sharp drop on the cam lobe that stops injection very rapidly.

DISTRIBUTOR PUMP SYSTEM

The distributor pump system shown in Figure 14-11 is found on small to medium-sized diesel engines and is often referred to as a rotary pump, due to the fact that its concept of operation is similar to that of the ignition distributor found on gasoline engines. A rotating member called a rotor within the pump distributes fuel at high pressure to the individual injectors in engine firing-order sequence. It is classified as a high-pressure system and is limited to engine sizes up to about 1.3 L per cylinder. Distributor pumps do not have the capability to deliver sufficient fuel volume or to create high-enough fuel injection pressures and delivery rates for heavy-duty large-displacement high-speed diesel engines used in trucks. The distributor pump concept draws fuel from the tank through a primary filter or fuel filter/water separator as shown in Figure 14-8, which illustrates the fuel system for a V8 engine.

The fuel lift pump pressurizes the fuel to between 3 and 5 psi (21 to 34 kPa) and delivers it through a secondary fuel filter and on into the distributor pump housing, where the fuel pressure is increased by the use of a vane-type transfer or charging pump mounted inside the end plate of the injection pump assembly (opposite the drive end). Fuel under pressure from the vane pump is delivered to a charging passage inside the injection pump at a maximum regulated pressure of approximately 130 psi (896 kPa). The fuel is then metered and timed for delivery to the individual

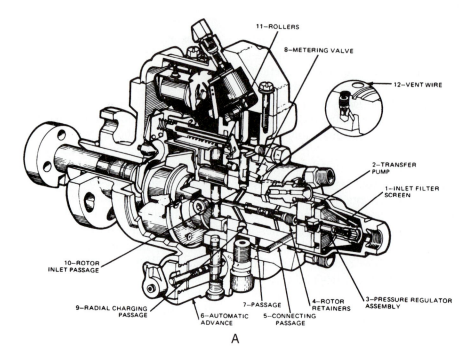

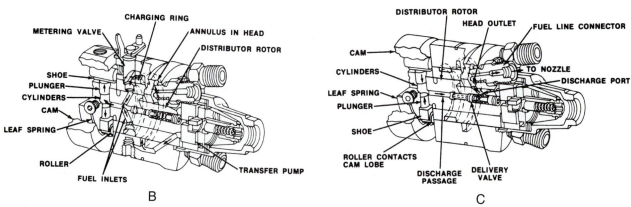

FIGURE 14–11 *(A) Features of a Stanadyne model DB2 mechanical distributor injection pump; (B) fuel flow during the pump charging cycle; (C) fuel flow during the pump discharge cycle. (Courtesy of Stanadyne Diesel Systems.)*

injection nozzles at pump pressures of from 3000 to 4000 psi (136 to 272 atm) on average. Each injection nozzle is directly connected to the pump hydraulic head by a high-pressure line. The adjustable nozzle release spring setting determines the actual injector opening pressure. A fuel return or leak-back line is also used to bypass fuel back to the secondary fuel filter assembly or to the fuel tank.

Distributor pumps are manufactured by Stanadyne Diesel Systems; Robert Bosch, whose VE model is widely used; Lucas-Varity Industries in England, with their legendary DPA (distributor pump assembly); and by Ambac in the United States. Both Bosch and Lucas have a number of licensees worldwide who manufacture these distributor pumps for use in small lightweight and medium-duty diesel engines, one being Zexel (Diesel Kiki) in Japan, and the United States.

Fuel Flow

Figure 14-11A illustrates the model DB2 Stanadyne mechanical injection pump and its major component parts. Flow through the injection pump is as follows: Fuel at lift pump pressure from the secondary fuel filter enters the injection pump at the hydraulic head end (injection line end). This fuel passes into the vane-type transfer pump (2) through a filter screen (1). To control maximum delivery pressure of the shaft-driven transfer pump, a spring-loaded pressure regulating valve will bypass fuel back to the inlet side of the transfer pump. This fuel pressure is set with the injection pump mounted on a fuel pump test stand and is usually limited to a maximum of 130 psi (896 kPa).

Transfer pump fuel flows through the center of the rotor and past the retainers (4) and into the hydraulic head of the injection pump. Fuel then flows up to the fuel metering valve (8), which is controlled by throttle position and governor action through connecting passage (5) in the hydraulic head to the automatic timing advance (6) and continues on through the radial passage (9) to this valve.

The pump rotor, which is turning at injection pump speed (one-half engine speed), allows the rotor fuel inlet passages (10) to align with the hydraulic head fuel charging ports. Fuel flows into the pumping chamber, where two rotor plungers are moved toward each other by their rollers (11), contacting a cam ring lobe. The rollers force the plungers inward to increase the pressure of the trapped fuel, which is directed out of the rotor discharge passage to the single spring-loaded delivery valve and then to the injection nozzle fuel delivery line. This occurs in firing-order sequence as the rotor revolves.

The purpose of the air vent passage (12) in the hydraulic head is to allow a percentage of fuel from the transfer pump to flow into the injection pump housing. This fuel is used to vent air from the system and also to cool and lubricate the internal pump components. This fuel flows back to the fuel tank via a return line.

Charging and Discharging Cycle

Charging Cycle
Rotation of the rotor allows both inlet passages drilled within it to register with the circular charging passage ports. The position of the fuel metering valve connected to the governor linkage controls the flow of transfer pump fuel into the pumping chamber and therefore how far apart the two plungers will be. The maximum plunger travel is controlled by the single leaf spring, which contacts the edge of the roller shoes. Maximum outward movement of the plungers will therefore occur only under full-load conditions. Figure 14-11B shows the fuel flow during the charging cycle. Any time that the angled inlet fuel passages of the rotor are in alignment with the ports in the circular passage, the rotor discharge port is not in registry with a hydraulic head outlet and the rollers are also off the cam lobes.

Discharging Cycle
The actual start of injection will vary with engine speed since the cam ring is automatically advanced by fuel pressure acting through linkage against it. Therefore, as the rotor turns, the angled inlet passages of the rotor move away from the charging ports. As this happens, the discharge port of the rotor opens to one of the hydraulic head outlets (see Figure 14-11C).

Also at this time, the rollers make contact with the lobes of the cam ring, forcing the shoes and plungers inward and thus creating high fuel pressure in the rotor discharge passage. The fuel flows through the axial discharge passage of the rotor and opens the spring-loaded delivery valve. Fuel then flows through the discharge port to the injection line and injector. This fuel delivery will continue until the rollers pass the innermost point of the cam lobe, after which they start to move outward, thereby rapidly reducing the fuel pressure in the rotor's axial discharge passage and simultaneously allowing spring pressure inside the injection nozzle to close the valve.

Delivery Valve Operation
To prevent after-dribble, and therefore unburned fuel with some possible smoke at the exhaust, the end of injection, as with any high-speed diesel, must occur crisply and rapidly. To ensure that the nozzle valve does in fact return to its seat as rapidly as possible, the delivery valve within the axial discharge passage of the pump rotor will act to reduce injection line pressure after fuel injection to a value lower than that of the injector nozzle closing pressure.

From some of the views shown so far you will recollect that the delivery valve is located within the rotor's axial passageway. To understand its function more readily, refer to Figure 14-12. The delivery valve requires only a stop to control the amount that it can

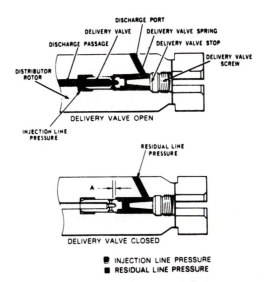

FIGURE 14-12 Distributor pump delivery valve action. (Courtesy of Stanadyne Diesel Systems.)

move within the rotor bore. No seals as such are required, owing to the close fit of the valve within its bore. With a distributor pump such as the DB2, each injector is supplied in firing-order sequence from the axial passage of the rotor; therefore, the delivery valve operates for all the injectors during the period approaching the end of injection.

In Figure 14-12 pressurized fuel will move the valve gently out of its bore, thereby adding the volume of its displacement to the delivery valve chamber, which is under high pressure. As the cam rollers start to run down the lobe of the cam ring, pressure on the delivery valve's plunger side is rapidly reduced and spring pressure forces the valve cuff to close the fuel passage off, thereby ending fuel injection at that cylinder.

Immediately thereafter, the rotor discharge port closes totally and a residual injection line pressure of 500 to 600 psi (3447 to 4137 kPa) is maintained. In summation, the delivery valve will seal only while the discharge port is open because the instant the port closes, residual line pressures are maintained by the seal existing between the close-fitting hydraulic head and rotor.

Fuel Return Circuit

A small amount of fuel under pressure is vented into the governor linkage compartment. Flow into this area is controlled by a small vent wire that controls the volume of fuel returning to the fuel tank, thereby avoiding any undue fuel pressure loss. The vent passage is behind the metering valve bore and leads to the governor compartment via a short vertical passage. The vent wire assembly is available in several sizes to control the amount of vented fuel being returned to the tank, its size being controlled by the pump's particular application. In normal operation, this vent wire should not be tampered with because it can be altered only by removal of the governor cover. The correct wire size would be installed when the pump assembly is being flow tested on a pump calibration stand.

The vent wire passage, then, allows any air and a small amount of fuel to return to the fuel tank. Governor housing fuel pressure is maintained by a spring-loaded ballcheck return fitting in the governor cover of the pump.

STANADYNE DS PUMP

Major manufacturers of distributor pump systems such as Lucas with its DPA, Robert Bosch with its automotive VE model, and Stanadyne with its well-known DB and DS distributor pumps are three of the major OEMs that have switched to electronic control for various models. One example of such an arrangement is illustrated in Figure 14-13 for the Stanadyne DS model, which is widely used on the General Motors turbocharged 6.5-L V8 pickup truck application.

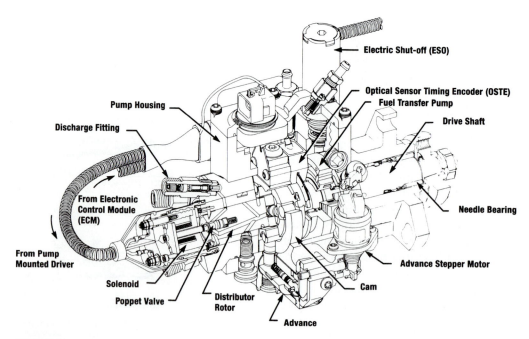

FIGURE 14–13 *Major features of the Stanadyne electronic model DS distributor pump used on General Motors 6.5-L V8 pickup truck application. (Courtesy of Stanadyne Diesel Systems.)*

The Stanadyne Model DS diesel fuel injection system offers electronic control of both fuel quantity and the start of injection timing. The mechanical governor and mechanical metering control system used on the DB2 automotive pump, for example, is replaced by a high-speed electrical actuator as shown in Figure 14-14. The DS pump is capable of handling up to 19 kW (25 bhp) per engine cylinder, with peak injection pressures to 1000 bar (14,500 psi).

As with all electronic engines, a number of electrical sensors send real-time engine operation information to the ECM (electronic control module). In addition, the injection pump speed and angular pulse train data are transmitted to the ECM. Custom algorithms process this information and send PWM (pulse-width-modulated) inject command signals to the pump-mounted solenoid driver. Additional input/output signals for other engine functions, such as glow plug control and EGR valves, is also initiated from the ECM. Figure 14-14 shows an electronic control system schematic used with the DS model pumps. Each injection is directly controlled by a solenoid instead of an intermediate analog mechanism. This type of system permits precise control of both injection timing and fuel quantity to optimize engine performance and emissions.

This DS pump model features a single high-speed solenoid to control both fuel and injection timing. A solenoid spill valve mounted in the hydraulic head area of the pump rotor, to minimize high-pressure volume, is a key to the higher injection pressures available from this pump model over its mechanical counterpart. The geometry of the internal pump cam ring has been designed to ensure higher injection pressures as well as the desired control characteristics relative to the start, duration, and end of injection. The higher injection pressure has been enhanced through a new drive design that features a larger-diameter zero-backlash drive shaft containing the cam rollers and four plunger tappets. In this way, the driving loads are isolated from the spinning distributor rotor. A higher gear-drive torque, as well as a belt-drive capability if desired, are accommodated with the larger-diameter drive shaft.

This DS pump model was the first to be offered in the U.S. light-truck consumer market; it was introduced in 1994 Chevrolet and General Motors light trucks. The pump provides electronic control of both the fuel quantity and start of injection timing. The governor mechanism and fuel metering commonly used on the DB2 mechanical pump models has been replaced with a high-speed electrical actuator. Sensors provide information to an ECM (electronic control module), which then computes the actual time in milliseconds that the fuel delivery and timing should be for any given condition of engine operation. Signals from the ECM instruct the pump-mounted driver electronics to supply the correct fuel injection PWM (pulse width modulation) signals.

Features of this electronic system can be seen in Figure 14-15; note the DS pump, the ECM, and the system sensors. These engine-mounted sensors send up-to-date operational data to the ECM. The pump speed and the angular pulse train data from the pump are also sent to the ECM. The programmed algorithms within the ECM process this information and send an appropriate inject command PWM signal to the PMD (pump-mounted driver). Some of the features of the DS pump are listed next:

- Shot-to-shot modification of fuel delivery and timing
- Complete governing flexibility with enhanced idle speed control
- Flexible controls for cold-engine operation
- Transient adaptation of fuel delivery and timing
- Complete flexibility of fuel metering and injection timing control

FIGURE 14–14 Basic operation of the model DS distributor pump, ECM, and system sensors which send up-to-date engine information to the ECM. Pump speed and the angular pulse train data from the DS pump are also sent to the ECM where customized algorithms process this information and send appropriate injection command signals to the PMD. (Courtesy of Stanadyne Diesel Systems.)

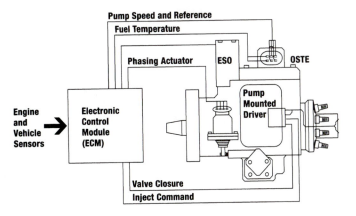

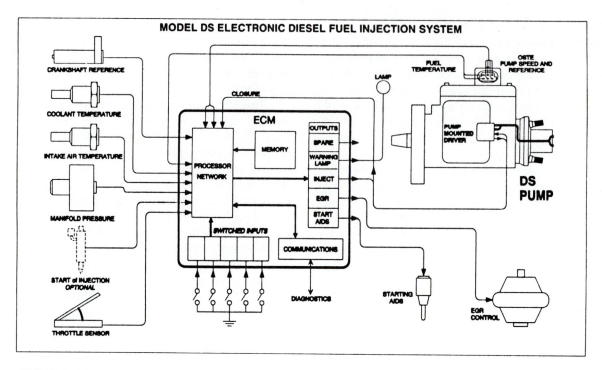

FIGURE 14–15 Model DS electronic diesel fuel injection system.

- Electronic spill control with a single 12-V solenoid actuator for timing and fuel control
- Pump-mounted solenoid driver with poppet valve closure detection
- High-resolution pump-mounted angular encoder
- Four pumping plungers driven by the lobes on the internal pump cam ring
- Headless rotor drive to isolate torque loads from the rotor

- Fuel oil lubricated
- Fuel inlet at the top of the pump housing for V-engine configuration and accessibility

Servicing of this DS model pump requires approximately 20 new service tools. Figure 14-16 is an example of a DS pump mounted on a fuel injection pump test stand; the pump is connected to a power supply/ECU. A conventional-type hand-held scan

FIGURE 14–16 Model DS distributor injection pump mounted on a fuel pump test stand and connected to a special diagnostic test equipment package, which also includes a hand-held DDR (diagnostic data reader—scan tool). (Courtesy of Stanadyne Diesel Systems.)

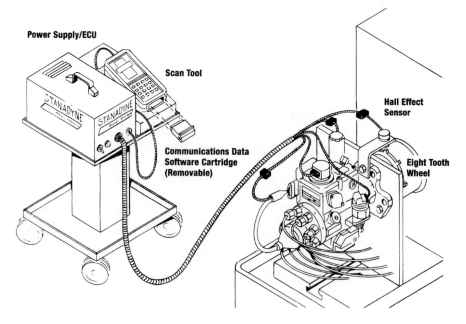

tool can also be used with the correct software data cartridge to monitor fault codes, and so on. Such a tool would be similar to that used on automotive gasoline engines and heavy-duty diesel engines with electronic unit injector systems.

LUCAS FUEL SYSTEMS

Lucas/Varity Industries PLC is the parent organization of Bryce, Simms, and CAV, all of which have been recognized fuel injection pump OEMs for many years. All three are now incorporated under the Lucas/Varity name. CAV began producing inline injection pumps under license from REF-Apparatebau in the late 1920s. A contract was signed in October 1931 whereby Robert Bosch became a 49% participant in CAV. This agreement was terminated due to World War II and the companies went their separate ways.

Today, Lucas is one of the world's leading suppliers of electronic and mechanical diesel fuel injection systems and components, supplying one-third of the growing European diesel car, van, and light-truck market with fuel injection systems. In the multiple-plunger inline fuel injection pump range, the Minimec, Majormec, and Maximec are very well known. In the smaller diesel engine line, the legendary CAV DPA (distributor pump assembly) has enjoyed unparalleled success for many years, with 24 million of these and the DPS-version pumps having been sold to date. Latest versions of the original DPA are now equipped with electronic controls, some of which are discussed in this section. In addition, Lucas produces small flange-mounted unit pumps for industrial, generator, and marine applications of 4 to 50 hp (3 to 37 kW), in one-, two-, three-, and four-cylinder configurations. Lucas injection pump products, nozzles, and injectors are produced throughout the world by a number of licensee companies. Caterpillar electronic injector systems were developed in conjunction with Lucas Industries.

The Bryce division of Lucas has for years produced single-cylinder plunger-type injection pumps for large-bore slow-speed engines. Today, Bryce continues in this field, now offering electronically controlled plunger pumps, or alternatively, an electronically controlled unit injector system. These single-cylinder heavy-duty jerk pumps range from a nominal stroke of 20 mm (0.78 in.) to 50 mm (1.968 in.), with a maximum pump plunger diameter from 22 mm (0.866 in.) to 50 mm (1.968 in.). The maximum fuel delivery output for these heavy-duty very-large-bore slow-speed industrial and marine engines can range from 2740 mm^3 per plunger stroke, to 39,250 mm^3 per stroke. Compare the delivery of 39,250 mm^3 [39.25 cm^3

(where 1000 cm^3 equals 1 liter)] to the injection quantity of approximately 205 mm^3 per stroke from an electronic unit injector typically used on a 400- to 450-hp (298- to 336-kW) high-speed heavy-duty truck engine, and you can readily appreciate the physical size difference and fuel requirements of these two engine systems.

Figure 14-17 illustrates an example of the electronic control system used by Lucas Bryce. In this system an electronically controlled plunger pump driven directly from the engine camshaft supplies fuel to the injector via a high-pressure pipe. The electric solenoids are operated by a heavy-duty electronic drive unit that is designed as an integral part of the system. Complementary electronic governors are available to suit specific applications.

Lucas Industries also owns Hartridge Test Products, one of the leaders in the manufacture of diesel fuel injection test and servicing equipment. This division, known as Lucas Assembly and Test Systems (Lucas A.T.S.), resulted from combining the U.K. business of Lucas Hartridge Ltd. with U.S.-based Allen Automated Systems to form one of the world's largest assembly and test system specialists.

Since the basic design and operation of Lucas inline and small flange-mounted pumps are similar to those of pumps manufactured by Robert Bosch Corporation, we do not discuss them in detail here. Refer to Chapter 19 for typical details.

DISTRIBUTOR PUMPS

The distributor pump systems now manufactured by Lucas are all based on the original DPA design. The DPA pump was a result of an agreement with Roosa Master (now Stanadyne Fuel Systems) in the United States, signed in 1956, that enabled CAV (now Lucas) to manufacture their own version of Vernon Roosa's distributor pump system. Today, Lucas's original DPA distributor pump is available in the DP200, DPC, DPCN, and EPIC versions. The DP200 direct-injection model is currently available for two-, three-, four-, or six-cylinder engines up to 1.3 L (79 in^3) per cylinder.

The DPC range of rotary fuel injection pumps was developed specifically for indirect-injection diesel engines for passenger cars and light vans with engine capacities up to 0.75 L (46 in^3) per cylinder. The DPCN model is based on the DPC but is controlled by an ECU for fully flexible timing and improved consistency.

DPA Fuel Injection Pump
The pump derives its name from the fact that its main shaft is driven and runs through the center of the pump housing lengthwise. Fuel is in turn distributed

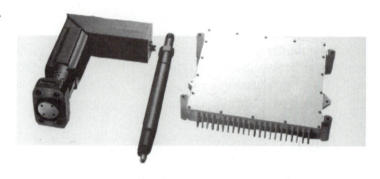

FIGURE 14–17 Lucas Bryce electronically controlled fuel system.

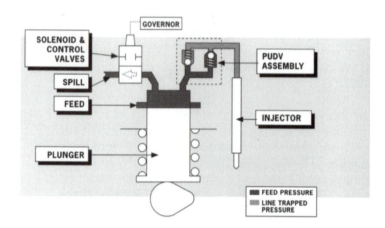

from a single-cylinder opposed plunger control somewhat similar to a rotating distributor rotor in a gasoline engine. The pump can be hub mounted or gear driven because its shaft is very stiff to eliminate torsional oscillation and ensure constant accuracy of injection.

Figure 14-18 shows a cutaway view of a typical DPA fuel injection pump with a mechanical governor. Figure 14-19 shows a DPA pump with a hydraulic governor. All internal parts are lubricated by fuel oil under pressure from the delivery pump. The pump can be fitted with either a mechanical or hydraulic governor, depending on the application; a hydraulically operated automatic advance mechanism controls the start of injection in relation to engine speed. The operation of the fuel distribution is similar to that found in Stanadyne distributor pumps in that a central rotating member forms the pumping and distributing rotor driven from the main drive shaft on which is mounted the governor assembly.

Fuel Flow

Mounted on the outer end of the pumping and distributing rotor is a sliding vane-type transfer pump that receives fuel under low pressure from a lift pump mounted and driven from the engine. This lift pump

pressure enters the vane-type pump through the fitting on the injection pump end plate the opposite the drive end and passes through a fine nylon gauze filter.

The vane-type pump has the capability of delivering more fuel than the injection pump will need; therefore, a pressure-regulating valve housed in the injection pump end plate allows excess fuel to be bypassed back to the suction side of the vane transfer pump. This valve is shown in Figure 14-20.

In addition to regulating fuel flow, the pressure-regulating valve also provides a means of bypassing fuel through the outlet of the transfer pump on into the injection pump for priming purposes. As seen in Figure 14-20 the regulating valve is round and contains a small free piston whose travel is controlled by two light springs. During priming of the injection pump, fuel at lift pump pressure enters the central port of the regulating valve sleeve and causes the free piston to move against the retaining spring pressure, thereby uncovering the priming port at the lower end of the sleeve, which connects by a passage in the end plate to the delivery side of the vane-type transfer pump, which leads to the injection pump itself.

Once the engine starts, we now have the vane-type transfer pump producing fuel under pressure, which enters the lower port of the regulating valve

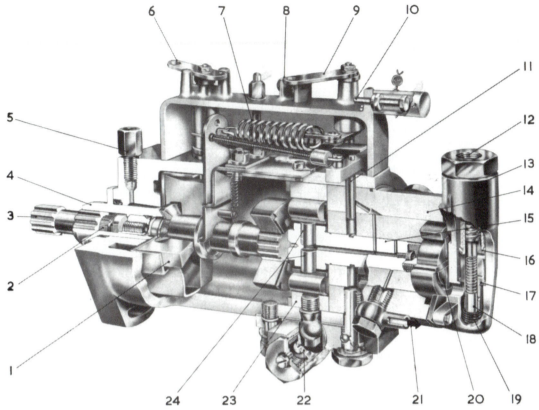

1. Governor Weights
2. Drive Hub Securing Screw
3. Quill Shaft
4. Drive Hub
5. Back Leak Connection
6. Shut-Off Lever
7. Governor Spring
8. Idling Stop
9. Control Lever
10. Maximum Speed Stop
11. Metering Valve
12. Fuel Inlet
13. End Plate Assembly
14. Hydraulic Head
15. Rotor
16. Nylon Filter
17. Regulating Valve Sleeve
18. Regulating Piston
19. Priming Spring
20. Transfer Pump
21. To Injector
22. Advance Device
23. Cam Ring
24. Plungers

FIGURE 14–18 DPA pump with mechanical governor. (Courtesy of Lucas CAV Ltd.)

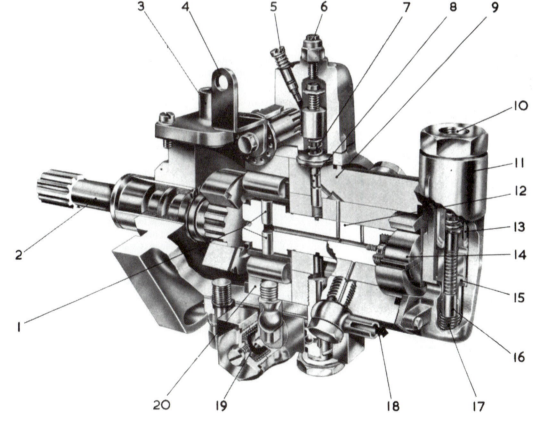

1. Plungers
2. Drive Shaft
3. Back Leak Connector
4. Control Lever
5. Idling Stop
6. Vent Screw
7. Governor Spring
8. Metering Valve
9. Hydraulic Head
10. Fuel Inlet
11. End Plate Assembly
12. Rotor
13. Nylon Filter
14. Transfer Pump
15. Regulating Valve Sleeve
16. Regulating Piston
17. Priming Spring
18. To Injector
19. Advance Device
20. Cam Ring

FIGURE 14–19 DPA pump with hydraulic governor. (Courtesy of Lucas CAV Ltd.)

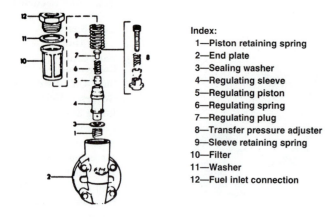

Index:
1—Piston retaining spring
2—End plate
3—Sealing washer
4—Regulating sleeve
5—Regulating piston
6—Regulating spring
7—Regulating plug
8—Transfer pressure adjuster
9—Sleeve retaining spring
10—Filter
11—Washer
12—Fuel inlet connection

FIGURE 14–20 *Pressure-regulating valve. (Courtesy of Lucas CAV Ltd.)*

and causes the free piston to move up against the spring.

As the engine is accelerated, fuel pressure increases, allowing the free piston to progressively uncover the regulating port, thereby bypassing fuel from the outlet side of the vane pump. This action automatically controls the fuel requirements of the injection pump. Figure 14-21 shows the fuel pressure-regulating valve assembled into its bore and its action during priming and regulating.

EPIC Distributor Pump

The EPIC (electronic pump injection control) model is a specially designed full-authority injection system for both direct- and indirect-injection engines. EPIC improves vehicle idling and reduces exhaust emissions. Figure 14-22 shows an external view of the EPIC pump

from both sides along with its ECU. The system features internal cam pumping and closed-loop control of fuel metering and timing. As with all electronically controlled fuel injection systems, signals from the various engine, pump, and vehicle sensors are converted to a number of maps stored in ECU memory. The ECU then sends signals to the pump actuators to implement the desired control strategy. Figure 14-22 illustrates a schematic of the EPIC and its control system. For more details on how electronic control systems function, refer to Chapter 15. Current developments for the high-speed direct-injection (HSDI) diesel car and van market are fully electronic high-pressure spill rotary pumps which generate injection pressures over 1000 bar (14,600 psi).

SUMMARY

Having reviewed this chapter, you should be conversant with the various types of mechanical and electronic fuel injection systems, and the names of the major engine OEMs that use these different systems. Test your knowledge of these different systems by visually determining what type of fuel injection system is being used on a variety of available engines/equipment.

SELF-TEST QUESTIONS

1. Technician A says that the peson credited with mass producing a high-pressure fuel injection system for diesel engines was
   a. Street
   b. Carnot

Index:
1—Retaining spring
2—Nylon filter
3—Regulating spring
4—Valve sleeve
5—Piston
6—Priming spring
7—Fuel passage to transfer pump outlet
8—Regulating port
9—Fuel passage to transfer pump inlet
10—Spring guide
11—Fuel inlet connection

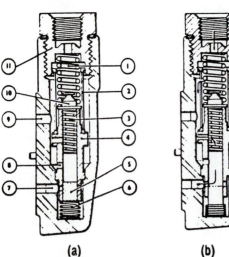
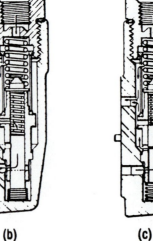
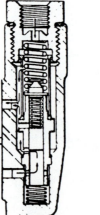

(a) (b) (c)

FIGURE 14–21 *Action of pressure-regulating valve: (a) rest; (b) hand priming; (c) running. (Courtesy of Lucas CAV Ltd.)*

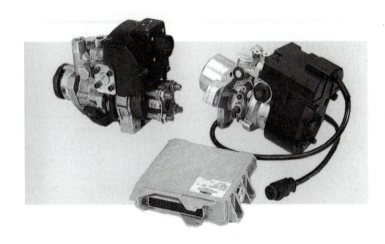

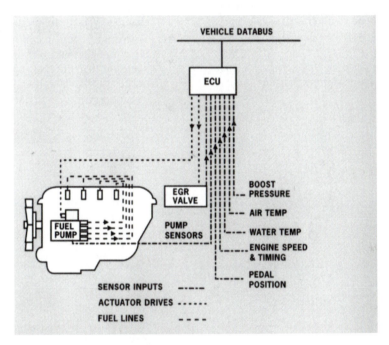

FIGURE 14–22 EPIC system.

c. Diesel

d. Bosch

2. Technician A says that fuel injection systems are generally classified as being either a high-pressure or a low-pressure design. Technician B says that all fuel systems operate on a high-pressure design. Which technician understands this difference best?

3. Technician A says that all fuel systems operate on the distributor pump concept. Technician B disagrees and says that a distributor pump system is just one type of fuel system. Who is correct?

4. Technician A says that with the exception of distributor pumps and Cummins PT systems, all PLN (pump–line–nozzle) and unit injector fuel systems operate on the jerk pump concept. Technician B disagrees. Who knows their basic operational theory best?

5. Technician A says that on a jerk pump system the model designation PF stands for "pump foreign," while technician B says that it stands for "pump fuel." Who is correct?

6. Technician A says that the designation PFR on a jerk pump means that the pump is driven remotely from the engine camshaft. Technician B says that it means that it has a roller tappet rather than a flat tappet as on the PF model. Which technician is correct?

7. Technician A says that PLN fuel systems deliver high-pressure fuel through steel-backed lines to the nozzles at pressures ranging on average between 2500 and 4300 psi (17,237 to 29,648 kPa). Technician B says that fuel pressures in the lines to the nozzles average between 500 and 900 psi (3447 to 6205 kPa).

8. Technician A says that as well as being more compact

than PLN systems, distributor pump systems are capable of delivering higher injection pressures. Technician B disagrees and says that PLN systems can produce higher injection pressures. Who is right?

9. Technician A says that unit injector fuel systems are capable of delivering higher injection pressures than is PLN systems. Technician B says that they deliver the same pressure. Who is right?

10. The function of a unit injector system is to
    a. time, atomize, meter, and pressurize the fuel
    b. time, atomize, meter, and vaporize the fuel
    c. pressurize, meter, inject, and vaporize the fuel
    d. pressurize, inject, atomize, and vaporize the fuel

11. True or False: The letters PT in Cummins mechanical fuel systems stand for "pressure–time."

12. True or False: Electronic controls permit closer regulation over the start and end of injection and, along with the various sensor inputs to the ECU/ECM, reduce exhaust emissions levels.

13. Technician A says that Detroit Diesel has been using unit injectors in their engines longer than any other engine OEM. Technician B says that Caterpillar has always used unit injectors in their engines. Who is correct?

14. Technician A says that PLN systems are classified as low-pressure fuel system: Technician B says that PLN systems are high-pressure fuel systems. Who is right?

15. True or False: Cummins PT fuel systems are classified as low-pressure fuel systems.

16. The letters HEUI mean
    a. hydrostatic engine unit injectors
    b. hydraulically actuated electronic unit injectors
    c. high-output engine unit injectors

17. Technician A says that *atomize* means to break the fuel down into very fine droplets for injection purposes. Technician B says that *atomize* means to inject a steady high-pressure column of fuel into the combustion chamber. Which technician is correct?

18. Technician A says that *meter* means to measure a quantity of fuel for injection purposes. Technician B says that it means that the fuel is correctly timed for injection purposes. Who is right?

Theory of Electronic Fuel Systems

OVERVIEW

This chapter deals with how electronic fuel injection systems operate. Details on how analog and digital signals are used, signal processing, sensor function and operation, ECM operation, waveforms, duty cycle, pulse width modulation signals, binary notation, SAE trouble codes, and how to access system trouble codes are discussed.

SYSTEM DEVELOPMENT

In this chapter we provide a simplified picture of how an electronically controlled fuel injection system operates without the specifics of a particular system. Details on particular systems are provided in subsequent chapters.

Environmental concerns about exhaust emissions from the internal combustion engine were the force that motivated diesel engine manufacturers to adopt *electronic engine control systems.* You may recollect from other discussions in this book that the adoption of electronics for diesels followed closely the process that was initiated for gasoline passenger car engines in the late 1970s and early 1980s. In the gasoline engine, the carburetor and contact breaker point ignition system was superseded by breakerless ignition systems and by either TBI (throttle body injection) or MPFI (multiport fuel injection).

Mechanically governed and mechanically controlled fuel injection systems on diesel engines had reached their limit of efficiency. The next logical technological move was to adopt a series of electrical engine sensors, an EFPA (electronic foot pedal assembly), and an on-board ECM (electronic control module) programmed to extract the optimum fuel economy and engine performance.

Initially, heavy-duty high-speed diesel engine electronic fuel injection systems were add-on items attached to existing PLN (pump–line–nozzle) systems such as those manufactured by Robert Bosch, Zexel, Nippondenso, Lucas, and Caterpillar. The first major OEM to release full-authority electronic controls was the Detroit Diesel Division of General Motors Corporation, now owned by Roger Penske and called Detroit Diesel Corporation. Detroit Diesel introduced the DDEC I (Detroit Diesel electronic controls) system in September 1985, DDEC II in September 1987, and DDEC III in September 1993. This EUI (electronic unit injector) system is employed on the company's two- and four-stroke-cycle engine models.

Caterpillar introduced its PEEC (programmable electronic engine control) system on its PLN fuel system for its 3406B truck engine in 1987. This was followed in 1988 by the release of its EUI system on the 3176 truck engine. The PEEC system on the 3406B and C engine models was superseded by the EUI system beginning in late 1993 and early 1994 with the introduction of the 3406E engine model. Both the 3500 and 3600 Caterpillar engines also employ EUI systems. Cummins introduced its first-generation ECI (electronically controlled injection) system in 1988. This was followed in 1990 by its Celect (Cummins Electronics) fuel system. The Celect system is available on Cummins' 14-L, M11, L10, and K series engine models. In 1994 Volvo introduced its VE D12 overhead camshaft 12-L truck engine equipped with VE, for Vectro (Volvo electronics) controlled unit injectors, which are similar to the DDEC system.

Mack has used a system known by the acronym VMAC (vehicle management and controls) on its PLN Bosch electronic fuel injection pumps for several years now. Robert Bosch, who is a major PLN OEM, recently purchased 49% of the Diesel Technology Equipment Division, Inc., of Detroit Diesel and now produces EUPs (electronic unit pumps) in addition to EUIs now used by Bosch's many engine OEMs in place of the long-used PLN fuel systems. Mercedes-Benz, the parent of Freightliner, and Detroit Diesel codesigned the stock engine used in the Century Class 8 trucks. This engine, known as the DDC series 55 (four-cycle), is a 12-L engine that incorporates EUPs controlled by the DDEC electronic system. John Deere also employ EUIs in their 10.5- and 12.5-L Power Tech engine models using an overhead camshaft for actuation. Another unique system is the HEUI (hydraulically actuated electronic unit injector) system, which was codesigned by Caterpillar and Navistar engineers. OEMs employing the HEUI system include Caterpillar, on their 3126, 3408E, and 3412E models, and Navistar, on their 444, 466, and 530 models. The Navistar 444 engine is used by Ford in a broad cross section of their vehicles.

From this information, it is apparent that the majority of engine OEMs are now committed to using electronically controlled diesel fuel injection systems. The trend at this time is to replace PLN systems with electronic unit injectors. Electronic diesel control means an advanced technology electronic fuel injection and control system that offers significant operating advantages over traditional mechanically governed engines. Electronic systems optimize control of critical engine functions that affect fuel economy, exhaust smoke, and emissions. These electronic systems provide the capability to protect the engine from serious damage resulting from conditions such as high engine coolant temperatures, high oil temperatures, and low engine oil pressure conditions.

FUEL SYSTEM STRUCTURE AND FUNCTION

Although there are unique differences in the electronic fuel systems employed by each OEM, overall there are more similarities than differences. Electronically controlled unit fuel injectors, with the exception of HEUI systems, are mechanically actuated. Each system employs a series of engine and vehicle sensors that are continually fed an electrical *input* signal from the ECM. Most sensors are designed to accept a 5.0-volt dc (direct-current) input signal from the ECM. Depending on the operating condition at the sensor, it will *output* a signal back to the ECM ranging between 0.5 and 5.0 V dc, although some systems can range as high as

5.25 to 5.5 V dc. The ECM then determines and computes a digital PWM (pulse width modulated) electrical signal based on predetermined calibration tables in its memory to control the time that each injector actually delivers fuel to the combustion chamber. This type of system allows tailoring of the start, duration, and end of fuel injection to ensure optimum engine performance at any load and speed. Fuel is delivered to the cylinders by the EUIs, which are driven by an overhead camshaft on Detroit Diesel series 50 and 60 engines, the Caterpillar 3406E, the Volvo VE D12, the John Deere 10.5-L and 12.5-L Power Tech models, and the Isuzu 12-L 6WA1TC, or by an in-block camshaft and pushrod on Caterpillar's 3176B, C10, C12, 3408E, and 3412E models; and Cummins' N14, M11, L10, and K models, to provide the mechanical input for sufficient pressurization of the fuel, resulting in injector spray-in pressures as high as 28,000 psi (193,060 kPa).

Figure 15-1 is a simplified schematic of an electronically controlled unit injector fuel system common to Caterpillar, Cummins, Detroit Diesel, and Volvo high-speed diesel engines. Figure 15-2 is a simplified line diagram of an electronic unit injector fuel system arrangement that shows the engine crankshaft TRS (timing reference sensor), the gear train SRS (synchronous reference sensor), the basic layout of the ECM components, the electronically controlled unit injector solenoid, most of the sensors used, and the operator interfaces, which indicate to the ECM when a function is desired. The number of engine/vehicle sensors and their location varies in makes and models of engines; in all, however, the ECM continually monitors each sensor for an *out-of-range condition*. When this occurs, a dash-mounted warning light system is activated and a trouble code is stored in ECM memory. This code can be extracted by the technician by means of a DDR (diagnostic data reader; see Figure 15-25).

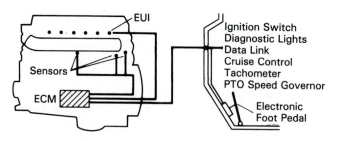

▨ ECM–Electronic Control Module
• EUI–Electronic Unit Injectors

FIGURE 15–1 *Simplified schematic of the engine-mounted ECM, sensors, and EUI (electronic unit injectors), plus the inputs and connections from the electronic foot pedal assembly and various switches for a DDEC system. (Courtesy of Detroit Diesel Corporation.)*

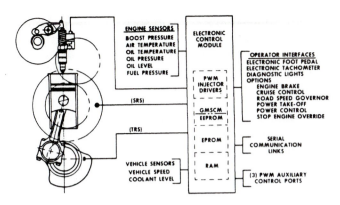

FIGURE 15–2 *Various inputs and outputs between the engine, sensors, and ECM of the DDEC system. (Courtesy of Detroit Diesel Corporation.)*

Engine Sensors and Location

Regardless of the make of electronically controlled heavy-duty diesel engine in use, they all employ engine sensors which are very similar in operation and even use identical sensors in some cases to monitor operating conditions using common technology. The various engine OEM sensors are located on the engine in similar positions. The exact location of these sensors can be seen in Figure 21-55 for Detroit Diesel, Figure 23-72 and Figure 23-73 for Caterpillar, Figure 22-85 for Cummins, and Figure 20-1 through 20-16 for Mack. The sensors and engine protective features employed by each engine OEM normally have the following elements (see Figure 21-55 for DDEC):

1. *TRS* (timing reference sensor): tells the ECM where the rotation of the engine is or when each cylinder is firing. Some OEMs (for example, Cummins) refer to this sensor as an EPS (engine position sensor; see Figure 22-85). Caterpillar employs an engine speed timing sensor (Figure 23-72 and Figure 23-73) that provides a PWM signal to the ECM, which the ECM interprets as a crankshaft position and engine speed reference.

2. *SRS* (synchronous reference sensor): advices the ECM when cylinder 1 is at TDC on the compression stroke (see Figure 21-55 for DDEC).

3. *TBS* (turbo boost sensor): provides information on intake manifold air pressure to the ECM and is used for control of white smoke and emissions.

4. *OPS* (oil pressure sensor): advises the ECM of the engine main oil gallery pressure. Engine protective features programmed into the ECM are calibrated to trigger an engine speed and power reduction feature when the oil pressure drops to a point lower than desired. If a dangerous oil pressure is sensed, the ECM warns the operator by flashing a dash-mounted red light; on some engine/vehicles it may be accompanied

by an audible buzzer. If the ECM is so programmed, automatic engine shutdown will occur after 30 seconds of low oil pressure. In some cases the system may be equipped with a manual override button to provide an extra 30 seconds of running time to allow the operator to pull a vehicle over to the side of the road safely.

5. *OTS* (oil temperature sensor): indicates the engine oil temperature at all times to the ECM. Normally, the ECM and engine protective features can be programmed to provide the same safety features as those described for a low oil pressure condition. However, a yellow dash-mounted warning light is triggered first when the oil temperature exceeds a safe, normal limit. Continued oil temperature increase to a preset maximum limit results in an engine power-down feature, followed by engine shutdown similar to that for the OPS. Many electronic engines employ this sensor at engine startup to advise the ECM to provide a fast idle speed, particularly during cold ambient conditions. In some engines the coolant temperature sensor provides the input signal to the ECM for this operating condition. This signal causes the ECM to vary the fuel injection PWM time to control white smoke on a cold engine. Normal idle speed is automatically resumed when the oil or coolant temperature reaches a predetermined limit or after a programmed engine running time.

6. *CTS* (coolant temperature sensor): used to advise the ECM of the engine coolant temperature. This sensor can be used to trigger an engine protection response; it has an automatic power-down feature and shutdown similar to that for the OPS and OTS. In addition, many heavy-duty trucks now employ this sensor to activate thermatic fan controls.

7. *CLS* (coolant level sensor): monitors the level of coolant in the radiator top tank or in a remote surge tank. Normally, this sensor is tied into the ECM engine protection system and initiates an automatic engine shutdown sequence at a low coolant level. In addition, the engine will fail to start when this sensor senses a low coolant level, and it will trigger a dash-mounted warning light.

8. *ACLS* (auxiliary coolant level sensor): indicates when the coolant level requires topping up. Positioned within the top radiator tank or remote surge tank, this sensor is located above the CLS.

9. *CPS* (coolant pressure sensor): normally employed on larger-displacement engines to closely monitor water pump/engine block pressure.

10. *CPS* (crankcase pressure sensor): usually found on larger-displacement engines in mining, stationary, and marine engine applications. This sensor can be profiled to monitor crankcase pressure direct; on two-stroke-cycle engines, it monitors air pressure

inside the air box of the two-stroke-cycle engine block. Caterpillar refers to this sensor as an *atmospheric pressure sensor*, which measures the atmospheric air pressure in the crankcase and sends a signal to the ECM.

11. *FPS* (fuel pressure sensor): usually monitors the fuel pressure on the outlet side of the secondary fuel filter. This sensor is used for diagnostics purposes.

12. *FTS* (fuel temperature sensor): provides fuel temperature information to the ECM and is normally located on the secondary fuel filter head. Changes in fuel temperature allow the ECM to adjust the PWM signal to the unit injectors, since warmer fuel expands, resulting in less horsepower.

13. *ATS* (air-temperature sensor): indicates intake manifold temperature to the ECM to allow the ECM to alter the injector PWM signal for emissions control.

14. *AAP* (ambient air pressure sensor): monitors altitude operation.

15. *EFPA* (electronic foot pedal assembly): indicates to the ECM the percentage of throttle pedal depression and therefore how much fuel is being requested by the operator. Current EFPAs are equipped with an IVS (idle validation switch) that indicates a closed throttle pedal condition and therefore that an idle speed is being requested.

16. *ITS* (idle timer shutdown): a programmable engine idle shutdown feature ranging from as low as 3 minutes to 24 hours, depending on the make of engine. For example, on a Caterpillar 3176B/3406E engine, 90 seconds before the programmed idle time is reached, the dash-mounted diagnostic lamp starts to flash rapidly. For the idle shutdown timer to function, the following operating conditions must be met:

- Idle shutdown timer feature has been programmed into the ECM.
- Vehicle parking brake must be activated/set.
- Engine must be at normal operating temperature.
- Vehicle speed must be at zero mph (km/h).
- Engine is running under a no-load condition.
- Parking brake switch has been installed to alert the ECM and the idle timer when to start the idle time-down feature.

17. *IAS* (idle adjust switch): located on the instrument panel and can be toggled to alter the hot idle rpm to eliminate shaky mirrors. Usually provides +100 and −25 rpm.

18. *EBC* (engine compression brake controls): compatible with cruise control features on trucks. While in the cruise mode, the engine brakes can be programmed to come on and off automatically to maintain a preset cruise speed. The engine brakes can be programmed to a set road speed above the cruise speed to improve the driveability of the vehicle.

19. *PGS* (pressure governor system): used on fire trucks to maintain a set water pressure by varying the engine rpm.

20. *SLS* (starter lockout sensor): indicates the engine condition to the ECM once the engine is running. This sensor prevents starter engagement to prevent grinding of the flywheel and starter pinion gears.

21. *VSS* (vehicle speed sensor): usually mounted over the vehicle transmission output shaft to provide the ECM with the speed of the vehicle. This signal is used for cruise control, vehicle speed limiting, and automatic progressive application of the engine Jake brakes to maintain a preprogrammed maximum vehicle speed. In addition, engine fan braking engages the cooling fan clutch automatically when the engine brakes are on *high*. This feature adds 20 to 45 bhp (15 to 33.5 kW) to the engine retardation for slowing down the vehicle.

22. *VSG* (variable-speed governor): supplied in the form of a hand throttle to maintain engine speed at a fixed rpm regardless of engine load; usually programmed within the ECM to provide a zero-droop condition (no speed change regardless of load).

23. *CEL* (check engine light): an amber or yellow light on the dash used to indicate to the operator that a system fault has been detected by the ECM. When activated, a trouble code is stored in the ECM memory. Depending on the severity of the condition, the engine may lose speed and power, but it will provide limp-home capability.

24. *SEL* (stop engine light): a red light on the dash that illuminates when a serious engine operating condition is detected. If the ECM has been programmed for automatic engine shutdown, the engine will shut down usually within a 30-second period. An optional feature such as an STEO (stop engine override) button can be provided to allow a temporary override condition so the operator can safely pull a truck or bus over to the side of the road.

25. *EPS* (engine protection system): a programmable feature within the ECM that provides a method to sense an out-of-range operating condition in the engine. When a sensor indicates to the ECM that the sensed condition is outside of the normal parameter (condition), the ECM systematically illuminates either the yellow or red warning lamp on the dash, and typically ramps down the engine speed and power setting. The degree of power reduction varies in different makes of engines, but it is usually from 100% to 70%; a further reduction down to about 40% occurs after the SEL (red) illuminates. Trigger sensors for this protection system usually include coolant temperature, oil temperature, oil pressure, and coolant level.

26. *VDL* (vehicle deceleration light): located on the rear of a truck or bus and illuminates when the driver takes his or her foot off the accelerator pedal, indicating that the vehicle is slowing down.

27. *PWM* (pulse-width modulation): the term used to describe the duration of time that the injector solenoid is energized and fuel is being delivered to the engine. Timed in milliseconds, or thousandths of a second, but measured in degrees of rotation of the engine crankshaft.

SENSORS

Basic Sensor Arrangement

Figure 15-3 is a simplified diagram of the basic sensor measurement system, where the sensor itself absorbs either a heat or pressure signal from a monitored engine condition. The sensor converts this signal into an electrical output and relays it to the signal processor. Within the signal processor, the sensor signal is amplified so that it can be sent to an analog or digital display; or alternatively, it may be used to activate a specific actuator on the engine or vehicle.

Signal processing can be accomplished with either analog devices or digital devices. Analog signals resemble the human voice and have a continuous waveform signal, whereas a digital signal forms a series of boxes to indicate an ON or OFF voltage condition. Analog signal processing involves amplifiers, filters, adders, multipliers, and other components; digital signal processing uses logic gates. In addition, digital processing requires the use of counters, binary adders, and microcomputers.

The IC (integrated circuit) can be analog or digital. The analog IC is one that handles or processes a wavelike analog electrical signal, such as that produced by the human voice; it is also similar to that shown on an ignition oscilloscope. An analog signal changes continuously and smoothly with time as shown in Figure 15-4. Its output signal is proportionate to its input signal.

Digital signals, on the other hand, show a more rectangular wavelength, as shown in Figure 15-5. These signals change intermittently with time, which means that, simply put, they are either on or off. This, of course, is quite different from the analog operating mode. The general characteristic of operation of the

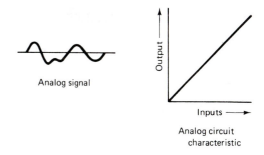

FIGURE 15-4 *Analog-wave signal shape.*

digital circuit can best be explained as follows: When the input voltage signal rises to a predetermined level, the output signal is then triggered into action. For example, assume that a sensor is feeding a varying 5-volt (V) maximum reference signal to a source such as a diode. In this condition the output signal remains at zero until the actual input signal has climbed to its maximum of 5 V.

This is why digital signals are classified as being either on or off. ON means that a signal is being sent, and OFF means that a signal is not being sent. For convenience sake, in electronics terminology, when a voltage signal is being sent (ON), the numeral 1 is used. When no voltage signal is being sent (OFF), this is indicated by the numeral 0. These numerals are used so that the computer can distinguish between an ON and OFF voltage signal.

Figures 15-6 and 15-7 show how this numeric system operates. Most sensors in use today in automotive applications are designed to operate on a 5-V reference signal. Anything above this level is considered as being in an ON, or numeral 1, condition, and any voltage below this value is considered as OFF, or 0 numeral, since the voltage signal is too low to trigger a diode response. Digital systems consist of many numbers of identical *logic gates* and *flip-flops* to perform the necessary computations.

A simplified example of an analog signal is that generated from a speedometer sensor that changes continuously as the vehicle speed increases or de-

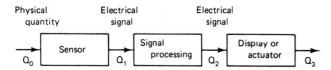

FIGURE 15-3 *Simplified sensor measurement operational system.*

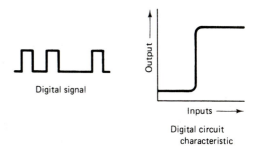

FIGURE 15-5 *Digital-wave signal shape.*

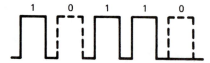

FIGURE 15-6 *Digital voltage signal in an* ON/OFF *mode (5 V reference or trigger signal).*

creases. An example of an applied digital signal that is either on or off can be related to the opening and closing of a car door. When open, the interior light comes on; therefore, the signal is at its maximum of 12 V. If, on the other hand, the door is closed, the signal is at 0 V.

Types of Sensors

Various engine/vehicle sensors are described in this chapter. The physical operating characteristics of each unit depend on the following design types: two-wire design, three-wire design, and pulse-counter design. Each of these operating types is illustrated and explained next to show how various sensors operate.

Two-Wire Design

Figure 15-8 illustrates the two-wire design type of sensor, which is basically a variable resistor in series with a known-fixed resistor contained within the ECM. Sensors that use the two-wire type of design are the CTS, OTS, FTS, MAT (manifold air temperature), and OAT (outside air temperature) units. All of these sensors operate on a varying resistance; their resistance varies inversely with temperature (thermistor principle).

Since most sensors in use in automotive applications use a base voltage input of 5 V (some use 8 V), the value of the variable resistor can be determined from the base voltage along with the known voltage drop across the fixed resistor.

The coolant and oil temperature sensors are mounted on the engine, while the fuel sensor is mounted on the fuel filter. Each sensor relays temperature information to the ECM. The ECM monitors a 5-V reference signal, which it applied to the sensor signal circuit through a resistor in the ECM. Note that these sensors are in reality a thermistor, which means that they change their internal resistance as the temperature changes. Specifically, when the sensor is cold, such as when starting up an engine that has been sit-

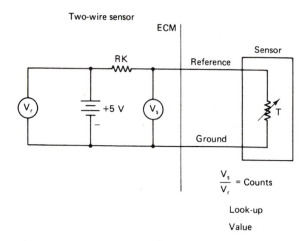

$$\frac{V_s}{V_r} = \text{Counts}$$

Look-up

Value

FIGURE 15-8 *Basic arrangement of a two-wire design sensor unit.*

ting for some time, the sensor resistance is high, and the ECM monitors a high signal voltage. As the engine warms up, however, the internal resistance of the sensor decreases and causes a similar decrease in the reference voltage signal. Therefore, the ECM interprets this reduced voltage signal as signifying a warm engine. The range of the coolant and oil temperature sensors varies with various engine/vehicle manufacturers, but normally it is between −10° and 300°F. At the low-temperature end of the scale, the resistance of the sensor tends to be about 100,000 ohm (Ω), while at the high range its internal resistance would have dropped to only 70 Ω. Figure 15-9 illustrates how a temperature of 150°F (65.5°C), which is an analog signal, is con-

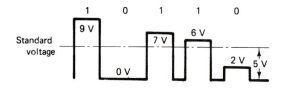

FIGURE 15-7 *Digital wave signal when the voltage values are either above or below the standard voltage references.*

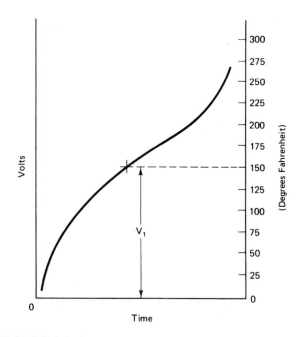

FIGURE 15-9 *Coolant temperature versus analog output voltage signal.*

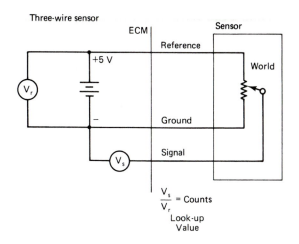

FIGURE 15–10   *Basic arrangement of a three-wire design sensor unit.*

verted from analog to digital within the A/D (analog/digital) converter. In Figure 15-9 we see a typical upward-moving sine wave which is representative of the changing voltage output signal from the oil or coolant sensor as the engine temperature increases because of the decreasing resistance value of the sensor. At a temperature of 150°F, the sensor analog output voltage is sampled by the A/D converter, which converts values into a *binary number value* or code.

Three-Wire Design

Figure 15-10 illustrates the three-wire design type of sensor arrangement, which is commonly in use in TPS (throttle position sensors), MAP (manifold absolute pressure), and BARO (barometric pressure sensors). These types of sensors have a reference voltage, a ground, and a variable wiper, with the lead coming off the wiper being the actual signal feed to the ECM. A change in the wiper's position automatically changes the signal voltage being sent back to the ECM.

Pulse Counters

Figure 15-11 illustrates the basic operation of a pulse counter. Sensors relying on this type of counting system are typically the VSS, the rpm or engine speed sensor, which could be a crankshaft- or camshaft-sensed Hall-effect type on various makes of vehicles, and also the distributor reference sensor on vehicles employing this style of ignition system.

Consider, for example, that many gasoline-powered cars and light-duty trucks today have a distributor-less ignition system. These systems rely on a crankshaft- or camshaft-mounted sensor, or both, to pick up a gear position, usually through the use of a raised tooth on the gear wheel. The resultant voltage signal produced is relayed by the sensor to the ECM, which then determines when to trigger the ignition pulse signal to the respective spark plug. On heavy-duty truck engines such as those employing the Detroit Diesel series 60 four-stroke-cycle DDEC engines, an electronic TRS (timing reference sensor) extends through an opening in the engine gear case and is positioned to provide a small air gap between it and the teeth of the crankshaft timing gear. The TRS sends a voltage signal to the ECM, which uses it to determine fuel injector solenoid operation/timing. This same engine employs an SRS (synchronous reference sensor) that is mounted to the rear of the engine gear case, where it is positioned to provide a small air gap between it and the rear of a bull gear driven from the crankshaft gear. The SRS sends a voltage signal to the ECM, which uses this information to determine engine speed.

The speed at which sensor signals are transmitted and monitored by the ECM microprocessor are usually updated a given amount of times in a second.

For those on request sensor values, the nominal response time in current ECMs used in heavy-duty trucks is 100 milliseconds.

FIGURE 15–11   *Pulse counter mode of operation.*

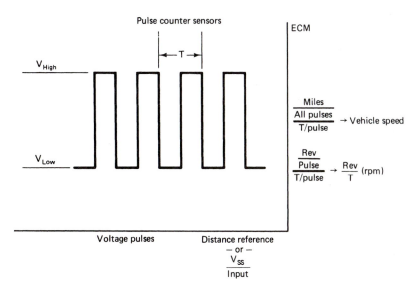

Oil Pressure Sensor Operation

To understand just how a typical sensor operates in a heavy-duty electronically controlled diesel truck engine, let's consider the oil pressure sensor as one example. The sensor outputs an analog signal, with the sensor resistance changing as a result of engine oil pressure changes. This oil pressure and sensor resistance change, in turn, creates changes in the sensor–resistor–battery circuit current flow. Any current increase will similarly create an increase in the voltage value across the resistor. Consequently, during engine operation, any oil pressure change is reflected by a sensor voltage output that the analog-to-digital subsystem will process accordingly.

Consider an oil pressure sensor with a sensor range between 0 and 65 psi (0 to 448 kPa) with a sensor output update rate of once per second and a resolution of 0.5 psi per bit. During engine operation, if the sensor failed, the check engine light would illuminate on the dash; if low oil pressure at the current engine speed is sensed, the check engine light will illuminate and the ECM would power down the engine. Unsafe oil pressure would result in the SEL (stop engine light) illuminating, followed 30 seconds later by an ECM-actuated engine shutdown procedure. If the engine is equipped with an SEO (stop engine override), the shutdown sequence can be delayed by holding the SEO button in for a couple more times only, after which the ECM shuts the engine off.

For ease of instruction, let's assume that the voltage across the oil pressure sensor is converted from an analog to a digital signal by an A/D converter in the form of a VCO (voltage-controlled oscillator), where the sensor voltage varies from 0 to 10 V. As you know from earlier information, the digital system is a square-wave signal typical of that shown in Figure 15-11. The amplitude (voltage strength) changes of the digital signals would have very fast ON/OFF reactions, varying from 0 to 5 V, with 0 V representing a logic number 0 and the 5 V amplitude representing a logic number 1.

Figure 15-12 illustrates a simplified system that represents this oil pressure sensor function. If a scale is selected to represent a change of engine oil pressure of from 0 to 65 psi (0 to 448 kPa), a change in voltage from 0 to 10 V can be used to duplicate/scale this change in oil pressure. If we assume that the VCO's output oscillates back and forth between 0 and 10 V based on changing engine oil pressure, the frequency of the voltage signal (how often it happens) in our scaled example would vary between 400 and 1000 hertz (Hz), or 400 to 1000 times a second, based on the 0 to 10 V input signal to the VCO. A change in voltage from 0 to 10 V would cause a change in frequency of 600 (= 1000 − 400) Hz in our example. The voltage output of the VCO is connected to one input of an AND logic gate. (For a description of an AND gate and its truth table combination refer to *Mid-Heavy Duty Truck Electrical and Electronic Systems* by Robert N. Brady published in 1991 by Prentice Hall, Upper Saddle River, NJ.)

Due to the operation of the AND logic gate shown to the immediate right of the VCO in Figure 15-12, the output of the VCO is connected to one input of the AND gate, while the other input is held to a logic level 1. This results in the output of the AND gate being a reproduction of the VCO's output. But when the second input from the VCO is at logic 0, the output of the AND gate would be a steady logic 0. Therefore, by actively controlling the logic levels on the second input, the VCO's output pulse can be gated through for a given amount of time, then blocked, then gated through again, with the process being repeated over and over.

For scaling purposes, let's consider that when a zero engine oil pressure exists, we will also have zero volts across the oil pressure sensor resistor. At 0 lb oil pressure, we will equate this to a frequency of 400 Hz. With the engine running and the oil pump creating 65 psi (448 kPa) of pressure, the voltage value is 10 V and the frequency is equivalent to a VCO output of 1000 Hz. If we also assume that the engine oil pressure rises linearly (gradual straight-line increase), there is a

FIGURE 15–12 *Simplified electronic oil pressure sensor system. (Reprinted with permission, copyright 1995, Society of Automotive Engineers, Inc.)*

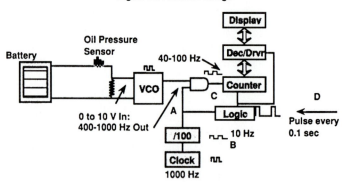

Digital Oil Pressure Gauge

direct relationship created between the oil pressure, the voltage, and the frequency. Since our scale runs between 400 and 1000 Hz to represent 0 to 65 psi (0 to 448 kPa), this means that over the 600-Hz range between these two numbers, we can scale the VCO's output frequency to represent any given oil pressure. For example, based on our graduated scale, a 32.5 psi (224 kPa) oil pressure would correspond to a signal of 5 V and a frequency halfway between 400 and 1000, which would be 700 Hz. Therefore, as you can see, it is quite easy to convert a given oil pressure at the sensor into a voltage input at the VCO, along with a frequency output from the VCO. The engine oil pressure sensor used on the DDEC system on Detroit Diesel's 71, 92, series 50, 55 and 60 heavy-duty truck diesel engines have an update rate of once per second; therefore, when the oil pressure is 65 psi (448 kPa), the VCO will be outputting a signal every second that is representative of this pressure. In our descriptive example, this would be equivalent to the VCO outputting 1000 square-wave pulses (digitally shaped) per second. For better resolution or monitoring of the changing oil pressure system, we could choose to set the logic gate up so that it is open for 0.1 second. This can be achieved by directing a signal to the second AND gate input, which has a logic 1 period equal to 0.1 second.

We can ensure this operating condition by employing a square-wave oscillating clock with a fixed frequency of 1000 Hz. The output can then be directed through a series of logic ICs (integrated circuits) that effectively divide the input count by 10, then by a further 10. Reference to Figure 15-12 indicates this clock system is identified as /100 above the 1000-Hz clock. This means that the 1000-Hz signal is divided by 100 to produce a square output wave with a 10-Hz frequency. Consequently, the signal would have a time period of 1/10 or 0.1 second.

If the logic gate pulses open for 0.1 second, it is closed, then opened once again on a continuing basis; then every time the logic gate is opened, 100 square waves will pass through as long as the oil pressure remains at 65 psi (448 kPa). If the engine speed is reduced, or the oil pressure were to drop to 32.5 psi (224 kPa), the VCO frequency would be reduced from 1000 to 700 Hz. This means that in a 0.1-second period, only 70 square-wave pulses will pass through the logic gate. When the 10-Hz signal is a logic 1 input, the VCO's output will pass through the AND gate. When the 10-Hz signal is logic 0, the AND gate's output is logic 0. Therefore, when the oil pressure is 65 psi (448 kPa), the internal digital clock counter will count 100 pulses in 0.1 second. At a pressure of 32.5 psi (224 kPa), it will count 70 pulses every 0.1 second. With zero oil pressure, the counter will register 40 pulses every 0.1

second. The clock counter's output is then input to a decoder/driver IC to drive a digital display that allows the truck driver to visually determine the engine oil pressure condition at a glance. Generally, the output of the decoder/driver is a latched output. This means that the output value changes only when a latch pulse, shown as item D in Fig. 15-12, is input to a latch input.

Electronic Foot Pedal Assembly

A unique feature of the electronic fuel system is that the foot throttle pedal assembly consists of a small potentiometer (variable resistor) rather than a direct mechanical linkage as is found on mechanical engines. This throttle arrangement is often referred to as a *drive by wire system*, since no mechanical linkage is used; only electrical wires transmit the position of the throttle to the ECM. The potentiometer is electrically connected to the ECM.

The throttle position sensor shown in Figure 15-13 contains a potentiometer (variable resistor) that is designed to output a voltage in direct response to the depression of the pedal. This sensor is designed to receive a 5-V input reference signal from the ECM. However, the output voltage is totally dependent on how far down the pedal is pushed for any given condition. When the throttle pedal is at its normal idle position, its voltage output is low; therefore, the signal sent to the ECM advises the system of its relative position, and the solenoid on each fuel injector is activated for a short pulse-width time. This results in a small delivery of fuel to each cylinder and therefore a low idle speed.

As the operator pushes the throttle pedal down, the voltage signal from the sensor increases, and when the ECM recognizes this voltage change, it sends out a signal to activate the solenoid on each fuel injector for a longer pulse width period. This results in a greater amount of fuel being delivered to the cylinders and therefore a higher speed. The actual quantity of fuel delivered and therefore the horsepower produced by the engine also depend on the engine coolant temperature, the turbocharger boost pressure, and both the oil pressure and temperature sensor readings. Each one of these sensors is continually relaying a voltage signal back to the ECM, which then computes the injector pulse width signal.

Newer models of the EFPA (electronic foot pedal assembly) feature an integrated idle validation switch/sensor that combines two electrical signal generators: the accelerator position sensor (APS) and the idle validation switch (IVS) in a single housing. The two components are isolated electrically but are actuated by a common mechanical link to the accelerator pedal. The

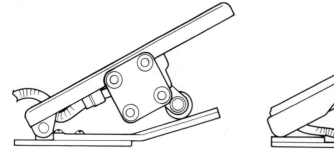
Bendix

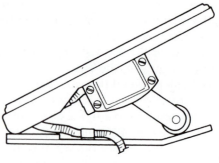
Williams

Electronic Foot Pedal Assemblies

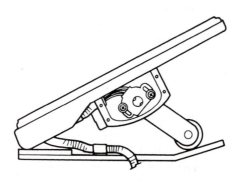

Throttle Position Sensor

FIGURE 15–13 EFPA (electronic foot pedal assembly) designs also showing the TPS (throttle position sensor). (Courtesy of Detroit Diesel Corporation.)

calibration between the two signals is set at the factory and will maintain uninterrupted adjustment throughout the life of the unit. The IVS provides verification independent of throttle pot movement that the pedal is, or is not, in the idle position. This scheme allows the ECM to detect potential throttle assembly problems. The IVS can be a separate mechanical or an integrated switch with the potentiometer.

Detroit Diesel, Caterpillar, and Cummins employ the same basic EFPA assembly, although the installation angle of the EFPA on its mounting plate varies to suit different truck floor pan installations. The pedal moves through approximately 20° from idle to WOT (wide-open throttle), thereby varying the voltage signal back to the ECM. The EFPA receives a 5-V input reference voltage signal from the ECM, and the return voltage signal is based on the percentage of throttle depression. Another feature of this EFPA with IVS and APS is that the automatic transmission shift point-control can be regulated by the integrated sensor. At a specified voltage, the transmission can be downshifted to a lower gear range. An engine retarder signal may be utilized to invoke an exhaust brake or other engine

transmission retarder device through the idle validation setting within the EFPA.

ELECTRONIC UNIT INJECTORS

In this section we describe briefly the operation of an electronically controlled unit injector. At this time, the high-speed heavy-duty electronic unit injectors employed by Detroit Diesel, Caterpillar, Cummins, Volvo, and Robert Bosch depend on an engine camshaft rocker arm activation system. The exception is the HEUI (hydraulically actuated electronic unit injector) codesigned by Caterpillar and Navistar for use on Navistar's T444E (7.3-L) medium-duty truck engine. See Chapter 23 for more details.

The electronic unit injector has an electric solenoid that receives a command signal from an ECM, which determines the start of injection as well as the amount of fuel metered. As we discussed earlier, a series of electronic engine and vehicle sensors are used to advise the ECM of the various operating conditions, much the same as those now in wide use on passenger cars.

System Operation

Figure 15-2 illustrates the basic arrangement of an EUI (electronic unit injector) system on a heavy-duty truck engine. This diagram shows a simplified layout of the system. Each system employs a throttle position sensor which contains a potentiometer (variable resistor) assembled into the pedal assembly. There is no direct connection between the throttle pedal and the injectors, since the position of the pedal sends out a signal to the ECM to let it know the percentage of throttle opening. In addition to the pedal position, the ECM receives input signals from a number of sensors, such as the engine turbo boost, intake manifold air temperature, fuel temperature, oil pressure, oil temperature,

coolant level or coolant temperature, engine speed, and vehicle road speed. Prior to startup, the engine receives signals from both a timing reference sensor and a synchronous reference sensor, so that the ECM knows the relative piston positions and can then initiate fuel delivery to the injectors. Some unit injectors, such as the Detroit Diesel two-stroke-cycle 71 and 92 models, the Caterpillar 3176, C10, C12, and 3116 engine models, along with the Cummins Celect system are operated through an engine-camshaft-actuated pushrod and rocker arm assembly (Figure 15-14A). On Detroit Diesel's series 50 and 60, the Caterpillar 3406E, the Volvo VE D12, and Deere's 10.5-L and 12.5-L Power Techmodels, an overhead camshaft operates

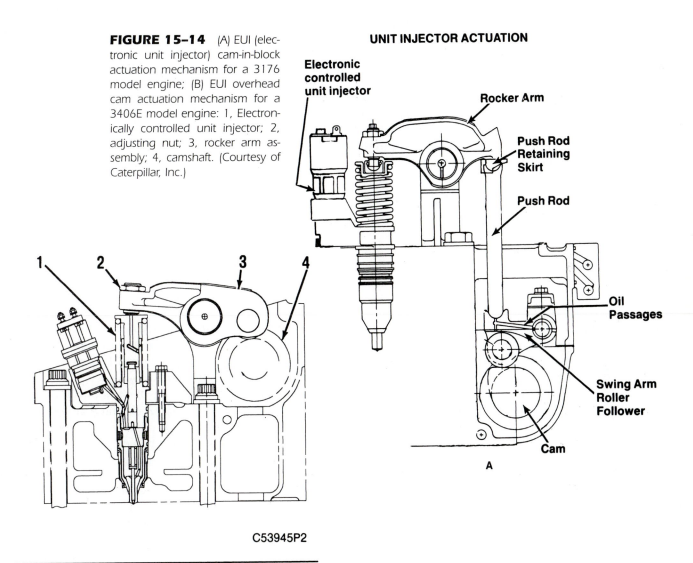

FIGURE 15–14 (A) EUI (electronic unit injector) cam-in-block actuation mechanism for a 3176 model engine; (B) EUI overhead cam actuation mechanism for a 3406E model engine: 1, Electronically controlled unit injector; 2, adjusting nut; 3, rocker arm assembly; 4, camshaft. (Courtesy of Caterpillar, Inc.)

UNIT INJECTOR ACTUATION

Electronic controlled unit injector

Rocker Arm

Push Rod Retaining Skirt

Push Rod

Oil Passages

Swing Arm Roller Follower

Cam

A

C53945P2

Unit Injector Mechanism
(1) Electronically controlled unit injector. (2) Adjusting nut.
(3) Rocker arm assembly. (4) Camshaft.

B

the unit injector rocker arm (Figure 15-14B). Each injector is controlled by an injector-mounted electric solenoid.

There is no mechanically operated fuel rack on any electronically controlled unit injector; therefore, the amount of fuel metered and the timing are controlled by the signal generated at the ECM, based on the various sensor outputs and the throttle position. This ECM signal to the injector, known as a PWM (pulse-width-modulated) signal, lasts for a given amount of crankshaft degrees. For a given speed, the longer the solenoid is energized, the greater the amount of fuel injected. Conversely, the shorter the PWM signal, the lower the volume of fuel injected into the combustion chamber. Generation of high-enough fuel pressure for injection purposes requires the action of the rocker arm assembly, as shown in Figure 15-14. Figure 15-15 illustrates the internal injector plunger, which is forced down by the rocker arm inside its barrel/bushing. Note that a small spill valve is shown to the right-hand side of the diagram; this spill valve is held open by a spring that will prevent any fuel pressure increase beyond that created by the fuel system's fuel supply pump. As the injector plunger moves down, fuel will simply flow or spill from this valve and return to the fuel tank. For injection to begin, this spill valve must be closed by a signal from the ECM energizing the

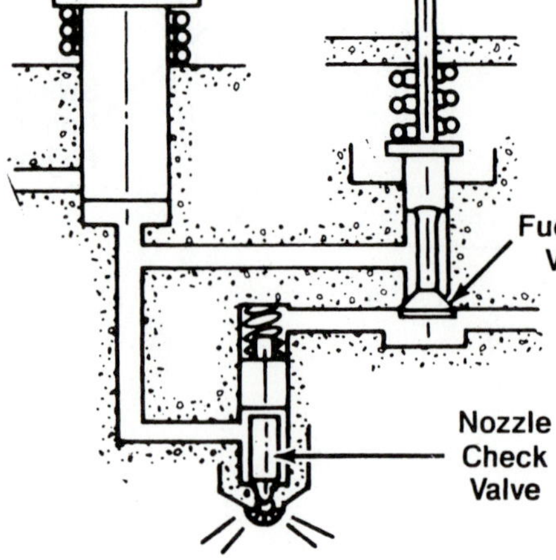

small electric solenoid, which sits on top of the injector. Once the solenoid is energized by the PWM signal from the ECM, the downward-moving injector plunger will create a rapid increase in the trapped fuel pressure below it. Once this pressure is high enough, the needle valve in the injector spray tip will be opened against its return spring, allowing fuel to be injected into the combustion chamber. Any time that the injector solenoid is de-energized, the small spill valve is opened by its spring, and fuel injection comes to an immediate end.

The basic difference between a mechanically operated and rack-controlled unit injector plunger, and the injector used on electronic-equipped engines, is that there is no helix on the electronic injector plunger; it is simply a solid plunger (Figure 15-16). Each one of the electronic unit injector systems is equipped with an electronic speed control system, which is a part of the solid-state circuitry contained within the ECM housing. On some systems, the ECM is cooled by routing diesel fuel through a cooling plate attached to the ECM mounting bracket to maintain the electronic components at an acceptable operating temperature.

Fuel Injector Operation

In the DDEC injector used with Detroit Diesel's series 50 and 60 engines, the fuel feed to the injector is similar to that found on other electronic engines. The fuel enters the injector through two fuel inlet filter screens around the circumference of the body between the third and fourth O-rings (seals) (Figure 15-17). All the injectors receive this fuel in the same manner, through the inlet manifold fitting. Fuel not required for combustion purposes, but which is used for cooling and lubrication of internal injector parts, exits the injector at the small fuel return hole located between the second and third O-rings and flows out of the restricted fitting connection shown in Figure 21-5B, where it returns directly to the fuel tank.

The actual identification of component parts is clearly shown in Figure 15-17 for the series 60 electronically controlled injector. The functions of the injector are the same as those for a non-DDEC-equipped unit:

- Creates the high pressure required for efficient injection. This is achieved by the action of the overhead camshaft pivoting the rocker arm through its roller follower to force the injector follower down against its external return spring. Therefore, a mechanical means is still required to force the internal injector plunger down to raise the trapped fuel to a high enough pressure to lift the needle valve at the bottom of the injector off its seat.

UNIT INJECTOR SCHEMATIC

FIGURE 15–15 *Basic concept of operation for an electronically controlled unit fuel injector. (Courtesy of Caterpillar, Inc.)*

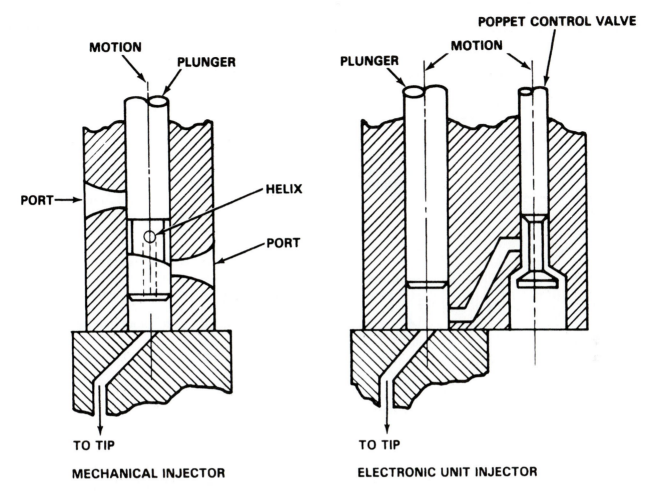

FIGURE 15–16 *Comparison of the unit injector plunger design differences between a mechanical and electronically controlled model. (Courtesy of Detroit Diesel Corporation.)*

- Meters and injects the precise amount of fuel required to handle the load. This quantity of fuel is determined by the ECM, which in turn continually receives input signals from the various engine sensors. The ECM sends out a pulse width signal to close the small internal poppet valve. This action allows the downward-moving plunger to increase the pressure of the fuel to lift the needle valve from its seat and injection begins. Injection lasts as long as the ECM is sending out a signal to energize the EUI (electronic unit injector) solenoid. As soon as the ECM deenergizes the solenoid, a spring opens the small poppet valve and the high fuel pressure that was holding the needle valve open is lost to the return line; therefore, injection ends. The longer the pulse width time, the greater the volume of fuel that will be injected.
- Atomizes the fuel so that it will penetrate the air mass within the cylinder and initiate combustion. This atomization is achieved by the downward-

moving plunger, which has to increase the fuel pressure to approximately 5000 psi (34,475 kPa) to lift the needle valve from its seat. The fuel is then forced through the multiple small holes (orifices) in the spray tip, which causes the fuel droplets to break down into a finely atomized state as they approach injection pressures of 28,000 psi (193,060 kPa).
- Permits continuous fuel flow in excess of that required for combustion purposes to ensure cooling and lubrication of all injector components.

The injection timing (start of injection) and metering (quantity) are controlled by the pulse width signal from the ECM through to the EUI. The longer the EUI solenoid is energized, the longer the small poppet valve will remain closed and the greater the amount of fuel that will be injected. In effect, by holding the poppet valve closed longer, we are lengthening the effective stroke of the downward-moving plunger, since it will always move down the same distance regardless

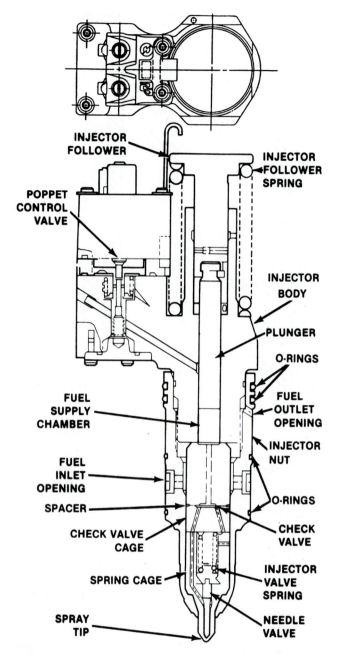

INJECTOR FOLLOWER

INJECTOR FOLLOWER SPRING

POPPET CONTROL VALVE

INJECTOR BODY

PLUNGER

O-RINGS

FUEL SUPPLY CHAMBER

FUEL OUTLET OPENING

INJECTOR NUT

FUEL INLET OPENING

O-RINGS

SPACER

CHECK VALVE CAGE

CHECK VALVE

SPRING CAGE

INJECTOR VALVE SPRING

SPRAY TIP

NEEDLE VALVE

FIGURE 15–17 *Cross-sectional view and identification of major parts of a series 60 engine electronically controlled unit injector assembly. (Courtesy of Detroit Diesel Corporation.)*

of the pulse width time. This is so because the lift of the camshaft lobe will always be the same.

When the poppet valve is closed by the EUI solenoid activation, which is called *response-time feedback,* the ECM uses the information to monitor and adjust fuel injection timing. This action ensures that there will be no injector-to-injector variation in the start of injection timing. The EEPROM (electrically erasable programmable read-only memory) chip set within the

ECM is programmed with a pulse width program for each particular engine and application; therefore, the maximum amount of fuel injected depends on this EEPROM information.

ELECTRONIC CONTROL MODULES

All electronically controlled engines incorporate an engine-mounted ECM or ECU (electronic control module or unit). Illustrations in this chapter indicate the location of various ECMs in different engine makes. The wiring harness connections to and from the ECM differ slightly in engine makes; however, all systems generally incorporate several types of wire harness:

- The engine harness connector to connect all of the sensors and switches to the ECM. This harness is supplied by the engine manufacturer to allow the engine to run.
- The injector harness to allow unit injector operation.
- The power harness to carry battery power to the ECM.
- An OEM harness to interface with all of the cab controls and ECM-controlled instrumentation.

Each engine manufacturer uses a generic ECM across its line of engines. Thus when the engine reaches the end of the assembly line, it is a simple matter to program it according to the end user's requirements and desired options as indicated on the sales order data sheet. Figure 15-18 illustrates how this is

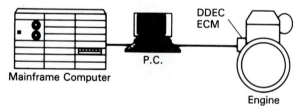

Mainframe Computer   P.C.   DDEC ECM   Engine

EEPROM CALIBRATION

Basic Rating	Customer Options
• BHP/RPM	• Engine Protection (Warning or Shutdown)
• Governor Features	• Road Speed/Cruise Control
• Low & High Idle	• Max Speed • Axle Ratio
• Droop	• Tires Rev./Mile • Transmission Data
	• Vehicle Speed Sensor
	• Power Control
	• Special Application Features

FIGURE 15–18 *Example of EEPROM (electrically erasable programmable read-only memory) end-of-line ECM program calibration for an electronically controlled heavy-duty diesel engine. (Courtesy of Detroit Diesel Corporation.)*

accomplished by connecting a PC (personal computer) to the engine ECM. Information stored in the factory mainframe computer downloads specific engine operating parameters through the PC and into the engine ECMs double-EE prom chip, more commonly identified by the letters EEPROM (electrically erasable programmable read-only memory). This information contains the engine calibration configurations such as maximum engine governed speed, governor droop characteristics, cruise control features, maximum vehicle road speed, transmission gear-down protection, PTO (power takeoff) operating features, idle shutdown timer, fuel injector information, horsepower rating, engine data list, diagnostic trouble codes, and engine/trip data. Once the vehicle or equipment is placed into service, a number of ECM operating parameters can be changed by an authorized OEM through use of a portable *programming station* similar to the one featured in Figure 21-53. This suitcase-mounted system includes a laptop computer and special telephone modem and engine hookup harnesses to allow connection to the factory mainframe computer when it is necessary to change engine horsepower settings, and so on. If an engine horsepower setting is altered, or if major alterations to the engine parameters are required while the engine is still under warranty, the OEM needs to know what changes are being made. This reprogramming feature can cost the engine user from several hundred to several thousand dollars, particularly if a higher horsepower setting is desired, because experience proves that higher horsepower engines tend to cost more because of service failures than do lower power-rated engines. The user pays extra dollars to cover the anticipated possible failure costs charged back to the OEM while the engine is under an extended warranty period.

A field service technician can access ECM information with the use of a hand-held DDR (diagnostic data reader) similar to the MPSI (Microprocessor Systems, Inc.) ProLink 9000 model shown in Figure 15-25. Access is controlled by the adoption of an electronic password, which is usually selected by the end user at the time of ordering the engine. Thousands of passwords are available and can be chosen by the owner or fleet management personnel. Without knowledge of the specific password (name or numbers), no changes can be made to the system operating parameters; therefore, system security is maintained. System security is usually offered to users in three forms:

1. *No password.* This option allows anyone to change selected options within a given range using a hand-held DDR connected to the DDL (diagnostic data link) of the engine ECM.

2. *Changeable password.* Only individual people with access to the password can make selected changes utilizing the DDR.

3. *System lockout.* A specific password is provided that allows only an authorized representative of the engine dealer to make changes to various options such as the horsepower or major engine settings.

ECM Operation

The ECM is the brains of the system. It continually receives input voltage signals from the various engine and vehicle sensors and computes these signals to determine the length of the EUI pulse width modulated signal. The longer the injector solenoid is energized, the greater will be the fuel delivered to the combustion chamber. Because of the high current switching requirements necessary for operation of the individual electronic unit injectors, the voltage signal from the ECM is sent to a series of drivers contained within the single ECM housing.

Introduction to Pulse-Width Modulation

Frequency is defined as the number of times in 1 second that a modulated electrical signal (voltage in this case) completes a cycle. Frequency is measured in units of hertz (Hz). *Cycles per second* and *hertz* are synonymous. For example, a signal modulating at a frequency of 10 Hz completes 10 cycles every second. An example of a modulated digital signal is illustrated in Figure 15-19.

In the case of engine controls, the electrical signal to the injection solenoids might have a frequency of 63 Hz during operation. This means that each second is divided into 63 segments or cycles during which the voltage will be ON for a period of time. The percentage of time the voltage is present inside each 1/63 second is called the solenoid's duty cycle. A 100% duty cycle indicates a maximum signal to the solenoid. A 0% duty cycle indicates a minimum or zero signal to the solenoid.

Pulse-width modulation is the ability of the ECU to vary the width (%) of the voltage ON time during a cycle. As the pulse width (or duty cycle) is increased, the solenoid is ON longer (see Figure 15-19).

Computer Programming

Although each computer contains the same major basic components for successful operation, the system must be programmed with a set of instructions that, in effect, tell the computer what it must do.

With its diodes, transistors, and resistors, the computer cannot accept a program that has been written in the normal everyday form of letters and numbers. Therefore, one function of a computer program is to

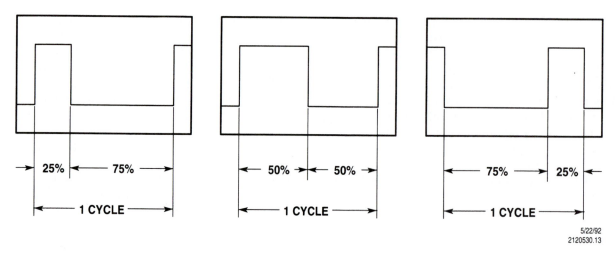

5/22/92
2120530.13

FIGURE 15-19 *Sample waveforms.*

transform data into a recognizable computer language so that the computer's solid-state devices can react to various commands. This requires that the input analog-voltage signals from the various sensor devices be converted into digital form (1's for ON and 0's for OFF).

Figure 15-20 illustrates, in simplified form, the wave sine for an analog signal and the rectangular box shape of the digital sine wave. The operation of both of these sine waves was discussed earlier.

Although we could take the regular digital numbers of 1 and 0 and program the computer, it would be very difficult to understand and use strings of 1's and 0's, particularly when we would need to use thousands of numbers. Therefore, to simplify this bulky system into a more manageable state, a special programming language has been developed.

Minicomputers in use in automobiles and trucks perform a limited number of calculations when compared to that of a large mainframe computer in an office or factory. Therefore, their programs are fairly simple to construct. A fixed program is built directly into the computer at the factory and is commonly referred to as hard wiring, because it is burned into the PROM (programmable read-only memory) or ROM (read-only memory) unit integrated chip by a laser beam in the latest systems. The PROM unit cannot be altered unless it is removed and replaced with another memory chip. EPROM (electrical PROM) or EEPROMs (electrically erasable PROMs) can be altered.

Binary Notation

Since the computer is constructed to understand only digital voltage signals, which are either in the ON (1) or OFF (0) mode, the many combinations of these numbers are represented in what is called *binary form*. What this means is that only the numerals 1 or 0 are used rather than the numbers from 0 through 9, which would represent 10 possible numbers.

To convert the decimal numbers into binary notation or form, a device within the minicomputer known as an *encoder* is required. In addition, to convert digital data (that is, binary numbers) into decimal form at any time, the computer also contains a *decoder*. Table 15-1 illustrates the system of numbers used with the binary system of notation. This is the system of numbers used to tell the computer what is going on at any time.

The binary system of numbers used with a computer is commonly called a *base 2 system*, while the conventional decimal system using 10 digits is known as a *base 10 system*. The word *decimal* is derived from the Latin word for *ten*.

The computer can interpret numbers only in the base 2 system. Since only zeros or ones (0's = OFF and 1's = ON) are continually produced by the various input sensors (analog-to-digital conversion done through

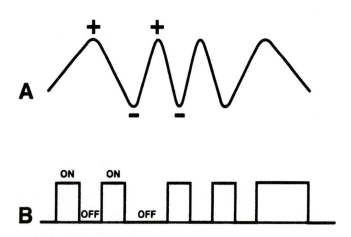

FIGURE 15-20 *(A) Analog signal; (B) digital binary signal.*

TABLE 15–1 *Minicomputer binary notation (base 2) system of numbering versus decimal (base 10) system*

Decimal base 10 system	Binary base 2 system
0	0000
1	0001
2	0010
3	0011
4	0100
5	0101
6	0110
7	0111
8	1000
9	1001
10	1010
11	1011
12	1100
13	1101
14	1110
15	1111
16	10000
255	11111111
256	100000000

an analog-to-digital converter within the computer unit), some form of equitable conversion system must be employed. Table 15-1 illustrates a comparison between a base 2 and a base 10 system. Note, for example, that the binary number 0011 is read and interpreted as the number "zero–zero–one–one," not as the number eleven.

Bits and Bytes

The digital signals created and interpreted in the computer are, as we now know, identified by binary numbers of 1 or 0, with 1 being an ON signal and with 0 representing an OFF signal (see Figure 15-20). These 1's and 0's are commonly referred to as *bits*, which is a word combination form contrived from the two words *binary digits*. A *bit* is the term used to indicate one unit of data or information and is indicated to the computer by the numeral 1 or 0. Each one of these digital numbers contains a very small unit of information. Therefore, to handle large amounts of usable information, the computer is designed to combine and handle these separate bits into words of different lengths known as *bytes* (Figure 15-21). Various computers are designed to handle information data in word lengths of 4, 8, 16, 32, or 64 bits.

The term *kilobyte* or the letter "K" indicates that the memory storage unit of the CPU can hold 1000 bytes.

Logic Circuits

Since microprocessors operate on digital signals, any analog signal must be converted to a digital signal so that the feedback information from any sensor can be readily understood and acted upon. Components within the computer are designed and programmed to recognize voltage signals by a number assigned to a specific input signal. Because of the many functions that the computer is asked to do, the various input signals are converted to a specific binary digit number through the use of logic gates, briefly discussed below. Operating conditions that are sensed by specific sensors attached to the engine/vehicle, output voltage signals that are fed into the on-board electronic control module (minicomputer), where the various solid-state devices, assisted by the different logic gates, are able to interpret these input data's binary digit (bit) representation of the analog sensor's amplitude. The electronic control module then outputs a voltage signal to the diesel fuel injectors, for example, to control how long they operate. In this way the amount of fuel delivered to the engine cylinders becomes proportional to the throttle position. Similarly, an output voltage signal

FIGURE 15–21 *Example of the translation of digital signals into binary form. (Courtesy of Allison Transmission Division; GMC Corp.)*

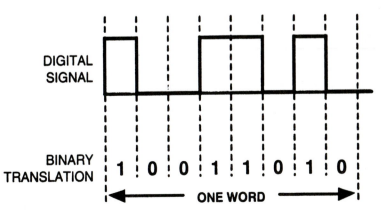

from the computer controls the injection timing and any other sensed components.

Paramount to the importance of ICs is the operation of the transistors. The converted digital voltage signals or circuits are known as *logic circuits*, and they consist of a series or combinations of varying types of systems and numbers, and interconnection patterns that are commonly referred to as *gates*. These gates are designed to accept voltage signals and logically make sense of them. In effect, they process two or more voltage signals. This is why they are called *logic gates*. They have the ability to make some sense out of all the various voltage feedback signals that are fed to the computer from the numerous sensors on the vehicle.

The various sensors used with each system were discussed earlier in this chapter. Sensors continually input voltage signals to the ECM when the engine is first cranked and is running. The idle rpm, fuel input, and therefore the horsepower developed at a given load/speed are determined by the injector solenoid pulse width signal, based on the various inputs from all the sensors used with the system.

The timers used are the basis for the fuel delivery system and have the following major functions:

- Time between cylinders (measured as crank degrees)
- Time from reference signal to injector solenoid turn on
- Solenoid response time
- Solenoid ON time
- Real-time program events

For each cylinder, a timer requests the beginning of injection (BOI), and the pulse width (PW) time (effective injector plunger stroke) is converted from degrees of crankshaft angle to a time reference.

Initiation of a cylinder injection sequence is started with the time delay between the beginning of the timing reference signal to actually turning the solenoid on. This time delay is estimated from the time between the last two sets of timing signals and subsequently reduced by the previously measured solenoid response time. Pulse width or injector solenoid ON time (fuel being injected) is determined by converting the requested crank angle degrees sensor signal to an equivalent time period plus the solenoid response time.

ECM Control Functions

The ECM receives the various sensor voltage signals and sends out a command pulse to the unit injector based on throttle position and engine speed. The peak torque rpm and actual torque shaping are determined by scheduling fuel pulse width (injector plunger effective stroke) based on engine speed at full throttle. The speed governor is designed to maintain a precise speed setting for all engine loads from the information stored in the calibration EEPROM. (See Chapter 17 for details on the electronic governor.) From this information, the governor has the ability to calibrate droop, which is the difference between maximum full-load and maximum no-load speeds. The system is designed for closed-loop control, whereby all sensors are providing input signals to the ECM so that the desired idle speed can be set for accessory performance and fuel economy; therefore, PTO (power takeoff) functions can be handled by establishing a new set speed when a load is applied to the engine.

On each system there is a built-in flexibility feature for calibrating droop from 0 to 150 rpm, to provide the best performance from engine speed/vehicle gearing. Zero droop can be programmed into the system to limit vehicle speed by setting the maximum full-load engine speed to match the maximum vehicle road speed. In addition, the system can be programmed for two-speed logic, whereby the maximum full-load rpm of the engine can be reduced any time that the transmission is in top gear. One or more switches can be used to indicate what gear the transmission is in, to limit vehicle speed or allow an extended rpm operating range in one or more gears for better fuel economy or performance improvement. The rated speed is determined by a switch input to the ECM. Improved cold starting of the engine is established by using a voltage signal from the engine oil temperature sensor to provide a 15% improvement over a nonelectronic engine.

Another feature of the electronic system is reducing white smoke on startup of a cold engine by increasing the idle-speed setting, along with advanced injection timing to allow faster engine warm-up. The idle speed is reduced and the injection timing is retarded as the engine warms up to ensure lower fuel consumption, reduced exhaust emissions, and lower combustion noise. If the ECM has been programmed to do so, a 3- to 100-minute idle shutdown can be incorporated into the electronic system. This shutdown timer starts its count once the engine is idling and the vehicle spring parking brakes are activated. An engine airflow turbocharged discharge pressure transducer sensor set for approximately 2 atm (29.4 psi) absolute, along with an engine speed sensor, provides improved engine acceleration as well as an improvement in engine torque because of the faster response of the electronic system. An air temperature sensor is also used to provide optimum timing for best fuel consumption based on changing air temperatures.

The electronic distributor unit (EDU) contained within the ECM functions as the high-current switching unit for actuation of the unit injector solenoids as well as monitoring the solenoid voltage waveform to sense valve closure. The EDU sources its current through a linearly controlled pass transistor circuit from the vehicle battery. Because of the high current generated by the current regulators, a cold plate using the engine fuel flow as the cooling medium provides a heat sink for the ECM on some electronic engine applications. The average current draw for various truck engine models is between 1 and 3 amperes (A) at idle speed to between 3 and 8 A at full-load engine rpm based on the number of cylinders and governed engine speed.

The cruise control interface system can use either the vehicle or the engine speed as the control input, while vehicle brake, set/coast, and resume/acceleration switch inputs provide drive commands. The engine brake operates when the ECM senses that the engine is in an unfueled state so that the engine brake can be applied. Output from the ECM is provided to interface with the engine braking system.

Each ECM contains two types of memory.

1. The EEPROM (electronically erasable programmable read-only memory) unit, which has been designed for use with a particular engine speed and horsepower setting, and coded for use in a particular truck based on its transmission and axle ratios as well as tire size, and so on. The EEPROM chip allows any engine to have its speed and horsepower settings changed without completely replacing the ECM.

2. The RAM (random-access memory) unit, which continually receives updated information from all the various engine/vehicle sensors to allow the ECM to be advised of any changes to the operating parameters for the engine vehicle during operation. In effect, the RAM unit becomes the working scratch pad of the ECM during engine operation.

ECM Safety Precautions
When working around electronic engines, major safety precautions must be observed.

Welding
Disconnect the vehicle batteries and the plug-in harnesses to the ECM to prevent any possibility of ECM damage during welding.

Electrical Shock
Never disconnect or connect any wires or harness connectors, particularly at the ECM, when the engine is running or when the ignition key switch is turned on. Also, remember that electronic unit injectors receive a PWM signal from the ECM that can range as high as

90 V when the engine is running. *Do not* come in contact with the injector terminals while the engine is running!

When handling an electronic part that has an electrostatic-discharge-sensitive sticker (Figure 15-22), follow these guidelines to reduce any possible electrostatic charge buildup on your body and the electronic part:

- Do not open the package until it is time to install the part.
- Avoid touching electrical terminals of the part.
- Before removing the part from its package, ground the package to a known good ground on the vehicle.
- Always touch a known good ground before handling the part. This should be repeated while handling the part and more frequently after sliding across the seat, sitting down from a standing position, or walking a distance.

Turbocharger Shield
It is sometimes necessary to operate an engine with the ducting to the intake side of the turbocharger disconnected. Never operate any engine without first installing a turbo "guard" similar to the one illustrated in (Figure 13-27).

ECM Diagnostic Access
All electronically controlled engines are designed to store or log a trouble code in ECM memory when a sensor is operating in an out-of-range condition. When a problem is sensed and relayed back to the ECM, the severity of the problem will cause either the yellow or red diagnostic instrument panel light to illuminate. When the yellow light is illuminated, there may be a rampdown (power reduction) of both engine power

NOTICE

CONTENTS SENSITIVE
TO
STATIC ELECTRICITY

HANDLE IN ACCORDANCE WITH STATIC CONTROL
PROCEDURES GM9107P AND GM9108P,
OR GM DIVISIONAL SERVICE MANUALS.

FIGURE 15–22 *Typical industry standard warning label/decal to indicate electrostatic discharge. (Courtesy of Detroit Diesel Corporation.)*

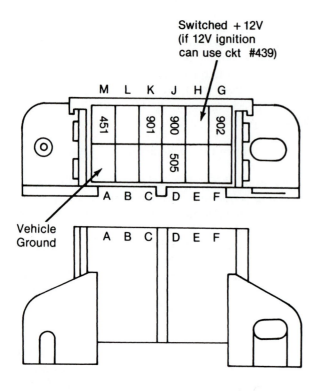

12 Pin DDL Connector P/N 12020043

FIGURE 15–23 Diagram of a DDEC I and DDEC II engine 12-pin DDL (diagnostic data link) connector normally located in the cab area of a heavy-duty truck to allow plug-in of the interface cable from the DDR. Trouble codes can be withdrawn by using the DDR or by using a jumper wire connected between terminals A and M of the DDL connector, then turning the ignition key on to monitor the flash codes. (Courtesy of Detroit Diesel Corporation.)

and speed. If the red light is illuminated, the sensed operating problem is serious enough to trigger an engine shutdown condition if the ECM has been programmed to do so. Some electronic systems are equipped with a *diagnostic toggle switch* that can be activated to cause the dash-mounted CEL to illuminate and to flash rapidly, thereby allowing the driver or technician to determine the *flash code number.*

In some electronic systems, the technician can use a *jumper wire* across two diagnostic connector terminals to cause any stored ECM trouble codes to "flash" the dash-mounted vehicle diagnostic light. See Figure 15-23 for one such example of a 12-pin DDL (diagnostic data link) connector generally located within the truck cab area (placement varies by OEM). This particular example is for a DDEC I or DDEC II Detroit Diesel system. Note that this procedure cannot be used on the DDEC III System! See Chapter 21 for information dealing with the DDEC III System. To extract a flash trouble code, with the ignition key switch off, insert a jumper wire between terminals A and M, which are clearly marked on the connector. When the ignition switch is turned back on, closely watch the dash-mounted yellow diagnostic light. An example of how to interpret stored flash trouble codes is illustrated in Figure 15-24. A flash code 13, for example, on a DDEC system (I or II) indicates that a coolant level sensor has detected low coolant. A code 21 on this system indicates that the TPS (throttle position sensor) has detected a high circuit voltage reading.

Some vehicles with electronic dashboards can provide a direct readout of engine diagnostic codes. This system, known as a ProDriver unit, can continually update the driver on engine and vehicle operating conditions, for example, an instant mpg/km per liter fuel consumption reading.

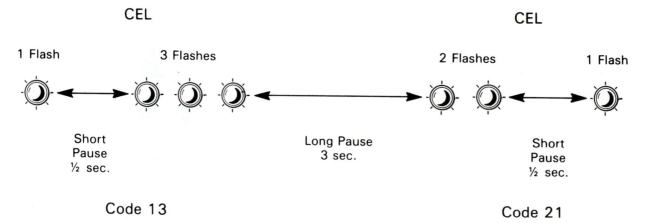

FIGURE 15–24 Example of how a stored DDEC I or DDEC II model ECM trouble code would cause the yellow warning light—CEL (check engine lamp)—on the vehicle dash to flash a code 13 and a code 21 when a jumper wire is installed across terminals A to M of the DDL shown in Figure 15-23. (Courtesy of Detroit Diesel Corporation).

Although flash codes are helpful, a more thorough analysis of system trouble codes and problem areas can be performed by the service technician using a handheld diagnostic reader, which is more commonly referred to as a DDR (diagnostic data reader). The type of diagnostic reader used to withdraw stored trouble codes varies in design among engine manufacturers; however, some major OEMs of diagnostic tools now offer a generic tool that can handle any make of engine, in addition to transmission and anti-skid brake electronic controls, simply by removing and inserting an electronic cartridge assembly into the handheld DDR. One such diagnostic tool (Figure 15-25) is manufactured by MPSI (Microprocessor Systems, Inc., Sterling Heights, MI). This tool is distributed through Kent-Moore Division, SPX Corporation. Refer to the sections in this chapter dealing with Caterpillar, Cummins, and Detroit Diesel for specifics on their special diagnostic tooling.

DIAGNOSTIC TOOLING

MPSI Diagnostic Tooling

MPSI (Micro Processor Systems, Inc.) is the major supplier of diagnostic tooling and equipment to the majority of engine OEMs. Their MPSI ProLink 9000 shown in Figure 15-25 connected to a printer is available with plug-in ProLink modules for every diesel engine OEM. It is also available with plug-in modules for semiautomated transmissions and Allison World Transmission models, as well as for ABS brake systems and similar systems.

FIGURE 15–25 *Hand-held ProLink 9000 model DDR (diagnostic data reader) connected to a miniprinter to capture a hard copy of engine operational data and logged trouble codes. (Courtesy of Detroit Diesel Corporation.)*

MPSI's latest diagnostic unit is the NGT (next-generation technology) model, which is similar in size and function to a mini laptop computer. This tool allows the portability desired by today's breed of new technician. Contained in a durable black case with a kick-out stand to support the tool for ease of viewing, the tool includes a backlit display similar to a laptop screen. Nine function keys and a pointing device are built into the unit to the right of the screen. Equipped with an RS232, RS485, parallel printer, PCMCIA, and module bays, this tool allows for installation of special interface electronics, such as oscilloscopes, digital volt-ohmmeters, gas and turbine analyzers, and vehicle data stream modules. For more information on the MPSI system, contact Micro Processor Systems, Inc., 6405 Nineteen Mile Road, Sterling Heights, MI 48078; tel: 313-731-6410, fax: 313-731-3348.

Diagnostic Tooling Principles

All electronic engine OEMs now offer dedicated software (disks) to facilitate diagnostic and programming information with their products using a laptop computer. Windows-based programs are available from each engine OEM which provide a point-and-click graphical interface for the technician. These software programs require an IBM-compatible (386 or higher) PC with a 25-MHz processor, 4 Mb of RAM, 10 Mb of hard disk space, a VGA monitor, a 3.5-in. floppy drive, DOS 5.0 or higher, Microsoft Windows 3.1 or higher, and an RS232 serial data port not used with a mouse or printer. For those maintenance facilities wishing to load an OEM software program onto a laptop computer, an internal fax modem, PCMCIA slot, and CD-ROM drive, as well as a 486 chip and higher levels of megahertz and RAM are necessary. All OEMs offer similar functions to fleets that want to implement an interactive maintenance system.

The DDR, which is connected to a DDL (diagnostic data link) connector located on the vehicle, can be used for troubleshooting and diagnostic purposes. It also can be used to provide unique capabilities such as these: running engine cylinder cutout, injector solenoid response times, injector calibration update, engine trip data, engine/vehicle speed calibration changes, cruise control speed setting changes, idle shutdown and transmission progressive shift changes, engine and engine protection configuration changes, parameter versus engine speed (or time), engine snapshot data, and limited ECM reprogramming when customer changes are desired and/or required within the operating conditions/parameters of the engine OEM.

By using any of the readily available DDRs from one of the major suppliers, the technician can access the ECM memory storage bank and monitor the sensor outputs and the diagnostic trouble codes. The technician can also confirm what ECM options have been programmed into the system, such as cruise control, automatic engine shutdown in the event of a major engine system problem, idle control time limit, and so on.

The DDR can be operated from the vehicle battery power supply, as can the printer (plug into the cigarette lighter). A 110-V power supply is also available to run the printer and is preferable when the DDR and printer are to be used for any length of time.

Technicians can extract and/or download ECM data into either a PC, laptop computer, or a small printer to produce a hard copy of the stored information within the ECM. A small printer is shown connected to a hand-held DDR in Figure 15-25.

ECM SAE Trouble Codes

The trouble code numbering system and interpretation stored in ECM memory are not the same in engines from different OEMs. For example, flash code 35 does not have the same meaning on Caterpillar, Cummins, Detroit Diesel, Mack, and Volvo engines. The SAE (Society of Automotive Engineers), through its technical standards committees, has been working with engine OEMs to arrive at a standard system of electronic coding and meaning. To encourage industry-wide acceptance of electronic serial data communication links between engines, SAE has created SAE-J reference standards, which are now in use.

- *SAEJ1587.* This standard enables the ECM to "talk" with diagnostic service tools, trip recorder and vehicle management information systems, electronic dash displays, and satellite communication systems. In other words, the J1587/J1708 data link provides sensor(s) and engine data to other vehicle modules.

- *SAE J1922 and J1939.* These two standards give the ECM the capability to communicate with and provide control data to other vehicle systems such as antilock braking systems, electronic transmissions, and antislip ASR systems (traction control devices). The on-vehicle communications harness assembly connects the ECM's J1922 and J1939 control data ports to other vehicle systems. The J1939 data link uses the CAN (controller area network) protocol.

- *SAE J1924.* This is a PC-software-compatible standard to allow the PC to interface with and translate the data link signal from the ECM. The software is installed as a TSR (terminate and stay resident) program.

When a technician uses a hand-held DDR similar to the one shown in Figure 15-25 to interpret stored ECM trouble codes, these codes are now displayed in the SAE technical standard format. Previously, stored trouble codes appeared on the DDR screen as a two- or three-digit number. The technician then referred to a flash code listing in the engine service manual or on a small plastic card provided by the OEM that allowed him or her to interpret the specific trouble code. The technician then referred to the trouble code number in the engine service manual and followed a step-by-step procedure to locate and correct the source of the problem. Although the technician can still follow this procedure, flash codes no longer appear on the screen of the DDR in newer electronic engine systems.

The flash codes have been replaced by parameter and system identification descriptions known as PID (parameter identifier) and SID (subsystem identifier) numbers. After the PID and SID numbers is an FMI (failure mode identifier), which defines the area where the fault has occurred. The following are summary descriptions of these numbers:

- *PID:* appears on the screen of the DDR as a single- or double-byte character to identify data of varying length, for example, the ECM data list of engine operating parameters, which would include items related to oil pressure, oil and coolant temperature, TPS (throttle position sensor), and so on.
- *SID:* appears only as a single-byte character to identify field-repairable or field-replaceable subsystems for which failures can be detected or isolated. Such a code would identify an injector problem.
- *FMI:* describes the type of failure detected in a subsystem and identified by the PID or SID. The FMI and either the PID or SID combine to form a given diagnostic code as defined by the SAE J1587 technical standard.

SAE Code Message Descriptions

All electronic systems now in use on heavy-duty trucks include SAE codes that can be extracted by using a DDR similar to that shown in Figure 15-25. In addition to their use on electronic engines, message identifier codes are also used with ABS (antibrake skid) and TCS (traction control systems), transmissions, vehicle navigation, and driver information systems. When a DDR is connected to any of these systems, message types by SAE code can appear from the serial data line when these aftermarket devices are used. Examples of the standard MIDs (message identifiers), PIDs (parameter identifiers), SIDs (subsystem identifiers), and FMIs (failure mode indicators) are given in this chapter for Caterpillar, Cummins, Detroit Diesel, and Mack engines. Listed below are standardized SAE codes in various key areas.

When illuminated on a DDR screen, the first set of SAE codes, identified as MIDs (message identifiers), indicate to the technician the vehicle system to which it refers. Once the system is identified, the technician can then use the DDR to access/enter that system to monitor trouble codes, perform a functional test, or reprogram the system. Once this has been done, the various SAE trouble codes that appear on the DDR screen (PIDs, SIDs, and FMIs) help in determining the area and cause of the problem.

Message Identifiers (MIDs)

128	Engine controller (used in V-MAC system)
130	Transmission
136	Brakes: antilock traction control
137–139	Brakes: antilock, trailers 1, 2, 3
140	Instrument cluster
141	Trip recorder
142	Vehicle management system (V-MAC MID)
143	Fuel system (FIC MID)
162	Vehicle navigation
163	Vehicle security
165	Communication unit: ground
171	Driver information system
178	Vehicle sensors to data converter
181	Communication unit: satellite

Parameter Identifiers (PIDs)

65	Service brake switch
70	Parking brake switch
83	Road speed limit status
84	Road speed
85	Speed control status
91	Percent accelerator pedal position
92	Percent engine load
100	Engine oil pressure
105	Intake manifold temperature
110	Engine coolant temperature
111	Coolant level
175	Engine oil temperature
182	Trip fuel
183	Fuel rate
184	Instantaneous MPG
185	Average MPG
190	Engine speed

Subsystem Identifiers (SIDs) Common to All MIDs

242	Cruise control resume switch
243	Cruise control set switch
244	Cruise control enable switch
245	Clutch pedal switch
248	Proprietary data link
250	SAE J1708 (J1587) data link

Subsystem Identifiers for MIDs 128 and 143

20	Timing actuator
21	Engine position sensor
22	Timing sensor
23	Rack actuator
24	Rack position sensor
29	External fuel command input

Subsystem Identifiers for MID 130

1–6	C1–C6 solenoid valves
7	Lockup solenoid valve
8	Forward solenoid valve
9	Low-Signal solenoid valve
10	Retarder enable solenoid valve
11	Retarder modulation solenoid valve
12	Retarder response solenoid valve
13	Differential lockout solenoid valve
14	Engine transmission match
15	Retarder modulation request sensor
16	Neutral start output
17	Turbine speed sensor
18	Primary shift selector
19	Secondary shift selector
20	Special function inputs
21–26	C1–C6 clutch pressure indicators
27	Lockup clutch pressure indicator
28	Forward range pressure indicator
29	Neutral range pressure indicator
30	Reverse range pressure indicator
31	Retarder response system pressure indicator
32	Differential lock clutch pressure indicator
33	Multiple pressure indicators

Subsystem Identifiers for MIDs 136–139

1	Wheel sensor ABS axle 1 left
2	Wheel sensor ABS axle 1 right
3	Wheel sensor ABS axle 2 left
4	Wheel sensor ABS axle 2 right
5	Wheel sensor ABS axle 3 left
6	Wheel sensor ABS axle 3 right
7	Pressure modulation valve ABS axle 1 left
8	Pressure modulation valve ABS axle 1 right
9	Pressure modulation valve ABS axle 2 left
10	Pressure modulation valve ABS axle 2 right
11	Pressure modulation valve ABS axle 3 left
12	Pressure modulation valve ABS axle 3 right
13	Retarder control relay
14	Relay diagonal 1
15	Relay diagonal 2

16   Mode switch: ABS
17   Mode Switch: traction control
18   DIF 1: traction control valve
19   DIF 2: traction control valve
22   Speed signal input
23   Warning light bulb
24   Traction control light bulb
25   Wheel sensor, ABS axle 1 average
26   Wheel sensor, ABS axle 2 average
27   Wheel sensor, ABS axle 3 average
28   Pressure modulator, drive axle relay valve
29   Pressure transducer, drive axle relay valve
30   Master control relay

Subsystem Identifiers for MID 162
1   Dead reckoning unit
2   Loran receiver
3   Global positioning system (GPS)
4   Integrated navigation unit

Currently, SAE FMIs list 15 numbers that are used in conjunction with either PIDs or SIDs. All of these numbers appear on the DDR screen used by the service technician to recall stored trouble codes from the ECM. Most of the FMIs that accompany either a PID or SID tend to be either a 3 or a 4, and they are included in the following list of the SAE numbers currently in use.

Failure Mode Identifiers (FMIs)
0   Data valid but above normal operational range (that is, engine overheating)
1   Data valid but below normal operational range (that is, engine oil pressure too low)
2   Data erratic, intermittent, or incorrect
3   Voltage above normal or shorted high
4   Voltage below normal or shorted low
5   Current below normal or open circuit
6   Current above normal or grounded circuit
7   Mechanical system not responding properly
8   Abnormal frequency, pulse width, or period
9   Abnormal update rate
10   Abnormal rate of change
11   Failure mode not identifiable
12   Bad intelligent device or component
13   Out of calibration
14   Special instructions
15   Reserved for future assignment by the SAE data format subcommittee

For example, the DDR illustrated in Figure 15-25, when connected to a DDEC III system, may display on its screen the following sequence:

Code p 91 3 = EFPA circuit failed high
3 = high voltage
4 = low voltage

When using the DDR, the screen will display (when prompted) whether there are *active* and *inactive* trouble codes stored in the ECM memory. Such a diagnostic request might display the following sequence for a DDEC III system:

[The engine serial number]
Diagnostic code list
NO ACTIVE CODES
INACTIVE CODES
Engine throttle sensor input voltage low
    PID:91 FMI:4 (flash code 22)
Engine oil pressure sensor input voltage low
    PID:100 FMI:4 (Flash Code 36)
Engine turbo boost sensor input voltage low
    PID:102 FMI:4 (flash code 34)
Coolant level sensor input voltage high
    PID:111 FMI:3 (flash code 16)

The foregoing information indicates to the technician that there are no active codes and four inactive codes. Note, however, that the flash codes would show on a DDEC II system DDR screen but not on a DDEC III system DDR screen! A dash-mounted flash code diagnostic request toggle switch can be activated on the DDEC III system to extract these types of codes.

Even though all engine manufacturers conform to the SAE technical standards, the flash codes are still different. Assume we are using a DDR and we uncover a PID/FMI number 100/01 on a Cummins, Caterpillar, or Detroit Diesel engine. This SAE code means that the engine ECMs have detected from the sensor input that a low oil pressure condition has been logged. The flash code on the Caterpillar would be a No. 46; on the Detroit Diesel, it would be No. 45; and on the Cummins, it would be No. 143. The PDI/FMI number 110/00 means a high coolant temperature warning; it would exhibit flash code No. 61 on the Caterpillar, a No. 44 on Detroit Diesel, and a No. 151 on the Cummins. The adoption of the standardized SAE fault codes ensures that all engine manufacturers using electronic fuel injection systems will display the same PIDs and FMIs regardless of individual flash code numbering systems.

Active/Inactive Codes

When an engine or vehicle speed sensor detects an out-of-range operating condition, the ECM receives a high or low signal based on the failure mode detected.

The ECM then logs a trouble code into its memory bank for extraction by the technician at a later date. For example, say the ECM was programmed to record a high engine oil temperature condition beginning at 250°F (121°C). When this condition is noted by the OTS (oil temperature sensor), the signal to the ECM will cause the yellow dash-mounted warning light to illuminate. This condition is known as an *active code* situation. If the ECM has been programmed for engine protection, the engine will usually start to lose speed and power to a level that was the average power occurring prior to the fault condition. If, however, the oil temperature continues to increase, at a preprogrammed point, the red SEL (stop engine light) on the dash will illuminate. Then a 30-second automatic ramp down (power reduction) will begin, followed by engine shutdown if the system has been programmed to do so. In some situations, if the fleet management or owners/operators have previously selected a temporary override option, the driver may push an STEO (stop-engine override) button on the dash to provide another 30 seconds of engine operation, so the vehicle can be pulled safely to the side of the highway.

In this same condition of high engine oil temperature, let's assume that the ECM is programmed to illuminate the dash-mounted yellow warning light at 251°F (122°C) and to shut the engine down at 261°F (127°C). The yellow light illuminates when the low-end temperature of the lube oil is reached, and a trouble code is stored in ECM memory. If the vehicle operating condition triggered this light when moving up a long hill and while heavily loaded, it is possible that once the hill is covered, the engine oil temperature condition would drop back into a normal operating range. This would cause the yellow light to go out; nevertheless, the trouble code would remain stored in ECM memory. This type of a condition is referred to as an *inactive code* (sometimes called a "historic" code). An active code indicates to the vehicle driver that an out-of-range condition has been detected, and an inactive code indicates to the service technician that a problem was detected by a sensor/ECM at some time during engine/vehicle operation. Most current ECMs are programmed not only to log and retain trouble codes, but also to record how many times they occurred and at what hours or miles.

Examples of the various trouble codes—PIDs, SIDs, and FMIs—are listed for Detroit Diesel, Caterpillar, and Cummins engines in their respective chapters.

Clearing Codes

After trouble codes have been stored in ECM memory and you want to remove them, you must select the menu option from the DDR that indicates to the technician whether you wish to erase all stored codes. All current electronic systems require this method. In some first-generation systems the stored trouble codes could be erased either by using the DDR or simply by removing the power supply fuses to the ECM for 10 seconds, then reinserting them. The disadvantage of these systems is that after an operator removes the codes, any record of troubles that may have occurred on a trip would be lost, and the service technician or fleet maintenance manager would have no knowledge of any engine or vehicle problems.

For a complete list of all current SAE codes used throughout the automotive and heavy-duty trucking industry, contact SAE (Society of Automotive Engineers) at 400 Commonwealth Drive, Warrendale, PA 15096-0001; tel: 412-776-4841, fax: 412-776-5760.

SUMMARY

The informational data in this chapter will provide you with a sound working knowledge that you can transfer to the more detailed chapters contained within this book dealing with Caterpillar, Cummins, Detroit Diesel, Mack and Bosch electronic fuel injection systems.

SELF-TEST QUESTIONS

1. Technician A says that the first major engine OEM to release electronic controls on their diesel engines was Caterpillar in 1987. Technician B says that Detroit Diesel was the first OEM to employ electronically controlled unit injectors in their two-stroke-cycle on-highway truck 92 series engines in September 1985. Which technician knows their electronics background best?

2. Technician A says that Caterpillar's first venture into electronic engine controls was with the introduction of the PEEC system on their 3406B truck engine. Technician B says that this occurred in 1985. Who is right?

3. Technician A says that EUIs (electronic unit injectors) are now being used by Detroit Diesel, Caterpillar, Cummins, Volvo, John Deere, and Mack. Technician B agrees, with the exception of Mack, which uses a Bosch electronic PLN system, while later engines use an EUP (electronic unit pump). Who is right?

4. Technician A says that the HEUI (hydraulically actuated EUI) fuel system is now in use by Navistar International and Caterpillar on selected engine models (3126, 3408E, and 3412E). Technician B says that only Caterpillar uses the HEUI system. Who is correct?

5. Technician A says that current users of EUP fuel systems include Mercedes-Benz/Detroit Diesel Series 55 engines now offered in the Freightliner Century Class heavy-duty trucks. Technician B agrees, but also says that Mack will use EUPs on their later-model E7 engines. Are both technicians right in their statements?

6. True or False: The term *CELECT* refers to "Cummins electronics."

7. True or False: The term *DDEC* refers to "Detroit Diesel electronic controls."

8. True or False: The term *VECTRO* refers to "Volvo electronics."

9. True or False: The term *VMAC* refers to "Vehicle management and control" and is a Mack-designed system.

10. Technician A says that most engine sensors receive an input signal from the ECM rated at 5 V. Technician B agrees but states that some engine OEMs also use 8 V, and in some cases 12-V sensor supply voltages. Are both technicians correct?

11. Identify the names of the components to match the following letters with respect to engine vehicle sensors:
    a. EFPA
    b. TRS
    c. SRS
    d. TBS
    e. ATS
    f. FPS
    g. FTS
    h. OPS
    i. OTS
    j. CTS
    k. CLS
    l. ACLS
    m. CPS
    n. CPS
    o. ITS
    p. IAS
    q. EBC
    r. PGS
    s. SLS
    t. VSG
    u. CEL
    v. SEL
    w. EPS
    x. VDL
    y. PWM
    z. EEPROM
    aa. DDR
    bb. RAM
    cc. CPU

12. Technician A says that some sensors operate on an analog signal, while others operate on a digital signal; however, analog signals must be converted to digital through a signal processor for the ECM to function. Technician B says that all engine and vehicle sensors operate as digital output signal processors. Which technician knows the theory best?

13. Technician A says that an analog signal varies in intensity over time, while a digital signal is either ON or OFF. Technician B says that digital signals vary in intensity over time. Who is right?

14. With the exception of a speed sensor signal or MPU (magnetic pickup unit), technician A says that sensors are designed to vary their voltage output based upon either a changing pressure or temperature signal. Technician B says that all sensors operate on temperature changes only. Who is correct?

15. True or False: Sensor output values depend on a changing resistance over time, generally ranging from 0.5 V to 4.5 V on 5-V types.

16. True or False: An AD converter is an analog–digital converter.

17. True or False: Pulse counters are generally used with speed sensors.

18. When the TPS within the EFPA is at a closed throttle (idle) position, the voltage signal return to the ECM is at its maximum value according to technician A. Technician B disagrees, saying that at a closed throttle, the voltage return signal to the ECM is at its minimum value. Who is right?

19. Technician A says that an oil pressure sensor is usually monitored for a changing value once per second. Technician B says that the OPS is monitored 10 times per second. Who is right?

20. True or False: A voltage rheostat and/or a potentiometer are basically used to control the voltage output of the TPS between idle and maximum position.

21. True of False: The percentage of throttle pedal depression, and therefore the fueling demand by the operator, is sensed by a changing output voltage to the ECM as the pedal is depressed.

22. Technician A says that EUIs still require mechanical actuation by a rocker arm assembly to raise the fuel pressure to a high-enough level to open the spray tip needle valve. Technician B disagrees, saying that an electronic signal to a solenoid does this job. Which technician knows the system operation best?

23. Technician A says that the PWM signal to the injector solenoid is used to close a small poppet valve to initiate the beginning of injection. Technician B says that a rocker arm determines the start of injection. Who is correct?

24. True or False: The quantity of fuel injected is determined by the duty cycle time of the signal sent from the ECM to the injector solenoid.

25. Technician A says that EUIs still require a plunger helix to allow variation of the start and end of injection. Technician B says that no plunger helix is necessary in an EUI. Who is right?

26. True or False: A DDR can be used to access the ECM, withdraw stored trouble codes, and reprogram certain ECM parameters.

27. Engine and vehicle computers operate on a binary system of measurement according to technician A. Technician B says that a base 10 system is used. Who is correct?

28. True or False: A *bit* is one unit of data or information.

29. True or False: A *byte* combines a series of bits into word lengths.

30. True or False: Within the CPU, a series of logic gates are used to add, multiply, subtract, divide, and compute the various sensor input signals to control engine and vehicle operation.

31. True or False: The RAM within the ECM is actually a working scratch pad when the engine is operating, to allow the ECM to be informed of changing sensor conditions which it can compare to preprogrammed operating parameters.

32. Technician A says that EUIs can create voltage signals between 90 and 105 V when the engine is running. Technician B says that the EUI voltage cannot exceed system voltage, being either 12 or 24 V. Who is correct?

33. True or False: Diagnostic access to stored ECM trouble or flash codes can only be extracted using a laptop computer.

34. Technician A says that each major engine OEM offers diagnostic programs based upon Windows for ease of troubleshooting. Technician B says that only a DDR can be used for troubleshooting. Which technician is correct?

35. Technician A says that the DDR and its miniprinter (see Figure 15-25) can be operated from the vehicle cigarette lighter if necessary. Technician B says that you can only operate the printer from a 110-V power supply. Which technician is correct?

36. True or False: Regardless of the different flash codes used by engine OEMs, SAE standardized code message descriptions are now in wide use.

37. Technician A says that the three standardized SAE trouble codes now in use for electronic systems include
    a. PID, FID, SMI
    b. PID, SID, FMI
    c. PID, FID, FMI

38. From your answer in Question 37, describe what each of the three SAE code letters mean?

39. Technician A says that the two most common numbers appearing after an FMI code are 3 and 4. Technician B disagrees and says that numbers 1 and 7 are more commonly flashed. Who is correct?

40. Technician A says that an FMI 3 indicates that voltage is above normal or shorted high. Technician B says that it means that voltage is below normal or shorted low for that circuit. Who is correct?

41. Technician A says that an "active" code is an out-of-range sensor/wiring condition that is currently affecting the engine operation. Technician B says that only "historic" (inactive) codes will affect engine performance. Which technician is right?

42. Technician A says that when a fault code is detected by the ECM, the yellow dash warning light will be illuminated and the engine may lose power based on the severity of the out-of-range condition detected. Technician B says that when any fault is detected, the red dash light will always illuminate. Who is right?

43. Technician A says that if the system has been programmed for automatic engine shutdown, once the red light illuminates, the engine will start to depower, and normally 30 seconds later, it will shut down. Technician B says that you can program the ECM to vary the shutdown time between 3 and 100 minutes. Which technician is correct?

44. Technician A says that to activate the idle shutdown on a heavy-duty truck, the spring parking brakes must be applied in order to permit the idle timer to start its count. Technician B says that the idle timer will function at any time regardless of whether the spring brakes are on or off. Who is right?

45. Technician A says that an operator can continue to drive a truck with the yellow warning light illuminated but may do so at reduced speed and power from ECM control. Technician B says that the vehicle should be pulled over as soon as possible, the engine shut off, and checked. Who is correct?

46. Technician A says that system trouble codes logged in ECM memory of current electronic systems can be erased by temporarily disconnecting the battery. Technician B says that codes can only be erased through connecting up the DDR. Which technician is right?

Diesel Fuel, Filters, and Fuel/Water Separators

OVERVIEW

Clean diesel fuel has always been paramount to obtaining long life from injection equipment. This is true even more with the introduction of electronically controlled diesel engines that operate with very high injection pressures. In this chapter we discuss the characteristics of diesel fuel, the construction, operation, maintenance, and service of fuel filters; fuel filter/water separators; and thermostatically controlled heaters, which are used in cold-weather operation.

DIESEL FUEL OIL GRADES

Diesel fuel oil is graded and designated by the American Society for Testing and Materials (ASTM); its specific gravity and high and low heat values are also listed by the API (American Petroleum Institute). Each individual oil refiner and supplier attempts to produce diesel fuels that comply as closely as possible with the ASTM and API specifications. Because of different crude oil supplies, the diesel fuel end product may be on either the high or low end of the prescribed heat energy scale in Btu per pound or per gallon. Therefore, diesel fuel oils available from one supplier may vary slightly from those provided by another. At this time, only two recommended grades of fuel are considered acceptable for use in high-speed heavy-duty trucks and buses in North America. These are the No. 1D and No. 2D fuel oil classifications. The No. 1D fuel is a lighter distillate than a No. 2D. However, No. 1D fuel has less heat energy per gallon than does a No. 2D grade. The No. 1D fuel also costs more per gallon to produce than a No. 2D grade. For this reason, No. 1D tends to be used more widely in city bus applications, while the heavier No. 2D fuel grade with its greater energy (Btu per gallon) content is widely used in heavy-duty high-speed truck diesel engine applications.

Grade No. 1D

The No. 1D fuel rating comprises the class of volatile fuel oils from kerosene to the intermediate distillates. Fuels within this classification are suitable for use in high-speed engines in service that involves frequent and relatively wide variations in loads and speeds, and also in cases where abnormally low fuel temperatures are encountered, because the No. 1D fuel provides easier starting qualities in cold-weather operation. Therefore, for heavy-duty high-speed diesel truck operation in continued cold-weather environments, No. 1D fuel may allow better operation than the heavier distillate No. 2D.

Grade No. 2D

The No. 2D fuel rating includes the class of distillate gas oils of lower volatility. They are suitable for use in high-speed engines in service that involves relatively high loads and uniform speeds, or in engines that do not require fuels having the higher volatility or other properties specified for grade No. 1D. No. 2D fuel is more widely used by truck fleets, due to its greater heat value per gallon, particularly in warm to moderate climates. Although the No. 1D fuel has better properties for cold-weather operation, many fleets still prefer to use the No. 2D grade in the winter. They employ fuel heater/water separators to provide suitable starting as well as fuel additive conditioners, which are added directly to the fuel tank.

Classifications of diesel fuels below grades No. 1D and 2D are not considered acceptable for use in high-speed automotive or truck engines; therefore, they will not be discussed here.

On a volume basis, typical No. 2D fuel has about 13% more heating value in Btu per gallon than does gasoline; No. 1D fuel, which is a lighter distillate and therefore less dense than No. 2D, has approximately 10% more Btu content per gallon than gasoline.

Fuel Grade and Engine Performance

Selection of the correct diesel fuel is a must if the engine is to perform to its rated specifications. Generally, seven factors must be considered in the selection of a fuel oil:

1. Starting characteristics
2. Fuel handling
3. Wear on injection equipment
4. Wear on pistons
5. Wear on rings, valves, and cylinder liners
6. Engine maintenance
7. Fuel cost and availability

Several other considerations are also relevant to the selection of a fuel oil:

1. Engine size and design
2. Speed and load range
3. Frequency of load and speed changes
4. Atmospheric conditions

SPECIFIC GRAVITY OF A FUEL

The lighter a fuel's SG (specific gravity), the less heat value per gallon it will have. Conversely, the heavier the SG of a diesel fuel oil, the greater will be its energy content in Btu per gallon. SG is the ratio of the diesel fuel's weight to the weight of an equivalent volume of water; usually this is designated as "sp. gr. 60/60°F," which indicates that both the diesel fuel and water are weighed and measured at 60°F (15.5°C). API measures diesel fuel with a special hydrometer and assigns a gravity degrees API rating to it. An example of the type of chart used to show various API-rated fuels is shown in the left-hand column of Table 16-1. The specific gravity shown in the second column from the left indicates the weight of an Imperial gallon of fuel compared with an Imperial gallon of water, which weighs 10 lb. The third column shows the weight in pounds of a U.S. gallon of fuel.

HEAT VALUE OF A FUEL

The fourth and fifth columns from the left-hand side of Table 16-1 illustrate the *high* heat values in Btu per pound and also in Btu per gallon. The sixth and seventh columns list the Btu/lb and the Btu/gallon for the *low* heat values of the fuel. In North America, the thermal efficiency or heat efficiency of an internal combustion engine that uses liquid fuel is determined on the basis of the HHV (high heat value) of the fuel used. This means that the products of combustion are cooled to their original temperature, water vapor is condensed, and the total heat released is known as the gross or HHV of the fuel. High heat value is termed in Btu/lb for liquid fuel and in Btu/cubic foot for gaseous fuels such as propane and compressed natural gas. However, if the water vapor from combustion is not condensed, the latent heat of vaporization (an indication of the cooling effect when liquids are vaporized) of the water is subtracted to give the fuel's net or LHV (low heat value). The heat value of any given diesel fuel fluctuates based on its specification as a No. 1D or a No. 2D grade. In addition, the heat energy value of the fuel varies slightly between a summer and a winter blend, even from the same refining supplier. Since the diesel fuel grade recommended by TMC/ATA (The Maintenance Council, American Trucking Associations) for heavy-duty high-speed diesel engines in highway truck/tractors is grade No. 2D, we will use this as a generally accepted fuel energy equivalent. A No. 2D grade diesel fuel with an API (American Petroleum Institute) gravity rating number of 36 at 60°F (15.5°C) would be as shown in Table 16-1.

The greater the Btu content per gallon of fuel, the greater the energy that can be released in the combustion chamber when that fuel is ignited. Consider that each Btu of fuel energy is capable of releasing the equivalent of 778 ft-lb of mechanical work. Therefore, if we multiply the total Btu/gal by this figure, we can determine the available work output that can be produced by the release of this heat energy. The total number of lb-ft of energy can then be divided by 33,000 ft-lb, which represents 1 hp/min. From this calculation we can equate just how much horsepower can be extracted from each gallon of diesel fuel.

Let us compare an API 34 fuel designation shown in Table 16-1, which has approximately 139,400 Btu/U.S. gallon with an API 36 with 138,200 Btu/U.S. gallon. The API 34 fuel can release 108,453,200 lb-ft of work output, while the API 36 fuel can release 107,519,600 lb-ft of work output. If we divide both totals by 33,000 lb-ft, which represents the work required

TABLE 16–1   *High and low heat values for API-rated diesel fuels*[a]

Gravity (°API)	Specific gravity at 60°F	Weight fuel (lb/gal)	High heat value		Low heat value	
			Btu/lb	Btu/gal	Btu/lb	Btu/gal
44	0.8063	6.713	19,860	133,500	18,600	125,000
42	0.8155	6.790	19,810	134,700	18,560	126,200
40	0.8251	6.870	19,750	135,800	18,510	127,300
38	0.8348	6.951	19,680	137,000	18,460	128,500
36	0.8448	7.034	19,620	138,200	18,410	129,700
34	0.8550	7.119	19,560	139,400	18,360	130,900
32	0.8654	7.206	19,490	140,600	18,310	132,100
30	0.8762	7.296	19,420	141,800	18,250	133,300
28	0.8871	7.387	19,350	143,100	18,190	134,600
26	0.8984	7.481	19,270	144,300	18,130	135,800
24	0.9100	7.578	19,190	145,600	18,070	137,100
22	0.9218	7.676	19,110	146,800	18,000	138,300
20	0.9340	7.778	19,020	148,100	17,930	139,600
18	0.9465	7.882	18,930	149,400	17,860	140,900
16	0.9593	7.989	18,840	150,700	17,790	142,300
14	0.9725	8.099	18,740	152,000	17,710	143,600
12	0.9861	8.212	18,640	153,300	17,620	144,900
10	1.000	8.328	18,540	154,600	17,540	146,200

Source: Bureau of Standards, Miscellaneous Publication *97, Thermal Properties of Petroleum Products,* April 28, 1933.

[a] It should be understood that heating values for a given gravity of fuel oil may vary somewhat from those shown.

to produce 1 hp/min, the API 34 fuel can produce an equivalent of 3286 hp divided by 60 to convert the total to horsepower developed in an hour, since all engines are computed on their ability to produce horsepower over a 1 hr period, we obtain 55 hp/hr. The API 36 fuel with its lower Btu heat content per gallon would produce slightly less at 54.3 hp/hr. However, on a 400-bhp engine, for example, that might consume 0.325 lb/hp-hr of diesel fuel, the engine would burn 130 lb of fuel in 1 hr. This figure is obtained by multiplying 0.325 × 400. If we divide the total fuel consumed in an hour by the weight of fuel per gallon, the API 36 fueled engine would consume 18.48 U.S. gal/hr, while the API 34 fueled engine would consume 18.26 U.S. gal/hr. Therefore, the engine running on the API 34 fuel would save 0.22 U.S. gal/hr. Projected over a 10 hr day, this is a savings of 2.2 U.S. gal. If the truck operates 7 days a week, we would save 15.4 U.S. gal/week. In a year, we would save 52 × 15.4 = 800.8 U.S. gal. Keep in mind, however, that we have to allow for heat, friction, and radiation losses from the engine,

as well as the driving habits of the operator and the terrain and ambient temperatures in which the truck operates. However, taking two trucks with identical specifications, all things being equal, the truck engine using the API 34 fuel should return slightly better fuel economy than the one using API 36. For more details on thermal efficiency of an engine, refer to the section on thermal efficiency in Chapter 3.

FUEL FILTRATION

No matter how carefully fuel is handled, contaminants find their way into fuel during transfer, storage, or even inside vehicle tanks. Indeed, water, an engine's primary enemy, condenses directly from the air during normal daily heating and cooling cycles. In addition to water, solid and semisolid (microbiological) particulate contamination is prevalent. Rust, sand, and other small particles routinely find their way into diesel fuel. Sometimes larger identifiable objects such as pebbles, leaves, and paint chips are present. The most common culprits of plugged fuel filter elements, however, are oxidized organic semisolid contaminants such as gums, varnishes, and carbon. To be effective, fuel filtration devices must provide adequate solid-particle retention efficiencies while maintaining large capacities for the natural organic contaminants found in diesel fuel.

In addition to contaminant challenges, there is the potential for paraffin wax crystal formation in the fuel during cold-weather operations. These crystals form (at the cloud point of a fuel) and cause filters to plug just as if they were fouled by contamination.

Water: An Engine's Worst Enemy

Water is commonly found in diesel fuel due mainly to condensation, handling, and environmental conditions. Water contamination, although ever present, is more pronounced in humid areas and marine applications. The presence of water in diesel fuel systems may cause the following problems:

- Water causes iron components to rust and form loose aggregated particles of iron oxide that contribute to injector wear.
- At the interface of water and diesel fuel, microbiological growth occurs rapidly under proper conditions. These microbes form a sludge that can actually hinder filter effectiveness and injection performance.
- Water contamination combines with various forms of sulfur contamination to form sulfuric acid. This strong acid can damage injection systems and engine components.
- Water inhaled by the injection system can displace lubrication provided by the fuel oil itself, causing galling and premature wear.

Typical primary filtration devices do not have the capability to remove water, so they leave the engine prey to pump and injector damage and reduced efficiency. It is essential, therefore, to effectively separate water from the fuel prior to the final stages of solid-particulate filtration. In the absence of a water separator, standard primary elements become waterlogged and ineffective. When waterlogged, they are especially susceptible to waxing in cold temperatures.

An *upstream* water separator can significantly enhance the performance and life of primary filter elements. Frequent replacement of primary filters is required when the volume of contaminants is significant. In such cases, engine damage may result because filters are not immediately available for replacement, or operators are not aware of the need to replace them.

Therefore, upstream filtration capacity, water separation capability, and a 30-μm rating can, when properly applied, as much as triple the service life of the filtration system.

In addition to keeping dirt particles out of the diesel fuel, water in the fuel must be avoided. Water will cause severe lack of lubrication, leading to possible seizure of injection system components. In some cases water can cause the injector tip to be blown off, due to the high engine temperatures encountered in the combustion chamber, which leads to the water exploding as it passes through the injector tip orifices, causing serious engine damage. This condition is more pronounced in direct-injection diesel engines with multiple-hole nozzles. Because of the noncompressibility factor of water and the extremely high injection pressures created, water must not be allowed to enter the diesel fuel system. Even when the engine is not running, water in the fuel system can rust precision-fitted parts, thereby causing serious problems. Clean fuel should contain no more than 0.1% of sediment and water. Auxiliary filtering equipment must be used when sediment and water exceeds 0.1%; therefore, it is advisable to use a fuel/water separator. Another problem of water in the fuel is, of course, that it can lead to fuel-line freeze-up in cold-weather operation.

Most diesel fuel systems today employ a fuel return line that runs back to the fuel tank; this line carries warm fuel that has been used to cool and lubricate the injection pump and nozzles. When this warm fuel settles in the tank, condensation can form, leading to water vapor. To minimize water vapor, many fleets fill their fuel tanks up at night to displace any warm air in the tank. To prevent fuel-line freeze-up due to minute water particles in the fuel, a fuel/water filter and optional heater can be used, as well as the addition of methyl or isopropyl alcohol in the ratio of 0.0125% or 1 part in 8000, which equates to about 1 pint of isopropyl alcohol (isopropanol) to every 125 gallons of diesel fuel.

Water is found in diesel fuel in three forms: absorbed, emulsified, and in a free state. Of the three, water in a free state is by far the easiest to remove from diesel fuel. This free water is generally removed from the diesel fuel by using a mechanical filter employing the process of centrifugal force. Pleated paper separator systems provide filtration and water separation, and although they perform much better than a mechanical separator, they are not as good as the true *coalescing filter*. Fuel/water filters operate on the principle of *coalescence* to remove emulsified and coarsely dispersed water from the fuel oil. The dictionary defines *coalesce* as "to cause to grow together, to unite so as to form one body or association."

Emulsified droplets of water are very small and thus take considerable time to separate from the fuel by gravitational means. On the other hand, coarsely dispersed water droplets are large enough to separate by gravitational means in a short period of time. In the process of coalescing, droplets of water enter the filter assembly where they form into large droplets or globules and become large enough to settle in the fuel/water separator sump by gravitational means. Smaller droplets are trapped in the filtering element. Factors affecting the design and performance of a coalescing element are viscosity, specific gravity, solubility, surfactants (surface-active agents) and additives, concentration of contaminants, the degree of emulsification, solids content, and filter pressure drop.

FUEL FILTERS

The use of a suitable filtration system on diesel engines is a must to avoid damage to the closely fitted injection pump and injector components. These components are manufactured to tolerances of as little as 0.0025 mm (0.0000984 in.); therefore, insufficient fuel filtration can cause serious problems. Six principal filter element media have been used for many years:

1. Pleated paper
2. Packed cotton thread
3. Wood fibers
4. Mixtures of packed cotton thread and wood fibers
5. Wound cotton or synthetic yarn
6. Fiberglass

Filtering ability varies among type of engines and manufacturers. On high-speed diesel engines, a primary filter and a secondary filter are generally employed. The primary filter is capable of removing dirt particles down to about 30 μm and the secondary down to 10 to 12 μm, although final filters with a rating of 3 to 5 μm are now more prevalent on truck diesel applications operating in severe-duty service. A micron is 1/1,000,000 of a meter, or 0.00003937 in.; therefore, 25.4 μm = 0.001 in. Fuel filters that employ wound cotton thread, pleated paper, or fiberglass media are typically rated only as low as 10 μm; therefore, current truck diesel engines often employ additional filtration in the form of either a fuel/water separator or injector filter. Some engines use only one fuel filter, but with a screen in the fuel tank to remove any larger dirt particles.

Pleated paper elements are made of resin-treated paper with controlled porosity. These fine pores hold solid contaminants but not water. Other factors related to the type of filtering media are the pressure drop across the filter and price of the replacement unit. Pleated paper elements are generally the lowest priced, and wound cotton yarn elements are more expensive. Fiberglass and cotton thread and wood fiber elements are usually the most expensive, but they offer the best protection and longest service life.

The degree of filtration is obviously related to the type and grade of fuel that has to pass through the filter; therefore, fuel filters are available with filter ratings of from as high as 60 to 70 μm down to an ultra-fine 0.5 to 3 μm. The makeup of typical filters used in midrange and heavy-duty diesel fuel filters is as follows:

- Nominal 15 to 20 μm rating, consisting of 60% superfine wood fiber and 40% white cotton thread
- Nominal 10 to 15 μm rating, consisting of 40% wood fiber and 60% white cotton thread
- Nominal 5 to 10 μm rating, consisting of 85% white cotton thread and 15% synthetic thread
- Nominal 3 to 5 μm rating, consisting of 50% cotton thread and 50% cotton linters
- Nominal 0.5 to 3 μm rating, consisting of ultrafine 60% ground paper and 40% fine wood chips

The fuel system can be equipped with either a primary or a secondary fuel filter, depending on whether a fuel filter/water separator is employed. When a primary filter is used, it is usually manufactured from a cotton-wound-sock type of material and is designed to handle dirt removal down to 25 to 30 μm in size. On the other hand, the secondary filter is made from specially formulated and treated paper and is usually designed to remove dirt particles down to between 10 and 12 μm in size. For severe heavy-duty operating conditions, however, the secondary fuel filter will remove particles down to between 3 and 5 μm in size.

Filter Change Intervals

The engine application and environmental conditions determine the best change interval for both primary and secondary fuel filters. Often filters are changed at a specific accumulated mileage, number of hours, time period, or amount of fuel consumed by the engine. Each engine or equipment manufacturer specifies this in its operator and service manuals. For example, the specification may be to change filters every 16,000 km (10,000 miles), 250 hours, or 6 months—whichever comes first.

In cases where low engine power is noticed, with no unusual color exhaust smoke, a fuel pressure gauge can be installed in the inlet and and outlet sides of the secondary filter head to determine if the filter is plugged. On the primary filter, a restriction check can be made of the fuel system on the suction side. This can be done by connecting an Hg (mercury) manometer or vacuum gauge to the outlet side of the primary filter head. Refer to Figures 13–42 through 13–45 which illustrate the use of manometers. Normally there is a small pipe plug that can be removed from the filter head so the vacuum gauge or manometer brass fitting can be installed. A small-bore rubber hose is then connected to the fitting, with the opposite end attached to the manometer. Start and run the engine at the recommended rpm, which is usually toward the high end of the speed range, and compare the reading on the manometer or vacuum gauge to the specs. For example, on both Caterpillar and Cummins engines, typical maximum allowable restriction is usually limited to 4 in. Hg on a clean system and 8 in. Hg with a dirty fuel filter. Detroit Diesel engines allow 6 in. Hg maximum on a clean system and 12 in. Hg on a dirty system. Values higher than this are indicative of fuel starvation due to plugged or collapsed hoses, hoses too small or kinked, plugging at the fuel tank inlet/suction pickup line, or a plugged filter. Also check for loose connections or fittings to determine if air is being drawn into the system.

When changing fuel filters, keep in mind that two types are commonly used: the S & E (shell and element) model or the SO (spin-on) type. The S & E model employs a steel canister that is retained in place by a bolt; the SO type is hand tightened. Fuel and lube oil filters are similar in external appearance and in liquid flow. Figures 11-6 and 11-7 illustrate an SO and an S & E lube oil filter. With the S & E type, the filter must be disassembled, washed in clean solvent, and reassembled with a new filter element and necessary gaskets. In the SO type, once the filter has been removed, it is discarded or recycled and a new unit is used. Figure 16-1 illustrates what to do before installing a new SO filter:

FIGURE 16–1 *Applying a coat of clean engine lube oil to fuel filter gasket; priming fuel filter with clean filtered fuel. (Courtesy of Cummins Engine Company, Inc.)*

1. Clean the filter head of any dirt.
2. Apply a light coating of clean engine oil to the captive filter seal.
3. Pour clean filtered diesel fuel into the element to prime it.
4. Install the filter by hand and tighten it according to the directions on the attached label, which usually indicate that the filter should be rotated an additional one-half, two-thirds, or one full turn after the gasket makes contact.
5. With S & E filters, use a torque wrench to correctly tighten the retaining bolt.
6. Inspect the filter for fuel leaks after starting the engine.

NOTE If the engine runs rough after changing a fuel filter, it is likely that air has been trapped in the fuel system. Bleed all air from the filter by loosening off the bleed screw. In the absence of a bleed screw, individually loosen all external injector fuel lines (see Figure 19-29c) until all air has been vented from the system and a steady flow of fuel is visible.

FUEL FILTER/WATER SEPARATORS

Due to the very fine tolerances of the injection components in today's diesel engines, not only is it necessary to ensure that a supply of clean fuel is maintained but also that no trace of water is allowed to enter the fuel injection system. For this reason, most diesel automotive, heavy-duty truck, stationary, and marine engine applications employ fuel filters with built-in water separators. Figure 16-2 is a typical schematic for a heavy-duty diesel fuel system with a fuel filter/water separator that functions as a *primary* filtration system. Additional fuel filters serve as secondary filters with a finer dirt removal capability. Depending on the engine size and the application, filters can be of the SO or bolted-canister type.

Although there are many manufacturers of fuel filter/water separators, the concept of operation in all cases is to separate the heavier water from the lighter diesel fuel, usually by centrifugal action of the incoming fuel within the specially shaped housing. Figure 16-3 illustrates the flow of diesel fuel into, through, and out of the heavy-duty filter/water separator for a Racor Turbine series model:

1. In the primary stage, liquid and solid contaminants down to 30 μm are separated out by centrifugal action created by the turbine centrifuge. Dirt and wa-

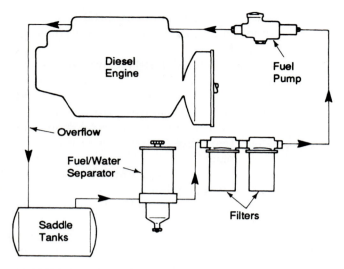

FIGURE 16–2 *Typical installation arrangement for using a fuel filter/water separator.*

ter, both being heavier than the fuel, tend to fall to the bottom of the clear bowl.

2. In the secondary stage, any minute particles of liquid contamination (lighter than the fuel) remain in suspension and flow up with the fuel into the lower part of the filter/separator shell where the minute particles tend to bead on the inner wall of the shell and the bottom of the specially treated filter element. Any accumulation of the water beads (heavier) will allow them to fall to the bottom of the filter/separator bowl.

3. In the final filtration stage, the fuel flows through the replaceable filter element where the minute solids down to a 2-µm particle size are removed to a 96% rating.

Filter replacement in this model is achieved by loosening off the large T-handle on top of the assembly and opening the drain valve to remove accumulated water and fuel contaminants from the clear bowl. The filter can then be replaced.

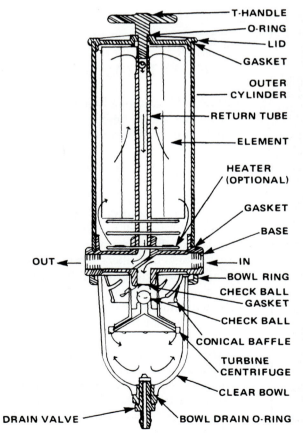

HOW THE RACOR FILTER/ SEPARATOR WORKS

The three stages of the Racor filter/ separator work in series to progressively clean the diesel fuel. Because virtually all water and particles of solid contamination are removed in the primary and secondary stages, the effective life of the fine micron replaceable element (the third stage) is 2-3 times longer than standard filters.

Primary Stage (Separation)

In the primary stage, liquid and solid contamination down to 30 micron are separated out by centrifugal action created by the turbine centrifuge. There are no moving parts in this highly efficient design. Because the contamination is heavier than the fuel, it falls to the bottom of the clear bowl.

Secondary Stage (Coalescing)

This stage functions when minute particles of liquid contamination (lighter than the fuel) remain in suspension and flow up with the fuel into the lower part of the filter/ separator shell. Here the minute particles tend to bead on the inner wall of the shell and the bottom of the specially treated replacement element. As the beads accumulate, they become larger and heavier and eventually fall to the bottom of the filter/separator bowl.

Final Stage (Filtration)

In this stage, the fuel flows through the replacement element where the minute solids are removed.

FIGURE 16–3 *Fuel flow through a Racor Turbine Series fuel/filter/water separator assembly. (Courtesy of Peterbilt Motors Company, a Division of Paccar, Newark, CA.)*

In some models of fuel filter/water separators, the first stage of the filter assembly directs the diesel fuel through a tube of fine nylon fibers that are designed to *coalesce* any water. The fuel containing emulsified water passes through the coalescer element. The element retards the flow of water droplets, allowing them to combine to form larger drops of water. The larger drops of water emerging from the coalescer then gravitate to the filter reservoir at the bottom of the filter. The fuel then passes through the second stage of the filter assembly paper element, which is specially treated to restrict passage of small water droplets.

Another widely used filter assembly is the Davco Fuel Pro 380 illustrated in Figure 16-4. This single filter system replaces both the primary and secondary fuel filter assemblies, thereby reducing filter usage by 75 percent. This filter model has now been adopted by several major diesel engine OEMs, who market the Fuel Pro 380 with their own brand name on it. In this unique heavy-duty filter model, a clear cover on the upper half of the assembly allows the operator or maintenance technician to see the filter condition, and to check for signs of air in the incoming fuel, as shown in Figure 16-5. In addition, as filter restriction increases through dirt entrapment in the filter pores, dirt collects on the filter from the bottom up and the fuel level rises on the clear filter cover, indicating the remaining life to the next service interval. Any water in the fuel falls to the bottom of the filter assembly where it can be drained away using the rugged no-leak quick-drain valve at the base. Within the filter housing, a thermostatically controlled electric preheater warms the fuel to prevent waxing and gelling in cold ambient operating conditions. The standard fuel preheater is rated at 250 W, 17 A. An optional 150-W 10-A model is also available. Many electric fuel heaters employ a PTC (positive temperature coefficient) ceramic heating element. A snap-disc thermostat in the heater assembly controls the operating temperature of the diesel fuel.

For severe cold weather operation, a Fuel pro 380 EF features two heat sources: electric preheat and a fluid heat tube (engine coolant). Figure 16-6 illustrates this combination heater system.

An optional engine coolant heater tube installed within the filter housing can also be used. The flow of engine coolant through this type of system is illustrated in Figure 16-6. A thermostat shuts off either the electric or engine coolant heater once the engine reaches a predetermined operating temperature. A check valve within the inlet port prevents fuel drainback when the engine is shut down. This feature prevents loss of fuel prime and hard starting conditions after shutdown. The check valve also prevents fuel losses when the filter assembly is changed.

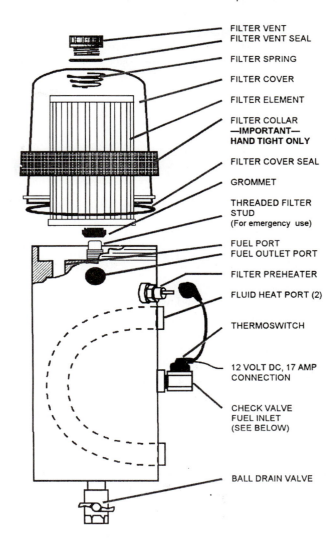

USE A BACK-UP WRENCH ON THE CHECK-VALVE WHEN INSTALLING OR REMOVING THE FUEL FITTING.

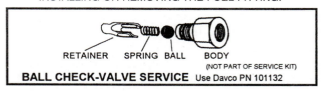

FIGURE 16–4 *Component parts and features for a Fuel Pro 380 fuel filter/water separator assembly. (Courtesy of Davco Manufacturing Corporation.)*

In the aluminum housing used with the Davco filter assembly, heat radiation from the filter is greater in warm weather than it is in some other filter housings. This reduces the temperature of the fuel and results in cooler fuel entering the system and in engines that run better with more power.

Another diesel fuel preheater system used on many heavy-duty truck applications is the *hot joint sys-*

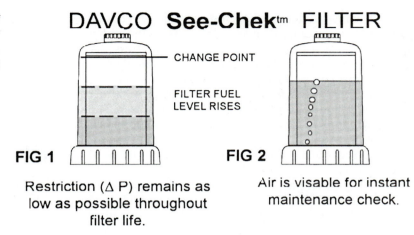

FIGURE 16–5 Features of the Davco See-Chek clear filter bowl used with the Fuel Pro 380. (Courtesy of Davco Manufacturing Corporation.)

DAVCO See-Chek™ FILTER

FIG 1
Restriction (Δ P) remains as low as possible throughout filter life.

FIG 2
Air is visable for instant maintenance check.

tem. This system is used with dual saddle-type fuel tanks that employ a balance line between the tanks on either side of the vehicle (Figure 16-7). The system prevents freeze-up at the fuel tank fitting in cold ambient operating temperatures, which would create serious engine starting problems. The hot joints can be wired to operate with an ON/OFF toggle switch (used with a 4-minute timer) or a thermoswitch. Each of the hot joints is typically protected by use of individual 15-A fuses or circuit breakers. If the ACC/IGN circuit will not handle 15-A, a 20-A relay can be used. An optional top-tank-mounted hot joint is also available. The hot joint heat probe shown in Figure 16-8 is thermostatically controlled for automatic operation from 40 to 60°F (4.5 to 15.5°C).

Figure 16-8 shows the *Fuel Manager* diesel filtration system. It includes an electronic water-in-fuel detection system to warn the operator or technician of excess water accumulation in the filter system. On diesel cars, pickup trucks, and light-duty trucks, this water sensor causes a light to illuminate on the vehicle dashboard. In many applications the operator can then simply activate a pushbutton drain valve located in the filter cover assembly or employ a mechanical lever system to automatically drain the accumulated water from the base of the filter assembly. The lamp extinguishes once the water has been drained, since the water acts as a ground system whereas the diesel fuel is more of an insulator.

FUEL HEATERS

Hot Line Fuel Heater

Some heavy-duty class 8 trucks and truck/tractors employ an advanced solid-state electric fuel heater that is actually constructed within the fuel line from the fuel tank to the filter assembly. Figure 16-9 illustrates this type of fuel heater system which is commonly called a *hot line system* (or a Thermoline, manufactured by the Racor Division of the Parker Hannifin Corporation). Figure 16-10 illustrates the wiring system used with a hot line system on a vehicle with a single fuel tank; a dual-saddle-tank system is also available. In a dual-tank arrangement, two hot line heaters are used (one for each tank) and a three-way dash-mounted selector switch is activated by the truck driver. The driver can activate either fuel tank's heater for a closed, single draw/single-return system; however both tanks cannot be heated at the same time. Placing the dash switch in the center, or OFF position, turns off all power to both hot line heaters.

Cold-Weather Operation

The properties of diesel fuel and its contaminants, especially water, may be altered drastically in cold weather. Depending on the quality of the diesel fuel, its cloud point (the point at which paraffin crystals precipitate) may be -17 to $7.2°C$ (0 to 45°F). Paraffin crystals (which are found in most diesel fuels) quickly coat filter elements and prevent fuel flow and vehicle operation. In addition, water contamination in the form of icy slush compounds the problem by slowing fuel flow even more quickly. It is desirable, therefore, to heat diesel fuel as close to the filter element as possible to reliquify wax and ice crystals.

Several methods are available to heat diesel fuel to maintain operation in cold weather. The two most common of these are (1) electric heaters and (2) coolant heaters. Both are inline units built into the diesel fuel filter/water separator.

For most low-flow applications [under 1.89 lpm (liters per minute), 0.5 gpm (gallons per minute)], an efficient 150- to 200-W electrical heater that is thermo-

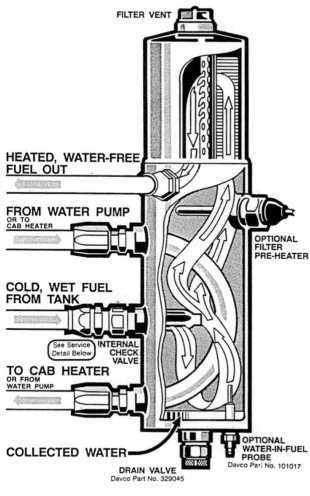

FILTER VENT

HEATED, WATER-FREE
FUEL OUT

FROM WATER PUMP
OR TO
CAB HEATER

OPTIONAL
FILTER
PRE-HEATER

COLD, WET FUEL
FROM TANK

See Service
Detail Below

INTERNAL
CHECK
VALVE

TO CAB HEATER
OR FROM
WATER PUMP

COLLECTED WATER

OPTIONAL
WATER-IN-FUEL
PROBE
Davco Part No. 101017

DRAIN VALVE
Davco Part No. 329045

BODY
NOT A KIT PART

BALL   SPRING   RETAINER

BALL CHECK-VALVE SERVICE
USE DAVCO KIT 101132

FIGURE 16–6 *Features and plumbing arrangement for a Davco Fuel Pro Model 321, which employs engine-heated coolant running through the filter body. (Courtesy of Davco Manufacturing Corporation.)*

statically controlled will economically provide immediate heat and maintain equipment operation. For higher-flow applications, the problem is more challenging. To ensure operation in cold conditions, a large amount of energy is required (for example, 1.5-gpm flow for a Cummins 350 to maintain operation). Several options are available: an efficient 350- to 500-W electrical heater; a 150- to 300-W startup heater in con-

junction with a coolant heater; and a combination coolant heater with an electrical heater. These options will prevent paraffin crystals from coating the filter medium and will assist in providing diesel fuel flow to the injection system in most cold-weather conditions. In extreme cold conditions (−76°C, −60°F) additional measures are required.

In a diesel engine, only a small percentage of the fuel that is delivered to the unit injectors is actually used for combustion purposes. As much as 80% is used for cooling and lubricating the injection pump and injector component parts. The high rate of return fuel has been filtered of its wax precipitants and has been warmed by the heat from the engine. On high-pressure inline injection pumps, most of the fuel is returned from the pump, not from the nozzles.

SUMMARY

This chapter has described diesel fuel grades, filter design and operation, fuel filter/water separators, thermostatically controlled heaters, and the maintenance/service of these items. This knowledge will help in troubleshooting the engine fuel system. For greater details on specific fuel systems and their operation, refer to the respective chapters within this textbook for a specific type of fuel system.

SELF-TEST QUESTIONS

1. Technician A says that material used in primary fuel filters generally consists of resin pleated paper, whereas technician B says that the primary filter is usually composed of cotton material. Who is correct?

2. Technician A says that a micron is one-ten-thousandth of a meter. Technician B says that a micron is equivalent to one-millionth of a meter. Who is right?

3. After the discussion in Question 2, technician A says that a micron can be written as 0.003937 in., whereas technician B disagrees, slaying that a micron is shown as 0.00003937 in. With whom do you agree?

4. Technician A says that the filtering capability of most primary filters used in regular service is rated as 30 μm. Technician B says that it is closer to 12 μm. Who is right?

5. Technician A says that secondary fuel filters used in what is classified as severe-duty service are generally rated at between 3 and 5 μm. Technician B disagrees, saying that this would cause too great a fuel flow restriction. Who is correct?

6. Technician A says that it is not necessary to use a separate primary filter when a good fuel filter/water separator assembly is used in the fuel system. Technician B disagrees, saying that you should always use a primary

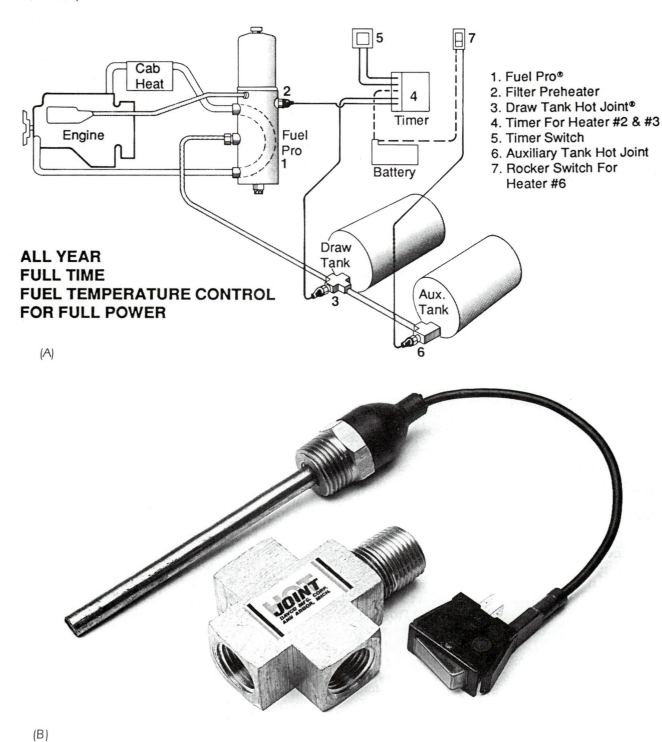

1. Fuel Pro®
2. Filter Preheater
3. Draw Tank Hot Joint®
4. Timer For Heater #2 & #3
5. Timer Switch
6. Auxiliary Tank Hot Joint
7. Rocker Switch For
   Heater #6

**ALL YEAR
FULL TIME
FUEL TEMPERATURE CONTROL
FOR FULL POWER**

(A)

(B)

FIGURE 16–7 (A) Typical system schematic, showing the diesel Fuel Pro and hot joints location on a heavy-duty truck with saddle tanks; (B) components of the Davco hot-joint assembly. (Courtesy of Davco Manufacturing Corporation.)

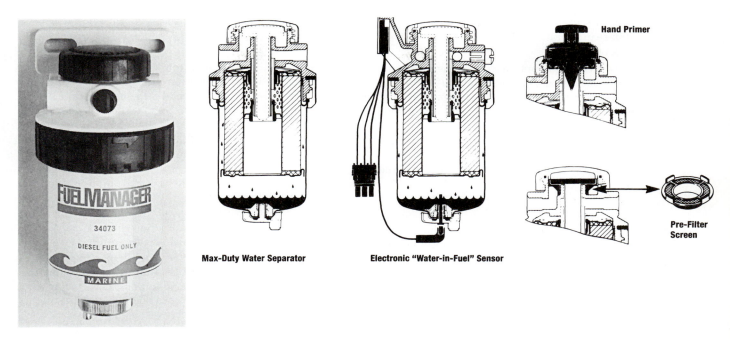

Max-Duty Water Separator   Electronic "Water-in-Fuel" Sensor   Hand Primer   Pre-Filter Screen

FIGURE 16–8 *Engine fuel manager diesel fuel filtration system. (Courtesy of Stanadyne Diesel Systems.)*

fuel filter, regardless of whatever else is used in the system. Who is correct?

7. Technician A says that water in the fuel will simply cause rusting of injection components. Technician B says that a slug of water can blow the tip off an injector. Who is correct?

8. Technician A says that water in a fuel tank can be caused by allowing the warm return fuel from the engine to cool in the tank. Technician B says that the only way that water can get into the tank is through improper handling of bulk fuel during fill-up. Who is right?

9. To minimize condensation in a fuel tank, you should
   a. always park the truck inside at night in a warm shop
   b. plug in a cylinder block coolant heater at night
   c. use a fuel tank heater
   d. instruct drivers to fill up the fuel tank at the end of each shift or at the end of the day if no shift work is performed

10. A truck fleet supervisor instructs a mechanic that if a fuel filter/water separator is not used on an engine fuel system, to prevent fuel line freeze-up add
   a. methyl or isopropyl alcohol
   b. liquid starting fluid as required

FIGURE 16–9 *Close-up view of Racor Thermoline diesel fuel line heater construction. (Courtesy of Parker Hannifin Corporation, Racor Division.)*

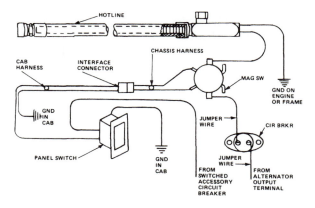

FIGURE 16–10 *Single hot line fuel heater arrangement for use on a heavy-duty class 8 truck/tractor. (Courtesy of Peterbilt Motors Company, a Division of Paccar.)*

   c. kerosene to cut the fuel's specific gravity

   d. antifreeze in the ratio of 1 pint to every 125 gallons of diesel fuel

11. Fuel filter water separators generally operate on the principle of coalescence. This simply means

   a. droplets of water entering the fuel/water filter form into large globules or droplets, where they settle in the reservoir

   b. water is broken down into tiny droplets to make it easier to spin them loose by gravitational forces

   c. preheating the water to make it easier to trap in the filter

12. Technician A says that the word *primary* and the word *secondary* are usually cast onto the fuel filter housing cover to prevent improper installation in the system. Technician B says that it doesn't matter, since the two fuel filters are the same physical size anyway. Who is correct?

13. Technician A says that fuel filters must be changed every 300 hours or 9000 miles. Technician B says that the filter change period can be determined by the truck fleet operating conditions. Who is correct?

14. Technician A says that fuel filters should be replaced when they become plugged. This can be determined when the engine loses horsepower. Technician B disagrees, saying that they should be changed at regular intervals to suit the operating conditions of the equipment. Who is correct?

15. Technician A says that to determine if the primary fuel filter is plugged you can make a fuel system restriction (vacuum) check. Technician B says that you should insert a fuel pressure gauge and determine the pressure drop through the filter assembly. What procedure would be acceptable?

16. True or False: A shell-and-element filter assembly is a throwaway type of unit.

17. A truck fleet mechanic says that after replacing diesel fuel filters you should always

   a. ensure that the filters have been filled up with clean filtered fuel

   b. fill the filters with unfiltered fuel since any dirt will be filtered out as it passes through the filter

   c. bleed (prime) the fuel system of all entrapped air

   d. fill up the fuel tank and crank the engine over until it starts

18. Technician A says that spin-on types of fuel filters should be tightened between one-half and two-thirds of a turn after the gasket contacts the base. Technician B says that the spin-on filter should be tightened securely with a strap wrench. Who is right?

19. Technician A says that if the engine runs rough or fails to run after changing the fuel filter assemblies, the most probable cause is a lack of fuel in the tank. Technician B says that it is more likely to be due to air trapped in the system. Who is correct?

20. True or False: Fuel filter/water separators contain internal heater units that must be switched ON/OFF in cold weather to prevent fuel line freeze-up.

21. Technician A says that water accumulation in a fuel filter/water separator must be drained off every day to prevent fuel filter damage. Technician B says that water accumulation has to be drained off only when the reservoir bowl is full or when the warning light on the vehicle instrument panel comes on. Who is correct?

22. Technician A says that all fuel filter/water separators contain a filter assembly that must be changed each time the regular fuel filters are changed. Technician B says that some models of fuel filter/water separators do not use a filter element at all and that the regular primary and secondary fuel filters are sufficient. Who is right?

23. Technician A says that a Thermoline unit is a heated fuel line that takes the place of the regular fuel line. Technician B says that a Thermoline unit is a fuel filter/water separator with a thermostatically controlled heating element. Who is correct?

24. The reason for using a fuel heater in winter is to

   a. increase the engine horsepower

   b. prevent waxing of the fuel filters, which would cause plugging

   c. stop any water in the fuel from freezing

   d. allow the engine to idle overnight without damage

25. Technician A says that fuel heaters are operated by warm coolant from the engine, whereas technician B says that only electrically operated fuel heaters are used. Who is correct?

17 Mechanical and Electronic Governors

OVERVIEW

The diesel technician today needs to understand fully the operation of both mechanical and electronic governor systems, because each controls fuel flow to the engine cylinders and consequently can affect the vehicle (or equipment or vessel) performance. In this chapter we discuss how both of these control systems function.

GOVERNOR FUNCTION

Since the speed of the engine is directly related to its power, speed must be maintained during operation. This is the job of the governor, which is considered the brain of the engine. The diesel engine governor controls the engine speed under various load conditions by changing the amount of fuel delivered to the engine cylinders. Governors, like engines, may be of many types and designs, but all will be designed to accomplish engine speed control under low-idle, high-speed, and full-load conditions.

If, for example, a truck engine did not have a governor, the operator would have to control the engine speed at idle manually, since the engine would not idle unattended. On the other end of the speed range, the top speed of the engine would have to be limited by the operator or the engine would overspeed and could cause engine damage. It is obvious that a governor on a truck engine is a much-needed component. Without it, the operator would have difficulty in controlling the engine properly.

This speed may be anywhere in the speed range from idle to high speed; then as the machine is oper-

ated, it may encounter a change in load many times a minute, causing the governor to change the fuel delivery accordingly. This fuel delivery change, in turn, maintains steady engine speed with sufficient power to pull the load. The operator could not possibly anticipate the rapid load change encountered by the engine to maintain a steady engine speed as well as sufficient power to pull the load.

WHY A GOVERNOR IS REQUIRED

The speed and horsepower capability of any internal combustion engine is regulated by the volume of air that can be retained within the engine cylinders and the volume of fuel that can be delivered and consumed during the engine power stroke. More than likely you have a driver's license, so you are aware of the fact that when you drive a car or truck equipped with a gasoline engine, *you* determine the rate of fuel supplied to the engine by manipulation of the gas or throttle pedal. Regardless of whether the engine is carbureted or fuel injected, throttle movement controls the flow of air into the engine cylinders and thus the desired fuel flow.

Therefore, a mechanical or electronic governor assembly is not necessary on a gasoline engine. Nevertheless, some gasoline engines in industrial and truck applications are equipped with a governor to control the maximum speed and power of the engine/vehicle. In addition, some models of passenger cars are equipped with an electronic ignition cutoff system to control the maximum speed of the vehicle. Remember, a governor is not a "must" with a gasoline engine as it is with a diesel engine.

Why then does a diesel engine require a governor assembly? The main reason has to do with the fact that the throttle pedal controlled by the operator does not regulate the airflow into the diesel engine but controls the fuel flow. Current gasoline engines in passenger cars have electronic controls for both the ignition and fuel systems and are designed to operate at air/fuel ratios that allow the engine to comply with existing U.S. EPA exhaust emissions standards. Through the use of an exhaust gas oxygen sensor, the air/fuel ratio is in *closed loop* operation (oxygen sensor receives an input reference voltage signal from the ECM and returns a system operating condition signal back to the ECM to complete the circuit). The oxygen sensor monitors the percentage of oxygen in the exhaust gases leaving the engine. The ECM then either leans out or enriches the air/fuel mixture to try and maintain a *stoichiometric* air/fuel ratio, which is between 14.6 and 14.7 parts of air to 1 part of fuel (gasoline).

Due to the unthrottled air supply condition, a diesel engine at an idle speed runs very lean, with air/fuel ratios being between 90 and 120:1, depending on the specific model of engine in question. Under full-load conditions, this air/fuel ratio is approximately 25 to 30:1.

Let's assume for instructional purposes that a given four-stroke-cycle diesel engine is designed to produce 400 bhp (298 kW) at 2100 rpm full-load speed. If we also assume that to produce this power, each fuel injector is designed to deliver 185 mm^3 of fuel into each cylinder for each power stroke, then by manual operation of the throttle we might assume that at an idle speed of 600 rpm, the fuel delivery rate to each cylinder might be only 18.5 mm^3 with the engine producing possibly 40 bhp (30 kW). A similarly rated two-stroke-cycle engine would inject approximately half as much fuel per power stroke, but since there are two power strokes for every one in the four-cycle engine, both engines will consume approximately the same amount of fuel.

If the vehicle is stationary and the throttle is placed into a WOT (wide-open throttle) position, the engine does not need to receive full fuel (185 mm^3) to accelerate to its maximum no-load speed. The engine can be accelerated with very little additional fuel being supplied to the cylinders, because with no load on the engine, we have to overcome only the resistance to motion from the engine components, as well as any accessory driven items that need more horsepower to drive them at this higher speed. In addition, if the engine has very little additional load from what it had at an idle rpm, the faster rotating flywheel will store enough inertia (centrifugal force generated at the higher speed) to keep the engine turning over smoothly at this higher no-load speed.

Once the engine obtains this higher no-load speed, in this example, say, 2250 rpm, the same amount of fuel (or slightly more) that was supplied at idle will basically maintain this higher speed. However, on a diesel engine, remember that manual operation of the throttle controls the fuel flow and *not* the airflow as happens on a gasoline engine. Therefore, by opening the throttle to a WOT position in this engine, we actually deliver 185 mm^3 of fuel to the engine cylinders, or *10* times more than we did at idle speed; but all we need to maintain this higher no-load rpm is basically the same volume of fuel that we used at idle (18.5 mm^3) at 600 rpm, or slightly more. If we generated 40 bhp (30 kW) at 600 rpm, at WOT we might develop an additional 10 to 15 hp (7.5 to 11 kW) to handle the increased power requirements of the various accessory items such as a fan, air compressor, or generator. We certainly do not require the 400 bhp (298 kW) rated power output of the engine under this operating condition.

Without a governor assembly, a WOT position grossly *overfuels* the engine in this high-idle no-load example by about 10 times its needs. Since we know from earlier discussions that the diesel engine always operates with an excess air supply, we have sufficient air to burn this full-fuel delivery rate. The result will be that with 10 times more fuel than necessary, the engine rpm will continue to climb in excess of a safe operating speed. Under such a nongoverned overfueled condition most diesels will quickly self-destruct as a result of valves striking piston crowns and connecting rods punching through the engine block as well as possible crankshaft breakage.

When a load is applied to a diesel engine, more fuel delivery is obviously required to generate the extra heat energy to produce the higher horsepower required. In our simplified example, this engine can produce 400 bhp (298 kW) at 2100 rpm WOT full-load operating conditions. It is only under such a condition that this engine needs its 185 mm^3 of fuel delivery to each cylinder. Refer to the engine performance curve charts illustrated in Chapter 3; you can see that the power produced by the engine increases with speed, since horsepower is considered as being the rate or speed at which work is done by the engine. To prevent the engine from over-revving and running away, we must have some type of control mechanism that will limit the amount of fuel injected to the engine cylinders under all operating conditions. In other words, we need either a mechanical or electronic governor assembly on the engine!

MECHANICAL GOVERNOR OPERATION

Regardless of governor type, most governors operate with many of the same basic components. These components should be understood before further governor

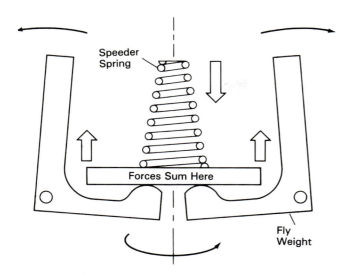

FIGURE 17–1 *Weight force versus spring force to achieve governor speed balance—often referred to as SOB (state of balance).*

study can take place. The basic mechanical governor (Figure 17-1) is a speed-sensing device that uses two main components: a set of engine-driven flyweights and a spring. Each of these components serves a purpose in *all* mechanical governors. The force of the spring is designed to move the fuel control linkage to an *increased* setting under all operating conditions. The centrifugal force generated by the engine-driven flyweights is designed to *decrease* the fuel control linkage setting under all operating conditions.

When the engine is stopped, the force of the governor spring is therefore attempting to place the fuel control racks into a full-fuel position. On some engines, the governor is arranged so as to provide excess

fuel for start-up purposes, whereas on some turbocharged engine models, a mechanical adjustment device limits start-up fuel to half-throttle to minimize exhaust smoke. In these simplified governor diagrams, we show the manual throttle control as being connected directly above the governor spring; in reality, seldom is this the case. Instead, additional linkage is used to transfer the manual operation of the throttle to the governor spring assembly.

Increasing the force of the governor spring through the throttle linkage when the engine is running manually increases the fuel rack setting, resulting in an increase in engine speed and power. As the engine accelerates, the centrifugal force generated by the rotating flyweights becomes stronger and the flyweights oppose the force of the spring. For a given throttle setting, the force applied to the spring will cause the weights to generate an equal and opposing force. When the spring force and weight forces become equal for a given engine load and speed, the governor is said to be in a *state of balance*, and the fuel racks will be held in a stationary position with the engine producing a specific horsepower at a given rpm.

Since the governor weights are engine driven, the governor assembly is said to be *speed sensitive*. An engine speed change due to a load increase or a load decrease will affect the rotational speed of the flyweights and, therefore, the state-of-balance condition that exists between the weights and the governor spring for any throttle setting position.

The only problem with the oversimplified governor assembly shown in Figure 17-1 is that we have no means by which we can change the engine speed setting by manipulation of a throttle. In the simplified diagram in Figure 17-2, there is a method shown by

FIGURE 17–2 *Concepts of basic governor reaction: (A) state of balance condition where the centrifugal force of the weights balances the spring force; (B) load decrease causes a speed increase, resulting in a decrease in the fuel setting; (C) load increase causes a speed decrease resulting in an increase in the fuel setting.*

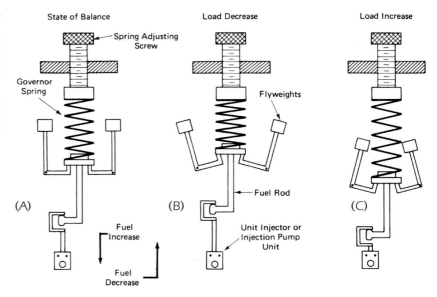

which we can vary the compressive force of the governor spring assembly, but the speed regulation of the engine would be limited by the force required to balance out this spring by the rotating governor flyweights and this system would not allow an engine speed change by a speed control lever when the engine is running.

To be able to change the fuel delivery to the engine manually, we have to introduce linkage that allows the truck driver to accelerate and decelerate the engine at will due to changing road, load, and speed conditions. Figures 17-3 and 17-4 illustrate simple examples of how we might achieve this with a single-spring all-range or variable-speed mechanical governor. This governor is capable of controlling the idle speed, the maximum speed, and all ranges in between. Take careful note of the connections between the components of this governor assembly. To increase the fuel injection pump rack setting, the following events must take place in Figure 17-3:

1. Press down on the accelerator pedal, shown as item I.

2. Throttle linkage H will move to the left-hand side of the diagram.

3. The vertical throttle linkage that extends down from the support bracket is supported above in two bushings, to allow the linkage to rotate each time the pedal is moved.

4. The lower end of the vertical throttle linkage is engaged with a sliding sleeve, shown as item G. Any throttle depression will therefore cause this sliding sleeve to move to the left against the compressive force of the governor spring F.

5. The mechanical linkage D will therefore move to the left-hand side of the diagram. As D moves, it will pull the injector control rack rod or in-line multiple-plunger pump control rack E to an increased or "open" fuel position.

6. The maximum fuel rack position is limited by the fact that linkage D will eventually butt up against the adjustable high-speed stop bolt K.

7. The position of the throttle pedal is determined by the truck driver or operator. When the sliding sleeve G is moved to the left, the governor tension spring F is placed under compression and the sliding sleeve C applies pressure to the toes of the flyweights, causing them to move inward slightly.

8. The operator has manually caused the fuel rack to move to an increased setting which allows the engine to accelerate, and it starts to develop additional horse-power due to the additional fuel supply to the combustion chambers.

9. When the operator halts throttle pedal movement, the now-faster rotating governor flyweights will reach a point where they attain a state of balance with the stronger governor spring. When this state of balance exists between the weight and spring forces, the engine will run at a steady speed.

10. In the simplified governor shown in Figure 17-3, this governor is capable of controlling the engine speed throughout the complete speed range and is therefore known as an all-range or variable-speed type. The idle speed is set by the position of the adjustable low-speed adjustment screw shown as item J. Turning the screw clockwise will increase the speed, while rotating it counterclockwise will decrease the speed.

FIGURE 17-3 Linkage connections from throttle to governor assembly for a multiple-plunger in-line injection pump type of system.

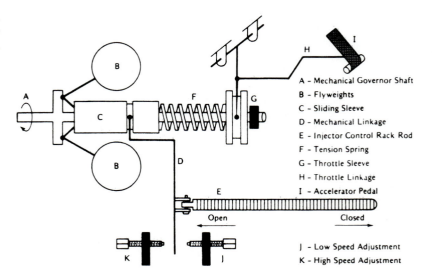

A – Mechanical Governor Shaft
B – Flyweights
C – Sliding Sleeve
D – Mechanical Linkage
E – Injector Control Rack Rod
F – Tension Spring
G – Throttle Sleeve
H – Throttle Linkage
I – Accelerator Pedal

Open   Closed

J – Low Speed Adjustment
K – High Speed Adjustment

FIGURE 17-4 *Basic mechanical governor linkage connections for a unit injector fuel system.*

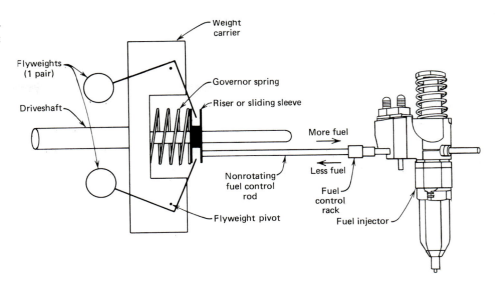

Starting and Idling the Engine

In Figure 17-3 the following sequence of events would occur during the initial cranking and starting procedures. With the engine stopped and the throttle linkage held in the idle position by the force of an external return spring, the tension spring F would expand and move the governor fuel control linkage D and E (rack) into a full-fuel position against the stationary flyweights. The throttle pedal would not move, since a yield link or telescopic link assembled into the throttle linkage can be used to prevent this from occurring. The expansion of the governor spring F allows the spring to give up some of its stored energy in moving the rack control linkage. When the engine is cranked over on the starter motor, shaft A will rotate and the weights B will attempt to move out against the tension spring F. As soon as the engine fires and runs, the accelerating flyweight force will start to compress the tension spring and push it to the right-hand side of the diagram. This action forces the linkage D and the rack E to move to a decreased fuel setting. The linkage movement D toward the closed fuel position will be limited by the setting of the low-speed adjustment screw J. As the weights compress the tension spring F, the spring force becomes stronger until the centrifugal force of the rotating flyweights is equal to that in the spring. When this position is obtained, the governor is said to be in a state of balance and the engine will run at a steady idle speed. To change the idle speed, the low-speed adjusting screw J is turned CW or CCW.

Load Increase at Idle

In Figure 17-3, when a load is applied to the engine at an idle speed, the state of balance between the weights and the tension spring F is disturbed in favor of the spring. This is because the engine speed will decrease with a load increase, causing the weights to move inward. The spring expands, giving up some of its energy in moving the fuel control linkage toward an open or fuel-increase position. The engine now receives additional fuel in order to develop additional horsepower to handle the increased load. The sensitivity of the governor mechanism determines just how quickly the engine will respond. As the engine develops more power, the weights will attempt to move outward again; however, since the spring is now longer and weaker than it was before the load was applied (expanded to increase fuel setting), the weights will obtain a new state of balance at a lower engine speed. This is known as the droop factor, because the engine will not return again to the same speed.

Load Decrease at Idle

If a load is removed from the engine at an idle rpm, the engine speed will tend to increase, causing the flyweights to move outward against the tension spring F. This action will push the sliding sleeve C and the linkage D, which is connected to the rack E, to the right-hand side of the diagram. Less fuel is delivered to the combustion chambers and the engine will now develop less horsepower. Due to the stronger initial weight force caused by the load decrease, the weights and tension spring obtain a new state of balance, but at a slightly higher speed, due to the force that was applied to the spring, which made it stronger. Again this is part of the governor's inherent droop factor.

Governor Action at the High-Speed End

The maximum speed of the engine is limited by the compressive force that can be applied to the tension spring F. Throttle pedal movement at I will force the throttle sleeve G to move the spring F, the linkage D, the rack E, and the sliding sleeve C to the left-hand side of the diagram. The maximum distance that the linkage D can move is limited by the high-speed adjustment screw K. This positive stop therefore limits the applied force to spring F from the throttle pedal. Regardless of where the truck driver places the governor linkage D between idle and maximum, the rotating governor flyweights B will be able to obtain a state of balance. Starting the engine under a no-load condition and then moving the throttle to its maximum (high idle) speed setting position will result in the engine obtaining a higher speed than it would under a full-load (rated) speed condition. The maximum no-load (high idle) speed of the engine is limited by the fact that the weights will start to compress the tension spring F, due to their higher rotative speed. Consider that if the engine were adjusted to produce a maximum no-load speed of 2310 rpm with a 10% sensitive governor, this means that the full-load or rated speed would be 2100 rpm. The initial placement of the throttle pedal into its maximum speed position compresses the tension spring F, which moves the fuel rack E to an increased fuel setting. As the engine accelerates, the weights are trying to develop enough force to oppose the spring. Since the weights are speed sensitive, as they reach a speed of 2100 rpm, they have enough force to start compressing the spring, which will move the rack E to a decreased fuel position. As they start to compress the spring, it becomes stronger, until a state of balance is obtained and the engine speed is limited in this case to no more than 2310 rpm no-load. If a load is now applied to the engine, its speed will decrease and the state of balance will be upset in favor of the tension spring F. The governor linkage D and the rack E will now be moved into an increased fuel position. If a full load is applied to the engine, it will settle at a rated speed of 2100 rpm. However, if less than full load is applied to the engine, the speed will settle down somewhere between the maximum no-load (high-idle) and the maximum full-load (rated) speeds. Therefore, the governor automatically compensates for changes in load and/or speed as a consequence of throttle movement or road terrain in a heavy-duty truck application.

GOVERNOR TERMS

All diesel engines must operate with a governor mechanism to control the speed and response of the engine under varying load and throttle opening conditions. As a foundation for our discussion of governor types and their operation, study the following governor terms; they are commonly used in reference to engine speed regulation.

Although most engine and fuel injection equipment manufacturers use the same general terms, phraseology fluctuates between specific engine manufacturers. Common meanings, and the different terms, will be discussed where applicable.

1. *Maximum no-load speed* or *high idle* is a term used to describe the highest engine rpm obtainable when the throttle linkage is moved to its maximum position with no load applied to the engine. This rpm can be adjusted to suit changing conditions or applications according to the engine manufacturer's limits and recommendations.

2. *Maximum full-load speed* or *rated speed* indicates the engine rpm at which a particular engine will produce its maximum designed horsepower setting as stated by the manufacturer.

3. *Idle* or *low idle speed* is the term used to indicate the normal speed at which the engine will rotate with the throttle linkage in the released or closed position. Normally, truck idle speed settings range between 500 and 700 rpm and are adjustable.

4. *Work capacity* describes the amount of available work energy that can be produced at the governor's terminal or output shaft. Each specific mechanical or hydromechanical governor assembly is designed to have enough work output to ensure that it can move the associated linkage that is connected to it. The work capacity is generally expressed in inch-pounds or foot-pounds.

5. *Stability* refers to the condition of the governor linkage after a load or speed setting change. The governor must be able to return the engine to a new speed/load setting without any tendency for the engine speed to drift up or down (fluctuate) before settling down at the new setting. Stability of a governor is usually indicated by the number of corrective movements it makes and the time required to correct fuel flow for any given load change.

6. *Speed droop*. An engine operating at WOT with no load on it will run at a higher speed than it does at WOT under full load! Why will the engine not run at the same speed loaded or unloaded? The answer has to do with the term *governor droop*, or how "sensitive" the governor assembly is to an engine speed change. How much speed will be lost or gained depends on the governor reaction. The difference between the engine MNL (maximum no-load) speed (high idle) and the MFL (maximum full-load) speed (rated) is known as governor droop. This can be determined as follows:

$$\text{droop} = \frac{\text{MNL} - \text{MFL}}{\text{MFL}} \times 100\%$$

$$= \frac{2250 - 2100}{2100} \times 100\% = 7.14\%$$

In this example, the droop is actually 150 rpm, which is a full-load droop speed. Regardless of the speed at which the engine is running, this droop percentage will remain constant; however, the rpm will change.

Seven percent of 2250 rpm versus 7% of 1200 rpm results in droop readings of 150 and 85 rpm, respectively. An engine idling at 600 rpm with no load would result in a speed loss of 42 rpm when fully loaded.

What causes droop? To describe this condition, let's refer to the three simplified diagrams illustrated in Figure 17-2. When the engine is stopped the weights are collapsed and the spring force pushes the fuel rack to the maximum position for startup purposes. When the engine is cranked and fires, the centrifugal force generated at the weights starts to compress the spring, while at the same time pulling the fuel rack to a decreased fuel setting. When the weight and spring forces are equal, the governor is said to be in a *SOB* (state of balance) condition. The position of the fuel rack is held at a position corresponding to this SOB. For example, with the throttle held at an idle position, the engine would run at this speed setting, which can be adjusted by a screw to change the spring force.

If in Figure 17-2A the weights and spring are at a SOB condition and the spring is compressed to 102 mm (4 in.), let's assume the spring has a stored energy (force) of 10 lb (4.5 kg). If we now apply a load to the engine at this fixed throttle position as shown in Figure 17-2C, the engine requires more power to maintain this SOB condition. The additional load will cause the engine speed to drop, which will upset the SOB condition between the weights and spring. This allows the spring to expand and give up some of its stored energy in moving the fuel racks to an increased position. Let's assume that the spring is now 108 mm (4.25 in.) long, with a stored energy of only 9 lb (4 kg); the centrifugal force generated by the rotating flyweights will be able to obtain a new SOB with this longer and weaker spring at a lower engine speed. The engine will now be running at a slower rpm, but with more fuel being delivered to the cylinders it will produce more horsepower to handle the additional load. The difference in engine speed due to this rebalancing between the weights and spring is what causes the "droop."

With the engine running at a fixed throttle position and a SOB condition similar to that shown in Figure 17-2A, we are now going to decrease the load as shown in Figure 17-2B. Once again we upset the SOB between the weights and spring in favor of the weights because the engine would now tend to pick up speed. As the weights fly outward due to the higher engine rpm, the spring is compressed as the fuel rack is pulled to a decreased fuel setting. Let's assume that the spring is now 95.25 mm (3.75 in.) long and has a stored energy of 11 lb (5 kg); with a shorter and stronger spring, the weights will have to rotate faster to maintain a new governor SOB condition. However, with the fuel rack at a decreased setting due to a lighter load, the engine now runs slightly faster

but produces less horsepower. Once again, droop has entered the speed change picture.

In a variable-speed (all-range) governor, the weights and spring can control any speed setting selected by the operator. In a limiting-speed (minimum/maximum) governor, however, the speed control is designed to operate only at the lower and higher ends of the speed zones. Between these speeds, the operator controls engine speed by manual operation of the throttle. Regardless of the type of governor employed on an engine and the speed at which it is running, a load increase or a load decrease situation results in governor reactions similar to those illustrated in Figure 17-2.

7. *Sensitivity* is an expression of how quickly the governor responds to a speed change. For example, a governor that responds to a speed change of 5% is more sensitive than a governor that responds with a 10% speed change. Once the governor has sensed a speed change, it must produce a corrective movement of the fuel control mechanism.

8. *Response time* is tied closely to the governor's sensitivity and is normally the time taken in seconds for the fuel linkage to be moved from a no-load to a full-load position.

9. *Isochronous* is the term used to indicate zero-droop capability. In other words, the full-load (rated) and no-load (high idle) speeds are the same.

10. *Speed drift* is usually most noticeable at an idle speed and more commonly referred to as *hunting* or *surging*, where the set speed tends to rise above or below the initial governed setting. Speed drift is usually easily adjustable by means of a buffer screw or a bumper spring on the governor housing.

11. *Overrun* is a term used to express the action of the governor when the engine tends to exceed its maximum governed speed. Generally, overrun occurs when the engine is driven by the vehicle road wheels, such as when descending a steep hill.

12. *Underrun* is simply a term used to describe the governor's inability to prevent the engine speed from dropping below a set idle, particularly when the throttle has been moved rapidly to a decreased fuel setting from a high idle or maximum full-load position. This can generally result in the engine stalling.

13. *Deadband* is the term used to describe a very narrow speed range during which no measurable correction is made by the governor.

14. *State of balance* is the common term used to describe the speed at which the centrifugal force of the rotating governor flyweights matches and balances the governor speeder spring force. This can occur at any speed in an all-range governor as long as the speed of the engine can develop sufficient horsepower to carry the load applied.

TYPES OF GOVERNORS

There are a number of different types or styles of governors used on diesel engines. Some of these are common to industrial, marine, and power generator set applications. Basic types of governors can be classified in the following six categories:

1. Mechanical centrifugal flyweight style, which relies on a set of rotating flyweights and a control spring; used since the inception of the diesel engine to control its speed. Millions of these are still used in one form or another on mechanically operated and controlled diesel fuel injection systems.

2. Power-assisted servomechanical style, which operates similarly to that described in 1 but also employs engine oil under pressure to move the operating linkage. Used on many engines, such as Caterpillar PLN products, in a variety of applications.

3. Hydraulic governor, which relies on the movement of a pilot valve plunger to control pressurized oil flow to a power piston, which in turn moves the fuel control mechanism. Commonly used on industrial, marine, and power generator set engine applications.

4. Pneumatic governor, which is responsive to the airflow (vacuum) in the intake manifold of the engine. A diaphragm within the governor housing is connected to the fuel control linkage, which changes its setting with increases or decreases in the vacuum.

5. Electromechanical governor assembly, which uses a magnetic speed pickup sensor on an engine-driven component to monitor the rpm. The sensor sends a voltage signal to an electronic control unit, which in turn controls the current flow to a mechanical actuator connected to the fuel linkage. Commonly used on stationary power plants and generator sets.

6. Electronic governor assembly, which uses a magnetic speed sensor to monitor the engine rpm. The sensor continuously feeds a signal back to an ECM (electronic control module). The ECM then computes this signal along with information from other engine/vehicle sensors, such as the throttle position sensor, turbocharger boost sensor, engine oil pressure and temperature, engine coolant level or temperature, and fuel temperature to limit the engine speed. The ECM actually alters the PWM (pulse-width-modulated) electrical signal to the electronically controlled injectors to control how long fuel is injected over a given amount of crankshaft degrees. This type of governor is typical of that now in use on Detroit Diesel, Caterpillar, Cummins, Mack, Volvo, and Mercedes-Benz engines.

The governors used on highway truck applications fall into one of two basic categories:

1. *Limiting-speed governors*, sometimes referred to as *minimum/maximum* models since they are intended to control the idle and maximum speed settings of the engine. Generally, there is no governor control in the intermediate range, which is regulated by the position of the throttle linkage by the driver/operator.

2. *Variable-speed* or *all-range governors*, which are designed to control the speed of the engine regardless of the throttle setting.

NOTE   A constant-speed-range governor assembly is another type of governor that allows the engine to go immediately to a fixed-speed setting after startup and stays there minus the droop unless it is capable of isochronous control. This type is used for industrial applications only.

ZERO-DROOP GOVERNORS

A *zero-droop governor*, or isochronous (single time) governor, is a governor that is capable of maintaining the engine speed the same, loaded or unloaded. This governor assembly is designed for adjustable droop through either an internal or external adjustment screw mechanism. The adjustable-droop feature may range from 0 to 10%, depending on the model of governor used. A zero-droop condition is one in which the engine runs at the same rpm loaded or unloaded. The adjustable-droop feature allows the internal governor linkage fulcrum point to be adjusted, so that after a load change the spring force is returned to the same length and strength. This ensures that the engine will continue to rotate at the same rpm.

A governor with adjustable droop is commonly used on a diesel power generator set. It is needed to ensure that when one or more engines are electrically tied together in a parallel arrangement, each engine can handle its share of the load in proportion to its gen-set rating. Generally, one engine governor is adjusted for zero droop to monitor the system, and the other engine governors are set to allow equal load sharing. Even if we select two identical model engines set at the same horsepower and driving equal sized gen-sets, mass production of parts prevents every engine from being able to produce the exact same horsepower at the same rpm. Variations in cylinder pressures and fuel delivery rates account for characteristic changes in both horsepower and acceleration. Adjustable-droop governors allow us to set up each engine for equal-load sharing capabilities.

ADJUSTABLE-DROOP GOVERNORS

In diesel engine applications that require closer speed regulation than that which can normally be achieved from the use of a mechanical governor assembly, a hydramechanical (oil pressure to move a power piston connected to the rack linkage is often used) or electronic governor can be selected.

It is often an advantage to employ a governor assembly that offers an adjustable-droop feature. This design allows the technician to tailor the desired droop rpm of the engine to suit many different engine and equipment applications.

One widely used example of a hydramechanical governor assembly is shown in Figure 17-5A, which illustrates a Woodward PSG (pressure-compensated simple governor) model. Manufactured by the Woodward Governor Company, one of the longest-established and best known prime mover governor control companies, Woodward products are used by every major engine OEM worldwide. In addition to hydramechanical models, Woodward also offers a wide range of electrohydraulic and electronic models for engines and gas turbines of all shapes, sizes, and power outputs, including jet aircraft engines.

PSG Model

The governor shown in Figure 17-6 uses engine lube oil or an oil supply from a separate pump whose lift should not exceed 12 in. (0.3048 m), and a foot valve should be furnished. Use a 20-μm filter with a minimum capacity of 2 gallons (7.57 liters). If the governor is mounted horizontally, the needle valve must be on the bottom and a 1/4-in. (6.35-mm) pipe tapped hole provided in the upper part of the governor case to drain oil away to the sump. Four check valves contained within the base plate of the governor permit rotation in either direction. Two of the passages can be plugged if rotation is only required in one direction. The oil pump within the governor is capable of producing either 75, 175, or 225 psi above inlet pressure and is controlled by the relief valve spring setting (517.12, 1206.62, or 1551.37 kPa oil pressure).

The PSG is normally isochronous (zero droop will be maintained as long as the engine is not overloaded). On power generator applications, when ac generating sets are tied in with other units, one governor can be set to zero droop by the droop adjusting bracket, which will regulate the frequency of the entire system. If speed droop is required, however, to permit load division between two or more engines driving genera-

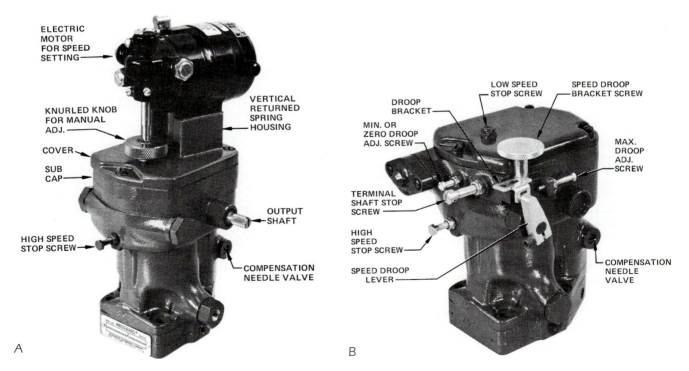

A

B

FIGURE 17–5 (A) PSG with vertical return spring and electric speed setting motor; (B) PSG with externally adjusted speed droop.

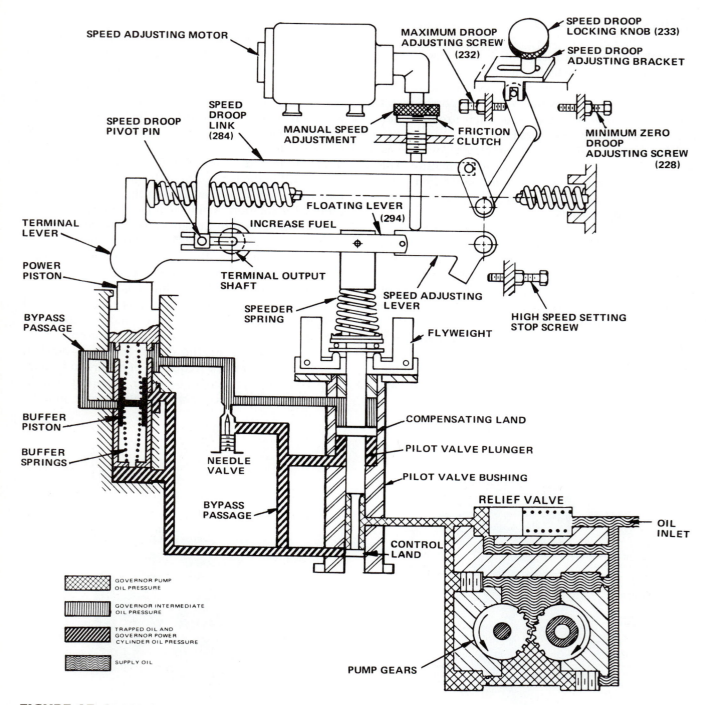

FIGURE 17–6 *PSG governor with horizontal internal return spring, externally adjustable droop, and electric motor speed setting. (Courtesy of Woodward Governor Co.)*

tors in parallel, the PSG can be adjusted between 0 and 7% droop.

The compensation system within the governor consists of an H-shaped buffer piston with a buffer spring located on either side of it, a needle valve, and a compensating land on the pilot valve plunger. This compensation system, then, is the major difference between the PSG and the SG.

Since the speeder spring force can be adjusted, it is the initial force of this spring that will determine at what rpm the engine will attain a state of balance between the weights and speeder spring.

Engine Stopped

As with the SG governor, the PSG would have the pilot valve plunger pushed all the way down owing to the force of the speeder spring. To shorten the cranking time, place the speed control or hand throttle lever connected to the terminal shaft in the full-fuel position, which takes control away from the governor for initial starting purposes. Once the engine starts, move the control lever back to the desired rpm until the engine warms up.

Engine Cranking (See Figure 17-7)

During cranking, the centrifugal force of the flyweights will oppose the speeder spring tension, and the instant the engine starts (depending on throttle position), the weights will attain a speed proportional to the amount of force within the speeder spring. In other words, if the throttle (terminal shaft) were left in the idle position, then the rotating flyweights would only have to produce enough centrifugal force to balance out the speeder spring force at this low speed. If, how-

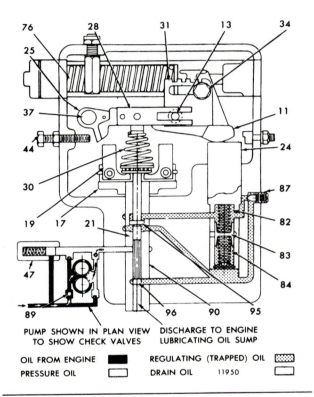

PUMP SHOWN IN PLAN VIEW TO SHOW CHECK VALVES   DISCHARGE TO ENGINE LUBRICATING OIL SUMP

OIL FROM ENGINE ■   REGULATING (TRAPPED) OIL ▨
PRESSURE OIL □   DRAIN OIL   11950 □

11.	Lever—Terminal	47.	Valve—Relief
13.	Shaft—Terminal (long)	76.	Spring—Terminal Lever Return
17.	Ball Head Assy.		
19.	Flyweight	82.	Spring—Buffer (upper)
21.	Plunger—Pilot Valve	83.	Piston—Buffer
24.	Piston—Servo-Motor	84.	Spring—Buffer (lower)
25.	Lever—Speed Adjusting	87.	Valve—Compensating Needle
28.	Lever—Floating		
30.	Spring—Speeder	89.	Valve—Check
31.	Bracket—Droop Adjusting	90.	Bushing—Pilot Valve
34.	Bolt—Droop Adjusting	95.	Land—Receiving Compensating
37.	Shaft—Speed Adjusting		
44.	Screw—Maximum Speed Adjusting	96.	Land—Pilot Valve Control

(a)

FIGURE 17-7A *Stable position of governor when load on engine is constant.*

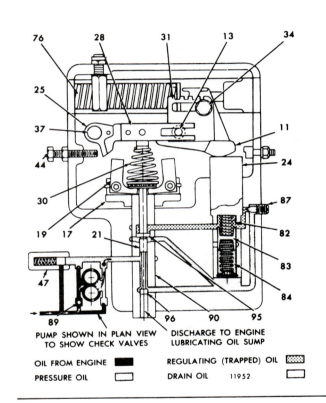

PUMP SHOWN IN PLAN VIEW TO SHOW CHECK VALVES   DISCHARGE TO ENGINE LUBRICATING OIL SUMP

OIL FROM ENGINE ■   REGULATING (TRAPPED) OIL ▨
PRESSURE OIL □   DRAIN OIL   11952 □

11.	Lever—Terminal	47.	Valve—Relief
13.	Shaft—Terminal (long)	76.	Spring—Terminal Lever Return
17.	Ball Head Assy.		
19.	Flyweight	82.	Spring—Buffer (upper)
21.	Plunger—Pilot Valve	83.	Piston—Buffer
24.	Piston—Servo-Motor	84.	Spring—Buffer (lower)
25.	Lever—Speed Adjusting	87.	Valve—Compensating Needle
28.	Lever—Floating		
30.	Spring—Speeder	89.	Valve—Check
31.	Bracket—Droop Adjusting	90.	Bushing—Pilot Valve
34.	Bolt—Droop Adjusting	95.	Land—Receiving Compensating
37.	Shaft—Speed Adjusting		
44.	Screw—Maximum Speed Adjusting	96.	Land—Pilot Valve Control

(b)

FIGURE 17-7B *Position of governor mechanism as load increases and engine speed tends to decrease*

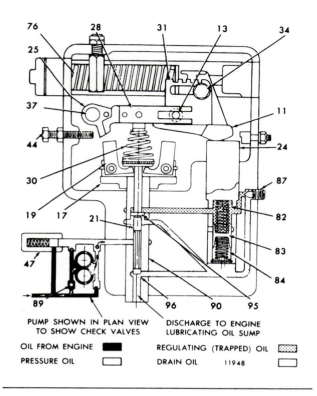

PUMP SHOWN IN PLAN VIEW
TO SHOW CHECK VALVES

DISCHARGE TO ENGINE
LUBRICATING OIL SUMP

| OIL FROM ENGINE | ■ | REGULATING (TRAPPED) OIL | ▨ |
| PRESSURE OIL | □ | DRAIN OIL   11948 | □ |

11.	Lever—Terminal	47.	Valve—Relief
13.	Shaft—Terminal (long)	76.	Spring—Terminal Lever
17.	Ball Head Assy.		Return
19.	Flyweight	82.	Spring—Buffer (upper)
21.	Plunger—Pilot Valve	83.	Piston—Buffer
24.	Piston—Servo-Motor	84.	Spring—Buffer (lower)
25.	Lever—Speed Adjusting	87.	Valve—Compensating
28.	Lever—Floating		Needle
30.	Spring—Speeder	89.	Valve—Check
31.	Bracket—Droop	90.	Bushing—Pilot Valve
	Adjusting	95.	Land—Receiving
34.	Bolt—Droop Adjusting		Compensating
37.	Shaft—Speed Adjusting	96.	Land—Pilot Valve
44.	Screw—Maximum Speed		Control
	Adjusting		

(C)

FIGURE 17–7C *Position of governor mechanism as load decreases and engine speed tends to increase*

ever, the terminal shaft were placed in the full-fuel position, the speeder spring force, being much greater, would require a greater weight force; this would only happen at the maximum engine rpm (state of balance).

As the engine is cranking, oil pressure would flow to the base of the piston toward the underside of the pilot valve plunger compensating land, and slowly bleed past the compensating needle valve to the upper area of both the buffer piston and pilot valve plunger land. This oil pressure due to the compensating needle valve would initially be higher on the underside of both the buffer piston and pilot valve plunger land.

As the buffer piston moves up, it would compress the upper buffer piston spring, which would in turn force up the power piston. The terminal and floating levers would move to the increased fuel position, their movement being determined by the initial terminal (throttle) lever position, which would control how fast the weights would have to rotate to balance out the preset speeder spring force.

As the buffer piston is moving up, the oil pressure on the underside of the pilot valve plunger (PVP) would be pushing up the pilot valve, thereby assisting the rotating flyweights to attain their state-of-balance position. As the oil pressure on the upper area of both the buffer piston and land of the PVP attains the same pressure as that on the bottom, the buffer piston and PVP will center, which will tie in with the state of balance being reached between the weights and springs. When this occurs, the engine will run at a steady-state speed. Figure 17-7A shows the position of the internal governor linkage anytime that a state of balance exists.

Load Increase

How quickly the governor responds to a load change is dependent on the droop bracket adjustment, and whether or not it responds without over or under corrections is tied into the compensating needle valve adjustment. Figure 17-7B shows the reaction within the governor during any load increase.

Refer to Figure 17-7B; with a load increase on the engine, the flyweights will tend to drop inward as the engine speed decreases. With the state of balance between the weights and speeder spring upset in favor of the spring, the pilot valve plunger will be forced down, which will allow pressurized oil from the pump to be directed to the underside of both the buffer piston and the receiving compensating land of the pilot valve plunger. The power piston has two diameters that are exposed to this pressurized oil from the base of the pilot valve plunger. The lower, smaller diameter is acted upon directly, and the upper annulus is connected through the bore in the power piston in which the buffer piston is carried.

The oil pressure will force the power piston up against the force of the terminal lever return spring, which can also be external if used with rotary motion of the terminal shaft instead of linear motion, such as would be used on some engines.

As the power piston moves up, it causes the terminal lever (11) to pivot around its support shaft (13) and compress the fuel rod return spring (76). This action causes the fuel rod to move the rack linkage toward an increased fuel setting. The movement of the terminal lever (11) will lift the droop-adjusting bracket (31) with it, since the droop bracket is connected to the terminal lever by bolt (34). Part of the droop bracket contains a pin that pivots in the slotted end of the speed-adjusting floating lever (28). Therefore, terminal lever rotation by power piston upward movement will lift the slotted end of the floating lever. This action will cause the force on the speeder spring (30) to be decreased, and this action will permit the rotating flyweights to move outward faster in an attempt to assist the PVP to recenter.

The fuel racks will therefore be moved to an increased fuel position. The pressurized oil, due to the compensating needle valve, will initially be greater on the underside of the buffer piston; therefore, it forces the buffer piston up, which compresses the upper buffer spring and relieves the pressure on the lower one. Since there is a higher initial oil pressure on the underside of the compensating land of the PVP, the PVP will be pushed up, thereby recentering the flyweights and closing off the supply port. This will stop the upward movement of the power piston, which has now made the necessary fuel correction.

If the droop bracket has been set for zero droop, the engine speed will remain constant regardless of load change; however, if the droop bracket were set to its maximum of 7%, the engine speed would drop 7% when a load is applied before the governor corrected.

The speed loss of the engine when a load is applied is dependent on the position of the speed droop adjusting bracket pin, which pivots within the slotted floating lever (28). By loosening off the bolt (34), or the speed droop locking knob bracket screw shown in Figure 17-5B, the technician can push the droop bracket and pin toward or away from the speeder spring (30). With the droop pin closer toward the speeder spring, the governor reaction will be more sensitive (less droop, therefore less speed loss). Moving the droop bracket and pin away from the speeder spring results in a slower governor reaction, and therefore we have a greater speed loss when a load is applied or removed from the engine under a fixed throttle condition. This reaction is caused by the fact that each time the power piston (24) moves up or down, the rotative action of the terminal lever (11) causes the slotted floating lever (28) to move with it. During upward movement of the power piston (increasing fuel) or downward movement (decreasing fuel), the speeder spring (30) force will be decreased or increased, respectively, due to the floating lever action. With the droop bracket pin position being adjustable, this means that the closer the pin is to the center of the spring, the quicker will be the reaction on the spring for a given power piston movement. Moving the pin away from the speeder spring will require a longer power piston stroke to cause a reaction at the speeder spring. Consequently, the en-

gine speed droop is proportional to the droop bracket pin placement within the slotted end of the speed-adjusting floating lever (28). Droop adjustment is strictly a trial-and-error setting; therefore, the technician must make an adjustment, then load and unload the engine fully to determine the governor response.

A simple method to understand how adjustable droop works is to refer to Figure 17-8A and Figure 17-8B. In both cases we show a fulcrum lever as being centered on the seesaw or teeter-totter, as well as in the center of the ship. If both kids weigh the same amount and sit equal distances from the fulcrum point, both will travel through the same arc of movement as they move up and down. If, however, one kid moves inward toward the center of the fulcrum point, they will move through a smaller arc of travel as they move up and down. Similarly, if the ship is moving through heavy seas and one deckhand stands an equal distance from the centerline of the ship (fulcrum point) at the bow while another deckhand stands an equal distance from the centerline but toward the stern of the vessel, both will move through the same arc of travel as the ship plows forward through the waves. If, however, one crew member moves closer to the centerline of the ship, they will move through a smaller arc of travel. Using this analogy, you can see why moving the governor droop bracket pin toward the centerline of the speeder spring will cause a reaction at the spring sooner (shorter power piston stroke equals less rack movement and less speed loss before the governor reacts).

Load Decrease

Figure 17-7C shows the governor linkage position when an engine load is removed. For a given (fixed) throttle setting, if a load is removed from the engine, engine speed will increase, which causes the flyweights to fly out farther, thereby overcoming the speeder spring force. This causes the PVP to lift, which opens the control port at its base, allowing trapped oil to drain from the base of the buffer piston and PVP compensating land. Terminal shaft return spring force will push the power piston in the decreased fuel direction, therefore reducing engine rpm. This reduced oil pressure on the underside of the buffer piston and receiving compensating land of the PVP will cause the higher (temporarily) oil pressure above to recenter the PVP, followed by recentering of the buffer piston as the oil bleeds through the compensating needle valve, and pressures above and below equalize. With a reduction in fuel input to the engine, a state-of-balance condition will again exist after the correction sequence.

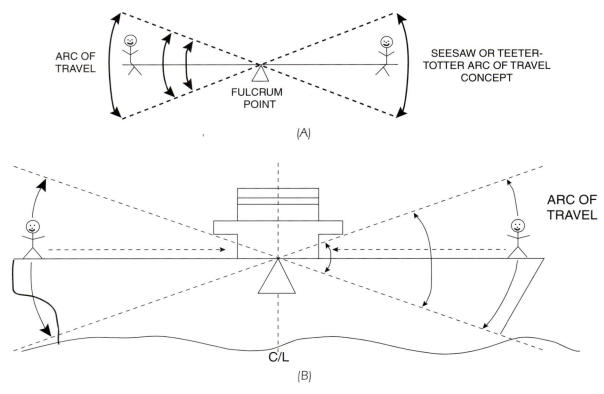

FIGURE 17–8 (A) How the arc of travel changes as children change their position toward or away from the center (fulcrum point); (B) how the individuals can change their arc of travel by moving toward or away from the C/L of the vessel as it pitches in rough seas. Relate both concepts to an adjustable droop level in a governor.

PSG Adjustments

Figure 17-5 shows all the available external adjustments. To adjust the droop setting on an external droop governor, refer to Figure 17-5B. On an internal droop model the top cover must be removed to get at the internal adjustment bolt (see Figure 17-7A, item 34). By moving the bracket in toward the center of the governor, the droop pin pivot point is changed, which will decrease the droop. Moving the droop bracket away from the center of the governor will increase the droop. This is effected by the reasons explained in the description of the SG model governor. All droop adjustments are done on a trial-and-error basis. Make sure that the engine is at normal operating temperature prior to any final adjustments.

Compensating Needle Valve Adjustment

With the engine at operating temperature, adjust the governor for no-load rated speed by manually moving the terminal shaft to its maximum position; then adjust the high-speed stop on the side of the governor housing to obtain the speed desired. Open the compensation needle valve between two and three turns until the engine or turbine begins to hunt or surge. With a recently installed rebuilt governor, this will be more noticeable than on a unit that has been in service, since you are bleeding the system of any entrapped air. Allow the unit to surge for at least 30 seconds. Gently close the needle valve until the hunting just stops; then manually disturb the engine or turbine speed to check that the engine will return to its original steady-state speed with only a small overshoot.

Closing the needle valve farther than necessary will slow down the oil bleed back between both sides of the buffer piston and PVP compensating land, resulting in a slow return to speed following a load change, whereas overcorrection can result if it is turned out too far.

Options

The PSG is available with a temperature-compensated needle valve that adjusts the compensated oil flow with the use of bimetal strips and a spring-loaded needle valve. Adjust it in the same manner as for the non-temperature-compensated valve.

Auxiliary Equipment (PSG)

In addition to those options available on the SG, such as an external electric motor for remote speed setting, the PSG can have the external droop adjustment, the temperature-compensated needle valve, spring-driven oil-damped ballhead, a torsion spring, and a pneumatic speed setting. Figure 17-9 shows such a setup, whereby remote speed adjustment is provided through a pneumatic speed setting assembly consisting of a diaphragm, housing, oil reservoir, adjusting screws, and pushrod that extends down through the governor cover and makes contact with the floating lever.

An internal return spring is also available as an option. Air signal pressure to the speed setting assembly is applied to an oil reservoir to dampen out oscillations of air compression. Oil pressure acting upon the diaphragm is transmitted to the floating lever by the push-rod, which will increase or decrease governor speeder spring force to produce a change in the speed setting.

ELECTRONIC GOVERNORS

The introduction of electronically controlled diesel fuel injection systems on Detroit Diesel, Caterpillar, Cummins, Volvo, Mack, and Mercedes-Benz heavy-duty high-speed truck engines has allowed the speed of the diesel engine to be controlled electronically rather than mechanically. In an electronic governor, the same type of balanced condition to that shown in Figure 17-1 for a mechanical governor occurs. The major difference is that in the electronic governor, electric currents (amperes) and voltages (pressure) are summed together instead of mechanical weight and spring forces. This is possible through the use of an MPS (magnetic pickup sensor), which is in effect a permanent-magnet single-pole device. This magnetic pickup concept is being used on all existing electronic

FIGURE 17-9 Pneumatic remote speed adjustment. (Courtesy of Woodward Governor Co.)

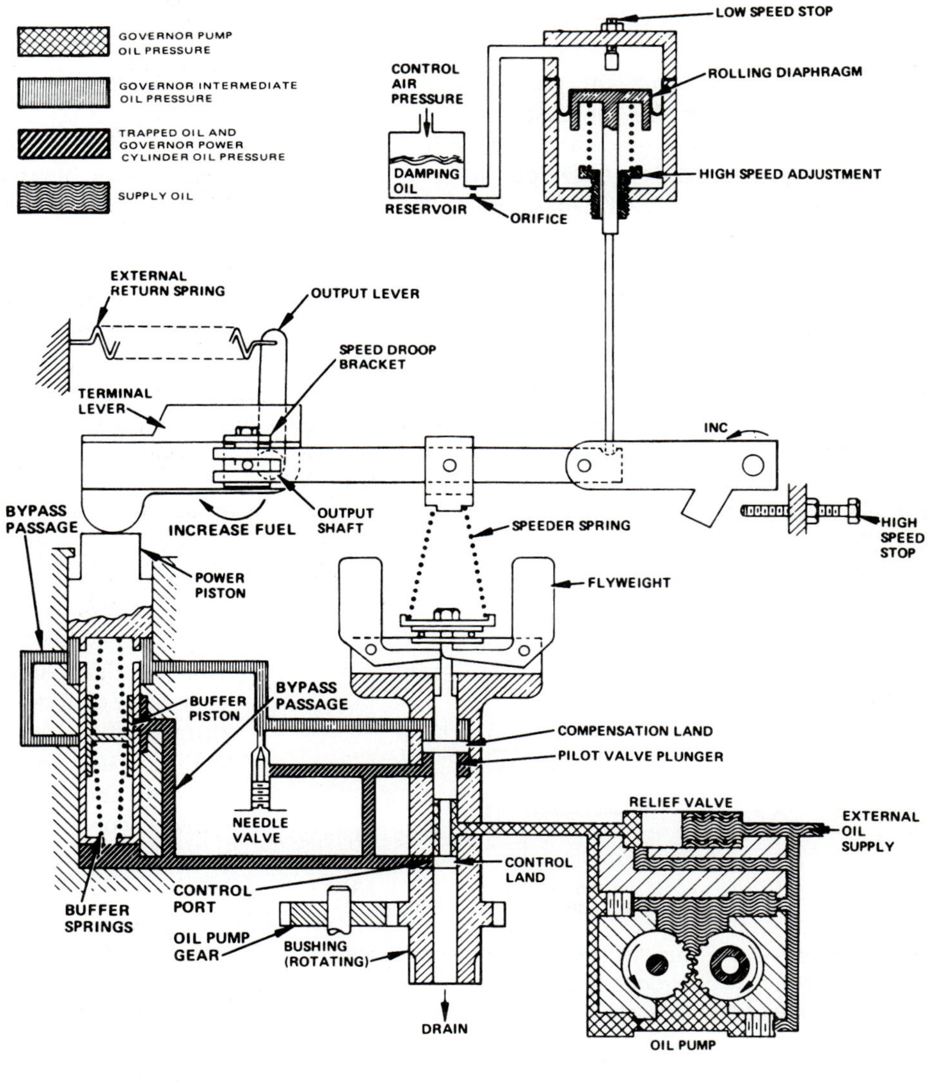

systems; therefore, its operation can be considered common to all of them. MPS are a vital communicating link between the engine crankshaft speed and the on-board computer, known as the ECM. The MPS is installed next to a drive shaft gear made of material that reacts to a magnetic field. As each gear tooth passes the MPS, the gear interrupts the MPS's magnetic field. This, in turn, produces an alternating current signal that corresponds to engine rpm. This signal is then sent to the ECM.

Figure 17-10 illustrates a simplified wiring diagram for a TRS (timing reference sensor) which is located on the engine block. Refer to Chapters 21 through 23 to see where this sensor is mounted on specific engines; usually this sensor picks up cylinder positions from a raised pin attached to either the crankshaft or camshaft gear. The sensor is installed so that a small air gap exists between the end of the sensor and the gear teeth or pickup pin.

The TRS generally receives a 5-V timing reference signal from the ECM and then returns a signal based on engine speed to the ECM, which then converts this signal to determine the speed of engine rotation. The rotation of the ferrous (metal) gear teeth past the end of the sensor causes the magnetic field or magnetic flux level to change every time a gear tooth passes through this electrically generated signal field since the air gap space is reduced. This action induces a voltage signal that is transmitted through the TRS return wire to the ECM. The shape and spacing of the gear teeth determine the electrical waveform of the sensor output voltage. The number of teeth on the gear determines the number of pulses per revolution of the gear. An 80-tooth gear, for example, rotating at 2100 rpm would produce 168,000 pulses per minute or 2800 pulses per second. This 2800 pulses per second in electronics terminology would be referred to as 2800 Hz (hertz), which is the frequency of the generated TRS signal. This TRS signal is used by the ECM to establish

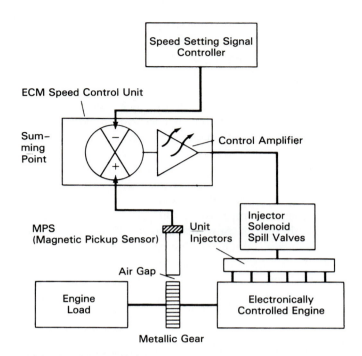

FIGURE 17-11 *Simplified schematic showing the concept of operation for a closed-loop control electronic governor assembly.*

the amount of fuel that should be injected into combustion chambers of the engine.

The components described above compose a closed-loop system of measurement, which is illustrated in Figure 17-11 in a simple line diagram. The output of the magnetic speed pickup sensor is connected to a speed sensor circuit inside the ECM. This circuit converts the ac magnetic pickup signal to a dc voltage whose level is proportional to the speed of the engine. An analog-to-digital converter within the speed control circuit provides this dc signal since the ECM circuitry is designed to operate only on dc signals. The dc voltage signal is compared to the speed reference voltage; therefore, if a difference or an error exists, the ECM output signal from the built-in amplifier causes the injector PWM signal to lengthen or shorten. This change to the PWM signal causes the injector fuel delivery cycle to last for a greater or shorter duration of crankshaft degrees, thereby changing the engine speed and fuel setting.

For the electronic governor system within the ECM to control the speed and fueling of the engine, it must know the following conditions:

- Speed of the engine
- Percentage of throttle depression
- Turbo boost/load on the engine
- Intake manifold temperature

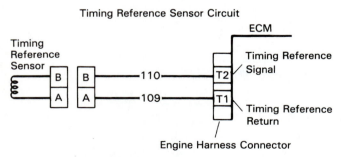

FIGURE 17-10 *Simplified example of a timing reference sensor circuit for an electronically governed engine. (Courtesy of Detroit Diesel Corporation.)*

An example of how an electronic governor control system operates on a heavy-duty high-speed truck engine is shown in Figure 17-12. The truck operator depresses the throttle pedal to the degree of fueling that he or she desires. The TPS relays a voltage signal to the ECM relative to the percentage of throttle pedal depression. Normally with a closed throttle, the TPS output signal will be in the range of 0.5 V, rising to a maximum value of approximately 4.5 V with a WOT (wide-open throttle). This desired engine speed signal is routed to the positive side of an ECM summing point. The actual engine speed obtained from the throttle input is determined from the engine timing sensor. This actual speed is relayed to the negative side of the summing point, where it is compared to the desired speed asked for by the operator. The ECM computes a corrected signal through its ALU chip and feeds this signal on to the least-win area. Two other signals are also fed into the least-win chip area: the FRC (fuel-ratio control) fuel position, which is tied into the engine turbocharger boost sensor, and the rated fuel position requirements needed to maintain the correct FRC position. The desired and actual engine speeds, FRC fuel, and rated fuel positions create a least-win signal, which dominates. In other words, the actual speed, turbo boost, and rated fuel position parameters are compared to determine if the speed asked for can be supported by sufficient turbo boost pressure versus that for the rated fuel position. This least-win

signal is fed on to the unit injector electric solenoid. In addition, the injector solenoid PWM (pulse-width modulation) signal is also factored in by other signals, based on desired engine timing, the coolant and oil temperatures of the engine, speed, engine load, atmospheric pressure, and intake manifold temperature. These signals are fed to another summing point, where a computed signal is generated and also sent to the unit injector solenoid control system. The injector PWM signal then determines the duration and required timing of each injector. In Chapter 21 we describe in greater detail the specific operation of an electronically controlled fuel injection system.

SUMMARY

A thorough understanding of this chapter, including commonly used governor terms, will broaden your perspective of the various governor functions, and prepare you with the knowledge and skills to effectively trace, diagnose, analyze and troubleshoot both mechanical and electronic engine control problems.

SELF-TEST QUESTIONS

1. Technician A says that a diesel engine requires the use of a governor because the air is not throttled into the engine. Technician B says that the governor is required to stop the diesel engine from stalling at an idle speed. Who is right?

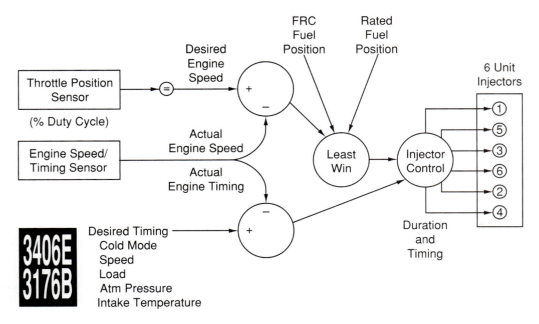

FIGURE 17-12 Electronic unit injector governor timing and injection control circuit arrangement schematic for the 3176B and 3406E engine models. FRC, fuel ratio control. (Courtesy of Caterpillar, Inc.)

2. Technician A says that mechanical and hydraulically assisted governors are speed-sensitive devices. Technician B says that they are load-sensitive devices. Who is correct?

3. Technician A says that at an idle speed, the air/fuel ratio in a diesel engine can be as high as 30:1, whereas technician B says that it is much higher, being as lean as 130:1. Who is correct?

4. Technician A says that the recommended idle speed of an engine can usually be found stamped on the exhaust emissions decal on the engine, whereas technician B says it will always be found on the governor ID tag itself. Who is right?

5. *High idle speed* is a term used by some manufacturers to indicate
   a. a higher-than-normal idle rpm used in cold-weather operation only
   b. the maximum no-load speed setting of the engine
   c. the maximum full-load speed setting of the engine
   d. the speed setting when the vehicle is stationary and a PTO (power takeoff) is being used.

6. Technician A says that the engine will use less fuel when running at a maximum no-load speed of, say, 2100 rpm than it will at a full-load speed of 1950 rpm. Technician B believes that it will use more fuel at the higher speed. Which mechanic knows the basic governor operation?

7. When the engine is running under full load (say, 1950 rpm) and its speed is slowly reduced to its peak torque speed of, say, 1200 rpm, why is the horsepower not constant if the engine is still receiving full-load fuel from the governor?

8. Why does the engine produce more torque under load at a lower engine speed (for example, at 1200 rpm) than it does at its full-load speed of, say, 1950 rpm if the governor is still supplying maximum fuel to the fuel injectors?

9. Technician A says that as the engine speed increases from its maximum full-load rpm to its no-load rpm, the governor will decrease the fuel delivered to the injectors. Technician B disagrees, saying that the governor would have to increase the fuel delivery rate to allow an increase in speed. Who is correct?

10. Technician A says that a state of balance condition in a mechanical governor can exist only when the engine is running at an idle speed. Technician B says that a state of balance condition can exist at any speed throughout the governor control range as long as the weight and spring forces are equal. Who is correct?

11. In a limiting-speed mechanical governor, the governor controls
    a. the idle speed
    b. the maximum speed
    c. all speed ranges between idle and maximum
    d. both a and b

12. Technician A says that governor droop is the difference in speed between the maximum no-load and maximum full-load engine rpm. Technician B says that it is the difference between high idle and rated speed. Who is correct?

13. Technician A says that governor droop is generally expressed as a percentage figure. Technician B says that droop is expressed as an rpm. Who is correct?

14. Technician A says that the term *governor sensitivity* is generally expressed as an rpm value, whereas technician B says that it is expressed as a percentage value. Who is right?

15. Technician A says that in a mechanical governor assembly, the force of the governor spring is always trying to increase the fuel delivery rate to the injectors. Technician B says that this is incorrect, and that the centrifugal force of the rotating flyweights are always attempting to increase the fuel to the engine. Who is correct?

16. A minimum/maximum governor is designed to control
    a. the idle and maximum speed of the engine
    b. the idle, intermediate, and maximum speed settings of the engine
    c. the idle and intermediate speed settings only
    d. the idle speed setting only

17. A variable-speed governor is designed to control
    a. idle speed
    b. idle, intermediate, and maximum speeds
    c. idle and intermediate speeds
    d. idle and maximum speed settings

18. Technician A says that when an engine using a mechanical minimum/maximum or limiting-speed mechanical governor is stopped and the engine is ready to start, the fuel control mechanism will be held in the full-fuel position. Technician B says that when the engine is stopped, the fuel control mechanism must be in the no-fuel position. Who is right?

19. True or False: The maximum engine speed settings are usually found stamped on the engine compliance/exhaust emissions label.

20. Technician A says that if an engine lacks power, the reason should be investigated. Technician B says that if an engine lacks power, the maximum speed setting of the engine should be increased until it performs according to specification. Who is correct?

21. Technician A says that if an engine was governed at a maximum full-load speed setting of 2100 rpm, then during operation, if the speed were allowed to increase to 2175 rpm, the engine would develop more horsepower. Technician B disagrees, saying that the horsepower would be less due to the action of the governor. Who is correct here?

22. Technician A says that if a truck running down a long steep incline is not slowed by use of an engine brake, retarder, or service brakes, engine overspeed can occur, causing damage to the engine. Technician B says that this cannot happen since the governor will automatically regulate the engine speed. Who is correct here?

23. Technician A says that to increase the truck road speed setting, the mechanical governor can be opened up and adjusted to raise the maximum no-load speed engine

rpm setting. Technician B says that this should never be done. Who is correct here?

24. Supply the missing words in the following statement: When a load is applied to an engine, the speed will ———— and the governor will ———— the fuel setting.

25. Supply the missing words in the following statement: When a load is decreased on an engine, the speed will ———— and the governor will ———— the fuel setting.

26. Technician A says that the term *isochronous* means that the governor is capable of a zero-droop setting, which means that the no-load and full-load speeds are the same. Technician B says that no engine can operate at the same speed loaded and unloaded; since it has to work harder under load, it will run slower. Who is right?

27. The letters MPS stand for
    a. magnetic pickup sensor
    b. mean position sensor
    c. motor point system
    d. motor position sensor

28. Technician A says that a rotating fiber gear tooth is used to interrupt the MPS field on a regular basis. Technician B disagrees, saying that the gear must be a metallic gear to operate. Who is correct?

29. Technician A says that the signal generated from the MPS is a dc signal, whereas technician B says that it is an ac signal. Who is correct?

30. Technician A says that the size of the air gap between the end of the MPS and the gear tooth determines the field strength and the proper operation. Technician B says that the width of the MPS gap has no bearing on its operation. Who is correct?

31. Technician A says that most sensors used on truck electronic governor systems receive a 5-V reference signal from the ECM to operate. Technician B says that they operate on the 12-V battery supply power source. Who understands the system best?

32. Technician A says that on the Detroit Diesel series 60 engine, the ECM uses the sensor value from the throttle pedal to determine the start and amount of fuel injection. Technician B says that the TRS (timing reference sensor) is used by the ECM to establish the amount of fuel that should be injected into the combustion chamber. Who is correct?

33. Technician A says that the frequency of electrical sensor signals is determined by the engine speed and number of teeth on the pickup gear. Technician B says that the ECM determines the frequency of sensor signal output. Who is correct here?

34. Technician A says that the maximum no-load engine speed on a mechanical governor can be altered. Technician B says that the engine maximum no-load speed should never be tampered with. Who is right?

35. Technician A says that the amount of droop (rpm loss) on all engines equipped with mechanical governors can be offset by setting the maximum no-load rpm higher than the full-load speed desired. Technician B says that both the full-load and no-load speeds are one and the same since the governor will compensate for any speed loss as the engine load is applied. Who is right here?

36. A state of balance in a mechanical governor means that
    a. the force of the weights and springs is equal
    b. the operator is controlling the engine speed
    c. the correct gear in the transmission has been selected to keep the engine at a steady speed
    d. the turbocharger boost and fuel delivery pressures are equal

37. Technician A says that the term *high idle* means the same as *maximum no-load* engine speed. Technician B says that it means the same as *rated* engine speed. Who understands the meaning of this terminology?

38. Technician A says that on a mechanical or hydramechanical governor, the fuel rack will be pushed into an increased fuel delivery position with a drop in engine speed from high idle to rated rpm. Technician B says that there will be less fuel delivered under such an operating condition. Who knows governor theory here?

18 Injection Nozzles

OVERVIEW

The fuel injection nozzle is a key component in the successful delivery and combustion of fuel. This chapter describes various types of nozzles, their function and operation, and the necessary checks, tests, inspection and adjustments needed to ensure a smooth-running engine, and one that complies with mandated EPA engine exhaust emissions.

NOZZLE STRUCTURE AND FUNCTION

All diesel engines require an injector for each cylinder to permit high-pressure fuel to be sprayed into the combustion chamber. PLN (pump–line–nozzle) inline and V-configuration injection pumps as well as distributor pump systems are equipped with injection nozzles, which are sometimes referred to simply as an injector. They are called nozzles because in both of these types of fuel systems, the timing, metering, and fuel pressurization is accomplished within the injection pump. The high-pressure fuel is then directed through a steel-backed fuel line to the nozzle, which is encapsulated within the body of the injector. The nozzle is simply a valve that opens to permit atomized fuel to enter the combustion chamber. The valve closes when the fuel pressure is no longer high enough to hold the nozzle needle valve open against an internal spring.

Engines equipped with unit injectors, such as Detroit Diesel, Caterpillar, Cummins, Volvo, and Navistar, are designed to time, atomize, meter, and pressurize the fuel within the body of the injector rather than within an injection pump housing. Details on the function and operation of unit injectors are given in Chapters 21 to 23. Nozzles and unit injectors both provide atomization of the fuel as it leaves the holes in the spray tip.

Figure 18-1 illustrates three typical nozzle and holder assembly wherein a needle valve is held on its seat at the base of the nozzle by spring pressure. The force of the spring can be altered either by rotating an internal adjusting nut or by the addition or removal of spring shims (5). This adjustment determines the required fuel pressure acting against the tapered face of the nozzle needle valve needed to lift the needle against the force of the spring. For example, if a nozzle has been adjusted so that it requires 4200 psi (28,959 kPa or 286 atm) fuel pressure to lift the needle valve, this is referred to as the opening or popping pressure of the nozzle. Once the needle valve is opened, fuel under high pressure from the injection pump can flow through a single hole or a series of small orifices within the tip of the nozzle body and into the combustion chamber. Figure 18-1 illustrates the commonly used nozzle types. Precombustion chamber (PC) design engines employ a single-hole nozzle, commonly referred to as a *pintle nozzle* (Figure 18-2), where the fuel is injected in a narrow cone-shape (Figure 18-3) into a small chamber outside the main cylinder. Pressurized gases then enter the main chamber through a connecting passage(s). Direct-injection (DI) engines commonly used on larger-bore heavy-duty engines use nozzles with multiple holes or orifices (Figure 18-4) where the fuel is injected directly into the open combustion chamber formed by the piston crown shape. The spray-in pattern covers a much wider angle than in a PC engine; DI-engines are much more widely used in today's engines than are PC designs.

358

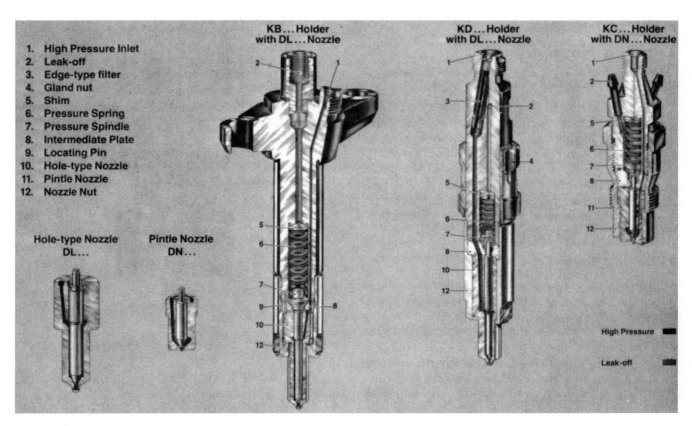

FIGURE 18–1 *Typical types of injector nozzles and holders. (Courtesy of Robert Bosch Corporation.)*

The popping pressure created within the nozzle is not high enough to permit successful atomization of the injected fuel; therefore, to increase the pressure of the injected fuel, and to break the fuel down into tiny droplets (atomization), one or more small holes or orifices are contained within the nozzle tip. Since a restriction to fuel flow is created by the size of the single or multiple holes in the nozzle tip, the fuel spray-in pressure into the combustion chamber is increased substantially. A simple method that can be used to un-

derstand this process is to consider a garden hose. If no nozzle is contained on the end of the hose, once the water is turned on, there is lots of flow, but at a reasonably low pressure. If, however, we place our thumb over the end of the hose, the result is an increase in water velocity (speed and direction of the fluid). This same process occurs at the tip of the nozzle.

The final atomized fuel spray-in pressure is dependent on the popping pressure, and the number and size of the holes used. In addition, the engine compression ratio, turbo boost, engine load and rpm, injection pump capability, and the cylinder bmep (brake

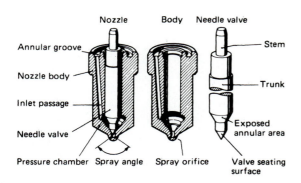

FIGURE 18–2 *Major parts of a pintle injection nozzle used with IDI engines. (Courtesy of Robert Bosch Corporation.)*

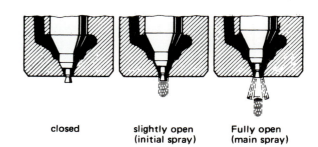

FIGURE 18–3 *Throttling pintle nozzle. (Courtesy of Robert Bosch GmbH.)*

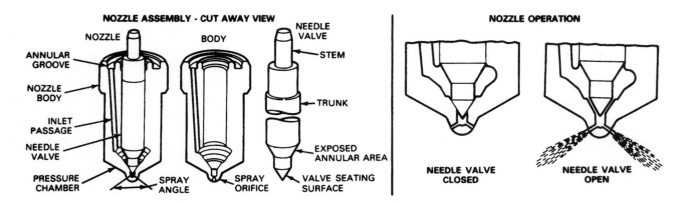

FIGURE 18–4 Cutaway view of the parts of a direct-injection multiple-hole nozzle; nozzle-closed and nozzle-open positions. (Courtesy of Robert Bosch Corporation.)

mean effective pressure) all factor into the actual nozzle spray-in pressure. For example, typical spray-in pressures for nozzles can range from as low as 9000 psi (62,055 kPa/621 bar) to as high as 19,575 psi (134,969 kPa or 1350 bar) in Bosch's P8500 model pump and matching nozzle in Mack's E7 engines. Later-model EVP (electronic unit pump) fuel systems (see Chapter 21) offer spray-in pressures from the nozzle tip of approximately 25,000 psi (172,375 kPa or 1724 bar). Higher spray-in pressures result in finer fuel atomization, better penetration of the compressed airmass, cleaner burning and lower exhaust emissions, and overall fuel economy improvement.

In a multiple-hole nozzle, each orifice is usually equally spaced around the circumference of the spray tip. Generally there are never fewer than four holes and there may be as many as 12 holes. Hole sizes vary between 0.006 and 0.060 in. (0.15 to 1.5 mm). A five-

hole nozzle is shown in Figure 18-5, where each atomized jet of fuel (1 through 5 in this example, spaced 72° apart) carries the atomized high-pressure fuel into the combustion chamber. The high-pressure air within the direct injected cylinder is subjected to a swirling action by the shape of the contoured piston crown as it moves up the cylinder on its compression stroke. This swirling air assists in rapid mixing of the atomized fuel with the hot air to initiate combustion of the fuel (see Chapter 4 for more details on the combustion phase).

In addition, the spray-in angle is chosen to provide optimum fuel penetration into the compressed airmass within the combustion chamber. Some OEMs quote their spray-in angle from the horizontal deck surface of the cylinder head, while others quote this angle from a vertical centerline passing through the nozzle body. Figure 18-4 shows one example of an in-

FIGURE 18–5 Computer tracing of the fuel spray from the five-hole nozzle clearly shows the air–fuel turbulence effect. (Courtesy of Mack Trucks, Inc.)

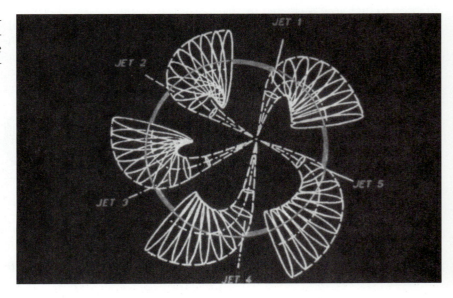

cluded spray-in angle as the fuel leaves the orifices of a multiple-hole nozzle.

NOZZLE IDENTIFICATION

Injection nozzles are simply hydraulic valves operated by fuel pressure. Fuel flow generated by the injection pump enters the nozzle holder at the fuel inlet and proceeds down the fuel inlet and into the annular area of the valve (see Figure 18-1). When the pressure of the fuel against the annular area of the needle valve exceeds the preset pressure of the pressure spring, the needle valve is raised from its seat. Then a metered amount of fuel is injected through the orifices on a hole-type nozzle or by the pintle on a pintle-type nozzle and into the combustion chamber.

During operation a small amount of fuel will leak through the needle valve to help lubricate and cool the valve. This fuel accumulates in the pressure spring area and is returned to the supply tank by a fuel return line.

NOZZLE COMPONENTS

1. *Nozzle holder.* The nozzle holder (Figure 18-1) is the main structural part of the injection nozzle. It provides a means of holding the nozzle to the engine cylinder head; it routes fuel from the injection pump to the nozzle; and it sometimes contains passageways for leakoff fuel coming from the nozzle and going back to the fuel tank or injection pump. Excluding occasional breakage or thread damage due to poor handling, the nozzle holder is very reliable. Information listed directly on the holder includes:

    a. Holder type number (varies with engine application)
    b. Holder part number (manufacturer's part number)
    c. Application part number (on some types)
    d. Nozzle opening pressure (on some types)

2. *Pressure spring.* The pressure spring determines the opening pressure of the nozzle valve. Tension of the pressure spring can be adjusted in most cases by an adjusting screw located above it, or by a shim pack.

3. *Cap nut.* The cap nut provides a dust seal for the nozzle holder and usually incorporates a connection for leakoff fuel. Some nozzles using a shim pack to set nozzle opening pressure do not require a cap nut.

4. *Retaining nut.* The retaining nut connects the nozzle body to the nozzle holder and also serves as a compression seal in the cylinder head.

5. *Pressure spindle.* The pressure spindle is a metal rod that transfers the force of the pressure spring to the nozzle valve.

6. *Nozzle valve assembly.* The nozzle is the heart of the injection nozzle assembly. The valve and body of the nozzle are lapped together and are not interchangeable. The valve has a special tapered seat that effectively seals off nozzle fuel pressure and does not allow any fuel to dribble into the combustion chamber.

In Figure 18-1, the nozzle employs a tapered face type of needle valve, which is held on a lapped nozzle seat in the spray tip by the action of a coil spring. Fuel under high pressure from the injection pump delivered to the nozzle through an internal fuel passage acts on the tapered needle valve face, causing the valve to lift upward in a multiple-hole design (see Figure 18-4), or move downward, depending on whether the nozzle is an inward- or outward-opening type (Figure 18-6).

When the fuel pressure from the injection pump decreases, the needle valve is returned rapidly to its seat by the action of the coil spring above the needle valve. This action effectively ends fuel injection to that cylinder. The action of the fuel pressure on the needle

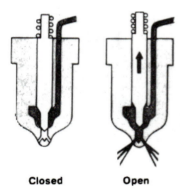

Closed   Open

INWARD-OPENING NOZZLE

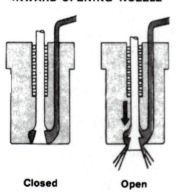

Closed   Open

OUTWARD-OPENING NOZZLE

FIGURE 18–6 *Operating concept of an inward-opening versus an outward-opening nozzle assembly.*

valve causes the term *closed differential hydraulically operated type* to be used in describing these types of nozzles.

Inward-opening nozzles are used with DI (direct-injection) engines, and the nozzle tip contains multiple holes or orifices. The outward-opening nozzle is common to IDI (indirect-injection) engines that use glow plugs to facilitate starting in cold-weather operation. The outward-opening nozzle used with some IDI engines employs a pintle or single-hole design. The nozzle and its spray tip are matched to one another at the time of manufacture and should not be intermixed when overhauling or repairing the injector.

The conical area at the base of the nozzle needle valve is ground to a slightly different angle with respect to the valve seat, which results in line contact seating, thereby creating a high-pressure sealing area to prevent leakage that could cause an increase in fuel consumption, unburned fuel, and thus smoke at the exhaust pipe, as well as carbon buildup around the nozzle tip, which can cause the nozzle to hang up or stay open. Plugging of the tip is also a possibility.

Similar nozzles can be used with various types of nozzle holders, depending on the application and make of engine. Examples of the coding used to identify Bosch fuel injection nozzles are given below, and are typical of the type of coding employed by most nozzle manufacturers. The nozzle code number is stamped or etched on the body of the injector, or in some cases can be found on a tag riveted to the body.

BOSCH NOZZLES

The Robert Bosch Corporation manufacturers a wide variety of nozzles and holders for use with its various injection pumps. The nozzle is the actual part of the complete injector that contains the holes where the fuel sprays into the combustion chamber, while the nozzle holder is the actual body of the injector that houses the nozzle itself. Figure 18-1 illustrates the basic types of nozzle holders produced by Bosch for trucks.

The nozzle holder is identified by a series of letters and numbers on the body. KBAL100SC2/13 would mean:

KB: type of nozzle holder (flange type)

A: spring location

L: long nozzle

100: installation length, in millimeters

S: shoulder diameter, which must match the shoulder diameter of the nozzle

C: nozzle locating pin placement when used

2/13: application information

DLLA150S633 would mean:

DL: hole-type nozzle

L: long nozzle

A: engineering information

150: spray-in angle in degrees (this is an included angle)

S: shoulder diameter, which must match the shoulder diameter of the nozzle holder

633: application information

INJECTOR NOZZLE SAC VOLUME

Depending on the year of manufacture and the particular engine in which it is used, many injectors and nozzles, regardless of whether they are used in DI or IDI engines, tend to retain a small percentage of fuel at the base of the nozzle. Since direct injection engine injectors and nozzles operate on the concept of a tapered needle type of valve held on its seat by spring pressure, some models will exhibit some retention of fuel underneath the nozzle seat. Multiple-hole nozzles are available with conventional sac hole, conical sac hole, or without sac hole for improved exhaust emissions regulations. Sac volume is the small percentage of diesel fuel that collects below the tapered needle tip in its holder, which tends to drop into the combustion chamber at the end of injection. Because it is in an unatomized state, it causes incomplete combustion and therefore some smoke or unburned hydrocarbons at the exhaust. To meet the stringent exhaust emissions regulations now in effect in both the United States and Europe, most hole nozzles are now manufactured with no sac volume below the tip.

Still further improvement in the RSV (reduced sac volume) nozzle and injection is being obtained through the use of a VCO (valve covers orifice) type of design. Both the RSV and VCO injection nozzles, together with a standard type of nozzle arrangement, are shown in Figure 18-7. The VCO orifice is typical of the type of needle valve and tip that can be found in current DDC two- and four-stroke-cycle high-speed heavy-duty engine injectors. Other manufacturers have incorporated this design in their later-model engines. Much research and development is currently under way to improve both injectors and fuel injection systems.

NOZZLE PROBLEMS

The service life of injection nozzles is directly attributable to the following conditions:

- Proper control of engine operating temperature to ensure complete combustion of injected fuel

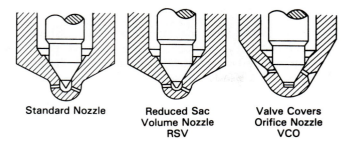

Standard Nozzle   Reduced Sac Volume Nozzle RSV   Valve Covers Orifice Nozzle VCO

FIGURE 18–7 *Various nozzle designs used to reduce hydrocarbon emissions from DI diesel engines. [Reproduced with permission of Society of Automotive Engineers, Inc., International, (copyright 1989), Warrendale, PA.]*

- Water- and dirt-free fuel supply
- Correct grade of fuel for ambient temperature conditions encountered.

Injection nozzle problems are usually indicated when one of the following conditions exists:

- Black smoke at the exhaust
- Poor performance and a lack of power
- Hard starting
- Rough idle and misfire
- Increased fuel consumption
- Combustion knock
- Engine overheating

A quick check of the nozzle operation when it is still in the engine can normally be performed by running the engine at the speed at which the problem is most noticeable. Loosen a high-pressure fuel line on inline Bosch pumps at each nozzle one at a time between one-half to one full turn (see Figure 19-29C). Cover the fuel line with a rag to prevent fuel spraying onto you or the engine compartment. With the fuel line loose, the injector will not be able to inject because insufficient fuel pressure will be present to lift the internal nozzle valve against the return spring. Under such conditions the cylinder will receive no fuel. The engine speed should decrease, and its sound should change, indicating that it is running on one less cylinder.

If one nozzle is found where loosening the high-pressure fuel line makes little or no difference either in the misfiring condition or visible black smoke concentrations at the exhaust pipe, that nozzle should be removed and checked on a pop tester for release or popping pressure, chatter, spray pattern, holding pressure, and leakage. If the nozzle passes these tests, the problem is either in the injection pump itself or there is low compression in that cylinder.

NOZZLE REMOVAL

The nozzle removal procedure will vary slightly between different engine makes depending on the type of nozzle design used. Some nozzles are retained in the cylinder head by being rotated into a screw thread. Others use a clamp and bolt, while others may use a retaining bracket and two bolts. Each nozzle has a fuel leakoff line that routes the internal fuel leakage past the needle valve stem back to the fuel tank. On some nozzles, a special puller clamp must be used to withdraw the nozzle and holder assembly from the cylinder head.

NOTE   Always obtain a suitable supply of plastic protective shipping caps, both male and female, prior to nozzle removal so that all open fuel lines or other lines can be plugged off during servicing to prevent any dirt or foreign material from entering either the fuel system or the cylinder bore once the nozzle has been removed.

Removal Procedure
    1.   Wash or steam clean the valve rocker cover area. (Do not apply direct steam pressure to the injection pump housing since as it is an aluminum alloy, its expansion rate is approximately twice that of the steel components within the pump, and severe damage to the pump can result, especially if the engine is running while you steam clean it.)
    2.   Disconnect all high-pressure injection lines at the nozzles.

NOTE   If individual lines are to be replaced, remove the support clamp from the set of lines containing the line to be replaced.

---

    a.   Disconnect the line(s) from the injectors.
    b.   Disconnect the line(s) from the fuel pump.

CAUTION   If removed, reinstall the support clamp in the original position and make sure the lines do not contact each other or another component.

---

    c.   Install the lines in the reverse order of removal.

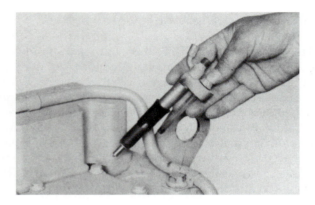

FIGURE 18–8 Removing injection nozzle from bore in the cylinder head. (Courtesy of CUMMINS Engine Company,

3. Disconnect all fuel return lines leading to the nozzles.

4. Remove the nozzle clamping nuts, studs, or special gland nuts.

5. Remove the nozzle from the cylinder head carefully (Figure 18-8). A pry bar or puller may be necessary in some cases.

The washer shown at the base of the nozzle in Figure 18-9 acts as a heat shield and should be replaced any time that the nozzle has been removed for any reason. The O-ring shown in this figure also seals the bore of the cylinder head to the nozzle body diameter. It should also be replaced after a nozzle has been removed.

NOTE Make sure that nozzle sealing washers come out with the nozzle. If not, remove them with a tapered, serrated tool, or form a hook-shaped tool from a piece of welding rod or other suitable material.

At this time all connections and openings should be covered with plastic caps or aluminum foil. Do not use tape or rags because of the danger of lint or gummy residue getting into the lines.

Place the nozzles in an area where they will not be damaged or take them immediately to a shop specializing in this work.

Bosch Nozzle Testing and Repair

The nozzle body holder or injector may differ slightly in outward appearance and the injector installation torque to the cylinder head may also differ; however, testing, inspection, and overhaul of these nozzles can be considered common for all engines that use a Bosch holder and nozzle, such as is shown in Figure 18-1. Figure 18-10 illustrates how nozzle tips can be identified by an etched part number.

Each manufacturer specifies that a particular injector nozzle pop tester be used with specific fittings for checking their engines' nozzles; however, there are a variety of nozzle pop testers available on the market that can be used to check any number of different nozzles, since all that is required is to adapt the correct fitting to the injector body for the various tests.

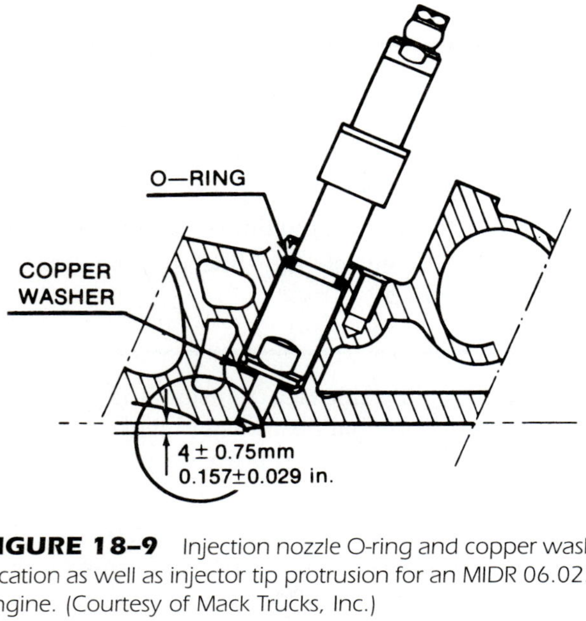

FIGURE 18–9 Injection nozzle O-ring and copper washer location as well as injector tip protrusion for an MIDR 06.02.12 engine. (Courtesy of Mack Trucks, Inc.)

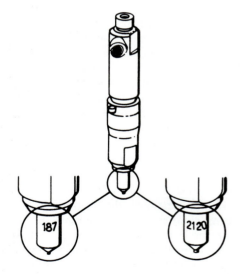

FIGURE 18–10 Nozzle tip identification number location. (Courtesy of Freightliner/Mercedes-Benz Truck Company, Inc.)

Before testing nozzles, *do not* clean them, especially at the spray tip, because if you remove any carbon that was affecting the nozzle spray pattern or release pressure, you will have removed the evidence. Test the nozzle just as it was when it was removed from the engine.

TESTING NOZZLES FOR PERFORMANCE

The nozzles should be removed from the engine and checked for correct opening pressure and spray pattern. Testing of Bosch nozzles follows the same basic routine as that for other manufacturers' nozzles. Tests that would be conducted to the nozzles with a pop tester are as follows:

1. Nozzle release pressure (popping pressure)
2. Nozzle spray pattern
3. Nozzle chatter
4. Nozzle tip leakage
5. Nozzle fuel leak-off

If the injection nozzle fails to pass any of these tests, it should be sent to the local fuel injection repair shop in your area for repair or exchanged for a new or rebuilt one. Use calibrating fluid rather than diesel fuel for testing the nozzles for the reasons given in this chapter for other nozzles. The same safety precautions should be exercised regarding eye protection and hand protection as for other nozzle test procedures.

CAUTION The fuel pressure buildup required to cause the injector nozzle to release fuel is commonly known as the popping pressure or release pressure. This fuel is forced out of the nozzle tip in a finely atomized spray due to the high-pressure buildup within the injector body and at the nozzle tip. This fuel pressure is high enough to cause penetration of the skin, leading to blood poisoning. Therefore, *never* place your hands or fingers into this spray area.

Pop testing machines come equipped with a protective receptacle, usually manufactured from a heavy transparent plastic that protects you from the high-pressure spray while still allowing you to see the spray pattern of the fuel. Most pop testers such as that shown in Figure 18-11 come equipped with a variety of fittings and lines to allow a number of different nozzles to be tested.

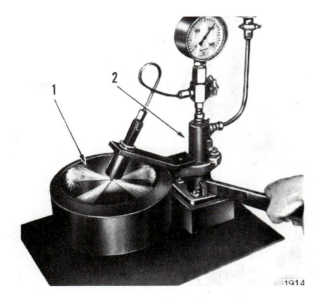

FIGURE 18-11 *Testing the spray pattern of an injection nozzle assembly. (Courtesy of Freightliner/Mercedes-Benz Truck Company, Inc.)*

NOTE Use only calibrating fluid that meets ISO specification ISO 4113, SAE 1968D, or SAE 208629 specs when checking a nozzle because it is more stable than diesel fuel, which can contain traces of water and sediment. Do not smoke or allow an open flame when testing nozzles, and always wear safety goggles.

Popping Pressure Test

1. Connect the nozzle and holder to a suitable pop tester as shown in Figure 18-11 and place clear plastic tubes to the injector overflow connections (fuel return lines) so that return fuel is not confused with injector leakage.

2. Leave the tester-to-nozzle holder fuel line loose and manually pump the tester handle until clear fuel free of air flows from the nozzle end of the tester fuel line; then tighten this fuel line nut.

3. Open the tester gauge shutoff valve if it is closed, and pump the tester handle fairly rapidly (about 45 to 55 strokes per minute) and note at what pressure the nozzle pops or releases fuel. Compare the nozzle opening or release pressure with the engine manufacturer's specifications.

4. Low popping/release pressure necessitates injector replacement or disassembly and repair. Nozzle opening pressure can be adjusted by adding or removing shims from above the internal nozzle valve

spring, or by loosening a nut under the nozzle holder cap and turning an adjusting screw. Figure 18-1 shows the location of the spring and shims. Shim thicknesses can vary between different Bosch nozzles and the make of engine that it is used with.

Nozzle Chatter Test

The nozzle needle valve will open and close as you pump the tester handle up and down. Some nozzles may chatter more than others, due to minor variations in seating angles, carbon deposits, and gum from combustion blowby. Lack of a nozzle chatter is no positive indication in itself that the nozzle is faulty, as long as it passes the other tests. While checking the release pressure of the nozzle, listen for a chatter or hissing sound, which is an indication that the internal nozzle valve is in fact free and moving within the nozzle bore. No chatter is generally accompanied by a poor spray pattern and/or low release pressure.

Lack of good chatter is usually caused by carbon or varnish buildup within the nozzle, which can restrict flow and act as a cushioning effect on the moving nozzle valve. Test for chatters as follows:

1. Close the shutoff valve to the pressure gauge to protect it.
2. Pump the handle quickly up and down until a chatter, hiss, or squeal is detected.

Nozzle Spray Pattern Test

Spray patterns for Bosch pintle nozzles are very similar regardless of the make of engine the nozzle is used in. Generally, pintle nozzles are designed to provide a concentrated spray angle that is fairly narrow or cone shaped. To determine accurately if the nozzle is spraying fuel as recommended, you can place a piece of paper toweling under the nozzle tip (about 12 in. or 30 cm below it) and when you pop the nozzle, look at the mark left on the paper. It should be circular in shape because of the concentrated spray angle. A wide or poorly dispersed spray pattern over the paper requires that the nozzle be disassembled and serviced or replaced. With a multiple-hole nozzle, pop the tester handle once and count the number of drops on the paper to confirm that there are no plugged holes. Check also that all drops on the paper are evenly spaced and at the same height.

NOTE   Some pop testers will not deliver fuel at a great enough velocity to obtain the correct spray pattern for proper analysis. Therefore, if the nozzle cannot be properly tested for spray pattern, yet passes the other tests, it should be considered acceptable unless performance problems occur with it in the engine.

Nozzle Holding Pressure Test

Although the nozzle may open at the correct pressure and have a suitable spray pattern, it must also be capable of preventing fuel dribble when it is not injecting fuel. Fuel dribble at the spray tip will result in nonatomized fuel dribbling into the combustion chamber, resulting in unburned fuel and smoke appearing at the exhaust. Using a lint-free rag or an air pressure nozzle, wipe or blow dry the complete nozzle tip and its holder (injector body).

This condition is best checked by bringing the nozzle pop tester up to a point usually 150 to 200 psi (1034 to 1379 kPa) below the nozzle popping or release pressure and while keeping pressure on the pump handle, inspecting the condition of the spray tip for signs of raw fuel leakage or a bubble/dribble of fuel at the spray tip, although a slight sweat is acceptable at the tip after 5 seconds as long as no fuel droplets appear. Inspect the other sealing surfaces on the nozzle holder (injector body) for signs of external leakage.

To check for fuel leak-off (internal leakage past internal parts), quickly operate the tester handle while looking at the nozzle return fuel outlet—which can be a single outlet at the top center of the nozzle holder, or the nozzle may have two separate fuel return lines. A few drips per pump handle stroke is acceptable, but a steady flow of return fuel indicates that there is wear between the internal injector parts and that the nozzle should be replaced. Table 18-1 lists typical nozzle problems.

NOZZLE DISASSEMBLY AND CLEANING

Extreme cleanliness must be exercised when repairing fuel injection nozzles as well as having access to the special tools and equipment necessary for successful completion of a repair procedure. To clean and decarbonize nozzles/holders properly, place them into a parts tray or basket. Both cold and hot cleaning solutions are available for cleaning purposes. Handle these with care; always wear eye protection. If special cleaners are unavailable, clean solvent or diesel fuel can be used with a small brass bristle brush. Do *not* use a hand-held steel wire brush or a bench grinder wire buffing wheel to clean up the injector components.

The cleaning of injection nozzles should be done in an area that is absolutely clean. Dirt and dust in the air, filings on benches, and greasy rags will contribute

TABLE 18–1   *Troubleshooting faulty nozzles*

Fault	Possible cause	Remedy
Excessive leak-off	Dirt between pressure face of nozzle, spring retainer, or plate and nozzle holder	Clean nozzle
	Loose nozzle retainer nut	Inspect lapped faces and tighten retainer nut
	Defective nozzle	Replace nozzle
Nozzle bluing	Faulty installation or tightening	Replace nozzle
	Insufficient cooling	Correct cooling system
Nozzle opening pressure too high	Incorrect shim adjustment	Replace nozzle
	Nozzle valve dirty or sticky or opening clogged	Clean nozzle
	Seized nozzle	Replace nozzle
Nozzle opening pressure too low	Incorrect shim adjustment	Readjust nozzle
	Nozzle valve spring broken	Replace spring and readjust pressure
	Nozzle seat worn	Install new or reconditioned nozzle
Nozzle drip	Nozzle leaks because of carbon deposit or sticking nozzle valve	Clean nozzle
	Defective nozzle	Replace nozzle
Spray pattern distorted	Carbon deposit on tip of nozzle valve	Clean nozzle
	Nozzle hole partially blocked	Clean nozzle
	Defective nozzle	Replace nozzle

Source: Robert Bosch Corporation.

to faulty nozzle operation and early failure. Tools and equipment necessary for the cleaning of nozzles are:

- Parts cleaner (solvent or ultrasonic type)
- Clean pans
- Lint-free towels
- Nozzle cleaning kit
- Nozzle holder
- Hand tools
- Clean diesel fuel

Shown in Figure 18-12 are the items included in most nozzle cleaning kits.

Cleaning Injection Nozzles

After nozzles are received for cleaning, clean the exterior with solvent to remove loose dirt and grease. Loosen the cap nut and nozzle retaining nut (Figure 18-13). Place nozzles in a suitable parts cleaner to loosen carbon and remove varnish. After soaking for a minimum of 1/2 hour, the nozzles should be rinsed in solvent.

Ultrasonic Nozzle Cleaner

Although loose carbon accumulations can be removed from the tips of injector nozzles by the use of a small brass bristle brush while soaking the part in calibrating fluid or solvent, often hard carbon cannot be removed successfully in this manner. To facilitate removal of hard carbon and varnish accumulations that tend to collect on nozzle components, it is best to use an ultrasonic cleaner, such as the one shown in Figure 18-14.

Ultrasonic Cleaning Method.   Ultrasonic cleaning units use sound waves or mechanical vibrations that are

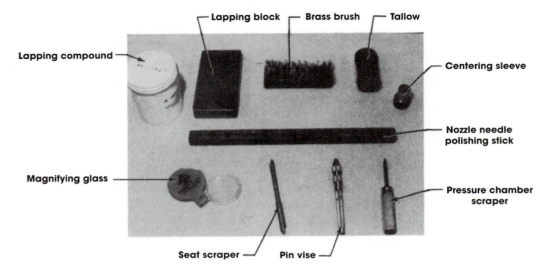

FIGURE 18–12   *Parts of a nozzle cleaning kit.*

above the human hearing range. Bransonic cleaners operate at frequencies around *55,000* cycles per second, or Hz. The sound waves are generated by the transducer, which changes high-frequency electrical energy into mechanical energy. This mechanical energy or vibration is then coupled into the liquid. This action forms millions of microscopic bubbles, which expand during the low-pressure wave and form small cavities. During the high-pressure waves these cavities collapse or implode, creating a mechanical "scrubbing" action that loosens solution. This action takes place approximately *55,000* times per second, making it seem as if dirt is blasted off the part.

Ultrasonic Cleaner Operating Checklist

- The tank should always be filled to about 1 in. from the top.

- Avoid contact with solutions and provide adequate ventilation.
- Ensure that the unit is grounded.
- When filling or emptying tank, unplug the line cord.
- The cleaner must not be overloaded.
- In the case of items containing working parts, parts should be cleaned individually and should be oiled immediately after cleaning.

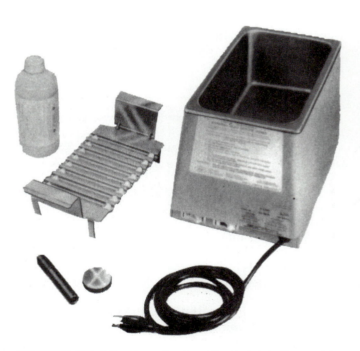

FIGURE 18–14   *Example of an ultrasonic injection nozzle cleaning kit. Cleaning solution is heated and ultrasonically agitated for fast cleaning of nozzle parts. (Courtesy of Kent-Moore Heavy Duty Division, Sealed Power Corporation.)*

FIGURE 18–13   *Loosening nozzle retaining nut.*

- The ultrasonic cleaner should never be immersed in water. After use, rinse tank with warm tap water and wipe dry.
- To avoid discomfort, do not place fingers in the machine when in operation.
- A certain amount of heat is generated during the ultrasonic cleaning process. Do not become alarmed if the bottom surface of the cleaner becomes warm.

Setup and Operation.   The ultrasonic nozzle cleaner, J29653-A, is featured in Figure 18-14. This unit consists of:

J29653-1	Cleaning tank and generator unit
J29653-2	1-lb container of cleaning powder
J29653-3	Nozzle disassembly tool
J29653-4	Parts tray

WARNING   Protect yourself from injury. Wear protective gloves and safety glasses, or other suitable face and eye protection, when mixing chemicals. Avoid contact with solutions and provide adequate ventilation.

1.   Mix the cleaning powder, Kent-Moore P/n J-29653-2 with warm tap water to make the solution (4 teaspoons to 3/4 gallon). The tank should always be filled to about 1 in. from the top.
2.   Plug the unit into a grounded outlet and turn on both switches.

NOTE   Allow the liquid to degas for a few minutes. Also, the cleaner will perform most effectively when the solution is between **120 and 140°F** (49 to 60°C).

3.   Position the tips and pintles in the tray; do not mix. The specially designed stainless steel tray holds nozzles in matched sets.
4.   Install the tray into the tank and place the lid on during the cleaning process. **Do not** place objects to be cleaned directly on the bottom of the cleaning tank.
5.   Remove the tips and pintles when clean (approximately 15 to 30 minutes). Cleaning times may vary, refer to the operator's manual for additional information.

Cleaning Procedure
1.   Always obtain a suitable container(s) prior to disassembly so that each nozzle and its components can be kept together. Do not intermix components between nozzles and holders.
2.   Wash the exterior of the injector body first to remove all dirt and loose carbon formation.
3.   Place the injector nozzle holder in a soft-jaw vise if the manufacturer's special tools are not available. Do not overtighten the vise; otherwise, nozzle damage can result.

   a.   Release pressure on the nozzle spring by removing the cap nut and loosening the pressure-adjusting screw (Figure 18-15).

CAUTION   Failure to remove spring pressure may result in dowel pin breakage when the retaining nut is loosened.

   b.   Invert the nozzle in the holder and remove the nozzle retaining nut and nozzle assembly. Be careful not to drop the nozzle needle!

4.   Disassemble the injector/nozzle components and lay them out in a tray or individual container per injector.
5.   Clean all disassembled parts in a cleaning solution.
6.   Inspect all components under a lighted magnifying glass or a lighted microscope. Check for signs of discoloration (overheated), nicks, scratches, and scuffing on the polished surfaces.
7.   To check the needle valve for freeness in its body after inspection, lightly dip the valve in calibrating fluid or clean filtered diesel fuel, and while holding the nozzle tip at a slight angle, insert the nozzle

FIGURE 18–15   *Loosening pressure-adjusting screw.*

FIGURE 18–16 *Polishing the end of the needle.*

into its tip holder. Pull the nozzle out about halfway and let it go. It should drop under its own weight. Repeat this check by turning the needle valve to different positions. If it does not drop under its own weight, replace the nozzle and tip (sleeve) assembly.

NOTE   Be certain that the nozzle needle is kept with the nozzle body from which it was removed, because nozzle needles are a selective fit in the nozzle body and cannot be interchanged from one nozzle body to another.

---

8.   Examine the needle carefully for scoring, blue spots, excessive wear, and corrosion. If any are found, discard the nozzle.

CAUTION   Never use steel wire bristle brush on precision nozzle parts. Always use brass wire brushes.

---

9.   Using the pintle cleaning block, polish the tapered end of the needle with mutton tallow (Figure 18-16). Place tallow on needle, insert needle in cleaning block, and rotate gently to polish the needle seat. Rinse off excess tallow in clean diesel fuel or calibrating oil.

CAUTION   Never use abrasives such as lapping compound, crocus cloth, or jewelers' rouge to polish the needle. Always use tallow.

---

10.   Using the brass brush, clean the nozzle body to remove loose carbon deposits (Figure 18-17).

11.   When cleaning orifice nozzles, clean the holes with the proper-size cleaning wire.

NOTE   Most nozzle valves will have the hole size stamped or etched on them. If the hole size is not stamped on the nozzle valve, refer to the manufacturer's specifications.

The cleaning wire should be fitted in a pin vise as shown in Figure 18-18, letting the wire protrude approximately 1/16 in. (1.5 mm). This lessens the dan-

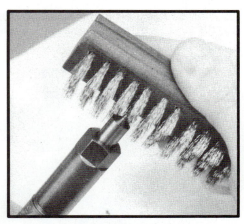

brass brush cleaning

A

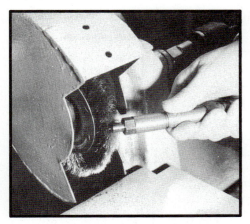

brass wheel cleaning

B

FIGURE 18-17 *Using a brass brush/wire wheel, thoroughly clean all carbon from the outside of the nozzle holder and nozzle before disassembling the nozzle holder: (A) brass brush cleaning; (B) brass wheel cleaning.*

FIGURE 18-18 *Cleaning orifices.*

ger of breaking wires off in the holes, since they are extremely hard to remove when broken. Most popular-sized wires are contained in the nozzle cleaning kits.

12. Using the special pressure chamber scraper shown in Figure 18-19, clean the chamber by rotating and exerting an upward pressure on the tool. Five or six turns are usually sufficient.

13. The nozzle valve seat scraper (Figure 18-20) is used to clean carbon from the valve seat. Two sizes are contained on the same tool for varying nozzle sizes. Rotate the tool to clean the seat.

14. Apply a small amount of tallow to a polishing stick and thoroughly clean and polish the valve seat in the nozzle body (Figure 18-21).

15. The surface of the nozzle body that contacts the nozzle holder as well as the holder surface must be lapped before reassembly.

CAUTION   Nozzles using dowel pins are not always lapped. If lapping is required, the dowels can be removed using diagonal pliers.

FIGURE 18-19 *Sectional view showing how the pressure chamber is cleaned.*

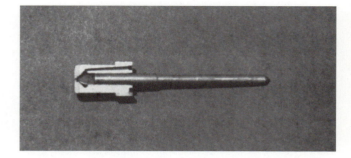

FIGURE 18-20 *Cleaning the valve seat.*

a. Place a small amount of nozzle lapping compound on the lapping plate. Hold the nozzle so that pressure will be exerted evenly on the entire surface. Move the nozzle smoothly and steadily in a figure 8 motion (Figure 18-22).

CAUTION   Do not rock the nozzle from side to side.

---

b. Lap only until the nozzle mating surfaces are clean and flat. Rinse the nozzle completely in clean diesel fuel to remove all traces of lapping compound.

c. Lap the nozzle holder in the same manner. Steady the holder near the lower end to prevent it from rocking.

16. Using a small screwdriver, scrape all loose carbon from the nozzle retaining nut and check for cracks and damaged threads. The sealing surface for the nozzle retaining nut may be cleaned up by rubbing it on the emery cloth.

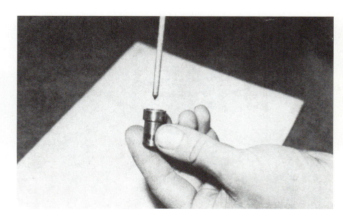

FIGURE 18-21 *Polishing the nozzle valve seat.*

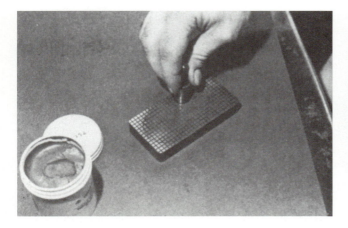

FIGURE 18-22 *Lapping the nozzle mating surface.*

INJECTION NOZZLE REASSEMBLY

1. Start reassembly by rinsing the nozzle needle and the body in clean diesel fuel and checking the valve fit (Figure 18-23). This can be done by holding the nozzle at a 45° angle and pulling the needle one-third of the way up. It should fall freely back to its seat. If it does not, remove the needle, rinse the parts, and try again.

2. Rinse the sealing surfaces of the nozzle holder and nozzle body in diesel fuel and assemble.

CAUTION Since no sealing rings of any type are used at this point, the mating surfaces must be absolutely clean. Do not use compressed air to clean the surfaces, as lint and dust will remain.

Make certain when assembling that locating dowels (if used) are in alignment with holes in the holder (Figure 18-24). On some nozzle types the spray tip is separate from the nozzle body and must be aligned by

FIGURE 18-23 *Checking nozzle valve for free operation.*

FIGURE 18-24 *Aligning the nozzle valve with the dowel pins, if used.*

means of timing lines (Figure 18-25). Hold the tip with a small wrench while snugging up the retaining nut.

3. On pintle nozzles, before final torquing of the retaining nut, the nozzle must be centered in the nut to ensure proper operation.

NOTE Do not center nozzles used with Bosch holders and retaining nuts, as they are self-centering.

To center the nozzle, a special sleeve (Figure 18-12) is used (supplied with nozzle cleaning kits). Carefully fit the centering sleeve over the nozzle body. The tapered end of the sleeve centers the nozzle within the retaining nut bore and on the holder. With the sleeve in place, tighten the nut finger tight. Make sure that the sleeve turns freely. Torque the nut to the manufacturer's specifications using a deep well socket.

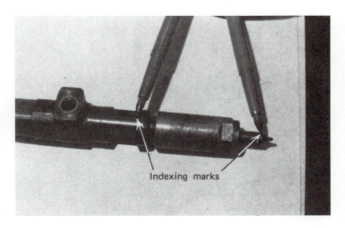

Indexing marks

FIGURE 18-25 *Using alignment marks to position spray holes.*

4. When all parts have been cleaned, inspected, and checked, reassemble the parts. Torque the components and retest the injector as in the tests discussed earlier.

5. To adjust the opening pressure, attach nozzle to the test stand and flush thoroughly by operating the handle. Adjust the opening pressure with the pressure adjusting screw or shims as required (Figure 18-26).

NOZZLE INSTALLATION

Nozzle and holder installation requires that you clean the bore in the cylinder head of any carbon or debris prior to installation. This can be done using a small round brush or, if necessary, use a carbon reaming tool or hard wooden round stick to remove accumulated carbon. To retain the copper washer in position on the nozzle, a small quantity of clean 15W-40 engine oil can be applied, or alternatively, drop the washer into the bore, ensuring that it is installed correctly, then gently lower the nozzle and holder into position.

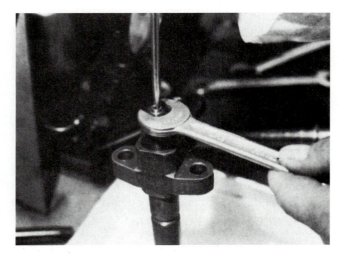

FIGURE 18–26 *Adjusting nozzle opening pressure.*

vere piston/cylinder damage and poor engine performance can result by the nozzle tip being either too far in or too far out. These washers should be replaced each time the nozzle is removed, then reinstalled.

Some manufacturers suggest that you coat the nozzle holder/sleeve with antisieze compound to prevent sticking/freezing in the bore. This will make it easier to remove at any future time. Torque the nozzle holder retaining nuts to the manufacturer's specifications. Attach the fuel leakoff line, then insert the high-pressure inlet fuel line into position, but leave it loose until you have bled the fuel system of all entrapped air. Once you have bled the fuel system, torque all nozzle fuel lines and check for any signs of leakage.

SUMMARY

If the procedures outlined in this chapter are followed, injection nozzle servicing is an easy task. When working with any type of nozzle not listed in this chapter, always refer to the manufacturer's technical manual. It will give the correct torques, opening pressures, operation, and any other pertinent data. If a question still exists, consult your instructor or contact your nearest fuel injection service shop for information.

SELF-TEST QUESTIONS

1. Name the two basic types of nozzles.
2. What is the purpose of the Pintaux nozzle?
3. Explain the difference between a standard pintle nozzle and the throttling pintle.
4. What does each of the following numbers and letters stand for: DN 12 SD 12?
5. State the difference between a nozzle and an injector.
6. Why do most pintle nozzles require centering on the nozzle body?
7. Explain in detail the procedures for removing and installing nozzles in the engine.
8. Why are orifice nozzles used with direct-injection engines?
9. List several reasons why nozzles should be cleaned regularly.
10. Why are retaining nut torque and nozzle hold-down torque so critical?
11. What is the purpose of dowel pins and timing lines in reference to nozzles?
12. What five tests are made on the nozzle test stand?
13. List all steps required in the cleaning of a regular throttling pintle nozzle.
14. Explain how a faulty nozzle can be located in the engine.

19 Robert Bosch Corporation Fuel Systems

COMPANY BACKGROUND

The name of Robert Bosch has been synonymous with fuel injection systems, both gasoline and diesel, for many, many years. After Robert Bosch had finished his apprenticeship with Thomas Edison in the United States, he opened his own precision mechanics shop in 1886. In 1892, Rudolph Diesel invented the diesel engine, but due to its size and weight, it was used mainly in stationary and marine applications. Not until Robert Bosch successfully designed and began mass producing diesel fuel injection systems in 1927 did use of this popular powerplant actually start to spread into all areas of the globe and into over 4200 different applications. The design concept and mode of operation of the different types of diesel fuel injection systems used by the various engine manufacturers is discussed in Chapter 14.

Today, the Robert Bosch Corporation is the largest manufacturer of fuel injection systems (both gasoline and diesel), with representatives in over 130 countries. Over 50% of all diesel fuel injection equipment sold in the free world is manufactured by Robert Bosch and its licensees. The original American Bosch Company, now part of Ambac International, was initially the American affiliate of Robert Bosch Corporation. Many companies worldwide now manufacture Bosch fuel injection equipment and products under a licensing agreement. Two examples are Zexel (Diesel Kiki) and Nippondenso in Japan, both of which supply fuel injection equipment to a wide range of OEMs (original equipment manufacturers). However, there is no longer any connection between Ambac and Bosch.

OVERVIEW

Robert Bosch Corporation is a leader world-wide in the manufacture of gasoline and diesel fuel injection systems. This chapter discusses the company's background and the vital role that Robert Bosch played in the success of the high speed diesel engine that we use today. Details are provided on the main types of Bosch injection pumps used by major engine OEM's, along with the function, operation, testing, inspection, adjustment, service and troubleshooting requirements. After reading this chapter you will be able to identify a number of Bosch fuel injection products, and describe how each fuel injection pump operates, as well as how to adjust, service and maintain it.

Bosch went to court in the United States and won a decision preventing any other company from using the name. There are many major diesel engine manufacturers worldwide who use Bosch fuel injection equipment and governor assemblies. Other injection pump manufacturers, such as Lucas CAV, were also licensees of Bosch but no longer have any tie-in with them. However, the CAV inline pumps do operate on the same basic concept as those produced by Bosch, as do the pumps manufactured by Ambac International. The name "Robert Bosch" is synonymous with success in diesel fuel injection equipment.

With the wide variety of inline pumps available from Bosch, almost every major truck manufacturer in existence that uses four-stroke-cycle engines in their product line, employ a Robert Bosch injection pump/governor. Well-known manufacturers such as Mack, Saab-Scania, Volvo, DAF, Hino, Isuzu, UD (Nissan), Mitsubishi Fuso, Navistar International, Ford, MAN, Mercedes-Benz, and Cummins are just some of the more prominent makes that use these Bosch fuel injection systems. Today, Bosch owns 49 percent of the Diesel Equipment Division of Detroit Diesel Corporation, allowing them access to DDC's DDEC technology.

PRODUCT OVERVIEW

Robert Bosch Corporation manufactures single-cylinder pumps, multiple-plunger inline and V-configuration pumps, and distributor pumps, nozzles, and mechanical governors for diesel engines, as well as electronic diesel control systems.

PF Jerk Pumps

Figure 19-1 illustrates a series of different-sized single cylinder PF jerk pumps. Some pumps are designed for use on small and medium-sized engines, while other pumps are designed for use with large-bore slow-speed, high-horsepower engines. These types of single-cylinder jerk pumps are mounted and timed to the engine. Some pumps employ a flat tappet at their base and are driven from a camshaft drive in the engine. Figure 19-2 illustrates a cross-sectional view of a small PFE 1Q pump, while Figure 19-3 shows a view of a larger PF 1D model.

Since the camshaft is foreign to these pumps, being contained within the engine, they are designated as PF models (the P stands for "pump" and the F for "foreign"). Some pumps in Figure 19-1 are known as PFR models (pump foreign with a roller tappet). A cross section of a PFR pump is shown in Figure 19-4. Based on the actual pump model, typically these pumps are capable of peak injection pressures ranging between 500 and 1000 bar (7350 to 14,700 psi).

The physical size of PF pumps can range from very small plunger sizes to suit single-cylinder portable diesel engines, to extremely large plunger diameters to suit very-large-displacement slow-speed diesel engines up to 60,000 hp (44,760 kW) in output.

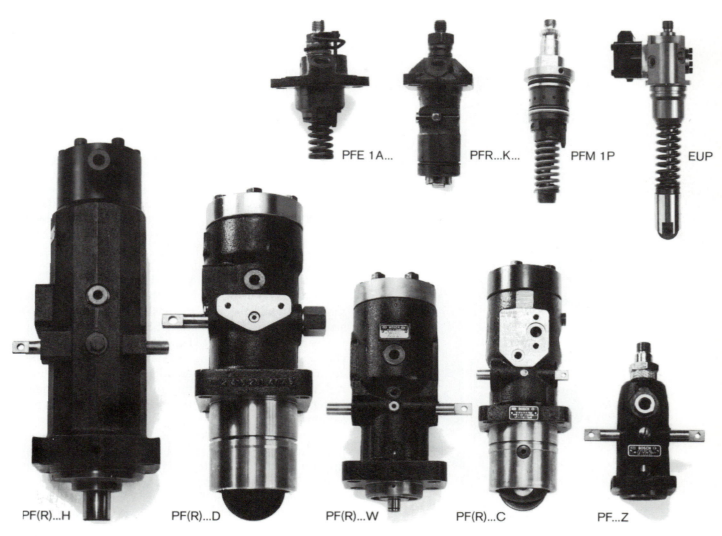

PFE 1A...   PFR...K...   PFM 1P   EUP

PF(R)...H   PF(R)...D   PF(R)...W   PF(R)...C   PF...Z

FIGURE 19–1 Individual jerk-pump model PF injection pumps. (Courtesy of Robert Bosch Corporation.)

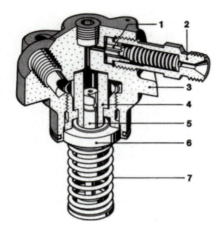

FIGURE 19–2 *Section through type PFE 1Q. 1, Delivery valve; 2, delivery-valve holder; 3, housing; 4, pump barrel; 5, pump plunger; 6, control sleeve; 7, plunger return spring.*

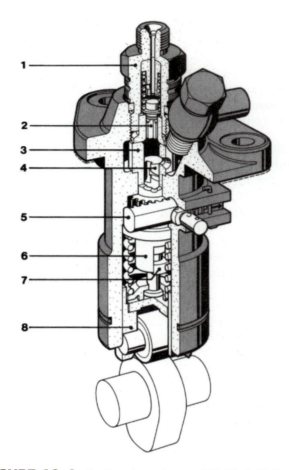

FIGURE 19–4 *Section through type PFR 1K. 1, Delivery-valve holder; 2, delivery valve; 3, pump barrel; 4, pump plunger; 5, control rod; 6, control sleeve; 7, plunger control arm; 8, roller tappet.*

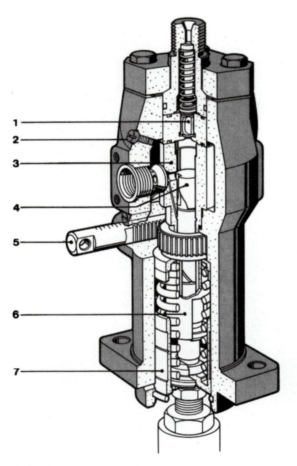

FIGURE 19–3 *Section through type PF 1D. 1, Delivery valve; 2, bleeder screw; 3, pump barrel; 4, pump plunger; 5, control rod; 6, control sleeve; 7, guide bushing.*

The PF pumps can have their tappet adjusting screw adjusted to set the LTPC (lift to port closure) dimension, while the PFR models can use either oversized rollers or shims placed below their mounting flange to set the correct LTPC specification. Later in the chapter we discuss timing of PF and PFR pumps to the engine, as well as how to set/adjust the individual fuel rod/rack linkage. Each pump functions to pressurize, meter, time, and atomize the fuel delivered to the injection nozzle.

When the engine camshaft drive lifts the flat tappet or roller (8) in Figure 19-4, the plunger (4) moves up in its mated barrel to close off the inlet fuel port. Trapped fuel above the plunger is then placed under increasing pressure as the plunger continues to move up. When the fuel pressure reaches approximately 690 to 1034 kPa (100 to 150 psi), the delivery valve (2) is opened against its return spring to allow fuel to exit the delivery valve holder (1), which is connected to the steel tubing leading to the injection nozzle. When the fuel pressure is raised to a high-enough level, the nozzle needle valve is lifted against the return force of its spring to permit high-pressure fuel to flow through the small orifices (holes) in the spray tip and into the combustion chamber. When the upward-moving plunger uncovers the spill port in the barrel, fuel pressure is released, and the nozzle return spring quickly closes the needle valve, ending injection. As the fuel in the nozzle line decreases, the delivery valve (2) is pushed back into the bore of the delivery valve holder. This action allows a volume of fuel equal to the retraction volume under the delivery valve to escape out of the fuel delivery line from the nozzle. Consequently, this lowers the fuel pressure in the delivery line to the nozzle, yet allows a residual pressure to be retained in the line (lower than the nozzle opening pressure) so that during the next injection cycle, the fuel within the line does not have to be repressurized from the very low transfer pump pressure level. Refer to Chapter 14 for more details on delivery valve operation.

Inline Injection Pumps

When the individual pumps are contained in a single housing with their high-pressure fuel outlets arranged in a straight line, the assembly is referred to as a PLN (pump–line–nozzle) system. Bosch and other pump OEMs call these pumps PE models (the P for "pump" and the E for "enclosed camshaft"), since they are mounted lengthwise within the base of the pump housing and driven from the engine gear train. As shown in Figure 19-5, these pumps can be mounted in one of three ways: base, cradle, or flange. The type of mounting is determined by looking at the drive end of the pump. When an inline pump is flange mounted, a third letter, S, is added to the designation, with the pump designated as a PES unit.

Inline pumps are referred to by their physical size, which relates to pumping plunger diameter, how much fuel they can deliver (quantity), and the pressure they can deliver to the nozzle. These pump sizes are M, A, MW, and P. Therefore, PES-A, PES-M, PES-MW, and PES-P indicate pumps with an enclosed camshaft of the size represented by the letter. Pump size examples are included in Figure 19-6.

Pump Designation

Identification of inline pumps can be done visually once you are familiar with the basic differences in design and component layout. Specific information can, however, be obtained from the pump nameplate, riveted to the housing as shown in Figure 19-6. In this example, the pump is listed as PE6P100A320LS825, which can be interpreted as follows:

PE: pump with an enclosed camshaft

  6: number of pumping plungers (six-cylinder engine application)

  P: pump size

100: pump plunger diameter (multiply times 1/10 mm = 10 mm)

  A: execution/original; A, first change; B, second change; C, third change

320: construction information

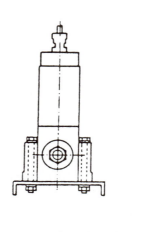
BASE MOUNTING

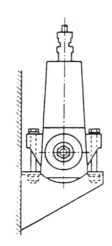
CRADLE MOUNTING

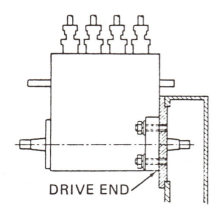
DRIVE END
FLANGE MOUNTING

FIGURE 19–5 *Three-types of mounting designs for inline PLN injection pumps.* (Courtesy of Robert Bosch Corporation.)

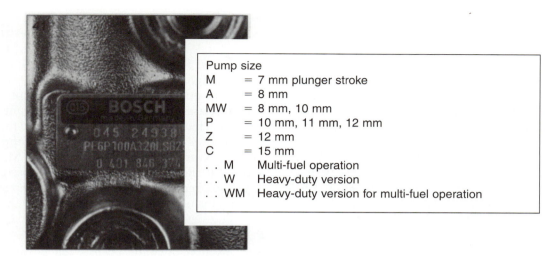

Pump size		
M	=	7 mm plunger stroke
A	=	8 mm
MW	=	8 mm, 10 mm
P	=	10 mm, 11 mm, 12 mm
Z	=	12 mm
C	=	15 mm
. . M		Multi-fuel operation
. . W		Heavy-duty version
. . WM		Heavy-duty version for multi-fuel operation

FIGURE 19–6 *Identification plate located on injection pump housing. (Courtesy of Robert Bosch Corporation.)*

L: direction of pump rotation L, left-hand or counterclockwise; R, right-hand or clockwise

S825: application information

In this example the pump can be either base mounted onto a support on the engine or can be bolted to a cradle on the engine. In a PES designation, the S indicates that the pump is flange mounted.

PUMP FEATURES

The following material describes the basic function and operation of the models M, A, MW, and P multiple-plunger inline pumps, which all operate on the same basic fundamental principle—that of a jerk pump.

The following four inline Bosch pumps are commonly used:

1. The M pump, the smallest inline pump that Bosch manufactures, which is designed for use on small passenger car and light-duty engines. We do not deal in detail with this pump in this book.

2. The A model pump, which was the original design concept created by Robert Bosch in 1923. This pump has undergone many product improvement changes and is still widely used on midrange to mid-heavy-duty high-speed diesel engines. This pump is limited to engines with an approximate cylinder horsepower not exceeding 36 hp (27kW).

3. The MW model pump, which operates on the same basic principle as the A unit; however, the MW employs an integrated flange element at the top of each pumping plunger. The MW pump can handle engines up to approximately 48 hp (36 kW) per cylinder.

4. The P model pump, which is the largest pump offered for use on high-speed heavy-duty truck engines, with a capability of handling up to approximately 98 hp (73 kW) per cylinder. This pump also employs an integrated barrel flange element similar to that for the MW model. The P pump is used extensively on diesel engines manufactured by such companies as Mack, DAF, MAN, Mercedes-Benz, Volvo, Ford, Scania, Hino, Isuzu, Mitsubishi, and Navistar International for use in their heavy-duty truck engines.

A-Size Pump

The A-size pump is illustrated in Figure 19-7 with its special features and major components shown. Still in wide use on a number of truck diesel engines, this pump is found on lighter-duty and mid- to midheavy-duty applications. An inspection plate on the side of the A pump housing can be removed to gain access to the individual pumping plunger and barrel elements when adjustments are required. Adjustments on the A model injection pump can best be established by referring to Figure 19-7 and reading the following description.

Adjusting the Pump

1. Individual pump plunger prestroke (lift to port closure) is set on the A pump by loosening off a tappet locking screw immediately above item 7 and rotating the hex nut. A depth micrometer or dial gauge can be used on the top of the pumping plunger to determine that all pump plungers have the same lift and clearance at the top of their stroke.

2. Fuel delivery for each pumping plunger is established by loosening a toothed clamp ring which is

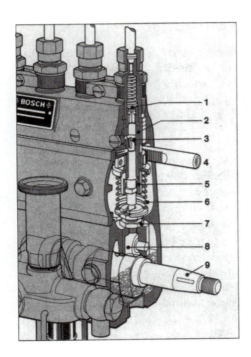

FIGURE 19–7 *Bosch A model multiple-plunger inline injection pump major internal components. 1, Delivery valve; 2, pump barrel; 3, pump plunger; 4, control rod/rack; 5, control sleeve; 6, plunger return spring; 7, tappet adjusting screw to alter lift to port closure dimension; 8, roller tappet; 9, camshaft. (Courtesy of Robert Bosch Corporation.)*

engaged with the fuel control rod (4) or rack. The clamping ring is assembled around the outside diameter of the control sleeve (5). By loosening the lock screw and moving this clamp ring and retightening its screw, its position in relation to the fuel rod/rack and the control sleeve (5) shown in Figure 19-7 can be changed. When the injector rod/rack (4) in Figure 19-7 is moved back and forward, the teeth on the rack, which are in mesh with the clamping ring, will also cause the control sleeve to rotate. At the base of the control sleeve (about halfway between 5 and 6) in Figure 19-7, you will notice that there is a projection on the pumping plunger which engages with slots on the control sleeve. Movement of the control sleeve (5) in Figure 19-7 will cause the plunger to be rotated and its "effective stroke" will be determined so that the amount of fuel delivered for a given rack setting can be adjusted to the manufacturer's specifications. The maximum amount of fuel is therefore adjusted by changing the setting of the individual clamping rings at each pump plunger. These adjustments for fuel delivery should be done only when the injection pump is on a test stand.

Both the M- and A-size pumps are pressure lubricated from the engine. The A-size pump contains a separate governor housing that is bolted to the end of the injection pump housing.

MW-Size Pump

The MW injection pump differs considerably from that of the M and A shown so far; however, the MW is very similar in design to the larger inline pump, the P-size unit. The MW pump was designed for higher injection pressures than the M and A units and is found on many automotive high-performance/high-output turbocharged engines produced by such manufacturers as Mercedes-Benz in its 300D and SD passenger cars, as well as by Volvo truck and marine engines, Navistar International, Mack Trucks, and Perkins diesel engines. Figures 19-8 and 19-9 illustrate the external and internal features of the MW model pump.

The MW pump uses a bolted flange/bushing installed into the top of the injection pump housing and does not have an access plate on the side of the pump housing that can be removed for individual pump adjustment as is the case with both the M and A pumps shown earlier. The bolted flange on top of the MW pump is slotted so that when loosened, the barrel and valve assembly can be rotated to ensure equal fuel delivery from each individual plunger and barrel assembly. In addition, each pump plunger prestroke can be set by the use of shims of varying thickness which are installed or removed from under each bolted flange on top of the pump housing.

The fuel control rod or rack, connected as shown in Figure 19-9, controls the rotation of each pumping plunger and therefore the start of the effective stroke (port closure) and the quantity of fuel delivered for a given throttle/rack setting. The rotation of the individual pump plungers is similar to the M model pump in that it employs a connection known as lever regulation, since the ball ends of the individual control levers engage with slots in the fuel control rod/rack.

Unlike the M and A model injection pumps, the MW model pump barrel (item 4 in Figure 19-8) extends above the top of the injection pump housing and is held in place by two retaining nuts and washers. The delivery valve and its holder (1) are screwed into the pump barrel (4) to form a compact, easy-to-service assembly. The pump is pressure lubricated from the engine's oil system. The MW pump has a separate governor assembly bolted onto the end of the injection pump housing.

P-Size Pump

The P-size injection pump, although not physically the largest unit manufactured by Robert Bosch, is the biggest pump that is used on high-speed heavy-duty type truck and industrial engine applications. Figure

FIGURE 19–8 Multiple-plunger inline pump model PES and major component ID features. 1, Delivery valve holder; 2, filler piece; 3, delivery valve spring; 4, pump barrel; 5, delivery valve; 6, inlet and spill port; 7, plunger helix; 8, pump plunger; 9, control sleeve; 10, plunger control arm; 11, plunger return spring; 12, spring seat; 13, roller tappet; 14, cam; 15, control rod/rack. (Courtesy of Robert Bosch Corporation.)

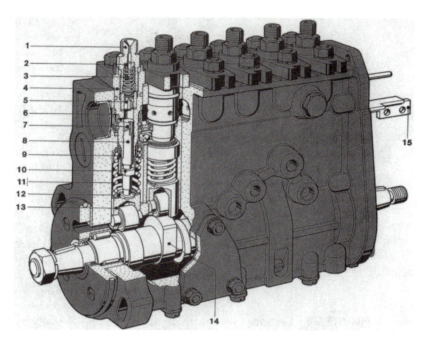

19-10 illustrates the model P injection pump in a cutaway view so that you can familiarize yourself with its features. Note that it contains a sheet-metal protection cover held in place by screws, mounted on top of the pump to keep dirt and debris away from the barrel flanges. It is this cover that will allow you to quickly identify the model P injection pump from other Bosch

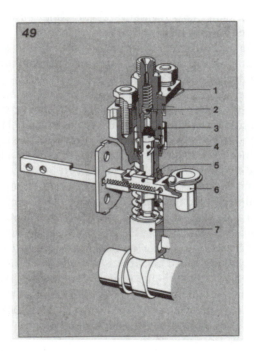

FIGURE 19–9 Partial section through a model MW inline injection pump. Index: 1, Bolted retaining flange for the plunger and barrel assembly; 2, delivery valve; 3, pump barrel; 4, pump plunger; 5, control rod/rack; 6, control sleeve; 7, roller tappet. (Courtesy of Robert Bosch Corporation.)

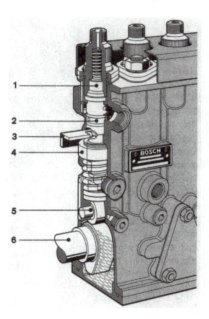

FIGURE 19–10 Sectional view through a model P inline injection pump. 1, Delivery valve; 2, pump barrel; 3, control rod/rack; 4, control sleeve; 5, roller tappet; 6, camshaft. (Courtesy of Robert Bosch Corporation.)

models. The model P pump uses a separate governor housing, bolted onto the end of the pump housing.

The P pump is similar in construction to the MW model pump illustrated in Figure 19-8, in that both pumps employ shims underneath the barrel flanges to adjust the individual plunger lift to port closure, which is commonly known as *prestroke* on Bosch pumps. Prestroke is when the upward-moving pump plunger moves from BDC to the point where it covers the inlet ports in the barrel. The start of fuel injection would begin shortly thereafter once the trapped fuel reaches a high enough pressure to open the delivery valve.

Current model P pumps are capable of very high injection pressures. For example, the P7100 model can produce 1050 bar (15,225 psi) on the pump side and 1250 bar (18,125 psi) on the nozzle side. The uprated P8500 model can produce 1150 bar (16,675 psi) on the pump side and 1350 bar (19,575 psi) on the nozzle side. Both pumps use a 12-mm-diameter plunger with a plunger lift of 12 mm and 14 mm, respectively.

In addition, both the model MW and P pumps use bolted barrel flanges on the top of the pump housing that can be rotated CW or CCW in order to alter the delivery rate of fuel from each pumping element. However, both adjustments should be performed only when the pump is mounted onto a fuel pump test stand where the necessary special tooling and equipment is readily available. Figure 19-11 shows the actual adjusting mechanism that alters the pumping element fuel delivery through the control rod (rack), which is connected to the throttle pedal through the governor assembly.

INLINE PUMP FUEL SYSTEM

The general fuel system arrangement employed with all inline multiple-plunger pumps can be considered common regardless of the make of engine on which it is employed. Figure 19-12 illustrates typical fuel injection pump external components, while the flow path

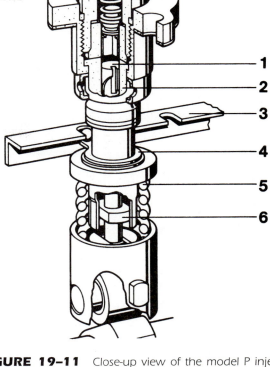

FIGURE 19–11 *Close-up view of the model P injection pump adjusting mechanism. 1, Plunger; 2, barrel; 3, control rod/rack; 4, control sleeve; 5, plunger return spring; 6, plunger control arm. (Courtesy of Robert Bosch Corporation.)*

of fuel from the tank to the supply pump is shown in Figure 19-13. The supply pump is referred to as a transfer or lift pump by some manufacturers. It is equipped with a small priming plunger that can have the plastic or metal handwheel on the top rotated CCW to loosen it, then by manually pulling/pushing the knob up and down, fuel can be drawn from the fuel tank to prime the filters or the injection pump. Some systems may use a primary fuel filter or combination fuel filter/water separator between the fuel tank and the supply pump. The supply pump typically delivers fuel at low pressure, usually in the re-

FIGURE 19–12 *Major external component parts identification of a multiple-plunger inline injection pump. (Courtesy of GMC Medium Duty Truck Division of General Motors Corporation.)*

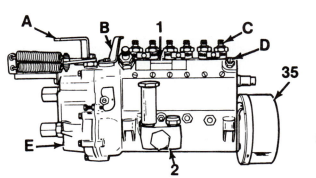

A. Accelerator Lever
B. Fuel Shut Off Lever
C. Number One Cylinder Delivery Valve Holder
D. Pump Bleed Screw
E. Governor
1. Identification Tag
2. Transfer Pump
35. Automatic Timer

The eight major components are:

1. Fuel Tank
2. Primary Fuel Filter
3. Fuel Supply Pump
4. Secondary Filter
5. Injection Pump
6. High Pressure Fuel Lines
7. Injection Nozzles
8. Governor

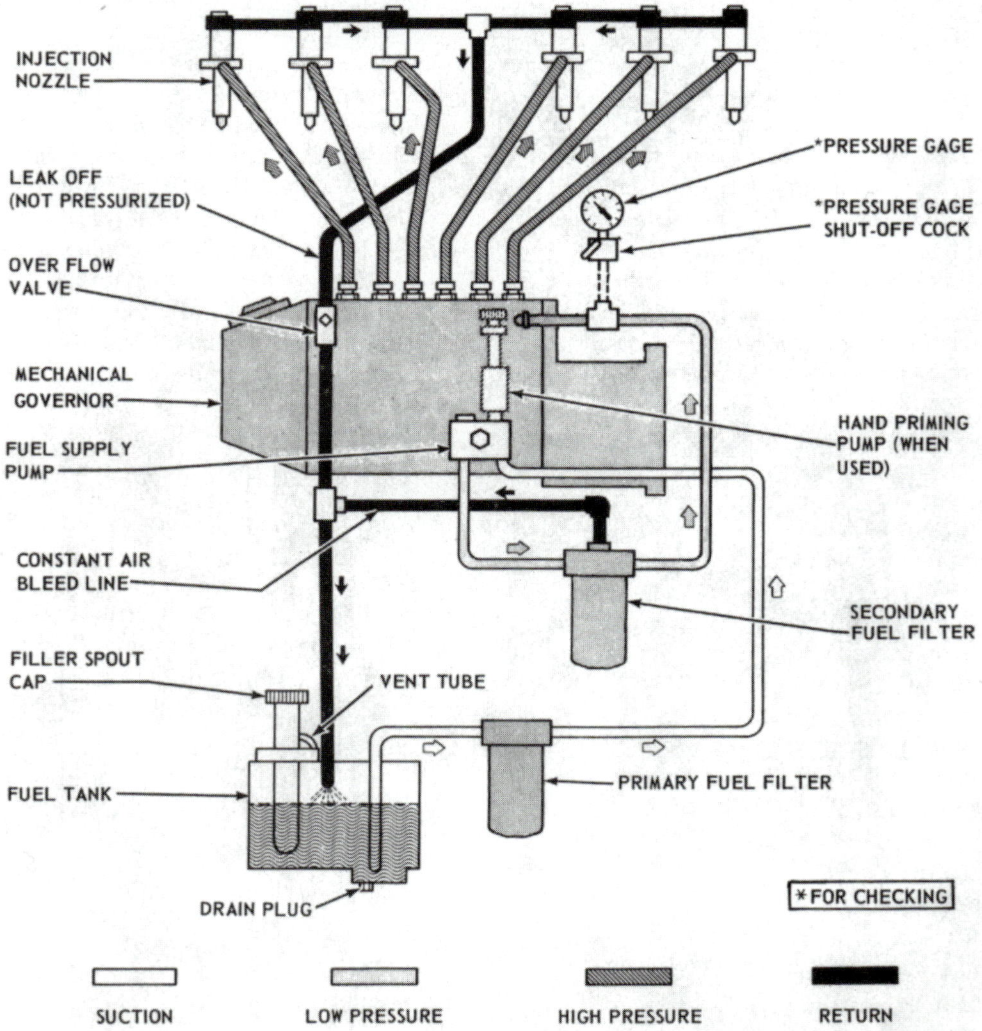

FIGURE 19–13 *Typical high-pressure multiple-plunger inline injection pump fuel system components layout. (Courtesy of Mack Trucks, Inc.)*

gion 19 to 44 psi (131 to 303 kPa) maximum. This fuel is pushed through the secondary fuel filter, where it passes to the inlet fitting on the injection pump. Many injection pumps employ a spring-loaded pressure relief valve (see Figures 19-13 and 19-14) to maintain a set operating pressure within the pump fuel gallery.

When the relief valve opens, fuel is routed back to the fuel tank. In this way warm fuel, used for cooling and lubrication purposes within the injection pump, is continuously recirculated back to the tank. A small spring-loaded overflow valve can also be used, which is shown in Figure 19-13 connected to the secondary

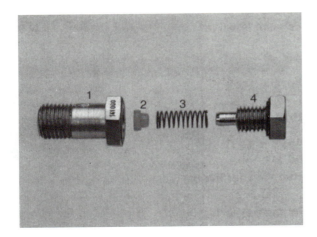

FIGURE 19–14 Exploded view of an inline injection pump pressure relief valve. 1, Valve body; 2, valve; 3, spring; 4, plug and seal ring. (Courtesy of Freightliner/Mercedes-Benz Truck Company, Inc.)

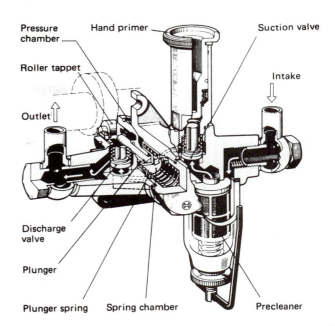

FIGURE 19–15 FP/K fuel supply pump. (Courtesy of Robert Bosch GmbH.)

fuel filter. Each injection nozzle also has a fuel return line connected to it to route regulated internal fuel leakage, which is also used for lubrication purposes, to return to the tank.

FUEL SUPPLY PUMP OPERATION

To ensure complete filling of the barrel assembly above the pumping plunger, the fuel gallery of the injection pump must be pressurized. A fuel supply pump is used to pump fuel from the fuel tank to the pump gallery (Figure 19-15).

FP/K Series Fuel Supply Pump
This is a single-acting plunger pump usually mounted on the side of the main injection pump and driven off the pump camshaft. The pump can be equipped with a preliminary filter enclosed in a sediment bowl and also a hand primer as shown in Figure 19-15. The hand primer is used to purge (bleed) air from the system if it has run dry or if the fuel filters have been changed.

Suction/Discharge Stroke of Fuel Supply Pump
On the suction stroke, the roller of the supply pump follows the camshaft inward, because of the force of the plunger spring (Figure 19-16a). As the plunger is moved inward, a low-pressure area is created. Atmospheric pressure then pushes fuel through the preliminary filter, past the suction valve, and into the suction chamber. At the same time, the opposite side of the plunger pushes fuel from the pressure chamber into the outlet line. The pressure in this line, varying from

14 to 28 psi (1 to 2 kg/cm^2), depending on engine application, will close the pressure valve.

Intermediate Stroke Position
As the injection pump camshaft continues to revolve, it forces the roller tappet of the supply pump outward, away from the injection pump, also pushing the plunger out (Figure 19-16b). Fuel trapped in the suction chamber will open the pressure valve and enter the pressure chamber. This fuel will also close the suction valve on the inlet line. This stroke completely fills the pressure chamber so that it can empty on the discharge stroke.

Double-Acting Supply Pump
In the double-acting supply pump shown in Figure 19-17, two additional nonreturn valves make the suction chamber and the pressure chamber of the single-acting supply pump into two combined suction and pressure chambers. The pump does not execute an intermediate stroke. On each stroke of the double-acting supply pump the fuel is drawn into one chamber and simultaneously delivered from the other chamber of the injection pump. Each stroke is, therefore, a delivery and suction stroke. In contrast to the single-acting supply pump, the fuel delivery can never be reduced to zero. For this reason, the delivery line or the fuel filter must be provided with an overflow valve through which the excess fuel can flow back to the fuel tank.

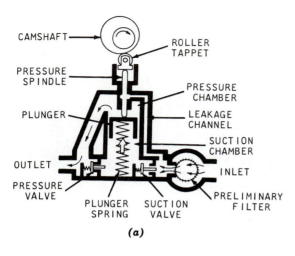

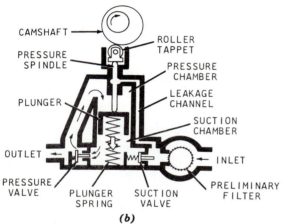

FIGURE 19-16 (a) FP/K transfer pump on inlet stroke; (b) FP/K transfer pump in intermediate position.

INJECTION PUMP OPERATION

All of the different models of Bosch inline multiple-plunger injection pumps operate on the fundamental principles described in Figure 19-18. This operating principle is commonly known as the *jerk pump* concept, since each pump plunger is moved up and down by the action of a gear-driven pump camshaft. For injection to begin, the pumping plunger must be lifted by the pump camshaft until it closes off the inlet fuel ports of the barrel. This term is commonly known in Bosch pumps as *lift to port closure* and refers to how far the plunger must move or lift to effectively close off both fuel inlet ports within the barrel. Figure 19-18 illustrates the action of the plunger to create an injection cycle for one pumping element. The lift to port closure dimension can be found in the Robert Bosch pump technical specifications for all models and applications. When setting this specification, the injection pump is normally mounted onto a pump test stand,

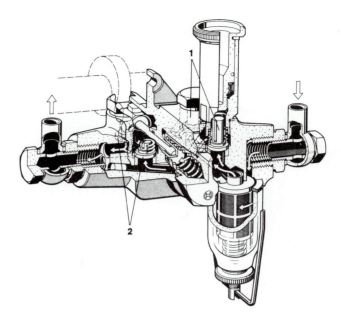

FIGURE 19-17 Supply pump, double acting. 1, Nonreturn valve (suction end); 2, nonreturn valve (pressure end).

where all of the other checks and tests can be accurately performed.

FUEL METERING (MEASUREMENT)

The key to a good fuel system is the method by which the fuel is controlled. Some common methods are the port and helix, inlet metering, and sleeve control types.

The port and helix (Figure 19-18) is probably one of the most common types of fuel control systems in use today. It is called spill port metering because it controls the amount of fuel pumped by opening a port and by spilling off high-pressure fuel.

Components
The port and helix pumping unit is composed of:
1. Barrel and plunger unit fitted or lapped together with a very small clearance between them to allow enough fuel to enter between the mating parts for lubrication.
2. Helix and vertical groove. If the pumping plunger unit did not have a helix or control groove machined on it, the pumping element would pump the same amount of fuel at all times, giving the operator no control over the engine.

Fuel Flow and Operation
1. With the helix and vertical groove, the pump output can be easily varied by turning the pumping plunger in relation to the barrel.
2. As the pumping plunger is forced upward and covers the inlet and outlet ports in the barrel, fuel is trapped above the pumping plunger.

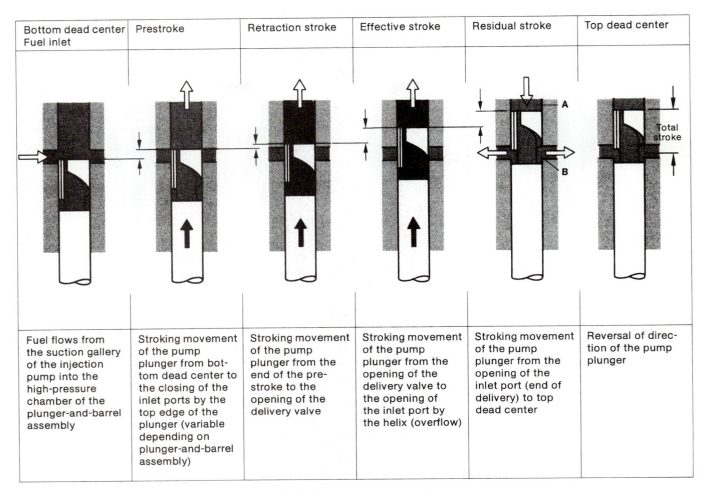

Bottom dead center Fuel inlet	Prestroke	Retraction stroke	Effective stroke	Residual stroke	Top dead center
Fuel flows from the suction gallery of the injection pump into the high-pressure chamber of the plunger-and-barrel assembly	Stroking movement of the pump plunger from bottom dead center to the closing of the inlet ports by the top edge of the plunger (variable depending on plunger-and-barrel assembly)	Stroking movement of the pump plunger from the end of the prestroke to the opening of the delivery valve	Stroking movement of the pump plunger from the opening of the delivery valve to the opening of the inlet port by the helix (overflow)	Stroking movement of the pump plunger from the opening of the inlet port (end of delivery) to top dead center	Reversal of direction of the pump plunger

FIGURE 19–18 *Phases of the injection pump plunger stroke to deliver fuel under pressure to the nozzles. (Courtesy of Robert Bosch Corporation.)*

3. The chamber and the vertical groove in the plunger are filled with pressurized fuel.

4. As the pumping plunger moves farther upward, the pressurized fuel opens the delivery valve that is mounted directly above the pumping element (Figure 19-18).

5. Fuel is then delivered to the injection nozzle via the fuel injection line.

6. End of delivery occurs when the helix uncovers an inlet port, allowing high-pressure fuel to rush down the vertical groove cut in the plunger. This lowers the pressure in the pumping chamber. Delivery to the cylinder stops, since the injection nozzle and delivery valve both close via spring pressure.

Metering Principle

The amount or volume of the fuel charge is regulated by rotating the plunger in the barrel as shown in Figure 19-19 to effectively alter the relationship of the control port and the control helix on the plunger. This is done by means of a rack and a control collar or control sleeve shown in Figure 19-20. The *rack* is basically a rod with teeth on one side, which is supported and operates in bores in the housing. The rack is in turn connected to a governor. The geared segment or control collar is clamped to the top of the control sleeve with teeth that engage the rack. The control sleeve is a loose fit over the barrel and is slotted at the bottom to engage the wings on the plunger so that as the rack is moved it will cause rotation of the collar, sleeve, and plunger.

The operation of Robert Bosch inline pumps is basically the same as that for CAV and Ambac inline pumps; however, let us quickly review the pumping plunger's operation and excess fuel device so that we thoroughly understand the principle.

The plunger within the barrel is moved up and down by the action of the rotating camshaft within the injection pump housing; it can also be rotated by the movement of the fuel control rack connected to the throttle and governor linkage. Anytime that the stop control is moved to the engine shut-down position,

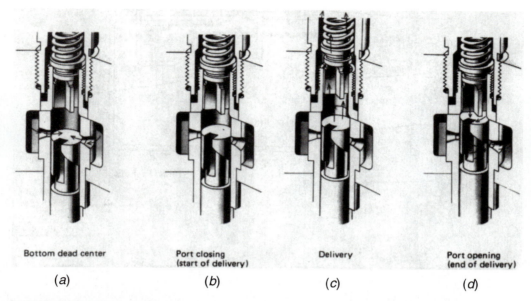

Bottom dead center	Port closing (start of delivery)	Delivery	Port opening (end of delivery)
(a)	(b)	(c)	(d)

FIGURE 19–19 Injection pump plunger operation; by providing a helical groove or land on the plunger and arranging to rotate it, the "effective" plunger stroke can be varied to control the quantity of fuel delivered per stroke. (Courtesy of Robert Bosch Corporation.)

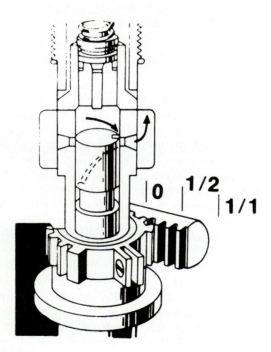

FIGURE 19–20 Rotating pump plunger by action of the control rack and gear segment to change the volume of fuel delivered per pump plunger stroke. (Courtesy of Robert Bosch Corporation.)

the plunger is rotated as shown in Figure 19-20 whereby the vertical slot machined in the plunger will always be in alignment with the supply or control port. Therefore, regardless of the plunger's vertical position within the barrel, fuel pressure can never exceed that delivered by the fuel-transfer pump. This pressure will never be able to overcome the force of the delivery valve spring, so no fuel can be sent to the injector nozzles.

During any partial fuel delivery situation, the amount of fuel supplied to the injector will be in proportion to the *effective stroke* of the plunger, which simply means that the instant the supply port is covered by the upward-moving plunger, fuel will start to flow to the injector. This will continue as long as the control port is covered; however, as soon as the upward-moving plunger helix uncovers this port, fuel pressure to the injector is lost and injection ceases. Therefore, we only effectively deliver fuel to the injector as long as the control port is covered; this is shown in Figure 19-21a for any partial throttle position. This will vary in proportion to the throttle and rack position from idle to maximum fuel.

When the operator or driver moves the throttle to its maximum limit of travel, the effective stroke of the plunger, due to the rotation of the plunger helix, will allow greater fuel delivery because of the longer

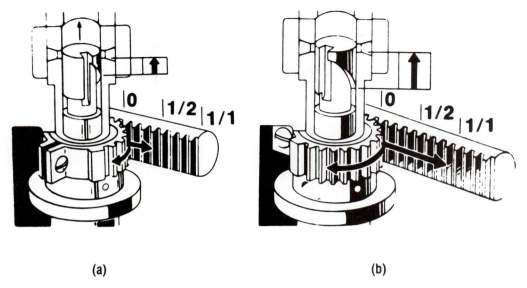

(a)   **(b)**

FIGURE 19–21   (a) Partial fuel delivery position; (b) Maximum fuel delivery position. (Courtesy of Robert Bosch Corporation.)

period that the control port is closed during the upward movement of the plunger by the pump camshaft. This is shown in Figure 19-21b.

Figure 19-22c shows a starting groove machined into the plunger; while Figure 19-23 shows a lower helix plunger with a retard notch. This groove is also referred to as an *excess fuel delivery and retard* notch. Excess fuel is possible only during starting, since while the engine is stopped the speed control lever is moved to the *slow idle* position, thereby moving the fuel rack to place the plunger in such a position that excess fuel can be delivered. The instant the engine starts, however, the governor will move the fuel rack to a position corresponding to the position of the throttle lever. The retard notch, also in alignment with the control port, delays port closing and therefore retards timing during starting.

HELIX SHAPES AND DELIVERY VALVES

Helixes

Plungers are manufactured with metering lands having lower or upper helixes (see Figure 19-22) or both to give constant port closing with a variable ending, variable port closing with a constant ending, or both a variable beginning and ending. With ported pumps, good control of injection characteristics is possible due to the minimum fuel volume that is under compression. However, a disadvantage of conventional port control pumps is the rising delivery characteristics as speed increases. This is caused by the fuel throttling

process through the ports, resulting in less fuel being bypassed before port closing and after port opening as the speed of the pump increases.

When the plunger is rotated so that the vertical slot on the plunger is in line with the control port (locating screw side), all the fuel will be bypassed; therefore, there will be no injection. With the rack in the full-fuel position, the plunger is able to complete almost its entire stroke before the helix will uncover the control port. Remember, as the plunger is rotated, it will uncover the port earlier or later in the stroke (Figure 19-21).

Some plungers employ a lower-right-hand helix, where the start of injection is constant with regard to timing; however, the ending is variable. In some applications it is advantageous to advance timing as the fuel rate is increased. This is achieved by the use of an upper helix, which gives a variable beginning and a constant ending. The helix may be cut on the left- or right-hand side of the plunger. It does not alter the injection characteristic except that the rack must be moved in opposite directions to increase or decrease fuel. There are other special adaptions, such as a short, shallow helix on top to give a slight retarding effect to the injection timing on engines that operate in the idle range for extended periods, and a double helix used by some manufacturers to provide rapid response with minimum rack movement.

With a lower helix design, the beginning of delivery is constant and the ending of delivery is variable. The reason for the helix being on opposite sides is that

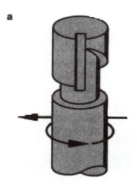

a

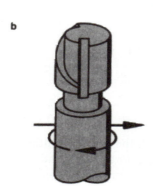

b

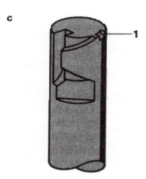

c   1

FIGURE 19–22 *Examples of typical inline injection pump plunger helix designs. (a) Lower helix; (b) upper helix; (c) upper and lower helix. 1, Starting groove. (Courtesy of Robert Bosch Corporation.)*

the one on the left would be employed when the governor is on the left or when the fuel rack is in front of the plunger. Figure 19-22b shows an upper helix design; the delivery has a variable beginning but a constant ending. Figure 19-22c shows plungers with both upper and lower helixes; both the beginning and ending of delivery are variable.

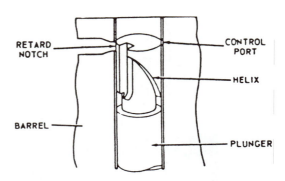

FIGURE 19–23 *Excess fuel delivery and retard notch.*

Delivery Valves

The main function of any delivery valve in the injection pump is twofold:

1. At the end of the plunger's upward fuel delivery stroke, the delivery valve prevents a reverse flow of fuel from the injection line.

2. Figure 19-24 illustrates the sucking action that occurs at the delivery valve piston portion which controls the residual pressure in the injection line so as to effectively improve the injected spray pattern of the fuel without fuel dribble and possible secondary injection. The sucking action that does occur at the delivery valve therefore effectively reduces the fuel pressure in the injection tube at the end of injection.

The delivery valve, or what is sometimes referred to as a discharge valve, is specially designed to assist in providing a clean, positive end to injection. Below the valve face is a collar that is a precision fit in the valve bore. When pressure is created in the pump above the plunger by the closing of the ports, the valve must be raised far enough off its seat for the collar to clear the bore.

At the end of injection when pressure in the pump chamber is relieved by the opening of the control port, the valve drops down on its seat assisted by spring pressure. A volume of fuel equal to the displacement volume of the valve is added to the line and nozzle, reducing this pressure and allowing the nozzle valve to snap shut without the cushioning effect of pressure retained in the line and nozzle, such as with the closing of an ordinary valve. This is commonly called *line retraction*, which lessens the possibility of secondary injection or after-dribble at the spray nozzle. It is accomplished by an antidribble collar (accurately fitted relief or displacement piston) located at the upper end of the valve stem just below the seat.

INLINE PUMP-TO-ENGINE TIMING

The purpose of this book is not to provide detailed information on the removal, installation, timing, repair,

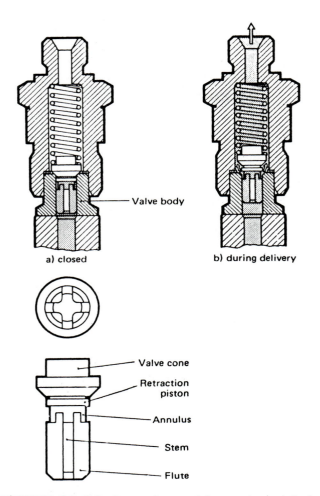

Valve body

a) closed   b) during delivery

Valve cone

Retraction piston

Annulus

Stem

Flute

FIGURE 19–24 *Pump plunger delivery valve nomenclature and cycle of operation. (Courtesy of Robert Bosch Corporation.)*

and troubleshooting of inline pumps for every model of engine. Due to similarity of design and application, the methods required to service and time these fuel injection pumps to typical midrange, midheavy, and heavy-duty on-highway trucks can be considered as being fairly similar to each other. Your guide when preparing to time an injection pump to the engine should always be the EPA exhaust emissions plate/label and tune-up specs decal. This decal is generally attached to the engine valve rocker cover and contains all the information you need.

Installation of an inline multiple-plunger fuel injection pump to an engine is a fairly straightforward procedure as far as actually mounting and bolting the pump into position is concerned. Prior to actual installation, however, it is necessary on some pumps to align a gear timing mark on the engine gear train with a matching mark on the fuel injection pump-driven gear. On other models of engine an external reference

timing mark, provided by the engine manufacturer, may be located on either the flywheel itself or on the crankshaft vibration damper or pulley located at the front of the engine. On some engines timing marks can be found on both the flywheel and vibration damper pulley, as illustrated in Figure 19-25A; OT stands for "overtop" and FB stands for "fuel begins." Figure 19-25B shows the pump to drive coupling alignment marks.

Generally, piston 1 is used as the reference cylinder on the compression stroke to align the marks with the stationary pointer, which is attached to either the engine gear timing cover at the front or at an accessory inspection plate cover on the flywheel. This is the procedure recommended by the majority of diesel engine manufacturers, with cylinder 1 being determined from the vibration damper/pulley end of the engine. Note, however, that the specific make of engine determines what cylinder to use while on its compression stroke. On some engines cylinder 1 is determined from the flywheel end (rear) of the engine; others may use cylinder 6 on its compression stroke as the reference point to align the injection pump-to-engine timing marks. Similarly, when timing an engine to an injection pump, pump 1 in the housing is always located at the end closest to the drive coupling.

The timing marks on the flywheel or vibration damper pulley may indicate TDC for both cylinders 1 and 6, or possibly for all engine cylinders. Remember the TDC mark on a four-stroke-cycle engine can occur once every 360°. Since the timing mark must be aligned only on the compression stroke, always remove the valve rocker cover to determine if free play exists at the valve operating mechanism on the cylinder being used as the reference point. Failure to do this can result in the piston being at TDC; however, it may be at TDC on the end of its exhaust stroke, which means that in fact the timing mark between the engine and injection pump would be 360° out of phase. This can be confirmed by checking for valve lash on the reference cylinder. If there is no valve lash, it is not on its compression stroke. Rotate the crankshaft manually another 360° to place the piston on its compression stroke.

Although we have discussed TDC for a particular cylinder, the static (engine stopped) pump-to-engine timing mark is always found on the engine exhaust emissions regulation plate or decal, which is usually attached to the valve rocker cover although on some engines it may be located elsewhere. Most engines have the static pump timing set for a number of degrees BTDC on the reference cylinder (No. 1); however, some engines use TDC as the actual pump-to-engine timing mark. On engines that have a BTDC

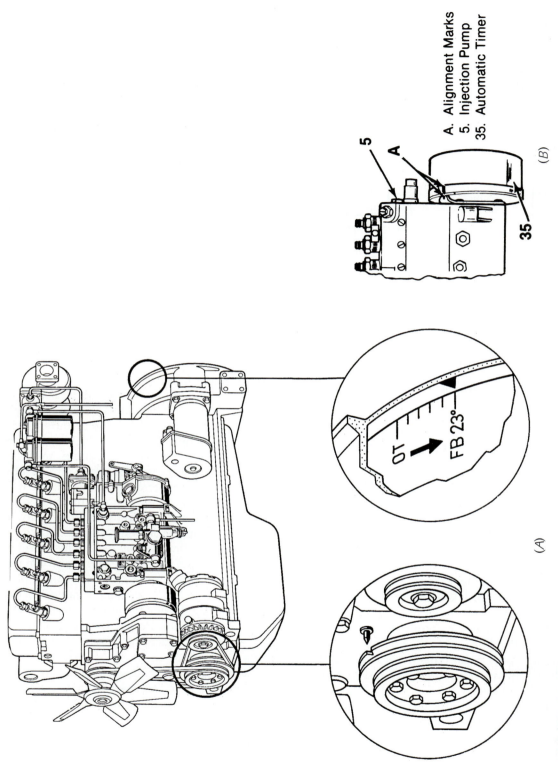

A. Alignment Marks
5. Injection Pump
35. Automatic Timer

(B)

(A)

OT

FB 23°

FIGURE 19–25 (A) Example of engine-to-pump timing marks, which can be referenced when spill timing the pump to the engine; (B) example of the actual timing marks for injection pump to drive coupling. (Courtesy of Robert Bosch Corporation.)

timing mark, say 26° BTDC, then while rotating the engine over manually in its normal direction of rotation from the front, the pump-to-engine timing mark of 26° BTDC would appear before the TDC mark. If the TDC mark appears before the 26° marking, you are turning the engine over backwards. On some engines this timing mark may also have the letters BT or BTC, meaning before top or before top dead center, to assist you in aligning the correct marks. The letters OT, meaning over top, also indicate that it is after TDC as shown in Figure 19-25A.

OVERVIEW: STATIC SPILL TIMING

When an injection pump is suspected of being out of time, or after the pump has been reinstalled onto an engine, a pump-to-engine timing procedure must be followed. A commonly employed procedure is known as *spill timing*. During this procedure the engine is stopped (static) and the pump-to-engine timing is performed by determining when the fuel is just starting to be delivered to cylinder 1. A small gooseneck-shaped line is attached to the top of the delivery valve holder so that the fuel flow can be monitored visually. An example of a gooseneck line or drip spout can be seen in Figure 19-26A.

Engine-to-pump timing can be determined by either a low- or high-pressure spill timing procedure. The low-pressure timing procedure involves using the hand priming pump attached to the transfer/lift pump shown in Figure 19-15, which supplies fuel to the No. 1 pumping plunger of the injection pump. Another low-pressure method uses regulated shop air to force the fuel through the injection pump. Both of these low-pressure spill timing procedures are commonly used and are reasonably accurate. The drawback of the low-pressure procedure is that the technician must first remove the pumping plunger spring-loaded delivery valve. The delivery valve components can be seen in Figure 19-26B. Removal is necessary because the low fuel pressure created is insufficient to lift the delivery valve against the spring force. For more precise pump-to-engine timing, a high-pressure spill timing procedure is recommended. The high-pressure procedure uses an electric-motor-driven fuel pump system that creates fuel pressure high enough to open the spring-loaded delivery valve in the top of each pumping plunger assembly.

Regardless of what spill timing method is used, when the engine-to-pump timing marks are not in alignment, and the piston in cylinder 1 is just starting its compression stroke, fuel will flow freely from the small gooseneck-shaped line attached to the No. 1 pumping plunger delivery valve holder shown in Figure 19-26A. This fuel flow occurs because the plunger is at the BDC (bottom dead center) position, which can be seen on the left-hand side of Figure 19-26C. This allows fuel under pressure from the injection pump gallery to flow in over the top of the plunger and exit out of the delivery valve holder at the top. As the engine is manually rotated in its normal direction of rotation, the injection pump camshaft will raise the pumping plunger (prestroke) until it closes off the fuel ports within the barrel. When this point is reached, fuel stops flowing out of the delivery valve holder, or the gooseneck-shaped fuel line if attached to the delivery valve holder. When the fuel from this line is reduced to 1 to 2 drops a minute (Figure 19-26D), this is the start of the static pump injection for that cylinder. The next step is to check the position of the engine flywheel or pulley timing marks to determine if the pump is correctly timed to the engine. If not, the pump or its drive coupling must be rotated to bring the engine and pump timing marks into proper alignment.

Method 1: Using High-Pressure Port Closing

Manually rotate the engine over in its normal direction of rotation, which is CW from the front, to place the No. piston 1 on its compression stroke. The exhaust emission label on the engine valve rocker cover lists the number of degrees BTDC that the static timing should be. Slowly rotate the engine over until the timing marks on the vibration damper are in alignment with the stationary pointer on the engine gear case. Refer to Figure 19-27a and connect the tooling from the high-pressure timer shown in Figure 19-27b to the injection pump as shown, then proceed through the sequence given below.

1. Cap or connect the injection lines on all injection pumping outlets other than the No. 1 cylinder, since this will be the reference unit for the spill-timing procedure.

2. Cap the valve return and bleed fitting from the nozzle drip line if it is connected to the injection pump overflow valve.

3. Connect the No. 6 Aeroquip high-pressure line from the portable PC stand to the injection pump gallery inlet (fuel supply).

4. Connect the No. 4 Aeroquip hose from the PC stand to the No. 1 cylinder injection pump delivery valve holder.

5. Ensure that the injection pump stop lever is placed and held in the normal running position; otherwise, no fuel will be able to flow from the No. 1 delivery valve assembly.

6. Activate the high-pressure PC stand so that fuel will flow into the injection pump fuel gallery.

7. Slowly turn the engine opposite to its normal

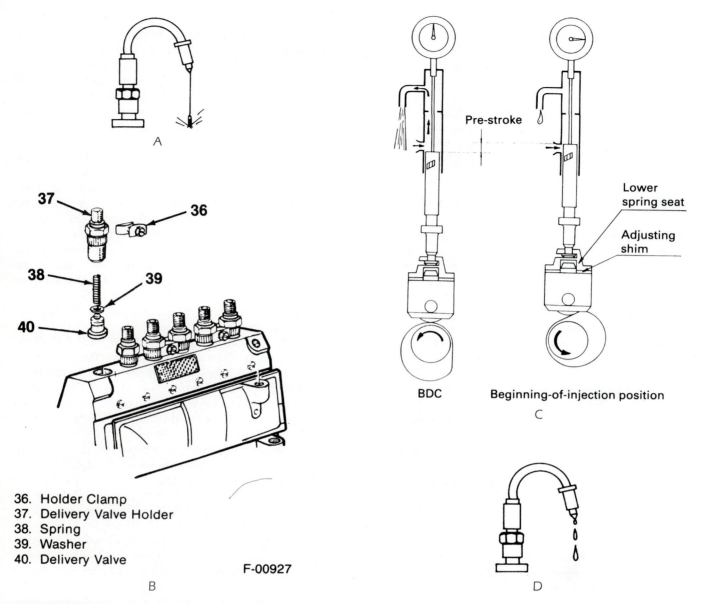

36. Holder Clamp
37. Delivery Valve Holder
38. Spring
39. Washer
40. Delivery Valve

F-00927

FIGURE 19–26 *(A) Gooseneck fuel line attached to the top of the No. 1 cylinder injection pump delivery valve holder (internal delivery valve/spring removed) showing a steady stream of fuel flowing from pumping chamber (barrel); (B) delivery valve components; (C) sequence to determine injection pump prestroke, or lift-to-port closure dimension using a dial indicator gauge and gooseneck fuel line to determine where and when the fuel flow stops; (D) stop crankshaft rotation when the fuel flow changes from a solid stream to the formation of drops. (Courtesy of Zexel USA.)*

direction of rotation, which is usually CCW from the front. This should cause fuel to spill from the end of the No. 1 delivery valve holder on the injection pump out of the gooseneck as shown in Figure 19-26A from the end of the test line running back to the fuel reservoir.

8.   Slowly rotate the engine in its normal direc-

tion of rotation, which is CW from the front, until the fuel flow from the end of the gooseneck line or from the test line connected to the No. 1 delivery valve holder is reduced as shown in Figure 19-26D to 1 to 2 drops per minute. This action confirms port closure for No. 1 pumping plunger.

9.   Inspect the flywheel timing marks and pointer,

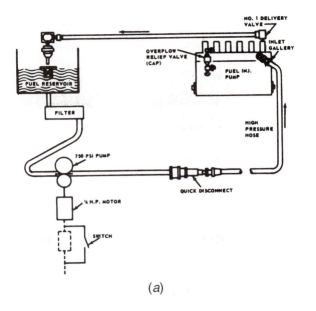

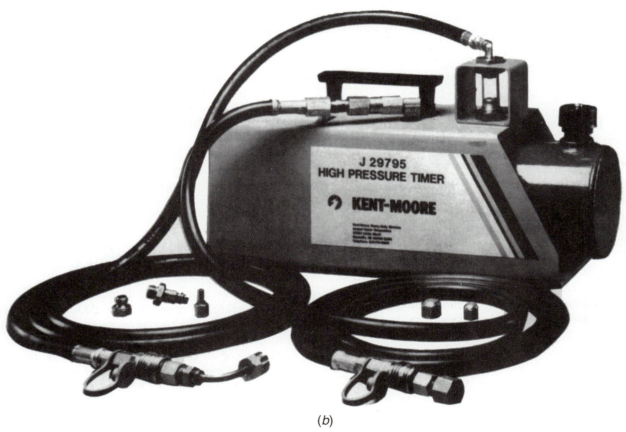

FIGURE 19–27 (a) High-pressure inline injection pump port closing fuel system hookup connections for spill timing purposes; (b) Model J 29795 high-pressure injection pump timer. [(a) Courtesy of Mack Trucks, Inc.; (b) courtesy of Kent-Moore Heavy Duty Division, (SPX Corporation.)]

or the marks on the crankshaft pulley/damper and stationary timing bracket located on the engine front cover. Compare these marks to the engine manufacturer's specs.

10.   If the injection pump is timed incorrectly, you can loosen the pump external flange mounting nuts and rotate the pump housing manually either CW or CCW until the fuel spilling from the No. 1 delivery valve holder occurs at the specified degrees BTDC. Tighten the external retaining nuts. On some pumps, timing must be adjusted by removing an access plate on the engine timing case cover to expose a series of internal retaining bolts on the pump drive gear. These bolts are installed through slotted holes to the pump drive hub (see Figure 20-28 for Mack). It is then necessary to loosen these bolts and rotate the engine over to change the timing, then retighten the bolts.

11.   Always recheck the pump-to-engine timing after making any necessary adjustments.

12.   Disconnect the special high-pressure spill timing components and reconnect all fuel lines, then bleed all air from the fuel system.

Method 2: Using Low Air Pressure

1.   Remove the No. 1 delivery valve holder from the injection pump and take out the delivery valve and spring.

2.   Install a suitable air line onto the IN fitting of the pump gallery.

CAUTION   Ensure that the air line is equipped with a separator and pressure regulator. Moisture-laden air can cause serious damage to injection pump parts.

---

3.   Attach a locally fabricated fixture to the delivery valve holder similar to that shown in Figure 19-28.

4.   Secure the stop lever in the running position.

5.   Activate the throttle lever several times and secure it in the full-load position.

6.   Turn on the air supply and just crack the regulator so that a steady flow of air bubbles is seen in the fixture jar without excessive turbulence.

7.   Rotate the crankshaft slowly in its normal direction of rotation. Observe the flow of air bubbles in the fixture jar, and the instant the bubbles stop, discontinue rotating the crankshaft.

8.   Check the position of the flywheel or vibration damper timing indicator. If properly timed, the indicator must register the recommended number of degrees as BTDC stamped on the valve rocker cover escutcheon plate.

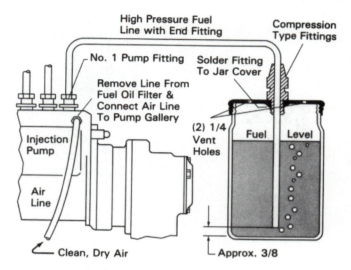

FIGURE 19–28   *Inline injection pump airflow spill timing check method. (Courtesy of Mack Trucks, Inc.)*

9.   If the timing checks out, repeat steps 7 and 8 to ensure accuracy.

10.   If the timing does not check out, bar the engine over in its normal direction of rotation until cylinder 1 is on the compression stroke and the timing mark indicates the correct number of degrees BTDC as recommended on the valve rocker cover escutcheon plate.

11.   Loosen the pump flange or gear retaining bolts and rotate the pump housing manually either CW or CCW until the flow of fuel from the gooseneck or test line slows from a steady stream to 1 to 2 drops per minute (Figure 19-26D). Tighten the retaining nuts or bolts.

12.   Perform the spill timing procedure once more to confirm that pump-to-engine timing is in fact correct.

13.   Remove the test equipment from the pump.

14.   Carefully reinstall the No. 1 pumping plunger delivery valve and components (Figure 19-26B), and torque the holder nut to specs.

15.   Bleed all air from the fuel system as shown in Figure 19-29A and B; start the engine and individually loosen and then tighten all high-pressure fuel lines at each nozzle, as shown in Figure 19-29C, to confirm that the engine is running correctly.

AIR IN THE FUEL SYSTEM

Once spill timing is complete and the fuel lines have been reinstalled, bleed the fuel system. Basically, bleeding of the system involves removing all entrapped air, which can be done by opening up the var-

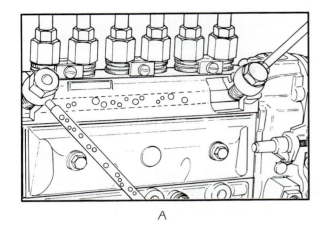

A

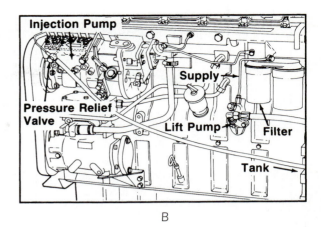

B

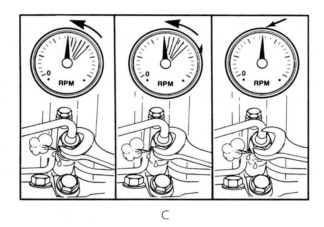

C

FIGURE 19–29 *Loosening a high-pressure fuel line at the injector nozzle to determine if the fuel injector is firing correctly. (Courtesy of Cummins Engine Company, Inc.)*

ious bleeder screws on the fuel filter housing and the injection pump housing, then using the hand priming pump (Figure 19-15) or the lift pump handle in Figure 19-29B to push fuel through the system. The pressure relief valve arrangement in the supply side of the fuel circuit creates a self-bleeding system for air introduced during replacement of the supply-side components (Figure 19-29B).

Once the injection pump is free of air, confirmed by the fact that no air bubbles are evident in the spilling fuel, each one of the fuel injector high-pressure lines can be left loose about one-half to one-full turn. The engine priming pump can be used again to push fuel through the lines; however, it is usually better to crank the engine over until fuel free of air flows from each line at the injector, after which time each line can be tightened up. Start the engine and check for any fuel leaks. If the engine still runs rough, rebleed the system. You can, however, loosen each fuel injector line one at a time to see if any air escapes as you

hold a rag around the line nut; then retighten it when you are sure that there is no air left in the system (Figure 19-29C).

Air from uncorrected leaks in the supply circuit will make the engine: hard to start, run rough, misfire, produce low power, and can cause excessive smoke and a fuel knock.

A source, which is often overlooked, for air to enter the fuel system is between the inlet of the prefilter and the suction tube in the tank. Fuel tanks that have the outlet fitting at the top will have a suction tube that extends down in the tank. Cracks or pinholes in the weld that joins the tube to the fitting can let air enter the fuel system.

CUMMINS C MODEL TIMING CHECK

The Cummins C model engine is a six-cylinder four-stroke-cycle unit with a displacement of 8.27 L (504.5 in^3) and is very widely used in a large number

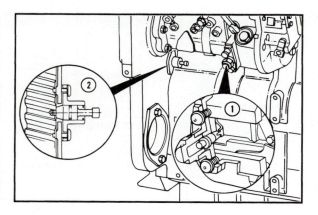

FIGURE 19–30 *Location of injection pump to engine timing pin. (Courtesy of Cummins Engine Company, Inc.)*

FIGURE 19–32 *Loosening injection pump drive gear nut. (Courtesy of Cummins Engine Company, Inc.)*

of applications. The engine is equipped with either a Bosch PES6A or PES6MW PLN system, as shown in Figure 19-29. The model of injection pump is determined by the particular engine power rating used. The engine-to-injection pump timing check is achieved using both an engine gear train timing pin and an injection pump camshaft timing pin (Figure 19-30) to confirm that the pump is timed to the engine correctly. To remove and replace the injection pump, follow the procedure described below.

Pump Removal

1. Locate TDC for cylinder 1. This can be done by barring the engine over slowly with the special flywheel ring gear turning tool, then pushing the TDC pin into the hole in the camshaft gear as shown in Figure 19-31.

2. Remove the engine front gear cover access cap

as shown in Figure 19-32; then, using a socket and breaker bar, remove the nut and washer from the front end of the fuel pump camshaft.

3. Attach a suitable gear puller as shown in Figure 19-33 and pull the fuel pump drive gear loose from the shaft.

4. Refer to Figure 19-34 and loosen/disconnect all the pump fuel lines as well as throttle linkage. If turbocharged, remove the AFC line between the pump and engine intake manifold. Remove the four 15-mm mounting nuts which secure the front end of the pump to the back side of the engine timing cover.

5. Grasp the injection pump and carefully remove it from the engine.

Pump Installation and Timing

1. Make sure that piston 1 is at TDC on its compression stroke. Refer to Figure 19-35 and bar the en-

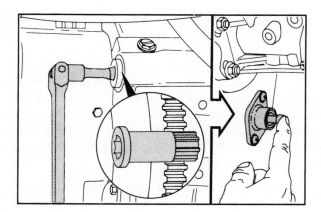

FIGURE 19–31 *Using special tool to bar engine over in order to install timing pin into backside of drive gear. (Courtesy of Cummins Engine Company, Inc.)*

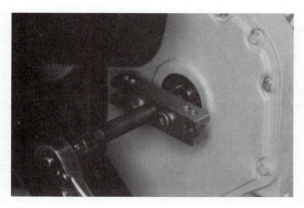

FIGURE 19–33 *Using a puller to loosen injection pump drive gear from end of pump camshaft. (Courtesy of Cummins Engine Company, Inc.)*

FIGURE 19–34 Removing injection pump from engine. (Courtesy of Cummins Engine Company, Inc.)

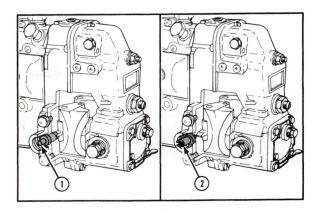

FIGURE 19–36 (1) Injection pump camshaft timing pin in engaged position; (2) timing pin in disengaged position. (Courtesy of Cummins Engine Company, Inc.)

gine over until the timing pin engages with the hole in the back side of the camshaft gear, as shown in the figure.

SERVICE TIP Although the injection pump is timed to piston 1 at TDC, the actual static timing will usually result in the pump being anywhere between 9 and 11.5° BTDC. The year of engine manufacture determines the actual pump-to-engine timing spec. Refer to the engine CPL plate and exhaust emissions decal to determine the actual timing spec.

---

2. Refer to Figure 19-36. The injection pump also has a timing pin (1) located in the governor housing in order to position the pump camshaft so that it will correspond to TDC for cylinder 1.

3. To access the pump timing pin, remove the 24-mm plug shown in Figure 19-37.

4. Remove the nylon timing pin as shown in Figure 19-38.

5. Carefully look into the access hole on the injection pump and note if the internal timing tooth is visible, as shown in Figure 19-39. If the timing tooth is not centered as shown, manually rotate the injection pump camshaft until the timing tooth is aligned as shown.

6. Reverse the position of the timing pin (see Figure 19-40) so that the slot in the pin will slide over the timing tooth in the pump as shown. Temporarily install the access plug over the pin to retain it in position.

7. Refer to Figure 19-41 and ensure that the O-ring seals at the drive end of the pump for the fill orifice and pilot are installed correctly and are not

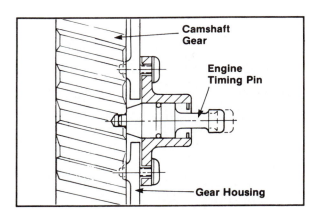

FIGURE 19–35 Closeup view of engine-to-injection pump timing pin. (Courtesy of Cummins Engine Company, Inc.)

Camshaft Gear

Engine Timing Pin

Gear Housing

FIGURE 19–37 Loosening or tightening the injection pump timing pin retaining nut. (Courtesy of Cummins Engine Company, Inc.)

FIGURE 19–38 *Removing captive injection pump camshaft timing pin from its location in retaining nut. (Courtesy of Cummins Engine Company, Inc.)*

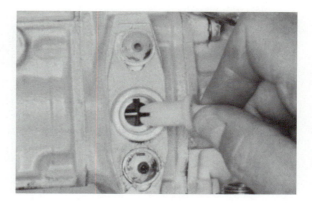

FIGURE 19–40 *Installing injection pump camshaft timing pin into access hole in pump housing. (Courtesy of Cummins Engine Company, Inc.)*

damaged. Lubricate the mounting flange with clean engine oil.

8. Carefully lift the injection pump into position as shown in Figure 19-34 so that the end of the pump camshaft slides through the central hole in the pump drive gear; then locate the pump flange over the four mounting studs on the engine cover.

9. Install the four 15-mm nuts over the flange studs and tighten these to a torque value of 43 N · m (32 lb-ft).

10. Refer to Figure 19-32 under step 2 for pump removal, and install the retaining nut and washer which were removed earlier. Using a socket and torque wrench, tighten this nut to 10 to 15 N · m (7 to 11 lb-ft). Be careful not to exceed this torque value at this time; otherwise, timing pin damage can result!

11. Disengage the engine timing pin as shown in Figure 19-35.

12. Remove the fuel pump timing pin plug and

reverse the nylon timing pin as shown in Figure 19-38. Install the pin, plug, and sealing washer, and torque the plug to 15 N · m (11 lb-ft).

13. Repeat step 10 using a torque wrench and final-tighten the pump camshaft retaining gear nut to 82 N · m (60 lb-ft) for a Bosch model PES6A pump, and to 90 N·m (66 lb-ft) for a Bosch PES6MW pump model.

14. Bleed the air from the fuel system as described in this chapter. Note that on later-model PES6MW pumps, to facilitate bleeding, loosen the vent screw shown in Figure 19-42, which is located close to the front of the pump on the side closest to the engine block. Place the governor speed control lever in the run position and crank the engine over until all signs of air have been vented (steady fuel flow). Tighten the vent screw. PES6A pumps equipped with a pressure relief valve as shown in Figure 19-29B are self-venting; however, each individual nozzle will still have to be bled of air as shown in Figure 19-29C.

FIGURE 19–39 *Injection pump inspection hole showing slotted camshaft timing location. (Courtesy of Cummins Engine Company, Inc.)*

FIGURE 19–41 *Inspect O-ring seals at both the fill-orifice and pilot. (Courtesy of Cummins Engine Company, Inc.)*

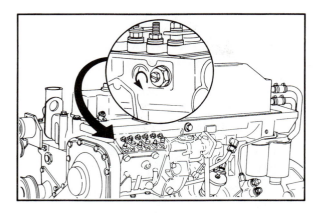

FIGURE 19–42 *Injection pump vent-screw location. (Courtesy of Cummins Engine Company, Inc.)*

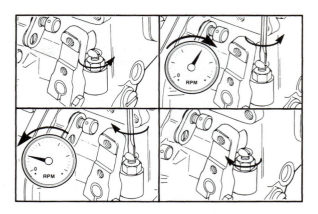

FIGURE 19–44 *RQV governor; idle adjustment screw location. (Courtesy of Cummins Engine Company, Inc.)*

Adjusting the Idle Speed

The idle adjustment screw location will vary based on the type of governor being used. Refer to the section dealing with Bosch mechanical governors to determine the actual idle screw location.

Once the engine is started, adjust the idle speed on industrial engines using an RSV governor by loosening the locknut and turning the screw (1), shown in Figure 19-43. CW rotation will increase the idle speed, and CCW rotation will decrease the idle speed. On automotive engines equipped with an RQV governor, refer to Figure 19-44 and using a 10-mm wrench and screwdriver, rotate the screw CCW to raise the engine speed and CW to decrease the idle speed.

1. Start and run the engine at its idle speed. Use a tach and note the idle rpm. Compare this to the spec stamped on the engine CPL plate.

2. If idle adjustment is required, loosen the lock-

nut and back out the bumper spring screw until there is no change in the idle speed.

3. Adjust the idle screw to obtain an idle speed approximately 20 to 30 rpm lower than that recommended and lock the retaining nut.

4. Slowly turn the bumper spring screw (2) shown in Figure 19-43 CW only enough to bring the desired idle rpm to a stable speed, then lock the retaining nut.

TIMING PF JERK PUMPS

Individual jerk pumps of the PF style similar to those shown in Figure 19-1 are found extensively on small, single, two- and three-cylinder diesel engines, as well as on very-large-displacement slow-speed heavy-duty deep-sea marine, railroad, and stationary applications. Timing of the individual pumps to the engine is done in the same basic procedure regardless of the OEM model. Use the following procedure as a general guide.

1. Refer to the flywheel markings on the engine to establish the base circle of the camshaft for the particular pump being installed.

2. Place the pump unit onto its mounting base, and bolt it down.

3. Check plunger movement through the inspection window, as shown in Figure 19-45. With the proper flywheel timing mark aligned with the stationary pointer on the engine, the timing line on the pump plunger and inspection window should be as shown in Figure 19-45c.

4. If the pump timing lines do not appear as in Figure 19-45c, double-check to ensure that the engine flywheel marks correspond to the pump cylinder.

5. To correct the timing, some pumps employ a

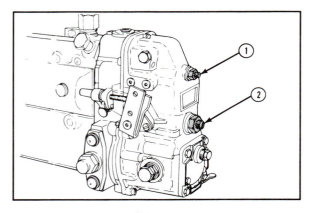

FIGURE 19–43 *RSV governor; item 1 is the idle screw; item 2 is the bumped spring screw. (Courtesy of Cummins Engine Company, Inc.)*

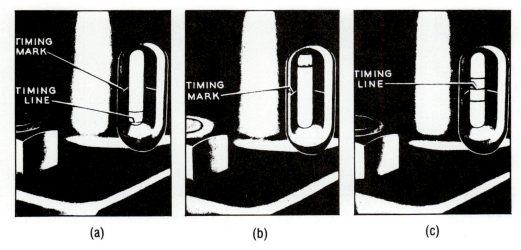

(a)   (b)   (c)

FIGURE 19–45 (a) PF/PFR type injection pump plunged timing line retarded; (b) injection pump timing line advanced; (c) injection pump timing line correctly aligned. (Courtesy of Cummins Engine Company, Inc.)

tappet adjusting screw to effectively raise or lower the plunger; however, some units require the use of selective shims under the pump base to correct this condition. Once adjusted, with the pump at the bottom and top of its stroke, the timing line on the plunger should stay in view, as shown in Figures 19-45a and b.

PF Rack Setting

Engines equipped with individual PF pumps usually have their fuel racks (control rods) interconnected by adjustable mechanical linkage to permit balancing the fuel flow to each nozzle and the combustion chamber. Some larger engines employ a micrometer-type knurled knob adjusting screw that the technician can rotate manually to obtain very fine adjustment of fuel delivery. On large, slow-speed engines, fuel delivery and cylinder balance are best achieved by monitoring the individual cylinder exhaust temperatures by looking at the pyrometer gauge(s) and adjusting the individual fuel rack adjustment knobs.

AUTOMATIC TIMING ADVANCE DEVICE

In the combustion process, diesel fuel takes a certain amount of time to ignite and burn. As the engine runs faster, the burn time remains the same, and much of the burning takes place after TDC (top dead center). This is called ignition lag and almost always results in lowered performance. To offset this ignition lag, fuel must be injected sometime before TDC to give good performance at rated speed. However, with this fixed advance of injection, engine performance is optimum at rated speed only. Engines that vary speeds over a wide range, that is, automotive vehicles, need injection timed correctly at all speeds. This is the function of the timing device.

The Bosch EP/S..DR(L) timing device is used on inline camshaft driven pumps (Figure 19-46). The EP/S..DR(L) is classified as an external, flyweight-operated device. Mounted at the front of the injection pump on the camshaft, the timing device is connected to the driving gear of the engine (Figure 19-46). Through the action of centrifugal force, the flyweights swing outward with increasing speed. Rollers mounted on the flyweights push against the cam plate (Figure 19-47), which is connected to the pump camshaft. This causes the camshaft to rotate a maximum of 8°, providing proper timing in relation to engine speed.

Stop pins limit the maximum amount of advance that can be obtained from any timing advance assembly. As with any automatic timing advance device, should the unit become worn or damaged, fuel injection timing will not be controlled correctly, resulting in poor engine performance and possible engine damage. Generally, if the timing advance unit were to stick in the full-advance position, the start of fuel injection would be too early at an idle speed, and severe combustion knock would result, together with a tendency for white smoke to appear at the exhaust stack. On the other hand, a timing advance unit that will not advance past the idle setting would result in late injection and the engine would be very sluggish, together with black smoke appearing at the exhaust stack through incomplete combustion.

FIGURE 19–46 *Component parts of a pump-mounted automatic timing advance unit for 344.912 and 344.937 engines. 1, Automatic timing advance unit (includes 2 through 10); 2, governor weight; 3, pin; 4, spring; 5, lock-tab; 6, capscrew; 7, segment plate; 8, injection pump gear; 9, spacer; 10, snap ring; 11, lock-washer; 12, round nut. (Courtesy of Freightliner/Mercedes-Benz Truck Company, Inc.)*

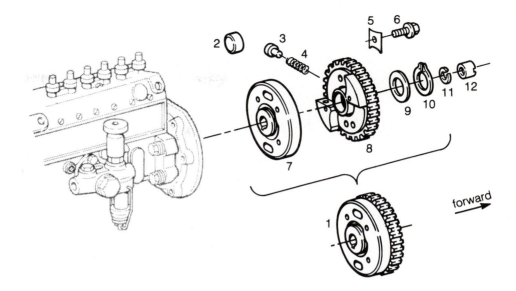

BASIC FUEL SYSTEM TROUBLESHOOTING

Information contained in this chapter deals with identification of the various models of Bosch pumps, governors, and nozzles, the general operation and function of each component, and the procedure re-

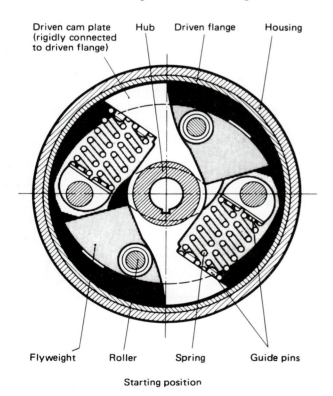

FIGURE 19–47 *Operation of automatic timing device. (Courtesy of Robert Bosch GmbH).*

quired to check and correct the injection pump-to-engine timing. Regardless of what make of engine a Bosch inline pump is used on, there are common procedural steps that are required to systematically pinpoint trouble areas in the fuel system. Figure 19-48 lists some of these typical problem symptoms, causes, and suggested remedies. In addition to this troubleshooting chart, the following information can be considered common to any make of engine employing the models A, MW, or P Bosch inline multiple-plunger injection pumps. When low power, rough idle, or stalling is reported on an engine with no unusual exhaust smoke color, the problem can most likely be traced to fuel starvation or low transfer pump delivery. To pinpoint the cause quickly, the following checks and tests should be performed:

1. Check the relief valve opening pressure. This relief valve is usually incorporated into the injection pump housing and return fuel line (Figures 19-14 and 19-29B).
2. Check the delivery pressure of the transfer pump.

SERVICE TIP Checks 1 and 2 above can be performed simultaneously.

---

3. Check the restriction to fuel flow at the suction side of the transfer pump (vacuum test).
4. Check the fuel delivery pressure to the injection pump inlet from the secondary fuel filters.

This troubleshooting chart uses columns labeled 1–11 (left to right) corresponding to the symptom headings:

1. Starting Problem at Idle
2. Engine Surges When Warm
3. Rough Engine Idle
4. Engine Misses When Under Load
5. Low Power/Excessive Fuel Consumption
6. Engine Power Cannot Be Shut Off
7. Excessive Performance (Idle or Maximum Rev Up Hot)
8. Poor Fog-Like Exhaust (White or Blue)
9. Incorrect Engine Does Pump Injection
10. Black Smoke Range
11. Low Power or Low Speed

#	Cause	1	2	3	4	5	6	7	8	9	10	11	Remedy
1	Tank empty or tank vent blocked	•	•		•								Fill tank/bleed system, check tank vent
2	Air in the fuel system	•	•	•	•								Bleed fuel system, eliminate air leaks
3	Shut off/start device defective	•					•						Repair or replace
4	Fuel filter blocked			•	•								Replace fuel filter
5	Injection lines blocked/restricted	•		•	•								Drill to nominal I.D. or replace
6	Fuel-supply lines blocked/restricted				•								Test all fuel supply lines—flush or replace
7	Loose connections, injection lines leak or broken				•	•							Tighten the connection, eliminate the leak
8	Paraffin deposit in fuel filter	•			•								Replace filter, use winter fuel
9	Pump-to-engine timing incorrect	•		•	•								Readjust timing
10	Injection nozzle defective			•	•	•							Repair or replace
11	Engine air filter blocked				•	•							Replace air filter element
12	Pre-heating system defective	•											Test the glow plugs, replace as necessary
13	Injection sequence does not correspond to firing order		•	•	•								Install fuel injection lines in the correct order
14	Low idle misadjusted					•	•						Readjust idle stop screw
15	Maximum speed misadjusted					•							Readjust maximum speed screw
16	Overflow valve defective or blocked							•	•				Clean the orifice or replace fitting
17	Delivery valve leakage								•				Replace delivery valve (max. of 1 on 4 cyl., 2 on 6 cyl.)
18	Bumper spring misadjusted (RS . . . governors)		•					•					Readjust bumper spring
19	Timing device defective				•	•			•				Repair or replace timing device
20	Low or uneven engine compression	•			•	•			•	•			Repair as necessary
21	Governor misadjusted or defective					•			•	•			Readjust or repair
22	Fuel injection pump defective or cannot be adjusted	•			•	•			•	•			Remove pump and service

Source: Robert Bosch Corporation.

aIt is assumed that the engine is in good working order and properly tuned, and that the electrical system has been checked and repaired if necessary.

FIGURE 19–48 Troubleshooting guide for diesel fuel injection system with Robert Bosch inline fuel injection pumps.

To perform the four tests listed above, several special tools are required, which can be found in most service shops:

- A fuel pressure gauge
- A vacuum gauge or mercury manometer
- Assorted fittings and lines to tap into the existing fuel system
- A length of clear plastic hose to note the presence of air bubbles

Many engine manufacturers supply special tool kits with all the necessary gauges and fittings to perform these tests. In addition, these special tools and fittings can be obtained from most reputable tool suppliers.

Test 1: Relief Valve and Pump Pressure Check

This test is a check to ensure that the injection pump relief valve is, in fact, opening at the correct pressure and that the transfer pump is performing correctly. If the relief valve is stuck open or is opening at too low a pressure, the fuel delivery pressure within the injection pump housing will be too low to sustain sufficient flow to the plunger and barrel of the individual pumping assemblies. On the other hand, if the relief valve is stuck closed or opens at too high a pressure setting, the fuel within the injection pump housing, which is also used for cooling and lubricating purposes, will run hot. This can result in a loss of horsepower due to the expansion of the fuel, since a less dense fuel charge will be delivered to the injectors and combustion chamber. In addition, fuel that is too hot can cause internal pump plunger damage due to its inability to properly cool and lubricate the component parts. Note that only 25 to 30% of the fuel delivered to the injection pump housing is actually used for combustion purposes. The remainder cools and lubricates the injection pump components.

Procedure

1. Refer to Figure 19-49 and disconnect the fuel line between the outlet side of the transfer pump which leads to the secondary fuel filters.

2. Connect a fuel pressure gauge tester similar to the one shown in Figure 19-49 into the fuel system between the transfer pump and secondary fuel-filters. Use suitable fittings to ensure that there will be no fuel leaks. The special tester gauge shown in Figure 19-49 is equipped with a clear fuel line to allow you to check for any signs of air bubbles in the fuel system. If you do not have a gauge similar to this one, insert a clear plastic fuel line into the system to allow you to monitor this condition.

3. Start and run the engine. Carefully note and record the fuel pressure reading on the gauge, which is an indication of the relief valve opening pressure. On most Bosch inline pumps this will run between 131 and 303 kPa (19 to 44 psi) at maximum no-load speed. Check the engine manufacturer's service manual for this specification.

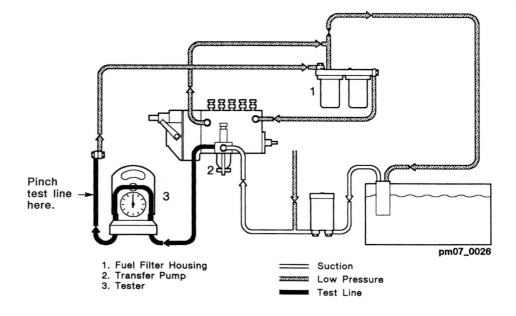

FIGURE 19-49 Fuel pressure gauge connected between the transfer pump outlet and secondary fuel filters. 1, Fuel filter housing; 2, transfer pump; 3, tester. (Courtesy of Freightliner/Mercedes-Benz Truck Company, Inc.)

Pinch test line here.

1. Fuel Filter Housing
2. Transfer Pump
3. Tester

===== Suction
〜〜〜 Low Pressure
▬▬ Test Line

pm07_0026

NOTE   If the engine runs rough or misfires, you may have to open the bleed screw on the filter and injection pump housing to vent any entrapped air from the fuel system.

4.   While the engine is running, take careful note of the fuel running through the special gauge or clear plastic line. If there is any sign of air bubbles, check the fuel-line connections for looseness or possible damage, including the fuel lines themselves.

5.   Pinch the fuel line hose in the area indicated in Figure 19-49 and carefully note the reading on the test gauge. This value actually indicates the transfer pump pressure, which should be at least equal to the OEM's minimum speed.

6.   When this test has been completed, stop the engine, disconnect the gauge tester, and reconnect the fuel system lines.

Test 2: Pump Vacuum Restriction Check

This test allows the mechanic/technician to determine if there is a high restriction to fuel flow to the suction side of the fuel transfer pump. If there is, the injection pump will not receive enough fuel. This will be accompanied by lack of power as well as possible rough idling and stalling. Either a vacuum gauge or a mercury manometer can be used to check the restriction to fuel flow. However, if a mercury manometer is teed into the fuel system in place of the special gauge (Figure 19-50) make sure that you hold or mount the manometer higher than the engine. Failure to do this can result in diesel fuel running back into the manometer when the engine is stopped. A low reading is what we are looking for here, since this indicates that the fuel lines and connections are offering a minimum restriction to flow at the suction side of the fuel transfer pump.

Procedure

1.   Refer to Figure 19-50 and connect the special gauge fixture or mercury manometer into the fuel system as shown between the suction (inlet) side of the fuel transfer pump and the fuel line from the primary fuel filter or fuel filter/water separator assembly.

2.   Start and run the engine at an idle speed and note the gauge or mercury manometer reading. Accelerate the engine up through the speed range and record the maximum gauge reading. Pinch the fuel line hose in the area indicated in Figure 19-50 and carefully note the reading on the gauge or mercury manometer. The value obtained indicates the fuel transfer pump vacuum, which should be between 50 and 80 kPa (7 to 12 psi). If using a mercury manometer, this value is equivalent to 14.25 to 24.4 in. on the scale. Refer to the metric conversion chart in Chapter 3 if using a metric-scale manometer.

SERVICE TIP   If the vacuum reading is too high, carefully inspect the fuel lines between the fuel tank and the transfer pump for signs of crimping, crushing, or physical damage. Also keep in mind that a plugged primary filter can cause a restriction to fuel flow.

FIGURE 19–50 *Vacuum tester connected between fuel transfer pump inlet side and the primary filter/fuel–water separator. 1, Fuel filter housing; 2, transfer pump; 3, tester. (Courtesy of Freightliner/Mercedes-Benz Truck Company, Inc.)*

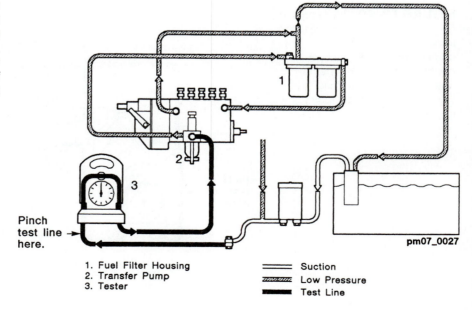

Pinch test line here.

pm07_0027

1. Fuel Filter Housing
2. Transfer Pump
3. Tester

———— Suction
〰〰〰 Low Pressure
▬▬▬ Test Line

3. Disconnect the gauge or manometer and re-connect the fuel-line fittings firmly. If either the transfer pump delivery pressure or vacuum (restriction) check is not within the engine manufacturer's specifications, proceed to remove and disassemble the transfer pump in order to carefully check the condition of the check valves inside the pump. If signs of wear or damage are evident, replace the valves or install a new exchange transfer pump assembly. If the fuel transfer pump and relief valve pressures as well as the vacuum check values are within the manufacturer's specifications, proceed to Test 3, described below.

Test 3: Secondary Fuel Filter Pressure Check

Refer to Figure 19-51 and disconnect the fuel line between the outlet side of the secondary fuel filter(s) and the inlet side of the fuel injection pump. Insert a special pressure gauge or, alternatively, a fuel pressure gauge and clear plastic line between the filters and injection pump as shown in Figure 19-51.

Procedure

1. Start and run the engine while carefully looking for any signs of air bubbles in the special gauge window or clear test fuel line. Remember, however, that there may be some air bubbles initially, due to the introduction of air into the fuel system while installing the test gauge. If the air bubbles do not disappear within a short period, try opening the bleeder screw on the fuel injection pump until all signs of aerated fuel disappears. If after bleeding the fuel system air bubbles still appear in the clear test fuel line, check the fuel filter seals for leakage, the fuel-line connections for tightness, and the fuel lines for damage.

SERVICE TIP   Keep in mind that all fuel lines and fittings on the outlet side of the transfer pump up to the injection pump and nozzles are under pressure; therefore, a fuel leak will be evident. Air introduced into the fuel system will generally be drawn into the fuel system between the suction side of the transfer pump and the fuel tank connections.

---

2. Normal fuel pressure on the test gauge should be between the minimum and maximum listed specs. If the earlier tests confirmed that the relief valve, transfer pump, and restriction check were within specifications, a low fuel pressure gauge reading at this time would indicate that the secondary fuel filters are plugged and require changing. If after changing the fuel filters, the fuel pressure is still low, double check the operating condition of the pressure relief valve.

3. If the fuel pressure reading is within specifications, stop the engine, remove the test gauge and lines, and reconnect and tighten the service fuel lines and fittings. Start and run the engine and bleed any air from the system. Check and correct any signs of fuel leakage. Similarly, if the fuel filters have to be changed, bleed the fuel system and make certain that there are no fuel leaks.

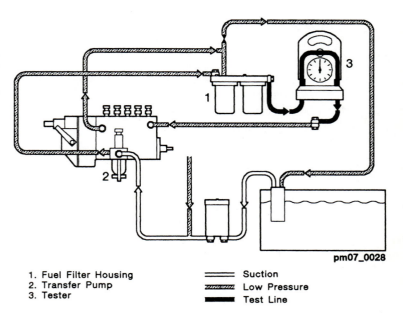

FIGURE 19–51 *Pressure tester gauge connected between the secondary fuel filters and the injection pump inlet. 1, Fuel filter housing; 2, transfer pump; 3, tester. (Courtesy of Freightliner/Mercedes-Benz Truck Company, Inc.)*

1. Fuel Filter Housing
2. Transfer Pump
3. Tester

Suction
Low Pressure
Test Line

pm07_0028

ROBERT BOSCH GOVERNORS

Robert Bosch governors used with inline pumps (M, A, MW, and P) can look the same externally; however, they are designed for different types of engine applications, and therefore engine speed control can be governed at different settings of the throttle. Types of governors manufactured by Robert Bosch Corporation and used on their inline injection pumps in truck applications are described below.

The letter designations used for these mechanical governors take the following forms:

    R: flyweight governor
    S: swivel lever action
    V: variable-speed (all-range) governor
    Q: fulcrum lever action
    K: torque cam control
    W: leaf spring action

For example, if the nameplate on a governor read EP/RS275/1400AOB478DL, this would mean:

    EP: found on older governors, no longer used
    RS: R/flyweight governor with swivel lever action, minimum/maximum (limiting speed) type of governor
   275: low-idle pump speed (this would be 550 rpm engine speed, four-cycle)
    /: also indicates min/max (limiting speed) governor
 1400: full-load rated speed (this would be 2800 rpm engine speed, four cycle)
    A: fits on A-size inline injection pump
    O: amount of speed regulation (droop percentage)
    B: execution—not used to indicate the original design on governors; A, first change; B, second change; and so on
 478DL: application and engineering information only

Types of Bosch Governors

Prior to studying the various types of truck governors manufactured by Robert Bosch in this section, it would be helpful to consider that although there are a variety of governor models, basically they fall into one of two main types and designs. The types are:

1. *Minimum–maximum governor:* often referred to as a limiting-speed unit since it governs only the low-idle and high-idle (maximum no-load speed) ranges
2. *Variable-speed governor:* an all-range governor that controls not only the low-idle and maximum speed ranges, but will maintain any speed range selected between these two ranges by the operator as long as the engine is not overloaded for a specific setting of the throttle

The concept of operation of the RSV and RQV governors is discussed in detail in this section; however, their design characteristics differ as follows:

1. The governor weights in the RQ and RQV models act directly against a coil spring which is assembled into the weights as shown in Figure 19-52.
2. The governor weights in the RS and RSV models act through mechanical linkage to transfer their motion to the coiled governor spring as shown in Figure 19-53.

Regardless of the type of governor used, all rely on the centrifugal force generated by the rotating flyweights acting through mechanical linkage to change the injection pump fuel rack position (see Chapter 17). Remember that weight forces are always trying to decrease the fuel rack position (less fuel), while the spring forces are attempting to increase (more fuel) the fuel rack position. If you remember this fact when you are studying the various governor models, you will soon be able to understand the various linkage differ-

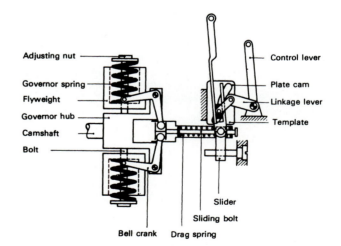

FIGURE 19–52 *Governor weight and spring arrangement in the RQ/RQV models. (Courtesy of Robert Bosch Corporation.)*

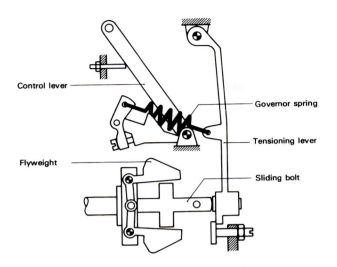

FIGURE 19-53 *Governor weight and spring arrangement in the RS/RSV models. (Courtesy of Robert Bosch Corporation.)*

ences between them and how they operate. The weight forces are nonadjustable; however, the spring tension can be altered in the RQ/RQV models by the adjusting nut shown in Figure 19-52 which is accessible through a plug in the governor housing. Similarly, the spring tension is adjustable in the RS/RSV models by a screw adjustment. Maximum engine speed is controlled by the tension on the governor springs, since the faster the engine rotates, the greater will be the force created by the rotating governor flyweights, which will reach a state of balance with the spring at a predetermined speed. If this speed is exceeded, the stronger weight forces will pull the fuel rack to a decreased speed position, thereby limiting the maximum speed of the engine.

RSV Governor Model

The RSV governor assembly is designed as an all-range (variable) governor which functions to control the engine idle and maximum speeds, in addition to allowing the operator to place the throttle at any position between idle and maximum where the governor will control the speed setting minus the droop (see Chapter 17 for a description of governor droop). The RSV governor is widely used on combination on- and off-highway truck applications, as well as farm tractors and industrial and marine units employing the M, A, MW, or P Bosch model inline multiple-plunger injection pumps. Although similar in external appearance to the RS limiting-speed (minimum/maximum) governor described in this section, the RSV does allow several adjustments at points outside the housing that

are not available on the RS unit. Figure 19-54 illustrates an external view of the RSV governor housing with the various external adjustments shown. These include:

- The idle-speed screw
- The auxiliary idle-speed spring or bumper screw
- The throttle lever linkage maximum speed adjusting screw

Components

Prior to describing the operation of the RSV governor, refer to Figure 19-54 which illustrates the major component parts and the associated linkage used with this governor model. Note that within the governor housing there are four springs used with this governor assembly:

- A starting aid spring
- The governor main spring
- An idle spring, sometimes referred to as a bumper spring
- A torque control spring

All of these springs are opposed by the rotating flyweights and act to provide governor control under various operating conditions. Figure 19-55 illustrates in simplified schematic form the various linkage component hookups within the governor.

RSV Governor Operation

Engine Startup. When the engine is stopped, the weights are collapsed and with the throttle linkage in the idle position, the fuel control rack is placed into its maximum (overfueling) position by the force of the starting spring pulling the linkage as shown in Figure 19-56. The main governor spring at this time adds almost no energy to the position of the fuel control rack because of the position of the control lever against the idle stop. When the engine is cranked over, the weights are attempting to move outward against the force of the idle spring and the starting spring in order to pull the control rack to a decreased fuel position to return the engine to an idle speed.

Engine Idling. When the engine fires, the centrifugal force of the rotating governor flyweights increases rapidly, with the engine in a temporary overfueling condition. As the weights transfer their motion through the sliding bolt, the guide lever moves to the right, causing the fulcrum lever to move in the same direction. If the throttle linkage has been moved by the operator to the maximum speed setting position before the engine starts, the speed will not return to idle unless the operator physically moves the speed control lever to the idle position. However, if the throttle was

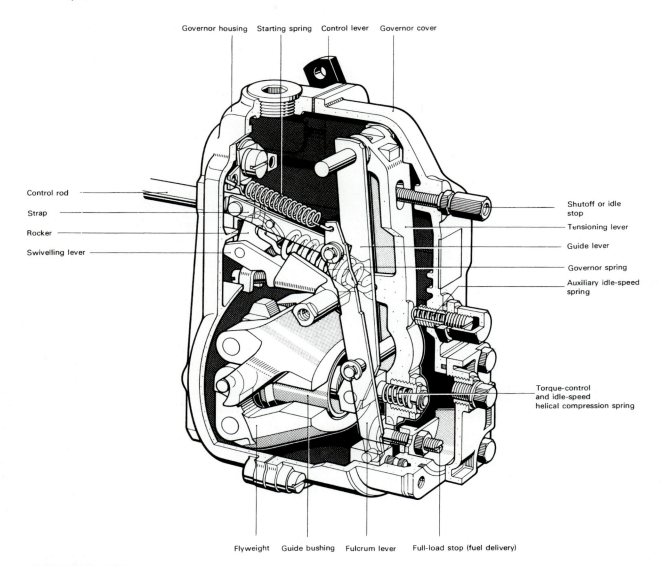

Governor housing   Starting spring   Control lever   Governor cover

Control rod

Strap

Rocker

Swivelling lever

Shutoff or idle stop

Tensioning lever

Guide lever

Governor spring

Auxiliary idle-speed spring

Torque-control and idle-speed helical compression spring

Flyweight   Guide bushing   Fulcrum lever   Full-load stop (fuel delivery)

FIGURE 19–54   *Schematic view of an RSV variable-speed governor model showing the major components. (Courtesy of Robert Bosch Corporation.)*

placed into its normal low-idle position, then once the engine starts, it will return to the idle speed. Regardless of the throttle position, through governor linkage, the fuel control rack is pulled to the right and the fuel delivery rate is reduced. At an idle speed, the tensioning lever now starts to bear against the auxiliary idle speed (bumper) spring. When the weight force and idle spring forces are equal, a state of balance occurs and the engine runs at a reduced fuel setting sufficient to keep the engine running at an idle speed. The idle speed can be adjusted through the screw adjustment shown in Figure 19-54.

Load On/Load Off at Idle.   With the engine running at an idle speed, if a load is applied, the rpm will drop and the centrifugal force of the flyweights is reduced. This upsets the previous SOB (state of balance) between the weights and the idle spring, and the stronger idle and main governor spring forces will move the governor linkage and control rack to an increased fuel setting to produce additional horsepower to prevent engine stalling. During this load increase, the action of the main governor spring holds the tensioning lever and fuel control rack away from the idle (bumper) spring. The engine will run at a slower rpm rate under this increased load, due to the governor droop characteristic of the spring, giving up some of its stored energy in moving the control rack to its new fuel setting. Therefore, the weights rebalance at a lower speed against a weaker spring.

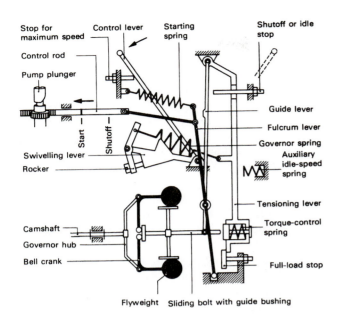

FIGURE 19–55 *RSV governor linkage schematic. (Courtesy of Robert Bosch Corporation.)*

If the load at idle is reduced, the weight forces increase as the engine picks up speed at this fixed throttle setting. The weights will force the sliding bolt and with it the guide lever to the right to cause a pivoting action at the fulcrum lever, which results in the fuel control rack being pulled to a decreased fuel setting. The tensioning lever is again forced against the idle (bumper) spring and the engine will run at a new SOB

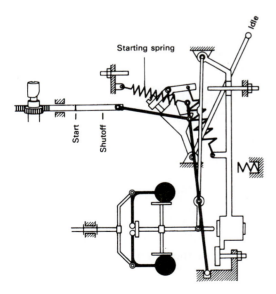

FIGURE 19–56 *RSV governor linkage/rack position during engine startup with the throttle in the idle position. (Courtesy of Robert Bosch Corporation.)*

speed which is higher than it was while the load was applied because of the droop characteristic of the governor spring.

High-Speed Governor Reaction. When the operator moves the speed control lever to the maximum position as shown in Figure 19-55, the internal swiveling lever attached to both this speed control lever and the main governor spring causes the main spring to add its greatest force to the tensioning lever. When the speed control lever butts against the full-load stop screw, the engine will receive its maximum fuel to produce its rated horsepower. In Figure 19-55 on a governor without a torque capsule spring, maximum fuel is controlled by weight action and spring forces; once the operator places the speed control lever in the full-fuel position, the engine accelerates. The difference is that when a torque control spring is used, as the engine speed increases the weight forces will start to compress the torque spring and the fuel rack would be pulled out of fuel. This results in a lower fuel delivery and therefore an engine with less rated horsepower at its governed speed than that of one without a torque capsule spring.

If the engine speed due to less than full-load conditions were to exceed the maximum full-load speed setting, the increased centrifugal force of the faster-rotating flyweights would pull the fuel rack to a decreased position. In this way the maximum engine speed is controlled and the fuel delivery is decreased in proportion to the decrease in load. If the engine were running at its full-load rpm, developing its rated horsepower, and the vehicle encountered a hill without the operator attempting to downshift the transmission, the engine speed would drop as a result of increasing load at the full throttle setting. On an engine with no torque spring, the horsepower would drop as the speed decreased and the rate of torque rise would be dependent on the volumetric efficiency of the engine at this full-fuel setting with a decreasing engine rpm. On an engine governor-equipped with a torque spring, as the engine speed drops, the weight forces decrease and the tension of the torque spring adds its force to that of the main governor spring. The result would be that the engine would receive a further increase in fuel as the speed drops. This action would result in a flatter horsepower curve and a higher torque curve in the engine.

Stopping the Engine. RSV governor-equipped engines can be stopped in one of two ways, depending on whether they have a governor control lever stop or a shutoff mechanism. Figure 19-54 illustrates an RSV governor with a governor control lever shutdown system. To stop the engine, this lever is moved all the way back to the right in the diagram, which causes lugs on the swiveling lever (connected to the main governor spring) to come into contact with the guide lever. As the guide lever is forced to the right, it pulls both the fulcrum lever and the fuel control rack with it and shutdown occurs. At the same time, the release of spring tension from the governor springs allows the weights to fly outward to further ensure a no-fuel situation, and the engine is now in the shutdown mode.

In some models engine shutdown is accomplished by the use of a special shutoff lever located at the top end of the housing. See Figure 19-12. Movement of this lever to the shutoff position causes the upper part of the fulcrum lever to move to the right as it pivots around the fulcrum point of the guide lever in Figure 19-54. This action forces the control rack to be pulled back by the strap to the shutoff position. When the shutdown lever is released, a return spring (not shown) would snap the lever back to the running position for the next engine startup procedure.

RQV Governor Model

The RQV governor is a variable-speed mechanical unit that employs the governor springs assembled into the weights in the same manner as that for other RQ models. As such, it controls idle speed, maximum speed, and any speed range in between at which the operator places the throttle linkage. Figure 19-57 illustrates the pear-shaped housing of the RQV governor, which is also found on all other RQ models.

The RQV governor is used with the models M, A, MW, and P Bosch inline multiple-plunger pumps, as well as on the VA and VE models of Bosch distributor pumps. Major truck engine manufacturers that use the RQV variable-speed governor are Deutz, Fiat-Allis, Navistar (International Harvester), Mack, Mercedes-Benz, and Volvo. The RQV is employed on vehicles with auxiliary drive, such as garbage compactor trucks, tanker trucks, and cement mixer trucks, to control the PTO (power takeoff) applications. Since the RQV is a variable speed (all-range) governor, it operates on the same basic principle as the RSV shown and discussed earlier in this chapter, the only difference being in the internal linkage arrangement. The RSV uses a starting and main governor spring, while the RQV has the springs assembled inside the weight carrier.

The difference between the RQ governor model and the RQV is that since the RQV is an all-range variable-speed unit, and the RQ is a minimum/maximum (limiting-speed) unit, the weights in the RQV will move out throughout the complete speed range, and

will not lose control between the end of the idle speed range and the start of high-speed governing such as occurs within the RQ model.

Prior to discussing the RQV governor action, refer to Figure 19-57 which illustrates the RQV governor differences from those of the RQ model. These differences, which should be noted in Figure 19-57 are:

- Spring-loaded sliding bolt
- Full-load stop
- Plate cam

Governing action is affected by adjustment of the flyweight springs, which are accessible through the pear-shaped housing access nut, and the leverage provided by the changing position of the pivot pin (piston within the bored and slotted fulcrum lever) which is itself connected through the linkage lever and shaft to the external control lever connected to the accelerator pedal or hand throttle linkage. The operating characteristic curve for the RQV governor is almost identical to that for the RSV governor model; therefore, refer to the description for the basic rack position under different operating conditions. In addition, the earlier discussion relating to the RSV governor characteristic curve can be applied to that of the RQV model.

RQV Governor Operation

The governor reaction of the RQV is similar to that for the RSV since both are all-range variable-speed models. Any load applied to the engine, whether it be at low-idle, maximum-rpm, or part-throttle position, will cause an upset in the SOB (state of balance) between the weights and springs, with the spring giving more rack under load, and the weights giving less rack when a load is removed. A new SOB is reached when the weight and spring forces are once again equal. The difference being that when a load is taken off the engine for a fixed throttle position, the new SOB will be at a slightly higher engine speed, and when a load is applied, the new SOB will be at a slightly lower speed because of the governor droop characteristic caused by the change in spring compression. A detailed description of droop is given in Chapter 17. Figure 19-58 illustrates the weight travel of the RQ governor at an idle speed. As you can see, the outer spring becomes the low-speed control, while all three springs would come into play as the engine is accelerated and the centrifugal force of the rotating governor flyweights increases.

The position of the governor linkage when the engine is operating at part-load speed is shown in Figure 19-59. Note carefully the position of the plunger helix. In these diagrams the governor rack movement will

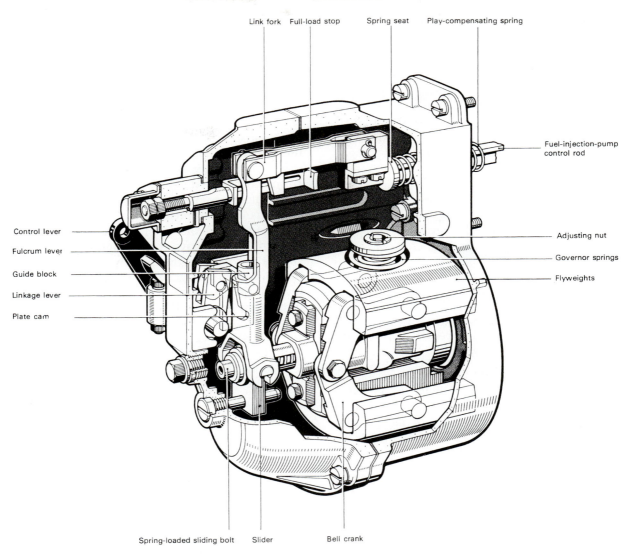

FIGURE 19–57 Schematic view of an RQV governor assembly. (Courtesy of Robert Bosch Corporation.)

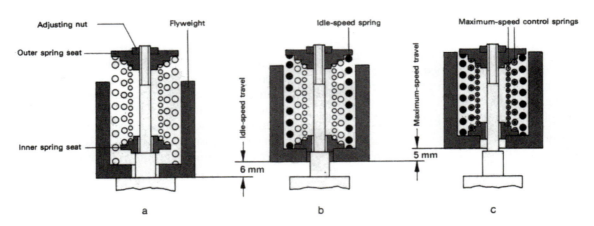

FIGURE 19–58 Flyweight travel and governor spring positions in the RQ mechanical governor assembly. (Courtesy of Robert Bosch Corporation.)

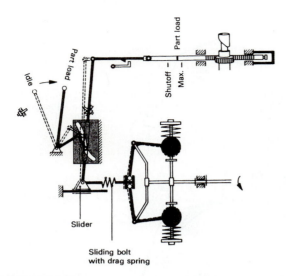

FIGURE 19–59 *RQV governor linkage position during part-load operation. (Courtesy of Robert Bosch Corporation.)*

rotate the plunger CCW (right to left) to expose more of the helix, which in effect lengthens the effective stroke of the plunger as it moves up within the barrel of the injection pump. Full rotation of the plunger would occur only when the engine throttle is placed into the maximum position with the engine running under full-load conditions. If the throttle were placed into its maximum position but there was no load on the engine, the engine would run faster, causing the stronger centrifugal force of the rotating governor flyweights to pull the sliding bolt in toward them. This in turn would move the slider and the pivoting lower end of the fulcrum lever toward the right, while the upper end pivoting around the guide pin would pull the rack to the left to decrease the fuel delivery. In this way the maximum no-load speed of the engine is controlled.

Engine overspeed, such as when a truck runs down a hill, can occur because of the direct mechanical connection between the drive wheels and the engine. However, the faster the engine rotated, the greater the weight forces developed, and they succeed in pulling the rack out of fuel. If a piston were to strike a valve during such an overspeed, the governor has still done its job. The problem is poor driver control.

Torque Control
In all engines used in highway vehicles, some form of torque control is desired to increase rack position during a decrease in engine speed under full-load control, such as when the truck climbs a hill. Earlier discussions of the RSV and RQ model governors described how this is accomplished. The system used in the RQV governor model is shown in Figures 19-57 and 19-59

with the torque control travel adjustment being accessible through a plug located at the top rear of the governor housing. Torque control occurs as a result of the interaction between the sliding bolt drag spring and the torque control spring. The position of the throttle lever will directly affect the control lever on the side of the governor housing. Therefore, if the throttle is placed at a high-speed position for starting, the drag spring is tensioned for the duration of the acceleration mode of the engine. As a result, the torque control spring is also compressed as the fuel rack strap connected to it pulls the torque spring control rod with it as the fuel rack moves to maximum fuel for starting. Once the rotating governor flyweights move out to this higher rpm range, however, the force on the sliding bolt drag spring is reduced and the compressive force of the torque spring is now strong enough to pull the fuel control rack back to lower fuel delivery after startup. Torque control adjustment can only be done with the pump/governor combination mounted on a test stand. The start of torque control is set by varying the tension adjustment screw of the torque control spring. In addition, the use of shims of different thicknesses will set the torque control travel.

RQV-K Governor Model
The RQV-K governor model has the same pear-shaped housing as both the RQ and RQV, but its control mechanism differs slightly. It also includes access to fine adjustments, which can be reached through the metal cover on top of the housing as well as behind a plate on the governor cover at the rear as shown in Figure 19-60. However, major adjustments to the RQV-K governor should be made only with the pump and governor combination on a test stand.

The RQV-K governor is mated to the P model Bosch inline multiple-plunger pump, with major users of this combination pump/governor being Navistar (International Harvester) and Mack trucks. The RQV-K is a mechanical variable-speed governor that can be fitted with any type of engine torque control arrangement to suit a wide range of desirable conditions. This flexibility of torque control allows the RQV-K to fill the different fuel injection requirements of the various engine users. Since the RQV-K uses the same basic flyweight assembly with three springs enclosed within the weight carrier as that in the RQV model, and operates in the same manner as described in this chapter for the RQV, you should have little trouble in systematically following the governor actions during startup, idle, part-load, and maximum speed/full-fuel control conditions. What we do need to consider, however, is the unique method employed in the RQV-K governor to maintain torque control.

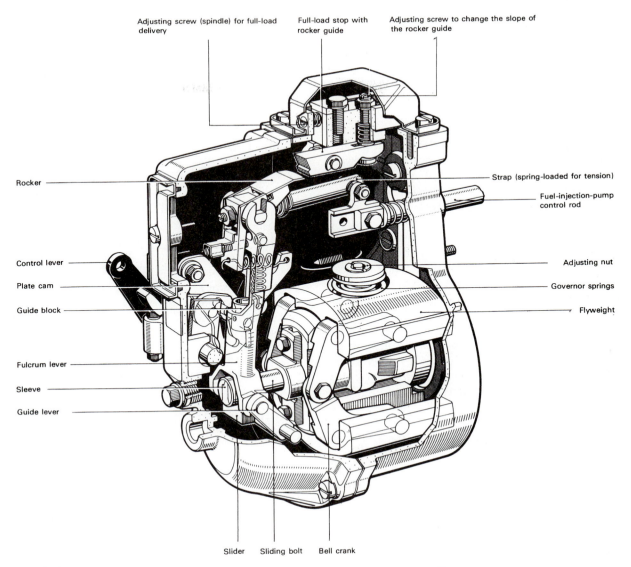

Adjusting screw (spindle) for full-load delivery

Full-load stop with rocker guide

Adjusting screw to change the slope of the rocker guide

Rocker

Control lever

Plate cam

Guide block

Fulcrum lever

Sleeve

Guide lever

Strap (spring-loaded for tension)

Fuel-injection-pump control rod

Adjusting nut

Governor springs

Flyweight

Slider   Sliding bolt   Bell crank

FIGURE 19–60 *Schematic diagram of a model RQV-K governor assembly. (Courtesy of Robert Bosch Corporation.)*

If you are already familiar with the governor linkage arrangement from the weight carrier through the fulcrum lever to the fuel control rack in the RQV models, reference to Figure 19-60 will allow you to identify the major component parts difference in the RQV-K model. Additional components used on the RQV-K that are not used on the RQV are listed below.

- A strap (spring loaded for tension), connected between the fuel control rod (rack) and the fulcrum lever
- An adjusting screw (spindle) for full-load delivery
- A full-load stop with a rocker guide

- An adjusting screw to change the slope (angle) of the rocker guide
- A rocker

Review Figure 19-60 and familiarize yourself with each of these five components and their relationship to other governor parts before proceeding, since the RQV-K rocker action becomes critical to your understanding of just how this torque control system functions with this type of governor.

RQV-K Governor Operation

With the engine stopped the weights are collapsed and the speed control lever, which is connected through external linkage to the throttle pedal on a truck, would be in the shutoff position. Refer to Figure 19-61 and note the control lever position, the guide block position within the slot of the plate cam, and the position of the rocker in relation to the rocker guide. Also note the fuel control rack identification mark, which is opposite the fuel shutoff indicator.

When the governor speed control lever is placed into the starting position, as with other Bosch governors, excess fuel delivery for ease of starting under all operating environments is desired. The fuel control rack would be moved 21 mm to the position shown in Figure 19-61. In this example, the rack movement at idle would sit between about 7 and 10 mm, depending on the load at initial startup. The rack position at full-load speed in this example is about 11 mm, which is about half of what is delivered during starting (excess fuel) and approximately 4 mm greater than at low-idle speed. If the engine load were increased beyond the horsepower capability of the engine such as when a vehicle climbs a hill, the engine speed would start to decrease without a transmission downshift. Consequently, the loss of speed would cause a reduction in the centrifugal force of the rotating flyweights and the three governor springs would start to expand against the governor linkage to move the rack to an increased position. The rocker would now sit in the base of the vee-shaped rocker guide, which means that the rack has been advanced as shown in Figure 19-62 to a position corresponding to about 13 mm of travel, which is about 2 mm greater than it was under full-load rated

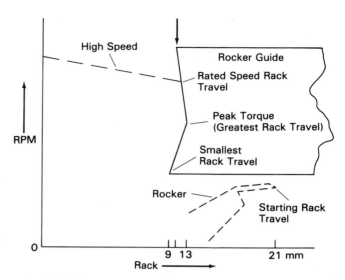

FIGURE 19–62 *Rocker guide cam shape for an RQV-K governor. (Courtesy of Robert Bosch Corporation.)*

speed conditions. This additional fuel delivery would provide a fairly flat (constant) horsepower curve plus a high rate of torque rise, with a reduction in speed from the no-load rpm position.

ANEROID/BOOST COMPENSATOR CONTROL

On engines using Robert Bosch injection pumps with a turbocharged engine, an aneroid/boost compensator control is used to prevent overfueling of the engine and hence black smoke during acceleration. This device controls the amount of fuel that can be injected until the exhaust-gas-driven turbocharger can overcome its initial speed lag and supply enough air boost to the engine cylinders. Such a device is used extensively by all four-stroke-cycle engine manufacturers today to comply with U.S. EPA smoke emission standards.

The aneroid is mounted on either the end or the top of the injection pump governor housing, with its linkage connected to the fuel control mechanism and a supply line running from the pressure side of the intake manifold (turbocharger outlet) to the top of the aneroid housing. Such a device is shown in Figure 19-63.

Figure 19-63A shows the position of the aneroid control linkage when the engine stop lever is actuated, which moves the aneroid fuel control link out of contact with the arm on the fuel injection pump control rack. Figure 19-63B shows the aneroid linkage position when the throttle control lever is moved to the slow idle position. This causes the starter spring to move

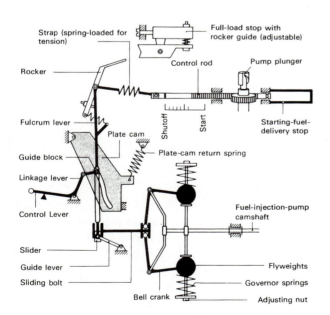

FIGURE 19–61 *RQV-K governor linkage schematic, engine stopped. (Courtesy of Robert Bosch Corporation.)*

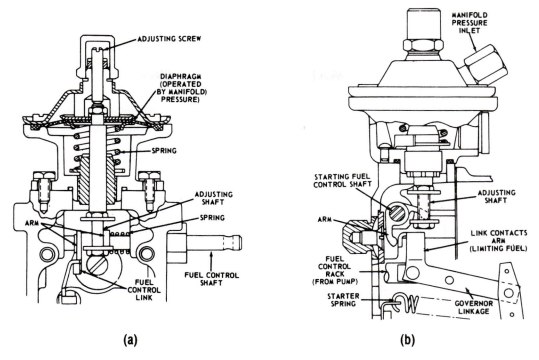

FIGURE 19–63 Governor aneroid control linkage component parts on an inline fuel injection pump. (Courtesy of Robert Bosch Corporation.)

the fuel control rack to the excess fuel position. Only during the cranking period is excess fuel supplied to the engine. This is because the instant the engine starts, we have the centrifugal force of the governor flyweights overcoming the starter spring tension, thereby moving the fuel control rack to a decreased fuel position. As this is occurring, the aneroid fuel control lever shaft spring will move the control link back into its original position. In Figure 19-63, the fuel control rack arm will contact the aneroid fuel control link, thereby limiting the amount of fuel that can be injected to approximately half-throttle and preventing excessive black smoke upon starting. The same lever will control the rack position at any time that the engine is accelerated, preventing any further increase in fuel delivery until the turbocharger has accelerated to supply enough boost air for complete combustion.

Boost Compensator Operation

Basically, the boost compensator ensures that the amount of injected fuel is in direct proportion to the quantity of air within the engine cylinder to sustain correct combustion of the fuel and therefore increase the horsepower of the engine. With the engine running, pressurized air from the cold end of the turbocharger passes through the (Figure 19-63b) connecting tube from the engine air inlet manifold to the boost compensator chamber. Inside this chamber is a diaphragm (Figure 19-63a) which is connected to a pushrod, which is in turn coupled to the compensator lever. Movement of the diaphragm is opposed by a spring, therefore for any movement to take place at the linkage, the air pressure on the diaphragm must be higher than spring tension. As the engine rpm and load increase and the air pressure within the connecting tube becomes high enough to overcome the tension of the diaphragm spring, the diaphragm and pushrod will be pushed down.

This movement causes the compensator lever to pivot, forcing the fuel control rack toward an increased fuel position. The boost compensator will therefore react to engine inlet manifold air pressure regardless of the action of the governor. When the turbocharger boost air pressure reaches its maximum, the quantity of additional fuel injected will be equal to the stroke of the aneroid boost compensator linkage, in addition to the normal full-load injection amount that is determined by the governor full-load stop bolt.

ALTITUDE PRESSURE COMPENSATOR

In naturally aspirated (nonturbocharged) diesel engines such as cars or trucks that can travel through varying terrain and altitudes, a means by which the fuel delivery rate can be altered is an important function of the governor and altitude pressure compensator. Since atmospheric pressure decreases with an increase in altitude, the volumetric efficiency of the engine will be less at higher elevations than it will be at sea level. On turbocharged engines, a boost compensator performs a function similar to that of the altitude compensator on nonturbocharged engines. Bosch refers to the altitude compensator as an ADA mechanism, and it is used in conjunction with either the RQ or RQV mechanical governor models. The ADA is located on the governor cover.

ROBERT BOSCH ELECTRONIC DIESEL CONTROL

Within the various chapters of this book are featured a number of high-technology diesel fuel injection control systems, with DDC's DDEC system (late 1985), Caterpillar's PEEC system (early 1987), and Cummins ECI system (1989) being mass-produced designs that have gained prominence since late 1985. The Robert Bosch Corporation offers electronic sensing and control of both its heavy-duty inline multiple-plunger pumps and its smaller model VE distributor pump assemblies used in automotive applications. As with the DDC and Cat systems, the high pressures necessary for injection purposes are still created mechanically by a reciprocating plunger within a barrel; however, control of the fuel rack position, and therefore of the quantity of fuel injected for a given throttle position and load, is determined by an ECU (electronic control unit) which has been programmed to output specific control signals to the governor/rack in relation to the accelerator position, turbocharger boost pressure, mass airflow rate, engine oil pressure, and temperature and coolant level.

The upgraded version of the Bosch P electronic model inline multiple-plunger injection pump, designated as the PDE, which is now in use in Europe on such OEM trucks as Mercedes-Benz, Volvo, and Saab-Scania, is also now in use in the United States. This pump incorporates several new design features for exhaust emissions–sensitive engines that need to comply with the EPA regulations. Newly developed pump plunger control-sleeve elements permit tighter control of prestroke regulation resulting in higher injection pressures of 1500 bar (21,796 psi) and precise control of injected fuel quantity and start of injection. Mack Trucks has already adapted the electronic pump to its heavy-duty line of E6 and E7 (electronic controlled) diesel engines. Robert Bosch continues to offer mechanically controlled governors and electronically controlled systems for monitoring and controlling engine performance.

Figure 19-64 illustrates an electronically controlled PLN system for a high-speed heavy-duty diesel engine. Modifications to the mechanical injection pump assembly are best viewed by reference to Figure 19-65. Note that although the pumping plunger (8) still operates within a barrel (2), it also moves through a control sleeve (3). The sleeve can be moved to allow an

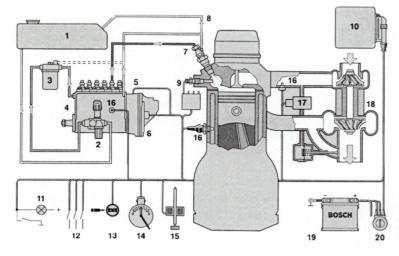

1 Fuel tank, 2 Supply pump, 3 Fuel filter, 4 In-line fuel-injection pump, 5 Timing device, 6 Governor, 7 Nozzle-and-holder assembly, 8 Fuel return line, 9 Sheathed-element glow plug with glow control unit, 10 Electronic control unit, 11 Diagnosis indicator, 12 Switches for clutch, brake, exhaust brake, 13 Speed selector lever, 14 Pedal position sensor, 15 Engine-speed sensor, 16 Temperature sensor (water, air, fuel), 17 Charge-pressure sensor, 18 Turbocharger, 19 Battery, 20 Glow-plug and starter switch.

FIGURE 19–64 Major components of a fuel injection system with an electronically controlled inline fuel injection pump. (Courtesy of Robert Bosch Corporation.)

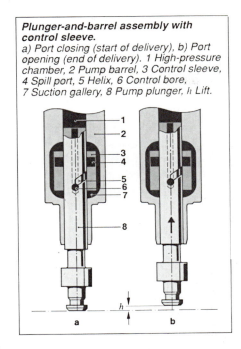

Plunger-and-barrel assembly with control sleeve.
a) Port closing (start of delivery), b) Port opening (end of delivery). 1 High-pressure chamber, 2 Pump barrel, 3 Control sleeve, 4 Spill port, 5 Helix, 6 Control bore, 7 Suction gallery, 8 Pump plunger, h Lift.

FIGURE 19–65 Components of an electronically controlled inline fuel injection pump plunger and barrel assembly. (Courtesy of Robert Bosch Corporation.)

adjustable prestroke to change the port closing, or to start injection. Compare this lift-to-port closure shown as *h* in Figure 19-65. By moving the control sleeve upward in the direction of fuel delivery—closer toward TDC as per Figure 19-65—the plunger has to lift through a greater distance (longer prestroke) before it is able to close the control bore (6); therefore, injection starts later. If the sleeve is closer to BDC, injection starts earlier, since the control bore enters the sleeve earlier. The actual fuel delivery rate can be altered by the design of the injection pump camshaft lobe.

The cutaway view of a six-cylinder engine injection pump in Figure 19-66 highlights the control sleeve design on the pumping plunger. Both the injected fuel quantity and the start of injection are electronically controlled by means of linear solenoid actuators. The injection sequence is controlled from an ECU (electronic control unit) which receives electrical inputs from a number of engine sensors (see Figure 19-64). Each sensor is fed a voltage input from the ECU in the region of 5 V, although this may be higher depending on the OEM using the system. Each sensor completes the electrical loop back to the ECU by sending an output signal based on its existing operating condition. Each temperature sensor, for example, is designed to

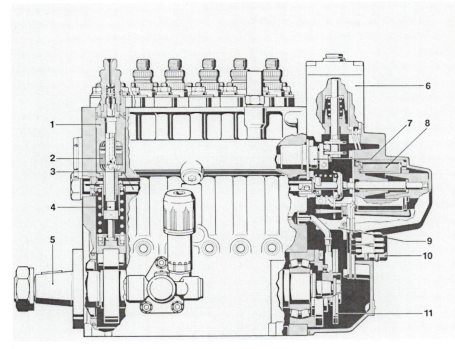

1 Pump cylinder, 2 Control sleeve, 3 Control rod, 4 Pump plunger, 5 Camshaft, 6 Port-closing actuator solenoid, 7 Control-sleeve setting shaft, 8 Rod-travel actuator solenoid, 9 Inductive rod-travel sensor, 10 Connector, 11 Inductive speed sensor.

FIGURE 19–66 Cutaway view of an electronically controlled inline injection pump illustrating main components. (Courtesy of Robert Bosch Corporation.)

have a fixed resistance value when cold; as it warms up, the resistance value decreases. An oil, fuel, or coolant temperature sensor may be designed to have 115,000 ohms (Ω) when cold and drop to 70 ohms (Ω) when it is at normal operating temperature. What this means is that if the ECU outputs a 5-V reference value to the sensor, the high resistance value will restrict the return signal to the ECU and the voltage value will be lower, usually in the region of 0.5 V. For any operating temperature, therefore, the return voltage signal value to the ECU will vary between 0.5 and 5 V. A pressure sensor, such as an oil or turbocharger boost, operates similarly to that described for the temperature sensors.

An inductive position sensor tells the ECU the position of the injection pump control rod/rack. An engine speed sensor (Figure 19-64, item 15) scans a pulse ring located to monitor the camshaft speed. A fuel temperature sensor monitors the fuel in the supply line to the injection pump. The accelerator pedal incorporates a variable resistor (potentiometer) so that the percentage of pedal opening can be relayed to the ECU. The throttle pedal is designed to show a high resistance value with a closed throttle at idle speed; consequently, the input voltage value of 5 V is reduced to approximately 0.5 V back to the ECU. At a WOT (wide-open throttle) position, the return voltage back

to the ECU is close to 5 V, or the same as the input value. In addition, an intake manifold air-temperature sensor indicates to the ECU the denseness of the air flowing into the engine cylinders based on temperature. If a turbocharger is used, a turbo boost sensor functions to tell the ECU basically the load under which the engine is operating. A high boost pressure means greater load, while low boost pressure indicates a lower load level. An alternator speed signal can also be employed to drive an electronic tachograph. This signal, in turn, can be used to indicate to the ECU the vehicle's road speed. The clutch pedal position is indicated by a switch, and the stop-lamp switch provides information relative to the brake pedal position.

From all of the various sensor inputs, the ECU calculates and adjusts the electrical current to the rack actuator system of the fuel injection pump. Figure 19-67 illustrates the sequence of events involved in the EDC (electronic diesel control) system. The ECU compares the actual plunger/barrel port closing signal for the start of injection from a needle-motion sensor installed in one of the injector nozzle holders with an operating value that has been programmed into the computer map. The port closing actuator system is then adjusted by varying the control current so that the actual requested throttle/fuel demands are met. The travel of

FIGURE 19–67 *Electronic open-loop and closed-loop control of the inline fuel injection pump with a control sleeve. (Courtesy of Robert Bosch Corporation.)*

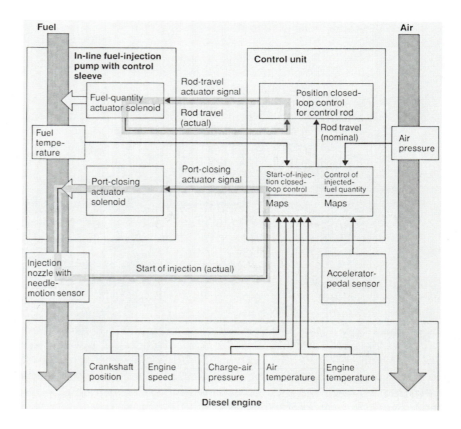

the injection pump rack electromagnet is directly proportional to the current demands of injection. The end of injection caused by port opening is varied on the electronically controlled pump in the same way it is for the mechanical system; that is, the pump plunger is rotated through rack movement.

DISTRIBUTOR PUMPS

Distributor pumps manufactured by Bosch include the VA and VE models (the V is from the German word *Verteiler*, and the second letter, A or E, indicates the specific model). The distributor pumps are used, for example, in Volkswagen cars and light trucks, Volvo and Peugeot cars, and International Harvester and Deutz farm tractors. Figure 19-68 illustrates that the VE pump has a horizontal control lever (throttle) and the timing piston (advance) cover is located near the bottom of the pump. The VA pump has two vertical control levers, with the timing advance piston cover located near the top of the pump.

ROBERT BOSCH MODEL VE INJECTION PUMP

The model VE fuel injection pump (Figure 19-68), takes its name from the German word *Verteiler*, which means distributor pump, although it is also commonly referred to as a rotary-type design that operates upon the same basic principle as that of a gasoline engine ignition distributor. Rather than employing high-tension pickup points inside a distributor cap, we have high-pressure fuel outlet lines to carry diesel fuel to each cylinder. On a gasoline engine, the ignition distributor feeds the high-tension spark via wire leads to each spark plug in engine firing-order sequence. In the diesel engine, the fuel injection pump delivers high-pressure fuel through steel-backed fuel lines to each cylinder's injector in firing-order sequence.

The E designation in the pump model refers to the particular model of rotary injection pump produced by Robert Bosch Corporation. The pump is available in two-, three-, four-, five-, six-, and eight-cylinder engine configurations to suit a variety of engines and applications. The VE injection pump is used widely on both passenger car and light-truck applications worldwide. The pump, although of Robert Bosch design and manufacture, is also manufactured under license by both Diesel Kiki and Nippondenso in Japan.

The product designation for VE pumps is similar to VA pumps with two notable exceptions. First, the plunger diameter is generally given in whole millimeters; and second, no execution letter is used. Let's break down a typical VE pump product designation—VE4/9F2500R16-2:

V: distributor pump type
E: pump capacity
4: number of high-pressure outlets
9: plunger diameter, in whole millimeters
F: flyweight governing
2500: full-load rated speed
R: direction of rotation (R, right; L, left)
16-2: engineering and application information

Let's look at just the letters and numbers that are important to us now: VE6/11F1800L19. This will be much simpler because there are fewer important letters and numbers to remember.

V: Distributor pump
E: Capacity
6: High-pressure outlets
11: Plunger diameter, 11 mm
L: Left-hand rotation

It is one of the most widely used distributor-type fuel injection pumps on the market today in automotive industrial and marine applications. Because of the various engine/vehicle manufacturers using this injection pump, minor differences or options may be found on one pump/engine that is not used on another; however, the design and operation of the VE pump regardless of what engine it is installed on can be considered common to all vehicles. The major differences would be:

1. The engine to injection pump timing.
2. The injection pump lift or prestroke (discussed later in this chapter).
3. The use of an altitude/boost compensator found on engines operating in varying altitudes and or equipped with a turbocharger. This device limits the amount of fuel that can be injected in order to comply with EPA exhaust emissions standards.
4. All VE pumps contain a vane transfer pump built within the housing of the injection pump assembly to transfer diesel fuel under pressures of from approximately 36 psi (250 kPa) at an idle rpm up to about 116 psi (800 kPa) at speeds of 4500 rpm into the hydraulic head of the injection pump. Some vehicles rely on this pump alone to pull fuel from the vehicle fuel tank; however, some vehicles employ an additional lift pump, usually electric-driven, between the fuel filter and the vane transfer pump to pull fuel from the tank and supply it to the vane transfer pump.

BOSCH Distributor-type fuel-injection pump type VE

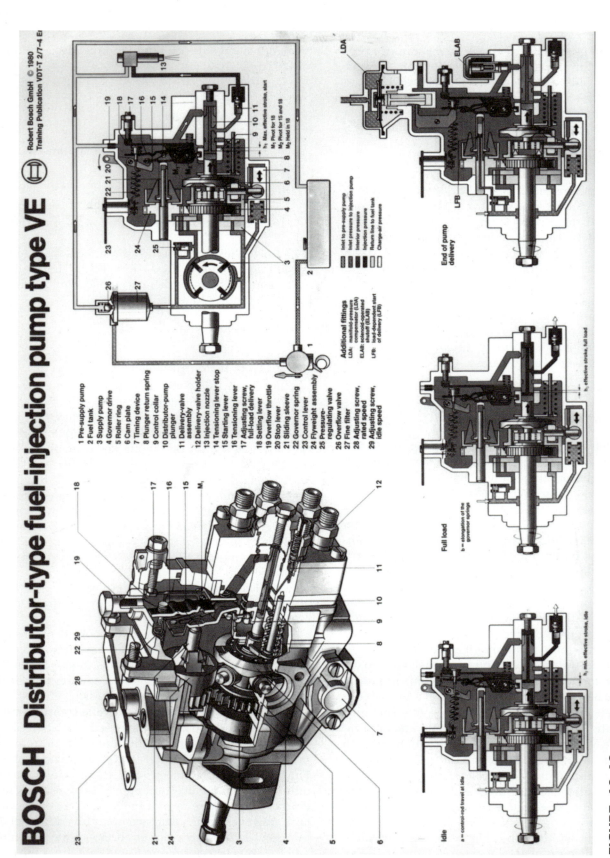

Robert Bosch GmbH © 1980
Training Publication VDT-T 2/7-4 E

1 Pre-supply pump
2 Fuel tank
3 Supply pump
4 Governor drive
5 Roller ring
6 Cam plate
7 Timing device
8 Plunger return spring
9 Control collar
10 Distributor-pump plunger
11 Delivery-valve assembly
12 Delivery-valve holder
13 Injection nozzle
14 Tensioning lever stop
15 Starting lever
16 Tensioning lever
17 Adjusting screw, full-load delivery
18 Setting lever
19 Overflow throttle
20 Stop lever
21 Sliding sleeve
22 Governor spring
23 Control lever
24 Flyweight assembly
25 Pressure-regulating valve
26 Overflow valve
27 Fine filter
28 Adjusting screw, rated speed
29 Adjusting screw, idle speed

Additional fittings

LDA: manifold-pressure compensator (LDA)
ELAB: electrically operated shutoff (ELAB)
LFB: load-dependent start of delivery (LFB)

Inlet to pre-supply pump
Inlet pressure to injection pump
Interior pressure
Injection pressure
Return line to fuel tank
Charge-air pressure

h_1 Max. effective stroke, start
M_1 Pivot for 18
M_2 Pivot for 15 and 18
M_3 Held in 18

LDA

ELAB

LFB

End of pump delivery

Full load

b = elongation of the governor springs

h_1 effective stroke, full load

Idle

a = control-rod travel at idle

h_1 min. effective stroke, idle

FIGURE 19–68 Bosch distributor injection pump VE–F operational diagram. (Courtesy of Robert Bosch Corporation.)

420

5. The VE pump is much more compact than the inline fuel injection pump used extensively on larger midrange and heavy-duty truck applications. The distributor pump uses approximately half as many component parts and usually weighs less than half that of an inline pump. Contained within the housing of the distributor pump are both a fuel transfer pump (vane type) and a governor mechanism.

Fuel Flow: Operation

Although minor differences may exist between the actual layout and fuel flow path from the vehicle fuel tank to the injection pump, Figure 19-68 illustrates a typical fuel flow arrangement used with the VE model pump as it applies to its use in passenger car and light pickup truck engines.

To start the engine, the operator must turn the ignition key on, which will electrically energize a fuel shutoff solenoid located on the injection pump housing just above the fuel outlet lines from the hydraulic head of the injection pump.

This solenoid is shown in Figures 19-68 and 19-69 and when energized is designed to allow fuel under pressure from the vane transfer pump to pass into the injection pump plunger pumping chamber. When the ignition key is turned OFF, the fuel solenoid is de-

energized and fuel can no longer be supplied to the plunger pumping chamber; therefore, the engine will starve for fuel and stop immediately.

Some vehicles use only the vane transfer pump, which is contained within the injection pump housing to draw fuel from the tank to the injection pump, while others may employ either a mechanical diaphragm or an electrically operated lift pump to draw fuel from the tank and deliver it to the vane transfer pump.

Also, most vehicles today employ a fuel filter/water separator plus a secondary fuel filter in the system between the fuel tank and the vane transfer pump.

The vane transfer pump is shown as item 3 in Figure 19-68. This pump is capable of producing fuel delivery pressures of about 36 psi (248 kPa) at an engine idle speed up to as high as 120 psi (827 kPa), although maximum pressures are generally maintained at around 100 psi (689.5 kPa). This fuel under pressure is then delivered through internal injection pump drillings to the distributor pump plunger shown as item 10 in Figure 19-68. All internal parts of the fuel injection pump are lubricated by this fuel under pressure; there is no separate lube oil reservoir.

Maximum fuel pressure created by the vane transfer pump, which is located within the injection pump body, is controlled by an adjustable fuel pressure regulator screw.

On four-stroke engines, the injection pump is driven at one-half engine speed and is capable of delivering up to 2800 psi (approximately 200 bar) to the injection nozzles; however, the adjusted release pressure of the nozzle establishes at what specific pressure the nozzle will open.

An overflow line from the top of the injection pump housing allows excess fuel that is used for cooling and lubrication purposes to return to the fuel tank through a restricted bolt readily identifiable by the word OUT stamped on the top of it.

Since the vane transfer pump is capable of either left- or right-hand rotation, take care when servicing this unit that you assemble it correctly. Take careful note of the various holes in Figure 19-68. Hole 1 in the eccentric ring is farthest from its inner wall compared to hole 2. When looking at the eccentric ring, this hole must be in position 1 for right-hand rotation pumps and to the left for left-hand rotation fuel injection pumps. Hole 3 should be on the governor side when the transfer pump is installed. Also the pump vanes should always be fitted with the circular or crowned ends contacting the walls of the eccentric ring.

Fuel under pressure from the vane transfer pump is then delivered to the pumping plunger shown in Figure 19-68 and also in Figure 19-70, where it is then

Electric shutoff (with pull solenoid).

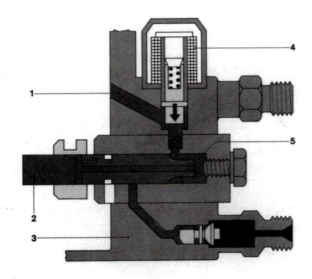

1 Inlet bore,	4 Pull (or push)
2 Distributor plunger,	solenoid,
3 Distrubutor head,	5 High-pressure chamber.

FIGURE 19–69 *VE injection pump plunger and barrel showing electric fuel shutoff. (Courtesy of Ford Motor Company.)*

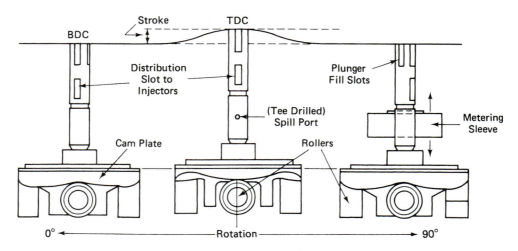

FIGURE 19–70   *VE injection pump distributor plunger location and design. (Courtesy of Volvo of America Corporation.)*

sent to the fuel injectors (nozzles). Let us study the action of the plunger more closely, since it is this unit that is responsible for the distribution of the high-pressure fuel within the system. Figure 19-71 shows the actual connection between the cam rollers and the pump plunger, which is also visible in Figures 19-68 and 19-70.

Notice that the plunger is capable of two motions: (1) circular or rotational (driven from the drive shaft), and (2) reciprocating (back and forth by cam plate and roller action).

Reference to Figures 19-68 and 19-71 shows that the cam plate is designed with as many lobes or projections on it as there are engine cylinders. Unlike Lucas CAV and Stanadyne distributor injection pumps, the rollers on the VE pump are not actuated by an internal cam ring with lobes on it, but instead the cam ring is circular and attached to a round cam plate. As the cam ring rotates with the injection pump drive-shaft and plunger, the rollers (which are fixed), cause the cam lobe to lift every 90° (for example) in a four-cylinder engine, or every 60° in a six-cylinder engine.

FIGURE 19–71   *High-pressure delivery. (Courtesy of Robert Bosch Corporation.)*

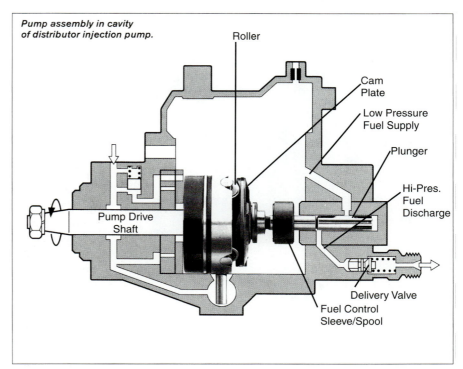

In other words, the rollers do not lift on the cam as in a conventional system, but it is the cam ring that is solidly attached to the rotating plunger that actually lifts as each lobe comes into contact with each positioned roller spaced apart in relation to the number of engine cylinders. With such a system then, the plunger stroke will remain constant regardless of engine rpm. At the end of each plunger stroke, a spring ensures a return of the cam ring to its former position as shown in Figure 19-68 (item 8). Therefore, the back-and-forth motion of the single pumping plunger is positive.

Anytime that the roller is at its lowest point on the rotating cam ring lobe, the pumping plunger will be at a position commonly known as BDC (bottom dead center); and with the rotating cam ring lobe in contact with the roller, the pumping plunger will be at TDC (top dead center) position, as shown in Figure 19-70. Distribution of fuel to the injector nozzles is via plunger rotation, and metering (quantity) is controlled by the metering sleeve position, which varies the effective stroke of the plunger.

If we consider the plunger movement, that is, *stroke* and *rotation*, Figure 19-72 depicts the action in a 90° movement such as would be found on a four-cylinder four-cycle engine pump. Even though there is a period of dwell at the start and end of one 90° rotation (one cylinder firing), the plunger movement during this time continues.

The sequence of events shown in Figure 19-72 is as follows:

1. The fill slot of the rotating plunger is aligned with the fill port, which is receiving fuel at transfer pump pressure as high as 100 psi (7 bar approximately), one cylinder only.

2. The rotating plunger has reached the *port closing* position. The plunger rotates a control spool regulating collar (see Figures 19-72, item 8, and 19-68, item 9). The position of the regulating collar is controlled by the operator or driver though linkage connected to and through the governor spring and flyweights. Because the plunger rotates as well as moving back and forth, the plunger must lift for port

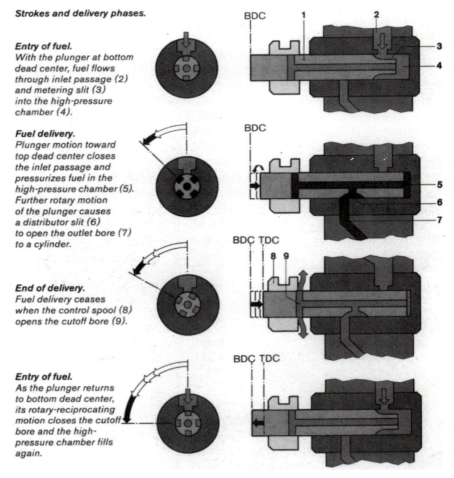

FIGURE 19-72 VE pump plunger movement in a four-cylinder, four-cycle engine through 90° pump rotation. (Strokes/Delivery Phases, courtesy of Robert Bosch Corporation.)

Strokes and delivery phases.

Entry of fuel.
With the plunger at bottom dead center, fuel flows through inlet passage (2) and metering slit (3) into the high-pressure chamber (4).

Fuel delivery.
Plunger motion toward top dead center closes the inlet passage and pressurizes fuel in the high-pressure chamber (5). Further rotary motion of the plunger causes a distributor slit (6) to open the outlet bore (7) to a cylinder.

End of delivery.
Fuel delivery ceases when the control spool (8) opens the cutoff bore (9).

Entry of fuel.
As the plunger returns to bottom dead center, its rotary-reciprocating motion closes the cutoff bore and the high-pressure chamber fills again.

closure to occur; then delivery will commence. Because the rotating plunger does stroke through the metering sleeve in the VE pump, this pump is classed as the *port closing* type. Therefore, even though the roller may be causing the cam–ring–plunger to lift, the position of the regulating collar determines the amount of travel of the plunger or *prestroke*, so the actual effective stroke of the plunger is determined at all times by the collar position.

3.   At the point of plunger lift (start of effective stroke), fuel delivery to the hydraulic head and injector line will begin in the engine firing order sequence.

4.   The effective stroke is always less than the total plunger stroke. As the plunger moves through the regulating collar, it uncovers a *spill port*, opening the high-pressure circuit and allowing the remaining fuel to spill into the interior of the injection pump housing. This then is *port opening* or spill, which ends the effective stroke of the plunger; however, the plunger stroke continues.

5.   With the sudden decrease in fuel delivery pressure, the spring within the injector nozzle rapidly seats the needle valve, stopping injection and preventing after-dribble, unburned fuel, and therefore engine exhaust smoke. At the same time, the delivery valve for that nozzle located in the hydraulic head is snapped back on its seat by spring pressure.

In a four-cylinder four-stroke engine, we would have four strokes within 360° of pump plunger rotation, which is of course equal to 720° of engine rotation. In summation, the volume of fuel delivered is controlled by the regulating collar position, which alters the (*effective stroke*) time that the ports are closed.

If there is an annulus or circular slot located on the right-hand side of the plunger in Figure 19-78, all distributor slits (item 6) are tied together; this is the reason that the plunger must lift for port closure to occur. Only after the annulus lifts beyond the fill port do we have port closure. Port closing occurs only after a specified lift from BDC.

Delivery Valve Operation

Contained within the hydraulic head (outlets) of the injection pump where the high pressure fuel lines are connected to the injection pump are delivery valves (one per cylinder) (Figure 19-73), which are designed to open at a fixed pressure and deliver fuel to the injectors in firing order sequence.

These valves function to ensure that there will always be a predetermined fuel pressure in the fuel lines leading to the fuel injectors. Another major function of these individual delivery valves is to ensure that at the end of the injection period for that cylinder there is no

Pressure valve.

a closed,	4 Valve body,
b open.	5 Shaft,
1 Valve holder,	6 Relief piston,
2 Valve seat,	7 Ring groove,
3 Valve spring,	8 Longitudinal groove.

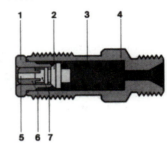

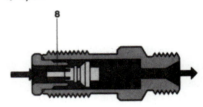

FIGURE 19–73   VE injection pump delivery valve operation. (Courtesy of Ford Motor Company.)

possibility of secondary injection and also that any pressure waves during the injection period will not be transferred back into the injection pump.

If secondary injection were to occur, the engine would tend to misfire and run rough. The delivery valves ensure a crisp cutoff to the end of injection when the fuel pressure drops off in the line and also maintains fuel in the injection line so that there is no possibility of air being trapped inside the line.

Fuel Return Line

All model VE pumps use a percentage of the fuel delivered to the injection pump housing to cool and lubricate the internal pump components. Since the diesel fuel will pick up some heat through this action, a bleed off or fuel return from the injection pump housing is achieved through the use of a hollow bolt with an orifice drilled into it as shown in Figure 19-74.

This bolt is readily identifiable by the word OUT stamped on the hex head, and if substituted with an ordinary bolt, no fuel will be able to return to the fuel tank from the injection pump.

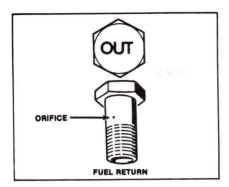

FIGURE 19–74 *VE injection pump fuel return bolt with restricted orifice. (Courtesy of Ford Motor Company.)*

Emergency Stop Lever

Should the fuel shutoff solenoid fail to operate when the ignition key is turned OFF, an emergency stop lever is connected to the injection pump housing and accessible underhood. This lever can be pulled to cut off fuel in the event of electric fuel solenoid failure. This lever is shown in Figure 19-68 as item 20.

Minimum/Maximum Speed Settings

The idle rpm and the maximum engine speed is controlled by adjusting two screws located on the top of the injection pump housing and shown as items 28 and 29 in Figure 19-68. Both of these adjustments should always be done with the engine at normal operating temperature.

Turning the idle speed adjusting screw clockwise will increase idle rpm. Turning the high-speed adjusting screw counterclockwise will increase the maximum speed setting of the engine. The minimum and maximum engine speed settings are listed on the vehicle emissions label/decal that is generally affixed under the hood in the engine compartment or at the front end of the engine compartment close to the radiator end.

Cold-Start Device

All vehicles equipped with the VE fuel injection pump are equipped with either a manually operated or automatic cold-start device (CSD). The year of vehicle manufacture and make establishes whether it has the former or the latter.

The main purpose of a cold-start device is to provide easier engine starting and warm-up properties. When the cold-start device is activated, the beginning of fuel injection is advanced through the movement of the injection pump cam roller ring in relation to the cam disc.

With a manually operated CSD such as shown in

Figure 19-75, a control cable, which is mounted inside the vehicle, is pulled out by the operator and turned clockwise to lock it in place. This action causes a lever connected to a cam (Figure 19-76A) to butt up against the injection pump advance piston and push it forward. Movement of the advance piston rotates the cam roller ring as shown in Figure 19-76A so that fuel injection will occur earlier in the cylinder BTDC. The manual CSD uses a ball pin shown as item 3 in Figure 19-76A to rotate the roller ring (6).

The automatic CSD operates on the basis of engine coolant temperature in contact with a thermo-valve that contains a wax element similar to a thermostat. Therefore this device shown in Figure 19-76B controls the linkage in both an engine-cold and engine-warm mode. Rotation of this linkage operates upon the timing control piston that will rotate the cam roller ring similar to the manually controlled system. The degree of timing advancement will vary between makes of engines and is determined by the engine manufacturer.

Governors for the VE Pump

The Robert Bosch VE distributor/rotary injection pump is available with one of two mechanical governors to control the speed and response of the engine. These two types of governors and their functions are:

1. *Variable-speed governor:* controls all engine speed ranges from idle up to maximum rated rpm. With this governor, when the throttle lever is placed at any position, the governor will maintain this speed within the droop characteristics of the governor. The variable-speed governor and its operation are illustrated in Figures 19-77A and 19-77B with its actual location in relation to the other injection pump components being clearly shown in Figure 19-68.

2. *Limiting-speed governor:* sometimes known as an idle and maximum speed governor since it is designed to control only the low and high idle speeds (maximum rpm) of the engine. When the throttle lever is placed into any position between idle and maximum, there is no governor control. Any change to the engine speed must be determined by the driver/operator moving the throttle pedal. This governor is shown in Figure 19-77C.

The variable-speed governor can be used on any application where all-range speed control is desired such as on a stationary engine or on a vehicle that drives an auxiliary power takeoff (PTO).

Operation of the Variable-Speed Governor

If you are not already familiar with the basic operation of a mechanical governor, it may be advantageous to you to review the description of operation given in Chapter 17.

FIGURE 19–75 *Manual cold-start device components, VE injection pump. (Courtesy of Ford Motor Company.)*

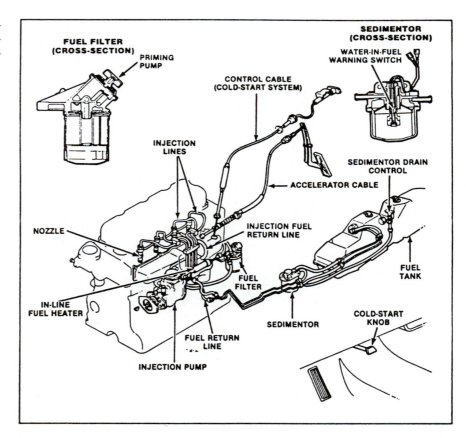

The thing to always remember is that the force of the governor spring is always attempting to increase the fuel delivery rate to the engine, while the centrifugal force of the governor flyweights is always attempting to decrease the fuel to the engine.

Anytime that the centrifugal force of the rotating governor flyweights and the governor spring forces are equal, the governor is said to be in a *state of balance* and the engine will run at a fixed/steady speed. You should also be familiar with the operation of the injection pump and how the *effective stroke* of the rotating pump plunger operates.

Engine Stopped
Refer to Figure 19-77(A). With the engine stopped there is no governor weight force and consequently the force of the idle spring (14) and the starting spring (6) force the governor linkage attached to the control spool (7) to a position whereby the effective stroke of the rotating pump plunger (9) will be at its maximum; therefore, during engine cranking, maximum fuel will be delivered to the cylinders.

Engine Cranking and Starting
As the engine is cranked over, the centrifugal force developed by the rotating governor flyweights (1 and 2)

will force the sliding sleeve (3) to the right in Figure 19-77A against the starting lever (5) and its spring (6). When the spring (6) is compressed, the lever (5) will butt up against a stop on the tensioning lever (4), which will now act directly against the force of the idle spring (14). Movement of the tensioning lever (4) will pull the speed control lever on top of the governor back until it bottoms on the idle speed adjusting screw (10).

Once the centrifugal force of the flyweights equals the preset tension of the idle spring (14), the engine will run at a steady speed. A state-of-balance condition exists between the weights and the idle spring. If the throttle lever is moved above the idle speed, the spring will be collapsed by the distance *c* shown on the right-hand side of Figure 19-77A.

Engine Acceleration
Refer to Figure 19-77A. When the engine is accelerated beyond the idle rpm, the centrifugal force of the rotating governor flyweights will force the sliding sleeve (3) to the right, and with the starting lever (5) up against the tensioning lever (4), the idle spring (14) will be compressed. Additional engine speed and therefore weight force will now cause lever (4) to pull against the larger governor spring (12).

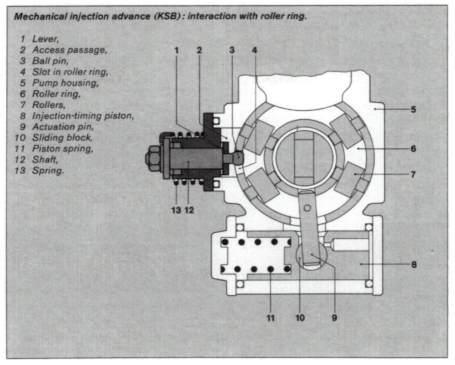

A

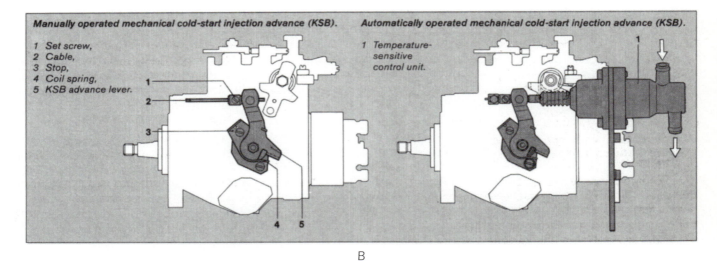

B

FIGURE 19–76 (A) KSB mechanical injection advance; (B) KSB cold-start mechanical injection advance linkage. (Courtesy of Robert Bosch Corporation.)

Refer to Figure 19-77B. Movement of the throttle lever causes the engine speed control lever (2) to move away from the idle speed adjusting screw and toward the full-load adjusting screw (11). The travel of the speed control lever is determined by the driver and just how fast he or she wants the engine to run. When the driver steps on the throttle, the previous state-of-balance condition that existed at idle is upset in favor of the governor spring (4). The control spool (10) is moved through lever (6) and (7) so that the effective stroke of the rotating pump plunger is lengthened by moving the control spool (10) initially to its right in Figure 19-77B under the heading "increasing engine speed."

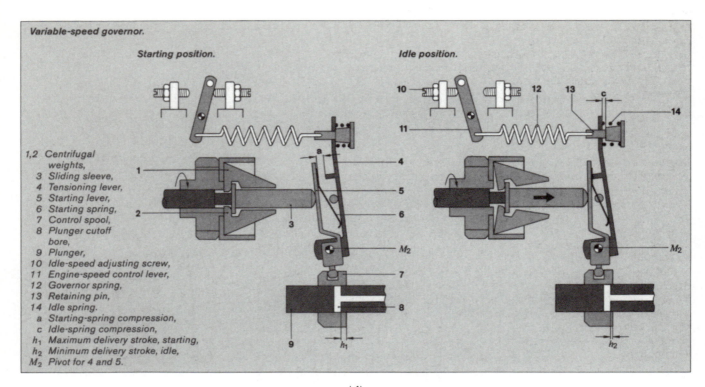

Variable-speed governor.

Starting position. **Idle position.**

1,2 Centrifugal
weights,
3 Sliding sleeve,
4 Tensioning lever,
5 Starting lever,
6 Starting spring,
7 Control spool,
8 Plunger cutoff
bore,
9 Plunger,
10 Idle-speed adjusting screw,
11 Engine-speed control lever,
12 Governor spring,
13 Retaining pin,
14 Idle spring.
a Starting-spring compression,
c Idle-spring compression,
h_1 Maximum delivery stroke, starting,
h_2 Minimum delivery stroke, idle,
M_2 Pivot for 4 and 5.

(A)

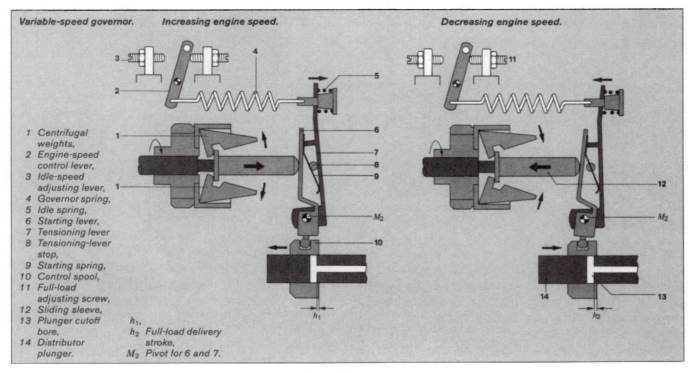

Variable-speed governor. **Increasing engine speed.** **Decreasing engine speed.**

1 Centrifugal
weights,
2 Engine-speed
control lever,
3 Idle-speed
adjusting lever,
4 Governor spring,
5 Idle spring,
6 Starting lever,
7 Tensioning lever
8 Tensioning-lever
stop,
9 Starting spring,
10 Control spool,
11 Full-load
adjusting screw,
12 Sliding sleeve,
13 Plunger cutoff
bore,
14 Distributor
plunger.

h_1,
h_2 Full-load delivery
stroke,
M_2 Pivot for 6 and 7.

(B)

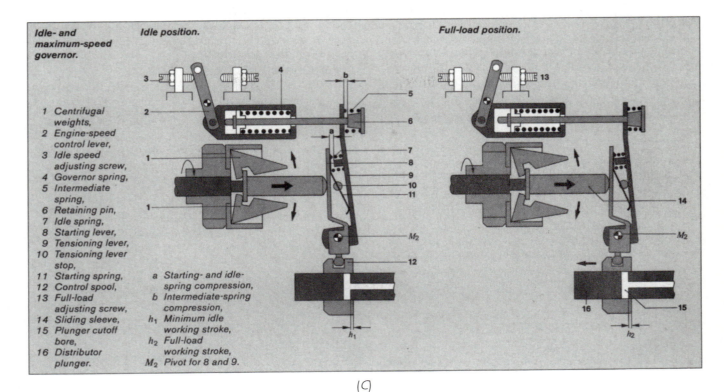

Idle- and maximum-speed governor.

Idle position.

Full-load position.

1 Centrifugal weights,
2 Engine-speed control lever,
3 Idle speed adjusting screw,
4 Governor spring,
5 Intermediate spring,
6 Retaining pin,
7 Idle spring,
8 Starting lever,
9 Tensioning lever,
10 Tensioning lever stop,
11 Starting spring,
12 Control spool,
13 Full-load adjusting screw,
14 Sliding sleeve,
15 Plunger cutoff bore,
16 Distributor plunger.

a Starting- and idle-spring compression,
b Intermediate-spring compression,
h_1 Minimum idle working stroke,
h_2 Full-load working stroke,
M_2 Pivot for 8 and 9.

(C)

FIGURE 19–77 VE Injection pump mechanical governor component arrangement: [A] variable-speed governor—starting/idle position; [B] speed increase/decrease position; [C] idle/maximum speed governor, idle/full-load position. (Courtesy of Robert Bosch Corporation.)

As the engine receives more fuel and accelerates, the centrifugal force of the rotating flyweights (1) will push the sliding sleeve (12) to its right as shown in Figure 19-77B causing levers (6) and (7) to stretch the governor spring (4). When a state-of-balance condition exists once again between the rotating weights (1) and the spring (4), the engine will run at a steady speed with the throttle in a fixed position.

If the throttle is placed in full-fuel, the speed control lever (2) will butt up against the full-load-adjusting screw (11), which will limit the maximum speed of the engine. Weight force at this point is greater than spring force; therefore, the sliding sleeve (12) will cause the starting (6) and tensioning lever (7) to pivot around the support pin M2.

The control spool (10) will be moved to the left as shown in Figure 19-77B under the heading "increasing engine speed," which will reduce the effective stroke of the rotating pump plunger. As a result, the engine will receive less fuel, thereby automatically limiting the maximum speed of the engine.

When the centrifugal force of the rotating governor flyweights (1) are equal to the governor spring force (4), the engine will run at a fixed rpm at maximum speed. If the engine was started and accelerated to its maximum rpm with the vehicle in a stationary position, the action of the governor weights would limit the maximum amount of fuel that the engine could receive by moving the control spool to decrease the pump plunger's effective stroke. When the engine is running under such a condition (maximum no-load speed), it is not receiving full-fuel.

Decreasing Engine Speed

If the driver moves the throttle to a decreased speed position, the engine speed control lever (2) will reverse the position of the control spool (10) through the levers (6) and (7). As the effective stroke of the pump plunger is reduced, the engine receives less fuel and therefore it will run at a lower rpm. For a fixed throttle position at this lower speed, once the centrifugal force of the weights equals that of the governor spring (4), a new state of balance will occur and the engine will run at a steady speed.

Load Increase

Since this governor will control speed throughout the complete engine speed range, for a fixed throttle position, the engine will deliver a specific horsepower rating. As long as the engine is not overloaded at a given rpm position, the governor can control the speed within the confines of its droop characteristic.

NOTE   Droop is the difference between the maximum no-load rpm and the full-load rpm. Obviously, the engine speed will be lower under full load than it will be at no load. Similarly, when a load is applied to the engine for a given speed setting, it will tend to slow down since it now has to work harder to overcome the resistance to rotation. A detailed explanation of droop can be found under the basic governor description in Chapter 17.

The reaction of the governor when a load is applied to the engine will be the same at any speed setting. A simplified description is as follows (Figure 19-77B):

1. Load applied at a given speed setting of the throttle, and engine slows down such as when going up a hill.

2. Upsets state of balance between weights (1) and spring (4) when above idle speed; if at idle, spring (5) in favor of the spring force.

3. Spring pressure is greater and therefore lever (6) and (7) acting through pivot point M2 moves the control spool (10) to its right to lengthen the effective stroke of the rotating pump plunger and supply the engine with more fuel to develop additional horsepower.

4. If the load on the engine continues to increase, the engine will receive more fuel to try to offset the load, but it will run at a slower rpm.

5. As long as the engine can produce enough additional horsepower, the governor will once again reach a state of balance between the weights and the spring, but at a slower speed than before the load was applied.

6. When the load was applied, the spring expanded (lengthened) to increase the fuel to the engine and in so doing lost some of its compression; therefore the weights do not have to increase their speed/force to what existed before to reestablish a new state of balance. The engine will produce more horsepower with more fuel but will be running at a slower rpm.

7. Regardless of the governor's reaction to increase fuel to the engine, if the load requirements exceed the power capability of the engine, the rpm will continue to drop. In an automotive application, the only way that the speed can now be increased is for the driver to select a lower gear by downshifting.

8. If the engine was running at an idle rpm and an air conditioner pump was turned on, the engine would tend to slow down (load increase). The governor through the spring force/less weight force would increase the fuel to the engine to prevent it from stalling.

Load Decrease

When the load is decreased at a fixed throttle position, we have the following situation:

1. Engine speed increases; weights fly out with more force and they will cause the sliding sleeve (12) in Figure 19-77B to move levers (6) and (7) against the force of the spring (4).

2. The reaction is the same as shown under the heading "increasing engine speed" where the control spool (10) will move to its left to decrease (shorten) the effective stroke of the pump plunger and reduce fuel to the engine until a new corrected state-of-balance condition exists.

3. With less load on the engine, it requires less horsepower and therefore less fuel and as the engine slows down, so do the weights until the state of balance is reestablished.

4. If a vehicle goes down a hill, the load is reduced. If the drive does not check the speed of the vehicle with the brakes, it is possible for the driving wheels to run faster than the engine. If the drive wheels start to rotate the engine, the governor weights will also gain speed and in so doing they will reduce the effective stroke of the pump plunger and the engine's fuel will automatically be reduced.

Limiting-Speed Governor Operation

The reaction in this governor is illustrated in Figure 19-77C and is the same as that described for the variable-speed governor above with the exception that there is no governor control in the intermediate speed range, which is the speed range between idle and maximum rpm.

Engine Stopped

The engine will receive maximum fuel for startup since the force of the starting spring (11) and the idle spring (7) will move the control spool (12) to a position where the pump plunger will obtain its maximum effective stroke.

Engine Cranking and Starting

As the engine is cranked, the centrifugal force of the governor weights (1) will force the sliding sleeve (14) to its right against the force of the starting spring (11) and the idle spring (7). As the starting levers (8) and (9) are moved to the right, the control spool (12) will be pulled back (left) to reduce the effective stroke of the pump plunger.

How far the spool (12) will be pulled back is established by the setting of the idle spring. When a state of balance exists between the weights (1) and the idle spring (7), the control spool (12) is held at a fixed position and the engine receives a fixed amount of fuel suitable for an idle rpm which is set by the adjusting screw (3).

Engine Acceleration

When the throttle is moved initially beyond the idle range, the weights will compress the idle spring (7), and the weight force will now act upon the force of the intermediate spring (5) for a short time. This spring (5) allows a reasonably wide idle-speed range, a large speed droop, and a soft or gradual transition from the low idle-speed range (governor control) to the point where the driver has complete control over the engine speed.

The intermediate spring (5) will be completely compressed (collapsed) shortly after the engine is accelerated from idle, and the throttle pedal now acts directly through the linkage to the sliding sleeve (14). There is not enough weight force to act upon the high-speed spring (4) until the engine speed approaches the high end. Engine speed is now directly controlled by the driver.

High-Speed Control

When the engine speed and therefore governor weight force is great enough, the centrifugal force of the weights will oppose the high-speed spring (4) until a state of balance occurs. When the weights and spring (4) come into play at the higher speed range, the maximum speed of the engine is limited by the fact that the weights as they fly out cause the sliding sleeve (14) to transfer motion through lever (8) and (9), which will compress the spring (4) and therefore move the control spool (12) to its left to shorten the effective stroke of the pump plunger. In this way, the engine receives less fuel and the maximum speed of the engine is therefore limited when the weights and spring (4) are in a state of balance. As load is applied and released from the engine (up hill) and (down hill), the governor will react in the same way that it did for the variable-speed governor described in detail earlier.

Automatic Timing Advance

The automatic advance mechanism employs the same principle of operation as that of CAV and Roosa Master Stanadyne distributor injection pumps. Fuel pressure from the transfer pump is delivered to a timing piston whose movement is opposed by spring pressure. At low engine speeds, the relatively low supply pump pressure has little to no effect on the timing piston travel. As engine speed increases, the rising fuel pressure will force the timing piston to overcome the resistance of the spring at its opposite end. At the center of the piston, as shown in Figure 19-76A, is a connecting pin extending up into the roller ring. The movement of the piston transmits this motion through the pin, which in turn rotates the roller ring in the opposite direction to drive shaft rotation, thereby advancing the timing of the cam plate lift from BDC to begin the plunger stroke. The timing piston travel should not be toyed with, but should be checked while the injection pump VE is mounted on a test bench.

Prestroke Compared to Nonprestroke Pumps

Some VE injection pumps use a plunger whereby all the fill ports are interconnected by an annulus, or circular passage, running around the circumference of the plunger as shown in Figures 19-71 and 19-78. With this type of plunger containing the annulus, the unit is known as a *prestroke* pump. With this type, the fill ports cannot close by plunger rotation alone. The plunger must lift for port closure to occur. Only after the annulus lifts beyond the fill port do we have port closure. The plunger must be adjusted for a specific lift from BDC for port closure to happen. With this type, fuel pressure buildup within the Tee-drilled plunger takes a few degrees longer than for the zero prestroke type, which does not have the annulus and wherein port closure occurs by plunger rotation alone: the plunger lifts from BDC after rotation from port closure.

Overhaul of the Injection Pump

Repair and major overhaul of any injection pump should only be undertaken by personnel trained in the diversified and intricate work of fuel injection equipment. Since special tools and equipment are required, which are not always readily available to everyone, refer to the Robert Bosch publication 46, VDT-W-460/100 B, Edition 1, *Repair of Distributor-type Fuel In-*

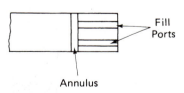

FIGURE 19–78 VE injection pump plunger annulus interconnection slot.

jection Pump 04604-VE-F. This is obtainable through your local Robert Bosch dealer or from one of the Robert Bosch licensees.

Bleeding the Fuel System

Anytime that fuel lines have been opened/loosened or the fuel system has been serviced, it will be necessary to vent all air from the fuel system in order to start the engine.

1. On engines equipped with an electric fuel lift pump, this procedure is relatively easy. However, if the fuel system does not have a separate lift pump, it will take a little longer because the vane transfer pump inside the drive end of the injection pump will have to pull the fuel from the tank to the pump on its own.

2. If the engine is equipped with an electric lift pump, make sure that all filter and injection pump vent screws are tight.

3. Turn the ignition key switch to the ON position to energize the fuel cutoff solenoid and allow the electric lift pump to operate for 1 to 2 minutes.

4. Crank the engine over, and if it starts and runs correctly without misfire or stumble, the system is properly bled of all air.

5. If the engine doesn't start, loosen the individual fuel line nuts (place a rag around the nut to absorb the spilled fuel) at the injectors and crank the engine over until air-free fuel appears at each line, then tighten them up.

6. If the engine is not equipped with an electric lift pump and only has a vane injection transfer pump, perform the sequence in step 5 while cranking the engine.

7. If the vehicle is equipped with a hand priming pump on the fuel filter/water separator, use this pump to bleed the filter first after opening the vent screw on top of the filter until air-free fuel appears. The inlet fuel stud on top of the injection pump housing can also be loosened off to vent air from the system right up to the injection pump. Place a drain tray underneath the fuel filter and pump to catch any leaking fuel. Step 5 can then be performed to bleed fuel up to the individual fuel injectors.

8. Once the engine starts and runs, if it is running rough, loosen each injector fuel line nut one at a time (engine idling) to bleed each unit with a rag placed around it then tighten the nut.

9. Wipe all spilled or bled fuel from the engine and compartment.

SPECIAL NOTE   On a fuel system that has been emptied completely by running the engine out of fuel, it may be necessary to perform additional bleeding of the system by cranking or attempting to run the engine as follows:

1. Loosen the fuel return fitting on the injection pump that is stamped OUT on the head of the hollow bolt (Figure 19-74).

2. Loosen the timing plug located in the center of the injection pump distributor head (Figure 19-79).

3. Loosen the fuel shutoff solenoid.

4. Loosen the injector pressure outlet valves.

CHECKING INJECTION PUMP STATIC TIMING

Contained within each engine chapter is a description of the various adjustments and timing checks for that particular engine. The following static timing check can be considered common to all model VE injection pumps with the major difference being in the dimension given by the manufacturer for a particular model engine. Several engines using the model VE pump will have the same setting while others will differ slightly.

Generally, a static timing check is required only when a new pump is being installed or when an engine has been rebuilt or the pump has been removed for one reason or another. A dynamic timing check (engine running) can be done with the use of special test equipment.

1. Manually rotate the engine over to place piston 1 at TDC on its compression stroke (both intake and exhaust valve closed). Align the timing mark on the crankshaft front pulley with the stationary pointer timing reference mark on the engine front cover.

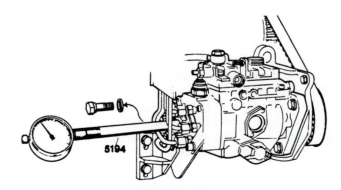

FIGURE 19-79 *Checking VE injection pump plunger lift/timing with dial gauge installed into hydraulic head of pump.*

2. Refer to Figure 19-79 and remove the center bolt from the injection pump hydraulic head along with its sealing washer. A dial indicator adapter is available for use with the particular engine that you are checking to allow the dial gauge to be held in position during the static timing check. One example of the timing gauge adapter is shown in Figure 19-80.

3. The adapter and dial gauge are installed onto the injection pump so that the plunger portion of the adapter projects into the injection pump. This will allow the dial gauge plunger to be in contact with the fuel injection pump plunger when installed. To do this correctly, ensure that the dial gauge shows at least 0.100 in. (2.54 mm) of preload on its face. Note, however, that VW recommends a preload of only 0.040 in. (1 mm), while Volvo on their D24 engine recommends 0.080 in. (2 mm) of gauge preload. The key here is that adequate preload be applied to the dial gauge to ensure that the pump plunger movement as you rotate the engine over during the static timing check will be felt/registered by the dial gauge plunger—otherwise a false reading will be obtained.

4. Manually rotate the engine in its normal direction of rotation until the dial gauge registers its lowest reading, then set the dial gauge to zero by rotating the face bezel to place the needle at zero.

5. Continue to rotate the engine manually in its normal direction of rotation smoothly until piston 1 is at TDC on its compression stroke. Some engine manufacturers supply a TDC aligning pin that is installed through a hole in the block to index with a hole in the flywheel so that the engine cannot be moved during this timing check (one example is the BMW 2.4-L six-cylinder turbocharged engine). If such a device is not available, ensure that either the timing marks between the crankshaft pulley/ damper and stationary timing pointer are in correct alignment or that the flywheel timing marks such as found on the VW and Volvo diesel engines are in alignment.

6. The measurement on the dial gauge face should be noted and compared with the engine manufacturer's specification. For example, if the static timing was given as 1 mm (0.03937 in.), the gauge should register this specification. If it doesn't, the injection pump-to-engine timing needs adjustment.

7. To change the injection pump-to-engine timing, loosen the injection pump housing retaining bolts and move the pump toward the engine if the measurement on the gauge is too small (this will advance the timing); move the pump housing away from the engine if the gauge reading is too large (this will retard the timing).

SPECIAL NOTE What you are actually doing when you move the injection pump toward or away from the engine is adjusting the pump plunger lift from the BDC position to the point of port closure by turning the cam ring away from or toward the rollers.

ADDITIONAL NOTE Certain engine manufacturers supply a special adjusting bracket that can be bolted onto the injection pump housing to facilitate accurate adjustment of the timing. This allows the pump to be held in position as you tighten the retaining bolts.

---

8. A specified tightening sequence is also given by various engine manufacturers to ensure proper seating of the pump-to-engine block.

9. Always rotate the engine over manually at least twice when you have completed your adjustment to double check that the setting is in fact correct. If the setting is incorrect, repeat steps 1 to 8.

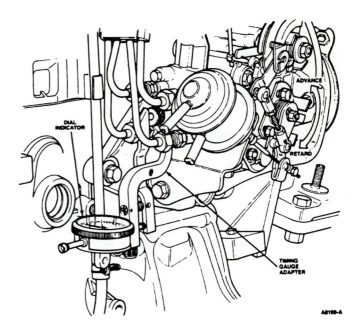

FIGURE 19–80 *Dial gauge and support bracket installed into VE injection pump to check pump to engine timing.*

ROBERT BOSCH VE INJECTION PUMP TROUBLESHOOTING

Problems related to the VE injection pump are basically similar regardless of the type of engine and vehicle that it is installed on. Figure 19-81 lists the typical types of problems that might be encountered on the engine when using a VE injection pump.

When an engine exhibits heavy smoke after a cold start, the cold-start device should be checked by monitoring the engine idle rpm. The cold-start device used with the VE pump is controlled by a wax-type thermostat arrangement shown in Figure 19-76 that responds to engine coolant as it warms up. When the vehicle attains its normal operating temperature, the cold-start device (CSD) does not operate.

Actual testing of the CSD can only be done properly with the injection pump mounted on a test bench (stand). However, a simple test of the CSD can be made on the engine as follows. Engine idle rpm should usually be about 200 rpm higher when the engine is cold compared to when it is at operating temperature. In addition, when the engine is at operating temperature, the cold-start device lever should not contact the lever on the injection pump as shown in Figure 19-76B. On vehicles equipped with an automatic transmission, an emergency stop lever is fitted to the side of the injection pump as shown in Figure 19-68. If the engine fails to shut off when the ignition key is turned OFF, there is a fault with the fuel solenoid located on the injection pump housing.

On a standard transmission equipped vehicle, the engine can be stopped by placing the transmission in gear with the engine idling and with your foot on the brakes, engaging the clutch to stall the engine.

On automatic transmission–equipped vehicles, refer to Figure 19-68, item 20, and pull the emergency stop lever. If the engine fails to start, the cause may well be the fuel solenoid on the injection pump as illustrated in Figure 19-68, (item ELAB) and Figure 19-69. Check the fuel solenoid valve by placing a voltmeter across its terminal and ground. A voltage of less than 10 V will fail to open (energize) this valve, while at least 8 V is required to keep the valve in an open state while the starter motor is cranking the engine.

ELECTRONIC DISTRIBUTOR PUMP

As early as 1985, Robert Bosch Corporation applied electronic controls to its mechanical VE distributor pump. Figure 19-82 illustrates a cross section of an electronically controlled distributor-type pump. As with any electronic system (see details in Chapter 15), a variety of sensors input a signal to an ECU (electronic control unit), which computes an output signal to the pump to manage fuel metering and/or timing. Metering is achieved by an electromagnetic actuator, timing by modulation of internal pump pressure via a solenoid. Figure 19-83 shows the arrangement required for the electronically controlled distributor pump system. To monitor and control the system effectively, the ECU electronic system is shown in graphic form in Figure 19-84. The distributor pump system produces a maximum injection pressure at the nozzles of approximately 1000 bar (14,600 psi) for high-speed automotive engine applications.

System Operation

The ECU receives continuous signals from the various engine sensors, based on changing operating conditions. The ECU then processes these signals and electronically controls the injected fuel quantity, start of injection, time-on of the glow plugs in IDI engine models, and exhaust gas recirculation rate. After initial start of a cold engine, the ECU operates the engine in an open-loop mode until the fuel temperature has reached a certain level. During open-loop mode, the ECU allows the engine to function from a preselected PROM (programmable read-only memory) chip. Switchover to the closed-loop control system occurs only after a given engine speed has been obtained. All sensor signals are now used by the ECU to closely control metering and timing.

Adjustment of the start of injection is determined by the ECU after consulting the input signal from the throttle pedal potentiometer, engine rpm, and intake manifold pressure. The ECU compares the actual start of injection measured by the small nozzle needle-motion sensor shown in Figure 19-85. Timing adjustment is performed within the ECU circuitry by using a clocked solenoid valve to modulate the fuel pressure on the inlet side of the timing-device piston until the start of injection has been reached.

To control exhaust emissions from the engine, an ECU signal to an exhaust gas valve permits graduation of recirculated exhaust gases to mix with the intake air to reduce NO_X (nitrogen oxide) emissions. Signals from an intake manifold airflow sensor to the ECU are used to control the exhaust gas recirculation rate. On turbocharged engine models, the boost pressure sensor signal also indicates to the ECU the percentage of engine load and torque so that timing and metering can be adjusted accordingly. On IDI engine models, glow plug ON time is controlled as a function

It is assumed that the engine is in good working order and properly tuned, and that the electrical system has been checked and repaired if necessary.

Starting Problem	Engine surges at idle	Rough idle when engine is warm	Engine misses under load	Low Power	Excessive Fuel Consumption	Engine cannot be shut off	Poor performance **or** black smoke **or** low power	Fog-like exhaust in full-load range (white or blue)	Incorrect idle or maximum speed	Engine does not rev up	Injection pump runs hot	CAUSE	REMEDY
●		●	●	●			●	●		●		Improper fuel (gasoline) in tank	Drain tank, flush system, fill with proper fuel
●	●		●	●				●		●		Tank empty **or** tank vent blocked	Fill tank/bleed system, check tank vent
●	●	●	●				●	●		●		Air in the fuel system	Bleed fuel system, eliminate air leaks
	●	●										Pump rear support bracket loose	Replace as necessary
●						●						Low voltage, no voltage **or** stop solenoid defective	Correct electrical faults/replace stop solenoid
●			●	●				●		●		Fuel filter blocked	Replace fuel filter
●			●	●			●	●				Injection lines blocked/restricted	Drill to nominal I.D. or replace
●			●	●				●		●		Fuel-supply lines blocked/restricted	Test all fuel supply lines—flush or replace
●			●	●								Loose connections, injection lines leak or broken	Tighten the connection, eliminate the leak
●			●					●		●		Paraffin deposit in fuel filter	Replace filter, use Diesel Fuel no. 1
●			●	●	●		●	●		●		Pump-to-engine timing incorrect	Readjust timing
		●	●	●	●		●					Injection nozzle defective	Repair or replace
				●	●		●					Engine air filter blocked	Replace air filter element
●												Pre-heating system defective	Test the glow plugs, replace as necessary
●		●		●	●		●					Injection sequence does not correspond to firing order	Install fuel injection lines in the correct order
					●				●			Low idle misadjusted	Readjust idle stop screw
				●					●			Maximum speed misadjusted	Readjust maximum speed screw
	●		●	●				●	●	●		Overflow fitting interchanged with inlet fitting	Install fittings in their proper positions
											●	Overflow blocked	Clean the orifice or replace fitting
●										●		Cold-start device not operating	Check bowden cable and lever movement
●		●		●			●			●		Low or uneven engine compression	Repair as necessary
●	●	●	●	●	●		●	●	●	●		Fuel injection pump defective or cannot be adjusted	Replace

FIGURE 19–81 *Troubleshooting guide for diesel fuel injection system with Robert Bosch distributor injection pump VE.*

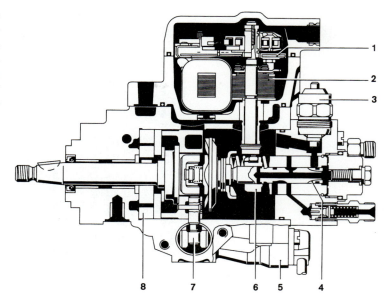

FIGURE 19–82 *Distributor fuel injection pump equipped for electronic diesel control. 1, Control collar position sensor; 2, actuator for fuel metering; 3, electric shutoff (redundant); 4, delivery plunger; 5, solenoid valve for injection timing; 6, control collar; 7, timing device; 8, feed pump.*

of engine operating temperature, speed, and injected fuel quantity in order to reduce HC (hydrocarbon) exhaust emissions shortly after engine startup. The service technician can access the ECU to withdraw stored trouble codes using a hand-held DDR (diagnostic data reader) similar to the one shown in Figure 15-25.

TESTING/SETTING INJECTION PUMPS

Introduction

Details on the testing and overhaul of all types of fuel injection pumps requires more space than can be provided in this textbook, consequently this section will

deal very briefly with the two major settings of a Bosch PLN injection pump, models A, MW and P. Prior to fuel injection pumps leaving the factory, or after a pump overhaul procedure has been performed, it is necessary to mount the injection pump onto a test stand similar to the one shown in Figure 19-86.

SPECIAL NOTE Both injection pump overhaul and the testing and adjustment procedure requires special tools, equipment and knowledge. Fuel injection technician specialists perform these tasks every day, therefore a regular heavy

FIGURE 19–83 *Fuel injection system with electronically controlled distributor fuel injection pump. 1, Fuel tank; 2, fuel filter; 3, VE pump; 4, injection nozzle with needle motion sensor; 5, fuel return line; 6, sheathed element glow plug, glow control unit; 7, shutoff device; 8, solenoid valve; 9, ECU; 10, diagnosis indicator; 11, speed selector lever; 12, accelerator pedal sensor; 13, road speed sensor; 14, temperature sensor (water, air, fuel); 15, EGR valve; 16, airflow sensor; 17, engine speed and TDC sensor; 18, battery; 19, glow plug and starter switch.*

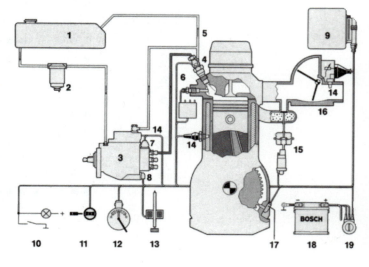

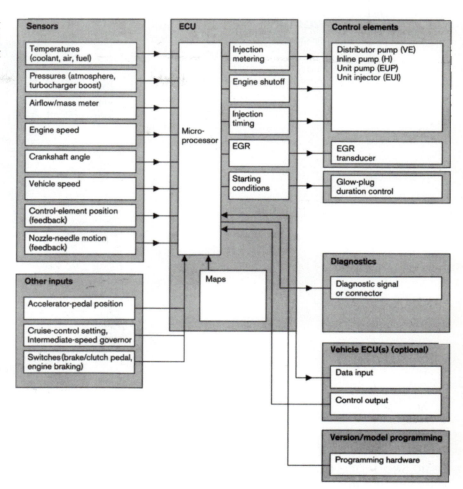

FIGURE 19–84 *Electronic control unit (ECU) operational schematic. (Courtesy of Robert Bosch Corporation.)*

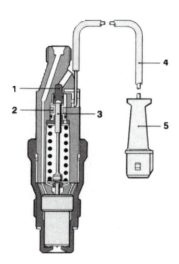

FIGURE 19–85 *Nozzle-and-holder assembly as shown with needle motion sensor (NBF). 1, Adjusting pin; 2, sensor winding; 3, thrust pin; 4, cable; 5, connector. (Courtesy of Robert Bosch Corporation.)*

duty equipment technician, commercial transport technician or diesel engine tech is not expected to perform this type of repair and testing. Local fuel injection specialist repair shops who are generally members of ADS (Association of Diesel Specialists) are best equipped with trained technicians to conduct these types of repairs and adjustments!

CAUTION DO NOT attempt to perform fuel injection pump LTPC (lift-to-port-closure), or calibration adjustments, on any fuel injection pump while it is mounted on the engine. Both injection pump and engine damage can result from untrained personnel performing either one of these adjustments!

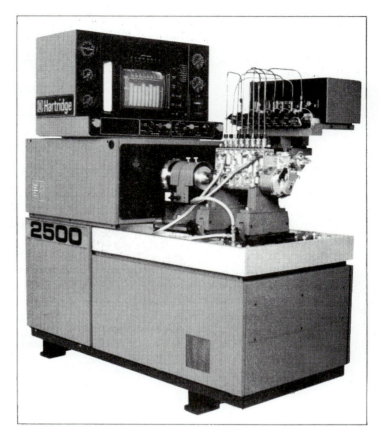

FIGURE 19–86 *Typical fuel injection pump test stand equipped with VDM (video display metering). (Courtesy of Hartridge Equipment Corporation, Virginia Beach, VA.)*

Basic Sequence of Adjustment

The following information is provided to give you a brief overview of the two most important adjustments required on Bosch models A, MW, and P PLN systems.

The two most important checks and settings on a PLN fuel system involves:

Step 1: Timing

Initial pump timing which generally involves adjusting each individual pumping plunger for a specified LTPC (lift to port closure) or prestroke shown in Figure 19-18. This adjustment ensures that as the injection pump camshaft rotates, that the plunger tappet or roller will be lifted at the correct number of degrees BTDC to establish initial injection timing. Adjustment of LTPC will depend upon the model of injection pump being used. For example on a Bosch 'A' model pump, LTPC is achieved by loosening off a tappet locknut, then rotating the adjustment nut CW or CCW to obtain the correct setting. This is illustrated in Figure 19-87. The LTPC dimension can be checked by using the dial indicator shown in Figure 19-88, or in Figure 19-89. The LTPC setting for Bosch

MW and P model pumps requires that split timing shims or one-piece timing shims be added or removed from below the pumping plunger barrel flange. These shims can be seen in Figure 19-90.

For example on a six-cylinder PLN system, the service technician would first begin by setting No. 1 pumping plunger LTPC. This can be achieved by using either a dial indicator mounted as shown in Figure 19-88 that is also equipped with a goose-neck (short bent fuel line), or a goose neck line alone mounted on top of the pumping plunger delivery valve holder. High pressure test stand fuel can be used; if low pressure fuel is employed you need to remove the pumping plunger delivery valve spring. This test illustrated in Figure 19-91 allows the technician to determine when LTPC has occurred, since the fuel will stop flowing from the end of the drip spout or goose neck line. Note in Figure 19-91 that in this particular pump example, shims within the tappet can be added or removed to achieve the correct LTPC dimension. Once this has been performed, the technician would manually rotate and then align a degree wheel mounted on the test stand and attached to the injection pump camshaft drive to the

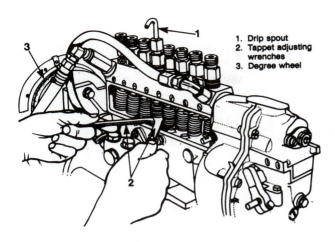

FIGURE 19–87 *Adjusting the tappet setting to correct for lift to port closure on a Bosch model A inline pump. (Courtesy of Robert Bosch Corporation.)*

1. Drip spout
2. Tappet adjusting wrenches
3. Degree wheel

FIGURE 19–89 *Injection pump plunger stroke measuring tool installed on the No. 1 pump plunger to determine plunger bumping clearance. (Courtesy of Diesel Kiki USA Co. Ltd.)*

"zero degrees" position. The degree wheel can be seen in Figure 19-88 on the lower right-hand side, where a small bar is used to rotate the degree wheel CW or CCW as desired. The remaining pumping plungers LTPC on a six-cylinder pump would then be set at succeeding 60 degree intervals; for example with a firing order of 1-5-3-6-2-4, number 5 would be set for LTPC at 60 degrees; 3 at 120 degrees; 6 at 180 degrees; 2 at 240 degrees; 4 at 300 degrees, which would then bring us back to 360 or zero degrees for No. 1. This process is commonly referred to

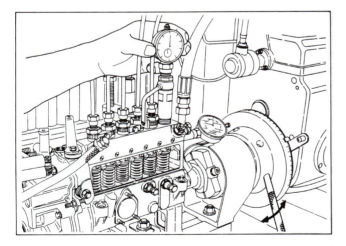

FIGURE 19–88 *Mounting a dial indicator onto the injection pump to measure the pump plunger lift. (Courtesy of Diesel Kiki USA Co. Ltd.)*

as "phasing." A four-cylinder pump would be set at 90 degree intervals.

Step 2: Calibration

Calibration of each pumping plunger is done to ensure that every cylinder receives the same quantity of metered and delivered fuel by lengthening or shortening the pump plungers effective stroke. This is obtained by loosening off the injection pump rack lock collar screw (see Figure 19-21) for 'A' model pumps, and then physically rotating this small collar by inserting a small pin punch into the holes drilled around the rack collar as shown in Figure 19-92. To change the fuel setting on both MW and P model Bosch pumps requires that the technician loosen off the barrel locating screws and then turn the barrel flange CW or CCW to obtain the desired fuel delivery. See Figure 19-93. Each pump manufacturer lists the allowable tolerance between cylinders in fuel delivery CC's while running the pump on the test stand over a specified number of strokes (typically 1000), with the fuel control rack set for a specified amount of travel. The rack travel is checked with the use of a dial gauge shown in Figure 19-88 and Figure 19-89 located on the side of the injection pump closest to the test stand drive end. Always refer to the pump Test Specification sheet for all dimensions and settings.

There are a variety of other injection pump and governor adjustments that must be performed on the test stand, however, space within this textbook does not permit us going into detail on how to perform

1. Delivery Valve Holder
2. Fill Piece
3. Delivery Valve Spring
4. Delivery Valve
5. Delivery Valve Gasket
6. Timing Shims
7. Spacer
8. O-rings
9. Delivery Valve Body
10. Flange Bushing
11. Barrel
12. Baffle Ring
13. Plunger
14. O-rings
15. Control Rack
16. Upper Spring Seat
17. Control Sleeve
18. Plunger Vane
19. Plunger Spring
20. Lower Spring Seat
21. Plunger Foot
22. Roller Tappet
23. Camshaft
24. Bearing End Plate
25. End Play Shim
26. O-ring
27. Bearing

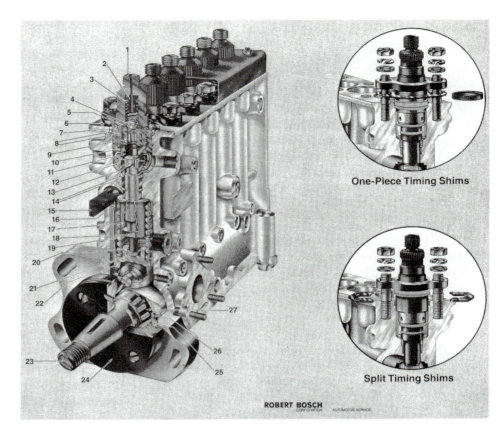

FIGURE 19–90 *Model P injection pump one-piece and split-timing shims concept used to alter lift to port closure. (Courtesy of Robert Bosch Corporation.)*

these. Have your instructor cover this with you, or arrange a tour of a local fuel injection repair shop for more details.

SUMMARY

With fully half of PLN fuel injection systems being of Bosch manufacture, this chapter has prepared you to understand the various models of Bosch fuel pumps; how to service, maintain, adjust, diagnose and troubleshoot these different models; and to appreciate the detailed function and purpose of a correctly adjusted and operating high pressure fuel system.

SELF-TEST QUESTIONS

1. The first successfully mass-produced diesel fuel injection pump system as we know it today was developed by
   a. Thomas Edison in 1886
   b. Rudolph Diesel in 1892
   c. Robert Bosch in 1927
   d. Charles A. Vandervell in 1938
2. Technician A says that only the model MW and P Bosch injection pumps are used on truck applications. Technician B disagrees, saying that the A model pump is also widely used. Who is right?
3. Technician A says that the letters PE in reference to a Bosch pump stand for "pump engine." Technician B says that they stand for "pump with an enclosed camshaft." Who is correct?
4. Technician A says that the letter S in a pump model, such as PES, means that the injection pump can either be base mounted or bolted to a cradle on the engine. Technician B says that the letter S in a pump ID implies that the pump is flange mounted. Who is right?
5. The four basic models of Bosch inline multiple-plunger pumps used in automotive or truck applications are the
   a. A, PE, S, and P
   b. M, A, MW, and P
   c. MW, PE, PES, and CW
   d. A, B, S, and MW

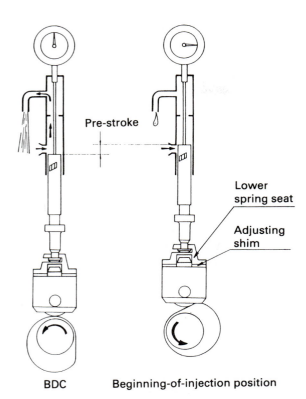

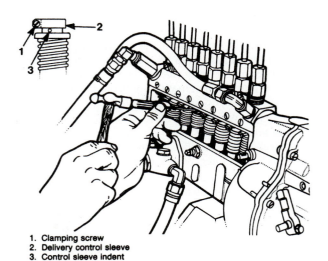

1. Clamping screw
2. Delivery control sleeve
3. Control sleeve indent

FIGURE 19–92 *Procedure used to adjust each pumping plunger for the same fuel delivery rate. (Courtesy of Robert Bosch Corporation.)*

BDC   Beginning-of-injection position

FIGURE 19–91 *Noting position where fuel flow stops and recording dial indicator reading. (Courtesy of Diesel Kiki USA Co. Ltd.)*

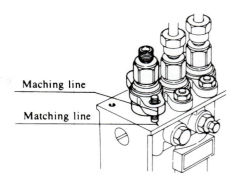

FIGURE 19–93 *Aligning the plunger block (barrel and flange assembly) to the injection pump housing. (Courtesy of Diesel Kiki USA Co. Ltd.)*

6. A P-size inline pump that is base mounted would be identified by the model coding
   a. PES4A
   b. PFR6A
   c. PF5R
   d. PE6P

7. Technician A says that the largest inline Bosch pump used in truck applications is the model P. Technician B disagrees, saying that it is the model PE. Who is correct?

8. Technician A says that the pump plunger lift in all Bosch inline pump models is determined by the pump camshaft. Technician B disagrees and says that the engine camshaft drives the pump and determines the plunger lift. Who is correct?

9. The term *prestroke* means
   a. The plunger stroke needed to supply excess fuel for startup
   b. The amount of lift required to reach port closure
   c. The amount of plunger rotation required to expose the retard notch for a cold-start condition
   d. The small lift designed into the camshaft for initial injection

10. Technician A says that fuel delivery begins when the plunger starts its lift. Technician B disagrees, saying that fuel delivery can begin only at port closure. Who is correct?

11. Technician A says that the amount of fuel delivered to the injectors can be altered by changing the effective stroke of the plunger. Technician B says that to do this, you would have to alter the camshaft lift. Who is correct?

12. Technician A says that in Bosch inline multiple-plunger pumps, injection ends when the barrel inlet port is uncovered. Technician B says that fuel injection ends when the pressure is relieved through the fuel return line. Who is right?

13. Technician A says that the fuel feed pump delivers fuel to the injectors. Technician B says that this is incorrect—

that the fuel feed pump simply transfers fuel at low pressure to the injection pump. Who is right?

14. Technician A says that the basic function of the injection pump is to pressurize and deliver fuel to the injectors. Technician B says that the pump pressurizes, times, and meters fuel to the injectors. Who is correct in his statement?

15. Technician A says that the term *phasing* is the term used to describe port closing at correct intervals by all pump plungers. Technician B says that it means equal delivery of fuel to all injectors. Who is correct here?

16. Technician A says that fuel metering depends on the speed of the engine and the camshaft lift. Technician B says that metering depends on the effective stroke of the plunger. Who is right?

17. Technician A says that with an upper helix plunger, prestroke is shorter to port closure. Not so, says Technician B; prestroke would be longer to port closure. Who is correct?

18. Technician A says that fuel delivery on a Bosch A model pump is balanced by adjusting the position of each control sleeve. Technician B says that fuel delivery is balanced by adjustment of the plunger lift. Who is right?

19. Technician A says that pump plunger prestroke on an A model pump is adjusted by installing tappet rollers of different diameters. Technician B says that a tappet adjustment screw is used for this purpose. Who knows the correct procedure?

20. Technician A says that pump plunger prestroke on the MW and P model pumps is done by rotating the barrel flange on top of the injection pump housing. Technician B says that it is obtained by removing or inserting shims underneath the barrel flange. Who is aware of the correct procedure here?

21. Technician A says that the MW pump is similar to construction and adjustment to the P model pump. Technician B says that the MW and A model pumps are basically the same. Who knows his or her Bosch pumps in this instance?

22. The P-8500 model injection pump is capable of injection pressures as high as
    a. 15,300 psi (1054 bar)
    b. 16,400 psi (1129 bar)
    c. 17,400 psi (1200 bar)
    d. 19,515 psi (1350 bar)

23. The two major checks and adjustments on an inline multiple-plunger fuel injection pump are
    a. phasing and calibration
    b. phasing and maximum speed adjustment
    c. calibration and governor overrun
    d. low- and high-speed fuel delivery rates

24. Technician A says that to alter the fuel delivery rate on Bosch model MW and P pumps, the barrel flange retaining nuts must be loosened and the barrel rotated either CW or CCW to suit. Technician B says that to change the fuel delivery rate, the rack flange collar screw must be loosened and the collar rotated. Who knows the correct procedure here?

25. Technician A says that when lift to port closure is done on a pump mounted on a test stand, to determine the degrees between individual cylinders, you simply divide 360° by the number of cylinders. Technician B says that regardless of the number of cylinders used, they are always set 60° apart. Who is correct?

26. Technician A says that when setting a pump for lift to port closure on a test stand, you should follow the firing-order sequence for best results. Technician B says that you can simply start with number 1 and proceed systematically through each additional cylinder number, such as 1–2–3–4–5–6. Who is correct?

27. Technician A says that the effective stroke of the pumping plunger is simply the lift from BDC to TDC established by the pump camshaft. Technician B says that effective stroke is the period of time during which the fuel inlet ports in the barrel are closed. Who is right?

28. Technician A says that the maximum amount of fuel rack movement is set by installing an adjustable fuel rod stop mechanism in the end of the fuel injection pump housing. Technician B says that rack movement is controlled by the governor. Who is right?

29. Technician A says that the delivery valve is located inside the injector, while Technician B says that it is located above the plunger and barrel within the injection pump. Who is correct?

30. Technician A says that the function of a delivery valve is to allow relief of the high fuel pressure in the fuel line at the end of injection. Technician B says that the delivery valve prevents a loss of fuel line prime between injection periods. Who is right?

31. Technician A says that a rough idle when the engine is warm could be caused by a leaking delivery valve. Technician B says that a rough idle could be caused by air in the fuel system. Who is right?

32. Technician A says that if the engine surges at idle, it could be caused by air in the fuel system or a misadjusted bumper spring. Technician B says that it could be due to pump-to-engine timing being incorrect. Who is the most analytical here?

33. Technician A says that failure of the engine to accelerate from an idle speed could be due to a defective timing device. Technician B says that it could be due to a plugged fuel filter. Who is right?

34. Technician A says that a low-power problem could be associated with a leaking delivery valve. Technician B says it is more likely to be a plugged fuel filter or loose connections in the fuel lines. Who is right?

35. Technician A says that an overheating injection pump can be caused by a defective or blocked overflow valve. Technician B says that the problem is a defective pump and that the pump should be removed for inspection. Who is correct?

36. Technician A says that poor engine performance, associated with low power and black smoke at the exhaust,

can be attributed to a plugged engine air filter. Technician B says that the cause could be a defective injection nozzle. Who is correct?

37. Technician A says that white smoke at the exhaust under full load can be caused by incorrect pump-to-engine timing. Technician B says that the cause is more likely to be air in the fuel system. Who is right?

38. Technician A says that excessive fuel consumption can be caused by incorrect pump-to-engine timing. Technician B says that a plugged fuel filter is more likely to be the cause. Who is right?

39. Technician A says that low or uneven cylinder compression can cause white smoke under load, whereas technician B says that low compression would cause black smoke and a lack of power. Who is right?

40. Technician A says that failure of the engine to shut off can be caused by a misadjusted or defective governor, whereas Technician B says that it can only be caused by a defective shutoff/start device. Who is right?

41. Technician A says that the best method to employ to check injection pump to engine timing is to spill-time it. Technician B says that it is best first to remove the pump and check the timing marks on the engine gear train to pump drive. Who is correct?

42. Technician A says that a Bosch RS governor is a minimum/maximum unit, whereas technician B says that it is a variable-speed design. Who is right?

43. Technician A says that mechanical governors use the force of springs to increase fuel delivery. Technician B says that this is achieved by the centrifugal force developed by the rotating governor flyweights. Who is correct?

44. Technician A says that the greatest amount of fuel is delivered during initial startup. Technician B disagrees, saying that the greatest fuel delivery occurs at the full-load speed. Who is correct?

45. Technician A says that in Bosch governors at breakaway, high-speed regulation pulls the rack to prevent engine stalling. Technician B says that breakaway prevents overspeed. Who is correct?

46. Technician A says that in an RQV-K governor, breakaway can occur at full load or part load. Technician B says that breakaway can occur only under a no-load condition. Who is correct?

47. In an RSV governor model at idle speed, the flyweights force the tensioning lever against the
    a. torque spring
    b. shutoff lever
    c. high-speed spring
    d. bumper spring

48. Technician A says that in an RSV governor, torque control increases rack travel with an increase in engine speed. Technician B disagrees, saying that rack travel is decreased. Who is right?

49. In an RSV governor model, adjusting the rocker screw on the swivel lever changes the tension on the

    a. bumper spring
    b. torque spring
    c. idle spring
    d. main spring

50. True or False: The torque spring adjustment in any governor is designed to tailor the horsepower setting of the engine between no-load and full-load rpm.

51. True or False: The function of the starting spring in Bosch governors is to assist the slow rotative speed of the flyweights to move the rack into a decreased fuel position to prevent overfueling.

52. Technician A says that the springs in an RQV governor model are contained inside the weight assemblies. Technician B says that he is confused—that it is the RS/RSV models which have this feature. Who is right?

53. RQV governor full load is limited by a
    a. mechanical stop
    b. boost/aneroid control
    c. torque spring
    d. fulcrum lever

54. Technician A says that in an RQV-K governor, there are three springs used for speed regulation. Technician B says that there are only two. Who is correct?

55. Technician A says that in an RQV-K governor, low-speed regulation is adjusted by changing shims. Technician B says that this is done by a screw adjustment. Who is correct?

56. In an RQV-K governor model, as the engine approaches full power, the rocker reduces rack travel according to the shape of the
    a. torque cam
    b. engine cam
    c. automatic timing device
    d. full-load stop bolt

57. In an RQV-K governor model, the spindle screw adjustment moves the torque cam in a straight line and also affects
    a. no-load rack travel
    b. full-load rack travel
    c. the torque curve rpm point
    d. breakaway

58. In an RQV-K governor, the torque cam can be adjusted by the spindle screw and the
    a. slope screw
    b. link screw
    c. low-idle screw
    d. high-idle screw

59. In an RQV governor model technician A says that turning the torque control spring screw changes how much torque control is applied. Technician B disagrees, saying that this adjustment determines "when" and not "how much" torque control is applied. Who is correct?

60. The aneroid boost compensator control used on some Bosch injection pumps/governors is connected to the
    a. cold-start device
    b. turbocharger/intake manifold line

c. altitude-sensing device

d. overspeed governor linkage

61. Technician A says that a pintle nozzle delivers a star-shaped spray pattern into the combustion chamber. Technician B says that a pintle nozzle is used on pre-combustion-chamber engines and exhibits a narrow spray pattern. Who is right?

62. Nozzles that produce wide spray angles and are used in direct injection engines are commonly known as
   a. pintle nozzles
   b. throttle pintle nozzles
   c. pintaux nozzles
   d. multiple-hole nozzles

63. For fuel to be injected into the combustion chamber, the high-pressure fuel from the injection pump must
   a. lift the spring-loaded needle valve inside the injector
   b. lift the delivery valve inside the injector
   c. lift the safety check valve inside the top of the plunger and barrel

64. At the end of the injection period, fuel dribble into the combustion chamber is minimized by
   a. the action of the delivery valve in the injection pump
   b. the needle valve snapping shut by spring pressure inside the injector
   c. plunger fuel spilling into the pump housing
   d. high-pressure fuel being rerouted back to the fuel tank

65. Technician A says that nozzle opening pressure is determined by the fuel pressure and rate of rise from the injection pump. Technician B says that it is determined by altering the spring force inside the injector. Who is right?

66. Technician A says that nozzle problems that create overfueling can cause black smoke. Technician B says that this will cause white smoke. Who is correct?

67. Technician A says that white smoke can be caused by nozzle problems which cause incomplete combustion. Technician B says that water in the combustion chamber will cause white smoke. Who is correct?

68. True or False: When checking the individual condition of the nozzles while still in a running engine, if you loosen a high-pressure fuel line to an injector and there is no change to the engine speed/sound, the injector is good.

69. Loose carbon around the nozzle tip can be removed with
   a. a steel wire bristle hand brush
   b. a brass bristle brush
   c. a powered bench grinder wire brush
   d. glass beading

70. Overtorquing an injector may cause
   a. the nozzle needle to bend
   b. leakage at the copper washer in the nozzle/cylinder head bore

c. cracking of the hold-down flange

d. binding of the fuel rack

71. Prior to disassembling an injector and loosening the nozzle nut, you should
   a. drain all fuel from the injector
   b. soak the nut in penetrating oil
   c. glass bead the assembly
   d. release the adjusting spring pressure screw

72. Technician A says that the nozzle body and needle valve can be purchased only as a matched set. Technician B says that it does not matter as long as the needle is free in the body. Who is right?

73. Technician A says that sealing of the component parts within the injector against high-pressure fuel leakage is obtained by lapping the parts together. Technician B says that O-ring seals are used for this purpose. Who is correct here?

74. True or False: Nozzle parts should always be assembled after they have been dipped in either clean test oil or clean diesel fuel.

75. Technician A says that if an injector is suspected of being faulty after testing it in the engine by opening the high-pressure line, it should be replaced. Technician B says that the injector should be checked in a pop tester first to determine its spray pattern and opening pressure. Who is correct?

76. Technician A says that injector sac volume is the small amount of fuel that is left below the needle valve after injection. Technician B says that sac volume is the amount of fuel metered and injected into the combustion chamber. Who is right?

77. On a separate piece of paper, list the four basic checks and tests that you would perform on an injector/nozzle to determine its suitability for reuse.

78. The best method used to clean nozzle parts is to employ
   a. a wire brush
   b. lapping blocks
   c. ultrasonic cleaning
   d. a brass bristle brush

79. Technician A says that a fuel system vacuum restriction check can be performed by installing a fuel pressure gauge into the secondary fuel filter assembly. Technician B says that you should use a mercury manometer or a vacuum gauge teed into the system between the fuel tank and fuel transfer pump for this test. Who is correct?

80. Port closing of the injection pump is accomplished by tappet screw adjustment on the
   a. M pump
   b. A pump
   c. MW pump
   d. P pump

81. Port closing of the injection pump is accomplished by shim adjustment on the
   a. M pump
   b. A pump

c. MW pump

d. P pump

82. Calibration on an injection pump is accomplished by loosening the bolted flange and rotating the bushing on the
    a. M pump
    b. A pump
    c. MW pump
    d. P pump

83. Technician A says that prior to removing the fuel injection pump from the engine you should align the FB (fuel begins) timing mark on the crankshaft damper and marked tooth on the injection pump drive gear. Technician B says that you should align the FB mark with the stationary pointer on the front timing gear cover. Who is right?

84. Technician A says that a spill-timing check is used to determine exactly when port closure occurs in the No. 1 pumping unit. Technician B says that spill timing determines the metering position of the rack. Who is correct?

85. Technician A says that it requires approximately 25 to 30 psi (172 to 207 kPa) of fuel pressure to lift the delivery valve from its seat in the injection pump. Technician B says that it is much higher, being about 150 psi (1034 kPa). Who is right?

86. Technician A says that manipulation of the fuel transfer pump priming handle can be used to create high-enough pressure to lift the delivery valve from its seat when spill timing. Technician B disagrees, saying that a special spill timing kit pump is required. Who is right?

87. Technician A says that the two common methods used to spill-time an injection pump to the engine is by removing the delivery valve from its holder or by using a high pressure pump kit. Technician B says that only a high-pressure pump kit can be used. Who knows the correct procedure?

88. Technician A says that to determine if cylinder 1 is at TDC on its compression stroke, you can check to see if both the intake and exhaust valve rocker arm have clearance. Technician B says that only the exhaust valve should have clearance; otherwise, you have cylinder 6 at TDC. Who is right?

89. Technician A says that when performing a spill timing check you should always rotate the engine CW from the front at least 90° to remove all gear backlash, then slowly, without jerking, rotate it CCW to align the FB mark with the stationary pointer. Technician B says that he agrees with the procedure, except that the engine should be rotated CCW from the front first, followed by CW rotation to align the timing marks. Who is right?

90. Technician A says that generally when the fuel injection pump is pushed toward the engine block, the timing will be advanced. Technician B says that it will be retarded. Who knows the basic theory here?

91. Technician A says that typical mechanical timing advance units employed on Bosch fuel injection pumps operate on the principle of weight advance. Technician B says that they operate on a spring advance principle. Who is right?

92. Technician A says that a timing advance unit that fails to operate would result in early injection and white smoke, whereas Technician B says that it would result in late injection, sluggish performance, and black smoke at the exhaust stack. Who is correct?

93. Technician A says that a timing advance unit stuck in the full advance position would result in early fuel injection at the lower engine speeds, associated with severe combustion knock and a tendency for white smoke. Technician B disagrees, saying that there would simply be a lack of power and excessive fuel consumption. Who is correct?

94. Technician A says that on any Bosch fuel injection pump, after reinstalling the pump onto the engine, it is not necessary to fill the pump housing with clean engine lube oil, due to the fact that it is pressure lubricated from the engine. Technician B disagrees, saying that the pumps used on Mercedes-Benz trucks should have $\frac{1}{2}$ quart of engine oil added to them. Who is right?

95. Technician A says that on Bosch injection pumps that employ a pressure relief valve on the pump housing, bleeding of the fuel system becomes unnecessary, due to the fact that the valve will open and expel all air from the system back to the fuel tank. Technician B disagrees, saying that you must bleed all air from the fuel system by opening the individual bleeder screws on the secondary fuel filter(s) and injection pump as well as the individual high-pressure fuel lines at each injector. Who is right?

96. Technician A says that it is acceptable to intermix or trade injector nozzles between different engines since they are of the same basic design. Technician B says that nozzles should never be intermixed between engines because of the difference in release settings and nozzle tips. Who is correct?

97. Technician A says that nozzle release pressures for injectors used in trucks are adjusted by adding or subtracting shims. Technician B says that they are adjusted by screw adjustment. Who is right?

98. Technician A says that you should never apply direct steam cleaner pressure to the injection pump housing, particularly when the engine is running; otherwise, serious damage can occur to the internal components. Technician B says that this is not true—that applying steam cleaner pressure would have no effect on the pump. Who is correct?

99. Technician A says that you should always check the thickness of the copper washer that is used below the injector in the cylinder head with a micrometer to ensure that the correct one is used. Technician B says that this is not necessary since these washers are stock units and are of the same thickness. Who is correct?

100. Technician A says that when installing a nozzle sleeve into the cylinder head, you should coat the inside diameter of the O-ring with silicone grease. Technician B says that you should use Permatex sealant instead. Who is right?

101. True or False: When removing injector high-pressure fuel lines, you must hold the line with a wrench above the cylinder head while you loosen the flare nut and locknuts.

102. Technician A says that the injection pump-to-engine timing specification can be found on the exhaust emission label attached to the engine. Technician B says that this contains only basic engine information and that you have to refer to the service manual. Who is correct?

103. Technician A says that when checking the static injection pump-to-engine timing specification, you have to employ a portable high-pressure port closing timer tool. Technician B says that you should use a low-air-pressure port closing method tool. Who is right?

Mack Electronic Fuel Systems

OVERVIEW

Mack Trucks, Inc., is a major user of Robert Bosch fuel injection pumps and governors on its engines. Although Robert Bosch fuel systems were discussed in Chapter 19, information in this chapter is specific to Mack diesel engines. Mack employs an electronically controlled fuel injection system commonly referred to as VMAC (Vehicle Management and Control). A study of the data here will help you understand how the system functions and operates, how to remove and install the pump, perform a timing adjustment, and how to systematically employ special diagnostic tooling and a laptop computer to effectively troubleshoot and maintain the system.

SYSTEM STRUCTURE AND FUNCTION

Mack's E6 and E7 engine models are inline six-cylinder units available with either nonelectronic fuel systems or in later versions a system known by the acronym V-MAC (vehicle management and control). This system is offered on the CH/CL, MH, RW, RB, and RD chassis models.

The E7 engine models at this time are rated at 325, 375, 400, 427, and 454 hp (242, 280, 298, 318, and 339 kW). Early-model V-MAC engines used a Robert Bosch Corporation P7100 injection pump capable of nozzle side injection pressures of 1250 bar (18,125 psi). Later-model V-MAC systems employ a Bosch P8500 injection pump capable of nozzle side injection pressures of 1350 bar (19,575 psi). A number of other engine-component-part enhancements were made to the 1994 and later E7 engines to improve performance, exhaust emissions, and fuel economy.

Details on the Robert Bosch EDC (electronic diesel control) system are given in Chapter 19. However, the V-MAC system using the P8500 injection pump differs from the EDC system in that it does not use a plunger and barrel assembly with a control sleeve. The V-MAC P8500 injection pump is similar to current production pumps using mechanical governors and is located on the right side of the engine. On the V-MAC pump, the mechanical governor is replaced by an actuator assembly. Therefore, operation of this system is somewhat similar to the Caterpillar 3406 PEEC fuel system which was used on 3406B and C models prior to the introduction of the EUI (electronic unit injector) on the 3406E engine model.

Figure 20-1 illustrates a schematic of the V-MAC system and components that utilizes two microprocessors: the V-MAC module supplied to Mack by Motorola, and a fuel injection control module manufactured by Robert Bosch Corporation. A variety of engine and vehicle sensors relay operating parameters and changing conditions to the microprocessors. Figure 20-2 illustrates the fuel injection control (FIC) and V-MAC module sensor inputs and outputs. The V-MAC module and the FIC module are both mounted on a panel underneath the vehicle dashboard in front of the passenger seat as shown in Figure 20-3. Access to both control modules is easily achieved by removing the panel retaining screws and carefully dropping the panel toward the passenger seat. Figure 20-4 identifies the V-MAC module as item 1; item 2 is the fuel injection control (FIC) module.

Performance Advantages
The V-MAC electronic system gives the driver more control over the engine's power, improves fuel economy, and is generally more reliable than the mechanical system.

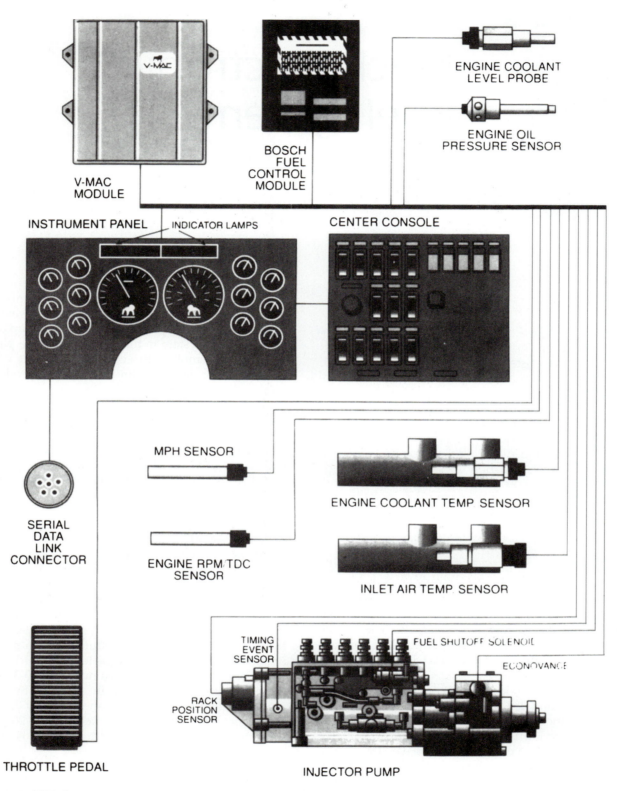

FIGURE 20–1 Schematic of V-MAC system components. (Courtesy of Mack Trucks, Inc.)

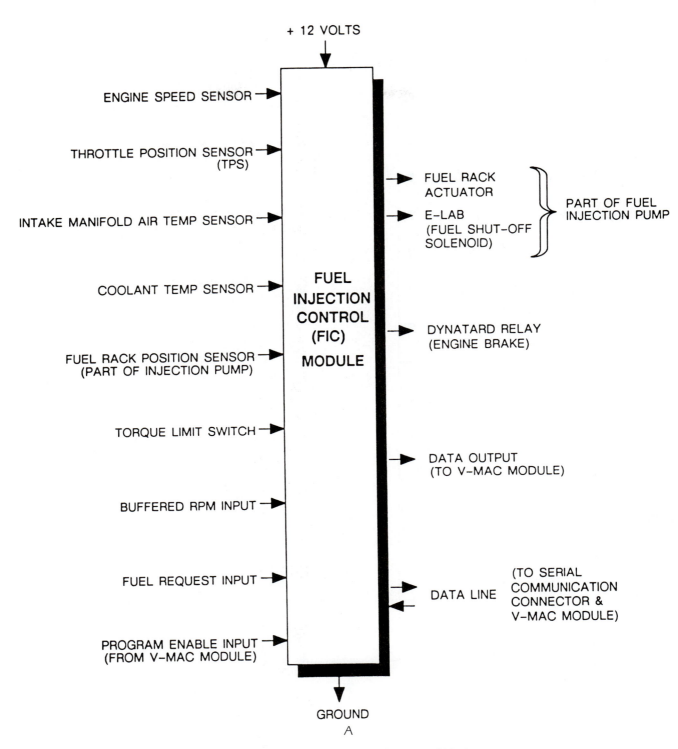

+ 12 VOLTS

ENGINE SPEED SENSOR →

THROTTLE POSITION SENSOR →
(TPS)

INTAKE MANIFOLD AIR TEMP SENSOR →

COOLANT TEMP SENSOR →

FUEL RACK POSITION SENSOR →
(PART OF INJECTION PUMP)

TORQUE LIMIT SWITCH →

BUFFERED RPM INPUT →

FUEL REQUEST INPUT →

PROGRAM ENABLE INPUT →
(FROM V-MAC MODULE)

FUEL
INJECTION
CONTROL
(FIC)
MODULE

→ FUEL RACK
ACTUATOR

→ E-LAB
(FUEL SHUT-OFF
SOLENOID)

PART OF FUEL
INJECTION PUMP

→ DYNATARD RELAY
(ENGINE BRAKE)

→ DATA OUTPUT
(TO V-MAC MODULE)

→ DATA LINE
←

(TO SERIAL
COMMUNICATION
CONNECTOR &
V-MAC MODULE)

GROUND
A

FIGURE 20–2 FIC and V-MAC module (A) inputs and (B) output. (Courtesy of Mack Trucks, Inc.)

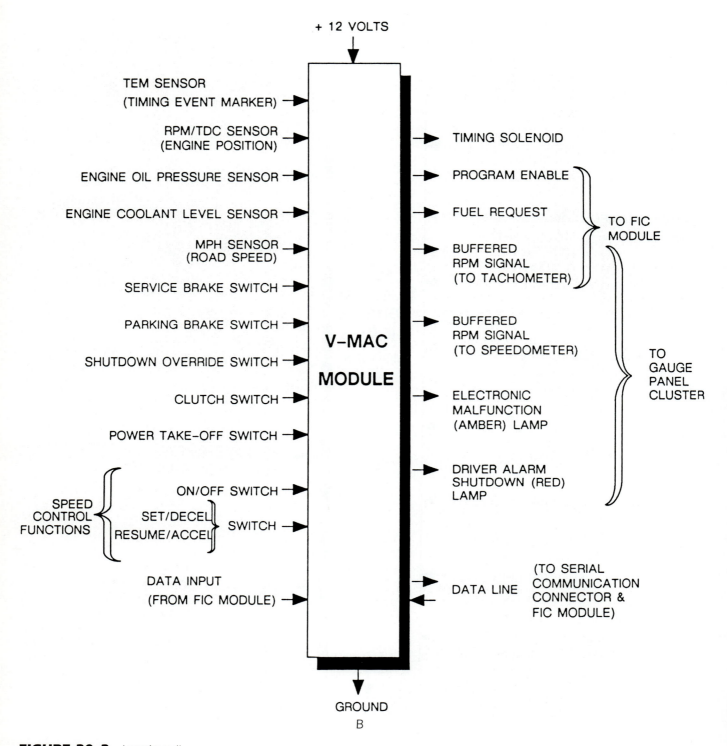

FIGURE 20–2 *(continued)*

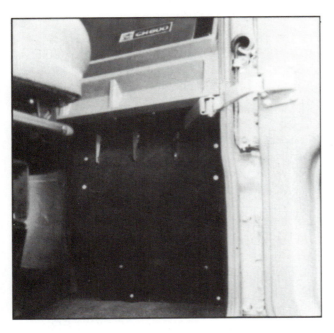

FIGURE 20–3 Location of V-MAC and fuel injection control (FIC) modules.

1. *Exhaust emission control.* The V-MAC system can control exhaust emissions with a much greater degree of accuracy than a mechanically-controlled system. The V-MAC module and FIC module work together to regulate fuel delivery and timing, which makes the engine run very clean and efficiently.

FIGURE 20–4 V-MAC module and fuel injection control (FIC) module.

2. *Road speed limiting.* To aid in increasing fuel economy the V-MAC system regulates top truck speed to a preset limit.

3. *Cruise control.* Controlled by the driver to any speed under the vehicle's preset road speed, the cruise control reduces driver fatigue and maintains a steady speed.

4. *Engine braking.* The V-MAC system will operate the Mack brake system Dynatard in conjunction with cruise control.

5. *PTO speed control.* The PTO speeds can be set by the driver by utilizing the cruise control switches. Two options are available: variable PTO speed control, which can be used to set PTO speeds at a point within predetermined limits, and single-speed PTO, which is preset to one speed.

6. *Low idle speed adjustment.* This can be programmed to provide an engine low idle speed of 500 to 750 rpm.

7. *Idle shutdown.* Designed to save fuel and reduce engine wear, the idle shutdown feature is designed to shut the engine off after a sufficient cool down period and can be programmed to fit the owner's requirements.

8. *Engine protection and self-diagnostics.* The system constantly monitors the engine oil pressure, coolant temperature, and coolant level. If a predetermined limit is reached by any one of these items the driver is warned by an amber light, which indicates an electronic malfunction, or by the red shutdown light, which indicates a problem exists that will shut down the engine.

When the engine is started, the system goes through a self-check and checks all lamps and sensors. If no faults exist in the system at this time, all lights will go out. If the self-test detects an active code, one of the lamps will stay lit. The system can be checked for active faults by using switches on the instrument panel.

Inactive faults can be detected by using the Pro-Link 9000, a hand-held tool which is connected to the truck's serial data link connector (see Figure 21-52). The 9000 can also be used to obtain access to V-MAC settings that require passwords.

9. *Engine warm-up.* Used to replace the hand throttle, the variable-speed control may be used to run the engine faster during warm-up.

V-MAC SYSTEM COMPONENTS

1. *Injection Pump.* Figure 20-5 illustrates a cross section of the Bosch P8500 injection pump used with later-model V-MAC systems. The pump camshaft lift of 14 mm (0.551 in.) provides higher injection rates for

FIGURE 20–5 *Main features of a Bosch P8500 PLN injection pump. (Courtesy of Robert Bosch Corporation).*

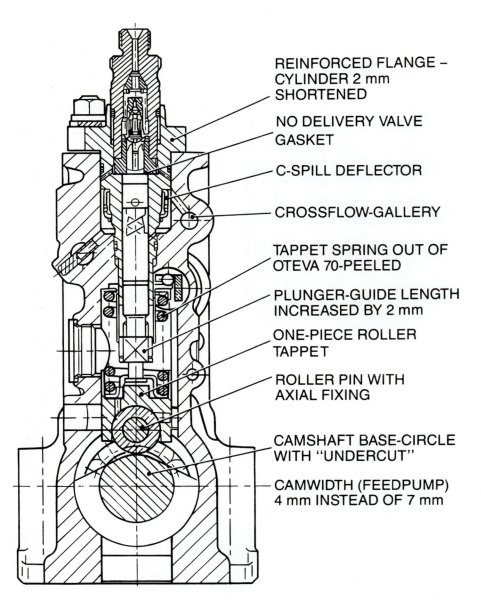

REINFORCED FLANGE – CYLINDER 2 mm SHORTENED

NO DELIVERY VALVE GASKET

C-SPILL DEFLECTOR

CROSSFLOW-GALLERY

TAPPET SPRING OUT OF OTEVA 70-PEELED

PLUNGER-GUIDE LENGTH INCREASED BY 2 mm

ONE-PIECE ROLLER TAPPET

ROLLER PIN WITH AXIAL FIXING

CAMSHAFT BASE-CIRCLE WITH "UNDERCUT"

CAMWIDTH (FEEDPUMP) 4 mm INSTEAD OF 7 mm

improved emissions and economy, as well as increased fuel delivery for a higher power capability. The pump camshaft base-circle geometry changes results in improved plunger lift velocity with higher injection pressures.

2. *V-MAC module.* The V-MAC electronic module shown as item 1 in Figure 20-4 provides control output for timing and speed control. In addition, it functions to monitor and log diagnostic fault codes and password processing for both the V-MAC and FIC module.

3. *Fuel injection control module (FIC).* The FIC module shown as item 2 in Figure 20-4 actually contains two microprocessors that function to control high-speed tasks such as injection pump fuel rack po-

sitioning as well as an rpm pulse reading. From these functions this subsystem can supply the basic control for the quantity of fuel being injected into the engine combustion chambers.

4. *Fuel rack actuator (FRA).* The fuel rack actuator (FRA) shown as item 1 in Figure 20-6 is located on the rear of the P8500 injection pump. The FRA employs an electric proportional solenoid used to provide a rack position force opposed by a return spring. The FRA solenoid position therefore directly controls the injection pump fuel rack position. An increase in current to the solenoid from the FIC module will move the rack to a higher fuel setting, while a decrease in current will move the rack to a lower fuel delivery setting. Anytime that electric power is removed from the FRA, the

FIGURE 20–6 Fuel rack actuator.

FIGURE 20–7 Fuel shutoff solenoid (ELAB).

return spring will move the rack to a fuel shutoff position. In addition, the FRA employs a rack position sensor to relay information to the FIC module so that it can control fuel delivery under all operating conditions. One other sensor is used within the FRA housing, which is an engine speed (rpm) magnetic pickup unit (MPU). The MPU generates voltage pulses in proportion to the rotative speed of a metallic wheel attached to the injection pump camshaft as it rotates past the end of the MPU. Refer to Figure 17-11, which describes how an MPU operates.

5. *Fuel shutoff solenoid (FSS)*. Should the actual fuel rack position differ from that asked for by the operator, the fuel injection control module will detect a rack position error and the fuel shutoff solenoid (FSS) or ELAB mounted on the injection pump housing (Figure 20-7, white arrow) will shut off the flow of fuel to the injection pump. This same solenoid is wired into the engine key start/stop switch, therefore turning the key off results in automatic engine shutdown. Note that in 1992 and later V-MAC engines, the fuel solenoid is replaced by a shutoff relay located in the electrical equipment panel of the vehicle.

6. *Econovance timing advance mechanism*. A hydromechanical injection pump timing advance device, which is incorporated into the injection pump drive, is located between the pump and the engine block (Figure 20-8). A description of an Intravance device is explained later in this chapter. Basically, timing is changed by rotating the injection pump camshaft ahead of the engine crankshaft as engine speed is in-

creased. However, in the V-MAC system an electric signal from the electronic control module operates an econovance control valve to control pressurized engine oil flow used to operate the econovance unit.

7. *Econovance control valve (ECV)*. Figure 20-9 shows the two components of the ECV within a single assembly mounted on top of the Econovance mechanism. The two components are:

- A proportional electric solenoid, which is an analog device, can be moved smoothly to any posi-

FIGURE 20–8 Econovance timing advance (current production).

FIGURE 20–9 *Proportional solenoid and hydraulic spool valve.*

FIGURE 20–10 *RPM/TDC sensor.*

tion within its designed range of travel by varying the electric current supplied to it by V-MAC.

- A hydraulic spool valve controls the amount of pressurized engine oil that can flow to the Econovance assembly. This hydraulic valve is controlled by the proportional solenoid.

8. *RPM/TDC engine position sensor.* This sensor, located at the forward side of the flywheel housing (Figure 20-10), generates a changing electric pulse signal and relays it back to the V-MAC module. Engine speed is used as the primary parameter to determine desired fuel injection timing. In addition, this sensor provides the crankshaft position data required for comparison with the timing event marker sensor input to the V-MAC module in order to calculate the current (actual) injection timing.

9. *Timing event marker (TEM) sensor.* Located at the outside rear of the P8500 injection pump, the TEM sensor determines when the timing bump on the injection pump speed sensor passes the end of the TEM (Figure 20-11). This signal indicates port closure of the No. 6 pumping plunger. This bump is used to orient the injection pump camshaft anytime that the injection pump is being installed on the engine after removal to set initial static injection timing.

10. *Vehicle road speed sensor.* The vehicle road speed sensor is located at the rear of the transmission housing (Figure 20-12). It operates as an MPU unit to sense the passage of a geared wheel assembled to the

transmission output shaft. The sensor pulse width signal is sent to the V-MAC module to control vehicle cruise control, or for vehicle road speed limiting.

11. *Coolant temperature sensor (CTS).* The CTS is located at the rear of the engine water manifold (item 1 in Figure 20-13). The CTS signal is used for cold-start enhancement by the fuel injection control module. On

FIGURE 20–11 *Timing event marker (TEM) sensor.*

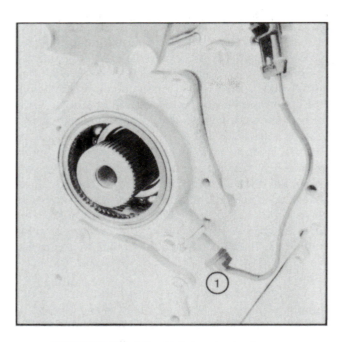

FIGURE 20–12 Mph (road speed) sensor.

a cold startup, a fast idle is initiated to allow faster warm-up and to control exhaust emissions. During normal engine operation, this sensor will monitor out-of-range coolant temperature conditions, radiator blockage, thermostat failure, overload, high ambient temperatures, and so on. If any of these conditions oc-

cur, a logged trouble code will be inserted into the V-MAC module.

12. *Intake manifold air temperature sensor (ATS).* The ATS is threaded into the intake manifold (Figure 20-13, item 2). It functions to calculate an accurate air/fuel ratio through the control module. This sensor signal is also used for engine timing control, particularly during engine warm-up to prevent white smoke at the exhaust from incomplete combustion of the fuel droplets. It also prevents misfire under light-load engine operation.

13. *Engine oil pressure sensor (OPS).* The OPS is threaded into the top of the oil filter assembly (Figure 20-14). It functions to relay a signal to the V-MAC control module. If the oil pressure falls outside normal operating parameters, a fault code will be logged into the module as well as activating a dash warning light.

14. *Coolant level sensor (CLS).* The CLS is located in the radiator top tank to monitor the coolant level (Figure 20-15). Low coolant will cause a fault code to be logged in the V-MAC module and activate a dash warning light.

15. *Throttle position sensor (TPS).* The TPS is often referred to as an electronic foot pedal assembly (Figure 20-16). Greater details on this unit can be found by referring to Figure 15-13. Basically, this drive-by-wire system is mounted into the throttle pedal. The percentage of throttle pedal depression (amount of requested fueling) is relayed to the fuel injection control module. Generally, the control module sends a 5-V signal to the TPS. At a closed throttle position (idle speed), the resistance through the TPS reduces this input voltage signal so that approximately 0.5 V is sent

FIGURE 20–13 Coolant temperature sensor and intake manifold air temperature sensors.

FIGURE 20–14 Engine oil pressure sensor.

FIGURE 20–15 *Coolant level sensor.*

back to the FIC module. At wide-open throttle, the TPS resistance value is decreased, allowing approximately 4.5 V to return to the control module. This return signal will vary based on the degree of throttle pedal depression; therefore, this changing voltage signal allows the control module to determine how much fueling is being asked for by the driver.

V-MAC SYSTEM TROUBLESHOOTING

The design of the V-MAC system will prevent the extraction of inactive fault codes from the dash-mounted malfunction lamp. This lamp will provide only "active" fault code readout (blink). To access all fault codes and perform other diagnostic functions, the V-

MAC system can be accessed in the same general way as that shown for other electronically controlled fuel systems shown in this chapter (Caterpillar, Cummins, Detroit Diesel) by using a ProLink 9000 DDR (diagnostic data reader) and printer as shown in Figure 20-17. Alternatively, a laptop computer similar to the concept shown in Figure 20-17 can be used along with V-MAC software.

If a ProLink 9000 system is not available or the technician wants to save some time in determining if any fault codes exist in the system, when active fault codes are detected by the ECM, these codes can be displayed on the electronic malfunction lamp on the vehicle dashboard by activating the system to create "blink" or "flash" codes similar to that shown in Figure 15-24. To activate the blink code lamp, proceed as follows:

1.   Turn the ignition key ON and wait about 2 seconds until the system bulb check is completed.

2.   If the electronic malfunction lamp does not illuminate after the check lamp goes out, there are no stored fault codes stored in computer memory.

3.   With the speed control ON/OFF switch in the OFF position, press and hold the SET/DECEL or the RESUME/ACCEL switch until the fault lamp goes OFF.

4.   The fault lamp will remain OFF for about 1 second.

5.   The V-MAC module will begin to flash a two-digit blink code. The two digits of the code will be separated by a 1-second idle time (lamp OFF) condition.

6.   Each digit of the blink code may consist of up to eight ON/OFF flashes. The ON and OFF time for each flash will be $\frac{1}{4}$ second, so be prepared to write down each code as it appears.

7.   Only one active fault code is flashed per request. There must be a separate request for each active fault code when multiple codes are stored. To request another fault code, hold in the SET/DECEL or RESUME/ACCEL switch until the fault lamp goes OFF. The blinking sequence will begin again after a 1-second delay.

8.   If the fault blinking request is repeated while V-MAC is in the process of blinking an active fault, that sequence will stop and the next active fault will be blinked.

9.   If an active fault is cleared while V-MAC is blinking that fault, the procedure will not stop.

10.   After every complete blinking sequence, the fault lamp will return to normal functions. It will remain ON for active faults and OFF for inactive faults.

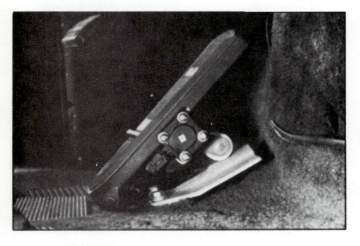

FIGURE 20–16 *Throttle position sensor.*

FIGURE 20-17 Interface devices.

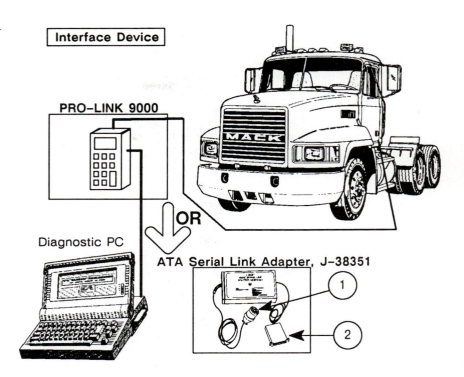

NOTE   When more than one active fault code is present, continue the blink code sequence until the first active fault is deployed to be certain that all faults have been recovered!

Mack Troubleshooting Connections

Although the technician can withdraw the active fault blink codes as described earlier, to utilize the diagnostic capabilities of the V-MAC system, greater information retrieval can be obtained by using the MPSI (Microprocessor Systems Incorporated) Pro-Link 9000 diagnostic tool or any IBM PC–compatible computer that will perform all the functions of the DDR (diagnostic data reader) ProLink 9000. The PC also allows

for enhanced diagnostics of the system and reprogramming of Mack propietary data.

Figure 20-18 illustrates the various ProLink connections where the DDR is connected at position 1 to an ATA (American Trucking Association) serial link adapter (4), which is available from Kent-Moore/SPX as part J38351. The adapter is in turn connected to a quick-connect wiring adapter at one end and to the V-MAC 9-pin serial cable (3) to the communication port located under the vehicle dash to the left of the steering column (Figure 20-19).

Although blink codes can be extracted as described, if using the ProLink 9000 or a laptop computer with Mack software, standardized SAE (Society of Automotive Engineers) trouble codes will provide the technician with enhanced diagnostics capability of the

FIGURE 20-18 Electrical connector required from handheld Pro-Link 9000 diagnostic tool to vehicle serial communication port. (Courtesy of Mack Trucks, Inc.)

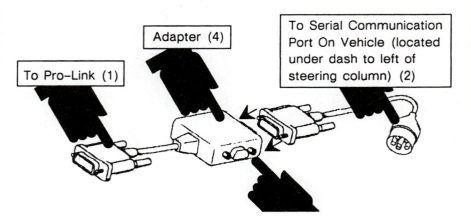

TABLE 20-1 SAE/ATA J1708 serial line standard terminology

Active blink	Fault code	Protocol identification	Assignment listing	Failure
1	1	PID 100/FMI 4	Engine oil pressure	Voltage below normal or shorted low
1	2	PID 100/FMI 3	Engine oil pressure	Voltage above normal or shorted high
1[a]	7	PID 111/FMI 3	Coolant level	Voltage above normal or shorted high
2	1	PID 110/FMI 4	Engine coolant temperature	Voltage below normal or shorted low
2	2	PID 110/FMI 3	Engine coolant temperature	Voltage above normal or shorted high
2	3	PID 105/FMI 4	Intake manifold air temperature	Voltage below normal or shorted low
2	4	PID 105/FMI 3	Intake manifold air temperature	Voltage above normal or shorted high
3	1	SID 21/FMI 8 (active)	Engine position (buffered rpm)	Abnormal frequency, pulse width, or period
		SID 31/FMI 8 (inactive)	Tachometer drive output (buffered rpm)	Abnormal frequency, pulse width, or period
3	2	SID 21/FMI 2	Engine position sensor (rpm/TDC)	Data erratic, intermittent, or incorrect
3	3	PID 190/FMI 2	Engine speed (injection, pump rpm)	Data erratic, intermittent, or incorrect
3	4	SID 22/FMI 2	Timing sensor (TEM)	Data erratic, intermittent, or incorrect
3	5	SID 20/FMI 7	Timing actuator	Mechanical system not responding properly, or out of adjustment
4	1	PID 84/FMI 4	Road speed (mph)	Voltage below normal or shorted low
4	2	PID 84/FMI 3	Road speed (mph)	Voltage above normal or shorted high
4	3	PID 84/FMI 8	Road speed (mph)	Abnormal frequency, pulse width, or period
4	4	SID 24/FMI 4	Rack position sensor	Voltage below normal or shorted low
4	5	SID 24/FMI 3	Rack position sensor	Voltage above normal or shorted high

5	1	PID 91/FMI 4	Percent accelerator pedal position	Voltage below normal or shorted low
5	2	PID 91/FMI 3	Percent accelerator pedal position	Voltage above normal or shorted high
5	3	SID 23/FMI 5	Rack actuator	Current below normal or open circuit
5	4	SID 23/FMI 7	Rack actuator	Mechanical system not responding properly, or out of adjustment
6	1	PID 183/FMI 8	Fuel rate	Abnormal frequency, pulse width, or period
		SID 29/FMI 8 (future)	External fuel command input	Abnormal frequency, pulse width, or period
6	2	SID 248/FMI 8	Proprietary data link	Abnormal frequency pulse width, or period
6	3	SID 250/FMI 8	J1708 (J1587) data link	Abnormal frequency, pulse width, or period
7	2	PID 118/FMI 7	Parking brake switch	Mechanical system not responding properly, or out of adjustment
7	4	SID 25/FMI 7	Shutdown override switch	Mechanical system not responding properly, or out of adjustment
N/A	N/A	PID 190/FMI 0	Engine speed (injection pump rpm)	Data valid but above normal operating range
Red and amber light and alarm		PID 110/FMI 0	Engine coolant temperature	Data valid but above normal operating range
Red and amber light and alarm		PID 100/FMI 1	Engine oil pressure	Data valid but below normal operating range
Red and amber light and alarm		PID 111/FMI 3	Engine coolant level	Voltage above normal or shorted high

[a]Red light and amber light and alarm.

FIGURE 20–19 *Serial communications port.*

V-MAC system. These SAE codes are the PID (parameter identifier), the SID (system identifier), and the FMI (failure mode indicator). Greater detail on these SAE codes is provided in Chapter 16. Codes that would appear in the V-MAC system when activated would include the items listed in Table 20-1.

Digital Multimeter

When fault codes are indicated through use of the blink codes or by using the ProLink 9000 or laptop computer, the technician needs to follow a test sequence to determine if the fault is caused by the sensor or associated wiring. This requires that a set diagnostic procedure be followed as specified in the V-MAC systems diagnostic manual, available from Mack Trucks, Inc. as part 8-201. This publication includes complete foldout wiring diagrams and step-by-step test sequences for different fault codes. Similarly, if a laptop computer and Mack software are used, the technician can follow the directions contained within the software program to trace a system fault systematically. When so indicated, a digital multimeter is used to measure voltage and resistance and to check for short and open circuits. Specifications for voltage and resistance can be found in the V-MAC diagnostic manual.

SERVICE TIP   Never disconnect or connect wiring harnesses or test equipment to the V-MAC system without ensuring that the ignition key is turned OFF. Once wire harnesses or test equipment has been connected/disconnected, you can safely turn the ignition key ON.

INJECTION PUMP REMOVAL

Should it become necessary to remove the P7100 or P8500 Bosch injection pump from a V-MAC-equipped engine, you should set the static injection timing prior to pump removal. This can be done by using the Kent-Moore J37077 timing light and tool sensor probe at the injection pump. This involves removing the TEM (timing event marker) sensor from the rear of the injection pump from the fixed timing port (Figure 20-20).

Setting the Timing

CAUTION   Thoroughly clean all residue from the fixed timing port threads (timing access window) before installing a tool sensor. This will prevent the possibility of a false reading.

1.   Clean the J37077 tool sensor probe points with compressed air before inserting it into the pump timing access window. This ensures that there will be no dirt or metallic contamination between the sensor probe points (Figure 20-21).

2.   Carefully install the timing position tool into the injection pump (Figure 20-22); ensure that the tool is aligned with the locating groove (12 o'clock) in the access hole.

3.   Slowly rotate the knurled nut CW on the timing tool to lock it in position (Figure 20-22). To check that the tool is seated, apply hand pressure to its end; if any movement is noted, remove and reinstall the tool.

FIGURE 20–20 *Removing the TEM sensor.*

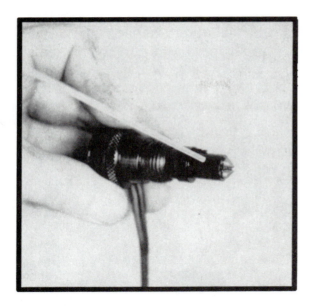

FIGURE 20–21 *Cleaning the sensor probe points.*

FIGURE 20–23 *Grounding the tool and turning it on.*

4.   Refer to Figure 20-23 and connect the fixed timing tool ground wire to a good connection on the engine. Press the tool power switch ON.

5.   Refer to the following information as a guide for the specific engine on which you are working.

6.   On standard transmission applications, you will need to remove the flywheel housing timing access cover as well as installing manual barring tool J38587 into the opening on the forward face of the flywheel housing to permit you to use a ½-in. drive ratchet to rotate the flywheel (Figure 20-42).

7.   Manually rotate the flywheel in a counter-

clockwise direction so that it is a minimum of 45° BTDC.

SPECIAL NOTE

- ON all P8500 V-MAC electronically controlled fuel injection systems, the injection timing is referenced to cylinder 1. The engine must be timed during the compression stroke of cylinder 1.
- ON all P7100 V-MAC electronically controlled fuel injection systems, the injection timing is referenced to cylinder 6. The engine must be timed during the compression stroke of cylinder 6.
- ON all P7100 non-V-MAC mechanically controlled fuel injection systems, the injection is referenced to cylinder 1. The engine must be timed during the compression stroke of cylinder 1.

FIGURE 20–22 *Turning the knurled surface clockwise.*

8.   Rotate the flywheel in a clockwise direction (viewed from the front of the engine = normal rotation) until both lights on the tester are illuminated. This sets the injection pump timing, and the pump can now be removed.

9.   A description of how to check fixed timing for a Mack E7 engine is the same for both a non-V-MAC- and a V-MAC-equipped engine. The procedural check is described later in this chapter; see the section "Mack Pump Timing Check (Non V-MAC)."

Pump Removal Procedure

1. If possible, steam clean the injection pump and nozzle area of the engine.

CAUTION Do not apply steam or high-pressure cleaner hot water directly to the pump housing if the engine is running and is hot, since the rate of expansion of the aluminum housing and the internal steel components are different. This can cause distortion and possible pump damage!

---

2. Disconnect the following lines:

- Supply pump outlet
- Overflow valve to tank
- Injection pump fuel inlet
- Supply pump inlet
- Injection pump lube oil supply
- Nozzle bleed-off line hose clamp

3. Loosen the injection pump rear support bracket nut located on the outboard No. 6 pumping element stud.

4. Loosen the front injection line support bracket nut located on the inboard No. 1 pumping element stud.

5. Loosen all six nozzle high-pressure lines at the pump.

6. Remove the fuel injection lines insulator bracket and clamp assembly.

7. Refer to Figure 20-24 and loosen the lower link support capscrew but do not remove it; remove

FIGURE 20–24 Loosening the lower capscrew.

FIGURE 20–25 Loosening the upper support capscrews.

the upper link support capscrew, then rotate the links to one side (toward the rear of the engine).

8. Refer to Figure 20-25 and loosen the two upper support bracket to injection pump capscrews (one outboard and one inboard).

9. Refer to Figure 20-26 and remove the three pump-to-Econovance mounting capscrews.

10. Refer to Figure 20-27 and remove the retaining capscrews from the injection pump drive access cover.

11. Loosen and remove the pump drive gear capscrews and gear as shown in Figure 20-28.

12. Disconnect the integral wiring harness connector from the engine harness connector as shown in Figure 20-29; *do not turn*. Also, do not use this connection as a support handle when lifting the injection pump clear of the engine.

13. Refer to Figure 20-30; securely grasp the injection pump housing and pull it from its mounting. If tight, tap the front of the pump housing with a plastic or rubber mallet to break the gasket seal.

FIGURE 20–26 Removing the three injection pump capscrews to the Econovance.

FIGURE 20–27 *Removing the remaining capscrews.*

FIGURE 20–29 *P8500 Governor cover.*

14. If the injection pump two-piece metal drive coupling shown in Figure 20-31 needs to be removed, use Kent-Moore special tool J28452A to hold the pump metal drive coupling securely while loosening the retaining nut as shown in Figure 20-31.

INJECTION PUMP INSTALLATION

Injection pump installation is basically the reverse procedure of removal. However, ensure that the engine flywheel has been turned to position the correct engine piston at TDC on its compression stroke prior to pump

installation. See "Special Note" under "Injection Pump Removal."

1. To facilitate ease of installation, refer to Figure 20-32 and install two dowel screws into the Econovance housing.

2. Install a new gasket over the studs and onto the Econovance housing.

3. To prevent possible dropoff of the injection pump outer drive coupling, install the coupling onto the Econovance mating gear as shown in Figure 20-33.

4. Refer to Figure 20-34 and loosen the three pump rear support bracket-to-engine block capscrews. Hand-tighten the screws, then loosen them about one-fourth turn each; this should permit the lower bracket to be moved from side to side for alignment purposes.

FIGURE 20–28 *Removing the capscrews and gear.*

FIGURE 20–30 *Removing the injection pump.*

FIGURE 20–31 *Loosening the coupling retaining nut.*

FIGURE 20–33 *Installing the outer coupling.*

5.   Loosen the rear outer and inner support bracket capscrews (Figure 20-25).

6.   Securely lift the injection pump into position, then align and slide the adapter over the two alignment dowel screws as shown in Figure 20-35.

7.   To fully engage the pump drive coupling, as you lift the rear of the pump housing, simultaneously rotate the Econovance hub as shown in Figure 20-36. This will allow the pump to be moved into engagement and against the drive housing.

8.   Refer to Figure 20-37 and install the lower pump mounting capscrew. Remove both alignment dowel screws and install the other two retaining capscrews. Torque all screws to 54 N · m (40 lb-ft).

9.   Reinstall and torque the two link support capscrews which were previously removed (Figure 20-24), and tighten them to 54 N · m (40 lb-ft) torque.

10.   Now tighten the three lower support bracket-to-block capscrews which were finger-tightened in step 4 (Figure 20-34). Torque these to 54 N · m (40 lb-ft).

FIGURE 20–32 *Installing the alignment dowels.*

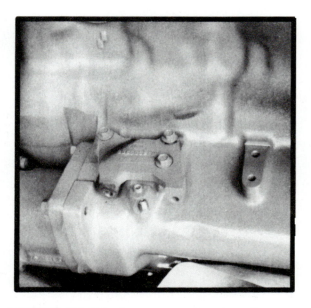

FIGURE 20–34 *Lower support bracket adjustment.*

FIGURE 20–35 *Aligning the pump over the dowels.*

FIGURE 20–37 *Securing the injection pump.*

11. Torque the inner and outer upper support bracket-to-pump capscrews shown in Figure 20-25 to 20 N · m (15 lb-ft).

12. Install the injection pump drive gear.

13. Perform a fixed engine timing check using Kent-Moore timing position sensor J37077, and follow the sequence described for Figures 20-22, 20-23 and 20-49.

14. Refer to Figure 20-38 and lubricate the engine timing cover O-ring with Lubrizol OS-50044 or equivalent. Install and tighten the cover retaining

capscrews (install the oil supply line clamp at the 12 o'clock position on the cover). Torque the capscrews to 40 N · m (30 lb-ft).

15. Prelube the injection pump on RE-30 governors by adding 3.5 oz of clean engine oil through the timing event marker location hole as shown in Figure 20-39.

16. Lubricate the V-MAC pump by removing the 10-mm plug located in the lower left side of the injection pump, and add 11 oz of clean engine oil.

17. Clean all oil residue from the timing event

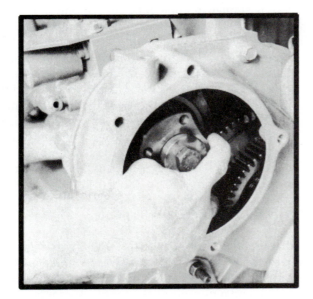

FIGURE 20–36 *Rotating the hub.*

FIGURE 20–38 *Lubricating the O-ring.*

FIGURE 20–39 *Prelubing.*

FIGURE 20–40 TEM.

marker and access window. Refer to Figure 20-40 and back off the TEM jam nut toward the pigtail. Carefully apply a bead of $\frac{1}{8}$ to $\frac{1}{4}$ in. (3.175 to 6.35 mm) of Silastic sealer or equivalent around the sensor threads at the jam nut. Failure to do this can result in an oil leak at the TEM sensor.

18.   Install and hand-tighten the TEM sensor into the pump access hole until it is seated in position. Screw down the jam nut by running it over the Silastic sealer. Torque the jam nut to 30 N · m (22 lb-ft). Wipe off any excess Silastic sealer with a dry cloth.

19.   Reconnect all fuel and oil lines and brackets that were removed earlier. Bleed the fuel system and start the engine. Inspect for signs of fuel or oil leaks.

ELECTRONIC UNIT PUMP SYSTEM

Mack's current six-cylinder E7 engine models are equipped with Robert Bosch PLN electronically controlled V-MAC engines rated at 454 hp (338 kW). Sometime in 1997, these engines are scheduled to use the Robert Bosch EUP (electronic unit pump) system on the 500-hp (373-kW)-rated model E7 engines. For details on how the EUP operates, refer to Chapter 21 (the series 55 DDC engine model employs this same system).

MACK PUMP TIMING CHECK (NON V-MAC)

Mack six-cylinder E6 and E7 model engines use Robert Bosch mechanically governed injection pumps. The E7 model is equipped with a Bosch P7100 pump and a

Bosch RQV-K mechanical governor. All 1991 E7 and later mechanically governed (non V-MAC) engines feature an injection pump plunger with a 6° light-load advance notch as well as a 6° start advance notch (Figure 20-41).

Pretiming Checks

To check the injection pump to engine timing on non-V-MAC engines, you will require the following special tools.

- Kent-Moore J38587 engine barring socket. (This tool is similar in appearance to the one shown in Figure 19-31 for the Cummins C engine timing check.)
- Kent-Moore J37077 fixed timing position sensor (light). Refer to Figure 20-42 which shows the barring socket in position and attached to a $\frac{1}{2}$-in. drive ratchet to facilitate turning over the engine crankshaft. In addition, note that the flywheel housing timing inspection cover has been removed. This permits the technician to see the flywheel timing degree marks in alignment with the stationary pointer.

PUMP INSTALLATION

Installation of the close-coupled P7100 Bosch injection pump on the E6 and E7 model engines is similar. It differs only in that the E6 pump requires a longer drive pump hub and a pump-to-cylinder block adapter. Follow this procedure.

FIGURE 20-41 *Features of PLN pumping plunger. (Courtesy of Mack Trucks, Inc.)*

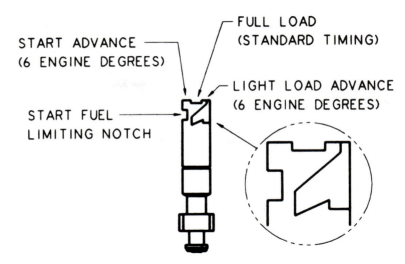

FULL LOAD
(STANDARD TIMING)

START ADVANCE
(6 ENGINE DEGREES)

LIGHT LOAD ADVANCE
(6 ENGINE DEGREES)

START FUEL
LIMITING NOTCH

1991 AND LATER PLUNGER DESIGN
MECHANICALLY GOVERNED PUMPS

1. Refer to Figure 20-42 and bar the engine over in its normal direction of rotation (clockwise) using the barring tool J38587 to place the No. 1 cylinder piston at TDC on its compression stroke (both inlet and exhaust valves fully closed). At this time the timing pointer on the flywheel or above the front crankshaft damper should indicate TDC No. 1. The 1991 production E7 engine flywheel shown in Figure 20-43 has a stamped timing scale consisting of a TC (top dead center) mark and 45° of engine travel for setting and checking pump-to-engine timing. In addition, the flywheel has three stamped locations 120° apart for valve set positions.

2. Lightly lubricate the pump-to-block mounting bore with clean engine oil as shown in Figure 20-44.

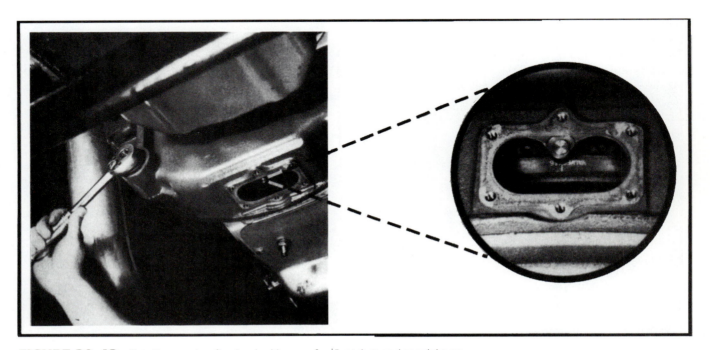

FIGURE 20-42 *Rotating engine flywheel with use of a $\frac{1}{2}$" ratchet and special turning tool. (Courtesy of Mack Trucks, Inc.)*

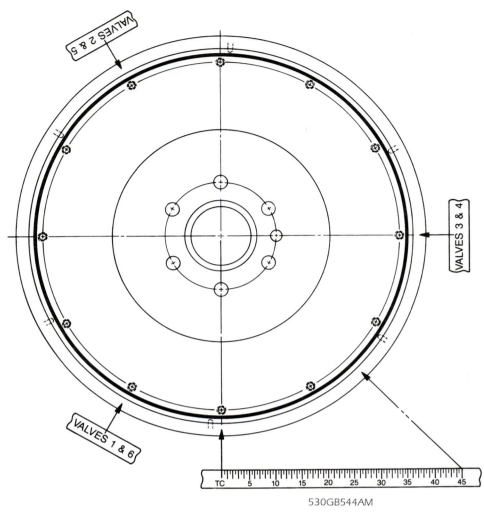

FIGURE 20-43 1991–E7 engine flywheel timing marks. (Courtesy of Mack Trucks, Inc.)

VALVES 2 & 5

VALVES 3 & 4

VALVES 1 & 6

TC 5 10 15 20 25 30 35 40 45

530GB544AM

FIGURE 20-44 Lubricating the pump-to-block mounting bore.

FIGURE 20-45 Injection pump to engine mounting. (Courtesy of Mack Trucks, Inc.)

3.   Refer to Figure 20-45 and install the injection pump/hub assembly over the mounting studs and carefully slide the pump forward until the pump is flush with the engine block.

4.   Install the washers and nuts to all pump mounting studs and tighten them to 60 N · m (45 lb-ft) with a torque wrench.

5.   Remove the 8-mm Allen-head plug screw shown in Figure 20-46 located in the RH rear of the pump (governor housing).

6.   Prior to installing the fixed timing probe J37077 into the access hole in the pump, look into the hole until you see the image illustrated in Figure 20-47. Note the small dark slot in the illustration at the 12 o'clock position.

7.   Refer to Figure 20-22 and carefully insert the J37077 timing probe into the pump fixing plate bore hole so that it aligns correctly. Gently run the knurled nut in until the timing probe is seated.

8.   Connect the fixed timing probe J37077 sensor tester electrical lead clamp to a good ground as shown in Figure 20-23 with the positive side connected to a 12-V battery.

9.   Push the press-on power switch of the tester.

10.   Slowly bar the engine over in a clockwise direction using the J38587 tool or with a socket attached to the pump camshaft retaining nut shown in Figure 20-48. Note that light A on the tester will illuminate first if the engine is being rotated in the correct direc-

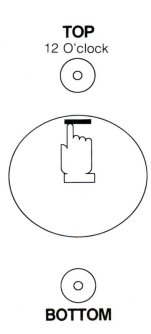

TOP
12 O'clock

FIGURE 20–47   *Locating the groove at 12 o'clock.*

tion. This also confirms that the injection pump is very close to port closure for cylinder 1.

11.   Continue to rotate the engine slowly until lamps A and B are both illuminated, as shown in Figure 20-49.

FIGURE 20–46   *Removing the fixing plate.*

FIGURE 20–48   *Rotating the pump in the clockwise direction.*

FIGURE 20–49 *Rotating the pump until both A and B lamps are lit.*

FIGURE 20–50 *Slots in gear centered about screw holes in hub.*

SERVICE TIP   Note that there is a very narrow band where only both lamps will illuminate, so gently bump the engine over as you approach this position!

---

12.   When both lights illuminate on the tester as shown in Figure 20-49, the injection pump is positioned at port closure for the No. 1 pumping plunger.

13.   Install the pump drive gear so that the slots in the gear are centered as shown in Figure 20-50 around the four bolt retaining holes in the hub. You can use alignment dowels to facilitate gear installation.

SERVICE TIP   Install a shop rag at the bottom of the gear and housing to prevent a retaining bolt from being dropped into the engine during installation.

---

14.   Thread the retaining bolts into position at this time until they are hand-tight only.

15.   Manually rotate the pump drive hub in a counterclockwise direction (see Figure 20-51) until the four gear retaining screws bottom in the ends of the slots. At this time both tester lamps should go out.

16.   With a socket and bar attached to the pump hub nut as shown in Figure 20-49, gently rotate the pump hub in a clockwise direction until the A and B tester lamps are both illuminated.

17.   Torque the injection pump gear retaining bolts to 55 N · m (40 lb-ft). During torquing, it is acceptable for both lamps A and B to go out.

18.   To confirm that the pump is correctly timed

FIGURE 20–51 *Rotating the pump hub counterclockwise.*

to the engine, refer to Figure 20-52 and rotate the engine in a counterclockwise direction approximately 45° (one-eighth turn). At this time tester lamps A and B should both go out.

19.   Slowly rotate the engine CW until lamps A and B both illuminate once again. Refer to Figure 20-53 and check to see if the timing indicator on the front cover and damper are aligned correctly. If the timing is not correct, repeat the timing procedure.

MACK INTRAVANCE/ ECONOVANCE SYSTEMS

Various models of Mack engines using AMBAC or Bosch PLN injection pumps employ an automatic timing device that operates from a set of weights to control oil pressure and therefore the degree of pump camshaft advancement. Earlier engines used the Intravance unit, while later model engines including the V-MAC 1 system employ an Econovance device.

Intravance Operation

The components of the Intravance unit are shown in Figure 20-54. This device forms a separate part of the injection pump camshaft and is dependent on engine oil pressure for its successful operation. The Intravance unit is said to be speed sensitive since it relies on a set of rotating flyweights to control the flow of pressurized engine oil into the components. At low engine speed, the centrifugal force of the weights are insuffi-

FIGURE 20–53 *Checking the timing.*

cient to overcome spring force; therefore, the internal control valve cannot move and prevents any engine oil from entering the unit. Consequently, the injection pump timing remains at its static position when the pump was installed on the engine.

As the engine is accelerated, the centrifugal force of the rotating flyweights becomes great enough to move them outward against the force of the spring. The weights pull the internal control sleeve toward the rear of the pump to permit pressurized engine oil to flow into the Intravance unit. The oil causes the splined sleeve (14) in Figure 20-55 to move forward. The splines on the sleeve are machined at an angle (almost like helical cut gear teeth); therefore, any forward movement of the sleeve will result in the cam (15) being rotated in direct proportion to the sleeve's forward movement. If straight spur cut splines were used, there would be no cam rotation! The cam advance is usually limited to a maximum of 20°.

As the engine speed decreases under load or by throttle movement, the centrifugal force of the rotating flyweights will be decreased. This allows the control valve to shift back, and the camshaft (15) attached to the pump will also move back as the oil drains from the sleeve area. Some Intravance models are designed with a dual-range system incorporating a special follow-up rod (8) and spring (6) (Figure 20-55) which operate in the 300 to 500 rpm range during engine startup. This permits engine timing to be retarded slightly for faster starting and to reduce white exhaust smoke.

FIGURE 20–52 *Rotating the engine counterclockwise.*

FIGURE 20–54 Cutaway view of Intravance. (Courtesy of AMBAC International Corp.)

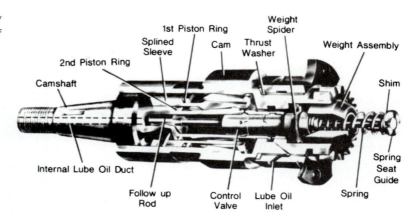

Econovance Operation

Beginning in 1990–1991 production, Mack model E7 V-MAC engines to serial number 1X were equipped with an Econovance timing device. This device consists of a splined drive sleeve, return spring and external oil supply line shown in Figure 20-28. This timing advance mechanism serves as a part of the fuel injection pump drive and is located between the engine cylinder block and the injection pump. Timing is altered by rotating the injection pump camshaft relative to the engine crankshaft. The system operates similar to the Intravance unit described, but rather than relying upon the centrifugal force of a set of flyweights to control timing advance, the Econovance system functions on a command from the electronic control unit.

The Econovance employs a helical spline machined into a sliding sleeve moved by engine oil pressure, which is in turn controlled by an electro-hydraulic actuator which converts the electrical output of the V-MAC module into a proportionate rate of oil flow to the Econovance. The proportional solenoid and hydraulic spool valve are shown in Figure 20-28. The solenoid is an analog device which can be moved to any position by varying the electric current supplied to it from the V-MAC module. The solenoid, in turn, is used to set the hydraulic spool valve at the position needed to control the flow of engine oil to the Econovance.

SUMMARY

This chapter has provided you with an overview and understanding of how the VMAC system functions. Coupled with your knowledge of how Robert Bosch fuel injection pumps operate, you should now have the skills to effectively maintain, service, repair, diag-

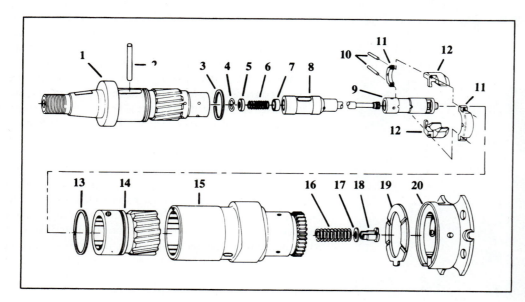

Parts List

(1) Drive Shaft
(2) Sleeve and Rod Pin
(3) Piston Ring
(4) Spring Ring
(5) Spring Seat
(6) Retard Spring
(7) Retard Piston
(8) Follow-up Rod
(9) Control Valve
(10) Weight Pin
(11) Weight Spider
(12) Weight
(13) Piston Ring
(14) Splined Sleeve
(15) Cam
(16) Advance Spring
(17) Washer(s)
(18) Spring Seat
(19) Thrust Washer
(20) Bearing Plate Assy.

FIGURE 20–55 Exploded view of Intravance.

nose, analyze, and troubleshoot a Mack engine equipped with electronic controls.

SELF-TEST QUESTIONS

1. Technician A says that later-model Mack six-cylinder E7 model engines employ a Robert Bosch P8500 injection pump model. Technician B says that all current E7 engines employ electronic unit injectors. Who is right?

2. True or False: Future Mack E7 engine models will use the Bosch EUP (electronic unit pump) system on E7 engines.

3. True or False: The V-MAC in the V-MAC system stands for "vehicle management and control."

4. Technician A says that the V-MAC module is a Motorola-supplied assembly. Technician B says that it is supplied by Delco Electronics. Who is right?

5. True or False: A fault in the V-MAC system triggered by an out-of-range operating condition in either the oil pressure, coolant temperature, or coolant level will activate an amber light followed by a red light.

6. Technician A says that fault codes can be accessed and retrieved from the V-MAC system by use of a MPSI Pro-Link 9000 DDR (see Figure 20-18). Technician B says that a laptop computer is the only method to extract stored fault codes. Who is correct?

7. Technician A says that the injection pump fuel rack actuator consists of a hydraulically actuated but electronically controlled solenoid. Technician B says that an electric proportional solenoid is used. Who is right?

8. True or False: An electric power loss from the fuel rack actuator will result in a spring returning the rack to a fuel shutoff position.

9. Technician A says that the V-MAC injection pump employs a hydromechanical injection pump timing advance device. Technician B says that injection timing advance is all performed by a PWM signal from the ECM. Who is right?

10. Technician A says that an engine position sensor located at the forward side of the flywheel housing generates an electric pulse signal and relays it back to the V-MAC module. Technician B says that the engine position sensor is located at the front of the engine and picks up a signal from the crankshaft gear. Which technician is correct?

11. Technician A says that a TEM (timing event marker) is located at the front of the injection pump. Technician B says that the TEM is located at the outside rear of the P8500 pump. Who is right?

12. Technician A says that the CTS signal is used to enhance engine cold startup by permitting a fast idle. Technician B says that the oil temperature sensor is used for this purpose. Who is right?

13. Technician A says that the air/fuel ratio control depends on a signal from the intake manifold air temperature sensor. Technician B says that only the turbo boost sensor can do this. Which technician is correct?

14. Technician A says that the fault code blink lamp on the dash can be activated by toggling the cruise control switches. Technician B says that a DDR must be used to determine blink codes. Who is right?

15. Technician A says that static injection pump timing on the V-MAC system can be performed using a special timing light and tool sensor probe at the injection pump. Technician B says this can only be done using a hand-held DDR. Who is right?

16. Technician A says that on all P8500 V-MAC injection pumps, injection timing is referenced to cylinder 6 while it is on the compression stroke. Technician B says that it is referenced to cylinder 1 on compression. Who is correct?

17. Technician A says that you can bar over an E6 or E7 engine by using a Kent-Moore J38587 socket installed at the flywheel housing. Technician B says that it is used at the front of the engine. Who is right?

18. Technician A says that pump timing and valve setting is facilitated by the fact that timing marks are located at both the engine flywheel and above the front damper. Technician A says that timing marks are only visible at the flywheel. Who is right?

19. Technician A says that when using the Kent-Moore fixed timing position sensor tool J37077, port closure for the No. 1 pumping plunger is confirmed when only one light illuminates on the tool. Technician B says that both lights must illuminate to confirm that plunger 1 is at the port closing position. Who is correct?

21

Detroit Diesel Corporation Fuel Systems

OVERVIEW

This chapter deals with both the function and operation of Detroit Diesel mechanical and electronic fuel systems. Detroit Diesel was the first major high speed engine OEM to adopt electronic controls, beginning in 1985 on their two-stroke cycle 92 Series engines. Today, DDC employs electronic fuel system and governor controls on their two- and four-stroke cycle heavy duty engines. Details on how to service, maintain, diagnose, analyze and troubleshoot mechanical and electronic DDC fuel systems is provided in this chapter.

COMPANY BACKGROUND

Detroit Diesel Corporation was organized in 1935 by a small but dedicated group of people whose objective was to design and build an engine to be used in trucks and buses produced by General Motors Corporation. Their company originated in the Cadillac Motor Car Division Plant in Detroit, Michigan. They were not the first manufacturer by any means to undertake such a venture; however, their aim was to produce a compact, lightweight diesel engine. They felt that the best way to do this task successfully would be to use a two-cycle rather than a four-cycle design. By March 1938, series 71 engines began production in the plant, which employed 360 employees. Engines were built in one-, two-, three-, four-, and six-cylinder models. In September 1970, the Detroit Diesel Engine Division and the Allison Division merged and formed the Detroit Diesel Allison Division of General Motors Corporation.

The series 53 engines were introduced in 1958, and the following year the 6V-53 appeared, followed in 1963 by the 8V-53. Due to the broad range of engines produced by DDC, the 2-53 and the 8V-53 were withdrawn from production in 1974. With the ever-increasing demand for more horsepower, DDC introduced the 149 series engines in 1967, and these are currently available in 8V, 12V, 16V and 20V configurations. The series 92 engine first appeared in 1974. The 92s are available in 6V, 8V, 12V, and 16V configurations. The model numbering sequence applied to all DDC two-cycle engines refers to the cubic inch displacement per engine cylinder. Therefore, as an example, an 8V-92 engine would have a total engine size of 8 times 92, which is 736 in^3 (12.07 liters).

DDC was the first major heavy-duty diesel engine manufacturer to adopt and release to the marketplace an electronically controlled fuel-injected system on its line of 71 and 92 series two-stroke-cycle highway truck engines, starting in September 1985. This electronic fuel control system, known as DDEC (Detroit Diesel electronic controls), is described in this chapter. In addition to their well-known line of two-stroke-cycle diesel engines, DDC also produces four-stroke-cycle diesel power units. Their first venture into the four-stroke field began in 1979 with the release of the midrange-duty 8.2-L (500-in^3) V8, which was designed at that time for Ford, which desired a reasonably inexpensive replacement engine for the large-displacement gasoline-powered engines in their truck line, particularly in the class 5, 6, and 7 ranges. This engine has subsequently been engineered into various other applications, particularly marine pleasure craft.

In the heavy-duty four-stroke-cycle end, DDC offers the series 60 inline six-cylinder model available in either an 11.1-L (677-in^3) or a larger 12.7-L (774-in^3)

version. Both engines are turbocharged and air-to-air aftercooled for heavy-duty class 8 truck application, and have overhead camshafts and heads with four valves per cylinder. The series 60 engines are equipped with DDC's DDEC (Detroit Diesel electronic controls) electronically controlled unit injector fuel system. The 11.1-L version is rated between 300 and 365 hp, while the larger 12.7-L unit is available from 365 to 500 hp, with higher ratings available in the future. The 8.5-L four-cylinder series 50, which is a four-cylinder version of the 12.7-L series 60 is rated between 250 and 315 hp. Series 50 and 60 engines are both also offered in electronically controlled natural-gas models.

The Series 55 model (a co-venture with Mercedes-Benz) is a six-cylinder, four-stroke truck engine of 12 L (730 cu. in) displacement, and uses EUP's (electronic unit pumps). In a co-venture with the German company "MTO," Detroit Diesel markets large displacement, high horsepower engine models known as the 2000 and 4000 units, which also use EUP's. *Note:* DDC is now owned by Roger Penske, well known for his racing successes!

ENGINE LABELS

All DDC engines are equipped with either an aluminum option plate on the rocker cover of older model units, or on engines manufactured since August 1985, a new paper-laminate engine option and emissions label is used (Figure 21-1). These labels provide the mechanic/technician with general engine information as well as detailed information regarding the horsepower setting of the engine, its fuel rate, maximum rpm, and valve and injector settings.

The emissions label is used mainly for highway-truck engine applications, although it may appear on various other application engines. It provides detailed information regarding confirmation with U.S. EPA emission regulations.

Bar code labels on the engine are printed in computer-readable form, with one bar identifying the engine serial number and the other listing the customer specification number when the engine was ordered initially. This allows a check at any time with the factory or DDC distributor/dealer as to what special options were originally ordered on that engine. The disclaimer label indicates that when the engine was manufactured, it complied with all government emission regulations and that DDC will not be held responsible for alterations to engine fuel settings, and so on; that would affect engine horsepower and/or emission certification. Items listed on an option plate or a paper-laminate label indicate that each of these items has been specially ordered for the particular model

and application of that engine. It is in reality a built-in parts book. When parts are required, the mechanic/technician simply refers to the type number on the label, along with the engine model and serial number, and you can then order parts through any DDC distributor/dealer worldwide, and along with the engine model number, you will be guaranteed the correct component part. The parts person simply cross-references the type number with a part number listing through a PC program.

FUEL SYSTEM FUNCTIONS

The fuel system employed by Detroit Diesel is commonly known as a low-pressure fuel system, owing to the fact that fuel delivered to the unit injectors averages 50 to 70 psi (345 to 482.6 kPa), compared to the average 2500 to 4000 psi (17,237 to 27,580 kPa) that passes through the fuel lines from the injection pump to the nozzles on fuel systems such as Ambac, Robert Bosch, ZEXEL–Diesel Kiki, Lucas CAV, Caterpillar, Nippondenso, and others.

The five main functions of the fuel system employed by Detroit Diesel are as follows:

1. To supply clean, cool fuel to the system by passing it through at least a primary and secondary filter before the pump and injectors

2. To cool the injectors as the fuel flows through them and returns to the tank (recirculatory system)

3. To lubricate the injector's moving parts, through the inherent lubricity of diesel fuel, which is basically a very light oil

4. To maintain sufficient pressure at all times through the action of the positive-displacement gear pump and the use of a restricted fitting located at the cylinder head return fuel manifold

5. To purge the fuel system of any air; the system is recirculatory in operation, therefore allowing any air to be returned to the fuel tank

FUEL SYSTEM COMPONENTS

Figure 21-2 shows a schematic view of a typical VEE fuel system used on a 6V two-cycle engine. Since the basic fuel system employed on all two- and four-cycle Detroit Diesel engines is identical as far as components used, the description of operation for one can be readily related to any other series of DD engine. An inline engine, for example, would use only one cylinder

Option labels attached to the valve rocker cover contain the engine serial and model numbers and list any optional equipment used on the engine.

With any order for parts, the engine model number with serial number should be given. In addition, if a type number is shown on the option plate covering the equipment required, this number should also be included on the parts order.

All groups or parts used on a unit are standard for the engine model unless otherwise listed on the option plate.

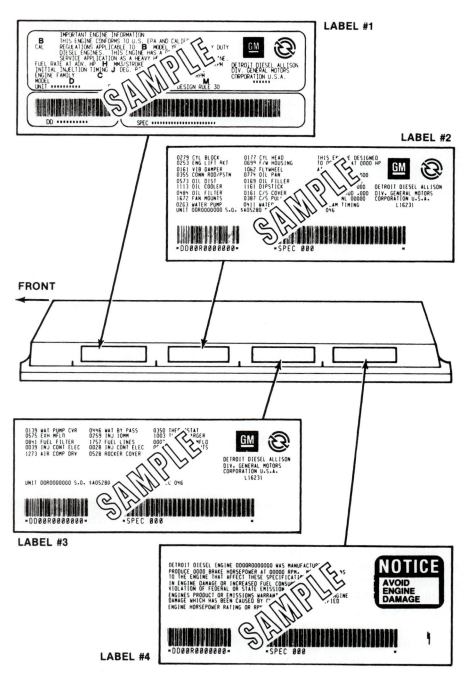

FIGURE 21–1 Rocker cover with option label.

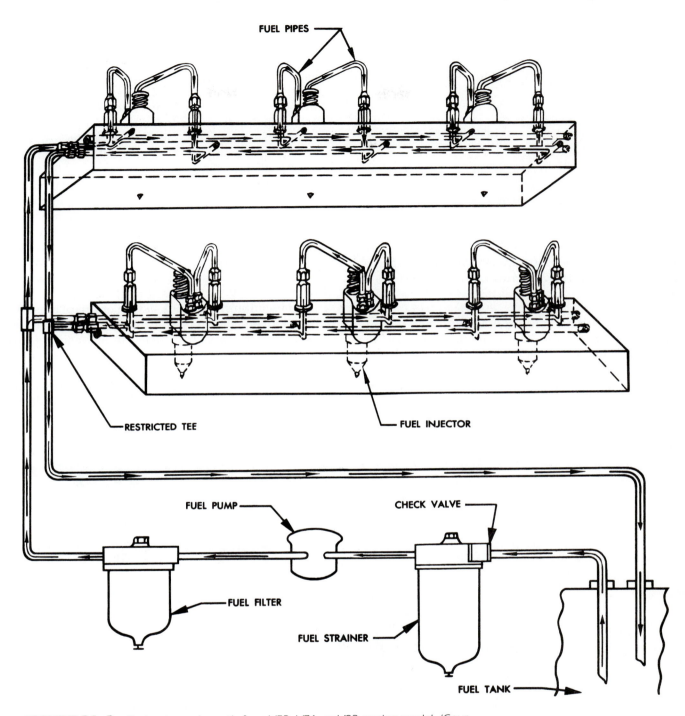

FIGURE 21–2 *Fuel system schematic for a V53, V71, or V92 engine model. (Courtesy of Detroit Diesel Corporation.)*

head, whereas a V-engine using two would have a fuel system as shown in Figure 21-2.

The basic fuel system in Figure 21-2 consists mainly of the following:

- Fuel injectors.

- Fuel pipes or jumper lines to and from the injectors (inlet and outlet).

- Fuel manifolds, which are cast internally within the cylinder head (older engines used external fuel manifolds running lengthwise along the head). Either way, the upper manifold is the *inlet* and the lower is the outlet or *return* on two-cycle models. To prevent confusion, the words *in* and *out* are cast in several places in the side of the head.

- Fuel pump (supply pump, not an injection pump).
- Fuel strainer or primary filter.
- Fuel filter (secondary).
- Fuel lines.
- One-way check valve.
- Restricted fitting on inline engines or a restricted T on V-type engines to maintain a minimum fuel pressure of 30 psi in the return fuel manifold.

FUEL PUMP

Figures 21-3 and 21-4 show the typical fuel pump used on all series 53, series 71, series 92, 8.2-L, and series 50 and 60 engines.

Fuel Flow: Two-Cycle MUI Models

The fuel pump draws fuel from the tank past the one-way nonreturn check valve into the primary filter, where the fuel passes through a 30-μm-filtering-capacity cotton-wound sock-type element. From the primary filter it passes up to the suction side of the fuel pump, where the fuel is then forced out at between 65 and 75 psi (448.2 and 517.1 kPa) to the secondary filter, which is a pleated paper element of 10-μm filtering capacity. Fuel then passes up to the inlet fuel manifold (upper) of the cylinder head, where it is distributed through the fuel jumper lines into each injector. All surplus fuel (not injected) returns from the injectors through the return fuel pipes, through the restricted fitting, which maintains adequate fuel pressure in the head at all times, then back to the tank. All Detroit Diesel engines are equipped with a fuel return line restricted fitting, the actual size varying with engine injector size and application; however, every restricted fitting has the letter R followed by a number that indicates its hole size in thousandths of an inch. Therefore, a fitting with R80 or R08 stamped on it would indicate an 0.080-in. (2.032-mm)-diameter hole drilled within the fitting.

These fittings may look like an ordinary brass fitting externally; therefore, care must be taken to ensure that in fact the proper restricted fitting, and not just any fitting, is installed into the return line. Use of too large a fitting can lead to low fuel pressure within the head manifolds and poor engine performance, whereas too small a fitting can lead to increased fuel

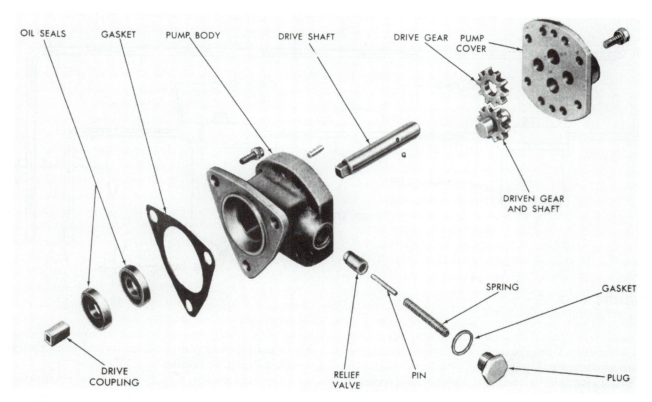

FIGURE 21–3 *Stackup of component parts of fuel pump. (Courtesy of Detroit Diesel Corporation.)*

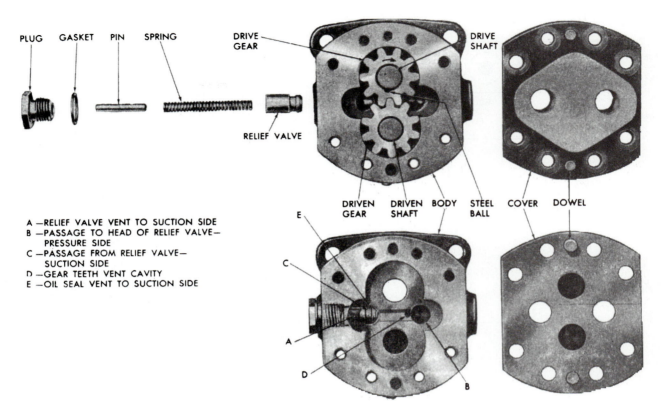

PLUG   GASKET   PIN   SPRING   DRIVE GEAR   DRIVE SHAFT

RELIEF VALVE

DRIVEN GEAR   DRIVEN SHAFT   BODY   STEEL BALL   COVER   DOWEL

A —RELIEF VALVE VENT TO SUCTION SIDE
B —PASSAGE TO HEAD OF RELIEF VALVE—
      PRESSURE SIDE
C —PASSAGE FROM RELIEF VALVE—
      SUCTION SIDE
D —GEAR TEETH VENT CAVITY
E —OIL SEAL VENT TO SUCTION SIDE

FIGURE 21–4 Exploded view of fuel pump relief valve and pump gearing. (Courtesy of Detroit Diesel Corporation.)

temperatures and some restriction against the fuel flow. The one-way check valve is used to prevent fuel from draining back to the tank from the primary filter and line when the engine is stopped.

The fuel pump is a positive-displacement gear-type unit that transfers fuel from the tank to the injectors at 65 to 75 psi (448.2 to 517.1 kPa). The standard pump has the ability to deliver $1\frac{1}{2}$ U.S. gallons/minute (5.67 L) or 90 U.S. gallons/hour (340.68 L), approximately at 1800 engine rpm.

Since the pump constantly circulates an excess supply of fuel to and through the injectors, the unused portion, which also cools and lubricates the injectors and purges the system of any air, returns to the fuel tank via the restricted fitting and fuel return line.

Series 50 and 60 Fuel System

Let's briefly look at the fuel system layout for the Detroit Diesel series 50 and 60 EUI (electronic unit injectors) engine models. Figure 21-5A illustrates that the fuel system is similar to that used with the MUI (mechanical unit injector) engines in that a gear-type fuel transfer pump driven from the rear of the air compressor assembly on truck applications creates the flow re-

quirements for the system. Fuel leaves the fuel tank and passes through either a primary fuel filter or fuel/water separator assembly to the inlet side of the fuel pump. This is the suction side of the fuel system; therefore, any loose fittings or connections will allow air to be drawn into the system, resulting in a rough running engine and a lack of power. From the outlet side of the pump, fuel under pressure flows through a cooling plate bolted to the ECM (electronic control module) on certain applications to maintain the internal operating temperature of the electronics components within the ECM at an acceptable level. This fuel cooler is not normally required on heavy-duty highway truck series 60 engines unless fuel temperatures are consistently above 140°F (60°C), although it is used on series 50 models in transit bus applications. Fuel now enters the secondary fuel filter and exits to the rear of the cylinder head, where it flows through an internally cast manifold to feed each EUI. Fuel that isn't required for injection purposes is used to cool and lubricate the internal components of the injector. Return fuel leaves the injector where it flows through an internal fuel return manifold cast within the cylinder head. Fuel leaves the head at the rear through a re-

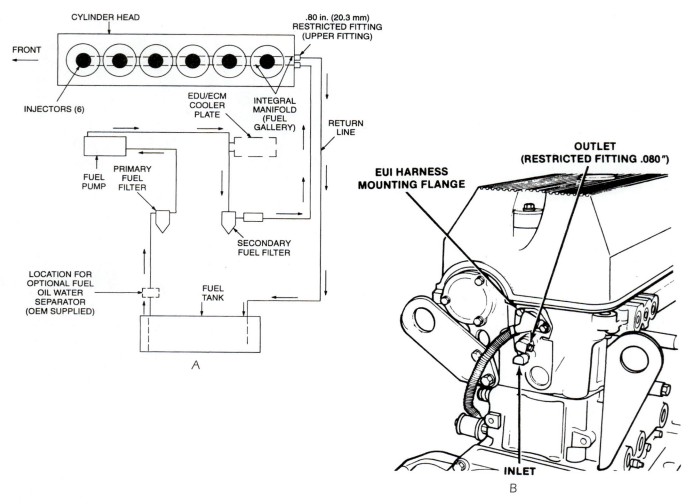

FIGURE 21–5 (A) Schematic layout of the fuel system for a series 60 four-stroke-cycle EUI engine model; (B) Series 60 engine model fuel gallery inlet and outlet fittings at the rear of the cylinder head. (Courtesy of Detroit Diesel Corporation.)

stricted fitting as shown in Figure 21-5B and returns to the fuel tank.

Identification of Fuel Pump Rotation

If you are in doubt as to a fuel pump's rotation, it can be identified as follows:

1. Stamped on the pump cover are the letters LH or RH, plus an arrow indicating the direction of rotation.
2. On inline engines, the fuel pump rotation can be determined by its location on the engine. When viewed from the flywheel end: left-hand-side location, LH pump rotation; right-hand-side location, RH pump rotation. All V71 and V92 engines use LH rotation pumps only; 149 engines use only RH rotation pumps.
3. A similar method would be to grasp the

pump in your left or right hand as it mounts on the engine with an overhand grip. Whichever thumb covers the relief valve indicates the pump's rotation.

The letters I/L (inlet) are also stamped on the pump cover; however, if not visible, the inlet side is the hole on the pump cover closest to the relief valve plug. The fuel pump body and cover are aligned by means of two dowels, and the body and cover are ground surfaces that contain no gasket between them, although a thin coat of sealant applied to these surfaces is recommended at installation. The relief valve bypasses fuel back to the inlet side of the pump when pressure reaches 65 to 75 psi (448.2 to 517.1 kPa).

Fuel drawn into the suction side of the pump fills the space between the gear teeth and the pump body, where it is carried around and discharged to the outlet cavity under an average pressure of 45 to 70 psi (310.2 to 482.6 kPa). Closer study of Figure 21-4 will indicate the characteristics of the pump shown.

Figure 21-3 shows an exploded view of the pump; the stackup of the component parts is clearly visible. The standard fuel pump gears are $\frac{1}{4}$ in. wide and contain 10 teeth, whereas the high-capacity pump that is available has gear teeth $\frac{3}{8}$ in. or $\frac{1}{2}$ in. wide, with this size stamped on the pump cover. The output of the $\frac{3}{8}$-in. gear pump is approximately 135 gph, and the $\frac{1}{2}$ in. unit is 175 to 180 gph U.S. Engine injector size, application, and rpm determine pump size. The drive gear is a 0.001-in. (0.0254-mm) press fit onto the shaft, and a gear retaining ball locates it on its shaft.

As shown in Figure 21-3, two oil seals are pressed into the pump bore from the flanged end for the following purposes:

- The seal closest to the drive fork prevents lube oil from entering the fuel pump.
- The inner seal closest to the pump gears prevents fuel oil leakage.

The installed seals do not butt up against each other but have a small space between them. Drilled and tapped into this cavity in the fuel pump body are too small holes, one of which is usually plugged; the other is open to allow any fuel or lube oil leakage to drain, thereby indicating damaged seals. Sometimes a small fitting and tube extend from one of these holes to direct any leakage to a noticeable spot. Acceptable leakage should not exceed 1 drop per minute.

A fuel pump with a star or the word *day* stamped on its cover indicates that the inner seal is reversed, and is used on *gravity feed* installations where the fuel tank is above the level of the fuel pump. The reversed inner seal (seal closest to the pump gears) prevents fuel seepage down the pump shaft and out the drain cavity hole, especially when the engine is shut down. *Never* plug both drain holes in the pump body between the oil seals; otherwise, any fuel leakage will cause crankcase oil dilution.

MINIMUM FUEL-LINE SIZES VERSUS RESTRICTION

All diesel engines, regardless of the make of manufacture, require a minimum size (diameter) of fuel line in order to keep the restriction to the suction side of the fuel transfer pump as low as possible. This minimum resistance to flow will ensure that the engine will not be subjected to periods of fuel starvation and lack-of-power complaints. The suction side of the fuel system extends from the fuel tank up to the inlet side of the

fuel transfer pump. Refer to Figures 21-2 and 21-5A, which illustrate the basic fuel system. Therefore, any fittings, connections, or fuel lines that are too small on the suction side of the system will create problems. The greatest amount of restriction to the system is generally caused by such items as fittings, one-way check valves, and the actual piping size itself.

A properly designed fuel system should have a maximum restriction with a clean primary filter installed of 6 in. Hg (mercury). This restriction can be checked by removing the small pipe plug from the left- or right-hand outlet side of the primary filter fuel strainer housing as shown in Figure 21-6. To connect the mercury manometer, remove the left-hand or right-hand filter outlet pipe plug, and install a suitable brass fitting. To this fitting would be connected a piece of rubber hose/tubing, with the other end attached to a mercury manometer. How to use manometers is discussed in detail in Chapter 13.

The restriction check, if possible, should be taken by connecting a suitable tee fitting to the inlet fitting of the fuel pump. However, it is often not convenient to access the pump on many applications; therefore, the primary filter, which is generally within 2 ft of the pump inlet, is acceptable (Figure 21-5). In addition, any loose fittings or connections on the suction side of the system will allow the pump to suck air into the system, resulting in low delivery. The engine will idle rough and stumble badly as you accelerate it and attempt to load it.

Air in the system can be checked during a fuel spill back when you can submerge the return fuel line under the spilled fuel in the container. Any air bubbles would be an indication that the system is not airtight on the suction side. Air in the system would also result in a low rate of spilled fuel. The fuel spill-back check is shown in Figure 21-20.

Another condition that can cause an increase in fuel system restriction is the height that the fuel pump is above the fuel tank, with every foot of lift causing a restriction increase of 0.8 in. Hg. Maximum allowable restriction in the fuel system with a dirty fuel filter should not exceed 12 in. Hg (mercury). The best guide for fuel-line size on any engine is to determine the size of the inlet to the transfer pump, then select the largest size fitting and fuel line that will fit this connection.

PRIMING THE FUEL SYSTEM

There are several ways in which to prime the fuel system. The degree of priming required depends on what caused the fuel loss in the first place. However, the priming of the fuel system on a Detroit Diesel engine is usually not as involved or as hard as it can be on

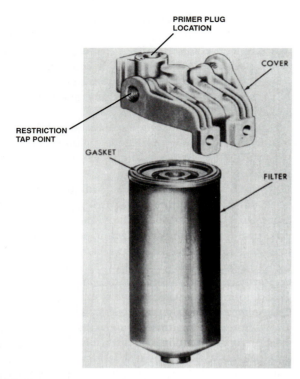

PRIMER PLUG
LOCATION

COVER

RESTRICTION
TAP POINT

GASKET

FILTER

FIGURE 21–6   Fuel filter. (Courtesy of Detroit Diesel Corporation.)

some high-pressure fuel systems, owing to the fact that since it is a low-pressure recirculatory type of fuel system, it will purge itself of air more readily than the conventional high-pressure type of system.

FILTER REPLACEMENT

Replace the primary and secondary fuel filters at the normal preventive maintenance change period.

Shell and Element Type Filters

1.   With the engine stopped and the drain tray under the filter canister, open the drain cock and lightly loosen the cover nut or bolt to facilitate free drainage of the fuel, then close the drain cock.

2.   Be sure to protect wiring harnesses or electrical equipment from fuel oil during the change period.

3.   Remove the shell and element, and remove and discard the cover nut retaining ring if used; discard the filter element and shell gasket or seal ring, the cover nut or bolt gasket, and cover bolt snap ring, if used.

4.   Wash out the shell in clean fuel oil and blow it dry with compressed air. Carefully examine the element seal and retaining ring to make sure that they are in position, since they cannot be replaced; if damaged or if the seat is not against the retaining ring, the shell assembly must be replaced.

5.   Thoroughly soak the element in clean fuel be-

fore installation, which helps to expel entrapped air and therefore makes for an easier initial engine start. Place the new element into the shell and push it down against its seat; then fill the shell two-thirds full with clean, filtered fuel.

6.   Place a new gasket or seal ring in the shell recess and a new gasket on the cover nut or bolt, and thread the nut or bolt into the shell. With the shell gasket in place, tighten the cover bolt or nut to prevent leakage. Remove the pipe plug at the top of the shell cover (Figure 21-6) and complete filling of the shell with clean fuel.

Spin-on Filters

1.   With spin-on types of filters (Figure 21-6), if no drain cocks are provided and water is a problem, a fuel–water separator should be employed. Unscrew the filter via the 1-in. (25.4-mm) 12-point nut at its base, discard it, fill the new unit two-thirds full with clean, filtered fuel, coat the seal gasket lightly with clean fuel oil, and after the filter contacts the gasket, tighten it two-thirds of a turn.

2.   The pipe plug on the inlet side of the filter cover in Figure 21-6 can be removed and using a suitable hand-operated pump the entire fuel system can be primed.

3.   Start the engine and check for fuel leaks.

ENGINE RUNS OUT OF FUEL

If an engine runs out of fuel, it is due strictly to carelessness on the part of either the equipment operator or the maintenance personnel. Downtime caused by this situation can be expensive, especially if it happens on the road or in a remote off-highway location. If you have to restart an engine due to this condition, check the sequence given earlier in this chapter on priming the fuel system.

Figure 21-6 shows the filler plug location employed in both the primary and secondary fuel filters that can be removed for the purpose of priming the fuel system when necessary. The problem in restarting an engine after it has run out of fuel stems from the fact that after the fuel is exhausted from the fuel tank, fuel is then pumped from the primary fuel strainer and is often partially removed from the secondary fuel filter before the fuel supply becomes insufficient to sustain engine operation. Therefore, these components must be refilled with fuel and the fuel lines rid of air in order for the system to provide adequate fuel for the injectors. This situation is not only avoidable, but expensive in terms of equipment downtime. On an engine that has run out of fuel, attempting to crank the engine over on the starter will not sustain engine firing. It will have to be primed.

NOTE   To facilitate starting after running out of fuel, do *not* spray ether (starting fluid) into the air intake to try to keep the engine running without adequate fuel. Severe damage to the injector plunger and bushing, as well as the spray tips, will result because they are running dry during this time. In addition, excess ether can cause cracked cylinder heads due to the high volatility of ether. Severe pressures can be created inside the combustion chamber.

Restarting Procedure

1.   It may not always be possible to fill the fuel tank completely, particularly if the vehicle/equipment is in a remote location; therefore, although it is desirable to have at least 25% of the tank capacity, or a minimum of 10 gallons in it, this may not always be possible. Obviously, the more fuel that is added to the tank, the easier it will be to prime the system.

2.   If clean, filtered fuel is available to you, remove both the primary and secondary fuel filters and fill them up. If nonfiltered fuel is available, remove the small pipe plug on top of each filter assembly and pour fuel into the assembly, or use a priming pump to force fuel positively through the system.

3.   The priming pump will allow you to force fuel through the fuel lines up to the injectors and therefore prime the complete system before attempting to restart the engine.

4.   It is helpful when the injectors have run completely dry to remove the No. 1 injector inlet jumper line, and prime the system with a prefiltered fuel supply. The inlet manifold and all injectors can be primed to assure quick startup of the engine after having poured or primed fuel into both the primary and secondary fuel filter assemblies.

5.   Crank the engine over until it starts, and with the fuel return line disconnected, allow fuel to pour into a container until all the air has disappeared and a steady flow of fuel is visible. If the air bubbles do not disappear, there is an air leak on the suction side of the fuel system (between the inlet on the pump and the fuel tank).

6.   Reconnect the fuel return line and run the engine to check for any signs of fuel leakage.

FUEL INJECTORS

Fuel Injector Mounting

The two-stroke DDC engine unit fuel injector is located in the cylinder head. The injector sits in a copper tube in the head, which is surrounded by water in all the two-stroke-cycle DDC engines for cooling purposes. The injector is located by a dowel pin on the underside of the body, and it is held in the head by a single bolt and clamp arrangement. The injector shown in Figure 21-7a is known as an *offset* body since the fuel inlet and outlet studs are offset to one another rather than being parallel or straight. This feature of the offset body is to allow sufficient clearance between the valves on four-valve-head engines.

The injector is actuated by a roller-type cam follower and pushrod threaded into the rear of the rocker arm. This threaded pushrod and locknut arrangement allows adjustment of the injector follower to body height (see the section "Tune-up Sequence"). Two fuel jumper lines supply fuel to the injector, with one being connected to an inlet fuel stud that is fed from the upper manifold in the cylinder head on 53, 71, and 92 engines, while the return fuel line is connected to a return fuel stud which directs fuel to the lower cylinder head manifold, through the restricted fitting, and back to the fuel tank. On the 8.2-L and series 60 four-stroke-cycle engines, the injectors are fed from an internal fuel manifold in the cylinder head. These injectors can be seen in the section dealing with these two engines.

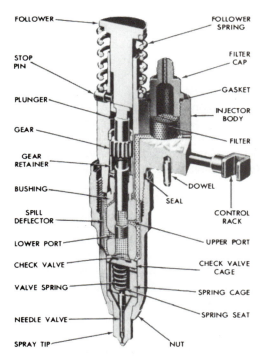

FIGURE 21-7A   Partial cutaway view of a mechanically operated needle valve unit fuel injector. (Courtesy of Detroit Diesel Corporation.)

FORMER
(5228587)

NEW
(5229778)

FIGURE 21-7B *Former and new service fuel inlet filters.*

NOTE   The inlet fuel stud on the unit injector is always the one directly above the fuel rack, or the one on the right hand side of the injector body when viewed from the rack control end. This is very important because only the inlet fuel stud contains a filter underneath it; therefore, if these fuel jumper lines are reversed, dirty fuel could enter the injector, creating serious damage. Figure 21-7b illustrates the early model stainless steel mesh fuel filter used in injectors through approximately the end of 1986. The current injector fuel filter consists of a black fiberglass-filled nylon screen cone fused to a nylon base. Both types of filters are capable of filtering dirt particle sizes down to 0.0045″ (0.114 mm) diameter. The nylon/fiberglass filter must be installed in the injector body with the pointed (cone) end up.

Clearly visible in Figure 21-7 is the injector fuel control rack connected to a control lever. A fuel control tube is connected to the governor by a fuel rod so that the speed of the engine can be changed by either manual operation of the throttle or by governor action. When the rack is moved in toward the injector body, fuel is increased, and when it is pulled out all the way, this is the fuel shutoff position.

Non-DDEC Unit Fuel Injector Function
The fuel injector, or what is often referred to as a *unit injector,* used by Detroit Diesel Corporation have some variations in basic injector model design and in the ac-

tual testing procedures used; however, the function and operation are the same for all.

These injectors were designed with simplicity in mind from both a control and an adjustment outlook. They are used on direct-injection, open-type, two- and four-cycle combustion chamber engines manufactured by DDC. No high-pressure fuel lines are required with these injectors, since the fuel from the fuel pump is delivered to the inlet fuel manifold cast internally within the cylinder head at a pressure of 50 to 70 psi or 345 to 482.6 kPa, and then to the injectors through fuel pipes.

Figure 21-7a shows a typical MUI (mechanical unit injector) employed by Detroit Diesel Corporation in their non-DDEC engines. Once the fuel from the pump reaches the injector, it performs the following functions:

1. *Times the injection.* Timing of the injector is accomplished by movement of the injector control rack, which causes rotation of the plunger within the injector bushing. Since the plunger is manufactured with a helical chamber area, this rotation will either advance or retard the closing of the ports in the injector bushing, and therefore the start and end of the actual injection period. Pushrod adjustment establishes the height of the injector follower above the body. This in turn establishes the point or "time" that the descending plunger will close the bushings' ports and therefore the start of the injection.

2. *Meters the fuel.* The rotation of the plunger by movement of the injector control rack will advance or retard the start and end of injection. If the length of time that the fuel can be injected is then varied, so will the amount of fuel be varied.

3. *Pressurizes the fuel.* Fuel that is trapped underneath the plunger on its downward stroke will develop enough pressure to force its way past the check valve and needle valve, as the case may be, and therefore enter the combustion chamber.

4. *Atomizes the fuel.* Fuel under pressure that forces its way past the check or needle valve must then pass through small holes or orifices in the injector spray tip. This breaks down the fuel into a finely atomized spray as it enters the combustion chamber.

Since the MUI is similar on all DDC engines with the exception of the plunger and spray tip, Figure 21-7 will allow you to identify the major components.

All current production Detroit Diesel Corporation engines employ the *needle valve* type of fuel injector. There are some minor variations in the spray-tip portion; however, they all operate on the same principle. The needle valve injectors have a popping pressure of between 2300 and 3200 psi, (15,858 to 22,753 kPa) required to lift the needle valve off its seat in the injector tip on standard injectors. High-VOP (valve opening pressure) models for between 2900 and 3900 psi (19,995 and 26,890 kPa). The final spray-in pressure penetrating the air mass in the combustion chamber is in the region of 20,000 to 25,000 psi (1360 to 1701 atm) with this type of injector, with the speed of penetration approaching 780 mph (1255 km/h).

Due to the higher pressures encountered on injector closing pressure, there is a much cleaner and crisper cutoff to the injection period with the needle valve injector. There is also no fuel left beneath the valve seat to dribble out into the combustion chamber because of the valve covers orifice design; this reduces the tendency for the engine to emit smoke (see Figure 21-8).

Phases of MUI Injector Operation

The amount, rate, and timing of fuel injection is controlled by the injector plunger design. Reference to Figure 21-7 shows that the top or neck of the plunger slides into a land area at the base of the injector follower.

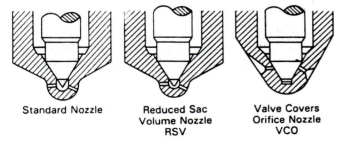

Standard Nozzle Reduced Sac Volume Nozzle RSV Valve Covers Orifice Nozzle VCO

FIGURE 21–8 *Nozzle designs to reduce hydrocarbon emissions from direct injection diesels.*

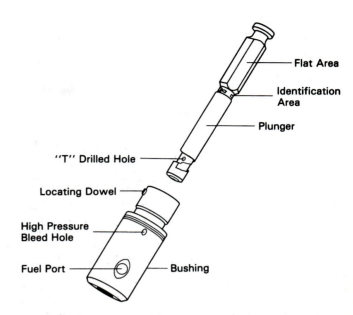

Flat Area

Identification Area

Plunger

"T" Drilled Hole

Locating Dowel

High Pressure Bleed Hole

Fuel Port

Bushing

FIGURE 21–9 *Identification of mechanical unit fuel injector plunger and bushing components. (Courtesy of Detroit Diesel Corporation.)*

The follower is forced down by the action of the rocker arm; therefore, the plunger will move the same distance on each stroke. A circumferential groove cut in the plunger determines the timing and the quantity of fuel injected. The upper edge of this groove is cut in the shape of a helix, with the lower edge either being straight or also cut in a helix. A flat on the upper portion of the plunger meshes with a flat on the inside diameter of the fuel control rack gear; therefore, when the fuel control rack is moved in or out it will cause the plunger to rotate, thereby changing the position of the helix and thus the output of the injector. Figure 21-9 shows a typical new DDC plunger and bushing. At the time of manufacture, the internal diameter of the bushings is measured with an air gauge, and the bushings are segregated into groups to the nearest 12 millionths of an inch. The plungers are also measured and segregated; therefore, the plunger and bushing are mated together to maintain a specified clearance that never exceeds 60 millionths of an inch.

The bushing actually has two ports, one on each side, with one being higher than the other. Anytime that both ports are uncovered by the plunger, fuel at pump pressure (50 to 70 psi; 345 to 482.65 kPa) is free to flow into and out of the bushing; therefore, no pressure beyond that being delivered by the pump is possible under this condition.

Figure 21-10 depicts the phases of injector operation through the vertical or downward movement of the plunger. In Figure 21-10a with the plunger at the top of its stroke, fuel at pump pressure is free to flow

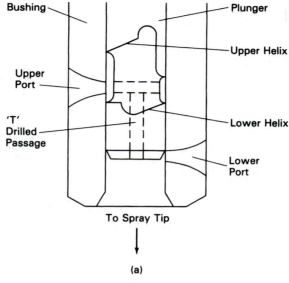

(a)

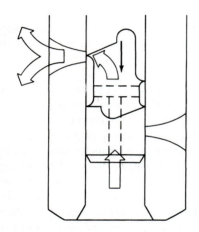

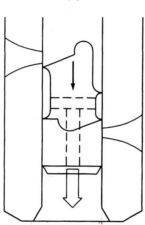

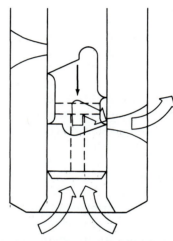

Injector Operation: The plunger descends, first closing off the lower port and then the upper. Before the upper port is shut off, fuel being displaced by the descending plunger may flow up through the "T" drilled hole in the plunger and escape through the upper port.

After the upper port has been shut off, fuel can no longer escape and is forced down by the plunger and sprays out the tip.

As the plunger continues to descend, it uncovers the lower port, so that fuel escapes and injection stops. Then the plunger returns to its original position and awaits the next injection cycle.

(b)

FIGURE 21–10 (a) Identification of plunger and bushing components; (b) sequence of events involved in the pumping cycle for a unit injector. (Courtesy of Detroit Diesel Corporation.)

into and out of the upper and lower ports of the bushing.

Figure 21-10 b illustrates the basic injector plunger operation as it is driven downward by the rocker arm acting on the injector follower. In order to change the amount of fuel delivered to the combustion chamber, we have to be able to lengthen or shorten the plunger's effective stroke. *Effective stroke* simply means that fuel is being injected. This is achieved by rotating the plunger within the bushing. When the fuel rack is moved, it causes the small gear shown in Figure 21-7 to rotate the plunger. The small flat area shown on the upper half of the plunger meshes with a flat within the bore of the gear. There is sufficient clearance, however, between the flats to allow the plunger to move/stroke through the bore of the gear as it is moved up and down by the rocker arm acting on the follower. The helix on the plunger will close the upper port earlier in its downward stroke when the rack is moved in toward the injector body. The upper port is covered later in the plunger's downward stroke when the rack is pulled away from the injector body. Consequently, the longer the effective stroke, the greater the amount of metered fuel that will be injected. Figure 21-11 illustrates the sequence of events as the plunger is rotated.

Fuel from the pump and cylinder head inlet manifold flows through the inlet fuel stud filter and drilled passages in the injector body, filling the cavity around the bushing. If the injector is not in an injection position, the fuel will flow through the upper and lower ports in the bushing and out of the injector return fuel stud.

When the injector rocker arm acting on the injector follower pushes it down (see Figure 21-7), the plunger will also move down, causing the upper and

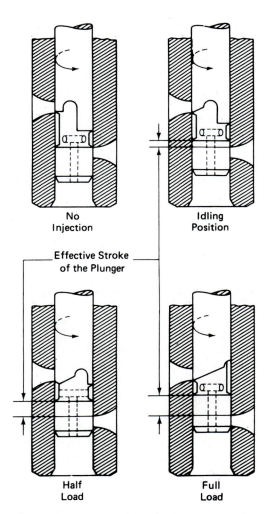

FIGURE 21-11 *Sequence of events involved when the plunger is rotated by rack/gear movement to change the "effective stroke." (Courtesy of Detroit Diesel Corporation.)*

lower ports in the bushing to be covered, thereby trapping fuel under the descending plunger. As the trapped fuel builds up pressure, it acts upon the tapered land of the needle valve. Between 2300 and 3900 psi (15,858 and 26,890 kPa) the needle valve begins to lift against the pressure of the spring, exposing the seat portion of the needle valve to this high-pressure fuel. With this pressure now working on an increased area, the needle valve will lift very rapidly, allowing the fuel to flow into the spray tip sac and on through the tiny holes in the spray tip into the combustion chamber. Since the fuel must force its way through these small holes, it is similar to turning on a garden hose with no nozzle on it. You will get lots of volume but little pressure; however, if you now place your thumb over the end of the hose, you will restrict the flow (less volume) but increase the pressure.

The size and number of the holes in the spray tip will vary between different unit injector models. For example, DDC 53, 71, and 92 series engines use injectors with between six and nine holes. The diameter of these holes can range from 0.0055 to 0.008 in. Therefore, the fuel will be injected at a pressure as high as 26,000 psi (179,270 kPa), causing the fuel to enter the combustion chamber in a finely atomized state. When the downward travel of the plunger ceases, fuel pressure drops off very rapidly, allowing the needle valve spring to seat the needle valve sharply and crisply, thus preventing any further injection.

Injector Sizes

To change the horsepower setting of any engine, either a two- or a four-stroke-cycle design, two common methods are used:

1. Increase the maximum governed speed of the engine.
2. Increase the fuel delivery rate at the same engine speed.

The speed at which the engine is governed is dependent on its actual application, since this determines whether the engine will be operating at its maximum output all the time or whether it will be changing both its load and speed on a regular basis. For example, a standby generator set, once it is brought on line after a utility power failure, may have to run at maximum load for some considerable length of time. A highway truck, on the other hand, is often moving up and down the speed range; therefore, both the rpm and the load is changing regularly.

The gen set would be classed as a *continuous duty cycle*, while the highway truck would be under what is known as the *intermittent continuous duty cycle*. Therefore, identical model engines, because of their application, may not produce the same horsepower or run at the same speed as a similar-size make and model of engine. Each manufacturer limits the actual fuel delivery allowed to an engine for a specific application, therefore installing larger injectors, or opening up the rack on a non-unit injector type of engine should never be done prior to checking with the local engine manufacturer's distributor/dealer. Each unit injector has either an identification tag pressed into the body of the injector on two-cycle engine models, or it will have a series of letters and numbers stamped onto either the body or the hold-down clamp on 8.2-L and series 50 and 60 engines, plus a bar-graph label.

All DDC unit injectors in use today are of the needle valve design. This is the valve contained within the injector spray tip that has to be opened by high-pressure fuel against a return spring to allow fuel delivery to the combustion chamber. This needle valve (NV) can be seen in Figure 21-7. Although all current injectors are of the NV design, they do not all use the same designation on the tag or body. For example, if we were to look at an injector with the tag N65 on it, this would mean that this injector would be an NV design and would flow 65 mm^3 of fuel out of its spray tip every time the rocker arm pushed the injector follower down, while the injector rack was in the full-fuel position.

An injector with the tag designation C65 simply means that it is a clean tip design with a constant end to injection. This was an improvement to the first N-type injectors, and it had less spray-tip "sac" volume; therefore, there was less after dribble at the end of the injection stroke. This resulted in a cleaner-burning engine with better fuel economy. The C injector also uses the needle valve spray-tip design. A B injector is simply a needle valve injector with a different plunger and bushing, as well as a different number of holes in the spray tip and was commonly used in California-certified automotive/truck engines. Several injectors are available with the same number on the ID tag, but they may employ a different letter designation.

The major difference between various designated injectors lies in the actual plunger and bushing designation as well as in the spray-tip assembly. The actual shape of the upper helix on the plunger determines the start of injection, while the lower helix establishes the end of injection. Therefore, installing the wrong designation plunger and bushing (P&B) will alter this timing characteristic. As an example, the spray-tip information 8-.0055-165-A indicates the following:

8: number of holes in the spray tip

.0055: diameter of each hole in the spray tip

165: included spray-in angle of the fuel leaving the tip (*included* meaning the angle between both sides of the centerline of the injector)

A: model designation (advanced) of the tip and angle

The number and size of holes in the spray tip affects the actual pressure of the fuel leaving the tip and entering the combustion chamber. Injectors of different sizes and model types should *never* be intermixed in the same engine. Poor performance as well as serious internal damage can result. Earlier we discussed the engine option plate and/or paper-laminate label, which contains all the various options on the engine. To determine the actual size and type of injector in an engine, simply refer to the type number opposite the INJECTOR stamped on the label, then cross-reference DDC current injector information to determine the actual injector that is in the engine. If the injector label type number does not agree with the actual injector tag on the injector that is in the engine, someone has changed out the injectors without advising the local DDC distributor/dealer, who would normally reprint a new label for the engine any time that any of the options listed on the label have been changed, either at an overhaul or a repair point. The engine emissions label will also indicate its fuel rate at advertised horsepower in cubic millimeters per stroke and key you in to the actual size of injector used. Any DDC dealer parts department can quickly supply you with an injector size/model from a type number stamped on the engine emissions label.

Horsepower Change

When the horsepower of a DDC engine is to be changed, this is generally done by increasing or decreasing the injector size in the engine as long as the maximum recommended injector size for that engine and application is not exceeded. Changing an injector from one size, say an N60 to an N65, for example, would result in an increase in horsepower, depending on the size and model of engine that it is in at the same governed rpm. Each successive move up the scale in multiples of 5 mm^3 will continue to increase the horsepower setting in a similar fashion.

The maximum no-load governed rpm for any engine is always stamped on either the engine rocker cover option plate and/or paper-laminate label on the newer engines. The tolerance on this speed setting is ±25 rpm and should not be exceeded under any circumstances, unless an engine is to be overhauled or placed into a different type of application. The local DDC distributor/dealer should be contacted in such a situation to ensure that you do not exceed the safe working limits for that engine, both in speed and injector size.

NOTE   In DDEC (Detroit Diesel electronic controls)-equipped engines, the EEPROM (electronically erasable programmable read-only memory) unit is designed for a particular engine and application; therefore, the governed speed of the engine and the fuel delivery rate are electronically controlled. This cannot be altered unless the DDEC I PROM is changed or the EEPROM is altered by the dealer/factory in DDEC II and DDEC-III. Again, this should *never* be attempted without first checking with your local DDC distributor or dealer.

Injector Timing

When a non-DDEC unit injector is assembled, a timing mark on the rack and the internal gear that the plunger slides through are aligned to provide initial timing. However, once the injector is installed into the engine, both on non-DDEC and DDEC engines a specific "timing height" of the injector follower above the body *must* be set with the use of a timing pin or dial gauge on all engine models, and only with a dial indicator on the 8.2-L four-stroke-cycle engine. This is discussed in detail under the tune-up procedure later.

The correct timing height *must* be set; otherwise, the engine will run rough and fail to perform properly under load. In addition, continued operation of an injector set at the wrong timing height can result in engine damage. The timing height is shown in Chapter 14 of all DDC service manuals; however, you can also refer to the engine option plate or paper-laminate label on the rocker cover to ensure that you do in fact know the correct dimension before performing this actual adjustment. The timing height determines just when the upper port in the MUI bushing will be closed and therefore the start of injection. It must be correct if the engine is to perform as originally designed.

Matched Injector Sets

Because of mass-production tolerances, all diesel engine manufacturers set a minimum and a maximum fuel delivery flow rate for their pumps (high-pressure inline injection pumps), while DDC specifies a high and a low flow rate for their unit injectors. This flow rate tolerance will vary, depending on the particular size of unit injector used on DDC engines. For example, the recommended acceptable flow rate for a 9290 injector when tested on a calibrator flow checking machine is between 85 and 91 cm^3. This means that any injector flowing within this minimum and maximum rate would be considered acceptable for that engine as long as it passed all of the other tests.

This injector flow rate, along with variations in cylinder compression pressures between engines, is one of the reasons that identical engines will often not produce the same horsepower. However, as long as the injectors fall within the recommended flow rates and the compression pressures are within specifications, each engine should fall within the stated manufacturer's published rated horsepower for its application ±5% due to mass-production tolerances. Some small difference in fuel consumption would also be noticeable between the engine using the high-end tolerance injectors versus the one fitted with the lower-flow-rate injectors. When an exchange set of unit injectors is obtained from any DDC distributor/dealer, always ask for a matched set. This will provide a smoother idle and acceleration under load than will a nonmatched set.

Balancing Injectors

In DDC engines, the term *balancing injectors* refers to the actual fuel rack adjustment that is required when new injectors are installed or when a tune-up is performed on the engine. This adjustment applies only to DDC engines fitted with mechanically operated injectors and a fuel control tube and rod connected to the mechanical governor, such as on a truck application. Engines equipped with the DDEC (Detroit Diesel electronic controls) fuel injection system do not have a mechanical connection between the governor within the ECM (electronic control module). For more information on the DDEC fuel control system, refer to the DDEC section in this chapter.

Injector Removal: Two-Cycle Engines

1.   Steam clean the valve rocker cover area and adjacent surroundings to prevent the entrance of dirt into the engine.

2.   Remove the valve rocker covers; loosen and remove the injector fuel pipes. Immediately install plastic shipping caps over all injector fuel cap studs and all other fuel connectors, and open fuel lines to prevent the entrance of any dirt.

3.   Crank the engine over, or bar it over, until the flats across the rocker arms (at the pushrod) are all in line or horizontal (53, 71, and 92 series only).

4.   Install plastic shipping caps over all fuel inlet and outlet holes.

5.   On 53, 71, and 92 engines, loosen and remove the two rocker shaft hold-down bolts; tip back the rocker assemblies clear of the valves and injector (see Figure 21-12).

FIGURE 21–12 *Using a small heel bar to remove the unit injector from the cylinder head. (Courtesy of Detroit Diesel Corporation.)*

6. On four-valve cylinder heads, remove the two exhaust valve bridges by lifting them from their guides (reinstall them on the same guide).

7. Remove the injector clamp hold-down bolt and clamp; then loosen both the inner and outer adjusting screws (earlier engines) on the injector rack control lever tube far enough to allow you to slide the lever away from the injector. Current engines have only one screw held by a locknut.

8. Insert a small heel bar or injector removal tool under the injector body, taking care not to exert any pressure directly on the control rack, and gently pry the injector from the cylinder head (Figure 23-12).

9. At this time, cover the injector hole in the cylinder head to prevent the entrance of foreign material. If you are removing the injector from a four-valve-head 53 series engine, there is no separate bridge mechanism. It is attached to the end of the rocker arm by a pin and is self-centering when in contact with the valve stems.

10. The exterior of the injector should now be cleaned with clean fuel oil and dried with compressed air prior to any additional tests.

Injector Installation: Two-Cycle Engines

If the cylinder head is off the engine, do not install the injector until the head has been replaced on the engine; however, the injector tube can be cleaned of carbon while the head is off, which will minimize the possibility of carbon particles dropping into the cylinder. If the cylinder head has been removed for any reason other than injector replacement, the injector copper

tubes in the head may be replaced if necessary; however, refer to the section on injector tube replacement for this function in all DDC service manuals.

If the cylinder head is on the engine, check the beveled seat on the injector tube where the injector nut seats for any signs of carbon deposits, which would prevent proper seating of the injector. To remove carbon deposits from 53, 71, and 92 injector tubes, use injector tube bevel reamer J5286-9. When using these reamers, be very careful to remove only the carbon and not the copper from the tube itself; otherwise, the clearance between the injector and the cylinder head will be altered, with possibly disastrous results.

> **NOTE** It is advisable to pack the flutes of the reamer with grease to retain the carbon removed from the tube and to prevent any carbon from dropping into the cylinder.

The injector should be filled with fuel oil through the inlet filter cap until it runs out of the outlet cap prior to installation into the cylinder head.

Installation Procedure

1. Insert the injector into the injector tube, making sure that the dowel pin on the underside of the injector body fits into the mating hole in the cylinder head.

2. Slide the injector rack control lever on the control tube on the head over until it sits into the injector control rack end.

3. Install the injector clamp and special washer (with the curved side toward the injector clamp), and bolt and tighten to 20 to 25 lb-ft (27 to 34 N · m) maximum on 53, 71, and 92 injectors.

> **CAUTION** Check to make sure that the injector clamp is centered over the follower spring prior to tightening; otherwise, the spring may contact the clamp during injector operation. In addition, overtorquing of the injector clamp bolt can cause the injector control rack to stick or bind.

4. On four-valve-head engines (71, 92) install the exhaust valve bridges over their guides and onto the valve stem tips (53 series four-valve-head engines have the bridge mechanism attached to the end of the rocker arms).

5. Move the rocker arm assemblies into position and tighten the hold-down bolts to the following specifications:

- *53 series engines:* 50 to 55 lb-ft (67.79 to 74.56 N · m)
- *71 and 92 series engines:* 90 to 100 lb-ft (122 to 135.58 N · m)
- *71 and 92 series engines* (only on the two bolts attaching a load limit or power control screw if used to the rocker arm shaft brackets): 75 to 85 lb-ft (101.68 to 115.24 N · m)

6.   Remove the shipping caps from the fuel inlet and outlet studs both at the injector and cylinder heads. Install the fuel pipes and tighten them as follows:

- *53, 71, and 92 series engines:* 12 to 15 lb-ft (16 to 20 N · m)
- *53, 71, and 92 series engines:* use of special fuel line socket J8932-01 to tighten the fuel lines is necessary

---

NOTE   Extreme care must be used so as not to bend the fuel pipes during installation; also, overtightening of the fuel pipe nuts can twist or fracture the flared end of the fuel pipe, resulting in leaks that cause lube oil dilution and damage to engine bearings.

---

7.   After all injectors have been installed, a complete engine tune-up as outlined in the section "Tune-up Sequence" will be necessary. In addition, the fuel system should be primed as described earlier in this chapter.

NOTE   If only one injector is removed from an engine, and the other injectors and the governor adjustment have not been disturbed, it is only necessary to adjust the valve clearance and time the injector for that one cylinder, and to position the injector rack control lever.

FUEL JUMPER LINE REUSE

All two-stroke-cycle DDC engines use an inlet and a return fuel jumper pipe to carry fuel from the inlet manifold to the injector, and then from the injector back to the return fuel manifold (see Figure 21-2.)

Each jumper pipe is attached to its respective fuel stud, which is itself threaded into the cylinder head to interconnect with either the inlet or the return fuel manifold.

A special socket tool, the Kent-Moore J8932-01, for use with 53, 71 and 92 series engines should be used to both loosen and tighten these fuel jumper lines.

Since these pipes are located underneath the valve rocker cover, if for any reason they were to leak during engine operation, the fuel oil would dilute the engine oil. Diluted crankcase engine oil can cause serious damage to engine bearings as well as creating a hazardous operating condition when the percentage of dilution approaches as little as 2%. Leaking fuel jumper pipes can usually be associated with improper removal or installation, which causes them to be bent, or when they have been overtightened. The recommended torque on these fuel lines is as follows for series 53, 71, and 92 engines:

1.   160 lb. in. (18.3 N · m) on standard uncoated jumper pipes.

2.   130 lb-in. (14.7 N · m) on the newer Endurion-coated fuel jumper pipes. Endurion is a gray-colored, modified manganese phosphate coating that reduces the friction between the nut and the jumper pipe flare. The Endurion-coated fuel pipe nuts are dull gray in color to distinguish them from the noncoated lines, which have a shiny, silvery look. Fuel jumper pipes on later DDEC-equipped engines (electronic fuel injection) do not have coated nuts, and these should be torqued to 145 lb-in. (15.6 N · m).

NOTE   Although both fuel pipe types can be used, to avoid over- or undertorquing these nuts at installation, it is recommended that you do *not* intermix these lines on the same cylinder head assembly.

---

3.   Jacob's brake jumper pipes 120 lb-in. (13.6 N · m) and jumper lines used with load-limiting devices also do not have coated nuts on the fuel jumper lines. These nuts should be torqued to 160 lb-in. (18.3 N · m). Also, do not attempt to straighten bent fuel jumper pipes, since this action will generally cause the pipe to weaken and eventually break, resulting in crankcase oil dilution. Carefully inspect the flared end of these fuel jumper pipes for signs of cracking, scored surface flaring, and overtightening before reinstalling them.

CARE AND TESTING OF UNIT INJECTORS

Unit injectors used in all DDC two- and four-stroke-cycle engines will provide many hours and/or miles/kilometers of successful operation if the fuel system filters are changed regularly and the system is kept free of any water. DDC covers the overhaul of its unit injectors in great detail in the respective engine service manuals; therefore, we will not attempt to repeat this procedure here.

NOTE   The mechanic/technician will not be expected to rebuild a unit injector at any time in the field, although he or she may be asked to determine from a few simple checks whether or not the injector is at fault and if a new or rebuilt exchange unit is required. This may involve removing it from the engine and performing a series of basic checks such as popping pressure and spray pattern. Every DDC distributor/dealer can supply the customer with exchange rebuilt unit injectors which have been brought up to factory standards, at a price considerably lower than the customer is able to achieve. In addition, each rebuilt injector comes with a six-month warranty; therefore, this is the accepted and preferred method when an injector is diagnosed as being at fault.

However, since many students and apprentices, as well as those mechanics/technicians involved with the maintenance and repair of DDC engines, require some knowledge of just what is involved in the repair of a unit injector, we discuss below some of the more commonly accepted tests required on the unit injector to determine its suitability for use.

Other than when the cylinder head is being removed for service, the engine is being repaired/overhauled, or the injectors are being changed at a predetermined service interval, perform the following checks before condemning the unit injector as faulty:

1. On two-stroke-cycle 53, 71, and 92 series DDC engines, with the engine running at an idle speed, push and hold the injector follower down with a large screwdriver or special tool. This action effectively prevents the lower port from closing, and therefore shorts the injector out, similar to a spark plug in a gasoline engine. When this is done, there should be a positive change to the operational sound of the engine, along with a reduction in rpm; otherwise, it is an indication that the injector was not operating correctly. A contact pyrometer placed on each individual exhaust manifold outlet will allow you to check the temperature of each cylinder. Generally, if this differs by more than 50°F (10°C) between cylinders, it can indicate a faulty injector, but then again it may be low compression in that particular cylinder.

2. On 8.2-L four-stroke-cycle engines, this action cannot be done, because the injector rocker arm pushrod is not threaded into the rocker arm assembly as it is on the two-stroke-cycle 53, 71, and 92 engines. If you attempt to hold the injector follower down, the pushrod will either fly out of the engine, or will fall out of its socket and bend itself. To check the injector on this engine, start and run the engine at an idle speed, and using injector flooding bar Kent-Moore J29522 or a modified slotted screwdriver, individually push one injector rack at a time to the full-fuel position (inward). This is known as flooding the cylinder, since full fuel is being delivered to the combustion chamber. If the engine does not pick up speed when you do this, the injector is faulty.

TECH TIP   You can manually push the injector rack into full-fuel with your finger. Take care, however, when doing this!

---

3. On DDEC-equipped engines (two- or four-stroke-cycle DDC), the injector follower is still mechanically operated by the rocker arm, although there is no injector rack. A small electrically operated solenoid controls the duration of fuel injection. Shorting out of these injectors can be done by selecting individual cylinders with the use of the DDR (diagnostic data reader) illustrated in Figure 21-52.

MECHANICAL INJECTOR TESTS

DDC unit injectors can be checked and tested on a pop tester stand for spray pattern and atomization. However, due to the design of the injector, the actual popping pressure or pressure at which the internal needle valve lifts from its seat against spring force can be done only by installing the internal parts on a special adapter. This requires that you loosen the injector body nut, remove the component parts below the injector bushing, and assemble these onto the special adapter along with the injector nut and seal. Only then can the actual injector popping pressure be determined on a special test stand.

In addition, the injector's delivery rate can be checked on a calibration test stand to determine if in fact the injector assembly is delivering the correct amount of fuel. There are several test stands and pop testers on the market that can be used to test DDC unit injectors. Some of these are Kent-Moore, Bacharach, and Hartridge equipment. Detailed unit injector tests are discussed next.

Injector Rack Control Freeness Test

The injector rack control freeness test can be done by two methods:

1. Simply turning the injector upside down while holding it in your hand to see if the rack actually falls under its own weight. Also apply some palm pressure to the top of the injector follower to see if the rack moves freely. If the rack fails to move with gentle pressure, a sticking/binding rack condition could occur when the injector is in the engine.

2. If available place the injector in tester J29584 and check rack freeness. With the injector control rack held in the *no-fuel* position, operate the handle to depress the follower to the bottom of its stroke. Then, very slowly release the pressure on the handle while moving the control rack up and down until the follower reaches the top of its travel. If the rack falls freely the injector passes the test. If the rack does not fall freely, loosen the injector nut, turn the tip, then retighten the nut. Loosen and retighten the nut a couple of times, if necessary. Generally, this will free the rack. Then, if the rack isn't free, change the injector nut. In some cases it may be necessary to disassemble the injector to eliminate the cause of the misaligned parts or to remove dirt.

Spray Pattern Test

The spray pattern test can be performed by installing the injector into a test stand such as the one shown in Figure 21-13. This test machine will allow you to clamp the injector into position hydraulically. The clear plastic shield can then be placed underneath and around the injector assembly. The tester pump handle is then operated manually to prime the injector only. To actually cause fuel to leave the spray tip, a separate handle that contacts the top of the injector follower must be manipulated to force the internal injector plunger downward. Rapidly activate the pump handle to achieve 40 to 80 strokes per minute. You can actually see the fuel distribution pattern from the end of the spray tip. Rapid operation of the handle will allow the fuel to spray in an atomized state from the tip. Generally, this fuel spray should be accompanied by a distinct "chatter" sound, which usually indicates that the injector needle valve is moving freely within the tip assembly. Any sign of a nonatomized fuel spray pattern from any of the tip holes would indicate a faulty injector. Another test that can be performed at this time is to place a piece of clean white paper towel around the inner circumference of the plastic spray shield. Pop the injector once, then count the number of fuel dots on the paper. Compare this to the number of holes in the spray tip to confirm if any holes are plugged. The number of holes are etched into the bottom of the

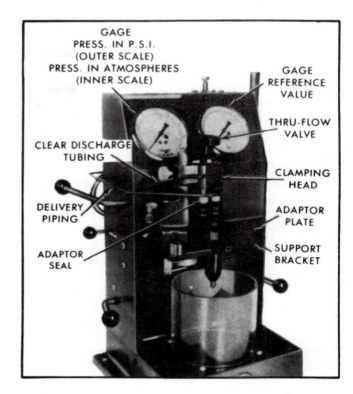

FIGURE 21-13 *Mechanical unit injector mounted into a Kent-Moore test stand J23010. (Courtesy of Detroit Diesel Corporation.)*

spray tip assembly. For example, a series of numbers that reads 8-0.006-165 indicates that the tip has eight holes. 0.006 in. (0.152 mm) each in diameter, and the included spray-in angle is 165°. Any drops of fuel that form on the end of the spray tip indicate a poor seat between the needle valve and the spray tip assembly. The start and end of injection should be sharp.

Injector Leakage Test

An injector leakage test can be performed while the injector is installed in position for the spray pattern and atomization test described in step 2. First dry off the injector with a clean, lint-free rag. Raise the tester pressure to between 1600 and 2000 psi (11,024 to 13,780 kPa). Check for fuel leakage at the injector filter cap gaskets, body plugs, and injector nut seal ring.

Operate the tester handle to raise the pressure to 1500 to 2000 psi (10,335 to 13,780 kPa). Time the pressure drop between 1500 and 1000 psi (10,335 to 6890 kPa). If the pressure drop occurs in less than 7 seconds using Kent-Moore fixture J23010, leakage is excessive between the lapped surfaces of the internal injector parts as well as between the plunger and the bushing.

Disassembling the Injector

1. Support the injector upright in injector holding fixture J22396 (Figure 21-14) and remove the filter caps, gaskets, and filters. Whenever a fuel injector is disassembled, discard the filters and gaskets and replace with new filters and gaskets. In the offset injector, a filter is used in the inlet side only. No filter is required in the outlet side.

2. Compress the follower spring (Figure 21-14). Then, raise the spring above the stop pin with a screwdriver and withdraw the pin. Allow the spring to rise gradually, and remove the plunger follower, plunger and spring as an assembly.

3. Using a deep socket J4983-01, loosen the nut on the injector body.

4. Lift the injector nut straight up, being careful not to dislodge the spray tip and valve parts. Remove the spray tip, spring cage, valve spring, spring seat, check valve cage and check valve. When an injector has been in use for some time, the spray tip, even though clean on the outside, may not be pushed readily from the nut with the fingers. In this event, support the nut on a wood block and drive the tip down through the nut, using tool J1291-02.

5. Refer to Figure 21-15 and remove the spill deflector. Then lift the bushing straight out of the injector body.

6. Remove the injector body from the holding fixture. Turn the body upside down and catch the gear retainer and gear in your hand as they fall out of the body.

7. Withdraw the injector control rack from the injector body. Also remove the seal ring from the body.

Since most injector problems are the result of dirt particles, it is essential that a clean area be provided on which to place the injector parts after cleaning and inspection. Wash all the parts with a suitable

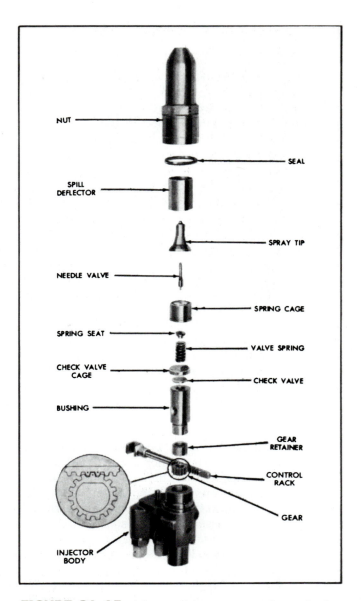

FIGURE 21–15 *Injector rack, gear, spray tip, and valve assembly details and relative location of parts.*

cleaning solvent and dry them with clean, filtered compressed air.

Testing the Injector

1. The spray tip test requires that all the parts above the bushing shown in Figure 21-15 be installed onto a special adapter (dummy bushing), and then secured in place with the injector nut and seal ring. Figure 21-16 illustrates the assembled adapter ready for test. When the tester handle is operated, the spray tip should open and release fuel at between 2200 and 3900 psi (15,158 to 26,890 kPa) on current two-stroke-cycle injectors. If the valve opening pressure is low and

FIGURE 21–14 *Removing the injector follower stop pin.*

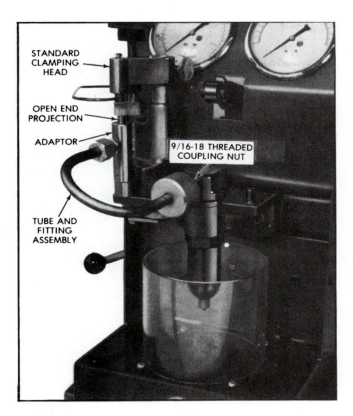

FIGURE 21–16 *Injector parts assembled to special adapter to determine the popping pressure (opening pressure) of the needle valve. (Courtesy of Detroit Diesel Corporation.)*

atomization is poor, you will have to replace the valve spring or spray tip assembly since the needle and tip are a matched pair. If the opening pressure is within the limits and atomization is good, pump the tester handle to bring the fuel pressure up to 1500 psi (10,335 kPa) and hold it for 15 seconds. Check to make sure that there are no fuel droplets or leakage at the spray tip.

2. The needle valve lift test requires that the spray tip be checked with a special gauge to determine if the needle valve lift is within 0.008 to 0.018 in. (0.203 to 0.457 mm). If the lift exceeds 0.018 in., replace the complete tip assembly. If it is less than 0.008 in., check for foreign material between the needle and seat. Figure 21-17 illustrates the spray-tip needle valve lift gauge.

3. Assemble all of the injected parts in the reverse order of disassembly. Anytime that an injector has been disassembled and the nut has been torqued to specs, the spray tip-to-injector nut concentricity must be checked by putting the injector into a special tool such as the one shown in Figure 21-18. The injector is rotated at least one full turn to ensure that the runout is no more than 0.008 in. (0.203 mm). If it is, re-

move the injector from the tester, loosen the nut and recenter the spray tip. Retorque the nut to between 75 and 85 lb-ft (102 to 115 N · m) and recheck the runout.

4. A fuel output test requires that the injector be installed into a test stand (calibrator) and checked for delivery rate according to the manufacturer's specifications. Figure 21-19 shows two typical MUI test machines.

Since detailed overhaul and testing of the unit injector is normally not performed in a truck shop by a mechanic/technician, but is undertaken by a fuel injection specialist either at the truck maintenance facility or at a local DDC distributor/dealer or fuel injection rebuild shop, the information given above will provide you with the ability to perform some of these checks and tests if special equipment is available to you.

FUEL SYSTEM TROUBLESHOOTING

One of the most common complaints received by the mechanic/technician is that the engine runs rough or lacks power. When this complaint is received, it can be caused by a number of conditions that often have nothing at all to do with the fuel system itself, but more often than not, it is the fuel system that receives the blame. Prior to condemning the fuel system as the cause of the complaint, you should always gather as much information as possible from the operator of the vehicle or equipment to assist you in systematically tracing the probable cause, or causes. However, it is always advisable to run the engine and closely monitor the color of the exhaust smoke, both at a no-load and a full-load condition, if possible.

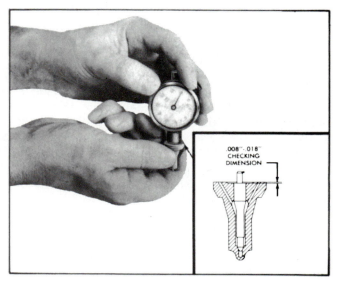

FIGURE 21–17 *Checking needle valve lift with special tool J9462-02. (Courtesy of Detroit Diesel Corporation.)*

FIGURE 21–18 *Checking assembled injector spray tip concentricity (runout) with a dial gauge. (Courtesy of Detroit Diesel Corporation.)*

The color of the exhaust smoke will quickly lead you to one or more of the engine systems. For example, gray-to-black smoke is usually an indication of air starvation, although it can also be caused by overfueling, which is not too common on today's engines. Blue smoke indicates oil being burned in the combustion chamber. This could be an internal engine problem, or even blower or turbocharger seal leakage. White smoke is generally associated with low compression or water in the cylinder; however, do not be misled on cold-weather startup, particularly on MUI engines when white smoke is evident. This is caused by the lower cylinder temperature due to the cold air which affects the ignition delay characteristic of the fuel. The unburned fuel particles quickly cool on entering the atmosphere and white smoke is created. If the white smoke is evident on startup but clears up within a short period of time (2 to 3 minutes or so on MUI engines), this is not the reason for the lack-of-power complaint.

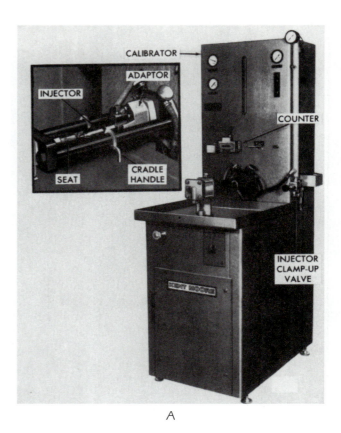

A

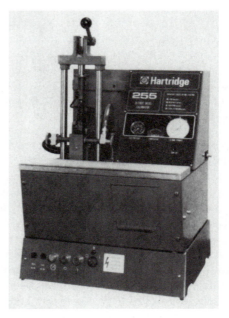

B

FIGURE 21–19 *(A) Injector calibrator; (B) Hartridge calibrator for Detroit injectors. (Courtesy of Lucas Hartridge, Inc.)*

NOTE Electronically controlled engines tend to clear white smoke 20 to 30 seconds after cold-weather startup.

If the white smoke fails to clear after the engine warms up, possible causes could be:

- Low cylinder compression
- The use of low-cetane diesel fuel
- Water in the combustion chamber from a leaking head gasket or a cracked cylinder head (can result in severe piston and con-rod damage due to the hydrostatic lock that will occur as the piston attempts to compress the trapped water)

DDC has determined that white smoke or misfire at an engine idle speed can be attributed in some cases to the idle fuel output being substantially higher or lower on one or more injectors than on the others. Cylinders receiving too little or too much idle fuel tend to white smoke, and idle quality suffers greatly due to these unbalanced firing impulses. On non-DDEC-equipped two-cycle engines only, it may be necessary after a tune-up and injector rack adjustment procedure to short out each individual injector by pushing and holding down the injector follower with a screwdriver to determine what cylinders are in effect firing with the engine idling. On those cylinders that are not firing, no change will be noticed in the engine rpm and sound when the nonfiring cylinder injector follower is depressed. It may therefore be necessary to adjust these particular injector racks while the engine is idling by turning the rack screw lightly to increase the fuel delivery to that cylinder. Series 92 engine racks should not be adjusted more than one-quarter turn (90°), while series 53 and 71 engine injector racks should not be adjusted more than one-eighth turn (45°).

NOTE On older engines employing two rack adjustment screws, the screw closest to the rack (inner) is the adjuster; the outer screw is a lock screw. On newer engines, only one rack screw is used on the injector control tube to rack.

After any such adjustment, slowly accelerate the engine a number of times, then allow it to settle down at the normal idle speed to determine if the idle is now smoother and the white smoke or roughness has disappeared. Should a rough idle or white smoke persist, further checks would be required to determine the cause.

With a lack-of-power complaint, black smoke is common and can generally be traced back to a high AIR (air inlet restriction) condition, or a combination high AIR and low blower or turbocharger boost condition. If a lack-of-power complaint is received with no visible smoke at the exhaust, this generally indicates that the engine is not receiving adequate fuel delivery. A check of throttle linkage travel should be made to determine whether or not the engine is actually receiving full-rack travel when the pedal is in its maximum fuel position.

NOTE On DDC engines equipped with the DDEC (Detroit Diesel electronic controls) fuel injection system, the throttle is a drive-by-wire (potentiometer/variable resistance) system; therefore, this check would not apply. The DDEC section in this chapter describes how to access the stored trouble codes within the computer, which will lead you to the general area of the problem. However, always eliminate the common causes, such as air inlet restriction, low turbo/blower boost, high EBP (exhaust back pressure), high crankcase pressure, fuel system restriction, and so on, before tackling the ECM (electronic control module) trouble codes.

Fuel Flow or Fuel Spill-Back Check

You may first want to check the fuel pump drive quickly by inserting the end of a small wire through one of the pump drain holes as you crank the engine over. Vibration or wire movement will indicate that the shaft is rotating. Sticking of the fuel pump relief valve toward the open or fuel bypass position can create low pump delivery pressure.

You may recollect from earlier discussions on DDC fuel systems that the system is termed a recirculatory one because of the high return of fuel back to the tank. This fuel must first pass through a *restricted fitting*, the size of which will vary among engines and injector size. Each fuel line restricted fitting is stamped with a number that signifies the actual hole size inside it. For example, an R80 fitting is a restricted fitting with an 0.080-in. (2.032-mm) hole size. The purpose and function of this fitting is to restrict the flow of fuel returning from the cylinder head fuel return manifold to ensure minimum fuel pressure within the cylinder head at the injectors of 30 to 35 psi (206.85 to 241.32 kPa). Normal fuel pressure is between 45 and 70 psi (310 to 483 kPa) from the pump.

Checking Procedure

1. Check first that you have the correct size of restricted fitting for your model and engine series. This can be found listed in section 13.2 in all DDC service manuals.

2. The amount of fuel spill back varies with the restricted fitting size. A general rule of thumb average for fuel spill back on engines employing a standard fuel pump is approximately related to the restricted fitting size. For example, an engine using a 0.055-in. (1.397-mm) restricted fitting should return 0.5 U.S. gallon (1.892 L) per minute minimum. An 0.080-in. (2.032-mm) fitting should return 0.8 U.S. gallon (3.028 L) per minute minimum at 1200 rpm or 0.9 U.S. gallon (3.406 L) per minute minimum at 1800 to 2300 rpm. In other words, if for some reason you did not have specifications readily at hand, by using the basic rules stated above you will be able to establish whether or not sufficient fuel is being circulated.

3. Disconnect the fuel return line at a convenient place that will readily allow you to run the fuel into a clean, adequately sized container (Figure 21-20).

4. You will need a watch with a second hand; if in a shop, a large wall clock with a second hand will

do. On nonturbocharged engines a fuel spill-back check is normally taken at an engine speed of 1200 rpm, although it can be checked out at 1800 rpm and beyond to ensure continuity of flow as per specifications. On turbocharged engines, the fuel spill back is normally taken at 1800 rpm, but it can also be taken at the higher rpm ranges as specified under fuel spill back to ensure continuity of fuel flow.

5. Start and run the engine at the specified speed for 1 minute, after which you can determine whether the system is receiving an adequate supply of fuel. While you are doing this check, immerse the fuel return line into the container to check for any sign of air bubbles rising to the surface. This would indicate that air is being drawn into the fuel system on the suction side of the fuel pump. Check all fuel line connections from the suction side of the pump back to the fuel tank, including the seal ring at the primary filter and at the strainer or fuel water separator if used. Remember, from the outlet or discharge side of the pump the fuel is under pressure; therefore, a fuel leak would occur from here on up to the cylinder head fuel manifold rather than sucking in air. When checking for air bubbles at the container during a fuel spill-back test, ensure that the fuel line is in fact submerged totally. Otherwise, agitation and aeration on the surface of the fuel may lead you to believe that the system is sucking air.

6. If the amount of fuel returned is less than specified in DDC manuals, replace the primary fuel filter, remove the pipe plug from the top of the secondary filter, and install a fuel pressure gauge. Start and run the engine again at 1200 or 1800 rpm, as the case may be, and measure the amount of fuel returned to the container. Also note what fuel pressure registers on the gauge at the secondary filter. Normal fuel pressure should be between 45 and 70 psi (310.27 to 482.65 kPa).

7. If the fuel return and pressure are still low, replace the secondary filter element and repeat the previous procedure.

8. If, after replacing the secondary filter, low fuel flow persists, then tee-in a vacuum gauge or mercury manometer at the primary filter outlet line or restriction tap point (Figure 21-5). Start and run the engine and note what the maximum restriction to fuel flow is. The maximum allowable on a system with new filters is 6 in. Hg (mercury), or 12 in. Hg on a dirty system. Check that the fuel line size is as recommended for your engine as stated by DDC. In addition, if the fuel tank is in excess of 20 ft (6.096 m) away from the pump, the next size of line should be used. Also, if you are lifting the fuel vertically more than 4 ft (1.219 m), you will have to go to a high-lift fuel system.

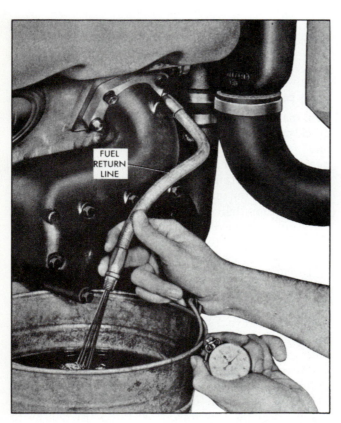

FUEL
RETURN
LINE

FIGURE 21–20 *Performing a fuel spill-back check for 1 minute at 1800 rpm. (Courtesy of Detroit Diesel Corporation.)*

9. If low fuel pressure and return still exist, tee-in to the fuel pump outlet; start and run the engine to establish what pressure the pump is producing. If it is suspected that the pump is faulty, temporarily replace it with a new or rebuilt unit and again perform the spill-back check to determine if the original pump was faulty. If an alternative pump is unavailable, loosen the pump relief valve plug and remove the bypass relief valve components to check that the valve is not stuck in the open position. If it is, attempt to remove the valve and clean the piston. You may also have to remove the pump from the engine and disassemble and clean it in order to free the stuck relief valve. If the gears are scored or damaged, a new pump will be required.

10. Another area that should be checked with a continued low spill back is the ECM (DDEC) for possible internal plugging or restriction within the cooler plate. To isolate the cooler plate, bypass it by simply connecting the inlet and outlet lines from the cooler plate and run the engine at its maximum no-load speed to determine if the fuel spill-back volume is within minimum acceptable rates. If it is, replace the cooler plate.

CAUTION If step 10 is performed, do *not* run the engine for longer than 5 minutes, since overheating of the electronics components within the ECM/DDEC can result.

NOTE To check if the pump drive shaft is rotating, insert a piece of small wire up through the pump flange drain hole, crank the engine momentarily, and note if the wire vibrates. If it does not, remove the pump and check the condition of the drive hub and coupling.

---

11. Although not a common problem, do *not* neglect checking out the fuel tank for foreign objects that may be blocking the fuel flow. There have been several instances in my own experience, especially around logging equipment, where an engine will run fine until the level in the tank drops low enough to allow a piece of wood chip or bark to be held against the fuel suction line and suddenly create a lack-of-power complaint, rough running, and even stalling.

12. Another possible problem area can be a plugged injector inlet filter. This is not common since most equipment owners usually change their primary and secondary fuel filters on a reasonably steady basis. If it is found that the injector filter is in fact plugged, it

is advisable to remove the injectors for service and replace them with a matched rebuilt set.

13. A quick check for plugged filters is to remove the fuel return jumper line from the injector. Install an old line onto the injector, which is bent to take fuel away from the head area. Crank the engine with the starter and note if a steady gush of fuel emanates from the fuel line. If not, the injector filter is probably plugged.

Checking Cylinder Compression Pressure: DDC Two-Cycle Engines

Since a certain amount of time is required to do a compression check on the engine, you should first analyze the color of the smoke coming out of the exhaust stack.

Checking Procedure

1. Refer to Figure 21-21. Remove the hand hole cover inspection plate from the side of the cylinder block. This allows free access into the air box area and the cylinder liner port area. Select a blunt (nonpointed) tool and push against the compression rings to check for free spring or tension. If there is no sign of this, the piston ring is stuck in its groove. An additional check would be to carefully note whether or not the compression rings have a visible groove all the way around the center circumference. This groove is placed there at the time of manufacture: If it is not visible, the rings are very badly worn. If it is visible in some spots but not others, irregular ring wear is evident. You can also check for damage to the piston ring lands and skirt area at this time.

2. If piston rings are badly worn in one or more cylinders, this would be noticeable as high crankcase

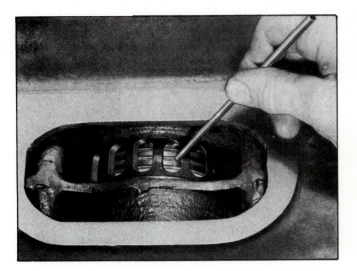

FIGURE 21–21 *Inspecting condition of piston rings through the liner ports on a DDC two-stroke-cycle engine. (Courtesy of Detroit Diesel Corporation.)*

pressure when using a water manometer. All rings badly worn would be reflected by blue exhaust smoke, lack of power, hard starting, and rough running.

3.   Prior to taking a compression check, it is imperative that the engine be at normal operating temperature. If only one cylinder is suspected of having low compression, start with it. If doing them all, start with cylinder 1.

4.   A cylinder compression check is taken on all DDC two-cycle engines at a speed of 600 rpm; therefore, you cannot hope to use a typical hand-held automotive-type gauge. Several suitable test gauges are readily available from well-known tool suppliers, or an old injector nut and body can easily be adapted for this purpose. A good machinist can easily make up a dummy-type injector for this also. Figure 21-22 shows the gauge installed ready for the compression check.

5.   To install the dummy injector and pressure gauge unit, it is first necessary to remove the fuel jumper pipes from the inlet and outlet of the injector. Place plastic shipping caps over the injector fuel holes. Remove the rocker arm hold-down bolts, and tip the assembly back. Loosen the injector clamp bolt and remove the injector.

6.   Install the proper adapter (dummy injector), and clamp it in place with the hose and gauge attached. Using an old fuel pipe, connect it between the fuel inlet and return manifold connections (all engines).

7.   It is advisable, if at all possible, especially on the larger-model engines, to use an old rocker cover that has suitable sections cut out of it to facilitate running the engine during the compression test. This will minimize oil throw-off.

8.   Start the engine and run it at 600 rpm until the

TABLE 21–1 *Typical engine compression pressure values for various DDC engine models*[a]

Engine at 600 rpm: sea level	Minimum	New parts
53 2 VLV, 4 VLV, and T	430	480
53N	540	590
71E 2 VLV, 4 VLV, and T	425	475
71N	515	565
V-71 2 VLV, 4 VLV, and T	425	475
V-71N	515	565
V-92	500	550
V-92T	450	500
8.2L and Series 60	48[b]	56[b]

Source: Detroit Diesel Corporation.
[a] The variation in compression pressures between cylinders must not exceed 25 psi at 600 rpm. Two-cycle engines only.
[b] Compression per cylinder at TDC is 48 psi minimum. Use cylinder leakage tester J29006 to determine psi.

pressure on the test gauge reaches its maximum point. Note and record the cylinder pressure. The pressure variation should not exceed 25 psi (172.37 kPa) between cylinders. To determine what the minimum acceptable pressure is for your engine, check the DDC service manual for your particular engine under section 13, operating conditions, or refer to Table 21-1. There are quite a variety of minimum acceptable standards, which vary with altitude.

9.   In addition to stuck or broken rings, compression leakage can occur at the cylinder head gasket, valve seats, injector tube, and in extreme cases through a cracked or holed piston.

SERIES 60 COMPRESSION LEAKAGE

The series 60 engine, which is a four-stroke-cycle engine, can have its compression pressure checked by the method described above, or by using a cylinder leakage test gauge arrangement such as that shown in Figure 21-23 must be used. This arrangement is similar to that used on DDC's 8.2-L V8 four-stroke-cycle engine; therefore, familiarity with this engine test arrangement will allow you to relate quickly to the sequence used for compression pressure checking of the series 50 and 60 engine.

A cylinder leakage check would be warranted by poor engine performance, particularly when either white or blue smoke is visible at the exhaust stack and other possible causes have been checked first. Loss of compression in an engine can usually be traced to either piston ring wear or leaking valves; however, it can

FIGURE 21–22 *Compression gauge and dummy injector in position for testing cylinder pressure. (Courtesy of Detroit Diesel Corporation.)*

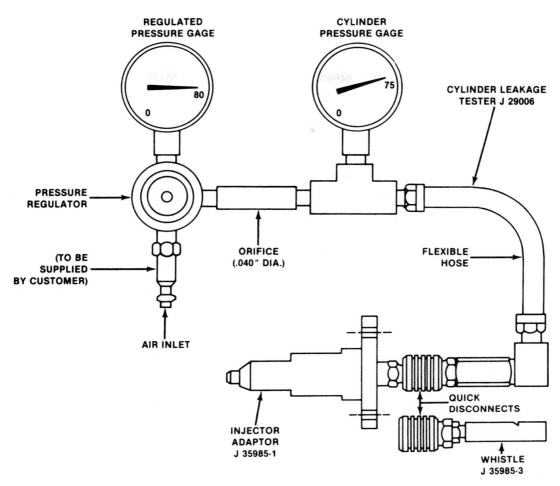

FIGURE 21–23 *Series 60 DDEC engine cylinder leak-down test gauges and tooling. (Courtesy of Detroit Diesel Corporation.)*

also be affected by broken rings, scored or worn cylinder walls, a leaking cylinder head gasket, a cracked cylinder head or liner, and possibly a hole in a piston assembly.

Cylinder Leak-Down Test

To effectively determine if one or more cylinders does have low compression, use the tool arrangement shown in Figure 21-23.

1. Start and run the engine until it reaches its normal operating temperature of 180°F (82°C).

SAFETY NOTE   Disconnect the battery ground cable(s) and isolate the starter motor at this time.

---

2. Stop the engine and proceed to:

a. Remove the air inlet ducting to the intake manifold.

b. Remove the rocker cover assembly.

c. Remove the oil filler tube cap.

d. Remove the radiator pressure cap.

e. Remove the exhaust piping from the turbocharger outlet.

f. Drain the cylinder head fuel galleries.

g. Remove all rocker arm assemblies.

h. Remove all electronic unit injectors.

3. Refer to Figure 21-24 and insert the special injector adapter into the injector hole tube of cylinder 1. This adapter, available as Kent-Moore tool J35985-1, is used in conjunction with TDC locating whistle J35985-3.

4. Secure the injector adapter and whistle in place by installing the EUI hold-down crab, washer, and bolt, and tightening the retaining bolt to 43 to 49 lb-ft (58 to 66 N · m).

5. Using a ¾-in. square breaker bar or ratchet assembly, install it into the mating hole in the crankshaft

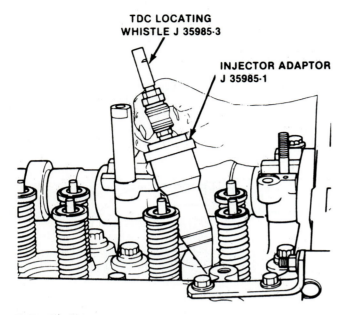

FIGURE 21–24 *Installing cylinder leak-down test tools on a series 60 DDEC engine. (Courtesy of Detroit Diesel Corporation.)*

pulley and slowly rotate the engine in a CW direction from the front.

6. As you rotate the engine, air in the cylinder will be expelled through adapter J35985-3, creating a sound just like a whistle. Slowly rotate the engine over until the sound starts to fade and then completely disappears when the piston reaches TDC. You may have to turn the engine crankshaft back and forward slightly to ensure that you have in fact reached true TDC.

7. Disconnect and remove the whistle from the injector adapter J35985-1.

8. Refer to Figure 21-25 and install the quick-disconnect coupling of cylinder leakage tester J29006 to the injector adapter in place in the cylinder head.

9. Connect a shop air line from a clean dry source to the regulator IN port of the cylinder leakage tester J29006. Shop air should be between 100 and 125 psi (690 to 862 kPa) with a maximum safe value not to exceed 150 psi (1025 kPa).

SAFETY PRECAUTION   If the engine is not at true TDC, it is possible for the crankshaft to rotate when air is applied into the cylinder; therefore, stay clear of any rotating assemblies as the air is being introduced through the regulator assembly.

---

10. With the shop air line connected as shown in Figure 21-25 carefully adjust the regulated air pressure gauge supply knob until 80 psi (552 kPa) registers on the gauge face.

NOTE   Should the engine start to rotate, true TDC has not been achieved. If this occurs, release the air pressure, disconnect the line, and repeat step 6. Do *not* attempt to turn the engine over while the air pressure line is attached to the adapter gauge set.

---

11. Allow the 80 psi regulated air pressure to remain in the cylinder for at least 60 seconds. Once the cylinder is full and the gauge has stabilized, note and record the reading on the cylinder pressure gauge.

12. Any air leakage from the inlet manifold, turbocharger exhaust outlet, oil filler tube, and adjacent injector tube holes on either side of the cylinder being tested will usually result in a lower-than-acceptable reading on the cylinder pressure gauge, due to problems at these areas.

13. For a cylinder to be considered acceptable during the leakage test, the cylinder pressure gauge must maintain 56 psi (386 kPa) or higher.

14. Minimum acceptable cylinder pressures are 48 psi (330 kPa); however, some power loss may be noticeable on an engine that has all cylinders at this minimum acceptable value.

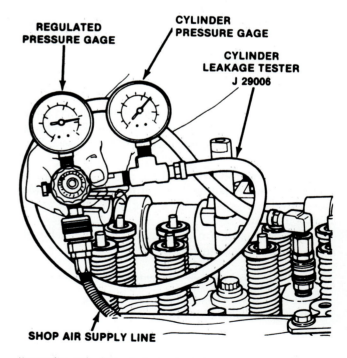

FIGURE 21–25 *Cylinder leakage test gauges J29006 in place on a series 60 engine to monitor the rate of compression leakage by introducing regulated compressed shop air into the cylinder. (Courtesy of Detroit Diesel Corporation.)*

TABLE 21–2 *Causes of low cylinder pressure readings*

Air is leaking from:	Possible cause
Air intake manifold	Intake valves not seating correctly
Turbo exhaust outlet	Exhaust valves burnt or not seating
Adjacent injector tube hole	Leaking or damaged cylinder head gasket
Air bubbles in radiator coolant	Leaking cylinder head gasket; cracked cylinder head or liner
Oil filler tube	Piston rings worn or stuck in their grooves (carbon), tapered cylinder liner bore, or a possible hole in the piston

15. Any cylinder that registers a reading lower than 48 psi (330 kPa) must be checked to determine where the compression pressure loss is. However, if a cylinder registers excessive leakage, disconnect the air line and after rotating the engine through 720° (two complete revolutions), repeat the TDC and pressure leakage test.

16. After testing all cylinders, you will be in a position to judge the mechanical state of the engine cylinders, rings, valves, and so on (see Table 21-2).

Determining the Problem

Several quick checks can be performed to determine specifically where the problem area might be.

1. Rap the tops of the intake and exhaust valve stems with a plastic or rubber mallet to ensure that the valves are not hanging up, and watch the gauge reading again.

2. Slowly and carefully rotate the engine crankshaft over in approximately 10° increments while watching the cylinder pressure gauge. If the gauge pressure rises as you turn over the engine, this usually confirms that there is wear in the upper part of the liner bore. However, if there is no change on the face of the cylinder pressure gauge, it confirms that the piston rings are worn or stuck in their grooves.

DDC TWO-STROKE-CYCLE ENGINE TUNE-UP: NON-DDEC ENGINES

The following information and sequences apply to the tune-up requirements for the two-stroke-cycle series 53, 71, and 92 truck engines equipped with a DDC mechanical governor. On DDC two-stroke-cycle engines equipped with the DDEC (Detroit Diesel electronic controls), there is no mechanical governor on the engine. There are also no fuel control rods, fuel control tubes, or injector racks; however, the valves and injector timing height adjustments are still required, so the sequence given here for non-DDEC-equipped engines can be followed. DDEC 1-equipped two-stroke-cycle engines were initially released to the market in September 1985 for on-highway truck series 71 and 92 engines. The series 60 four-stroke-cycle engines discussed in this chapter are all equipped with DDEC fuel systems.

Tune-up of a diesel engine is not based on the same criteria as for automotive-type gasoline engines. Until 1972 there was no set interval at which a full tune-up had to be performed, with the performance of the engine being the controlling factor in actually undertaking the full tune-up. However, with the 1972–1973 model year, all diesel engine manufacturers had to comply with the EPA requirements regarding exhaust emissions. This has forced engine manufacturers to check and correct as necessary (to comply with emissions warranty requirements) such items as injector timing, valve lash, idle and no-load speeds, and throttle delay or fuel modulator settings.

All DDC mechanical governors are easily identifiable by a nameplate attached to the governor housing; the following letters are typical examples.

- *DWLS:* double-weight limiting speed (mobile equipment)
- *SWLS:* single-weight limiting speed (mobile equipment)

When performing a necessary tune-up on an engine, do *not* back off all the necessary adjustments. It is only necessary to *check* these for a possible change in the settings. If, however, a cylinder head or the governor or injectors have been removed and overhauled or replaced, several initial adjustments are necessary before the engine can be started. These adjustments would consist of the first four items in the DDC tune-up sequence, the only exception being that the valve clearance is greater on a cold engine.

Prior to listing the tune-up sequence steps, it should be noted that if a supplementary governing device such as a mechanical throttle delay piston or a fuel modulator unit is used on a turbocharged engine, these should be loosened-off before the engine tune-up is performed; otherwise, they will interfere with the injector rack control adjustments. A tune-up should always be performed with the engine at normal operating temperature, which is generally within the range 170 to 195°F (77 to 91°C). This is commonly known as a *hot set* and is the correct method for a tune-up.

Of course, if an engine has had major service work performed on it, or the engine has been reassembled after an overhaul, a hot set cannot be performed until the engine has been started. Therefore, it is necessary for the mechanic/technician to perform a *cold set*. The only difference between a cold set and a hot set is that the exhaust valve clearance on a cold engine is always a wider specification. This spec can be seen on the engine emissions label.

NOTE It is important when performing a hot set to keep the engine temperature at or higher than 170°F; therefore, it may be necessary to start and run the engine several times during the hot set to ensure that all adjustments are being done at the same temperature.

CAUTION Before starting the engine after any governor or speed control adjustments, always check to ensure that when the governor STOP lever is placed into the stop position, the injector racks do in fact move to the fuel-shutoff position; otherwise, engine overspeed could result.

Each DDC engine is certified to be in compliance with federal and California emissions regulations established for the model year in which it was manufactured. In addition, DDC engines comply with both the Australian Design Rule 30 and those imposed by the European Economic Community. To comply with these regulations, engine tune-up is dependent on the following five physical characteristics:

1. Fuel injector type
2. Maximum full-load engine speed
3. Engine camshaft timing (standard or advanced)
4. Fuel injector timing
5. Supplementary governing device to limit exhaust smoke emissions, particularly on turbocharged heavy-duty on-highway truck vehicles

TUNE-UP SEQUENCE

The tune-up sequence *must* be followed exactly as given; otherwise, you can affect other adjustments which have already been performed. On TT-equipped governor engines, back off the belleville washer retainer nut as shown in Figure 21-26 and 21-43 prior to performing the complete tune-up. Also, on engines equipped with either a mechanical throttle delay piston or a fuel modulator piston, loosen the retaining bolts holding these accessories to prevent any interference when setting the fuel racks and other adjustments.

Tune-up Procedure
1. Check and adjust the exhaust valve bridge adjustment.
2. Check and adjust the exhaust valve clearances.
3. Check and adjust the injector follower timing height above the injector body.
4. Check and adjust the governor gap.
5. Position/adjust the injector rack control levers.
6. Check and adjust the maximum no-load speed.
7. Adjust the engine idle speed.
8. If the engine is equipped with a TT (tailor torque) governor assembly, adjust the belleville washers to obtain the recommended TT horsepower setting for that specific model of engine. Refer to the TT governor description/adjustment in this chapter.
9. Adjust the buffer screw.

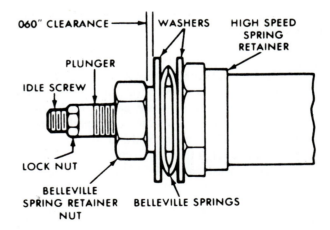

FIGURE 21–26 *Adjusting nut backed off to allow a minimum clearance of 0.060 in. (1.52 mm) between the belleville washers prior to setting the TT horsepower setting on a two-stroke-cycle V92 engine, or prior to performing a tune-up. (Courtesy of Detroit Diesel Corporation.)*

10. Adjust the starting aid screw on turbocharged engines only.

11. Adjust either the throttle delay mechanism or the fuel modulator on turbocharged engines only.

12. Check that the throttle linkage is allowing full fuel; otherwise, adjust it.

Exhaust Valve Bridge Adjustment

The purpose of the exhaust valve bridge is to allow the rocker arm to push it down and open two exhaust valves at once; therefore, they are used only on four-valve-head engine models. Generally, unless cylinder head work has been done, they do not require adjustment; however, these should be checked and reset if they are incorrect. Each bridge should always be reinstalled on the bridge guide from which it was removed, since it takes up a wear characteristic peculiar to its own guide.

If the cylinder head has been rebuilt or has been off of the engine for any reason, the valve bridges can be adjusted once the head has been torqued into position, prior to bolting the rocker arm assemblies back down. However, if you have to check and adjust them on an engine that is in service, the following procedure should be followed.

Procedural Check

1. Rotate the engine over to place the injector follower all the way down on the cylinder to be checked.

2. Obtain two pieces of 0.0015-in. (0.038-mm) brass shim stock or feeler gauge material that have been cut to approximately $\frac{3}{16}$ in. (4.75 mm) in width.

3. Lift up on the bridge slightly to allow you to slip each 0.0015-in. strip of feeler gauge between the bridge and both exhaust valve stem tips.

4. Apply light, even pressure to the bridge assembly in the center and check the drag on both feeler gauge strips between the bridge and each valve.

5. If both feeler gauges have the same drag, the bridge is properly adjusted. However, if they do not have the same drag, the fuel jumper lines have to be removed along with the rocker arm bracket hold-down bolts to gain access to the individual cylinder bridges.

Once the individual rocker arms have been removed, adjust the individual bridges.

Bridge Adjustment Procedure

1. Place the valve bridge in a *soft-jaw* vise or, if available, bridge holding fixture J21772, and loosen the locknut on the bridge adjusting screw. Back out the adjusting screw several turns.

NOTE Failure to follow the sequence noted above can result in damage. If the locknut is loosened or tightened with the bridge in place, the

---

twisting action involved can result in either a bent bridge guide or a bent rear valve stem.

---

2. Install the bridge back onto its respective bridge guide.

3. While firmly applying pressure to the bridge, as shown in Figure 21-27, turn the adjusting screw clockwise until it lightly contacts the valve stem. Carefully turn the screw an additional one-eighth to one-quarter turn and run the locknut up finger-tight.

4. Install the bridge in a soft-jaw vise and, while using a screwdriver to hold the adjustment screw, tighten the locknut to 20 to 25 lb-ft (27.1 to 33.87 N · m) torque.

5. Using engine oil, lubricate the bridge and guide, and reinstall it in its original position.

6. Select two 0.0015-in. (0.0381-mm) feeler gauges (pointed-finger type), or cut two thin strips that will fit under the bridge at each valve stem tip. Apply finger pressure to the pallet (center) surface of the valve bridge, and check to see that both feeler gauges are in fact tight. If they are not tight, readjust the screw as outlined previously.

7. Adjust the remaining valve bridges in the same manner.

8. Ensure that when the rocker arm assemblies are swung into position, the valve bridges are properly positioned on the rear valve stems; otherwise, damage to the valve and bridge mechanism is a possibility.

Exhaust Valve Clearance Adjustment

The writer assumes that the person involved in a typical tune-up on one of these engines has had some

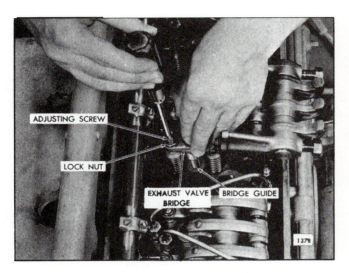

FIGURE 21–27 *Valve bridge adjustment procedure on a four-valve-head two-stroke-cycle engine model. (Courtesy of Detroit Diesel Corporation.)*

training in the basics of engine construction and general overhaul and therefore is in a position to interpret the data and sequence that follows.

On any engine, whether a gasoline or diesel engine, correct valve clearance is very important to ensure smooth efficient operation of the engine. On DDC two-cycle units, all valves are *exhaust* since the cylinder liner ports take the place of the intake valves. Therefore, insufficient valve clearance on these engines can result in a loss of compression since the valves will be held off their seats. In addition, this will cause misfiring cylinders and eventually burned valve seats and seat inserts, due to the fact that the valve is unable to dissipate its heat through good seat contact. On the other hand, excessive valve clearance will result in noisy operation, especially at the lower speed ranges. In both cases there will be a noticeable loss of power.

Valve adjustment is thus necessary any time the head has been removed and replaced or the valve mechanism has been disturbed in any way. The initial setting is done with the engine cold, and must be checked and reset when the engine has reached its normal operating temperature. If the exhaust valve bridges require adjustment, see the earlier section for the procedure.

The sequence for exhaust valve adjustment is the same for series 71 and 92 engines. The only difference on the four-valve-head 53 series engine is that it uses a pivoted bridge attached to the end of the rocker arm assembly; therefore, the valve clearance is checked under only one valve stem to bridge since it will self-center during operation of the engine.

Series 53, 71, and 92 engines employ pushrods that are threaded into the ends of the rocker arm as-

sembly; therefore, the exhaust valve clearance adjustment is always made at the pushrod. *Do not disturb the exhaust valve bridge adjustment screw* unless the cylinder head has been removed for servicing or the bridge adjusting screw has been loosened for any reason.

Since a two-cycle engine requires only 360° of crankshaft rotation for each power stroke per cylinder, as opposed to 720° on a four-cycle engine, all the exhaust valves can be adjusted in firing-order sequence in one full turn of the crankshaft. Every DDC service manual shows the particular engine firing order under general engine specifications at the front of the manual.

On all series of DDC engines the following must be kept in mind when working with firing-order sequence:

1. Engine rotation is always determined from the front of the engine as CW (clockwise) or RH (right-hand) rotation, or CCW (counterclockwise), which is LH (left-hand) rotation.
2. Also determined from the front of the engine is the cylinder numbering sequence. For example, 1–2–3–4 on the LB and 1–2–3–4 on the RB.
3. On all V-type DDC engines the LB (left bank) or RB (right bank) is determined from the rear or flywheel end of the engine.

Table 21-3 lists some firing orders for some engines within a given series.

53, 71, 92, 149 Exhaust Valve Clearance Adjustment

1. It is imperative that all loose dirt be either steam cleaned from around the valve rocker covers or at least washed with solvent to prevent the entrance of

TABLE 21–3   Typical engine firing orders

Engine	Right-hand rotation	Left-hand rotation
8.2L	1L–8R–4R–3L–6R 5L–7L–2R	
6–71	1–5–3–6–2–4	1–4–2–6–3–5
6V–71 and 92	1L–3R–3L–2R–2L–1R	1L–1R–2L–2R–3L–3R
8V–71 and 92	1L–3R–3L–4R–4L–2R–2L–1R	1L–1R–2L–2R–4L–4R–3L–3R
Series 60	1–5–3–6–2–4	1–6–2–4–3–5
Series 12V–149	1L–5L–3R–4R–3L–4L–2R–6R–2L–6L–1R–5R	1L–5R–1R–6L–2L–6R–2R–4L–3L–4R–3R–5L
Series 16V–149	1L–2R–8L–6R–2L–4R–6L–R5–4L–3R–5L–7R–3L–1R–7L–8R	1L–8R–7L–1R–3L–7R–5L–3R–4L–5R–6L–4R–2L–6R–8L–2R
Series 20V–149	1L–5L–10L–4R–3R–9R–4L–3L–6R–9L–2R–6L–8R–7R– 2L–8L–7L–1R–5R–10R	

both dirt and foreign matter into the engine during and after their removal. The area around the governor should also be cleaned at this time.

2. On all two-cycle DDC engines there is no flywheel or accessory timing marks to line up, such as on Caterpillar and Cummins diesel engines. It is only necessary to observe the position of both the injector and valve rocker arms on the cylinder that is to be adjusted.

3. The governor speed control lever should be placed in the *idle* speed position, and the *stop* lever, if provided, should be secured in the stop position.

4. To rotate the engine crankshaft, either the starting motor can be used or preferably an engine barring tool, such as J22582; a $\frac{3}{4}$-in. (19-mm) square drive socket set with suitable socket to fit over the crankshaft pulley bolt will also do.

CAUTION When using either a barring tool or socket on the crankshaft bolt at the front of the engine, do *not* turn the crankshaft opposite its normal direction of rotation as this may loosen the bolt.

---

5. To determine which valves or injector is in a position to be adjusted, do the following: To set the valves on any given cylinder, the center rocker arm, which is the injector arm, must be all the way up when viewing the rocker assembly from the pushrod side.

6. Loosen the exhaust valve rocker arm pushrod locknut (53, 71, 92); on 149 series engines, loosen the locknut on the top of the rocker arm. From Table 21-4 select the proper feeler gauge for the particular engine that you are working on (see also engine emissions label).

NOTE It is advisable to use go/no go feeler gauges for this purpose, which will ensure that all the valves are in fact set to the same clearance (see Figure 21-28).

---

7. Place the correct gauge between the valve bridge pallet on four-valve heads or between the valve stem and rocker arm on two-valve heads. Assume that you were setting a four-valve-head 71 series engine *cold*. You would require a 0.015 to 0.017 in. (0.381 to 0.431 mm) go/no go feeler gauge for this purpose. Adjust the pushrod with a $\frac{5}{16}$-in. (7.93-mm) wrench on the square shoulder until the 0.017-in. (0.431-mm) portion of the gauge can be withdrawn with a smooth pull, and tighten the locknut with a $\frac{1}{2}$-in. (12.7-mm) wrench.

8. If the adjustment is correct, you should now be able to push the 0.015-in. (0.381-mm) part of the feeler gauge through the rocker arm area freely, but the 0.017-in. (0.431-mm) portion should not pass through. You should feel the shoulder of the feeler between the two sizes actually butt up against the rocker arm pallet. If necessary, readjust the pushrod.

TABLE 21–4   *Valve clearance specifications for various DDC engine models*[a]

Engine	Cylinder head	Cold setting in.	mm	Hot setting[b] in.	mm
Series 53	Two-valve	0.011	0.28	0.009	0.23
	Four-valve	0.026	0.66	0.024	0.61
Series 71	Two-valve	0.012	0.31	0.009	0.23
	Four-valve	0.016	0.41	0.014	0.36
Series 92	Four-valve	0.016	0.41	0.014	0.36
Series 8.2L	Intake	0.012	0.31	0.011	0.28
	Exhaust	0.014	0.36	0.012	0.31
Series 60	Intake	0.008	0.20		
	Exhaust	0.020	0.51		
Series 149	Four-valve	0.016	0.41	0.012	0.31

Source: Detroit Diesel Corporation.
[a] Use tool J9708-01.
[b] Hot setting should be made when the engine is at normal operating temperature [160 to 185°F (71 to 85°C)]. It may be necessary to run the engine between adjustments to maintain the temperature.

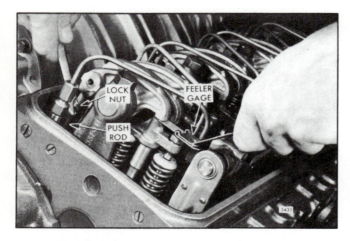

FIGURE 21–28 *Adjusting the valve clearance by rotation of the square shoulder on the pushrod on a two-stroke-cycle engine model. (Courtesy of Detroit Diesel Corporation.)*

Fuel Injector Timing

Although the injector plunger is timed by the fact that it meshes with a flat on the internal rack gear inside the injector body, which is in turn timed to the fuel control rack by a dot on the gear which is centered between two dots on the injector fuel rack, the actual effective length that the plunger moves down in its bushing is controlled by the height of the injector follower above the injector body. This is adjusted by turning the injector pushrod CW or CCW, as the case may be, to arrive at this dimension.

TECH TIP This dimension is given in section 14, engine tune-up, in all DDC service manuals; current timing pin dimensions can also be found stamped on the valve rocker cover emissions decal. Be certain that you select the proper timing pin gauge; otherwise, serious damage could result to the engine, not to mention poor performance.

All the injectors can be timed in firing-order sequence during one full revolution of the crankshaft similar to the valves on all two-cycle DDC engines. Four-cycle engines would require two revolutions of the crankshaft.

The sequence for injector timing is as follows:

1. The governor speed control lever should be in the *idle* position. If a stop lever is provided, secure it in the *stop* position.

2. The crankshaft can be rotated as explained in step 4 for exhaust valve adjustment.

3. To determine which injector is in a position to be checked or adjusted, do the following: Turn the engine over until the exhaust valves are fully depressed

(completely open) on the cylinder on which you wish to set the injector.

4. Insert the small end of the timing pin (gauge) into the hole provided in the top of the injector body, with the flat portion of the gauge facing the injector follower as shown in Figure 21-29. An optional dial gauge is also available for setting injector timing height.

5. Gently push the shoulder of the gauge by holding the knurled stem with the thumb and forefinger (see Figure 21-29) toward the follower; there should be a slight drag between the gauge and follower. You can also turn the gauge around in a circular motion to determine this same feel.

6. If this cannot be done, loosen the injector pushrod locknut and adjust it until the drag of the gauge (slight feel) has been determined; then hold the pushrod and tighten the locknut.

7. Recheck the feel, and if necessary, readjust.

8. When hot setting this adjustment, wipe off the top of the injector follower and place a clean drop of oil on it. When properly adjusted, the gauge should just wipe the oil film from the follower when the slight drag is felt and the pin gauge is rotated.

9. Time the remaining injectors in the same fashion.

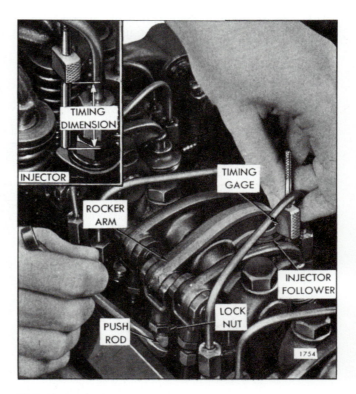

FIGURE 21–29 *Using the correct injector timing height gauge to adjust the distance between the top of the injector follower and the injector body on a two-stroke-cycle engine model. (Courtesy of Detroit Diesel Corporation.)*

Governor Gap Adjustment

Figures 21-30 to 21-32 illustrate where to check this gap on all double- and single-weight limiting-speed governors. However, prior to performing a governor gap adjustment, make sure that the following conditions are met:

1. Adjust the idle speed to the normal idle rpm that the engine will run at when it is operating.

2. Clean and remove the governor cover and gasket.

3. Back out the buffer screw prior to checking/adjusting the gap. ($\frac{5}{8}$ in. from the locknut).

4. Back out the starting aid screw on turbocharged engines.

5. Loosen the throttle delay or fuel modulator clamp.

6. On TT (tailer torque) engines, loosen the belleville washer retainer adjusting nut to provide a clearance of 0.060 in. (1.5 mm) between the nut and the washers as shown in Figure 21-26.

7. It is necessary to bar the engine over manually on DWLS V governors in order to insert the wedge spreading tool J35516 (Figure 21-31) between the larger low-speed weights and the riser shaft. On DWLS governors the gap should be between 0.003 and 0.019 in. (0.076 to 0.48 mm); otherwise, set it to 0.008 in.

(0.2 mm). On SWLS governors, the wedge tool is not necessary, since the weights are not touched. The gap is checked and set between the low-speed spring cap and the high-speed spring plunger to 0.170 in. (4.31 mm) on inline engines, and to 0.200 in. (5 mm) on V-engines with the engine stopped (Figure 21-32). On variable-speed governed models (SWVS):

a. Place the speed control lever in the *maximum speed* position.

b. Insert a 0.006-in. feeler gauge between the spring plunger and the plunger guide (Figure 21-41). If required, loosen the locknut and turn the adjusting screw until a slight drag is noted on the feeler gauge.

Injector Racks Setting and Adjustment

Since all the injector racks are connected to the fuel control tube and then to the governor via the fuel rod or rods, they must be set correctly to ensure that they are all equally related to the governor. Their positions determine the amount of fuel that will be injected into the individual cylinders and therefore assure equal distribution of the load. Properly adjusted injector rack control levers with the engine at full load will ensure the following:

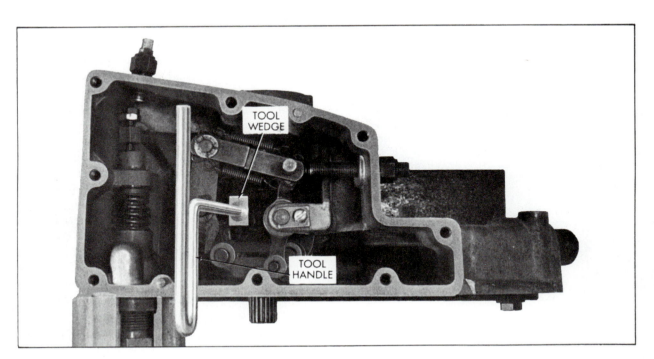

FIGURE 21–30 *Special wedge tool J35516 inserted between the double-weight mechanical limiting-speed governor low-speed weight and the riser shaft to measure the governor gap between the low-speed spring cap and high-speed spring plunger of a two-stroke-cycle V-design engine. (Courtesy of Detroit Diesel Corporation.)*

FIGURE 21–31 *Close-up view of wedge tool J35516 inserted between the low-speed weight and riser shaft of a double-weight limiting-speed governor on a V-design two-stroke engine. (Courtesy of Detroit Diesel Corporation.)*

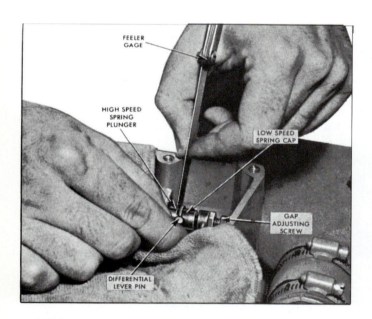

FIGURE 21–32 *Using governor gap adjusting screw which is threaded into the bellcrank lever to set the DW limiting-speed governor gap between the low-speed spring gap and the high-speed spring plunger, which should be between 0.003 and 0.019 in. (0.076 to 0.48 mm); otherwise, adjust it to 0.008 in. (0.20 mm) on all V71 and V92 two-stroke-cycle engines. (Courtesy of Detroit Diesel Corporation.)*

1. The speed control lever at the maximum speed position
2. The governor low-speed gap closed
3. The high-speed spring plunger on its seat in the governor control housing
4. The injector fuel control racks in the full-fuel position

Failure to set the racks properly will result in poor performance and a lack-of-power complaint.

The governor's location on the engine will control which injector rack is set first. On those engines with the governor located at the front, cylinder 1 injector rack would be set first, whereas with the governor mounted at the rear (flywheel end), the rear cylinder injector rack would be set first.

For V-design engines, the right and left banks are determined from the rear, and the cylinder numbering sequence is determined from the front. Therefore, all V-engines with the governor located at the front have the No. 1 left bank injector rack set first, since it is the closest (shortest rack) to the governor. On those V-design engines (6V-53) with the governor located at the rear, the No. 3 left-bank injector rack would be set first.

With this in mind, prior to setting the first injector rack, do the following:

1. Disconnect any linkage attached to the governor speed control lever (hand or foot throttle cables or rods).

2. Back out the idle speed adjusting screw until there is no tension on the low-speed spring (limiting speed governors only). When approximately $\frac{1}{2}$ in. (12.7 mm) or 12 to 14 threads are showing beyond the locknut when the nut is against the high-speed plunger, the tension of the low-speed spring will be low enough that it can be easily compressed. This allows closing of the low-speed gap without possible bending of the fuel rod or rods or causing the yield link (used with throttle delay engines) spring mechanism to yield or stretch.

NOTE   Failure to back out the idle speed adjusting screw as stated may result in a false fuel rack setting and the problems associated with this.

---

3. If the engine is equipped with a throttle delay mechanism, this would have been removed or the U-bolt clamp loosened prior to checking the governor gap.

4. Similarly, the buffer screw should *still be backed out* approximately $\frac{5}{8}$ in. (15.875 mm) as it was prior to setting the governor gap.

5. Also, the belleville spring retainer nut on engines so equipped (Figure 21-26) should have the 0.06-in. (1.524-mm) clearance as shown.

6. On turbocharged or fuel-squeezer engines employing a starting aid screw, *do not touch it* at this time. Leave it backed out.

NOTE   When the injector racks are adjusted properly, the effort expended in moving the throttle from an idle to maximum speed position should be uniform throughout its travel. Any increase in effort while doing this could be caused by the following: (a) injector racks adjusted too tight, causing the yield link to separate; (b) binding of the fuel rods; or (c) failure to back out the idle screw.

---

7. On earlier-model engines, loosen all the inner and outer adjusting screws of each injector rack control lever at the control tube (Figure 21-33). The newer engines employ only one adjusting screw (the inner one) with a locknut on it (Figure 21-34). On V-design

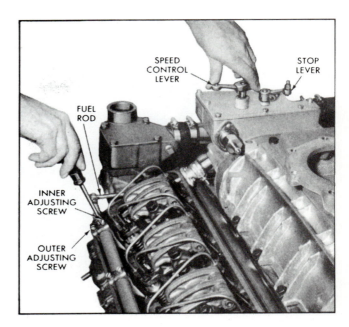

FIGURE 21–33 *Positioning the No. 1 LB injector rack control lever while gently holding the governor speed control lever (throttle) in the full-fuel position. On earlier-engine-model two-screw assemblies, the inner screw is an adjuster, while the outer screw is a lock screw. (Courtesy of Detroit Diesel Corporation.)*

engines, loosen the screws on both banks. Be sure that all the injector rack control levers are free on the control tube. Make sure that the screws are backed off at least $\frac{3}{16}$ in.

8. *V-design engines only.* Remove the clevis pin from the fuel rod at the right bank injector control tube lever (LB still connected to the governor).

9. On *limiting-speed* governors, move the speed control lever on top of the governor housing to the maximum speed position and hold it there with light finger pressure, as shown in Figure 21-33; on single-screw systems alternatively, hold the speed control lever in the full-fuel position with the aid of a light spring, as shown in Figure 21-34.

10. With the (throttle) speed control lever being held lightly in the full-fuel position, turn down the inner adjusting screw (two-screw type) or adjusting screw (one-screw type) until the No. 1 left bank injector rack is almost against the injector body and is observed to roll up (Figure 21-35) or an increase in effort to turn the screwdriver is noted. Tighten the screw approximately one-eighth turn more on the single-screw type; then lock it securely with the adjusting screw locknut. On the two-screw type, turn the inner adjusting screw down on the No. 1 LB of V-design engines, or the screws on the rack closest to the governor on inline engines, until a slight movement of the control

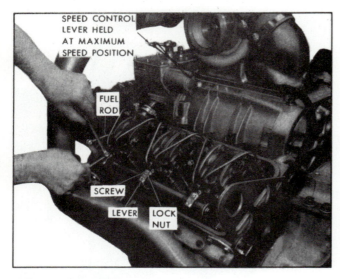

FIGURE 21–34 *Positioning the No. 1 LB injector rack control lever while gently holding the governor speed control lever (throttle) in the full-fuel position on a later-model two-stroke-cycle engine. There is only one adjusting screw, which is locked by the use of a small hex nut. (Courtesy of Detroit Diesel Corporation.)*

tube lever is observed or a step-up in effort to turn the screwdriver is noted. Turn down the outer adjusting screw until it bottoms lightly on the injector control tube; then alternately tighten both the inner and outer adjusting screws one-eighth turn each until snug. Finally, torque the screws to 24 to 36 in.-lb (3 to 4 N · m) to avoid damage to the injector control tube.

CAUTION While turning down the inner adjusting screw (one- or two-screw type), if you go too far, you will feel the speed control lever (limiting-speed governor) move. If this happens,

you have gone too far, and the rack is being forced out of the full-fuel position. Therefore, adjust the screw until very slight movement can be felt at the speed control lever; then back the screw off slightly.

At this time the No. 1 LB rack on V-design engines, or the closest rack to the governor on inline engines, should be in the full-fuel position with the governor linkage and control tube assembly in the same position they will attain while the engine is operating at normal operating temperature under full load.

11.   To be sure that you have in fact adjusted the rack correctly, hold the speed control lever (limiting-speed governor) in the maximum fuel position. Refer to Figure 21-36 and press down on the injector rack clevis with a screwdriver blade, which should cause the rack to tilt downward; when the pressure of the screwdriver blade is released, the control rack should bounce or spring back upward. If the injector rack does not have a good bounce or spring, it is too loose; to overcome this condition, back off the outer adjusting screw very slightly and tighten the inner one an equal amount. On single-screw units, loosen the locknut, turn the adjusting screw clockwise slightly, and retighten the locknut. Recheck the rack condition for bounce.

To ensure that the rack is not set *too tight*, do the following. Move the speed control lever (limiting speed) from the idle to the maximum speed position. While doing this, if the injector rack becomes tight on the ball end of the rack leg (see Figure 21-35) before the

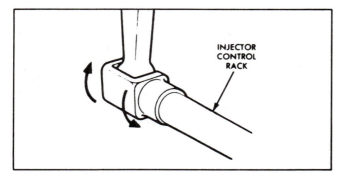

FIGURE 21–35 *Location to determine if injector rack bounce exists (no free play) between the ball end of the rack leg and the injector rack linkage. (Courtesy of Detroit Diesel Corporation.)*

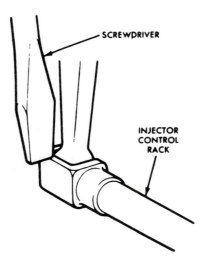

FIGURE 21–36 *Using a small screwdriver to check the injector rack after adjustment for signs of a good bounce (light springback) on a two-stroke-cycle engine model. (Courtesy of Detroit Diesel Corporation.)*

end of the lever travel, the rack also needs readjusting. To correct this condition, either loosen the screw locknut or the *inner* adjusting screw on the rack slightly and tighten the outer screw a similar distance, or back out the one-screw type and tighten the locknut. Recheck the rack bounce and movement. If an engine has been in service for a considerable period of time, the ball end of the rack leg sometimes becomes slightly scuffed. This can prevent a good bounce when setting the racks; if you encounter this problem, loosen both rack screws and slide the rack leg lever to the side of the injector, swing it upward, and lightly rub the ball end with fine emery cloth.

12. On all inline engines the first rack that has been set is the one closest to the governor. On V-design engines the No. 1 LB is the closest to the governor, with the exception of the 6V-53, which has the No. 3 LB closest. In either case, once the first rack has been adjusted, this now becomes the *master rack*, since it has been set to the governor. To adjust the remaining injector rack control levers on the engine, proceed as follows:

a. *Inline engines.* Remove the clevis pin from the fuel rod at the injector control tube lever; hold the injector control racks in the full-fuel position by means of the lever on the end of the control tube.

b. *V-design engines.* Remove the clevis pin from the fuel rod at the LB injector control tube lever. Install the clevis pin in the fuel rod at the right-bank injector control tube lever and adjust the No. 1 RB rack the same way as for the No. 1 LB in step 10. To verify that both No. 1 racks are adjusted the same, insert the clevis pin at the LB fuel rod. Move the speed control lever (LSG) to the maximum speed position and check the drag on the clevis pin at each bank. In addition, check the bounce on each No. 1 rack. If they are not the same, the No. 1 RB rack has to be readjusted, since the No. 1 LB was the first one set to the governor and is therefore the master rack. To increase drag or bounce on the No. 1 RB rack, turn the rack adjusting screw clockwise on the one-screw setup, or the *inner* screw clockwise on the two-screw setup, after slightly loosening the *outer* screw. Turn the screws counterclockwise to decrease pin drag or bounce.

13. To adjust the remaining injector racks on each bank, you can remove both clevis pins from each bank and:

a. Hold the LB injector control racks in the full-fuel position by means of the lever on the end

of the control tube (same setup as for the inline engines); or

b. Hold the governor speed control lever lightly in full-fuel by hand or leave the spring shown in Figure 21-34 attached; then

c. Tighten or run down the adjusting screw (inner) of the No. 2 LB injector rack control lever until the rack clevis rolls up or a step up in effort to turn the screwdriver is noted. If you feel the control tube lever move, back off on the adjusting screw slightly and turn it clockwise gently until you are satisfied that the rack is positioned correctly. While holding the control tube in the full-fuel position, compare the bounce on the No. 2 LB rack with that of the No. 1 LB rack. They should be the same; if not, readjust No. 2.

CAUTION Do not alter the adjustment of the No. 1 LB rack at any time. Remember that it is the master rack and has already been set to the governor.

---

d. Adjust the remaining racks on the LB in the same fashion, checking the bounce of each rack with the No. 1 setting every time. They should all have the same bounce when you are finished. Repeat the same procedure for the RB injector rack adjustments, always bearing in mind that the racks on each bank are set to the No. 1 rack on that bank. Therefore, *do not alter the No. 1 LB or RB setting to suit the others.*

14. When all the injector control racks have been adjusted, install the clevis pins in each fuel control tube to fuel rod if step 13a was used. Move the governor speed control lever to the maximum fuel position. Check each injector control rack for the same bounce or spring condition and also the drag on each clevis pin at each bank. If they are not the same, further checks and adjustments will be required. If one clevis is tight and the other not, one bank will invariably run hotter than the other, indicating that it is doing most of the work.

15. Once you are satisfied that you have adjusted each bank equally, secure the clevis pin with a cotter pin at each bank.

16. On limiting-speed governors, turn in the idle screw adjustment until the screw projects approximately $\frac{3}{16}$ in. (4.762 mm) from the locknut, which will permit starting of the engine.

17. On inline engines the injector racks are adjusted in the same fashion as for those on the V-design engines, the only difference being that you do not have two separate banks to adjust. Also, once the first rack

has been set to the governor, do not readjust it to suit another rack's bounce.

18.   Replace the valve rocker cover or covers if the engine is going to be run for any reason, after making sure that the racks will move to the no-fuel position when the stop lever is activated.

Series 149 Rack Setting

Series 149 engines have injector racks that are set slightly different than in 53, 71, and 92 series engines. The 149 racks are designed to have a light drag (but no bounce such as found on 53, 71, and 92 engines). When setting 149 racks, proceed as described below.

1.   Remove the valve rocker covers and governor cover.

2.   Disconnect the left-bank fuel rod (left and right banks determined from the rear) from the captive pin located on the end of the fuel control tube at the cylinder head area. This is done by removing the small circular spring clip from the groove on the end of the pin with a pair of needle-nose pliers, then sliding the fuel rod off the pin. Place a rag below the pin so that if you drop the clip, it won't be lost.

3.   Loosen off all injector rack control screws. Early engines employed a two-screw arrangement, while later engines employed only a single screw and locknut as shown in Figure 21-37.

4.   Refer to Figure 21-38 and manually grasp and hold the operating lever so that it forms a 90° angle.

5.   Set the No. 1 RB rack screw(s) to place the rack in the NO-FUEL position. Use the outer screw to do this on two-screw arrangements. On single-screw arrangements, set this screw in the same manner as for the outer screw on two-screw sets.

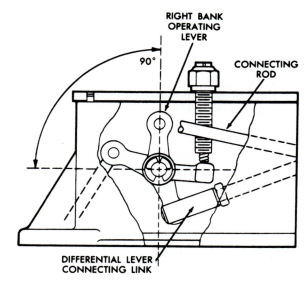

FIGURE 21–38 *Governor operating lever in position to adjust No. 1 R. B. rack (current governor).*

6.   Turn the No. 1 right-bank injector outer screw CW to place the rack in the NO-FUEL position. If movement is felt at the operating lever during this procedure, this will force the operating lever out of its 90° position. Make sure that this doesn't happen.

7.   Release the operating lever in the governor housing and manually grasp and rotate the right-bank fuel control tube away from you to place it in the FULL-FUEL position.

8.   Refer to Figure 21-39 and check the No. 1 RB rack for the condition illustrated by lightly grasping the end of the injector rack. There should be no end play, and the rack should exhibit a light drag around the fuel lever ball end.

9.   Leave the RB fuel rod connected. Walk around to the left bank and reconnect the fuel rod back onto the captive pin and install the spring clip retainer.

10.   If necessary depending on the type of engine application, stand on a stool or small ladder to allow you to reach up into the governor housing and push the differential lever away from you. Hold this lever lightly in this position.

11.   Turn down the inner or single adjusting screw on the LB control tube to place the rack in the FULL-FUEL position. If you rotate the screw too far, you will feel the differential lever pushing back against your fingers, and the rack will move out of the FULL-FUEL position.

12.   When you have set the rack correctly, step down. Push the LB fuel control tube away from you and check the No. 1 LB rack in the same manner as you did for the No. 1 RB rack. This was shown in Figure 21-39.

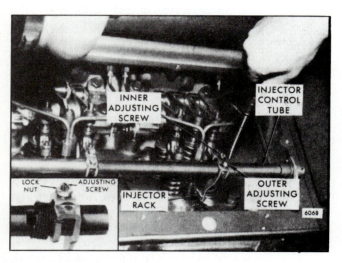

FIGURE 21–37 *Positioning the No. 1 injector rack control lever.*

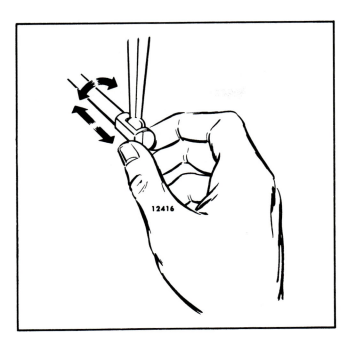

FIGURE 21-39 *Checking movement of injector control rack.*

13. Carefully compare the feel and drag of the No. 1 LB rack, then walk around to the RB and recheck the No. 1 RB rack setting. If the No. 1 RB rack is loose, you have tightened the No. 1 LB screw too far. If the No. 1 RB is tighter than that for the No. 1 LB rack, retighten the No. 1 LB screw slightly until the No. 1 LB and No. 1 RB are both set the same.

14. The No. 1 LB and No. 1 RB racks now become the master racks for each bank.

15. Replace the governor cover, making sure that the speed control lever pin on the cover engages with the slotted end of the differential lever. Install and tighten the retaining bolts.

16. Place the throttle lever into the FULL-FUEL position and lock it in place.

17. Proceed to adjust the remaining rack screws on each succeeding injector from the front to the rear of the engine. Do one bank at a time. If a two-screw arrangement is used, always use the inner screw to set the remaining racks into the FULL-FUEL position. After setting each additional rack, always compare it to the No. 1 rack on that bank. If the No. 1 rack is loose after setting the No. 2 rack, reset No. 2. Similarly, a loss of drag at the No. 1 rack after setting any others requires that you readjust that rack until it feels the same as the No. 1 (master rack). Never alter the No. 1 rack setting on either bank to compensate for the setting at another rack!

18. When all racks have been set, release the speed control lever from its FULL-FUEL position. Check for any signs of bind or sticking.

19. Move the STOP/RUN lever to the RUN position and back to the STOP position manually to ensure that the racks will in fact move to the NO-FUEL position to ensure proper engine shutdown when desired. Failure of the racks to move to the STOP position would require readjustment of the racks if no other reason can be found as to why the racks are jamming.

Maximum No-Load Engine Speed Adjustment: Limiting-Speed Governors

The type of engine application determines the maximum governed speed of the engine, and this is set on the engine prior to leaving the factory. For a variety of reasons, and to ensure that the engine speed will not exceed its recommended no-load speed, which is stamped on the engine's *option plate* or emissions paper-laminate label on the valve rocker cover, it is necessary to check and set the maximum no-load engine speed.

Adjustment Procedure

1. Make sure that the buffer screw is still backed out $\frac{5}{8}$ in. (15.875 mm) from the governor housing and locknut. If not, interference can occur while adjusting the maximum no-load speed.

2. On limiting-speed governors (Figure 21-40), loosen the spring retainer locknut and back off the high-speed spring retainer nut approximately five full turns. With the engine operating at normal operating temperature of 160 to 185°F (71 to 85°C), and with no load on the engine, place the speed control lever in the

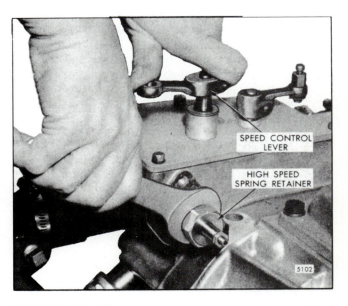

FIGURE 21-40 *Adjusting the engine's maximum no-load speed. Rotate the high-speed nut CW to increase and CCW to decrease the setting. Manually place the speed control lever (throttle) in the full-fuel position to check the speed setting. (Courtesy of Detroit Diesel Corporation.)*

full-fuel position. Turn the high-speed spring retainer nut clockwise until the engine is running at the recommended no-load rpm.

CAUTION On fuel-squeezer engines, the belleville springs must be readjusted any time that the no-load speed has been altered. The engine's no-load speed must be set 150 rpm above the rated speed prior to adjusting the belleville springs.

NOTE Hold the high-speed spring retainer nut and tighten the locknut. Limiting-speed governors used on industrial engines, and some 53 engines, use shims at the bellcrank end of the governor spring to vary the speed, similar to a variable-speed governor.

Minimum No-Load Speed: Variable-Speed Governor

To adjust the maximum no-load speed on a variable-speed governor requires that you remove the spring cover bolts. Within the cover are shims and stops which limit the maximum force that can be applied to the single governor spring. Each 0.001-in. (0.0254-mm) shim will increase or decrease the engine speed by approximately 1 rpm. Figure 21-41 illustrates the governor spring and adjustment components for the variable-speed (all-range) governor.

Idle Speed Adjustment

See Figure 21-42. The idle speed for an engine will vary with its particular application; therefore, always check the governor ID plate or emissions label for the recommended idle range. The recommended idle speed for non-EPA-certified engines with limiting speed governors is 400 to 450 rpm on the majority of these units, but may vary with special engine applications. EPA-certified minimum idle speeds are 500 rpm for trucks and highway coaches and 400 rpm for city coaches. After the maximum no-load speed has been adjusted properly, the idle speed can be set.

Adjustment Procedure

1. Ensure that the engine is operating at the normal operating temperature of 160 to 185°F (71 to 85°C) and that the buffer screw is still backed out, to avoid contact with the differential lever.

2. On earlier engines, the idle screw had a slotted end for screwdriver adjustment; however, later engines have an Allen head screw for idle adjustment. Loosen the idle screw locknut, and turn the idle speed adjusting screw either CW to increase the rpm or CCW to reduce the rpm until the engine operates at approximately 15 rpm below the recommended idle speed.

NOTE You may find it necessary to use the buffer screw (turn it in) to eliminate engine roll or surge so that you can establish what the engine idle speed is at this time. Once this is established, *back out the buffer screw* to its previous setting, which should be $\frac{5}{8}$ in. (15.875 mm).

---

3. Hold the idle screw and tighten the locknut.

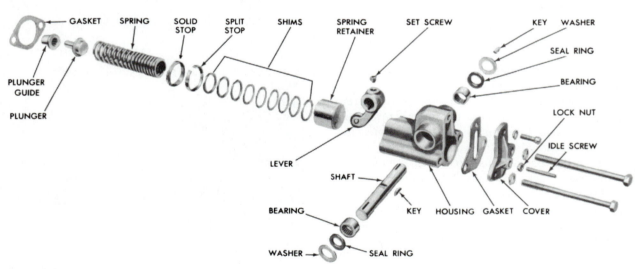

FIGURE 21-41 *Variable-speed spring housing details and relative location of*

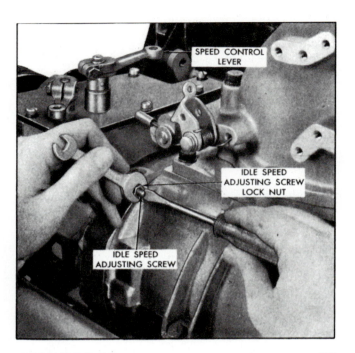

FIGURE 21–42 *Adjusting the idle speed; turn screw CW to increase and CCW to decrease the speed. (Courtesy of Detroit Diesel Corporation.)*

TT Belleville Washer Adjustment

Tailored torque (TT) governor assemblies are basically mechanical limiting-speed governors that have been modified specifically for use on DDC two-stroke-cycle highway truck engines. The operation of the governor during its startup phase, idling, load increase and decrease at idle, acceleration up through the intermediate speed range, maximum no-load speed control, and load-on and load-off conditions is the same as for the single- and double-weight limiting-speed governor assemblies. Where the TT governor differs from the standard limiting-speed governor is in the amount of fuel

that is delivered at the maximum full-load speed rpm. In other words, a TT-equipped governor restricts the fuel delivery at the maximum full-load rated horsepower speed, with the result that compared with a non-TT governor engine, an identical model TT governor engine would produce less horsepower. This is achieved through the use of a shorter high-speed spring which is also nonprogressively wound, in conjunction with a pair of belleville washers.

Figure 21-43 illustrates the component parts of the TT governor spring pack, with the belleville spring washers clearly shown. *Belleville washers* are basically thin sprung-steel washers that have a cupped or dished shape. When they are assembled into the governor, they would be installed as shown in Figure 21-26 so that the cupped sides face each other in assembled form.

When the belleville washers are installed in the governor as shown in Figure 21-26 and adjusted, they exert a compressive force against the high-speed spring as it attempts to pull them together. You will note in Figure 21-43 and 21-26 that the high-speed plunger is threaded, whereas the high-speed plunger on a non-TT engine is not. The reason for these threads on the TT governor is to allow the belleville washers to have their compressive force adjusted by rotating the retainer nut shown in Figure 21-26.

TT Governor Operation

Operation of the TT governor is similar to that for the non-TT limiting-speed assembly, the major exception being the adjustment of the belleville washers, since the tension applied to these washers is what determines the horsepower setting of the engine. Remember that a TT engine is identical to a non-TT engine except for the fact that it employs belleville spring washers. For example, let's consider an 8V-92TA and an 8V-92TTA; the TA engine, with 90-mm^3 injectors

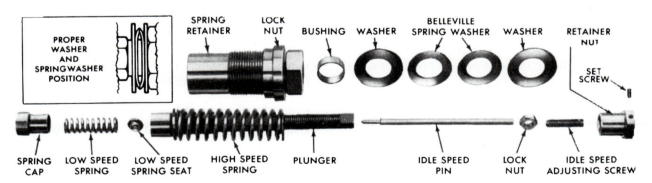

FIGURE 21–43 *Exploded view of the limiting-speed mechanical governor high- and low-speed spring assemblies showing the placement of the belleville washers on a TT (tailored torque) two-stroke-cycle V92 engine model. (Courtesy of Detroit Diesel Corporation.)*

running at 2100 rpm full load produces 475 bhp (354 kW), whereas the TTA engine produces only 400 bhp (298.4 kW) at the same speed.

It is possible to adjust the belleville spring washers so that the engine will in fact produce more than its TT rating of 400 bhp, as well as less; therefore, when the belleville spring washers are adjusted, this setting must be carefully checked to ensure that the recommended TT rating of 400 bhp is achieved. It is easy to alter the belleville spring washer setting to squeeze a few extra horsepower out of the engine, but the minute you do this, you will alter the following characteristics of the TT engine:

1. Higher horsepower means the engine will use more fuel than normal.
2. The torque at this higher horsepower will also be higher; therefore, when the engine speed drops below its maximum full-load setting of 2100 rpm, the rate of torque rise will not be as high, since you are already starting at a higher level because of the higher horsepower setting.

Remember that the purpose of a TT engine, which is sometimes referred to as a "fuel squeezer" engine, is to have a higher rate of torque rise as the engine rpm drops from its maximum full-load speed of 2100 rpm down to its peak torque point at 1300 rpm. It can achieve this high percentage of torque rise only if the belleville spring washers are adjusted to provide 400 bhp at 2100 rpm, and as the engine speed is reduced because of additional load, the horsepower will remain constant down to 1600 rpm, with a high rate of torque rise occurring at the same time, to offer the benefit of less downshifting. Before describing the two methods of adjusting the belleville spring washers, let's look at what actually causes this change to occur.

In Figure 21-43, when the high-speed spring starts to push the high-speed plunger back against the decreasing governor weight force (load = slower speed), the belleville spring washer retaining nut, which is threaded onto the right-hand side of the high-speed plunger, will also be moving left inside the bore of the high-speed spring retainer.

NOTE   The 0.06-in. (1.52-mm) clearance shown in Figure 21-26 is not an adjustment specification. Any time that the belleville spring washers are to be adjusted, or an engine tune-up is to be performed, the belleville spring retainer locknut is backed off (CCW) to allow a 0.06-in. gap in order to remove any possibility of interference from the

spring force of the belleville washers during rack setting, and to allow a starting point prior to adjusting the engine's TT horsepower setting.

Refer to Figure 21-43 now. As the high-speed plunger moves to the left in this diagram by spring force, the belleville spring washer retaining/adjusting nut on the right will start to compress the belleville spring washers. The point to which the washers are compressed will depend on this retainer nut adjustment. If the retainer nut is backed out, then as the high-speed plunger moves to the left (high-speed spring force) due to decreasing engine speed and weight force, it will allow the racks to be pushed into the full-fuel mode sooner, resulting in an increase in horsepower. However, if the retainer nut is rotated clockwise on the threaded high-speed plunger, then it in fact pulls the high-speed plunger back to the right, because the nut is acting against the surface of the high-speed spring retainer, which is itself threaded and locked to the governor housing. Turning the retainer nut clockwise allows it to act as a puller. Therefore, the engine horsepower will be decreased, because as the high-speed plunger is pulled back to the right, the racks receive less fuel. This would be the same reaction that would result from the weights compressing the high-speed spring.

Clockwise rotation of the retainer nut makes the belleville washers stronger; therefore, this force assists the high-speed weights in opposing the high-speed spring force at the full-load rpm, resulting in less fuel being delivered to the engine, which will produce less horsepower. Counterclockwise rotation of the retainer nut weakens the belleville spring washers at the maximum full-load rpm setting, and they offer less assistance to the high-speed weights in keeping the high-speed spring compressed; therefore, the engine will receive more fuel at the full-load rpm point, resulting in a higher horsepower setting. In review, then, turning the belleville retainer/adjusting nut clockwise results in a decrease in the engine horsepower setting, while turning it CCW (counterclockwise) will increase the engine horsepower setting.

Belleville Spring Adjustment: Limiting-Speed Governors, Highway Vehicles

This adjustment applies only to those engines that have the limiting-speed governor; therefore, on-highway vehicles using turbocharged engines with this governor setup are classed as fuel-squeezer engines. For example, the term *TT* in an engine model designation, such as 8V-92 TT, simply means that the engine is a V8 engine with 92 in.^{3} (1507.6 mm^3) of displacement per cylinder and is equipped with a governor for TT (or tailored torque) horsepower (kW) adjustment.

TT horsepower adjustment is accomplished at the moment by two methods, depending on the equipment available: (1) by an established idle drop method and (2) by use of an established power reduction factor. Regardless of the method used, to obtain satisfactory results the engine must be in good mechanical condition and properly tuned; therefore, do *not* attempt belleville spring governor adjustment until a thorough engine tune-up has been completed.

Method 1: Idle Drop
This method is an effective, accurate means of setting TT horsepower (kW). The idle drop method employs a reduction in engine rpm in order to position the belleville washers and both the governor low- and high-speed springs. The correct positioning of these components results in obtaining the desired fuel-squeezer horsepower (kW).

NOTE   Use of the engine's mechanically driven tachometer for this purpose is inadequate. An accurate tachometer is *mandatory* (use Kent-Moore tool J26791 or one of the latest-style electronic hand-held digital tachs when using the idle drop method). Each 1-rpm error in setting the idle drop will result in a 2- or 3-hp error.

Adjustment Procedure
1.   Do a complete engine tune-up. Set the no-load speed as specified according to the engine type, injector size, and the governor part number.
2.   Disconnect the accelerator linkage from the governor speed control lever on top of the governor housing if this has not already been done.
3.   Run the engine until a stabilized engine operating temperature between 160 and 185°F (71 to 85°C) is obtained.
4.   Refer to available information through a local DDC dealer or service bulletin, and using the engine type, injector size, and governor part number, obtain the initial and specified idle drop numbers for the rated TT horsepower (kW) and rated engine speed at which the engine is to operate.
5.   Set the initial idle rpm by the use of the idle adjusting screw to that determined in step 4. For example, one engine would be adjusted to 915 rpm by use of the idle screw, then reduced to 848 rpm according to step 6.
6.   With the governor speed control lever in the idle position, turn the belleville spring retainer nut

(Figure 21-26) clockwise on the plunger until the specified idle drop rpm is achieved. Secure the retainer nut with the locking screw. When the specified idle rpm is achieved, the engine is power controlled to the TT horsepower (kW) rating.

NOTE   It is imperative that the idle speeds be adjusted to the exact rpm and also be steady with no fluctuation. If they are not, check for any binding or rubbing in the fuel control system at the governor, fuel rods, injector control tubes, and racks.

7.   Lower the idle speed to the normal specified operating idle rpm, using the idle adjusting screw.
8.   Adjust the buffer screw and starting aid screw (see the buffer screw and starting aid screw procedure later in this section).

Method 2: Power Reduction Factor
This method differs from the idle drop method in that it consists of setting the TT engine horsepower (kW) to a specific percentage below full throttle horsepower (kW) as observed on an engine, chassis, or output shaft dynamometer. The desired horsepower within a reasonable tolerance can be obtained based on the following variations:

- Dynamometer calibration
- Driveline efficiency
- Fuel grade and temperature
- Air density
- Tire slippage

Adjustment Procedure
1.   Perform the standard engine tune-up.

NOTE   The throttle delay piston must be removed and the belleville spring retainer nut must be backed out until there is approximately 0.060 in. (1.524 mm) clearance between the washers and retainer nut (Figure 21-26) prior to operating the engine on the dynamometer.

2.   Set the no-load speed as required by the engine type, injector size, and governor part number. This can be found stamped on the valve rocker cover option plate on the engine.
3.   Run the engine until the coolant temperature is above 170°F (77°C).
4.   Using an engine, chassis, or output shaft dynamometer, measure and record the *full-throttle* horse-

power (kW) at 100 rpm below rated engine speed with the belleville washers loose, as shown in Figure 21-26.

IMPORTANT   Satisfactory power adjustment can be obtained only if the full throttle horsepower (kW) and adjusted horsepower (step 4) are obtained with the engine cooling temperature in both instances being the same. (If a thermatic or air-operated fan is used, note whether it is engaged or disengaged.)

---

5.   Select the power reduction factor from DD Service Information Bulletin 35-D-87 dated December 1987 (contact any DDC distributor/dealer for this information) for proper engine type, desired rate horsepower, and rated engine speed.

6.   Multiply the horsepower (kW) recorded in step 4 by the factor selected in step 5. Record this value.

7.   Adjust the belleville spring retainer nut clockwise so that the observed horsepower is reduced to that recorded in step 6 at 100 rpm below the rated engine speed, with the governor speed control lever in the maximum speed position and the fan in the same mode of operation as step 4. Verify that the engine is obtaining the specified adjusted horsepower TT within 5% at *rated* engine speed. If the adjusted TT horsepower (kW) cannot be obtained at rated engine speed, governor *droop* interference may be the cause. If necessary, to eliminate droop interference, readjust the engine no-load speed from 150 to 175 rpm above rated engine speed and repeat the power reduction factor method.

8.   Check the idle speed and readjust if necessary.

9.   Adjust the buffer screw and starting aid screw.

Buffer Screw Adjustment

Buffer screw adjustment on DDC engines must be done carefully to avoid any unnecessary increase to the normal engine idle range and to the maximum no-load speed. Prior to buffer screw adjustment, the specified engine idling speed must be properly set to within 15 rpm of that desired. Use an accurate electronic digital tachometer for this purpose.

CAUTION   Running the buffer screw in too far can cause a runaway engine.

With the idle speed properly set, adjust the buffer screw as follows:

1.   With the engine having been adjusted to its recommended idle speed and running at normal operating temperature, refer to Figure 21-44 and turn the buffer screw in so that it lightly contacts the differential lever inside the governor housing. This is easily determined by the fact that the engine speed will pick up slightly, and the roll or surge in the engine will level out.

NOTE   Be very careful that you do not increase the engine idle speed more than 15 rpm with the buffer screw adjustment. This is why an accurate tachometer must be used.

---

2.   Move the speed control lever to the maximum fuel position to check the no-load speed. If it has increased more than 25 rpm, you have gone too far on the initial adjustment; back off the buffer screw until this increase in the no-load rpm is less than 25 rpm.

3.   Hold the buffer screw with a screwdriver and tighten the locknut.

Booster Spring Adjustment

All DDC engines equipped with a SWVS (single-weight variable-speed) governor assembly employs a throttle booster spring, which is located as shown in Figure 21-45. This spring is designed to assist the rapid return of the throttle to an idle position when the operator releases the throttle linkage. If the booster spring linkage has been disturbed at an engine overhaul or during an engine tune-up procedure, perform

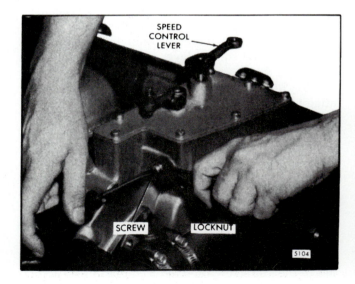

FIGURE 21–44 *Adjusting the buffer screw CW to remove any roll/hunt from the two-stroke-cycle engine at idle. Never increase the idle speed by more than 15 rpm by buffer screw adjustment. (Courtesy of Detroit Diesel Corporation.)*

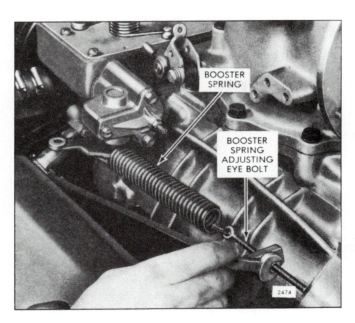

FIGURE 21–45 *Adjusting the booster spring.*

an adjustment to the booster spring after having adjusted the idle speed as follows.

1.   Move the speed control lever to the IDLE speed position.

2.   Refer to Figure 21-45 and loosen the booster spring retaining nut on the speed control lever. Loosen the locknuts on the eyebolt at the opposite end of the booster spring.

3.   With the speed control lever in the IDLE position, move the bolt in the slot of the speed control lever until the center of the bolt is on or slightly over center (toward the IDLE speed position) of an imaginary line through the bolt, lever shaft and eyebolt. Hold the bolt from turning and tighten the locknut.

4.   Start the engine and move the speed control lever to the MAXIMUM speed position and release it. The speed control lever should return to the IDLE speed position. If it does not, reduce the booster spring tension. If it does, continue to increase the spring tension until the point is reached that it will not return to idle. Then reduce the spring tension until it does return to idle and tighten the locknut on the eyebolt. This setting will result in the minimum force required to operate the speed control lever.

5.   Connect the linkage to the governor levers.

DETROIT DIESEL FOUR-STROKE-CYCLE ENGINES

A rather unique rocker arm mechanism arrangement is that employed by Detroit Diesel in its series 50 and 60 engines (Figure 21-46). The arrangement allows for two long and two short rocker arm assemblies without having to resort to a valve bridge mechanism to open the two intake and two exhaust valves per cylinder. Note the internal oil holes to lubricate the self-centering adjusting screw button, rocker shaft, and roller follower, as well as the various profiles of the camshaft lobes for the intake, exhaust, and unit injector. As you can see, the actual cam lobe profiles are quite different for each system.

Since the engine has a firing order of 1–5–3–6–2–4, refer to Figure 21-47. Bar the engine over manually until one of the injector followers has just started to move down. This procedure allows all of the valves and injectors to be set in two complete crank rotations (720°). Refer to Figure 21-48 and adjust all four valves (two intake and two exhaust) on this cylinder using the procedure illustrated. From the information provided in Figure 21-47, set the fuel injector height on the mating (companion) cylinder. For example, if we had just set the valve lash on cylinder 1, we would now set the injector on the cylinder 6. The unit injector is adjusted for a listed dimensional height (indicated on the engine decal) from the top machined surface of the follower to the injector body by using a *timing pin* which fits into a drilled hole in the injector body as shown in Figure 21-49. Adjust the injector height as illustrated in Figure 21-50 until a slight drag is felt on the flag of the gauge as it passes over the top of the injector follower. Tighten the locknut when done and recheck the injector height.

SERVICE TIP   Some experienced technicians like to place a small amount of clean engine oil onto the injector follower. When the timing height gauge is rotated over the follower, a small half-circle shape, which is visible as the oil is wiped off, confirms that the injector is correctly set. Other technicians simply rely on feel as the gauge is moved backward and forward over the follower, which is machined with a small chamfer on its circumference.

NOTE   DDC recommends that after a new or overhauled engine has been in service for a given time period, both the valve lash and the injector heights on all series 50/60 engines should be checked and reset if necessary. For truck engines, the time for checking is at 60,000 miles (96,000 km) or 24 months, whichever occurs first. On stationary and industrial engine applications, check at 1500 hours or 45,000 miles (72,000 km). Failure to check these clearances and settings may result

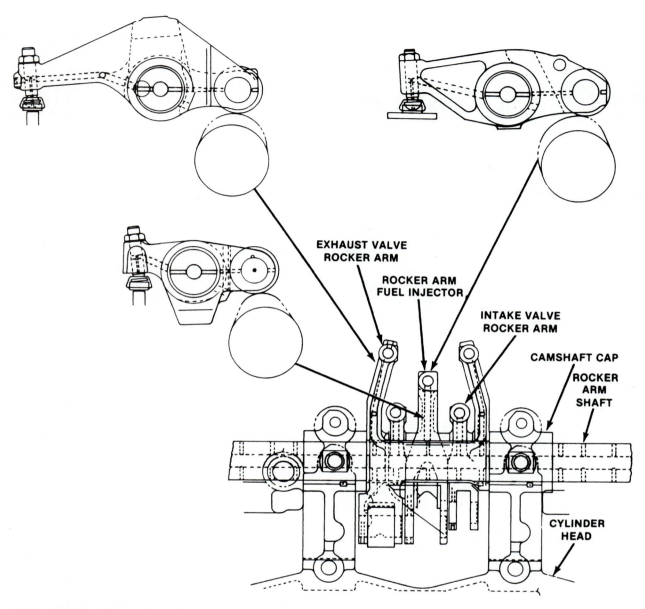

FIGURE 21–46 Unique overhead camshaft valve and injector operating mechanism components used on the series 50 and 60 electronic engine models. Note that there is no need for valve bridges with this design. (Courtesy of Detroit Diesel Corporation.)

in gradual loss of engine performance and reduced fuel efficiency.

DETROIT DIESEL ELECTRONIC SYSTEMS

SPECIAL NOTE   The information contained within this section dealing with the DDEC (Detroit Diesel Electronic Controls) systems is designed to provide an overview of the system operation and the special diagnostic tools that can be used to troubleshoot the system. It is *not* intended to supplant the excellent printed literature and audiovisual materials readily available from Detroit Diesel. If you intend to perform service diagnostics on DDEC systems, you should acquire the following service publications from your local Detroit Diesel service dealer: Publication 7SA708, *DDEC III Application and Installation Manual*; Publication 6SE492, *DDEC III Troubleshoot-*

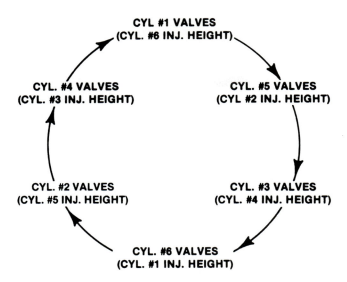

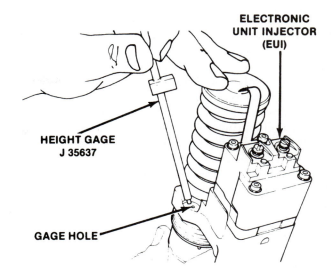

FIGURE 21–47 *Timing circle chart that can be used to check and adjust all of the valve and injector settings on a DDC series 60 four-stroke-cycle engine. (Courtesy of Detroit Diesel Corporation.)*

FIGURE 21–49 *Location of the injector timing height gauge pin hole to check and adjust the injector-body-to-follower dimension, which can be found on the engine decal attached to the valve rocker cover. (Courtesy of Detroit Diesel Corporation.)*

ing Guide, which contains all of the system trouble codes, wiring diagrams, and step-by-step diagnostic troubleshooting procedures to quickly and effectively analyze system problems; and an engine service manual related to the particular Detroit Diesel engine that you will be working on; for example, the series 60 service manual is available under Publication 6SE483.

In September 1985 Detroit Diesel Corporation was the first major engine OEM in the world to release electronic unit fuel injection controls in a high-speed diesel engine. This system was known as DDEC I (Detroit Diesel Electronic Controls) and was followed in September 1987 by the more advanced DDEC II system. In

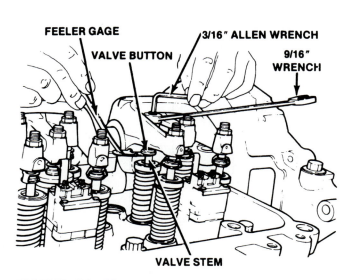

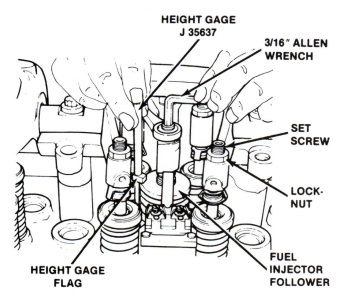

FIGURE 21–48 *Setting the valve clearance adjustment on a series 50 or 60 overhead cam design engine model. The valve clearance specs can be found on the decal attached to the valve rocker cover. (Courtesy of Detroit Diesel Corporation.)*

FIGURE 21–50 *Using an Allen key and wrench to adjust and lock the electronic unit injector screw after setting the fuel injector body to follower height dimension. (Courtesy of Detroit Diesel Corporation.)*

September 1993, DDC released its third-generation system, known as DDEC III. DDEC IV is due in late 1997.

DDEC III: Evolution and Advantages

DDEC III evolved as a result of a unique set of events: requests from customers for additional electronic engine features and more information; the need to meet increasingly stringent air quality standards; improvements in microprocessor capabilities; and significant strides in the electronics industry.

The DDEC III development team included engineers working together from Detroit Diesel, Motorola Inc., and Pi Research, Ltd. Motorola, one of the world's leading providers of electronic equipment, systems, components, and services, designed the hardware and manufactures the electronic control module. Pi Research, headquartered in Cambridge, England, is known for its dashboard display and on-board sensors designed for cars such as those that race in the Indianapolis 500. This experience, combined with development of DDEC II, allowed Pi Research to write the DDEC III software and assist in numerous hardware designs.

The DDEC III computing capability is eight times faster and memory capacity is seven times larger than that of DDEC II; the result is faster engine information response, expanded features, and more precision from the engine control systems. DDEC III represents a major step in providing management information to the fleet operator.

One of the benefits of the extra memory capacity provided by DDEC III is the ability to have multiple ratings in one engine. Multiple ratings enable customers to order one engine with up to four ratings. When the customer orders an engine, the truck manufacturer selects the rating that meets the customer's specification. The DDEC III also allows several control functions to be incorporated into one ECM, thereby reducing cost and complexity while improving system reliability. The ECM can control the engine brakes, so a separate brake controller is not necessary. The fan can be engaged by the ECM based on a variety of input signals that could call for fan operation. The low coolant system no longer needs its own control module because it is managed by the DDEC III ECM.

Reprogramming of DDEC software is now much easier than it was in the DDEC I or DDEC II systems. All software can now be reprogrammed using the in-cab six-pin connector, illustrated in Figure 21-51, through advances to DDEC memory chips. Connecting either the DDR shown in Figure 21-52 or the re-

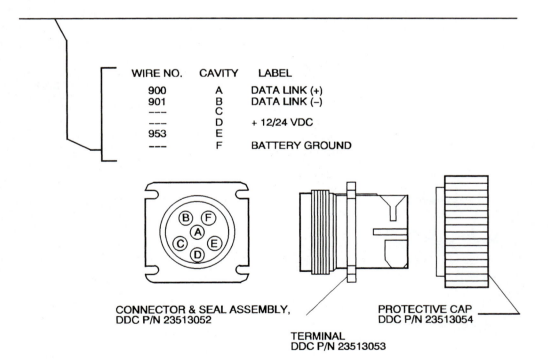

FIGURE 21–51 DDEC III ECM six-pin diagnostic connector used to connect the DDR shown in Figure 21-52 to enable the technician to access engine data, stored SAE standard trouble codes, conduct various engine tests, and to reprogram the ECM when desired by the customer. (Courtesy of Detroit Diesel Corporation.)

programming unit shown in Figure 21-53 reduces reprogramming time and improves reliability, because removal of the ECM or wire harness connector is no longer required.

Media Signal and Baud Rate

When a field service or shop technician is required to reprogram the engine ECM, interface with the factory mainframe to change engine horsepower settings during the warranty period, or to download information from the engine to a company office PC, (see Figure 21-54), he/she can use the laptop computer shown in Figure 21-53. It is of value for the technician to understand just how this is done. From our discussion of data related to Figure 15-20, there are two possible ways to classify the signal sent on a line. These, as you know, are analog and digital.

To interface with the factory mainframe computer, the technician requires the use of a modem to hook up the engine ECM and laptop computer through the telephone lines. Because digital impulses can't be sent over the analog phone lines, conversion of the ECM digital signals to the continuous-wave form (analog) is called modulation. Translation from continuous waves

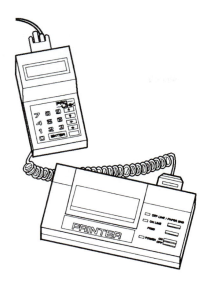

FIGURE 21-52 *Hand-held ProLink 9000 model DDR (diagnostic data reader) connected to a miniprinter to capture a hard copy of engine operational data and logged trouble codes. (Courtesy of Detroit Diesel Corporation.)*

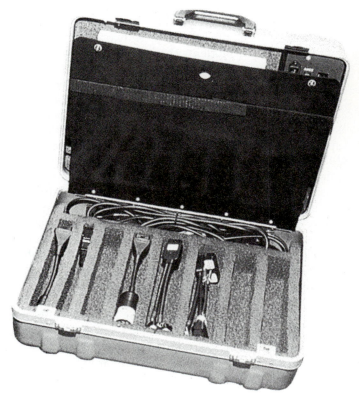

FIGURE 21-53 *Portable technician briefcase with a laptop computer, special adapters, and electronic controls to allow ease of ECM reprogramming. (Courtesy of Detroit Diesel Corporation.)*

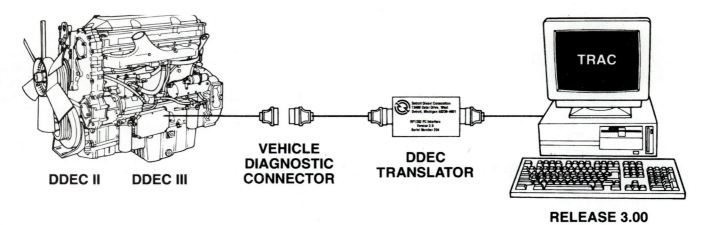

FIGURE 21–54 Hookup required to the engine ECM for downloading or data extraction system of stored ECM and data hub information. Hookup allows translation to a PC software file for electronic engine and vehicle management control. (Courtesy of Detroit Diesel Corporation.)

back to digital impulses is termed demodulation. A single device called a modem (coined from the words 'modulation' and 'demodulation') takes care of both operations. Therefore when a PC terminal sends a remote CPU (central processing unit) a message that must be carried over an analog line, a modem is needed at both the sending end to convert from digital to analog, and at the receiving end to convert from analog to digital. Modems that are not hard-wired to specific equipment and that have an acoustic cradle to accept a phone headset are called acoustic couplers.

When using a modem, or sending data across phone lines, the speed of data communication is measured in bits per second (bps). The slowest rates of speed are referred to as narrowband transmission. Medium speed lines, which are commonly used in the telephone network, are capable of voice-grade transmission. The highest rates of speed, referred to as wideband transmission, are possible only with coaxial cable, fiber optic cable and microwaves. The 'baud rate' is a term used to indicate the speed at which data travels between computers, and is measured in bits per second (bps). Therefore a long file which takes 10 minutes to travel from one computer to another at 1200 baud, will take 5 minutes at 2400 baud, $2\frac{1}{2}$ minutes at 4800 baud, and half-as-much again at 9600 baud. A 1200 baud modem cannot send or receive data at a faster rate, but a 2400 baud modem can work at the higher or lower speed. If you are familiar with using a PC on the Net, or when using the E-mail format, most modems today are set for a speed of transmission of 28,800 bps or faster. Therefore if long distance phone charges are involved, speed of transmission may be a consideration.

Engine Sensors and Location

Figure 21-55 illustrates the location of various DDEC III engine sensors, and they are described here:

1. Air temperature sensor located in the intake manifold allows the ECM to adjust engine timing to reduce white smoke on startup, improve cold starts, and provide engine protection should the intake manifold air become too hot.

2. Turbo boost sensor monitors turbocharger compressor discharge pressure and provides data to the ECM for smoke control during engine acceleration.

3. Oil pressure sensor activates the engine protection system when the oil pressure falls below a normal oil pressure at a given engine rpm. A dash-mounted warning light can be used to warn the driver of a low oil pressure condition.

4. Oil temperature sensor tells the ECM the engine operating temperature; oil temperature is a closer reflection of engine operation than is coolant. This information optimizes idle speed (fast idle at cold startup) and injection timing to improve cold startability and reduce white smoke. In addition, this sensor activates the engine protection system if the oil temperature is higher than normal. A dash-mounted warning light can be used to warn the driver of a high oil temperature condition.

5. Fuel temperature sensor, usually located at the secondary fuel filter, provides a signal to the ECM to calculate fuel consumption for instant readout at the push of a button on a truck instrument panel such as the Detroit Diesel ProDriver option. The ECM also utilizes the fuel temperature signal to adjust the unit injector PWM time for changes in the fuel density with a change in temperature.

DDEC III
How It Works. . .

The major components of the system consist of the electronic control module (ECM), the electronic unit injectors (EUI) and the various system sensors. The purpose of the sensors is to provide information to the ECM regarding various engine performance characteristics. The information sent to the ECM is used to instantaneously regulate engine and vehicle performance.

■ **Air Temperature Sensor**

■ **Electronic Unit Injector (EUI)**

■ **Coolant Temperature Sensor**

■ **Electrical Connectors**

■ **Fire Truck Pump Pressure Sensor**

■ **The SRS and TRS Sensors**

FIGURE 21–55 *The DDEC III system—how it works and the various sensors needed for the electronic control system to function and operate properly. (Courtesy of Detroit Diesel Corporation.)*

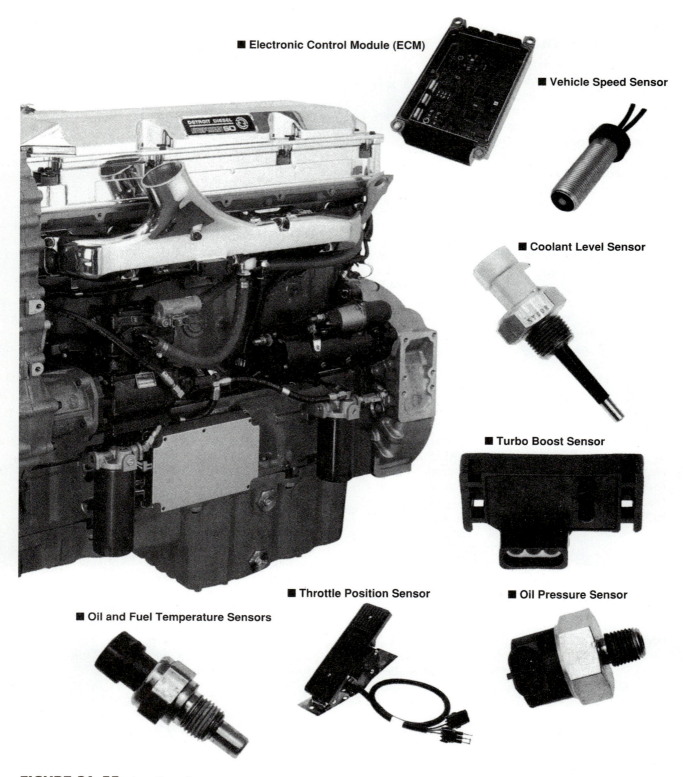

■ Electronic Control Module (ECM)

■ Vehicle Speed Sensor

■ Coolant Level Sensor

■ Turbo Boost Sensor

■ Throttle Position Sensor

■ Oil Pressure Sensor

■ Oil and Fuel Temperature Sensors

FIGURE 21–55 *(continued)*

6. Coolant level sensor, mounted on the radiator top tank, triggers the engine protection feature when a low coolant condition is sensed. An additional coolant level sensor located higher in the radiator top tank indicates, through either a dash-mounted warning lamp or the ProDriver readout module, that the engine coolant is low, but not enough to activate the DDEC engine protection feature.

7. Coolant temperature sensor, located on the right side of the engine, also triggers the engine protection system if the coolant temperature exceeds specified limits. A warning light can be provided on the dash to inform the driver when this situation occurs.

8. SRS (synchronous reference sensor) provides a once per cylinder signal to the ECM.

9. TRS (timing reference sensor) provides a 36 per crankshaft revolution signal from a toothed wheel bolted behind the crankshaft gear. Working in conjunction, the SRS and TRS tell the ECM which cylinder is at TDC for firing purposes. Precise monitoring of piston position allows for optimum injection timing, resulting in excellent fuel economy and performance with low emissions.

10. Vehicle speed sensor is usually mounted over the vehicle transmission output shaft to provide the ECM with the speed of the vehicle. This signal is used for cruise control, vehicle speed limiting, and automatic progressive application of the engine Jake brakes to maintain a preprogrammed maximum vehicle speed. In addition, engine fan braking engages the cooling fan clutch automatically when the engine brakes are on *high*. This feature adds 20 to 45 bhp (15 to 33.5 kW) to the engine retardation for slowing down the vehicle.

11. On fire truck applications, a fire pump water pressure sensor is used to monitor the pressure governor system. The signal back to the ECM changes engine rpm to allow the fire water pump to maintain a steady water pressure during pumping operation.

12. Throttle position sensor is located within the body of the electronic foot pedal assembly (which was featured in Figure 15-13). An idle validation switch within the throttle sensor assembly tells the ECM when the throttle is at an idle position. In addition, as the operator depresses the pedal or hand throttle on a marine application, the percentage of throttle opening is relayed to the ECM. Throttle response is fast and accurate. Later model throttle sensors are self-calibrating (idle validation) and require no maintenance.

On larger model Detroit Diesel two-stroke-cycle 149 series engine models, a crankcase pressure sensor and a coolant pressure sensor are two additional sensors unique to these models. On the smaller model 71 and 92 two-cycle engines, the sensor locations vary from those on the series 50 and 60 engines but function in the same manner. In addition, the 71 and 92 engines usually mount the ECM above and in front of the engine blower assembly; the SRS and TRS sensors pick up their signals from the left front camshaft accessory drive pulley. On 149 engines two ECMs are used, a "master" and "slave" to handle the additional electrical loads on these larger displacement engine models.

The DDEC system has several additional features:

1. Throttle inhibit system can disable the accelerator pedal on a passenger bus application when the doors are open or on a fire truck when the pressure governor fire pump is active.

2. A deceleration light typically used on buses can be mounted on the dash and at the rear of the vehicle to indicate that the vehicle is slowing down when the operator takes his or her foot off of the throttle pedal.

3. A starter motor lockout is commonly used on buses to prevent starter activation after the engine is already running.

4. A green cruise control light illuminates when "cruise" is selected to alert the driver of this condition.

5. A fan clutch override switch can engage the cooling fan at any time when either the engine oil, coolant, or intake manifold temperatures exceed their preset values.

6. A low DDEC voltage light illuminates on the dash when the ECM records a voltage less than 10 V on either a 12- or 24-V vehicle system. This light is typically used on fire truck applications.

Engine Protection System

An engine protection system is programmed into the ECM and operates based on out-of-range operating conditions from the individual engine and vehicle-mounted sensors. On the DDEC III system, the ECM initiates the protection procedure when it receives an out-of-range signal from the oil pressure, oil temperature, coolant temperature, coolant level, and intake manifold air temperature sensors. The system can be programmed for one of three protection features: shutdown, rampdown, or warning.

A warning feature alerts the driver by illuminating a yellow dash-mounted warning light with 100% engine power still available. For example, the oil temperature sensor may be programmed to illuminate the light at 250°F (121°C). If the oil temperature continues to increase, a gradual loss of engine power will occur down to approximately the 70% level, at which time the red dash light will illuminate, for example, at 260°F (127°C). The operator must then choose to pull the vehicle over and shut it down. If the vehicle or marine unit is equipped with a ProDriver feature such as the one illustrated in Figure 21-56, oil temperature can be monitored by the push of a button.

A ramp-down condition alerts the driver also by illuminating the yellow dash warning light and reducing the engine power from 100% to 70%, at which time the red dash light will illuminate and the engine power will quickly be reduced to a 40% level.

A shutdown condition occurs similarly to the rampdown mode, except that 30 seconds after illumination of the red light, the ECM has been programmed to automatically shut the engine down.

When toggled or pushed, an STEO (stop engine override) switch located on the instrument panel will allow the engine to return to a 70% power level every 30 seconds while the engine is running. In other words, the operator must activate this switch manually after the red light is illuminated and before the 30-second time interval expires; otherwise, the engine will shut down and will not restart.

Engine Diagnostics

The DDEC III system provides an indication of engine and vehicle malfunctions by illuminating the yellow CEL (check engine light) or red SEL (stop engine light) at any time that a sensor or system fault is detected.

When the yellow CEL is illuminated, it signifies that a fault has been detected; however, the fault is not serious enough to activate the automatic engine shutdown feature if it has been programmed within the ECM. The condition should be diagnosed as soon as possible; if the vehicle is equipped with a ProDriver diagnostic system similar to the one shown in Figure 21-56, the operator can determine what the fault condition is. This allows the operator to contact a service facility or the home service base and report the problem to the service/maintenance personnel.

Any faults that are stored in ECM memory can be accessed in one of three ways:

1. Connect a DDR (diagnostic data reader) such as the model shown in Figure 21-52 to the DDL connector of the vehicle (see Figure 15-23 for DDEC II systems). For DDEC III systems, depending on the vehicle or equipment in which the engine is installed, the diagnostic connector shown in Figure 21-51 may be located in several areas; therefore refer to the vehicle/equipment service manual for the exact location. On heavy-duty trucks, this connector is usually within the cab area and located under the dash or behind a side kick panel.

2. Use a jumper wire on DDEC II systems simi-

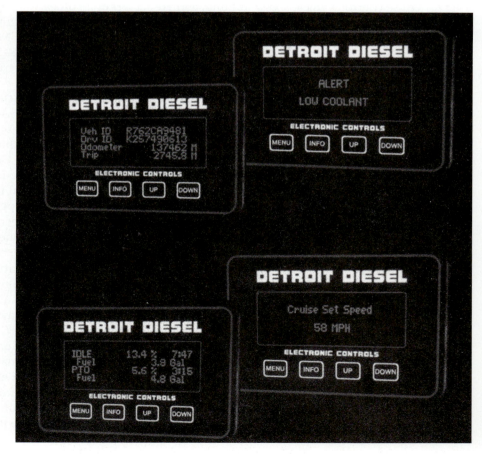

FIGURE 21-56 Example of how an instrument-panel-mounted ProDriver diagnostic readout screen might appear to a truck driver or service technician. (Courtesy of Detroit Diesel Corporation.)

lar to that described earlier and shown in Figure 15-23 across terminals A to M on the 12-pin connector to activate the yellow CEL flash codes. On DDEC III systems, flash codes *cannot* be activated in this manner; instead, a diagnostic request switch mounted on the dash must be toggled.

3. Connect a PC or a laptop to the ECM vehicle diagnostic connector on either a DDEC II or a DDEC III system as illustrated in Figures 21-53 and 21-54. The use of a DDEC translator device converts the SAE J1708 standard to an RS232 serial output protocol. Refer to Figure 21-52, where the small printer shown is connected to the RS232 serial port on the side of the DDR. This same PC hookup can be employed with Detroit Diesel software called TRAC (Trip Record Access) release 3.00, which is a programmed package that extracts operational data stored in the ECM. These data can be used to automate fleet record keeping or analyzed to evaluate fleet performance in key areas such as miles (kilometers) driven, engine hours, fuel consumed, total idle/PTO time, total idle fuel used. Fault codes and ECM setup parameters can also be reviewed to aid in troubleshooting when necessary.

Remember that there are two types of trouble codes that can be stored and extracted from the ECM memory system. When an inactive code is logged in ECM memory, it is "time stamped" with the following information: (1) the first occurrence of each diagnostic code in engine hours on all engine applications; (2) the last time that each diagnostic code occurred in engine

hours; (3) the number of STEO actions recorded during a trouble code condition; and (4) the total time in seconds that the diagnostic code was active.

SPECIAL NOTE   When disconnecting or connecting ECM or sensor wire harnesses, the ignition switch power *must* always be in the OFF position to prevent serious damage to the various circuits. The ignition system is fuse protected; nevertheless, make certain that no power is on when connecting or disconnecting diagnostic equipment or special tester tools.

ECM and Special Tools

Figure 21-57 illustrates the DDEC II ECM with all of the wiring harness connectors at one end. Figure 21-58 shows the DDEC III ECM which has wiring harness connectors on both ends of the electronic control module.

If it becomes necessary to trace a wiring circuit fault in a DDEC system, open up the alligator-style wiring harness protective cover by prying it apart with your hands. Each wire is identified by an ink-stamped number that corresponds to the system wiring diagram. In addition, each ECM connector pin is identified in the DDEC system wiring diagram as to the wire number to which it connects. Thus it is a reasonably easy task for the service technician to trace all wires for

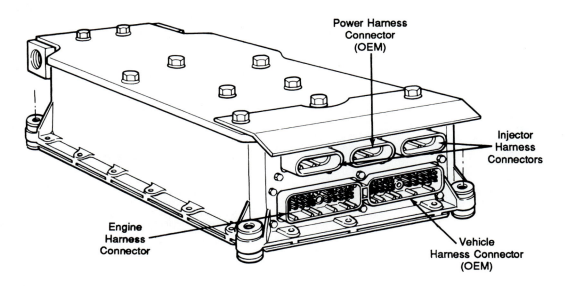

Electronic Control Module (ECM)

FIGURE 21–57 DDEC II ECM and engine/vehicle interface electrical connectors. (Courtesy of Detroit Diesel Corporation.)

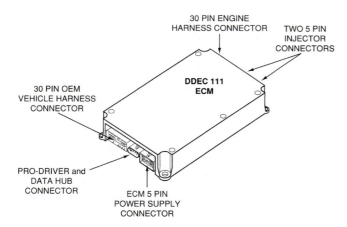

FIGURE 21–58 *DDEC III ECM and engine/vehicle interface electrical connectors. (Courtesy of Detroit Diesel Corporation.)*

possible faults. However, *never* attempt to pierce the insulation on any wire to probe for a reading with a multimeter. Breaking the insulation causes serious problems from corrosion and/or short circuits. When it becomes necessary to trace the wiring circuits and/or possible faults in wire harness connectors, or within the ECM, refer to Figure 21-59, which illustrates a BB (breakout box) designed specifically for this purpose. When connected into the system, the probes of a multimeter can be inserted into the lettered and numbered BB sockets that correspond to the engine wiring diagram connections. Readings can then be safely taken according to the BB directions or diagnostic step-by-step procedure for tracing a specific trouble code in the engine service manual.

Figure 21-60 illustrates a Kent-Moore special DDEC jumper wire set with its various probe connectors that are designed for insertion into either the ECM female or male connection points and harness connectors. Multimeter leads can then be inserted into the opposite ends of these special probe connectors to safely determine a voltage or resistance value. This reading can then be compared to the service manual specs.

Should it become desirable to check the various DDEC system sensors individually, refer to Figure 21-61, which illustrates a special Kent-Moore sensor tester. Simply disconnect the snap wire harness connector from one or more sensors and attach the correct mating sensor tester harness. Rotate the sensor tester dial knob to the sensor that you want to check; then insert the multimeter test leads into the two probe holes on the tester to read the sensor value and compare it to service manual specs.

DIAGNOSTIC TOOLING

All electronic engine OEMs now offer dedicated software (disks) to facilitate diagnostic and programming information with their products. Using a laptop computer similar to that shown in Figure 21-53, Windows-based programs are available from each specific engine OEM, which offers a point-and-click graphical interface for the technician. These software programs require an IBM-compatible (386 or higher) PC with a 25-MHz processor, 4 Mb of RAM, 10 Mb of hard disk space, a VGA monitor, a 3.5-in floppy drive, DOS 5.0

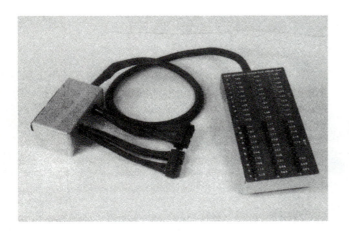

FIGURE 21–59 *ECM breakout box (J35634) for use in testing and troubleshooting possible DDEC system problems. (Courtesy of Kent-Moore Division, SPX Corporation.)*

What's A Break-Out Box?
It's a hand held device which allows the technician to "Break-Out" or access electronic circuits so they can be checked for proper voltage, resistance, and continuity.

Why Use The Break-Out Box?
• The Break-Out Box allows complete interrogation of any DDEC circuit (engine or vehicle) from one convenient device at a comfortable position away from the engine compartment.
• No need to probe the back of the harness connectors or pierce wire insulation to pick-readings.
• All testing is done after "one" initial hook-up of the Break-Out Box. No individual jumper wires to install in male and female connectors. No chance of error in locating the proper circuit.

How Is The Break-Out Box Used?
• Simply disconnect the vehicle and engine harness at the Electronic Control Module (ECM) and connect to the Break-Out Junction Box. The vehicle and engine connectors from the junction box are then connected to the ECM.
• The probes from a Volt/Ohm Meter (such as Kent-Moore J 34039-A) are then inserted into the proper sockets to take readings with ignition on and with or without engine running.

Specifications
• Uses same connectors as found in DDEC.
• Six foot cable between junction box and probe panel.
• Sixty socket probe panel with connector cavities marked to correspond with vehicle and engine connectors (DDEC II) and J1A and J1B (DDEC I).
• Includes handy reference card to identify connector cavities.

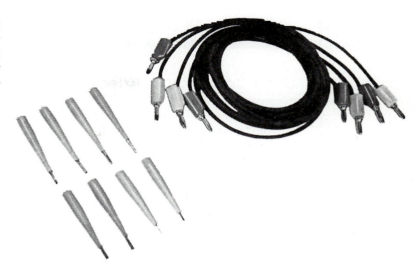

FIGURE 21–60 Model J35751 DDEC jumper wire kit for effective electrical troubleshooting and problem diagnosis. (Courtesy of Kent-Moore Division, SPX Corporation.)

or higher, Microsoft Windows 3.1 or higher, and an RS232 serial data port not used by a mouse or printer. For those maintenance facilities wishing to load an OEM software program onto a laptop computer, an internal fax modem, PCMCIA slot, CD-ROM drive, 486 chip, and greater levels of MHz and RAM are necessary. All OEMs offer similar functions to fleets that want to implement an interactive maintenance system.

Detroit Diesel Software

Detroit Diesel's group of data hub products consists of five parts which are: (1) data logger, (2) ECM data pages, (3) ProManager 2.0, (4) ProDriver, and (5) TRAC. All of these software products are designed to

FIGURE 21–61 DDEC engine sensor tester tool used to isolate possible faulty sensors or wire harness faults. Sensors can be checked on or off the engine. Tester requires a 12-V battery power source and the use of a digital multimeter. (Courtesy of Kent-Moore Division, SPX Corporation.)

operate with each other or separately depending on fleet requirements. ProDriver (Figure 21-56) is a dash-mounted on-board computer, while TRAC is data extraction software designed to format ECM information for a spreadsheet program such as Lotus or Excel. The other three parts listed above are intended to interact between vehicle/engine and technician to provide diagnostic and troubleshooting capabilities. The data logger can store up to three months of vehicle data when joined to ProManager 2.0 software versus the 14-day capacity for the data pages option. The data logger and the ECM data pages can be installed in each tractor of fleets running DDEC III engines that need the combined functions of both systems. A typical diagnostic connector hookup to a Detroit Diesel series 60 engine is shown in Figure 21-54. Contact any Detroit Diesel dealer or distributor for more information on this software.

Diagnostic Codes

In accordance with SAE industry-wide technical standardization trouble codes, all engine OEMs now employ the same PIDs, SIDs, and FMIs to indicate the same problem area with their systems. Refer back to the section in Chapter 15 titled, "ECM SAE Trouble Codes" for a description of these.

ECM flash codes, which were described and shown in Figure 15-24, are shown in Figure 21-62 for DDEC systems. Keep in mind that these flash codes appear on the DDR screen in DDEC I and DDEC II systems but not on DDEC III systems, which reveal only the PIDs, SIDs, and FMIs. Flash codes can be extracted from DDEC III systems only if a diagnostic request switch has been wired into the ECM system. Figure 21-62 lists SID-PID-FMI trouble code to flash code cross-references used on DDEC III systems for SAE standard J1587.

DDEC III   Flash Codes   SAE Faults

TO READ CODES: Use the diagnostic data reader or depress and hold the diagnostic request switch with the ignition on, engine at idle or not running. Press and hold the switch. Active codes will be flashed on the stop engine light, followed by the inactive codes being flashed on the check engine light. The cycle will repeat until the operator releases the diagnostic request switch.

Flash Code	DDEC III Description
11	VSG input low
12	VSG input high
13	Coolant level circuit low
14	Intercooler, coolant or oil temp. circuit high
15	Intercooler, coolant or oil temp. circuit low
16	Coolant level circuit high
17	Bypass position circuit high
18	Bypass position circuit low
21	TPS circuit high
22	TPS circuit low
23	Fuel temp. circuit high
24	Fuel temp. circuit low
25	No codes
26	Aux. shutdown #1or #2 active
27	Air temp. circuit high
28	Air temp. circuit low
31	Aux. output short or open circuit (high side)
32	SEL short or open circuit
33	Boost pressure circuit high
34	Boost pressure circuit low
35	Oil pressure circuit high
36	Oil pressure circuit low
37	Fuel pressure circuit high
38	Fuel pressure circuit low
41	Too many SRS (missing TRS)
42	Too few SRS (missing SRS)
43	Coolant level low
44	Intercooler, coolant or oil temp. high
45	Oil pressure low
46	Battery voltage low
47	Fuel pressure high
48	Fuel pressure low
52	A/D conversion fail
53	EEPROM write or nonvolatile checksum fail
54	Vehicle speed sensor fault
55	J1939 data link fault
56	J1587 data link fault
57	J1922 data link fault
58	Torque overload
61	Injector response time long
62	Aux. output open or short to battery
63	PWM open or short to battery
64	Turbo speed circuit failed
67	Coolant pressure circuit high or low
68	IVS switch fault, open or grounded circuit
71	Injector response time short
72	Vehicle overspeed
75	Battery voltage high
76	Engine overspeed with engine brake
81	Oil level or crankcase pressure circuit high
82	Oil level or crankcase pressure circuit low
83	Oil level or crankcase pressure high
84	Oil level or crankcase pressure low
85	Engine overspeed
86	Water pump or baro. pressure circuit high
87	Water pump or baro. pressure circuit low
88	Coolant pressure low

SAE Fault	Flash Code	DDEC III Description	SAE Fault	Flash Code	DDEC III Description
p 052 0	44	Intercooler temp. high	s 009 0	61	Injector #9 response time long
p 052 3	14	Intercooler temp. circuit high	s 009 1	71	Injector #9 response time short
p 052 4	15	Intercooler temp. circuit low	s 010 0	61	Injector #10 response time long
p 072 3	17	Bypass position circuit high	s 010 1	71	Injector #10 response time short
p 072 4	18	Bypass position circuit low	s 011 0	61	Injector #11 response time long
p 073 3	86	Pump pressure circuit high	s 011 1	71	Injector #11 response time short
p 073 4	87	Pump pressure circuit low	s 012 0	61	Injector #12 response time long
p 084 0	72	Vehicle overspeed (fueled)	s 012 1	71	Injector #12 response time short
p 084 11	72	Vehicle overspeed (absolute)	s 013 0	61	Injector #13 response time long
p 084 12	54	Vehicle speed sensor fault	s 013 1	71	Injector #13 response time short
p 091 3	21	TPS circuit high	s 014 0	61	Injector #14 response time long
p 091 4	22	TPS circuit low	s 014 1	71	Injector #14 response time short
p 092 0	58	Torque overload	s 015 0	61	Injector #15 response time long
p 094 0	47	Fuel pressure high	s 015 1	71	Injector #15 response time short
p 094 1	48	Fuel pressure low	s 016 0	61	Injector #16 response time long
p 094 3	37	Fuel pressure circuit high	s 016 1	71	Injector #16 response time short
p 094 4	38	Fuel pressure circuit low	s 020 3	81	Dual fuel BOI input failed high
p 098 0	83	Oil level high	s 020 4	82	Dual fuel BOI input failed low
p 098 1	84	Oil level low	s 021 0	41	Too many SRS (missing TRS)
p 098 3	81	Oil level circuit high	s 021 1	42	Too few SRS (missing SRS)
p 098 4	82	Oil level circuit low	s 025 11	26	Aux. shutdown #1 active
p 100 1	45	Oil pressure low	s 026 3	62	Aux. Output #1 short to battery
p 100 3	35	Oil pressure circuit high	s 026 4	62	Aux. Output #1 open circuit
p 100 4	36	Oil pressure circuit low	s 040 3	62	Aux. Output #2 short to battery
p 101 0	83	Crankcase pressure high	s 040 4	62	Aux. Output #2 open circuit
p 101 1	84	Crankcase pressure low	s 047 0	61	Injector #17 response time long
p 101 3	81	Crankcase pressure circuit high	s 047 1	71	Injector #17 response time short
p 101 4	82	Crankcase pressure circuit low	s 048 0	61	Injector #18 response time long
p 102 3	33	Boost pressure circuit high	s 048 1	71	Injector #18 response time short
p 102 4	34	Boost pressure circuit low	s 049 0	61	Injector #19 response time long
p 103 8	64	Turbo speed circuit failed	s 049 1	71	Injector #19 response time short
p 108 3	86	Baro. pressure circuit high	s 050 0	61	Injector #20 response time long
p 108 4	87	Baro. pressure circuit low	s 050 1	71	Injector #20 response time short
p 109 1	88	Coolant pressure low	s 051 3	31	Aux. Output #3 open circuit
p 109 3	67	Coolant pressure circuit high	s 051 4	31	Aux. Output #3 short to ground
p 109 4	67	Coolant pressure circuit low	s 052 3	31	Aux. Output #4 open circuit
p 110 0	44	Coolant temp. high	s 052 4	31	Aux. Output #4 short to ground
p 110 3	14	Coolant temp. circuit high	s 053 3	62	Aux. Output #5 short to battery
p 110 4	15	Coolant temp. circuit low	s 053 4	62	Aux. Output #5 open circuit
p 111 1	43	Coolant level low	s 054 3	62	Aux. Output #6 short to battery
p 111 3	16	Coolant level circuit high	s 054 4	62	Aux. Output #6 open circuit
p 111 4	13	Coolant level circuit low	s 055 3	62	Aux. Output #7 short to battery
p 121 0	76	Eng. overspeed with eng. brake	s 055 4	62	Aux. Output #7 open circuit
p 168 0	75	Battery voltage high	s 056 3	62	Aux. Output #8 short to battery
p 168 1	46	Battery voltage low	s 056 4	62	Aux. Output #8 open circuit
p 172 3	27	Air temp. circuit high	s 057 3	63	PWM #1 short to battery
p 172 4	28	Air temp. circuit low	s 057 4	63	PWM #1 open circuit
p 174 3	23	Fuel temp. circuit high	s 058 3	63	PWM #2 short to battery
p 174 4	24	Fuel temp. circuit low	s 058 4	63	PWM #2 open circuit
p 175 0	44	Oil temp. high	s 059 3	63	PWM #3 short to battery
p 175 3	14	Oil temp. circuit high	s 059 4	63	PWM #3 open circuit
p 175 4	15	Oil temp. circuit low	s 060 3	63	PWM #4 short to battery
p 187 3	12	VSG input high	s 060 4	63	PWM #4 open circuit
p 187 4	11	VSG input low	s 061 11	26	Aux. shutdown #2 active
p 187 7	11	VSG interface not responding	s 230 5	68	IVS switch fault, open circuit
p 190 0	85	Engine overspeed	s 230 6	68	IVS switch fault, grounded circuit
p 251 10	--	Clock module abnormal rate	s 231 12	55	J1939 data link fault
p 251 13	--	Clock module failure	s 238 3	32	SEL short to battery
s 001 0	61	Injector #1 response time long	s 238 4	32	SEL open circuit
s 001 1	71	Injector #1 response time short	s 239 3	32	CEL short to battery
s 002 0	61	Injector #2 response time long	s 239 4	32	CEL open circuit
s 002 1	71	Injector #2 response time short	s 240 2	--	FRAM checksum incorrect
s 003 0	61	Injector #3 response time long	s 248 8	55	Proprietary link fault (master)
s 003 1	71	Injector #3 response time short	s 248 9	55	Proprietary link fault (slave)
s 004 0	61	Injector #4 response time long	s 249 12	57	J1922 data link fault
s 004 1	71	Injector #4 response time short	s 250 12	56	J1587 data link fault
s 005 0	61	Injector #5 response time long	s 253 2	53	Nonvolatile checksum incorrect
s 005 1	71	Injector #5 response time short	s 253 12	53	EEPROM write fail
s 006 0	61	Injector #6 response time long	s 253 13	--	Incompatible cal version
s 006 1	71	Injector #6 response time short	s 254 0	--	Failed external RAM
s 007 0	61	Injector #7 response time long	s 254 1	--	Failed internal RAM
s 007 1	71	Injector #7 response time short	s 254 6	--	Entered boot via switches
s 008 0	61	Injector #8 response time long	s 254 12	52	A/D Conversion fail
s 008 1	71	Injector #8 response time short			

FIGURE 21–62 Listing of DDEC III system flash codes and SAE standard fault codes. (Courtesy of Detroit Diesel Corporation.)

Using the MPSI DDR

The MPSI ProLink 9000 DDR illustrated in Figure 21-52 is designed to provide the service technician with a number of functions. It contains an operational soft-touch *keypad* (with 16 keys) similar to that illustrated in Figure 21-63. The MPSI reader can be used with all current heavy-duty diesel electronic systems. However, since each engine and vehicle manufacturer has chosen its own computer operating system, the ProLink 9000 DDR can have its software cartridge changed to suit the engine or transmission type. The slip-in cartridge can be easily removed or installed from the rear of the DDR with light pressure.

Figure 21-63 lists the MPSI DDR reader functions that can be used to access the engine ECM. The DDR shown in Figure 21-52 contains 10 numeric keys and 4 arrow keys. See closeup in Figure 21-63. The up and down arrow keys can be used to scroll through the digital screen readout displays, while the right and left arrow keys can be used to toggle back and forth between

DDEC III   MPSI Reader Functions

Engine Selections

ENGINE DATA LIST

Active Codes	Intercooler Temp	Cruise Set Speed
Inactive Codes	Oil Pressure	SRS Received
Engine RPM	Fuel Pressure	Idle Speed RPM
Pulsewidth	Baro Pressure	Engine Governor
Turbo Boost	Crankcase Pressure	% Torque Limit
TPS Counts	Coolant Pressure	Half Engine
TPS Percent	External Pump	Engine Brake
VSG Counts	Oil Level	Fuel Rate
VSG SETRPM	Coolant Level	Fuel Economy
BOI	Bypass Valve	ISD Option
Oil Temp	Engine Load	PWM #1
Coolant Temp	Torque	PWM #2
Fuel Temp	ECM Volts	PWM #3
Air Inlet Temp	Vehicle Speed	PWM #4

DIAGNOSTIC CODES
Active Codes
Inactive Codes
Clear Codes

CALIBRATION CONFIGURATION
Engine & Engine Protection Configurations
VSG & Cruise Control Configurations
Idle Shutdown & Progressive Shift Configurations
ECM Input & Output Configurations

FUEL INJECTOR INFORMATION
Cylinder Cutout
Response Times
Calibration Update
Change Injector Password

ENGINE/TRIP DATA

Fuel	Idle Hours	VSG Hours
Engine Hours	Idle Fuel	Cruise Hours
Miles	Engine Brake Hours	Fuel Economy,
		(MPG - km/L)

CALIBRATION CHANGES
Reprogram Options
Change Password

SWITCH/LIGHT STATUS
ACTIVATE OUTPUTS
MID MESSAGES BEING RECEIVED

Pro-link Selections

RS-232 SERIAL PORT	**CUSTOM DATA LIST**
PRINTER OUTPUT	Display Standard
Engine Data	Display Custom
Diagnostic Codes	Edit Custom
Calibration Configuration	Reset Custom
CCO Test Results	
Snapshot Data	**CONTRAST ADJUST**
Injector Response Times	
Trip Data	**ENGLISH/METRIC**
Total Engine Data	
TERMINAL OUTPUT	**SNAPSHOT**
P.C. INTERFACE	
PORT SETUP	**RESTART**

choices on the display. The Function key is used to choose one of the functions listed in Figure 21-63. The Enter key must be pressed once you have selected a function from the readout window screen to confirm your choice or instruct the DDR to continue to the next step.

NOTE Within the DDR ProLink is a 2-A fuse; failure of the unit to power up and display information on the window screen may indicate a blown fuse.

DDR operation requires connection of a special cable with a 15-pin terminal to the top of the housing,

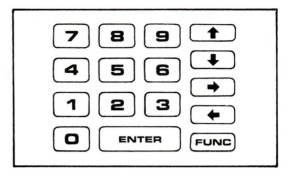

FIGURE 21–63 DDEC III system MPSI DDR (see Figure 23-52) ProLink 9000 selections available by using the various function keys on the hand-held tool. (Courtesy of Detroit Diesel Corporation.)

as shown in Figure 21-52. Once installed, lightly tighten the two captive plastic thumbscrews to secure the cable connection. If a printer is being used, connect it as shown in Figure 21-52.

Troubleshooting with the DDR
Always make sure that the ignition switch/key is OFF before connecting or disconnecting the DDR connec-

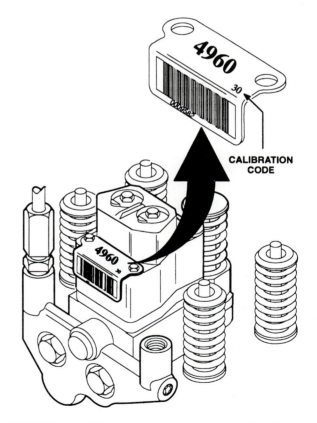

FIGURE 21–64 Electronic unit injector calibration code location on the load plate for all DDEC III systems. (Courtesy of Detroit Diesel Corporation.)

FIGURE 21–65 *Step-by-step sequence that would be followed on the hand-held ProLink 9000 diagnostic data reader when recalibrating new or rebuilt DDEC III electronic unit injectors. (Courtesy of Detroit Diesel Corporation.)*

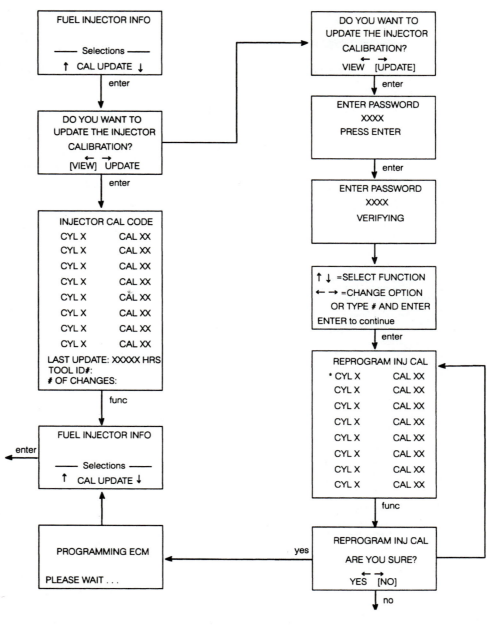

Injector Calibration with the DDR

Injectors in the 1994 later-production DDEC III engines have performance *bar codes* and are individually programmed into the ECM after installation. This feature is shown in Figure 21-64, where the injector load plate has a bar code label on it plus a calibration code number that can range from 00 to 99. This number must be entered into the ECM using the DDR when injectors are replaced. By doing so, we can ensure a cylinder balancing feature to help control engine horsepower variability in each cylinder. This variability occurs due to mass production tolerances that result in variations in cylinder compression pressures, fuel injector delivery volume, and so on. Use of the calibration number results in improved engine response

tors. When the DDR is connected to the ECM diagnostic data link connector, the technician can select any of the items listed in Figure 21-63. Scroll through the selections illuminated on the DDR screen with the up and down arrows. When you see the function you want, you may have to use the left and right arrow keys to place the brackets [ ] around your selection when prompted to do so on the screen. Then you have to press the Enter key. As you select a given function, the DDR screen prompts you about what to do next. If you want to extract stored trouble codes, or short out engine cylinders automatically or by cylinder selection, you can do so using the Function and Enter keys. After a short practice period with the DDR, you will become relatively comfortable using it.

and fuel efficiency because the ECM is able to accurately compute many factors, including each injector's performance, and meter an exact fuel quantity into each cylinder.

Figure 21-65 illustrates the procedure required when the DDR is used to recalibrate injectors; the following description explains the procedure in more detail. When using the DDR to calibrate injectors, select ENGINE from the screen and hit the Enter key. Using the arrow keys, scroll to FUEL INJECTOR INFO on the screen and press the Enter key. Scroll with the arrow keys again until CAL-UPDATE appears on the DDR screen and press the Enter key. From DO YOU WANT TO UPDATE THE CALIBRATION select [VIEW] and hit the Enter key. The DDR screen will display the various injector calibration codes. Compare the two-digit calibration numbers shown on the injectors (see Figure 21-64) with the numbers shown on the DDR screen. If no changes are required, press the Function key and turn off the ignition; then disconnect the DDR.

If some of the injector codes differ from those shown on the DDR screen, press the Function key to return to the FUEL INJECTOR INFO menu. Select UPDATE and press the Enter key. Type in the four-digit update injector calibration password for the DDR and press Enter. If this feature is not password protected, type 0000 and press the Enter key. A message will appear telling you to use the up and down arrow keys to SELECT FUNCTION (in this case the cylinder number), and TYPE # (the injector calibration code). An asterisk (*) will highlight the first cylinder number in the list. Using the arrow keys, scroll to the cylinder requiring the code change and type in the new two-digit injector calibration code number; then press the Enter key. Repeat the same procedure for each cylinder that requires a change to the injector code number. Note, however, that the Enter key must be pressed before the DDR will allow selection of another cylinder number!

When all cylinders have been updated with the required new injector calibration code numbers, press the Function key. Select YES from the display and press Enter to reprogram the ECM with the revised injector calibration codes. Turn the ignition key to the OFF position and wait a minimum of 5 seconds before starting the engine.

NOTE Always replace removed injectors back into the same cylinder after a service operation; otherwise, correct cylinder balance will not occur. If you have placed injectors back into a different cylinder from which they were removed, they will have to be rechecked with the DDR as just described and updated.

OPTIMIZED IDLE

Introduction
On long haul trucks with sleeper cabs, it is advantageous for the operator to be able to have the engine electronic controls automatically stop and restart the engine, particularly in cold weather operation for heater operation and in hot weather for air conditioning operation. Figure 21-66 illustrates the OI (optimized idle) dash-mounted electronic controls panel. The OI system when engaged is designed to automatically stop and restart the engine to maintain oil temperature, battery voltage, and cab temperature. The DDEC system will stop the engine when the oil temperature reaches 104°F (40°C), and restart the engine when the oil temperature drops to 60°F (15°C). The system will also start the engine when the battery voltage drops to 12.2 volts with the minimum run time for a low battery condition being programmed in for 20 minutes. In cold weather the programmed idle speed is set for 1100 rpm, while in hotter weather the idle is set for 1000 rpm.

Advantages
The OI feature has the following advantages:

1. Maintains the engine oil temperature at factory set limits.

2. Ensures a fully charged battery. A plus at anytime, but even more so in cold weather operation.

3. Maintains the cab and sleeper compartment at a preselected operator temperature from an optional thermostat.

4. Idle time reduction; improved fuel economy and engine reliability resulting in longer life to overhaul.

5. No cold starts thereby providing maintenance savings.

6. It eliminates warm-up time and fuel usage.

7. Increased driver satisfaction through use of the in-cab thermostat.

8. The optimized idle system is more cost/weight effective than existing pony packs (small auxiliary engine and heating system mounted behind the cab).

9. Reduces both air and noise pollution.

FIGURE 21-66

10. Can be added to existing DDEC 111 equipped engines.

OI On/Off Conditions

When the operator desires to use the OI (Optimized Idle) feature, the following conditions must be met:

- Engine running at an idle with the ignition switch ON.
- Hood or cab closed.
- Transmission in neutral and in high-range (if so equipped).
- If a vehicle cruise control switch is used, it must be in the ON position "after" the vehicle is idling.
- When OI is ON, a dash-mounted active light will illuminate.

To disable optimized idle, turn off the ignition switch. or use the drive-away feature which will automatically disable the system. This simply involves releasing the parking brake(s) and/or placing the transmission lever into gear. When the engine returns to base idle, the system OI active light will turn off. During OI operation, the variable speed engine governor, cruise VSG, and the foot pedal will not function, therefore if operation of these features is desired, OI must be disabled.

The system operates in the engine mode until the in-cab thermostat is turned on by the operator pressing any button. The thermostat may be turned off by pressing and holding the MODE button for three seconds. The in-cab thermostat set point range for OI activation is between 60–85°F (15–29°C), with comfort zone choices being adjustable between 4, 7, and 10°F (2, 4, and 6°C). The OI system will provide continuous run temperatures when the ambient temperature is less than 25°F (−4°C), and in hot weather when ambient temperatures are higher than 100°F (38°C), and an air conditioning fan is desired. The heater or A/C fan will cut-in 30 seconds after engine start. An extended idle system operation will occur for 45 minutes, then cycle for 15 minutes on/15 minutes off until the cab thermostat is satisfied, or the system is disabled.

If the OI system fails to start the engine, a CEL (check engine light) and logged ECM trouble code will be set. The maximum start attempts are limited to two, and the maximum cranking time to 8 seconds. The time between automatic start attempts is 45 seconds.

ELECTRONIC UNIT PUMP SYSTEM

A derivative of the basic Bosch PLN (pump–line–nozzle) system is the recently introduced camshaft driven and electronically controlled EUP (electronic unit pump) illustrated in Figure 21-67. Now used as the base fuel system on the Detroit Diesel series 55, jointly developed with Mercedes-Benz, parent company of Freightliner Corporation, the series 55 engine will be the stock offering in Freightliner's new Century class heavy-duty trucks. Weighing approximately 2100 lb (953 kg), this engine will be targeted to run against both the Cummins M11 and the Cat 3176 C-10 and C-12 models in the range 365 to 400 hp (272 to 298 kW). The engine is a derivative of MB's own OM447LA and/or 457 engine models, having a displacement of 12 L (730 in^3), a compression ratio of 16.25 : 1, a firing order of 1–5–3–6–2–4, and rotates CW from the front. The current engine is rated at 365 hp (272 kW) at 2000 rpm, produces 1450 lb-ft (1966 N · m) of torque at 1100 rpm, and is controlled by Detroit Diesel's own DDEC III system. The various sensors used on the engine are similar to those found on DDEC systems to send a return signal back to the ECM for EUP fueling control. The engine is being manufactured in the United States at DD's own engine assembly plant.

The individual EUPs for each cylinder are mounted along the camshaft side of the engine block at an angle, where their roller follower is camshaft actuated. Figure 21-68 illustrates the basic fuel system arrangement for the series 55, which employs a gear-driven pump similar in both design and operation to that used on the series 60 DD engines. The camshaft roller follower within the unit pump body raises a plunger within a barrel to create the high pressures necessary for injection. The basic parts of the unit pump are shown in Figure 21-69, where item 1 is the electric solenoid which receives a PWM (pulse-width-modulated) signal from the DDEC III ECM. Operating in the same way as a DDEC EUI, the actual time of one cam revolution is about 60 ms.

Injection can occur only when the solenoid valve is closed and the camshaft is lifting the internal plunger within the EUP body. Low-pressure fuel spill occurs when the solenoid valve is open and the plunger is moving downward by the force of the spring (item 4). Fuel delivered from the EUP flows through a small-bore high-pressure fuel line and into the nozzle, item 5 shown in Figure 21-70. The nozzle tip contains eight holes (orifices) and requires approximately 4500 to 5000 psi (31,027 to 34,475 kPa) to open it against spring pressure, resulting in a spray-in pressure around 26,000 psi (1769 atm).

Troubleshooting and diagnosis of the EUP system can be done in a manner similar to the DDEC system by using a DDR (Figure 21-52) to withdraw stored trouble codes within the ECM and to perform a cylinder cutout sequence automatically or by selected cylinder.

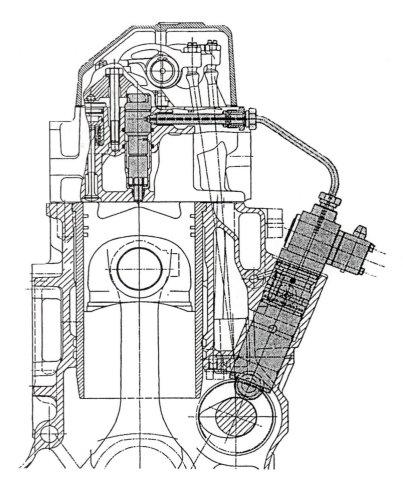

FIGURE 21–67 *Camshaft-driven electronically controlled unit pump illustrating a short pipe connected to the in-head injector. This design results in a "stiff" injection system for low exhaust emissions. (Courtesy of Detroit Diesel Corporation.)*

SPECIAL NOTE   Mack's current six-cylinder engines, which are equipped with Robert Bosch PLN electronically controlled V-MAC engines, are scheduled to use the EUP system on the 500-hp (373-kW) model E7 engines due in late 1997.

VALVE ADJUSTMENT FOR MERCEDES-BENZ/DETROIT DIESEL SERIES 55 ENGINE MODELS

The series 55 Detroit Diesel engine offered as the stock engine in Freightliner's new Century class heavy trucks, is derived from MB's own OM447LA engine but is manufactured by Detroit Diesel and is equipped with DD's own DDEC III electronic controls fitted to EUPs (electronic unit pumps). The individual four-valve head designs also include a smaller fifth valve in the cylinder head which is hydraulically activated by oil pressure, and electronically controlled by a signal from the DDEC III ECM. This fifth valve is opened to activate the engine compression brake.

Valve adjustment on these engines is achieved through the conventional locknut and screw adjustment shown in Figure 21-71. To adjust the valves accurately on this engine which uses a 1–5–3–6–2–4 firing order, refer to Figure 21-72, which illustrates that two main steps are used to adjust all the intake and exhaust valve lash clearances. Begin by rotating the engine crankshaft over by the insertion of a $\frac{3}{4}$-in. (19-mm) breaker bar or ratchet into the square hole in the center of the crankshaft pulley.

Locating the TDC-Compression No. 1 Piston

Rotate the crankshaft until piston 1 is at TDC on its compression stroke. Since there is no timing marks on either the engine flywheel or on the front crankshaft damper/pulley, true TDC can be determined by

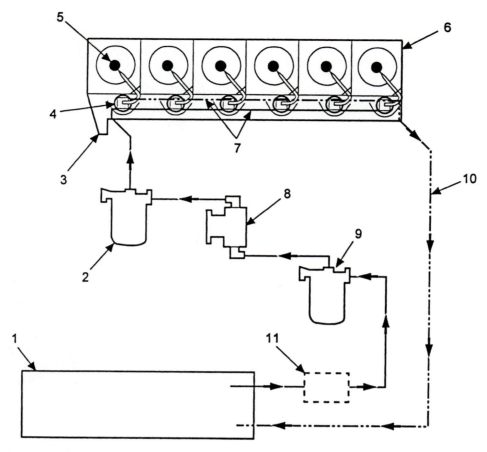

FIGURE 21–68 *Series 55 fuel system schematic diagram. 1, Fuel tank; 2, secondary fuel filter; 3, cylinder block; 4, electronic unit pump (EUP); 5, injector nozzle; 6, cylinder head; 7, integral block (fuel galleries); 8, fuel pump; 9, primary fuel filter; 10, return line; 11, location for optional fuel/oil water separator. (Courtesy of Detroit Diesel Corporation.)*

removing the SRS (synchronous reference sensor) located as shown in Figure 21-73 at the flywheel housing. Remove the single retaining bolt and rotate the engine over CW from the front until the SRS pin is visible and centered when viewed through the SRS access hole. TDC No. 1 can now be determined by grasping the rocker arms and feeling for clearance or by checking that the pushrods on cylinder 1 can be rotated freely. If none of these two conditions exist, No. 6 cylinder valves would be in a position to be adjusted; therefore, rotate the crankshaft through another 360° (one full turn) to place the valves on cylinder 1 into the correct position. With the No. 1 piston at TDC-compression, proceed as described below:

1. Match-mark the vibration damper and front cover with a piece of chalk or felt-tip pen to provide a TDC No. 1 compression reference mark.

2. Valves that can be checked and adjusted with piston 1 at TDC-compression would include those shown in step 1 of Figure 21-72. This includes the intake valves on cylinders 1, 2, and 4 and the exhaust valves on cylinders 1, 3, and 5.

SERVICE TIP An alternative method that you can employ to set the valves listed in step 2 is to rotate the crankshaft over until the exhaust valves on cylinder 2 are fully open. When adjusting the valves, some technicians prefer to use a sequence known as the "12 system," which has six sets of intake and six sets of exhaust valves (two intake and two exhaust per cylinder). With this procedure we number the intake and ex-

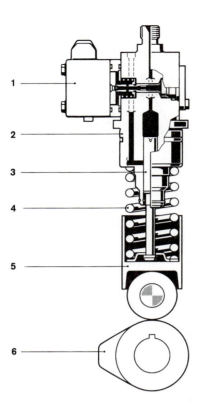

FIGURE 21–69 *Electronically controlled unit pump. 1, Solenoid valve; 2, barrel assembly; 3, plunger; 4, plunger return spring; 5, roller tappet; 6, engine camshaft. (Courtesy of Robert Bosch Corporation.)*

haust valve sets from the front to the rear of the engine. Therefore, starting with cylinder 1 we have valve sets 1 and 2 on through to cylinder 6, which would have the valves numbered as 11 and 12. With the cylinder 2 exhaust valves fully open, set the clearances for valve sets 1, 2, 3, 6, 7, and 10 as in Figure 21-74A.

3. Insert a feeler gauge as shown in Figure 21-71 between the end of the rocker arm pallet and the valve bridge. The intake valve clearance is 0.016 in. (0.406 mm), while the exhaust is 0.020 in. (0.508 mm).

4. To adjust the clearance, loosen the locknut (item 4) and rotate the adjusting screw (item 3).

5. Tighten the locknut and recheck that the clearance is correct; otherwise, reloosen the locknut and readjust.

6. Rotate the crankshaft over another 360° (one full turn) to place cylinder 6 at TDC-compression. At this time the cylinder 1 valves will be on the rock. The

intake valves are just starting to open and the exhaust valves are almost closed.

7. Valves that can be checked and set with piston 6 at TDC-compression include those shown in step 2 of Figure 21-72. This includes the intake valves on cylinders 3, 5, and 6 and the exhaust valves on cylinders 2, 4, and 6.

SERVICE TIP   An alternative method to set the valves listed in step 7 is to rotate the crankshaft over until the cylinder 4 intake valves are fully open, and using the 12 sequence described in the Service Tip following procedural step 2. Set the valve sets on 4, 5, 8, 9, 11, and 12 as in Figure 21-74B.

---

8. Check and adjust the valve clearances shown in step 2 of Figure 21-72, in the same manner as described in procedural steps 3, 4, and 5.

SUMMARY

A detailed description and analysis of how DDC fuel injection systems, both mechanical and electronic function and operate, along with information of how-to service, maintain, diagnose, analyze and effectively use special diagnostic tooling, has provided you with expanded knowledge and capabilities to understand fuel system operation, and will permit you to function as an effective fuel system troubleshooter and diagnostic technician.

SELF-TEST QUESTIONS

1. DDC engines use a fuel system known as a
   a. high-pressure system
   b. low-pressure recirculatory system
   c. common-rail system
   d. distributor pump system

2. Identify the basic functions of a DD fuel system:
   a. supplies clean fuel, and cools and lubricates the injectors
   b. purges the system of air and maintains adequate pressure
   c. self-primes, lubricates, and supplies pressure
   d. both a and b are correct

3. Technician A says that installing too small a fuel inlet/suction line from the fuel tank can result in a high fuel system restriction to the suction side of the fuel transfer pump. Technician B says that too small a line can cause lack of power under load. Who is right?

FIGURE 21–70 *Series 55 fuel injector flow diagram. 1, Cylinder block; 2, cylinder head; 3, nozzle hold-down crab; 4, M10 bolt; 5, injector nozzle; 6, internal injector fuel line; 7, high-pressure fuel line; 8, electronic unit pump. (Courtesy of Detroit Diesel Corporation.)*

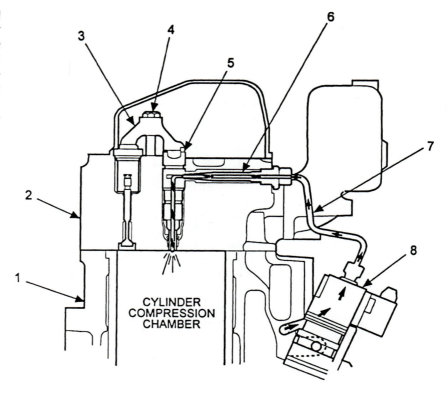

4. Technician A says that he would perform a fuel system restriction check by performing a fuel spill-back check. Technician B says that he would use a mercury-manometer at the primary filter. Who knows the correct procedure?

5. Technician A says that if air is drawn into the fuel system, it can occur only between the fuel tank and inlet side of the fuel pump. Technician B says that you could also suck air at the secondary fuel filter if the gasket is not sealing properly. Who is right?

6. Technician A says that normal fuel system pressure on a DDC engine is between 30 and 45 psi (207 to 310 kPa). Technician B says that this is too low and that it should be between 50 and 70 psi (345 to 483 kPa). Who is right?

7. Technician A says that the fuel system restricted fitting is installed at the fuel inlet manifold. Technician B disagrees, saying that it is located at the fuel outlet/return fuel manifold. Who is correct?

8. Technician A says that the purpose of the fuel system restricted fitting in all DDC engines is to maintain a minimum pressure of 35 psi (241 kPa) at the inlet fuel manifold. Technician B says that the restricted fitting is to limit the fuel flow to the injectors to limit the engine horsepower. Who understands the purpose of this fitting?

9. Technician A says that the size of the restricted fitting orifice is stamped on the brass fitting. Technician B says that all restricted fittings on DDC engines are the same. Who is correct here?

10. Technician A says that a fuel spill-back check is used to confirm that the fuel pump pressure is up to specs. Technician B says that this check can confirm whether there is air in the system and if the fuel filters are plugged. Who is right?

11. Technician A says that an RO8 or R8O stamping on a fuel system restricted fitting indicates that the orifice size is 0.080 in. Technician B says that it means that the orifice size is 0.8 mm. Who is correct in this instance?

12. Technician A says that the fuel inlet manifold on two-stroke 71 and 92 series engines is always the upper fuel manifold on the cylinder head. Technician B says that the inlet manifold is the lower one. Who is correct?

13. Technician A says that the fuel inlet manifold on the series 60 four-stroke-cycle engine is always the lower

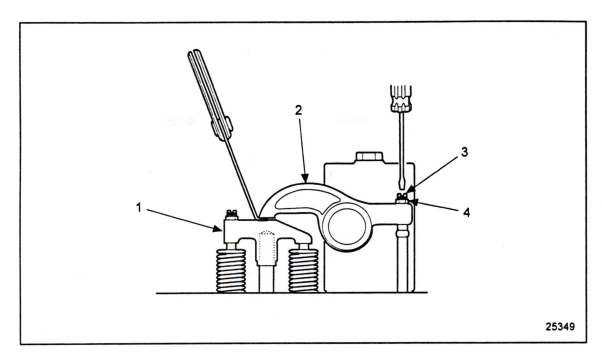

FIGURE 21–71 *Valve clearance adjustment. 1, Valve bridge; 2, rocker arm assembly; 3, adjusting screw; 4, locknut. (Courtesy of Detroit Diesel Corporation.)*

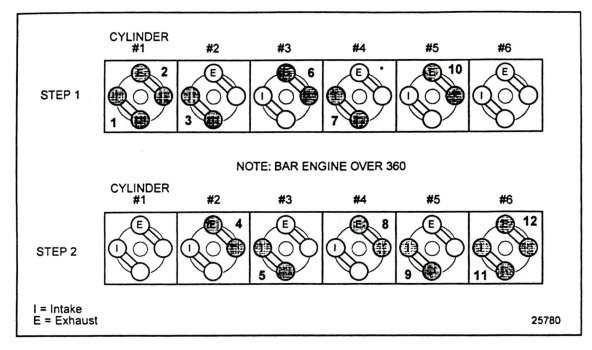

Valve Adjustment Sequence

FIGURE 21–72 *Valve adjustment sequence, Series 55 engine. (Courtesy of Detroit Diesel Corporation.)*

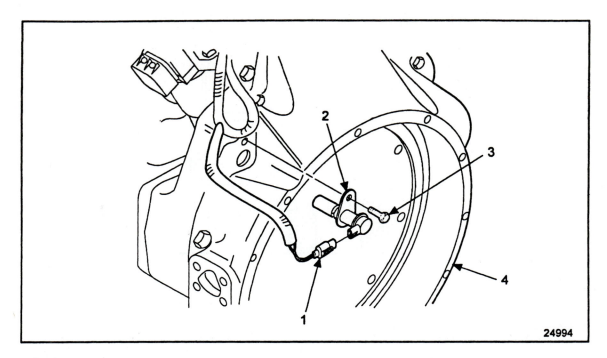

FIGURE 21–73 *Location of SRS (synchronous reference sensor) in a Series SS engine. (Courtesy of Detroit Diesel Corporation.) 1, SRS connector; 2, SRS sensor; 3, bolt; 4, flywheel housing.*

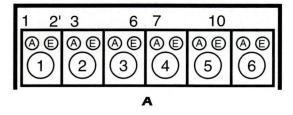

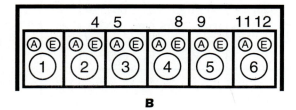

FIGURE 21–74 *a) Valves to adjust when No. 2 cylinder exhaust valves are fully open. b) Valves to adjust when No. 4 cylinder intake valves are fully open. (Courtesy of Detroit Diesel Corporation.)*

manifold on the cylinder head. Technician B says that the inlet is always the upper manifold. Who knows their basic fuel system knowledge?

14. Fuel pump rotation can be identified by
   a. an arrow etched on the pump housing
   b. an arrow stamped on the pump cover
   c. both an arrow and LH or RH stamped on the pump cover
   d. the letters LH or RH stamped on the pump cover

15. Technician A says that to quickly determine if the fuel pump drive has sheared or broken, you can perform a fuel spill-back check to establish how much fuel is being circulated. Technician B says that you can gently insert a small piece of wire up through the seal drain hole and feel for movement as the engine is cranked over. Who is right?

16. Technician A says that the fuel pump relief valve will open and bypass fuel between 45 and 65 psi (310 to 448 kPa). Technician B says that the bypass relief valve opens between 65 and 75 psi (448 to 517 kPa). Who is correct?

17. Technician A says that if the fuel pump relief valve was stuck open, low fuel pressure would exist and a lack of horsepower would occur, particularly under heavy load. Technician B says that the engine would tend to stall at idle. Who is right?

18. Technician A says that the word *primary* and the word *secondary* are usually cast onto the fuel filter housing cover to prevent improper installation in the system. Technician B says that it doesn't matter, since the two fuel filters are the same physical size anyway. Who is correct?

19. Technician A says that fuel filters must be changed every 300 hours or 9000 miles. Technician B says that the filter change period can be determined by the truck fleet operating conditions. Who is correct?

20. Technician A says that spin-on fuel filters should be tightened one full turn after the gasket contacts the filter base. Technician B says that they should only be turned approximately two-thirds of a full turn. Who is correct?

21. Technician A says that the four functions of the unit injector used in DDC engines is to time, atomize, meter, and pressurize the fuel. Technician B says that the four functions are to time, meter, inject, and atomize the fuel. Who is correct?

22. Technician A says that you cannot intermix DDC unit injectors in the engine. Technician B says that you can since they will physically fit. Who is correct?

23. Technician A says that the basic horsepower on DDC mechanical engines (non-DDEC) can be changed by installing a larger or smaller injector size. Technician B says that to change the horsepower setting, you have to increase the maximum full-load engine speed. Who is right?

24. Technician A says that to change the horsepower setting on a DDC electronically controlled fuel injection system engine (DDEC), you would have to alter the EEPROM (electrically erasable programmable read-only memory) in the ECM. Technician B says that you would have to physically remove the existing PROM chip and install a new one that has been recalibrated for a new setting. Who is correct?

25. Technician A says that overtorquing a mechanically controlled unit injector (non-DDEC) can result in a binding rack condition. Technician B says that it could cause injector misfire. Who is right?

26. Technician A says that metering of the fuel inside a mechanical (non-DDEC) unit injector is accomplished by the position of the rack, which alters the helix position and therefore the fuel delivery rate. Technician B says that the length of the plunger effective stroke does this function. Who is right?

27. Technician A says that the injector popping pressure is the pressure required to atomize the fuel. Technician B says that it is the pressure required to lift the internal needle valve. Who is right?

28. Technician A says that the fuel delivery rate in DDEC-equipped engines is controlled by rocker arm movement and the governor linkage connection. Technician B says that the ECM regulates the fuel delivery by a PWM (pulse-width-modulated) electrical signal. Who is correct?

29. Numbers stamped on the injector tip indicate
    a. date of production and injector type
    b. number of holes, diameter of the holes, and the included spray-in angle
    c. delivery rate, injector type, and spray angle

30. Technician A says that to time the injector on both non-DDEC- and DDEC-equipped engines, you have to set the height between the injector body and the top of the injector follower to a given specification. Technician B says that you have to do this only on non-DDEC engines, since the DDEC injectors are electronically controlled. Who is right?

31. Technician A says that in a *matched* set of injectors, they all flow at the same fuel rate when tested on a calibration test stand. Technician B says that all the injectors are set to the same timing height. Who is correct?

32. Technician A says that spray tips are generally blown off of an injector by high fuel delivery pressures. Technician B says that this is usually a direct result of water in the fuel. Who is right?

33. Technician A says that excessive carbon buildup on the injector tip is usually an indication of low popping pressure and poor atomization, whereas Technician B says that water in the fuel will cause this. Who is right? (Self-research)

34. Technician A says that on non-DDEC-equipped truck engines, the mechanical governor is a limiting-speed (minimum/maximum) design. Technician B disagrees saying that it is usually an all-range variable-speed type. Who is correct?

35. Technician A says that a governor gap must be set into the governor assembly discussed in Question 34. Technician B says that this is not necessary since the injector rack adjustment will establish this gap. Who is correct?

36. Technician A says that the maximum no-load engine speed should be set according to the engine option plate/decal and can be altered by rotating the high-speed governor spring nut CW or CCW. Technician B says that the engine maximum no-load speed should never be tampered with. Who is right?

37. Technician A says that the amount of droop (rpm loss) on all DDC engines equipped with mechanical governors can be offset by setting the maximum no-load rpm approximately 7% higher than the full-load speed desired. Technician B says that both the full-load and no-load speeds are one and the same since the governor will compensate for any speed loss as the engine load is applied. Who is right here?

38. Technician A says that the minimum recommended idle speed can be found listed on the EPA exhaust emissions label. Technician B says that it is stamped on the governor cover plate. Who is correct?

39. Technician A says that when adjusting a buffer screw on a non-DDEC-equipped engine, you can rotate the screw until a steady idle speed is obtained. Technician B says that you should never increase the idle speed more than 15 rpm; otherwise, the maximum no-load speed can be altered. Who is aware of the function of the buffer screw?

40. Technician A says that to increase the idle speed on a non-DDEC-equipped engine, you have to rotate the adjusting screw CW to increase the compressive force on the internal spring. Technician B says that you must back the screw out CCW to raise the idle speed. Who is right?

41. Technician A says that on a TT-equipped non-DDEC engine, to decrease the engine horsepower setting, you have to rotate the belleville washer adjusting nut CCW. Technician B says that you would have to rotate this adjusting nut CW. Who is right?

42. Technician A says that engine tune-up must be performed every 50,000 miles (80,465 km) to ensure that the engine exhaust emissions comply with EPA regulations. Technician B says that tune-up is required only when a low-power complaint is received and the air and fuel systems are mechanically sound. Who is correct?

43. Technician A says that when performing a tune-up on a V71 or V92 engine, the first injector rack to be adjusted should always be the No. 1 left bank. Technician B says that it does not make any difference whether you start with No. 1 on the left bank or No. 1 on the right bank. Which mechanic knows his tune-up procedure correctly?

44. Technician A says that failure to back out the idle and buffer screws as well as the belleville washers on a TT engine (non-DDEC) can result in incorrectly adjusted injector racks. Technician B says that if you back out the idle screw, the injector rack settings will be too loose. Who is aware of the correct procedure here?

45. On a non-DDEC engine equipped with a mechanical governor, the throttle delay cylinder functions to
    a. minimize exhaust smoke during acceleration
    b. delay the governor action during slow acceleration
    c. increase the governor response time
    d. reduce engine torque in the high-speed range

46. Technician A says that when timing an injector on a two-stroke-cycle DDC engine, the exhaust valves should be fully closed. Technician B says that the exhaust valves should be fully open. Who is correct?

47. Technician A says that when setting the injector on a series 60 four-stroke-cycle engine, the valves and injector cannot be set at the same time on the same cylinder.

Technician B says that the injector can only be set when the intake and exhaust valves are in position to be set on its companion cylinder. Who is right here?

48. Technician A says that to clear the ECM trouble codes from DDEC II or DDEC III memory, you simply have to pull the inline system fuses for 10 seconds. Technician B says that you have to employ an electronic DDR (diagnostic data reader). Who is correct?

49. Technician A says that stored ECM trouble codes can be determined by shorting out jumper pin A to M on the 12-pin DDL truck connector and watching the CEL illumination flashes. Technician B says that you must use the DDR (diagnostic data reader) of DDEC I or II systems for DDEC III systems. Who is right?

50. Technician A says that diesel fuel is used to cool the ECM in some DDEC systems. Technician B says that engine coolant is routed through the ECM housing for this purpose. Who is correct?

51. Technician A says that if a DDEC-equipped engine shuts down repeatedly after idling for 5 minutes, this is a normal condition controlled by the ECM. Technician B says that this indicates a plugged primary fuel filter and the engine is simply using the fuel volume contained within the secondary filter assembly. Who is right?

52. A bus driver with a DDEC-equipped coach complains that the engine fails to rev up when the coach is parked and idling with the passenger door open. Technician A says that this is a normal condition. Technician B says that this is an abnormal condition. Who is correct?

53. Technician A says that the throttle pedal on a DDEC system uses a sensor which is basically a variable potentiometer that changes the voltage output signal proportional to throttle depression. Technician B says that the throttle pedal is connected to mechanical linkage running to a TPS sensor and then to the electronic governor in front of the blower on two-stroke-cycle engines. Who is correct?

54. Technician A says that when the CEL (check engine light) on the dash illuminates, a trouble code has been logged into ECM memory and that the driver should have the DDEC system checked at the first available opportunity. Technician B says that when the CEL illuminates, within 30 seconds the engine/ECM will initiate an engine shutdown sequence. Who is correct here?

55. Technician A says that the SRS and TRS must be adjusted on all DDEC-equipped engines. Technician B says that this has to be done only on DDEC-equipped two-stroke-cycle 71 and 92 series engines. Who is right?

56. Technician A says that the EUI (electronic unit injectors) used on the DDEC systems can be effectively cut out in the engine by using a DDR tester. Technician B says that you have to use a large screwdriver and hold the injec-

tor follower down while the engine is running in order to check their operation. Who is right?

57. Technician A says that when checking the DDEC system wiring for either a resistance or voltage value, it is acceptable to puncture the wiring to gain a good connection. Technician B says that you should never do this since this will expose the weatherproof connections to the elements. Who is correct?

58. Technician A says that the DDR (diagnostic data reader) can be used to reprogram part of the engine calibration in the ECM. Technician B says that this can be done only by connecting the DDR to a factory computer interface hookup. Who is correct?

59. A fuel system problem is generally indicated when
   a. black smoke emanates from the exhaust stack
   b. white smoke emanates from the exhaust stack
   c. the engine loses power with no abnormal exhaust smoke
   d. high crankcase pressure is apparent

60. Technician A says that high fuel system operating temperatures will result in high horsepower. Technician B says that this will result in a loss of horsepower. Who is correct?

61. Technician A says that a low fuel spill-back rate with normal fuel pressure would indicate air in the fuel system. Technician B says that this is probably due to too small a restricted fitting. Who is right?

62. Technician A says that too large a restricted fitting can cause a loss of fuel pressure at the injectors. Technician B says that this can cause a high fuel spill-back rate. Who is correct?

63. Technician A says that to check an injector for a misfiring condition in a non-DDEC 71 or 92 engine, you can run the engine at idle and simply depress the injector follower (hold it down). Technician B says that you should individually push each injector rack into the full-fuel position and see if the engine picks up speed. Who knows the correct procedure?

64. Technician A says that the DDL connection for the DDR on the DDEC III system incorporates a six-pin Deutsch connector. Technician B says that it is a 12-pin connector, the same as DDEC II systems. Who is right?

65. Technician A says that the DDR shown in Figure 21-52 can be used to interface with the ECM on all DDEC systems without having to change the snap-in module on the backside. Technician B says that this can only be done if the latest DDEC III module is in place on the DDR, since the module for DDEC II will not handle the DDEC III system. Who is correct?

66. True or False: A portable laptop computer (see Figure 21-53) must be used to reprogram the ECM.

67. Technician A says that the DDEC III system employs an ATS (air temperature sensor) which was not used on DDEC I and DDEC II systems. Technician B says that all DDEC systems, I, II, and II, all used the ATS. Who is right?

68. True of False: Automatic engine shutdown of a DDEC-equipped engine will usually be tied into an out-of-range operating condition in either the oil pressure, oil temperature, and coolant level sensors.

69. Technician A says that the ProDriver permits the operator to detect problems with the engine and DDEC system. Technician B says that only the DDR can tell you this. Who is right?

70. Technician A says that the DDEC III system is four times faster and contains a memory capacity three times larger than the DDEC II had. Technician B says that DDEC III is eight times faster and seven times more powerful than DDEC II. Who is right?

71. Technician A says that if any injectors are changed in a DDEC III system, the DDR should be used to recalibrate the ECM information to provide a proper cylinder balance. Technician B says that this is not necessary. Who is right?

72. True of False: The series 55 DDC engine is a shared design with Mercedes-Benz but the engine is manufactured in Detroit by DDC.

73. True or False: The series 55 engine employs the DDEC system to control the EUPs (electronic unit pumps).

74. True or False: The series 55 DDEC-equipped engine employs an overhead camshaft.

75. True or False: The series 55 DDEC-equipped engine has the SRS in the same place as on the series 50 and series 60 engines.

76. Technician A says that only the DDEC III system is programmed to illuminate standardized SAE trouble codes to the DDR. Technician B says that all DDEC systems will send SAE codes to the DDR. Who is right?

77. Describe the meaning of the following SAE code letters:
   a. PID
   b. SID
   c. FMI

78. Technician A says that the most common FMI codes are the numbers 3 and 4. Technician B says that codes 7 and 10 are more common. Who is right?

79. List the names of the five DDC data hub software products.

80. Technician A says that an active code can cause the engine to shut down. Technician B says that only a historic code can initiate this action. Who is right?

81. Technician A says that if it is suspected that a problem exists within the ECM, a breakout box can be used. Technician B says that only the DDR can detect this problem. Who is right?

82. Technician A says that the DDEC III system can be programmed to allow automatic progressive engine compression braking (Jacobs or PacBrake) when in the cruise mode to maintain the set cruise speed, particularly when descending an incline. Technician B says

that the compression brake needs to be manually activated by the operator to cause this to happen. Who is right?

83. Technician A says that automatic engine fan engagement during cruise control on a DDEC III–equipped vehicle would indicate a fan relay problem. Technician B says that this is a normal occurrence and is tied in with automatic compression brake engagement. Who is correct?

84. True or False: The SRS provides a once-per-cylinder signal to the ECM.

85. True or False: The TRS provides a 36-per-crankshaft revolution signal from a toothed wheel bolted behind the crankshaft gear.

22

Cummins Fuel Systems

OVERVIEW

This chapter describes how both mechanical PT and Cummins Celect electronic fuel systems function and operate. Additional data deals with how to service, maintain, diagnose and effectively troubleshoot performance complaints on these types of engines. This information, coupled with your understanding of how an electronic fuel injection system operates from information supplied earlier in Chapter 15, will broaden your knowledge of these very important types of fuel systems.

COMPANY BACKGROUND

The Cummins Engine Company was founded in 1919 by Clessie Cummins and has grown to become one of the world's largest independent manufacturers of diesel engines. The company has established an excellent reputation over the years of producing an engine that is used in a wide variety of applications worldwide. The company presently has over 2900 distributors and dealers in 98 countries offering sales and service facilities for their product. In addition, there are parts and engine manufacturing facilities in 11 locations around the world. In the United States the main research and engineering center is located in Columbus, Indiana; an additional technical center is located in Essen, West Germany.

Over the years Cummins has produced a series of innovations, such as the first automotive diesel, in addition to being the first to use supercharging and then turbocharging. All cylinders are commonly served through a low-pressure fuel line. The camshaft control of the mechanical injector times the injection throughout the operating range without the timing lag problems of high-pressure, remote-mounted plunger pump systems.

To meet the U.S. EPA (Environmental Protection Agency) exhaust emissions standards proposed for even more stringent regulations, Cummins offers the Celect (electronically controlled injection) system on both their M11, L10 and 14-L on-highway truck engines. Since the Celect system did not start production until November 1989, there are literally hundreds of thousands of Cummins products still in the marketplace with PT (pressure–time) fuel systems. In this chapter we discuss the operation and basic maintenance of the PT system first, then discuss the basic operating concept of the newer Celect system. In addition to the PT and Celect systems, Cummins B series engines employ a Bosch VE distributor pump, while their C series engines use a Bosch inline multiple-plunger pump. Information on the inline pump is given in Chapter 19.

ENGINE MODEL IDENTIFICATION

As with any engine manufacturer's product, identification of the actual series and model engine is an important part of the technician's job for ordering parts and for service information. Cummins uses an engine data plate affixed to the side of the engine front timing cover on their engines, regardless of the engine series and model. The engine data plate contains specific information about the engine, such as the serial number and control parts list (CPL).

PT FUEL SYSTEM

The PT fuel system illustrated in Figure 22-1 is exclusive to Cummins diesel engines, being introduced in 1951; it employs injectors that meter and inject the fuel, with this metering based on a pressure–time principle.

549

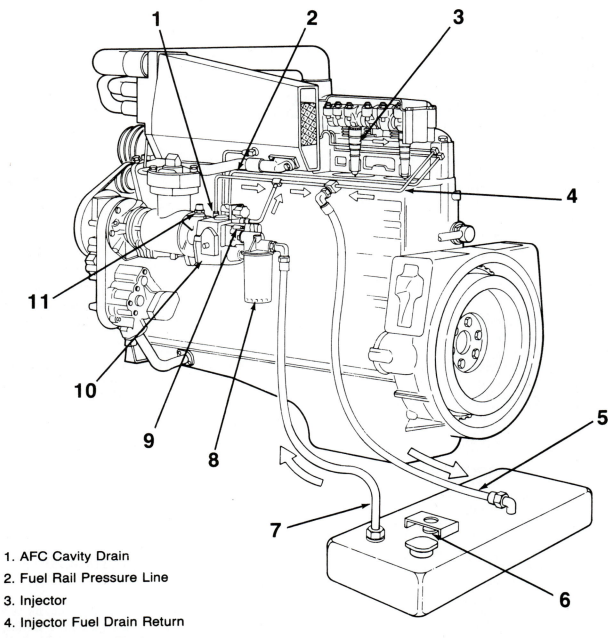

1. AFC Cavity Drain

2. Fuel Rail Pressure Line

3. Injector

4. Injector Fuel Drain Return

5. Fuel Return to Tank

6. Fuel Tank Breather

7. Fuel Inlet Supply

8. Fuel Filter

9. Gear Pump Coolant Drain

10. Fuel Pump

11. Tachometer Drive

FIGURE 22–1 *Basic PT fuel system layout and identification of major components.* (Courtesy of Cummins Engine Company, Inc.)

Fuel pressure is supplied by a gear-driven positive-displacement low-pressure fuel pump, and the time for metering is determined by the interval that the metering orifice in the injector remains open. This interval is established and controlled by the engine speed, which therefore determines the rate of camshaft rotation and consequently the injector plunger movement, which is pushrod and rocker arm actuated.

Since Cummins engines are all of the four-cycle type, the camshaft is driven from the crankshaft gear at one-half engine speed. The fuel pump turns at engine speed. Because of this relationship, additional governing of fuel flow is necessary in the pump.

Although the camshaft is turning at one-half engine speed, when the engine is running at 2100 rpm; the cam is turning 17.5 times every second, therefore, the fuel pump varies pressure to the injectors in proportion to engine rpm.

The flyball type of mechanical governor controls fuel pressure and engine torque throughout the entire operating range. It also controls the engine's idling speed and prevents engine overspeeding in the high-speed range. The throttle is simply a shaft with a hole; therefore, the alignment of this hole with the fuel passages determines pressure at the injectors.

A single low-pressure fuel line from the fuel pump serves all injectors; therefore, the pressure and the amount of metered fuel to each cylinder are equal.

The main components of the PT fuel system that control the pressure at the injectors are shown in Figure 22-1. The PT fuel pump assembly is coupled to the air compressor drive on the engine, which is driven from the engine gear train. The fuel pump main shaft in turn drives the gear pump, governor, and tachometer shaft assemblies.

System Operation

Figure 22-2 describes the PT system flow and injector function and operation. The fuel metering process in the PT system has three main advantages:

1. The injector accomplishes all metering and injection functions.

2. The injector injects a finely atomized fuel spray into the combustion chamber at spray-in pressures exceeding 20,000 psi (1360 atm).

3. A low-pressure common-rail system is used, with the pressure being developed in a gear-type pump. This eliminates the necessity for high-pressure fuel lines running from the fuel pump to each injector, similar to that found in a multiple-plunger inline injection pump system.

To understand the sequence of events pertaining to actual injection of fuel by the injector, a study of the injector operating mechanism is necessary.

Downward movement of the injector plunger forces metered fuel into the cylinder as shown in Figure 22-2. Since the shape of the camshaft lobes is directly related to the start and end of injection, let us take a look at this first. Figure 22-2 shows a cross-sectional view of the camshaft. The injector cam shape is based on two circles, an inner and an outer circle.

To follow this a stage further, let's go back to basics for a minute, and using a circle to represent 720°, as when using a polar valve timing diagram, the 720° circle can represent two rotations of the engine crankshaft. We can then place or superimpose one cam lobe shape in the center of this circle and illustrate injector push tube and injector plunger travel.

Figure 22-2 actually shows the motion transfer from the camshaft lobe, to the push tube and rocker arm, then the injector plunger.

Having studied Figure 22-2 you should now be familiar with the basic camshaft positions; Figure 22-3 shows that during the *intake* stroke, the follower roller moves from the outer cam base circle across the retraction ramp to the inner or lower base circle, which will allow the injector push tube to follow it down. Injector plunger return spring pressure lifts the plunger as the lowered push tube permits the rocker arm lever to tilt backward. As the injector plunger lifts (see Figure 22-3 start upstroke) it allows fuel at low pressure to enter the injector at port A and flow through the inlet orifice (B), internal drillings, around the annular groove in the injector cup, and up passage D to return to the fuel tank. The amount of fuel flowing through the injector is determined by the fuel pressure before the inlet orifice (B). Fuel pressure is determined by engine speed, governor, and throttle.

As the injector plunger continues its upward movement, metering orifice C is uncovered and a charge of fuel is metered to the cup, the amount being controlled by fuel pressure. Passage D is blocked, momentarily stopping fuel circulation and isolating the metering orifice from any fuel pressure pulsations (see Figure 22-3, upstroke complete).

As the camshaft continues to rotate and the cylinder's piston is coming up on *compression*, the follower roller crosses the inner base circle, thereby holding the plunger up for metering, and as it reaches the camshaft lobe injection ramp, the upward-moving push tube working through the rocker arm assembly forces the injector plunger toward injection. Refer to Figure 22-3 (downstroke); you will notice that the downward-moving plunger closes off the metering orifice, thereby cutting off fuel entry into the cup. At this instant, the drain outlet (D) is uncovered; fuel that was not metered to the cup can now leave the injector up passage E, and fresh fuel enters the balance orifice.

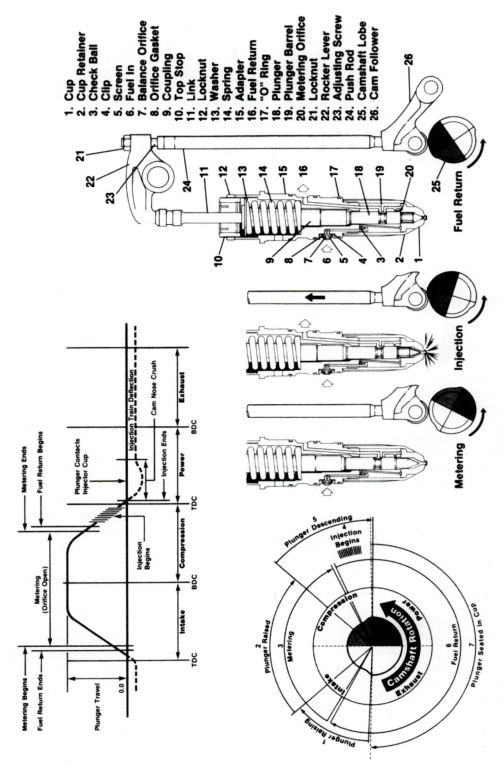

FIGURE 22-2 Fuel injection cycle PT (type D): top stop injector. (Courtesy of Cummins Engine Co., Inc.)

1. Cup
2. Cup Retainer
3. Check Ball
4. Clip
5. Screen
6. Fuel In
7. Balance Orifice
8. Orifice Gasket
9. Coupling
10. Top Stop
11. Link
12. Locknut
13. Washer
14. Spring
15. Adapter
16. Fuel Return
17. "O" Ring
18. Plunger
19. Plunger Barrel
20. Metering Orifice
21. Locknut
22. Rocker Lever
23. Adjusting Screw
24. Push Rod
25. Camshaft Lobe
26. Cam Follower

**Start upstroke
(fuel circulates)**

Fuel at low pressure enters the injector at (A) and flows through the inlet orifice (B), internal drillings, around the annular-groove in the injector cup and up passage (D) to return to the fuel tank. The amount of fuel flowing through the injector is determined by the fuel pressure before the inlet orifice (B). Fuel pressure in turn is determined by engine speed, governor and throttle.

**Upstroke complete
(fuel enters injector cup)**

As the injector plunger moves upward, metering orifice (C) is uncovered and fuel enters the injector cup. The amount is determined by the fuel pressure. Passage (D) is blocked, momentarily stopping circulation of fuel and isolating the metering orifice from pressure pulsations.

**Downstroke
(fuel injection)**

As the plunger moves down and closes the metering orifice, fuel entry into the cup is cut off. As the plunger continues down, it forces fuel out of the cup through tiny holes at high pressure as a fine spray. This assures complete combustion of fuel in the cylinder. When fuel passage (D) is uncovered by the plunger undercut, fuel again begins to flow through return passage (E) to the fuel tank.

**Downstroke complete
(fuel circulates)**

After injection, the plunger remains seated until the next metering and injection cycle. Although no fuel is reaching the injector cup, it does flow freely through the injector and is returned to the fuel tank through passage (E). This provides cooling of the injector and also warms the fuel in the tank.

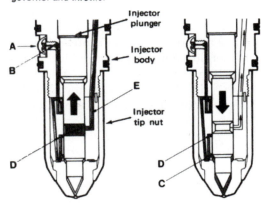
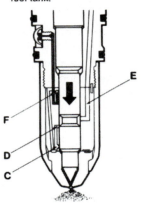
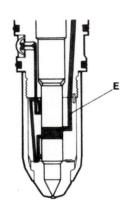

FIGURE 22–3 Descriptive operation of PT injector plunger during the fuel metering and injection period. (Courtesy of Cummins Engine Company, Inc.)

As the plunger continues down into its seating position in the cup, it forces the fuel under great hydraulic pressure through tiny holes (for example, eight holes 0.007 in. or 0.177 mm in diameter), creating a fine fuel spray for penetration of the air mass to assure complete combustion of fuel in the cylinder.

At the completion of the plunger downstroke after injection has ceased, the plunger remains seated until the next metering and injection cycle. The end of injection occurs as the roller follower reaches the nose of the cam; this ensures that the plunger remains seated in the cup because the follower is riding evenly around the concentric outer base circle of the cam lobe. During this time, however, as shown in Figure 22-3, downstroke complete, fuel is allowed to flow freely through the injector and lubricate and cool internal parts. The fuel picks up some heat during this time, which warms the fuel in the tank, which is helpful during cold-weather operation.

Injection Sequence

The injector nozzle is manufactured in two separate pieces and is composed of the *cup* and the *cup retainer*, the cup being the lower part of this assembly. The fuel charge into the cup is determined by the fuel rail *pressure* (P) at the injector body metering orifice, and the *time* (T) that this orifice is uncovered during the upstroke of the injector plunger, as shown in the second diagram from the left in Figure 22-3. The inlet orifice (B) in this diagram is adjustable by burnishing and therefore provides a positive method of being able to balance (same flow rate-calibration) all injectors. In this way, one basic injector assembly can be used in a wide range of engines and horsepower settings simply by changing the injector orifice size.

Fuel that enters the injector at the adjustable orifice is high enough in pressure to unseat the small checkball, which has the express purpose of preventing the reversal of fuel flow as the plunger is pushed downward by the rocker arm across the metering orifice during deceleration and engine shutdown. Fuel delivered to the injector cup occurs during the latter part of the engine's intake stroke and the early part of the compression stroke. As cylinder compression builds, this heated air enters the cup through the small holes drilled in the cup tip, which creates a mixture of air and fuel within the cup prior to actual injection. To ensure that fuel injection pressures will be high enough prior to the point of injection, the plunger is already moving downward before the piston has reached the end of its compression stroke. When the fuel pressure exceeds the combustion chamber air charge pressure, a pilot discharge of fuel within the cup will initiate ignition prior to the main fuel charge being injected.

Injection pressures created with this type of mechanical injection system are in excess of 20,000 psi (1360 atm) which compares well with those found in DDC and Caterpillar unit injector systems both of which are capable of maximum pressures of 20,000 psi (1360 atm) plus. These injection pressures are higher than those developed in hydraulically actuated injectors such as inline pump types and those found with distributor-type injection pumps. The point at which the descending rocker-arm-actuated plunger makes contact with the metered fuel charge is dependent on the "pressure and time" concept for a given load and engine speed. The level of fuel metered into the cup at idle is less than that at rated speed, while there is more fuel metered into the cup at the peak torque point.

Based on this metering principle, the point of injection will be automatically retarded at part-load conditions and advanced for larger fuel charges at higher speeds and loads. In other words, a larger metered fuel charge in the injector cup means that the plunger will start to pressurize the fuel charge earlier in its downward stroke, thereby advancing injection. Injection will cease once the plunger bottoms in the cup and the drain groove on the plunger will be aligned with the drain passages in the injector barrel, allowing fuel to flow through this drain groove and return back to the fuel tank.

Cummins Big Cam model engines employ a larger-diameter camshaft to provide more precise control of injector plunger movement, to ensure a shorter fuel injection period, higher injection pressures, reduced emission levels, and improved fuel economy. The top stop injectors used by Cummins are used to limit the upward travel of the plunger to allow momentary unloading of the injection train components during the actual fuel metering cycle. This provides improved lubrication, resulting in reduced wear and longer operating periods between actual injector adjustments, as well as better overall average fuel economy and therefore emissions control.

PT FUEL PUMPS

All PT fuel systems are equipped with an identification tag riveted onto the pump housing, which provides the necessary information to the service technician when a new exchange pump is required, or

alternatively, it provides the fuel injection rebuild specialist with the necessary information required to find the correct component parts and the fuel pump calibration information required when rebuilding and testing the pump. Always quote this pump code information when parts are required, or when attempting to procure an exchange unit from a local Cummins dealer or fuel injection shop.

Prior to 1977, PT systems employed a simple mechanically governed pump that employed either a limiting-speed or a variable-speed governor assembly depending on the requirements of the vehicle. In 1977 Cummins introduced the existing PT pump, which was known as the PTG-AFC (PT pump with a governor and an air/fuel control attachment), in place of its earlier aneroid control system, which was remotely mounted from the PT pump. The AFC system is assembled within the PTG-AFC pump. The AFC pump provides a more completely combustible air/fuel mixture by continuously monitoring turbocharger air boost pressure and proportionally responding to load and acceleration characteristics. The PT pump achieves this by varying the fuel rail pressure delivered to the injectors. The PT pump fuel pressure is set on a test stand and is determined by the actual engine model demands, with the fuel pressure usually being adjustable between 130 and 250 psi (896 to 1724 kPa).

Figure 22-4 illustrates a typical PTG-AFC fuel pump, which is normally equipped with a limiting-speed governor assembly. A PTG-AFC/VS designation indicates that the pump is equipped with a variable-speed governor assembly. Figure 22-5 illustrates a PTG-AFC/VS pump. The P in the name "PT fuel system" refers to the actual fuel pressure that is produced by the gear pump and maintained at the inlet to the fuel injectors. The T is obtained from the fact that the actual time available for fuel to flow into the injector assembly (cup) is determined by the engine speed as a function of the engine camshaft and injection train components. Actual flow into the combustion chamber from an injector is therefore not only a function of both pressure and time, but is also the actual flow area within the injector. For this reason, injectors are calibrated for a given flow at rated engine speed where the maximum horsepower will be obtained.

Within the pump assembly a fuel pump bypass button of varying size can be installed to control the actual maximum fuel delivery pressure of the gear pump before it opens and bypasses fuel back to the inlet side of the pump. In this way, the actual horsepower setting of the engine can be altered fairly easily (more on this later). Figure 22-6 illustrates the main

1. Tachometer Drive
2. AFC Fuel Return
3. AFC Air Supply
4. Priming Plug
5. Fuel to the Injector
6. Shutoff Valve Electric Connection
7. Gear Pump Fuel Return
8. Fuel Inlet Connection
9. Idle Speed Screw Location
10. Fuel Rate (Pressure) Screw

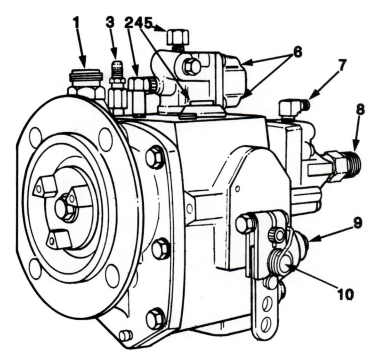

FIGURE 22–4 *PT (type G) AFC fuel pump connection and adjustment locations. (Courtesy of Cummins Engine Company, Inc.)*

1. Tachometer Drive
2. AFC Air Supply
3. Fuel to the Injectors
4. VS High Speed Screw
5. VS Low (Idle) Speed Screw
6. Gear Pump Fuel Return
7. Fuel Inlet Connection
8. Idle Speed Screw Location
9. Fuel Rate (Pressure) Screw

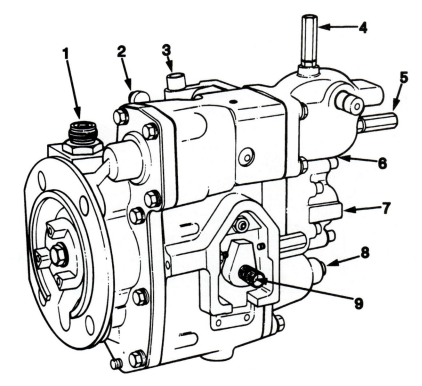

FIGURE 22–5 *PT (type G) AFC-VS fuel pump connections and adjustment locations. (Courtesy of Cummins Engine Company, Inc.)*

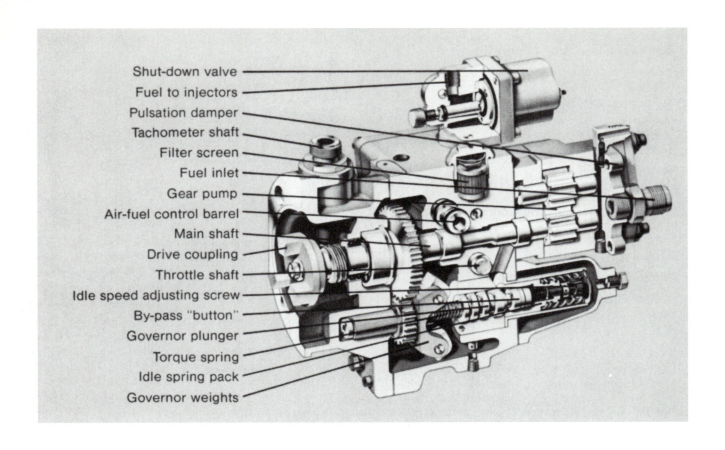

- Shut-down valve
- Fuel to injectors
- Pulsation damper
- Tachometer shaft
- Filter screen
- Fuel inlet
- Gear pump
- Air-fuel control barrel
- Main shaft
- Drive coupling
- Throttle shaft
- Idle speed adjusting screw
- By-pass "button"
- Governor plunger
- Torque spring
- Idle spring pack
- Governor weights

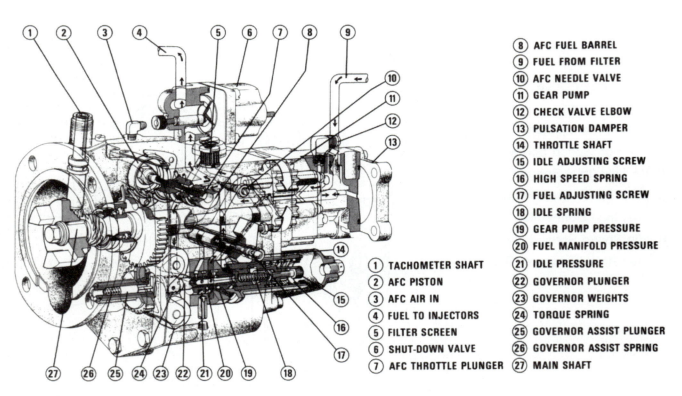

1. TACHOMETER SHAFT
2. AFC PISTON
3. AFC AIR IN
4. FUEL TO INJECTORS
5. FILTER SCREEN
6. SHUT-DOWN VALVE
7. AFC THROTTLE PLUNGER
8. AFC FUEL BARREL
9. FUEL FROM FILTER
10. AFC NEEDLE VALVE
11. GEAR PUMP
12. CHECK VALVE ELBOW
13. PULSATION DAMPER
14. THROTTLE SHAFT
15. IDLE ADJUSTING SCREW
16. HIGH SPEED SPRING
17. FUEL ADJUSTING SCREW
18. IDLE SPRING
19. GEAR PUMP PRESSURE
20. FUEL MANIFOLD PRESSURE
21. IDLE PRESSURE
22. GOVERNOR PLUNGER
23. GOVERNOR WEIGHTS
24. TORQUE SPRING
25. GOVERNOR ASSIST PLUNGER
26. GOVERNOR ASSIST SPRING
27. MAIN SHAFT

FIGURE 22–6 Schematic view of a PT-G AFC fuel pump with "standard" automotive governor and component identification. (Courtesy of Cummins Engine Company, Inc.)

components of the PT-AFC pump assembly. The major functions of the PTG-AFC fuel pump assembly are as follows:

- To pull and transfer fuel from the tank and filter
- To develop sufficient fuel pressure to the rail (common fuel passage) to all of the injectors (see item 2 in Figure 24-1)
- To provide engine idle speed control (governing)
- To limit the maximum no-load and full-load speed of the engine (governing)
- To allow the operator to control the throttle position and therefore the engine's power output
- To control exhaust smoke emissions to EPA specifications under all operating conditions.
- To allow shutdown of the engine when desired

A major feature of the PT pump system is that there is no necessity to time the pump to the engine, since the pump is designed simply to generate and supply a given flow rate at a specified pressure setting to the rail (common fuel line passage) to all injectors. The injectors themselves are timed to ensure that the start of injection will occur at the right time for each cylinder.

Basic PT Pump Flow

The basic flow of fuel into and through the PT pump assembly will vary slightly depending on the actual model of PT pump. For this reason, Figure 22-1 illustrates a diagram of this flow through a PTG-AFC pump without any reference to any of the components involved, since it does allow you to trace this path by following the arrows alone. Simply put, fuel enters the pump on the right-hand side (see item 8, Figure 22-4) and flows down into the gear pump, where the fuel is pressurized and sent to a small internal fuel filter. From there it flows down into the lower section of the pump, then on up into the AFC section and up into the outlet passages through the electric fuel shutoff valve (see item 6, Figure 22-4).

Simplified Fuel Flow

We begin our discussion of the PT system fuel flow by describing the simplified fuel path through the PT pump without regard to specifics at this time, since this will allow you to trace quickly how the fuel travels from the tank to the injectors for combustion purposes. Figure 22-7a illustrates the general PT pump component parts and their identification. Figure 22-7b illustrates what happens when the truck driver cranks the engine over on the starter motor and the engine fires and runs at an idle speed. What happens is that fuel from the vehicle saddle tanks is drawn by the gear

pump (2) through fuel passage C and into the primary fuel filter assembly (1). This filter is usually a combination fuel/filter/water separator on most heavy-duty truck/tractors. The filtered fuel then flows through a small filter screen (3) which is located within the PT pump assembly, and then flows down into the internal governor sleeve (4). The position of the governor plunger (5) determines the actual fuel flow through the various governor plunger ports, which are identified as items 16, 17, and 18. The position of the mechanically operated throttle determines the amount of fuel that can flow through the throttle shaft (19). Fuel from the throttle shaft is then directed to the AFC needle valve (20). The position of the AFC control plunger (21) within the AFC barrel (22) determines just how much throttle fuel can flow into and through the AFC unit and on to the engine fuel rail, which feeds the injectors. The AFC plunger position is determined by the amount of turbocharger boost pressure in the engine intake manifold, which is piped through passage B to the AFC unit within the PT pump body. At engine startup, the boost pressure in passage B is very low; therefore, fuel flow is limited. Fuel under pressure flows through the electric solenoid valve (25), which is energized by power from the ignition switch (26). This fuel then flows through the fuel rail pressure line, shown as item 2 in Figure 22-1 and into the injectors (3). A percentage of the fuel from both the PT pump and the injectors is routed back to the fuel tank in order to carry away some of the heat that was picked up, cooling and lubricating the internal components of the pump and injectors. Figure 22-7c illustrates the fuel flow during normal driving; Figure 22-7d shows the path of flow during the start of high-speed governing, and Figure 22-7e illustrates the fuel flow path during complete high-speed governing operation.

Detailed Pump Flow

Now that you have a good solid understanding of the actual path of flow through the PT pump, let's discuss in more detail exactly how the speed and power developed by the engine is achieved and controlled. Within the PT system, fuel delivery between idle and maximum speed ranges to the injectors is normally controlled by manual operation of the throttle by the operator. Fuel under pressure is then allowed to flow through the idle passage at low engine speed as well as through the throttle shaft. At higher engine speeds, the idle passage is blocked off and fuel flows through the main supply passage to the throttle shaft, then on to the injectors in a PTG pump, or in a PTG-AFC pump, the fuel from the throttle shaft first flows to and through the AFC unit, and then onto the injectors.

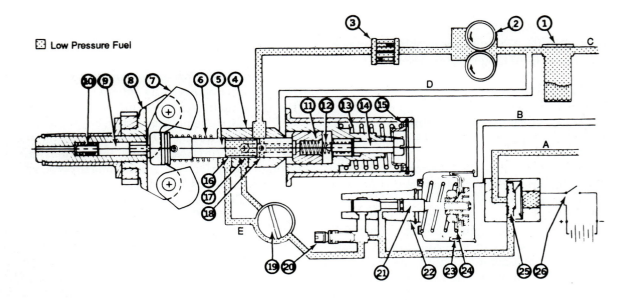

☒ Low Pressure Fuel

1	PRIMARY FUEL FILTER	17	MAIN GOVERNOR PORT
2	GEAR PUMP	18	GOVERNOR DUMP PORTS
3	FILTER SCREEN	19	THROTTLE
4	GOVERNOR SLEEVE	20	AFC NEEDLE VALVE
5	GOVERNOR PLUNGER	21	AFC CONTROL PLUNGER
6	TORQUE CONTROL SPRING	22	AFC BARREL
7	GOVERNOR WEIGHTS	23	DIAPHRAGM (BELLOWS)
8	GOVERNOR WEIGHT CARRIER	24	AFC SPRING
9	WEIGHT ASSIST PLUNGER	25	SOLENOID VALVE
10	WEIGHT ASSIST SPRING	26	IGNITION SWITCH
11	IDLE SPRING PLUNGER	A	FUEL TO INJECTORS
12	IDLE SPEED SPRING	B	AIR FROM INTAKE MANIFOLD
13	MAXIMUM SPEED GOVERNOR SPRING	C	FUEL FROM TANK
14	IDLE SPEED ADJUSTING SCREW	D	BY-PASSED FUEL
15	MAXIMUM SPEED GOVERNOR SHIMS	E	IDLE FUEL PASSAGE
16	IDLE SPEED GOVERNOR PORT		

(a)

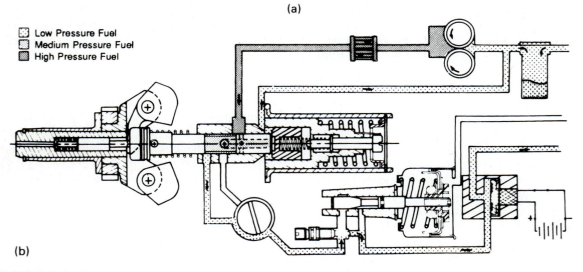

☒ Low Pressure Fuel
▨ Medium Pressure Fuel
■ High Pressure Fuel

(b)

FIGURE 22–7 Fuel flow through a PT-G AFC fuel pump. (a) Engine stopped; (b) starting and idling; (c) normal driving; (d) beginning of high-speed governing; (e) complete high-speed governing. (Courtesy of Cummins Engine Company, Inc.)

558

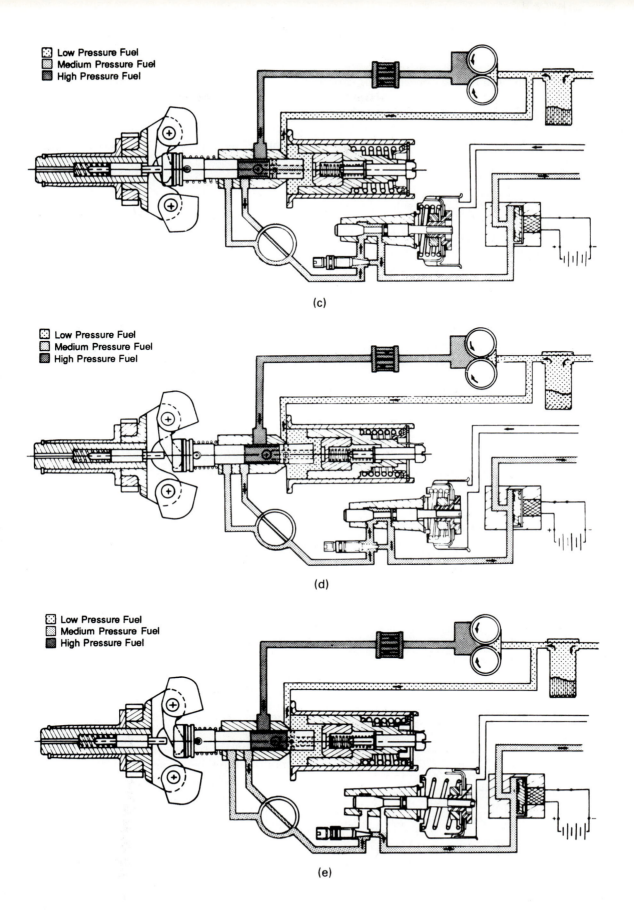

Low Pressure Fuel
Medium Pressure Fuel
High Pressure Fuel

(c)

Low Pressure Fuel
Medium Pressure Fuel
High Pressure Fuel

(d)

Low Pressure Fuel
Medium Pressure Fuel
High Pressure Fuel

(e)

Manipulation of the throttle by the operator will vary the rail pressure to the injectors. At wide-open throttle the rail pressure will be higher than at half-throttle or at an idle speed. The throttle shaft illustrated in Figure 22-8 is cylindrical in shape and is hollow throughout approximately half its overall length in order that a fuel adjusting screw can be screwed into this bore horizontally. This screw in turn will restrict the flow of fuel leaking through the vertical hole drilled through the throttle shaft, and therefore the maximum flow area of the throttle shaft passage when the throttle is in its wide-open position.

When the operator rotates the throttle shaft through mechanical linkage, this fuel rate setting acts as a variable-area orifice since the vertical hole within the shaft indexes with the outlet passage to the injectors, as shown, for example, in Figure 22-8 at an engine idle speed. When the operator accelerates the engine, the throttle shaft will rotate CCW in Figure 22-9 to expose more of the outlet passage to this fuel flow.

Throttle leakage becomes very important to successful operation of the engine. At a closed throttle position there must be adequate fuel leakage through the throttle shaft to keep the fuel lines filled with fuel to the injectors to ensure both cooling and lubrication. However, this amount of leakage is insufficient on its own to keep the engine at an idle speed; therefore, the

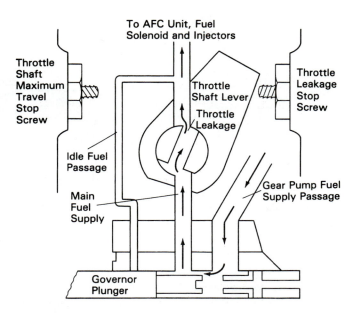

FIGURE 22–9 PTG-AFC fuel pump open throttle and adjustment screw location for throttle leakage and maximum throttle travel. (Courtesy of Cummins Engine Company, Inc.)

governor plunger allows fuel to flow to the idle passage to supplement that flowing from throttle leakage. Throttle leakage is controlled by adjustment of a setscrew located behind the throttle shaft cover on newer engines, or externally on earlier engines. This screw can be seen in Figure 22-9. Insufficient or too much throttle shaft leakage will result in the conditions listed in Table 22-1.

Fuel entering the PT pump's governor plunger and barrel assembly flows around and into the plunger area, where the plunger rides freely in the carrier and sleeve, which is being lubricated by this fuel. Fuel flowing into the plunger travels in both directions and will therefore follow the route of least resistance. Figure 22-10 shows that spring pressure on the right-hand side holds the idle plunger against the end of the governor plunger until fuel begins to flow, at which time they are pushed apart enough for some fuel to escape.

In the cutaway section shown in Figure 22-8 the amount of fuel being bypassed depends on resistance to its flowing out in other directions through the idle

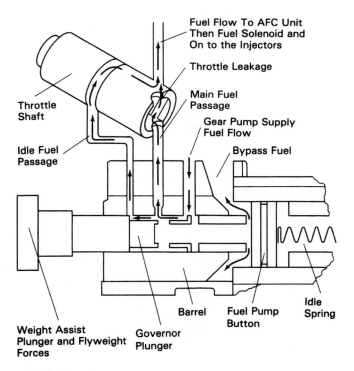

FIGURE 22–8 PTG-AFC pump idle fuel flow and throttle leakage paths. (Courtesy of Cummins Engine Company, Inc.)

TABLE 22–1   Throttle leakage setting problems

Too high	Too low
Slow deceleration	Hesitation on acceleration
Injector carboning	Injector plunger damage

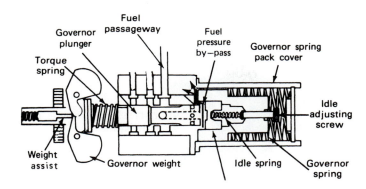

FIGURE 22–10 *PTG governor. (Courtesy of Cummins Engine Company, Inc.)*

and throttle openings in the plunger and barrel assembly. To simplify this action of how the fuel flow is controlled, the fuel pressure as it reaches the governor plunger is caused by the restriction to this flow by placing the surface of the idle plunger against the end of the governor plunger. Such a condition can be likened to that created when you place a thumb over the end of a garden hose minus the nozzle. Water pressure builds up in the water behind your thumb owing to restriction caused by your thumb over the end of the hose; therefore, water that does escape has an increased velocity or greater force and direction.

Under this condition, fuel is held in the governor plunger by the surface of the idle plunger, which is under spring pressure; therefore, as the volume of fuel flow increases, fuel will eventually push the idle plunger back if no other outlet is found. There are, however, two other outlets for governor plunger fuel, which are shown in Figures 22-8 and 22-9.

Figure 22-9 shows (1) the *idle* port (or drilling), which allows fuel to escape during *low* speeds, and (2) the *throttle* port, through which fuel escapes during times of higher speeds or loads. Whether or not fuel is routed through these two other passages is controlled by just how they are aligned with fuel from the governor plunger, and how hard it is for the fuel volume to push the idle plunger surface away from the end of the governor plunger. The throttle shaft system then does the following:

- Forms the idle fuel passageway
- Controls fuel flow for selecting the desired engine speed
- Controls minimum circulation to the injectors (throttle leakage)

Let's study these three functions a little more closely.

1. *Idle passage.* Idle fuel flow is controlled by the pump governor. The throttle shaft idle passage is always open to fuel pressure.

2. *Manual fuel control passage.* As mentioned earlier, fuel for engine operation must pass through the throttle shaft, which is aligned at this time with the passage in the pump body. Rotation of the throttle shaft causes misalignment of fuel passages and restricts fuel flow, thereby reducing fuel manifold pressure available to the injectors. Figure 22-9 shows that two throttle stop screws limit throttle movement. The *rear* screw allows adjustment of maximum fuel passage opening. The *forward* screw limits the closed throttle position. On AFC fuel pumps the front throttle stop screw is for throttle travel adjustments and the rear screw is for throttle leakage adjustments.

3. *Throttle leakage.* Adjustment of the forward throttle stop screw sets the engine idle speed by controlling the amount of fuel flowing to the injectors with a closed throttle. This throttle leakage also does the following:

a. Maintains fuel manifold rail pressure required at the injector metering orifice for immediate acceleration when desired

b. Purges air and gases from the injector

c. Lubricates the injector

Remember that the amount of fuel that will be delivered to the injectors at an idle speed through the idle fuel passage is controlled by the idle spring plunger fuel pump button resting against the governor fuel control plunger in its barrel, as shown in Figure 22-8. This is in turn controlled by the idle spring tension on the back side of the button, while the fuel plunger is pushed against the button by the forces of the weight assist plunger and centrifugal forces developed by the rotating governor weights at the opposite end. When a state of balance is achieved between these opposing forces, a steady fuel pressure and flow rate through the idle fuel passage, as well as throttle leakage, will maintain a steady predetermined idle speed of the engine. A plunger button with too large a number allows the fuel pressure to act on a larger area; this will reduce the pressure at which fuel begins bypassing, thereby lowering the system supply pressure. Alternatively, using a smaller button number than recommended will result in fuel bypassing at a higher pressure, thereby raising the supply pressure.

In all truck engine PT fuel pumps the fuel delivered to the injectors (rail pressure) is controlled by use of a selected idle spring plunger button such as those illustrated in Figure 22-11. In Figure 22-11, for example, a No. 7 button (part 141624) has a counterbore di-

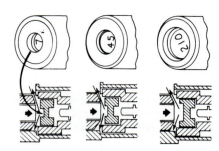

FIGURE 22–11 *Different sizes of idle spring plungers used to control the amount of fuel and horsepower setting of the engine. (Courtesy of Cummins Engine Company, Inc.)*

FIGURE 22–12 *Governor weight assembly showing the location of the weight-assist plunger. (Courtesy of Cummins Engine Company, Inc.)*

ameter of between 0.2135 and 0.2165 in. (5.42 to 5.50 mm), while the No. 45 button (part 138862) has a counterbore size of 0.2885 to 0.2915 in. (7.33 to 7.40 mm). The largest button shown in this figure is No. 210 (part 145963) with a counterbore dimension between 0.4185 and 0.4215 in. (10.63 to 10.70 mm). The smallest button is a size No. 5 (part 141623), with a dimension between 0.2085 and 0.2115 in. (5.30 to 5.36 mm), and the largest is a No. 237 (part 145974), with a counter-bore size between 0.4735 and 0.4765 in. (12.03 to 12.10 mm). Button sizes increase in increments of 0.005 in. (0.127 mm) from the smallest to the highest. Therefore, when an engine seems to be lacking power, and all possible areas have been checked out to satisfaction, be certain that the correct idle spring plunger button size is being used, since either too small or too large a fuel pump button can drastically alter the fuel rail pressure, and therefore the power output of the engine.

Basic Governor Plunger Control

Since what happens to the fuel flow is dependent on the forces that change the amount of restriction to flow, we have to look at how these forces are created and consequently controlled. The governor weight assembly applies force to push the governor plunger back toward the idle plunger surface. The weight assembly is driven through gears from the engine via the engine's gear train and fuel pump mainshaft, as shown in Figure 22-7. The weights are supported and pivot on pins contained in the weight carrier assembly shown in Figure 22-12.

Note that there are more than one set of weights available for these pumps; if the wrong weights are used, it will be impossible to calibrate the pump properly. A change of weights will entirely change the action of the governor plunger. The weights are so positioned that when the engine is running, centrifugal force throwing them outward causes their feet to push against the front end of the governor plunger on each side of the drive tang, causing the plunger to spin in

the barrel assembly. Since governor weight force is proportional to engine speed, at an idle rpm plunger movement by weight force is small; therefore, a short weight-assist plunger exerts pressure against the governor plunger at an idle speed to allow fuel pressure for startup and idle.

The main function of the weight-assist plunger and spring assembly is to add its spring force to that of the governor flyweight centrifugal force when the engine is running at a closed throttle idle speed. For a given throttle leakage setting, the rail pressure to the injectors is determined by the position of the governor plunger cutoff shoulder over the idle passage. The combined forces of the weight-assist plunger spring and the centrifugal force being developed by the rotating governor flyweights at an idle speed are opposed by the idle spring located at the opposite end of the pump plunger. When a state of balance exists between these opposing forces, the engine will run at a predetermined idle rpm. Therefore, the forces developed by the rotating governor flyweights and the weight-assist plunger spring are attempting to force the fuel plunger to a position that will close off the idle fuel passage, while the force of the idle spring at the opposite end of the plunger is attempting to push it to open the idle fuel flow passage. The amount that the weight-assist plunger protrudes through its bore against the governor weights is determined by installing or removing shims between it and its spring assembly.

When checking a PT pump on a test stand, should the fuel pressure not be as specified at the recommended Cummins *check-point speed*, the pump must be disassembled and the weight-assist plunger protrusion checked. The weight-assist plunger protrusion must be decreased to lower the fuel pressure, while increasing its protrusion will raise the fuel pressure at the check point speed.

NOTE After any adjustments to the governor weight-assist plunger, both the idle fuel pressure and the pump high-idle (no-load speed) governor cutoff point should be rechecked.

It should be noted that when the engine speed approaches either high-idle (no-load rpm) or rated (full-load) speed, the weight-assist plunger and spring no longer affect the position of the governor fuel plunger, since the rotating flyweights have moved away from them. The idle fuel passage will have been closed by the centrifugal weight force pushing the fuel plunger forward in the barrel, and the idle spring no longer affects the operation, since the fuel pump button has also bottomed in the idle plunger guide.

AFC PUMPS

The PTG-AFC fuel pump, which is used on later-model on-highway truck engines, is an acceleration exhaust smoke control device built internally into the pump body. The AFC (air/fuel control) assembly is shown in Figure 22-13 with the major components identified. The AFC (air/fuel control) unit is designed to restrict fuel flow in direct proportion to engine air intake manifold pressure during engine acceleration,

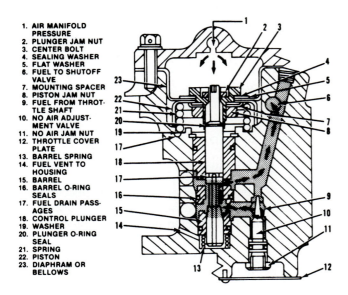

1. AIR MANIFOLD PRESSURE
2. PLUNGER JAM NUT
3. CENTER BOLT
4. SEALING WASHER
5. FLAT WASHER
6. FUEL TO SHUTOFF VALVE
7. MOUNTING SPACER
8. PISTON JAM NUT
9. FUEL FROM THROTTLE SHAFT
10. NO AIR ADJUSTMENT VALVE
11. NO AIR JAM NUT
12. THROTTLE COVER PLATE
13. BARREL SPRING
14. FUEL VENT TO HOUSING
15. BARREL
16. BARREL O-RING SEALS
17. FUEL DRAIN PASSAGES
18. CONTROL PLUNGER
19. WASHER
20. PLUNGER O-RING SEAL
21. SPRING
22. PISTON
23. DIAPHRAM OR BELLOWS

FIGURE 22-13 Cross section of AFC unit in fuel pump and component parts identification. (Courtesy of Cummins Engine Company, Inc.)

under load, and during lug-down conditions. It is somewhat similar in function to the aneroid control used on older-model Cummins diesel engines.

Since a turbocharger is exhaust gas driven, the speed of the turbo is related to exhaust gas flow, which is in turn controlled by engine speed and load conditions. With no direct mechanical drive then to the turbocharger, during acceleration turbo speed lags behind the almost instantaneous fuel-delivering capability of the pump and injectors, thereby creating a temporary air starvation situation until the turbocharger can accelerate and supply enough additional airflow. Before this can happen, however, we are supplying an overrich fuel-to-air mixture, which causes excessive exhaust smoke. Therefore, the AFC provides a more controlled combustion of fuel to air by constantly monitoring turbocharger air pressure and responding proportionally to load or acceleration changes.

AFC fuel control is monitored within the fuel pump. This necessitates running a line from the underside of the intake air manifold air pressure hole to a No. 4 fitting located in the pump AFC cover plate (see Figure 22-13). Both parts (a) and (b) of Figure 22-14 are plan views (top) of the AFC unit. View (a) is a cross section of the control plunger in the *no-air* position; view (b) shows the control plunger in the *full-air* position. Current production Cummins engines are equipped with the PT-type G AFC fuel pump. Those engines not requiring an AFC feature simply have a specially designed plug screwed into the pump housing in place of the AFC barrel assembly.

The aneroid control unit that was used on earlier Cummins engines was designed to function as an ON/OFF fuel bypass device. The AFC unit acts as both a fuel pressure and flow restrictor to provide the correct air/fuel delivery rate to the engine during acceleration.

Operating Principles

The main pump operation is very similar for both the PTG and PTG-AFC; however, the major difference is that which occurs between the fuel pump throttle shaft and the shutdown valve on the AFC pump. In the straight PTG pump unit, fuel passes directly from the throttle shaft through a passage to the shutdown valve, while in the PTG-AFC pump, the fuel passes through the AFC unit after leaving the throttle shaft and before it reaches the shutdown valve on top of the pump body.

Fuel enters the AFC control after leaving the governor and passing through the throttle shaft. When no air pressure is supplied from the turbocharger, the AFC plunger closes off the primary fuel flow circuit

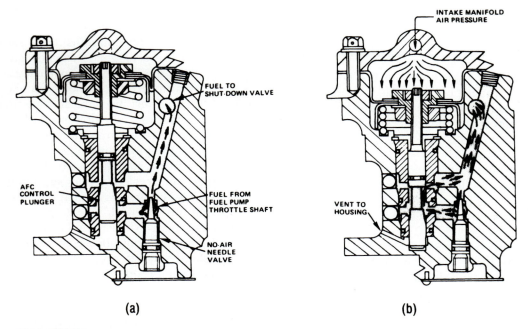

FIGURE 22–14 *AFC fuel pump flow: (a) without turbocharger boost; (b) with tur-bocharger boost. (Courtesy of Cummins Engine Company, Inc.)*

(see Figure 22-14a). A secondary passage controlled by the position of the no-air needle valve supplies fuel for this condition, such as engine cranking, or at initial acceleration of the engine. The no-air needle valve is located directly above the throttle shaft under the throttle cover plate.

As intake manifold pressure increases or decreases, the AFC throttling plunger reacts to deliver a proportional increase or decrease in fuel, which prevents the air/fuel mixture from getting overrich and causing excessive exhaust smoke. The AFC plunger is positioned by action of the intake manifold air pressure acting against a piston and diaphragm opposed by a spring to a proportionate amount of travel (see Figure 22-14b).

Therefore, when a full-throttle lug-down condition occurs, fuel flow through the AFC unit is unrestricted. The AFC unit also controls fuel flow after deceleration in traffic, during gear shifts, running downhill with a closed throttle, or on a downgrade operation on the light-load portion of the governor droop curve.

Fuel Pump Cooling Kit

Some PT fuel pumps employ a cooling kit elbow, which is basically a fitting with a spring-loaded check valve inside it. This fitting would be located in the fuel inlet line (Figure 22-4, item 7). In many automotive applications where long downhill runs are encountered,

little fuel is actually being circulated through the system when the throttle is in a closed position; therefore, a percentage of the hot fuel within the pump is bled back through the check valve elbow and line to the fuel tank, thereby allowing cooler fuel drawn from the tank to be circulated through the PT pump assembly by its own built-in gear pump. The spring-loaded valve within the elbow opens only when fuel pressure is high enough to lift the check valve from its seat. Therefore, when the engine is stopped, the check valve is seated by the spring, which ensures that no fuel or air can drain from the injector return line through the pump.

PTG-AFC PUMP FLOW REVIEW

You have learned from studying this chapter that in the letters PT, P is the fuel pressure at the injector inlet and T is the time allowed for the fuel to actually flow. The quantity of fuel injected per cycle is therefore dependent on:

1. The fuel rail pressure, which is dependent on the pressure regulator settings within the PT pump assembly, since the point at which the supply pressure is bypassed back to the inlet side of the gear pump is itself determined by

the size of the fuel pump button recess and the spring force behind it

2. The flow time, which is related to engine speed

3. The size of the flow area (injector orifice size/calibration)

The uniqueness of the Cummins PT fuel system is such that the conditions listed in Table 22-2 would be typical of the sequence of events occurring in a model NTC-350 (855-in^3/14-L) six-cylinder engine.

SPECIAL NOTE   The example above is used only to illustrate that in the PT fuel system, at a higher engine speed, there is less time to meter the fuel; therefore, the engine will receive less fuel per injection stroke at its rated horsepower setting than it will at its peak torque point, because at the lower engine speed there is more time to meter the fuel. The greatest fuel usage, however, will occur at rated horsepower (full-load speed), since there are a greater number of injection cycles at this higher speed, although the actual quantity injected is lower due to the shorter metering time. Fuel consumption of current Cummins electronically controlled engines is superior to that shown. The actual fuel consumption is dependent on the specific engine model. For example, technological improvements to the Big Cam series of engine has resulted in continued improvements in the fuel economy.

From the information stated in this chapter and reference to Figure 22-7 you now know that the fuel

TABLE 22–2   *Example of fuel rate usage and number of injection cycles per hour*

	Peak torque speed, 1300 rpm	Rated engine speed, 2100 rpm
Fuel injected per cycle (lb)	0.00038	0.00030
Number of actual injection cycles per hour	234,000	378,000
Total fuel consumption per hour [lb (U.S. gal)]	89 (12.5)	115.5 (16.2)

delivered to the injectors is dependent on the following conditions:

1.   The speed of the engine, which drives the gear pump located at the rear of the PT fuel pump assembly

2.   The governor assembly, which on the standard automotive governor provides: (a) pressure regulation, (b) idle speed governing, and (c) maximum speed governing. At an idle speed, governor weight force is minimal; therefore, the idle fuel supply passage in the pump barrel is held open by a balance between the rotating governor weights, assisted by the weight-assist spring at the end opposite the governor idle spring force. Remember that the weights and assist spring are always trying to close the idle spring passage, while the idle spring force is attempting to open it. In addition, a regulated amount of throttle shaft leakage is added to the idle fuel to maintain a steady idle speed. At maximum engine speed, the idle fuel passage is completely blocked off by the fact that the stronger governor weight force compresses the idle spring and pushes the plunger against the force of both the torque spring and main governor spring.

3.   Rail pressure (to injectors) is controlled by regulating the fuel pressure supplied to the governor assembly. This fuel pressure is dependent on the "supply pressure," which is in itself regulated by a bypass regulator, which allows the fuel pump button (see Figure 22-11 for examples of button sizes) to separate from the governor plunger when the fuel pressure acting on the button becomes high enough to overcome the spring force behind it. Fuel is then bypassed to the suction side of the gear pump.

4.   A larger recess in the fuel pump button will result in a lower supply pressure and therefore a lower rail pressure to the injectors, since the larger recessed area reduces the pressure at which the fuel starts bypassing back to the suction side of the gear pump.

5.   A smaller recess in the fuel pump button will result in a higher supply pressure and therefore a higher rail pressure to the injectors, since the smaller recessed area increases the pressure at which the fuel starts bypassing back to the suction side of the gear pump.

NOTE   The supply pressure is therefore controlled by the force acting on the button and the actual area of the button recess. Therefore, a change in the engine horsepower can be achieved by changing the actual fuel pump button size, which is stamped in the recessed area.

---

6. The rail pressure is the supply pressure minus the total pressure drop across the other fuel system components.

7. For any given engine speed, the rail pressure controls the quantity of fuel metered per cycle at each injector, and therefore both the engine torque and horsepower levels.

8. When the engine exceeds its rated (full-load) rpm, governor weight force pushes the plunger forward in the barrel to the point where the fuel supply pressure to the injectors is decreased by the shoulder on the plunger restricting the main fuel passage. This is known as the governor *breakpoint*.

9. If the engine speed exceeds its no-load rpm (high idle), the governor weight force will push the plunger forward inside the barrel until all fuel to the main passage to the injectors is cut off by the shoulder on the plunger. This is known as the governor *cutoff point*.

10. The difference between the engine's rated speed (full-load rpm), and its high-idle speed (no-load rpm), is known as *droop*. For more information on this term, refer to Chapter 17. On Cummins engines using the PT fuel system governor, the difference between the rated and high-idle speeds is approximately 12%. Therefore, if a required full-load (rated) speed of 2100 rpm were desired, adding 12% to this speed would mean that the maximum no-load (high-idle) rpm would be 2352, which is obtained by adding 252 rpm to 2100.

11. Fuel from the throttle shaft flows to the AFC section of the pump. When there is little or no air pressure (idle speed or transient engine operation) being applied to the AFC diaphragm from the intake manifold line, the AFC return spring will force the AFC fuel control plunger into a position where no fuel can flow through the AFC plunger to the main supply line to the injectors. Under this operating condition, fuel to the injectors (rail pressure) is routed through the AFC no-air adjusting screw needle valve. When the engine speed is increased and the turbocharger boost (manifold) pressure increases as a load is applied to the engine, this air pressure acting on the AFC diaphragm will overcome the return spring force and push the AFC fuel plunger forward, allowing supply pressure now to be routed through to the main fuel delivery solenoid passage along with whatever volume is flowing through the "no-air" needle valve. In this way, rail pressure will be increased, and the injectors are capable of metering sufficient fuel to allow an increase in engine horsepower. In non-AFC-type PTG pumps, the fuel from the throttle shaft would flow directly to the fuel control solenoid and then to the injectors.

MANUAL FUEL SHUTOFF

All Cummins engines are equipped with an electric fuel shutoff solenoid valve, which is mounted on top of the fuel pump body. See item 6 in Figure 22-4. A closer view of this solenoid shutdown illustrates a knurled thumbscrew (not numbered) just to the right of item 2. The thumbscrew allows manual control of the fuel flow/shutoff at any time a problem may exist in the normal electric fuel control solenoid assembly. Rotating this knurled thumbscrew clockwise (into the solenoid) will allow the flow control valve to be placed in an open position, therefore allowing fuel to flow to the injectors. If, at any time, the engine fails to shut down in the normal manner, the knurled thumbscrew can be manually rotated in a counterclockwise direction, which will close off the fuel supply to the injectors, and engine shutdown is therefore assured. When the knurled thumbscrew is turned CW into the solenoid body, it forces a flexible metal diaphragm or shutdown disk back against the tension of a cupped-type spring washer and opens up the fuel passage through the shutdown solenoid to the rail and injectors. Fuel is prevented from flowing to the injectors any time the knurled thumbscrew is rotated CCW, since the spring washer would force the diaphragm forward and close off the fuel passage.

PT PUMP CHECKS AND ADJUSTMENTS

Service and adjustment of the PT fuel pump assembly is best performed by removing the pump from the engine, mounting it on a test stand, and setting all adjustments as in the correct fuel pump spec sheet listed in the PTG-AFC *Fuel Pump Calibration Values Manual*, 3379352-01, for all PT pumps.

Details on how to perform the disassembly, reassembly, and testing of the PT pump are described in this chapter. However, it is often possible for the service technician to perform a series of checks, tests, and on-engine adjustments of the PT fuel pump by connecting a portable fuel flow rate measuring device to the engine. This special tool is shown in Figure 22-9.

"On Engine" Checks and Adjustments

During normal engine operation, in addition to the normal routine service/maintenance procedures such as fuel filters, it may become necessary to perform a number of checks and adjustments to the PT fuel system, particularly as road miles or hours accumulate on the engine. Regardless of whether the engine is an NT 855-in^3 (14-L) model, an L10, M11, a larger K engine, or a small V unit, since it uses a PT fuel pump, the same basic procedures will apply to the various checks and adjustments of the fuel system. Examples of such checks and adjustments include the following:

- Engine idle speed adjustment
- Engine maximum speed adjustment (high idle)
- Fuel system restriction and oil leak checks
- Fuel rail pressure check
- Turbocharger boost pressure check
- Engine fuel rate check/adjust
- Throttle linkage adjustment
- Remove/install the PT fuel pump assembly
- Adjust the road speed governor (truck applications)
- Engine power check (requires an engine or chassis dynamometer)
- AFC—no air valve setting
- PT pump throttle shaft leakage
- Throttle response time check (highway truck)
- Stall test (off-highway unit)

Each of the checks and tests above is described in detail below for both a PTG-AFC and a PTG-AFC-VS pump, with the exception of the last five items, which are external to the pump or must be done on a test stand.

The actual location of various adjustments and major PT pump components can be seen in the various figures in this section as well as by referring to the various figures illustrated so far in this chapter that pinpoint the exact location of such items. When a complaint of low power is received, always systematically check out the color of the engine exhaust smoke first to determine whether the problem may lie in a system other than the PT fuel pump or system.

Table 22-3 lists typical fuel system specification limits for a typical N14 engine equipped with a PT fuel pump system. Refer to these values when performing the checks/tests listed above. Minor spec variations exist between other engine series.

Idle Speed Adjustment

The location of the PT pump/engine idle speed adjustment screw will vary slightly between pumps depending on whether the pump in use is an older PTG, a PTG-AFC, or a PTG-AFC-VS. Examples of the idle and maximum speed adjusting screws for these particular PT pumps can be seen by referring to Figures 22-4 and 22-5, shown earlier in this chapter. Prior to checking the engine idle speed, run the engine until it attains its normal operating temperature (above 160°F/70°C coolant). In addition, you should hook up an accurate tachometer to the PT pump tach drive, or

select a digital or optical tachometer so that you can accurately set the idle rpm. In addition, a remote starter switch can be hooked up to the starter motor to assist you in starting the engine while you are achieving this setting. Figure 22-15 illustrates the idle adjustment tool and location for an AFC pump, and Figure 22-16 shows the location for an AFC-VS pump assembly.

Idle Adjustment: PTG-AFC

1. Refer to Figure 22-15 and with the engine already at operating temperature, remove the access plug at the bottom of the pump housing.

2. Install special idle adjusting tool 3375981 into the access hole by threading its fitting into position. This tool is equipped with a small sealing ring to prevent air from being drawn into the pump during this adjustment with the engine running.

NOTE   Special tool ST-984 can also be used for this purpose. One can readily be manufactured by selecting a small, round, straight-bladed screwdriver, a small O-ring that is a snug fit over the round shank, and a male and female brass tube fitting combination that will fit into the pump access hole as shown in Figure 22-15.

---

3. Start and run the engine at high idle for about 30 seconds to ensure that all air has been removed from the fuel system.

4. Allow the engine to return to a low idle speed and ensure that the pump throttle lever is at its normal low-speed position.

5. With the special idle adjusting tool engaged with the internal idle screw, turn the tool CW to increase the tension on the idle spring and therefore raise engine idle rpm, or CCW to decrease idle spring tension and lower engine idle rpm. The engine idle speed should be between 650 and 725 rpm on current PTG-AFC pumps on Big Cam engines, and between 675 and 725 rpm on L10 engines. The idle speed is stamped on the engine CPL data plate.

SPECIAL NOTE   Another way of setting the idle speed on PTG pumps is to obtain the pump code, look up the recommended fuel pressure at idle, and with a fuel pressure gauge hooked up to the rail (item 2 in Figure 22-1) adjust the idle screw until the specified pressure is reached. Due to the variety of applications and environments in which Cummins engines operate, you may find

TABLE 22–3 *Fuel System Specifications*

Basic application requirements	
Engine idle speed	650 to 725 rpm
Fuel inlet maximum restriction	
Clean fuel filter	100 mm Hg (4.0 in. Hg)
Dirty fuel filter	200 mm Hg (8.0 in. Hg)
Fuel drain line maximum restriction	
Without check valves	65 mm Hg (2.5 in. Hg)
With check valves	165 mm Hg (6.5 in. Hg)
Fuel check valve between fuel filter and fuel pump	
Minimum opening pressure	2.1 kPa (0.3 psi)
Fuel check valve between fuel pump and cylinder head	
Opening pressure	21 to 55 kPa (3 to 8 psi)
Engine minimum cranking speed	150 rpm
Fuel check valve in fuel drain line	
Opening pressure	13 to 25 mm Hg ($\frac{1}{4}$ to $\frac{1}{2}$ psi)
Derate engine fuel rate for high altitude	4% per 300 m (1000 ft) above 3600 m (12,000 ft)
Derate engine fuel rate for hot weather	2% per 11°C above 38°C (1% per 10° above 100°F)
Shutoff valve solenoid coil resistance	
6VDC	1.72–2.02 Ω
12VDC	7.0–8.0 Ω
24VDC	28–32 Ω
32VDC	49.5–56.5 Ω
36VDC	54.5–61.5 Ω
48VDC	105–125 Ω
115VDC	645–735 Ω

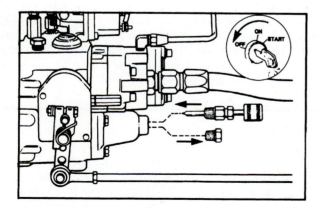

FIGURE 22–15 Idle-speed adjustment on a PTG-AFC fuel pump. (Courtesy of Cummins Engine Company, Inc.)

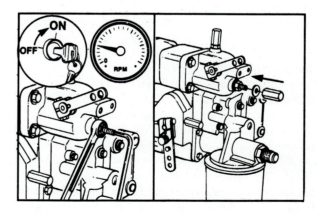

FIGURE 22–16 Idle-speed adjustment on a PTG-AFC/VS fuel pump. (Courtesy of Cummins Engine Company, Inc.)

it impossible to obtain a specified rail pressure setting when adjusting the idle screw. If the fuel system does not have a high restriction and no lack-of-power complaint had been lodged, it is possible that high weight-assist settings are being used; therefore, it may be necessary to add one or more idle spring seat washers to the end of the adjusting screw.

6. When the correct idle adjustment has been obtained, stop the engine and remove the special adjusting tool.

7. Install the small pipe plug into the hole in the pump body.

8. Start and run the engine until it operates smoothly, which will ensure that all air has been removed from the system, and recheck the idle speed.

NOTE Should it become necessary to remove the idle spring assembly from the pump, it first requires that you remove the end plug from the pump housing via a snap ring on PTG pumps, or alternatively, by unbolting the governor spring pack retainer cover from the pump housing on PTG-AFC pumps.

Idle Adjustment: PTG-AFC-VS

The procedure for the PTG-AFC-VS pump is the same as that for the PTG-AFC, with the exception that the idle adjustment screw is located as shown in Figure 22-16.

1. The engine should be at least at 160°F (70°C) coolant temperature.

2. Refer to Figure 22-16 and remove both the idle screw lock and jam nuts at the rear of the VS cover and throw away the old copper washers, since new ones should be installed.

3. Install a new copper washer along with the idle screw jam nut.

4. Start and run the engine with the VS lever held in the idle position.

5. Insert an Allen (hex) wrench into the end of the idle adjusting screw and rotate it CW to increase the speed, or CCW to decrease the speed.

6. While holding the Allen wrench firmly, tighten up the jam nut with a combination wrench.

7. Install a new copper washer over the idle screw and up against the jam nut.

8. Thread the locknut onto the idle screw and tighten it into position.

NOTE To remove the idle spring assembly from a PTG-AFC-VS fuel pump, remove the throttle linkage at the pump lever first, then refer to Figure 22-17, and after removing the four retaining bolts from the cover, withdraw the idle and high-speed spring component parts, which consist of the housing cover, gasket, throttle lever plunger, high-speed spring and shims, plunger assist spring, spring guide, and idle spring.

High-Idle Adjustment: PTG-AFC-VS

Adjustment of the high idle on the PTG-AFC-VS unit is straight-forward, as shown in Figure 22-18. Obtain the maximum high-idle speed from the CPL data place on the engine, or from the sales literature data sheet or engine service manual.

Adjustment Procedure

1. The engine should be at its normal operating temperature, or at least with a coolant temperature of 160°F (70°C).

2. With the engine stopped, refer to Figure 22-18 and remove the lock and jam nuts from the top screw on the VS cover. As with the idle adjustment, discard the used copper washers, since new ones should be installed.

3. Install a new copper washer and jam nut onto the high-idle screw.

4. Start the engine, allow the oil pressure to increase, then manually rotate the VS lever CW to place the engine at its maximum no-load (high-idle) rpm.

5. With an Allen (hex) wrench installed into the high-speed adjusting screw, note the speed on the tachometer and adjust the screw to obtain the specified

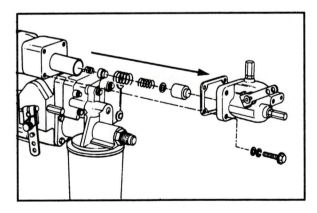

FIGURE 22–17 *Removal of the PTG-AFC/VS fuel pump governor spring pack assembly. (Courtesy of Cummins Engine Company, Inc.)*

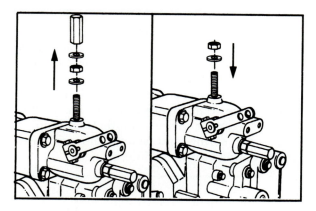

FIGURE 22–18 *High-idle adjustment on a PTG-AFC/VS fuel pump assembly. (Courtesy of Cummins Engine Company, Inc.)*

rpm, then tighten the jam nut with a combination wrench while holding the Allen wrench firmly in position.

6. Recheck the high-idle speed.

7. Install a new copper washer and the locknut and tighten.

High-Idle Adjustment: PTG-AFC Pump
Adjustment of the high-speed spring on the PTG and PTG-AFC fuel pumps is done by removing the four bolts that retain the spring pack assembly cover to the bottom rear of the fuel pump housing. Figure 22-7 illustrates the high-speed spring assembly location (item 13). The spring cover is the one shown in Figure 22-15 through which you can adjust the idle screw. The engine's maximum speed can be changed by adding or removing shims from behind the spring. Generally, each 0.001-in. (0.0254-mm) shim added to the spring will increase the engine speed by approximately 2 rpm, while removal of these same shims will decrease the speed accordingly.

BASIC PT FUEL SYSTEM TROUBLESHOOTING

Generally, when an engine lacks power, or fails to obtain its maximum rated speed, a number of conditions can be the cause. However, an experienced mechanic/technician will first perform a number of simple checks to lead him or her into the general area of the problem. For example, a quick check of the color of the engine exhaust smoke can confirm whether the problem is in the fuel system or elsewhere in the engine. For example, a high air inlet restriction due to such a simple thing as a plugged air cleaner will result

in the engine starving for air, with the result that it will lack power, as well as overheating. This condition would be reflected by gray/black smoke in the exhaust stream. Blue smoke is generally an indication of a mechanical defect in either the turbocharger (seals) or the engine pumping oil, while white smoke can be caused by low temperatures on initial startup from cold. If white smoke continues after the engine has warmed up, it is possible that low compression exists in one or more cylinders (misfiring). Low power with no unusual smoke color at the exhaust is cause to check out such items as the following:

1. Are the engine cylinders receiving full fuel when the throttle and lever are placed into the maximum position? Check and adjust the linkage if necessary.

2. Is the engine fuel pump starving for fuel? Check the fuel system for signs of starvation, restriction, air in the fuel, and so on.

In the following section we discuss how to check out the fuel system systematically for signs of possible faults, by performing checks on:

1. Fuel system restriction
2. Air in fuel
3. Air leaks

Fuel System Restriction Check
To minimize the restriction to the suction side of the fuel transfer pump, the fuel line size *must* be as large as possible to the inlet connection on the pump body. Do not employ smaller lines than that of the fuel connection at the pump inlet. Smaller lines can lead to additional restriction to the transfer pump inlet. Unnecessary bends or elbows will also create additional restriction to fuel flow. The maximum allowable inlet restriction to the suction side of the fuel transfer pump on Cummins PT pump-equipped engines is 4 in. Hg (mercury) or 100 mm when a new clean primary filter has been installed, or alternatively, when checking the restriction on an engine already in service (dirty filter), the maximum allowable reading should not exceed 8 in. Hg or 200 mm on either a vacuum gauge or a mercury manometer connected as shown in Figure 22-19.

Checking Procedure
1. A vacuum gauge or a mercury manometer can be used for this check. In addition, the restriction check can be taken at either the primary filter, which is generally mounted close to the pump, or alternatively, at the fuel supply hose close to the pump itself.

2. Refer to Figure 22-19, which illustrates a

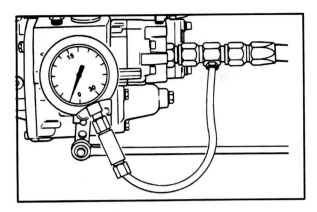

FIGURE 22–19 *Checking PT fuel system for excessive restriction using ST-434 vacuum gauge. (Courtesy of Cummins Engine Company Inc.)*

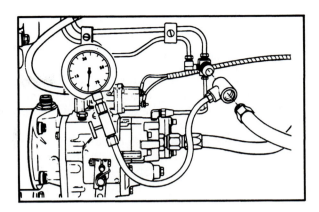

FIGURE 22–20 *Checking PT fuel pump drain line restriction. (Courtesy of Cummins Engine Company Inc.)*

Cummins ST-434 vacuum gauge installed into the fuel pump inlet line. This gauge or a manometer could also be used at the primary filter.

SPECIAL NOTE To obtain an accurate reading at the vacuum gauge, it is imperative that you tie or hold the gauge so that it is level with the actual gear fuel pump, as shown in Figure 22-19.

---

3. Start and run the engine at idle, then slowly accelerate the engine until it reaches its rated rpm under load, if possible. If you cannot load the engine down to rated speed, check it at its high-idle rpm. Compare the reading obtained with the specifications listed above, namely a maximum of 4 in. Hg with a clean filter or a maximum of 8 in. Hg with a dirty filter (unit in service).

4. Replace the fuel filter if the restriction is beyond the limit for a dirty filter. If the filter has been changed and the restriction is still excessive, carefully check the fuel lines for kinks or bends, a possible collapsed inlet hose, and so on.

Fuel Drain Line Restriction Check

Refer to Figure 22-20 and after disconnecting the fuel drain line, install fuel pressure gauge ST-1273 using the adapters from the ST-434 vacuum gauge kit to connect up the fuel pressure gauge.

Checking Procedure

1. With the pressure gauge connected as in Figure 22-20, start and run the engine up to rated speed at full load if possible and ensure that the drain line is free flowing (no crimps).

2. While holding the pressure gauge level with the connection, monitor the reading. The maximum allowable restriction at the drain line should not exceed 2.5 in. Hg (mercury) or 65 mm on a system with no check valves, while the allowable maximum on a fuel system equipped with check valves should not be higher than 6.5 in. Hg (165 mm).

3. If the readings are higher than allowable, remove the fuel tank filler cap first, then repeat the check. Acceptable readings with the cap removed would indicate a plugged or faulty filler cap or tank vents.

4. Readings still above the allowable maximum with the fuel tank filler cap removed would require you to carefully check the condition of the fuel drain lines for a restriction caused by a kink, bends, or a collapsed hose internally.

Air Leak in Fuel Suction Line Check

An air leak in the fuel pump suction side will result in low fuel delivery as well as air being circulated through the fuel system to the injectors. The engine will not only lack power but will run rough at idle and possibly stall as a load is applied. Four main methods can be used to check for suction leaks in the fuel system:

1. Installing a temporary fuel return line submerged into a partially filled beaker (container) of diesel fuel

2. Inserting a sight glass, ST-998, into the line between the gear transfer pump and the primary filter

3. Installing a clear plastic line between the filter and the pump

4. Pressurizing the fuel system (low pressure) between the tank and the gear pump

Method 1

1. To check for air being drawn in on the suction side of the system, refer to Figure 22-21 and remove the pump drain line from the check valve; then plug off the drain line.

2. Install a temporary hose or suitable short fuel line over the pump check valve as illustrated on the right-hand side of Figure 22-21.

3. Submerge the temporary hose into a beaker or container that contains some diesel fuel.

4. Start the engine, then run it to its maximum high-idle speed no load.

5. Any air bubbles appearing in the fuel container shown in Figure 22-21 at the temporary fuel return line are confirmation that there is, in fact, a suction leak between the pickup at the fuel tank and the inlet to the gear-type fuel transfer pump.

6. Carefully inspect and check all fuel-line connections, as well as the primary filter fittings and seals, for signs of looseness.

NOTE   If it is hard to determine just where the suction leak might be, disconnect the fuel line at both the fuel tank and the pump. Seal off one end and using a small pressure pump attached to the opposite end, apply a couple of pounds of pressure to the system to establish where the leak is actually located. If no problem is located after checking the fuel line connections, carefully inspect the condition of the pickup fuel line inside

the fuel tank for damage. On a road speed governor-equipped engine/pump, remove the air supply tube first, then check and correct any air leaks in the suction side of the system.

Method 2

1. Refer to Figure 22-22, and after loosening the fuel suction line at the transfer pump, install the sight glass, ST-998, as illustrated.

2. Start the engine and run it up to its maximum high-idle speed no load.

3. Any bubbles appearing in the sight glass at this time will confirm that air is in fact being drawn into the fuel system suction side.

NOTE   Small leaks will be evidenced by a milky appearance of the fuel, while a substantial suction leak reflects itself as positive air bubbles flowing through the sight-glass window.

4. Check and correct for suction leaks as in method 1.

Fuel Pump Air Leak Check

It is possible for the PT fuel pump itself to draw air into the system. If all previous checks for air leaks were negative on the suction side of the system, refer to Figure 22-23 and with the engine running, loosen the fuel outlet line above the fuel solenoid on the PT pump assembly to vent any trapped air that might be in the system. However, if this air continues to vent after a few seconds, the PT fuel pump should be removed from the engine and repaired as necessary. This

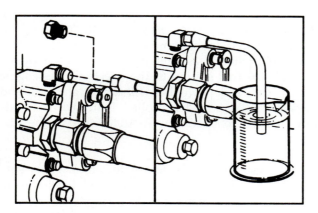

FIGURE 22–21   Left side of figure shows removal of the fuel pump suction drain line; right side of figure illustrates a temporary test line installed from the pump to a clear container to note the presence of any air bubbles. (Courtesy of Cummins Engine Company, Inc.)

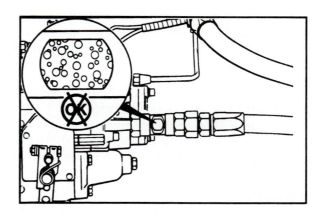

FIGURE 22–22   Use of a sight glass (ST-998) in the suction line to the fuel pump to determine the presence of air with the engine running. (Courtesy of Cummins Engine Company Inc.)

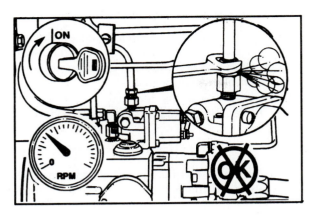

FIGURE 22–23 *Venting air from the PT fuel pump outlet line. (Courtesy of Cummins Engine Company Inc.)*

air leak could be caused by a leak through the seal rings within the road speed governor housing, or alternatively, at the AFC unit itself.

Checking Procedure

1. To check the condition of the PTG-AFC fuel pump assembly, refer to Figure 22-24 and start by removing the AFC air inlet line, which runs from the air intake manifold on the engine.

2. Install Cummins pressure pump 3375515 to the AFC line connection as shown in Figure 22-24.

NOTE If this pressure gauge is unavailable, make up a suitable attachment using shop air from a regulated air valve assembly.

---

3. With the engine stopped, gradually apply 25 psi (170 kPa) of air pressure to the AFC air supply line.

4. When using shop air as a supply, ensure that you shut off the air supply once this pressure is obtained.

5. Carefully note the position of the pressure gauge needle for at least a 10-second period. Any loss in pressure indicates that the line and/or connections are leaking.

6. Carefully inspect the line and connections and tighten if required, then recheck the AFC unit.

7. A pressure loss with no indication of leaks at the line or connections would lead us to the actual AFC unit as a possible suspect.

8. After disconnecting the AFC fuel return line at the top side of the fuel pump, apply 25 psi (170 kPa) of air pressure to the AFC air supply line. This will cause the internal AFC bellows to move.

9. Refer to Figure 22-25 and note if a small puff of air or a small amount of diesel fuel comes out the top of the pump AFC return line. A continuous flow of air from the top of the fuel pump is an indication that the AFC bellows is faulty; therefore, the pump should be removed for repair.

10. No air or fuel emanating from the AFC fuel return line connection, together with no sign of an air pressure loss at the gauge assembly, could be caused by a restriction at the check valve connection in the AFC cover plate. Therefore, remove and clean, or replace this check valve, if necessary, as shown in Figure 22-26.

PT Pump Fuel Rail Pressure Check

The gear-type fuel transfer pump located within the PT pump body is designed to produce its maximum fuel (rail) pressure at rated engine speed. Rated engine speed is the maximum full-load rpm at which the

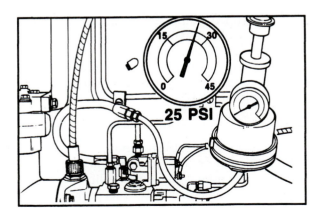

FIGURE 22–24 *Pressure gauge and hand pump installed into the AFC fuel line connection. (Courtesy of Cummins Engine Company Inc.)*

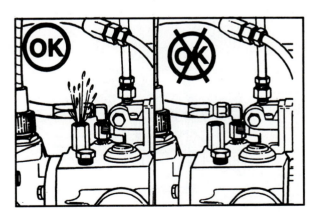

FIGURE 22–25 *Detecting a small puff of air or diesel fuel from the AFC fuel return line. (Courtesy of Cummins Engine Company Inc.)*

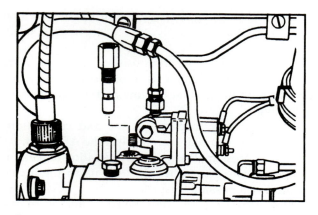

FIGURE 22–26 *Removal of the pump check valve from the AFC cover plate for cleaning/inspection purposes. (Courtesy of Cummins Engine Company Inc.)*

engine will produce its maximum designed horsepower. The turbocharger will produce its maximum rated boost pressure at this same full-load rpm. Low pump rail pressure will adversely affect the engine horsepower, since the PT fuel system operates on a pressure–time principle; therefore, reducing the fuel rail pressure will result in a lower flow rate to each fuel injector and a loss of horsepower.

Figure 22-27 illustrates the location of the Cummins ST-435 pressure gauge attached to the fuel shutoff valve after the small access plug has been removed.

The PT pump is to be checked on a Cummins-certified fuel pump test stand to verify that the pump is within Cummins specs for the CPL the engine is built to. The pump will be sealed after setting or verifying the calibration.

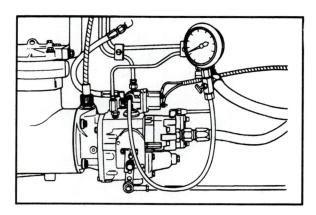

FIGURE 22–27 *ST-435 gauge installation at the fuel shutoff valve to monitor fuel system pressure. (Courtesy of Cummins Engine Company Inc.)*

NOTE *Do not* readjust a fuel pump on the engine after having set the rail pressure and flow on a pump stand. When calibrating a pump there is but *one pressure/flow* per code! Refer to current Cummins publications for fuel pump calibrations. Table 22-4 lists some fuel pump code spec examples.

If a Cummins-certified pump stand is not available on site, send the pump to the nearest Cummins authorized location to be tested. If this cannot be done before overhaul completion, use a truck or chassis dyno or conduct a Compuchek run to verify pump rail pressure.

To determine the maximum fuel rail pressure accurately, the engine must be subjected to its full-load rated speed by one of the following conditions:

1. Place the vehicle on a chassis dynamometer.

2. Disconnect the vehicle driveline and install a portable-type Go-Power dynamometer to the transmission output shaft.

3. Place the engine alone onto a stationary dynamometer.

4. On a piece of mobile industrial equipment, the machine can be "stall tested" with a fuel rail pressure gauge in position, and the time to stall is monitored along with the rail pressure reading.

5. If no dynamometer is available for a truck application, the vehicle can be road tested and with the throttle wide open, the brakes can be applied to reduce the engine speed to its normal rated rpm while monitoring the rail pressure gauge inside the cab.

Only if the overhauling location does not have access to any of the equipment noted above will a "snap-rail" test be allowed. Failure of a pump to pass any test will require that the pump be calibrated properly on a Cummins-certified pump stand. *Always* seal a pump before the truck leaves your shop, for your protection. The throttle shaft ball must also be in place. Sealing a pump after setting or verifying calibration only confirms that the pump was tested or set within Cummins specs at that time.

NOTE To determine the fuel pump rail pressure for a particular engine, you have to consult the applicable Cummins fuel pump calibration manuals after having obtained the fuel pump calibration code number on the fuel pump data plate. Each fuel pump/engine horsepower setting has been assigned a given fuel rail pressure for its year of manufacture and engine application rat-

TABLE 22–4. Fuel pump code specifications

	Pump Code E742-A	E743-B
Date Control parts list	JUN87 0447	APR87 0447
Tool (hp @ rpm)	461–479 @ 1800	523–545 @ 2100
Engine fuel (psi)	114–126	150–166
Torque rise (% curve)	2	23
No air snaprail (psi)		
Fuel rate (lb/hr)	161–167	193–201
Auto governor setting	1890–1910	2190–2210
V.S. governor setting	1830–1850	2130–2150
Max governor check (rpm—psi)	2106—15	2330—15
Throttle leakage (Co-Pph)	110	110
Throttle travel	26	26
Idle speed (psi @ rpm)	—	—
Idle speed (cc @ rpm)	250 @ 700	190 @ 775
Intake mfd. press. (in.—Hg)	27—35	41—49
Calibration (psi @ rpm)	119 @ 1800	167 @ 2100
Calibration flow	507	599
Check point (psi @ rpm)	68–94 @ 1500	123–129 @ 1500
Check point flow	432	506
Check point (psi @ rpm)	— @	— @
Check point flow		
Weight-assist setting—spring	.750—143854	.800—143854
Idle plunger code—Part No.	45—138862	30—141633
Auto idle spring	3018767	3018767
Auto governor spring	3000937	143252
Gear pump size	1.000	1.000
Auto governor weights	146437	146437
Auto governor plunger	3009380	3009380
Torque spring—shirne	.000	142867—.000
V.S. governor max. spring	109686	107787
V.S. governor idle spring	70776	153240
V.S. governor weights	163826	163826
V.S. governor plunger	212350	212350
V.S. governor sleeve	212146	212148
A.F.C. (in./Hg—psi)	7—3.4	17—8.3
A.F.C. (rpm)	1600	1600
A.F.C. (psi—flow)	35—275	82—350
A.F.C. spring	179630	3000592
A.F.C. no air setting (rpm)	1600	1600
A.F.C. no air (psi—flow)	76—360	76—400
Certified-year-by	9999	9999
Certified by	CONS	CONS
Engine model	KTA 19 P	KTA 19 C
Notes	(1)	(2)

(1) Use with wet exhaust manifold. Use fuel pump part 3021960.
(2) Use fuel pump part 3021960.

ing. If this information is unavailable to you, contact your local Cummins dealer or diesel fuel injection company rebuilder. Failing this, check the rail pressure on an engine known to be good that has the same pump code and use this as a guide.

To determine if a Cummins fuel pump is within Cummins specs, use the on-engine recheck limits in the latest Cummins fuel system publications. See example below:

CPL 1211   NTC-400   Pump code is 6039

Calibration set point on stand is 184 psi (1267 kPa) at @ 2100 rpm.

On-engine recheck limit is 175 to 193 psi (1207 to 1331 kPa) at @ 2100 rpm.

Allowable deviation of ±2 psi = 173 to 195 psi (1193 to 1344 kPa) maximum.

If the pump tested beyond the maximum rail pressure of 195 psi (1344 kPa), it is considered as being overfueled and must be set back to the calibration set point.

Snap Pressure No-Load Test

If an engine complaint is lack of horsepower and you have confirmed that the air inlet restriction, exhaust back pressure, and fuel filter restrictions are within published specs, you can perform a snap-rail pressure check. This is done by connecting a fuel pressure gauge (Figure 22-27) into the fuel solenoid tap point and running the engine under no-load. On AFC-equipped pumps, the air line from the intake manifold must be disconnected and a regulated air supply connected to the pump. Adjust the air supply to approximately 24 to 24.5 psi (165 to 169 kPa) before making the check.

Test Procedure

1. Start and run the engine.
2. Loosen the gauge connection to bleed any entrapped air from the line and gauge; otherwise, a false reading can be obtained.
3. Grasp the throttle linkage, and quickly accelerate the engine manually from idle to wide-open throttle.
4. Read the gauge carefully during acceleration.
5. Repeat this process several times to gain a mean average fuel pressure value.
6. The fuel pressure should be within published pump specifications listed in the calibration sheet.
7. If the snap pressure reading is low, you may need to change the throttle restriction or the idle spring plunger button.

8. If the no-load high-idle engine rpm is incorrect, you may have to add or remove shims from the main governor spring.

FUEL RATE: PTG-AFC PUMP

Each PT fuel pump installed on a Cummins engine has been calibrated to ensure maximum engine performance at a particular full-load (rated) rpm with a stated burn rate of fuel per horsepower per hour. The quantity of fuel that a particular engine should consume at its rated power setting can be found by referencing the fuel pump code, then looking up the fuel rate in pounds per hour in the Cummins *Fuel Pump Calibration Values Manual*, part 3379352-01, for all PT fuel pumps. The maximum fuel rate can best be checked with the engine on a dynamometer, or if it is in a vehicle, on a chassis dynamometer. Although a dynamometer test will confirm the actual fuel rate at rated horsepower, a truer test as to actual fuel consumption is best accomplished over a given period with the engine operating in its actual application environment. On the dynamometer test, fuel rail pressure is checked after ensuring that the restriction to the suction side of the gear transfer pump is within the allowable specifications of 4 in. Hg (101.6 mm) with a clean fuel filter, and not more than 8 in. Hg (203.2 mm) with a dirty filter. In addition, air inlet restriction should be within allowable specifications and turbocharger boost pressure can be checked as illustrated in Figure 22-28 by installing pressure gauge ST-1273 into the air compressor air inlet line.

The fuel flow meter measuring device illustrated in Figure 22-29 is available from Cummins as part 3376375. This portable machine is designed to function the same as a fixed test stand shown in Figure 22-30. In

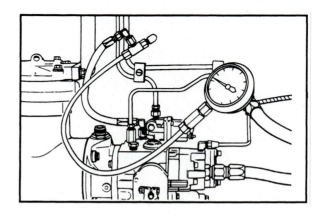

FIGURE 22–28 Connection point into the air compressor inlet line for ST-1273 gauge in order to check turbocharger boost pressure. (Courtesy of Cummins Engine Company Inc.)

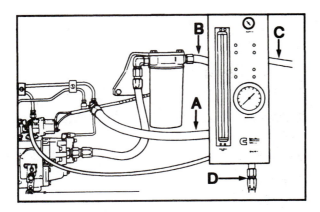

FIGURE 22–29 *Fuel rate measuring device connected to the engine. (Courtesy of Cummins Engine Company Inc.)*

Figure 22-29 the letter A indicates that this is the fuel return line from the engine to the fuel measuring device, the letter B is the fuel inlet line to the fuel filter inlet, the letter C is the return line from the measuring gauge to the fuel tank, and the letter D indicates the fuel inlet line to the fuel measuring device from the fuel tank suction line. An accurate tachometer should be used when measuring the fuel consumption of the engine to ensure that the engine rpm is at the specified rated speed per the engine CPL data plate.

With the engine loaded to its specified rated speed and horsepower, in addition to checking the fuel rate in pounds per hour, also check the turbocharger boost pressure per Figure 22-28, the engine fuel rail pressure per Figure 22-27 and the gear pump inlet restriction per Figure 22-19. If a chassis dynamometer is used, or a driveline dynamometer, make sure that you operate the vehicle in top gear (high range) at a speed of 50 mph (80 km/h).

Fuel Rate Adjustment

On current PTG-AFC fuel pumps, fuel rate adjustment is accomplished by removing the tamper-resistant ball from the end of the throttle shaft (Figure 22-31). Place a center punch mark at the center of the ball to facilitate use of a $\frac{3}{16}$-in. (0.1875-in.) or 4-mm drill bit. Once the hole has been drilled in the ball, insert an easy-out bit extractor or small slide hammer in order to pop the ball free from the end of the throttle shaft. Should you be unable to remove the ball from the end of the shaft, the complete throttle shaft assembly will have to be removed from the PT pump. This can be achieved on an AFC pump only after the snap ring located inside the pump housing has been removed, which involves removing the front drive housing. In addition, the cover plate surrounding the throttle shaft and lever, which has CUMMINS PT written on it, must also be removed by removing the driven-in screws or rivets.

FIGURE 22–30 *Cummins PT fuel pump test stand. (Courtesy of Lucas-Hartridge Company.)*

CAUTION Should it become necessary for any reason to replace the throttle shaft, remember that the shaft is matched to the pump housing bore. Therefore, always note the color code on the removed throttle shaft along with its size, so that the same dimension shaft is used. At this time there are five different sizes of throttle shafts used in Cummins engines.

Actual adjustment of the fuel rate can best be seen by referring to Figure 22-32, which shows the slotted end of the internal adjusting screw within the hollow throttle shaft. Some PTG-AFC pumps use an Allen-

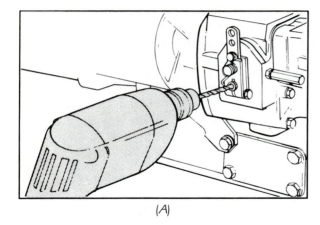

(A)

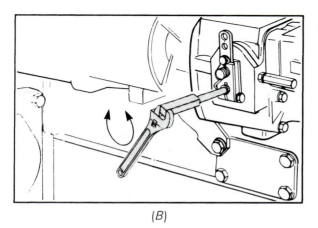

(B)

FIGURE 22–31 (A) Drilling the throttle shaft tamper resistant ball to gain access to the fuel rate adjusting screw. (B) Using on "easy-out" extractor tool to remove the throttle shaft ball. (Courtesy of Cummins Engine Company Inc.)

head screw in place of a slotted screwhead. Rotating this screw CW will lower the engine fuel rate, while turning the screw CCW will increase the fuel rate. After any fuel rate adjustment, always install a new ball into the end of the throttle shaft assembly to prevent unauthorized tampering with the fuel setting, as well as keeping dirt and foreign material out of the pump. Special tool 3375204 should be used to install a new ball into the end of the throttle shaft.

CAUTION   In Figure 22-32 note that the throttle shaft adjustment screw should *never* be turned CCW (out) to a dimension closer than 6 mm ($\frac{1}{4}$ in.; 0.250 in.) from the end of the shaft; otherwise, it is actually possible for the fuel pressure to force this plunger out of the hollow throttle shaft.

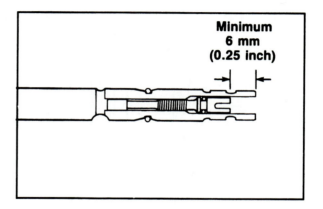

FIGURE 22–32   Minimum dimension to which the throttle shaft adjusting screw should be backed out. (Courtesy of Cummins Engine Company Inc.)

NOTE   If the engine fuel rate cannot be adjusted to the correct specification per the listed value, the fuel pump should be removed, disassembled, repaired, and set up on a fuel pump test stand to ensure correct calibration values.

In addition to the throttle shaft fuel rate adjusting screw illustrated in Figure 22-32, which is the method found on current PTG-AFC fuel pumps, earlier PT pumps used a slightly different system than this. In earlier-model PT pumps, to alter the fuel rate, the throttle shaft assembly was removed by first removing a large snap ring in order to withdraw the throttle shaft completely from the pump housing. In this type of earlier PT system, there was no adjusting screw within the hollow throttle shaft; instead, there was a restrictor shaft assembled into it.

To change the fuel flow rate, the internal restrictor shaft could be taken out by removing a socket head plug from the end of the throttle shaft along with its associated shims. Fuel rate (pressure) was increased by the addition of shims, while the removal of shims lowered it. This was due to the fact that the internal restrictor shaft (plunger) covered more or less of the flow hole within the hollow throttle shaft.

The amount that the internal restrictor plunger covers the throttle shaft fuel supply hole can readily be seen by looking into the hole. Best results are, of course, obtained with the PT fuel pump mounted on a calibration test stand assembly so that the actual rate of flow can be adjusted according to the fuel pump code and the Cummins test specifications. Flow of fuel through this hole in the throttle shaft with a closed throttle at an idle speed is required to keep sufficient fuel flowing to the fuel injectors to prevent stalling.

At wide-open throttle (high-idle) and at rated (full-load) speed, the idle passage has been completely cut off; therefore, fuel to the injectors is whatever flows through the throttle shaft hole. Keep in mind, however, that it is the size of the recess in the fuel pump button in PTG and PTG-AFC pumps that actually regulates the maximum fuel pressure and therefore the engine horsepower setting. In PT-R pumps a spring-loaded pressure regulator is used to control the maximum fuel pressure and therefore the point at which bypass fuel occurs.

Fuel Consumption Check

If an engine has been tested on a dynamometer and the fuel rate has been adjusted according to the fuel pump data code and the specifications listed in the *Fuel Pump Calibration Values Manual*, Bulletin 3379352-01, vehicle fuel consumption can be checked.

Checking Procedure

1. Weigh the test fuel tank (see step 2) when it is filled with the same grade of fuel that is normally used in the vehicle's main fuel tanks. As a rule of thumb, No. 2 diesel fuel weighs 7.03 lb per U.S. gallon or 0.844 kg per liter. The API gravity rating of the fuel being used will alter its specific gravity and also its weight per gallon. To calculate accurately just how much fuel is being used per mile or kilometer covered by the vehicle under test, it is extremely important that you use a scale that is capable of measuring within a range of at least $\frac{1}{10}$ of a pound (0.045 kg).

2. Install a test fuel tank remote from the main fuel supply system that is capable of allowing the vehicle to run for at least a 50-mile (80-km) test route.

3. Run the vehicle under the same type of conditions that would be encountered in normal service. In other words, ensure that all tire pressures are inflated according to the tire manufacturer's specifications, that all brakes are properly adjusted, and that the engine is in an acceptable state of mechanical performance. Closely monitor the coolant temperature, oil pressure and temperature, and exhaust temperature during the road test to ensure that no unusual conditions of operation are being encountered.

4. In addition to using the vehicle odometer on the instrument panel, refer to the hubdometer if the vehicle is so equipped to check the accuracy of both instruments. If different from the normal vehicle routing, the test route selected can lead to variations in previously recorded driver fuel usage reports. If possible, mileage signs along the test route, which have been measured off and posted, can be used to verify the accuracy of the odometer readings.

5. After the test route has been completed, stop the vehicle/engine, remove the test fuel tank, and weigh the tank and its contents on the same scale as used in step 1.

6. To compute just how much fuel has been used and to arrive at the fuel consumption in miles per gallon or liters per kilometer, use the following equations:

$$\frac{\text{weight}}{0.844} = \text{liters} \quad \text{then} \quad \frac{\text{kilometers}}{\text{liters}} = \text{kilometers/liter}$$

$$\frac{\text{weight}}{7.03} = \text{U.S. gallons} \quad \text{then} \quad \frac{\text{miles}}{\text{gallons}} = \text{miles per gallon (mpg)}$$

NOTE   Although the test above is an acceptable mode of operation, generally at least three test drives should be undertaken to arrive at an average for any given vehicle in a fleet. In addition, a recognized type 11 fuel economy test according to the Society of Automotive Engineers, the RCCC, and ATA should be performed if any inaccuracies cannot be accounted for in the fuel test listed above in steps 1 to 6.

The SAE type 11 test involves the following conditions:

1. Perform the fuel economy test using both a test vehicle and a control vehicle, which will compensate for changes in traffic conditions.

2. Weigh the fuel and the tank per step 1 stated above, or alternatively, drain the regular vehicle fuel tank, and fill it with a previously measured accurate amount of fuel; then after the test, drain the tank into a calibrated container and subtract the remaining volume from that which was added earlier to compute the miles per gallon or kilometers per liter.

3. The two vehicles *must* stay close together in order to experience the same traffic flow conditions as well as weather conditions; however, do not allow one vehicle to hug-in behind the other, since wind resistance will be substantially reduced and will create a major change in the outcome of the test.

4. The test course should be between 40 and 50 miles (65 to 80 km) in length.

5. Each truck trailer should be sealed before the test to ensure that no tampering with laden weights occurs.

6. Each truck should be driven on a "warm-up" test run to record the difference in elapsed time be-

tween each test run. Variations should not exceed ±0.5%, which, simply stated, would be no more than plus or minus 15 seconds over a 50-mile (80-km) route.

7. The amount of fuel used by the test truck between each of its three test drives *must* fall within a 2% range: for example, 6 mpg versus 6.12 mpg. This difference can be attributed either to weather/wind conditions, or to changes in the density of traffic.

8. The same experienced drivers should be used in all three tests, and the vehicle speeds should be representative of typical day-to-day fleet operation.

9. During the road tests, monitor and record the following conditions:

    a.   Ambient temperature
    b.   Relative humidity
    c.   Barometric pressure
    d.   Wind velocity
    e.   Wind direction

In any future fleet fuel tests, if the variables in item 9 change, a positive comparison between earlier results cannot be made.

THROTTLE CHECKS

Throttle Linkage Length

In many instances of a lack-of-power complaint, service personnel overlook checking the throttle linkage length. This can be affected by cab movement, the twists and bending of the linkage as the cab is tilted back and forward during servicing. On conventional-type cabs on highway vehicles, it is easier to check this out than on a cab-over unit; however, with the foot pedal of the throttle hard on the cab floorboards and the throttle linkage disconnected at the fuel pump, you should be able to connect the linkage with the hole in the pump throttle bracket (also being held in full fuel) without having to back up on the throttle bracket. If you cannot, adjust the linkage as needed, but do *not* loosen the throttle lever clamp on the throttle shaft bracket.

Throttle Travel

The throttle travel is generally set on a fuel pump test stand at the time of calibration pressure adjustment. The arc of travel of the throttle lever should be set with Cummins ST-3375355 or, if unavailable, a protractor will do. The throttle lever idle position centerline should be 27 to 29° from a vertical position toward the gear pump (Figure 22-33a).

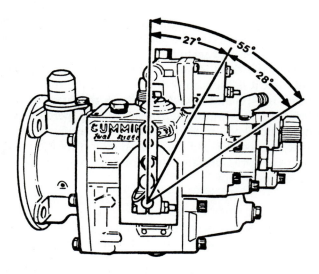

THROTTLE LEVER TRAVEL

A

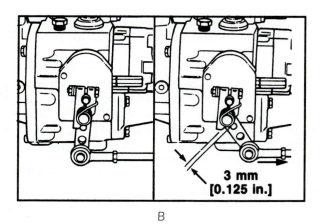

B

FIGURE 22-33 Throttle lever breakover check dimension. (Courtesy of Cummins Engine Company Inc.)

Throttle Lever Breakover Check

Once the throttle lever travel has been adjusted, it is necessary to ensure that the correct amount of "breakover travel" exists in the linkage as illustrated in Figure 22-33B. Adjust the linkage so that the throttle lever breaks over between 0.125 and 0.250 in. ($\frac{1}{8}$ to $\frac{1}{4}$ in.) or the equivalent of 3 to 6 mm in metric measurement when the lever is in the full-throttle position. The throttle lever stop must make contact with the rear throttle stop screw when this dimension has been set.

PT FUEL PUMP REMOVAL AND INSTALLATION

PT fuel pump removal is a straightforward task that presents no special problems for the truck shop mechanic since it is not necessary to time the fuel pump to the engine.

1. With the engine stopped, clean off the area immediately surrounding the pump and the air compressor to which the PT pump is bolted.

2. Disconnect the vehicle batteries to prevent any possibility of someone inadvertently cranking the engine over while you are in the process of conducting your repairs.

3. Remove the following components from the pump assembly:

    a. Fuel shutoff wire
    b. Throttle lever linkage

NOTE   Refer to Figure 22-34 for items c to i, shown as numbers 1 to 7 in the illustration.

---

    c. Fuel drain line from the cylinder head (1)
    d. Gear pump cooling drain line (2)
    e. Gear pump suction line (3)
    f. AFC fuel drain line (4)
    g. Fuel supply line to the injectors (5)
    h. AFC air supply hose to the intake manifold (6)
    i. Tachometer drive cable (7)

4. Remove the four retaining capscrews (two on each side of the PT pump housing) that hold the PT pump to the air compressor assembly as shown in Figure 22-35.

5. Remove and scrape the old gasket from the pump mounting flange.

6. Carefully inspect the pump drive coupling spider for signs of wear or other damage.

7. Install a new drive coupling and a gasket.

8. Reverse the removal procedure for successful installation.

AFC NO-AIR VALVE SETTING

On PTG-AFC pumps, fuel inside the pump assembly flows from the throttle shaft (throttle leakage) along with idle fuel passage flow at idle rpm and onto the AFC assembly. At opening throttle conditions, idle fuel is eventually cut off and fuel flows through the main passage from the governor plunger and on through the throttle shaft. When the engine is running at an idle speed or at high-idle (no load), there is very little turbocharger boost pressure acting on the diaphragm within the AFC unit. Consequently, the internal return spring within the AFC unit moves the AFC plunger back against the diaphragm and closes off the possibility of fuel flowing to and through the fuel solenoid and onto the rail that supplies the injectors. Under such an operating condition, the only fuel that can feed the injectors is that which flows from the throttle shaft to the AFC unit, which then passes through the adjustable no-air needle valve, which is item 10 shown in Figure 22-13 as well as various other PTG-AFC pump diagrams in this chapter. A closer view of the AFC unit during a no-air situation (no tur-

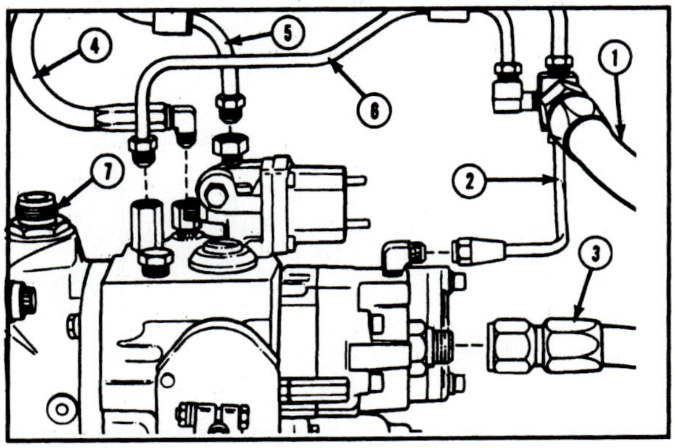

FIGURE 22-34 *Components that must be removed to remove the PT fuel pump assembly. (Courtesy of Cummins Engine Company Inc.)*

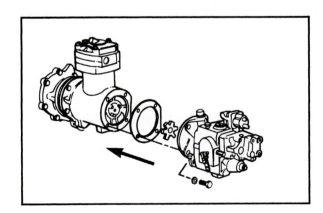

FIGURE 22-35 *Removal of four PT pump retaining bolts from the air compressor housing. (Courtesy of Cummins Engine Company Inc.)*

bocharger boost) and during maximum turbocharger boost pressure is illustrated in Figures 22-14 a and b, respectively. The NO-AIR valve setting therefore refers to the AFC needle valve adjusting screw, which determines the maximum fuel rail pressure and flow rate to the injectors when the AFC internal spring places the AFC plunger into the no-fuel position under any operating speed condition where there is no turbocharger pressure (boost).

AFC No-Air Valve Setting Adjustment

To properly complete an adjustment to the AFC NO-AIR valve setting, on the vehicle or equipment place the machine into one of the following operating conditions:

1.   On a chassis dynamometer for a truck so that the engine can be loaded down to 1600 rpm with the transmission in the highest possible gear.

2.   An over-the-road test where the vehicle can be placed into a loaded condition which represents 1600 rpm during a wide-open throttle situation, obtained through application of the vehicle brakes.

3.   In off-road equipment or vehicles equipped with an automatic transmission or torque converter, the time taken to stall test the unit is used.

Each of these procedures is described below. Regardless of the method chosen and used, the following initial checks and preparation are required.

1.   Obtain the PT pump code AFC NO-AIR rail pressure for 1600 rpm loaded, which is available from the Cummins *Fuel Pump Calibration Values Manual*, part 3379352-01, by referencing the fuel pump code number. See Table 22-4 for some examples.

2.   The fuel pressure monitored on the engine with a pressure gauge *must* be within 7 psi (48 kPa) of the no-air pressure setting that would be listed in the specs if the pump were being run on a calibration test stand.

3.   Install a rail pressure fuel gauge such as that illustrated in Figure 22-27 to the electric fuel shutoff solenoid. Cummins gauge ST-435 is shown.

4.   Install a tachometer that can be driven from the PT pump tach point, or use an accurate tachometer to monitor the engine speed to 1600 rpm.

5.   Remove the AFC air supply line from either the air intake manifold or the air compressor inlet tube, depending on the hookup used. Then install a suitable plug cap into the air manifold hole.

6.   Start and idle the engine for a few minutes, then slacken off the fuel pressure gauge fitting to bleed any entrapped air from the line.

7.   The engine *must* be at normal operating temperature for this test.

Operating Condition 1:
Chassis Dynamometer Procedure
With the vehicle securely chained down to a chassis dynamometer, accelerate the engine up through the gears until the transmission is in the highest possible gear. Maintain the throttle pedal in a wide-open position while load is applied to the dyno to place the engine speed at 1600 rpm. Check the AFC no-air rail pressure on the test gauge and compare it to the spec sheet for your pump code and engine. If it is incorrect, an adjustment as described below under AFC no-air valve setting is required.

Operating Condition 2:
Vehicle Road Test
Drive the vehicle over the road with the throttle wide open in top gear and apply the vehicle brakes to reduce the engine speed to 1600 rpm and check the AFC no-air rail pressure on the gauge. If the pressure is incorrect, adjust according to the AFC no-air rail pressure setting described below.

Operating Condition 3:
Stall Test Off-Road Equipment
After performing all the pre-stall test checks, such as: (1) oil level, (2) coolant level, (3) no-load engine speed, and (4) blocking of the vehicle front and back, obtain the manufacturer's stall speed rpm and also the time required to reach the stall speed from an idle rpm. When the stall speed is reached, check the rail pressure on the fuel gauge and compare to the spec sheet. If adjustment is required, adjust as described below.

1.   Remove both the throttle lever and the throttle shaft cover plate.

2.   Reinstall the throttle lever (only) over the shaft as per Figure 22-36.

3.   Refer to Figure 22-36 and using Cummins tool 3375140, adjust the AFC NO-AIR valve to the correct

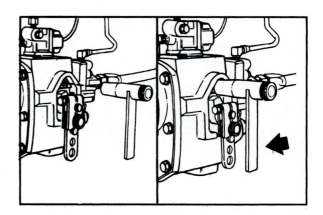

FIGURE 22–36 *Installing and adjusting AFC NO-AIR valve setting with Cummins special tool 3375140. (Courtesy of Cummins Engine Company Inc.)*

pressure listed in the fuel pump code manual, then tighten the locknut to 30 to 45 in.-lb (3.4 to 5.1 N · m) torque.

NOTE   After loosening the AFC NO-AIR screw locknut by turning the handle of special tool 3375140, CW rotation of the knurled knob on the end of the tool will result in a decrease in the rail pressure, while turning it CCW will increase it.

---

4.   Always recheck the AFC no-air rail pressure after any adjustment, and reset it if necessary.

5.   Remove the throttle lever from the shaft; install the pump cover plate and throttle lever again.

INSTALLING THE CUMMINS PT PUMP TO THE ENGINE

1.   Inspect the drive spider for cracks and wear. Replace if any wear or cracks are evident.

NOTE   Black drive spiders are used in six-cylinder engines; white plastic drive spiders are used in V8 engines.

---

2.   Using a new gasket, mount the pump onto the pump mounting flange.

NOTE   Cummins pumps are not timed, so you need not be concerned about engine or pump drive shaft position.

---

3.   Install mounting bolts and tighten.

4.   Connect all fuel lines and tighten.

NOTE   The Cummins fuel system does not have to be bled, since it will pump the air into the return line and back to the tank.

---

5.   Connect the wire to the shutdown valve and tighten. Make sure the manual override screw on the shutdown valve is screwed all the way out.

6.   Change fuel filter if any doubt exists about when it was last changed.

7.   Start and run the engine. Check the following:

a.   Fuel leaks

b.   Engine low idle

c.   Engine high idle

d.   Throttle linkage

TROUBLESHOOTING THE CUMMINS FUEL PUMP

The following procedures should be used as a guideline when troubleshooting the Cummins fuel pump on the test stand (1 to 7) and on the engine (8 to 13).

1.   If the pump will not pump fuel after initial installation on the test stand (no flow shown in flow meter), the following procedures should be followed:

a.   Loosen the fuel inlet line, recheck all fittings, and retighten.

b.   Determine if the shutoff solenoid is in run position.

c.   Make sure the pump rotation is correct.

d.   Check the fit between idle spring plunger and governor plunger. It may be necessary to change one or both to obtain a good fit between them.

e.   Check the gear pump suction to determine if the gear pump is worn out.

f.   Make sure the gear pump is installed correctly on the main pump body.

2.   Check to see if there is aeration of fuel in the flow meter. This indicates an air leak somewhere on the suction side of the gear pump.

NOTE   Any leakage at various places on the PTG AFC housing can cause suction leaks, since the PTG AFC housing is on the suction side of the gear pump during operation. Later-model pumps utilize a pressurized housing.

The following parts, if defective, will permit air leaks into the pump:

a.   Determine if the tachometer drive seal is leaking. Check by putting a small amount of diesel fuel into the tachometer drive coupling with the pump running. It should not be sucked into the pump.

b.   Check all pump housing gaskets and retighten all capscrews.

c. Remove the throttle shaft and check the O-ring on the throttle shaft. Replace the O-ring if necessary.

d. Check the drive shaft seals. Using an oil can, squirt a small amount of oil into the weep hole between the seals. The oil should not be sucked away. If it is, the inside or back seal is leaking.

3. If the governor cutoff is not correct, each of the following should be examined:

a. Check the governor for wear. Replace if needed.

b. Determine if the governor plunger is sticking in its barrel.

c. Determine if the proper number of shims are on the governor spring.

4. If the throttle leakage cannot be adjusted so that it comes back to the same setting after being moved, examine the following items:

a. Determine if the throttle shaft is worn or scored.

b. Check the governor plunger to see if it is worn.

5. If the fuel manifold pressure cannot be adjusted correctly, determine if the following items are in proper working order:

a. See if the idle spring plunger is correct.

b. Check the gear pump suction and determine if the gear pump is worn.

c. Check the governor plunger to see if it is worn.

d. Determine if the throttle shaft is worn.

6. If check points (on calibration chart) do not meet specifications, check the following items:

a. Is the torque spring correct?

b. Is the weight-assist plunger adjusted correctly?

c. Are the governor weights correct for application?

d. Is the gear pump worn?

7. If the pump operation is noisy, determine which of the following parts is worn:

a. Is the governor worn?

b. Is the governor drive gear worn?

c. Is the gear pump worn or scored?

8. If the engine will not run, check the following:

a. Check for operation of the electric shutdown valve.

b. Change the fuel filter if any doubt exists about whether it may be plugged.

c. Make sure that all lines leading to the pump are tight.

d. Check the fuel inlet line for restriction by blowing back through it with an air hose.

e. Remove the tach drive cable and crank the engine; the tach drive should turn at this time. This is a good indication that the pump is or is not turning.

f. If the pump is not turning, check the drive spider or splined sleeve.

9. If the engine runs but is low on horsepower, examine the following items to detect the problem:

a. Check the fuel filter and change if necessary.

b. Check the snap pressure.

c. If the throttle travel is not correct, check to make sure the throttle is in the wide-open position with the accelerator pedal all the way down.

10. The engine often does not decelerate properly. This is a common complaint after a pump has been overhauled and calibrated on the test stand, since each engine may require a different amount of fuel during deceleration.

a. If engine deceleration is too slow, turn the throttle stop screw counterclockwise $\frac{1}{8}$ to $\frac{1}{4}$ in.

NOTE   Check the position of this screw before moving it and then move it a small amount. If no change occurs, put the screw back in its original position and lock the locknut.

---

b. Make sure that the throttle return spring is returning the throttle to the idle position.

c. There should be no binding or sticking of the accelerator linkage.

11. If the engine stalls or underruns as it slows down to idle, check the following items to determine the problems:

    a. Is the idle adjusting screw correctly adjusted?

NOTE The idle screw is adjusted by removing the pipe plug in the governor spring pack cover and inserting a screwdriver through the opening to engage the screw. Turning the screw in increases idle speed, and turning it out decreases idle speed. (See Figure 22-15.)

---

    b. Is there a suction leak at the fuel inlet line?
    c. Is the fuel filter restricted?
    d. Is the throttle leakage screw adjusted correctly?

12. If the engine high idle is incorrect, check each of the following items:

    a. Add or subtract shims from the governor spring as needed.

    b. Check throttle travel.
    c. Check the governor to determine if it is worn or incorrect.

13. If there is excessive black smoke from engine under load, examine the following items:

    a. Check the snap pressure and adjust the throttle restriction if required.
    b. Determine if the correct governor idle spring plunger button has been used.

If additional information on Cummins PT pump overhaul and calibration is required, consult your instructor or Cummins fuel system service manual.

PT INJECTORS

The operation of the PT injector was described in detail in Figures 22-2 and 22-3. Current PT-equipped engines employ what is known as a PT *top stop* injector assembly, which is shown in Figure 22-37b to distinguish it from a conventional non-top stop PT type D injector [Figure 22-37a]. The PT-D top stop injector was designed to allow better engine oil lubrication and

FIGURE 22–37 Index: (a) PT type D injector components; (b) PT type D top stop injector components. (Courtesy of Cummins Engine Company Inc.)

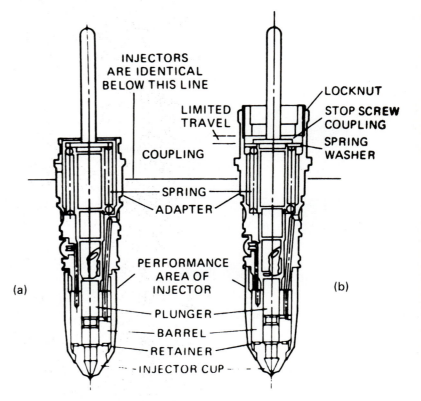

cooling to the injector ball and socket joints, thereby reducing wear in the injector operating mechanism and permitting longer life and service intervals between injector adjustments. A stop nut (item 5 in Figure 22-38) is adjusted to limit injector travel; therefore, the injector train component parts are unloaded during the metering portion of the fuel supply cycle. In addition, hardened injector plunger couplings and spring retainers are now used with this type of injector assembly to prevent wear from occurring on the bottom side of the coupling flange and on the top side of the spring retainer. Hardened couplings are identified by a gray metallic color, while nonhardened couplings are black in color.

The top stop injector operates similar to a standard injector, with the exception that the upward travel of the injector plunger is controlled or limited by an adjustable stop that is set prior to installing the injector in the engine. Proper installation and adjustment of the injector permits the plunger spring load to be carried up against the stop. The top stop injector is designed to operate with no lash; therefore, any wear in the system beyond normal limits can increase push tube load if the injector is reset, because of the shorter top stop travel after adjustment.

Injector Identification
Current Cummins injectors are identified by the part number stamped on them Figure 22-39. This number can then be used to further identify the injector by re-ferring to the injector specifications book. The following information will be used during injector rebuild:

1. Flow code refers to the amount of fuel in cubic centimeters that an injector should deliver will be tested
2. The number of the injector cup (Figure 22-40)
3. Barrel and plunger number
4. Adjustable orifice range

Components
The Cummins PTD and PTD top stop injectors are composed of the following component parts (Figure 22-41):

a. Body
b. Cup
c. Plunger
d. Plunger return spring
e. Balance orifice
f. Barrel and plunger (PTD) only (high and low flow)
g. Injector link

The injector's function is to time, meter, inject (pressurize), and atomize the fuel. Fuel is supplied to the injector from the passageways in the cylinder head. Fuel then flows through the injector in this order (fuel flow given is for PTD injector):

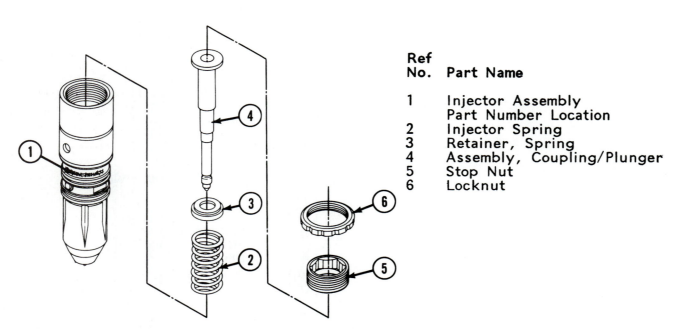

Ref No.	Part Name
1	Injector Assembly Part Number Location
2	Injector Spring
3	Retainer, Spring
4	Assembly, Coupling/Plunger
5	Stop Nut
6	Locknut

FIGURE 22–38 Exploded view of a PT type D top stop injector. (Courtesy of Cummins Engine Company Inc.)

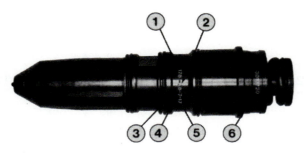

FIGURE 22-39 *F60200: Size location on injector adapter. 1, 178: Injector flow; 2, A: 80% flow; 3, 8: Number of Holes; 4, 7: size of holes (0.007); 5, 17: Degree of Holes; 6, Assembly Number.*

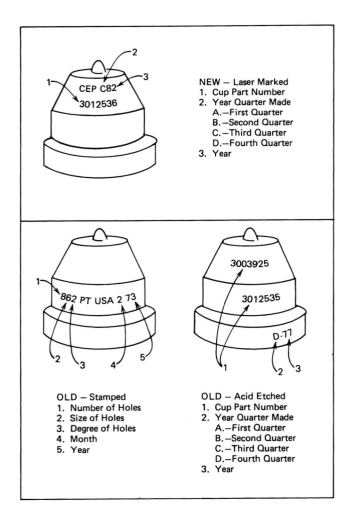

FIGURE 22-40 *Identification of injector cups (Courtesy of Cummins Engine Company, Inc.)*

1. Fuel is supplied to the injector balance orifice from the fuel passageways in the cylinder head.
2. Fuel then flows through the injector as shown and described in Figure 22-3.

Direct Fuel Feed PT Injectors

In addition to the standard PTD injectors discussed in this section, beginning with the Big Cam III model NT 855-in³ (14-L) inline six-cylinder engines, and carrying over into the Big Cam IV models, an injector identified as a DFF (direct fuel feed) unit was incorporated into the PT fuel system. Figure 22-42 illustrates the DFF type of injector alongside a standard unit. The DFF injector, which was tried and tested first in the K model engines, prevents fuel from entering the injector cup during the off mode when the engine is motoring, thereby reducing injector maintenance by preventing carboning of the plunger tip. This design change can be seen in the diagram, with the operation being similar to that described in this section.

Locating a Misfiring PT Injector

On Cummins PT fuel system–equipped engines, removal of an injector may be required if it is determined that the engine has a cylinder misfire and other conditions have been eliminated as the possible cause. Check each injector for operation in a PT-equipped fuel system engine as follows:

1. Run the engine until it has attained a coolant temperature of at least 160°F (70°C).
2. Remove the valve rocker lever covers.
3. Install a Cummins special tool ST-1193 rocker lever actuator over the injector rocker lever as shown in Figure 22-43.
4. With the engine running at its normal idle rpm, push the combination wrench shown in Figure 22-43 toward the water manifold side of the engine to hold the injector plunger down. This will stop the fuel flow through the injector.
5. If the engine rpm decreases, the injector was firing and is good.
6. If there is no change in the engine sound and there is no reduction in rpm, the injector is defective and should be replaced.

PT Injector Removal and Installation

Removal and installation of one or more injectors may be required any time that a cylinder head is to be serviced, diesel fuel leakage is evident into the lube oil through damaged injector O-rings, or the injector requires servicing.

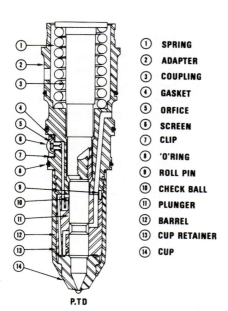

①	SPRING
②	ADAPTER
③	COUPLING
④	GASKET
⑤	ORFICE
⑥	SCREEN
⑦	CLIP
⑧	'O'RING
⑨	ROLL PIN
⑩	CHECK BALL
⑪	PLUNGER
⑫	BARREL
⑬	CUP RETAINER
⑭	CUP

P.TD

1. Cup
2. Cup Retainer
3. Barrel
4. Plunger
5. Check Ball
6. Adapter
7. Screen Clip
8. Fuel Screen
9. Fuel In
10. Orifice Plug
11. Orifice Gasket
12. Coupling
13. Fuel Out
14. O-ring
15. Link
16. Spring
17. Retainer
18. Locknut
19. Top Stop Screw

PT (type D) Top Stop Injector cross-section

FIGURE 22–41 *Several different Cummins injectors. (Courtesy of Cummins Engine Company, Inc.)*

Removal Procedure

1. Steam clean the rocker cover area of the engine prior to injector removal to ensure that no dirt is allowed to fall into the rocker arm and valve operating mechanism.

2. Remove the rocker cover assemblies.

3. It may be necessary to rotate the engine over via the accessory drive pulley to remove the spring tension from the injector rocker lever prior to attempting to back off the rocker lever adjusting screw.

4. Loosen the injector rocker arm adjusting screw locknut on the cylinder required, then back out the adjusting screw far enough to allow the injector pushrod to be moved to the side or removed from the engine. If it is removed, match-mark it so that it can be reinstalled in the same cylinder position on the engine later.

5. Grasp and rotate the injector rocker lever upward, then remove the injector link.

6. Refer to Figure 22-44 and after loosening and removing the two injector clamp capscrews, lift out the injector hold-down clamp.

7. Obtain Cummins injector slide hammer puller 3376497 and install it onto the injector body as illustrated in Figure 22-45, then slide-hammer the injector free from its bore in the cylinder head.

8. Once the injector has been removed from its bore, it is important that you remove any carbon accumulations from the injector copper sleeve in the cylinder head with the use of a clean, soft, lint-free cloth wrapped around a wooden stick so as not to scratch or damage the copper sleeve. In addition, Cummins offers the chip removing unit, ST-1272-11, to remove any carbon accumulation from the top of the piston crown.

Each injector has three external O-rings, located about halfway down the body, which are used to seal lube oil from entering the injector bore area as well as preventing diesel fuel leakage into the rocker box area and dribbling into the combustion chamber. The O-ring seals should be renewed any time the injector has been removed from the cylinder head for any reason.

NOTE   Current Viton O-rings are color coded red (K engines) and green and are used in all positions on the injector.

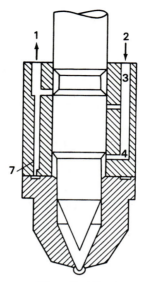
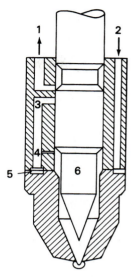

Direct Fuel Feed
1. Fuel Drain
2. Fuel In
3. Supply Drilling
4. Metering Orifice

Standard PTD
5. Fuel Groove in Barrel
6. Plunger Minor Diameter
7. Vent Drilling

FIGURE 22–42 *Direct fuel feed and standard PT type D injector barrel comparison.(Courtesy of Cummins Engine Company, Inc.)*

Installation Procedure

1. O-rings should be installed over the injector into the retaining grooves so that they do not twist when in position; therefore, take care that they are rolled into position without any sign of such a twist.

2. Lubricate the injector body O-rings with STP, Alemite CD2, or equivalent lubricant, or if not available, use clean SAE 30 engine oil.

3. Prior to installing the injectors, check the bores in the cylinder head for signs of burrs or sharp

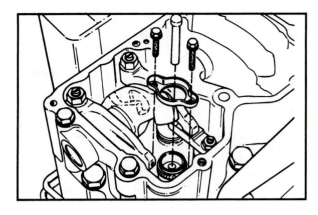

FIGURE 22–44 *Removing one-piece injector hold-down clamp. (Courtesy of Cummins Engine Company, Inc.)*

edges that could nick, cut, or tear the O-ring as it enters the bore.

4. Carefully insert the injector into its bore in the cylinder head.

5. Refer to Figure 22-46 and use a clean blunt object such as a hammer handle on the injector adapter body (not on the injector plunger or link) to push it into position.

6. Seat the injector in its bore by giving a quick, hard push. As the injector seats fully, a snap should be heard and felt.

7. Install the hold-down clamp that was removed (Figure 22-44) along with the two capscrews.

8. Alternatively tighten each capscrew in 50-in.-lb (6-N · m) increments until a final torque of 144 to 168 in.-lb (16 to 19 N · m) has been achieved.

9. Install the injector link into each injector.

10. Install the pushrod which was match-marked earlier for that injector rocker arm.

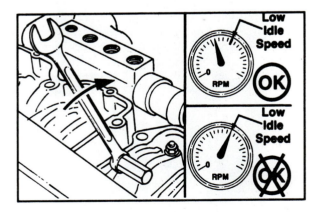

FIGURE 22–43 *Using special tool ST-1193 to short-out an injector. (Courtesy of Cummins Engine Company, Inc.)*

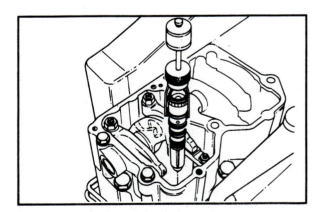

FIGURE 22–45 *Using a slide hammer and attachments to remove a PT injector from its bore in the cylinder head. (Courtesy of Cummins Engine Company, Inc.)*

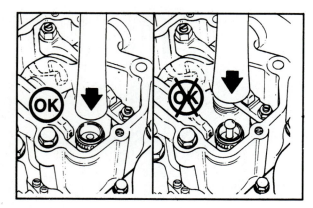

FIGURE 22–46 *Using a clean hammer handle shaft to facilitate pushing the PT injector fully home in its bore. A distinct click/snap should be heard as the injector is pushed fully home. (Courtesy of Cummins Engine Company, Inc.)*

11.   Turn in the rocker arm adjusting screw until it seats in the pushrod socket just enough to hold the pushrod in place.

12.   Adjust all crossheads, valves, and injectors according to the tuneup section of this chapter.

Injector Disassembly, Cleaning, and Inspection

Assume that the injectors are removed from the engine and are ready to be disassembled, cleaned, and repaired.

NOTE   Before disassembly of the injector, rinse it in solvent and blow it off with compressed air. Remove body O-rings and discard them. Then proceed with the following steps:

Disassembly of PTD Standard and "Top Stop" Injectors

PTD injectors are disassembled in much the same way as PTB and PTC injectors except that they must be installed in a loading fixture before disassembly.

1.   Remove the plunger link if not done previously.

NOTE   The plunger link on the PTD injector is simply lifted out of the plunger coupling. No snap ring is used to hold it in place. On top stop injectors, the plunger stop nut must be removed.

---

2.   Remove the plunger.

3.   Remove the spring from the plunger.

4.   Install the injector in the loading fixture, and install the cup retaining nut wrench and body holding fixture (Figure 22-47).

CAUTION   Do not attempt to disassemble the injector without torquing the injector in the holding fixture or damage to the injector may result.

---

5.   Torque the hold down screw to the required torque.

6.   Loosen the cup retainer nut.

7.   Remove the injector from the holding fixture.

8.   Remove the cup retainer or nut and catch the check ball as barrel and plunger assembly come apart.

9.   Remove the balance orifice.

Cleaning PTD and PTD Top Stop Injectors

If injectors and injector parts have not been rinsed with cleaning solvent, do so before placing them in the cleaning solution.

1.   Place all injector parts in a basket and soak them in a cleaning solvent like carburetor cleaner. An alternative method of cleaning is to use an ultrasonic cleaner.

FIGURE 22–47 *Cummins injector holding fixture.*

2. After the carbon has been removed or loosened by one of the methods mentioned above, flush the parts thoroughly in a clean parts washing solution.

3. Blow off all parts with clean, dry, compressed air.

Parts Inspection: PTD and PTD Top Stop

Parts inspection is one of the most important procedures in rebuilding and repairing injectors. As experience is gained, parts inspection becomes routine.

Injector Testing and Calibration

Injector testing and calibration must be done after injector overhaul to ensure correct injector and engine operation. Also if Cummins leakage tester 3375375 is available, the following leak checks should be performed if they were not performed during parts inspection.

1. Cup to plunger seat test
2. Barrel and plunger test
3. Check ball leakage test

If the 3375375 tool is not available, some other method of leak checking should be devised, since leak checks are very important to correct injector operation. After the injector has been leak checked and is ready to be calibrated, consult the injector calibration and flow tables for the correct injector flow. This calibrator simulates operation of the injector in the engine and allows for accurate testing and flow matching of injectors. (Figure 22-48).

check the injector data for orifice range. If a larger-than-recommended size is required to obtain flow, the injector barrel and plunger are probably worn and must be replaced. Test and calibrate all injectors.

Setting the Top Stop Injectors: Off Engine

PTD-TS (top stop) injectors *must* be adjusted for a given plunger travel if they are to operate correctly when installed in the engine. Two models of TS injector off-engine setting fixtures are available. Early-model PTD-TS models used a fixture with a mechanical dial gauge, while all PTD-TS, STC (HVT), and Hyperbar TS injectors manufactured after November 1986 used Cummins tool 3822696, which is shown in Figure 22-49. For details on how to use the DIGI-MATIC TS setting fixture, refer to *Cummins Service Tool Instruction Bulletin 3377598*. Although somewhat similar to the earlier injector setting fixture, the procedure is more detailed and far more accurate.

Operating Instructions. After the leakage testing of the injector is complete, the injector can be assembled to the point where the plunger top stop, or plunger travel setting can be made. This is done by removing the injector plunger, installing the spring retainer and spring(s), and then installing the plunger again.

Setting the Top Stop Plunger Travel. The plunger travel must be set for all top stop injectors. This includes all PT (type D) top stops, both old and new STC and HVT injectors, and future Hyperbar injectors. The instructions for setting the plunger travel are as follows:

1. Install the top stop screw and locknut.
2. Place the holding bracket, part 3822726, into the fuel groove flats of the injector (Figure 22-50).

3. Place the long K injector plunger link, part 205462, into the injector.
4. Install the injector into the fixture. Slide it all the way into the lower plate of the fixture, centering it over the injector stop nut. The holding bracket will fit into the lowest machined slot in the lower plate. The L10 adapter, if present, will fit into the center machined slot in the lower plate. The L10 adapter or

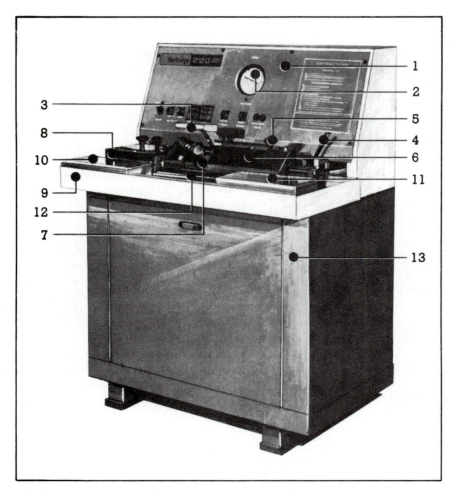

General arrangement of the HA 290

Key
1. Facia panel with instruments, controls and operating instructions
2. Dial indicator — injector output display
3. Fuel arm
4. Pressure select valve
5. Rotary control valve
6. Guard
7. Anti-splash flap
8. Cambox
9. Top tray
10. Stowage box — cams, box spanner, T bar etc.
11. Stowage box — adaptors and links
12. Work tray
13. Base with front access door

FIGURE 22-48 *General arrangement of the HA290 PT injector test stand. (Courtesy of Cummins Engine Company, Inc.)*

flange on the injector body, whichever is applicable, will rest against the ledge at the top of the machined area in the lower plate (Figure 22-52).

5. Adjust the injector stop nut up against the injector cup and tighten it to 11 to 13 N · m (100 to 115 in.-lbs) torque. Use a 32-mm (1¼-in.) open-end crowsfoot wrench (Figure 22-52).

6. Turn the overcenter clamp handles so that they point downward. This will allow the full 11.3-kg (25-lb) deadweight system to be used.

7. Lower the weight and center plunger by placing the upper toggle switch in the LOWER position.

8. Bottom the plunger in the cup by placing the lower toggle switch in the LOAD position. If the ram of the main air cylinder does not travel down and seat the plunger in the cup, refer to the troubleshooting chart.

9. Press the PSET button, then press the LOAD button on the presetter. Wait a few seconds until the preset value, a downward arrow, and an "in" symbol appear on the indicator display. If this does not happen, refer to the troubleshooting chart.

10. Release the plunger from the cup by placing the lower toggle switch in the UNLOAD position. Read the top stop setting on the indicator display.

11. If the reading is not within ±0.013 mm (0.0005 in.) of the desired top stop setting, adjust the stop screw up or down until the reading is correct. Use the adjusting tool, part 3375165, for NT-855 injectors. Use the adjusting tool, part 3376868, for the L10 injectors. The setting tolerance is ±0.013 mm (0.0005 in.) from nominal. The recheck tolerance is ±0.076 mm (0.0030 in.) from nominal.

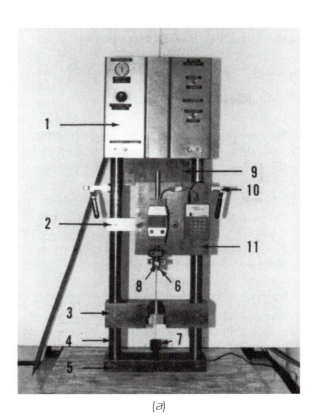

(a)

Ref. No.	Part No.	Description	Qty.
1		Control Panel	1
2		Upper Plate	1
3		Lower Plate	1
4		Side Rails	2
5		Bottom Plate	1
6		Center Plunger	1
7	3822745	Injector Stop Nut	1
8		Indicator Arm	1
9		20 lb. Dead Weight	1
10	3375391	Overcenter Clamp	2
11		Measurement System Mounting Plate	1
12	3822727	L-10 Adapter	1
13	3822726	Holding Bracket	1
14	205462	K Injector Plunger Link	1
15	3025181 or 3052233	K-STC Injector Plunger Link	1
16	3822730	DIGIMATIC Indicator	1
17	3822731	DIGIMATIC Presetter	1
18		Connecting Cord	1
19		Power Cord	1
20	3822733	Presetter Mounting Screws	2

(b)

FIGURE 22–49   *(A) Top-stop injector setting fixture; (B) list of top-stop injector setting fixture parts; (Courtesy of Cummins Engine Company, Inc.)*

FIGURE 22–50   *Install holding bracket.*

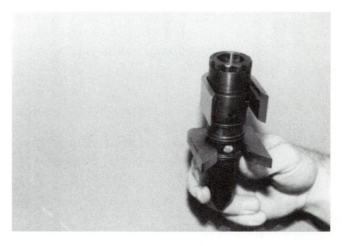

FIGURE 22–51   *Install L10 setting stand adapter and holding bracket.*

FIGURE 22–52 Install injector into fixture.

NOTE   The stop screw on STC injectors can be adjusted up or down by inserting a small Allen wrench into one of the oil feed holes and turning the stop screw (Figure 22-53).

---

12.   Recheck the top stop setting by repeating steps 8 to 11.

13.   Tighten the locknut to 75 N · m (55 ft-lb) torque. For L10 injectors, use the crowsfoot wrench, part 3376867. For the old-style HVT injectors, use the crowsfoot wrench, part 3822526. For all other injectors, use the crowsfoot wrench, part 3375166.

14.   Recheck the top stop setting by repeating steps 8 to 10. Make sure that the locknut did not

FIGURE 22–53 Adjusting STC stop screw.

change the setting when it was tightened. Reset the top stop if it is not within ±0.013 mm (0.0005 in.) of the desired setting.

15.   Raise the weights and center plunger by placing the upper toggle switch to RAISE.

16.   Remove the injector from the stand by reversing the installation process.

17.   The injector is now ready for flow testing on the calibration test stand.

Setting the Tappet Top Stop Total Travel.   After the injector flow calibration is complete, the injectors that contain the tappet top stop hardware must have the total travel set. STC injectors and future Hyperbar injectors will have the tappet top stop hardware. To set the total travel on these injectors, proceed as follows:

1.   Install the injector plunger link, tappet, clamping ring (if present), oil-feed locknut, and tappet top stop cap into the injector (Figure 22-54).

NOTE   See Bulletin 3379664-06, or later editions, for top stop and total travel settings.

---

2.   Place the holding bracket, part 3822726, into the fuel groove flats of the injector (Figure 22-50).

3.   Install the injector into the fixture (Figure 22-52).

4.   Torque the injector stop nut to 11 to 13 N · m (100 to 115 in.-lb) (Figure 22-52).

5.   Place the short K-STC injector plunger link that came with the fixture, part 3025181 or 3052233, into the top of the injector tappet (Figure 22-55).

NOTE   Do not use the short link that comes with the injector, as it can cause false readings.

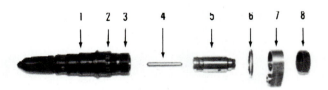

FIGURE 22–54 STC injector (NT-855) hardware. 1, Injector body; 2, locknut; 3, Stop screw; 4, injector plunger link; 5, tappet; 6, clamping ring; 7, oil-feed locknut; 8, tappet top stop cap.

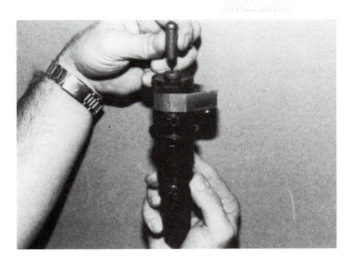

FIGURE 22–55 Install K-STC link.

CAUTION Turn the handles of the overcenter clamps so they point upward. This will allow only 2.3 kg (5 lb) of the deadweight system to be used. This is very important.

---

6. Lower the weight and center plunger by placing the upper toggle switch to LOWER.

7. Bottom the plunger in the cup by placing the lower toggle switch in the LOAD position. If the ram of the main air cylinder does not move down and seat the plunger in the cup, refer to the troubleshooting chart.

CAUTION If the indicator shows a slow change, there is oil trapped in the tappet. If the indicator is still changing after 20 seconds, remove the tappet, separate the tappet sleeve from the tappet plunger, and pour out the excess oil. Reassemble the tappet and injector, and repeat the setting procedure (Figure 22-56).

---

8. Press the PSET button, then the LOAD button on the presetter. Wait a few seconds for the downward arrow and the correct preset value to appear. If they do not appear, refer to the troubleshooting chart.

9. Release the plunger from the cup by placing the lower toggle switch in the UNLOAD position.

10. Read the display. If the display is not within ±0.013 mm (0.0005 in.) of the setting desired, adjust the top stop cap up or down until the correct display is shown. The top stop cap can be turned with your fingers.

FIGURE 22–56 Disassembled tappet. 1, Tappet plunger; 2, spring; 3, tappet sleeve.

11. Recheck the setting by repeating steps 7 to 10.

12. Turn the oil-feed locknut up against the top stop cap. Hold the top stop cap with a crowsfoot wrench, part 3375166. Tighten the locknut to the top stop cap to 75 N · m (55 ft-lb) torque. The oil-feed locknut can be held with a 38-mm (1½-in.) open-end or adjustable jaw wrench. See Figure 22-57.

13. Repeat steps 7 to 9 to make sure the top stop setting did not change when the top stop cap was torqued. If the travel is not within ±0.013 mm (0.0005 in.) of the desired setting, reset the tappet top stop.

14. Raise the weight and plunger off the injector by placing the upper toggle switch in the RAISE position.

15. Remove the injector from the fixture by reversing the installation procedure.

FIGURE 22–57 Torque locknut to top stop cap.

16. Remove the K-STC injector plunger link which was installed in step 5. Replace it with the original injector plunger link and retaining ring. For a reference on which link is used for each type of injector, see Service Parts Topic 86T6-5.

ENGINE-TO-INJECTOR TIMING

Once an engine has been assembled, basic piston-to-camshaft timing is established through alignment of the timing marks between the crankshaft and camshaft gearing. Injector timing must be checked and set if any of the following are changed: camshaft, timing gears, cam follower box gaskets, cam followers, or cam follower box. However, we now have to ensure that the actual start of injection occurs at a specific amount of degrees BTDC; therefore, this involves a series of checks and adjustments and if the actual injection timing does not match that specified on the CPL (control parts list) data plate located on the side of the engine front engine timing cover. Once the injection timing code has been noted on the CPL data plate, it is necessary to refer to the Cummins *CPL Manual*, part 3379133, which lists all the various codes and respective injector push tube travel specifications for all engine models and CPL codes.

NOTE   The injection timing check confirms that the distance existing between the injector plunger and the injector cup when measured with a dial indicator is correct when the piston is 19° BTDC, which is equal to a measurement of 0.2032 in. or 5.161 mm BTDC. The timing is correct when the reading on the piston travel dial indicator and the push tube dial indicator are as in the specs listed in the Cummins *CPL Manual* 3379133. The injection timing code on the CPL engine data plate can be cross-referenced to the specs in this manual for all Cummins engines. Therefore, the injection timing relates to the amount of push tube travel remaining before the plunger bottoms in its cup when the engine piston is 19° BTDC on its compression stroke.

Engine-to-PT-Injector Timing Example
To remove any confusion about why injection timing is so important to the successful operation of the engine, Figures 22-58 and 22-59 illustrate graphically just how the piston position and injector push tube movement relate to one another. If we were to assume for discussion purposes that the engine injector push tube spec-

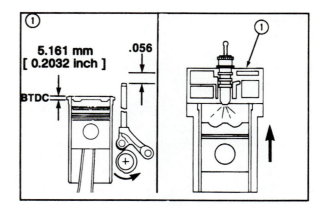

FIGURE 22–58   Early fuel injection as a result of too small a push tube lift BTDC. (Courtesy of Cummins Engine Company, Inc.)

ification was listed as 0.066 in. (1.67 mm) in the CPL manual for a particular engine when the piston was 0.2032 in. (5.161 mm) from TDC on its compression stroke, which is equal to 19° BTDC, any reading less than this 0.066 in. would indicate that timing is advanced or "fast," since it would place the injector plunger closer to bottoming in its cup with the piston in its correct position of 19° BTDC. In effect, fuel would be injected too early, as shown in Figure 22-58 with an example reading of 0.056 in. (1.42 mm).

Figure 22-59 illustrates the result of "slow" or retarded timing with an example push tube reading on the dial indicator of 0.076 in. (1.93 mm) instead of the correct 0.066 in. (1.67 mm). In this situation, the start of injection would occur too late (piston closer to TDC).

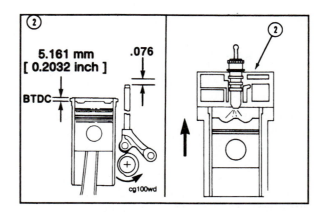

FIGURE 22–59   Late fuel injection as a result of too large a push tube lift BTDC. (Courtesy of Cummins Engine Company, Inc.)

Changing Injection Timing

CPL codes on the engine data plate for injection timing are either a single or double alphabetical letter that relates to a specification numeral listed in the CPL manual. Injection timing can be changed on the NT 855 series of engines by removing the cam follower housing and increasing or decreasing the thickness of the gasket used. On V-type, K series, and L10 engine models, injection timing is changed by removing the camshaft gear and installing an "offset key" to alter the timing dimension. Advancement or retardation of injection timing is accomplished by altering the position of the injector cam follower roller in relation to its position on the camshaft lobe when the piston is 19° BTDC on its compression stroke.

Figure 22-60 illustrates how a thicker or thinner cam follower housing gasket on an NT 855 engine would alter the push tube lift in relation to the piston position. In addition an offset key can be installed into the slotted keyway on the engine camshaft to change the timing. Figure 22-61 represents two different offset keys for an 855 (14-L) model engine; if the arrow on the key is pointing toward the engine, the injection timing is retarded, while if the arrow is pointing away from the engine, the timing is advanced. Table 22-5 lists the timing change for the different camshaft keys used.

NOTE   On 855 model engines, since three cylinder heads are used to cover the six cylinders, we also have three cam follower housings. This means that the injection timing check must be done for all three cam follower housings by performing the timing check on one cylinder for

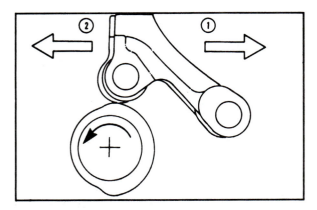

FIGURE 22–60 *Changing injector push tube lift by varying the thickness of the cam follower gasket on an NT engine. (Courtesy of Cummins Engine Company, Inc.)*

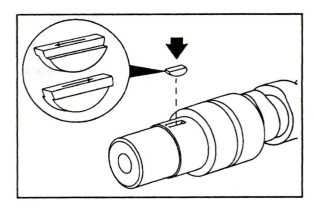

FIGURE 22–61 *Changing injector push tube lift timing by the use of an offset engine camshaft key. (Courtesy of Cummins Engine Company, Inc.)*

each housing. Therefore, prior to performing the injection timing check, remove the fuel injectors from cylinders 1, 3, and 5.

To establish that the injector will in fact inject fuel into the combustion chamber at the proper number of degrees BTDC during the compression stroke, two dial indicators are required. One dial indicator measures the relative piston position in the cylinder, and the other establishes the actual injector push tube lift and duration. Cummins timing fixture, 3375522 (Figure 22-62), is required on the engine for this purpose, or a suitable alternative.

SERVICE TIP   To prevent a possible false reading of the dial indicator setup shown in Figure 22-62, it is always advisable to check the cam follower housing capscrews located on the side of the engine block on 14-L six-cylinder engines. These bolts should be tightened to between 30 and 35 lb-ft (41 to 48 N · m), starting from diagonally opposite corners, moving to the two diagonally opposite corners then finishing in the middle of the six-bolt pattern.

Injector Timing Fixture Installation

1. Select the proper injector timing fixture adapters for the engine to be checked, from the special tool kit (see Figure 22-62).

2. Attach the correct adapters to the fixture hold-down screws.

3. Tighten the jam nuts against the adapters to lock them in place.

TABLE 22–5   *Examples of engine camshaft keys that can be used to change the Initial engine/injection t ming value*

¾-in. Key part no.	Offset		Timing change	Change in pushrod travel at 19° BTDC	
	in	mm		in	mm
3021601	None		None	None	
3021595	0.0060	0.15	Retard	0.0030	0.07
3021593	0.0075	0.19	Retard	0.0037	0.09
3021592	0.0115	0.29	Retard	0.0057	0.14
3021594	0.0185	0.47	Retard	0.0092	0.23
3021596	0.0255	0.65	Retard	0.0127	0.32
3021598	0.0310	0.79	Retard	0.0155	0.39
3021597	0.0390	0.99	Retard	0.0195	0.49
3021600	0.0510	1.30	Retard	0.0255	0.65
3021599	0.0115	0.29	Advance	0.0057	0.14
3022352[a]	0.0185	0.47	Advance	0.0092	0.23
3022353[a]	0.0310	0.79	Advance	0.0155	0.39

Source: Cummins Engine Company, Inc.
[a] For mechanical variable timing (MVT) engines.

4. If your engine does not require adapters, simply remove the jam nuts from the hold-down screws, which will allow the hold-down screw threads to be screwed into the rocker housing. Note that rocker-box removal is not necessary.

5. Slide both dial indicators to the upper end of their support brackets, which will prevent possible indicator damage when you install the timing fixture onto the cylinder head.

6. Carefully install the timing fixture over the cylinder to be checked. (The injector has, of course, been removed from the cylinder previously.) Position the timing tool so that the extension rod attached to the main fixture dial indicator passes through the injector tube hole on into the cylinder.

7. Screw the hold-down screws into the tapped hole or studs of the cylinder head to secure it in place. (Make sure that the timing tool is straight.)

8. Refer to Figure 22-62. Rotate the swivel bracket so that the plunger assembly of the other dial indicator can be located into the injector push tube socket and tighten the capscrew.

9. Engage the dial-indicator plunger rod into the push tube socket and slide the plunger rod bracket down until the spring is compressed approximately 0.050 in. (1.27 mm). Align the edge of the pushrod plunger bracket with the vertical scribe mark on the fixture.

10. With the timing fixture in position, rotate the crankshaft in the normal direction of engine rotation, which is CW from the front. If both dial indicator plunger rods on the timing fixture move together in the upper direction, this will confirm that the piston is moving up the cylinder on its compression stroke.

11. Continue to rotate the engine crankshaft CW slowly until the dial indicator piston plunger rod stops moving.

12. Carefully position the piston dial indicator over the plunger rod in its fully compressed or bottomed state. Slowly allow the dial gauge plunger rod to move up until a reading of 0.025 in. (0.63 mm) is obtained and lock the gauge assembly in position.

13. Slowly rotate the engine from the front in a backward and forward motion until you have determined the rock point of the dial gauge needle pointer. Gently turn the crankshaft CW until the pointer stops moving. Loosen the dial indicator bezel retaining screw and rotate the gauge to place the pointer at the zero position (see Figure 22-63).

14. Rotate the engine over CW from the TDC position until it is 90° ATDC. Position the injector dial indicator over its plunger rod until it is fully compressed, then gently allow it to rise until a reading of 0.025 in. (0.63 mm) registers on the dial gauge and lock it in place. Zero the indicator pointer by loosening the gauge bezel retaining screw, then rotate the bezel until

Ref. No.	Detail No.	Description	Qty.
1	3376212	Adapter (K-6, KV, NH 5-1/2 bore)	2*
2	3376213	Adapter (NH 5-1/8) 1/2 X 13 thread	2*
3	3376214	Adapter (NH 5-1/8) 1/2 X 20 thread	2*
4	3376215	Adapter (V6-V8)	1*
5	3376216	Adapter (J & C)	2*
6	3376408	Dial Indicator	2
7	3376409	Spindle Extension	1
8	3376451	Knob	1
9	3376452	Handle Assembly	1
10	3376453	Bracket	1
11	336454	Support Assembly	1
12	3376611	Extension Assembly	1

* Adapters are used by pairs; however are sold by the piece when ordered separately.

Part No. 3376625 Kit must also be purchased to time 10 Litre engines. 3376625 Kit includes 3376217 Adapter, 3376218 Adapter and 3376180 Setting Gauge.

The Timing Fixture is designed to determine the injector push tube travel in relation to the piston travel.

FIGURE 22–62 Part 3375522 injection timing fixture tools. (Courtesy of Cummins Engine Company, Inc.)

the pointer is opposite the zero reading. Lock it in this position (see Figure 22-64).

15. Refer to Figure 22-65 and rotate the engine CCW from the front until the piston dial gauge registers between 0.425 and 0.450 in. (10.8 to 11.4 mm). This dimension represents a piston position approximately 45 crankshaft degrees BTDC. The reason for this action is to ensure that all gear backlash will be removed when we go to the next procedural step.

16. Slowly rotate the engine CW and stop at a position equal to about 30° BTDC. Very gently nudge the engine CW until the piston dial indicator registers 0.2032 in. (5.161 mm) (see Figure 22-66).

17. Look now at the pointer needle value regis-

tered on the injector push tube dial indicator assembly. This value is read from zero in a counterclockwise direction. Compare the injector dial indicator value with the specification for your engine, which can be found in:

a. An engine shop manual
b. Engine CPL (control parts list) publications
c. The timing code for your engine, listed on the CPL data plate located at the side on the gear train cover at the front of the engine

18. If the reading you obtain on the injector push tube dial indicator is greater than specified, the en-

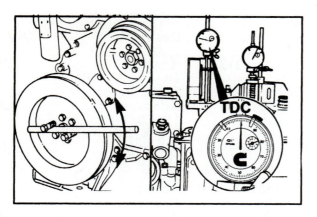

FIGURE 22–63   Placing the piston at TDC and zeroing-in the dial indicator. (Courtesy of Cummins Engine Company, Inc.)

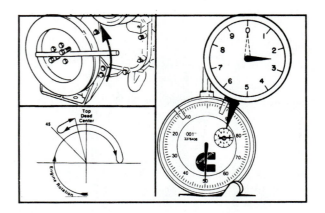

FIGURE 22–65   Piston follower indicator rod at 45° BTDC. (Courtesy of Cummins Engine Company, Inc.)

gine/injector timing is said to be "slow." If the reading is less than specs, the timing is said to be "fast."

19.   To alter an incorrect injector dial indicator reading, we must add or remove gaskets as shown in Figure 22-67 from behind the pivoted cam follower roller boxes located on the side of the engine block. This action changes the lift of the injector push tube, which is basically a pivoted roller follower. With this in mind, the following conditions will hold true:

a.   To decrease the dial indicator reading value, we would add cam follower housing gaskets which would advance the injection timing in relation to the piston position.

b.   To increase the dial indicator reading value, we would remove gaskets from behind the

cam follower housing. This would have the effect of retarding the injection timing in relation to the piston position.

20.   Each 0.007 in. (0.18 mm) of gasket thickness will affect injection timing by approximately 0.002 in. (0.05 mm) of dial indicator travel on all 2.5-in. (63.5-mm) cam models. Gaskets for the NH/NT 855 2.5-in. cam model engines are available in the following nominal thicknesses:

a.   0.007 in. (0.18 mm)

b.   0.017 in. (0.43 mm)

c.   0.017 in. (0.43 mm), Print-O-Seal gasket

d.   0.022 in. (0.56 mm)

e.   0.030 in. (0.76 mm)

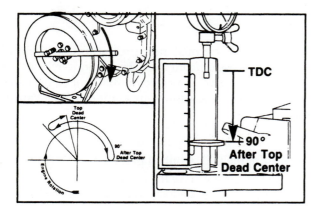

FIGURE 22–64   Piston at 90° ATDC and positioning the push tube dial indicator rod. (Courtesy of Cummins Engine Company, Inc.)

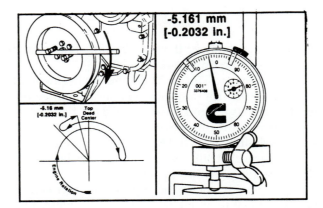

FIGURE 22–66   With piston at 19° BTDC, note the dial indicator reading. It should be 0.2032 in. or 5.161 mm. (Courtesy of Cummins Engine Company, Inc.)

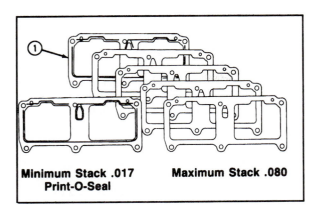

Minimum Stack .017
Print-O-Seal

Maximum Stack .080

FIGURE 22–67 *Minimum and maximum acceptable cam follower housing gasket thickness stackup for NT 2.5-in.-diameter camshaft models. (Courtesy of Cummins Engine Company, Inc.)*

SPECIAL NOTE   One Print-O-Seal gasket *must* be used on each cam follower housing. Increasing the gasket thickness will *advance* injection timing, while decreasing gasket thickness will *retard* injection timing.

CAUTION   On 2-in. (50.8-mm) cam model engines, each 0.007 in. (0.18 mm) of gasket thickness will alter the reading on the dial indicator gauge by approximately 0.001 in. (0.025 mm). Gasket selection sizes for the 2-in. cam model engines are 0.007, 0.015, 0.022, 0.030, and 0.037 in. or 0.18, 0.38, 0.56, 0.76, and 0.76 mm.

21. Table 22-6 lists the various cam follower housing gaskets available for the NH/NT type 855 engines along with the approximate change to the dial indicator (push tube) travel with the piston 19° BTDC on its compression stroke.

22. Figure 22-67 illustrates that the minimum thickness of gasket stackup that can be used on 2.5-in. (63.5-mm) cam models should never be less than 0.017 in. (0.43 mm), while the maximum stackup should never exceed 0.080 in. (2.03 mm). With a Print-O-Seal gasket (item 1), the sealing bead should always be toward the cam follower housing for effective sealing.

NOTE   On 2-in. (50.8-mm) cam models, the minimum amount of gasket thickness stackup is 0.015 in. (0.38 mm), while the maximum amount is 0.125 in. (3.175 mm).

CAUTION   If injection timing cannot be achieved according to the specification listed in the *CPL Manual 3379133* with either the minimum or maximum recommended gasket thickness stackup, an offset camshaft key similar to that shown in Figure 22-61 *must* be installed, then the injection timing procedure repeated to determine what cam follower housing gaskets are now required.

NOTE   Use of an offset key will allow the camshaft lobe profile to be rotated slightly while ensuring that the engine gear train timing remains

TABLE 22–6 *Cam follower housing gasket thicknesses and part numbers that will change the initial engine/injection timing value*

Gasket part no.	Thickness		Change in pushrod travel at 19° BTDC	
	mm	in.	mm	in.
3020000 (Print-O-Seal)	0.36–0.51	0.014–0.020	0.09–0.13	0.0035–0.005
3020001	0.15–0.20	0.006–0.008	0.04–0.05	0.0015–0.002
3020002	0.36–0.51	0.014–0.020	0.09–0.13	0.0035–0.005
3020003	0.51–0.61	0.020–0.024	0.13–0.15	0.005–0.006
3020004	0.69–0.84	0.027–0.033	0.18–0.20	0.007–0.008

Source: Cummins Engine Company, Inc.

stationary. Cam keys on the NH/NT 855 engines are available in $\frac{3}{4}$-in. (19-mm) and 1-in. (25.4-mm) sizes, with the $\frac{3}{4}$-in. offset keys interchangeable with the 1-in. straight keys; however, $\frac{3}{4}$-in. straight keys cannot be interchanged for 1-in. offset keys. To retard injection timing, the top of the offset key *always* points in the direction of camshaft rotation. The greater the amount of key offset, the greater the degree of injection timing retardation. This rule can be applied to all Cummins engine models.

VALVE AND INJECTOR ADJUSTMENT

The term *tuneup* generally refers to the need to check and adjust the valve crossheads, the valve and injector clearance, as well as performing any minor repairs to the fuel injection system and other engine systems. Once the engine injection timing has been checked according to the description given earlier in this chapter, the basic tuneup checks and adjustments can be carried out. These adjustments should be performed when the engine is cold, which is considered to be at 140°F (60°C) or less, since temperature variations across cylinders can affect valve and injector clearances. If adjustment is checked during troubleshooting or between the specified 60,000-mile (96,558-km), 1500-hour, or 1-year service intervals, valve and injector adjustment should not be required. Valve and injector adjustments are listed on the engine CPL data plate.

NOTE   On NH/NT 855 engines, the injector is always set before the valve crossheads and the valve clearance. The exception to this procedure is on the L10 engine, where Cummins recommends that to compensate for rocker lever shaft deflection, all valves and valve crossheads be adjusted before adjusting any injectors.

Prior to 1971, NH and NT 855 model engines and small vees required what is known as a *torque setting method*. We will deal only with later-model engines conforming to the U.S. Federal Clean Air Act that use what is known as DIM (dial indicator method) of injector adjustment. Since the valve crosshead and valves can be adjusted on one cylinder while the injector is being set on another cylinder, prior to proceeding into the sequence for valve crosshead, valve, and injector adjustment, the engine cylinder numbering sequence should be known, as well as the ability not

only to recognize the VS (valve set) marks on the engine accessory drive pulley, but also to understand just what valves and injectors can be checked and adjusted at VS mark A, B, or C.

The accessory drive pulley VS marks are the most widely used reference markings now in use on Cummins engines and the ones that we shall refer to in this discussion; however, timing marks can also appear on the engine flywheel, and in some older-model engines, timing marks were also visible on the crankshaft pulley. The accessory drive pulley will rotate in a CW direction when viewed from the front of the engine, and the markings would be representative of a CW rotating engine with a firing order of 1–5–3–6–2–4.

Three VS marks appear on the accessory drive pulley—A, B, and C (see Figure 22-68)—with the respective injector and valves that can be adjusted for each mark shown in Table 22-7. When aligned with the stationary mark on the engine housing, the three letters A, B, and C on the accessory drive pulley indicate the following:

1. When A is aligned, pistons 1 and 6 are both 90° ATDC; however, one cylinder will be on its power stroke, while the other will be on its intake stroke.

2. When B is aligned, pistons 2 and 5 are both 90° ATDC; however, one cylinder will be on its power stroke, while the other will be on its intake stroke.

3. When C is aligned, pistons 3 and 4 are both 90° ATDC, again with one cylinder being on its power stroke, while the other is on its intake stroke.

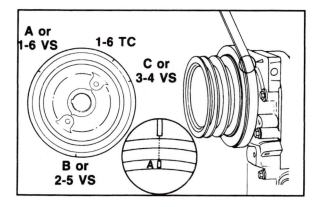

FIGURE 22–68 *Accessory drive pulley VS (valve set) markings and stationary pointer location on the engine gear case cover of a CW rotating NT-855 (14-L) engine. (Courtesy of Cummins Engine Company, Inc.)*

TABLE 22–7   Injector and valve adjustment sequence chart, NT engines[a]

Bar engine in direction of rotation	Pulley position	Pulley	
		Injector	Valve
Start	A	3	5
Advance to	B	6	3
Advance to	C	2	6
Advance to	A	4	2
Advance to	B	1	4
Advance to	C	5	1

Source: Cummins Engine Company, Inc.
[a] Firing order: 1–5–3–6–2–4.

NOTE   Early Cummins engines had the numbers 1 and 6 in place of the letter A, 2–5 for the letter B, and 3–4 for the letter C.

The reason the three VS marks are repeated twice in Table 22-7 is to allow you to set all valves and injectors in two complete revolutions of the engine (720°). One does not, of course, have to start with the A mark, but if you do, always check to see whether the valves are fully closed (clearance) on cylinder 5 or 2, since the ones with the clearance would be the ones to set in conjunction with its mated cylinder for the injector shown in the chart. If you start at another VS mark, simply follow through the engine firing order according to the arrangement shown in Table 22-7.

Engine Firing Orders

Both the injector and valve adjustments can be performed in two complete revolutions of the engine crankshaft, or 720°. Since it is always easier to perform these adjustments in the firing order of the engine, the following information will be helpful. Regardless of whether the engine is an inline L10 or NT 14-L model, or one of Cummins's earlier Vs, engine rotation is determined from the front. Cylinder numbers also start from the front, with cylinder 6 being closest to the flywheel. If you are working on a V-design engine model, the left and right banks are determined from the flywheel end. Typical firing orders are:

- NT 14-L and L10 CW rotating engines:1–5–3–6–2–4
- V6 CW rotating engine: 1–4–2–5–3–6
- V8 CW rotating engine: 1–5–4–8–6–3–7–2

Valve Crosshead Adjustment

Prior to adjusting the valve crossheads, the valve clearance, or the injector setting, refer to Figure 22-69 and after removing the rocker housing cover plates, torque the housing capscrews to 60 lb-ft (80 N · m) in the tightening sequence shown. In addition, always check that the injector clamp capscrew hold-down torque is 13 lb-ft (18 N · m) on NT 855 engines. The valve crosshead (bridge) is located on both sides of the injector (see the right-hand diagram in Figure 22-69. The function of the valve crosshead is to open two intake or two exhaust valves at the same time; therefore, there are two crossheads per cylinder. To operate correctly, the crosshead must sit square on its guide stud in the cylinder head. Crosshead adjustment should always be checked before attempting to set the intake or exhaust valve clearance. The adjustment procedure is similar for all models of Cummins engines.

1.   Refer to Table 22-7 and follow the VS timing mark procedure to determine which crosshead to check on what cylinder. This would be the cylinder on which the values would normally be set. Valves are fully closed.

2.   Loosen the crosshead screw locknut one full turn.

3.   Check that there is no bind between the crosshead and its guide.

4.   Apply light finger pressure on the center pallet surface of the crosshead, then gently run down the adjusting screw until it just touches the valve stem. Be careful that you do not go too far; otherwise, the crosshead will actually be raised from the other valve stem. If this occurs, it is possible for the crosshead to swing sideways on its guide during engine operation, causing possible damage as it jams between the valve spring retainer and stem.

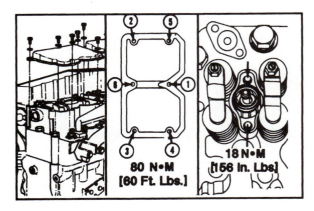

FIGURE 22–69   *Torquing sequence for rocker housing and injector hold-down clamp capscrews. (Courtesy of Cummins Engine Company, Inc.)*

5. When the locknut is tightened, it is very important that you do not allow the adjustment screw to move from its set position. To assist you with this procedure, a special Cummins torque wrench adapter ST-669 is availabe for NT 855 engines and shown in use on the right-hand side of Figure 22-70.

6. The torque on the crosshead locknut when using the ST-669 adapter, or when using a combination wrench and screwdriver, is shown in Table 22-8.

Valve Adjustment

To properly check and adjust the valve clearance, refer to Figure 22-68, which indicates what valves can be checked and adjusted in relation to a given VS (valve set) alignment mark between the accessory drive pulley and the cast-in stationary pointer on the engine gear cover. Remember, any time that you align one set of VS timing marks, the letter A (1–6), B (5–2), or C (3 or 4) represents two cylinders in a position corresponding to 90° ATDC.

We cannot adjust the valves or injector for either one of the coupled cylinders that correspond to the VS mark since the camshaft is not in its correct position. Reference to Table 22-7 indicates what valves and injector can be set relative to these VS positions. You must follow this guide; otherwise, valves and injectors will not be adjusted on the correct point of the camshaft lobe.

Only *one* particular cylinder's valves can be set when a VS alignment mark is opposite the stationary pointer, since only one cylinder will have its camshaft lobe in a position to ensure that both valves are closed. To check which cylinder this is, refer to Figure 22-71, which illustrates the three rocker arm levers for an NT 855 six-cylinder engine, with item 1 in the figure representing the *exhaust* rocker lever, item 2 being the *in-*

TABLE 22–8   *Crosshead locknut torque chart*

	Torque	
	lb-ft	**N · m**
Less Jacobs brake		
with adapter	25	35
without adapter	30	40
With Jacobs brake model 401 adjusting screw (exhaust crosshead only)		
With adapter	22	30
Without adapter	25	35

jector rocker lever, and item 3 being the *intake* valve rocker arm lever.

For example, with the A VS mark aligned, we would check both cylinders 5 and 2 to determine which can have the valve lash checked and set. The cylinder that has clearance between both the intake and exhaust valve rocker arm lever's and the crosshead pallet surface is the one that can have its valve clearances checked and set. The recommended valve lash is stamped on the *engine* CPL data plate, located on the side of the engine gear cover. For an NT 855 model engine, this specification is:

- Intake valve lash: 0.011 in. (0.028 mm)
- Exhaust valve lash: 0.023 in. (0.058 mm)

For an L10 model engine, this specification is:

- Intake valve lash: 0.014 in. (0.36 mm)
- Exhaust valve lash: 0.027 in. (0.69 mm)

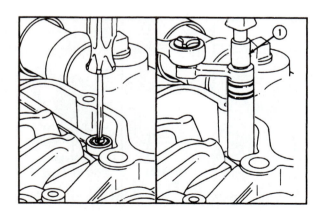

FIGURE 22–70 *Using ST-669 torque wrench adapter for tightening valve crosshead locknut. (Courtesy of Cummins Engine Company, Inc.)*

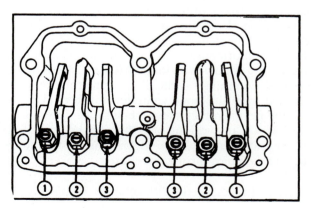

FIGURE 22–71 NT-855 engine rocker lever identification. *(Courtesy of Cummins Engine Company, Inc.)*

Two methods can be used when adjusting the valve clearance of an NT 855 engine:

1.   The *torque wrench method* has proven to be the better of the two, since not only does it eliminate the need for a feeler gauge, but consistently removes the variation found in acceptable degrees of feeler gauge tightness or looseness. With the rocker arm lever locknut loose, tighten the adjusting screw down to 6 in.-lb (0.68 N · m) using Cummins inch-pound torque wrench assembly, 3376592. Refer to Figure 22-72 and if you are using the ST-669 torque wrench adapter illustrated on the right-hand side of the diagram, tighten the locknut to 35 lb-ft (45 N · m). If you are using a screwdriver and combination wrench, tighten the locknut to 45 lb-ft (60 N · m), as shown on the left-hand side of the diagram.

2.   The *feeler gauge method*, if used, can be improved by employing a go/no go type of feeler gauge. For the intake valve clearance, a 0.010-in. (0.254-mm) go, 0.012-in. (0.30-mm) no-go gauge should be used, while for the exhaust valve clearance on the NT 855 engine, a 0.022-in. (0.55-mm) go, 0.024-in. (0.60-mm) no-go gauge can be used.

Types of Injectors

Prior to performing an injector adjustment on an engine, you must first determine whether the engine is equipped with a non-top stop injector or a top stop injector. When an engine is equipped with a top stop injector, the CPL data plate on the engine gear cover will have the words T. S. ZERO after the injector travel stamping, followed by the words INCH LASH. If the engine is fitted with a non-top stop injector, a setting dimension such as 0.187 in. (4.74 mm) may appear on the CPL data plate after the injector travel stamping. The CPL data plate should always be our guide when it is necessary to adjust injector settings, since each engine does not use the same injector setting, unless of course it is equipped with a top stop injector, which has a zero-lash setting. Since most Cummins PT engines are now equipped with the top stop injector assembly (see Figure 22-37), it is mandatory that the injector be adjusted for a given preload when it is removed from the engine as shown in Figure 22-49.

NT 855 Top Stop Injector Adjustment: On Engine

If the top stop injector has been adjusted while it is out of the engine by the preload method described using Cummins special tool shown in Figure 22-49, it is now necessary to check the injector for a zero-lash setting in the engine. If injector adjustment is required at the normal maintenance interval, it will also be adjusted for a zero-lash condition while in the engine.

Injector Adjustment: Top Stop

To check and set the top stop injector zero-lash condition, refer to Table 22-7, which indicates what injectors can be set when a given VS mark is aligned with the stationary pointer on the engine housing.

1.   Rotate the accessory drive pulley clockwise to place either VS mark A, B, or C opposite the stationary pointer.

2.   Check the coupled cylinders according to Table 22-7 to determine which cylinder is on its power stroke (valves closed and lash exists), then proceed to adjust the correct injector as per the chart.

3.   Loosen the injector rocker arm locknut, then turn the adjusting screw back down (CW) until all clearance is removed from the valve train components. This can be confirmed by rotating the injector push tube until you can no longer turn it.

4.   Tighten the injector adjusting screw one complete turn or 360° to ensure that the injector link assembly is seated, and that all oil has been squeezed from the contact surfaces. Note that this procedure does not bottom the plunger in the injector cup, but it does partially compress the top stop injector internal spring.

5.   Slowly loosen the injector adjusting screw as shown in Figure 22-73 until the injector spring retainer washer just touches the top stop screw. The injector rocker lever is now in an unloaded position.

6.   Using the small Cummins T-handled wrench 3376592, torque the injector adjusting screw to 5 to 6 in.-lb (0.56 to 0.68 N · m).

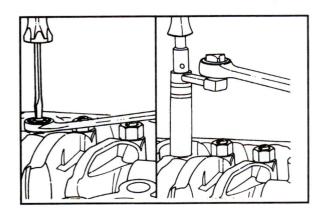

FIGURE 22–72 *Tightening valve rocker arm adjustment locknut. (Courtesy of Cummins Engine Company, Inc.)*

CAUTION   If this special tool is not available, you must use an inch-pound torque wrench with a scale that does not exceed 12 in.-lb (1.36 N · m)

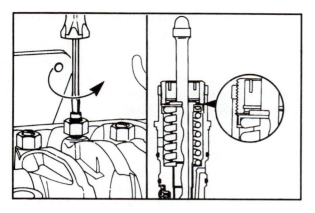

FIGURE 22–73 *Loosening injector adjusting screw until the injector spring retainer washer just touches the top stop screw. Final adjustment to top stop injector, 5 to 6 in.-lb torque. (Courtesy of Cummins Engine Company, Inc.)*

because if you overtorque the injector setting, increased stress on the injector train components and camshaft lobe will result. Other results are bent pushrods and higher exhaust particulate and smoke levels. In addition, misadjusted injector plunger travel will result in an increase in fuel consumption since travel distances and time contribute to effective metering at the injector fuel port in the PT fuel system. Therefore, when fuel is delivered late, the result is incomplete combustion, resulting in both carbon buildup internally within the engine and black exhaust smoke. Properly adjusted top stop injectors result in less frequent settings because it improves injector train and joint lubrication, thereby causing less wear on the camshaft and associated parts, as well as improving exhaust emission levels.

7.   To tighten the injector adjusting screw locknut after setting the screw to 5 to 6 in.-lb of torque without disturbing this important setting, use Cummins special torque wrench adapter ST-669, shown in Figure 22-72 on the right-hand side of the diagram, to lock the nut to 35 ft-lb (45 N · m) while holding onto the adjusting screw with the installed ST-669 screwdriver handle. If this tool is not available, use a combination wrench and screwdriver as shown on the left-hand side of Figure 22-72.

Non-Top Stop Injector Adjustment: Dial Indicator Method

On earlier-model engines equipped with other than top stop injectors, refer to the CPL data plate which is located on the engine front gear cover at the side. The CPL plate lists the actual injector setting height dimension for the engine. Remember that all top stop injectors are set to a zero-lash setting; however, all other injector types are set and adjusted with a dial indicator to the specification shown on the CPL data plate. We will use an NT 855 (14-L) engine as an example for the DIM (dial indicator method) of injector adjustment in this description. Cummins recommends that you use their injector setting kit 3375842, illustrated in Figure 22-74, which contains all the tools necessary for the injector setting.

Injector Setting

Before setting any injectors, refer to Figure 22-69 and check the torque on the rocker boxes and injector hold-down capscrews as shown.

1.   To set the injectors in sequence, refer to Table 22-7, which you used for checking and setting the valves.

2.   Rotate the engine over to place one of the accessory drive pulley VS marks in alignment with the stationary pointer cast into the gear cover (see Figure 22-68).

3.   With the rocker covers removed, and either the A, B, or C VS mark aligned with the pulley, determine from Table 22-7 which cylinder has clearance between the valve rocker arm and the crosshead, then set the recommended injector.

4.   Mount the dial indicator from the kit 3375842 onto the support bracket as shown in Figure 22-75 so that the dial indicator extension will rest on top of the injector plunger flange. This is more clearly shown within the small circle at the top left of Figure 22-75.

CAUTION   Be sure that the dial indicator extension completely clears the injector rocker lever when installed; otherwise, a false reading/setting will be obtained as well as possible damage to the dial indicator.

5.   Tighten the finger screw (1) as well as the hold-down capscrew (2) shown in Figure 22-75 to secure the dial gauge and bracket assembly in position.

6.   To preload the dial indicator prior to checking the injector setting, refer to Figure 22-75 and loosen off the clamp knob to the right of item 1 and below item 2. Carefully lower the dial indicator stem extension onto the injector plunger flange until the stem is fully compressed.

7.   Slowly allow the stem of the dial indicator to rise approximately 0.025 in. (0.63 mm), then tighten the lock knob securely. Double check that the dial in-

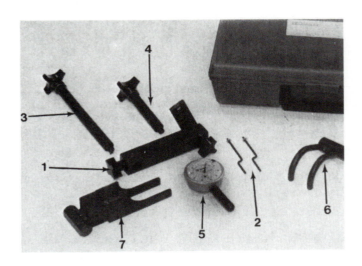

Engine Series: NT, V-903 (5-1/2 bore)

Ref. No.	Detail No.	Description	Qty.
1	*ST-1170-5111	Bracket Assembly	1
2	*ST-1170-5112	Indicator Tip Assembly	2
3	*ST-1170-5113	Long Mounting Shaft	1
4	*ST-1170-5114	Short Mounting Shaft	1
5	*3375006	Dial Indicator	1
6	ST-1193	Rocker Lever Actuator (NH)	1
7	3375790	Rocker Lever Actuator (V-903)	1
8	3377978	Instruction Card	1

*These items make up ST-1170 Assembly or can be ordered separately.

This kit is a combination of tools required to adjust injector travel.

FIGURE 22–74 Cummins NT engine injector setting kit 3375842. (Courtesy of Cummins Engine Company, Inc.)

FIGURE 22–75 Preloading the dial indicator for injector check/setting. (Courtesy of Cummins Engine Company, Inc.)

dicator extension is still in contact with the injector plunger flange.

8. Select the double hook-type tool ST-1193 from the tool kit and install it so that it rests over the injector rocker arm lever as shown in Figure 22-76.

9. With the box end of a combination wrench placed over the rocker lever actuating tool as shown in Figure 22-76, push back and forward on the injector plunger three or four times to ensure that all lube and fuel oil has been removed from the injector. On the last activation of the tool, allow the rocker lever to return gently to its upward position to prevent any disturbance at the dial indicator.

10. Pull the injector actuating tool ST-1193 as shown in Figure 22-76 toward the front of the rocker arm assembly, and while holding it in this position, rotate the bezel on the dial indicator to place the pointer needle at zero, and lock the bezel there with its screw.

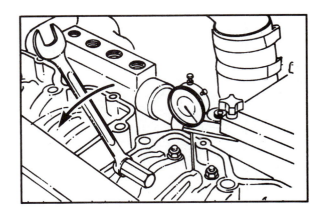

FIGURE 22–76 Using rocker lever actuator tool ST-1193 to depress the injector plunger. (Courtesy of Cummins Engine Company, Inc.)

11. Slowly and carefully release the ST-1193 injector rocker lever actuator and read the dimension on the dial gauge.

12. Compare this dimension with the specification on the CPL data plate for your particular engine, or with the following specifications:

a. *Big Cam engine:* setting should be 0.228 in. (5.79 mm)

b. *NTE Big Cam engine:* setting should be 0.225 in. (5.71 mm)

13. If the reading on the dial indicator is not within the recommended CPL data plate range, injector adjustment is necessary; therefore, proceed to steps 14 to 17. Allowable tolerance is 0.001 in. (0.0254 mm).

14. Loosen the injector rocker arm adjusting screw locknut located at the rear of the rocker arm, and rotate the adjusting screw either CW or CCW until the recommended dimension is obtained on the dial indicator.

15. Hold the adjusting screw with a screwdriver or the Cummins torque wrench adapter ST-669 as shown in Figure 22-77. Torque the screw to 35 lb-ft (45 N · m) if using the adapter, or to 45 lb-ft (60 N · m) when using a screwdriver and a combination wrench.

16. To check the injector setting after tightening the locknut, actuate the rocker lever again, several times, with tool ST-1193 (Figure 22-76). Allow the rocker lever to return slowly to its upward position, then place and hold it down so that the injector plunger is bottomed. The dial gauge should still be on the zero setting. If not, activate the rocker arm several more times. If the gauge is not on zero, rotate the bezel to zero the pointer needle with the rocker arm and injector plunger bottomed.

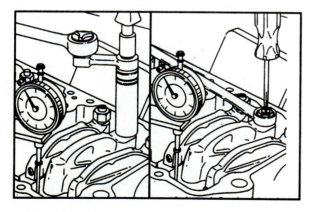

FIGURE 22-77 Tightening the injector adjusting screw using either an ST-669 torque wrench, or a screwdriver and combination wrench. (Courtesy of Cummins Engine Company, Inc.)

17. Slowly allow the rocker arm to return to the top of its stroke, and read the dial gauge to confirm that the setting is still according to specifications.

STEP TIMING CONTROL SYSTEM

The STC (step timing control) system introduced in 1986 is used on NH/NT 855 engines with the PT fuel system and is designed to allow the engine to operate in advanced injection timing during startup or light-load conditions, and return to normal injection timing for medium- or high-load conditions. The STC system operates similar to the earlier HVT system, the major difference being that the HVT system required electricity to operate the fuel pressure switch and the oil flow control valve, whereas the STC system uses a completely mechanical fuel rail pressure controlled oil control valve. The STC system performs the following functions:

During Advanced Timing

- Reduces cold-weather white smoke (hydrocarbons)
- Improves cold-weather idling characteristics
- Improves light-load fuel economy
- Reduces injector tip/cup carboning

During Normal Timing

- Increases engine durability
- Reduces nitrous oxide emissions

The STC system consists of a direct fuel-feed injector (see Figure 22-42) of the top stop design which uses two plunger springs and a hydraulic top stop tappet. The tappet assembly illustrated in Figure 22-78 is dependent on engine oil for its operation.

Advanced injection timing occurs when the STC tappet is filled with engine oil. This action lengthens the tappet in the same basic way as that for a gasoline engine hydraulic valve lifter, and therefore effectively increases the injector plunger length for each degree of rotation of the camshaft lobe. Simply put, this means that the injector plunger will be advanced in its effective stroke; therefore, fuel is pressurized and injected earlier than normal into the combustion chamber. This earlier start, or advancement of injection, will create higher-than-normal cylinder pressures and temperatures, with the result being that there will be less white smoke and improved engine performance. The STC tappet operation is similar to that used for the HVT tappet assembly. In the STC system during normal timing, no oil is allowed into the injector tappets; therefore, the tappet piston will collapse before the injector plunger starts to inject fuel because the injec-

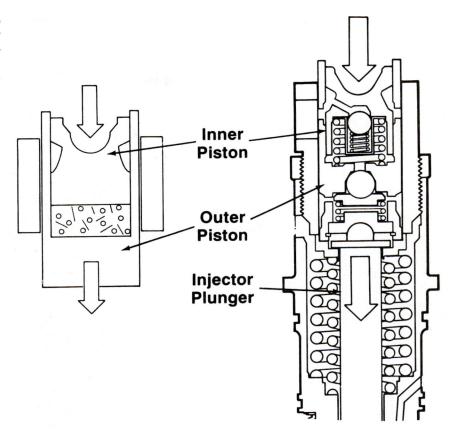

FIGURE 22–78 *STC (step timing control) top stop injector components. (Courtesy of Cummins Engine Company, Inc.)*

Inner Piston

Outer Piston

Injector Plunger

tor lobe profile on an STC engine camshaft is designed with a greater lift than a conventional engine camshaft.

During advanced camshaft timing, when the tappets are filled with pressurized engine oil, the start of injection will occur earlier, as the injector plunger is lifted sooner per degree of camshaft rotation by the longer tappet assembly (filled with oil). This action causes the plunger to bottom in the injector cup before the cam lobe obtains peak lift. The result of this action is that the added pressure on the tappet will unseat the internal load-cell check ball and permit oil to escape; therefore, the tappet collapses. In summation, in the STC system the tappet collapses before the plunger begins to move when in normal timing, but the tappet collapses after the plunger is finished moving (bottomed in the cup) when in the advanced timing mode of operation.

Tappet Assembly Oil Flow

When the injector cam follower roller is on the inner base circle of the engine camshaft, the injector plunger is at the top of its stroke/travel, and the metering orifice is uncovered inside the injector body to allow fuel to flow into the injector cup. As the injector follower rides up on the camshaft lobe (outer base circle), the metering orifice will close as the plunger descends, and the plunger will seat in the cup forcing fuel into the combustion chamber. During this same period, the drain port in the injector body is open to allow fuel to flow from the drain groove back to the fuel tank to carry heat away from the injector.

Figure 22-78 shows a sectional diagram of the STC tappet assembly. When fuel pump pressure is less than a predetermined value such as during startup and light loads, the system oil control valve is open to allow engine lube oil to flow to an oil manifold which supplies the STC injector tappets. When oil pressure exceeds approximately 10 psi (69 kPa), it moves the tappet inlet check ball off its seat, and oil flows between the inner and outer pistons of the tappet. As the injector cam rotates, the rocker arm will force the inner piston of the tappet down, causing oil pressure trapped below it to increase and force the outer piston (tappet) down as shown in Figure 22-79. This tappet movement also causes the injector plunger to move down. Therefore, any time that the tappet is filled with oil, the injector plunger will move down earlier, causing fuel injection timing to be "advanced." During advanced timing, oil is trapped

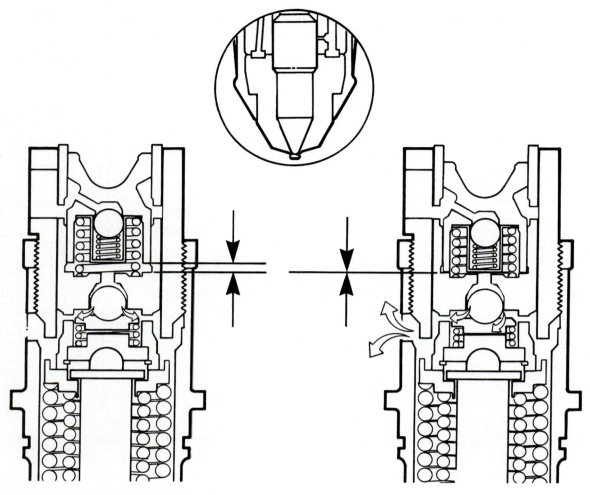

FIGURE 22–79 *STC top stop injector tappet assembly components during loaded and unloaded positions. (Courtesy of Cummins Engine Company, Inc.)*

in the tappet by the inlet check valve ball and the load cell check ball.

At the end of the injection cycle, injector force will increase the oil pressure inside the tappet to hold the injector plunger firmly seated in the cup. This causes the tappet oil pressure to rise to between 1100 and 1500 psi (7585 to 10,343 kPa), which unseats the load cell check ball (lower one in Figure 22-79) in the tappet, and oil drains through holes in the injector adapter and returns to the oil pan through drain passages in the cylinder head and engine block as shown in Figure 22-79. Meanwhile, with the continuing camshaft lift, the plunger makes contact with the socket and sleeve assembly (tappet) and maintains injector plunger seating force.

When the engine fuel pressure exceeds a predetermined value, the oil flow control valve is closed to prevent any pressurized engine lube oil from entering

the tappet and altering the timing. During this condition, static oil will remain in the oil supply manifold and oil lines without affecting operation of the STC tappets. With this oil pressure being lower than 10 psi (69 kPa), no STC can occur. Since no oil is trapped within the tappets inner and outer pistons, injection timing returns to a "normal" mode. With tappet oil removed, the camshaft lift must be greater to force the tappet's inner piston against the outer piston, which results in a later start to fuel injection for both an increase in engine durability and the reduction of nitrous oxide emissions.

NTCC CARB (California Air Resources Board) Engines
Starting with the 1988 model year, all 14-L (55-in^3) highway truck engines were built to conform to CARB emissions limits regardless of the U.S. state or Cana-

dian province in which they will be used. Therefore, 1988 and later engines use only one STC (step timing control) system, resulting in all NTC 365-, 400-, and 444-hp engines using STC, while NTC 315- and 350-hp engines employ fixed timing systems. This arrangement has reduced the engine CPL (control parts list) to only four different CPLs for 14-L engines. All CARB Big Cam III MVT (mechanical variable timing) models were available only until 1988, when they were superseded by the STC system. For your information, MVT was used only on the Formula 400 (BC III), the NTCC-350, the Formula 350, and NTCC-315 Power Torque, the Formula 315, the NTCC-300, and the Formula 300 engines, meeting CARB emissions levels prior to 1988. Prior to 1988, STC was used on the NTC-444, the NTC-400, Formula 400, NTC-365, and Formula 365 for 49-state-certified engines as well as on CARB NTCC-444, NTC-400, and NTC-365 models. Operating characteristics for both valves are as listed in Table 22-9.

The reason for the closer switching points in the NTCC valve is related to the differences in the NTCC fuel pump and injectors, in order to meet engine performance standards. The STC oil control valve assembly Figure 22-80 utilizes a "class fit" (mated plunger and barrel assembly) AFC plunger which allows pressurized engine oil flow to the injector tappets until the PT fuel pressure exceeds those listed above. This would be at 370 kPa (53 psi) on NTC engines, and at 170 kPa (25 psi) on NTCC engines. When these pressures are reached, the plunger will shift and block off the internal oil flow passage, resulting in the engine moving into a normal timing mode of operation as shown in Figure 22-81. When the fuel pressure decreases to the set point of 170 kPa (25 psi) for NTC engines, or to 140 kPa (20 psi) for NTCC engines, the STC plunger spring forces the oil valve back to open the oil flow passage, and pressurized engine oil again flows to the injector tappets, placing the engine back into the advanced timing mode of operation as shown in Figure 22-81.

As a safety feature, the STC oil control valve is designed to ensure that normal timing is "locked in" any time that the engine C brake is operating. Figure 22-82 shows the arrangement used to maintain normal engine timing when the C brake is engaged. A sensing line from the brake housing to the STC oil control valve permits oil pressure to act upon the valve diaphragm. A minimum oil pressure of 40 kPa (6 psi) will shift the plunger into the normal timing position, thereby blocking off any oil flow to the injector tappets. This feature is necessary to allow C brake operation while removing any undue stress from the valve train and camshaft mechanism. Therefore, in the STC system, when injector fuel rail pressure is low, injector timing will be advanced, while during operating conditions that allow medium to high rail pressure, or C brake engagement, the injector timing will be placed into a normal mode of operation.

Setting the STC Overhead

Since its introduction in 1986, the setting procedure for the PT-D STC injector has been changed to a camshaft OBC (outer base circle) method, where the crush of the injector plunger to cup is set by tightening the injector rocker lever adjusting screw to a prescribed in.-lb (N · m) torque value. The early method required that the technician use a special STC tappet clearance tool; however, this procedure resulted in engine performance degradation as internal and external wear caused a loss of injector plunger to cup crush, which led to plunger carboning, decreased injector fuel flow, and more retarded injection timing. Therefore, this procedure is no longer valid.

Cummins recommends that valves and injectors be adjusted every 96,000 km (60,000 miles), 1500 hours, or once a year (whichever comes first) on engines equipped with PTD-STC injectors. The current adjustment procedure requires setting both the valves and injectors of N14 engines on the camshaft OBC (outer base circle).

TABLE 22–9   Fuel rail pressure required to cause a timing shift

Model	Part number	Shifts into normal timing as rail psi increases		Shifts into advanced timing as rail psi decreases		Rail psi drain line	Plunger spring part number
		kPa	psi	kPa	psi		
NTC	3056564	370	53	170	25	Yes	3041069
NTCC	3056565	170	25	140	20	No	3042420

FIGURE 22–80 External view of the STC control valve assembly. (Courtesy of Cummins Engine Company, Inc.)

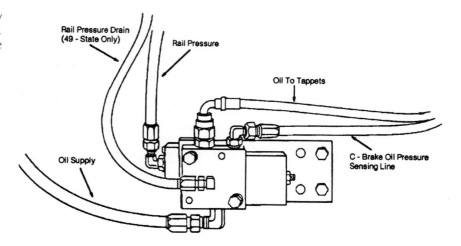

NOTE   Do not attempt to use the OBC method on early-model L10 STC engines, since doing so will result in engine damage.

The procedure required for N14 engines follows.

1.   Refer to Figure 22-68 which illustrates the accessory drive pulley VS (valve set) timing marks. When any of these VS marks are aligned with the stationary pointer on the engine front cover, the coupled pistons are actually 90° ATDC. One piston would be on its power stroke, while the other would be on its intake stroke.

2.   Table 22-10 shows the position at which the accessory drive pulley should be placed to set both the injector and valves for a given cylinder.

3.   To determine what cylinder valves and injector can be set, let's assume that the A mark is aligned. Since the engine is a four-stroke-cycle model, two complete revolutions of the crankshaft are required to set and adjust all valves and injectors. Manually grasp the intake and exhaust valve rocker arms for both cylinders 1 and 6. Whatever rocker arms are loose when you move them confirms that this cylinder is on its power stroke and therefore in the OBC camshaft

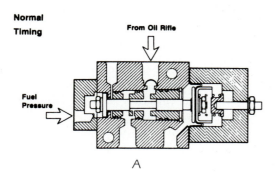

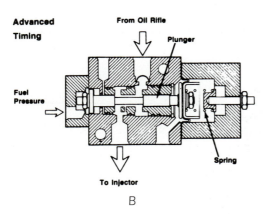

FIGURE 22–81 (A) STC oil control valve NORMAL timing position; (B) STC oil control valve ADVANCED timing position. (Courtesy of Cummins Engine Company, Inc.)

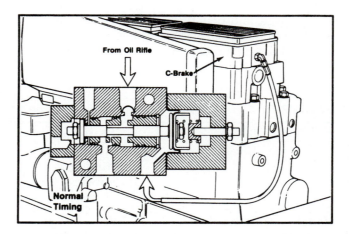

FIGURE 22–82 STC oil control valve position during engine C-brake (compression) operation. (Courtesy of Cummins Engine Company, Inc.)

TABLE 22–10 Outer base circle (OBC) injector and valve adjustment sequence[a]

Bar engine in direction of rotation	Pulley position	Set cylinder Injector	Valve
Start	A	1	1
Advance to	B	5	5
Advance to	C	3	3
Advance to	A	6	6
Advance to	B	2	2
Advance to	C	4	4

[a]Firing order: 1–5–3–6–2–4.

position. Prepare to adjust both the injector and valves for this cylinder. Let's assume that it is No. 6.

SERVICE TIP If the engine or cylinder heads have been removed for overhaul, the injector and valve adjusting screws will be loose. Therefore, the easiest method to determine which cylinder is on its power stroke is to watch the intake and exhaust valve push tubes carefully (or lightly place two fingers on the top of each tube). When both the intake and exhaust valve push tubes move downward, this confirms that

the valves are closed and that the piston is on its power stroke. You can also look visually to see if both push tubes are level when viewed from the side.

4. Refer to Table 22-11, which lists the engine model, engine CPL number, and the specifications for both the injector and valve adjustments, as well as for the C-brake. Let's assume that the CPL stamped on the CPL plate on the side of the engine front timing cover indicates a CPL No. 821. We will therefore set the No. 6 STC injector to 105 in.-lb (12 N · m).

5. Select an accurate inch-pound (N · m) torque wrench and loosen the No. 6 injector rocker arm locknut similar to that shown in Figure 22-73.

NOTE The injector adjusting screw may be a slotted type on non-C-brake engines, or employ a hex-head screw on C-brake engines. Therefore, obtain the correct type of torque wrench socket prior to adjustment.

6. Use a screwdriver and lightly run the injector adjusting screw down until a slight step up in effort is felt. Do this three or four times to settle down the linkage and to squeeze any oil out. Then back the screw off until it is loose.

TABLE 22–11 Valve adjustment specifications

Engine model	Engine CPL	Injector adjusting screw torque in.-lb	N · m	Intake valve lash	Exhaust valve lash	C-brake lash
NBCIV	621.633, 903, 904, 805	105	12	0.014	0.027	0.016
86BCIV	910, 827, 1185, 1188, 1210, 1211, 1256, 1280,	90	10	0.014	0.027	0.016
N14	1374, 1380, 1395, 1405, 1507	125	14	0.014	0.027	0.023

7. Refer to Figure 22-83 and place the torque wrench into position over the injector adjusting screw. Carefully tighten the injector adjusting screw until the torque wrench clicks, or if using a dial-type wrench, watch the torque wrench. Tighten the screw until 105 in.-lb (12 N · m) is obtained.

8. Hold the adjusting screw with either tooling method shown in Figure 22-77. Tighten the locknut to 54 N · m (40 lb-ft) on New Big Cam IV engines, or to 68 N · m (50 lb-ft) on 1988 Big Cam IVs.

9. Proceed to set the intake and exhaust valves on the same cylinder as that for the injector just completed. Refer to Table 22-11 for the correct valve set clearance. Torque the valve rocker arm locknuts to the same spec as for the injector described in step 8.

10. If the engine is equipped with a C-brake, check and adjust the slave piston to exhaust valve crosshead with the VS pulley mark in the same position as that used for the valve adjustment. Either the IBC shown in Table 22-7 can be followed or the OBC method shown in Table 22-10. The C-brake clearance can be found on the C-brake data plate or Jacobs brake label. On Big Cam 14-L engine models, this is usually 0.46 mm (0.018 in.). Use either a feeler gauge or a dial indicator for this procedure.

CUMMINS ELECTRONICS

SPECIAL NOTE The information contained in this section dealing with the Cummins Celect

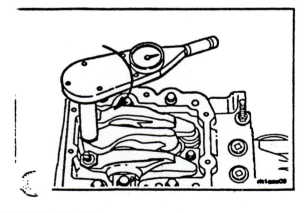

FIGURE 22–83 Torquing injector rocker-arm lock nut. (Courtesy of Cummins Engine Company, Inc.)

(Cummins Electronics) system is designed to provide an overview of system operation and the special diagnostic tools that can be used to troubleshoot the system. It is *not* intended to supplant the excellent printed literature and audiovisual materials readily available from Cummins. If you intend to perform service diagnostics on Cummins Celect-equipped engines such as the L10, M11 and N14, you should acquire the following service publications from your local Cummins dealer: Bulletin 3810389, *Celect Fault Code Manual*; Bulletin 3810389, *Celect Fault Code Manual*; Bulletin 3810469, *Troubleshooting and Repair Manual, CELECT System, N14 Engines* (or order for an L10 or M11 engine); *Celect Wiring Diagram* (plasticized); and the engine service manual for your engine model.

Cummins Engine Company first ventured into engine electronics in the 1980s with its Pace and PT/Pacer systems. Basically those had an add-on cruise control system, plus an engine monitoring system that could be used with Cummins mechanically controlled PT (pressure–time) fuel system on its 444-hp (331-kW) 855 in^3 (14-L) six-cylinder heavy-duty truck engines.

In late 1988, Cummins released its first-generation electronically controlled injection system, known as ECI (electronically controlled injection). This was followed in April 1990 by the current Celect (Cummins Electronics) system, which was released on the L10, and in mid-1990 on the N14 series of on-highway truck engines. This system is also now in use on the M11 which will supersede the L10, as well as on the larger industrial, marine, and off-highway K series engines. Figure 22-84 is a schematic of the Celect system as applied to a six-cylinder engine configuration.

Celect Fuel System Flow

The fuel pump shown in Figure 22-84 is driven from the rear of the air compressor on an N14 engine. Refer to Figure 22-85 to see more clearly the location of the fuel system components. The fuel pump is a gear type and operates similarly to the gear transfer pump that was used on earlier PT (pressure–time) fuel systems. Figure 22-86 is a cross-sectional view of the fuel pump and the flow through the housing, and Figure 22-86 illustrates the basic fuel flow into and through the electronically controlled injector. Fuel is drawn from the tank by the pump where it can pass through a primary fuel filter or fuel/water separator filter assembly before it flows into and through a cooler plate bolted to

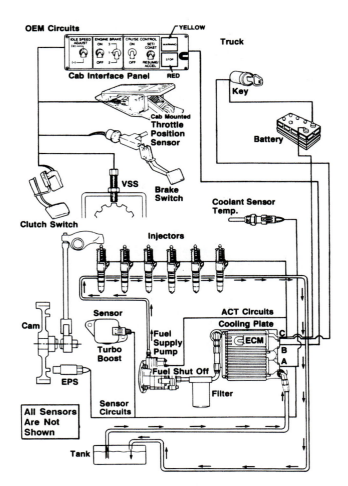

FIGURE 22–84 *Celect (Cummins electronics) system layout and basic fuel flow path for a six-cylinder heavy-duty diesel engine. (Courtesy of Cummins Engine Company, Inc.)*

fuel systems. When the ignition key is switched on, this solenoid is energized. Turning the key switch off deenergizes the fuel pump solenoid to allow engine shutdown by blocking further fuel flow out of the pump assembly.

CAUTION The electric fuel shutoff solenoid located on top of the gear type fuel transfer pump outlet shown in Figure 22-86 is supplied with voltage from the ECM supply circuit. The rating for the ECM (electronic control module) is either 12 or 24 V. The technician should *never* supply a voltage to this solenoid in excess of the ECM rating on either the CELECT or CELECT Plus systems. Cummins tests have shown that voltages as low as 1 to 2 V higher than the rating can cause extensive damage to the internal components of the ECM. These higher voltage ratings cause current to be sent into the ECM on pin 16 of actuator connector C (see Figure 22-97) to destroy the electronics.

Fuel from the gear pump flows into the rear of the cylinder head on N14 engines, where a common rail allows all injectors to receive fuel through the cast manifold within the cylinder head. The pump is designed to circulate an excess amount of fuel to and through the injectors, so that fuel not used for injection purposes is used to cool and lubricate the internal components, as well as to purge any air from the fuel system and injectors. Fuel from the inlet manifold enters the injector as shown in Figure 22-86 at the left center of the body through a small circular filter screen similar to that for the PT injector systems. Fuel is then directed up to and around a small poppet valve. This poppet valve is electrically controlled by a signal from the ECM. Injection can occur only when this PWM signal closes this small internal poppet valve as the injector pushrod is activating the injector rocker arm assembly. Rocker arm motion is required to raise the trapped fuel pressure within the injector body to a high enough level to lift the needle valve from its seat in the spray tip (cup). Therefore, the start of injection, the quantity of fuel metered, and the duration of injection are electronically controlled by the ECM.

The injector is mechanically operated by a rocker arm and pushrod assembly. The injector contains three O-rings for fuel sealing purposes and it is held in the cylinder head by use of a hold-down clamp and bolt.

the rear of the ECM assembly. The purpose of directing fuel through the cooling plate is to ensure that the electronics package components are maintained at an acceptable operating temperature level during engine operation. Fuel then flows through a filter and on to the inlet side of the gear transfer pump. The system pressure and flow rate will vary proportionally to engine speed; therefore, the maximum system operating pressure is 150 psi (1034 kPa) at rated engine speed. Within the fuel pump, a spring-loaded bypass valve opens to bypass fuel back to the suction side of the pump to regulate fuel pressure. Fuel under pressure is directed through the electric solenoid on top of the fuel pump, which is similar to that used in the earlier PT

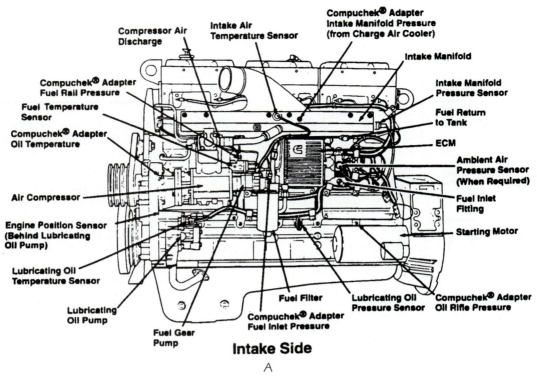

Intake Side

A

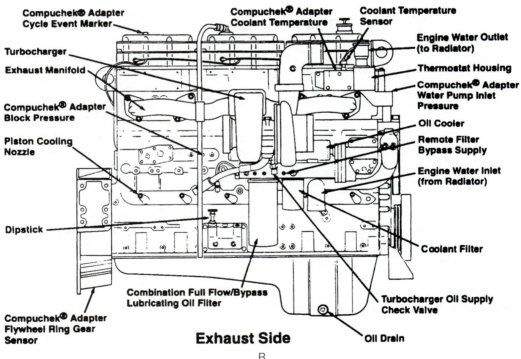

Exhaust Side

B

FIGURE 22–85 *Intake and exhaust side views, N14 Celect engine. (Courtesy of Cummins Engine Co., Inc.)*

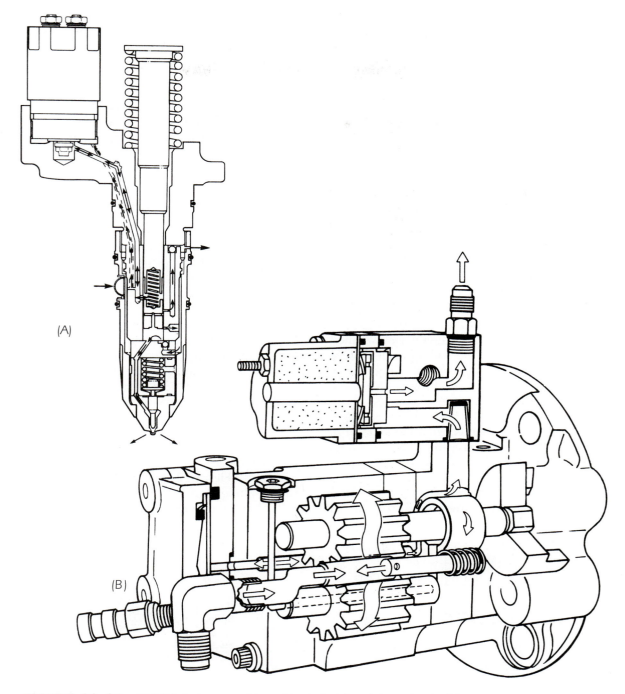

FIGURE 22–86 (A) ECI injector assembly and basic fuel flow into and out of the body; (B) Celect engine gear fuel supply pump. (Courtesy of Cummins Engine Company, Inc.)

The injector requires rocker arm actuation of the plunger to create the high fuel pressures necessary for injection purposes. To control both the start of injection timing and the quantity of fuel metered, the ECM sends out a PWM (pulse-width-modulated) electrical signal to each injector. The initial PWM signal determines the start of the injection, while the duration of this signal determines the start of the injection, while the duration of this signal determines how long the injector can effectively continue to spray fuel into the combustion chamber as the plunger is forced down by the rocker arm assembly. A shorter PWM signal means that the effective stroke of the injector plunger will be decreased, while a longer PWM signal means that the effective stroke will be increased. Simply put, this means that the longer the duration of the PWM signal, the greater the amount of metered fuel that will be delivered to the combustion chamber. The greater the fuel rate, the greater will be the developed horsepower. The start of injection and the duration of the PWM signal is determined by the ECM based on the various input sensor signals and the preprogrammed PROM information within the ECM. Each PROM is designed for a specific engine/truck combination based on the desired horsepower setting and rpm, the tire size, and gear ratios used in the vehicle.

Figure 22-87 illustrates the basic design arrangement of the ECI injector assembly in schematic form. Contained within the injector is a timing plunger, a return spring, and an injector control valve, which is the key to the operation, since this electrically operated valve receives an energize/deenergize voltage control signal from the ECM, which determines the actual start of injection. The length of time that this solenoid is energized determines the quantity of metered fuel which will actually be injected to the combustion chamber. Also within the injector body is a metering spill port which must be closed to allow injection, a metering check valve, fuel supply passages, the closed nozzle subassembly, the metering piston, the bias spring, and the spill-timing port. When the injector receives a signal from the ECM, the small injector control valve will close and the metering phase begins while the metering piston and timing plunger are bottomed in the injector.

Study Figure 22-87 first so that you can associate the differences between the ECI injector and the standard PTD injector. Once you know these differences, it will make it easier for you to understand the operation of the ECI unit since pushrod and rocker arm actuation are still necessary to create the high pressures necessary for injection purposes.

Simplified ECI Operation

Figure 22-88 illustrates in a much more simplified version the major operating components required to effectively meter and time the fuel delivery rate to the combustion chamber. The same components that were shown earlier in Figure 22-87 are laid out slightly different in this diagram; however, this simplified diagram will allow you to better understand the system's operation. The following sequence of events occur as described:

1. In Figure 22-88, both the metering piston and timing plunger are bottomed in the injector. Note carefully that the injector solenoid-operated control valve

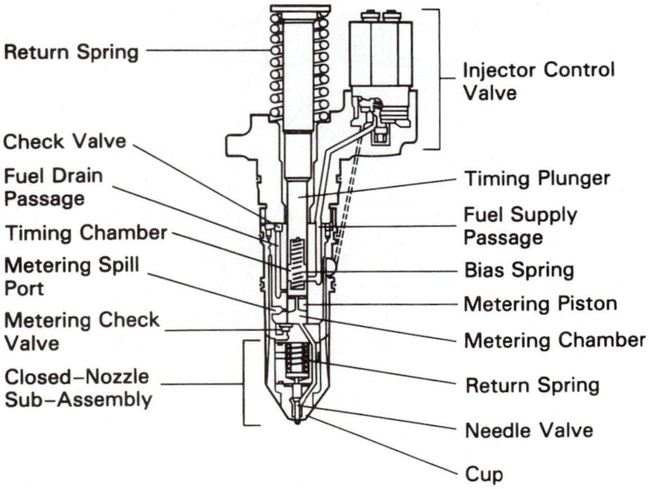

Return Spring
Check Valve
Fuel Drain Passage
Timing Chamber
Metering Spill Port
Metering Check Valve
Closed-Nozzle Sub-Assembly

Injector Control Valve
Timing Plunger
Fuel Supply Passage
Bias Spring
Metering Piston
Metering Chamber
Return Spring
Needle Valve
Cup

FIGURE 22-87 *Basic component identification of an ECI injector assembly. (Courtesy of Cummins Engine Company, Inc.)*

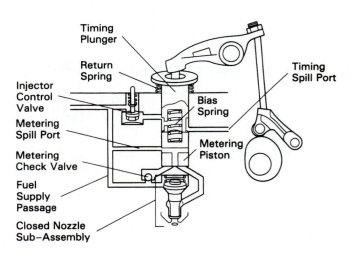

FIGURE 22-88 *Basic gear train and major operating parts of an ECI injector assembly. (Courtesy of Cummins Engine Company, Inc.)*

is held closed by the action of a small spring. This is the *start* of the metering action.

2. As the engine camshaft rotates, the injector pushrod cam follower roller will ride down the cam ramp, thereby allowing the rocker arm and pushrod to be forced up and down by the energy of the timing plunger return spring as shown in Figure 22-89. Fuel at gear pump pressure of approximately 150 psi (1034 kPa) can now flow into the fuel supply passage and unseat the small lower check valve. This action allows the metering chamber to be charged with pressurized fuel as long as the timing plunger is being pulled upward by the force of the large external return spring. This fuel pressure acting on the bottom of the metering piston forces it to maintain contact with the timing plunger within the bore of the injector body.

3. Metering ends when the ECM energizes the injector control valve, thereby causing it to open. Pressurized fuel can now flow through the open injector control valve into the upper timing chamber, which will effectively stop any further upward travel of the metering piston. This action is shown in Figure 22-90. To ensure that the metering piston remains stationary, the small bias spring in the timing chamber holds it stationary while the timing plunger continues to move upward due to camshaft rotation. The fuel and bias spring forces acting on the metering piston will ensure that adequate fuel pressure is maintained below the piston to keep the small lower metering check ball (valve) closed. This sequence of events will allow a precisely metered quantity of fuel to be trapped in the metering chamber. Note that this quantity of trapped fuel is what will actually be injected into the combustion chamber.

4. As long as the timing plunger moves upward

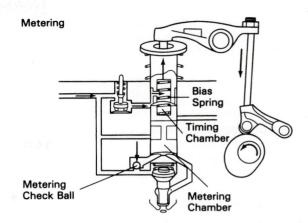

FIGURE 22–90 *End of metering; ECM energizes the injector control valve, causing it to open. (Courtesy of Cummins Engine Company, Inc.)*

due to the rotating camshaft lobe action and the force of the external return spring on the ECI injector, the upper timing chamber will continue to fill with pressurized fuel.

5. When the engine camshaft lobe starts to lift the injector cam follower roller, the pushrod moves up and the rocker arm reverses this motion to push the timing plunger downward. On the initial downward movement the injector control valve remains open and fuel flows from the timing chamber and through the control valve to the fuel supply passage. In other words, a small amount of fuel spills from the timing chamber. Figure 22-91 illustrates the action. When the ECM closes the control valve, fuel is trapped in the timing chamber; this fuel will act as a solid hydraulic link between the timing plunger and metering piston; therefore, the metering piston is forced to move down-

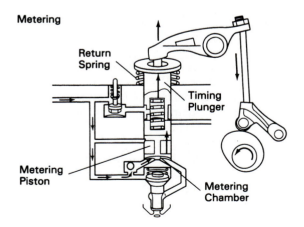

FIGURE 22–89 *Initial engine camshaft rotation to provide charging of the ECI injector with pressurized fuel. (Courtesy of Cummins Engine Company, Inc.)*

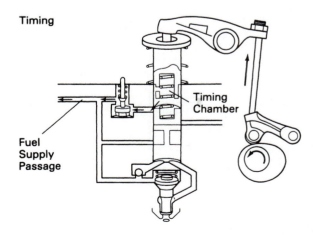

FIGURE 22–91 *ECI injector timing action. (Courtesy of Cummins Engine Company, Inc.)*

ward with the descending timing plunger being moved by rocker arm action. The downward movement of the timing plunger therefore causes a rapid increase in the trapped fuel within the metering chamber. At approximately 5000 psi (34,475 kPa) the tapered needle valve in the tip of the injector will be lifted up against the force of its return spring and injection begins.

6. Injection will continue until the spill passage of the downward-moving metering piston uncovers the spill port as shown in Figure 22-92. Fuel pressure within the metering chamber is lost and the needle valve will be forced back on its seat by its return spring. This in effect terminates injection. Immediately after the metering spill port has been uncovered, the upper edge of the metering piston also passes the timing spill port (Figure 22-93) to allow fuel within the upper timing chamber to be spilled back to the fuel drain as the timing plunger completes its downward movement. The injection cycle has now been completed.

You can now appreciate that the start of injection is controlled by the ECM closing the small injector control valve. The point in the compression-cycle when the control valve closes thereby varies the actual start of injection timing. Opening of the small injector control valve terminates metering and therefore controls just how much fuel will be trapped and injected. In this manner the ECI system through ECM action allows the engine power to be closely tailored to changing demands. Both fuel economy and exhaust emission can be improved substantially.

ECM Connectors

The ECM has three wire harnesses plugged into it to control the Celect system. Figure 22-94 illustrates these three individual wire harnesses:

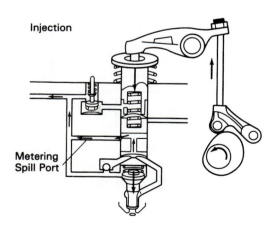

FIGURE 22–92 *Start of injection; injection ends when the metering spill port is opened. (Courtesy of Cummins Engine Company, Inc.)*

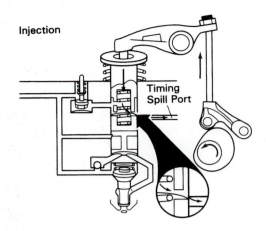

FIGURE 22–93 *Spilling fuel from the timing port after injection ends. (Courtesy of Cummins Engine Company, Inc.)*

1. The sensor harness identified as A receives electrical signals from all of the engine-mounted sensors, which are shown in Figure 22-85. The sensors tell the ECM the current state of the engine operation regarding throttle position, air intake manifold temperature, ambient pressure, turbocharger boost temperature, engine piston position from a sensor located to monitor a pin attached to the engine camshaft gear, engine coolant and oil temperature, and oil pressure. Some engines are equipped with a fuel pressure and fuel temperature sensor.

2. The OEM (original equipment manufacturer such as a truck builder) harness identified as item B is wired to all of the vehicle instrument panel control switches. These include the cruise control switch and the vehicle speed sensor which monitors the transmission output shaft rpm, an instant readout of fuel consumption, engine compression brake controls, and the cab interface panel. This harness is not supplied by Cummins but by the truck or equipment manufacturer.

3. The actuator harness identified as item C controls the injector solenoids.

The three ECM harness connectors cannot be inadvertently installed into the wrong position. This is ensured by the fact that each connector has a different *key design feature* as illustrated in Figure 22-94 so that each connector is readily identifiable by the letter A, B, or C. Note also that each connector pin is identified by a number that can be traced back through the system wiring diagram. Figure 22-95A illustrates the wires that are connected to the oil temperature sensor ECM connector A. This example shows wires 3 and 6. If this sensor and wires were operating outside a designed limit, the ECM would log a fault code 215 (SAE-PID =

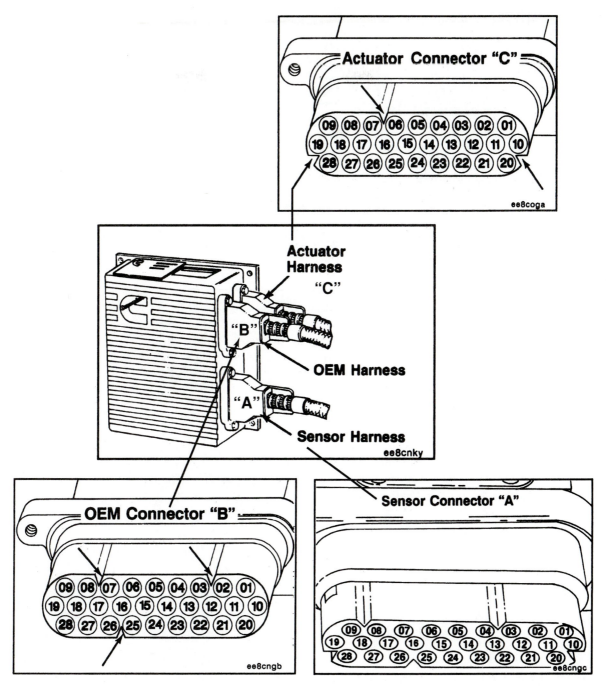

FIGURE 22–94 *Location and identification of the three main ECM wire harness connections and pin numbers of the Celect (non-Plus) system. (Courtesy of Cummins Engine Company, Inc.)*

parameter identifier 175, and FMI = failure mode identifier 1).

Figure 22-95B illustrates the OEM-ECM connector B. This example shows wires 17 and 26, which are the two wires connected to the engine tachometer. Figure 22-95C illustrates the ECM actuator harness C. This example shows how the battery is connected into the

system, some of the fuses used, and some of the typical multimeter readings that might be obtained when checking the system. By using these wiring diagrams and a *breakout box* similar to that shown for the DDEC system in Figure 21-59, or by using special pin-out jumper wires inserted into specific numbered connector holes, a multimeter can be employed to check any

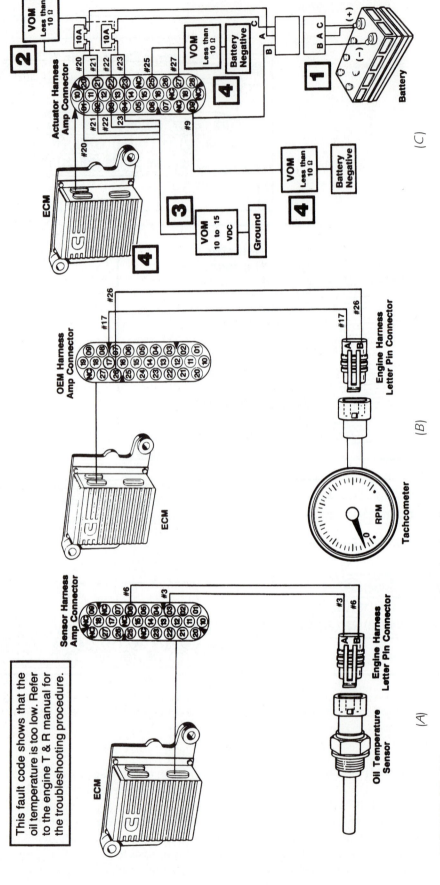

FIGURE 22-95 (A) Sensor harness example showing the oil temperature sensor wiring—fault code 215 (PID 175, FMI 1); (B) OEM wiring harness connection showing the wiring to the electronic engine tachometer—fault code 234 (PID 190, FMI 0); (C) actuator harness connector illustrating typical wire connections—fault code 434 (SID 251, FMI 4). (Courtesy of Cummins Engine Company, Inc.)

wire system for a voltage or resistance value. Then compare the values to Cummins' specs.

Sensors

The sensors used on Celect engine models vary in physical shape based on the year of manufacture of the engine. The 1991 model L10 and N14 engines employed a square flange mount design sensor, which can be seen in Figure 22-85. In June 1993, the L10 and M11 entered production with threaded pressure sensors for oil, turbo boost, and ambient air temperature. The N14 engines implemented the same sensor change in July 1993. These threaded pressure sensors have the same internal components as the flange mount design but in a different shell. This sensor shape change did not require a change to the sensor harness on the L10 engine models, but on the N14 engines the oil pressure sensor was relocated to the oil rifle (gallery), which created the need for a new sensor harness. In addition, the ambient air pressure sensor was relocated to the rear of the ECM. Note that it is not necessary to convert the remaining sensor(s) to the threaded design in these engine models. Cummins does offer, however, a threaded sensor kit to update an earlier engine model from the flange to the threaded design.

Both the M11 and N14 1994 engine models entered production with the threaded pressure sensor design. Note that the flange mount design must *not* be installed on a 1994 model M11 or N14 engine. In the 1994 engines, the threaded turbo boost sensor is a higher set unit, ranging from 0 to 50 psi (0 to 348 kPa), whereas the earlier flange model ranged from 0 to 32 psi (0 to 222 kPa). *Do not* interchange the 32-psi sensor with the 50-psi model. The 1994 model has a unique round wire harness instead of the oval shape of the 1991 model.

Celect Plus

To many people the word *electronics* simply encompasses household conveniences and various forms of entertainment. In the trucking industry, however, the word takes on a whole new meaning. Where Cummins products are concerned, the catch phrase is *Celect Plus*. The C in *Celect* stands for "Cummins," the "elect" stands for "electronics," and the "Plus" means that you get everything that you need plus more.

Behind the Celect Plus name tag the engines have been vastly improved.

- *More responsive*. At any speed, step on the throttle and the high-horsepower engine answers immediately.
- *Increased load starting*. With higher clutch engage-

ment torque, you'll notice a lot more "pull" the instant you let out the clutch.
- *Improved high-speed performance*. This added power is something that heavy haulers and on/off-road truckers really appreciate.
- The CELECT Plus Advanced Electronic Control Module (ECM) provides enhanced customer features and improved engine controls.
- *Higher fuel efficiency*. With more advanced electronic engine controls and hardware improvements, these high-horsepower engines deliver more miles per gallon than do competitive products.
- *Proven durability*. Based on the performance of over 50,000 high-horsepower engines already on the road, this engine is setting new standards for durability.
- *Higher resale value*. An outstanding reputation for long life-to-overhaul, along with easy uprating capability to higher horsepower means maximum resale value.
- *Improved cold startability*. Celect Plus monitors engine temperature, which allows timing adjustments during cold conditions.
- *Engine warm-up protection*. This feature keeps you from seriously damaging your engine by not allowing it to run at high rpm levels until it is ready.

Under the Celect Plus umbrella, Cummins has developed many features and parameters that make the driving experience more enjoyable. Some of these features are:

- *Road speed control*. This feature lets you set the maximum road speed, which limits vehicle top speed and increased fuel efficiency.
- *Gear-down protection*. For more efficiency, this feature encourages driving in top gear by setting a lower speed limit in the lower gears.
- *Idle shutdown*. This allows you to set a time between 3 and 60 minutes, that the engine will shut off automatically if there is no driver activity.
- *Cruise control*. This is an automotive cruise control, so it delivers maximum convenience and reduces driver fatigue.
- *Cruise control auto resume*. This makes driving easier because the cruise control does not need to be reset after a gear change.
- *Automatic engine brake with cruise control*. Celect Plus can be programmed to activate engine brakes at speeds above the set cruise speed.

Celect Plus also has much to offer in the management area. From diagnostics to trip reports, Celect Plus gives you a list of comprehensive standard features.

- *Trip information.* This feature gives you access to vital operational data. Celect Plus provides information about how an engine is being operated under various conditions such as idling, PTO, and when pulling a load (Figure 22-96). You can use the in-depth information about vehicle operation, including areas such as fuel, braking, and shifting, to improve your productivity and efficiency. You can access this information through a variety of Cummins electronic products and download directly to a PC.

- *Engine protection system.* This system automatically derates an engine whenever conditions exceed acceptable preset limits.

- *Maintenance monitor.* This feature alerts you when key fluids and filters are due to be changed. This helps service stay on a regular schedule and keeps your vehicles running right.

The Celect Plus ECM 3096662 (M11 and N14 engine models) requires three 28-pin AMP connectors with modified keying on each connector to ensure that older Celect engine models/ECMs are not installed mistakenly on Celect Plus engines. Figure 22-97 illustrates the A (sensor), B (OEM), and C (actuator) harness connectors used on the Celect Plus ECMs. The sensor harness and actuator harness have been combined to form the engine harness with a sensor connector and an actuator connector.

The Celect Plus system also employs a new intake manifold temperature sensor known as an ETAT (exposed thermistor air temperature) sensor, which has a faster response time to air-temperature changes and can only be used on Celect Plus engines and specified transit bus calibrations. The new ETAT sensor is exposed to airflow through the caged plastic housing. In addition, Celect Plus engines employ a new factory-installed AAP (ambient air pressure) sensor, which is a flange-mounted design mounted to the engine with two capscrews.

FIGURE 22–96 *Dash-mounted Celect Roadrelay digital readout instrument. (Courtesy of Cummins Engine Co, Inc.)*

Electronic Protection System

The purpose of the Celect engine protection system is similar to that found on DDC and Cat engines, that is, to prevent and/or limit damage to the engine when it operates outside specific temperature and pressure parameters (conditions). The system is always active; however, one customer-selectable feature of the system is the option to shut down the engine if an *out-of-limit condition* is detected. Should the ECM not be programmed for this shutdown feature, the engine will simply derate in both speed and power. The shutdown protection feature can be activated at any time by connecting one of Cummins' electronic diagnostic tools (Compulink, Echek, or INSITE). Sensors that provide information to the ECM on the Celect system for engine protection include coolant temperature, coolant level, oil pressure, oil temperature, and intake manifold temperature.

When an out-of-limit condition is detected, several activities occur. A dash-mounted engine protection lamp illuminates to warn the driver that an out-of-parameter condition has been detected. As long as the problem exists, this warning lamp remains lit. In addition, within the ECM memory storage system, a *fault code* is logged into memory; it indicates the specific fault detected, the time of the occurrence, and the elapsed time and maximum value of the out-of-limit condition. Low coolant level and low oil pressure are two main faults that will immediately cause the ECM to derate the engine speed and power, and if so programmed, they will initiate the engine shutdown sequence. First a dash light begins to flash. When the operator sees this, he or she has 30 seconds to pull the vehicle over to the side of the road or come to a controlled stop. If the sensors detect that the coolant level or oil pressure is once again within a safe operating limit, the system will reset itself and the process will start again if operating conditions warrant.

It is possible during engine/vehicle operation for the engine protection system (coolant, oil, and intake manifold temperature) to cause the engine protection lamp to illuminate without shutting the engine down. For example, when climbing a long steep hill fully loaded in warm weather, the engine oil temperature condition may reach a level beyond 250°F (121°C). This would cause the warning light to illuminate and remain lit as long as the oil temperature remains above the low out-of-range condition of 250°F. However, if the oil temperature climbs to, say, a high-end safe operating limit of 260°F (137°C), the light will start flashing and the engine will automatically start a sequence of speed and power reduction, followed 30 seconds later by an automatic engine shutdown.

During an engine derate caused by a low out-of-

FIGURE 22-97 *Celect Plus ECM 28 PIN AMP connectors. (Courtesy of Cummins Engine Co, Inc.)*

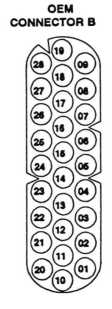

SENSOR CONNECTOR A   OEM CONNECTOR B

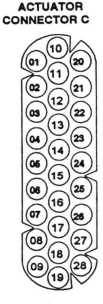

ACTUATOR CONNECTOR C

range sensor condition, the power and speed reduction helps to protect the engine and provide "limp-home" capability by reducing the engine speed. Information stored in the ECM can be extracted by the service technician to help reconstruct the sequence of events which led to the derate or engine shutdown action.

DIAGNOSTIC TOOLING

All electronic engine OEMs now offer dedicated software (disks) to facilitate diagnostic and programming information with their products. Using a laptop computer similar to that shown in Figure 21-53. Windows-based programs are available from each specific engine OEM, which offers a point-and-click graphical interface for the technician. These software programs require an IBM-compatible (386 or higher) PC with a 25-MHz processor, 4 Mb of RAM, 10 Mb of hard disk space, VGA monitor, 3.5-in. floppy drive, DOS 5.0 or higher, Microsoft Windows 3.1 or higher, and an RS232 serial data port not used by a mouse or printer. For those maintenance facilities wishing to load an OEM software program onto a laptop computer, an internal fax modem, PCMCIA slot, CD-ROM drive, as well as a 486 chip and greater levels of MHz and RAM are necessary. All OEMs offer similar functions to fleets that want to implement an interactive maintenance system.

Cummins Software

A family of integrated software from Cummins known as Intelect is used to support Celect (Cummins Electronics), Celect RoadRelay, and Cadec-equipped engines. A Windows-based software program from Cummins known as Insite operates by plugging the laptop computer via the RS232 serial port cable into the engine's SAE J1708 connector located behind the dash. A component of Insite software called Inquire acts as an automated data extraction program to translate engine language into text. The Insite program gives maintenance personnel access to:

- All available diagnostic information from the ECM
- Trip information (for example, sudden decelerations and brake actuation frequency)
- Engine parameter adjustment options
- A guide of correct diagnostics for inexperienced technicians
- Troubleshooting graphics and tips
- Complete wiring and sensor location diagrams
- A glossary of technical terms
- The Shop Talk system, which provides repair tips
- ECM security enhancement
- Automatic storage of information in a database for future use

Cummins recently introduced a Celect Plus fuel system for use on both M11 and N14 engine models with expanded electronics capability. Features of the Celect Plus system are discussed below.

Celect Plus Service Tools

- Compulink: reprogrammable cartridge software: Version 2.0, Celect Plus 1.0
- Echek: Cartridge 4.0 part 3885819

- ESDN: Version 3.0 part 3885783
- Insite: Version 2.0 Celect Plus 1.0 part 3885810

Celect Plus Service Literature

- *Shop Manual M11 Series Engines*; Bulletin 3666075
- *CELECT Plus Troubleshooting and Repair Manual*; Bulletin 3666130
- *Operation and Maintenance Manual, N14 Plus Series Engines*; Bulletin 3666136
- *Troubleshooting and Repair Manual, M11 Series Engines* (STC, CELECT, CELECT Plus models); Bulletin 3666139
- *Troubleshooting and Repair Manual, N14 Plus, N14 (1994 Certifications) Series Engines*; Bulletin 3666142
- *Operation and Maintenance Manual, M11 Plus Series Engines*; Bulletin 3666143
- *CELECT Plus Compulink 1.0 Cartridge Manual*; Bulletin 3666144
- *CELECT Plus, CELECT - Echek - 4.0 Cartridge Manual*; Bulletin No. 3666145
- *CELECT Plus Wiring/Fault Code Diagram*; Bulletin 3666146
- *INSITE CELECT Plus User's Manual*; Bulletin 3666147
- *Shop Manual N14 Engines*; Bulletin 3810487
- *ESDN Version 3.0 User's Manual*; Bulletin 3885786

Celect Plus ECM Calibration Process

The nonreprogrammable Compulink cartridge cannot be used to download Celect Plus calibrations. Celect Plus calibration size necessitates the use of only the reprogrammable cartridge (RPC). The ESDN Application Version 2.51 does not support Celect Plus calibrations. Celect Plus calibrations are supported only on the ESDN 3.0 platform (part 3885783). Insite 2.0 (part 3885810) and ESDN 3.0 will support Celect Plus calibration downloads without the use of Compulink. Celect Plus ECM calibrations can only be performed using the engine-mounted service tool data link.

Electronic Control Modules.

The ECM must be tested for proper SC code/CPL match at overhaul. If they are not set correctly, do so. Only the customer parameters may be adjusted once the SC code is set. Print out a copy of the ECM and engine electronic data plate and retain with the overhaul documents. If your shop does not have a printer, write the SC code and ECM serial number from the electronic data plate on the work order as documentation. The purpose of this is to protect all parties involved. Record the SC code and ECM serial number on the NOW certificate.

Celect Data Link

The system is equipped with an ATA (American Trucking Association) and SAE (Society of Automotive Engineers) data link that conforms to SAE/ATA Practice Specifications J1708 and J1587 and is therefore compatible with industry standards. The data link performs ECM communications with external devices, including service tools, PC data base, mini-trip recorders, and smart dashes. When accessed by use of a diagnostic reader, the data link can update and broadcast certain engine operating performance information for external use by the vehicle system. Broadcast parameters would include such items as road speed, engine speed, cruise control and PTO status, engine brake status, and stored fault codes. Approximately 26 to 28 software modules are associated with the data link functions, allowing all diagnostic functions to be obtained via the data link. In addition, the SAE J1922 proposed data link standard, which is designed as a central interface between the engine and other electronically controlled vehicle and drive-train systems, can be used. This data link will eliminate the use of redundant sensors and actuators. This new J1922 standard will allow communication of critical control parameters to the other devices. Parameters will define the full throttle torque curve, idle speed, peak torque speed, and high idle speed. In addition, dynamic parameters such as the percent utilization of full load, engine speed, throttle pedal position, PTO/cruise control, and engine brake status will be updated to the ECM every 50 milliseconds.

Troubleshooting the Celect System

To troubleshoot the Celect system, special diagnostic tooling can be used to access the information stored within the ECM memory. This can be done by using Cummins Compulink, Echek, or Insite electronic equipment. In addition, several major tool and equipment manufacturers offer generic diagnostic handheld tools that can be used on all of the various makes of electronic engines in use today. A specific test cartridge must be inserted into the DDR similar to the one shown in Figure 22-98 for the Echek system or the MPSI 9000 model shown in Figure 21-52.

SPECIAL INFORMATION For more details on troubleshooting the Celect system, Cummins offers through its dealers a series of videotapes, slides, and information booklets. Obtain the three following Cummins publications: *Bulletin 3666018,* a plasticized wiring diagram foldout; *Bulletin 3810389 (Celect Fault Code Manual),* a guide to a given procedure for any fault code

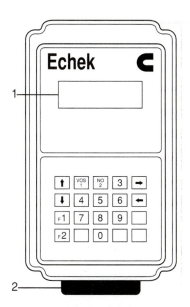

FIGURE 22–99 Procedure required to activate and use the step forward or step backward to a fault code number. When choosing to engage the instrument-panel-mounted idle speed, adjust + or − toggle switch. (Courtesy of Cummins Engine Company, Inc.)

1 —

2 —

FIGURE 22–98 Hand-held diagnostic Echek reader for use with Cummins Celect engines. Note the digital display window (1), which shows data and messages to the user and the various available memory cartridges (2), which contain the necessary software to test Cummins and other electronic engines when connected to the diagnostic data link. (Courtesy of Cummins Engine Company, Inc.)

called up from the ECM; and *Bulletin 3810469 (Troubleshooting and Repair Manual CELECT System N14 Engines)*—a similar publication is available for both the L10 and M11 engines as well as the larger K engine models.

Approach *electronic* engine troubleshooting in a systematic manner just as you would for a mechanically equipped and governed engine. Plugged fuel filters or air filters will result in the same basic complaints on either engine type, namely, a lack of power and visible exhaust smoke. This book cannot provide the test sequences that should be followed to successfully troubleshoot all of the various trouble codes for a Cummins engine. Refer to the Cummins Celect troubleshooting manual and follow closely the *troubleshooting trees* in the performance of each repair; these will guide you through a sequence of possible causes and symptoms.

Vehicle Cab Interface Panel

The dash-mounted cab interface panel illustrated in Figure 22-99 can be activated by the driver through a series of small toggle switches. This panel contains several elements:

1. An idle speed adjust switch can be used to ad-

just the engine idle speed between 550 and 800 rpm. Each time the switch is moved briefly to either the + or − position, the idle speed changes by approximately 25 rpm.

2. The engine compression brake control switch has an ON/OFF position to activate either a Jacobs or Cummins C brake system. The other toggle switch used with the engine brake control can be placed into position 1, 2, or 3. In position 1, on NT (14L) engines, only two cylinders are activated; position 2 activates the compression brake on four cylinders, and position 3 allows all six engine cylinders to provide compression braking.

3. The cruise control panel has two toggle switches; one of these is simply the ON/OFF switch. The second one is actually the cruise control position select switch that the truck driver actually uses to set and adjust the cruise control speed while driving. This toggle switch can be used to set and adjust the engine speed while the PTO is in operation. Take careful note that some truck manufacturers may choose to employ a labeling system with a cruise control system that reads SET/ACCEL and RESUME/COAST instead of what is shown in the example of Figure 22-99 which is SET/COAST and RESUME/ACCEL. The cruise control switch operates in the same manner as that found on most passenger cars equipped with a cruise control feature. The cruise control will not operate if the brake pedal has been depressed. In addition, the cruise control will not operate below 30 mph (48 km/h).

To adjust the cruise control set speed up, move the control select switch briefly to the ACCEL position once for 1-mph increments, or twice to this same position for 2-mph increments. To reduce the speed, use the

COAST select switch in the same manner just described. The engine PTO is controlled from the cruise control switches while the vehicle is in a parked position, although there are certain Cummins-approved applications that allow the vehicle to move up to 6 mph (10 km/h) during PTO operation.

4. On the right-hand side of this control panel are two warning lights. One of these is yellow in color and is labeled WARNING, while the lower one is red in color and is labeled STOP (see Figure 22-99). When the yellow warning light is illuminated during engine operation, this indicates that a Celect system problem has been detected and recorded in ECM memory. The vehicle can still be operated since the problem is not serious enough to warrant engine shutdown; however, the driver should have the system checked out at the earliest available opportunity. Should the red stop light illuminate during engine operation, the truck driver should bring the vehicle to the side of the road as soon as possible, shut off the engine, and make the necessary adjustments to have a service technician from the closest Cummins dealer determine the reason for the engine shutdown.

To withdraw stored trouble codes from ECM memory without using the Compulink or Echek system, a diagnostic switch that can be either an ON/OFF design or a jumper connection cap located in the cab instrument panel area similar to that illustrated in Figure 22-99 can be used. Activation of the diagnostic system will cause the yellow and red fault lights to illuminate and flash a specific code sequence that indicates a given trouble code number. As a means of confirming that both the yellow warning and red stop lights are operational, each time the ignition key is turned on while the diagnostic switch is off, both lights should illuminate and then go out after approximately 2 seconds. Both lights will remain off until a fault code is detected, at which time either the yellow warning light (can still operate the vehicle) or the red stop light (bring the vehicle to a halt and shut the engine off) will illuminate. To check the ECM memory for stored fault codes, the ignition key switch should be off; place the dash-mounted diagnostic toggle control switch into the ON position. Now turn the ignition key switch on.

SPECIAL NOTE   If no fault codes are stored in ECM memory, the yellow warning and red stop lights will simply illuminate. However, if active fault codes are in ECM memory, both the yellow and red lights will begin to flash the code of the recorded faults.

Figure 22-100 illustrates a similar example of the sequence that the yellow and red warning lights would go through to indicate a code. The system will continue to flash the same codes until the system is instructed to move to another function. To show any other fault codes in ECM memory, refer to Figure 22-99 and move the idle INC/DEC + or − toggle switch momentarily to the INC position. If you desire to back up to the previous fault code, move the idle toggle control switch to the DEC (−) position momentarily. Should there be only one active fault code stored in ECM memory, the system will continue to display the same fault code continually. When finished withdrawing fault codes, simply turn the diagnostic toggle switch off as well as the ignition key switch off.

ECI Cylinder Misfire Test

SPECIAL NOTE   When attempting to diagnose a Celect engine cylinder misfire condition, *do not* touch or remove the injector electric wire leads, since this can cause you to receive a serious electric shock!

To check the electronically controlled injectors individually for signs of a suspected misfire condition, two individual procedures can be used.

1. Use the same basic procedure as that for a mechanically controlled Cummins engine by inserting rocker lever actuator Cummins part 3823609 or a wrench on an injector rocker lever as illustrated in Figure 22-76. The engine must be running at a speed between 800 and 1000 rpm using the throttle pedal. Do *not* use the idle or PTO controls to raise the engine speed. Hold the injector plunger down while the en-

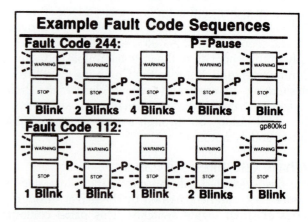

FIGURE 22–100   Fault code sequence example. (Courtesy of Cummins Engine Company, Inc.)

gine is running, which will stop fuel flow to the injector. If the engine rpm decreases when an injector plunger is held down, the injector is good. This same procedure can be used to detect smoking cylinders. If the exhaust smoke disappears when a cylinder is cut out, this cylinder is the one causing the exhaust smoke problem.

2. Use the Cummins Compulink, Echek handheld diagnostic data reader illustrated in Figure 22-98 or the Insite unit plugged into the engine OEM harness access connector, which is usually located inside the vehicle cab. Make sure that the ignition key switch is off. The diagnostic connector location differs on different makes of trucks. Turn the ignition key switch back on. By selecting the desired menu command and depressing the correct keys on the face of the Echek tool, with the engine running, the ECM will cycle the engine through an automatic cylinder cut-out sequence to allow you to determine if a specific injector is misfiring. This is the preferred method. An Echek handheld diagnostic tool provides you with the ideal diagnostic capability to effectively troubleshoot the system. The keypad used with the Echek system feeds a command pulse into the Echek and then into the Celect ECM to extract stored trouble codes or to cause the engine to react to a specifically chosen test parameter condition.

Celect Fault Code Information

Figure 22-101 provides information dealing with Celect fault codes. A number of different SAE standard fault codes, which have been stored in ECM memory, can be extracted by the technician using either the Compulink, Echek, or Insite diagnostic tools. In addition, if the vehicle is equipped with a cab interface panel (see Figure 22-99) it can be used to obtain flash codes from ECM memory. Details on SAE (SIDs, PIDs, and FMIs) were discussed in detail in Chapter 15.

Celect-Valve and Injector Adjustment

The procedure required to set and adjust the valves and injectors on the ECI-Celect-equipped L10 and N14-L engines is similar to that for a PT-equipped Cummins engine. Refer back to Figure 22-68, which illustrates the position of the accessory drive pulley markings at the front of the engine. Manually rotate the crankshaft over CW from the front to align the A or 1–6 VS (valve set) mark on the accessory drive pulley with the stationary pointer on the engine gear cover.

The Celect engines can have both the valves and injectors set at the same time on any one cylinder. With the A or 1–6 VS mark aligned with the gear case pointer, check to see if both the intake and exhaust valves are closed on cylinder 1 or 6. This can be con-

firmed by the fact that when you manually pull up and push down on the valve rocker arms, they should both rattle or indicate that free play exists between the end of the rocker arm and valve crosshead assembly. At the same time the injector plunger should be at the bottom of its stroke. Once you have determined whether the cylinder 1 or 6 injector and valves are ready to be adjusted, refer to Table 22-12, which illustrates the respective accessory drive pulley location to perform both valve and injector adjustments.

NOTE The engine should be at a temperature not higher than 140°F (60°C) when performing injector and valve adjustments.

Adjustment Procedure

1. If we assume that you are starting with the No. 1 cylinder, the A or 1–6 VS mark on the accessory drive pulley will be aligned with the stationary pointer.

2. Bottom the injector plunger three to four times by installing an inch-pound (N·m) torque wrench with a slotted screwdriver adapter in the adjusting screw slot. Turn the torque wrench until it obtains a value of 25 in.-lb (2.82 N·m). This action will remove all fuel from below the plunger so that we can obtain an accurate setting.

3. Gently turn the injector rocker arm adjusting screw down until it just bottoms.

4. Carefully back out the injector adjusting screw 120°, which is the equivalent of two flats on the locknut.

5. Hold the screw and tighten the locknut to between 40 and 45 lb-ft (54 to 61 N·m).

TABLE 22–12 ECI-equipped engine injector and valve adjustment sequence[a]

Bar engine in direction of rotation	Pulley position	Set cylinder injector and valves
Start	A	1
Advance to	B	5
Advance to	C	3
Advance to	A	6
Advance to	B	2
Advance to	C	4

Source: Cummins Engine Company, Inc.
[a] Firing order: 1–5–3–6–2–4.

LAMPS: R = Red   Y = Yellow   EP = Engine Protection Lamp
ABBREV: SH = Sensor Harness   AH = Actuator Harness   OH = OEM Harness

FAULT CODE LAMP	PID(P) SID(S) FMI	EFFECT
115 R	P190 2	Current to injectors turned off. Engine dies.
121 Y	P190 10	None. Possible fueling or timing shift.
122 Y	P102 3	Derate to no-air setting.
123 Y	P102 4	Derate to no-air setting.
131 R	P091 3	Severe derate (power and speed). Power to get off road, or limp home if throttle pedal is held down.
132 R	P091 4	Severe derate (power and speed). Power to get off road or limp home if throttle pedal is held down.
135 Y	P100 3	No engine protection for oil pressure.
141 Y	P100 4	No engine protection for oil pressure.
143 EP	P100 1	Progressive power derate with increasing time after alert.
144 Y	P110 3	Possible white smoke. Fan on if ECM controlled. No engine protection for coolant temperature.
145 Y	P110 4	Possible white smoke. Fan on if ECM controlled. No engine protection for coolant temperature.
151 EP	P110 0	Progressive power and speed derate with increasing temperature.
153 Y	P105 3	Fan clutch engaged if ECM controlled. No engine protection for manifold air temperature.
154 Y	P105 4	Fan clutch engaged if ECM controlled. No engine protection for manifold air temperature.
155 EP	P105 0	Progressive power and speed derate with increasing temperature.
212 Y	P175 3	No engine protection for oil temperature.
213 Y	P175 4	No engine protection for oil temperature.
214 EP	P175 0	Progressive power derate with increasing temperature.
221 Y	P108 3	Power derate by 15%.
222 Y	P108 4	Power derate by 15%.
234 R	P190 0	Fuel shutoff valve closed. Opens when RPM falls to 2000.
235 EP	P111 1	Progressive power derate with increasing time after alert.
241 Y	P084 2	Engine speed limited to "Max. Engine Speed W/O VSS" Compulink value. Cruise control, progressive shift, gear down protection and road speed governor will not work.
243 Y	P121 4	ECM turns off engine brake supply voltage. Engine brakes can't be activated.
245 Y	S033 4	ECM turns off fan clutch supply voltage. Fan won't turn on. Possible engine overheat if ECM controlled fan in use.
254 R	S017 4	ECM turns off fuel shutoff valve supply voltages. Engine dies.
255 Y	S026 3	None on performance. Fuel shutoff valve or fan clutch or brake enable supply voltage stays on.

FIGURE 22–101 Celect fault code SAE information listing for use with Cummins engines. (Courtesy of Cummins Engine Company, Inc.)

SPECIAL NOTE On N14-L engines, two flats (120°) on the locknut will be equivalent to 0.020 in. (0.51 mm) of clearance, while on the L10 engines, two flats are equal to 0.023 in. (0.58 mm). Cummins specifies that this lash must be between 0.018 and 0.025 in. (0.46 to 0.64 mm). This adjustment can be performed as stated above, or a dial indicator can be used if desired.

6. Once you have adjusted the injector, set the valve lash on that same cylinder to the specifications listed on the engine CPL data plate, which is located on the side of the engine gear case cover.

SUMMARY

This chapter has established a foundation on which you can expand your knowledge of electronic fuel systems and controls. Details of how to use diagnostic tooling and equipment should now be fairly familiar. Cummins, as a major heavy duty diesel engine OEM, has committed to expanding the use of electronic fuel system controls to its broad range of diesel engines. Although still found on earlier model Cummins en-

FAULT CODE LAMP	PID(P) SID(S) FMI	EFFECT
311 Y	S001 6	Speed derate to 1400-1600 RPM. Current to injector is shut off.
312 Y	S005 6	Speed derate to 1400-1600 RPM. Current to injector is shut off.
313 Y	S003 6	Speed derate to 1400-1600 RPM. Current to injector is shut off.
314 Y	S006 6	Speed derate to 1400-1600 RPM. Current to injector is shut off.
315 Y	S002 6	Speed derate to 1400-1600 RPM. Current to injector is shut off.
321 Y	S004 6	Speed derate to 1400-1600 RPM. Current to injector is shut off.
322 Y	S001 5	Speed derate to 1400-1600 RPM. Current to injector is shut off.
323 Y	S005 5	Speed derate to 1400-1600 RPM. Current to injector is shut off.
324 Y	S003 5	Speed derate to 1400-1600 RPM. Current to injector is shut off.
325 Y	S006 5	Speed derate to 1400-1600 RPM. Current to injector is shut off.
331 Y	S002 5	Speed derate to 1400-1600 RPM. Current to injector is shut off.
332 Y	S004 5	Speed derate to 1400-1600 RPM. Current to injector is shut off.
333 Y	S254 12	Speed derate to 1400-1600 RPM.
335 R	S254 12	Unpredictable - possible no start (no power to either fuel solenoid or injectors).
341 R	S254 12	Unpredictable - possible no start (no power to either fuel solenoid or injectors).
342 R	S253 12	Engine won't start (no power to fuel solenoid).
343 Y	S254 12	None on performance.
351 Y	S254 12	Possible no noticeable effects. Possible reduced performance.
352 Y	S254 4	Cruise control/PTO, engine brakes don't work. 431 fault code - Compulink shows all switches open... OR... derate to no air and simultaneous logging of fault codes, 123, 141, 145, 154, 213, 222 and 422.
411 Y	S249 3	Control device may not work properly.
412 Y	S250 3	Compulink or Echek may not work properly.
413 Y	S249 9	Control device may not work properly.
414 Y	S250 9	Compulink or Echek may not work properly.
415 EP	P100 1	Progressive power and speed derate with increasing time after alert.
422 Y	P111 2	No engine protection for coolant level.
431 Y	P091 2	None on performance.
432 R	P091 11	Engine will only idle.
433 Y	P102 2	Derate to no-air setting.
434 Y	S251 4	Possible no noticeable performance effects. Possibility of engine dying or difficulty in starting engine.

gines, the PT mechanical fuel system, unique to Cummins engine products, is now being supplanted by their well known Celect system.

SELF-TEST QUESTIONS

1. Cummins diesel engines used in current on-highway truck applications consist of the following models:
   a. A, B, C, L10, and 14-L units
   b. L10 and 14-L units
   c. B, C, and L10 units
   d. B, C, L10, M11, and 14-L units

2. Technician A says that all Cummins engines use the PT fuel system. Technician B disagrees, saying that the PT and Robert Bosch inline multiple-plunger pump systems as well as a distributor pump of Bosch or CAV manufacturers are used on the various series of engines. Which technician is up to date with his information?

3. Technician A says that the CPL data plate indicates the control parts list for the engine. Technician B says that the CPL plate means "Cummins pump list." Who is correct?

4. Technician A says that the letters PT stand for "pressure timed" system. Technician B says that it stands for "pump timed." Who is right?

5. Technician A says that the PT system is a high-pressure fuel system capable of delivering pressures as high as 3000 psi (20,685 kPa) to the injectors. Technician B disagrees, saying that the PT system is basically a low-pressure fuel system and delivers a maximum pressure of 225 psi (1551 kPa) to the injectors. Who is correct?

6. Technician A says that the Cummins PT Pacer system is an electronically controlled fuel injector system. Technician B disagrees, saying that it is the Celect system that has these features. Who is correct?

7. Technician A says that the amount of PT fuel flow at idle is controlled by the size of the idle spring plunger. Technician B says that fuel flow at idle is controlled by the throttle position. Who is correct?

8. Technician A states that fuel pressure in the PT system is produced by a gear-type pump. Technician B says that it is produced by a plunger-actuated pump from the injection pump housing. Who is correct?

9. Technician A states that fuel flow to the PT injectors is controlled by the idle spring. Technician B says that the throttle control shaft provides an external means of manually restricting or interrupting the fuel flow to the injectors. Who is right?

10. Technician A says that if the fuel solenoid was faulty, the engine could be started and stopped by manual rotation of the PT pump thumbscrew on the top of the pump. Technician B says that you would have to replace the solenoid. Who is correct?

11. Technician A says that the idle and maximum speeds of the engine with a PT fuel system are controlled by the position of the throttle shaft. Technician B says that this is true to some extent, but he believes that the internal pump spring pressures actually do this. Who is right?

12. Technician A says that to adjust the engine idle speed on a PT system, you would have to remove the pipe plug on the end of the pump spring housing, insert a screwdriver, and rotate the adjusting screw CW to increase the speed and CCW to decrease it. Technician B says that this is not necessary; you simply have to adjust the external throttle shaft lever stop screws to alter the idle speed. Who is right?

13. If the idle speed were adjusted on a minimum/maximum PT pump governor without using an O-ring or special tool ST-984 or 3375981, technician A says that air can be drawn into the pump, resulting in an inaccurate idle speed adjustment. Technician B says that engine oil used to lubricate the pump would spray lube oil all over the engine compartment if you do not use the correct special tool. Who is right?

14. Technician A says that if the idle speed is set too low on a PT pump, the engine would stall. Technician B says that poor load pickup would result. Who is correct?

15. Technician A says that too high an idle speed on a PT pump would result in a complaint from the truck driver of difficult gear engagement. Technician B says that engine overspeed could occur. Who is correct?

16. Technician A says that the maximum speed adjustment on a PT pump is done by the use of shims under the high-speed governor spring. Technician B says that it is achieved by screw adjustment. Who is right?

17. Technician A says that the purpose of throttle leakage in a PT pump is to lubricate internal pump components as well as the throttle shaft. Technician B says that throttle leakage is to keep the fuel lines and supply and injector drillings full of fuel during closed throttle deceleration. Who is correct?

18. Technician A says that too much throttle leakage in a PT pump will result in slow engine deceleration, while technician B says that it will cause engine overspeed. Who is right?

19. Technician A says that insufficient throttle leakage in a PT pump will result in engine response hesitation after closed throttle motoring. Technician B says that it will result in stalling after decelerating to idle speed. Who is correct here?

20. Technician A says that the term *cutoff* as applied to a PT fuel system means that when fuel manifold pressure reaches its peak, governor action will cause this pressure to drop by 1 to 2 psi (7 to 14 kPa). Technician B says that cutoff means to physically stop the engine when overspeed occurs. Who is correct?

21. Technician A says that to manually stop the engine, you can rotate the PT pump thumbscrew outward. Technician B says that you should turn the thumbscrew inward. Who is correct?

22. Technician A says that the letters AFC following a PTG pump designation stands for "air fuel control." Technician B says that it stands for "aftercooler fuel control." Who is correct?

23. The injector supply pressure in a PTG-AFC fuel pump is determined or preset by
    a. the size of the injector supply orifice
    b. the relief valve pressure in the transfer pump
    c. the recess size of the idle plunger
    d. throttle leakage

24. Technician A says that the AFC valve is located above the governor in the top of the PT fuel pump housing. Technician B says that the AFC valve is located external to the fuel pump in a separate housing. Who is right?

25. Technician A says that after installing a new or rebuilt PT pump onto the engine, you should squirt some clean lube oil into the gear pump inlet hole to aid in fuel pickup. Technician B says that this is not necessary; simply loosen the fuel line above the fuel shutdown solenoid and crank the engine. Who is correct?

26. Technician A says that after a PT fuel pump has been calibrated and installed on the engine, there is no need for any further adjustment. Technician B says that the idle speed may have to be reset since parasitic loads will change this test stand setting. Who is correct?

27. Technician A says that to change the fuel rate on a PTG-AFC system, you have to remove the ball from the end of the throttle shaft, then rotate an internal adjusting screw CW or CCW to achieve the desired setting. Technician B says that you simply remove the large snap ring from the throttle shaft lever retainer cover, disassemble the throttle shaft, and install or remove shims as necessary. Who is up to date on their PT pump systems?

28. Technician A says that the throttle snap method of checking fuel manifold pressure is an accurate method to do this check. Technician B says that the engine should be at its rated speed when doing this check. Who is right?

29. Technician A says that the Cummins PT governor controls engine speed by controlling the fuel supply to the engine by regulating the fuel pressure. Technician B says that the governor mechanically limits the fuel flow. Who is correct?

30. At an idle speed, technician A says that the PT governor weights pull the idle speed plunger backward to allow fuel flow. Technician B disagrees, saying that the weights push against the plunger in order to compress the idle spring and position the plunger recess. Who is right?

31. Technician A says that during high-speed governing in the PT fuel system, idle fuel flow is cut off completely and fuel flows through the main passage only. Technician B says that you still need idle passage fuel flow to supplement that from the main passage. Who is correct?

32. Technician A says that the difference between a PT limiting-speed governor and a variable-speed governor is that the VS governor uses only one fuel passage. Technician B disagrees, saying that you still need two fuel passages, one for idle and one for maximum speed. Who is correct?

33. Technician A says that if dirt in the fuel was to score the PT governor plunger, low fuel pressure to the injectors would result. Technician B says that this could lead to conditions of excessive throttle leakage and slow engine deceleration. Who is correct?

34. Technician A says that the function of the governor weight-assist plunger in the PT system is to act as a surge damper during idle by preventing the governor plunger from bouncing against the flyweight feet. Technician B says that it ensures adequate fuel pressure during closed throttle operation (starting), especially in cold weather. Who understands the function of the weight-assist plunger?

35. The function of the PT governor torque control spring is to
    a. oppose the governor weight force and shape the fuel pressure curve
    b. assist the governor weight force and establish the start of torque control
    c. oppose the governor weight force and cut off fuel at high idle
    d. assist the governor weight force and add fuel at high idle

36. Technician A says that a slow deceleration to idle speed and failure to idle at a low enough speed could be caused by a high weight-assist setting, excessive throttle leakage, or a scored governor plunger. However, technician B says that this would be caused by a weak idle plunger spring or a throttle linkage problem. Who is right?

37. Technician A says that air leakage in the line from the intake manifold to the AFC fuel pump connection would result in no movement of the AFC control plunger, accompanied by a lack-of-power complaint. Technician B says that there would still be some movement of the AFC control plunger; however, a restriction to fuel flow would exist at wide-open throttle and a lack of power would exist. Who is correct?

38. Technician A says that at rated rpm under load the AFC portion of the PT pump does not affect the fuel flow at all. Technician B says that the AFC system limits the preset fuel flow rate. Who is right?

39. Technician A says that during continued high-speed or downhill motoring in a PTG-AFC pump, the governor would be in a cutoff position and that fuel is bypassed within the fuel pump allowing fuel to flow at reduced pressure through the main supply passage to the injectors. Technician B says that cutoff does exist, but that fuel to the injectors comes only from that flowing around the no-air needle valve. Who is correct?

40. Technician A says that metering takes place in the PT injector when the plunger is held down. Technician B disagrees, saying that metering can occur only when the plunger is held up. Who is right?

41. Technician A says that the amount of fuel injected depends on the time that the metering orifice is uncovered and the pressure on the fuel. Technician B says that the

amount of fuel injected is dependent on the size of the injector balance orifice. Who is right?

42. Technician A says that the advantage of a PTD top stop injector is that the upward travel of the injector plunger is controlled by an adjustable stop. Technician B says that this is true, but he believes that the major advantage is that the injector train component parts are unloaded during the metering portion of the fuel supply cycle. Who is correct here?

43. Technician A says that the PT-D top stop injector is designed to operate with no lash. Technician B says that there has to be some lash; otherwise, excessive push tube load and component wear will occur. Who is right?

44. Technician A says that all of the valves and injectors can be adjusted in one complete revolution of the crankshaft. Technician B disagrees and says that two complete revolutions of the crankshaft are necessary. Who is correct?

45. The three VS (valve set) marks A, B, and C stamped on the accessory drive pulley on an L10 or 14-L engine relate to cylinder numbers:
    a. A = 1–6, B = 2–5, C = 3–4
    b. A = 1–3, B = 2–5, C = 4–6
    c. A = 2–5, B = 3–4, C = 1–6
    d. A = 3–4, B = 1–2, C = 5–6

46. Technician A says that injection timing relates to the amount of push tube travel remaining before the injector plunger bottoms in its cup with the piston BTDC on its compression stroke. Technician B says that injection timing relates to the alignment marks between the PT pump and the engine crankshaft. Who is right?

47. Technician A says that the injection timing specification can be found stamped on the engine CPL plate. Technician B says that you have to obtain the PT pump part number and then cross-reference the Cummins PT fuel pump specifications booklet. Who is right?

48. Technician A says that when checking injector push tube travel, if the dial indicator reading was less than that specified, the timing would be slow or retarded. Technician B says that this would be indicative of fast or advanced timing. Who is correct here?

49. Technician A says that on 14-L NT and L10 model engines, the injection timing can be changed by adding or subtracting cam follower housing gasket thickness. Technician B says that you would change the timing on an L10 by installing a different offset camshaft key. Who is right?

50. Technician A says that increasing the gasket thickness on the cam follower housing will advance injection. Technician B says that this action will retard the timing. Who is correct?

51. Technician A says that when adjusting the valve clearance on a 14-L NT model engine, the preferred method is to use a feeler gauge. Technician B says that the torque method of valve adjustment is more accurate. Who is correct?

52. Technician A says that the injector plunger travel on a PT-D top stop injector is changed by loosening the rocker arm locknut and rotating the adjusting screw. Technician B says that it has to be changed by rotating the injector adjusting nut within the body. Who is correct?

53. Technician A says that the Cummins Compuchek system is a vehicle cruise control system. Technician B disagrees, stating that Compuchek is simply a diagnostic test tool to monitor engine operating conditions. Who is correct?

54. Technician A says that engine cylinder balance can be checked on a Cummins engine by using the Compulink system. Technician B disagrees and says that you have to perform an engine compression check in order to determine cylinder compression and therefore cylinder balance. Which technician understands the functions of the Compuchek or Compulink system?

55. Technician A says that a simple gear pump controls fuel system pressure in a Celect system. Technician B says that the Celect fuel system pressure is controlled by the size of the fuel pump button recess as in the PT system. Who is correct?

56. Technician A says that the Celect system operates at an approximate fuel pressure of 200 psi (1379 kPa). Technician B says that this is too high and that it is usually around 140 to 150 psi (965 to 1034 kPa). Who is correct?

57. Technician A says that diesel fuel routed through the ECM cooling plate functions to keep the internal solid-state components at a safe operating temperature. Technician B says that the purpose of the cooling plate is to allow ECM warm-up in cold ambient temperatures. Who is correct here?

58. Technician A says that the purpose of the EPS (engine position sensor) on a Celect system is to monitor engine rpm. Technician B disagrees and says that its function is to provide both a piston position and engine speed condition to the ECM. Who is right?

59. Technician A says that on a Celect-equipped engine, only the engine coolant temperature sensor signal to the ECM will determine the engine idle speed at startup. However, technician B states that it is the engine oil temperature sensor signal that determines the initial idle speed at startup. Who is correct?

60. Technician A says that when an oil or coolant sensor signal on the Celect system is outside normal operating parameters, the ECM will lower the engine's maximum speed automatically. Technician B says that only a low coolant level sensor will do this. Who knows the Celect system best?

61. Technician A says that the TPS (throttle position sensor) on the Celect system is mounted on the PT fuel pump housing, whereas technician B says that it is located within the throttle pedal in the vehicle cab. Who is correct?

62. On a Celect-equipped engine, technician A says that any time the throttle pedal is in any position but idle,

both the PTO and engine brakes will be deactivated. Technician B says that depressing the throttle pedal past idle will allow the cruise control feature to be overridden. Are both technician correct, or only one of them?

63. The term *PWM* (pulse-width modulated) refers to the
    a. duration in crankshaft degrees that the injector actually delivers fuel
    b. length of signal duration from the engine position sensor
    c. percentage of throttle depression
    d. fuel pressure created in the fuel rail to the electronically controlled injectors.

64. Technician A says that each time the idle speed adjust switch is toggled once on a Celect engine, the idle rpm will increase by approximately 50 rpm. Technician B says that the speed change is closer to 25 rpm. Who is right?

65. Technician A says that the maximum fuel system pressure in the Celect system is controlled by a spring-loaded bypass valve within the gear pump. Technician B says that a restricted fuel return fitting in the fuel rail to the injectors controls the fuel pressure. Who is right?

66. On a Celect-equipped engine, technician A says that the injector is manually operated by a rocker arm and pushrod similar to that used on a PT system to create the pressures necessary for injection. Technician B says not so, that the injector is operated by an electric solenoid to create the high fuel pressures necessary for injection purposes. After all, he asks, isn't that what electronic fuel injection is all about? Which technician understands how the Celect system operates?

67. Technician A says that in order for injection to occur within the Celect injector, a metering spill port must be closed. Technician B says that there is no metering spill port and that injection begins and ends based on the PWM signal to the injector from the ECM. Who is correct?

68. Technician A says that metering ends in the Celect injector when the small electric control valve is opened by a signal from the ECM. Technician B says that fuel metering is controlled by gear pump pressure. Who is right?

69. Technician A says that fuel system performance checks of the Celect system can be performed only by using a hand-held electronic diagnostic data reader. Technician B says that a fuel supply restriction check, fuel drain line restriction check, and cooling plate restriction check can be performed in a similar manner to that for a PT-equipped engine. Which mechanic/technician is correct?

70. Technician A says that removal of a Celect injector from the cylinder head should be done only after the rocker boxes have been removed, and then only by use of a special hydraulic puller. Technician B says that the injector can be removed in a similar manner to that for a PT injector by employing a similarly designed type of injector puller. Which technician is correct here?

71. Technician A says that the valves and injectors adjustments on a Celect-equipped engine follow the same basic procedure as that on a PT-equipped engine. Technician B says that no injector adjustment is required since the injector is electronically controlled. Which technician is correct?

72. Technician A says that the Celect injector can be checked for a misfire condition in the same manner as for a PT injector. Technician B says that an electronic diagnostic data reader is required to effectively short out the ECM signal to the injector solenoid. Who is right?

73. Technician A says that Cummins C series engines employ a PT fuel system, whereas technician B says that they use a Robert Bosch (inline) multiple-plunger pump with a mechanical governor assembly. Who is right here?

23

Caterpillar Fuel Systems

OVERVIEW

Descriptive information in this chapter covers several of the major mechanical fuel systems employed by Caterpillar on various Cat engine products. Additional information describes how the Cat electronic unit injector and HEUI systems function and operate. Diagnostic tooling required for electronic engine maintenance, diagnosis, analysis and troubleshooting is also provided, as is adjustments and checks for the mechanical fuel systems.

COMPANY BACKGROUND

Caterpillar Tractor Company, now known as Caterpillar, Inc., was formed on April 15, 1925 as the result of a merger between two well-known U.S. west coast firms, the Holt Manufacturing Company and the C.L. Best Gas Traction Company. Both of these companies were formed in 1869. Caterpillar's Engine Division was started in 1931 as the Special Sales Group and was formed into the Engine Division of Caterpillar in 1953. Today "Caterpillar" and "Cat" are registered trademarks of this well-known company.

SYSTEM STRUCTURE AND FUNCTION

Caterpillar has used a variety of different styles of fuel systems over the years on its different engine series. These systems include the following:

1. *Forged body fuel system:* individual pumping plunger elements contained in a bolted and flanged body attached to the top of the fuel injection pump housing. Used on earlier-model Cat engines.

2. *Compact body fuel system:* similar in external appearance to some Bosch PLN systems where individual pumping plungers and barrels are contained within a common housing. Each pumping element can be removed individually from the main injection pump housing. Used across the line of Cat engine products for many years.

3. *New scroll fuel system* (NSFS): an update of the compact body system. The NSFS incorporates a more robust design to permit higher injection pressures; used initially on the 3406B and 3406C mechanical model engines.

4. *Sleeve metering fuel system* (SMFS): designed for use on the 3208 and earlier-model 3300 series engines. This design incorporates a sliding sleeve through which the pumping plunger strokes. The sleeve position determines the effective stroke and therefore the quantity and timing of the fuel delivered.

5. *Mechanical unit injector* (MUI) *system:* used on the 3116, 3500, and 3600 engines. The MUI operates similar to that described for a DDC unit injector. The major difference is that with the Cat MUI, the rack movement is opposite that for the DDC models.

6. *Electronic unit injector* (EUI) *system:* rocker arm activated, but controlled by energizing an electric solenoid which receives its signal from an ECM (electronic control module). This system is used on the 3176, C10, C12, 3406E, 3500, and 3600 engines.

7. *Hydraulically actuated electronic unit injector* (HEUI) *system:* currently in use on the 3126, 3408E, and 3412E engine models.

The general concept of operation of Cat's PLN fuel systems is similar to that described for Bosch injection pumps, while the MUI and EUI systems are similar to that described for DDC's unit injectors. In this chapter we discuss briefly the NSFS, EUI, and HEUI fuel systems.

NEW SCROLL FUEL SYSTEM: 3306 AND 3406 ENGINES

Injection Pump Operation

The *new scroll* fuel system was introduced in 1979 and was targeted initially for the 3300 series engines. Since that time Caterpillar has applied the new scroll system to the 3300 and 3406B truck engines. As mentioned earlier in the introductory comments dealing with the various types of fuel systems that have been and are now in use on Caterpillar diesel engines, the major reason for using the new scroll fuel system was to create higher injection pressures for use on direct-injection engines, which offer approximately 10% fuel economy improvement over precombustion-type engines. The ability to meet long-term EPA exhaust emission regulations and better overall engine performance, as well as the ability to provide greater parts commonality between different series of engines and lower overall heat rejection, allow new scroll engines to use smaller cooling systems than those of previous engines. In addition, service personnel will be able to use the same special tooling and test procedures to tune up, adjust, and troubleshoot fuel systems on different engines.

A schematic of the new scroll fuel system flow is shown in Figure 23-1, which illustrates the injection nozzle mounted straight up and down in the cylinder since it is located underneath the rocker cover. This is common to the 3406 engine; however, the injection nozzle in the 3300 series engines is mounted outside the rocker cover and is installed at an angle of 15° to position the nozzle tip in the center of the piston. The new scroll injection pump is shown in Figure 23-2, while the actual flow through the pump barrel is illustrated by the arrows in Figure 23-3. In the new scroll system shown in Figure 23-3, two ports are used: the bypass closed port (4) and the spill port (1). Fuel is supplied from the transfer pump to an internal fuel manifold in the injection pump housing at approximately 35 psi (240 kPa). When the pump plunger is at the bottom of its stroke, fuel at transfer pump pressure flows around the pump barrel and to both the bypass closed port (4) and spill port (1), which are both open at this time to allow fuel flow into the barrel area above the pump plunger.

The major advantage of separate fill and spill ports to the plungers is that hot fuel (after the injection period) is not discharged on one stroke and reused on the next stroke such as is the case with the older forged body system and the compact body system. Pump plunger movement is similar to that used in Robert Bosch inline pump systems, in that it is moved up and down by the action of a roller lifter (9) riding on the injection pump camshaft (10), which rotates at one-half engine speed as shown in Figure 23-2. The plunger can also be rotated by the use of a rack and gear as in the compact body system described earlier. As the injection pump camshaft rotates and the plunger rises, some fuel will be pushed back out of the bypass closed port (4) until the top of the plunger eventually closes both the bypass port and the spill port.

NOTE When both ports are covered by the plunger, this is the start of the *effective stroke*, which means that fuel is effectively being placed under pressure and injection will begin. Further plunger movement will cause an increase in the trapped fuel pressure, and at approximately 100 psi (689.5 kPa) the check valve (2) will open and fuel will flow into the fuel injection line to the injection nozzle.

The fuel pressure of 100 psi (689.5 kPa) is insufficient to open the injection nozzle; a pressure of between 1200 and 2350 psi (8300 to 16,200 kPa) is required to open it on 3304/3306 engines and between 2400 and 3100 psi (16,500 to 21,390 kPa) on 3406B engines. Fuel-line pressures of 15,000 psi (103,425 kPa) can be maintained with the scroll system, with an injection pump camshaft lift of 0.012 in. per camshaft degree. However, as the plunger continues to move up in its barrel, this fuel pressure is reached very quickly.

A high-pressure bleed-back passage and groove machined around the barrel are in alignment during the effective stroke to bleed off any fuel that leaks between the plunger and barrel for lubrication purposes; otherwise, engine oil dilution would result. When the upward-moving plunger scroll (helix) (14 in Figure 23-3) uncovers spill port (1), the fuel above the plunger goes through the slot (15) between the solid part of the plunger and the scroll (helix), along the edge of the scroll and out the spill port (1) and a hollow dowel back into the fuel manifold within the injection pump housing. The instant that the scroll uncovers the spill port, injection ceases, and although the plunger can still travel up some more, this is simply to allow most of the warm fuel (due to being pressurized) to spill back out into the manifold.

As the plunger travels down in the barrel, it will once again uncover the bypass closed port (4) and cool fuel will again fill the area above the plunger for the next injection stroke. When the pump spill port is opened as shown in Figure 23-3, pressure inside the barrel is released and the check valve (2) is seated by

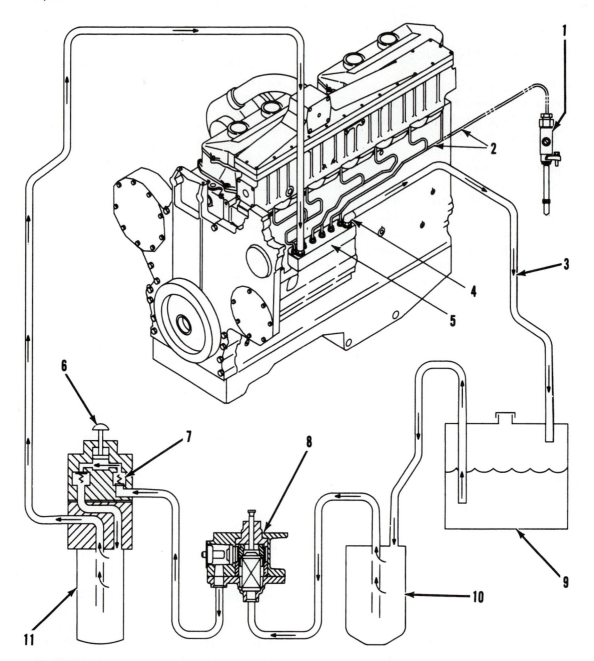

FIGURE 23–1 3406B engine fuel system flow schematic and identification of major components. 1, Fuel injection nozzle; 2, fuel injection lines; 3, fuel return line; 4, constant bleed orifice (part of the elbow); 5, fuel injection pump housing; 6, fuel priming pump; 7, check valves; 8, fuel transfer pump; 9, fuel tank; 10, primary fuel filter; 11, secondary fuel filter. (Courtesy of Caterpillar, Inc.)

its spring (13). Within the check valve assembly is a reverse-flow check valve (11) which will be opened by the fuel pressure within the fuel injection line as long as this pressure remains above 1000 psi (6895 kPa). High-pressure fuel which returns through the pump barrel will flow out through the spill port (1) and a hollow steel dowel pin, which prevents erosion of the pump housing. This fuel deflects off a pulse deflector

within the injection pump housing to protect the aluminum fuel manifold from erosion due to the high-pressure fuel spillage.

The return fuel from the fuel injection line will cease as soon as the fuel pressure drops to 1000 psi (6895 kPa), when the reverse-flow check valve spring (12) will seat the valve. This action will keep the injection line filled with fuel at 1000 psi approximately for

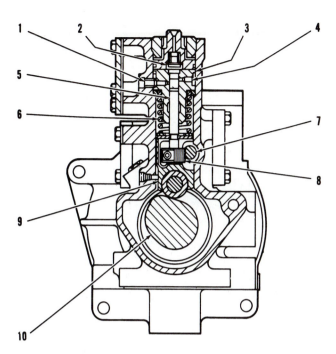

FIGURE 23–2 Cross-sectional view of a new scroll fuel injection pump. 1, Spill port; 2, check valve; 3, pump barrel; 4, bypass port; 5, pump plunger; 6, spring; 7, fuel rack; 8, gear; 9, lifter; 10, cam. (Courtesy of Caterpillar, Inc.)

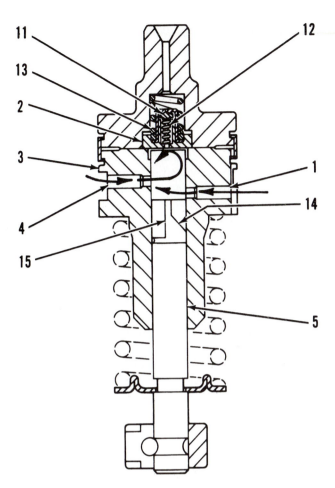

FIGURE 23–3 New scroll pump barrel and plunger assembly showing both the spill and bypass ports open. 1, Spill port; 2, check valve; 3, pump barrel; 4, bypass port; 5, pump plunger; 11, orificed reverse-flow check valve; 12, spring; 13, spring; 14, scroll; 15, slot. (Courtesy of Caterpillar, Inc.)

the next injection period. The reverse-flow check valve controls the fuel-line hydraulics to provide a consistent, smooth engine power curve. If the engine is stopped, the fuel-line pressure will bleed down through the action of a small groove machined into the bottom face of the reverse-flow check valve. The amount of fuel delivered to the injection nozzle is controlled by the length of the plunger's effective stroke.

The plunger stroke itself will not change since the injection pump camshaft always has a constant lift; however, *effective stroke* refers to the period of time that the bypass closed port remains closed, because as long as it stays closed, fuel trapped above the plunger can be pressurized. The effective stroke is controlled by closure of the bypass closed port and opening of the spill port; the longer the period of time that these ports are closed, the greater the amount of fuel injected (longer injection period in actual crankshaft degrees). This closure time is established by rotation of the pump plunger by the rack and gear arrangement. This rotation of the plunger causes the injection to start earlier or later by the fact that the helix or scroll on the plunger will uncover the spill port earlier or later in the upward-moving plunger's stroke, thereby "effectively" metering a given quantity of fuel for any particular rack position.

An orifice bleed valve allows approximately 10

U.S. gallons (40 L) of fuel per hour along with any air in the system to return to the fuel tank. This action allows a continual bleed-off of hot fuel from the fuel manifold that has spilled back from the end of injection, and which is also used for lubrication purposes, to carry this heat back to the tank and let cooler transfer pump fuel flow into the manifold. On engines equipped with this orifice bleed valve, it will not be necessary to bleed the fuel system or use the hand priming pump after changing the fuel filters, since any air in the system will be vented back to the fuel tank through this valve. However, if the system has been completely drained of fuel, it will be necessary to loosen the fuel injection lines at the injection nozzle on the 3300 engines (external) or the fuel line at the valve rocker cover on 3400 engines in order to bleed any entrapped air from the system. To stop the engine the pump plunger is simply rotated so that the slot on the pump plunger is always "inline" with the spill port regardless of the pump plunger's position (vertically) within the barrel. The scroll-metered plungers are driven through steel roller lifters by the action of the heat-treated steel pump camshaft.

Fuel Shutoff Solenoid

The engine can be equipped with an electrical solenoid which is usually mounted on the rear of the fuel injection pump below the air/fuel ratio control unit. This solenoid can be used to move the fuel rack to a no-fuel position and thereby effectively stop the engine when the ignition key is turned off. The solenoid is available in two modes: One mode offers *energize to run*; the other option is *energize to shutoff*. In the energize-to-shutoff solenoid, a special kill button is pressed and held until the engine stops, then it is released. In the energize-to-run solenoid, when the ignition key is turned ON, the solenoid is electronically energized to allow rack movement toward the fuel ON or OFF direction. When the ignition key is turned OFF, the solenoid is deactivated and rack movement toward the fuel-on direction is prevented, causing the engine to shut down. Generally, a diode is used between the two electric terminals of the energize to run a solenoid to eliminate electric spikes that could possibly damage other electronic circuitry in the vehicle electrical system.

FUEL TRANSFER PUMP

With the introduction of the new scroll fuel injection system to the 3406 B and C models, the gear-type fuel transfer pump that had been used for many years with the compact body injection system was superseded by the use of a piston-type transfer pump for use on the new scroll system. Current new scroll fuel systems employ a single-piston, double-acting pump with three one-way check valves, as shown in Figures 23-4 and 23-5. The transfer pump is bolted onto the low side of the injection pump housing and is capable of delivering up to 51 U.S. gallons (192 L) per hour at 25 psi (172 kPa). There is no requirement for a pressure relief valve in this transfer pump, due to the fact that maximum pressure is controlled automatically by the force of the piston return spring (1), shown in the operating schematic.

Pushrod 1 in Figure 23-4 is activated by an eccentric on the injection pump camshaft which causes the pushrod to move in and out as the engine is running. Refer to Figure 23-4 which shows that pushrod 1 will also cause piston 2 to move down against the force of the piston return spring (5) as the eccentric on the injection pump camshaft forces the pushrod down inside the transfer pump housing. The downward-

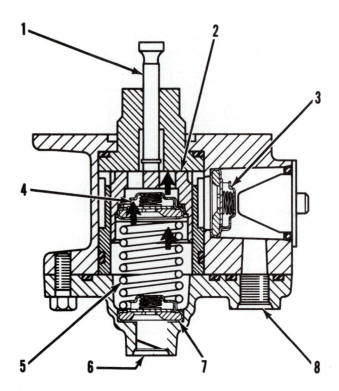

FIGURE 23–4 Fuel transfer pump—start of downstroke (arrows indicate fuel flow direction). 1, Pushrod; 2, piston; 3, outlet check valve; 4, pumping check valve; 5, pumping spring; 6, pump inlet port; 7, inlet check valve; 8, pump outlet port. (Courtesy of Caterpillar, Inc.)

moving piston will cause the inlet check valve (7) and the outlet check valve (3) to close, while the pumping check valve (4) will open to allow fuel below the piston to flow into the area immediately above the downward-moving piston.

As the injection pump camshaft eccentric rotates around to its base circle or low point, the transfer pump spring (5) pushes the piston (2) up inside its bore, which causes check valve 4 to close; however, both the inlet check valve (7) and the outlet check valve (3) will be forced open. Fuel above the piston will now be forced through the outlet check valve (3) and flow through the pump outlet port (8) at approximately 35 psi (240 kPa), as shown in Figure 23-5. While this action is taking place, fuel will also flow through the pump inlet port (6) and the inlet check valve (7) to fill the area below the piston (2), and the pump will repeat the cycle described above.

GOVERNOR

The governor assembly used with the new scroll fuel system is a hydramechanical servo-type unit, illustrated in Figure 23-6. The reason for using a servovalve

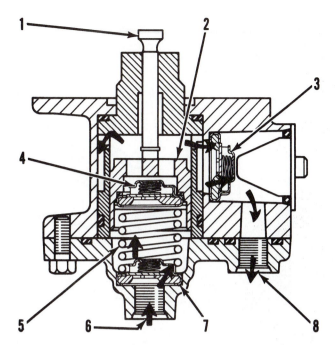

FIGURE 23–5 *Fuel transfer pump—start of upstroke (arrows indicate fuel flow direction). 1, Pushrod; 2, piston; 3, outlet check valve; 4, pumping check valve; 5, pumping spring; 6, pump inlet port; 7, inlet check valve; 8, pump outlet port. (Courtesy of Caterpillar, Inc.)*

with the new scroll governor assembly is that without this unit to provide a boost, both the governor spring and flyweights would have to be very large, heavy, and cumbersome to move the injection pump rack and overcome the resistance of the gear segments and plungers within the barrels. With the use of the servo assist, little force is required to move both the accelerator and the governor control lever, and rapid rack movement and throttle response time can be achieved.

Basically, the governor assembly consists of three separate components:

1. The mechanical components of the governor, such as the weights, springs, and linkage (Figure 23-7).
2. The governor servo (Figure 23-6), which provides hydraulic assistance through the use of pressurized engine oil to provide rapid throttle response and to reduce the overall size requirements of the governor flyweights and springs.
3. The dashpot assembly, which is designed to provide stability to the governor during rapid load/throttle changes (Figure 23-6).

Prior to reading the explanation of the governor operation, take a minute to become familiar with the component parts and their arrangement to each other. If you are already familiar with the basic operation of a mechanical governor, you can proceed to the description of operation. If, on the other hand, you are not familiar with the operation of a basic mechanical governor, it may be of assistance to you at this time to study the description of operation in Chapter 17, where we discuss in detail how a basic mechanical governor operates.

SPECIAL NOTE Bear in mind that the centrifugal force of the governor flyweights are always attempting to decrease fuel to the engine, while the force of the governor spring is always attempting to increase fuel to the engine.

Governor Oil Flow
Figure 23-6 illustrates the location of the governor in relation to the fuel injection pump assembly, as well as the oil flow path for both the injection pump and the governor. The governor mounting base contains both a small oil inlet hole and a larger oil drain port. Engine oil under pressure enters the governor end of the housing and flows up to the governor servo valve and to the hydraulic air/fuel control unit on turbocharged engines. A percentage of this oil drains down to the bottom of the governor housing for lubrication of governor components and to supply oil to the dashpot unit. Drain oil flowing over the governor weights allows the weights to throw oil up and around over the remaining governor components. The oil drain hole maintains the oil at a fixed level at all times.

Pressurized oil also flows to and through the fuel injection pump camshaft via a centrally drilled oil hole where cross-drilled passages feed the camshaft journals as well as the front camshaft bearing. The oil drains out of the front of the pump housing and over the engine gear train on its way back to the engine crankcase.

AUTOMATIC TIMING ADVANCE UNIT

The automatic fuel injection timing advance unit used with the new scroll fuel system differs from that used with the earlier compact body fuel system. The timing unit used with the new scroll system is a combination of a hydraulic variable timing unit and a mechanical unit. The major difference is that the new scroll fuel system timing unit is adjustable by use of a setscrew that limits the degrees of allowable advance. Figure 23-8 shows the new scroll fuel system automatic timing advance unit.

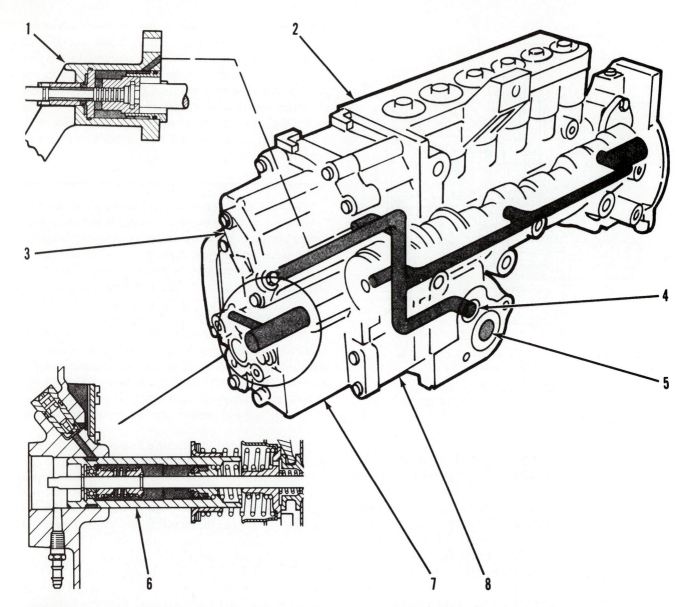

FIGURE 23–6 New scroll fuel injection pump and governor oil flow passages. 1, Servo; 2, fuel injection pump housing; 3, cover; 4, oil supply from cylinder block; 5, oil drain into cylinder block; 6, dashpot; 7, governor rear housing; 8, governor center housing. (Courtesy of Caterpillar, Inc.)

Before discussing its operation, refer to Figure 23-9, which illustrates the assembled automatic timing advance unit in position at the front of the engine with its timing gear cover removed. Figure 23-10 shows the timing advance unit removed; the toothed gear in the center of the diagram is actually the forward end of the fuel injection pump camshaft, which has left-hand helical cut teeth machined onto it. This camshaft gear is actually shown as item 5 in the operational diagrams.

Figure 23-11 shows the carrier (8), which is illustrated as item 4 in the operational diagrams. Note that the carrier is machined with external straight spur cut gear teeth, while the inner hub area contains helical splines (teeth) that will engage with the teeth on the forward end of the fuel injection pump camshaft.

Unit Operation

Figure 23-8 illustrates the automatic timing advance unit in the nonoperational position (no advance provided); however, the engine is running. The timing advance unit relies on the centrifugal force created by the four weights shown as item 2 and on pressurized engine oil delivered through the centrally drilled camshaft, which will enter the timing advance unit at

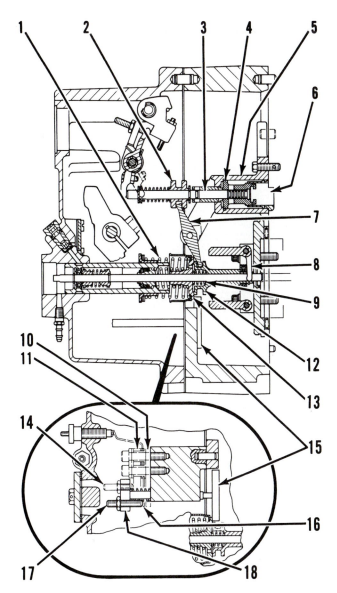

FIGURE 23–7 *3406B mechanical governor schematic. 1, Governor spring; 2, sleeve; 3, valve; 4, piston; 5, governor servo; 6, fuel rack; 7, lever; 8, flyweights; 9, overfueling spring; 10, load stop bar; 11, stop bar; 12, riser; 13, spring seat; 14, torque rise setting screw; 15, stop bolt; 16, torque spring; 17, fuel setting screw; 18, stop collar. (Courtesy of Caterpillar, Inc.)*

its right-hand side as shown in the diagram through a drilled hole shown in the center of the spool (12). The pressurized engine oil is used to force a carrier (4) back and forward within the confines of a ring (10) bolted to the timing gear (3), which is in mesh with the engine gear train at the front of the engine. To allow the pressurized engine oil to work on the carrier (4), a set of four flyweights opposed by a spring (8) moves a control spool back and forth within the bore of the body (13).

Advancement

When the engine speed becomes fast enough to create a strong enough centrifugal force at the flyweights (2), they will pull the spool valve (12) to the left while simultaneously compressing the small spring (8). The movement of the spool (12) allows pressurized engine oil to flow out of the centrally drilled pump camshaft and through the body (13). This oil will now act on both the body (13) and the carrier (4). When the oil pressure becomes greater than the force of the large spring (1), both the body and the carrier will move to the left in the diagram. This action will allow the carrier (4), with its straight-cut outer splines (gear teeth) and its helically cut inner splines, to exert a twisting force through the inner splines, which are in mesh with the helical cut teeth on the forward end of the pump camshaft (5). The pump camshaft will therefore be rotated in relation to the timing gear (3), which is driven from the engine gear train, thereby providing maximum injection timing advance in relation to the speed of the engine. For further clarification, the advancement takes place between the inner splines, shown in Figure 23-11 and the teeth of the camshaft, shown in the center of Figure 23-10.

Timing advancement will continue as the engine speed increases until the moving parts, particularly the spool (12), butts up against the adjustable setscrew (7). The body (13) will stop moving when the oil pressure on the body and the carrier (4) is equal to the force of the large spring (1), which will take place as the oil ports begin to close. Adjustment of the setscrew (7) will determine and limit the amount of automatic timing advancement. This setting can vary for different Caterpillar engines and can be obtained by referring to the service supplement for the particular engine.

Deceleration

When the engine speed decreases, the centrifugal force of the flyweights (2) will allow the force of the smaller spring (8) to push the spool valve (12) to the right in the diagram, which will block the oil supply from the camshaft and simultaneously drain the previously trapped oil out of the automatic timing advance unit. The force of the large spring (1) will now push the carrier (4), the body (13), and the spool valve (12) to the right, which will cause the inner splines on the carrier (4) to retard the injection timing as it rotates the camshaft in the opposite direction with a decrease in engine speed.

Update

Later 3406B engines, starting with engine serial number 7FB55250 and effective with fuel injection pump serial number 66120, are equipped with an orifice

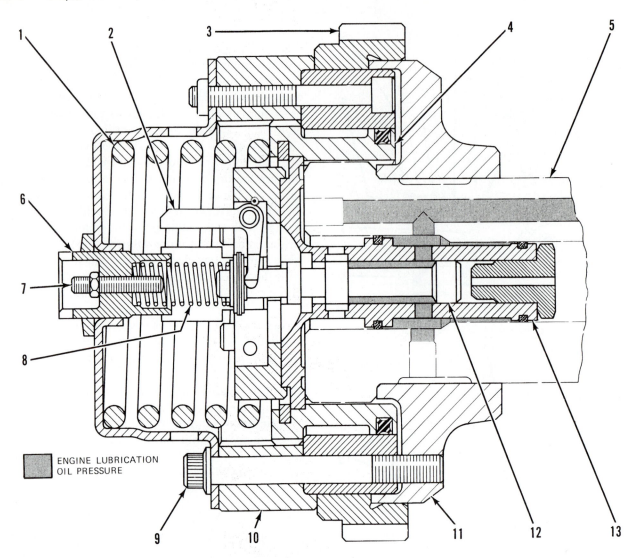

FIGURE 23–8 *Automatic timing advance unit before timing advance begins. 1, Spring; 2, flyweights; 3, timing gear; 4, carrier; 5, fuel injection pump camshaft; 6, screw; 7, setscrew; 8, spring; 9, bolt; 10, ring; 11, ring; 12, spool; 13, body. (Courtesy of Caterpillar, Inc.)*

screen assembly, 7C2568, in the timing advance unit. The new screen assembly is located within a single tapped hole in the end of the fuel pump camshaft. The purpose of this orifice screen in these later-model engines is to reduce both the engine noise and total vehicle noise during full-load acceleration situations by restricting the actual oil flow to the timing advance mechanism. This in turn increases the time required before full advance will occur. Because of this longer time interval to reach full advance, the technician must allow at least 30 seconds at each specific rpm test point when using either the 6V3100 or 8T5300 engine timing indicator groups.

STATIC ENGINE TIMING

Locating Top Dead Center: 3406B Engine

It often becomes necessary to locate the No. 1 piston at its TDC compression position, such as when checking the static fuel injection pump-to-engine timing. Finding TDC on all 3400 series engines follows a similar pattern in that an injection pump timing pin and a flywheel timing bolt are used to check this condition. Piston 1 is the reference cylinder for checking injection pump-to-engine gear train timing.

Although the engine can be rotated over manually from the front of the crankshaft, Caterpillar offers

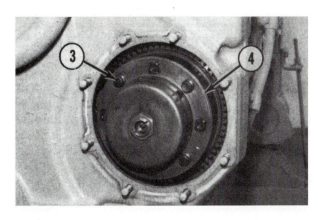

FIGURE 23–9 *Automatic timing advance unit component identification on a 3406B engine and retaining bolts position. 3, Retaining bolts; 4, automatic timing advance mechanism. (Courtesy of Caterpillar, Inc.)*

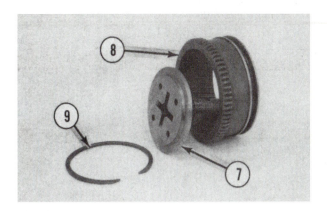

FIGURE 23–11 *View of the automatic timing advance unit showing both the internal helical splines and the straight-cut spur gear teeth. 7, Body; 8, carrier; 9, lock ring. (Courtesy of Caterpillar, Inc.)*

an engine turning tool, 9S9082, which can be inserted into a hole in the forward side of the flywheel housing to facilitate turning the engine over during the timing check or when setting valves, and so on. This tool can be seen in Figure 23-12 along with the flywheel timing bolt (1); Figure 23-13 illustrates the normal stored location of this timing bolt in the forward side of the flywheel housing on the left-hand side. An optional hole for installing the timing bolt during a No. 1 piston TDC check can be found on the forward side of the flywheel housing on the right-hand side of the engine.

To check the static timing of the injection pump to the engine, piston 1 must be placed at TDC on its compression stroke.

Location Procedure

1. Refer to Figure 23-13 and remove bolt 1 and its diagonally opposite unit so that the access plate can be removed.

2. With the access plate removed, turning tool 9S9082 can be inserted through this hole to engage with the flywheel ring gear as shown in Figure 23-12 with a $\frac{1}{2}$-in. square drive ratchet.

3. Refer to Figure 23-13 and remove the pipe plug (2) from the flywheel housing.

4. Install the timing bolt (1 in Figure 23-12) and install it into the pipe plug hole.

5. Slowly rotate the engine with the turning tool and ratchet until the timing bolt slides into its mating threaded hole in the flywheel.

6. If you miss the hole and reverse the engine rotation, always come back at least 30° before coming forward again, to ensure that all gear train backlash will be eliminated.

7. To ensure that piston 1 is at TDC on its compression stroke, remove the front valve rocker cover and check that both the intake and exhaust valve

FIGURE 23–10 *Automatic timing advance unit removed to show the internal ring gear, item 5. (Courtesy of Caterpillar, Inc.)*

FIGURE 23–12 *3406 engine turning tool 9S9082 and timing bolt location. 1, Timing bolt; 5, 9S9082 engine turning tool. (Courtesy of Caterpillar, Inc.)*

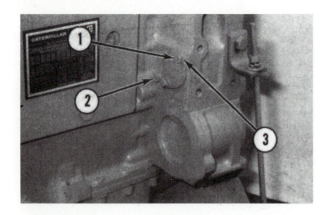

FIGURE 23–13 3406 engine timing bolt and storage location on left side of engine. 1, Timing bolt; 2, timing bolt location; 3, storage location. (Courtesy of Caterpillar, Inc.)

rocker arms have free play. This confirms that all valves are closed and that the piston is on TDC compression.

NOTE   If both rocker arms do not have clearance, the piston is at TDC but is 360° off. It is, in fact, just finishing the exhaust stroke and starting the intake with a valve overlap condition evident.

---

8.   Remove the timing bolt from the flywheel, rotate it another 360°, and reinsert it into the threaded hole in the flywheel.

9.   Piston 1 is now at TDC compression with all valves closed.

Static Timing Check

The static timing check is confirmed when piston 1 is at TDC compression, the timing bolt will screw into the threaded hole in the flywheel, and at the same time, the injection pump timing pin will slip into engagement with the injection pump camshaft slot.

1.   With piston 1 at TDC compression, remove the flywheel timing bolt.

2.   Using turning tool 9S9082, manually rotate the flywheel opposite its normal rotation, which is clockwise from the front. Therefore, pull the $\frac{1}{2}$-in. drive ratchet upward when standing at the side of the engine to turn the flywheel CCW when viewed from the front. Turn the flywheel back between 30 and 45°.

3.   Refer to Figure 23-14 and remove the plug (2) from the injection pump housing.

4.   Refer to Figure 23-15 and install timing pin 6V4186 into the hole in the injection pump housing.

5.   Slowly rotate the engine in its normal direc-

tion of rotation, which is CW from the front (CCW from the rear), until the injection pump timing pin 6V4186 drops into engagement with the machined slot in the pump camshaft. Gently rotate the engine until the pin is tight.

6.   If you can now install the timing bolt into the threaded hole in the flywheel, the static pump timing is correct.

7.   If you cannot install the bolt into the flywheel housing, the timing is incorrect and should be remedied by moving to step 8.

SPECIAL NOTE   On 3406B truck engines starting with engine serial number 4MG3600 and up, a new timing advance holding tool, illustrated in Figure 23-16 is required to hold the timing advance at the bottom of its travel (retarded position) when pin timing the fuel injection pump to the engine. Failure to employ this special tool on engines with these serial numbers will result in an inability to perform pin timing correctly.

---

8.   Remove the cover from the front right-hand side of the gear train timing housing to expose the automatic timing advance assembly as illustrated in Figure 23-9.

9.   Loosen the four bolts, item 3 shown in Figure 23-9, and with the injection pump timing pin still in position, remove the flywheel timing bolt.

10.   Rotate the flywheel with the 9S9082 turning tool and ratchet opposite its normal rotation (either CCW when viewed from the front, or CW when viewed from the flywheel end) approximately 45°.

11.   Select two of the four bolts that were loosened in step 9 that are 180° apart, and tighten them carefully to a torque reading of 27 lb-in. (not lb-ft!) (which is 3 N · m), in order to apply a small degree of clamping force to the automatic timing advance unit.

12.   Rotate the flywheel, now in its normal direction of rotation (CW from the front and CCW from the rear), until the flywheel timing bolt can just be installed into its mating threaded hole.

13.   Tighten the four automatic timing advance unit bolts to a torque of 41 to 46 lb-ft (55 to 62 N · m).

14.   Remove the flywheel timing bolt and the timing pin from the injection pump housing.

15.   To double check the static timing, rotate the flywheel opposite its normal rotation about 45° (one-eighth turn).

16.   Slowly rotate the flywheel in its normal rotation until the timing pin drops into the camshaft slot of the injection pump.

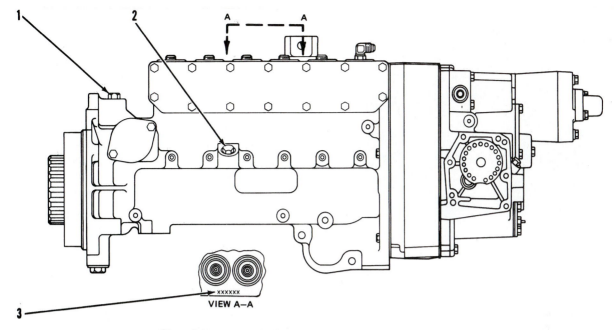

(1)   Location for rack centering pin.

(2)   Location for timing pin.

(3)   Location of stamped part number and serial number for FUEL INJECTION PUMP AND GOVERNOR GROUPS.

See FUEL SETTING AND RELATED INFORMATION FICHE for the correct fuel injection timing.

Injection sequence (firing order) 1,5,3,6,2,4

Rotation of Fuel Pump Camshaft
(when seen from pump drive end) .... counterclockwise

FIGURE 23–14   *View of injection pump showing location of rack centering pin (1) and timing pin (2). View A–A, location of stamped part number and serial number for fuel injection and governor groups. Injection sequence firing order 1–5–3–6–2–4. Rotation of fuel pump camshaft when seen from drive end is CCW. (Courtesy of Caterpillar, Inc.)*

FIGURE 23–15   *Timing pin, item 2, 6V4186 installed into injection pump access hole. (Courtesy of Caterpillar, Inc.)*

17.   Carefully rotate the flywheel again in its normal rotation to ensure that there is no gear lash left in the gear train and see if the flywheel timing bolt will thread into position. If it does, the static timing is indeed correct.

18.   If it does not, repeat the procedure.

DYNAMIC ENGINE TIMING

Dynamic Timing Charts

The specific timing curve information for various models of Caterpillar truck engines is readily available, upon request, through any local Cat dealer. The static (engine stopped) and dynamic (engine running) timing characteristics for the same model of engine

FIGURE 23–16 Timing advance holding tool 1U8271 for use on 3406B engines from 4MG3600 and up. (Courtesy of Caterpillar, Inc.)

will be different for each horsepower setting and are also based on whether or not the engine is JWAC (jacket water aftercooled) or ATAAC (air-to-air aftercooled). Figure 23-17 illustrates a sample engine information plate for a 3406B, 400-hp engine model with a static fuel timing specification of 18.0° BTC (before top dead center). Other information on this plate includes the full-load static fuel rack setting dimension, the full-torque static fuel dimension, and the A/F (air/fuel) ratio dynamic setting. Timing charts that list all of the dynamic timing specifications for the most popular models of truck engines are available from Caterpillar in pads of 50. These charts will eliminate the need for you to graph your own during a dynamic timing check.

NOTE To obtain the correct dynamic timing chart for your engine, the OT microfiche at your local Cat dealer must be checked for the timing advance part number as well as the occurrence number listed under the parts section of the microfiche, and the static timing listed under the fuel system section. Dynamic timing can be checked with the use of Caterpillar special tool group 8T5300, and dynamic rack movement can be checked on a running engine with the 8T1000 electronic position indicator group, which is shown in Figure 23-18.

Dynamic Rack Setting Measurement Tools

For many years the acceptable method employed when checking/setting fuel injection pump rack movement on all Caterpillar engines was to use a mechanical dial indicator. The only problem associated with this type of instrument is that it is subject to rapid oscillation due to engine vibration and mechanical reactions through mechanical governor control linkages, and so on. Consequently, when using mechanical dial indicators, the mechanic/technician had to be alert when attempting to read such a dynamic (engine-running) maximum rack reading, since it generally will occur only for an instant once the engine throttle is moved to the full-fuel position.

Figure 23-18 illustrates Caterpillar special service tool 8T1000, which is an electronic position indicator tool which can be used when calibrating, monitoring, and testing all Caterpillar fuel injection pumps.

This tool is battery operated and is capable of measuring linearly (in a straight line) with a digital readout as well as retaining a storage memory. This

CAT				3406B	
SER. NO. 7FB38516		DATE DELIVERED			
MODIFICATION NO.			DLR CODE		
AR NO. 4W4109		PERF SPEC 0T4953		MAX ALT	22550 M
OEM NO. 34A49PSI/051134B					
FULL LOAD STATIC FUEL	2.60 mm		FULL TORQ. STATIC FUEL	3.10 mm	
POWER	400 HP	0298.0 kw	A/F RATIO DYNAMIC	-02.00 mm	
BARE ENG. HI IDLE RPM	2339	FULL LOAD RPM	2100	FUEL TIMING	18.0 BTC
					9L6531 13

FIGURE 23–17 Sample 3406B engine information plate. (Courtesy of Caterpillar, Inc.)

FIGURE 23–18 8T1000 electronic position indicator instrument to check rack movement. (Courtesy of Caterpillar, Inc.)

memory is capable of storing the minimum, maximum, and difference values of the measurement being taken; therefore, it offers features that are not available in a mechanical dial indicator arrangement, which will often fail when used repeatedly when measuring dynamic (engine running) rack readings. The electronic design of the 8T1000 tool ensures that gauge fluttering such as occurs with a mechanical dial gauge is totally eliminated when using it on a running engine. Both static (engine stopped) and dynamic (engine running) readings can easily be monitored in either the inch or metric scale with the 8T1000 unit. Another feature of the 8T1000 unit is that it has a floating zero; therefore, by pressing a touch switch, the digital display can be set to zero anywhere within the measurement range of the linear moving probe. The digital display will then show the distance and direction (+ or −) that the probe shaft moves from this floating zero position.

Dimensions of the unit are such that it has a 1-in. (25.4-mm) measurement range with a 0.375-in. (9.52-mm)-diameter mounting stem and a 0.750-in. (19-mm) body diameter, which allows it to be used and mounted with standard Caterpillar dial indicator fixtures and accessories. In addition, extension cables allow the mechanic/technician to use this tool from a remote location, which provides tremendous flexibility when working around equipment. Detailed information on the use, calibration, and operation of the 8T1000 electronic position indicator group is available from Caterpillar dealers in special instruction form SEHS8623.

Tool Installation and Prechecks

To check the dynamic (engine running) timing between the engine and the injection pump, several special tools have been used over the years for various types of Caterpillar fuel systems. The 1P3500 injection timing light, similar to that used on a gasoline engine, was one such early example. On later engines, however, such as those using the new scroll fuel system, timing indicator group 6V3100 was used, then superseded by 8T5300. Although tool 6V3100 can be used, the later 8T5300 tool group is recommended for use with the new scroll fuel system and can be adapted to other Caterpillar engines.

Operational instructions for the use of the 8T5300 timing indicator can be found in Caterpillar form SEHS8580, along with printed directions included inside the lid of the timing indicator box. Basically, the timing indicator group employs a TDC magnetic pickup probe inserted into the flywheel housing timing bolt hole, which indicates when piston 1 is at TDC, although No. 6 can be used if desired. In conjunction

with this feature, a fuel injection pump transducer inserted between the No. 1 or No. 6 injection pumping element and nozzle fuel injection line monitors and senses the high fuel pressure, to activate an electrical contact switch within the transducer which is relayed to the engine timing indicator. In this way, the dynamic (running) engine-to-injection pump timing advance can be closely checked and compared to specifications. If the dynamic timing is incorrect, the automatic timing advance unit located at the front of the engine can be adjusted to correct the timing.

Adjusting the Dynamic Timing: 3406B Engine

1. Stop the engine and remove the ATA (automatic timing advance) cover at the right front side of the engine gear train timing cover to expose the timing unit as shown in Figure 23-19.

2. Refer to Figure 23-19 and loosen the locknut (10) on the front of the ATA unit and turn the screw (11) clockwise to increase the speed where the timing advance starts, then tighten the locknut (10) to 50 to 61 lb-ft (70 to 85 N · m).

NOTE   Rotating the adjusting screw (11) will increase the spring force in the timing unit; therefore, higher engine speed is required before the timing will start to advance (weights have to turn faster to create greater centrifugal force). One full turn (360°) of the screw (11) will alter the start of timing advance by about 50 rpm. Once this has been done, we must also reset the point at which the timing advance stops. Rotating the setscrew

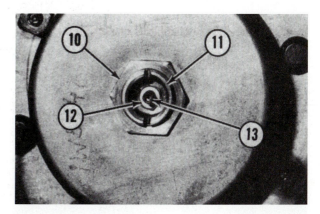

FIGURE 23-19 *Automatic timing advance unit for a mechanical pump 3406B engine showing the lock and adjusting screw location at the front of the engine. 10, Locknut; 11, screw; 12, locknut; 13, setscrew. (Courtesy of Caterpillar, Inc.)*

(13) one full turn (360°) will alter the end of timing advance by about 30 rpm.

3. To adjust the point at which the ATA stops, loosen off the locknut (12) and turn the setscrew (13) clockwise to decrease the speed where timing advance stops. Tighten locknut 12 to 20 to 22 lb-in. (2.25 to 2.50 N · m). Use special tool 6V2106 for this purpose (see Figure 23-20).

4. After any adjustments, install the ATA cover back onto the engine front cover, and run the engine to recheck the timing with 8T5300 timing indicator.

5. If the ATA unit fails to fall within the specifications and cannot be adjusted within specifications, repair or replace the ATA unit.

Fuel Rack Setting Procedure: 3406B Engine

The injection pump rack can be checked/set with the pump either on or off of the engine; however, since most times when the rack is suspected of being out of adjustment, it is on a vehicle (low-power complaint), the following procedure describes the check/setting while on the engine.

NOTE For many years the accepted method of checking the injection pump control rack movement was by installing a mechanical dial indicator onto the correct special brackets bolted into position on the pump housing. This method created a problem, particularly when a dynamic or engine running rack dimension was required, since the engine vibration and rapid oscillation of the dial indicator needle not only made it hard to read, but was also tough on the life of the dial gauge. Consequently, Caterpillar now recommends that the technician use the 8T1000 electronic position indicator group illustrated in Figure 23-18, which employs a digital readout and can be used for precision linear measurement of both static and dynamic engine rack movement in place of the previous mechanical dial indicator assemblies.

Setting Procedure

1. Refer to Figure 23-14 and remove the rack centering pin plug (2) from the injection pump housing. Also remove the two bolts on the inspection plate to the left of this plug to facilitate installation of the rack setting tools shown in Figure 23-21.

2. Refer to Figure 23-21 and install the rack position tools and mechanical dial indicator as illustrated or install the 8T1000 electronic tool shown in Figure 23-18 using the correct components for your particular model engine. To check/set the rack on the 3406B engine, set up the dial indicator as follows:

a. Place the collet 5P4814 (7) onto the bracket assembly 6V6109 (4).

b. Refer to Figure 23-22, which shows the slot in the fuel injection pump rack (9), and position the mechanical dial indicator or the 8T1000 electronic tool arm so that it sits in the mid-travel position to ensure contact with the rack slot. Place the 6V6109 bracket assembly (4)

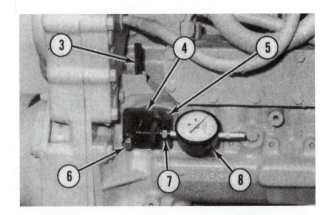

FIGURE 23-21 3406B engine mechanical dial indicator and rack centering pin installed on injection pump. Note that the 8T1000 electronic indicator shown in Figure 23-18 can be used in place of, and is preferable to, the mechanical dial indicator. 3, 6V4186 timing pin; 4, 6V6109 bracket assembly; 5, 2A0762 bolt [¼ − 20 NC × 15.88 mm (0.625 in.)]; 6, 8H9178 ground body bolt [¼ − 20 NC × 25.4 mm (1.00 in.)]; 7, 5P4814 collet; 8, 6V6106 dial indicator. (Courtesy of Caterpillar, Inc.)

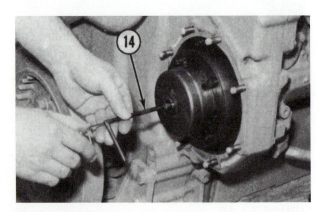

FIGURE 23-20 Adjusting the automatic timing advance unit with 6V2106 tool group (item 14). (Courtesy of Caterpillar, Inc.)

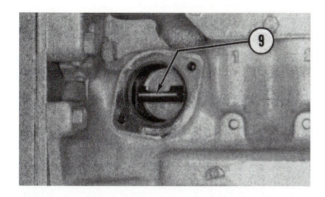

FIGURE 23–22 *View of timing slot (item 9) in 3406B engine fuel injection pump rack. (Courtesy of Caterpillar, Inc.)*

into position on the injection pump housing as illustrated in Figure 23-21.

c. Insert bolt 8H9178 (6) through the bracket assembly followed by bolt 5, as shown in Figure 23-21.

d. Slide the mechanical or electronic dial indicator into position on the collet as shown in Figure 23-21.

e. Thread the small contact point 9S8903 onto the 6V2030 extension, then thread them both onto the dial indicator (8).

f. Carefully tighten the collet by hand just enough to hold the dial indicator firmly without causing binding in the movement of the spindle and needle.

3. Truck engine applications of the 3406B employ an electric fuel shutoff solenoid just below the air/fuel ratio control unit at the rear of the injection pump housing. This shutoff must be removed so that special tooling can be installed for the rack position check as shown in Figure 23-21. If the engine was not equipped with an electric fuel shutoff solenoid, remove the small cover plate that would be in position here.

4. Refer to Figure 23-23 and install item 10, adapter plate 6V6151, to the mounting hole where the fuel shutoff solenoid was located earlier.

5. Manually rotate the governor speed control (throttle) lever as shown in Figure 23-23 to the left (CCW), which will place it into the normal low-idle position.

6. Install the timing pin 6V4186 (3) illustrated in Figure 23-21 through the access hole in the injection pump housing so that you feel it make contact with the rack.

7. Refer to Figure 23-23 and using item 11, which is the 6V7942 hook, slide it through the adapter

plate so that you feel it push the sleeve and fuel rack to the fuel-shutoff position, and that the timing pin does in fact engage with the slot in the rack.

8. Rotate the governor speed control lever (throttle) into its maximum (full-load) position by turning it to the right (CW) and lock it in this position with the aid of a spring, or tie it there.

9. Using the hook that was used in step 7 (item 6V7942), pull the sleeve and rack assembly through the servo unit (12) against the rack timing pin as shown in the cutaway governor diagram in Figure 23-24.

10. While holding light pressure on the hook, carefully zero the dial indicator assembly in the collet, making certain that both the large and small needles on the gauge are in the zero position; otherwise, turn the bezel and adjust the dial gauge in the collet until they are. Tighten the collet and bezel.

11. Remove the timing pin (3) shown in Figure 23-21 from the rack and injection pump housing, as well as the hook (11 in Figure 23-23).

12. Remove the light spring or untie the governor speed control lever (throttle) from its previous full-load position.

13. Refer to Figure 23-25 which illustrates the 6V7941 governor linkage compressor assembly. Adjust this rod as shown in the diagram to set up a dimension of 1 in. (25.4 mm) between the knurled end of the rod and its body.

14. Install the preadjusted compressor rod into the governor housing as illustrated in Figure 23-26.

15. Using circuit tester 9S4627 or equivalent (15 in Figure 23-27) connect the clip-end lead to the insulated terminal (16) on the housing, and the other one to any good clean electrical ground.

16. Manually rotate the governor speed con-

FIGURE 23–23 *Pushing the injection pump rack into the fuel shutoff position with hook 6V7942 (item 11). Item 10 is a 6V6151 adapter. (Courtesy of Caterpillar, Inc.)*

FIGURE 23–24 Pulling the rack against the timing pin using hook 6V7942 (item 11). Item 12 is the servo valve. (Courtesy of Caterpillar, Inc.)

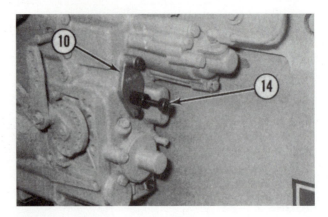

FIGURE 23–26 Governor linkage compressor rod installed into the rear of the governor housing in preparation for static rack setting. Item 10, 6V6151 adapter; 14, a 6V7941 compressor assembly. (Courtesy of Caterpillar, Inc.)

trol lever (throttle) CW to place it in its full-load position.

17. Slowly and carefully turn the knurled end of the governor linkage compressor rod assembly shown in Figure 23-27 (item 13) clockwise until the tester light (15) just starts to flicker. Very slowly increase the knurled knob until the tester light goes out completely.

18. Continue to turn the knurled knob on the compressor rod (13) until the dial indicator gauge needles move 2 mm (0.080 in.) in the negative (−) direction. This involves two complete revolutions of the large needle pointer on the gauge face.

NOTE   Minus readings are read to the left of the zero rack position, while positive readings are read to the right of the zero rack position.

CAUTION Should a noticeable increase in pressure be required to rotate the compressor rod (13), do *not* continue to try to turn it inward, since damage to the governor components occur due to this excessive force.

---

19. Refer to Figure 23-28 and remove the adjustment screw cover (17) from the lower rear of the governor housing.

20. To effectively determine the actual rack setting, slowly rotate the compressor rod (13 in Figure 23-27) counterclockwise until the test light just begins to illuminate, since this is the point at which the full static rack setting is reached. This reading on the dial indicator should be within ±0.25 mm (0.010 in.) of the

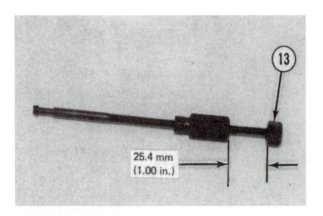

FIGURE 23–25 Mechanical governor linkage compressor rod 6V7941 (item 13) preadjustment dimensions. (Courtesy of Caterpillar, Inc.)

25.4 mm (1.00 in.)

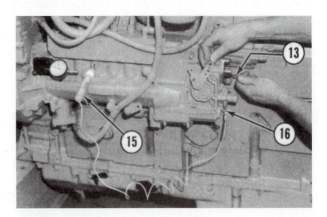

FIGURE 23–27 Checking static fuel rack setting point with a circuit tester connected into the system. 13, Rod (part of 6V7941 compressor assembly); 15, 8S4627 circuit tester; 16, insulated terminal. (Courtesy of Caterpillar, Inc.)

FIGURE 23–28 *Mechanical governor adjustment screw access cover. 17, Adjustment screw cover. (Courtesy of Caterpillar, Inc.)*

setting listed on the engine information plate or, alternatively, that listed in the fuel setting and related information microfiche literature available from your local Caterpillar dealer technical services department.

SPECIAL NOTE   In step 20 above, when the compressor rod (13) is backed out CCW, there will be a noticeable small amount of dial gauge needle movement within the first half-turn or so of the rod. During the next 1.5 turns of the rod, the dial gauge will show no movement, after which the needle would begin to rotate again until the desired setting is reached. To ensure that this reading is correct, rotation of the compressor rod (13) must be done *gradually*, not quickly. Therefore, repeat steps 17 through 20, to ensure that the correct measurement has been established.

---

21. Once the static fuel setting has been determined, the compressor rod (13 in Figure 23-27) should be turned out until the needle pointer on the dial gauge stops moving, after which the rod should be rotated CCW an additional two turns.

22. Push in on the rack stop collar accessible through the adjustment screw cover shown in Figure 23-28, (item 17), to ensure that the linkage is settled in the right position. Whatever reading is now visible on the dial indicator is the full torque static rack setting. This specification is located on the engine information plate on later 3406B engines; on earlier-model engines, you will have to consult the fuel setting and related information microfiche literature through your local Caterpillar dealer. The dial indicator reading must be within ±0.25 mm (0.010 in.) of the specified dimension; otherwise, adjustment is required.

23. To adjust either the injection pump static fuel rack setting or the full torque static setting correctly, refer to the following section, in which we discuss and use examples of just what is required to change the rack setting to specification.

Determining the Required Fuel Rack Adjustment

Once you have obtained the recommended static fuel rack setting and full torque static setting specification for your particular engine, based on your reading in steps 20 and 22 above, you must calculate whether the setting has to be changed by rotating the adjustment screws illustrated in Figures 23-29 and 23-30 CW (clockwise) or CCW (counterclockwise). Caterpillar special tool group 6V2106, shown as item 19 in Figures 23-29 and 23-30 is recommended for this purpose, since this tool arrangement allows you to both loosen/tighten the locknuts and rotate the adjustment screws. Should it be necessary to change the setting of both the static fuel rack setting and static full torque setting, rotate the torque rise adjustment screw (20 in Figure 23-30) CCW the same number of turns as that for the static fuel rack setting adjustment screw (18 in Figure 23-29) determined from Table 23-1. However, if only the static fuel rack setting is going to be decreased, it is not necessary to adjust/rotate the static full torque adjustment screw at this time.

GOVERNOR BALANCE POINT CHECK

The term *balance point* or *set point* refers to the condition that exists at the engine speed when the fuel setting screw or pin is just lightly touching either the

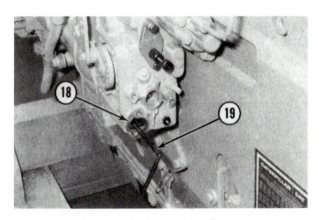

FIGURE 23–29 *Fuel rack setting adjustment screw location. 18, Fuel setting screw; 19, 6V2106 rack adjustment screw. (Courtesy of Caterpillar, Inc.)*

FIGURE 23–30 *Fuel rack torque setting adjustment screw location. 19, 6V2106 rack adjustment tool group; 20, torque rise setting screw. (Courtesy of Caterpillar, Inc.)*

torque spring or fuel rack stop bar. In addition, the balance point check of the engine can be used to determine and diagnose engine performance. The full-load speed or engine rpm is the speed at which the engine will produce its rated horsepower. The position of the rack (adjustable) is what determines the actual horsepower rating of the engine; the application of the engine is the determining factor in setting an engine to a particular horsepower rating or level. The governor

TABLE 23–1 *Amount of change for each part turn of the fuel setting adjustment screw on a 3406B engine*

Amount of change

in.	mm	Turns of adjustment screw
0.118	3.0	$3\frac{3}{4}$
0.110	2.8	$3\frac{1}{2}$
0.102	2.6	$3\frac{1}{4}$
0.094	2.4	3
0.087	2.2	$2\frac{3}{4}$
0.079	2.0	$2\frac{1}{2}$
0.071	1.8	$2\frac{1}{4}$
0.063	1.6	2
0.055	1.4	$1\frac{3}{4}$
0.047	1.2	$1\frac{1}{2}$
0.039	1.0	$1\frac{1}{4}$
0.031	0.8	1
0.024	0.6	$\frac{3}{4}$
0.016	0.4	$\frac{1}{2}$
0.008	0.2	$\frac{1}{4}$

Source: Caterpillar, Inc.

balance point is set by adjustment of the high-idle speed setting and the static fuel rack setting.

Checking the Balance Point

To check the engine balance point on an early scroll or compact body type of fuel system, you will require a circuit tester similar to 8S4627 and an accurate tachometer similar to 6V3121. On engines equipped with the new scroll fuel system you will require the 8T5300 engine timing indicator group along with the 6V4060 engine set point indicator group (Figure 23-31). Both the 8T5300 and 6V4060 indicator groups can be used in conjunction with the new IU5470 engine pressure group.

The balance point for the engine is always 20 rpm higher than the engine full-load speed. At this point the following conditions exist:

1. The engine is just leaving the overrun (governed) condition but has not quite reached the lug or nongoverned position.
2. Where the load stop pin or the rack stop collar just comes lightly into contact with the torque spring or stop bar (makes contact approximately 10% of the time).
3. Just prior to the point (rpm) where the engine will receive its maximum amount of fuel per pump stroke allowed by the governor, and where the engine has maximum power output.
4. Immediately before the engine rpm point where any increase in load on the engine will cause the engine to enter a lug (nongoverned) situation, with *lug* being defined as the condition whereby a small increase in load will cause a decrease in engine rpm.

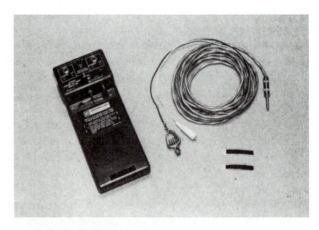

FIGURE 23–31 *6V4060 engine set point tool indicator group. (Courtesy of Caterpillar, Inc.)*

NOTE The fuel rack setting and high-idle speeds must be set correctly prior to adjustment to the engine balance or set point.

Balance/Set Point Procedure

Connect the 8T5300 multitach group to the engine tach drive or use one of the locally available electronic digital tachometers to closely monitor the speed of the engine. If the 8T5300 multitach and 6V4060 set point tool groups are available, install the multitach on the 6V4060 set point indicator and connect the set point indicator rack contact cable to the fuel injection pump. Detailed instructions for the use of these special tools can be found in Caterpillar special instruction forms SEHS7807 and SEHS7931, respectively.

If using the circuit tester 8S4627, connect it to the fuel pump as described earlier in checking and adjusting the rack setting, and to the brass terminal screw 16 as shown in Figure 23-27. The engine should be at normal operating temperature for this check.

Procedure

1. Rotate the governor control linkage to place the engine at its high-idle (maximum no-load rpm) speed and carefully record the speed shown on the multitach or electronic digital tach being used.

2. If using the engine set point indicator 6V4060, the "engine 1 over run" light should be illuminated.

3. Carefully/slowly add load to the engine while at its high-idle rpm until either the circuit tester light just starts to illuminate or, alternatively, the "engine 1 over run" light just goes out. In both cases this is the set or balance point of the engine; therefore, carefully record this rpm.

4. Repeat steps 1 and 3 a minimum of five times while recording the speeds attained in step 3.

5. Add up the rpm/speeds attained in steps 3 and 4 and divide by 5 to determine the average set/balance point figure. Subtract 20 rpm from the average speed that you obtained by calculation, which will give you the full-load speed setting of the engine.

6. Decrease the engine speed, and allow the engine to cool for a few minutes prior to shutting it down.

7. Compare the readings that you obtained in steps 1 and 5 with the specification stamped on the engine information plate, or given in the Caterpillar fuel rack setting information, which lists the maximum high-idle and full-load speeds for the particular engine.

8. Should the engine's full-load speed not be correct, adjustment of the governor high-idle speed screw as shown earlier is required to establish the correct full-load engine rpm.

9. Both the full-load and high-idle speeds *must* be within the tolerance specified by Caterpillar. This tolerance is ±10 rpm for the set point, and ±50 rpm for the high-idle speed with the engine in chassis, or ±30 rpm on a bare engine.

NOTE Should the engine's high-idle rpm be outside the published Caterpillar specification, yet the engine's full-load rpm be correct, it is possible that the problem could be associated with either a weak or an incorrect governor spring.

Set Point (Balance Point) Adjustment

If the set point is incorrect, remove the governor cover to gain access to the locknut (4) and adjustment screw (5) illustrated in Figure 23-32. Adjustment of the set point is achieved by loosening the locknut and turning the adjustment screw either CW or CCW to achieve a setting which is basically at the midtravel point of the allowable published tolerance listed above.

After any adjustment, always check and recheck the high-idle rpm to ensure that you have not exceeded the top end of the published tolerance figure. High-idle speeds in excess of the published figure could be a result of an incorrect governor spring or a flyweight problem, and high-idle readings lower than the published spec could be caused by excessive parasitic loads (accessories) or by a governor spring and flyweight problem.

FIGURE 23–32 Engine rack set point adjustment screw location. 4, Locknut; 5, adjustment screw. (Courtesy of Caterpillar, Inc.)

TORQUE CONTROL GROUP: 3406B/400-HP ATAAC

On the 3406B ATAAC (air-to-air aftercooled) 400-hp setting on-highway truck engine at 1800 rpm, a new torque control group has been available since December 1986. This torque control group 2W6660 replaces the former 2W8628 group to provide increased fuel delivery within a narrow 200-rpm speed range immediately below the rated (full-load) rpm of 1800. This results in an improvement in the overall engine response without any change occurring in either the full-load or full-torque static fuel settings. Figure 23-33 illustrates this new torque control group and its components, the only difference between this group and the earlier one being in the torque spring and shim parts. This new torque control group can be installed in place of the former group to provide increased engine response.

AIR/FUEL RATIO CONTROL

All turbocharged Caterpillar mechanical engines use an air/fuel ratio control unit to ensure that the amount of fuel delivered to the combustion chambers will be in proportion to the amount of airflow being supplied from the turbocharger assembly under varying loads and speeds. In this way, excess exhaust smoke is avoided, and EPA emissions are assured as well as good fuel economy and engine performance. The exception to this would be on all engines equipped with electronic engine control.

The air/fuel ratio control used with the new scroll fuel system is a little different in appearance from that used on earlier compact body fuel systems. However,

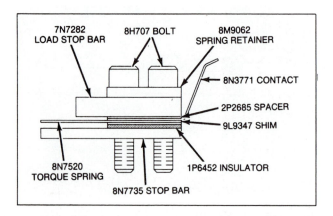

FIGURE 23-33 Location of the components in the 2W6660 torque control group. (Courtesy of Caterpillar, Inc.)

its function and basic operation are the same. It is mounted on the rear of the governor housing. Figures 23-34 and 23-35 illustrate the various operating positions of the hydraulic air/fuel ratio control unit, which are designed to prevent overfueling of the engine. It accomplishes this by limiting fuel rack movement until the turbocharger air boost pressure to the inlet manifold is sufficiently high to ensure complete combustion of the injected fuel. Without the air/fuel ratio control unit, the inherent lag in all exhaust-gas-driven turbochargers would allow more fuel than air and consequently would result in incomplete combustion through overfueling and black smoke at the exhaust gases.

AFC Operation
Engine Stopped
When the engine is stopped, no restriction exists between the air/fuel ratio control and the fuel injection pump rack; therefore, the condition within the air/fuel ratio control would appear as shown in Figure 23-34. In this position the stem (6) is fully extended; therefore, the operator can move the throttle linkage to any setting, or leave it at the low-idle position, and the overfueling spring (9 in Figure 23-7) will allow extra fuel for initial startup.

Engine Running at Idle
Once the engine is started, the governor will control the engine speed as discussed in the earlier governor description. The action within the air/fuel ratio control would be as shown in Figure 23-35. With the engine running, pressurized engine oil will flow through passage 5 and chamber 10, where the oil will flow through passage 9 and into the internal valve (3) and on out the drain passages in the stem (6). The turbocharger air pressure must be high enough to move the internal diaphragm assembly (2) to the right. A small line connects the air inside the engine inlet manifold to the air/fuel ratio control unit. When the diaphragm moves to its right, valve 3 will also move right and close oil passage 9, which allows the oil pressure to increase in chamber 10. Piston 8 and stem 6 move to their left into an operating mode until the engine is stopped as shown in Figure 23-34.

Engine Acceleration
When the operator increases the throttle position, the air/fuel ratio stem (6) will limit the movement of the throttle/governor lever (11) toward the increased fuel position since the pressurized engine oil in chamber 10 resists the movement of stem 6. As the turbo-charger boost pressure increases, the diaphragm (2) and valve (3) will move to the right. Valve 3 opens oil passage 9

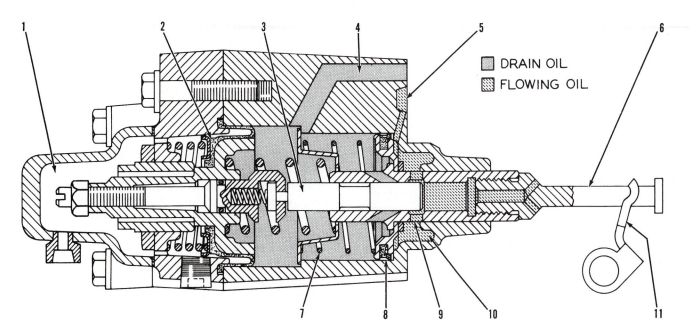

FIGURE 23–34 AFC (air/fuel ratio) control with the engine running after startup. 1, Inlet air chamber; 2, diaphragm assembly; 3, internal valve; 4, oil drain passage; 5, oil inlet; 6, stem; 7, spring; 8, piston; 9, oil passage; 10, oil chamber; 11, lever. (Courtesy of Caterpillar, Inc.)

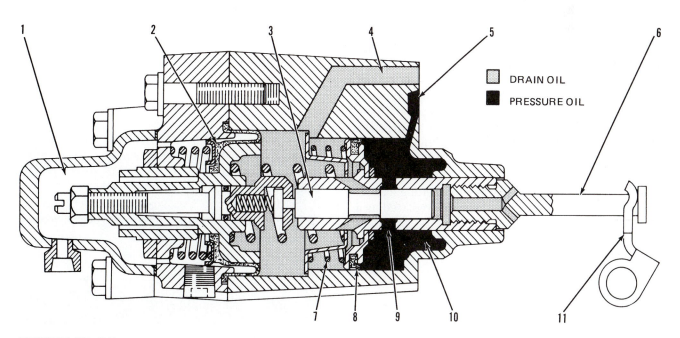

FIGURE 23–35 AFC control in the activated position. 1, Inlet air chamber; 2, diaphragm assembly; 3, internal valve; 4, oil drain passage; 5, oil inlet; 6, stem; 7, spring; 8, piston; 9, oil passage; 10, oil chamber; 11, lever. (Courtesy of Caterpillar, Inc.)

657

and drains oil from chamber 10 through the oil passage (4). This action reduces the oil pressure behind piston 8, and spring 7 will move piston 8 and stem 6 to the right until the oil passage (9) is closed by valve 3. The throttle lever can now be moved without resistance until the fuel rack is in the full-fuel position.

NOTE When intake manifold pressure is approximately 50% of the turbocharger's maximum boost or higher, full-fuel rack travel is available because the stem of the air/fuel ratio control is extended, and does not interfere with rack movement. Therefore, rapid acceleration under load is assured at a rate that will permit complete combustion, together with low exhaust smoke emissions.

Update: New 3406B Fuel Ratio Control Unit

Later 3406B truck engines, with serial numbers beginning with 7FB, use the fuel ratio control unit item 7W5318. This unit is less expensive to manufacture, as well as being simpler in design and operation. This new unit can be adapted to earlier engines with a minor amount of rework. The new unit is initially set/activated after engine startup as soon as engine oil pressure is high enough to act on a lever assembly within the governor housing. Once this governor lever has been tripped/set by engine oil pressure, the unit operates on turbocharger boost (intake manifold) pressure.

There is no need to adjust the static control linkage with this new unit such as described in this chapter for the earlier units, since all ratio control setting checks are done with the engine running (dynamically). These settings are performed simply by loosening a two-bolt retaining plate which secures the unit in place on the governor housing, then rotating the air/fuel ratio housing in either a CW direction to create a more negative setting, or by turning the housing CCW to effect a more positive setting. No repairs are possible on this new unit; it is replaced as a complete assembly should problems be apparent during service that cannot be corrected by simple adjustment.

Air/Fuel Ratio Control
Adjustment: 3406B Engine

This procedure lists the recommended routine for this adjustment, and where differences exist, they will be noted and you would then proceed to the next recommended step or would follow the sequence, depending on the serial number of the engine you are servicing. If it has been determined from the previous air/fuel ratio performance check that the air leakdown rate is less than 3 psi (21 kPa) over a 30-second period, after having applied a maximum pressure of 10 psi (69 kPa), and if an adjustment is in fact required on the engine, proceed as follows.

1. Refer to the engine information plate (new models) or obtain from your local Caterpillar technical services department, via the fuel setting and related information microfiche records, the actual dynamic (engine running) air/fuel ratio control setting for the particular engine on which you are working. To obtain this information, provide the engine serial number if it is not on the engine information plate.

2. Install and position either the rack position mechanical dial indicator tool group as shown in Figure 23-21 or if available, install in place of the mechanical dial indicator the 8T1000 electronic position indicator group discussed earlier and illustrated in Figure 23-18.

3. Refer to Figure 23-36 and remove the air line (15) first, then the cover from the air/fuel ratio control unit.

NOTE Step 4 applies only to earlier-model 3406B engines, which used a stop and a nut on the air/fuel ratio control unit. When these older-model air/fuel ratio control units are rebuilt, both the stop and the nut should not be used again. Step 5 applies only to CARB-certified engines.

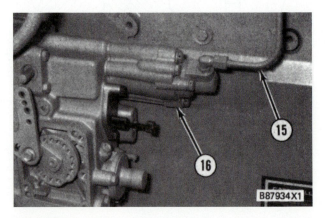

FIGURE 23-36 Removing AFC air line and housing. 15, air supply line; 16, fuel ratio control. (Courtesy of Caterpillar, Inc.)

4. Refer to Figure 23-37 and loosen nut 4, then rotate the stop (5) CW until it actually comes into contact with the shoulder on the retainer (8). Then rotate the stop CCW two complete turns and tighten the nut (4).

5. On CARB-certified engines only, refer to Figure 23-37 and adjust the air/fuel ratio preload by loosening nut 4 and rotating the stop (5) CCW between 2 and 3 complete turns.

6. On all 3406B engines, if the engine is not already at normal operating temperature, start and run it until it is.

7. Refer to Figure 23-37 and activate the air/fuel ratio control by pushing in manually on the valve extension (7).

NOTE   Steps 8 to 10 apply to CARB-certified engines only.

---

8. On CARB-certified engines only, with the engine running at 900 rpm, quickly snap the governor control lever to its maximum fuel position and record the measurement on either the mechanical dial indicator or 8T1000 electronic position indicator, then release the governor throttle control lever. Turn the stop (5 in Figure 23-37).

9. On CARB engines repeat step 8 until the dial indicator or 8T1000 electronic position indicator reads 1.0 ± 0.15 mm (0.040 ± 0.006 in.) greater than the dimension recorded in step 8.

10. If necessary, turn the stop (5) CW until the adjustment is obtained, then tighten the nut (4). Recheck the setting once more to ensure that you have it right.

11. On *all* engines, refer to Figure 23-37 and while holding retainer 8 in position, loosen the nut (6).

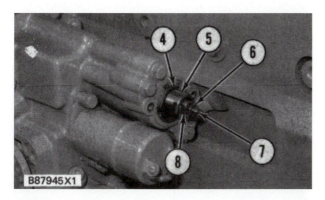

FIGURE 23–37 *3406B engine AFC adjustment components identification. 4, Nut; 5, stop; 6, nut; 7, valve extension; 8, retainer. (Courtesy of Caterpillar, Inc.)*

It is necessary to hold item 8 firmly to prevent the internal diaphragm from rotating any time that nut 6 is loosened or tightened.

12. Refer to Figure 23-37 and rotate item 7, the valve extension, to obtain the correct setting. Turning the extension CW will provide a more positive setting on the dial indicator or 8T1000 electronic position indicator tool, while turning it CCW provides a more negative setting of the measurement tool.

13. After each adjustment to the air/fuel ratio control, always check the dynamic (engine running) setting by running the engine to 900 rpm, snapping the throttle quickly into its full-fuel position, and holding it there while you record the travel on either the dial indicator or 8T1000 electronic position indicator tool.

NOTE   The 8T1000 electronic position indicator group tool is the preferred tool to use for this reading, since the mechanical dial indicator will register this maximum reading only briefly, then will tend to vibrate fairly severely. The 8T1000 tool, on the other hand, has a memory that can quickly be recalled by the push of a button to allow you to see for certain what the maximum reading was during the wide-open throttle setting.

---

14. Once the correct air/fuel ratio control setting has been obtained, tighten the nut (6 in Figure 23-37), then with the engine running at 900 rpm, quickly snap the throttle into its full-fuel position and double check that the setting has not changed.

15. Install the gasket and cover onto the air/fuel ratio housing and torque the retaining bolts to 9 ± 3 N · m (7 ± 2 lb-ft).

16. Using the air pressure regulator, valve, and fitting, apply a maximum pressure of 69 kPa (10 psi) to the fuel ratio control unit at fitting 15 in Figure 23-36 to fully extend the air/fuel ratio control so that we can obtain a true dynamic (engine running) full-torque rack setting.

17. Repeat the process described in step 13.

18. Should you not be able to obtain the recommended dynamic full-torque rack setting according to the engine information plate or Caterpillar spec, the air/fuel ratio control unit is in need of repair or replacement.

19. Once you have finished this setting, rewire and seal the air/fuel ratio control unit, install the air line (15), which was removed in step 3, and remove the dial indicator or 8T1000 electronic position indicator tool group.

Air/Fuel Ratio Control Linkage Adjustment: Engine 3406B

This adjustment is required only if, when performing the air/fuel ratio control adjustment described in this chapter for the 3406B engine, you got as far as step 18 and were unable to obtain the desired setting. Then you would proceed to check and adjust the system as described below. The tools needed for this linkage adjustment are contained within the Caterpillar 6V6070 tool group.

SPECIAL NOTE   The tools would be set up as illustrated in Figures 23-21 to 23-26 and you would follow procedural steps 1 through 14 listed in the section "Fuel Rack Setting Procedure: 3406B Engine."

FUEL INJECTION PUMP ASSEMBLY: 3406B ENGINE

Pump Removal

1. Steam clean the engine, particularly in the area of the engine front timing cover and around the air compressor and injection pump housing.

2. Disconnect the batteries to prevent any possibility of the engine being cranked over.

3. Make sure that the vehicle spring brakes are applied. Block the wheels to prevent possible movement forward or reverse.

4. Bleed all air from the vehicle's compressed-air tanks. Ensure that all compressed air from the air compressor governor air line has also been vented to zero.

5. Refer to Figure 23-9 and remove the automatic timing advance assembly from the front of the engine.

6. Refer to Figure 23-38 and remove:

a. The fuel line from the fuel transfer pump

b. The fuel line from the injection pump housing

c. The intake manifold aftercooler air line to the air/fuel ratio control

7. Remove from the top of the injection pump housing all of the high-pressure fuel lines that connect to the injector nozzles.

8. Refer to Figure 23-39 and remove the air line (5) and the compressor coolant line (6). Use a suitable container to catch coolant that will vent from this hose.

9. Since the 3406B injection pump and governor

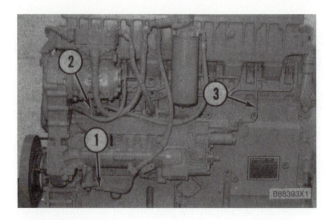

FIGURE 23–38   Removal of fuel line. 1, Fuel line; 2, aftercooler air line; 3, to the AFC housing. (Courtesy of Caterpillar, Inc.)

assembly weighs 125 lb (57 kg), sling the pump to an overhead hoist with a webbing harness as shown in Figure 23-40.

10. Refer to Figure 23-40 and remove the retaining bolts (7).

11. Refer to Figure 23-41 and remove the two nuts and bolts (8 and 9). Check that the webbing sling is attached securely and carefully pull the injection pump and housing clear of the engine.

Pump Installation

Pump installation follows the reverse procedure as that described above for removal. However, once the pump has been reinstalled onto the engine, it will have to be timed. Refer to the section "Dynamic Engine Timing" as well as to the section "Automatic Timing Advance Unit."

FIGURE 23–39   Removal of air line. 5, 6, compressor coolant line. (Courtesy of Caterpillar, Inc.)

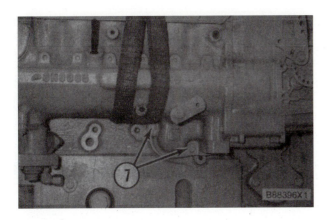

FIGURE 23–40 *Web sling supporting injection pump prior to removal of retaining bolts (item 7). (Courtesy of Caterpillar, Inc.)*

Individual Injection Pump Removal

1. Clean the area around the top of the injection pump housing to prevent any possibility of dirt entering the housing.

2. Disconnect the vehicle batteries to prevent any possibility of the engine being cranked over during this service procedure.

3. Center the fuel injection pump rack as described in this chapter and shown in Figures 23-14 and 23-21.

4. Remove the high-pressure injection line from the pump that is to be removed.

5. You will require the Caterpillar special tool set 6V7050 compressor group, the 8S4613 wrench, and the 8S2244 pump extractor.

CAUTION The pump plunger/barrel assembly is under strong spring pressure when installed

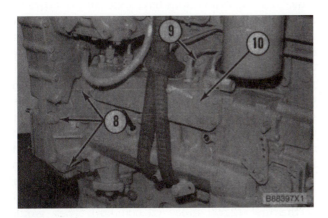

FIGURE 23–41 *Removal of nuts. 8, bolts; 9, to allow injection pump; 10, removal. (Courtesy of Caterpillar, Inc.)*

into the injection pump housing. This is why the 6V7050 compressor assembly is required, as shown in Figure 23-42. The compressor handle must be pushed down until it locks into position prior to loosening the pump bushing retainer (4).

6. Refer to Figure 23-42 which illustrates the injection pump rack centering pin (1) in position. Also shown are wrench 8S4613(2), compressor tooling 6V7050 (3) in its locked position, and the individual pump retainer bushing (4), which has been loosened by wrench 8S4613 (2).

7. Once the pump retainer bushing (4) is clear of its bore, slowly release the 6V7050 compressor assembly handle until all spring force from the plunger/barrel assembly has been removed.

8. Remove all the special tools shown in Figure 23-42 from the top of the pump housing.

9. Refer to Figure 23-43 and install the special pump extractor 8S2244 onto the pump threads.

10. Carefully pull the extractor and pump assembly straight up and out of the housing.

11. Remove the pump spacer from within the bore of the housing.

Individual Injection Pump Installation

Prior to reinstalling an individual pumping unit back into the main injection pump housing, the rack must be centered as described for pump removal (see Figure 23-21). You will require the same special tools that were used for pump removal, shown in Figures 23-42 and 23-43.

1. Ensure that the lifter for the pump to be in-

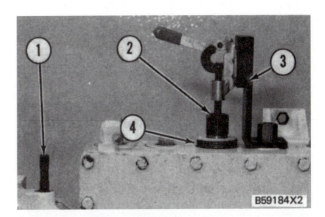

FIGURE 23–42 *Removal of an individual injection pump assembly using special tool group. 1, 6V4186 timing pin; 2, 8S4613 wrench; 3, 6V7050 compressor group; 4, retainer housing. (Courtesy of Caterpillar, Inc.)*

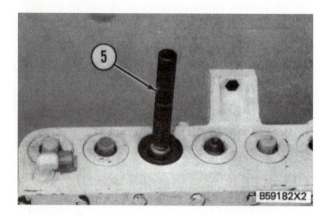

FIGURE 23–43 *Withdrawing an individual injection pump assembly from its bore using special extractor tool 8S2244. (Courtesy of Caterpillar, Inc.)*

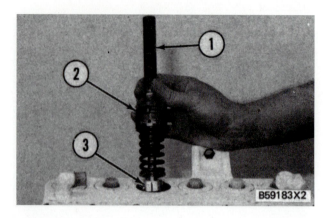

FIGURE 23–45 *Preparing to install an individual injection pump into its bore in the housing using special extractor tool 8S2244 (item 1). 2, Pump barrel; 3, gear segment. (Courtesy of Caterpillar, Inc.)*

stalled is at the bottom of its travel. This can be checked by looking into the bore and noting if the cam lobe is on its base circle or lowest position.

2. Install the spacer into the pump bore that was removed in step 11 during disassembly/removal.

3. Ensure that the slot/groove in the pump gear segment is aligned with its pin in the side of the lifter and barrel groove. Refer to Figure 23-44 and make certain that the pump barrel groove (5) is aligned with the dowel in the bore of the injection pump housing.

4. Using the extractor tool (8S2244) that was used during the removal procedure, carefully lower and guide the assembled pumping plunger and barrel into position in the housing (see Figure 23-45)

5. Unscrew the extractor. Place a new O-ring in position under the pump bushing (4 in Figure 23-42).

6. Install the special tooling shown in Figure 23-42 position over the pump assembly.

7. Slowly and carefully depress the 6V7050 compressor handle to push the pump into the bore of

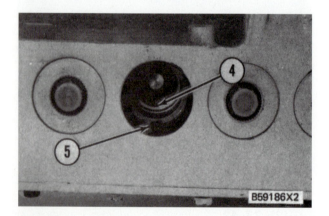

FIGURE 23–44 *Internal view of individual injection pump bore, highlighting the pin. 4, Dowel; 5, location. (Courtesy of Caterpillar, Inc.)*

the housing. If the handle does not move smoothly, it usually indicates that something is not aligned; invariably, you will find that it is the pump gear segment, groove in the barrel, and pin in the bore. Repeat the alignment procedure if necessary.

8. Once the compressor handle has locked in position, ensure that the O-ring seal is in position in its bore.

9. Use special wrench 9S4613 to tighten the pump retainer bushing.

10. Remove the compressor tooling group and tighten the retainer bushing to 160 ± 11 lb-ft (215 ± 15 N · m).

VALVE ADJUSTMENT: 3406 ENGINE

At one time there was no specific number of hours or miles in which it was considered necessary to check and adjust the intake and exhaust valves on the engine. Ongoing evaluations have determined, however, that the greatest rate of change to the valve lash clearance occurs within the first few hundred hours of operation in a new or rebuilt engine. For this reason, Caterpillar no longer recommends adjusting the valves at the time of a predelivery check, since insufficient hours have accumulated on the engine to create any substantial change. However, with the emphasis on longer engine life as well as increased fuel economy, Caterpillar now recommends that this adjustment be performed at the following time intervals: On highway truck engines, the valves should be adjusted at the first oil change on a new or rebuilt engine, or at the first 12,500 miles (20,000 km). They would then be checked and adjusted every 100,000 miles (161,000 km), or once per year. This supersedes the old recommendation whereby there was no valve adjustment until 50,000 miles or 80,000 km.

In addition to the valve lash adjustment, it is also imperative that you check and adjust the valve bridges, which are designed to open two valves on each cylinder at the same time. Since valve and valve mechanism components do not always wear evenly, this results in the bridge going out of adjustment. Bridge adjustment should always be done before the actual valve lash is checked and adjusted.

Valve Bridge Adjustment

If an engine has been overhauled or the cylinder head has been worked on, the bridges can be set prior to installing the rocker arm assemblies; however, if the bridges are being checked on an engine already in service, it is not necessary to remove the rocker arm shaft to perform the bridge adjustment. With the valves closed for the cylinder being checked, simply push down on the top of the rocker arm immediately above the center of the bridge to check and perform the adjustment listed below.

1. Place the bridge assembly in a soft-jawed vise and loosen the adjusting screw locknut. This makes it easier than trying to do it while in place on its dowel.

2. To remove all friction, apply a small amount of oil on both the bridge support dowel on the cylinder head and in the actual bore of the bridge itself.

3. Place the bridge over its dowel, with the bridge adjusting screw facing toward the engine exhaust manifold.

4. Back out the bridge adjustment screw several turns.

5. Apply light pressure with your finger on top of the bridge pallet to keep it in contact with the valve stem tip.

6. Lightly turn down (CW) the bridge adjustment screw until it just makes contact with the valve stem tip.

7. Rotate the adjustment screw another 30° CW, which should cause the bridge to sit square on its dowel as well as allowing for any clearance that might exist in the adjustment screw threads.

8. Hold the adjustment screw firmly in this position and torque its locknut to 22 ± 3 lb-ft (30 ± 4 N · m).

NOTE   If the engine rocker arms are not in position, such as during reassembly of the head, it is easier to remove the bridge after lightly snugging the locknut up, place it in a soft-jaw vise, and perform the torque procedure on the locknut.

9. Apply clean engine oil between the bridge pallet and the end of the rocker arm assembly if reassembling a rebuilt head.

Valve Clearance Adjustment

Once the valve bridges have been set, the valve lash clearance can be checked and adjusted. The firing order for the 3406 engine is 1–5–3–6–2–4 with the No. 1 cylinder being at the front of the engine.

NOTE   When checking the valve clearance between the end of the rocker arm and the bridge pallet, adjustment is not necessary if the clearance falls within the following specifications:

Valve Clearance: Engine Stopped (Tolerance)

- Exhaust: 0.027 to 0.033 in. (0.69 to 0.84 mm)
- Intake: 0.012 to 0.018 in. (0.30 to 0.46 mm)

However, if the engine cylinder head has been removed for service work, the valve clearances should be set to the following specifications:

Valve Clearance: Engine Stopped and Resetting to Spec

- Exhaust: 0.030 in. (0.76 mm)
- Intake: 0.015 in. (0.38 mm)

If setting the valve clearance to spec, it can be checked using either a go/no go feeler gauge or a straight feeler gauge, although go/no go gauges are easier to use and generally result in a more accurate setting. Check the valve clearance between the rocker arm and bridge pallet.

Adjustment Procedure

1. Rotate the engine over manually in its normal direction of rotation from the front, which is CW, to place the No. 1 piston at TDC on its compression stroke. This ensures that both the intake and exhaust valves are closed. This can be confirmed by the fact that clearance will exist between the end of each rocker arm and the pallet of the valve bridge. TDC for piston 1 can be accomplished as described earlier in this chapter and shown in Figure 23-12, where the engine can be rotated by the use of a $\frac{1}{2}$-in. drive ratchet and special turning tool 9S9082, until the timing bolt will enter the hole in the engine flywheel.

2. With the piston 1 at TDC on its compression stroke, check and adjust the intake valve clearance on cylinders 1, 2, and 4, and the exhaust valve clearance on cylinders 1, 3, and 5, by loosening the rocker arm

adjusting screw locknut, and rotating the screw until the correct feeler gauge clearance is obtained.

3. Torque the locknut to 22 ± 3 lb-ft (30 ± 4 N · m) after each adjustment setting and recheck that the clearance is still correct.

4. Remove the flywheel timing bolt, then manually rotate the engine one full turn or 360° until the bolt will again reenter the hole in the flywheel. The No. 6 piston is now at TDC on its compression stroke.

5. Adjust the intake valves for cylinders 3, 5, and 6, and the exhaust valve clearance for cylinders 2, 4, and 6.

CAUTION Be sure to remove the timing bolt from the flywheel when all adjustments have been performed, and install it back into position in the flywheel housing as shown in Figure 23-13.

3114 AND 3116 MECHANICAL MODEL ENGINES

Released into full-scale production in the 1988 model year, the Caterpillar 3114 and 3116 model engines both have a displacement of 1.1 L (67 in.^{3}) per cylinder, from a bore of 105 mm (4.12 in.) and a stroke of 127 mm (5.00 in.). The 3114 is a four-cylinder design and the 3116 is a six-cylinder four-stroke-cycle design. Both engines have been designed as 6000-hour life-cycle engines between overhaul, with extensive use of aluminum alloy being used throughout the engine to ensure a lightweight design. This is reflected in the weight of the 3114—400 kg (800 lb)—and the 3116—493 kg (1085 lb). The horsepower range of the 3114 is between 80 and 140 hp (60 to 104 kW), while the 3116 is rated between 165 and 250 hp (123 to 187 kW). Depending on the specific truck application, the maximum full-load governed speed will not exceed 2600 rpm. Therefore, these engines will be found in a number of light- and medium-duty truck applications into the 1990s. Both engines use a mechanically operated unit injector system similar to the design that has been used in Detroit Diesel Corporation engines since their initial inception in 1938. The Cat 3114/3116 injector looks more like the 8.2-L V8 midrange DDC engine unit injector, in that it has a captive hold-down clamp which is part of the injector assembly. Combustion is of the direct injection design with a compression ratio of 16.5:1 in order to gain the maximum performance and fuel economy, and to meet the strict EPA exhaust emission requirements.

Depending on the engine application, the 3114/3116 engines can be equipped with a one-piece aluminum alloy trunk-type piston, where peak cylinder pressures do not exceed 1700 psi (11,722 kPa). In applications where peak cylinder pressures approach 1900 psi (13,100 kPa) a two-piece crosshead aluminum alloy piston is used to provide longer piston and ring life expectancy.

The 3114/3116 engines have been designed to compete directly with Cummins B model engines, which have a displacement of 3.9 L and 5.9 L, respectively, in both a four- and six-cylinder engine configuration. However, the Cummins B series employ a Robert Bosch model VE or CAV DPA distributor-type injection pump mated to pencil-type nozzles. The Cat engine uses a high-mounted camshaft to reduce the overall length of the pushrods as well as using a roller cam follower design. The Cat 3114 engine also employs a balancer mechanism mounted below the engine block, as does the Cummins B series engine. The Cummins B series employs a low-mounted camshaft and therefore uses longer pushrods with flat-type slipper follower tappets.

The GMC Truck Division of General Motors Corporation is a large user of the 1.1-L Caterpillar engines in their line of Topkick and Chevrolet Kodiak medium-duty trucks. GMC's heavy-duty truck line is now part of the Volvo GMC truck line, owned 80% by Volvo and 20% by General Motors.

NOTE Both 3114 and 3116 engines are manufactured as 100% metric fastener designs.

Fuel System

The fuel system used with 3114/3116 engines is very similar to that used on all Detroit Diesel Corporation engines; therefore, if you are familiar with the DDC fuel system, you will have a ready frame of reference. Figure 23-46 illustrates a basic fuel system schematic that identifies the major system components. The fuel system employs a plunger-type transfer pump mounted above and forward of the engine governor on the right-hand side of the engine looking from the front. This fuel pump is similar to the plunger pump used on other Caterpillar engines. For details on the design and concept of operation, see Figures 23-4 and 23-5. Although no primary fuel filter per se is used with these engines, a fuel filter/water separator can be installed if desired between the fuel tank and the fuel transfer pump.

The fuel flow in Figure 23-46 operates as follows: Fuel in the tank is pulled through a small inline type of screen (1) or a fuel filter/water separator if used into the fuel transfer pump (2). Fuel is pressurized inside

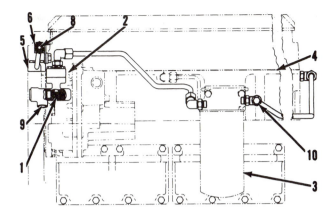

FIGURE 23–46 Fuel system components located on the left-hand side of the 3116 engine. 1, Screen; 2, fuel transfer pump (integral with governor); 3, main filter; 4, cylinder head; 5, pressure regulating orifice; 6, check valve; 8, outlet (fuel return to tank); 9, inlet (fuel from tank). (Courtesy of Caterpillar, Inc.)

the pump at an idle speed to a minimum of 7 to 9 psi (48 to 62 kPa), while at higher speeds this fuel pressure will increase to as high as 57 psi (393 kPa), although normal-running fuel pressures tend to be between 30 and 35 psi (207 to 241 kPa). The higher the engine's rated speed, the higher will be the fuel pressure. The 3114/3116 engines can be governed between 2000 and 2800 rpm, depending on the application. The outlet pressure of the fuel transfer pump must be a minimum of 29 psi (200 kPa) when the engine is running at full-load speed. Fuel under pressure is directed out of the pump through an external fuel line to the fuel filter (3), which has a 5-μm rating.

Filtered fuel leaves the filter and passes through a steel line to the rear of the engine, where it enters the center of the cylinder head (4). A common-rail-type fuel passage that runs the length of the head internally feeds all unit injectors at the same fuel pressure. The fuel delivered to the injectors serves the purpose not only of supplying fuel for injection purposes but also for both cooling and lubrication of the injector components. There is always an excess amount of fuel delivered over and above that required for injection purposes to ensure that adequate cooling and lubrication occurs regardless of engine load and speed. Fuel not required for injection purposes exits the cylinder head at the front of the engine and passes through a regulating orifice (5) and a check valve (6) prior to returning to the fuel tank (7). The orifice (5), which is located in the fuel return housing, functions in the same manner as that of the restricted fitting used in all DDC engine fuel systems, in that is ensures that there will be sufficient fuel pressure in the cylinder head fuel

gallery to supply the injectors under all operating conditions, but particularly when the engine is operating at a low idle speed. The check valve (6) is there to prevent fuel drain back to the tank when the engine is shut down; therefore, it is similar in function to the one-way check valve used on the suction side of many high-speed diesel fuel systems to prevent loss of fuel prime when the engine is shut down. Later-model 3114 and 3116 engines use a new fuel return valve in the fuel filter lines group. The valve uses spring force against an O-ring seal and seat. This provides a positive seal against fuel siphoning when the engine is not operating. The former valve could allow the fuel to siphon back to the tank making it hard to start the engine.

Unit Injector

Due to the similarity in function and design, a detailed description of the unit fuel injector will not be covered here. We will describe the basic design and functional operation of the injector; however, for detailed unit injector operation and maintenance, refer to Chapter 21. Figure 23-47 illustrates the mechanical unit injector used with the 3114/3116 engines. The injector is actuated by a pushrod and rocker arm concept similar to that for the 3176 electronically controlled unit injector. The unit injectors are manufactured by Lucas CAV for Caterpillar, and their main function is to:

1.   Time the fuel delivery by setting the injector tappet follower height above the injector hold-down clamp. The initial timing is, of course, controlled by the engine crankshaft-to-camshaft gear timing.

2.   Meter the quantity of fuel delivered to the combustion chamber by moving the fuel rack out from the body for more fuel, or toward the injector body for less fuel. This action rotates the plunger within the barrel and advances or retards the start of injection by placing the helix (scroll) on the plunger closer or farther from the point of barrel port closure. The rack movement on the Cat 3114/3116 engines is exactly opposite that for DDC unit injectors.

3.   Pressurize the fuel within the injector to a high-enough pressure to open the internal needle valve against its spring, so that fuel can be forced through the small orifices (holes) in the spray tip and into the combustion chamber. The injector tappet follower is forced down by the action of the self-centering button on the end of the rocker arm. The rocker arm is, of course, activated by a pushrod lifted by engine camshaft rotation.

4.   Atomization of the fuel occurs due to the fact that approximately 3500 psi (24,133 kPa) is required to lift the internal needle valve from its seat. This fuel pressure is then forced through a series of very small

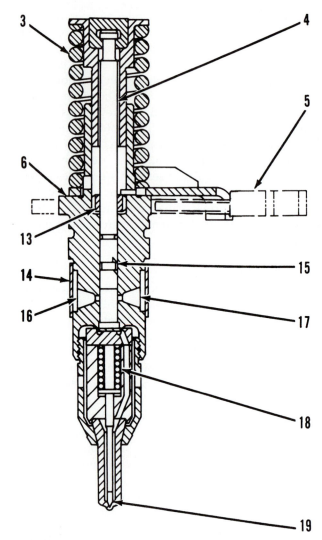

FIGURE 23-47 *Cross-sectional view of a mechanically operated unit fuel injector, 3116 engine. 3, Tappet spring; 4, plunger; 5, rack; 6, barrel; 13, gear; 14, sleeve filter; 15, helix; 16, lower port; 17, upper port; 18, spring; 19, check (needle valve). (Courtesy of Caterpillar, Inc.)*

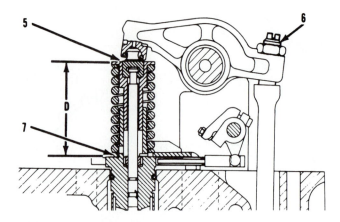

FIGURE 23-48 *3116 mechanically operated unit fuel injector timing dimension setting height D between top of follower and injector body. (Courtesy of Caterpillar, Inc.)*

In order to perform this check and adjustment correctly, you should have access to the following special Cat tools:

1. 1U6680 governor and fuel system adjusting tool group
2. 6V6106 dial indicator
3. 1U6677 injector timing fixture
4. 1U8702 injector timing block
5. 5P4160 dial gauge contact point
6. 1U6678 calibration fixture group

Checking Procedure
1. Place the engine at TDC on cylinder 1 according to the description given under the procedure for finding TDC.
2. Due to the fact that two crankshaft positions are required to check all injectors, refer to Table 23-2 which will guide you to the correct piston position (No. 1 at TDC compression or exhaust).
3. The injection timing height can be done with the rocker arms in place or removed from the engine using either a mechanical or digital gauge.
4. Figure 23-49 illustrates the injector timing fixture in position on the calibration fixture so that the dial gauge can be effectively adjusted. Make sure that all components are clean.
5. With all of the necessary tools assembled in position as shown in Figure 23-49, refer to the engine information plate on the valve rocker cover to obtain the specified injector fuel timing (height) dimensions in millimeters.
6. Carefully write the fuel timing spec down on a piece of paper; subtract the length of the 1U8702 injector timing block (item 3 in Figure 23-49), which is

orifices (holes) in the injector tip, which will result in a rise in fuel pressure to as high as 22,000 psi (151,690 kPa) spray-in pressure. This high fuel pressure breaks the fuel down into a finely atomized state similar to a fine mist, to ensure penetration of the compressed air mass within the piston bowl (crown).

Unit Injector Fuel Timing
This check is required to determine if the height of the injector tappet follower is according to the correct spec above the unit injector shoulder as shows in Figure 23-48. This check is similar to that for DDC 8.2-L engine unit fuel injectors in that a dial gauge is used instead of a timing pin.

TABLE 23–2 *3114/3116 Engine crankshaft positions for fuel timing and valve clearance setting[a]*

3114 Engine	
Check/adjust with No. 1 piston on TC compression stroke[b]	
Intake valves	1–2
Exhaust valves	1–3
Injectors	3–4
Check/adjust with No. 1 piston on TC exhaust stroke[b]	
Intake valves	3–4
Exhaust valves	2–4
Injectors	1–2
Firing order	1–3–4–2
3116 Engine	
Check/adjust with No. 1 piston on TC compression stroke[b]	
Intake valves	1–2–4
Exhaust valves	1–3–5
Injectors	3–5–6
Check/adjust with No. 1 piston on TC exhaust stroke[b]	
Intake valves	3–5–6
Exhaust valves	2–4–6
Injectors	1–2–4
Firing order	1–5–3–6–2–4

Source: Courtesy of Caterpillar, Inc.
[a]SAE standard (counterclockwise) rotation engines as viewed from the flywheel end.
[b]Put the No. 1 piston at the top center (TC) position and make the identification for the correct stroke. Refer to "finding top center position for No. 1 piston." After the top center position for a particular stroke is found and adjustments are made for the correct cylinders, remove the timing bolt and turn the flywheel counterclockwise 360°. This will put the No. 1 piston at the top center (TC) position on the other stroke. Install the timing bolt in the flywheel and complete the adjustments for the cylinders that remain.

FIGURE 23–49 *3116 injector calibration fuel timing fixture. 2, 1U6677 timing fixture; 3, 1U8702 timing block; 4, 1U6678 calibration fixture; 9, 1U8869 digital dial indicator; A, bolt; B, collet sleeve; C, locating pin. (Courtesy of Caterpillar, Inc.)*

62.00 mm from the fuel timing dimension. For instructional purposes let's assume that the fuel timing spec was 64.40 mm. If we substract 62.00 mm from this, we have a value of 2.40 mm, which is assigned a (minus) reading.

7.   If using a mechanical dial gauge, use the red figure scale on the dial indicator only. Carefully move the dial indicator stem in the collet sleeve (item B in Figure 23-49) so that the dial indicator needle pointers register a value of 2.40 mm on the red or negative scale. Tighten the collet, then recheck that the reading is still at 2.40 mm. The digital dial gauge is set up in a similar manner using the ON/OFF and PRESET buttons, plus the correct contact point on the end of the gauge stem plunger.

8.   Wipe the top of the unit injector tappet follower clean, as well as the shoulder.

FIGURE 23–50 *Special tool 1U6677 injector timing fixture installed in place over the unit injector. 2, 1U6677 timing fixture; 6, adjustment screw; 8, valve cover base; 9, 1U8869 digital dial indicator. (Courtesy of Caterpillar, Inc.)*

9. Refer to Figure 23-50, which illustrates the dial indicator in position with the timing fixture over an injector. This is done by removing bolt A from the timing fixture in Figure 23-49 so that the bracket, dial indicator, and collet are free from the test fixture base. Carefully install the fixture into position as shown in Figure 23-50. This can be determined by noting that the locating pin C and bolt A easily engage with the holes in the top face of the valve cover base (8); then tighten the bolt.

10. Carefully lower the collet sleeve B until the long pin contacts the shoulder (7) of the unit injector shown in Figure 23-48.

11. Observe the reading on the dial indicator pointers at this time. If the pointers indicate 0.00 or are within 0.05 mm, no adjustment is required.

12. If unit injector timing height adjustment is necessary, loosen the injector pushrod adjustment screw locknut in Figure 23-48, item 6.

13. Carefully rotate the adjustment screw (6) until the dial indicator pointers read 0.00 mm.

14. Tighten the adjusting screw locknut (6) to a torque value of $25 \pm 7\,\text{N} \cdot \text{m}$ (18 ± 5 lb-fit). The recheck the dial indicator value to ensure that a 0.00-mm reading still exists.

15. Repeat this procedure on half of the unit injectors according to the procedure given in Table 23-2 then pull the flywheel timing bolt and rotate the engine another 360° and do the rest.

16. Make sure that you remove the timing bolt from the flywheel when finished and insert the access plug.

Unit Injector Synchronization

This check and adjustment will ensure that all unit injector rack control linkage is set up the same to ensure

even fuel distribution to all cylinders. We will use the first and second special Caterpillar tools listed above for the fuel timing check/adjustment, plus three additional ones. These tools are as follows:

1. IU6680 governor and fuel system adjusting tool group
2. 6V6106 dial indicator
3. IU6675 injector spring compressor
4. IU6679 injector group
5. IU6673 wrench

Synchronization of the injector rack is required any time that it has been removed and replaced. Normally when checking the rack setting, the No. 1 injector is not touched since it becomes the reference or master rack when comparing the rest of the injector's rack linkages. However, if the injectors, including No. 1, have been removed, all injector rack linkages must be reset/synchronized. Due to the small clearance that exists when the rocker arms are in position on the engine, it is recommended that all rocker arm assemblies be removed prior to this check.

SPECIAL TIP   The electrical fuel shutoff solenoid must be latched into its RUN position before checking the rack linkage. Otherwise, there will be no rack movement. In addition, each injector spring tappet follower must be compressed slightly with a special tool; otherwise, the rack will bind and you will be unable to move the rack for the check/adjustment.

Synchronization Procedure

1. To effectively latch the electrical shutdown solenoid for the rack linkage check, stop the engine and turn off the ignition key switch.

2. Refer to Figure 23-51, which illustrates the latching-type electrical solenoid. Using a pair of pliers, grasp and pull out the center rod (3) until you feel it click into the run position.

3. If a nonlatching type of electrical solenoid (energize to run type) is used, remove it completely to allow free rack movement during the check and adjustment.

4. With the rocker arm assemblies removed, install the IU6675 flat injector spring compressor shown as item 6 in Figure 23-52. Thread the hold-down bolt into the cylinder head rocker arm assembly hole.

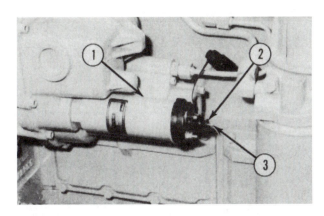

FIGURE 23–51 Location of 3116 engine fuel shutoff solenoid. 1, Solenoid; 2, ferrule; 3, center rod. (Courtesy of Caterpillar, Inc.)

NOTE   There is one injector spring compressor for each cylinder. Install all of them into position for the check.

---

5.   Once the injector spring compressors have been installed, oil the top of the compressor, then tap it lightly with a plastic or rubber hammer above the injector. This will seat the compressor and ensure that the injector rack will move freely.

6.   Refer to Figure 23-53 and remove the bolt (7) that is close to the injector. This will allow us to install the injector synchronization tooling shown in Figure 23-54.

7.   Install the dial indicator into the tool fixture as shown in Figure 23-54, but do not tighten the dial indicator just yet.

8.   Make sure that no dirt exists on the tooling

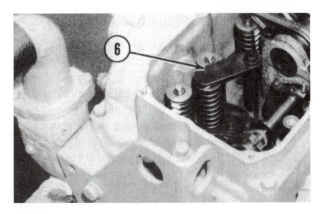

FIGURE 23–52 Installing injector spring compressor over No. 1 injector. 6, 1U6675 Injector spring compressor. (Courtesy of Caterpillar, Inc.)

FIGURE 23–53 Showing injector spring compressor in position for checking procedure. 6, 1U6675 Injector spring compressor; 7, bolt. (Courtesy of Caterpillar, Inc.)

or rack closest to the tooling to ensure that a false reading will not be recorded.

9.   Install the tooling into position as shown in Figure 23-55 and bolt it into position where the small bolt was previously removed as item 7 in Figure 23-53.

10.   With the tooling in position, make sure that the lever (10) does in fact contact the end of the rack (12) as shown in Figure 23-56.

11.   The rack must be checked in the zero fuel or shutoff position. Manually push the end of the rack (11) toward the injector body until the rack stop (14) touches the injector body (13) as shown in Figure 23-56. Hold it there.

12.   Adjust the dial indicator until the two small dial pointers are set at zero, then tighten the collet screw. Manually rotate the bezel until the large pointer is zeroed and tighten the bezel screw.

13.   Release the rack and refer now to Figure

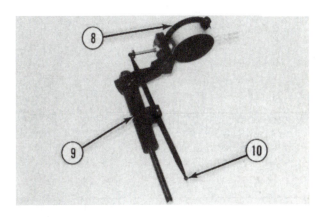

FIGURE 23–54 Mechanical unit fuel injector, 3116 engine synchronization tooling. 8, 6V6106 dial indicator; 9, 1U6679 indicator group; 10, lever (part of 1U6679 indicator group). (Courtesy of Caterpillar, Inc.)

FIGURE 23-55 *Special injector synchronization tooling installed in position on the 3116 engine. 8, 6V6106 dial indicator; 9, 1U6679 indicator group. (Courtesy of Caterpillar, Inc.)*

23-57. Manually push down on clamp 9 to rotate the rack outward to the fuel ON position, then quickly release it. This action simply confirms that there is freedom of movement and no bind in the linkage, and it also settles the linkage into its normal operating position.

14. Refer back to Figure 23-56 and push the injector rack (11) of No. 1 injector toward the injector body until the rack stop (14) touches the injector body. *Hold it here* by hand, which is the zero or fuel shutoff position.

15. Refer to Figure 23-57 and while holding No. 1 rack in the NO-FUEL position, push down, then release rack lever 6 of the particular injector being checked. Do this several times to confirm that there is no bind in the rack linkage.

16. The dial indicator *must* record a value of between +0.01 and 0.05 mm each time that you repeat

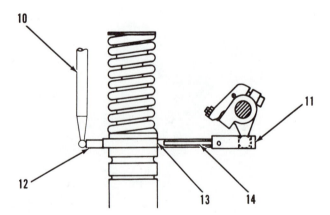

FIGURE 23-56 *Initial setup of special tooling to check injector rack settings. 10, Lever (part of 1U6679 indicator group); 11, rack head; 12, rack bar; 13, injector base; 14, rack stop. (Courtesy of Caterpillar, Inc.)*

the check at the injector rack linkage as stated in step 15.

17. On any injectors that do not fall within the 0.01 to 0.05 mm value, adjustment is required as described in step 18.

CAUTION Make sure that any rack adjustment is accomplished only by loosening item 8 in Figure 23-57. Do *not* under any circumstances attempt to loosen the socket head screws that are filled with sealant shown on the opposite side of the rack bar since these particular screws are factory set to the rack control shaft; therefore, if they are tampered with at any time it is impossible to reset them to the factory setting. This action would result in poor engine performance, and engine damage could occur as a result of the imbalance of fuel delivery to the different cylinders.

---

18. Use special Caterpillar wrench IU6673 to effectively loosen the locknut and back off the setscrew (5) CCW (see Figure 23-57).

19. With the dial indicator in position as shown in Figure 23-55, hold the rack head of the No. 1 injector in the fuel shutoff position, which is all the way toward the injector body.

20. Push down and quickly release the rack lever (Figure 23-57) of the injector being adjusted to its synchronized position. Using wrench 1U6673, turn the setscrew CW until the dial indicator reads +0.01 to 0.05 mm; then tighten the locknut.

21. Double check your setting by repeating the movement of the rack linkage two or three times to confirm your reading.

22. If other injectors require adjustment of the rack linkage, repeat the same steps. When complete, remove all tooling and install all rocker arm assemblies and prepare the engine to run again.

23. Refer back to Figure 23-51 and manually pull ferrule 2 on the shutoff solenoid (1) until it is unlatched.

Fuel (Power) Setting
The horsepower setting of an engine is dependent on its airflow and pressure delivery, the speed of the engine, and the amount of fuel delivered to the combustion chambers. Since the amount of airflow is related to the turbocharger installed on the engine, and the maximum speed is determined by the maximum full-load speed set in the governor as recommended by the engine manufacturer, the fuel delivery rate is generally one setting that has to be checked and possibly ad-

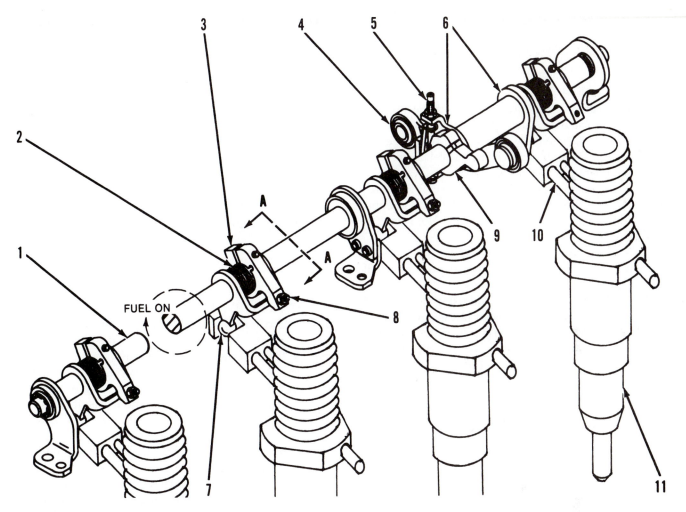

FIGURE 23–57 Fuel injector and rack control linkage on a 3116 engine. 1, Shaft; 2, spring; 3, clamp; 4, link; 5, fuel setting screw; 6, lever assembly; 7, lever assembly; 8, synchronization screw; 9, clamp; 10, rack; 11, injector. (Courtesy of Caterpillar, Inc.)

justed on the 3114/3116 engine models. This is achieved on these two engines by a fuel setting screw that limits the unit injector rack position and therefore limits the power output of the engine. The individual unit injector racks must be adjusted/set (synchronized) prior to performing the fuel setting check. Figure 23-57 illustrates the location of the fuel setting screw (5) on the injector control linkage between injectors 1 and 2.

You cannot perform the fuel setting check without the use of various special Caterpillar tools, which are listed below. Some of these special tools are used in other areas of this section for checks and adjustments. The required tools are as follows:

1. 1U6680 governor and fuel system adjusting tool group
2. 1U6675 injector spring compressor

3. 1U6679 indicator group
4. 1U6673 wrench
5. 6V6106 dial indicator
6. 6V6 pliers
7. 1U7305 insertion tool
8. 1U6681 holding tool

NOTE   This adjustment can be performed with the No. 1 rocker arm assembly either in position or removed. When removed, greater room is afforded for the installation of the various special tools. We will also have to install the unit injector tappet spring compressor bracket shown in Figure 23-52 to free the rack up for this check and adjustment. If the rocker arm assemblies are left in place for this check, the injector spring compressor 1U6675 is not required; however, a screwdriver will be required to push the rack head toward the injector.

Setting Procedure

1. With the engine stopped and the ignition key switch turned off, latch the solenoid as shown in Figure 23-51; if the engine is equipped with an energize-to-run solenoid, remove it completely for this check/adjustment.

2. Refer to the section "Unit Injector Synchronization" and repeat procedural steps 6 to 12, mounting the dial indicator in position on the No. 1 unit injector and rocker arm assembly.

3. After completing steps 6 to 12 as mentioned in step 2, refer to Figure 23-58 and remove the small spring clip (9) using a pair of pliers.

4. Refer to Figure 23-59 and using a soft-jawed pair of pliers such as those listed in the special tools list as 6V6, slide the sleeve (11) out of the governor and toward the engine cylinder head. It will take a little bit of pressure and back-and-forward movement to accomplish this. Do *not* use hard-jawed pliers since damage can occur to the sleeve and oil leakage can result later due to wiper seal damage.

5. Refer to Figure 23-60 and insert the long, thin-pin 1U7305 (14) into and through the link pin (13) of the governor control linkage so that equal lengths of the pin are visible on both sides of the link pin.

6. We must now install the tapered-wedge holding tool 1U6681 in position. This is best seen by referring to Figure 23-61. Insert the 1U6681 holding tool (15) between the sleeve (11) and the small diameter (B) of the long, thin pin 1U7305 which was installed in step 5. This pin is shown as item 14 in Figure 23-61.

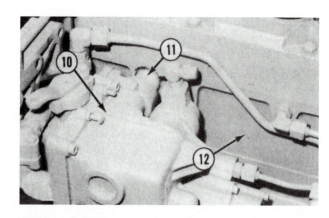

FIGURE 23–59 *Moving governor sleeve collar out of position. 10, Governor; 11, sleeve; 12, cylinder head. (Courtesy of Caterpillar, Inc.)*

7. Push the holding tool (15) down until the small diameter (B) of pin 14 contacts the face (A) of the governor (10). With this tooling in position, we are now at the governor calibration point.

8. Refer to Figure 23-57 and push down manually on the injector rack lever and release it. Do this several times to ensure that no bind exists. It also centers the linkage.

9. Read the engine information plate data from the rocker cover to determine the correct engine fuel setting value in millimeters.

10. Figure 23-62 illustrates the dial indicator in position to check the No. 1 injector rack movement. If the reading on the dial indicator is correct according to the engine information plate or available Caterpillar microfiche data, no adjustment is necessary to the fuel setting screw (5 in Figure 23-57).

11. If fuel setting screw adjustment is required,

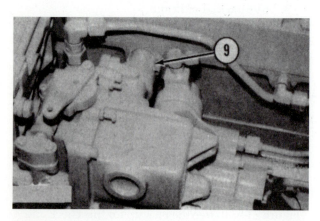

FIGURE 23–58 *Removal of spring clip (9) from linkage at governor. (Courtesy of Caterpillar, Inc.)*

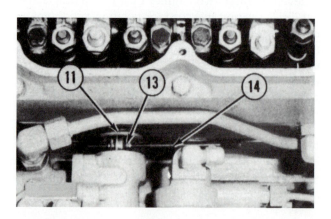

FIGURE 23–60 *Inserting long, thin link pin into and through governor control linkage. 11, Sleeve; 13, link pin; 14, 1U7305 insertion tool. (Courtesy of Caterpillar, Inc.)*

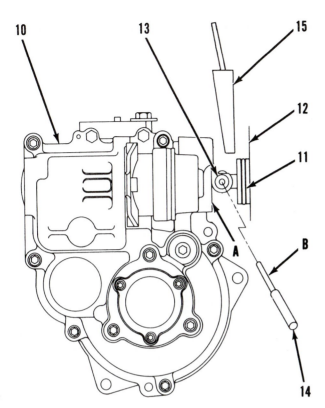

FIGURE 23–61 *Rear view of governor assembly showing position of special tooling to adjust racks. 10, Governor; 11, sleeve; 12, cylinder head; 13, link pin; 14, 1U7305 insertion tool; 15, 1U6681 holding tool; A. face of governor; B, small diameter of tool. (Courtesy of Caterpillar, Inc.)*

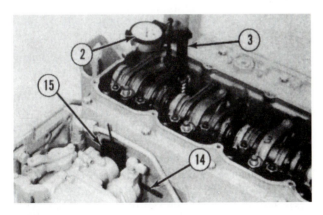

FIGURE 23–62 *Checking No. 1 injector rack control movement with a dial indicator. 2, Dial indicator; 3, 1U6679 indicator group; 14, 1U7305 insertion tool; 15, 1U6681 holding tool. (Courtesy of Caterpillar, Inc.)*

use special tool wrench 1U6673 to loosen the fuel setting screw locknut.

12. Rotate the fuel adjusting screw CW or CCW until the correct value is recorded on the face of the dial indicator to that shown on the engine information plate. Turning the screw CCW will result in greater fuel delivery, while rotating the screw CW will result in a lower fuel delivery rate and therefore less horsepower.

13. After any fuel setting screw adjustment, always double check the dial indicator setting by quickly pushing down and releasing the No. 1 rack lever.

14. Remove all of the special tooling and prepare to install the rocker arm assemblies and all other items that were removed.

15. Remember to reset the electric shutdown solenoid, as explained in step 23 of the section "Unit Injector Synchronization."

Governor Operation and Adjustment

The mechanical servo-assisted governor used on 3114/3116 engines is very similar in operation to the mechanical servo-governor used on both the 3208 and 3406B engines described in this chapter. The 3114/3116 governor assembly is gear driven from the engine at the front as shown in the schematic of Figure 23-63. The mechanical governor is an all-range or variable-speed type assembly in that the governor will control any speed setting determined by a throttle position from low to high idle (maximum no-load rpm). This is easily accomplished by the fact that two springs are used inside the governor mechanism. The low-speed spring is shown as item 6, while the high-speed spring is shown as item 7 in Figure 23-63. For detailed information on the basic operation of all mechanical governor assemblies, refer to the information contained in Chapter 17.

RECALL INFORMATION The most important thing to remember about the basic operation of all governors is as follows:

1. The governor spring pressure is always attempting to increase the fuel setting.

2. The centrifugal force developed by the rotating governor flyweights is always attempting to decrease the fuel setting by opposing the force of the springs, which is determined by placement of the throttle lever.

3. For any given throttle lever setting, the centrifugal force of the flyweights can match the

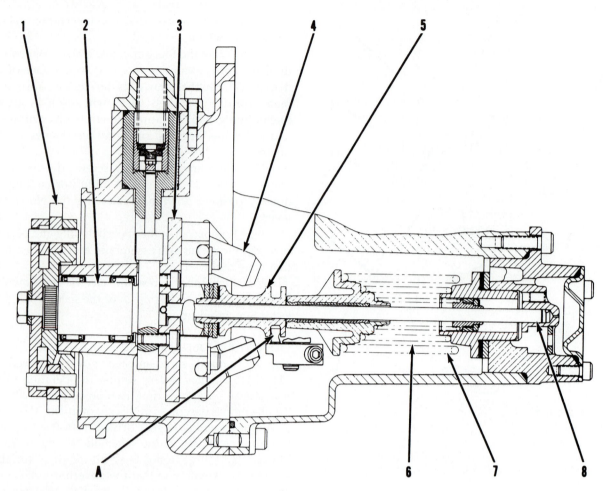

FIGURE 23–63 *Schematic view of the mechanical governor assembly. 1, Governor drive gear; 2, shaft; 3, flyweight carrier; 4, flyweights; 5, riser; 6, low idle spring; 7, high-idle spring; 8, shaft; A, pin. (Courtesy of Caterpillar, Inc.)*

force of the springs. When this action occurs, the governor is said to be in a state of balance (SOB). As long as the engine speed for a given throttle position is able to develop sufficient power to handle the load, the weight and spring forces will remain equal.

4. An increase in load for a given (fixed) throttle position will cause the engine to slow down, and the centrifugal force of the engine-driven governor flyweights will decrease. This upsets the SOB and the governor springs will cause the fuel linkage to move toward an increased fuel setting to allow the engine to develop more power to handle the additional load.

5. A decrease in load for a given (fixed) throttle position will cause the engine speed to increase, and the centrifugal force of the rotating governor flyweights will increase. This upsets the SOB that had existed between the weights and springs in favor of the weights. The weight action will compress the governor springs, thereby moving the linkage to a decreased fuel setting. The engine will now develop less power to handle the decreased load.

6. In both steps 4 and 5 a corrected state of balance will occur as the weights and springs reach a new position. The engine will not run at the speed it did prior to load increase or load decrease, due to the inherent droop characteristic of the mechanical governor. Droop is the difference in engine speed between the maximum full-load and maximum no-load (high-idle) speed settings. For more information on droop, refer to Chapter 17.

Governor Operation

If you look more closely at Figure 23-63, the governor flyweight carrier (3) will always rotate at drive ratio speed since it is connected to the drive gear (1). The faster the engine speed, the farther the flyweights will move outward, due to an increase in centrifugal force. The toes of the flyweights bear against a three-piece self-centering thrust bearing which transfers the weight movement to the horizontal riser shaft (5). The horizontal movement of the riser shaft (5) bears against the low- and high-speed spring seat located between the riser shaft and the low- and high-speed springs, shown as items 6 and 7 in the diagram. With this arrangement, the weights and springs are attempting to oppose one another at all engine speeds. However, keep in mind from the recall information discussed in items 1 to 6 above the various reactions that will affect the governor operation.

If you study Figure 23-63 more closely, "key in" on item A, which is identified as a pin. When the riser shaft moves to the right in the diagram due to weight action, this pin will also move. If the spring forces move the riser shaft (5) to the left, the pin A will also move to the left. Let's transfer the position of this pin A to another governor diagram, which will make it easier to explain the actual linkage action during operation. In Figure 23-64, locate item 18 (the riser lever); at the left-hand side of this lever is the small pin that was shown as item A in Figure 23-63. Remember that weight movement of the spring force can cause this small pin to move either toward the springs or toward the weights. With this in mind, the position of the unit injector racks can be moved to any position by one of two methods:

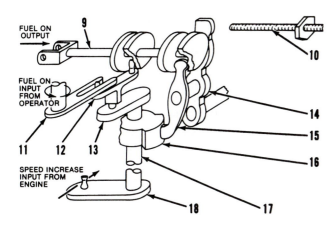

FIGURE 23–64 Governor linkage operating schematic. 9, Governor output shaft; 10, limit lever setscrew; 11, throttle lever; 12, fulcrum lever; 13, pivot lever; 14, limit lever; 15, torque lever; 16, torque cam; 17, pivot shaft; 18, riser lever. (Courtesy of Caterpillar, Inc.)

1. The operator physically moving the throttle lever, which is connected to item 11 in Figure 23-64. The movement of the throttle lever (11) will transfer its motion through item 12, the fulcrum lever, which will cause the governor output shaft (9) connected to the racks to move. Depending on which way the operator moves the throttle pedal on a truck application (either down or up), the governor output shaft (9) can increase or decrease the unit injector rack position. When the throttle is moved down, the racks will be pulled away from the injector body to increase the fuel delivery to the combustion chamber. Allowing the throttle pedal to come up will move the unit injector racks toward the injector body, thereby decreasing the fuel delivery.

2. With the engine running at a fixed throttle position, a state of balance will exist between the centrifugal forces of the flyweights and the opposing force of the low- and high-idle springs. Removing a load from the engine when the throttle is in a fixed position will upset the state of balance in favor of the weights, which will want to rotate faster. This would cause the riser shaft to move the pin A, and the riser lever 18 in Figure 23-64 would rotate and transfer motion up through the linkage to item 12, the fulcrum lever. This lever will pivot around the fixed slotted throttle lever; the pin on item 12, which is positioned in the slotted lever, allows this to happen. When item 12, the fulcrum lever, moves to the right in the diagram due to weight action, its opposite end will move to the left. If you look closely at item 12 in Figure 23-64, you will notice that there is a pin that engages with the governor output shaft (9). Therefore, shaft 9 must move to the left, which is to a decreased fuel position to offset the decrease in load. The engine receives less fuel and the engine will tend to slow down, allowing the centrifugal force of the flyweights to decrease until a new corrected state of balance again exists between the weights and the springs. In reality, the engine will run at a slightly higher rpm than it did prior to the governor reaction, due to the droop factor. Take careful note that this was all done automatically by the governor; the operator did not move the throttle from its previous fixed position. For a description of droop, see Chapter 17.

If the engine was running at a fixed throttle position and the load was increased, weight force decreases and the springs will move the riser shaft and pin A back toward the weight carrier. This causes the riser lever (18 in Figure 23-64) to move exactly as shown in the diagram. The resultant motion transfer up through the governor linkage will now move the governor output shaft (9) to an increased injector rack setting. This delivers more fuel to the engine to develop the additional power required to handle the load increase. Once again, a new corrected state of balance will exist between the weights and springs, but the engine will run at a slightly lower rpm than before the governor reaction, due to the droop factor of the governor (see the droop description in Chapter 17).

Figure 23-65, which illustrates the basic governor levers, shows more clearly the location and interaction that exists with regard to the throttle lever. The throttle lever is connected by mechanical linkage from the foot pedal in the cab of the truck to this lever.

Air–Fuel Ratio Control

The 3114/3116 truck engines employ an FRC (fuel ratio control) which functions and operates in the same manner as shown in Figure 23-34 for the 3406B engine series. Basically, the air/fuel ratio control has an inlet port (item 2 in Figure 23-66) connected to the engine intake manifold. Turbocharger boost pressure flowing through this line acts on a diaphragm that causes the FRC governor linkage to move in proportion to the degree of boost pressure. This therefore ensures that the amount of fuel increase to the engine cylinders is lim-

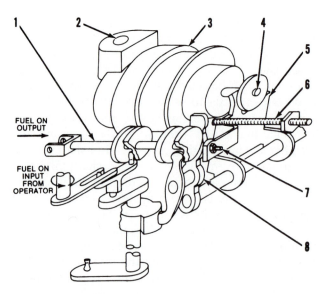

FIGURE 23–66 *Mechanical governor and connections to the air/fuel ratio control unit. 1, Governor output shaft; 2, inlet port; 3, fuel ratio control; 4, retainer shaft; 5, FRC lever; 6, limit lever setscrew; 7, FRC lever setscrew; 8, limit lever. (Courtesy of Caterpillar, Inc.)*

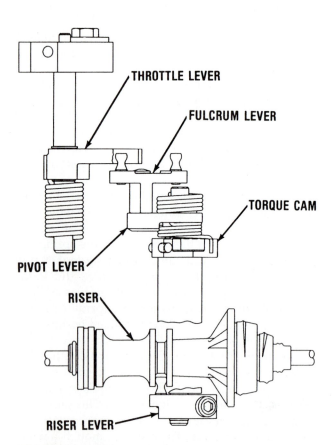

FIGURE 23–65 *Major operating components and linkage arrangement in the 3116 engine governor assembly. (Courtesy of Caterpillar, Inc.)*

ited by turbo boost. In this way overfueling is avoided and excessive black smoke at the exhaust stack is eliminated. If you study Figure 23-66, you can see how the FRC linkage is connected to the mechanical governor linkage. The governor will still react as described above; the only difference is that the rate of engine acceleration and increased fuel delivery is controlled directly by the amount of turbocharger airflow/boost.

Governor Servo

The governor is equipped with a hydraulic servo assist mechanism which acts to move the governor linkage by the aid of pressurized engine oil. Figure 23-67 illustrates this mechanism. The main component here is item 1 (valve), which allows pressurized engine oil to flow into or to drain from behind the piston, shown as item 2. In the fuel-on direction shown in Figure 23-67, valve 1 will move to the left, opening outlet B while closing oil passage D. Engine oil under pressure enters at A and forces piston 2 and clevis 5 to the left. The oil behind piston 2 will pass along passage C, along valve 1, and out of oil outlet B.

During a state of balance, when the centrifugal force of the rotating governor flyweights and the spring forces are equal, valve 1 will not move. Oil pressure from A pushes piston 2 until oil passage D is opened. Oil drains through passage D, along valve 1, and through outlet B. A governor reaction that causes a fuel decrease (less load on the engine) moves valve 1 to the right to close oil outlet B while opening passage

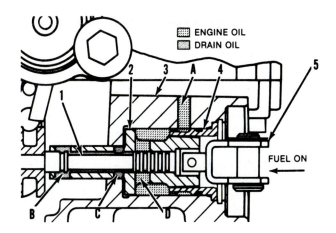

ENGINE OIL
DRAIN OIL

FUEL ON

FIGURE 23–67 *Governor servo mechanism (fuel-on direction). 1, Valve; 2, piston; 3, cylinder; 4, cylinder sleeve; 5, clevis for fuel injector rack control linkage; A, oil inlet (shown out of position); B, oil outlet; C, oil passage; D, oil passage. (Courtesy of Caterpillar, Inc.)*

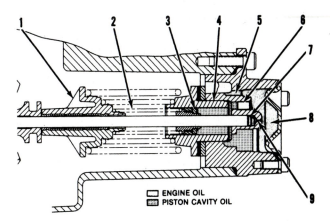

ENGINE OIL
PISTON CAVITY OIL

FIGURE 23–68 *Governor dashpot linkage arrangement. 1, Spring seat; 2, dashpot spring; 3, piston; 4, seat; 5, overflow passage; 6, orifice plug; 7, oil passage; 8, reservoir; 9, passage. (Courtesy of Caterpillar, Inc.)*

D. This allows pressurized oil from A to both sides of the piston (2). Since the piston area is greater on the left than on the right, the piston (2) and clevis (5) move to the right.

Governor Dashpot

The purpose of a dashpot is to act as a type of shock absorber to the governor mechanism when rapid throttle movements due to operator action, or due to a governor reaction (load on or off), occur. These rapid movements can induce a tendency for the governor linkage to oscillate at a high frequency. This action would result in a high-speed surge condition in the engine. To counteract this tendency, a hydraulic dashpot is used, mounted on the end of the governor assembly opposite the weight end. Figure 23-68 illustrates the dashpot.

Engine oil under pressure is fed to the dashpot through passages 7 and 9 to fill reservoir 8. Excess oil drains through passage 5. If the operator upsets the SOB between the weights and springs, or the governor reacts to a load increase or load decrease, the spring seat (1) will force the dashpot spring (2) to move the piston (3) in seat 4. If the operator moves the throttle pedal to an increased fuel setting, or if the governor reacts to a load decrease (engine wants to speed up), piston 3 will move to the right. Any oil in the piston cavity will be subjected to increased pressure as it is forced through the small orifice plug (6) and out into the reservoir (8). During an engine speed decrease, caused either by the operator allowing the throttle pedal to come up, or to the governor reaction during a load increase, item 3, the piston, will now move to the left in the diagram, resulting in an oil pressure de-

crease in the piston cavity. We now have a reversal of our earlier reaction, in that oil is now pulled through orifice 6 from the reservoir (8). The orifice (6) restricts the oil flow, thereby effectively slowing or dampening the movement of the piston (3) and spring seat (1). This action therefore effectively dampens the governor linkage movement to prevent any possible oscillation.

Low-Idle Setting

The only external adjustment that can be performed on the governor assembly is the low-idle setting via a setscrew and locknut, illustrated in Figure 23-69. Although another screw is shown in this figure, it does not limit the maximum speed of the engine but acts simply to prevent the throttle lever from moving too far in the high speed range; otherwise, damage to the internal governor linkage would result due to excessive movement.

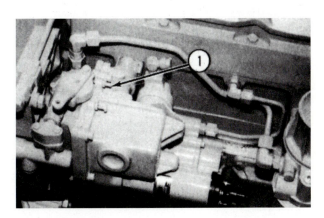

FIGURE 23–69 *Position of governor low-idle adjustment screw (1). (Courtesy of Caterpillar, Inc.)*

Valve Clearance Adjustment

Adjustment of the intake and exhaust valves on 3114/3116 engines is a straightforward procedure and the various valves can be set with the No. 1 piston on the compression and exhaust strokes to accommodate all cylinders. Table 23-2 lists what position the No. 1 piston should be at for the various valve adjustments.

Valve Clearance

- Intake valves: 0.38 ± 0.08 mm (0.015 ± 0.003 in.)
- Exhaust valves: 0.64 ± 0.08 mm (0.025 ± 0.003 in.)

CATERPILLAR ELECTRONIC FUEL SYSTEMS

SPECIAL NOTE   The information contained within this section dealing with the Caterpillar EUI (electronic unit injector) fuel system is designed to provide an overview of the system operation and the special diagnostic tools that can be used to troubleshoot the system. It is *not* intended to supplant the excellent printed literature and audiovisual materials readily available from Caterpillar. If you intend to perform service diagnostics on Caterpillar engine products, you should acquire the service publications from your local Caterpillar service dealer.

Caterpillar introduced its first electronic control system in early 1987 on its 3406B model heavy-duty highway truck engine series, which was known by the acronym PEEC (programmable electronic engine control). This system retained the conventional PLN (pump–line–nozzle) system that had been in use by Caterpillar for many years. This first system was retained through the 3406C model until the introduction in late 1993 of the 3406E model, which uses an overhead cam design and EUIs similar to those used by Detroit Diesel. Caterpillar, however, first released its EUI system in 1988 on its on-highway truck 3176 model engine, which is now in its second generation and is known as the 3176B.

Caterpillar truck engine models that employ EUI controls are the 3176B, C10, C12, and 3406E. Cat's smaller 3116 and 3126 truck models, and the larger-displacement 3408E and 3412E industrial and marine engines, use a HEUI (hydraulically actuated electronic unit injector) system. Both the newer model C-10 and C-12 engines fit above the existing 3176B and below the larger-displacement 3406E in Cat's on-highway engine range. Figure 23-70 lists the basic specs for the 3176B, C-10, C-12, and 3406E models. The 3176B, C-10, and C-12 models share a common cylinder block, but with the elimination of the aluminum spacer deck that was used on the 3176 model. This lowers overhaul costs and eliminates a joint from the engine. There are a number of major components in common between the C-10 and C-12, but with major updates.

Both the C-10 and C-12 have a one-piece solid aluminum front housing versus the two-piece clamshell type used on the 3176B. The same fuel pump is used on the 3176B, C-10, and C-12; it has been relocated to the front of the engine from its rear mount on the 3176. The C-10 and C-12 electronic fuel system is basically the same as that for the 3176B engine, which is a Caterpillar/Lucas design, with the electronic control module being common to all Cat electronic truck engines. The ECM includes a full range of programmable options, more data storage capacity, and rapid data retrieval using industry-

Engine Model	Cat 3176B	Cat C-10	Cat C-12	Cat 3406E
Disp.	10.3 L	10.3 L	12.0 mm	14.6 mm
Bore	125 mm	125 mm	130 mm	137 mm
Stroke	140 mm	140 mm	150 mm	165 mm
HP range	275–365	280–370	355–410	310–550
Max HP	380	385	425	550
Torque range	975–1350 lb ft	975–1350 lb ft	1350–1550 lb ft	1150–1850 lb ft
Weight	1945 lb	2050 lb	2070 lb	2867 lb
Fuel system	EUI	EUI	EUI	EUI

FIGURE 23–70 Engine specifications for Caterpillar heavy-duty on-highway truck engines equipped with electronic controls. (Courtesy of Caterpillar, Inc.)

available tools such as the Argo Mobile Data Terminal or via direct link to a PC.

The C-10 and C-12 engines use a redesigned front gear train with a new air compressor drive using a larger drive gear bolted to the air compressor driveshaft. The C-10 uses a Schwitzer turbocharger, and the C-12 employs a Garrett model. The cylinder head remains largely the same on the 3176B, C-10, and C-12 using a four-valve design. The C-10 and C-12 camshaft has been located into a midmount cylinder block position versus the earlier aluminum spacer deck location of the 3176 models. Other changes for the C-10 and C-12 models include 8% larger crank main bearings, and 4% wider con-rod journal bearings. A stainless steel versus copper (3176) injector sleeve and beefed-up valve train components appear in the C-10 and C-12 models. Other differences between the C-10 and C-12 are that the C-12 uses different pistons, liners, connecting rods, crankshaft, turbocharger, oil cooler, and injector tips, due primarily to the larger displacement. Both the C-10 and C-12 employ two-piece articulated Metal Leve pistons with a forged steel crown and cast aluminum skirt, similar to that shown in Figure 9-3B.

EUI Operation

The EUI operates similar to that shown in Figure 15-15; the visual difference is that the 3406E unit has its solenoid mounted at an angle. The 1994 and later EUIs were manufactured with preradius nozzle orifices to eliminate erosion, reduce emissions, and decrease engine performance variability.

The operation of the EUI on engines is the same, except that the activation of the injector follower is different. On the 3176B engine, the camshaft is block mounted and employs a short pushrod, as shown in Figure 15-14a. On the 3406E engine, which uses an overhead camshaft located in the cylinder head, a roller follower attached to the rocker arm is actuated by the camshaft directly, as shown in Figure 15-14B. Keep in mind that all of the sensor inputs, as well as the position of the EFPA (electronic foot pedal assembly) sending signals to the ECM, are what determines the start, duration, and end of injection. The length of the PWM signal from the ECM to the injector solenoid controls the fuel delivery rate and the power developed by the engine. The EUI on the 3406E engine produces a fuel spray-in pressure similar to that of the series 50 and 60 Detroit Diesel models, which is approximately 28,000 psi (193,060 kPa); for the 3176B engine, the spray-in pressure is approximately 25,500 psi (175,822 kPa).

EUI Electronics

For the 1994 and later model years, all engines used new ADEM (advanced diesel engine management) electronic controls, which provide fleet managers with such information as tracking trip and lifetime data through stored data from the ECM. Figure 23-71 illustrates the ECM layout for the 3176B and 3406E with its dual microprocessors, which have reduced calculation times for critical engine control parameters and improved engine efficiency and performance response. The same ECM is installed in the 3176B–3406E C-10 and C-12 series engines. The ECM continues to be diesel-fuel cooled to greatly reduce damaging thermal (heat) cycles and increase reliability/durability under the most extreme operating temperatures.

Information from the ECM can be displayed on an optional dash display DDR (Figure 21-52) or downloaded to a PC (Figure 21-54). A generic ECM is used across all applicable engine lines so that the ECM can be programmed for the specific application of the engine. This new ECM has eight times the memory capacity, processes data from twice as many sensor inputs, and makes calculations four times faster. Engine/vehicle parameters that can be monitored are total miles, average fuel consumption, and speed and load factors. This information can be used for management software to help determine precise maintenance intervals. With dual microprocessors, engine performance, response, and fuel economy are improved. Fault codes are logged in memory, and the ECU also records engine parameters immediately before a fault and shortly after it has occurred. The ECM processes information supplied by a fuel temperature sensor located in the fuel manifold and makes adjustments to compensate for fuel warming, thereby avoiding the possibility of a power loss. If fuel temperature exceeds 150°F (65.5°C), the ECM logs a fault code.

For vehicle PTO operation, the rate of speed increase can be controlled. As an option, the Caterpillar "softcruise" speed control system modulates fuel delivery above and below the set speed, particularly when a truck is running over rolling terrain, to eliminate abrupt fuel cutoffs, and it helps to keep turbo boost spooled up for the next hill. The ECM is soft mounted to the engine and cooled by diesel fuel piped through a cooler plate to ensure that radiated engine heat does not affect the operation of the electronics components. Mounted within the ECM is the engine's *flash memory chip*, which contains the engine's control software. The flash memory technology enables software to be downloaded directly to the ECM and eliminates the need for the replaceable "personality module" for individual engine ratings as was the case with the earlier 3406B and C PEEC and 3176A engines. New

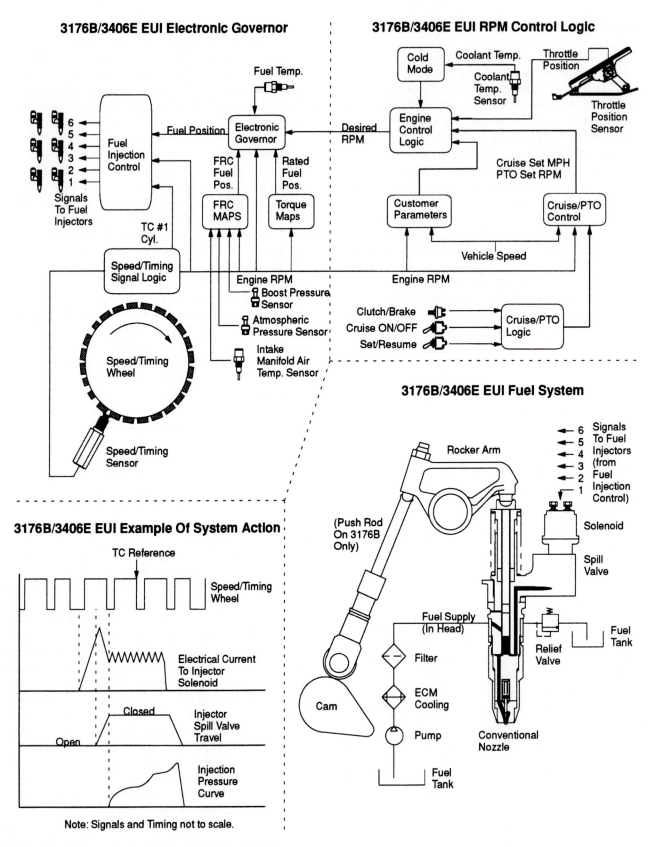

FIGURE 23–71 3176B/3406 EUI electronic sytem.

software previously stored in 3176A personality modules can be downloaded directly to the ECM via a PC. All sensors are connected to the ECM by two Deutsch 40-pin connectors. One of the 40-pin connectors provides the electrical interface between the engine and vehicle.

Figures 23-72 and 23-73 show the sensor and component locations for both a 3406E/3176B electronic system that allows you to visually trace the system components and wiring arrangement. The sensors shown along the bottom row of Figure 23-73 receive a 5-V input signal from the ECM. Their output voltage value varies between 0.5 and 4.5 V based on the changing resistance value at the sensor, and whether it is a pressure or temperature type. The PMTPS (pedal-mounted throttle position sensor) shown in Figure 23-74 receives an 8-V input signal from the ECM. Other switches operate on a 12-V battery supply. Injector solenoids are pulsed on and off by ECM voltage signals. A good injector solenoid exhibits a resistance value between 0.5 and 2.0 Ω (20 kΩ), while the resistance value from either injector solenoid terminal to the injector case should always be greater than 20,000 Ω (20 kΩ). Other 1994 changes in the ECM include SAE J1922 power-train data link to allow the engine to communicate with ABS (antibrake skid), new automatic transmissions, and traction control ASR systems. A pedal-mounted TPS (throttle position sensor) similar to that shown in Figure 15-13, which is basically the standard EFPA now used by all heavy-truck OEMs, replaces Caterpillar's own earlier and bulkier TPS system. The newer ECM system also provides either 12- or 24-V Jacobs brake control and speedometer and tachometer inputs to eliminate OEM sensors. The system also includes both an SAE J1708/J1587 satellite communications interface and improved diagnostics. As with other competitive systems, the Caterpillar system provides a programmable droop feature up to 150 rpm above the truck engine limit to provide fewer transmission shifts in rolling terrain, driver comfort, and improved fuel economy. Another improvement is the incorporation of the previously external truck speed buffer into the ECM to minimize the need for cleaning up the signal from the OEM-provided truck speed sensor. The ECM continuously monitors battery voltage and logs a diagnostic code if battery voltage decreases below an acceptable limit. This provides a continuous health check of the wiring and pinpoints system problems that may affect engine operation.

The previous transducer module used on the 3406B and 3406C engine PEEC systems has been eliminated, because new technology sensors allow remote mounting of these units, thereby doing away with needed hose connections. The radiator engage/disengage fan system is automatically turned on when the engine retarder *high mode* is applied to provide increased engine braking. The ECM continuously monitors coolant temperature, intake manifold air temperature, the engine compression brake position and the air-conditioning system pressure to determine if and when the radiator fan should be activated.

An electronic full-range governor features a programmable low idle rpm (600 to 750 rpm), with a factory setting of 600 rpm and 20 rpm overrun. There is no need for a mechanical air/fuel ratio control system, since the intake manifold air temperature sensor, turbo boost pressure sensor, and atmospheric pressure sensor allow electronic control of engine fuel delivery.

Update Information

Refer to Figure 23-73 on later-model 3406E (5EK) (NOV95) truck engines. The turbocharger boost sensor (2) has been moved from its earlier location (between cylinder 5 and 6) on the air compressor side of the engine block to a location just above the air compressor. In addition, the electronic unit injector wire harness connector (J5/P5, item 3) has been relocated from its earlier position on the valve cover base between cylinders 4 and 5, to a location between cylinders 2 and 3. The P3/J3 wire harness connector has been relocated toward the front of the engine from the rear. In addition, the vehicle speed signal no longer loops through the P24/J24 connector; however, this connection will still be used solely for timing purposes, by connecting the special diagnostic timing probe tool to the P24 connector.

Additional changes to these engines include personality module changes which provide customer-programmable starter motor lockout when the engine is running; a temperature-based idle shutdown to allow continuous idling when outside air temperatures create the need for cab heating or cooling; and extended range idle shutdown between 3 and 1440 minutes (24 hours). A vehicle electrical shutdown feature reduces the chance of accidental truck battery discharge when accessories such as headlights are left on after idle shutdown. A customer-programmable parameter determines the lowest vehicle speed at which the engine retarder can be active. A quick vehicle stop recorder logs any rapid-deceleration situation. This new software supports SAE-J1939 data link communications between the ECM and the transmission or other drive-train components. A real-time clock has been added to "time stamp" critical events and snapshot data. An electronic oil temperature gauge is provided as a dash-mounted digital display. An auto-retarder feature in the truck cruise control mode allows low-to-medium

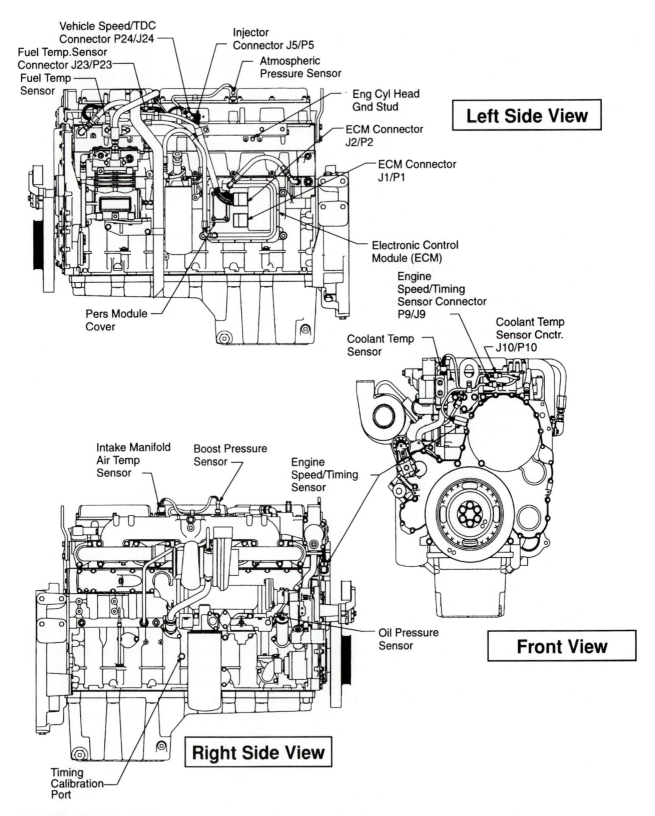

FIGURE 23–72 3176B Sensor and connector locations. (Courtesy of Caterpillar, Inc.)

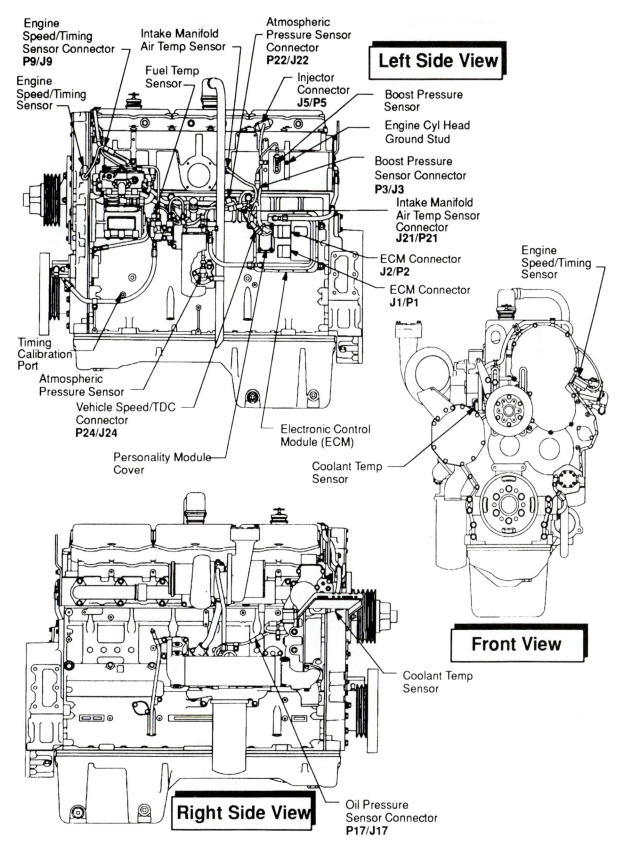

Engine
Speed/Timing
Sensor Connector
P9/J9

Intake Manifold
Air Temp Sensor

Atmospheric
Pressure Sensor
Connector
P22/J22

Left Side View

Engine
Speed/Timing
Sensor

Fuel Temp
Sensor

Injector
Connector
J5/P5

Boost Pressure
Sensor

Engine Cyl Head
Ground Stud

Boost Pressure
Sensor Connector
P3/J3

Intake Manifold
Air Temp Sensor
Connector
J21/P21

ECM Connector
J2/P2

ECM Connector
J1/P1

Timing
Calibration
Port

Atmospheric
Pressure Sensor

Vehicle Speed/TDC
Connector
P24/J24

Personality Module
Cover

Electronic Control
Module (ECM)

Engine
Speed/Timing
Sensor

Coolant Temp
Sensor

Front View

Coolant Temp
Sensor

Right Side View

Oil Pressure
Sensor Connector
P17/J17

FIGURE 23–73 *3406E Sensor and connector locations. (Courtesy of Caterpillar, Inc.)*

683

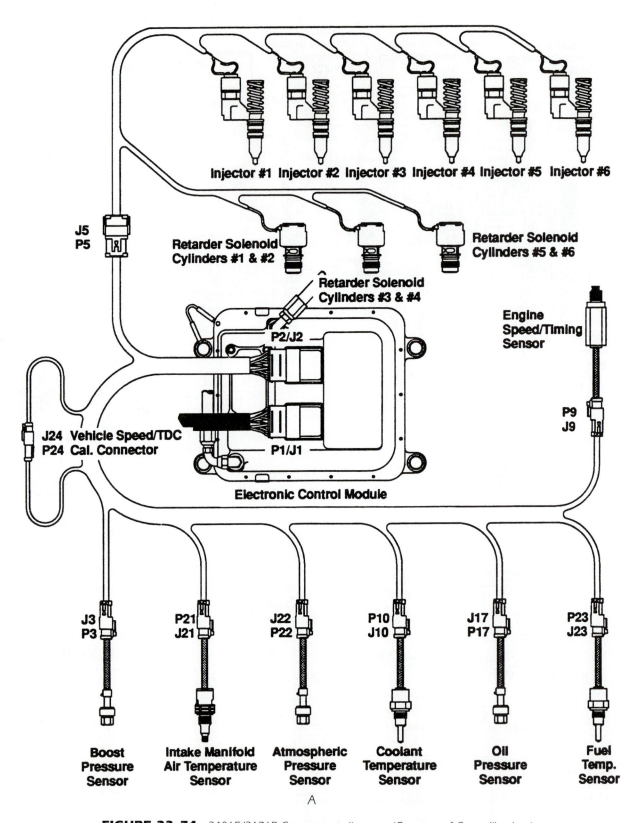

FIGURE 23–74 3406E/3176B Component diagram. (Courtesy of Caterpillar, Inc.)

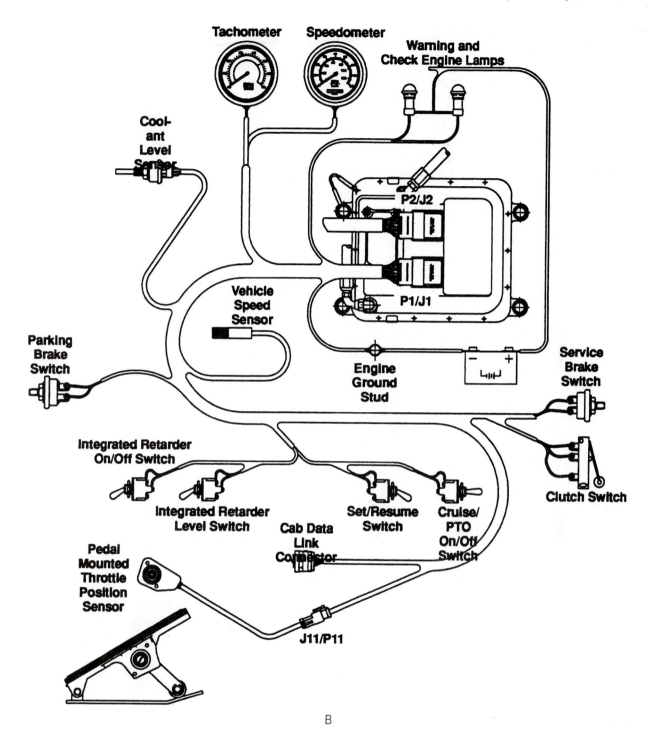

Tachometer   Speedometer   Warning and Check Engine Lamps

Coolant Level Sensor

P2/J2

P1/J1

Vehicle Speed Sensor

Parking Brake Switch

Engine Ground Stud

Service Brake Switch

Integrated Retarder On/Off Switch

Clutch Switch

Integrated Retarder Level Switch   Cab Data Link Connector   Set/Resume Switch   Cruise/ PTO On/Off Switch

Pedal Mounted Throttle Position Sensor

J11/P11

B

and medium-to-high retarder levels when the vehicle speed exceeds the cruise set speed. The engine fan can be engaged for additional power retardation.

Fuel System Layout

Although similar in function and operation, the fuel systems used on the 3176B and 3406E EUI-equipped engines differ slightly in layout. Figure 23-75A and B illustrate the location of the major fuel system external components and the actual fuel flow through the system for the 3176B model. Figure 23-76A and B represent the fuel system arrangement and flow for the 3406E. In Figure 23-76B you can see that the fuel supply to the system's electronically controlled unit injectors (3) is provided by a gear fuel pump (9) which pulls fuel from the tank (12). Within the pump body, a check valve (11) allows fuel flow around the gears when the fuel priming pump (item 2 in Figure 23-76a) located on top of the filter housing is used, for example, when priming the fuel system after the filters have been changed or service work has been performed on the system.

Also within the fuel pump body is a pressure regulating valve (item 10 in Figure 23-76b) to limit and protect the system from extreme pressure. Fuel under pressure from the pump (91 psi, 630 kPa, at rated speed) is directed through cored passages in the distribution block (8), around the hand-priming pump (7), and into the fuel filter (6), which is rated at 5 μm (0.00020 in.). Fuel enters a cooler plate bolted to the ECM (5) to maintain the operating temperature of the electronics components within the ECM at an acceptable level. Fuel leaves the ECM and enters the fuel manifold (2) at the rear of the cylinder head, where it is distributed equally to all injectors from the common-rail design. An amount of fuel over and above that required for injection purposes is circulated through the EUIs. Fuel not required for injection purposes is used for cooling and lubrication of the EUIs (3) as well as purging any air from the system. Fuel then leaves the cylinder head through the fuel return manifold (4) and is directed back into the fuel distribution block (8), where a regulating valve is designed to maintain sufficient pressure within the fuel return manifold to ensure that the EUIs remain filled with fuel. This warm fuel then travels back to the fuel tank (12), where it cools before being recirculated through the system. Minimum fuel transfer pump flow for the 3176B engine is 3.5 L (0.93 U.S. gallon) per minute at 1800 engine rpm. On the 3406E, the minimum pump flow is quoted as being 3.2 L (0.83 U.S. gallon) per minute at a speed of 840 rpm with a delivery pressure of 310 kPa (45 psi).

The fuel pump for the 3176B engine is located as shown in Figure 23-75a at the left rear corner of the engine. It is mounted to a spacer block and is driven by the camshaft through a pair of helical gears. On the 3406E engine shown in Figure 23-76a, the fuel pump is located at the left front corner of the engine, where it is mounted to the timing gear cover (plate) and is driven from the engine gear train.

The 3176B and 3406E fuel systems are very similar; the normal fuel pressure for both engines is 91 psi (630 kPa). A low-fuel-pressure condition would be 75 psi (517 kPa); check the fuel filters for plugging. A high system pressure would be 100 psi (690 kPa) or higher; remove the fuel regulating valve from the adapter behind the return fuel line fitting and check for debris plugging the orifice holes. The injector popping pressure on the 3406E is 5003 ± 275 psi (34,474 ± 1896

kPa), while it is 5500 psi (37,931 kPa) for the 3176B. Both injector solenoids receive a 90-V signal from the ECM to determine the start of injection.

System Troubleshooting

When an operational complaint is lodged by an operator on any electronic engine, always keep in mind that the engine fuel system or a mechanical problem may be the cause for the complaint. Always consider that simple items such as a plugged air filter, plugged fuel filters, or high exhaust back pressure can be the reason for a low power complaint. To help a truck driver determine the cause on a 3176B or a 3406E engine, refer to the engine performance chart shown in Table 23-3.

This chart is also helpful for the service technician to use before performing a series of checks and tests to pinpoint the problem. By using the various special tools and diagnostic equipment illustrated in Figure 23-77, then referring to the various SAE standard codes listed in Table 23-4, the service technician can systematically determine the cause of the performance complaint. For more details on the SAE standardized trouble codes, refer to the earlier section "ECM SAE Trouble Codes."

Both the 3176B and 3406E engines are equipped with an ECM that is programmed to offer three levels of engine protection during operation. These three sit-

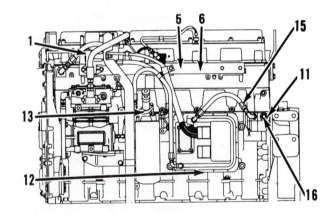

Fuel System Components
(1) Adapter (siphon break). (5) Fuel return manifold. (6) Fuel supply manifold. (11) Fuel transfer pump. (12) Electronic control module (ECM). (13) Fuel priming pump. (14) Fuel filter. (15) Fuel outlet (to ECM). (16) Fuel inlet (from tank).

A

FIGURE 23–75 (A) Component location and identification for model 3176B electronic engine external fuel system; (B) fuel system schematic and flow. (Courtesy of Caterpillar Inc.)

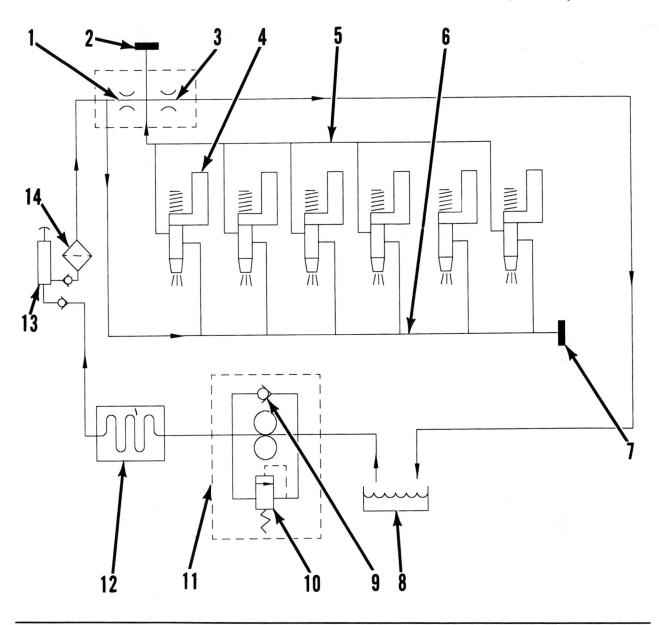

Fuel System Schematic
(1) Siphon break passage. (2) Vent plug. (3) Pressure regulating orifice. (4) Electronically controlled unit injectors. (5) Fuel manifold (return path). (6) Fuel manifold (supply path). (7) Drain plug. (8) Fuel tank. (9) Check valve. (10) Pressure regulating valve. (11) Fuel transfer pump. (12) Electronic control module (ECM). (13) Fuel priming pump. (14) Fuel filter (secondary).

B

uations are triggered by sensor values that change based on engine operating conditions. The ECM programming feature will initiate the following type of engine protection actions: a dash-mounted *warning* light, an engine *derate* or *shutdown*, and engine *shutdown*. Table 23-5 indicates the PID-FMI (parameter identifier-failure mode identifier) sensor-induced trouble code condition that will cause each one of these conditions to occur.

All electronic diesel engines today are password protected by factory-inserted alpha/numeric (letter/number) codes. Factory passwords are calculated on a computer system available only to Caterpillar dealers to protect the customer-selected engine operating parameters. Passwords are selected by the end user or customer.

Both the 3176B and 3406E electronic systems have some ability to self-diagnose. When a problem is detected, a diagnostic code is generated and the diagnostic *check engine lamp* is turned on, and in most cases the

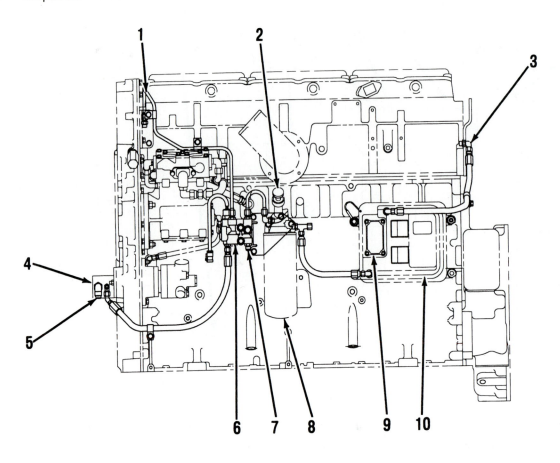

Component Locations
(1) Fuel return line. (2) Fuel priming pump. (3) Fuel inlet line. (4) Fuel transfer pump. (5) Fuel inlet from fuel tank. (6) Distribution block. (7) Fuel return to tank. (8) Fuel filter. (9) Personality module. (10) Electronic control module (ECM).

A

FIGURE 23–76   (A) Component location and identification for model 3406E engine, external fuel system; (B) Fuel system schematic and flow path. (Courtesy of Caterpillar Inc.)

code is stored in permanent memory within the ECM for extraction by a service technician. Codes that present current faults are known as *active* because they indicate an existing problem. *Logged* codes stored in ECM memory may have been temporary conditions and record "events" rather than actual failures. By using the ECAP (electronic control analyzer programmer) diagnostic tool shown in Figure 23-77, all stored trouble codes, engine operating parameters and conditions, shorting out of individual injectors, and fault tracing can be performed. When a diagnostic code occurs, the ECM records the time when this happened in engine hours as well as the engine operating parameters for 9.6 seconds before and 3.4 seconds after the code was detected.

When using the ECAP, which is powered by vehicle 12-V supply, always ensure that the ignition key switch is off during connector hookup or when test wires are being disconnected. The ECAP is connected to the system through the DDL (dash data link) connector by means of one of the adapters shown in Figure 23-77. The ignition key can be turned on to power up the ECAP, which will operate with the engine running or stopped as long as the key is on.

The ECAP window screen presents you with a choice of functions. Select one simply by pressing the desired control keys or scroll through the ECAP menu until you find the operating parameter or condition that you want to enter. You can reprogram the ECM personality module by connecting up a communica-

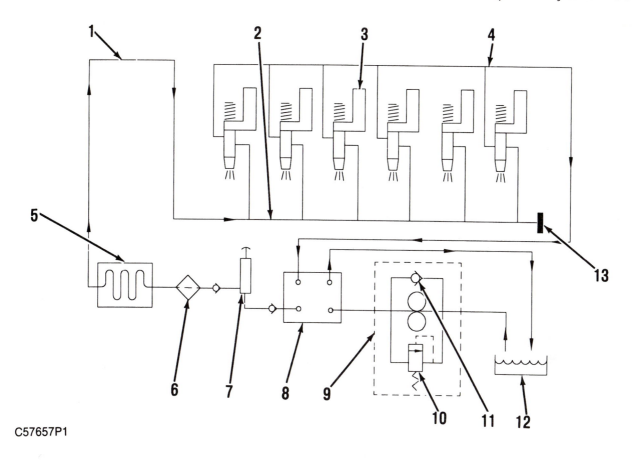

C57657P1

Fuel System Schematic
(1) Fuel supply line. (2) Fuel gallery (supply path). (3) Electronically controlled unit injectors. (4) Fuel gallery (return path). (5) Electronically controlled module (ECM). (6) Fuel filter. (7) Fuel priming pump. (8) Distribution block. (9) Fuel transfer pump. (10) Pressurized regulating valve. (11) Check valve. (12) Fuel tank. (13) Drain plug.

B

tion adapter and PC as illustrated in Figure 23-78. Figure 23-79 is an example of what a service technician may encounter on the information screen of the ECAP when it is powered up and he or she has selected "system configuration parameters." By pressing the up and down arrows on the ECAP keyboard pad, the technician can scroll through the information for that selected menu. As with the DDR used on the DDEC system, with continued exposure you will master the use of the ECAP tool and be able to diagnose performance complaints quickly.

The built-in MI (maintenance indicator) calculates service intervals for PM 1 (preventive maintenance 1), PM 2 (preventive maintenance 2), and coolant flush/fill maintenance procedures. The customer has the option of programming a specific number of hours or miles (kilometers) or even, based on engine oil sump quantity, the optimal PM 1 time interval. Note, however, that the PM 2 and coolant flush intervals are not programmable but are based on the recommended mileage or hours from the operation and maintenance manual. Within the ECM, the maintenance indicator sends a signal via the SAE J1587 data link to a hand-held service tool similar to that shown in Figure 21-52, to a dash display (see Figure 21-56 or to the fleet management program and indicates that maintenance is due 3000 miles (4828 km) prior to the estimated service. Once the MI has been alerted, it can be reset using the hand-held or ECAP service tool (see Figure 23-77) or the dash display controls.

A trip data system that includes two trip data registers is an optional item that allows the driver to view a dash-mounted display with a reset feature and permits the owner/fleet user to download stored data

TABLE 23–3 Diagnostic flash code/engine performance relationship: 3176B/3406E

Diagnostic Flash Code	Engine misfire	Low power	Engine speed reduced	Engine shutdown	Shut down vehicle[a]	Service ASAP[b]	Schedule service[c]
01—Idle shutdown override							✓
02—Event recorder data lost							✓
12—Coolant level sensor fault[d]							✓
13—Fuel temperature sensor fault							✓
14—Retarder solenoid fault							✓
19—A/C high-pressure switch open circuit							✓
21—Sensor supply voltage fault[d,e]		✓					✓
24—Oil pressure sensor fault[d]		✓					✓
25—Boost pressure sensor fault[e]							✓
26—Atmospheric pressure sensor fault[e]							✓
27—Coolant temperature sensor fault[d,e]							✓
28—Check throttle sensor adjustment							✓
31—Loss of vehicle speed signal			✓				✓
32—Throttle position sensor fault			✓			✓	
34—Engine rpm signal fault	✓		✓	✓		✓	
35—Engine overspeed warning							
36—Vehicle speed signal fault							✓

38—Intake air temperature sensor fault[d,e]							✓
41—Vehicle overspeed warning							
42—Check sensor calibrations		✓					✓
46—Low oil pressure warning		✓	✓	✓	✓	✓	
47—Idle shutdown occurrence				✓			
51—Intermittent battery power to ECM	✓	✓		✓		✓	
53—ECM fault	✓	✓	✓	✓		✓	
55—No detected faults							
56—Check customer/system parameters		✓	✓				✓
58—Powertrain data link fault							✓
59—Incorrect engine software							✓
61—High coolant temperature warning		✓		✓		✓	
62—Low coolant level warning		✓		✓		✓	
64—High intake air temperature warning							✓
65—High fuel temperature warning							✓
72—Cylinder 1 or 2 fault	✓	✓				✓	
73—Cylinder 3 or 4 fault	✓	✓				✓	
74—Cylinder 5 or 6 fault	✓	✓				✓	

[a]Shut down vehicle: Drive the vehicle cautiously off the road and get immediate service. Severe engine damage may result.
[b]Service ASAP (as soon as possible): The driver should go to the nearest qualified service location.
[c]Schedule service: The driver should have the problem investigated when convenient.
[d]Reduces the effectiveness of the engine monitoring feature when active.
[e]May affect the system only under specific environmental conditions, such as engine startup at cold temperature, cold weather operation at high altitudes, etc.

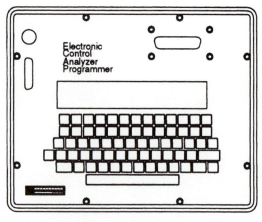

8T8697 ECAP Service Tool
NEXG4522 Service Program Module (SPM)

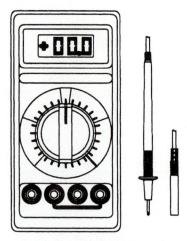

6V7800 or 6V7070 Digital Multimeter

8C9801 PWM Signal Adapter Group

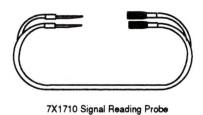

7X6370 3–Pin Breakout "T"

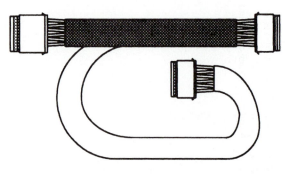

7X1715 40–Pin Square DRC Breakout "T"

7X1710 Signal Reading Probe

FIGURE 23–77 Electronic engine service diagnostic tools for use with the 3176B and 3406E engine models. (Courtesy of Caterpillar, Inc.)

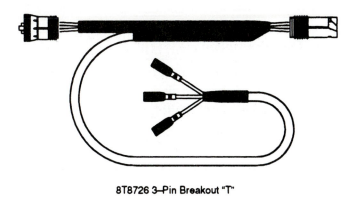

8T8726 3-Pin Breakout "T"

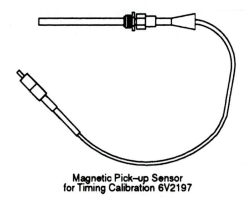

Magnetic Pick-up Sensor
for Timing Calibration 6V2197

TABLE 23–4 *3176B and 3406E engine models SAE standard diagnostic troubleshooting code description and flash code numbers*

PID—FMI	Flash code	Code description
1—11	72	Cylinder 1 fault
2—11	72	Cylinder 2 fault
3—11	73	Cylinder 3 fault
4—11	73	Cylinder 4 fault
5—11	74	Cylinder 5 fault
6—11	74	Cylinder 6 fault
22—13	42	Check timing sensor calibration
41—03	21	8-V supply above normal
41—04	21	8-V supply below normal
71—00	01	Idle shutdown override
71—01	47	Idle shutdown occurrence
84—00	41	Vehicle overspeed warning
84—01	31	Loss of vehicle speed signal
84—02	36	Invalid vehicle speed signal
84—08	36	Vehicle speed out of range
84—10	36	Vehicle speed rate of change
91—08	32	Invalid throttle signal
91—13	33	Throttle sensor calibration
100—01	46	Low oil pressure warning
100—03	24	Oil pressure sensor open circuit
100—04	24	Oil pressure sensor short circuit
100—11	46	Very low oil pressure
102—00	25	Boost pressure reading stuck high
102—03	25	Boost pressure sensor open circuit
102—04	25	Boost pressure sensor short circuit
102—13	42	Boost pressure sensor calibration
105—00	64	High intake manifold air temperature warning
105—03	38	Intake manifold air temperature sensor open circuit
105—04	38	Intake manifold air temperature sensor short circuit

(continued)

TABLE 23–4   (Continued)

PID—FMI	Flash code	Code description
105—11	64	Very high intake manifold air temperature
108—03	26	Atmospheric pressure sensor open circuit
108—04	26	Atmospheric pressure sensor short circuit
110—00	61	High coolant temperature warning
110—03	27	Coolant temperature sensor open circuit
110—04	27	Coolant temperature sensor short circuit
110—11	61	Very high coolant temperature
111—01	62	Low coolant level warning
111—02	12	Coolant level sensor fault
111—11	62	Very low coolant level
121—05	14	Retarder solenoid low/high open circuit
121—06	14	Retarder solenoid low/high short circuit
122—05	14	Retarder solenoid medium/high open circuit
122—06	14	Retarder solenoid medium/high short circuit
168—02	51	Low or intermittent battery power to ECM
174—00	65	High fuel temperature warning
174—03	13	Fuel temperature sensor open circuit
174—04	13	Fuel temperature sensor short circuit
190—00	35	Engine overspeed warning
190—02	34	Loss of engine rpm signal
228—03	19	A/C high-pressure switch open circuit
232—03	21	5-V supply above normal
232—04	21	5-V supply below normal
244—02	02	Event recorder data lost
249—11	58	Powertrain data link fault
252—11	59	Incorrect engine software
253—02	56	Check customer or system parameters
254—12	53	ECM fault

Source: Caterpillar, Inc.

into a PC from the ECM. Typical items that can be monitored or recorded include these:

- Start engine hours, current engine hours, trip hours
- Start miles, current miles, trip miles (kilometers)
- Current/total trip time, idle time
- Fuel consumed at idle
- Average load factor
- Average speed
- Average mpg (L/100 km), average fuel rate

In addition, with a diagnostic tool connected to the data link, the technician can monitor or record engine rpm, mph (km/h), fuel rate in gph (L/h), fuel rate with correction factor, average engine load factor, mph in increments of 5 mph (8 km/h); and engine rpm in increments of 100 rpm. Using programmable data screens, the technician can record additional engine and vehicle parameters such as coolant temperature, oil pressure, and cruise operation.

Breakout Cable Assemblies

Figure 21-59 showed a *breakout box* that can be used on the DDEC systems to check system wiring and harness

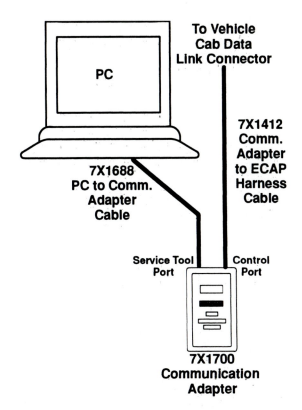

**To Vehicle
Cab Data
Link Connector**

PC

**7X1412
Comm.
Adapter
to ECAP
Harness
Cable**

**7X1688
PC to Comm.
Adapter
Cable**

Service Tool   Control
Port   Port

**7X1700
Communication
Adapter**

FIGURE 23–78 *Optional diagnostic tooling required to reprogram the engine ECM for the 3176B and 3406E engine models. (Courtesy of Caterpillar, Inc.)*

connections with the aid of a multimeter. Wiring and harness connections on Caterpillar's 3176B and 3406E engine models can be checked using the various wire harness breakout T's shown in Figure 23-77 to speed up electrical troubleshooting. These cables allow the probe tips of a multimeter to be safely inserted into the tip jacks to obtain a signal from any harness wire. The 7X6370 three-pin breakout T-harness is inserted in series between a 3176B/3406E harness jack and plug to permit voltage measurement on an operating system. The 8T8726 T-harness is only required to check a remote-mounted throttle position sensor, which receives a battery signal between 11 and 13.5 V.

HEUI FUEL SYSTEM

Existing EUI systems currently in use by Caterpillar, Cummins, Detroit Diesel, Volvo, and John Deere on their high-speed heavy-duty engine models utilize a camshaft-actuated rocker arm assembly to force the injector follower and fuel plunger downward. This action is required to raise the trapped fuel within the injector barrel to a high enough pressure to open the injector needle valve within the spray tip assembly.

However, a rather unique electronically controlled injection system now in use by both Caterpillar and Navistar International Transportation Corporation on their diesel engine product line is a system known by the letters HEUI (hydraulically actuated electronically controlled unit injection). The system is commonly referred to in the industry by the term HEUI, pronounced as in the name "Hughie." In this system, which was codesigned by Caterpillar and Navistar, no camshaft-actuated rocker arm is needed to raise the fuel pressure within the injector to the high levels needed to open the needle valve within the spray tip assembly.

In place of a rocker arm, the HEUI system employs high-pressure lube oil acting on an intensifier piston designed into the top end of each injector. Figure 23-80 illustrates a schematic arrangement of the components required with the HEUI system. Currently, the HEUI system is used by Navistar on their T444E V8 engine model. This engine is widely used by Ford in a number of their pickup and midrange truck models as well as by Navistar in their own product lineup. In addition, Navistar employs the HEUI system on their inline six-cylinder DT-466 model as well as in their 530E engine series. Caterpillar employs the HEUI system in their 3116, 3216, 3408E, and 3412E engine models.

System Operation

The design of the HEUI system permits enhanced performance through improved fuel economy and lower exhaust emissions by controlling the rate of injection hydraulically rather than mechanically, which depends on engine speed. Because the HEUI injector plunger does not move until the injector solenoid is energized by a signal from the ECM, plunger movement is not limited to the speed or duration of the engine cam lobe as it is in a mechanically actuated EUI system. Therefore, timing control is more precise. Within the injector body an intensifier piston multiplies hydraulic force between 3000 and 21,000 psi (20.7) to (143.8 MPa) on the fuel plunger.

Components required with the HEUI system are illustrated in Figure 23-81, with the five major items consisting of:

1. ECM (electronic control module)
2. IDM (injector drive module)
3. HPOP (high-pressure oil pump)
4. RPCV (rail pressure control valve)
5. HEUI injectors

TABLE 23-5 Engine ECM warning and protection system PID-FMI trouble code features that will initiate various operating parameters on 3176B and 3406E engines

Programmed to Warning

PID—FMI	Flash code	Code description	Warning lamp	45 mph max.	160 hp max.	1350 rpm max.
100—01	46	Low oil pressure warning	Solid	No	No	No
100—11	46	Very low oil pressure	Solid	No	No	No
105—00	64	High intake manifold air temperature warning	Solid	No	No	No
105—11	64	Very high intake manifold air temperature	Solid	No	No	No
110—00	61	High coolant temperature warning	Solid	No	No	No
110—11	61	Very high coolant temperature	Solid	No	No	No
111—01	62	Low coolant level warning	Solid	No	No	No
111—11	62	Very low coolant level warning	Solid	No	No	No

Programmed to Derate or Shut Down

PID—FMI	Flash code	Code description	Warning lamp	45 mph max.	160 hp max.	1350 rpm max.
100—01	46	Low oil pressure warning	Solid	No	No	No
100—11	46	Very low oil pressure	Flash	Yes	Yes	Yes

PID—FMI	Flash code	Code description	Warning lamp	Time to shutdown	Start time		
105—00	64	High intake manifold air temperature warning	Solid	No	No	No	No
105—11	64	Very high intake manifold air temperature	Solid	No	No	No	No
110—00	61	High coolant temperature warning	Flash	Yes	Yes	No	No
110—11	61	Very high coolant temperature	Flash	Yes	Yes	No	No
111—01	62	Low coolant level warning	Solid	No	No	No	No
111—11	62	Very low coolant level warning	Flash	Yes	Yes	No	No

Programmed to Shut Down

PID—FMI	Flash code	Code description	Warning lamp	Time to shutdown	Start time
100—01	46	Low oil pressure warning	Solid	No	No
100—11	46	Very low oil pressure	Flash	30 sec.	18 sec.
105—00	64	High intake manifold air temperature warning	Solid	No	No
105—11	64	Very high intake manifold air temperature	Solid	No	No
110—00	61	High coolant temperature warning	Flash	No	No
110—11	61	Very high coolant temperature	Flash	20 sec.	60 sec.
111—01	62	Low coolant level warning	Solid	No	No
111—11	62	Very low coolant level	Flash	30 sec.	80 sec.

Source: Caterpillar, Inc.

```
                    Read System Configuration Parameters
      Selected Engine Rating
         Rating #:                                     1         # 4
         Rating Type:                          Standard
         Rated Power:                               445  HP
         Rated RPM:                                1700  RPM
         Rated Peak Torque:                        1650  LB FT
      more... Press  ↑ or ↓ to move through the rest of the parameters.

         Rated Peak Torque RPM:                     1200  RPM
         Top Engine Limit–RPM Range:           1620–2120  RPM
         Test Spec:                             0T1234
               with BrakeSaver:                 0T5678
         Last Service tool to change system parameters:    TMCA1000
         Last Service tool to change customer parameters:  TMCA1000
         Full Load Setting:                           10      # 0
         Full Torque Setting:                         10      # 0
         Personality Module Code:                      1      # 0
         Personality Module P/N:              12T4321–02
         Personality Module Release Date:         OCT91
         Electronic Control Module S/N:       XXX–000000
         Vehicle ID:                          1234509876      #2
         Engine Serial Number:                XXX 01234
         Total  Tattletale:                           60
```

FIGURE 23–79 *ECAP screen: System configuration parameters.*

The ECM is a variant of Ford's own EEC-IV control module, and is a microprocessor that monitors a variety of engine sensors to determine the optimum fuel rate and injection timing for any operating condition. The injector drive module, which functions as an electrical relay, sends a precisely controlled current pulse to energize each injector solenoid. This pulsing signal, commonly referred to as a PWM (pulse-width modulation) signal, is described in greater detail in Figures 15-19 and 15-20. To supply high-pressure engine oil to the oil manifold(s) to feed the injector intensifier piston for the purpose of driving down the fuel plunger, a seven-piston fixed-displacement Rexroth axial piston pump is employed. Figure 23-82 illustrates a schematic of the high-pressure oil system used with the HEUI system. In the schematic, the high-pressure oil pump is gear driven and draws oil through both a filter and an oil cooler from the engine oil sump.

The oil circuit consists of both a low- and a high-pressure section: The low side from the engine oil pump operates at pressures of approximately 43.5 psi (300 kPa), and the high side, which provides the oil to the injector intensifier piston, operates in the range 3103 to 18,961 kPa (450 to 2750 psi), depending on the speed of the engine.

The high-pressure lube oil is controlled by the RPCV (regulator pressure control valve), which opens and dumps oil directly back to the engine oil pan. The RPCV is an electrically controlled dump valve that controls the pump output pressure. A variable signal current from the ECM determines pump output pressure. Figure 23-83 illustrates a cross section of the RPCV valve. With the engine stopped, the internal valve spool is held to the right by a return spring and the oil drain ports are closed. At engine startup the ECM signal to the RPCV permits the solenoid to generate a magnetic field to allow the armature to exert a force on the push pin and poppet. The combination of spring force and oil pressure flowing into the spool chamber continues to hold the spool valve to the right to ensure that the drain ports are held closed. Therefore, all oil flow is directed to the pressure rail manifold or manifolds cast into each cylinder head until the desired oil pressure is obtained.

Once the engine fires and runs, the ECM sends a signal to the RPCV, and the injection control pressure sensors monitor actual gallery pressure. The ECM then compares the actual rail pressure to the desired rail pressure and adjusts the electrical signal to the RPCV to obtain the desired rail pressure. Within the RPCV valve, the pressure in the spool chamber is controlled

FIGURE 23–80 *Fuel system schematic for a model 3408E/ 3412E engine equipped with a HEUI (hydraulically activated electronic unit injector) arrangement. (Courtesy of Caterpillar Inc.)*

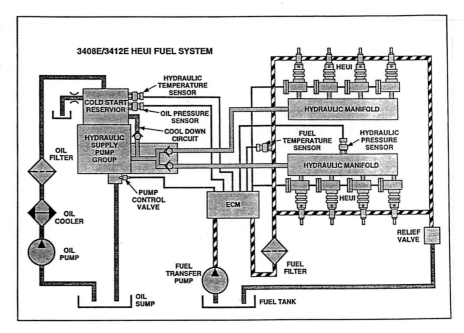

by adjusting the position on the poppet and allowing it to bleed off some of the oil in the spool chamber. The position of the poppet is controlled by the strength of the magnetic field based on the ECM signal. Therefore, the spool position determines how much area of the drain ports is open to control the rail pressure oil.

The HEUI injector operation involves three stages:

1. Fill cycle
2. Injection cycle
3. End of injection

Figure 23-84 illustrates the main components within the HEUI injector. During the fill cycle, the internal spring below the intensifier piston returns all components to their nonactuated positions, as shown in Figure 23-85. Fuel at a pressure of approximately 40 psi (274 kPa) unseats the plunger fill check valve, allowing the plunger cavity to fill with fuel. The fill cycle ends when the intensifier piston is pushed to the top of its bore, permitting the check valve to close. Since the solenoid of the injector is deenergized (no signal from the ECM), no high-pressure lube oil from the rail manifold can enter the injector. There is, however, fuel pressure within the plunger cavity since with the engine running, this fuel will be at approximately 40 psi (276 kPa).

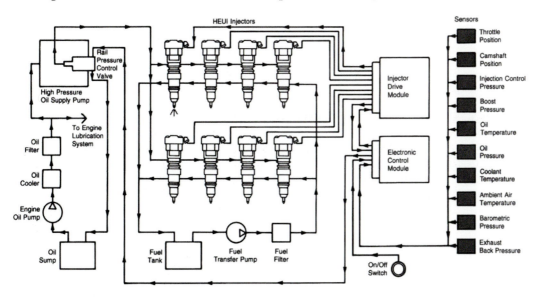

FIGURE 23–81 *International HEUI (hydraulically activated electronically controlled unit injection) fuel system operation.*

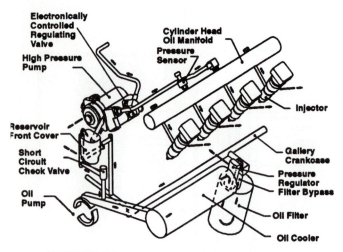

FIGURE 23–82 Lube oil side of fuel system.

When it is determined by the ECM, based on various sensor input signals, to inject fuel from a specific injector, the ECM sends a fuel delivery control signal to the injector drive module, which handles the needed current for activation of the injector solenoids. This electrical signal causes the injector solenoid armature to overcome the spring tension that is holding the poppet valve closed. When the poppet valve opens, it simultaneously closes off any path to drain for the oil and allows high-pressure oil to flow around the poppet valve and into the top of the intensifier piston, as shown in Figure 23-86. The high-pressure lube oil acting on the surface area of the intensifier piston will push the fuel plunger down. When the fuel pressure attains a pressure of approximately 2700 psi (18,495 kPa), it will lift the injector needle valve off its seat against its spring force (popping pressure), and

injection into the combustion chamber will begin. The injector spray-in pressure will range between 3000 and 21,000 psi (20.6 to 145 mPa), depending on engine load and speed requirements.

Injection ends when the ECM PWM solenoid signal is shut off. This action causes the injector poppet valve spring to close the poppet and shut off the flow of high-pressure lube oil. The distance between the intensifier piston and the bottom of its bore is controlled, which is known as *stroke limiting*. This protects against increasing maximum fuel delivery above designed rates. Once the poppet valve is seated by its return spring, the upper land of the poppet opens the high-pressure oil cavity to drain. This permits the fuel pressure within the plunger cavity to exert an upward force on the plunger and the intensifier, halting any further downward movement of the intensifier and plunger. With plunger motion stopped and the check valve still open, the remaining fuel pressure pushes a minute amount of fuel through the spray-tip orifice holes. This will cause a large pressure drop to the needle valve closing pressure value at approximately 1600 psi (11 mPa), to firmly close the needle valve on its seat, effectively ending injection.

When the plunger fill check valve closes, the fill cycle shown in Figure 23-85 will begin again by allowing fuel pressure at 40 psi (276 kPa) to unseat the check valve and fill the plunger cavity with fuel. The injection cycle is now ready to repeat.

Diagnostics
A Caterpillar ECAP (electronic control analyzer and programmer), shown in Figure 23-77, can be used to withdraw stored ECM trouble codes and to troubleshoot and diagnose system malfunctions. Other hand-held DDRs (diagnostic data readers), similar to

FIGURE 23–83 Cross section of a HEUI fuel system RPCV (rail pressure control valve) actuator. (Courtesy of NAVISTAR International Transportation Corporation.)

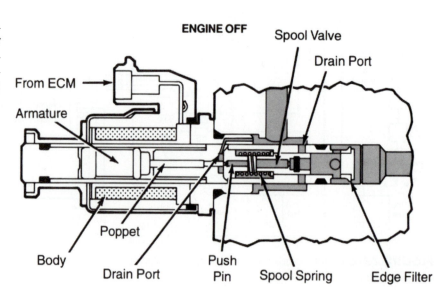

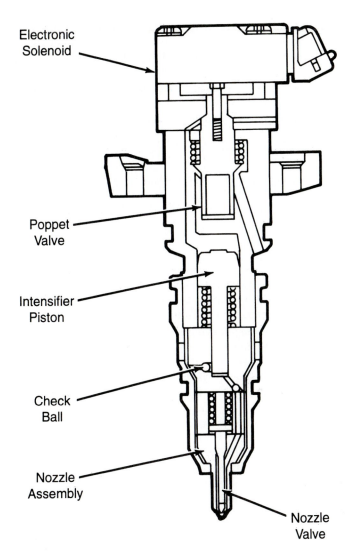

Electronic
Solenoid

Poppet
Valve

Intensifier
Piston

Check
Ball

Nozzle
Assembly

Nozzle
Valve

FIGURE 23-84 *Cross section of a HEUI fuel injector. (Courtesy of NAVISTAR International Transportation Corporation.)*

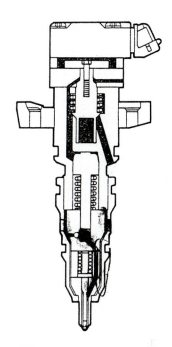

FIGURE 23-85 *HEUI fuel fill cycle. (Courtesy of NAVISTAR International Transportation Corporation.)*

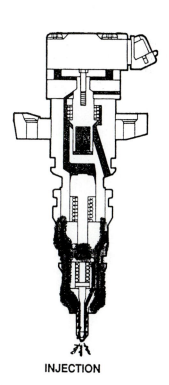

INJECTION

FIGURE 23-86 *HEUI injection cycle. (Courtesy of NAVISTAR International Transportation Corporation.)*

the one shown in Figure 21-52 can also be used on the HEUI system.

SUMMARY

The description of Caterpillar mechanical and electronic fuel injection systems in this chapter has rounded out your knowledge of the advantages of using electronic controls on today's diesel engines. Many similarities exist between the types of EUI systems used by Caterpillar, Cummins, Detroit Diesel, Volvo, and Mack. The diagnostic tooling employed by each major diesel engine OEM has more similarities than differences. A review of each of these major fuel systems can be readily applied to your main-tenance and diagnostic capabilities as a diesel technician.

SELF-TEST QUESTIONS

1. Technician A says that the 3208 V8 engine model uses an electronically controlled unit injector fuel system. Technician B says that the 3208 engine model uses a sleeve metering fuel system. Who is up to date on his Caterpillar engine models?

2. Technician A says that the 3114 and 3116 engines each has a cylinder displacement of 1.1 L (67 in³). Technician B says that they have 1.4 L (85 in³) and 1.6 L (98 in³) displacement per cylinder, respectively. Who understands the model designation identification sequence?

3. Technician A says that the 3406B truck engine was the first Caterpillar vehicle engine to receive electronic controls. Technician B believes that it was the 3176 engine model. Who is correct?

4. Technician A says that the 3300 series truck engine also uses a mechanical unit injector fuel system. Technician B says that this engine uses the new scroll fuel injection pump, as does the 3406B engine. Who is correct?

5. Technician A says that the letters PEEC in relation to a Caterpillar engine stand for "programmable electronic engine controls," whereas technician B says that they stand for "programmable electrical engine combustion." Who is up to date on terminology?

6. Technician A says that the basic concept of design/operation of a Caterpillar multiple-plunger injection pump is similar to that for Robert Bosch systems. Technician B says that is not so. Who is correct?

7. The conventional term used by Caterpillar in their injection pumps for the *helix* is the word
   a. port
   b. plunger
   c. barrel
   d. scroll

8. Describe the meaning of the following letters in relation to Caterpillar fuel systems:
   a. SMFS
   b. CBFS
   c. NSFS
   d. PEEC

9. Technician A says that the new scroll fuel injection pump was designed to allow greater fuel delivery volume for higher engine horsepower settings. Technician B says that the new scroll fuel system was designed for higher injection pressures and shorter injection duration. Who is correct?

10. Typical injection pressures for the NSFS are approximately:
    a. 10,000 psi (688 bar)
    b. 12,000 to 14,000 psi (826 to 964 bar)
    c. 15,000 to 16,000 psi (1033 to 1102 bar)
    d. 18,000 to 20,000 psi (1239 to 1377 bar)

11. Technician A says that the SMFS uses a spill sleeve collar to control the effective stroke of the pumping plunger. Technician B says that this is incorrect since it is not a distributor-type pump. Who is correct?

12. Technician A says that Caterpillar now only uses direct-injection combustion chamber engines in their line of highway truck engines. Technician B disagrees, saying that for cold-weather operation, a PC (precombustion) engine is still available with glow plug controls. Who is correct?

13. Technician A says that mechanical governors used on Caterpillar truck engines are speed sensitive. Technician B says that they are load sensitive in order to be able to respond to highway operating conditions such as hills. Who is correct?

14. Technician A says that the AFC (air/fuel control) unit is designed to limit injection pump rack travel, thereby eliminating exhaust smoke. Technician B says that the AFC is designed to act as a wastegate for the turbocharger to limit boost under load. Who is correct?

15. Which of the following two ports are used in the NSFS injection pump?
    a. inlet port
    b. bypass closed port
    c. outlet port
    d. spill port

16. Technician A says that normal fuel transfer pump pressure in the NSFS is 25 to 30 psi (172 to 207 kPa), whereas technician B thinks that it should be closer to 35 psi (241 kPa). Who is correct?

17. Technician A says that for fuel to flow from the injection pump into the fuel injection line, at least 100 psi (690 kPa) of fuel pressure is needed to open the pump check valve in an NSFS. Technician B says that it requires 350 psi (2413 kPa) to open this check valve. Who is right?

18. Technician A says that the amount of fuel delivered to the nozzle in a Caterpillar multiple-plunger injection pump is determined by the lift of the pump camshaft. Technician B says that it is determined by the effective stroke of the pumping plunger. Who knows what he or she is talking about here?

19. Technician A says that the purpose of a reverse-flow check valve in an NSFS is to provide a consistent, smooth engine power curve by controlling fuel-line hydraulic action. Technician B says that the reverse flow check valve in the NSFS is designed to allow fuel line pressure bleed down once the engine has stopped. Who is correct?

20. Technician A says that on later-model 3406B engines using the NSFS, it is not necessary to have to bleed the fuel system after changing the fuel filters when an orifice bleed valve is used on the pump. Technician B disagrees, saying that if you do not bleed air from the fuel system, the engine may fail to start or run rough. Who is correct?

21. Technician A says that the automatic timing advance unit used on 3406B engines is nonadjustable. Technician B says that you can adjust the automatic timing device on 3406B engines. Who is right?

22. Technician A says that the fuel transfer pump used with the NSFS is a gear-type unit, whereas technician B says that the transfer pump is a piston-type transfer pump. Who is correct?

23. Technician A says that there is no need for a pressure relief valve with the 3406B engine fuel transfer pump, due to its design characteristics. Technician B says that to operate correctly, all transfer pumps require a pressure relief valve. Who is right?

24. Technician A says that current Caterpillar mechanical governors used on the 3406B engines is a hydramechanical servo type. Technician B says that they are straight mechanical used in conjunction with an AFC unit. Who is correct?

25. Technician A says that the governor springs are always attempting to pull the fuel rack to a decreased fuel position. Technician B says that it is the centrifugal force of the rotating governor flyweights that pull the rack to a decreased fuel position. Who is right?

26. Technician A says that the purpose of the servo spool valve in an NSFS governor is to transfer engine oil pressure to the servo piston to move the fuel control rack. Technician B says that the servo piston controls the AFC unit. Who is right?

27. A state of balance in a governor means that
    a. the force of the weights and springs is equal
    b. the operator is controlling the engine speed
    c. the correct gear in the transmission has been selected to keep the engine at a steady speed
    d. the turbocharger boost and fuel delivery pressures are equal

28. To increase the fuel delivery rate to the engine cylinders on an NSFS, you have to
    a. speed up the engine
    b. lengthen the effective stroke of the pumping plungers
    c. apply more force to the governor linkage
    d. adjust the fuel injection pump camshaft for greater lift

29. Technician A says that the term *high idle* means the same as *maximum no-load* engine speed. Technician B says that it means the same as *rated* engine speed. Who understands the meaning of this terminology?

30. Technician A says that on a Caterpillar mechanical or hydramechanical governor, the fuel rack will be pushed into an increased fuel delivery position with a drop in engine speed from high idle to rated rpm. Technician B says that there will be less fuel delivered under such an operating condition. Who knows his governor theory here?

31. The function of a governor dashpot is to
    a. ensure smoother governor response with rapid throttle movements
    b. prevent oscillation of governor parts with a load increase
    c. prevent oscillation of governor parts with a load decrease
    d. balance out the weight and spring forces

32. Technician A says that the basis of operation of a governor dashpot is to use oil on one side and a spring on the other. Technician B says that oil pressure is used on both sides of the dashpot piston. Who is right?

33. Technician A says that if the dashpot needle valve is adjusted to allow too much oil flow, it can create an engine hunting condition. Technician B says that it will cause the governor response to be slower than normal. Who is correct?

34. Technician A says that any time that the intake manifold pressure is approximately 50% of the turbocharger's maximum boost or higher, the AFC unit will allow full fuel rack travel. Technician B disagrees, saying that the rack can only move proportional to turbo boost pressure.

35. Technician A says that the electric fuel solenoid used on 3406B engine fuel injection pumps is an energize-to-run hookup, whereas technician B says that it is an energize-to-shutoff system. Who is right?

36. Technician A says that dynamic (running) engine to pump timing can be checked using Caterpillar special tool group 8T1000. Technician B says that you would use special tool 8T5300. Who is right?

37. Technician A says that if the engine lacks power with no unusual exhaust smoke color, the problem is probably due to fuel starvation. Technician B says that it is more likely a faulty injector. Who is right?

38. To determine if an injection nozzle is misfiring on an NSFS, you should
    a. loosen the high-pressure fuel line nut while the engine is running to check the engine sound and speed drop
    b. loosen the high-pressure fuel line nut while the engine is running to check the engine sound and speed pickup rate
    c. remove the nozzle from the engine and install it into a pop tester
    d. block off the fuel supply line from the injection pump and run the engine at an idle speed

39. When using a contact pyrometer to determine each engine cylinders exhaust temperature, technician A says that a low reading on one cylinder could be due to insufficient fuel delivery. Technician B says that it could be caused by low cylinder compression. Who is right?

40. Technician A says that a high pyrometer reading at one cylinder could be an indication of too much fuel being

delivered due to orifice wear in the nozzle tip. Technician B says that a high pyrometer reading is more likely to be due to too little fuel, creating a lean-fire condition. Who is right?

41. Technician A says that dirty fuel or water in the fuel can lead to enlargement of the spray-tip orifices, which will cause the spray-in angle to flatten out. Technician B says that it will cause seizure of the engine. Who is right?

42. True or False: Carbon should be removed from a nozzle tip with a brass bristle brush, *not* with a wire brush.

43. To remove a pumping plunger element from an NSFS injection pump, you should
    a. place piston 1 at TDC (compression)
    b. center the fuel rack
    c. remove the AFC unit
    d. remove the governor

44. On a 3406B engine the flywheel timing bolt
    a. is located in the forward side of the flywheel housing
    b. is located in the injection pump housing
    c. is located in the rocker cover recess
    d. is a special order bolt

45. Technician A says that when performing a static timing check on a 3406B engine, piston 1 should be at TDC (compression). Technician B says that piston 6 is the reference cylinder since it is closer to the flywheel. Who is right?

46. Technician A says that when performing a dynamic rack setting procedure on a 3406B engine, a small mechanical dial indicator can be used to record the rack movement. Technician B says that you should use Caterpillar service tool 8T1000, which is an electronic position indicator. Who is right?

47. Technician A says that rotating the adjusting screw in the automatic timing advance unit of a 3406B engine will alter the weight travel internally. Technician B says that the adjustment screw will change the spring force in the timing unit. Who is right?

48. Technician A says that the rack setting on a 3406B engine is controlled by a stop bar, whereas technician B says that it is done with a torque spring arrangement. Who is right?

49. The term *balance* or *set point* on a Caterpillar engine refers to the condition that exists when the fuel setting screw or pin is just lightly touching the
    a. governor speed control lever internally
    b. torque spring or stop bar
    c. AFC plunger control tip
    d. rack centering pin

50. Technician A says that if the balance/set point is incorrect on a 3406B engine, to gain access to the adjustment screw you would remove the electric shutdown solenoid. Technician B says that you would remove the small governor access cover. Who is correct?

51. Technician A says that the use of the electronic controls on both the 3176 and 3406B engines does away with the need for an AFC unit. Not so, says technician B; you still need the AFC unit. Who is right?

52. The letters PWM in reference to an electronic unit injector engine stand for
    a. power width module
    b. pulse-width modulated
    c. pressure working motor
    d. pneumatic with magnetic controls

53. Technician A says that the letters TPS stand for "throttle position sensor," while technician B says that they stand for "throttle power switch." Who is right?

54. The throttle pedal on an electronically controlled engine such as the 3406 and 3176 is basically a(n)
    a. variable potentiometer
    b. hydraulic/pneumatic cylinder
    c. on/off relay switch
    d. mechanical/electrical circuit breaker

55. Technician A says that the term *PROM* stands for "programmable read-only memory," whereas technician B says that it stands for "power road override module." Who is correct?

56. Technician A says that an EEPROM unit is an "electrically erasable programmable read-only memory," whereas technician B says that it is an "electric engine power road override module." Who is correct?

57. Technician A says that to prevent unauthorized adjustment of the engine power setting on electronic engines models, an electronic password is required. Technician B says that you can alter the engine horsepower setting by removing and installing another PROM assembly. Who is right?

58. Technician A says that the control module determines injection timing, fuel delivery rate, and governor reaction/setting. Technician B says that this is done by manipulation of the TPS. Who is right?

59. Technician A says that to withdraw stored trouble codes from computer memory in the engines that you require special Caterpillar diagnostic equipment. Technician B says that you can also activate and use the flashing trouble lamp mounted on the vehicle dash. Who is correct?

60. Technician A says that the normal fuel delivery pressure to the unit injectors on a 3176 engine is between 45 and 70 psi (310 to 483 kPa). Technician B says that it is higher and runs at approximately 91 psi (630 kPa). Who is correct here?

61. Technician A says that a relief valve that sticks open in the return fuel manifold of a 3176 engine will cause the engine to run at a fast idle speed. Technician B says that this would cause the engine to run rough, misfire, and fail to pick up the load. Who is correct?

62. True or False: The time taken for the electronic unit injector fuel spill valve to close in a 3176 engine is approximately 1 millisecond.

63. Technician A says that the 3114/3116 engines employ a mechanically operated and controlled unit fuel injector system, whereas technician B says that they use an electronic unit injector. Who is right?

64. Technician A says that the 3114/3116 engines employ a gear-type fuel transfer pump, whereas technician B says that a plunger-type fuel transfer pump is used. Who is correct?

65. Technician A says that the minimum fuel pump transfer pressure on the 3114/3116 engines is 29 psi (200 kPa). Technician B disagrees, saying that it should be at least 35 psi (241 kPa); otherwise, the engine will run rough, misfire, and fail to pull the load. Who is correct here?

66. Technician A says that moving the unit injector fuel rack toward the injector body in a 3114/3116 engine will result in increased fuel being delivered to the combustion chamber. Not so, says technician B; this action will decrease the fuel rate to the cylinders. Who is right?

67. Technician A says that the injector racks on a 3114/3116 engine must be checked with the aid of a dial gauge. Technician B disagrees, saying that you can do this by hand just as well. Who is right?

68. Technician A says that the 3114/3116 truck engines are equipped with a limiting-speed mechanical governor assembly. Technician B disagrees, saying that it uses an all-range or variable-speed governor assembly. Who is right?

69. Technician A says that the 3114/3116 engine uses a hydraulic servo-assist mechanism with a dashpot. Technician B disagrees, saying that a straight mechanical governor is used. Who is correct?

70. True or False: The only external governor adjustment that can be performed on a 3114/3116 engine is the low-idle setting.

Electrical Fundamentals and Batteries

OVERVIEW

Today's breed of technician must have a solid foundation in electrical concepts and the fundamentals of electronics systems. In this chapter we describe the basics of electrical flow, and how a typical electrical system functions and operates. The battery system supplies the needed electrical power to feed all of the electrical components used on an engine and piece of equipment. Details on how to service, maintain, test and troubleshoot a basic electrical system and battery are given here.

ELECTRICITY

What is electricity? We all experience its effects and use it every day of our lives. It lights our homes and shops, starts our car or truck, and powers many labor-saving devices, such as electric drills, saws, and impact wrenches. It is largely taken for granted because it is so dependable and easy to use. Most people know very little about it. To become a successful heavy-duty diesel technician you will have to understand some basic electrical principles.

Electricity can be defined as the flow of *electrons from atom to atom* in a conductor. To further understand this action we must discuss briefly the nature of matter and atoms.

All *matter* is made up of *atoms*, this matter may be a solid such as copper, which is used in electrical wiring, a liquid such as the oil in the diesel engine, or a gas such as the air we breath. Not all *atoms* are the same. Different *elements*, such as copper, aluminum, and others, have different atoms. Even though they

differ, all contain electrons and protons (Figure 24-1), and each element will have atoms of different structures. Understanding this atomic *structure* and its actions will help us understand how electricity works.

Let us examine an atom of the simplest element hydrogen. The hydrogen atom has one electron and one proton (Figure 24-2). The proton is in the center of the atom and is positive (+), while the electron is negative (−) and maintains an orbit around the proton forming a circular-shaped shell. Simple electrons such as hydrogen will have one shell with one electron, while more complex electrons will have several shells and many electrons.

The element copper will be of particular interest to us in our study of electricity because it is one of the principal elements used in heavy-duty electric circuits and components. The structure of a copper atom is shown in Figure 24-3. With its atomic number of 29, the copper atom will have 29 protons and 29 electrons. As in other atoms, the protons are at the center, while the electrons encircle the protons in four rings or shells, with each shell containing fewer electrons. Located at different distances from the proton and of different diameters, the shells all contain electrons. The innermost shell contains 2 electrons, the next ring contains 8 electrons, and the third ring contains 18 electrons. The outermost shell contains only one electron.

This atomic structure makes copper a good conductor of electricity because it has only one electron in its outer ring. Elements such as copper, with fewer than four electrons in their outer ring, are all classified as good conductors. Elements that have more than four electrons in their outer ring are considered insulators. Elements that have exactly four electrons in the outer shell are considered semiconductors.

As stated earlier, the protons and electrons in an

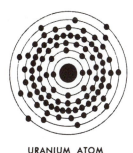

URANIUM ATOM

FIGURE 24–1 Typical atom. (Courtesy of Delco Remy America.)

atom have electrical charges, the proton being positive and the electron negative. Each atom of an element has a positive center with the negative electrons in orbit around it. (The movement of electrons from atom to atom in an element is called *electron flow*.)

Charges that are alike, such as positive protons, do not attract each other, while unlike charges such as a proton (+) and electron (−) do attract. This electrical attraction is what holds the atom in an element together. The core of protons exerts an attraction on the electron in the outer ring and holds them in orbit.

As long as the attraction from the center of the atom (positive charge) is equal to the negative charge of the orbiting electrons, the atom will maintain a neutral electrical charge. If this neutral charge is changed, the electrons orbiting in the outer ring may leave one atom and move to another. We can change the neutral charge of the atom by applying an electrical charge to the element containing the atom such as a copper wire.

Elements such as copper, which have fewer than three electrons in the outer shell of their atom, have a tendency to allow their electrons to move easily from one atom's outer shell to the next atom's outer shell. Other elements or compounds that have more than five electrons in their outer shell do not allow electrons to move from shell to shell. Such elements are known as nonconductors of electricity.

Electron movement in a copper wire will be from

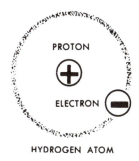

PROTON

ELECTRON

HYDROGEN ATOM

FIGURE 24–2 Hydrogen atom. (Courtesy of DRA.)

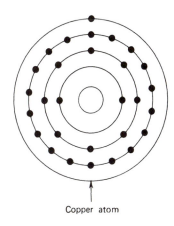

Copper atom

FIGURE 24–3 Copper atom. (Courtesy of Delco Remy America.)

atom to atom, but unless it is directed it will not be current flow. By applying a positive charge to one end of the wire and a negative charge to the other end of the wire, the negatively charged electrons will be attracted to the positive charge (Figure 24-4). Each atom will then be giving up electrons to the positive end of the wire and receiving electrons from the negative end of the wire. This movement of electrons, or current flow, will continue as long as the positive and negative charges are maintained.

PRINCIPLES OF SIMPLE ELECTRICAL CIRCUITS

Our study of electrical circuits must include current, voltage, and resistance.

Current

Current is the flow of the negatively charged electrons in a conductor. This flow of current is measured in amperes (A). One ampere of current is 6.28 billion billion electrons passing one point in the conductor in 1 second (Figure 24-5).

Current Flow

Two theories exist regarding current flow.

1. *The conventional theory* of current flow has long been accepted and used in explaining electricity

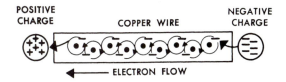

POSITIVE CHARGE   COPPER WIRE   NEGATIVE CHARGE

ELECTRON FLOW

FIGURE 24–4 Electrons flowing in copper wire. (Courtesy of DRA.)

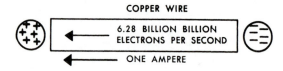

FIGURE 24–5 *Measurement of electron flow. (Courtesy of DRA.)*

as it is applied to heavy-duty vehicles. It states that current flow is from positive to negative in the electrical circuit. The conventional theory is still in use today and should be used when studying electrical circuits in heavy-duty vehicles.

2. *The electron theory* of current flow is used in the explanation of electricity as it is applied to electrical appliances and electrical engineering. It states that current flow is from negative to positive in the electrical circuit. It is used in electronic programs to teach current flow and electrical principles. In most cases it cannot be used in our study of electricity in heavy-duty vehicles, since all training charts and diagrams are drawn using the conventional theory.

Types of Current

1. Alternating current (ac) electricity is used primarily in household and industrial-type use. Sixty-cycle electricity is in common use, the 60 representing how many times per second the current flow changes direction.

2. Direct current (dc) is current that flows in one direction only and is used in heavy-duty vehicles to power the starter, to supply current for the lights, to charge the battery, and to power all the other electrical components.

Voltage (Electromotive Force)

Voltage applied to a circuit creates an imbalance in the atoms causing the electrons to flow. Sometimes called *electromotive force* (EMF), voltage can be produced mechanically by generators or chemically by batteries. Current flow does not exist without voltage. If the vehicle battery is discharged and can produce no voltage, current will not be forced to flow into the starter motor to crank the engine. A 12-volt (V) battery has a voltage potential of 12 V; if no electrical component is connected between the battery terminals, the battery voltage will remain at 12 V.

Resistance

In an electrical circuit, resistance to electron flow is caused by each atom resisting the loss of electrons and the collisions of atoms and electrons moving through the wire.

Conductors

All types of conductors have resistance, and depending on the element or compound used, will be in different amounts. Resistance is measured in ohms (Ω), *1 ohm is the resistance that will allow 1 ampere to flow when the potential is 1 volt.* Several factors determine the resistance in the conductor portion of a circuit.

1. Type of material (element or compound used).
2. Length of the conductor; since a given length of wire has a certain resistance, adding length to the wire will obviously add resistance.
3. The temperature of the wire. The hotter the conductor, the greater resistance to electron flow.
4. Cross-sectional area or size. A larger-diameter wire will provide a greater area for current to flow.

As we discussed, resistance in an electrical circuit can be controlled by the type and construction of various elements. This control or design of electrical circuits gives the designer control over current flow and is used throughout heavy-duty electrical systems. Based on a common voltage of 12, electrical units are designed to control current flow by resistance. If it were not for this resistance, electrical components and circuits would be uncontrollable. Starting motors, which have very little resistance, allow a large current flow compared to a small 12-V light bulb, which will have a large amount of resistance. The regulation of alternator charging circuits is all based on the resistance of the system, which is determined by the circuit (conductors and the battery).

Semiconductors

As stated earlier, semiconductors are elements whose atoms have exactly four electrons in their outer ring. When designed into an electrical device such as a diode or transistor, they become very useful. Electronic control units utilized to control electronic fuel injection systems and alternator regulators are two good examples of the use of semiconductor components.

LAWS RELATING TO VOLTAGE, CURRENT FLOW, AND CIRCUIT RESISTANCE

The interaction between voltage, current flow, and resistance are important to today's heavy-duty technician, since more and more of the entire vehicle and engine are controlled and operated by electrical circuits.

To fully understand this relationship, we must discuss one important law of electrical circuits: Ohm's law.

Ohm's Law

Ohm's law states that 1 ohm is the resistance of a circuit in which a potential difference of 1 volt produces a current (flow) of 1 ampere. It can be seen that Ohm's law expresses the relationship between the following three properties:

1. *Voltage or electromotive force (EMF) or (E).* Called system pressure.
2. *Current or inductance (I).* Current is the flow of electricity in a circuit. The amount of flow (measured in amperes) is dependent on voltage and resistance.
3. *Resistance (R).* Resistance to flow is measured in ohms. The amount of resistance in a circuit is determined by the type of conductor and the electrical component. In equation form, Ohm's law can be expressed three different ways:

$$E = I \times R \text{ (amperes} \times \text{ohms)}$$
$$I = E \div R \text{ (volts} \div \text{ohms)}$$
$$R = E \div I \text{ (volts} \div \text{amperes)}$$

If any two values are known, the third can be calculated using the equations outlined above.

Using Ohm's Law to Figure Circuit Values

It can be seen from Figure 24-6 that if one value in the circuit equation is missing, we can use the known two to calculate the missing value. All electrical circuits that we work with in heavy-duty electrical and electronics will be either series, parallel, or series–parallel.

Series Circuit

A series circuit is a circuit in which a single path or conductor connects all parts of the circuit. In addition, all current must flow through one path to return to the source voltage. Figure 24-7 is a simple series circuit with a voltage potential of 12 with 3 A flowing through a 4-Ω resistor.

If the current in this circuit were not known (Figure 24-8), it could be calculated using Ohm's law. To help us

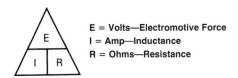

E = Volts—Electromotive Force
I = Amp—Inductance
R = Ohms—Resistance

FIGURE 24–6 *Ohm's law triangle with definition.*

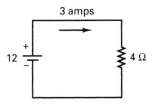

FIGURE 24–7 *12-V circuit with voltage, amperage, and resistance.*

visualize this, we use the triangle shown in Figure 24-9. Since we do not know the current flow, we will leave its space in the triangle blank and fill in the values that we know, 12 V and 4 Ω. This gives us 12 ÷ 4, which equals 3. We now know that we have 3 flowing in this circuit.

Now let's assume that we did not know the resistance value in the circuit (Figure 24-10). The equation would be 12 V ÷ 3 A, with 4 Ω as the answer. If the voltage value was missing in our simple circuit (Figure 24-11), the equation would be 3 A × 4 Ω = 12 V.

If the series circuit contains two resistors (Figure 24-12), we should add the resistance values together, *since the sum of all the individual resistors equal the total resistance in a series circuit.* In the example in Figure 24-12, we know that the voltage is 12 and the two resistors added together equal 8 Ω of resistance; our equation (Figure 24-13) would be 12 Ω, ÷ 8 the answer being 1.5 A. Similarly, if we did not know the voltage, it would be an easy task to calculate it using Ohm's law.

Further use of Ohm's law can include calculating the voltage drop across a resistor or electrical accessory. In Figure 24-14 the resistance of the first resistor is 2 Ω, and if we know that the current flow is 1.5 A, our equation would be 2 × 1.5 = 3 V drop across the first resistor. The second resistor is 6 Ω, so the equation would be 6 × 1.5, which equals 9. The two voltage drops equal the voltage available in the circuit, which is 12 V.

From our study of series circuits we know that three facts exist regarding a series circuit:

1. *Current flow* in the circuit and all resistors or accessories will be the same, since there is only one path for current to flow.

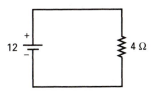

FIGURE 24–8 *12-V circuit with resistance and no current flow.*

FIGURE 24–9   *Ohm's law triangle.*

2. *Voltage drop* across each resistor in the circuit will be proportional to the resistance of the resistor. Therefore, if each resistor has a different value, the voltage drop across it must be different. Also, the total circuit resistance is equal to the sum of all resistors in the circuit.

3. The voltage drop in the circuit must always equal the source voltage. When 12 V is available, the voltage drop in the entire circuit will be 12 V.

Parallel Circuits

In a series circuit, current leaving the positive battery post had no choice but to follow one path back to the negative battery post. Parallel circuits differ from series circuits in that there is more than one path for the current leaving the positive battery terminal to return to the battery. Like series circuits, parallel circuits are known to have certain characteristics that we must recognize before we can understand how they work.

1. The voltage is the same across each resistor. This means that all resistors in a parallel circuit have the same voltage available.

2. Current flow through each resistor will depend on its resistance value. Also, the total resistance in a parallel circuit will be less than in a series circuit, since more than one path back to the battery exists.

3. Total current flow will equal the sum of the flow in all circuits or branches of the circuit.

In a parallel circuit (Figure 26-15), two parallel resistors are connected to a 12-V battery. Using Ohm's law, we can calculate the current through each resistor and the total current flow.

FIGURE 24–10   *Ohm's law triangle.*

FIGURE 24–11   *Ohm's law triangle.*

1. Resistor 1, with 2 Ω of resistance, gives us the equation 12 V ÷ 2 Ω = 6A.

2. Resistor 2, with 4 Ω of resistance, gives us the equation 12 V ÷ 4 Ω = 3, giving us an amp flow of 3 A through the resistor.

3. The amp flow through the first resistor and the second resistor represents total current flow through the circuit, which is 9 A.

4. To eliminate calculating each resistor separately, we can find the equivalent resistance by using one of the following methods.

NOTE   Equivalent resistance is the resistance of the parallel resistors in the circuit.

---

a. The value of any two resistors in parallel is equal to the product divided by the sum:

$$\frac{2 \times 4 = 8}{2 + 4 = 6} = 1.33 \ \Omega \text{ equivalent resistance}$$

To use this method for more than two resistors, calculate the resistance value for each two resistors until you have calculated the final average resistance.

b. The value of any number of resistors in parallel can easily be determined using another method, which is

$$\text{Equivalent resistance} = \frac{1}{\dfrac{1}{R_1} + \dfrac{1}{R_2} + \dfrac{1}{R_3}}$$

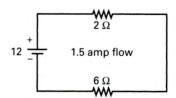

FIGURE 24–12   *Circuit with two resistors.*

FIGURE 24–13 *Ohm's law triangle.*

c. Using this formula, we can easily compute the equivalent resistance in the circuit of Figure 24-16, which has three resistors.

d. To determine the equivalent resistance, our first equation would be

$$\frac{1}{1/2 + 1/4 + 1/6} = \frac{1}{0.5 + 0.25 + 0.16}$$
$$= \frac{1}{0.91}$$
$$= 1.09$$

1.09 represents the equivalent resistance of the three resistors. Current flow in the circuit is determined by dividing 12 by 1.09, which gives us 11 A flowing in the circuit.

Series–Parallel Circuits

As implied by the name, series–parallel circuits have a combination of series and parallel circuits. A typical series–parallel circuit is shown in Figure 24-17.

1. In Figure 24-17 current flows through the first resistor, which is in series with the two parallel resistors.

2. To calculate current flow, we must first calculate the equivalent of R_2 and R_3.

3. Using the first method, which we described earlier, our calculation would be

$$\frac{6 \times 6}{6 + 6} = \frac{36}{12} = 3 \text{ equivalent resistance}$$

4. Now that we know what the equivalent resis-

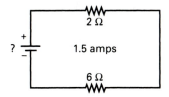

FIGURE 24–14 *Circuit with two resistors.*

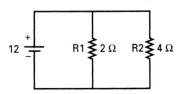

FIGURE 24–15 *Parallel circuit.*

tance of the two parallel resistors is, we can calculate the total resistance by adding 3 + 2 = 5.

5. Using the total resistance of 5, we divide this into 12 to obtain current flow, which is 2.4 A.

The relationship among voltage, amperage, and resistance is true for all electrical circuits. Once this relationship is understood by the technician, electrical circuit and component troubleshooting become easy.

PERMANENT MAGNETS AND ELECTROMAGNETS

Permanent Magnets

Almost everyone has had some experience with magnetism, especially permanent magnets. The magnetic base on a dial indicator is a good example of a permanent magnet. Permanent magnetism was first discovered in iron called lodestone. It was discovered that this iron ore has polarity. This means that one end is attracted to the earth's north pole and the other end is attracted to the south pole. All magnets, permanent and electro, have polarity. Further discoveries indicated that a permanent magnet (Figure 24-18) has a force field surrounding it that tends to attract other iron, hence the name *magnet*.

This force field is utilized in all electrical components of diesel engines. Since the control of this force field is an essential part of component operation, permanent magnets are not used in diesel engine components because they cannot be controlled. Electromagnets are used in most diesel engine electrical components because they can be controlled by regulating the amount of electrical power applied to them.

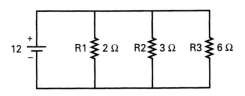

FIGURE 24–16 *Parallel circuit with three resistors.*

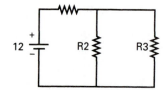

FIGURE 24–17 *Series–parallel circuit.*

Electromagnets

Much like permanent magnets, electromagnets are pieces of iron with wire wrapped around them. To make the magnet work, current must be flowing through the wire. To better understand how an electromagnet works, we must first look at a straight conductor or wire. If current is passed through this wire, a magnetic field is created around the wire (Figure 24-19). The direction of this magnetic field can be determined using the *right-hand rule for a current-carrying conductor*. To determine the force-field direction around a straight conductor by using this rule, grasp the conductor with your right hand, letting the thumb point in the direction of current flow through the conductor. The other four fingers of your right hand will then point in the direction that the magnetic lines of force travel in to encircle the conductor (Figure 24-20). These magnetic lines of force will encircle the conductor as long as current is flowing through the wire. The lines of force are stationary and do not move. The size of the force field is dependent on the amount of current being passed through the conductor.

If a straight current-carrying conductor is wound to create a coil of wire, the magnetic field around each loop of wire is added together to create an electromagnet (Figure 24-21). This electromagnet has polarity that can be determined by using the *right-hand rule for an electromagnet* (Figure 24-22). To identify the polarity of an electromagnet by using the right-hand rule, let your

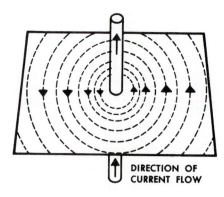

FIGURE 24–19 *Force field encircling a straight conductor. (Courtesy of Delco-Remy of America.)*

fingers encircle the coil in the direction the wire is wrapped and current is flowing. The thumb then will point to the north pole of the electromagnet.

Since a simple coil of wire would not be a very strong magnet, many coils are used, and in most cases a soft-iron bar is placed in the center of the coil to increase its strength. This increase in strength occurs because the force field can pass through the soft-iron core much more easily than it could pass through the air.

Once the two right-hand rules as applied to a straight conductor and an electromagnet are understood, the electrical components used on a diesel engine will be understood more easily.

ELECTROMAGNETIC INDUCTION

As stated earlier, electron flow in a conductor is current flow. To get this current flowing, voltage is needed. The most common method used in diesel engine components is electromagnetic induction. This

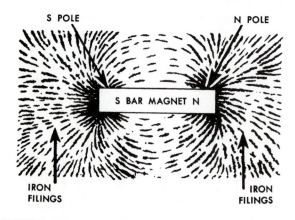

FIGURE 24–18 *Permanent magnet with force field. (Courtesy of Delco-Remy of America.)*

FIGURE 24–20 *Right-hand rule applied to a current-carrying conductor. (Courtesy of Delco-Remy of America.)*

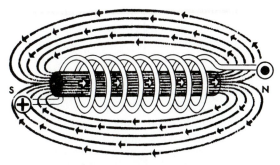

IRON CORE INCREASES FIELD STRENGTH

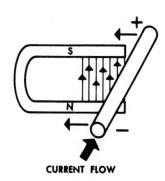

CURRENT FLOW

FIGURE 24–23 Electromagnet induction. (Courtesy of Delco-Remy of America.)

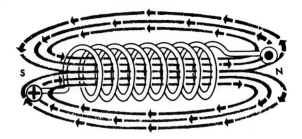

FIGURE 24–21 Typical electromagnet. (Courtesy of Delco-Remy of America.)

principle is widely used to produce current flow in a conductor. Figure 24-23 shows the three items needed to produce voltage by electromagnetic induction:

1. Conductor
2. Magnetism
3. Movement

A voltage is induced in the conductor as the conductor is moved through the force field. This principle is used in dc generators to produce voltage and current flow.

A simple dc generator could be constructed by placing a loop of wire, which serves as a conductor, be-

tween two electromagnets. The loop of wire is then rotated and voltage is induced into the wire. This principle is illustrated in Figure 24-24. Ac generators (alternators) use the same basic principle but apply it differently. In this application the conductors are stationary and the magnet rotates, moving the magnetic field across the conductor, creating current flow. These two principles are explained further in Chapter 25.

TEST INSTRUMENTS

Many types of testing equipment are available to test electrical circuits, charging systems, and batteries. Two of the most common are the multimeter and ampere/volt tester units.

Multimeter (Volt-Ohmmeter)
The multimeter (Figure 24-25) can be used to check a multitude of electrical components and circuits. Multimeters are one of two types, analog (meter with a hand) or digital. The multimeter can usually be used to read ac voltage, dc voltage, ohms, and amperes. In addition, some meters have a special diode check position.

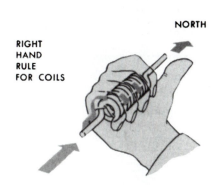

RIGHT HAND RULE FOR COILS

NORTH

FIGURE 24–22 Right-hand rule for an electromagnet. (Courtesy of Delco-Remy of America.)

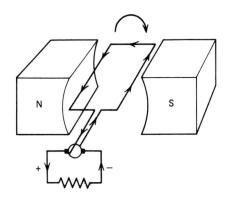

N   S

FIGURE 24–24 Generator principle. (Courtesy of Delco-Remy of America.)

FIGURE 24–25 Multimeter.

Ampere/Volt and
Adjustable Carbon Pile (AVR)

Many different combination testers used to test amperes and volts are available (Figure 24-26). Ampere/volt testers are used to test batteries, charging systems, voltage regulators, starters, solenoids, and other electrical circuits.

Most heavy-duty shops will have a tester similar to this to check and test electrical circuits and components. Utilization of this type of tester allows testing of components such as the alternator and starter on the vehicle. All heavy-duty technicians who are involved in

electrical testing must be able to use an AVR (Figure 24-26). The tester leads and controls are used as follows:

1. Load leads (heavy-duty leads connected to the battery or batteries) allow the tester to apply a current draw to the batteries being checked. These cables also provide power to the tester as well as sense the voltage in the circuits.

2. The ampere (current) pickup clips onto any size wire or cable that will allow it to close completely. It is polarity-sensitive, so it must be installed with the arrow in the direction of current flow to show a positive reading on the amp meter.

3. Small external voltage leads are used to make voltage drop tests and other tests where a voltmeter is required. They plug into external voltage jacks.

4. The amperage display is a digital and bar graph-type display capable of displaying from 0 to 1200 A. The bar graph readings will be from 100 to 500 in 10-A increments.

5. The voltage display is also digital with a bar graph, digital range from 0 to 0.99.9 V in 0.1-V increments, and bar graph range from 0 to 30 V in 0.5-V increments.

6. The load indicator will be displayed when the carbon pile is engaged.

7. The time indicator keeps track of the time that load is applied and will display 15 seconds after time has elapsed, since this is the time commonly used to load test batteries.

FIGURE 24–26 Close-up of the features of the VAT-60 digital unit. (Courtesy of Sun Electric Corporation.)

8. External and battery volt keys are used to select either external battery voltage (at the battery) or internal battery voltage at the machine.

9. The external or internal battery volts indicator will display *external* when external key is pushed or *internal* when the internal key is pushed.

10. The amperes zero key is used to zero the amperage display before load is applied to the batteries or alternator is tested.

11. The load control knob controls the amount of current load applied to the system with the carbon pile.

12. The alternator diode test indicator shows the condition of alternator diodes by indicating good, marginal, or bad.

13. The digital amperes display indicates the amperage of the system or battery being tested.

14. The volts display is a digital readout of the voltage of the system or battery being tested.

The multimeter and the AVR tester are two common pieces of test equipment that all diesel technicians must become familiar with.

BATTERIES

The electricity produced in the charging system must be stored for use during starting. This job is handled by the battery (Figure 24-27). Batteries used in diesel-powered equipment are lead acid batteries and may be of three different types: conventional, low-maintenance, and maintenance-free.

Battery Construction

Lead acid batteries are made up of cells that are separated from each other by compartments (Figure 24-28). Each individual cell contains negative and positive plates separated by porous separators and electrolyte (a mixture of water and acid). The negative and positive plates are connected by a molded strap across the top of the cells. This strap connects the cells in series, meaning that they are connected negative–positive through the entire battery.

Every battery contains a number of cells; 6-V batteries contain three cells and 12-V batteries contain six cells. Each cell has a voltage potential of 2 V. Since the

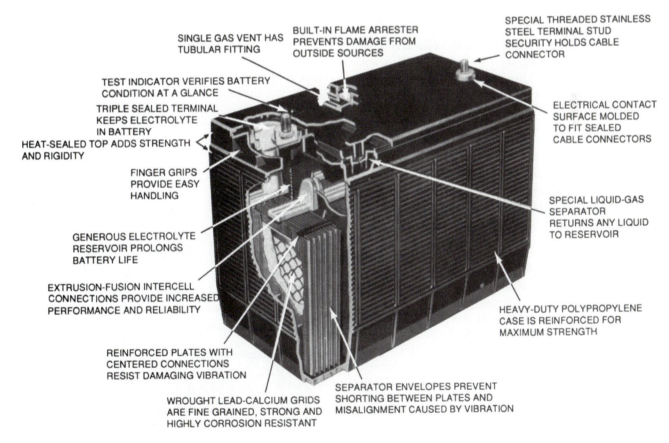

FIGURE 24–27 *Cross-sectional view of an 1100 series Delco heavy-duty 12-V maintenance-free truck battery. (Courtesy of Delco-Remy of America.)*

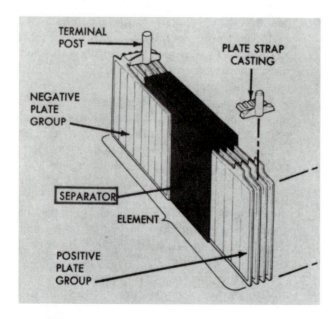

FIGURE 24–28 *Battery cell construction. (Courtesy of Delco-Remy of America.)*

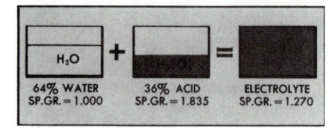

FIGURE 24–29 *Battery solution contents. (Courtesy of Delco-Remy of America.)*

cells are connected in series, three 2-V cells will have a total voltage of 6 V, while six 2-V cells will have a total voltage of 12 V.

All the cells are contained in a hard-rubber case. Early battery cells were placed in the case connected together and the spaces between the cells filled with tar to seal the battery. These batteries were called soft-top batteries. The soft-top battery created some problems, since the tar was soluble in gasoline or diesel fuel. Current batteries are constructed with a hard rubber top and are called hard top batteries. Each cell has an opening through which the battery is filled. This opening is covered with a cell cover or cap. One style of battery manufactured today is completely maintenance free and does not have any cell openings or cell covers.

Battery Operation

As stated previously, the battery cells are filled with water and sulfuric acid. Chemical action between this electrolyte solution and the cell plates produces electricity. This chemical action will eventually discharge the battery, since the active materials in the cells are reacting as the battery discharges.

The electrolyte in a fully charged battery consists of a solution of sulfuric acid in water that has a specific gravity of approximately 1.270 at 80°F (27°C). The solution is approximately 36 percent sulfuric acid (H_2SO_4) and 64 percent water (H_2O) (Figure 24-29).

When the battery is connected into a completed electrical circuit, current begins to flow from the bat-

tery. This current is produced by chemical reactions between the active materials in the two kinds of plates and the sulfuric acid in the electrolyte. The chemical reactions during discharge are shown in Figure 24-30.

In a battery electrical energy is produced by chemical reaction between the active materials of the dissimilar plates and the sulfuric acid of the electrolyte. The availability and amount of electrical energy that can be produced by the battery in this manner are limited by the active area and weight of the materials in the plates and by the quantity of sulfuric acid in the electrolyte. After most of the available active materials have reacted, the battery can produce little or no additional energy. The battery then is said to be *discharged*. Before the battery can be further discharged, it must be recharged by being supplied with a flow of direct current from some external source. The charging current must flow through the battery in a direction *opposite* to the current flow from the battery during discharge. Therefore, the positive terminal of the charging unit

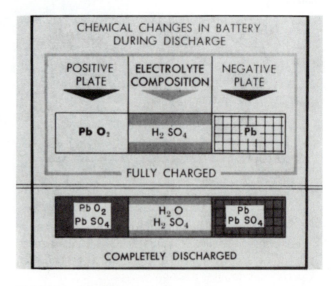

FIGURE 24–30 *Chemical action during battery discharge. (Courtesy of Delco-Remy of America.)*

should be connected to the positive terminal of the battery. This causes a reversal of the discharge reactions and the battery becomes recharged.

When the battery is in a charged condition, the active material in the positive plate is essentially lead peroxide (PbO_2). It is chocolate brown in color. The active material in the negative plate is spongy lead (Pb), which is gray in color.

The lead peroxide (PbO_2) in the positive plate is a compound of lead (Pb) and oxygen (O_2). Sulfuric acid is a compound of hydrogen (H_2) and the sulfate radical (SO_4). During discharge, oxygen in the positive active material combines with hydrogen in the electrolyte to form water (H_2O). At the same time, lead in the positive active material combines with the sulfate radical, forming lead sulfate ($PbSO_4$).

A similar reaction takes place at the negative plate, where lead (Pb) of the negative active material combines with the sulfate radical to form lead sulfate ($PbSO_4$). Thus lead sulfate is formed at both plates as the battery is discharged.

The material in the positive plates and negative plates becomes similar chemically during discharge as the lead sulfate accumulates. This condition accounts for the loss of cell voltage, since voltage depends on the difference between the two materials.

As the discharge continues, dilution of the electrolyte and accumulation of lead sulfate in both plates eventually cause the reactions to stop. However, the active materials are never completely used up during a discharge. This is because the lead sulfate formed on the plates acts as a natural barrier to diffusion of electrolyte into the plates. When the cell can no longer produce the desired voltage, it is said to be discharged.

The chemical reactions that occur in the cell during charging are essentially the reverse of those occurring during discharge, as shown in Figure 24-31. The lead sulfate on both plates is separated into lead (Pb) and sulfate (SO_4). At the same time, the oxygen (O_2) in the electrolyte combines with the lead (Pb) at the positive plate to form lead dioxide (PbO_2), and the negative plate returns to the original form of lead (Pb).

In normal operation the battery gradually loses water from the cells due to disassociation of the water into hydrogen and oxygen gases, which escape to the atmosphere through the vent caps. If this water is not replaced, the level of the electrolyte falls below the tops of the plates. This results in overconcentration of the electrolyte and also allows the exposed active material to dry and harden. Thus, if the water level is not properly maintained, premature failure of the battery is certain to occur. Since water loss is more rapid during high-temperature operation than at low tempera-

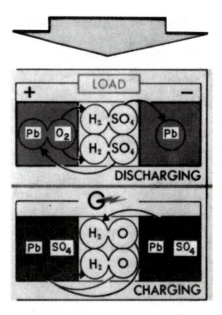

FIGURE 24–31 *Chemical action during battery charge cycle. (Courtesy of Delco-Remy of America.)*

tures, the electrolyte level should be checked more frequently during the summer months.

It has been noted that water plays an important part in the chemical action of a storage battery. Colorless and odorless drinking water is satisfactory, but when obtained from a faucet it should be allowed to run for a few minutes before using.

Battery Testing

Testing batteries requires a certain degree of know-how and equipment. Work at becoming a proficient battery tester, since this is one place where many technicians have problems. It has been estimated that approximately 50 percent of the batteries that are replaced are replaced needlessly. This unnecessary replacement of batteries could be avoided if battery tests were taken with more accuracy and less guesswork. Unfortunately, batteries sometimes have to be tested in a short period of time because many customers will not or cannot allow their vehicle to stand idle while the battery is being charged at a slow charge rate to determine if it is usable or not. In situations like this a quick, accurate test applied in a systematic approach is needed. Battery testing becomes confusing, however, because of the many different recommended procedures. The following information attempts to sort out and clarify some of them:

Visual Inspection

Battery visual inspection plays an important part in making the decision of the battery's condition. Inspect the battery visually for the following:

1. Check the date the battery was put into service, since an old battery has a better chance of being worn out. The date the battery was put in service is usually stamped on the battery or indicated on a tag fastened to the top of the battery.

2. Check for cracks in the battery case and/or cover. A cracked battery case may have been caused by freezing of electrolyte, improper hold-down clamp or brackets, plugged vent caps that prevent venting of the hydrogen gas given off during charging, battery explosion, and excessive charging.

3. Check battery top for acid and dirt accumulation. This accumulation can allow the battery to discharge across the top by making a connection through the dirt from the positive to negative cell of the battery. Clean this accumulation from the battery by washing it with a mixture of baking soda and water.

4. Remove the vent caps and inspect the color of the electrolyte. Discolored electrolyte indicates cell problems. Note also the odor of the electrolyte. A very toxic odor indicates the cell is sulfated and will not take a charge.

5. Check electrolyte level. Electrolyte level is important if the battery is going to function normally, since cell capacity is reduced greatly when it is low on water.

6. Check battery posts for looseness and signs of abuse, such as partially melted posts caused by arching the battery from terminal to terminal.

NOTE   If the battery is installed in the vehicle when making the inspection, check the cables and cable clamps for corrosion and correct size. Most 12-V applications will require a 4- or 6-gauge cable (Figure 24-32). Also check the cables for corrosion or fraying.

Battery Voltage and Specific Gravity Tests
The state of charge of the battery can be checked using a voltmeter across the positive and negative terminals, or on batteries with removable cell caps an SG (specific gravity) test of the electrolyte can be performed to determine if all cells are producing the same voltage. If one cell is low, it will tend to pull down the remaining

cells, and battery failure will soon occur. On maintenance-free types of batteries similar to the one shown in Figure 24-27, an inspection test window can visually determine the state of battery charge as in Figure 24-33.

SG can be checked by using either a squeeze bulb type of hydrometer shown in Figure 24-34, or by employing a refractometer tool, which is shown in Figure 24-35. Figure 24-36 describes how to use the refractometer in a safe and efficient manner. The hydrometer compares the SG of the battery electrolyte to that of water, which is assigned an SG value of 1.000, meaning that 1 Imperial gallon (4.546 L) weighs 10 lb (4.5 kg). A U.S. gallon (3.785 L) weighs only 3.746 kg. All hydrometers measure the SG between an expanded scale of 1.100 and 1.300.

Bulb-Type SG Test.   To test the battery electrolyte:
1. Remove the cell cap and squeeze the bulb of the hydrometer, expelling the air.
2. Insert the hydrometer pickup tube in the cell of electrolyte and release slowly, drawing electrolyte into the float bulb chamber.
3. Draw in only enough electrolyte to cause the float to rise.
4. Read the number or letter directly at the electrolyte level.
5. Correct this reading for temperature depending on the type of hydrometer you have.
6. Squeeze the bulb to force the electrolyte back into the cell and then flush the hydrometer with water.

CAUTION   Be careful when handling a hydrometer filled with acid. Avoid splashing acid on your clothing or getting it into your eyes.

---

7. After determining what the cell's specific gravity is, make your decision about the cell, based on the following: If the specific gravity reading is 1.215 or more, the state of charge is satisfactory. Refer to Table 24-1, which lists the SG of battery electrolyte, compares it to an open-circuit voltage reading, and permits you to determine the actual equivalent state-of-charge condition.

FIGURE 24–32 Cable Sizes.

NO. 0 GAUGE   NO. 1 GAUGE   NO. 2 GAUGE   NO. 4 GAUGE   NO. 4 GAUGE   NO. 6 GAUGE   NO. 8 GAUGE

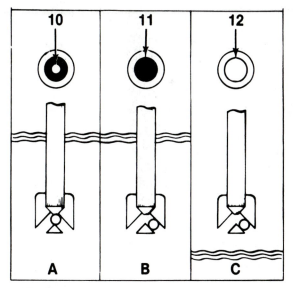

10. Green
11. Dark
12. Clear
A. 65% or Above State of Charge
B. Below 65% State of Charge
C. Low Level Electrolyte

FIGURE 24–33 *How to interpret a built-in battery hydrometer. (Courtesy of GMC Trucks.)*

NOTE   To double-check the state of charge, make a capacity test, outlined later in this chapter.

If the reading is 1.215 or less, recharge the battery.

NOTE   The difference in specific gravity between cells should not exceed 0.050. If it does, one or more cells are probably defective. Replace the battery.

Battery Load Tests (High-Rate Discharge Test)

One of the most accurate ways of performing a high-rate discharge test on a battery is to use the AVR tester (discussed earlier in this chapter).

NOTE   Make sure that the battery temperature is between 60 and 100°F (16 and 38° C) when testing.

NOTE   If the battery has just been charged, remove the surface charge by loading the battery to 200 to 300 A for 15 seconds. Then wait 15 seconds for the battery to recover before testing.

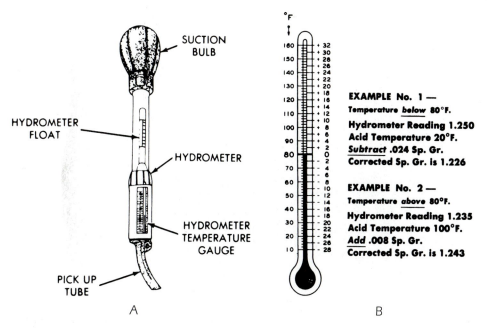

EXAMPLE No. 1 —
Temperature below 80°F.
Hydrometer Reading 1.250
Acid Temperature 20°F.
Subtract .024 Sp. Gr.
Corrected Sp. Gr. is 1.226

EXAMPLE No. 2 —
Temperature above 80°F.
Hydrometer Reading 1.235
Acid Temperature 100°F.
Add .008 Sp. Gr.
Corrected Sp. Gr. is 1.243

FIGURE 24–34 *(A) Bulb-type hydrometer unit; (B) reading the battery electrolyte hydrometer.*

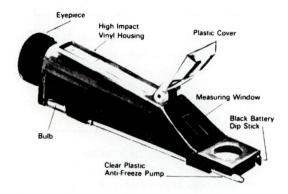

Eyepiece
High Impact
Vinyl Housing
Plastic Cover
Measuring Window
Black Battery
Dip Stick
Bulb
Clear Plastic
Anti-Freeze Pump

FIGURE 24–35 Refractometer battery electrolyte tester. (Courtesy of Kent-Moore Division, SPX Corporation.)

1. Connect the tester to the battery with respect to polarity, as shown in Figure 24-37.

2. Operate the tester to obtain an ampere draw of half the cold cranking amperes.

3. Maintain this load for approximately 15 seconds.

4. If the battery is in good condition, the battery voltage should stay above 4.8 V for a 6-V battery and 9.6 V for a 12-V battery.

5. If the battery voltage meets the recommended voltage after the discharge test, the battery is generally good and will perform satisfactorily. Charge the battery and put it back in service.

6. If the battery fails the test on the basis of voltage, do not condemn the battery until it has been charged and rechecked.

NOTE   The procedure above is a common test in most shops. The danger in this test is that the technician may make a hasty decision and replace a perfectly good battery. Always recharge the battery and make a second test to ensure that you are getting an accurate test.

Three-Minute Charge Test

The 3-minute charge test is made on batteries to determine if cells are sulfated to the point where they will not accept a charge and the battery must be replaced.

NOTE   A sulfated battery means that the sulfate compound on the battery plates, which is normally returned to the electrolyte during charg-

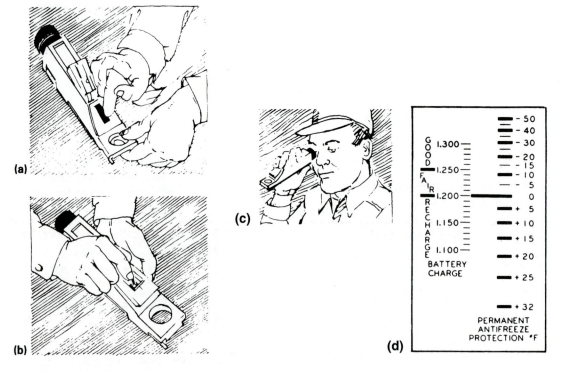

(a)

(b)

(c)

(d)

G O O D   1.300
F A I R   1.250
1.200
R E C H A R G E   1.150
1.100
BATTERY CHARGE

- 50
- 40
- 30
- 20
- 15
- 10
- 5
0
+ 5
+ 10
+ 15
+ 20
+ 25
+ 32

PERMANENT ANTIFREEZE PROTECTION °F

FIGURE 24–36 (a) Preparing Duo-Chek refractometer battery electrolyte tester for a reading; (b) placing drops of battery acid onto Duo-Chek tester; (c) viewing/reading the refractometer scale shown in (d). (Courtesy of Kent-Moore Division, SPX Corporation.)

TABLE 24-1   *Specific gravity and voltage*

Open-circuit voltage reading	Corresponding specific gravity	State of charge	
1.95	1.100	1.100 to 1.130	discharged
1.96	1.110		
1.97	1.120		
1.98	1.130		
1.99	1.140		
2.00	1.150		
2.01	1.160		
2.02	1.170	1.170 to 1.190	25% charged
2.03	1.180		
2.04	1.190		
2.05	1.200	1.200 to 1.220	50% charged
2.06	1.210		
2.07	1.220		
2.08	1.230	1.230 to 1.250	75% charged
2.09	1.240		
2.10	1.250		
2.11	1.260	1.260 to 1.280	100% charged
2.12	1.270		
2.13	1.280		
2.14	1.290		
2.15	1.300		

ing, is not doing so and the battery will not accept a charge.

To make the 3-minute charge test, proceed as follows:

1. Connect the battery charger to the battery with respect to polarity.
2. Connect a voltmeter to the battery terminals.
3. Set the charger for a 3-minute charge.

NOTE   Charge a 12-V battery at approximately 40 A and a 6-V battery at approximately 75 A.

---

4. After charging for 3 minutes, with the charger operating read the voltmeter.
5. The battery is acceptable if voltage is less than 15.5 V on a 12-V battery or less than 7.75 V on a 6-V battery. The battery can be recharged and put back in service.

NOTE   The voltages given are with the battery at 70°F (21°C).

---

6. The battery is not acceptable if voltage is more than 15.5 V for a 12-V battery and more than 7.75 V for a 6-V battery.
7. Depending on how much time is available, you may place the battery on a slow charge (1 A) for a 24-hour period; in many cases the battery will respond to this slow charge and be acceptable after charging. If this time is not available, replace the battery.

The 3-minute charge test, like all other battery tests, is not 100 percent fail safe, but after you have gained some experience in making these tests, you will be able to test a battery and make sound recommendations on its continued use or replacement.

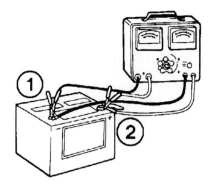

FIGURE 24–37 *Load testing a battery with a VAT (volt-amp tester): block-to-block, red-to-red.*

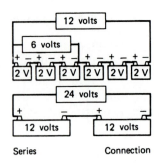

Series   Connection

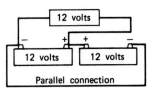

Parallel connection

FIGURE 24–38 *Series and parallel battery connections.*

NOTE   Manufacturers of freedom-type batteries do not consider the 3-minute charge test a valid test.

Battery General Maintenance

The diesel technician will be called on to perform general maintenance on batteries. Some of these maintenance procedures are as follows:

Battery Charging

Slow Charge.   To slow charge a battery properly, charge the battery at 1 A for approximately 12 to 16 hours. Slow charging is recommended if you think the battery is sulfated.

Quick Charge.   To quick charge a battery properly, charge a 12-V battery at 40 A and a 6-V battery at 75 A for approximately 1 hour. This will not charge the battery completely, but it should be sufficiently charged so it can be put back in service. To charge the battery completely, the fast charge must be followed with a slow charge.

NOTE   During fast charging do not charge the battery at a rate that will cause the battery cell temperature to rise beyond 125°F (52°C).

Charging More Than One Battery at a Time.   A number of batteries of the same voltage can be charged at the same time by connecting them in parallel (Figure 24-38), positive to positive and negative to negative. Two batteries may be charged hooked in series if the charger has the capability. Two 6-V batteries

hooked in series can be charged the same way as one 12-V, since two 6-V batteries in series equal one 12-V.

Filling Dry-Charged Batteries

Most batteries, with the exception of maintenance-free batteries (sealed), will need to be filled with acid before putting them in service. These batteries are dry charged at the factory and are shipped without electrolyte.

1.   Carefully fill each cell with electrolyte.

CAUTION   Make sure to wear protective goggles and gloves to prevent injury when filling the battery with electrolyte.

2.   After filling, charge the battery at a rate of approximately 30 to 40 A until the electrolyte has a specific gravity reading of 1.240 or higher with an 80°F (27°C) temperature.

Installing the Battery into the Vehicle

Special care should be taken when installing a battery so that it will provide trouble-free power for a long period of time.

1.   Check the battery box for rocks, corrosion, and foreign objects. Also make sure that the battery box or compartment is solid, since a loose battery compartment can ruin a battery in a short time.

2.   Check all battery cables to make sure that they are free of corrosion. Replace any bolts that show signs of deterioration.

3.   If you have two or more batteries in one vehicle, place the batteries in the compartment in a manner

that will enable you to connect the cables. Install hold-down brackets or clamps.

4. Install and tighten cables on the batteries. Coat cables with a special battery cable preservative or a spray paint.

After installing the battery or batteries, check the starter operation to make sure all cables are connected correctly.

Battery Troubleshooting

It is not enough to be able to determine what is wrong with a battery and whether it should be replaced; an effort must be made to determine why the battery failed. Some of the common reasons for battery failure are:

1. *Overcharging.* In many cases the voltage regulator in the charging system is not functioning correctly and the battery is continuously being overcharged. The first symptom of this condition is excessive use of water in the battery.

2. *Undercharging.* The voltage regulator may be set to cause the battery to be in a low undercharged condition at all times. Undercharging the battery can cause the battery to become sulfated.

3. *Battery too small for application.* A battery that does not have sufficient capacity for the vehicle load will fail quickly, since the battery will be discharged in large amounts and may not have time to charge adequately before it is again called on to deliver large amounts of current, such as during engine starting.

4. *Improper or lack of maintenance.* If the battery is not properly maintained as outlined in the battery maintenance section, the battery will age prematurely and fail much sooner than normal.

If you have any further questions concerning battery service and testing, consult your instructor or the information supplied with your battery tester.

SUMMARY

In this chapter we have explained the theory of electricity used in automotive electrical components and discussed theory, testing, and maintenance of batteries. If you master the material in this chapter, you are well on the way toward becoming a proficient electrical technician.

SELF-TEST QUESTIONS

Fundamentals of Basic Electricity

1. Technician A says that a simple hydraulic system can be used to understand the basic concepts of an electrical system. Technician B sees no correlation between the two. Who is right?

2. Technician A says that a smaller-diameter wire will offer less resistance to electrical flow than will a larger wire. Technician B says that a larger-diameter electrical wire will offer less resistance to flow than will a smaller wire. Who is correct?

3. Technician A says that the battery acts as the electrical reservoir of power in a system. Technician B says that the alternator is the power source in the electrical system. Who is right?

4. Technician A says that in the conventional theory system of electricity, power flows from the positive side of the battery to the negative side. Technician B says that in the conventional theory power flows from the negative side and back to the positive side. Who is right?

5. Technician A says that to complete an electrical circuit, power has to flow only from the positive side of the battery to the load. Technician B says that power must flow from the positive battery terminal, through the load, and back to the negative side of the battery to complete the circuit. Which technician is correct?

6. The concepts of electrical pressure, electrical current, and electrical resistance are fundamental to basic electricity. What is the term used for electrical pressure in a circuit? What is the term used for electrical current? What is the unit in which electrical resistance is measured?

7. Technician A says that electrons flow from a negatively charged substance to a positive one. Technician B says that electrons will only flow from a positively charged substance to a negatively charged one. Who is right?

8. Technician A says that an open in an electrical circuit means that electricity can flow through the circuit. Technician B says that an open circuit stops power flow in an electrical circuit. Which technician understands basic electricity better?

9. Technician A says that a VOM (volt-ohmmeter) can be used to measure only volts and ohms in an electrical circuit. Technician B says that a multimeter or VOM can be used to check all three conditions listed in your answer for Question 6. Who is correct?

10. Technician A says that Ohm's law can be used to determine an unknown value in an electrical system as long as one of the other values is known. Technician B says that you need to know two of the three values in order to find the third using Ohm's law. Who is right?

11. In Ohm's law the letter *I* indicates voltage according to technician A. Technician B says that the letter *I* indicates amps. Who is right?

12. Technician A says that all atoms contain particles made up of minute positive and negative electrical charges. Technician B says atoms contain only negative charges. Who is correct?

13. Technician A says that contained within the center of an

atom are particles called neutrons. Technician B says that these particles are known as protons. Which technician is right?

14. Technician A says that protons are positively charged particles. Technician B says that protons are negatively charged. Who is correct?

15. Technician A says that neutrons have neither a positive nor a negative charge, but are neutral. Technician B says that they must have either a positive or negative charge. Who is right?

16. Technician A says that the opposing charges of protons and neutrons tend to attract one another. Technician B says that protons and electrons are attracted to each other. Who is right?

17. Technician A says that voltage is what pushes the current through the circuit. Technician B says that it is amperage that does this. Who is correct?

18. Technician A says that a charge of electricity is created when numerous electrons gather in one area. Technician B says that a charge of electricity can be created only when a large group of protons gather in one area. Which technician knows electrical theory better?

19. Technician A says that electrical energy applied to one end of a wire is transmitted to the opposite end at the speed of sound, or approximately 780 mph (1255 km/h). Technician B says that the energy is transmitted at the speed of light, about 186,000 miles per second (299,330 km/sec). Which technician has a more solid understanding of electricity?

20. Technician A says that the number of electrons required to produce one amp of flow is 6.28 million passing a given point in one second. Technician B says that the number is 6.28 billion. Who is right?

21. Technician A says that oppositely charged particles oppose each other. Technician B says that oppositely charged particles attract one another and similarly charged particles repel one another. Which technician is correct?

22. Technician A says that EMF (electromotive force) is a term used to describe the force required to pull an electron out of orbit and cause it to flow in a conductor. Technician B says that EMF means electrical-magnetic-furons. Which technician is right?

23. Technician A says that a conductor is a material that offers low resistance to electron flow. Technician B says that a conductor is any material that conducts electrical energy into a heat sink to prevent a short circuit. Who is right?

24. Technician A says that an insulator retains electrical energy from operating a load. Technician B says that an insulator is any component that offers very high resistance to electron flow. Which technician is correct?

25 On a separate piece of paper, list four good insulators of electricity.

26. On a separate piece of paper, list three good conductors of electricity.

27. Technician A says that resistance is the opposition to the free flow of amps. Technician B says that resistance opposes the flow of volts. Which technician is correct?

28. Technician A says that using too small a wire between the starter motor and the battery would cause a high voltage drop and possible melting of the wire. Technician B says that a large diameter wire would draw too many amps and damage the starter motor solenoid and motor windings. Which technician is correct?

29. Technician A says that an ohmmeter can be used to check circuit resistance. Technician B says that a voltmeter should be used to check resistance. Which technician is right?

30. Technician A says that an alternator produces AC (alternating current) to directly charge the battery. Technician B says that the battery can only be charged with DC (direct current). Which technician is correct?

31. Technician A says that when electricity flows through a wire, a magnetic field is created around the wire. Technician B says that no magnetic field can exist without using a magnet. Who is right?

32. Technician A says that the strength of a magnetic field can be increased by reducing the flow of current through a wire. Technician B says that we can increase the strength of the magnetic field by use of an iron core and additional coils of wire wrapped around the core. Who is right?

33. Technician A says that a coil with an iron core is, in effect, an electromagnet. Technician B says that it would form a solenoid. Who is right?

34. Technician A says that reluctance in an electrical circuit is the same as resistance. Technician B says that reluctance is due to the resistance that a magnetic circuit offers to lines of force or flux. Who is right?

35. Technician A says that electromagnetic induction is created when voltage is induced in a conductor that moves across any magnetic field. Technician B says that to create electromagnetic induction you need to place bar magnets against one another with like poles together. Which technician is right?

36. On a separate piece of paper, list the three main factors that determine the magnitude or amount of induced voltage in an electrical conductor.

37. Technician A says that many wires wrapped around an iron core similar to a starter motor are commonly referred to as an armature. Technician B says that this would form what is commonly referred to as a stator. Which technician is correct?

38. Technician A says that, in an alternator, the magnets rotate, while the wire windings are stationary. Technician B says that the wire windings rotate and the magnets are stationary. Who is right?

39. Technician A says that in a typical ignition coil, the primary winding consists of many turns of small-diameter copper wire. Technician B says that it is the secondary

winding that has the smaller-diameter wire, while the primary uses larger-diameter wire. Which technician is correct?

40. Technician A says that the voltage produced in an ignition coil is proportional to the number of wires used between the primary and secondary windings. Technician B says that the voltage is related strictly to the battery voltage. Which technician is correct?

41. Technician A says that all vehicle electrical circuits operate on the series principle. Technician B says that both a series and a parallel circuit arrangement can be found on heavy-duty trucks and equipment. Who is right?

42. Technician A says that in a parallel circuit, current can flow only along one path from the battery and return back to the battery. Technician B says that there are two or more paths for current to flow through. Which technician knows circuit types better?

43. Technician A says that in a parallel circuit, the amount of current in each path must be the same. Technician B says that current in each path may be different and depends upon the amount of resistance in each path. Who is correct?

44. Technician A says that when a series-parallel circuit is employed, 24 V cranking and 12 V charging can be sourced. Technician B says that you must use the same voltage starter motor and alternator system. Which technician is correct?

45. Technician A says that an open circuit in a series-wired system will prevent power flow to all accessories after the location of the open. Technician B says that an open in a series circuit will not affect any other electrical accessories. Which technician is correct?

46. Technician A says that the total resistance in a parallel circuit is less than that of any individual resistor used in the circuit. Technician B says this is impossible. Which technician is right?

47. Technician A says that a short circuit can be caused by a pinched or cut wire, or by a faulty electrical device. Technician B says that a short can only be caused by a faulty fuse. Which technician is correct?

48. Technician A says that a faulty fuse can only be determined by visual inspection. Technician B says that an ohmmeter can be used to confirm a faulty fuse. Which technician is correct?

49. Technician A says that a maxifuse can be used to replace a fusible link. Technician B says that this should not be done. Which technician is correct?

50. Technician A says that an autofuse is most often used between the battery and fuse block inside the vehicle. Technician B says that the autofuse is commonly used to protect the wiring between the vehicle cab fuse block and the electrical system components. Which technician is correct?

51. Technician A says that a manual circuit breaker must be replaced when it is opened by a circuit overload. Technician B says that you simply have to reset it. Which technician is right?

52. Technician A says that a cycling circuit breaker opens when excessive heat is generated by high current flow. Technician B says that when this occurs the circuit breaker needs to be replaced. Who is right?

53. Technician A says that a fusible link offers a one-time protection and must be replaced when it melts. Technician B says that you simply have to replace the circuit fuse. Which technician is correct?

54. Technician A says that a higher number on a wire indicates smaller wire diameter. Technician B says that a higher number indicates a larger diameter. Which technician is correct?

55. Technician A says that circuit wiring is easily identified from one end of the wire to the other by the numbers printed along its length. Technician B says that you would need to use an ohmmeter to trace a wire from one end to the other. Who is right?

56. Technician A says that relays are remotely controlled switches used in high-current circuits and in circuits controlled by sensors. Technician B says that all relays must be triggered manually. Which technician is correct?

57. On a separate piece of paper identify the meaning of the electrical symbols in Figure A.

A

58. Identify the circuit malfunctions shown in Figure B.

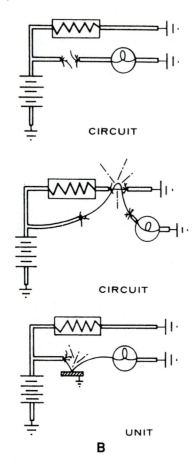

CIRCUIT

CIRCUIT

UNIT

B

59. Technician A says that 8M Ω indicates a value of 8,000 ohms of resistance. Technician B says that 8M Ω means 8,000,000 ohms of resistance. Who is right?

60. Technician A says that a voltmeter must be connected into an electrical circuit in parallel with the existing circuit. Technician B says to connect the voltmeter in series. Who is right?

61. Technician A says that if you are using an analog-type multimeter and the needle swings in the wrong direction, the leads are connected in a reverse direction. Technician B says that this would indicate a faulty multimeter. Who is right?

62. Technician A says that when checking for continuity in a circuit, continuity is confirmed when the ohmmeter value shows a finite value. Technician B says that the ohmmeter should register infinity. Which technician understands the meaning of infinity better?

63. Technician A says that if you are using a digital multimeter, it should have a minimum resistance value of 1 megohm to prevent damaging diodes or transistors in a circuit. Technician B says that the minimum value should be at least 10 megohms. Who is right?

64. Technician A says that an ammeter should be connected into an electrical circuit in series. Technician B says that you should connect it in parallel only. Who is correct?

65. Technician A says that an unpowered test light is used in a powered circuit. Technician B says that the unpowered test light should be used only on an unpowered circuit. Who is right?

66. Technician A says that a jumper wire can be used to locate grounds in a circuit. Technician B says that a jumper wire is typically used to locate opens in a circuit. Who is right?

67. Technician A says that it is advisable to use a fused jumper wire to prevent possible circuit damage. Technician B says it is not necessary to use a fused jumper wire since the vehicle's own fuses and circuit breakers will protect any wires or accessory items from damage. Who is right?

68. Technician A says that a breakout box is used to connect between the male and female connectors of an ECM safely and effectively. Technician B says that a breakout box is used to break open an ECM and check for damaged or burned components. Which technician is familiar with the specific use of a breakout box?

Batteries

1. Technician A says that battery cases are always constructed from hard rubber. Technician B says that in addition to hard rubber, both polypropylene and plastic are used. Who is correct?

2. Technician A says that a battery cell-pack consists of positive and negative plates with a separator in between. Technician B says that if there were a separator plate, you wouldn't be able to get any electricity from the cell. Which technician is correct?

3. A maintenance-free battery contains no antimony in its cell-plate makeup according to technician A. Technician B says that no lead or calcium is used. Who is right?

4. Technician A says that battery electrolyte is a mixture of water and lead peroxide. Technician B says that it also contains diluted sulfuric acid. Who is right?

5. When a lead-acid battery becomes discharged according to technician A, the percentage of water in the electrolyte increases. Technician B says that the percentage of hydrogen increases. Which technician is correct?

6. Technician A says that in a fully charged battery, the electrolyte consists of approximately 64% water and 36% acid. Technician B says that you require at least 80% acid and 20% water for the battery to function correctly. Which technician understands the basic concept of operation of a fully charged battery better?

7. Technician A says that within the battery, the chemical reaction occurs among the sulfuric acid, the sponge lead in the negative plate, and the lead sulfate in the positive plate. Technician B says that it is between the sulfuric acid and the lead peroxide in the positive plate. Who knows chemical theory better?

8. Technician A says that the chemical reaction within a discharging battery causes the negative plate to gain electrons and remain in a negative state of charge. Tech-

nician B says that the positive plate loses electrons, while the negative plate will gain electrons. Who knows basic electricity fundamentals better?

9. Technician A says that the electrolyte in a fully charged battery at 80°F (27° C) has a specific gravity of approximately 1.240. Technician B says that it should be closer to 1.270. Who is right?

10. Technician A says that a specific gravity of 1.240 means that the battery electrolyte is heavier than water. Technician B says that it means the electrolyte is lighter than water. Who is right?

11. Technician A says that a fully charged battery would exhibit a voltage of approximately 2.1 to 2.2 V per cell, providing a reading between 12.6 and 13 V for a 12 V battery. Technician B says since it is a 12 V battery, each cell only can produce 2 V. Which technician is correct?

12. Technician A says that a battery specific-gravity reading of 1.235 at 80°F (27°C) converted to voltage would be equivalent to approximately a 65% state of charge. Technician B says that it would be closer to a 75% charged state. Which technician is correct?

13. Technician A says that a battery specific-gravity reading of 1.150 at 80°F (27°C) corresponds to a voltage reading of approximately 2.0 V per cell. Technician B says that it would represent 2.1 V per cell. Which technician is right?

14. Technician A says that the cranking ability of a fully charged battery at 32°F (0°C) is equivalent to approximately 50%. Technician B says it would be closer to 65%. Which technician is correct?

15. Technician A says that as battery electrolyte temperature rises, its specific gravity increases. Technician B says the specific gravity decreases. Who is right?

16. Technician A says that when using a hydrometer to check the specific gravity of battery electrolyte, you have to add or subtract 0.002 point to the scale for every 5° temperature change above or below 80°F (27°C). Technician B says that you need to add or subtract 0.004 point for each 10°F change above or below 80°F (27°C). Which technician is correct?

17. Technician A says that the reason you need to continually add water to a non-maintenance-free battery is due to spillage from the vent caps during handling. Technician B says it is due to gassing of the electrolyte during normal operation, a result of the normal chemical reaction. Who is right?

18. Technician A says that freezing of a fully charged battery electrolyte would not occur unless the ambient temperature were to drop to approximately −83°F. Technician B says that you would never experience such a low temperature and believes that the electrolyte could freeze at about −20°F (−29°C). Which technician is correct?

19. Technician A says that a battery in a low state of charge with a specific gravity of 1.160 (2.01 V per cell) would freeze its electrolyte at about 0°F (−18°C). Technician B says that it would freeze at about 0°C (32°F). Who is right?

20. Technician A says that to prevent battery electrolyte freezeup you can add a weak antifreeze solution to the water when topping up the cells. Technician B says you should never add antifreeze to a battery. Which technician is correct?

21. Technician A says that when a battery is in a fully discharged state, the electrolyte consists of approximately 17% pure sulfuric acid and 83% water. Technician B says that the percentages are opposite to what technician A states. Who is right?

22. Technician A says that when a battery cell gasses, a mixture of hydrogen and nitrogen exists. Technician B says that it is a mixture of hydrogen and oxygen. Which technician is correct?

23. A good state of charge of a maintenance-free battery can be confirmed by viewing the built-in hydrometer, which should appear yellow in color according to technician A. Technician B says that it should appear green in color. Who is right?

24. Technician A says that battery amperage is usually increased by increasing the size of the cell-plate area. Technician B says that its voltage is increased in this way. Which technician is correct?

25. Technician A says that to create 24 V starting on a truck, the batteries must be connected in series. Technician B says that you should connect them in parallel. Who knows basic electricity better?

26. Technician A says that connecting batteries in parallel results in greater voltage. Technician B says it provides the same voltage but increases the amperage available. Who is right?

27. Technician A says that a series-parallel switch will provide 24 V starting and 12 V charging power. Technician B says it is the other way around. Who is correct?

28. Batteries are rated by either the SAE (Society of Automotive Engineers) or the BCI (Battery Council International) according to technician A. Technician B says that the ASTM (American Society for Testing and Materials) does this. Which technician is correct?

29. Batteries are generally rated, according to technician A, by their reserve capacity and cold cranking amps. Technician B says that they are rated by their amp-hour capacity. Which technician is correct?

30. Technician A says that the battery positive terminal is always red in color and the negative is blue. Technician B says that the positive terminal is red and the negative terminal is black. Who is right?

31. Technician A says that on post-type batteries the − terminal is physically larger than the + terminal. Technician B says that the + terminal is always the larger of the two. Who is right?

32. Technician A says that a battery should never be boost-charged if its specific gravity is higher than 1.225. Technician B says that you can boost-charge at any specific gravity level. Who is correct?

33. Technician A says that boost-charging results in apply-

ing a full charge to the weak cells. Technician B says that you simply provide a surface charge condition to each battery cell. Which technician is correct?

34. Technician A says that batteries can only be charged when they are connected in series. Technician B says that they can be connected either in series or in parallel depending upon the type of charger being used. Who is right?

35. Technician A says that when disconnecting a battery, you should always remove the negative grounded cable clamp first. Technician B says you should always remove the positive cable first. Which technician is correct?

36. Technician A says that when reconnecting battery cable clamps, you should always connect the positive cable last. Technician B says you should connect the negative ground cable last. Who is right?

37. Technician A says that spilled battery electrolyte is best neutralized by using baking soda mixed at the rate of 1.5 cups to each gallon of water. Technician B says you should use a high-pressure washer for this purpose. Which technician is correct?

38. Technician A says that the only time that sulfuric acid should be added to a battery is when a dry battery is being activated for service. Technician B says that sulfuric acid can be added to a set battery in service, when its specific gravity is less than 1.200. Which technician is correct?

39. Technician A says that the state of charge of a battery can only be determined by using a voltmeter. Technician B says that a hydrometer or a voltmeter can be used on a conventional screw-in cell connector. Who is right?

40. Technician A says that an open-circuit voltage reading is the voltage obtained across the battery terminals with no load on the battery. Technician B says that it is achieved when a light-load test is applied to the battery. Which technician is correct?

41. Technician A says that when using a voltmeter to check a battery immediately after charging, you should take care not to create a spark since this could cause the battery to explode. Technician B says this is impossible, and that you would need to strike a match or be smoking for this to happen. Which technician is correct?

42. Technician A says that battery cable sizes for heavy-duty trucks using high-output starter motors are generally a No. 0 AWG size. Technician B says that you should select an AWG 00 size. Which technician is correct?

43. Technician A says that voltage drop through a battery cable for a heavy-duty truck should not exceed 0.01 V per 100 A. Technician B says that it should not exceed 0.075 V at 100 A. Who is right?

44. Technician A says that when removing tight battery cable clamps from the battery post, it is proper procedure to place a large screwdriver under the clamp and force it upwards. Technician B says that you should use a battery clamp puller to do this to avoid damaging the battery case and loosening the post. Which technician has better work habits?

45. Technician A says that clean clamps and terminals should always be reassembled using a good grade of commercially available grease. Technician B says you should always assemble these parts dry, otherwise arcing may occur. Who is right?

46. Technician A says that when filling battery cells with water, you should bring the level only to the bottom of the split guide ring. Technician B says you should fill each cell as close to the top as possible, since a loss of electrolyte during charging will occur anyway. Which technician has better work habits?

47. Technician A says that when load-testing threaded top terminal battery post models, you should simply clamp good jumper cables to each terminal securely. Technician B says you should always install special adapters first, followed by load clamps. Who is right?

48. Technician A says that if a 12 V battery is low, particularly in cold weather operation, it is acceptable to apply 24 V to the system for no longer than 15 seconds. Technician B says you should never apply 24 V to a 12 V battery system. Which technician is correct?

49. Technician A says that when jump-starting a vehicle, you should always connect the jumper cable clamps to the discharged battery first, and to the good battery last. Technician B says that you should connect to the good battery first, and then to the discharged battery. Which technician knows the procedure better?

50. Technician A says that it is a good idea during jump-starting to connect the ground cable to a solid connection on the engine block rather than to the negative discharged battery post. Technician B says that this would create a poor ground condition; attach the cable to the negative battery post. Which technician is correct?

51. Technician A says that on lighter-duty vehicles that use a fusible link in the ground junction point and the starter motor ground post, a direct short circuit over 150 A will cause the fusible link to melt, creating a break in the ground circuit and a no-crank condition. Technician B says that the engine will crank, but it will not start. Which technician is correct?

52. Technician A says melting of the fusible link in Question 51 can be caused by a direct short between the battery + cable and frame. Technician B says it could be due to an improper hookup of booster cables during jump starting. Are both technicians correct, or is only one?

25 Alternator Charging Systems

OVERVIEW

In order to maintain the battery and electrical system in a proper state of charge, it is necessary to use a gear- or belt-driven alternator charging system. This chapter describes the function and operation of a typical heavy duty alternator. Both brush and brushless designs are described, along with the testing, diagnosis, analysis, inspection, disassembly and repair of the alternator assembly.

ALTERNATOR FUNCTION

The name *alternator* originates from the fact that this engine-driven component (belt or gear) is designed to produce an alternating current that when rectified will supply the battery or batteries with a direct-current flow to maintain them in a full state of charge. Often referred to as a *generator*, the alternator is part of the charging system on any car or truck. The alternator forms part of the basic heavy-duty electrical system.

Figure 25-1 shows a typical charging circuit used on a diesel engine. Every vehicle has different current requirements, so different-size alternators are required. The amperage rating of the alternator may be from 35 to 100 A. If the alternator had an amperage rating of 45 A and the system requirements were 55 A, the battery would quickly be discharged, since the additional 10 A would be supplied from the battery. When replacing an alternator, always make sure you have the correct amperage.

ELECTRICAL SYSTEM LOADS

Typical electrical loads placed on the batteries and charging system of a vehicle will vary depending on the classification of truck. A tractor/trailer will have more marker lights, parking lights, and stoplights than those on a straight-body medium-duty truck. The options specified for any given vehicle determine the maximum electrical load that the alternator/battery charging system must handle. In addition, even though medium- and heavy-duty trucks often use the same electrical accessories, the construction of the component is usually more rugged on a diesel powered class 8 highway tractor than in a gasoline-powered midrange straight-body truck, which necessitates a heavier current (amperage) draw. Table 25-1 illustrates typical electrical accessories and their respective amperage ratings.

TYPES OF ALTERNATORS

In diesel-powered trucks and equipment, two main types of charging system alternators are used:

1. The slip-ring and brush type
2. The brushless type

Figure 25-2 illustrates a widely used Delco 21-SI (system integral) heavy-duty brush generator and identification of the major component parts. The 21-SI offers high output to 160 A, a built-in integrated-circuit regulator designed for low parasitic draw, and it provides excellent RFI (radio-frequency interference) suppression. A specially designed bridge provides protection for other electronic devices on the vehicle by

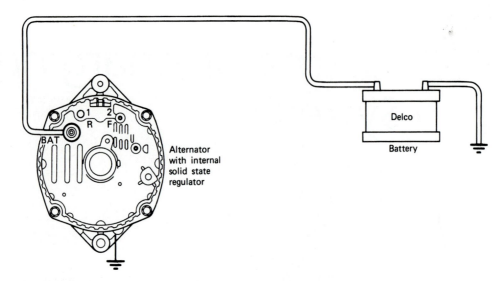

FIGURE 25–1 Alternator charging circuit. (Courtesy of Delco Remy Division of General Motors Corporation.)

TABLE 25–1   Amperage ratings for electrical accessories

Device	Amperes	Hours used per 12-hour shift	Ampere-hours per 12-hour shift
Ignition, engine	0.4	12	4.8
Auxiliary heater fan	9.0	12	108
Air dryer, heated	5.0	12	60
CB radio	3.0	12	36
Defroster fans	8.8	12	105.6
Clearance lights	4.14	12	49.68
Headlights, single high	9.94	10	99.4
Heated mirrors	20	10	200
License plate lights	1.4	10	14
Marker lights	5.5	10	55
Panel and meter lights	3.63	10	36.3
Fuel filter, heated	30	12	360
Stop lights	9.0	0.5	4.5
Turn lights	13.9	0.5	6.9
		Subtotal	1140.18
		Plus 25% safety factor	285.05
		Total	1425.23[a]

[a] The truck in this example needs a total of 1,425 amps of power generated by the alternator during the 12-hour period to match the demand.

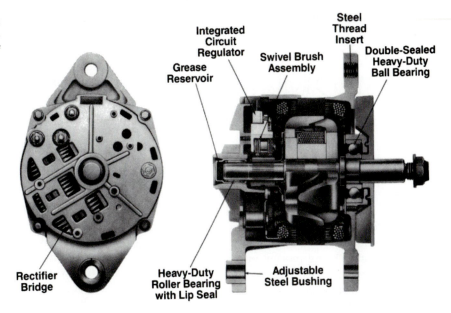

FIGURE 25–2 Features of a Delco 21-S1 heavy duty brush-type generator. (Courtesy of Delco-Remy America.)

effectively clamping voltage surges up to 40 V. The swivel brush holder design minimizes brush side wear, bounce, hang-up, and erosion. The 21-SI is available between 65 and 160 A in a 12-V model or between 50 and 70 A on a 24-V model.

Figure 25-3 illustrates a 26-SI heavy-duty brushless generator with a stationary field coil and no brushes or slip rings. This design features increased service life over brush units. The absence of moving electrical connections eliminates sparks from brush/slip ring contact. A special diode-trio/capacitor assembly provides superior RFI suppression. The 26-SI's electronics are protected in two ways. Standard load dump protection guards the generator against voltage spikes caused by loose connections or interruptions in the charging line and total environmental

sealing against dirt, road salt, and other corrosives. The 26-SI features either 85 A at a 12-volt rating or 50 or 75 A at a 24-V rating. For larger amperage outputs, a Delco 30-SI model brushless generator rated at 105 A at 12 V, 75 or 100 A at 24 V, or 60 A at 32 V is available. The SI Delco generators use a diode trio and rectifier bridge to change stator ac voltage to dc voltage at the alternator output.

ALTERNATOR OPERATION

From electrical fundamentals you will recall that the flow of electricity (the flow of electrons) is called current. This is a measure of the quantity of electron flow, similar to water flow in a water system, although it is measured in gallons per minute or liters per minute.

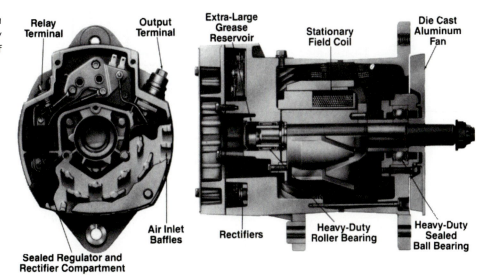

FIGURE 25–3 Features of a Delco 26-S1 model heavy-duty brushless generator. (Courtesy of Delco-Remy America.)

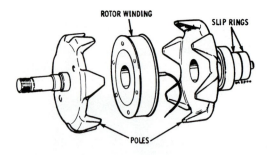

FIGURE 25-4 *Alternator rotor assembly. (Courtesy of Motorola Automotive and Industrial Electronics Group.)*

The electrical unit used for measuring current is the ampere. Remember, however, that current cannot flow without pressure being present in the system.

The electrical pressure is known as voltage, which is the effort needed to force the current through the wire carrying conductors and electrical accessories. The unit of electrical pressure is the volt. Also recollect from basic electrical fundamentals that both electricity and magnetism are involved in an electrical system. If we pass current through a wire, an electromagnet is produced. The strength of this magnetic field is proportional to the amount of current flowing in the wire; the greater the current, the stronger the magnetic field.

Figure 25-4 shows a basic alternator rotor assembly, which is the only moving component of the alternator (driven by a belt and pulley, or gear driven). A rotor winding consisting of many turns of insulated wire wound around an iron spool is contained within the rotor assembly; when current is passed through this field winding, we produce an electromagnet and also a magnetic field.

The structure of the rotor assembly consists of the field winding, two iron segments that contain individual poles or interlacing fingers whose number can vary between makes, a support shaft (which is rotated), and two slip rings on which brushes ride on one end of the rotor shaft and are attached to the leads from the field coil.

The rotor field winding current flow has a direct bearing on the strength of the pole pieces (north and south) of the rotor assembly. A certain residual magnetism is retained in these pole pieces at all times. However, by controlling the strength of the generator rotor field winding current, we can control the output voltage of the alternator. In this respect, the alternator is said to be externally excited because the field current is supplied from the battery and ignition switch through resistors, diodes and transistors at a voltage of between 1.5 and 2.5 V, on average. Figure 25-5 shows the circuit for a typical slipring and brush-type alternator. Generator field current is supplied through a diode trio connected to the stator windings. A capacitor, or condenser, mounted to the end frame protects the rectifier bridge and diode trio from high voltages, and suppresses radio noise. The direction of current

FIGURE 25-5 *Alternator excitation circuit, slip rings, and brushes. (Courtesy of Motorola Automotive and Industrial Electronics Group.)*

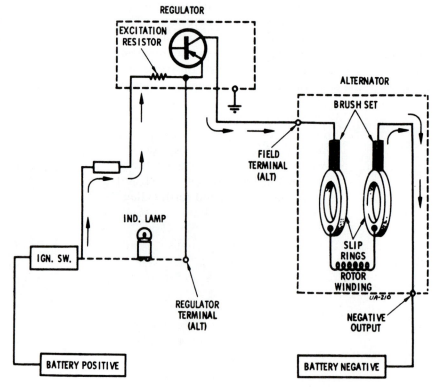

flow in the rotor field winding will produce a north magnetic pole in each finger of one-half of the rotor segment, and a south magnetic pole in each finger of the other half of the rotor segment.

To use the force of this rotating magnetic field produced by the rotor effectively, we need to mount a series of copper wires within the magnetic field that will absorb the electrical energy from the lines of force; for this purpose we commonly use a *stator*. The basic stator is a simple loop or loops of wire arranged in such a fashion as to allow the magnetic lines of force from the spinning rotor to cut across this wire.

As this action occurs, electrical pressure or voltage is produced in the loop or loops of wire (the stator, which is stationary); the greater the speed of rotor rotation, the greater will be the voltage induced within the stator windings. Stators currently used in all alternators generally consist of a laminated iron frame and three stator or output windings which are wound into the frame slots. The stator laminations are insulated with an epoxy coating prior to installation of the windings. The assembly is then varnish-coated for added insulation and to prevent movement of the windings. The stator assembly is then sandwiched between the opposite ends of the alternator to form part of the generator frame. Battery current that flows through one slip ring into the field windings of the rotor leaves the field coil through the other slipring and brush and returns to the battery through the ground return path (see Figure 25-5).

When all components are assembled to produce the alternator, the rotor turns freely within the inner diameter of the stator. However, a very small air gap does exist between the rotor poles and the stator laminations to prevent contact between the rotor and stator; otherwise, physical damage could occur.

Movement of the rotor will alternately allow each pole finger (north and south poles) to pass each loop in the stator windings, thereby inducing a voltage and subsequent current flow in the stator windings. The voltage induced within the stator windings will therefore be constantly alternating between these north and south poles. This oscillating or back-and-forth voltage will cause the current (amperes) within the stator windings to flow in one direction, then the other. This type of current is known as alternating current (or ac). The alternating current is changed into direct current through the diodes. This dc voltage appears at the generator output BAT terminal.

Finally, we require a voltage regulator to control the ac output of the alternator. The ac output is dependent on the quantity of current flow through the rotor field coil windings; therefore, to ensure and maintain a constant-voltage output, alternators commonly em-

ploy a solid-state voltage regulator built into the alternator housing itself. This voltage regulator measures the output voltage and automatically adjusts the field current to keep the output voltage constant as the load changes due to vehicle electrical system demand.

THREE-PHASE STATOR WINDING

The three-phase stator windings are mounted to the stator assembly as shown in Figure 25-6. Phase 1 forms the inner winding row, phase 2 the middle winding row, and phase 3 the outer winding row. Each winding set has a coil per rotor pole, or two coils per pole pair (360°) connected in series opposing. All windings are spaced 120 electrical degrees (not mechanical) apart with respect to the rotor poles and are terminated in a delta or wye (Y) arrangement.

STATOR WINDING DESIGNS

To enable the generated current within the alternator windings to be coordinated in a useful manner, the individual windings must be connected together to produce a steadier current output as well as allowing the generated alternating current (ac) to be converted or rectified to direct current (dc) for battery-charging purposes. This is achieved by connecting the alternator windings together into either:

1. A star or wye connection (both terms are used and they have the same meaning)
2. A delta connection

Figure 25-7 illustrates these two types of stator windings.

Three ac voltages are available from a delta-connected stator, which is like having three individual single-phase units wired together. However, in the Y-connected stator, the voltages produced consist of the voltages in two loops of wire added together, which will be approximately 1.7 times as large in mag-

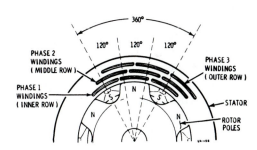

FIGURE 25–6 Stator winding assembly. (Courtesy of Motorola Automotive and Industrial Electronics Group.)

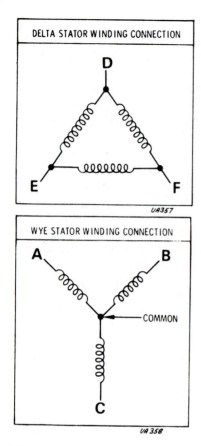

FIGURE 25–7 *Delta-wound and wye (Y)-wound stator windings. (Courtesy of Motorola Automotive and Industrial Electronics Group.)*

nitude as any one individual loop voltage. Three ac voltages, however, are available from the Y-connected stator spaced 120° apart.

The difference in output obtainable from an alternator with the same stator, but with a delta versus a wye winding, is that the delta stator will produce a higher output at the top end of the speed range, while the wye winding will produce current equal to a delta winding at the low speeds at a lower rpm.

RECTIFICATION OF AC VOLTAGE

To convert ac voltage to dc voltage in an alternator, six silicon diodes are used. These diodes function as one-way check valves to allow current flow in only one direction. Three of these diodes are positive (+), while the other three are negative (−), in order to rectify the alternating current voltage produced in each of the windings (three-phase).

If a battery is connected up backwards, such as connecting the positive battery post cable to a vehicle ground, or if any negative connection on an alternator is subjected to positive battery flow, the internal

diodes within the alternator, which have very little resistance value, would simply have too much current impressed through them. This would immediately destroy the diodes, requiring that the alternator be removed for major repair. To protect the alternator against such damage, some manufacturers install a polarity diode along with a fuse into the circuit so that if the battery is connected up backwards, the polarity diode fuse will blow, thereby protecting the alternator diodes. The battery should be connected up in the right direction, the blown fuse replaced, and the engine started. The polarity diode is usually located between the ground circuit and the alternator isolation diode. The fuse is located between the two.

GENERATOR CONTROL CIRCUIT

The amperage created within a three-phase Y- or delta-connected stator is very similar. Next we describe how this is achieved. A delta-connected stator wound to provide the same output as a Y-connected stator will provide a smooth voltage and current output when connect to a six-diode rectifier. For convenience, the three-phase ac voltage curves obtained from the basic delta connection for one rotor revolution are illustrated in Figures 25-8 to 25-12 and have been divided into six periods, as shown in Figure 25-8.

During period 1 (Figure 25-9), the maximum voltage being developed in the stator is in phase BA. To determine the direction of current flow, consider the

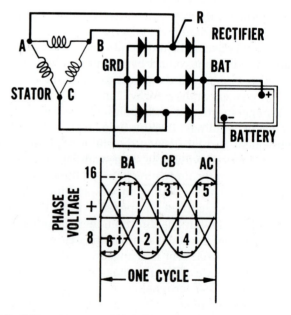

FIGURE 25–8 *SI generator wiring schematic showing the six rectification diodes and the accompanying sine-wave action. (Courtesy of Delco Remy Division of General Motors Corporation.)*

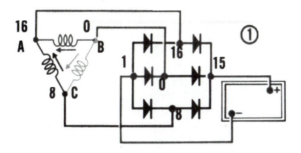

FIGURE 25–9 Period 1 (phase BA) action in an SI generator. (Courtesy of Delco Remy Division, General Motors Corporation.)

instant at which the voltage during period 1 is at a maximum, and assume this voltage to be 16 V. Since the curve is above the horizontal line, the voltage potential at A is plus 16, and at B is zero. From the curve it can be seen that the voltage of phase CB is 8 V and below the horizontal line, so C is 8 V and B is zero. Similarly, the voltage of phase AC is 8 V. Since AC is below the horizontal, A is 8 V positive with respect to C. This checks, since A is 16 and C is 8. These voltage potentials are shown in the illustration. The current flow through the rectifier is exactly the same as for a Y-connected stator, since the voltage potentials on the diodes are identical.

An inspection of the delta stator, however, reveals a major difference from the Y stator. Whereas the Y stator conducts current through only two windings throughout period 1, the delta stator conducts current through all three. The reason for this is apparent, since phase BA is in parallel with phase BC plus CA. Note that since the voltage from B to A is 16 V, the voltage from B to C to A must also be 16 V. This is true since 8 V is developed in each of these two phases.

During period 2 (Figure 25-10), the maximum voltage developed is in phase AC, and the voltage potentials are shown on the illustration at the instant the voltage is maximum. Also shown are the other phase voltages, and again, the current flow through the rectifier is identical to that for a Y stator, since the voltages across the diodes

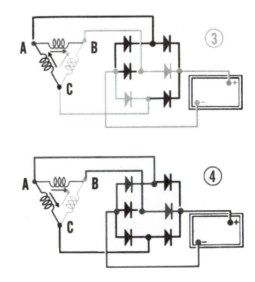

FIGURE 25–11 Periods 3 and 4 reaction in an SI model generator. (Courtesy of Delco Remy Division, General Motors Corporation.)

are the same. However, as during period 1, all three delta phases conduct current as illustrated.

Following the same procedure for periods 3 to 6 (Figures 25-11 and 25-12) the current flow directions are shown. These are the six major current flow conditions for a delta stator.

BRUSHLESS GENERATOR OPERATION

The operation of a brushless generator similar to either the 26-SI, 30-SI or 33-SI Delco models is best described by reference to Figure 25-13. The only movable parts

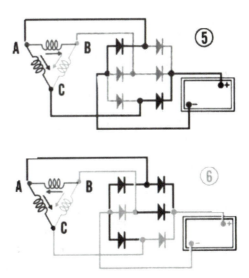

FIGURE 25–12 Periods 5 and 6 (current flow indicated by arrows) in an SI generator. (Courtesy of Delco Remy Division, General Motors Corporation.)

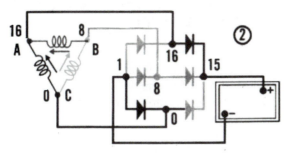

FIGURE 25–10 Period 2 (phase AC) action in an SI generator. (Courtesy of Delco Remy Division, General Motors Corporation.)

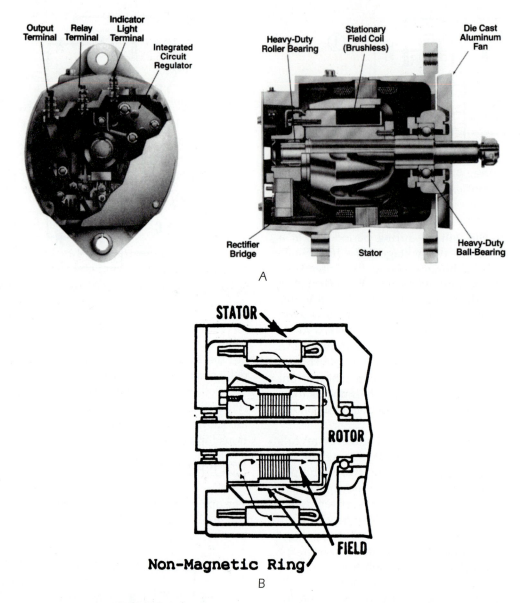

FIGURE 25–13 *33-SI heavy-duty brushless generator.*

are the bearings and the iron rotor. To generate volt-ages in the stator windings, the spinning rotor, which is supported on bearings at each end, causes alternate north and south magnetic lines to cut across the stator windings. A main feature of the brushless construction is the nonmagnetic ring that attaches one set of rotor poles to the other set.

The stationary field coil is mounted with screws to the end frame, and the rotor is located to fit between the stator and field coil. If we consider that the field coil produces a north pole at the right-hand side of the coil, the magnetic lines of force cross the air gap between the field coil and the rotor to make all the right-hand rotor poles all north poles. The magnetic lines of force cannot

penetrate the nonmagnetic ring: therefore, they pass through the very small air gap into the stator and then across the very small air gap into the left-hand south magnetic poles of the rotor. The magnetic lines then cross the air gap between the rotor and field coil, into the field coil, to complete the magnetic path. Therefore, as the rotor spins, the magnetic lines cut across the sta-tor to induce voltage in the stator windings.

VAT TESTER

One of the most important and helpful test instru-ments that the mechanic technician can access and which all well-equipped service shops have is what is commonly called a VAT tester. The letters VAT simply stand for "volt/ampere tester" (Figure 24-26). One is the well-known and long-used analog (swinging needle gauge) model, while the later VAT model employs digital readout gauges.

HEAVY-DUTY ALTERNATOR TEST: ON VEHICLE

When a problem is reflected in the starting/charging system through complaints of hard starting or low power to operate accessories, there are a couple of checks that can be performed fairly quickly to confirm whether the problem is actually in the batteries, starter motor, alternator, or associated wiring. Simple causes such as high circuit resistance in a number of wiring connections can lead the mechanic/technician to suspect either battery or starter problems, with some suspicion that the problem might also be in the alternator or voltage regulator. High circuit resistance will cause a voltage loss to the batteries, and this can be caused by corrosion, loose or dirty terminals, or damaged wiring or connections.

The first step in pinpointing any starting/charging system problem is to note whether the lack of power occurs only during a cranking/starting attempt. If it does, you can refer to Chapter 24 for batteries or to Chapter 26 for starting motors. Visually check and feel the battery connections and all other wire terminals and connections between the battery, starter, and alternator. If nothing unusual is noted, perform a load test on the batteries according to the instructions. Replace any faulty batteries and clean and tighten all battery connections. What we want to do now is to perform a charging circuit voltage drop and alternator output test.

For purposes of discussion, we select a heavy-duty truck equipped with four 12-V batteries in parallel using a Delco 42MT starter motor and a Delco SI brushless generator.

1. With the engine stopped, connect a carbon pile load tester (make sure that the carbon pile control knob is in the OFF position) between the alternator output terminal and the ground of the alternator housing. The alternator output terminal is at battery voltage.

CAUTION Care must be exercised when connecting the carbon pile to the alternator output terminal to ensure that the pile clamp does not touch a ground circuit such as the alternator body or other metal bracket that may be in close proximity.

---

2. Battery voltage can be monitored simply by connecting the red voltmeter lead to the + battery post and the black lead to the − battery post, as shown in Figure 25-14 at position A.

NOTE Determine the alternator part number then refer to OEM test specs and pick out the rated output in amperes for the alternator model in question. Some alternators have the rated output stamped on the alternator housing or on a name tag attached to the housing.

---

3. Slowly rotate the control knob on the carbon pile until the built-in ammeter registers the alternator rated output in amperes. If the carbon pile does not have an ammeter, connect a separate ammeter into the system so that amperage draw can be monitored.

4. Quickly note and record the battery voltage on the voltmeter while the carbon pile is drawing the recommended amperage, then turn the carbon pile control knob OFF.

5. Disconnect the voltmeter from position A in Figure 25-14 and reconnect it to position B. This requires that the red voltmeter lead (+) be attached to the alternator (BAT) output terminal and that the black lead (−) be attached to the alternator housing for ground purposes.

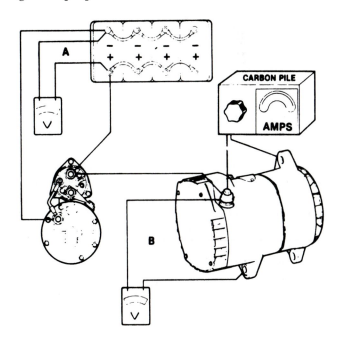

FIGURE 25–14 Step 1: electrical test hookup to check the charging circuit voltage drop condition with a voltmeter connected in position A, then in position B. (Courtesy of Detroit Diesel Corporation.)

CAUTION   Do not connect the voltmeter leads to the carbon pile leads; otherwise, when the carbon pile is turned on, the high amperage will damage the voltmeter and its leads.

6.   Slowly rotate the carbon pile control knob once again until the ammeter registers rated alternator output according to the note between steps 2 and 3 above.

7.   Quickly note and record the voltage at the alternator (BAT) output terminal, then turn off the carbon pile by rotating the control knob OFF or to the MIN position.

8.   The system voltage drop can now be determined simply by subtracting the voltage reading that was obtained at the alternator BAT terminal in step 7 from that recorded previously in step 4.

9.   If the reading determined in step 8 is greater than 0.5 V for a 12-V system, or 1.0 V for a 24-V system, proceed to step 10. If, however, the voltage drop is within specifications, proceed directly to the alternator output test described after step 16.

10.   With the carbon pile still connected but in the OFF position, connect a digital scale voltmeter, since we want to read precisely what the voltage drop is on either the + or − side of the charging circuit.

11.   Refer to Figure 25-15 and connect the digital voltmeter red (+) lead to a battery positive terminal. Connect the black (−) lead of the voltmeter to the alternator (BAT) output terminal. If the batteries are too far away from the alternator, hook up a jumper wire to extend the voltmeter leads.

12.   Slowly rotate the carbon pile load control knob until the ammeter registers rated alternator output once again.

13.   Quickly note and record the voltmeter value, then turn the carbon pile load control knob OFF.

14.   Refer to Figure 25-15 step 2, and connect the voltmeter leads to the negative side of the charging circuit, which involves placing the red (+) lead to the alternator housing and the black (−) lead to the battery negative terminal.

15.   Rotate the carbon pile load control knob slowly until the ammeter registers the alternator rated output in amperes, then quickly read and record the voltmeter reading. Turn off the carbon pile by rotating the control knob.

16.   Add the positive circuit voltage loss to that for the negative circuit loss. This combined value should not exceed 0.5 V for a 12-V system, or 1.0 V for a 24-V system.

Once you have determined where the voltage loss is, correct by removing the necessary connections and

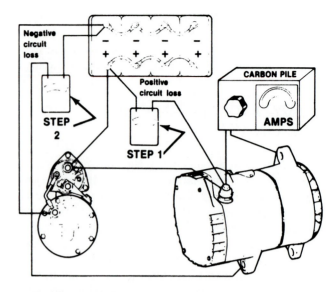

FIGURE 25–15   *Step 2: electrical test hookup to check the charging circuit voltage drop condition. (Courtesy of Detroit Diesel Corporation.)*

cleaning and tightening them again. Recheck the system voltage drop again, then proceed to the alternator output test.

ON-VEHICLE ALTERNATOR OUTPUT TEST

This check will quickly confirm if the problem is in either the alternator or voltage regulator.

1.   Make sure that the engine is at shop ambient temperature prior to conducting this test.

2.   Refer to Figure 25-16 and select a starting/charging system analyzer, such as a Sun Electric VAT tester model, that contains both an ammeter and a voltmeter and, usually, a built-in carbon pile.

3.   Connect the voltmeter leads to one of the 12-V batteries, making sure that the red lead goes to a + connection and that the black lead goes to a − connection.

4.   Place the tester inductive pickup plastic clamp around the alternator output wire (Figure 25-17).

5.   Connect the carbon pile leads or a separate carbon pile if the tester is not equipped with one so that it spans one battery on a 12-V parallel-connected system. If the system is a 24-V arrangement, connect the carbon pile leads across one 12-V battery and the voltmeter across the normal 24-V battery connection.

6.   Make sure that all vehicle electrical accessory load switches are off.

7.   Make sure that the carbon pile load control knob is off.

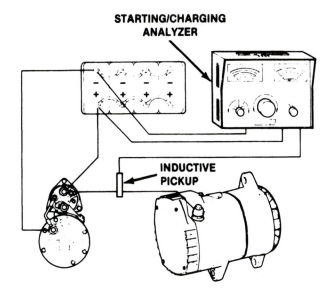

FIGURE 25–16 *Using a VAT tester inductive pickup to monitor the alternator rated output value. (Courtesy of Detroit Diesel Corporation.)*

8. Start the engine and accelerate it to a fast idle, between 1000 and 1200 rpm maximum.

9. Turn the carbon pile on and slowly rotate the control knob to cause the alternator to produce its rated amperage output. Read and record the voltage value.

10. The voltage value should not exceed 15 V on a 12-V system, or 30 V on a 24-V system, although 28 V is usually stated and accepted as maximum. If the voltage exceeds these limits by more than 1 V, and the alternator output is not within 10 A, a voltage adjustment can be attempted on Delco 25-S1 and 30-S1 models by removing the alternator rear cover and accessing the voltage potentiometer adjusting screw.

FIGURE 25–17 *Model J35590 current clamp. (Courtesy of Kent-Moore Division, SPX Corporation.)*

11. Failure of the alternator to function to rated amperage and voltage after any voltage adjustment would require that the voltage regulator be replaced.

12. Voltage that exceeds the limit by more than 1 V and that cannot be lowered by adjustment would require that the generator be removed for inspection and repair.

TROUBLESHOOTING LEECE-NEVILLE ALTERNATORS

To effectively troubleshoot Leece-Neville alternators, refer to Figure 25-18 and systematically test the charging system in the steps listed. To check battery overcharge, undercharge, and wiring and belt tension is a simple procedure (to check the batteries refer to the information in Chapter 24). To check the diode trio on alternators so equipped, refer to Figure 25-19, and after removing the diode trio from the alternator, connect the ohmmeter test leads as shown. The diode trio is okay when a LOW resistance reading is observed in one direction and a HIGH resistance is observed in the other; otherwise, replace it.

Full Field Test

1. Start and run the engine at about 1000 rpm with all electrical accessories OFF. Measure the output voltage across the alternator terminals and write it down for reference.

2. Refer to Figure 25-20 and attach a short jumper wire to the alternator as illustrated; use a piece of 50-mm (2-in.) stiff wire such as a paper clip. Insert the wire in the full field access hole and hold it firmly against the brush terminal inside the housing (this action also flashes the field).

3. With the jumper in place as shown, connect a "digital" voltmeter across the alternator terminals and run the engine at approximately 1000 rpm. Compare the reading with that obtained in step 1.

4. With the jumper still connected and the wire in place, connect an ac voltmeter across terminals 1 and 2, 1 and 3, and 2 and 3 to be able to read the voltages. If they are all the same, they are considered to be "balanced."

5. Remove the jumper wire. If the voltage in step 3 is higher than in step 1, and the voltages measured in step 4 are balanced, the stator and alternator are okay; therefore, move to the voltage regulator adjustment procedure.

6. However, if the voltage in step 3 is higher than that in step 1 and the voltages measured in step 4 are not balanced, the alternator stator or rectifier is defective.

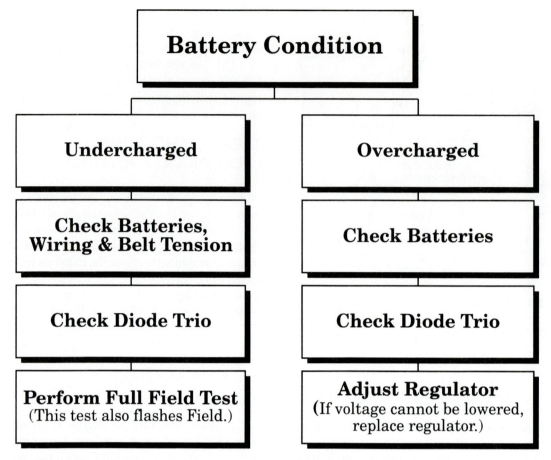

FIGURE 25–18 *Self-check chart to systematically determine charging system complaint.*

Voltage Regulator Adjustment

Inspect the alternator to determine if it has:

A. A flat cover plate similar to that shown in Figure 25-21 which indicates that it is a fully adjustable regulator

B. A finned, curved cover plate which indicates that a three-step regulator is used

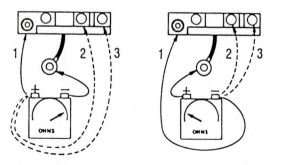

FIGURE 25–19 *Checking alternator diode-trio. (Courtesy of Leece-Neville, PEI.)*

Type A Procedure

1. Ensure that the battery is at least 95% charged and that all wire connections and the drive belt tension is correct.

2. With all electrical accessories OFF, start and run the engine at 1000 rpm.

3. Connect a digital voltmeter to the alternator outputs.

4. Remove the plastic screw from the regulator as illustrated in Figure 25-21 and insert a small slotted screwdriver into the access hole until it engages with the adjustment screw.

5. Exercise care during this adjustment process so as not to place undue force on the adjustment screw.

6. Rotate the screwdriver CW to raise the voltage and CCW to lower the voltage setting, which should be set between 14.0 and 14.2 V (28.0 to 28.4 V on a 24 V charging system). Replace the small plastic screw back into the cover plate.

Type B Procedure

1. With the engine stopped, disconnect the battery ground cable.

FIGURE 25–20 *Performing a field test. (Courtesy of Leece-Neville, PEI.)*

2. Refer to Figure 25-22 and remove the No. 10-32 nuts and lockwasher from the voltage regulator terminal and disconnect the diode trio if so equipped.

2. Remove the four regulator cover retaining screws.

3. If dirt or corrosion is evident, clean the brush contact pads with No. 600 or finer sandpaper.

4. Inspect and reinstall the brushes.

5. If voltage regulator adjustment is required after pad cleaning, remove and reinstall the adjustment strap in one of three positions:

- Between terminals A and B (low)
- Between terminals A and C (medium)
- Between terminals B and C (high)

Each strap change within these three settings will alter the voltage output by approximately 0.4 V.

FIGURE 25–21 *Voltage regulator adjustment. (Courtesy of Leece-Neville, PEI.)*

FIGURE 25–22 *Inspecting voltage regulated brush contact pads in preparation for voltage adjustment. (Courtesy of Leece-Neville, PEI.)*

DUVAC (DUAL-VOLTAGE ALTERNATOR CONTROL) CONTROL SYSTEM

The Duvac control system is designed to direct the alternator to charge in either the 12 or 24-V mode depending on the needs of each individual battery circuit in the coupled system. The Duvac control is normally off as a silicon-controlled rectifier creates an open between terminals A and 1 of the Duvac module (Figure 25-23). The alternator B+ wire terminal (green wire of the Sure Power Regulator) is the power source for the alternator field coils. Its connection point is determined by the rated voltage of the alternator. For 12-V alternators, this terminal is directly connected to the A+ terminal of the voltage regulator. For 24-V alternators, this terminal is connected to a 24-V point. If, however, the alternator is equipped with an integral voltage regulator, some modification of that regulator is required if it is not totally removed from the system. Sure Power Industries can supply details on this necessary change.

When the alternator begins to charge, the Duvac regulator system directs the current through the entire battery system in series. At the same time, Duvac monitors the voltage of the B half of the battery system, which is providing some of the power required for the vehicle's 24-V loads. When the B battery is fully charged, a voltage sensor in the Duvac control unit turns the Duvac on as shown in Figure 25-23. The B battery is then bypassed temporarily, and the current is directed to the A battery, which is providing the other 12-V half needed for the 24-V loads as well as the entire 12-V portion of 12-V accessories.

As long as the Duvac control is on, the charging system will be in the 12-V mode, and charging current

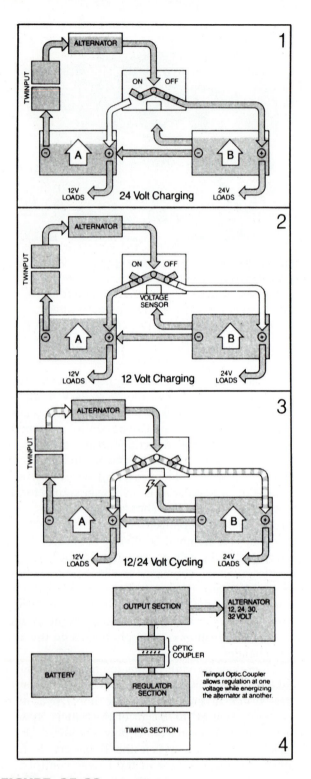

FIGURE 25–23 (1) DUVAC 11 system 24-V charging schematic; (2) DUVAC 11 12-V charging schematic; (3) DUVAC 11 12/24-V cycling schematic; (4) DUVAC 11 optic coupler system schematic. (Courtesy of Sure Power Industries, Inc.)

will bypass the B battery. If this condition were to continue, the B battery would be run down. To avoid this undesirable situation, a twinput regulator with an internal timing circuit is employed. The output section of this regulator delivers power to the alternator fields through a power transistor. The alternator output voltage is regulated by turning a transistor off approximately 1500 times per second. In addition, every 55 to 60 seconds, the regulator timing circuit takes control and turns off the power transistor for about 2 seconds, thereby lowering (interrupting) the alternator excitation field voltage to almost zero. When this happens, the alternator stops charging and current stops flowing through the SCR (silicon-controlled rectifier) in the Duvac module, causing it to turn itself off. After 2 seconds the field voltage is restored, and the alternator once again begins to charge but with the Duvac module now operating in the 24-V mode, where it monitors the B battery and charges it as necessary, as shown in Figure 25-23. It is important to note that the "twinput regulator" cycles only to ensure that the Duvac has the opportunity to change charging modes, not to cause it to change. Since the regulator timing circuit is totally separate from the Duvac switching process, it will cycle every 55–60 seconds regardless of what charging mode the Duvac is in. If the Duvac, due to the state of charge of the "B" battery, stays in the 24 volt mode throughout the 55–60 second timing period, the regulator will cycle just the same. Therefore all of the batteries in the system are properly balanced, regardless of how different each load is on the individual battery. This 12 volt load on a 24 volt system is possible due to the use of an optic coupler design illustrated in diagrammatic form in Figure 25-23 (4) for the "twinput regulator" system. In summation, the Duvac control determines whether the alternator should charge at 12 or 24 volts regardless of its specified voltage, while regulating one 12 volt "B" battery portion of the entire battery system.

For more detailed information on the Duvac system, contact Sure Power Industries, Inc; 10189 S W. Avery, Tualatin, OR 97062.

ALTERNATOR DRIVE BELTS

Charging system problems are often assumed to be caused by the alternator, the regulator, or the associated wiring, when in many cases the cause may be an improperly adjusted drive belt system. Drive belts used on medium- and heavy-duty trucks can be either a poly-vee design or a multirib belt design. In addition, only one drive belt may be used, although dual or triple arrangements are also commonly used on heavy-duty truck applications.

A loose drive belt will slip in the pulley groove, resulting in a low rotational speed of the alternator rotor, the end result being that the current output from the generator will remain too low for the batteries to maintain a full state of charge. The vehicle electrical load will shortly drain the battery cranking power and the batteries' ability to operate all of the various electrical accessories. Many heavy-duty truck alternators employ double-groove pulleys to distribute the power requirements of the belts over a greater-cross-sectional surface area. In this way the drive belts can be made less wide as well as being cheaper. It also offers the advantage of still being able to drive the alternator should one belt break.

When it is necessary to adjust an alternator drive belt(s), a belt tension gauge should always be used to ensure the longest belt life as well as minimizing possible damage to the alternator support bearings should the belt be adjusted too tightly. Drive belts that are too loose can result in slippage, tearing, burning, grabbing and snapping as well as chirping or a high-pitched squeal particularly when the engine is accelerated under load. More drive belts fail as a direct result of being too loose than of being too tight. If the drive belt(s) are adjusted too tightly, they can cause excessive side loading, particularly on multiple-drive belt hookups. High-drive-belt tension has been shown to cause crankshaft bearing damage and in severe cases can contribute to crankshaft breakage. It will also cause excessive side thrust not only on the alternator bearings, but also to other drive accessories that share the same belt drive arrangement. Even if no direct damage is noticeable on these accessories, too much belt tension will definitely stretch and weaken the belts.

Regular inspection of drive belts and mounting bracket bolts should be a part of any vehicle maintenance check, with many fleets doing belt inspection at each engine oil change or at a specific mileage based on their operating conditions. When drive belts are worn, an adjustment will not stop them from slipping, and they can cause pulley damage if left in position. If an inspection reveals wear in any drive belt, replace it! Different engine manufacturers state that once a drive belt has made one complete revolution, it is considered to be a used belt, whereas others state that once a belt has been in operation for 10 minutes, it would be considered a used belt. Regardless of these differences, belt installation and adjustment remains the same. Most manufacturers quote a new unused belt tension as well as a used belt tension specification in their respective service literature.

Although there are a number of commercially available belt dressings in rub-on or spray-on form, most belt and engine manufacturers advise against us-

ing these since most of them contain chemicals that can soften the belt material. Note that any time that multiple-belt drives are to be replaced, all belts should be replaced as a matched set since if only one new belt is installed, it will absorb all of the tension, resulting in early failure.

INSPECTION AND OVERHAUL OF SYSTEM COMPONENTS

It is assumed that the alternator has been removed from the engine.

Alternator Disassembly and Overhaul
Remove the alternator from the engine by disconnecting all wires and attaching bolts.

1. Match-mark the alternator end frames and center section for reference during reassembly.

NOTE The following disassembly procedure is general in nature and may have to be supplemented by using the service manual for the specific alternator being worked on.

---

2. Remove the through bolts that hold the alternator together.
3. Remove the drive end frame drive pulley and rotor as an assembly. It may be necessary to pry the drive end frame drive pulley and rotor away from the stator and rear end frame using a screwdriver.

CAUTION Caution must be used when prying on the end frame with a screwdriver, as damage to the end frame could result.

NOTE When the rotor is removed, the brushes and brush springs will fall out of place. The brushes are attached to the alternator with small wires and will not fall out completely. The springs are not attached to anything and may be lost if you are not careful.

---

4. Remove the stator from the slip ring end frame by disconnecting the three stator leads that are connected to the diodes.
5. Place the rotor, which has the drive pulley and drive end frame on it, into the vise and clamp it securely.

CAUTION Tighten the vise on the rotor just tight enough so that you can remove the pulley retaining nut. Tightening the vise tighter than this may damage the rotor.

6. Using the correct-size socket, remove the pulley retaining nut, the washer, pulley, fan, and spacer.

7. Next remove the drive end frame from the rotor shaft.

NOTE You may have to tap on the rotor shaft slightly with a plastic hammer to remove it from the drive end bearing.

8. The alternator is now completely disassembled with the exception of the diode heat sink, which does not have to be removed unless a bad diode is found during testing.

Alternator Component Testing

1. Check all bearings and bushings for roughness or scoring.

NOTE Ball bearings are used in the front end frame of an alternator and should be spun by hand to check for roughness. If any roughness is felt, replace the bearing. Needle bearings are used in the slip ring end frame and are usually replaced as a matter of practice if the alternator has many hours of use on it.

2. Check brushes for wear. If they are worn over half of the original length, they should be replaced with new ones.

3. Check pulley groove for wear. If worn excessively, replace the pulley.

4. Check the stator windings with an ohmmeter for:

   a. *Grounds.* Touch one lead of the ohmmeter to the slip ring and the other to the rotor shaft. The ohmmeter should read overload.

   b. *Opens.* Use an ohmmeter connected between each pair of windings at the lead connections. The ohmmeter should read very low resistance.

   c. *Shorts.* If all other checks on the stator prove it to be all right and the alternator still does not work, replace the stator. Many times a shorted stator can be identified by the color of the windings. Burned or blackened windings usually indicate a shorted winding. It is very difficult to perform an accurate check on the stator for shorts due to the very low resistance of the windings.

5. Check the rotor with an ohmmeter for:

   a. *Grounds.* Touch one lead of the tester to the shaft and the other lead to the slip ring. There should be no continuity between the rotor shaft and slip ring.

   b. *Shorts.* Using a battery and ammeter in series with the two slip rings, touch one lead from the battery to one slip ring. Connect one ammeter lead to the other battery post and then touch the other ammeter lead to the other slip ring (Figure 25-24). Current flow should be as specified in specification sheet.

CAUTION Do not touch the ammeter lead from the ammeter to the face of the slip ring. As the wire is disconnected from the slip ring, a spark will be created and the slip ring surface will be damaged.

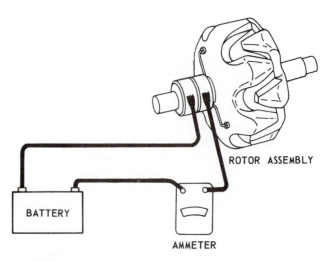

FIGURE 25–24 Testing rotor with ammeter and battery. (Courtesy of Delco-Remy of America.)

c. *Opens.* The rotor is easily checked with an ohmmeter for opens by touching the two test leads to the two rotor slip rings. (There should be continuity.) After testing the rotor electrically, the slip rings should be checked for wear. The brushes will wear grooves in the slip rings after a long period of use. These grooves must be removed before the alternator is reassembled to prevent premature brush wear. The rotor should be mounted in an armature lathe to recondition the slip rings.

NOTE   Slip rings should be reconditioned to 0.002 in. (0.05 mm) out-of-round.

CAUTION   Remove only enough metal from the slip rings to clean them up because they are very thin and may be ruined.

---

6. Check the diodes by using a multimeter. Set to read ohms or in the diode check position, if your multimeter has one.

NOTE   Diodes are mounted in different alternators in many different ways. It can be expected that removal and checking of diodes will differ from alternator to alternator and the specific repair manual should be followed in this area. The following checking procedure is general in nature.

---

a. Isolate the diode you are checking from the other diodes. Touch one lead from the ohmmeter to the alternator lead and the other test lead to the diode case. If the ohmmeter indicates continuity, switch the leads and the meter should indicate an open circuit (overload).

b. If the diode passes the electrical tests, check the diode lead for looseness in the diode case. If the lead is loose, the diode should be replaced.

Regulators

As stated previously, regulators are the brain of the system. They are designed to sense the demands on the system and adjust the system output to the demand.

Regulators for alternators are usually solid state although some early alternators did use the vibrating-relay-type regulators similar to the one used with dc generators. In most cases solid-state regulators are not adjustable and, if the generator voltage is not correct, the regulator must be replaced. Exceptions to this would be some Delco alternators that have a high-low voltage adjustment (Figure 25-25).

Alternator Assembly and Testing

1. Install the front bearing into the front bearing housing and install the bearing retainer.
2. Install the rotor into bearing and then install the cooling fan and drive pulley.
3. Install and tighten the drive pulley retaining nut and lock washer.
4. Clamp the rotor into a vise and torque the drive pulley nut.
5. Install the brushes or brush assembly into the slip ring end frame and insert the brush-holding device.

NOTE   Some alternators are assembled before the brushes are installed. Follow the manufacturer's recommendation closely in this area.

---

6. Install stator assembly onto the slip ring end frame and connect the leads.
7. Install the rotor and drive end frame into the stator and slip ring end frame.
8. Install the bolts that hold the alternator end frames together.

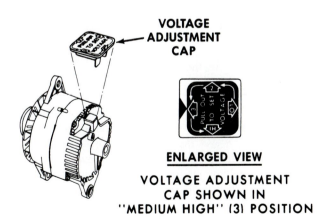

VOLTAGE ADJUSTMENT CAP

ENLARGED VIEW

VOLTAGE ADJUSTMENT CAP SHOWN IN "MEDIUM HIGH" (3) POSITION

FIGURE 25–25 *High-low voltage adjustment on regulator. (Courtesy of Delco-Remy of America.)*

9. Testing:
   a. Mount the alternator on a test stand or engine.
   b. Test output by running the machine or engine.
   c. If alternator was tested on test stand, mount the alternator on the engine and connect all wires.
   d. Run and test alternator.

SUMMARY

This chapter has covered the operating principles, overhaul, and troubleshooting of generators and alternators. You will find that charging system repair is easy once you master the basics. As you gain experience on charging circuits, the troubleshooting and repair of electrical circuits are what you will look forward to.

SELF-TEST QUESTIONS

1. Technician A says that the word *alternator* is derived from the alternating electrical current produced within the windings. Technician B says that the alternator produces DC current in its winding, which is then rectified to AC to charge the battery. Which technician is right?

2. Technician A says that the two main components within an alternator are the stator and rectifying diodes. Technician B says that it is the rotor and the stator assembly. Which technician is correct?

3. Technician A says that battery power on brush-type alternators is supplied to the field windings by a voltage regulator. Technician B says it is supplied through a slip ring. Which technician is right?

4. Technician A says that the stator windings within the alternator are wired to produce three-phase power. Technician B says that single-phase power is used. Who is correct?

5. Technician A says that the stator frame is generally made from a solid iron core, while technician B says that it is manufactured from a series of metal laminations. Which technician knows the core construction better?

6. Technician A says that the term *claw-pole* rotor indicates that a series of interlacing fingers of opposite polarity are used. Technician B says that it is a rotor consisting of two north and two south pole magnets. Who is right?

7. Technician A says that alternating current means that amps flow in one direction, and then reverse direction within the stator windings throughout each cycle. Technician B says that current flows in one direction for one cycle, followed by flow in the opposite direction on the succeeding cycle. Who is right?

8. Technician A says that commonly employed stator windings employ six windings. Technician B says that only three are used. Which technician understands the concept of operation better?

9. Alternating current, according to technician A, in Delco SI-type alternators is normally rectified by the use of a diode-trio and rectifier bridge. Technician B says that 12 diodes are required to do this, plus a voltage regulator. Which technician understands the circuit better?

10. Technician A says that magnetic lines of force tend to flow from the south to the north pole. Technician B says that they flow from north to south. Who is right?

11. Technician A says that connecting the battery cables backwards (reverse polarity) can result in alternator diode damage. Technician B says that the alternator is immune to reverse-polarity hookup. Which technician is correct?

12. Technician A says that a reverse-polarity diode is usually located between the hot side of the circuit and the isolation diode. Technician B says that it is located between the ground circuit and the isolation diode, with a fuse installed between the two. Who is right?

13. Technician A says that the purpose of a diode is to allow current flow in one direction only. Technician B says that it functions to permit current flow in both directions. Who is right?

14. Technician A says that within the alternator, the magnetic field is represented by a stationary rotor. Technician B says that the rotor spins and the stator windings do not move. Which technician understands the concept of operation better?

15. Technician A says that the individual stator windings are all connected together. Technician B says that they must be separate for the three-phase design to operate correctly. Which technician is correct?

16. Technician A says that all alternators use the same design of stator winding connection. Technician B says that both a delta and a Y connection are used. Who is right?

17. Technician A says that a delta-wound stator produces a higher output at the top end of the speed range than does a Y design. Technician B says that the delta produces a higher output at the low-speed end. Which technician understands these design differences better?

18. Technician A says that if one winding of a delta-wound stator is damaged, no power will flow from the alternator. Technician B says that this would occur only in a Y-wound stator design. Who is right?

19. Technician A says that although alternator field current supply will vary between makes and models, typical average current supply to a heavy truck alternator will range between 10 and 15 A. Technician B says that this would only range between 3.5 and 7 A average. Which technician knows the system operation better?

20. Technician A says that to protect the alternator system against high-voltage spikes in the stator, a number of transistors within the diode-trio are used. Technician B says that a number of zener diodes are employed within the rectifier bridge. Which technician is correct?

21. Technician A says that the terms *forward-biased* and *reverse-biased* imply that a diode will conduct current in only one direction or the other; this is known as *half-wave rectification*. Technician B says that this is *full-wave rectification*. Who is right?

22. Technician A says that in temperature-compensated voltage regulators, voltage will decrease with an increase in temperature and will increase with a decrease in temperature. Technician B says that it would function exactly opposite. Who is correct?

23. Technician A says that disconnecting the batteries while the engine is running allows you to determine if the alternator output is sufficient to handle the loads. Technician B says you should never disconnect the batteries on a running engine, since this can lead to diode damage. Which technician is correct?

24. Technician A says that grounding the generator field circuit on a running engine can cause diode burnout. Technician B says that it will cause increased generator output. Which technician is correct?

25. Technician A says that if an uninsulated starting motor is used, a ground strap must be used, otherwise faulty alternator operation can occur. Technician B says that a ground strap must be used on an insulated starter motor. Which technician is correct?

26. Technician A says you should always disconnect the batteries and isolate the alternator if arc welding is to be performed on the vehicle frame. Technician B says this is not necessary since the alternator is insulated and fuse protected. Who is right?

27. Technician A says that a carbon pile tester is used to apply a variable load to the battery and starter motor. Technician B says it is used to apply a variable load to the battery and alternator charging system. Which technician is correct?

28. Technician A says that the most important precaution prior to hooking up a carbon pile tester is to ensure that the control knob is in the OFF position. Technician B says that it can be full on as long as the ignition switch is off. Which technician is right?

29. Technician A says that the voltage regulator switches field current on and off at a fixed frequency of about 60 cycles per second. Technician B says it is much faster—closer to 400 cycles per second. Which technician is correct?

30. Technician A says that a generator isolation diode operates a charge indicator lamp by being wired in series with the alternator output. Technician B says that it is wired in parallel. Which technician is right?

31. Technician A says that when you check alternator diodes, a good diode should exhibit one high and one low ohmmeter reading as the leads are switched during testing. Technician B says that both values should be the same, otherwise the diode is faulty. Which technician is correct?

32. Technician A says that diodes that allow current flow in one direction are shorted; no current flow in either direction signifies an open diode. Technician B agrees with the second part of this statement, but says that diodes that allow current flow in both directions are shorted. Which technician is correct?

33. Technician A says that diodes should be checked with a 110 V test lamp or high-voltage test equipment. Technician B says that only a multimeter with a minimum 10 megohm resistance value should be used for this check. Who is right?

34. Technician A says that alternator resistance values will vary between makes and models, but that generally if the resistance value is between 5 and 50 ohms, it is serviceable. Technician B says that it should read between 300 and 400 ohms. Which technician is correct?

35. Technician A says that a strong acid odor from an alternator usually confirms that the shaft bearings have been overheated. Technician B says that it indicates overheating and probably insulatation or wiring damage. Who is right?

36. Technician A says that alternator drive belts that are too loose can cause slippage and a high-pitched squeal or chirp noise when accelerated under load. Technician B says that the only result would be a slipping belt. Which technician knows troubleshooting better?

37. Technician A says that alternator drive belts that are too tight, particularly on a double-belt setup, will result in excessive side loading and early bearing failure. Technician B says that the belts will simply roll in their pulley grooves. Who is right?

38. Technician A says that more drive belts fail as a result of being too loose than of being too tight. Technician B believes that too-tight drive belts result in more belt failures. Which technician do you think is correct?

39. Technician A says that on a two-belt drive system, if one belt fails, only one belt need be replaced. Technician B says that both belts must be replaced. Who is right?

40. Technician A says that it isn't necessary to loosen drive belts when the vehicle is to be placed in storage for an extended period of time. Technician B says that if you don't do this, lumpy belts can result, leading to vibration when the engine is restarted. Which technician is correct?

41. Technician A says that alternator drive belts that show signs of worn sides, or have exhibited squeak, squeal, or whine during operation could indicate that the drive pulley is misaligned. Technician B says these symptoms indicate a belt that has been slipping. Which technician is correct?

42. Technician A says that when installing a new alternator drive belt, it is acceptable to place the new belt into position and pry it over the pulley with a large screwdriver. Technician B says that you should never do this since it can stretch or tear the new belt: loosen the belt adjusting bracket or alternator assembly. Which technician has better work habits?

43. Technician A says that you should always adjust drive belt tension with a belt tension gauge. Technician B says

that as long as you set the belt deflection to between $\frac{3}{8}$ and $\frac{1}{2}$ in. (9.5–12.7 mm) there should not be any problems. Which technician is correct?

44. Technician A says that belt squeal and squeak that disappears once the engine warms up is usually due to moisture in the pulley grooves on cool or cold mornings. Technician B says it indicates a belt tension problem and possible misalignment. Who is right?

45. Technician A says that a high-pitched whine is usually an indication of a belt that is too tight. Technician B says it is more than likely due to bearing damage to one of the alternator support bearings. Which technician is right?

46. Technician A says that excessive drive belt glazing can usually be traced to oil or grease on the belt or pulley grooves. Technician B says this would be due to too-tight belt tension. Who do you think is right?

47. Technician A says that cracking at the belt base, fabric rupture, cover tears, gouged edges, worn sides, cord damage, belt flip-over, or belt disintegration can be traced to too little tension in the belt adjustment. Technician B says it would be caused by too much tension, pulley wear, damage, or misalignment. Which technician is correct?

48. Technician A says that a brushless alternator employs no slip rings, but relies upon a rotor with permanent magnetism, diodes, and resistors. Technician B says that although there are no brushes, the slip rings are in contact with a variable resistor collector ring. Which technician is correct?

26 Electric Starting Motors

OVERVIEW

In order to crank the diesel engine for starting purposes, an electrical starter motor is necessary to provide the correct voltage and amperage to provide a fast enough cranking speed to initiate combustion. The starter motor, therefore, relies on a fully charged battery system, which itself is charged from the alternator assembly. This chapter describes the function and operation of both an electrical and compressed air starter motor. Details are supplied with respect to how to maintain, service, repair, diagnose, analyze and troubleshoot the electrical starter motor assembly.

STARTER MOTOR FUNCTION

The purpose of an engine starter motor is to rotate the engine flywheel ring gear by the use of either an electric or compressed air-driven starter assembly. The starter drive gear must be rotated fast enough to permit the engine to fire and initiate combustion. After the engine starts, the motor must disengage automatically to prevent damage to the drive pinion assembly.

Because of the higher compression ratio and heavier components used with a heavy-duty high-speed diesel engine, the electric starter motor can be designed to operate on either 12 or 24 V. However, if a 24-V starter motor is used along with a 12-V alternator charging system, then either a series–parallel switch or a battery equalizer system must be used to permit the electrical system to function at these two different voltages. Most heavy-duty truck diesel engines are now equipped with high-torque 12-V starters; however, many buses/coaches, industrial, and marine applications operate with 24/32-V starter motors and generator charging systems.

ELECTRIC STARTER SYSTEM STRUCTURE

Figure 26-1 illustrates two external views of a heavy-duty truck high-speed diesel engine starter motor assembly, while Figure 26-2 shows a cross-sectional view of the internal components for the starter motor shown in Figure 26-1b.

To support engagement of a heavy-duty starter motor, an electrical system similar to that shown in Figure 26-3A using an external magnetic switch is required. However, newer models may employ a system similar to that shown in Figure 26-3B, where an IMS (integral magnetic switch) is used.

The purpose of the individual system components are as follows:

1. *Starting motor.* A dc electric motor that converts electrical energy into cranking power to rotate the engine for starting.

2. *Solenoid switches.* An electrical magnetic switch that makes and breaks the circuit between the starter and battery. It also shifts the starter drive in and out of the flywheel ring gear.

3. *Cables.* Large cables are required to transmit the huge amount of current needed by the starter motor to crank the engine.

4. *Battery.* The battery provides the source of power to operate the starter motor. In many systems more than one battery is required, since one battery does not contain sufficient amperage to turn the starter.

5. *Thermostatic connector.* Both systems shown in Figure 26-3 feature the use of a thermostatic connector

FIGURE 26–1 (a) Typical 37-MT motor. (42-MT is similar); (b) end view of 42-MT motor showing thermostat connector. (Courtesy of Delco-Remy of America.)

which is designed to open the electrical circuit to prevent cranking when the temperature of the starter motor windings reach a predetermined temperature. This action will inhibit cranking for between 1 to 6 minutes, after which time the thermostat will close and allow cranking action once again. This lengthens starter motor life substantially!

12- AND 24-VOLT CIRCUITS

Heavy trucks and equipment can be equipped with either a 12- or 24- V high-torque starter motor. Figure 26-4A illustrates the typical hookup required when more than one battery is employed in an electrical system. In a parallel hookup, all the positive terminals are

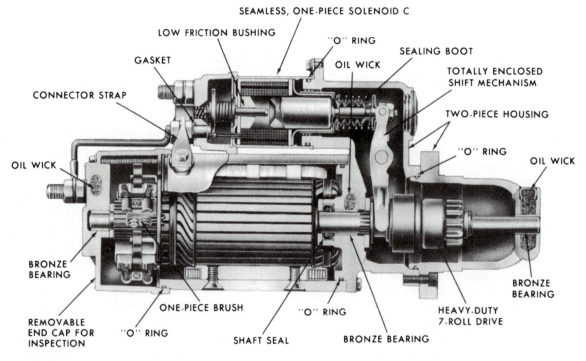

FIGURE 26–2 Cross-sectional view, typical 42-MT motor. (Courtesy of Delco-Remy of America.)

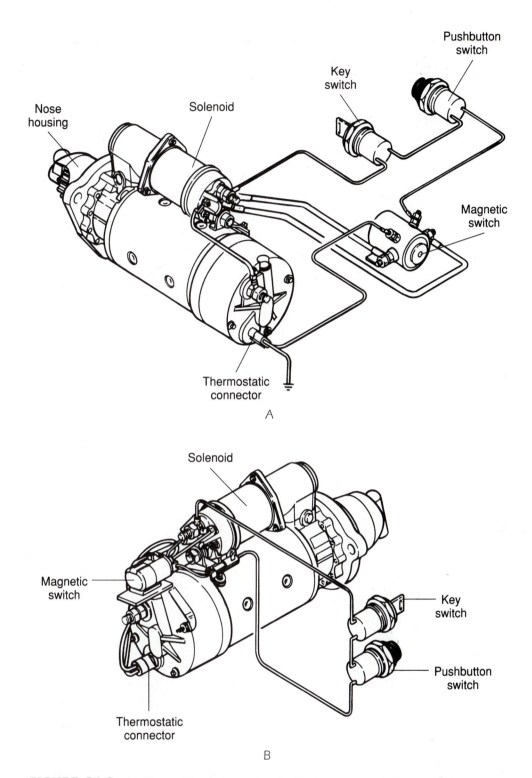

FIGURE 26-3 (A) Heavy-duty starter motor electrical system employing a remote mounted magnetic switch. (B) starter electrical system using an integral magnetic switch. (Courtesy of Delco-Remy America.)

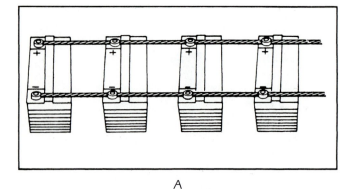

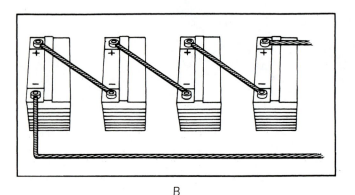

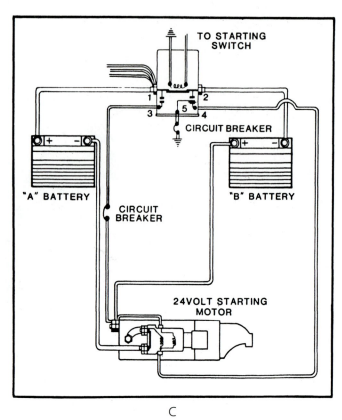

FIGURE 26–4 *(A) Battery parallel arrangement; (B) battery series arrangement; (C) Series–parallel arrangement. (Courtesy of Snap-on Tool Corp.)*

connected together and all the negative terminals are connected together as shown in the diagram. This wiring arrangement results in the amperage of all batteries being added together; however, the voltage is the sum of only one battery, or 12 V.

When a 24-V starter motor is used, the batteries must be connected in a series hookup as shown in Figure 26-4B. The positive terminals are connected to the negative terminal of the opposite battery. This wiring arrangement results in 24 V, with the amperage being the sum of only one battery. When a 24-V starter motor is used along with a 12-V charging system, it is necessary to employ a series–parallel switch arrangement similar to that shown in Figure 26-4C.

AIR STARTER SYSTEM

Another popular starting system is an air starter powered by compressed air from the vehicle or equipment reservoirs, which in turn are charged from an engine-driven air compressor assembly. Figure 26-5 illustrates the basic components required for an air starter motor system.

ELECTRIC STARTER MOTOR COMPONENTS

An exploded view of a heavy-duty Delco 42MT starter motor is shown in Figure 26-6. The major components shown function as follows:

1. *Field frame.* The field frame provides a place to mount the fields and also the front and rear bearing housing.

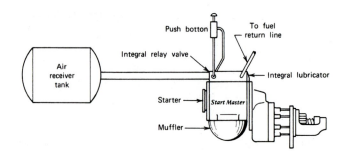

FIGURE 26–5 *Air-starting motor. (Courtesy of Stanadyne Diesel System.)*

FIGURE 26–6 Exploded view of a Delco heavy-duty model 42MT starter motor assembly. (Courtesy of GMC Trucks.)

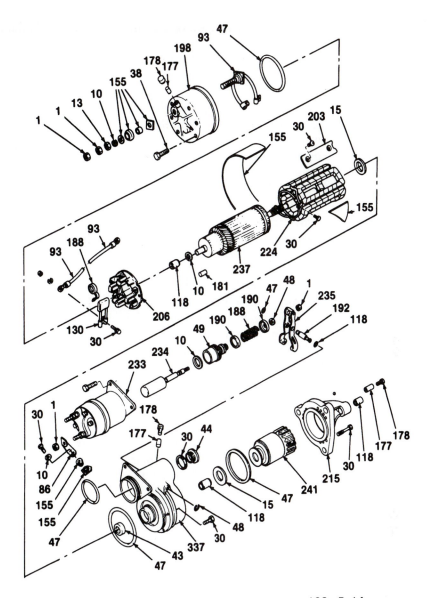

1. Nut	49. Rubber boot	198. End frame
10. Washer	86. Connector	203. Pole shoe
15. Spacer washer	93. Lead	206. Brush plate
30. Retaining screws	118. Bushing	215. Drive housing
30. Inspection plug	130. Brush	224. Coil
washer (mated to	155. Insulator	233. Solenoid
item 44)	177. Oil wick	234. Plunger
38. Screw and washer	178. Oil reservoir	235. Shift lever
43. Oil seal	181. Pin	237. Armature
44. Inspection plug	188. Spring	241. Drive assembly
47. O-ring	190. Spring retainer	337. Shift lever housing
48. Retainer ring	192. Shift lever shaft	

2. *Brush end bearing housing.* This housing provides a place for the commutator end bushing or bearing.

3. *Armature assembly.* This assembly is composed of many conductors (heavy copper ribbons) mounted between iron laminations on an iron shaft. On one end of the armature is the commutator, and on the other end is the starter drive.

4. *Starter drive.* It is mounted onto the armature shaft and transmits the power of the starting motor to the flywheel. On all drives is a pinion that engages the flywheel ring gear when the starter motor is operating. To allow the starter motor to turn faster than the engine it is cranking, a gear reduction of approximately 15 to 1 is utilized. The pinion mechanism must be designed to disengage from the flywheel or overrun after

the engine starts; otherwise, the starting motor would be rotated by the engine at too fast a speed and cause damage to the starter. Many different types of starter drives are used today; some of the most common ones are listed here:

    a. *Posi-torque.* As the name implies the posi-torque drive is designed to eliminate slippage. Designed like a ratchet, it will not slip under load but will ratchet if engaged when the engine starts (Figure 26-7A).

    b. *Sprag clutch drive* (Figure 26-7B). The sprag clutch is an overrunning clutch that locks the pinion to the armature shaft in one direction and allows it to rotate freely in the other direction. It is composed of inner and outer shells that are locked together by sprags. It is engaged by the starter solenoid through a shift lever. Figure 26-7C shows two widely used starter motor drives.

5. *Brushes.* They are made from a carbon and graphite mixture, are square or oblong in shape, and connect the starter commutator segments to the generator terminals. They are called brushes because they brush the commutator segments to make contact.

6. *Drive end housing.* The starter housing that provides a means of mounting the starter onto the engine.

7. *Bearings and bushings.* The starter armature is supported in the field frame by bushings or bearings.

Starter Operating Principle

To understand the electrical principle on which a cranking motor operates, consider a straight wire conductor located in the magnetic field of a horseshoe-shaped magnet with current flowing through the wire as shown by the arrow in Figure 26-8. With this arrangement there will be two separate magnetic fields: one produced by the horseshoe magnet and one produced by the current flow through the conductor.

Since magnetic lines leave the north pole and enter the south pole, the direction of the magnetic lines between the two poles of the horseshoe magnet will be upward as shown in Figure 26-9. The current-carrying conductor will produce a magnetic field consisting of concentric circles around the wire in the direction illustrated. The net result is a heavy concentration of magnetic lines on the left-hand side of the wire and a weak magnetic field on the right-hand side of the wire.

This condition occurs on the left side where the magnetic lines are in the same direction and add together; it occurs on the right-hand side where the magnetic lines are in the opposite direction and tend to cancel each other out.

With a strong field on one side of the conductor and a weak field on the other side, the conductor will tend to move from the strong to the weak field, or from left to right, as shown in Figure 26-9. The stronger the magnetic field produced by the horseshoe magnet and the higher the current flow in the conductor, the greater will be the force tending to move the conductor from left to right. The resultant force illustrates the electrical principle on which a cranking motor operates.

A basic motor is shown in Figure 26-10. A loop of wire is located between two iron pieces and is connected to two separate commutator segments or bars. Riding on the commutator bars are two brushes that are connected to the battery and to the windings located over the pole pieces.

With this arrangement, current flow can be traced from the battery through the pole piece windings to a brush and commutator bar, through the loop of wire to the other commutator bar and brush, and then back to

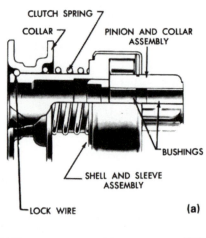

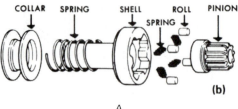

A

FIGURE 26–7 A: Roller starter motor clutch drive: (a) cutaway view; (b) exploded view; B: (a) sprag clutch assembly; (b) disassembled view of heavy-duty sprag clutch drive assembly; C: (a) intermediate-duty drive clutch ID; (b) heavy-duty drive clutch ID. (Courtesy of GMC Truck Division of General Motors Corporation.)

COLLAR — SPRAGS — PINION

SHELL — RETAINER CUPS

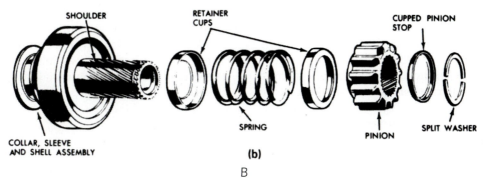

SHOULDER — RETAINER CUPS — CUPPED PINION STOP

COLLAR, SLEEVE AND SHELL ASSEMBLY — SPRING — PINION — SPLIT WASHER

(b)

B

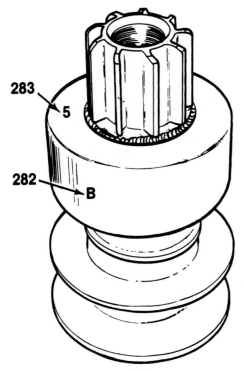

283
5
282
B

282. Month; Jan. (A), Feb. (B)
283. Year; 1984 (4), 1985 (5)

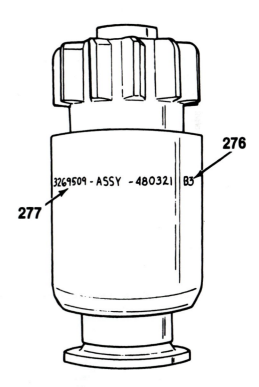

276
277
3269509 - ASSY - 480321 B3

276. Build Date
277. Part Number

C

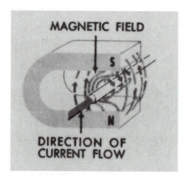

FIGURE 26–8   Magnetic field and conductor. (Courtesy of Delco-Remy of America.)

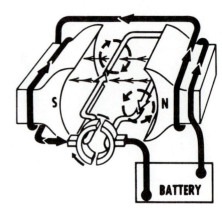

FIGURE 26–10   Simple starter motor. (Courtesy of Delco-Remy of America.)

the battery. The resulting magnetic fields impart a turning or rotational force on the loop of wire as illustrated in Figure 26-11.

When the wire loop has turned one-half turn, the commutator bars will have interchanged positions with the two brushes, so that the current through the wire loop will move in the opposite direction. But since the wire loop has exchanged positions with the pole pieces, the rotational effect will still be in the same clockwise direction as previously shown in Figure 26-11.

SOLENOID SWITCH COMPONENTS AND OPERATING PRINCIPLES

Components
A starter solenoid (Figure 26-12) is made up of the following component parts:

1. *Terminal bolts.* Bolts to which the battery cable and motor terminal are connected.

2. *Contact plate.* The plate that makes the contact between the terminal bolts.

3. *Pull-in coil.* A coil within the solenoid that helps engage the solenoid shift lever (grounded in the starting motor).

4. *Hold-in coil.* A coil within the solenoid that holds the solenoid in the engaged position (grounded to solenoid case). Or solenoid insulated ground terminal.

5. *Plunger.* The iron core of the solenoid, which is connected to the starter shift lever.

Switch Operation
The solenoid switch is used to engage the starter pinion and close the circuit between the starter and the battery. When the starter switch on the vehicle instrument panel is closed, the solenoid operates as follows:

1. The hold-in and pull-in coils work together to pull the solenoid plunger into the solenoid.

2. As the plunger is pulled into the solenoid housing, the contact plate shorts the pull-in coil and the hold-in coil holds the switch engaged (Figure 26-13).

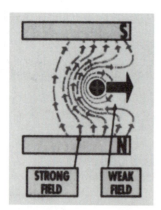

FIGURE 26–9   Magnetic field between two magnets. (Courtesy of Delco-Remy of America.)

FIGURE 26–11   Force exerted on starter conductors by force field. (Courtesy of Delco-Remy of America.)

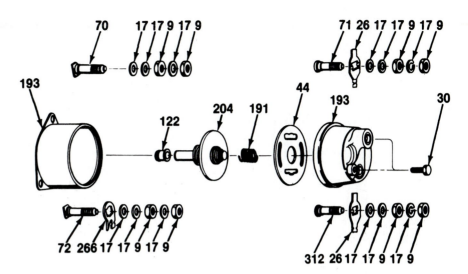

FIGURE 26–12 Exploded view of Delco starter motor model 42MT solenoid components. (Courtesy of GMC Trucks Division, General Motors Corporation.)

9. Terminal Nut	71. Solenoid Terminal Stud	204. Contact
17. Terminal Washer	72. Motor Stud	266. Clip
30. Screw	122. Plunger Rod Bushing	312. Terminal Stud
44. Gasket	191. Contact Spring	
70. "BAT" Terminal Stud	193. Solenoid Housing	

NOTE   The pull-in coil circuit during engagement is from switch to coil to starter motor for ground. After engagement the solenoid plate contacts the solenoid inner terminals. This circuit has much less resistance than the pull-in coil circuit. As a result the pull-in coil is shut off.

3. In addition to closing the circuit between the battery and starter with the contact plate, the solenoid operates the drive shift lever, which moves the drive into the flywheel.

4. The switch remains in this position until the starter switch on the instrument panel is released, causing the solenoid to disengage the shift lever and break the contact between the battery and starter.

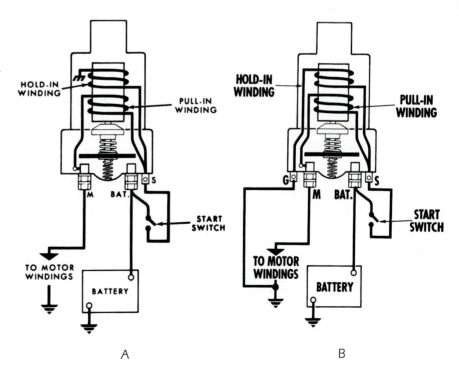

FIGURE 26–13 (A) Solenoid circuit (hold-in winding grounded internally); (B) solenoid circuit with ground return terminals. (Courtesy of Delco-Remy of America.)

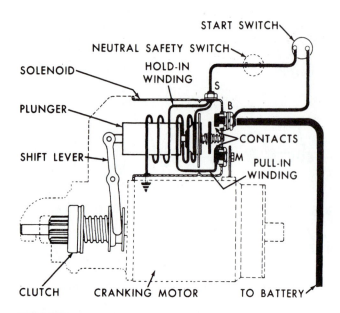

FIGURE 26-14 *Operation of hold-in and pull-in coil.* (Courtesy of Delco-Remy of America.)

When this happens, the starter stops turning and the pinion is disengaged from the flywheel (Figure 26-14).

ELECTRIC STARTER TROUBLESHOOTING

When a problem exists with the starter motor, the fault may lie either in the motor itself or in the wiring circuit. Figure 26-15 lists problems associated with slow cranking or a clicking or chattering solenoid. Figure 26-16 lists possible causes for no cranking and/or no sound from the solenoid when the starter switch is engaged. Often a low-voltage supply to the starter is one of the main causes of failure to crank. Figure 26-17 illustrates the use of a voltmeter connected into the starter motor circuit to determine the voltage drop (available cranking voltage). Perform the voltage check as follows:

1. A starter motor voltage drop check can quickly confirm whether or not the starter should be removed for service. Figure 26-17 illustrates a typical quick check that can be performed with the starter motor in position on the engine.

2. Place the positive (red) lead of a voltmeter against the solenoid BAT terminal and the negative (black) volmeter lead against the starter motor ground terminal.

3. Close the starter switch (key or button) to crank the engine while noting the voltage reading on the face of the meter.

4. If the voltage is 9 V or less on a 12-V starter system while cranking at normal room temperature of 60 to 70°F (15 to 21°C), check the resistance and voltage loss between the interconnecting cables of the batteries.

5. While cranking the engine, touch the voltmeter leads to the positive and negative posts or stud nut of each battery. There should not be more than 0.5-V difference between any two battery readings; otherwise, there is high resistance level between connections. A starting circuit resistance check procedure is listed below.

Typical starter circuit voltage drops are established by the use of a voltmeter connected across sections of the circuit in parallel, then isolating the problem area.

Starter Motor Bench Check
If a starter motor problem cannot be traced while on the engine, remove the starter and perform a bench check according to the hookup shown in Figure 26-18. During this bench check, mount the motor into a starter motor holder or clamp it tightly into a vise. Tests that can be performed include voltage and amperage draws, resistance checks, solenoid operation, cranking speed, and breakaway torque using a special pinion drive torquemeter.

Solenoid Disassembly and Testing
The starter motor solenoid handles the battery power required to energize the enclosed shift mechanism connected to the starter motor pinion. Figure 26-2 shows the connection, while Figure 26-12 illustrates the typical component parts for a heavy-duty solenoid assembly. Often when a starter motor problem exists, the cause may lie within the solenoid unit. The solenoid can be tested for internal shorts or open circuits using a multimeter or test lamp across the windings. An example of how to perform a solenoid check is illustrated in Figure 26-19A and B for both three- and four-terminal models.

Checking Procedure
1. To check the solenoid for grounds, connect a test lamp between the solenoid case and each terminal one at a time.

2. There should be no test light illumination if the solenoid is operating correctly. However, if the test light does illuminate, the terminal is grounded and the solenoid should be replaced.

3. To check the solenoid hold-in and pull-in windings, disconnect all of the wire leads from the solenoid and make the test connections as shown in Figure 26-19.

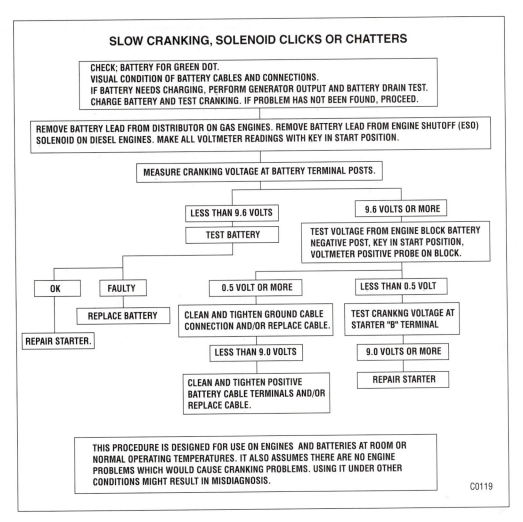

FIGURE 26–15 *Slow cranking system diagnosis. (Courtesy of GMC Trucks, GMC Corp.)*

SPECIAL PRECAUTION Serious damage to the solenoid pull-in winding can occur if during this test you allow current to flow for longer than 15 seconds. The carbon pile must be used to limit the voltage to that specified in the manufacturer's printed data. Note also that the current draw to the winding will decrease as the winding temperature increases.

4. Turn the load switch on and adjust the carbon pile to lower the battery voltage to the value shown in test specs for the solenoid switch.

5. Carefully note the amperage reading; a higher reading than specified is indicative of a shorted or grounded winding, a low-amperage reading indicates excessive resistance.

6. The winding resistance value can be read di-

rectly by using a digital ohmmeter capable of measuring in tenths of an ohm, since typical values for the pull-in winding will be between 0.14 and 0.16 Ω. Values for the hold-in winding on heavy-duty Delco starters is usually between 0.65 and 0.70 Ω. A low resistance value reading usually indicates that there is an internal short circuit, while no reading indicates an open circuit. If a coil resistance value is not available, you can determine this by using Ohm's law, divide the voltage by the current (ampere) value.

If the solenoid fails any of the tests above, disassemble it and inspect all components for signs of overheating, burning, and damage to the internal contacts, such as the disk plate.

Cranking with a low-battery condition will cause the solenoid to overheat, resulting in possible welding (closing) of the contacts, which will result in the starter circuit being continuously energized and the engine attempting to crank steadily. Alternatively, the pinion

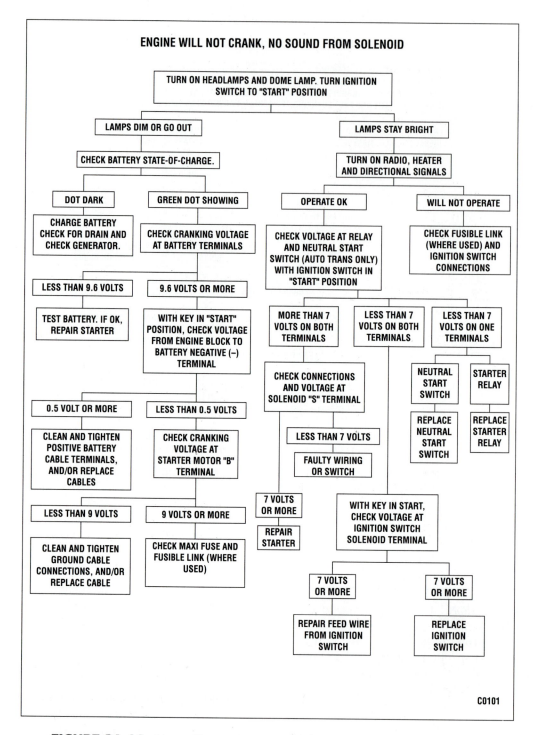

FIGURE 26-16 No cranking system diagnosis. (Courtesy of GMC Trucks, GMC Corp.)

may not engage with the ring gear, but the starter will continue to motor without cranking the engine. Disassembly of the solenoid is straightforward, usually requiring only the removal of the cover screws and attachments to expose the internal components. An example of a disassembled solenoid for a heavy-duty starter is shown in Figure 26-12.

Generally, the part that requires the most attention is the circular solenoid contact disk, identified as item 204. This circular disk comes into contact with the terminal stud that is connected to the battery power when energized. If the contact disk and terminals are not badly burned, the disk and terminals can be cleaned up. The disk can be turned over and the ter-

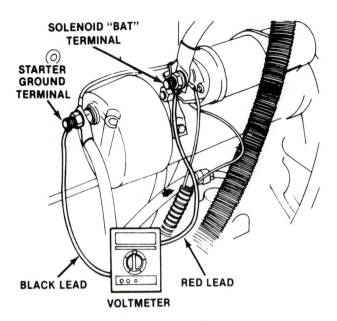

FIGURE 26–17 Voltmeter connections at the starter motor to determine the available cranking voltage. (Courtesy of Detroit Diesel Corporation.)

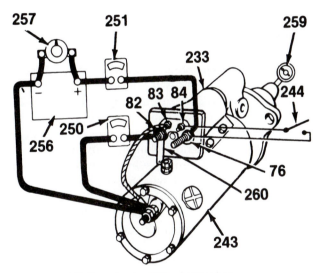

76. "BAT" Terminal	251. Ammeter
82. "MTR"	256. Battery
83. "GRD"	257. Carbon Pile
84. "SW"	259. RPM Indicator
233. Solenoid	260. Connector Strap
243. Starting Motor	
244. Switch	
250. Voltmeter	

FIGURE 26–18 No-load test hookup on heavy-duty starter motors with ground terminals. (Courtesy of GMC Trucks Division, General Motors Corporation.)

minals rotated 180° to provide an unworn surface. First you have to remove the contact disk.

Removing the Contact Disk

1. Remove the small spring from the end of the disk, then carefully compress the contact cushion spring.

2. Remove the small roll pin from the plunger pin.

3. Remove the spring retainer, spring, and plunger pin from the disk.

4. Replace or turn the disk over to expose a new clean surface, and reinsert the small pin.

5. Install the spring, retainer, small roll pin, and spring in front of the disk.

Typical damage occurs to the disk due to attempting to crank the engine over with batteries that are in a state of low charge. This results in serious damage to the solenoid contact disk as a result of repeated attempts to start the engine with low battery power.

Pinion Clearance Check

Once the starter has been completely reassembled, it is necessary to check and adjust the solenoid plunger and shift lever movement so that the pinion drive mechanism will shift the gear drive into proper engagement with the flywheel ring gear once the starter switch has been closed.

SPECIAL NOTE   Heavy-duty starter motor drives have a provision to adjust the pinion clearance if it is incorrect; however, there are no provisions for adjusting the pinion clearance on starter motors using an intermediate-duty clutch.

To check and adjust the solenoid plunger and shift lever movement, clamp the starter field frame into a vise.

1. To check the pinion clearance, disconnect the motor field coil connector from the solenoid motor terminal.

2. Connect the necessary battery voltage to match the solenoid rating (either 12 or 24 V) from the solenoid switch terminal to the solenoid frame or ground terminal (Figure 26-20).

3. To minimize power flow through the solenoid, momentarily flash a jumper lead from the solenoid motor terminal to the solenoid frame or ground terminal. This will immediately energize the solenoid and shift the pinion gear and clutch drive into the cranking position, where it will remain as long as the jumper wire is held in place.

4. Manually push the pinion or drive back toward the commutator end to eliminate all free play.

5. Using a feeler gauge, measure the distance

FIGURE 26-19 (a) Testing solenoid windings (three-terminal solenoid); (b) testing pull-in windings on three- and four-terminal solenoids.

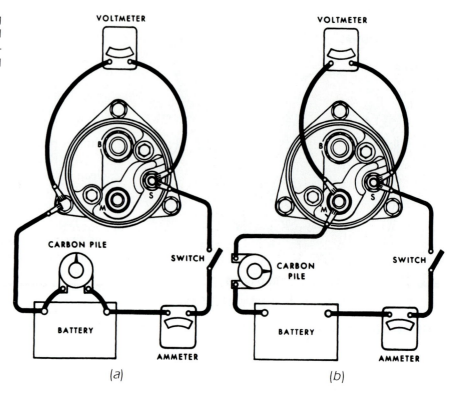

(a)   (b)

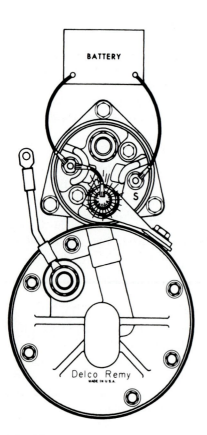

FIGURE 26-20 Connections for checking pinion clearance (seven-roll drive).

between the drive gear pinion and the nose cone retainer (Figure 26-21). Note that the clearance limits for different starter drive types will vary.

6. After any starter rebuild, solenoid lever adjustment is invariably required; therefore, disconnect the battery power temporarily if you have not already removed the shift lever housing access plug (Figure 26-21).

7. To adjust the pinion clearance to within the published limits, use a socket, short extension, and ratchet drive to access the solenoid plunger adjustment nut.

8. Using the jumper wire again, energize the starter pinion drive and with hand pressure against the pinion, recheck the pinion-to-nose cone clearance as shown in Figure 26-21. Rotate the shaft adjusting nut clockwise or counterclockwise until an acceptable clearance value is obtained.

9. Always recheck the clearance at least once more to confirm that there is sufficient free play between the pinion gear and nose cone.

10. Reinstall the access plug from the shift lever housing and tighten it securely.

SPECIAL NOTE   Always perform a no-load test on the starter after assembly and after completing the pinion clearance check. Details of this test were discussed and shown earlier in this chapter.

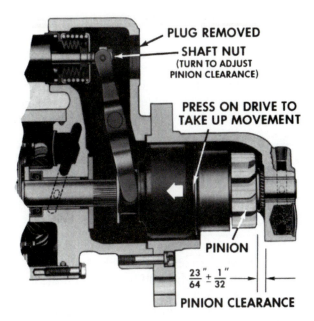

FIGURE 26-21 Checking pinion clearance (drive shown in Figure 26-2).

DISASSEMBLY, INSPECTION, AND OVERHAUL OF ELECTRIC STARTERS AND COMPONENTS

Starter Disassembly

It is assumed that the starter has been removed from the engine. If not, disconnect the battery ground cable and remove the starter from the engine. Disassemble the starter in the following manner:

1. Match mark the end housing to the end frame with a center punch or chisel (Figure 26-22).
2. Remove the bolts that hold the commutator end frame and the field frame together.

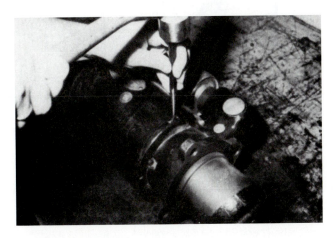

FIGURE 26-22 Match-marking starter housings.

NOTE Depending on which type starter you have, the bolts may be threaded into the main field frame or may be through bolts that reach through the field frame housing and thread into the shift lever housing.

3. At this point the front bearing end frame can be removed from some starters without further disassembly, while other starters must have the brushes disconnected before the end frame can be removed.
4. Remove the bolts that hold the lever and nose housing to the main field frame.
5. Withdraw the nose and lever housing along with the armature from the field frame assembly.

NOTE The solenoid plunger is still connected to the shift lever and will slide out of the solenoid when the lever housing is removed.

6. To remove the armature from the lever housing and drive assembly of a starter that does not use through bolts, simply lift the armature from the lever housing and drive.
7. On starters that use through bolts to attach the lever housing to the main frame, the bolts that hold the nose housing to the lever housing must be removed. This allows the nose housing to be removed, providing access to a snap ring and collar that must be removed before the armature can be withdrawn from the lever housing.
8. Remove the solenoid housing from the starter field frame.

Starter Component Testing and Inspection

1. Visually inspect the starter armature commutator for roughness, burned spots, and ridging. If these problems are noticed, the commutator should be turned in a commutator lathe.

NOTE Do not turn the commutator until you have made the electrical checks on the armature in case it is bad electrically and will have to be replaced.

2. Place the armature in an armature growler and check for:

   a. *Shorts.* Perform this check by turning the growler switch on and placing the hacksaw blade crossways on top of the armature center. The hacksaw blade should not vibrate. If it does, the armature is shorted and must be replaced.

NOTE Before condemning an armature that tests shorted, check the commutator carefully for pieces of copper between the segments. A piece of copper wedged between the segments will short the armature. Clean the grooves between the segments and recheck the armature.

---

b. *Grounds.* The armature can be checked for grounds by using the growler test light. Touch one probe of the test light to a commutator bar and the other probe to the armature shaft (Figure 26-23). The test light

should not light. If it does, the armature must be replaced.

c. *Opens.* The armature can be checked for opens by using the meter on the growler. Place the armature on the growler and turn on the power switch. Place the meter probe on two adjacent commutator bars.

NOTE   On some armatures it may be necessary to place the test probe on one bar; then skip one bar, and place the other probe on the next bar to get a reading.

Turn the armature to obtain the highest reading. Generally the probes will have to be placed on the armature below the center line to obtain a reading.

In addition to the growler check, open circuits may be detected by visually inspecting the commuta-

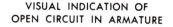

VISUAL INDICATION OF OPEN CIRCUIT IN ARMATURE

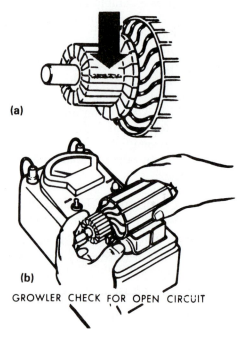

(a)

(b)

GROWLER CHECK FOR OPEN CIRCUIT

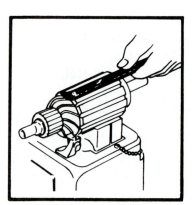

(c) GROWLER CHECK FOR SHORT CIRCUIT

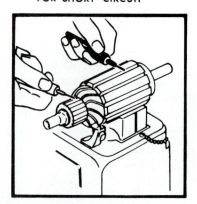

(d) TEST LAMP CHECK FOR GROUND CIRCUIT

FIGURE 26–23 (a) Visual check of armature commutator; (b) growler check of armature for an open circuit and a short circuit; (c) short-circuit check; (d) test lamp check of armature for a grounded circuit. (Courtesy of Delco-Remy of America.)

tor bars. The bar that has an open circuit is usually burned and easily spotted.

3. *Testing field coils* (fields not removed from the starter).

NOTE   Before testing the field coils, make sure that they are disconnected from ground or the starter solenoid, since such a connection will cause an incorrect reading during the test.

The field coils should be tested for:

a. *Open circuits.* Using a test light or ohmmeter, test the field circuit for opens by placing one probe on one end of the field brush connection and the other probe on the starter terminal connection (Figure 26-24). The light should light or the ohmmeter should show continuity if the fields are good. If not, the fields are open.

NOTE   To ensure complete testing of the field circuit, touch all field brush connections with the one test probe while holding the other test probe on the starter connector terminal.

---

b. *Field ground circuit test.* Test the field circuit for grounds with a test light or ohmmeter. Touch one probe of the test light to a field connection and the other probe to the ground. The test light or ohmmeter should not show any ground. If it does, the field circuit is grounded to the starter case and must be repaired or replaced. If the test light does not light, the field is not grounded and can be considered good. If the fields are grounded and require replacement, follow this procedure:

(1) With a large screwdriver or square drive handle, remove the screws that hold the field pole pieces in place (Figure 26-25).

NOTE   Sometimes the screws that hold the pole pieces in place will not be easily removed with a screwdriver. In some cases a special removal tool may be available. If no such tool is available, an

impact screwdriver works very well. If none of these methods is available, a small pin punch ($\frac{1}{4}$ in. or 6 to 7 mm) and hammer can be used to jar them loose.

---

(2) After the screws have been loosened, remove them with a screwdriver.

NOTE   Before removing the fields and pole pieces, match mark them to the housing with a marking pencil for reference during reassembly.

---

(3) Remove the fields and field pole pieces.
(4) Install the field pole pieces into the new fields if new fields are to be installed and install the assembly into the starter main frame with reference to match marks. Tighten the pole screws securely.

4. The insulated brush holder must be tested for grounds as follows: Using a test light or ohmmeter, touch one probe of the test light to the insulated brush holder while touching the other probe to the brush end frame (Figure 26-24). The light or ohmmeter should not show continuity. If it does, the brush holder is grounded and must be repaired.

5. All bearings and bushings should be checked closely for wear and roughness. If any questions or doubt remains about a bearing or bushing, replace it.

NOTE   Special grease has been developed for use in starter bushings or bearings and should be used instead of wheel or chassis lubricant. This grease is available from starter parts suppliers.

---

6. *Insulated terminal testing.* The starter insulated terminal should be checked for grounds with a test light or ohmmeter. If the terminal is grounded, remove it and check the insulation; replace if visually damaged or cracked. Replace bolt and check for grounds.

7. *Solenoid disassembly and inspection.* The starter solenoid on a diesel engine starter performs two im-

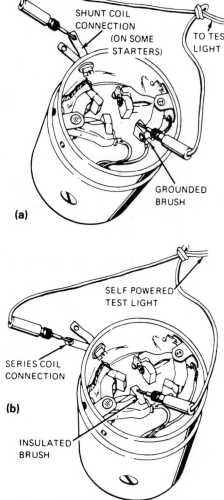

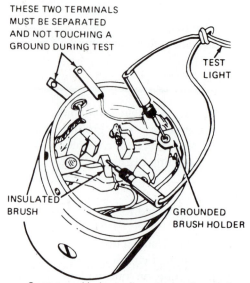

On starters with shunt coil, separatte series and shunt coil strap terminals during this test. Do not let strap terminals touch case or other ground. Using a test lamp place one lead on the grounded brush holder and the other lead on either insulated brush. If the lamp lights, a grounded series coil is indicated and must be repaired or replaced.

(c)

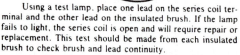

Using a test lamp, place one lead on the series coil terminal and the other lead on the insulated brush. If the lamp fails to light, the series coil is open and will require repair or replacement. This test should be made from each insulated brush to check brush and lead continuity.

FIGURE 26–24   (a) Testing the shunt coil for an open condition; (b) testing the series coil for an open condition; (c) testing the series coil for a ground condition. (Courtesy of GMC Trucks.)

portant jobs: (1) engaging the starter drive pinion and (2) closing the circuit between the starting motor and battery. To disassemble and check the starter solenoid, proceed as follows:

    a. Remove the screws that hold the solenoid cover onto the solenoid.

    b. Lift the cover from the solenoid.

    c. Inspect the contact plate and contact bolts.

    d. Replace the contact bolts and contact plate if they show wear, pitting, or burning.

    e. Replace the solenoid cover and install and tighten the screws.

Reconditioning or Turning the Starter Commutator

When the starter motor is disassembled, the copper commutator end bars should be carefully inspected for signs of scoring, or possible ovality. Scoring is generally caused by the high pressure contact of the spring loaded brushes, which tends to create friction. This leads to minute brush and commutator particles being dragged around during starter motor engagement. Entrapment of metal particles between the commutator segments can cause shorting. Ovality of the round commutator end can be caused by worn armature bearings or bushings, permitting the armature to ro-

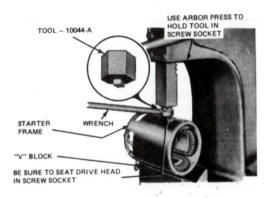

FIGURE 26–25 *Starter motor pole shoe retaining screws removal. (Reprinted with Ford Motor Company's permission.)*

tate off center. This can also cause slow cranking, or failure of the starter to rotate.

If the commutator bars are rough or scored, the armature can be placed in a lathe and brought back to a true and new surface by machining. Remove only enough material to provide a new smooth surface. If only minor irregularities exist, rather than machining, sandpaper can be used to repolish the commutator in the lathe. After machining or polishing, the insulation between the commutator bar segments should be inspected for depth. Some OEMs advise against recutting the insulation after polishing or machining, and suggest that the armature be replaced. However, it is often necessary to lightly do this to ensure that shorting does not occur between individual commutator bar segments. Carefully follow the service manual specs to ensure that if undercutting is performed, that the depth of cut is maintained within specifications. Figure 26-26 shows a starter motor armature undercutting tool that allows the armature to be placed be-

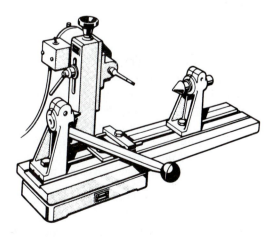

FIGURE 26–26 *Starter motor commutator undercutting machine. (Courtesy of Robert Bosch Corporation.)*

tween two centers. An adjustable cutter tool permits accurate undercutting of the insulation between the commutator bar segments.

At the completion of both commutator polishing/machining, and undercutting procedures, carefully clean the commutator and armature areas of any metal filings. Place the armature into a test growler (Figure 26-23) and recheck it to ensure that it is serviceable!

SUMMARY

This chapter, and performing hands-on tasks, has provided you with the skills required to effectively maintain, service, repair and troubleshoot the electric starter motor system. Coupled with your knowledge of the alternator charging system and battery systems, you should be capable of effectively maintaining all of these three electrical systems.

SELF-TEST QUESTIONS

1. Technician A says that starter motors for heavy-duty trucks can be driven by either electricity or compressed air. Technician B says that air starters are only used on off-highway and industrial equipment. Which technician is correct?

2. Technician A says that battery power to rotate the starter motor armature flows through a set of brushes into the commutator. Technician B says that the power flows through a solenoid and to the motor drive gear assembly. Who is right?

3. Technician A says that all heavy-duty on-highway trucks operate with 12 V starter motors. Technician B says that some are equipped with 24 V starter motors. Which technician is correct?

4. Technician A says that when a 24 V starter motor is used, the batteries must be connected in parallel. Technician B says they must be connected in series and use a series–parallel switch arrangement. Who is right?

5. Technician A says that all starter motors employ a direct gear drive arrangement from the armature to the flywheel ring gear. Technician B says that gear-reduction starters also are used to increase the torque. Which technician is correct?

6. Technician A says that the starter motor nose cone can usually be unbolted and rotated to one of several positions to provide mounting flexibility. Technician B says that each starter motor is designed for only one engine application. Which technician is correct?

7. Technician A says that starter motors can be designed for either CW or CCW rotation. Technician B says that all starter motors drive the flywheel ring gear in a CW direction. Who is right?

8. Technician A says that all starter motor circuits must use a magnetic switch. Technician B disagrees, saying

that some systems use a magnetic switch, but others use a heavy-duty solenoid. Which technician is correct?

9. Technician A says that the starter motor drive pinion is engaged or pulled into engagement with the flywheel ring gear by centrifugal force as it is rotated. Technician B says that shift linkage connected to the solenoid assembly performs this function. Which technician is correct?

10. Technician A says that when the starter switch is closed, a set of magnetic switch contacts closes and the solenoid pull-in windings are connected to the battery source. Technician B says that once the switch is closed, the solenoid hold-in windings connect the motor to the batteries. Who is right?

11. Technician A says that once the starter drive pinion engages with the flywheel ring gear, the hold-in windings allow full battery power to flow to the brushes and through the armature windings, and then to rotate the drive pinion. Technician B says that it is the pull-in windings of the solenoid that provide this action. Which technician understands the motor operation better?

12. Technician A says that once the engine fires, centrifugal force will cause drive pinion disengagement. Technician B says that positive drive pinion disengagement is provided by the heavy-duty roller clutch used with the drive pinion. Who is right?

13. Technician A says that you should never engage the starter motor for periods longer than 15 seconds. Technician B says that you should not exceed a 30-second cranking time without allowing a cool-down period. Which technician is correct?

14. Technician A says that if a starter motor fails to operate or engage the flywheel ring gear after several cranking attempts, but will operate once again after a cool-down period, you should remove and overhaul it. Technician B says it is probably equipped with a thermostatic switch to avoid overheating. Which technician do you think is right here?

15. Technician B says that starter motor cool-down time after attempting to start the engine for a 30-second crank time should be 2 minutes. Technician B says that a 30-second cool-down time is sufficient. Who is right?

16. Technician A says that a starter motor that fails to engage unless the clutch pedal is depressed indicates that the electrical system is fitted with a neutral safety switch. Technician B believes it indicates that a short exists in the electrical system to the starter motor through the battery cable contacting the clutch linkage. Which technician do you think is correct in this case?

17. Technician A says that heavy-duty starter motors generally contain between 4 and 6 field pole shoes in their housing. Technician B says all starters contain only three pole shoes. Who is right?

18. Technician A says that starter motor rotation is provided by creating opposing magnetic fields around the starter motor. Technician B says that rotation is achieved by creating a stronger magnetic field strength on one side of the armature wires than on the other. Which technician understands the principles of operation better?

19. Technician A says that starter motor torque is greatest when the engine just starts to fire and run. Technician B says the starter motor torque will be greatest during initial engagement with the flywheel ring gear, when it is known as *breakaway torque*. Which technician understands the term *torque* better?

20. Technician A says that the pole piece windings are arranged in a series design. Technician B says that they are wound in a parallel design. Who is right?

21. Technician A says that a starter motor magnetic switch simply opens and closes the circuit from the battery to the motor. Technician B says that the magnetic switch is designed to move the starter pinion drive linkage into engagement with the flywheel ring gear. Which technician understands this function better?

22. Technician A says that the solenoid mounted on top of the starter motor assembly functions to open and close the circuit between the batteries and the starter motor. Technician B says that the solenoid functions both to open and close this circuit and to shift the internal plunger to move the drive pinion into engagement with the flywheel ring gear. Which technician do you think is right?

23. Technician A says that the motor solenoid terminal marked *S* connects the battery power to one side, then through the pull-in winding to ground on the other side to complete the circuit. Technician B says that the battery power flows to the hold-in winding instead. Who is right?

24. Technician A says that on a heavy-duty starter motor circuit, once the drive pinion is fully engaged, the solenoid disc in contact with the B and M terminals now requires less magnetism, and the pull-in winding is shorted to stop current flow through it. Technician B says that the pull-in winding must stay energized to keep the starter motor turning. Which technician understands the system operation better?

25. Technician A says that the solenoid contact disc is positively released from engagement with both terminal studs by the reverse polarity created once the engine fires. Technician B says that the contact disc is released only when the key or pushbutton switch is released, and a small spring kicks the disc back. Who is right?

26. Technician A says that a chattering noise from the starter and failure to crank the engine is probably due to low voltage at the solenoid from undercharged batteries. Technician B says that high circuit resistance or a faulty solenoid could also be the cause. Are both technicians correct, or is only one?

27. Technician A says that starter motor shift solenoids will draw between 45 and 90 A, depending on the starter type and size. Technician B says that 25 to 30 A is more common. Who is right?

28. Technician A says that repeated attempts to crank the engine with low battery voltage will simply result in a no-start condition. Technician B says that this can cause burning of the solenoid contacts. Which technician is correct?

29. Technician A says that if a starter motor continues to motor after the engine has started and the key switch or push button has been released, the problem is probably due to failure of the solenoid or wiring to open the circuit. Technician B says that this problem would be due to the drive pinion overrunning clutch not disengaging. Which technician do you think is correct?

30. Technician A says that a rumble or growl from the starter motor as it is coasting to a stop after starting the engine could be caused by a defective pinion drive clutch. Technician B says it is more liable to be a bent or unbalanced starter motor armature. Which technician do you think is correct?

31. Technician A says that a high-pitched whine during cranking before the engine fires, although the engine cranks and fires okay, is probably due to misalignment. Technician B says that this problem is due to too great a distance between the starter pinion and the flywheel. Which technician is right?

32. Technician A says that voltage readings across the solenoid coil terminals of a heavy-duty 12 V starter motor should be at least 11 V. Technician B says that 10.5 V would be acceptable. Who is correct?

33. Technician A says that voltage readings across the solenoid coil terminals of a 24 V starter motor should be at least 21 V. Technician B says it should be nothing less than 22 V. Which technician is right?

34. Technician A says that starter motors can be bench-checked to test them for a no-load operation while you monitor the pinion rpm, current draw, and voltage. Technician B says that this can only be performed on a special test stand. Who is right?

35. Technician A says that you can bench-check a heavy-duty starter motor by placing it in a vise, locking the drive pinion with a special adapter, then engaging the motor to stall-test the unit for a specific torque output. Technician B says that you can only stall-test torque converters, not starter motors. Which technician is correct?

36. Technician A says that if an ammeter registers a high current draw, but the starter fails to rotate, you should check for broken brush springs. Technician B says that you should check for a direct ground circuit in either the field windings or the terminal connection. Who do you think is right?

37. Technician A says that if an ammeter shows no current draw on an inoperative starter motor, the problem could be high insulation between the armature commutator bar segments. Technician B says that the problem could be worn brushes or weak or broken brush springs. Are both technicians right here, or is only one?

38. Technician A says that a starter motor that exhibits a low rotative speed and a low current draw probably has shorted field coils. Technician B says that it probably has high internal circuit resistance. Who is correct?

39. Technician A says that a high current draw when checking a starter motor, accompanied by a high rotative speed, can normally be traced to shorted field coils and a possible shorted armature. Technician B thinks this is due to an open field circuit in the solenoid. Who do you think is right?

40. Technician A says that a disassembled starter motor should have its armature checked for shorts, opens, and grounds by using a growler test unit. Technician B says that you can do this simply by using an ohmmeter. Which technician is right?

41. Technician A says that when a flat steel strip placed lengthwise along an armature mounted in a growler vibrates, it indicates a grounded circuit. Technician B says it indicates a short. Who is right?

42. Technician A says that starter motor brushes should be replaced when they have worn down approximately 50%. Technician B says that brushes only need to be replaced when they have worn down 70%. Which technician is correct?

43. Technician A says that the starter motor pinion clearance can be adjusted by shims on a heavy-duty model. Technician B says that this adjustment is obtained by a nut located inside the solenoid assembly. Which technician is correct?

Index

771